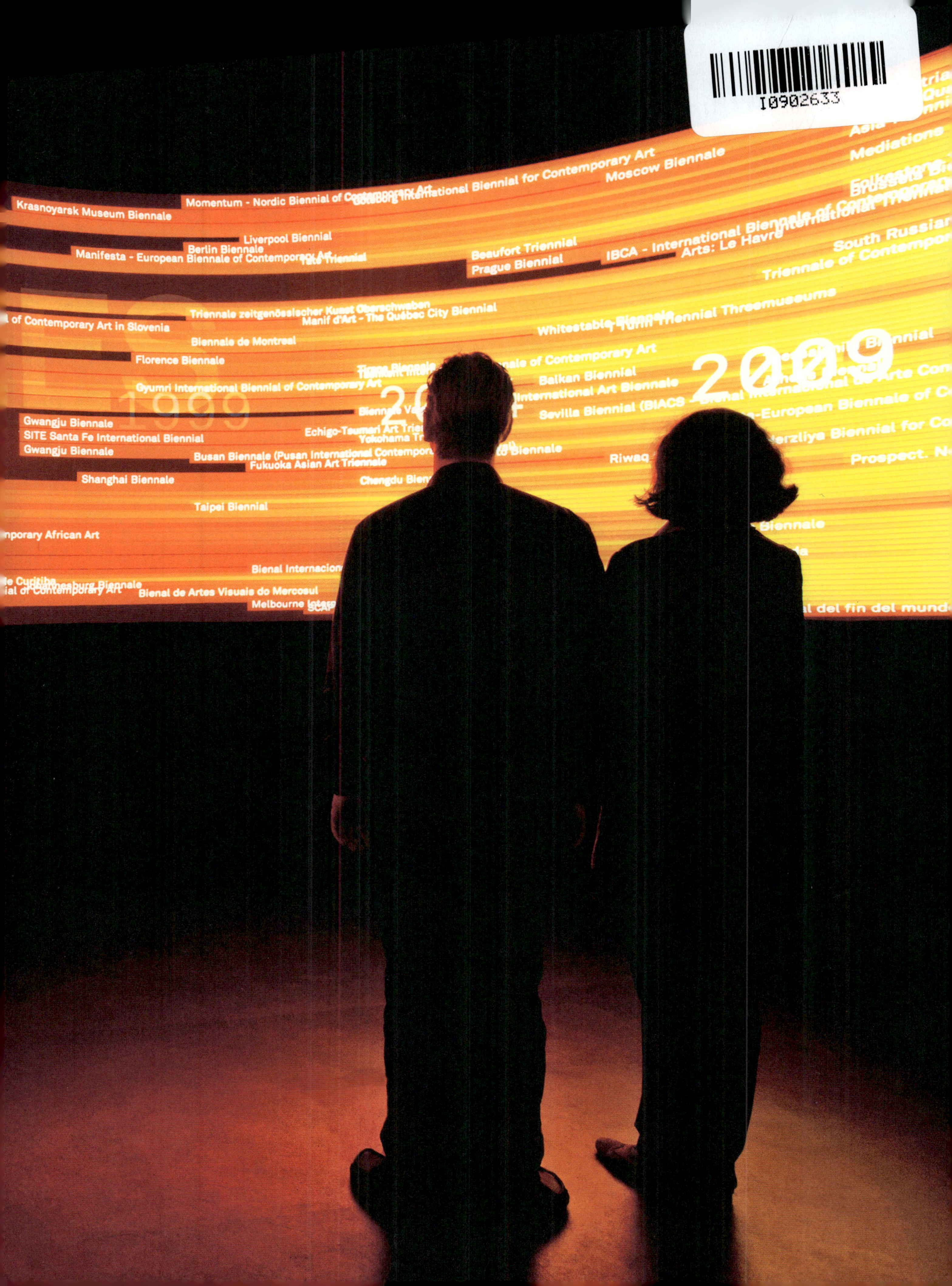

Krasnoyarsk Museum Biennale
Momentum - Nordic Biennial of Contemporary Art
Moscow Biennale
Liverpool Biennial
Berlin Biennale
Manifesta - European Biennale of Contemporary Art
Beaufort Triennial
Prague Biennial
IBCA - International Biennale of Contemporary
Arts: Le Havre
South Russian
Triennale of Contempor
Mediations
Triennale zeitgenössischer Kunst Oberschwaben
Manif d'Art - The Québec City Biennial
of Contemporary Art in Slovenia
Whitestable Biennale
Biennale de Montreal
Florence Biennale
Balkan Biennial
Gyumri International Biennial of Contemporary Art
International Art Biennale
Sevilla Biennial (BIACS
1999
2009
Gwangju Biennale
SITE Santa Fe International Biennial
Gwangju Biennale
Echigo-Tsumari Art Triennale
Busan Biennale (Pusan International Contempor
Fukuoka Asian Art Triennale
Riwaq
Herzliya Biennial for Co
Prospect. N
Shanghai Biennale
Chengdu Bien
Taipei Biennial
nporary African Art
Biennale
Bienal Internacion
Johannesburg Biennale
Bienal de Artes Visuais do Mercosul
Melbourne Intern
al del fin del mundo

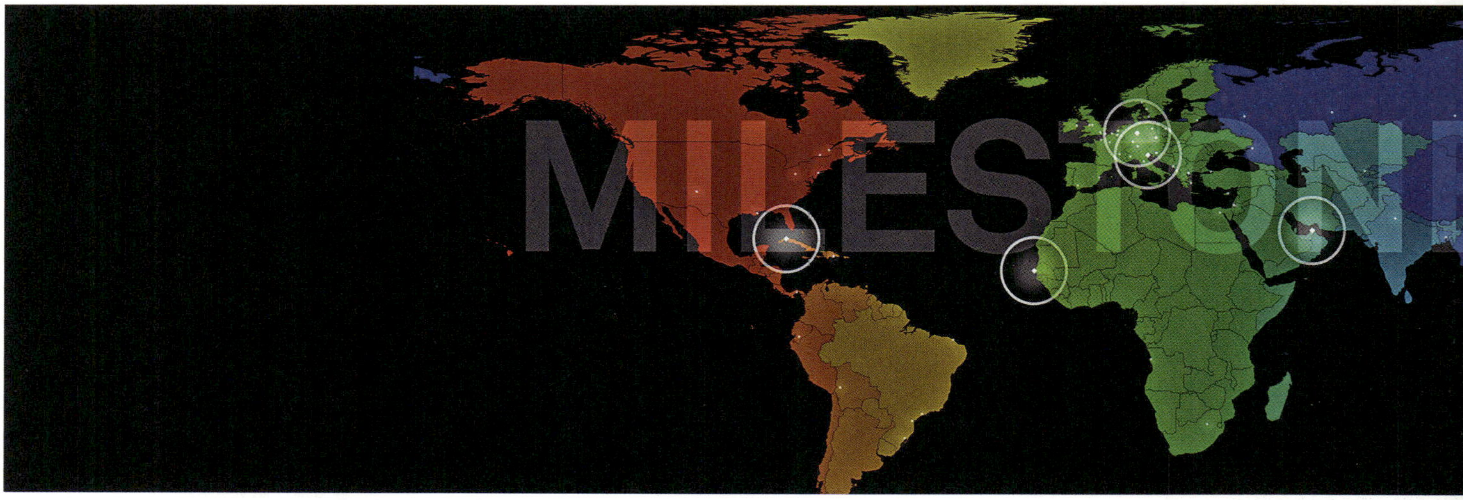

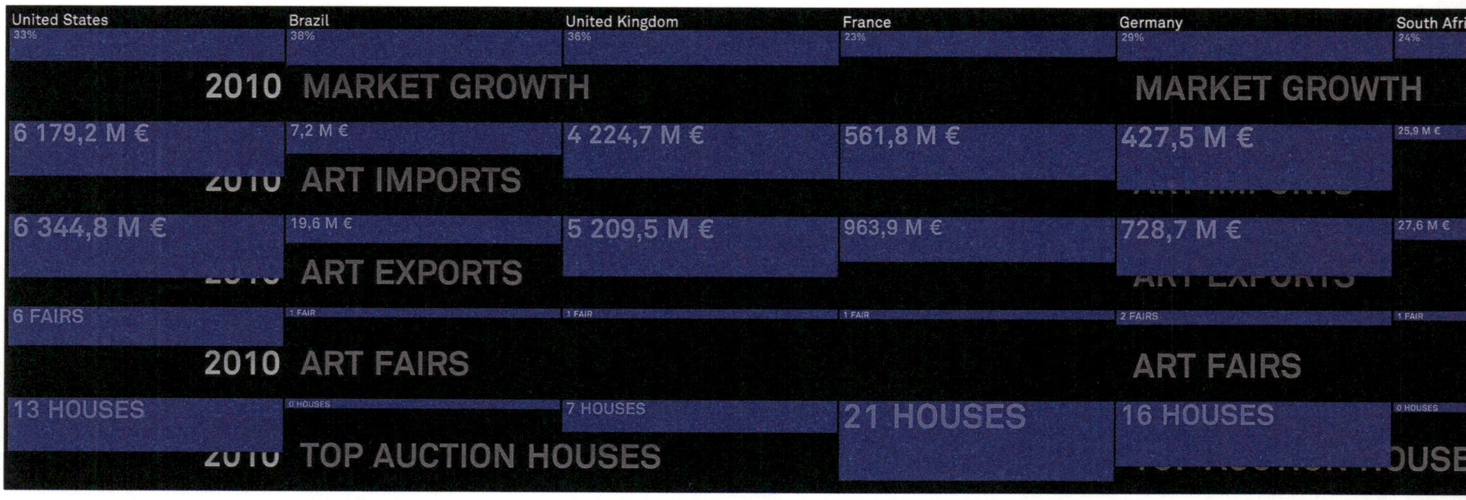

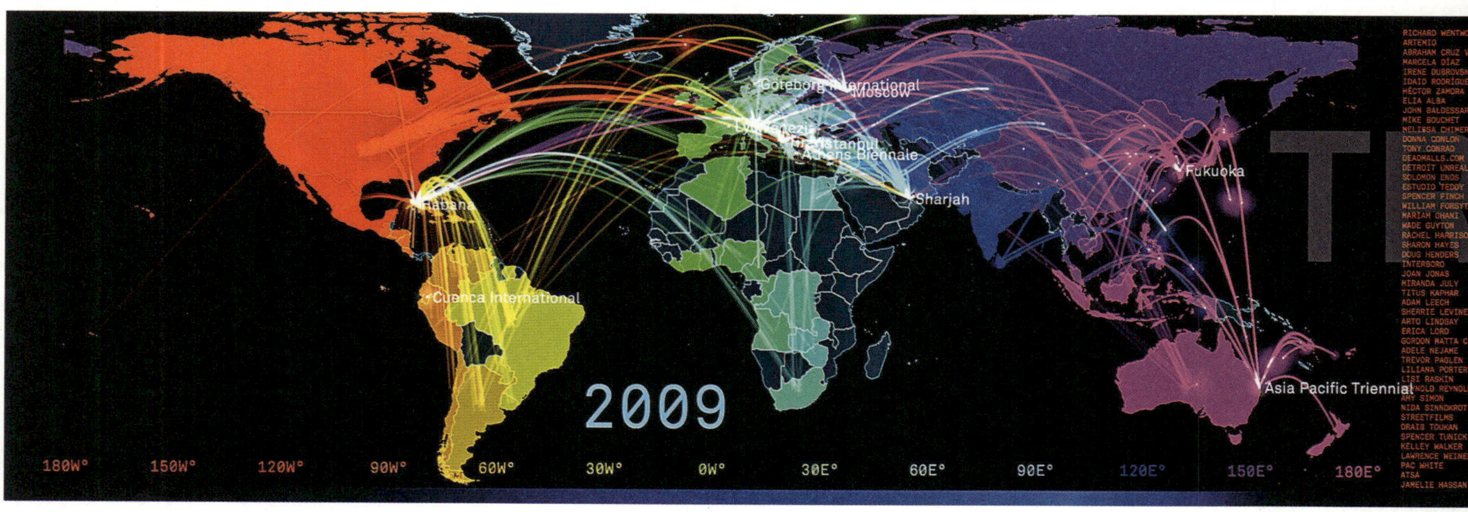

trans_actions: The Accelerated Art World 1989–2011, 2011, installation for PanoramaScreen, screen shots

Previous page: *The Accelerated Art World 1989–2011*, 2011, installation view

Following pages: Views into the exhibition *The Global Contemporary. Art Worlds after 1989*, ZKM | Karlsruhe, 2011–2012

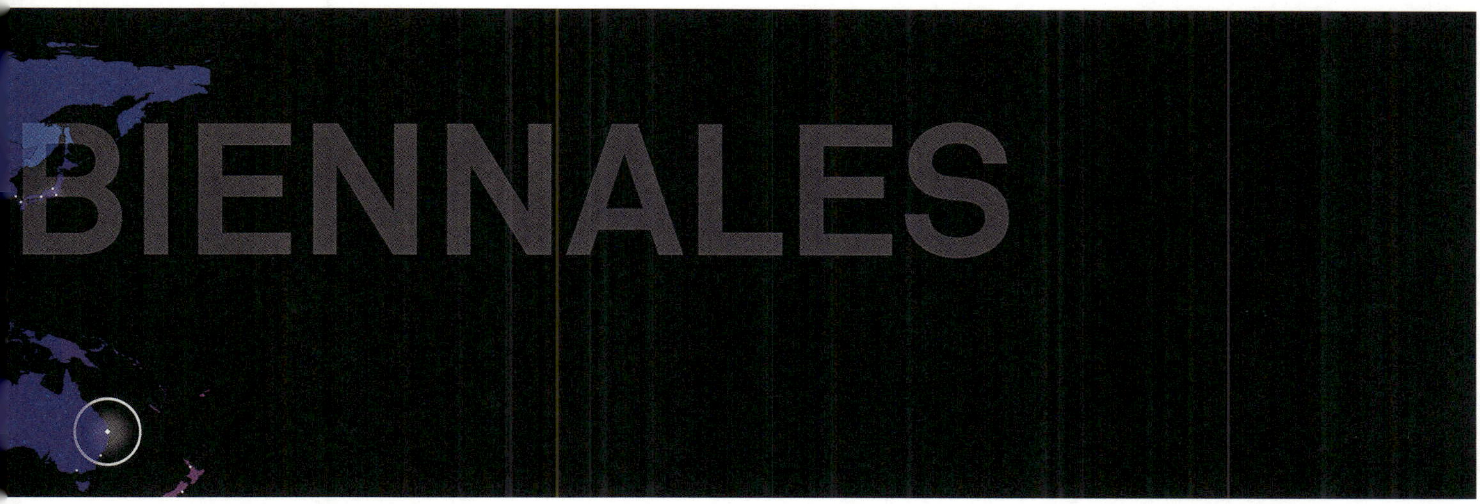
BIENNALES

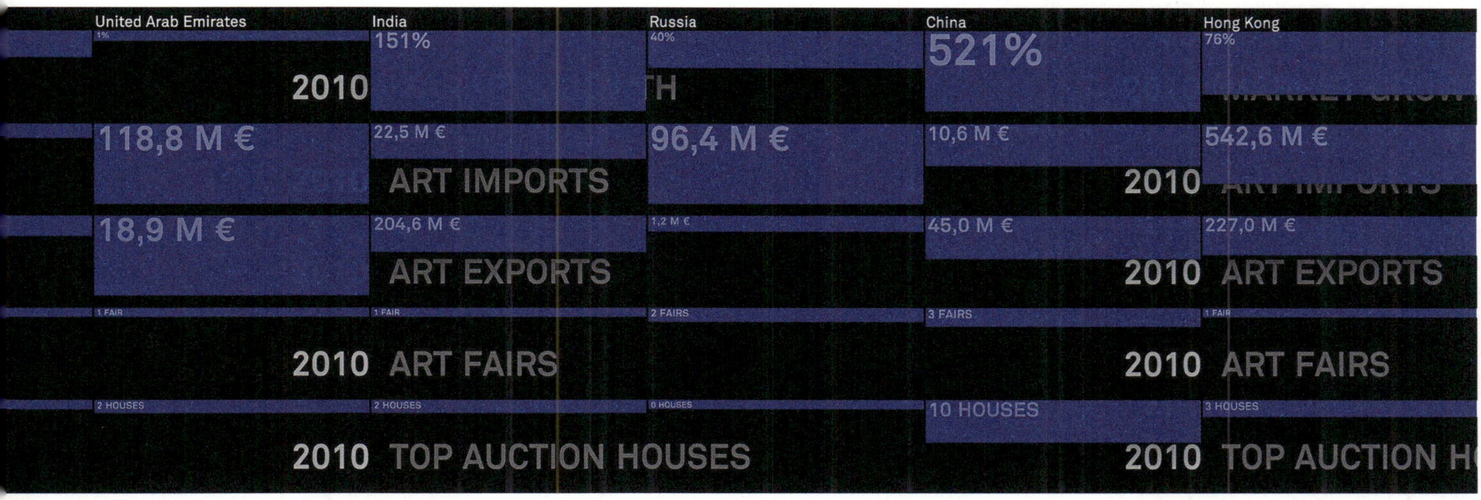
United Arab Emirates
1%
2010
118,8 M €
18,9 M €
1 FAIR
2010 ART FAIRS
2 HOUSES
2010 TOP AUCTION HOUSES
India
151%
22,5 M €
ART IMPORTS
204,6 M €
ART EXPORTS
1 FAIR
2 HOUSES
Russia
40%
96,4 M €
1,2 M €
2 FAIRS
0 HOUSES
China
521%
10,6 M €
45,0 M €
3 FAIRS
10 HOUSES
Hong Kong
76%
542,6 M €
2010
227,0 M €
2010 ART EXPORTS
1 FAIR
2010 ART FAIRS
3 HOUSES
2010 TOP AUCTION H

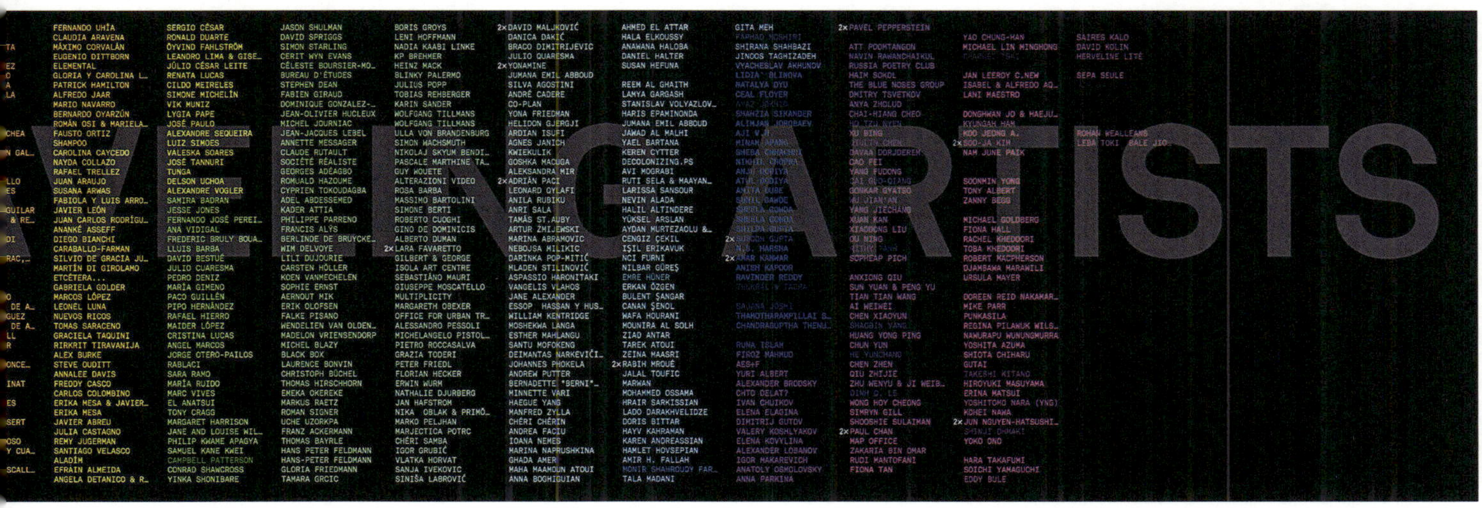
ARTISTS

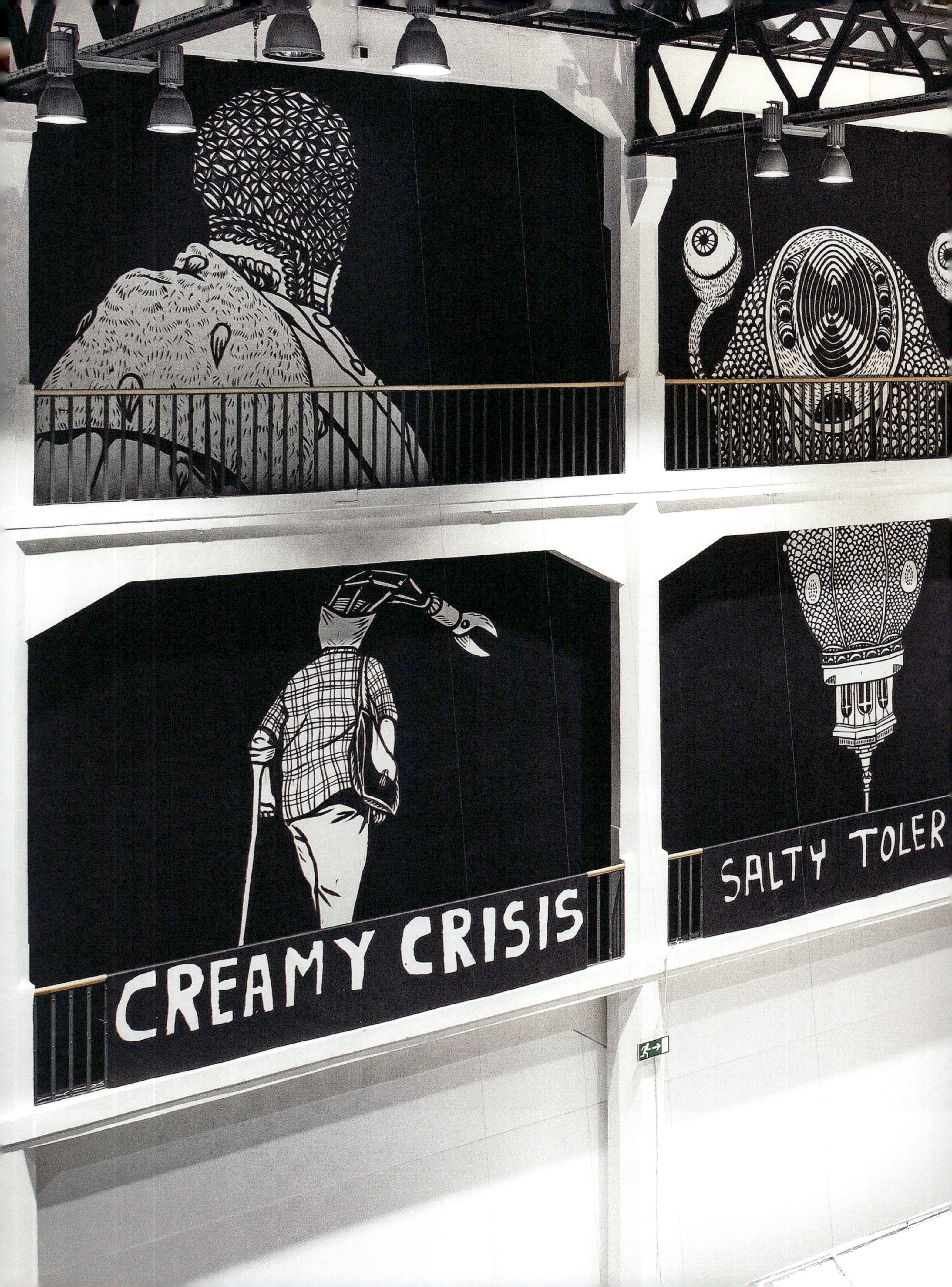
CREAMY CRISIS
SALTY TOLER

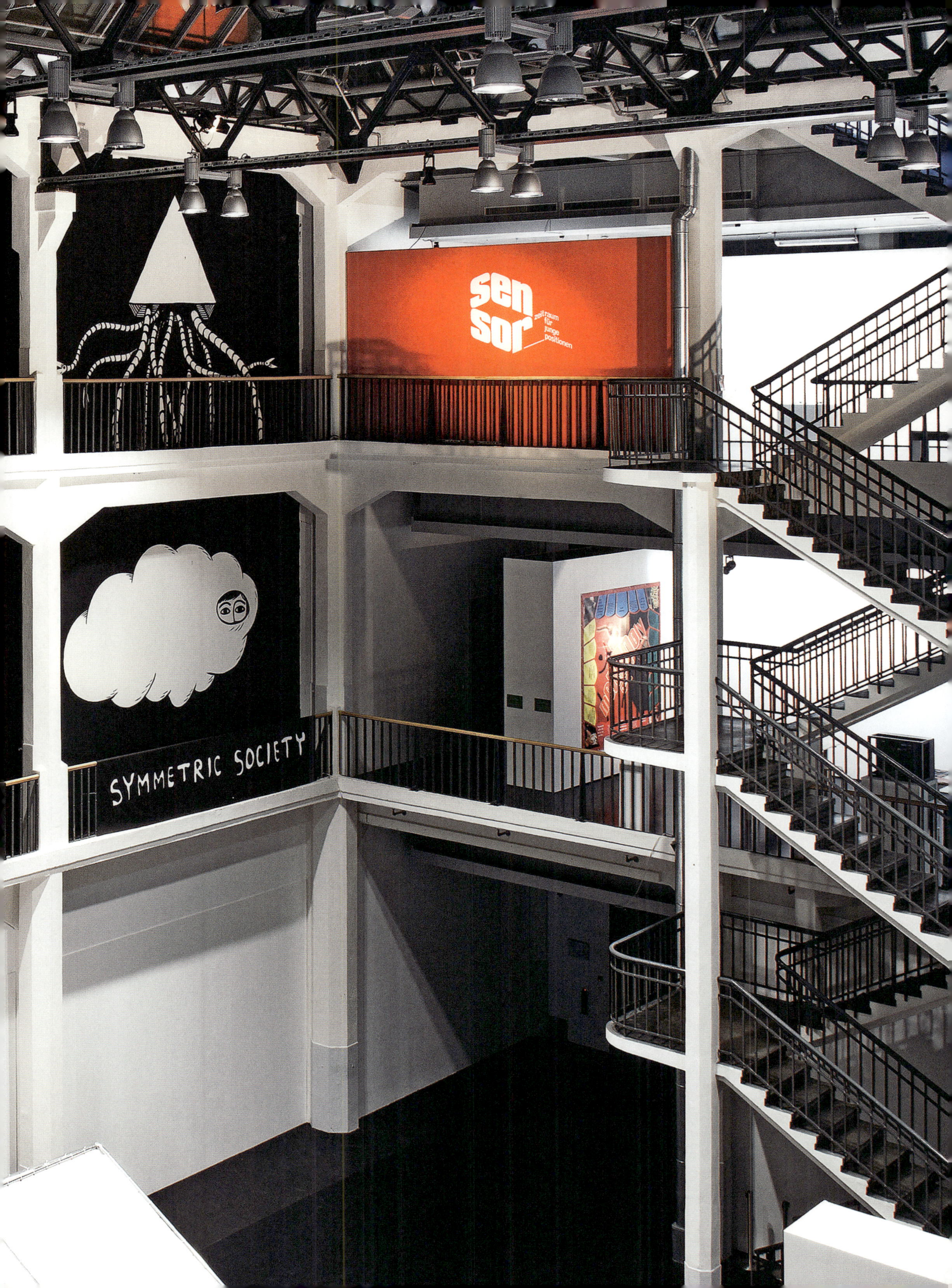
sen sor
zeit raum für junge positionen
SYMMETRIC SOCIETY

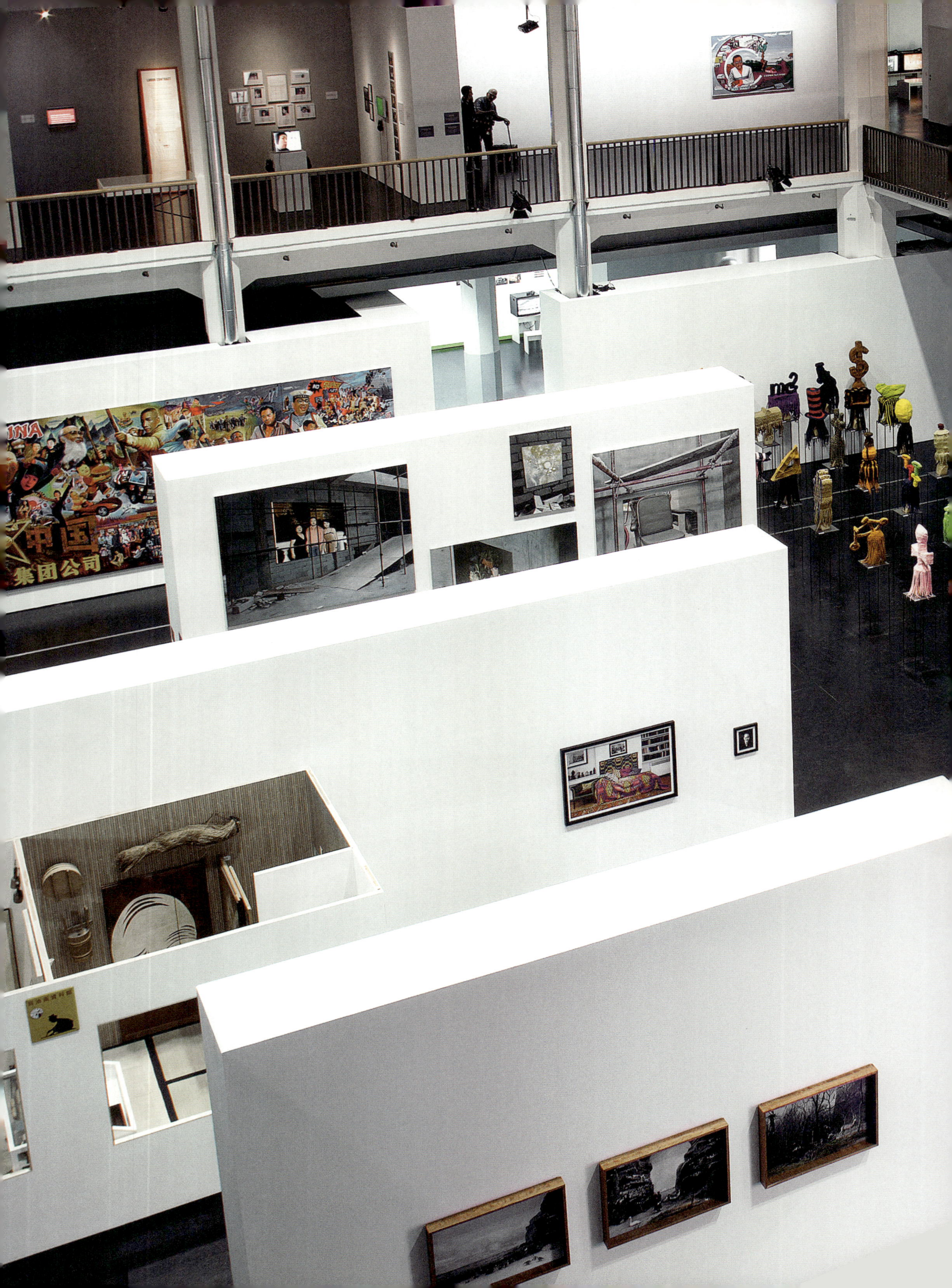
中国
集团公司

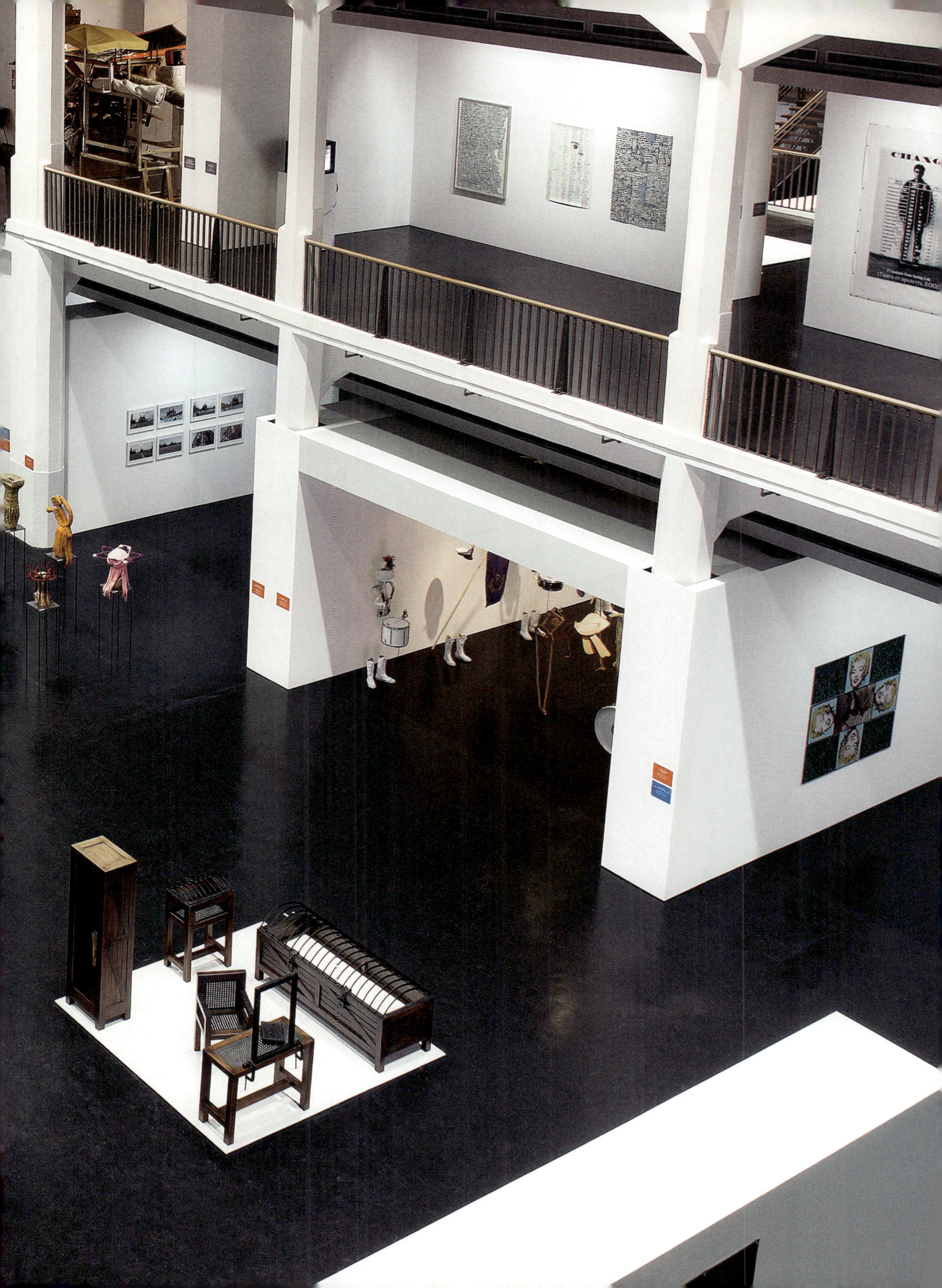

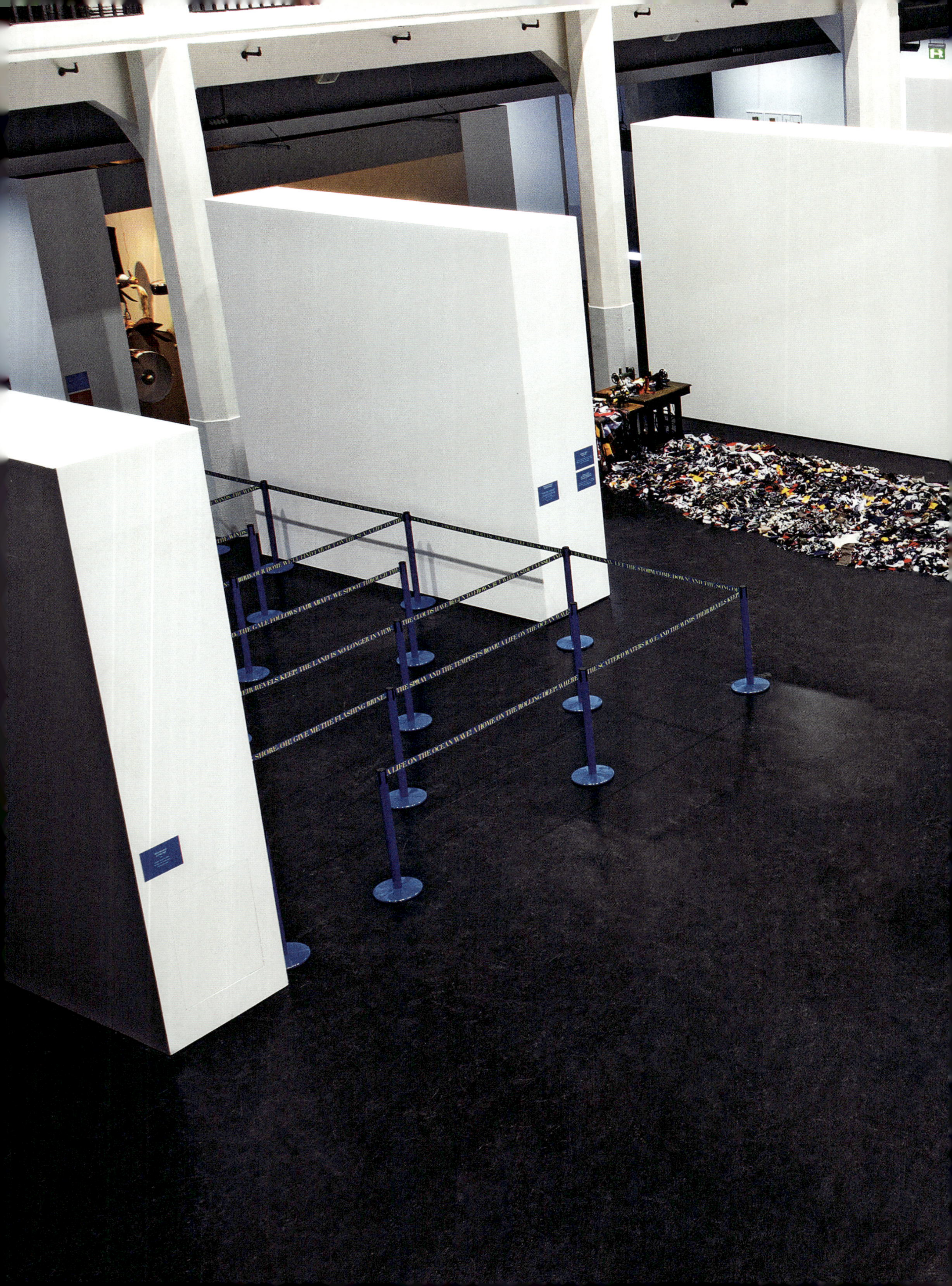

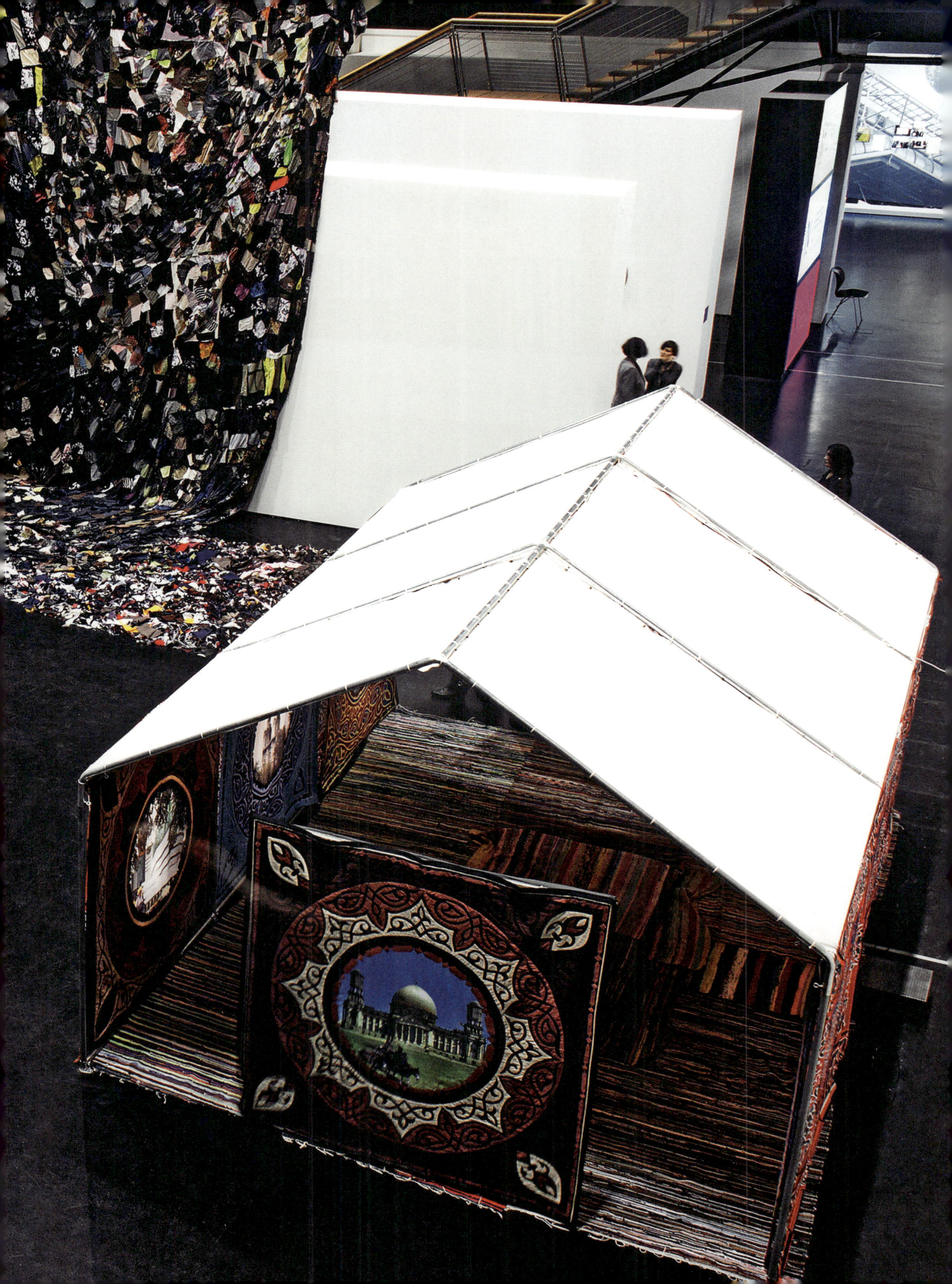

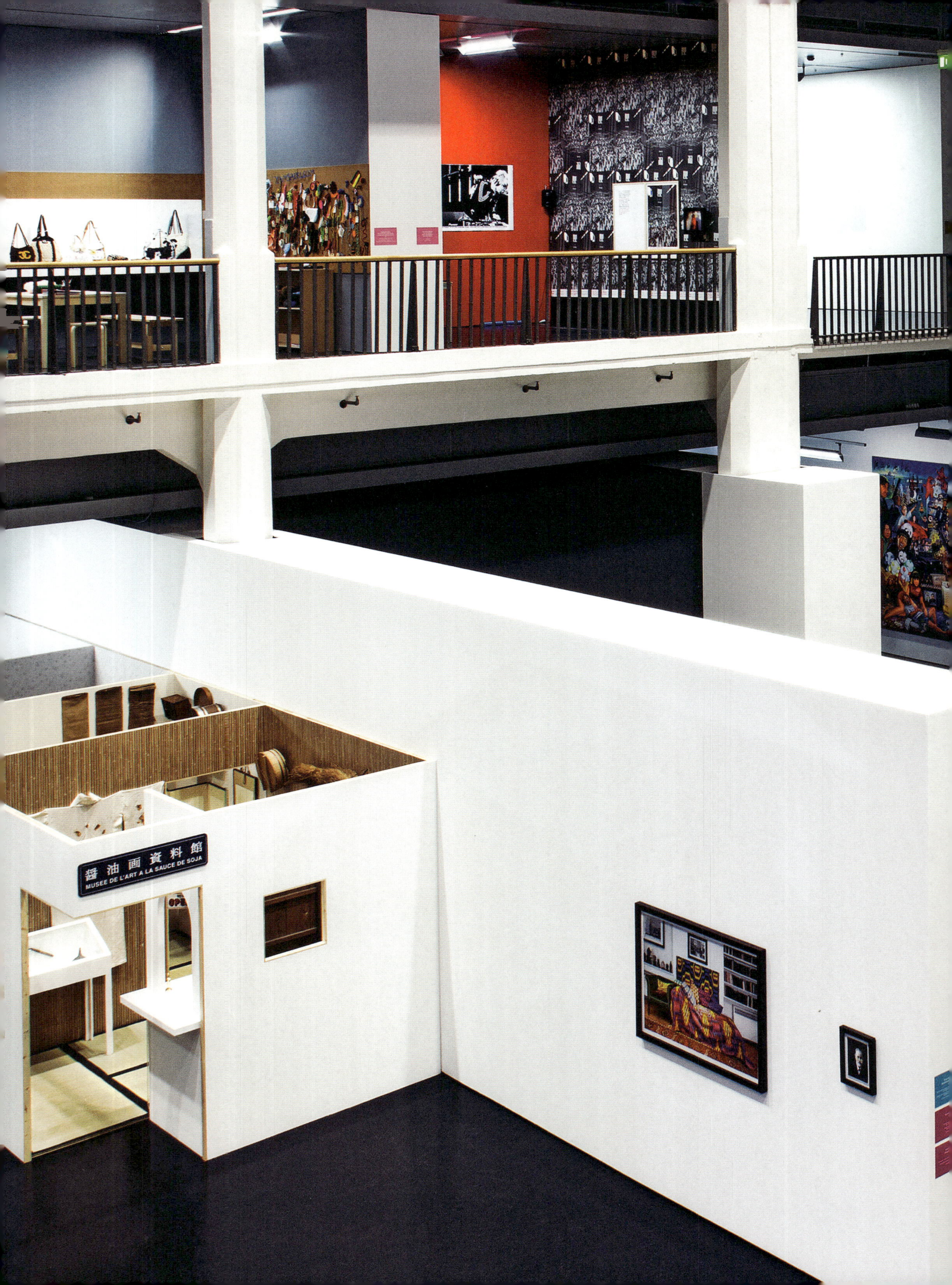
醤油画資料館
MUSÉE DE L'ART À LA SAUCE DE SOJA

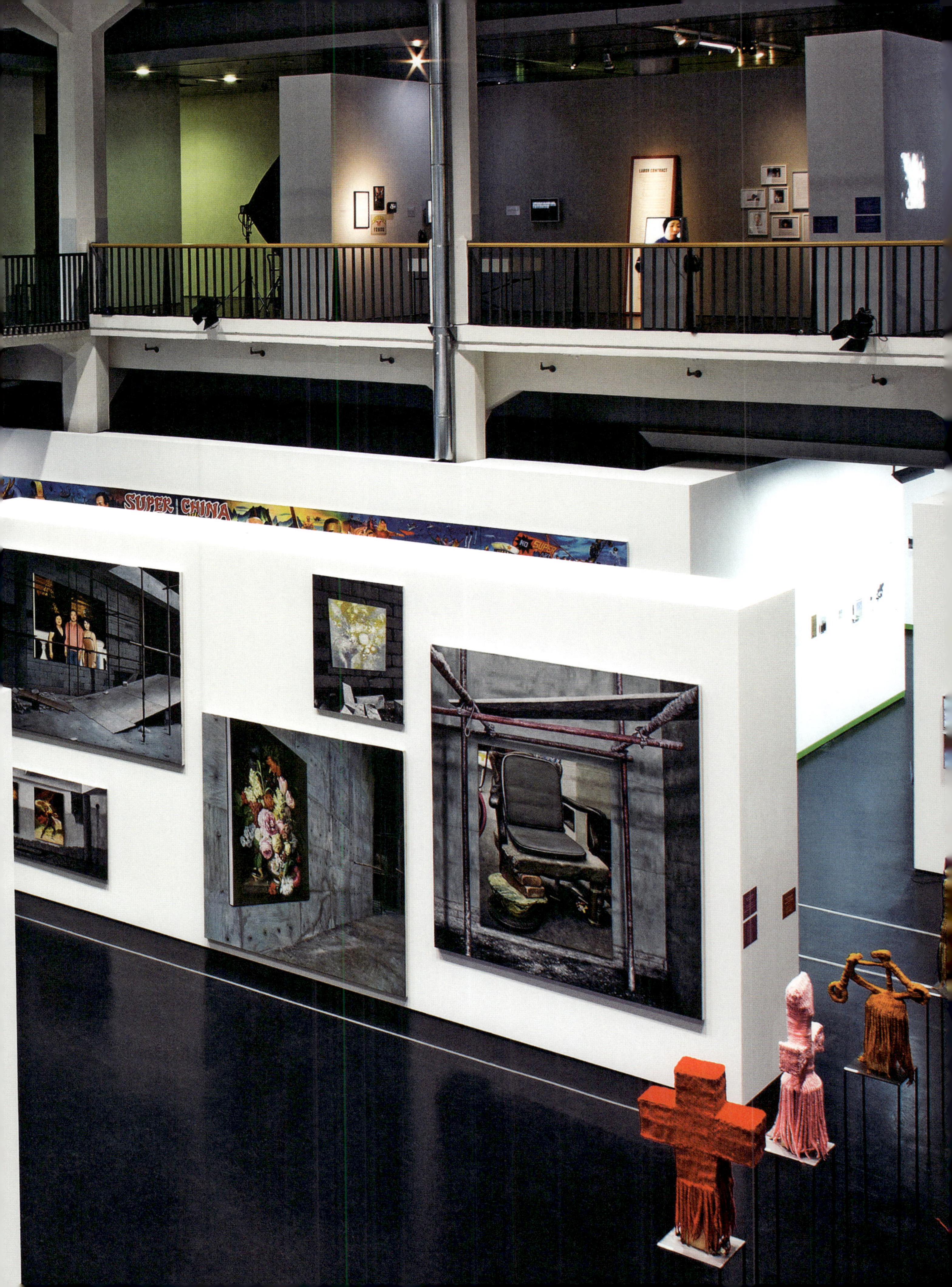
SUPER CHINA

The Global Contemporary and the Rise of New Art Worlds

edited by Hans Belting, Andrea Buddensieg, and Peter Weibel

Published by ZKM | Center for Art and Media Karlsruhe, Germany
The MIT Press, Cambridge, MA / London, England

Contents

Contents

Eight Views from an Exhibition

Acknowledgments

After the exhibition *The Global Contemporary. Art Worlds after 1989* at ZKM ended in February 2012, our next task was to prepare the present volume, which is conceived as a companion guide to the topic of the exhibition and furthermore seeks to contextualize its aims. The ZKM team again brought off a miracle by realizing such an ambitious exhibition project, and we then had the pleasure of working together with a very congenial group of colleagues on this book.

First of all, we would like to extend our warmest thanks to the members of the ZKM | Publication Department (Jens Lutz, Miriam Stürner, Maraike Steding, Luise Pilz) on whose capable shoulders rested the bulk of the editing work and who once again demonstrated their professional excellence. We are deeply indebted to Sara Giannini who not only collaborated with us on the concept for the *Room of Histories*, but also made an enduring contribution to its explanatory texts as well as organizing the picture research and correspondence. The book profited greatly from the work of the designers: Renata Sas for the general layout, and Boris Dworschak for the *Room of Histories*. For their kind cooperation our grateful thanks go to the authors of the texts, who for the most part contributed an essay written especially for this occasion, and to Gloria Custance for professional and careful editing. Clare McAndrew gave us invaluable assistance by sharing her material with us for the art market section in the *Room of Histories*. Jane Morris, the chief editor of *The Art Newspaper* in London, kindly gave us permission to republish our GAM website column with "Global News from *The Art Newspaper*."

We are sincerely grateful to the Federal Cultural Foundation of Germany for supporting both the exhibition and the publication of the present book. Last but not least, neither the exhibition nor the book publication could have been realized without the generous support of the ZKM's founders, the city of Karlsruhe and the State of Baden-Württemberg. The Hubert Burda Foundation helped us with a Felix Burda fellowship dedicated to the preparatory stages of the publication.

A special thanks to Ernst Gärtner and his team at Eberl Druck for their professional advice and excellent support in seeing the book through to completion. We would also like to thank Roger Conover, Executive Editor at MIT Press, who encouraged our project when he generously accepted the book for the program of MIT Press.

The Editors

Preface

German Federal Cultural Foundation

With the upheavals coming in the wake of globalization and its attendant movements over the past twenty years, the era that witnessed the prevalence of Western canons in art history has come to a close. A global, contemporary art of diverse origins has now taken its place. But what are the implications for museums? According to what guidelines will they function in the future, and what roles are they to play? These are some among the opening questions posed by the "Global Art and the Museum" research project initiated a good five years ago at the ZKM | Center for Art and Media Karlsruhe, and which has recently culminated in the large-scale exhibition *The Global Contemporary. Art Worlds after 1989* followed by the present publication *The Global Contemporary and the Rise of New Art Worlds.*

As a project and worldview, together with its pretension to universality, modernity was inseparably bound to a claim of hegemony in economics, politics, and culture. "Art" was one of its core domains. Only the countries of the "West" were considered to be modern while all others were at least one step "behind." Under pressure of the historical events of the past two or three decades, but also following objections raised by ever larger groups within their own countries, this arrogant worldview then evolved into a more subtle position. Rather than a single modernity we now have the "multiple modernities" of which Israeli sociologist Shmuel Noah Eisenstadt has spoken: their legacy and the question of the role of art and culture have to be negotiated locally in every culture. This is, perhaps, one of the most important lessons of the "global turn."

New museums of contemporary art have been opening around the world. Curators and art historians, formerly devoted solely to Western art history are now focusing increased attention on the local traditions of non-Western cultures in an endeavor to understand the new art now exerting an impact upon many current collections and exhibitions. These are "postethnic" positions, which, while drawing on the formal language and intellectual tradition of their respective countries of origin, are at the same time embedded within international discourses. The artists are in constant interaction with one another through such international events as biennials, artist-in-residence programs, and by way of the new class of jet-setting curators. But they all search in their own way for a social position, their own history and identity, whether in Oceania, China, New York, or in Saxony-Anhalt.

And not only are the collections and museums of the art world obliged to react to these global developments: such developments no less affect the self-image of a funding institution such as the German Federal Cultural Foundation. The value and specific form of the international characteristics of artistic projects play a central role in our funding activities, as do the relationships between international artistic standards and local traditions and requirements. It is for such reasons that we are thrilled, also for entirely selfish reasons, about this exhibition and about the further course of research and discussions inspired by the project.

We are grateful to everyone involved, but especially to Andrea Buddensieg, Hans Belting, and Peter Weibel, the general curators of the exhibition and editors of this publication, for the energy and vision with which they engage in these important questions. We trust that the persons involved will enjoy the great success this ambitious project deserves.

Hortensia Völckers,
Executive Board / Artistic Director
Alexander Farenholtz,
Executive Board / Administrative Director

Globalization and Contemporary Art

Peter Weibel

One effect of globalization is that encounters between different cultures, religions, and languages, as well as between different ethnic and national identities, have intensified. At the moment there are two main hypotheses offered to explain the resulting conflicts and rifts: one hypothesis, formulated by Samuel P. Huntington, is that civilizations meet in a clash,[1] that is, as hostile antagonists or protagonists. The other suggestion is that there is hope for a "confluence of cultures," a proposition put forward in Ilija Trojanow and Ranjit Hoskoté's book *Kampfabsage* (2007).[2] My own explanatory model, by contrast, starts from a theory of rewriting.

This theory proceeds from the observation that liberal democratic terms such as *integration* and *assimilation* in fact center on the pair of terms *inclusion/exclusion*. Hence the point is not to ascertain that those who do not integrate or assimilate are excluded by society. The point is not to establish that specific sections of the population are excluded from participating in social function systems. Nor is the point to define the problems that arise as a result of class rule. All these variants play down the problem of exclusion, for inclusion can only exist if exclusion is possible. Inclusion and exclusion are inherent in and of relevance to the system, which is why I organized a first exhibition on the thematic complex of globalization, migration, and postcolonialism back in 1996 with the title *Inklusion : Exklusion* (steirischer herbst, Graz) and conceived a "museum of global art."

The theorem particularly concerns the West and one of its greatest inventions: modernity. For Europe and North America - or rather for the European-North American axis - globalization is the first case in history where *they* do not apply this binary opposition to other peoples and states, but where it can be applied to them. Up to now, Europe and North America have always been able to define who was included in the respective national, economic, or military alliance, and hence who was automatically excluded. Now, for the first time they find themselves in the situation - or at least potentially in a situation - where other states determine who is included and excluded. Thus for the West globalization means applying the rule of inclusion/exclusion to itself. This is creating unrest and anxiety in the West. For the application of the inclusion/exclusion mechanism to the West itself calls into question the West's dominance over the entire world.

What were the prerequisites for this hegemony of the West? I would say it was the Borromean rings of economics, politics, and art under the sign of "creative destruction" (Joseph A. Schumpeter), that is, innovation. The most common answer, however, is the development of sovereign nation-states and the capitalist mode of production. The spread of the capitalist economy within the framework of globalization as far as China is quite evident. The spreading of the territorial system of nation-states is also on the increase. Even in Europe, once medium-sized states such as Yugoslavia are breaking up into a number of small states under the pressure of globalization. Here, too, the global expansion of the idea of the nation-state is now being applied to Europe itself in the form of renationalization. Hence the powerful forces that once led to the global hegemony of the West - namely, the nation-state and capitalism - are threatened from within. Modernity was nothing other than a cultural expression of these two forces and itself a part of European expansion. In this sense, it follows that globalization has merely continued the work and the process of colonization, which was based on the obliteration and exploitation of the Other. As long as these processes of modernization, colonization, and globalization only concerned the rest of the world but not Europe itself, Europe naturally regarded this as legitimate. Only now, when the consequence is apparent that these forces are threatening Europe itself - namely, that as the Other Europe will be expunged - are the negative sides of modernization, colonization, and globalization recognized.

1 **See: Samuel P. Huntington,** *The Clash of Civilizations and the Remaking of World Order*, Simon & Schuster, New York (NY), 1996.

2 **Ilija Trojanow, Ranjit Hoskoté,** *Kampfabsage: Kulturen bekämpfen sich nicht - sie fließen zusammen*, Blessing, Munich, 2007.

Significantly, the contours of a postmodern order and a postmodern culture were sketched in the 1980s as escapism, as a reaction to emerging conflicts. The ideas of postmodernism were the first dubious and desperate attempts to untie the Borromean knot of the nation-state, capitalism, and modernity. Failure was inevitable because postmodernism did not accept the axiom of the mechanism of inclusion and exclusion upon which modernity is fundamentally based.

If we follow the theory of Niklas Luhmann, as outlined in his 1997 book *Die Gesellschaft der Gesellschaft*,[3] then we must acknowledge with him that problems of exclusion are inevitable consequences of the functional differentiations of the social system, and that modernity - and in particular modern art - is precisely the result of such a functional differentiation. The differentiation of social systems upon which modern society is built make the reinforcement of deviations, and hence of exclusions, unavoidable. Only the difference between inclusion and exclusion makes it possible to construct identities; that is, closed subsystems. In this sense the inclusion/exclusion difference is a metadifference that is responsible for all the other distinctions within a social system. Whether identity is national, religious, ethnic, linguistic, or cultural, every construction of identity is the result of such operations of distinction and exclusion, because that is the process by which it is determined; it is immaterial whether the members of the functional system believe in the same God or not, speak the same language or not, belong to the same ethnic group or not. Only when this difference has been ascertained can the identity of the group be defined. The difference operation is the prerequisite for the construction of identity. Thus it follows that inclusion and exclusion are also the metadifference for the distinction between just and unjust, moral and immoral, culture and barbarism.

Ultimately, differentiating implies applying the mechanism of inclusion/exclusion. Because modernity is the result of differentiation, it also applies rules of inclusion/exclusion. This is the reason why there is no simple solution for counteracting tendencies to exclude. All liberal-democratic projects, all assertions of modernity that promise to keep the space of social and cultural inclusion open sooner or later avail themselves of the mechanism of exclusion. One of the collateral effects of those modern societies that are unavoidably built on mechanisms of exclusion, though without knowing or being aware of it, is the growing world of alterities that protest these exclusions.

In the age of globalization, however, in which the legitimacy of differentiated systems and subsystems is called into question by encounters with other functional systems, a critique of the mechanisms of inclusion and exclusion has arisen. Let there be no misunderstanding: globalization is, on the one hand, the result and the product of Western modernity, but at this historical moment globalization is turning against the very author of globalization. Hence it does not argue about belonging to a culture, nation, or civilization - as is still articulated in hegemonic terms in the concept of integration or assimilation - but concentrates on monopolizing the mechanisms of inclusion and exclusion. Those who integrate, subjugate themselves to the dominant culture. In essence they extinguish themselves as the Other.

Other cultures do not wish to subjugate themselves to the monopoly of the West - that is, to reject their own culture through mechanisms of inclusion and exclusion. Other peoples and civilizations fight against this monopoly and want to decide themselves who and what is included or excluded. As a result of this contention about the monopoly over mechanisms of inclusion and exclusion, a new epoch began after 1989, because the year 1989 signified the end of the Western monopolies. The rise of art from Arabia, Asia, Africa, and South America, amongst others, in Western institutions is nothing other than the legitimate attempt by other cultures, nations, and civilizations to strip the West of its monopoly on exclusion. As Hans Belting once wrote, "the definition of modern art [...] was based on a double exclusion."[4] These artists from Arabia, Asia, Africa, South America, and elsewhere, do not want to integrate into Western culture; at most they want to break down these mechanisms of exclusion. In this respect they differ from Western modernism. Global art after the collapses of 1989 does not ask for inclusion nor can it naïvely demand the elimination of all mechanisms of inclusion and exclusion; it would, however, like to break up the Western monopoly. In that respect, these new art worlds create new mechanisms of inclusion and exclusion, which I would like to describe with the term *rewrite* rather than *clash* or *confluence*.

The idea of rewriting is based on the assumption that every system consists of a finite number of elements and of a limited number of rules as to how these elements are connected and can be sequenced. These rules are called rewriting rules. In language, they constitute grammar. In society, they can be called codes of behavior, or marriage laws, or traffic laws, or rules for cooking. If we consider society as a

3 **Niklas Luhmann**, *Die Gesellschaft der Gesellschaft*, Suhrkamp, Frankfurt am Main, 1997.

4 **Hans Belting**, "Contemporary Art as Global Art: A Critical Estimate," in: *The Global Art World. Audiences, Markets, and Museums*, ZKM | Karlsruhe, Hatje Cantz, Ostfildern, 2009, p. 55.

system, then it is possible to apply the idea of rewriting programs to it. It is also the case that rewritings can take place in society. What has been happening in nature for millions of years is a constant process of rewriting. This process is called evolution. It would be absurd to assume that social systems are less complex than natural systems. So let's take as given that social systems are subject to rewriting rules, as are all other systems. So what we have been calling integration, assimilation, inclusion, and exclusion are, from this perspective, merely processes of rewriting. How precisely these rewriting processes of cultures, economic systems, and states occur under pressure from globalization was an essential focus of the exhibition *The Global Contemporary. Art Worlds after 1989* at the ZKM | Center for Art and Media Karlsruhe. This exhibition showed how historical, ethnic, and cultural characteristics are rewritten by the global cultural and economic transformations that are taking place. The world of art offers a glance at these global rewriting processes through a magnifying glass, as it were. The global world system has transformed the global art system.

The Colonial Condition of Modernity. Extrinsic Causes of the Transformations of the Art World

The end of European expansion, that is, the end of the colonial condition, signified the end of modernity. In the twentieth century, the world was subdivided into three social zones. The industrialized nations of Europe, North America, plus Australia, New Zealand, and Japan formed the "First World." The former communist societies in the USSR and Eastern Europe were considered the "Second World." The "rest of the world," which is not white, was called the "Third World," although it contained the majority of the world's population.

The countries of the Third World, from Brazil to India, were almost all colonies of the West from the seventeenth to the early twentieth century. In other words, the Third World is a product of colonization, of the colonial condition. The process of colonization profoundly and enduringly shaped the global map in social and cultural terms. The affluence of the industrialized nations of the First World is causally related to the poverty of the agricultural Third World. In the global colonial condition, agrarian societies form the necessary complement to the industrialized societies. The industrial nations of the First World need the Third World's natural resources (oil, gas, metals, etc.). For this reason, a simple distribution system was enforced; the North industrializing, the South remaining agrarian. The Third World is thus also having to shoulder the burden of mitigating climate change. The asynchrony between the developing countries and the so-called developed nations is thus not due to chance or nature, but a politically controlled and engineered fact. The First and Third World are intimately bound up with each other. The Third World's role is to provide the raw materials, and the First World trains the trading network. The Third World makes commodities and the components available; the First World furnishes the capital and the manufacturing facilities. The division between industrialized nations and agrarian societies is weighing increasingly heavily on today's global society, and without doubt it is a product of colonization. Colonization may only have a five-hundred-year history, but it also has a present because its impact persists. Postcolonialism can be understood as an emerging awareness of the consequences of centuries of colonization of the larger part of the world by the smaller part. The permanent state of the colonial condition is a highly industrialized First World at the cost of the Third World, which is kept in an agrarian state as a resource supplier that cannot make use of its own raw materials, and as a market that buys goods from the First World. Europe subsidizes its farmers and fishermen to ensure that products from Africa remain too expensive, for example, to stop imported chickens and fish from being cheaper than those farmed or caught locally. The First World has little interest in the industrialization of the Third World. Using the World Bank's controlling mechanisms and guiding instruments, the Third World countries are artificially kept in the status of agrarian nations. Emission trading in response to global climate change is today a very visible expression of this policy.

For the colonies were never an end in themselves, but always a means to increase the wealth of the mother country. The rise of the modern capitalist world system depended on colonization, and colonization included slavery. The prosperity of the white immigrants in the colonies rested on the misery of the colored indigenous populations. The affluence in the dominating countries in particular required additional hands to provide the so-called unskilled labor, and these hands were dragged in violently from all over the world. The transatlantic slave trade was thus part of the colonial condition, followed by racism, which to this day is responsible for the problems of immigration, of migration. Capitalism, colonialism, slavery, and racism together form a dynamic quadrupel, whose elements cannot be treated in separation. Together, they created five hundred years of Western hegemony. This hegemony has created a global geography that is based on the structure of exclusion. The capitalist world system and its colonial conditions have constructed a social space in which the "white" nations of the North are included and the "colored" nations of the South with their religions and cultures are excluded. The division into First and Third Worlds is itself such an exclusion. Exclusions for ethnic, religious, ideological, economic, or political reasons are central and dominating strategies of the Western world.

The development of the idea of modernity needs to be considered in this historical context, for modernity is itself part of European expansion. The exclusion strategies of the economic world system also apply to the world system of art. Both modernity and modernism are the result of this Western hegemony. The Third World's cultural exclusion, and until recently, namely 1989, of the Second World as well, is part of the capitalist world system. Since the Berlin Wall came down in 1989 and the Soviet Union's implosion, new art worlds have thus been coming into existence in which the Second and Third Worlds play a central role. Their artists are even conquering the metropolises, museums, biennial, and league tables in the First World. Two sociological analyses are of especial import in this context: Anthony Giddens' theories, that hinge on postmodernism relativizing or concerning itself with the contradictions of modernity, and the theories of Immanuel Wallerstein, who hopes in the Marxist sense that capitalism's inner contradictions will lead to its implosion. Giddens believes two organizational structures are of especial relevance for the development of modernity: the nation-state and the systematic capitalist mode of production. The power of these two complexes has led the West's dominance to spread across the entire globe. A fundamental result of modernization is the globalization that extinguishes the Other.[5] Giddens speaks of the "two main thrusts that drove the spread of modern institutions. The one is the expansion of the capitalist economy, the other the expansion of the territorial system of nation-states."[6]

Starting from the fact that in modernity not only contradictions are visible, but also developmental trends that carry the potential for radical social transformations within them, Giddens develops his "utopian realism," a critical theory of late modernity in which the trends and corrections already latent in modernity become more radical. Instead of the global threat that the interaction of the capitalist global economy could pose, the international division of labor, the system of nation-states and a military world order, Giddens hopes that we will see the contours of a liberal and open, postmodern order emerge. Postmodernism, therefore, takes the place of modernity at the historical juncture when capitalist production and the colonial condition come to an end.

The thought of Immanuel Wallerstein is profoundly informed by the search for the roots of inequality and the battle against the institutions that support inequality in the world. Thus one of his most important books is entitled *World Inequality*,[7] which rephrases the French Revolution's call for equality under the changed conditions of historical capitalism. Wallerstein also accords the nation-state an important role. In the nineteenth century, the claim to equality was coupled with the idea of the nation-state. Every nation had the same right to be free, and within each nation everyone had the same right to liberty, to affluence, and so on. Yet in the twentieth century it soon became clear that such justifications did not suffice. The nation-state was no longer an autonomous unit. Today, the economy is global and extends far beyond the nation-state. This is why Wallerstein also speaks of a "capitalist world economy" and the "modern world system" as logically linked. An Australian company operates multiplex cinemas throughout Europe. A Swedish company builds furniture all over Europe. Banks do business from Hong Kong to London. In other words, globalization is a product of trade, which knows no national borders. Today, globalization means producing and distributing goods to all corners of the globe. Should tax regimes, wages, and so on be too high in one country because of the influence of trade unions, a company simply relocates to neighboring or remote low-wage countries. American products such as computers and smartphones then get manufactured in the land of the ideological enemy, for example, in China. Thus the battle against inequality can not be fought successfully within a nation-state, but only within the global system as a whole.

The modern global system is a capitalist world economy as a result of European expansionism.[8] The capitalist global economy arose in the sixteenth century in Europe on the back of the accumulation of capital, mechanisms of inequality (unequal exchange), and the division of labor. It is immensely important - if the global economy is to function - for the world labor force to be ethnicized, for a correlation to be established between ethnicity and economic role; for example, at the international level by imposing low wages on non-European, Asian, or African workers, or at the national level on immigrants. The visible classification of labor power and ethnic groups provides the index for income

5 See: **Anthony Giddens**, *The Consequences of Modernity*, Stanford University Press, Stanford (CA), 1990, pp. 174ff; translated from the German.

6 **Anthony Giddens**, *Kritische Theorie der Spätmoderne*, Passagen Verlag, Vienna, 1992, pp. 33ff; translated from the German.

7 **Immanuel Wallerstein (ed.)**, *World Inequality. Origins and Perspectives on the World System*, Black Rose Books, Montreal, 1975.

8 See: **Immanuel Wallerstein**, *The Politics of the World-Economy*, Cambridge University Press, Cambridge, 1984. Immanuel Wallerstein, *The Modern World-System*, Academic Press, New York (NY), 1974.

distribution, often justified by appealing to "traditions" that were in reality socially constructed. This institutionalized racism (and it goes beyond xenophobia) is one of the most significant pillars of historical capitalism.[9] Racism serves as an all-embracing ideology to justify inequality.[10] The second key ideology that serves to maintain capitalism is that of universalism. "The belief in universalism has been the keystone of the ideological arch of historical capitalism."[11] While the ideology of racism as a mechanism served to control the direct producers (the laborers) worldwide, the ideology of universalism shored up control of the bourgeoisie. The concept of a neutral universal culture that the ruling cadres of the respective countries all tended to deploy, functioned as the pillar of the global system. The ideology of progress and modernization supported this collection of ideas in forming a universalized whole. Universal culture, a knowledge of the same languages, literary and visual works all became the fraternal signs by which the capital accumulators of the world recognized one another. This universal culture was something that one needed to assimilate to, and historically it aided the expansion of capitalism worldwide. It guaranteed global sales markets for standardized goods, including those of the entertainment and culture industry, for example the worldwide distribution of American movies. In other words, universalism served colonialization and servitude.

The ostensibly contradictory trends of capitalism, ethnicization, and universalism complement one another at different levels for they serve one and the same goal, the accumulation of capital. Ethnicization means the allocation of groups to specific lower rungs of the wage hierarchy. Sexism and racism and other discriminatory practices were all used to justify paying lower wages for certain tasks within end-to-end production chains. According to Wallerstein, households are the smallest units in the world economic system. Domestic labor is just as devalued as the work of a Thai - in order to lower production costs or, by dint of low wage costs, to maximize profits. Ethnicization thus means assigning people to groups whose social status is low or is made low to justify paying them a lower wage.

Ethnicization is therefore a strategy of particularization: groups are isolated from others and are thus constructs. Segments and segregation are created in order to legitimate inequality. The designation "white" or "upper class" is a social construct. Races are created socially by the dominant social forces as are classes, or peripheries and provinces in order to defend the center (where the production and commodity chains converge).[12]

My hypothesis relies neither on Wallerstein's conflict model nor on Giddens' appeasement model, but focuses on a confluence of cultures through rewriting programs.

Modernity, and by extension modern art, were part of European expansion, part of the expansive universal ideology, part of historical capitalism's ideology of progress. Eurocentric culture as part of the capitalist world system that arose around 1500 in Europe is increasingly being questioned by the colonized countries. Contemporary art in the global age addresses the opportunities for a gradual transformation of the culture of this capitalist world system and the attendant difficulties and contradictions as well as the opportunities for developing an understanding of other cultures and their equality, assuming that such art takes such qualities seriously and is worthy of its name.

We are at present witnessing the beginning of a transformation process that needs and utilizes the plethora of biennials in Asia, South America, and the Arab world to take form, whereas modern art, naturally, is defending its position hysterically in the capitalist world system's fairs and auctions by charging high prices. The art that is part of this transformation process can be considered as contemporary, because modern art is not.

Speculum Artis. Intrinsic Reasons for the Transformations of the Art World

Any exhibition can, by virtue of its focus, function like a magnifying glass on the contemporary art world, as art itself is a magnifying glass on the contemporary world.

What we observe through these magnifying glasses are above all transfers and transformations, translations and changes, within the art world and with the world, on a global scale. We recognize there is a new cartography of art as an effect of globalization. New continents and countries, from the Asian to the Arab world, enter the art world. But with this attention shift, we experience not only a remapping of the cartography of art, but also a rewriting of art itself. The canon of modern art linked more or less to the West, to the European-North American axis, is loosening. It may be,

9 **See: Immanuel Wallerstein**, *Historical Capitalism*, Verso, London, 1983.

10 **See: W. E. B. Dubois**, *The Philadelphia Negro: A Social Study*, 1899, where for the first time a Black sociologist showed how the Blacks' social space was hierarchically constructed in terms of unequal wages (for the same activities as those performed by whites).

11 **Wallerstein 1983**, p. 81.

12 **See: Etienne Balibar and Immanuel Wallerstein**, *Race, Nation, Class. Ambiguous Identities*, Verso, London, 1991.

as the eminent art historian T. J. Clark has declared[13] that we are saying farewell to the epoch of modern art at the threshold of the twenty-first century.

We can observe and name at least several transformations. The starting point of these transformations is the evidence that in the global art world everything is contemporary. From the names of museums to titles of auction catalogs the word "modern" is substituted by the word "contemporary." With a fine nose for the zeitgeist the artist Tino Sehgal instructed his performers, the attendants of the German pavilion at the Biennale di Venezia 2005, to sing for every visitor: "Oh, this is so contemporary!" They did not say: "Oh, this is so modern!" We cannot claim that all the art, which is produced now in Asia or Africa, is modern according to the canon of the West. But this art is truly contemporary. To speak about art as contemporary art is already the effect of global transformations. We can therefore decide between external agents of transformations, like economic and political causes, and internal agents which can be tracked in the art system itself. When contemporary art changes the Western canon, it must be possible to identify reasons for these transformations both inside and outside of the art system.

The Paradigm of the Media

It is evident that the most influential paradigm in twentieth century art was the covert hegemony of photography. Famous painters like Francis Bacon, Gerhard Richter, or Andy Warhol have painted photographs or have derived their paintings from photographs. From Constantin Brancusi and Man Ray to Erwin Wurm, sculptors have been influenced by photography. Photographic documents are the remnants of Land art, Performance art, and other genres. Photography was the beginning of a long chain of new technical media of images: film, video, television, computer. The new paradigm of twenty-first century art is the global web, especially since the Web 2.0 revolution: access by all to all media at all times. "Anybody anything anytime anywhere" is the imperative of the new, digital age.[14] The media experience has become universal. "Understanding Media" (M. McLuhan, 1964) is the prerequisite for understanding the world. We experience the world through media. "Whatever we know about society, or indeed about the world in which we live, we know through the mass media."[15] With an iPod everyone can make his own radio program: podcasting instead of broadcasting. With videocasting everyone can make his or her own TV program. With the Net everyone has become a broadcaster.

The advent of new media, new materials, and new technologies has produced a tremendous effect on contemporary art production. Beyond the market and the museums a huge generation of young artists, designers, and architects all over the world have created a new culture, new visual and acoustic worlds in a new architecture. These productions are normally suppressed by art institutions and therefore the general public has no idea what contemporary art is really about. Contemporary artists all over the world, from Chile to China, work in all media. It would not be correct to neglect one medium (painting) at the expense of another (computer). An exhibition on contemporary art should include all media, all genres, and all disciplines, from Sound art to Performance art, from installation to painting, from sculpture to Net art, all contemporary forms of time-based and space-based art, because contemporary artists have expanded their vocabulary in all directions and into all media. The equality of materials and media is the artistic equation of our time. This media justice could also be defined as the postmedia condition, since today everything is a medium, from a car to a painting. The triumph of media is not the existence of a new media art, but their influence and effect on classical art, from painting to sculpture.[16] The postmedia condition is defined by two phases: the equivalence of all media and the mixing of media.

At the end of the twentieth century, after a battle of one hundred years, the equivalence of the media was finally achieved. Media art, from photography to film, became accepted as a genuine medium of art by collectors, curators, and museums. In this phase each medium has unfolded its own intrinsic material and conceptual qualities and possibilities. Painting has demonstrated the intrinsic value of paint by flowing and dripping techniques. Photography has demonstrated its ability to portray the object world realistically. Film has demonstrated its narrative capability. Video has demonstrated its critical subversion of the mass medium of television. Digital art has demonstrated its powers of imagination in virtual worlds. This phase is more or less completed.

The second phase, which is happening now, is the mixing and crossing of the media. Video, for example, triumphs with the narrative imagination of film by using multiple projections instead of one screen, and telling a story from many perspectives at the same time rather than from just one perspective. Video artists establish a strong relationship

13 See: T. J. Clark, *Farewell to an Idea. Episodes from a History of Modernism*, Yale University Press, New Haven (CT), 1999.

14 See: The publication of a series of books by Cynthia Davidson under the titles *Anywise* (1996), *Anybody* (1997), *Anyhow* (1998), *Anytime* (1999), *Anymore* (2000), and *Anything* (2001), MIT Press, Cambridge (MA).

15 Niklas Luhmann, *The Reality of the Mass Media*, Polity Press, Cambridge, 2000, p. 1.

16 See: Rosalind E. Krauss, *"A Voyage on the North Sea." Art in the Age of the Post-Medium Condition*, Thames & Hudson, London, 2000.

to the mass media. They refer to Hollywood stars and Hollywood genres. The mass media play a new role in video art. The border between art and film has blurred. Art as film and film as art has created a new genre. With the availability of new digital cameras and graphics programs, photography is abandoning the realistic world and inventing unseen, virtual worlds. Sculpture can consist of a photo or a videotape. Sculpture can be articulated in any medium: photography, video, or language. Language on LED screens can be a painting, a book, and a sculpture. Video and computer installations can be a piece of literature, architecture, or a sculpture. Photography and video art, originally confined to two dimensions, achieve spatial and sculptural dimensions in installations. Paintings refer to photography or digital graphics programs and use both. The computer graphics programs are called paint programs because they refer to painting. Film is proving to be increasingly dominant in documentary realism, which takes its critique of the mass media from video. The Web supplies dialogs and texts for all media in its chatrooms. The Web can produce self-generative pictures and words.

This mixing of the media has led to extraordinary major innovations in each of the media and in art. No single medium is dominant any longer; instead, all of the different media influence and determine each other. The array of all media forms a universal medium. Most artistic practices are not subordinated to the task of representing reality, but instead make references to media. Most artistic productions use media in reference to other media.

References have replaced reality. Naturally, the effect of this tendency is also a counterreaction: a reenactment of reality, a remaking of historic events, a reentry of history into the present. The reality check is also part of contemporary art practices.

The Substitution of Representation by Reality

However, the media of representation, from painting to video, have not only been transformed, but also substituted. Therefore, in contemporary art we find a mix of representation and reality, and sometime we find only reality, particles of reality, a doubling of reality as art.

Around 1913 the classical program of art, defined by Leonardo da Vinci to "render visible the universal essence of things"[17] by means of the science of painting like line, point, plane, volume, shadow, and light, was disbanded. The end of representing the world of visible things was declared. One school banned the object entirely from painting and just represented the formal elements of painting (lines, points, planes, ...). This representation of the means of the medium painting, starting with Kazimir Malevich and finding in Wassily Kandinsky's book the programmatic title *Point and Line to Plane: Contribution to the Analysis of the Pictorial Elements* (1926), we call abstract art and it dominated painting and sculpture in the twentieth century. But another school declared just the opposite: this school, starting with Marcel Duchamp, introduced the real object into the art system. The representation of reality was declared to be at an end. Instead, two different, even opposite strategies of representation followed: the representation of the means of art and the representation of things. The object as painterly representation was banned, but the real object was introduced. Between this bracket, between this binary opposition, modern art happened and developed. Everything that formerly had been representation was substituted by reality: painted landscapes became Land art; painted still lifes became collages, assemblages, installations, environments of real things; painted portraits became Body art; genre paintings became performances, events, happenings; painted waterfalls were substituted by real artificial waterfalls, painted fire was substituted by real fire. Real air, real earth, and real animals were exhibited and, finally, real people. The classical program of art, representation, came to an end with modern art. Representation was completely substituted by reality, by the reality of the elements of representation or the reality of things.

Slowly a third school arose in the twentieth century, beginning with photography - the reality of media. This school was in conflict with the doctrine of modern art, because photography, film, and video were still media of representation, although they could be combined with real things and real people in installations. Therefore media were very fitting to transform the doctrine of modern art. Media art rewrote modern art by bridging the gap between representation of artistic means and representation of objects. They created a new reality: media reality.

The Performative Turn (The Participation of the Public)

In 1967 Richard Rorty published his famous book *The Linguistic Turn. Essays in Philosophical Method.*[18] This "linguistic turn" summarized a worldview from anthropology (Claude Lévi-Strauss) and psychoanalysis (Jacques Lacan) in which the structure of language formed a universal model. The product of this linguistic turn was Conceptual art. In the 1980s we experienced the return of the image. Therefore, in 1992, W. J. T. Mitchell coined the term "the pictorial turn,"

17 **Leonardo da Vinci**, quoted in: Laura L. Bass, *The Drama of the Portrait: Theater and Visual Culture in Early Modern Spain*, Penn State Press (PA), 2008, p. 36.

18 **Richard Rorty (ed.)**, *The Linguistic Turn. Recent Essays in Philosophical Method*, University of Chicago Press, Chicago (IL), 1967.

which was published in 1994 in his book *Picture Theory*.[19] Also in 1994, the German art historian Gottfried Boehm spoke of the "iconic turn" in his essay "Die Wiederkehr der Bilder" [The Return of the Images].[20] This sequence of turns reminds us a little bit of the sequence of modernity, postmodernity, and second modernity (Heinrich Klotz and Ulrich Beck[21]), or altermodernity (Nicolas Bourriaud[22]). But the decisive book was published in 1961: *How to Do Things with Words* by J. L. Austin, which announced the "performative turn."[23] Since the experimental music of the 1950s (from John Cage to Henri Pousseur) and the experimental poetry (Umberto Eco), the public has been invited to participate in the creation of artworks. The artist is not the sole contributor to the work, there is also the spectator. Marcel Duchamp stated in 1957 in his famous lecture on the creative act: "All in all, the creative act is not performed by the artist alone; the spectator [...] adds his contribution to the creative act."[24] modern art is much more than just abstract painting. The real rupture with classical art is the introduction of real objects, real movements, real time, and finally real people into the art system. In the beginning it was only the artist, who acted in the artwork, but soon the act of performance was transferred by, for example, Happenings, to the spectator and the audience. Since the end of the 1950s, we live - maybe unnoticed - in the age of the performative turn. The arts, from music to sculpture, are immensely influenced by the performance of the public. The performative turn in the arts mirrors the slow dispersal of representative politics by performative politics. This performative turn has an influence on our notion of creativity, on the behavior of the masses, and on our concept of art. First and foremost, we experience the emancipation of the audience: the visitor becomes a user.

The very terms "user innovation" or "consumer-generated content" bear witness to the birth of a new kind of democratic art in which everyone can participate. The model platform for this participation is the Internet, where everyone can post his or her texts, photos, or videos. For the first time in history there is an "institution," a "space" and a "place" where the lay public can offer their works to others with the aid of media art, without the guardians of the art world. Until now, of course, the products of the masses' creativity have been censured. Only museums and other state-owned or privately controlled zones like art magazines or galleries could define what art is and what good art is. They defined and stipulated what could be exhibited. They defined legitimate art. Now the gate is open for illegitimate art.[25] With the advent of picture machines like the photographic camera, painters lost their monopoly on image making. And now, with the existence of the Internet as a global distribution system, art in general has lost its monopoly on creativity. After the expanded arts (George Maciunas), we are living in the epoch of expanded creativity. Everybody is an artist (Joseph Beuys, 1970) and everybody is creative (on the Web). Art loses its image monopoly and its monopoly on creativity. The mass media lose their control function. On the Internet everybody is a distributor. Public activism was already a major factor in revolutionary art practices in the 1960s. Now we have a triumphant comeback of performance practices and strategies, due to public and private activism in the political, social, and artistic spheres performed on social Web platforms and in public spaces.

Rewritings

Some people perceive the transformations of the global world from the perspective of a clash.[26] Some people see these transformations from the perspective of confluence.[27] Our perspective is that we are experiencing an epoch of rewriting programs: rewriting art history, rewriting political and economic history on a global scale. Translations and transfers from one culture to another, in a multilateral and multipolar world, no longer create the hegemony of an international art, but the reevaluation of the local and the regional. We are witnessing the reentry of forgotten and unforeseen parts of geography and history, we experience how historic concepts and events are reenacted. Contemporary art and the contemporary world are part of a global rewriting program. We observe how Indian art rewrites European art and how European art rewrites Indian art, how European art rewrites Asian art and how Asian art rewrites North American art. We are witnessing a new cartography of art in the making. What we see today is a rewriting of technologies, economies, politics, cultures, and art forms. We intend to expose the traces of these rewriting programs in global art that articulate the confluences and influences of cultures. In this sense we are living in a postethnic age; we encounter the postethnic state of art.

19 **William J. Thomas Mitchell**, *Picture Theory. Essays on Verbal and Visual representation*, Chicago University Press, Chicago (IL), 1994.

20 **Gottfried Boehm**, "Die Wiederkehr der Bilder," in: Gottfried Boehm (ed.), *Was ist ein Bild?*, Wilhelm Fink Verlag, Munich, 1994, pp. 11-38.

21 **Ulrich Beck, Anthony Giddens, and Scott Lash (eds.)**, *Reflexive Modernization: Politics, Tradition and Aesthetics in the Modern Social Order*, Stanford University Press, Stanford (CA), 1994; Heinrich Klotz, *Die Zweite Moderne: Eine Diagnose der Kunst der Gegenwart*, C. H. Beck, Munich, 1996.

22 **Nicolas Bourriaud (ed.)**, *Altermodern: Tate Triennial*, Tate, London, 2009.

23 **John Langshaw Austin**, *How to Do Things with Words*, Clarendon Press, Oxford, 1962.

24 **Marcel Duchamp**, *The Creative Act*, 1957, available online at: http://www.ubu.com/papers/duchamp_creative.html, accessed 12/11/12.

25 **See: Pierre Bourdieu**, *Un art moyen. Essai sur les usages sociaux de la photographie*, Minuit, Paris, 1965.

26 **See: Huntington 1996.**

27 **See: Trojanow and Hoskoté 2007.**

From Art World to Art Worlds

Hans Belting and Andrea Buddensieg

The concept of a global production of contemporary art was discussed for the first time in the Paris exhibition *Magiciens de la terre* in 1989. Its date coincided with the end of the Cold War which also meant the emergence of the New Economy with its multinational corporations. In subsequent years the spread of worldwide biennials changed contemporary art's geography forever. A new generation of artists not only claimed international recognition but proclaimed coevalness in a worldwide *koine* of art. Copresence with the western art scene replaced their nonpresence, which had been a result of exclusion. Today's art presents itself not only as new art, but also as a new kind of art, an art that is expanding all over the globe. Art no longer aims at the avant-garde position of modern art, but presents itself as contemporary, in a chronological, symbolical, and even ideological sense. Thus, twenty-first century art testifies to worldwide contemporaneity without limits of the kind imposed by the western privilege of history.

The last remaining stronghold of the western art concept is the notion of a single and independent art world which is believed to survive even today as a global art world, again in the singular. But, in fact, this belief is contradicted by the recent emergence of several art worlds that coexist and compete in the wake of the global practice of contemporary art. The mapping of new art regions with a transnational character, such as the Asia-Pacific region or the one in the Middle East, is clear proof of the formation of specific art worlds where art meets different conditions and cultural traditions. Their claims to be contemporary have emerged as their all-defining feature (see: this volume pp. 100ff). With respect to the plurality of worlds, as a contemporary condition, anthropologists have today developed a pertinent model. Marc Augé describes their new fieldwork as "an anthropology of contemporaneous worlds"[1] and argues that the contemporary "is made up of several worlds" (see: this volume pp. 246ff). The global reality is, in fact, no longer synonymous with the all-encompassing term "world," but is composed of a multiplicity of worlds. This conclusion is not only valid for societies and cultures at large, but also includes the newly established art worlds. The resulting multiplicity of art worlds is in part explained by the observation that *art* production is turning increasingly into *culture* production, especially in such places where art is still a new experience and needs the support of local traditions of visual production.

Contemporary art today means art after modernism, just as it once meant modern art. Modern art always had the purpose of distinction and absolute power. Modern history separated the world, since it wasn't everyone's history. Hence the term "contemporary" serves as a beacon to guide artists past old borders. Artists from developing countries take up positions against the modernist legacy simply because they feel compromised by its colonial history. The West always wanted to stay modern, even when it was proclaiming postmodernism in order to remain modern in other ways. Likewise, Nicolas Bourriaud's concept of "altermodernity"[2] once again lays claim to leadership. But what happens to all those who were never modern and could only assert the right of alternative modernities?

Global art differs not only from modern art, but also from world art (see: this volume pp. 178ff) with which it is still so often identified. World art continues to mean the art of all ages and peoples that the West musealized in colonial times, thus safeguarding a mainstream concept of art. Contemporaneity was excluded from world art, since the latter seemed to lack the experience of modernity. Whereas the term "world literature" also includes contemporary literature, world art has become synonymous with the world legacy of art, which is why it was first shown in curiosity cabinets and then in colonial museums, but not in art mu-

1 See: **Marc Augé**, *An Anthropology of Contemporaneous Worlds*, Stanford University Press, Palo Alto (CA), 1999.

2 **Nicolas Bourriaud**, *The Radicant*, Lucas & Sternberg, New York (NY), 2002, pp. 25ff.

seums. World art, therefore, no longer covers today's art production. In the museum, for a long time physical ownership included the right of interpreting what it owned. But the new art worlds are opposing and replacing the colonial history of world art.

Today we experience a new kind of mapping, in which the label of identity serves as distinction. Yet migration has for a long time accelerated the new global mobility of cultures. Arjun Appadurai, who coined the term "ethnoscapes," argues against a geographical definition of cultures, since the majority of their main representatives are already living in the diaspora.[3] Salman Rushdie, in his essay "Imaginary Homelands"[4] from 1981, sees people in the diaspora as rooted "[...] in ideas rather than places, in memories as much as in material things."[5] Diaspora, once an important issue for Africans and Afro-Americans, has again become an experience for Chinese artists who went into exile after the events of 1989. In general, the concept of diaspora, however, is losing its distinction between homeland and abroad with the emergence of multicultural societies. An unprecedented mobility has also reached the lives of artists who enjoy fellowships for artist-in-residence programs and train in international art academies. In addition, the use of electronic communication has changed their working habits and allows them to cooperate with other artists who live on different continents. In this situation, artists often appropriate fictional identities, with which they respond to other environments and escape the racist prejudice of being "different."

Since globalization creates a new world map of art, it raises the question as to how such a map might be drawn and what should be marked on it. This issue results in a hectic competition in which new art regions struggle for their profile. More than one hundred biennials, in which *traveling* curators operate as global agents, present packages of international plus regional art to a cosmopolitan audience in ever-new venues. This is the quintessential constellation of art's globalization. The new professional profile of curators, who are increasingly trained in so-called Curatorial Studies, helps to promote art as a critical practice that represents global issues for a local audience.

But globalization, on the other hand, is a power struggle where markets, in the end, become an obstacle to the world's growing together. It has roots both in modernization and in colonialization and, consequently, contemporaneity is an attempt to break free of these roots. Temporality, as the experience of time, and contemporaneity, as simultaneity, do not necessarily mean the same thing. The experience of time might differ in traditional cultures where people feel to live in their own time. Unlike traditional cultures, the modern West broke with its own past and in the same spirit, colonized time as world time.

The polycentric *practice* of art flagrantly contradicts the old claim to a single, universally valid *idea* of art. But the expanding art markets, on the other hand, tend to regulate such an art practice and trade art as a new kind of currency or branding for an international clientele. As a result, many artists increasingly express open or covert criticism of the art market, or deliberately avoid a profile that conforms to the market. One of these strategies is to place the production of one's own work in the hands of copyists who devalue the status of the "original." Thus, *Liu Ding's Store* (see: this volume, pp. 266ff and pp. 422–423) offers objects for made-up prices in order to expose the market's real prices as fiction and to oppose the rules of the art trade.

As was to be expected, expanded art production leads to a crisis of the art concept whose limits cannot be extended at will. In fact, the global practice of art deliberately accepts the loss of a binding concept in favor of penchants for national, cultural, and religious connotations of art. Artists often address an audience without proper art experience and are expected to respond to cultural traditions that have not already been filtered through modernity and colonialization. At the same time, art also turns against a privilege of representation that was limited to the West and excluded any other art in that capacity. Representation always meant more than just representation of the visual world, but included representation of social and political realities. Curating art after the global turn means translating art for new audiences. Wherever artists work without the protection of a proper art scene, they easily trigger conflicts with censorship. In the same way, the Internet is considered a threat by authoritarian regimes when it strives for freedom of expression.

This book undertakes the attempt to draw a first conclusion in discussing globalization, which has produced a new kind of contemporary art over the past twenty years. It presents the results of the exhibition *The Global Contemporary. Art Worlds after 1989* that opened on September 17, 2011 at the ZKM | Center for Art and Media Karlsruhe, Germany. Rather than being an exhibition catalog, the book incorporates benefits reaped from the exhibition experience. Even the exhibition itself was conceived as a work in progress. Throughout its duration, it constantly changed as the result of an artist-in-residence program, which provided

3 See: **Arjun Appadurai**, *Modernity at Large: Cultural Dimensions of Globalization*, University of Minnesota Press, Minneapolis (MN), 1996.

4 See: **Salman Rushdie**, *Imaginary Homelands: Essays and Criticism, 1981–1991*, Granta, London, 1991.

5 **Rushdie 1991**, p. 124.

guest artists with an opportunity to bring in their own viewpoints. The exhibition, for its part, grew out of the project GAM - Global Art and the Museum, for which the research was initiated by the ZKM in 2006. Two columns of the GAM website www.globalartmuseum.de regularly present a "Monthly Guest Author" and "The MoCA of the Month." In the latter case, we selected museums which reveal changes that have been going on in global art production for the past 20 years. Three volumes presenting the results of conferences at the ZKM, such as "Where Is Art Contemporary" (2007) and seminars such as "Contemporary Art and the Global Age" (2009) or "Global Studies" (2010 and 2011) have been published on the theme to date.[6]

The book is introduced by an interview, which Manthia Diawara conducted with Édouard Glissant during a boat trip from Southampton to New York in 2009, shortly before Glissant's death. The poet and philosopher from Martinique always drew on his personal experience of "creolization" in the archipelago of the Caribbean when he explained the role of culture and identity in today's world. We are all "inhabitants of the archipelago" (see: this volume, pp. 35ff). In the interview, he resumes the main ideas of his last book *Philosophie de la Relation* (2009)[7] in which he turns against the modernist myth of the universal. "Relation is made up of all the differences in the world," and creolization is the sign of a "state of perpetual change" (see: this volume, p. 38). It marks "a permanent process that supersedes historical avatars" (see: this volume, p. 38). Glissant deserves a place of honor as the last of the great generation of African and Afro-American writers who have created the postcolonial spirit in cultural theory.

Rasheed Araeen, the Pakistan-born London artist and art critic, holds a prominent place in the documentary section. On the eve of globalization, in 1987, he founded the magazine *Third Text* as a critical forum, for a long time the only one, for *Third World perspectives* on art and culture, to quote the subtitle of the first decade. The goal was to discuss "the institutional closures of the art world and the artists they excluded."[8] Soon, the periodical also became the focus of a new kind of cultural theory that was not yet acceptable in mainstream circles. For the exhibition, Araeen contributed the installation *The Reading Room, 1979–2011*, which presented a complete set of *Third Text* editions as the artist's alternative "critical practice" to express himself. His editorial activity persistently centered on the need for the recovery of the other, neglected story of modern art.

This volume is divided into three sections. One part, *The Room of Histories*, contains a documentation on the globalization of art, whose space served as an introduction to the exhibition (see: this volume, pp. 49–176). A second part includes essays, largely written for this occasion, which provide general perspectives on the state of the arts today. These have been divided into thematic groups such as the change from a single art world to a plurality of competing art worlds (see: this volume, pp. 177–321). A new role is being played by anthropology, which is gaining increasing significance in the discussion of contemporary art. This is no longer the role of "the artist as ethnographer" which Hal Foster had described as the "ethnographic turn" in 1996.[9] Today, art production with its cultural diversity addresses the curator as an ethnographer. At the same time the ethnographer acts as an art critic. For this reason, we also invited anthropologists to offer their own views on today's art practice. The essays deal with general themes, but also with the situation in specific geographic areas. A third part provides eight different views from the exhibition. They relate to the thematic units which have structured the exhibition at ZKM. Artists were selected with respect to their contribution to these thematic units. The sections carry the following titles: "World Time: The World as Transit Zone," "Real Worlds and Picture Worlds," "World Art: The Curiosity Cabinet in Postcolonial Times," "Boundary Matters: The Practice of Art After Modernity," "Networks & Systems: Globalization as Subject," "Art as Commodity: The New Economy and the Art Markets," "Lost in Translation: New Artists' Biographies," and finally the "Artist-in-Residence Program."

The *Room of Histories* is an attempt to illustrate, in a graphic manner, the production and distribution of art (biennials, art fairs, institutions) in today's world. Using aids such as timelines, maps, and catalogs, the documentation serves to put individual aspects of the globalization process into focus. In our book, we have tried to recover the visual experience that awaited the visitor in the exhibition. Beginning with a timeline for the year 1989 and an overview of the current global vocabulary, the *Room of Histories* is divided into seven sections. The first is dedicated to exhibitions

6 **See: Andrea Buddensieg and Peter Weibel (eds.)**, *Contemporary Art and the Museum. A Global Perspective*, Hatje Cantz, Ostfildern, 2007; Hans Belting and Andrea Buddensieg (eds.), *The Global Art World. Audiences, Markets, and Museums*, Hatje Cantz, Ostfildern, 2009; Hans Belting, Jacob Birken, Andrea Buddensieg, and Peter Weibel (eds.), *Global Studies. Mapping Contemporary Art and Culture*, Hatje Cantz, Ostfildern, 2011.

7 **See: Édouard Glissant**, *Philosophie de la Relation. Poésie en étendue*, Gallimard, Paris, 2009.

8 **Sean Cubitt**, "In the Beginning: *Third Text* and the Politics of Art," in: *The Third Text Reader on Art, Culture and Theory*, Continuum Books, London, New York (NY), 2002, pp. 1–8, p. 3.

9 **Hal Foster**, The Return of the Real: the Avant-garde at End of the Century, The MIT Press, Cambridge (MA), 1996, p. 182.

that made history. The second section introduces nineteen recent "Art Spaces," that have changed the traditional profile of the art museum in various parts of the world. The section "Branding" presents the breakneck development of new art markets, above all in Asia, with the help of statistics and diagrams that owe much to the advice of the economist Clare McAndrew from Dublin. The section "Mapping" offers an overview of a new geography of art that emerges as the result of the worldwide expansion of biennials. The documentation includes a selection called "Global News from *The Art Newspaper*" which features a critical collection from the magazine *The Art Newspaper* that was presented and commented on the GAM website over the span of two years (2009-2011). Finally, the project *trans_actions*, which was commissioned by the ZKM, represents a new tool for visualizing the temporal and spatial data of biennials and art markets via a cinematic projection on ZKM's *PanoramaScreen*.

We would like to convey our sincere thanks to Peter Weibel who had the vision to initiate the research project GAM at the ZKM. He also was the driving force behind the *The Global Contemporary* exhibition in his capacity of its main curator. As early as 1996, he curated the exhibition *Inclusion : Exclusion*, which was one of the very first projects to address the global issue in the art scene, at the Neue Galerie in Graz, Austria. The advisory board proved to be of great importance for the selection of artists and the choice of thematic units in the ZKM show. It is therefore a pleasant duty to thank N'Goné Fall (Dakar, Paris), Patrick D. Flores (Manila), Carol Yinghua Lu (Beijing), and Jim Supangkat (Djakarta) for a vital exchange of ideas during our meetings in Karlsruhe. The exhibition was initially conceived as a traveling project that would begin in Karlsruhe and take on a different profile, as it changed curators with each new venue - in other words, it would be an ongoing process on a global scale. However, it was not possible to realize the project in this manner at the time. Therefore, it is our hope that this book will travel instead and familiarize the reader with an exhibition unseen and incomplete by its own definition.

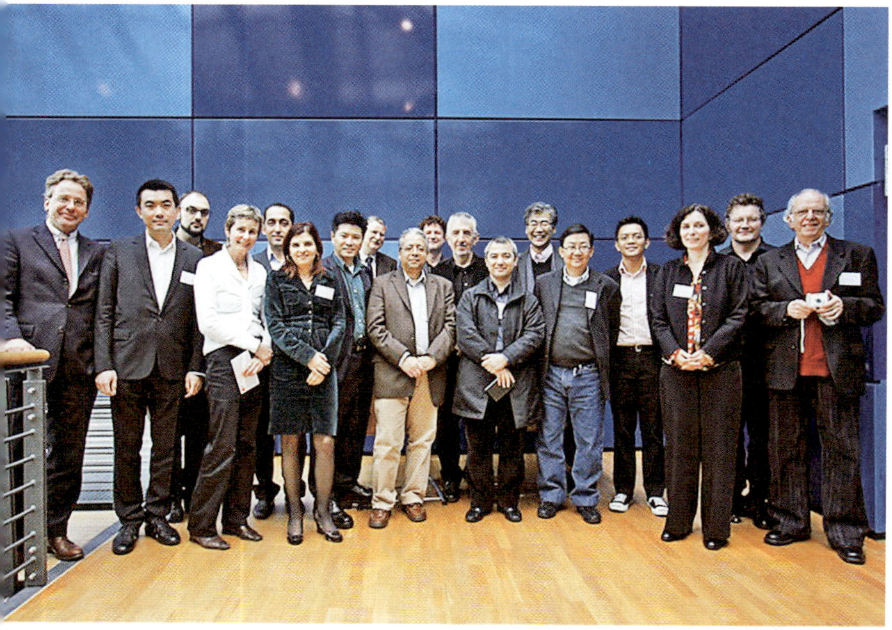

1

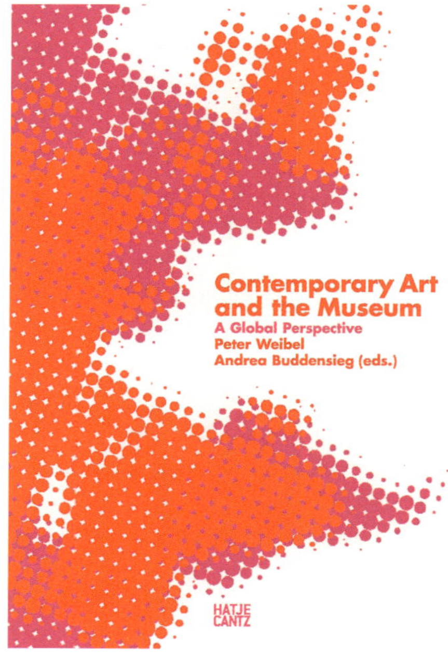

2

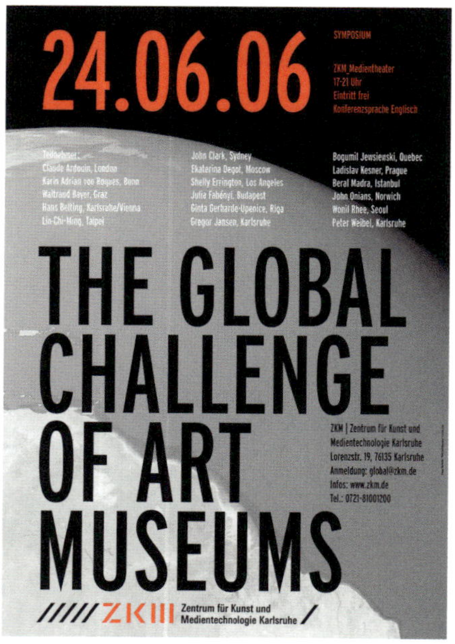

3

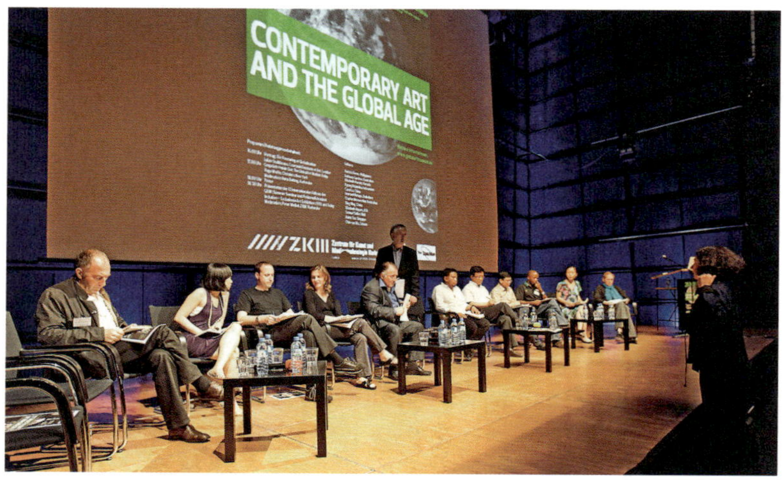

4

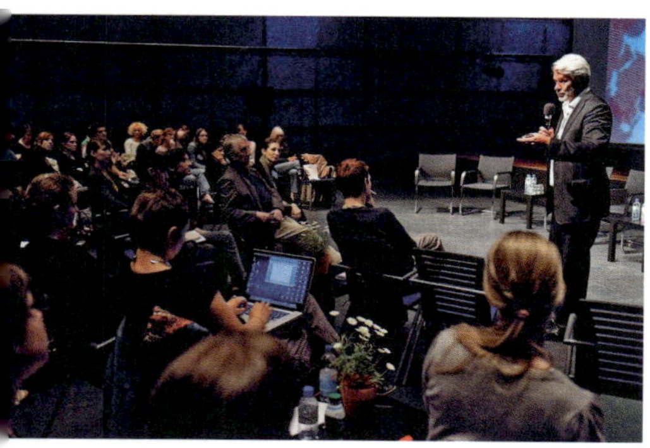

5

1 **Conference "Where is Art Contemporary? The Global Challenge of Art Museums II,"** ZKM | Karlsruhe, October 19–20 ,2007

Participants from left to right: Hans-Joachim Petersen, Eugene Tan, Miguel A. Hernández, Koeki Claessens, Ebrahim Melamed, Mirjam Shatanawi, Wonil Rhee, Michael Hübl, Claude Ardouin, Gregor Jansen, Hans Belting, Rafael Sámano, Fumio Nanjo, Oscar Ho Hing Kay, Ramón Lerma, Andrea Buddensieg, Colin Richards, Ángel Kalenberg

2 **First publication of the GAM series:** Peter Weibel and Andrea Buddensieg (eds.), *Contemporary Art and the Museum*, ZKM | Karlsruhe and Hatje Cantz, Ostfildern, 2007

3 **Poster** of the conference "The Global Challenge of Art Museums," June 24, 2006, at ZKM | Karlsruhe

4 **ZKM Summer Seminar "Contemporary Art and the Global Age,"** June 21– July 1, 2009

Public panel discussion at ZKM, June 28, 2009 with the participants, from left to right: Charles Merewether, Adele Tan, Anthony Gardner, Elizabeth Harney, Peter Weibel, Hans Belting, Agung Hujatnika, Ding Ning, Patrick D. Flores, Jesmael Mataga, Carol Yinghua Lu, Elizabeth Rogers

5 **ZKM Global Studies, "Art and Visual Media Today,"** June 18–20, 2010

Chris Dercon giving a lecture.

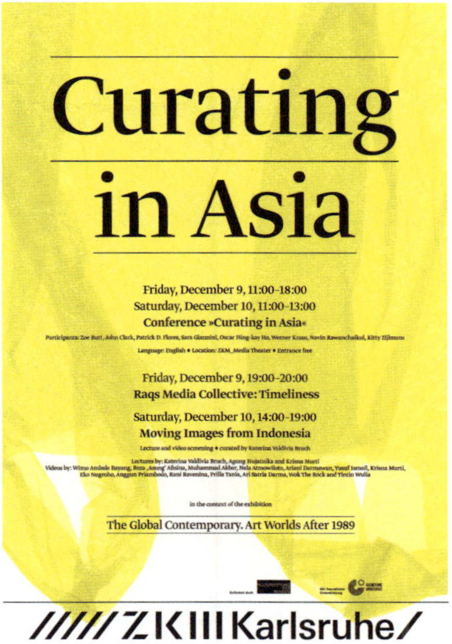

6

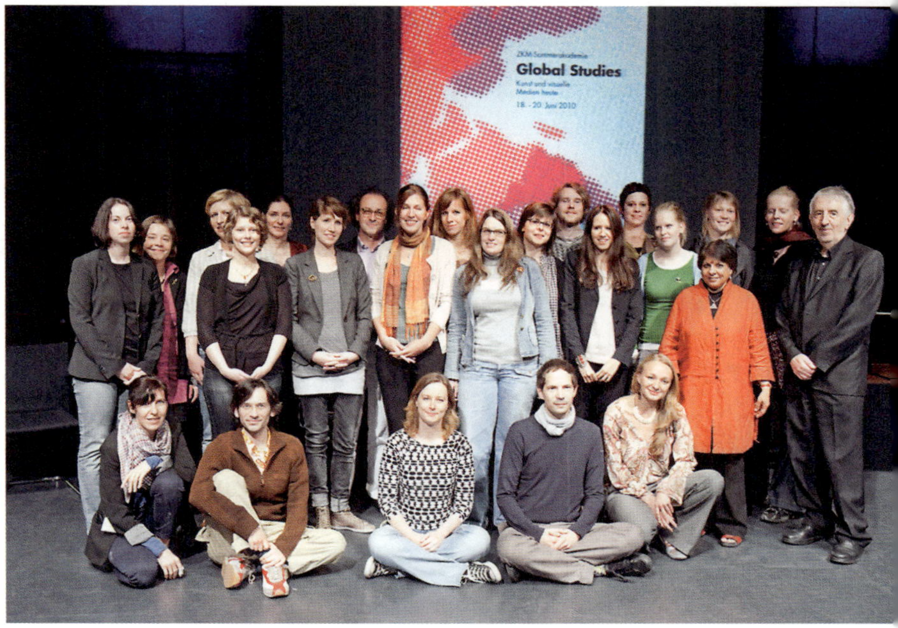

7

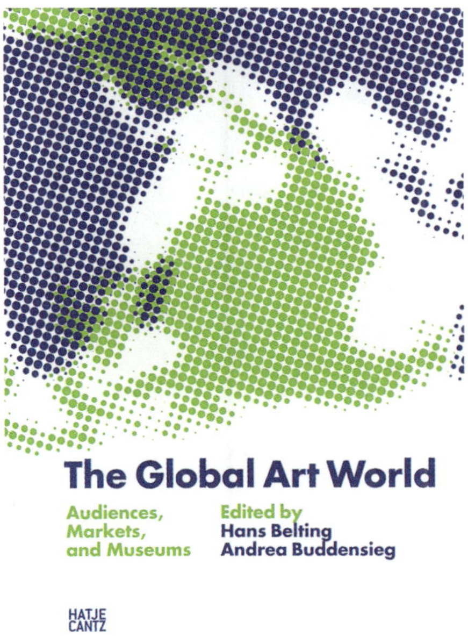

8

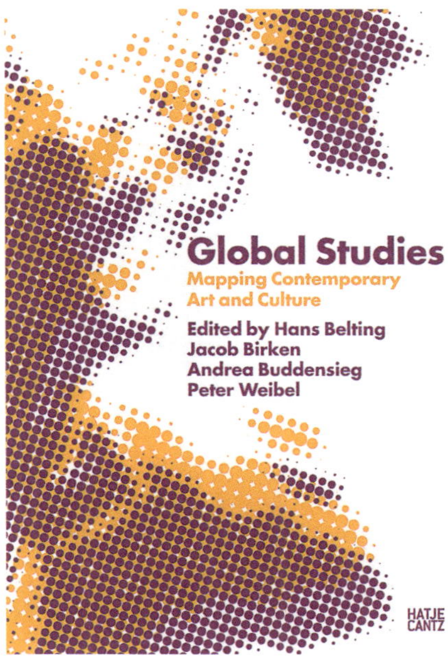

9

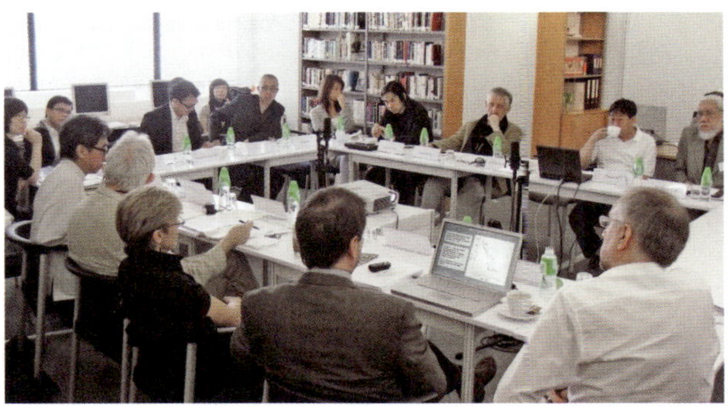

10

6 **Poster** for conference "Curating in Asia" at ZKM | Karlsruhe, December 9–10, 2011.

7 **ZKM Global Studies "Art and Visual Media Today,"** June 18–20, 2010

Participants from left to right: Anne Linden, Nadine Siegert, Barbara Wolner, Julia Binter, Andrea Buddensieg, Henrike Plegge, Thomas Fillitz, Noemie Jäger, Nicole Müllerschön, Chrischona Schmidt, Birgit Hopfener, Sebastian Baden, Rania Gaafar, Cathrine Bublatzky, Anna Grasskamp, Monica Juneja, Ulrike Heine, Isabel Seliger, Hans Belting in the front: Antonia Marten, Jacob Birken, Daniela Wolf, Markus Hafner, Irina Vogelsang

8 **Second publication of the GAM series:** Hans Belting and Andrea Buddensieg (eds.), *The Global Art World. Audiences, Markets and Museums*, ZKM | Karlsruhe and Hatje Cantz, Ostfildern, 2009.

9 **Third publication of the GAM series:** Hans Belting, Jacob Birken, Andrea Buddensieg and Peter Weibel (eds.), *Global Studies. Mapping Contemporary Art and Culture*, ZKM | Karlsruhe and Hatje Cantz, Ostfildern, 2011.

10 **GAM Platform III "A New Geography of Art in the Making"** at Goethe-Institut Hong Kong

Participants at the table from bottom right: David Clarke, James Elkins, Jane DeBevoise, John Clark, Johnson Chang Tsong-zung, Nathalie Boseul Shin, Patrick D. Flores, Zhuan Huang, Ju Lie, Claire Hsu, Kuroda Raiji, Hans Belting, Oscar Ho Hing Kay, Jim Supangkat

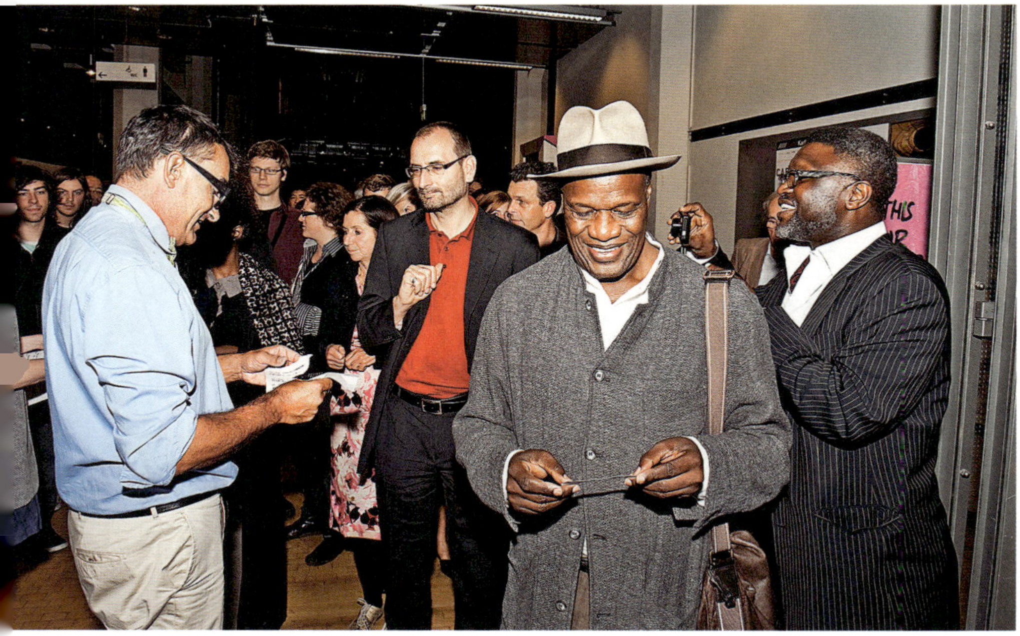

11

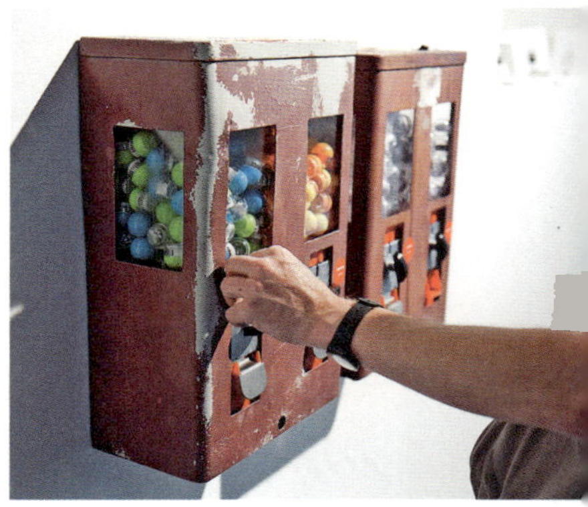

12

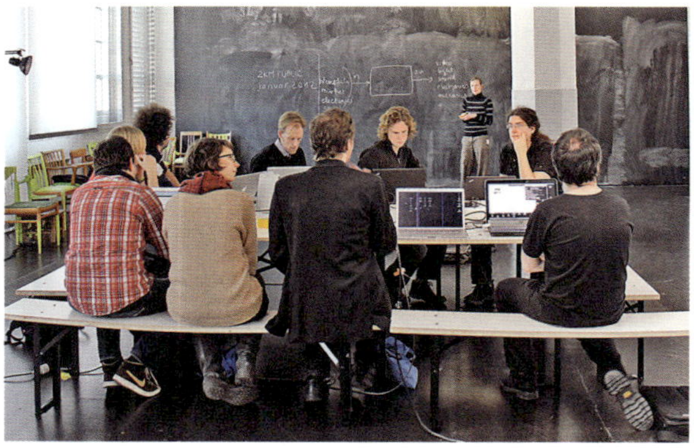

13

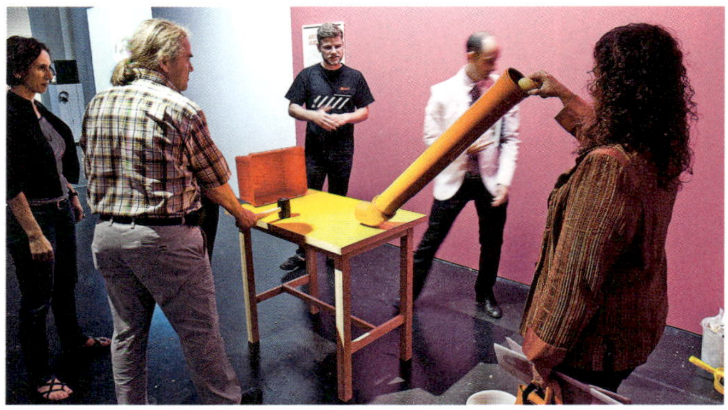

14

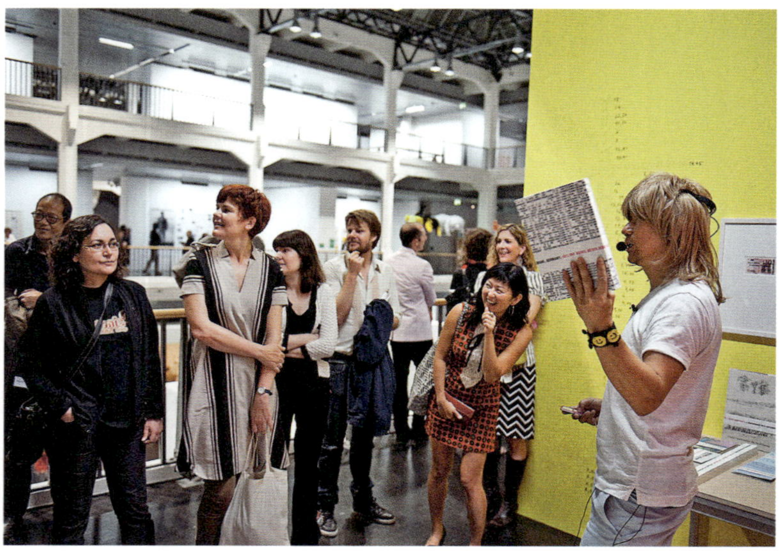

15

11 **Opening of the exhibition** *The Global Contemporary. Art Worlds after 1989*. In the front Thierry Geoffroy inviting Manthia Diawara and Mansour Ciss Kanakassy for a biennalist action.

12 **In the frame of the educational program** of the exhibition, a group of students participating in the project *Cultural.Explorers!* shared their knowledge on the topic of globalization and offered it for sale via chewing-gum dispensers in the exhibition.

13 **Antidatamining Workshop** "Global Databases & Manipulation Strategies" by RYBN in the studio of the exhibition *The Global Contemporary*, January 13–15, 2012.

Workshop in the context of the seminar "Globalization, Contemporary Art and Forms of Artistic Mediation," a project on the Interface of School and Museum in cooperation with the University of Education Karlsruhe.

14 **Opening of the exhibition** *The Global Contemporary. Art Worlds after 1989*. Visitors testing SUPERFLEX' interactive installation *FREE BEER & COUNTER-GAME STRATEGIES*

15 **Opening of the exhibition** *The Global Contemporary. Art Worlds after 1989*. Surasi Kusolwong's performance *50% OFF BOOKS (Never Mind Kapital = Never Mind Kunst)*

Conversation with Édouard Glissant aboard the RMS Queen Mary 2

Manthia Diawara (August 2009)

Manthia Diawara
We're traveling aboard the Queen Mary 2, on our way to New York from Southampton. Why a ship, when it would have been easier and faster to travel on a plane?

Édouard Glissant
Ever since I started having heart trouble, I've been unable to take long-distance flights. And since it's eight and a half hours from Paris to Fort-de-France, I'm obliged to take the boat, and this one is pretty much the only one that makes regular trips. It's all quite ambiguous, because you'd think that a boat is a sign of comfort and ease, but in my opinion it's quite the opposite. It's a sign of catching up the time lost; the time that you cannot let slip away or run away, the times that you become caught up in things - you can't flee or run anywhere. It seems to me that on any kind of boat you can be closer to yourself, while in a plane you're really detached from yourself - you're not yourself, you're something else. And I'm saying this jokingly - and I'm not alone in this - it's not normal for a person to be suspended in the air even if man's always dreamed of being a bird. Accordingly, I take this boat regularly when I have to go to Martinique or New York.

Diawara
I gather that crossing the Atlantic in a ship also gives you time to think about the past, the present, and the future. It recalls for me not only the slave ships, but also the New World and an important landmark for the creation of the African diaspora.

Glissant
That's another matter. It's also a paradox, because this is an ultra-comfortable, super-luxurious ship... and when you lean over the ship's railing, you can't stop thinking about the Africans at the bottom of the sea. It's not the same route, but you think about it just the same. It seems to me that it's another way of meditating on what's happened in the world. Christopher Columbus had left for what was called the New World and I'm the one who returned from it [laughs]. And being on this boat - well, it's not exactly revenge, which would be the stupidest thing to say - but it's a turn of events to know that my ancestors had left for the New World in terrible conditions very much unlike these. There is a return, because right from the start, the whole setup - Africa/middle of the ocean/arrival - is an enslaving, colonialist setup: it's the moment when the African diaspora became a forced diaspora. And the return occurs when slavery and domination disappear. That's why I said that Columbus leaves, but I'm the one who returns. I don't mean myself, Édouard Glissant. What I mean is that those who were forced to leave as slaves do not return as slaves, but as something else: a free entity, not only free but a being who has gained something in comparison to the mass of humanity. And what has this being gained? Multiplicity! In relation to the unity of the enslaving will, we have the multiplicity of the antislavery will. That is what we've gained, and that is the true return.

Diawara
A boat connotes a departure from point A and an arrival at point B - in this context, it is a departure for the Africans who are captured for the first time and pushed onto a boat. What does departure mean to you?

Glissant
It's the moment when one consents not to be a single being and attempts to be many beings at the same time.

In other words, for me every diaspora is the passage from unity to multiplicity. I think that's what's important in all the movements of the world, and we, the descendants, who have arrived from the other shore, would be wrong to cling fiercely to this singularity which had accepted to go out into the world. Let us not forget that Africa has been the source of all kinds of diaspora - not only the force of diaspora imposed by the West through the slave trade, but also of millions of all types of diaspora before - that have populated the world. One of Africa's vocations is to be a kind of foundational unity, which develops and transforms itself into a diversity. And it seems to me that, if we don't think about that properly, we won't be able to understand what we ourselves can do, as participants in this African diaspora to help the world to realize its true self, in other words its multiplicity, and to respect itself as such.

Diawara
The middle of the Atlantic, just like the middle in every narrative, represents a moment of uncertainty before the moment of arrival or change, or rupture. What is the mid-point of the Atlantic for you?

Glissant
First, we must think about the following. When the caravels arrived on the African coasts, the Africans had never seen a covered boat. They didn't understand this boat that wasn't open. Their politics was a politics of the open boat, not the closed one. And furthermore, when they were transported across the ocean, they didn't understand this river without a shore on both sides, so the Middle Passage was truly the unknown: no shore to their right, no shore to their left, and nothing in front of them - the complete unknown. The first chapter of my book *Poetics of Relation* describes this situation, saying that what characterizes the Africans' situation in this adventure is the abyss, the abyss of the unknown, the abyss of the ocean floor, of course, but also the two nonexistent shores, the unknown that lies before, the unknown country at which they will arrive; nobody knew what was awaiting these people who were already slaves.

The Africans in the New World - African-Americans, but also the Antilleans, Brazilians, etc. - escaped the abyss and carry within them the abyss's dimension. And I think the abyss's dimension is not, contrary to what one might believe, the dimension of unity, but rather the dimension of multiplicity. And we have to bring all that together, explore it so that we can see where we're going.

Diawara
Where we're going? Are we arriving somewhere? Still, a story has a point of arrival. So what is that arrival point for us?

Glissant
For me, the arrival is the moment when all the components of humanity - not just the African ones - consent to the idea that it is possible to be one and multiple at the same time; that you can be yourself and the Other; that you can be the Same and the Different. When that battle - because it is a battle, not a military but a spiritual one - when that battle is won, a great many accidents in human history will have ended, will be abolished.

Diawara
In the Anglophone world, scholars and artists, following Paul Gilroy, have been using the concept of the "Black Atlantic" to attempt to give similar explanations of the condition of the people of the African diaspora. What do you think of the theory of the Black Atlantic?

Glissant
I respect the work of these thinkers who are African-Americans for the most part. I think that, deep down, in the idea of the Black Atlantic there is more of a persistence of that kind of unity than they would have us believe. I think that part of the African genius - not the Black race's - is multiplicity. The diaspora is exploding forth everywhere; it is not concentrated in a single area. So for me the Atlantic is a continent, not an archipelago. And we are inhabitants of an archipelago. When the colonizers attacked Africa, it wasn't a continent, but an archipelago. Consider that NATO stands for North Atlantic Treaty Organization. I believe the arrival of the Africans within the phenomenon of slavery is not about the Atlantic, but the Caribbean. That's where they arrived: in Louisiana, the islands, Cuba, Jamaica, Martinique, and it spread from there across the new continent. And the Caribbean is the source, the origin of the plantation system that began to contain and signify the existence of the Blacks. So I'm not an Atlanticist, nor am I continental. I think that the "archipelagization" of the deportation of the Africans is a reality, a precious one. That is why, for all the esteem I have for the theoreticians of the Black Atlantic, I don't agree with their thesis.

Diawara
Do you address the same critique of unity to Négritude?

Glissant
Yes, but bear in mind that, historically, Négritude was an absolutely necessary movement. When Négritude intervened in the history of Black people, above all in

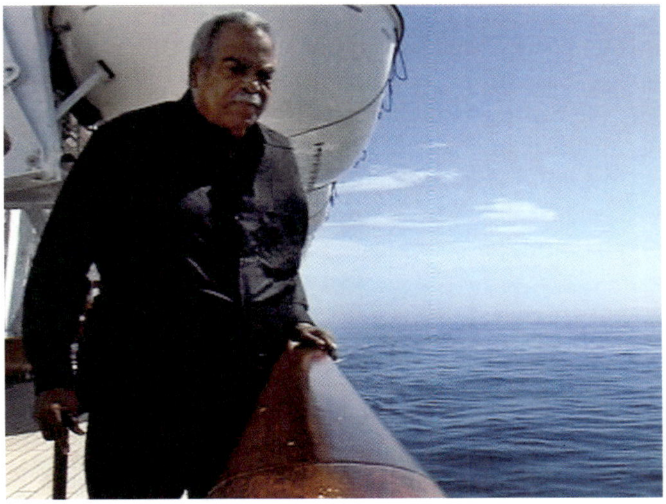

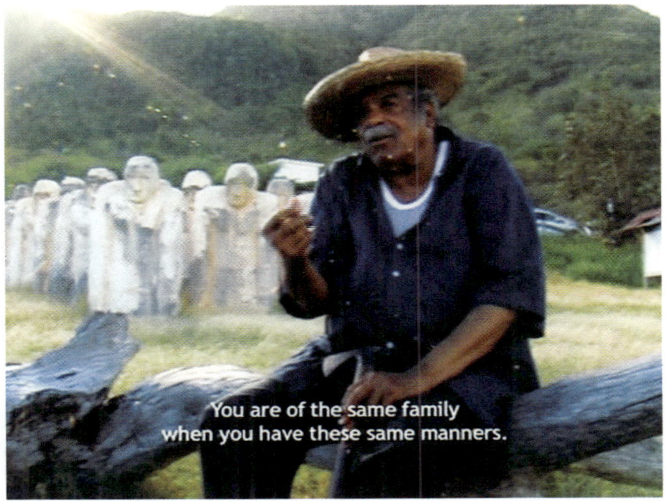

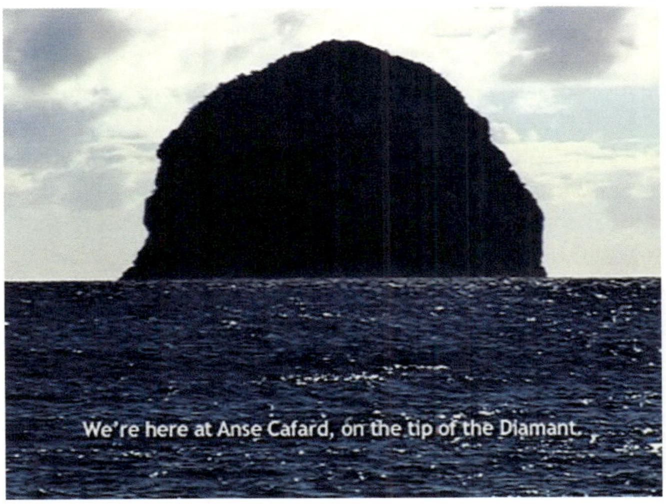

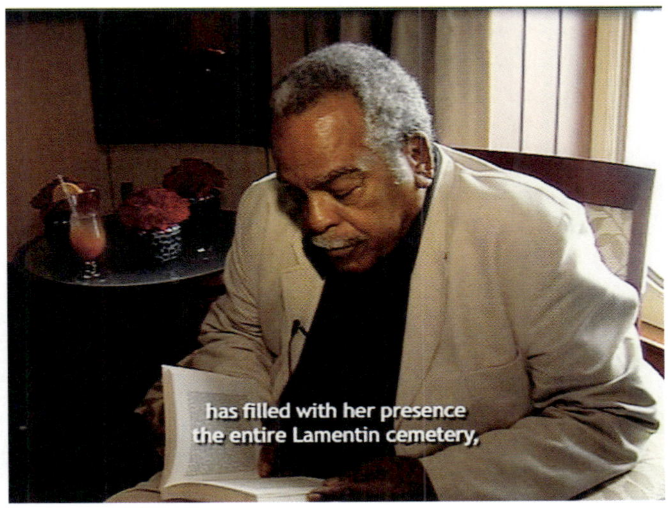

Manthia Diawara, *Édouard Glissant: Un monde en relation*, 2009, video, color, sound, 50 min., video stills

the history of Black people in the New World, it did so to restore balance to our souls and our spirituality, something that appeared quite improbable to us, because we held ourselves in contempt, we had no consideration for ourselves, and we knew nothing of African civilizations and cultures. In other words, Négritude was utterly necessary. I have always been hesitant to subscribe to Négritude completely, because I thought that it was nonetheless a kind of general idea. Blacks are not all the same. A Black from Brazil and a Black from the United States are not the same. So we have to establish nuances, we have to bring out the specific richness of each. There's African-American richness, Brazilian richness, Martinican richness, Cuban richness, etc., and we shouldn't try to bring everything under the same uniform model. Paradoxically, I think that in its beginnings at least, the theory of Négritude was greatly inspired by French intellect, because that intellect is generalizing, given to generality, whereas the British, Anglophone intellect is empiricist and not very interested in general ideas. That's why from the start Anglophone Africans were not at all partisans of Négritude. Wole Soyinka said the most unbelievable things about Négritude when he spoke of "tigritude," the tiger lives his tigritude and doesn't need to proclaim it, etc. All this because even as Anglophone Africa was fighting for the rights of Black people, there wasn't a felt need for a theory of Négritude as a generalizing unity that would encompass everyone. One day, a commander of a liberation army told me: "Wherever Black people are suffering, Négritude is completely necessary. But whenever they pick up a rifle, they no longer need it." In other words, it's a general idea that can be conceived within suffering, but when you particularize yourself by affirming the multiplicity of your being, you no longer need this general theory.

Diawara
Was the Créolité movement an answer to the paradoxes of Négritude, or is it just another form of "Atlanticism"?

Glissant
I don't think it's an answer, no. I believe that the Créolité movement is like Négritude: it has some real justifications, namely, that a large number of the African population, in particular the Brazilians, Antilleans, Caribbeans, were formed on the basis of a mixed reality, or a will towards that reality. You can't say that the Caribbean is not *mestizo.* What's important is that Caribbean *mestizaje* is African.

Like Négritude Créolité has a dual aspect. It's necessary because you can't deny that the Caribbean's *mestizo.* But you can't say that it's a Chinese or White *mestizaje*, because Africa and Africans have a vocation for diaspora and *mestizaje.* But when they mix, they don't stop being themselves. That's what nobody wants to admit. For some people, you're either Black or you're mixed, that is, not Black. Now that's not true. In Africa, there is a need for diaspora and multiplicity. Anyway, in Africa itself the nations and tribes mix with each other. Today, there's no such thing as a unified Peul or Senegalese people. For example, there's very intense *mestizaje* between Senegal and Mali. So this aspect of Créolité is valuable.

The other aspect, which is not valuable, is this: when you say "Créolité" you fix its definition of being once and for all in time and place. Now I think that being is in a state of perpetual change. And what I call "creolization" is the very sign of that change. In creolization you can change, you can be with the Other, you can change with the Other while being yourself, you are not one, you are multiple, and you are yourself. You are not lost because you are multiple. You are not broken apart because you are multiple. Créolité is unaware of this. It becomes another unity like Frenchness, Latinity, etc., etc. That is why for a long time now I have developed the idea of creolization, which is a permanent process that supersedes historical avatars. It's difficult to admit this because we're afraid of losing ourselves. We tell ourselves: if I change, then I'll lose myself. If I take something from the Other, then my own self will disappear. We absolutely must abandon this error.

And that's why it seems to me that the history of Africans in the New World is exemplary. It's a history that takes into account the history of the world, because in this very moment the whole world is creolizing itself, and there are no longer nations or races that are untouched by others. And what racists fear most of all is mixing. They don't allow for it. And that, I think, is the battle we need to wage, despite everything happening in the world, all those fundamentalisms of all shapes and sizes. I believe we are on the way to winning that battle.

Diawara
I am fascinated by your definition of creolization as a continuous process. Do you think that we can talk about the African diaspora in the same sense?

Glissant
There was an African diaspora millions of years ago which gave birth to the various humanities, because Africa is the cradle of humankind. And there have been other diasporas out of Africa: for example, the forced diaspora brought about by slavery; and today there is also a coerced diaspora caused by poverty and destitution, emigrants, and emigrations. Consequently, we can say that in the African condition there is a kind of vocation to go elsewhere. And when

there is a mixture of Africa and something else - well, it's Africa that's dominant, because of that vocation, not for racial or historical reasons.

Diawara
The word diaspora was borrowed from the Jews. African-Americans have been very much inspired by the Jewish experience, be it the literal return of Jews to Israel today or the history of the Old Testament. So what are the similarities and differences?

Glissant
Outside of the similarity of suffering, I don't think they resemble each other very much. It seems to me that in Jewish errantry, there has been an extraordinary suffering that may be found in the displacement of Africans towards the New World. All kinds of comparisons can be made on this point. Beyond that, there's no similarity. When the Jews made their diaspora in the world, they always preserved their cultural instruments: the Torah, the Talmud, etc. The Africans had lost everything; they had nothing, not even a song. In jazz, Black Americans had to recompose, through memory and through extraordinary suffering, the echo of what Africa had for them. Jazz came about not through a book but through a flight of memory. That's why jazz is valid for everybody, because it's a reconstruction within a distraught memory of something that had disappeared and had now been regained. It required a terrifying effort. That's why jazz at the beginning was so tragic. If you look at the faces of the great jazz musicians, they are very tragic, and that's something everyone can see. The same goes for Bob Marley and reggae: it's valid for everyone, but in the end what we have here is a fundamental difference, and we need to be aware of that.

The arts created by the Blacks of the diaspora - contrary to what's believed - are not indigenous to them; they are arts of mixture, of adjustment to situations. For example, music from, let's say, Tyrol, to take a well-known example, is linked in the ancestral order to the use of a musical instrument from that place. What's fantastic about jazz is that there's an African music that expresses itself with an incredible beat through the piano, which is an instrument played by Beethoven and Bach. And if you think about it, the same thing applies to most of the other areas.

What's happening is that music is becoming more and more diverse. We're now beginning to understand that European liturgies, Arab music, Indian music, Japanese music are valid for everyone. But only now are they like this, because there's this amazing mixture, this incredible complexity. And because of that, it's of fundamental importance in today's world to say that everything is happening in a rhizome world; that is, roots that intertwine, mix, and mutually assist each other. And I think that somewhere in all this is the drama of New World Blacks, whether in Brazil to the south, in the Caribbean at the center, or in the Americas of the north, which has begun to make this multiplicity of the world comprehensible. That's why it's so important, and that's why I believe that the truth that is increasingly coming to light about Black reality in the New World is the truth of multiplicity, the truth of the step towards the Other. Well, it's all quite simple to summarize things in formulas. But I myself like the idea that I can change through exchanging with the Other without losing or distorting myself. It's only recently that it's been possible to believe this, and I think it's one of the truths of the present world.

Diawara
And that's where your theory of "Relation" comes in.

Glissant
Yes, because within Relation... now I'm going to try to say something that I hold dear on this terrain. I believe that Relation is the moment when we realize that there is a definite quantity of all the differences in the world. Just as scientists say that the universe consists of a finite quantity of atoms, and that it doesn't change - well, I say that Relation is made up of all the differences in the world and that we shouldn't forget a single one of them, even the smallest. If you forget the tiniest difference in the world, well, Relation is no longer Relation. Now, what do we do when we believe this? We call into question, in a formal manner, the idea of the universal. The universal is a sublimation, an abstraction that enables us to forget small differences; we drift upon the universal and forget these small differences, and Relation is wonderful because it doesn't allow us to do that. There is no such thing as a Relation made up of big differences. Relation is total; otherwise it's not Relation. So that's why I prefer the notion of Relation to the notion of the universal.

Diawara
Definitely. Now, another question - why is it that nowadays architects, museum curators, and young musicians are so interested in Édouard Glissant's work?

Glissant
I can try to tell you why, and it's out of modesty, not vanity, that I say this. It's because reality has caught up with and imposed what I've been saying for twenty or thirty years now amidst general incomprehension. Forty years ago in Mexico, in a conference with Octavio Paz at the National

Autonomous University of Mexico, I demanded the right to opacity. There's a basic injustice in the worldwide spread of the transparency and projection of Western thought. Why must we evaluate people on the scale of transparency of the ideas proposed by the West? I understand this, I understand that, and the other - rationality. I said that as far as I'm concerned, a person has the right to be opaque. That doesn't stop me from liking that person, it doesn't stop me from working with him, hanging out with him, etc. A racist is someone who refuses what he doesn't understand. I can accept what I don't understand. Opacity is a right we must have. And the audience said: But what kind of barbarism is this? We have to understand, and if we don't, etc., etc. And I can assure you that twenty or thirty years later in the same auditorium, in the same city, there was a meeting, and quite pleasantly I reminded them of what I had said twenty or thirty years before, and everyone in the room said, we have to demand the right to opacity at the UN. Why? Because people came to understand that what was barbaric was imposing one's own transparency on the Other. I always tell psychoanalysts: If I don't accept my own opacity for myself, I've essentially defeated myself, but I can accept my own opacity and say: I don't know why. I don't know why, but I detest this person or like this other person. I can like this person not for any particular quality or reason, but just because I do. Does anyone know why he dislikes cauliflower or that other green vegetable...

Diawara
Broccoli?

Glissant
Everyone likes broccoli, but I hate it. But do I know why? Not at all. I accept my opacity on that level. Why wouldn't I accept it on other levels? Why wouldn't I accept the Other's opacity? Why must I absolutely understand the other in order to live next to him and work with him? That's one of the laws of Relation. In Relation, elements don't blend just like that, don't lose themselves just like that. Each element can keep its - not just its autonomy but also its essential quality - even as it accustoms itself to the essential qualities and differences of others. After thirty years, people understood that, but before, they never stopped saying how stupid it was. Then, the very movement of the world enables us to understand, because after seeing on TV the aborigines of Australia, Japanese, Parisians from the hood, Inuits from Alaska, we've understood that we can't understand everything and that there are things that remain within themselves. As a result, the world catches up with this sort of reflection on its complexity, on mixture, etc., and people end up accepting the idea.

Diawara
Beautiful. I'm thinking about a concept that's popular in Anglo-Saxon countries, not just in philosophy, but especially in the definition of cultural identity: the notion of the Other. In France, it's more nuanced; you use *alterité*. The Other has become the minority - the Black, the homosexual, the Chicano, the woman, etc. What do you think of that notion of the Other?

Glissant
Well, that doesn't interest me; it's so obviously false that I can't see why anybody would discuss it. I don't think that genuinely Anglo-Saxon thought would go that far. But we were talking about what's specific in the definition of the Other. Whether in the Francophone, Anglophone, Arab, Chinese, Japanese world, what's specific in the definition of the Other is that this Other is not just considered different. The Other is considered as contrary. Now, in the world, there is no contrary. The dialectic of differences is something I agree with, but not the dialectic of contraries, because the dialectic of contraries assumes that there's a truth over here, and its contrary over there. Now I don't believe there is a truth...

Diawara
Or a model...

Glissant
... or a model, yes, that's it... a luminous transcendence. I don't believe in that. I say that nothing is true and everything is alive. We've already gone over this - what that means is that nothing is absolutely true. There isn't one absolute truth, but truths. Everything is alive; everything is a Relation of differences, not contraries, but differences. Accordingly, the dialectic is not a linear approach towards that which is contrary. The dialectic is a total rhizome of what's different.

This Text is reprinted from: Tanya Barson and Peter Gorschlüter (eds.), *Afro Modern. Journeys through the Black Atlantic*, exhib. cat., Tate Gallery, Liverpool, 2010, pp. 58-63.

Translated from the French by Christopher Winks.

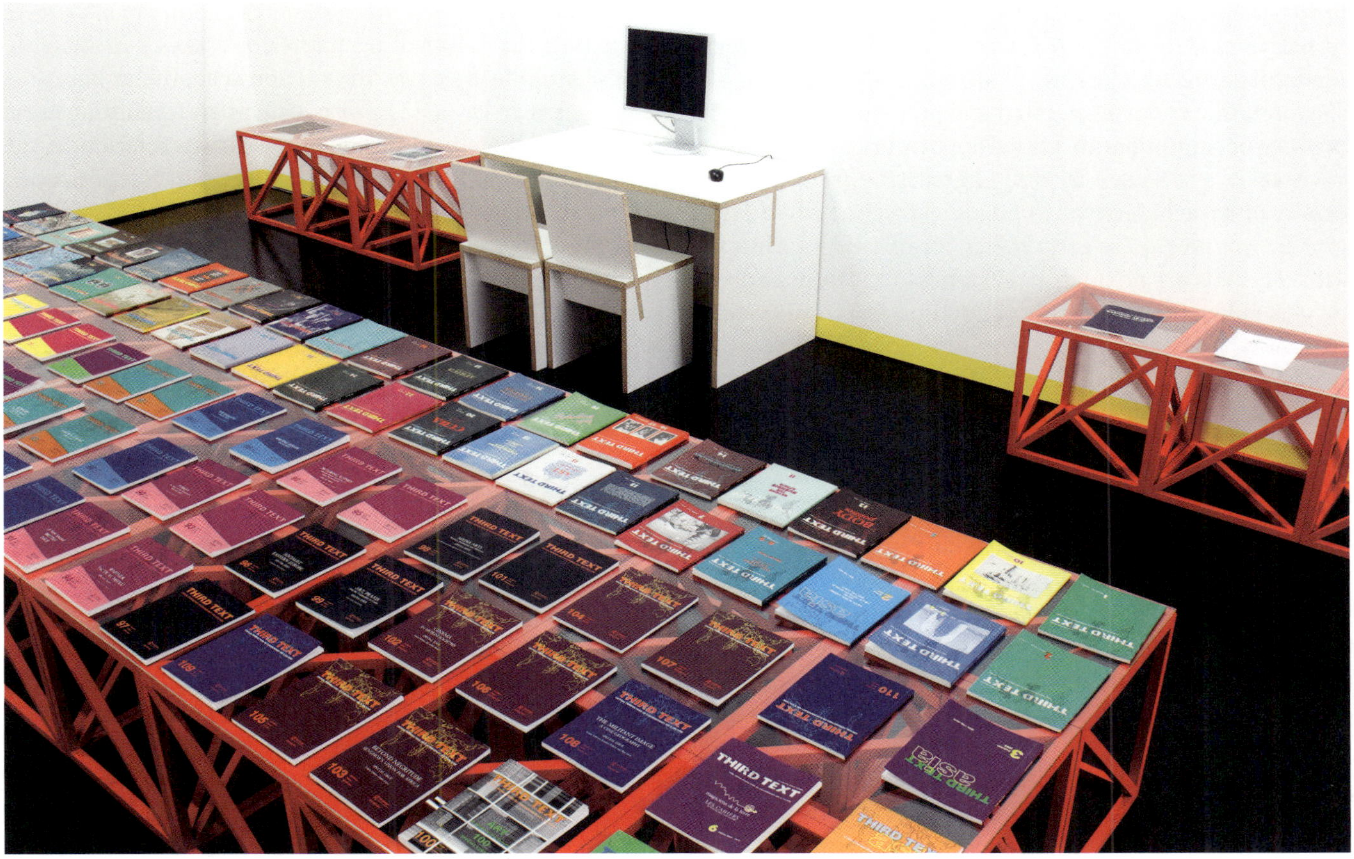

Rasheed Araeen, *The Reading Room, 1979-2011*, installation view *The Global Contemporary. Art Worlds after 1989*, ZKM | Karlsruhe, 2011-2012

Rasheed Araeen: Artist and Critic

Andrea Buddensieg

Rasheed Araeen is well-known as the founder and editor of the influential journal *Third Text*[1] that initiated a new discussion about modern and contemporary art in a global context. This achievement must also be understood against the background of Araeen's career as an artist in Britain who had emigrated from Karachi, Pakistan, in 1964. His editorial and the artistic activity are fueled by the same vision. This became apparent again when Araeen conceived his installation *The Reading Room, 1979-2011* for the exhibition *The Global Contemporary* (see: this volume, pp. 98-99), where he aimed to document his editorial work in a most original way. The cubes of his work *Vienna 36: Zero to Infinity* (1968-2009) were used to display a complete set of *Third Text* from 1987 until 2011. It was a great pleasure for us to welcome him to the opening of the exhibition in which he participated in various discussions. With his presence in the art world since the 1960s Araeen made an important contribution to the change which we all too superficially refer

1 **The subtitle of the journal** was *Third World Perspectives on Contemporary Art & Culture* before it changed to *Critical Perspectives on Contemporary Art & Culture* in 1999.

to as the "global turn." Insisting on the need to recover alternative modernities which were ignored by mainstream modernism for far too long, Araeen is undoubtedly one of the forefathers who propagated and prepared the road for a practice of contemporary art without frontiers.

Araeen, a graduate in civil engineering from the University of Karachi, arrived in London at a time when Minimal art was still at the early stages of formation within the art scene. His art production evidences that from early on he was obliged to pursue the general project of his visibility as artist in a dominantly Western art world or, in other words, to follow his intention to develop alternative strategies for questioning and changing the narrow limits of the "system."[2] In her text for Araeen's solo exhibition at the Aicon Gallery in 2010, Anna Malik demonstrates how Araeen's work "signals an attempt to maintain the universal, antisubjective impulses of Constructivism as it continued into Minimalism in the post-war period."[3]

His installation *Zero to Infinity*, a prominent work from his early period, was conceived in 1968 when he sent in drawings for a proposal for what he then called *Bio-Structural Play* to the Institute of Contemporary Arts (ICA) in London, which was rejected. Already in 1966 he had begun to develop the idea "of skeleton cubes with their sides bisected by diagonals as the basis of new sculpture, resulting in symmetrically and serially organized lattice structures."[4]

In a recent text entitled "My Own Story: Or, A Journey of the Idea," Araeen said that he left Karachi "because I felt terribly constrained by the nature of modernity I was surrounded by in my country."[5] His fascination with the work of Anthony Caro led him to abandon painting and become a sculptor. But he was looking for "an original path of Minimalism."[6] For some years he "worked with the idea, using lattice-type structures, that symmetrical configuration rather than composition should be the basis of new sculpture" to challenge "the exclusivity of fixed object-based art."[7] At that time his concept already postulated "a constant transformation within and through the public domain."[8]

Such was the case with *Chakras, The Floating Discs* (1969–1970) where water was to carry away his objects, even out into the open sea. Sixteen equal-sized circular discs colored fluorescent red in the symmetrical order of 4 × 4 were floated on the water of St. Katherine's Docks in London. An essential feature was interaction with the public, who were meant to launch the discs. It was an important move to abandon the closed profile of the art installation in the Minimalist sense. Instead, Araeen's intention was to open the creative act in terms of real movement. In a commentary that he wrote in 1974 in the context of restaging the work in Jheel Park, Karachi, he stated that the "changing relationship is my basic concern [...], the significance of which does not lie in mere beautification of the environment but to create an *environment* that reflects new IDEAS and CONCEPTS."[9]

In 2010 Araeen recapitulated the history of his work *Zero to Infinity* which, although it was conceived in 1968, in that year was only realized in a small version consisting of four cubes, namely *Char Yar* [Four Friends] painted red, blue, yellow, and green.[10] Meant as a "single sculpture," this "structural unit of four equal-sized cubes was subjected to a process of constant arranging and rearranging; it produced innumerable transformations within its own framework."[11] Over thirty years later, in 2004, he at last realized his idea at 291 Gallery, London, with 100 open cubes painted blue (each 50.8 × 50.8 × 50.8 cm) "which are initially laid out on the ground as a Minimalist sculpture (10 × 10), then dismantled by a public participation,"[12] and were now titled *Zero to Infinity*. As a constantly changing installation, the work offers the possibility to group and regroup the cubes freely revealing changing symmetries and asymmetries instead of maintaining a fixed form within an exhibition. The work changed its name to *Zero to Infinity* when a first draft of a commentary was written in the late 1990s. In 2007 the work was purchased by Tate Britain where 25 of its cubes served as a square Minimalist formation and performance of dismantling and rearranging at the show *Minimalism and Beyond: Rasheed Araeen at Tate Britain.*[13] A second version, *Vienna 36: Zero to Infinity* (1968–2009) with 36 cubes painted in red, was developed for the exhibition *The Death of the Audience* at the Secession in Vienna in 2009, and later became part of the ZKM_Collection where it entered the installation *The Reading Room.*

2 **Rasheed Araeen**, "The *Third Text* Story: Writing/Publishing as a Collective Work," in: *Third Text Asia*, no. 1, 2008, p. 133.

3 **Anna Malik**, "The New Generation Sculpture, Minimalism and the Work of Rasheed Araeen," in: *Rasheed Araeen: Before and after Minimalism 1959–1974*, Aicon Gallery, London, 2010, n. p.

4 *Rasheed Araeen: Before and after Minimalism 1957–1974*, 2010, n. p.

5 **Rasheed Araeen**, "My Own Story: Or, A Journey of the Idea," in: *Art Beyond Art: Ecoaesthetics: A Manifesto for the 21st Century*, Third Text Publications, London, 2010, pp. 20f.

6 **Araeen 2010**, p. 22.

7 **Araeen 2010**, p. 24.

8 **Araeen 2010**, p. 25.

9 **Rasheed Araeen**, *Making Myself Visible*, Kala Press, London, 1984, pp. 64f (emphasis Araeen).

10 See: "**Zero to Infinity: A Breaking of Symmetry**," in: Araeen 2010, pp. 43ff.

11 **Araeen 2008**, p. 133.

12 **Araeen 2010**, p. 43.

13 See: *Minimalism and Beyond:* Rasheed Araeen *at Tate Britain*, Third Text and Tate Britain, London, 2007, n. p.

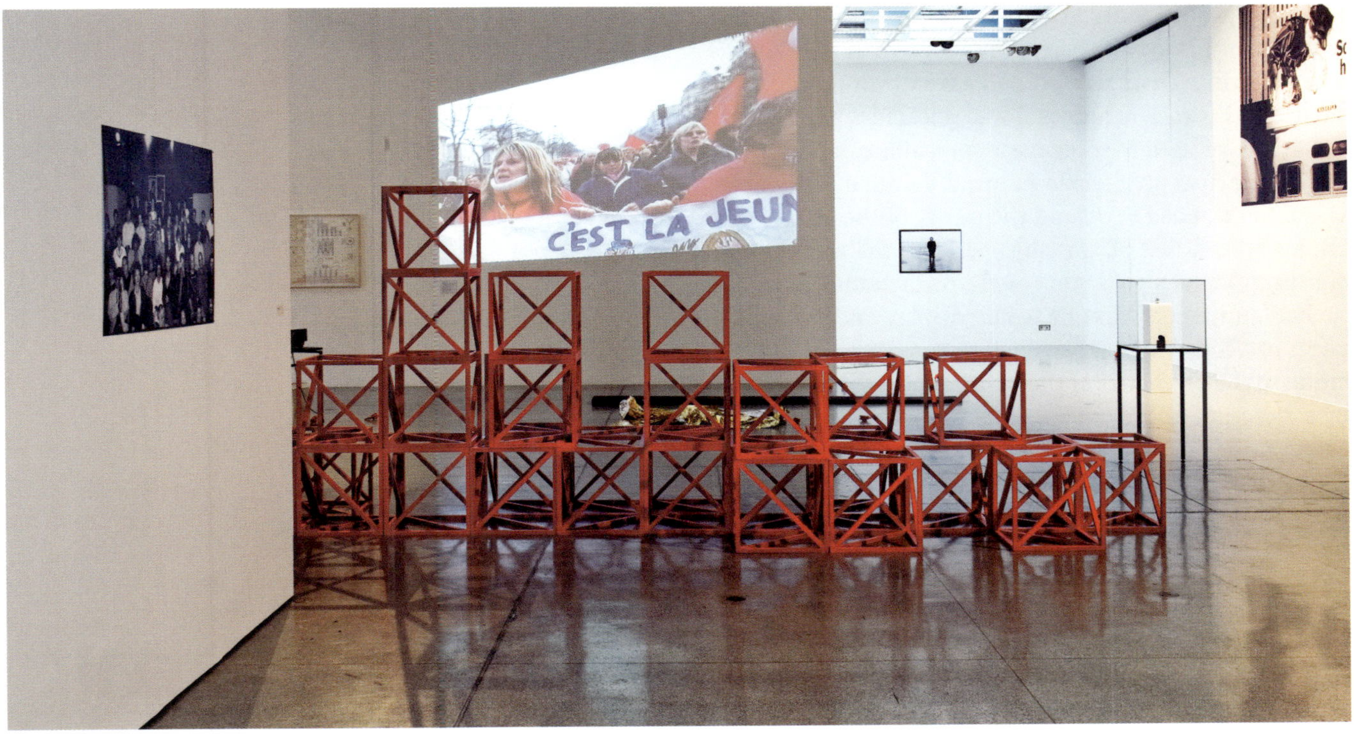

Rasheed Araeen, *Vienna 36: Zero to Infinity*, 1968–2009, 36 cubes painted in red, installation view, Secession, Vienna

> "The real aim of the work is to show that it is possible to confront and challenge the established view of things or the status quo within the formal framework [...]. This challenge is not carried out by an individual, but is realized through a process that recognizes the collective creativity of people, so as not only to redefine and construct radically new premises of art but also the role of the artist as well as of the public in its conception and execution."[14]

Araeen's ongoing work reveals the consistency with which he pursues his credo as an artist also in his critical writing. Though he chooses very different strategies to express his program, there is always the attempt to promote what he calls the idea, as the artist's task, an idea which must remain visible behind the changing faces of the different strategies. The concept of "nominalism" that he explains as "art of resistance,"[15] was chosen to develop the idea "to produce art in a radically different context,"[16] and thereby also to turn it against the traditional museum. Art should become a "critical practice,"[17] destined to overcome the barrier between art and life. His conception of the "everyday"[18] or "nominal" did not aim at an aestheticized object. He turned "the institutional space of the art world"[19] into the target of his critique. On the whole, Araeen never ceases to promote art as an idea rather than an exhibition commodity, an idea located in the artist's imagination.

Araeen, in fact, no longer intended to act in a museum space or as an exhibition artist. His true arena would become the public space. It was there that he wanted to carry conflicts out into the open that would remain silent in the art space. Thus, he became a penetrating critic of the present art museums in general. In this sense, he doubted the possibility that "significant art [could exist] within the bourgeois institution,"[20] that is, in a museum. It was the public space where he wanted to act both with his publications and with his art production intended for public sites.

In 2001, the Kunsthaus Bregenz in Austria invited artists to publish their institutional critique of today's art museum. Among the 33 artists who contributed to the volume *The Museum as Arena*,[21] Araeen was one of the few with a non-Western origin. He was not interested in the

14 **Araeen 2010**, p. 48.
15 **Rasheed Araeen**, "The Art of Resistance: Towards a Concept of Nominalism," in: *Third Text*, vol. 16, no. 4, December 2002, pp. 451ff.
16 **Araeen 2002**, p. 454.
17 **Ibid.**
18 **Ibid.**, p. 455.
19 **Ibid.**, p. 465.
20 **Rasheed Araeen**, *The Strange Ways of Artistic Imagination*, London, March 2005, unpublished manuscript.
21 **See: Christian Karavagni (ed.)**, *The Museum as Arena: Artists on Institutional Critique*, exhib. cat. Kunsthaus Bregenz, Verlag der Buchhandlung Walther König, Cologne, 2001.

fashionable postmodern rhetoric. Instead, he published the outcome of his private correspondence with the Ikon Gallery in Birmingham, which had asked him to join an exhibition in 1980. His proposal was rejected when the other ten artists refused to show their work alongside his.[22] Their opposition not only made cultural conflicts evident, but was also intended to defend the purity of the gallery space where Araeen had proposed to perform the slaughter and consumption of a goat. Along with the actual performance, he had announced that he would display and tear up "the pages of a contemporary art history book."[23] Thus, his opposition to the aesthetics of the white cube was also informed by a rejection of the official story of Modernist art and its avant-garde history.

By that time he had already "decided to engage the system simultaneously at several levels by making art works, performing, starting a magazine, writing polemics and letters, printing postcard and broadsheets, contributing to conferences, and initiating a research project to change the content of teaching in British art schools."[24] When he spoke about his own journal *Third Text*, he stated that "the emergence of writing [...] as an integral part of my activity as an artist was due to a realization that art objects alone could not adequately and critically reflect upon the world, let alone penetrate the system and question it."[25] He called it an attempt to "demolish the boundaries that separate art and art criticism." And he had discovered that he only could expect to be different when he acted differently and addressed his own case also in writing. Writing was tantamount to raising his voice against the hegemonic discourse of the art world. This discourse had confined him to an ethnic stereotype that prevented him from becoming an artist in his own right in the first place.

The first book he published with texts of his own in 1984 was entitled *Making Myself Visible*. Visibility there raised the question of who becomes visible and where. The publication placed his artistic work side by side with most of the texts he had written up to that point. In the editorial he addresses "the question of identity for the Third World artist."[26] Previously he had published the "Black Manifesto," which in 1978 appeared in the first issue of *Black Phoenix*,[27] the new magazine he had started, which, however, only lasted for three issues. The term "Black Artist," regardless of skin color, meant the "other" in the art world. In the Manifesto, he discussed the question, "how are Third World people trying to enter the modern era or/and create their own contemporary history?"[28] The term "ethnic artists," Araeen reminded the readers of *Third Text* in his essay "From Primitivism to Ethnic Arts,"[29] was coined by Naseem Khan,[30] whose father had emigrated from the Punjab in the 1930s. Araeen delivered a riposte to her book *The Art that Britain Ignores* in an essay entitled "The Art Britain *really* Ignores," reprinted in his 1984 book.[31] Rejecting the notion of ethnic artists he instead demanded "a common physical and intellectual space into which all people - irrespective of race, color or creed - can enter and take part in art activity."[32]

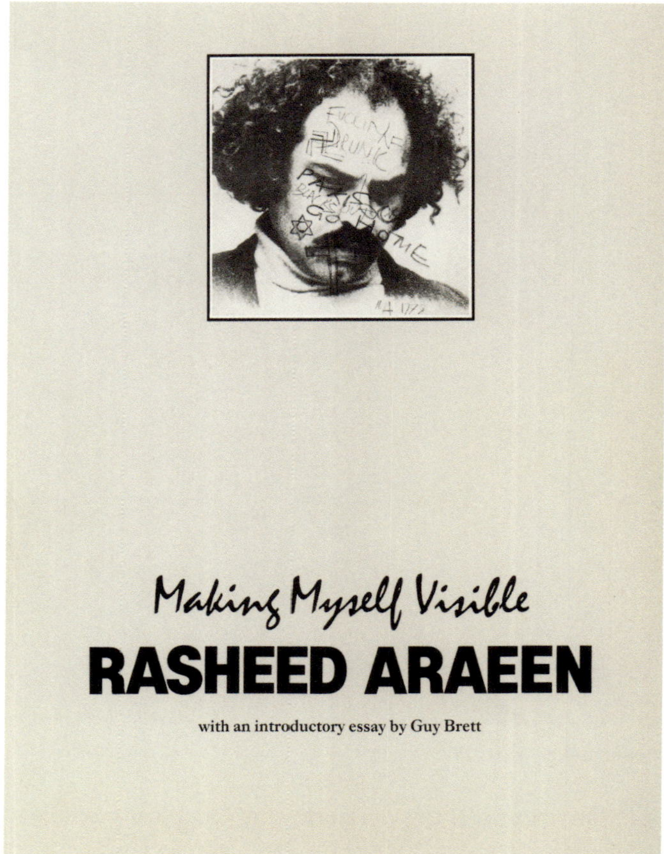

Rasheed Araeen, *Making Myself Visible*, Kala Press, London, 1984, book cover

22 **This correspondence is also published in: Araeen**, 1984, pp. 135ff. The exhibition *Imagination is the Venom Passing Slyly Through the Vein* at Ikon Gallery, 1980, showed works by Brian Catling, Stephen Cochrane, Stephen Dilworth, David Duly, Tom Gilhespy, Richard Mackness, Jayne Parker, Iain Sinclair, Elaine Shemilt, and Sue Wood.

23 **Araeen 1984**, p. 137.

24 **Guy Brett**, "Introduction," in: Araeen 1984, p. 7.

25 **Araeen 2008**, p. 132. See also the following quote.

26 **Araeen 1984**, p. 5.

27 **See: Araeen 1984**, p. 73.

28 **Araeen 1984**, p. 73.

29 **Rasheed Araeen**, "From Primitivism to Ethnic Arts," in: *Third Text*, vol. 1, no. 1, Autumn 1987, p. 7.

30 **See: Naseem Khan**, *The Art Britain Ignores: The Arts of Ethnic Minorities in Britain*, A Report to Arts Council of Great Britain, Calouste Gulbenkian Foundation and Community Relations Commission, London, 1976.

31 **See: Rasheed Araeen**, "The Art Britain *really* Ignores," in: Araeen 1984, pp. 100–105.

32 **Araeen 1984**, p. 105.

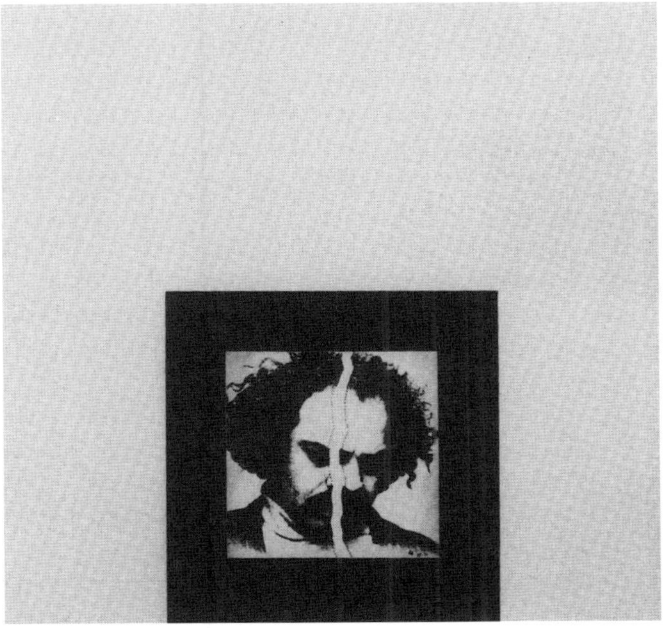

Rasheed Araeen, *Art/History*, 1980–1981, mixed media

He was determined to resist total assimilation. In his 1989 exhibition, *The Other Story*, in which he presented "Afro-Asian Artists in Post-War Britain" at the Hayward Gallery in London, he insisted upon telling the story of all those "who defied their otherness" within the modernist space.[33] He realized the deliberate falsity of the modernist story and agreed with Edward Said that one should "tell other stories than the official sequential or ideological ones produced by institutions of power."[34]

It is in keeping with his new strategy that the cover of his 1984 book shows a self-portrait. As a matter of fact, Araeen had produced a series of self-portraits after 1978, the year of the "Black Manifesto," at a time when politics with immigrants in Britain had taken a violent turn. The self-portraits, which come as a surprise after his abstract works, are not only different in that they are figurative. They show a non-Western face that raises problems of identity in the art world. Sometimes his face seems to have been attacked by an invisible crowd. In one case, the face is torn into two halves, much as the title is split into *Art* and *History*.[35] The fissure implies that Araeen could do art, but would still not enter official modernist art history. As in other instances, the strategy is ironical and subversive. The face that appears on the cover of the 1984 book represents one who struggles to "make myself visible." The graffiti across his face give the impression that his head is subjected to acts of aggression. The title of an earlier work raises the question: "How Could One Paint a Self-Portrait!"[36] given the uncertainty of the artist's identity. The picture was made for John Moore's Liverpool Biennial in 1978, but was returned by the committee with its decision "not accepted," which Araeen then pasted onto the work. In fact, under such auspices a self-portrait is in itself a contradiction.

The so-called *Ethnic Drawings*[37] counterbalance the portraits with texts in Araeen's mother tongue Urdu that reveal a cultural dilemma. In one of the four drawings, the face is an empty surface that fills up with writing. In another, the face is blinded and carries English words among others in Urdu. The artist wanted to "satirise those who by adopting their stereotypes (ethnicities) seek their careers in the West."[38] There is a lot of irony involved when Araeen admits a dualism between his ego and his supposed ego. The wide and surprising range in his use of the self-portrait proves the complexity of his strategy to "make myself visible" even as late as the 1980s when globalization was already imminent.

In fact, Araeen participated in the 1989 exhibition *Magiciens de la terre* with his sculptures and a new type of work that had already made its first appearance in his 1987 retrospective at the Ikon Gallery in Birmingham.[39] Each work in this group consists of a matrix of nine panels whose serial arrangement seems to refer to his early Minimalist production, this time including photographs, silk screens, texts, and paint. *Golden Calf*, (see: this volume, p. 344) which dates from 1987 juxtaposes, as Desa Philippi writes in the Birmingham catalog, "Andy Warhol's portrait of Marilyn Monroe [...] with the silkscreened photographs of what appears to be a crowd of mourning Iranian women, while the center is occupied by the single image of a dead Iranian soldier lying in a pool of blood."[40] The photograph of the Iraq-Iran war was taken from an Iranian newspaper, and the four Marilyn Monroes against the reality of politics and war look like idols from an indifferent art world. The Western art fetishes, as free trade commodities, are contrasted with the contemporary world.

33 **See: Rasheed Araeen,** *The Other Story. Afra-Asian Artists in Post-war Britain*, exhib. cat. Hayward Gallery, London; Wolverhampton Art Gallery; Manchester City Art Gallery and Cornerhouse, 1990.

34 **Edward Said**, "Opponents, Audience, Constituencies and Community," in: Hal Foster (ed.), *The Anti-Aesthetic: Essays on Postmodern Culture*, Bay Press, Port Townsend (WA), 1983, p. 158. Quoted in: Araeen 1989, p. 9.

35 **See: Araeen 1984**, image of *Art/History*, p. 147.

36 **Rasheed Araeen**, *How Could One Paint a Self-Portrait!*, 1978–1979, mixed media, 122 × 102 cm, image in: *From Modernism to Postmodernism. Rasheed Araeen. A retrospective: 1959–1987*, exhib. cat. Ikon Gallery, Birmingham and John Hansard Gallery, The University Southampton, 1988, n. p. In 1979, the work had been exhibited in a group exhibition at Serpentine Gallery, London, see: Guy Brett, "Introduction," in: Araeen 1989, p. 10.

37 **See: Araeen 1984**, pp. 158f.

38 **Quoted from a letter of Rasheed Araeen** that he wrote to the editors in November 2005.

39 **See:** ***From Modernism to Postmodernism*** **1988**, n. p.

40 **Desa Philippi**, "Impatience of Signs," in: *From Modernism to Postmodernism* 1988, n. p.

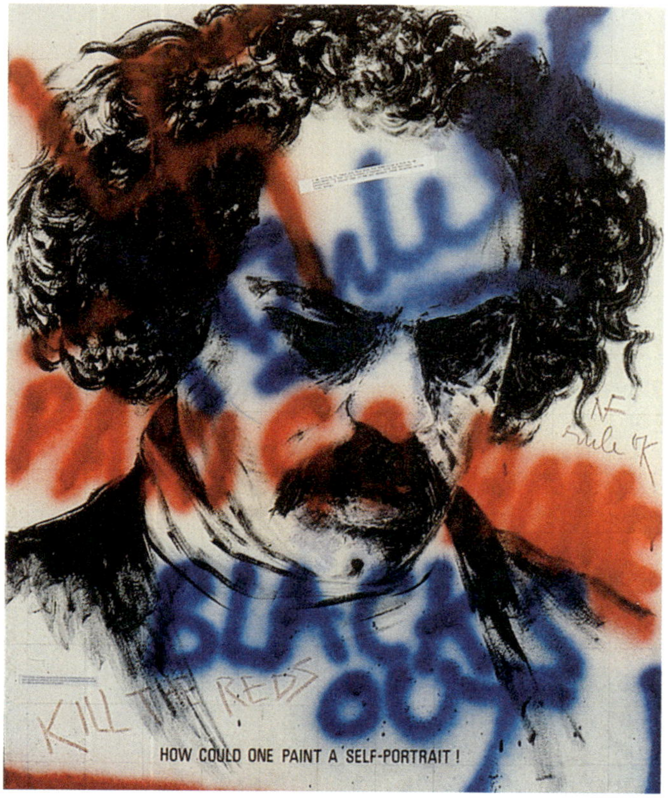

Rasheed Araeen, *How Could One Paint a Self-Portrait!*, 1978–1979, mixed media, 121.9 × 101.6 cm

The four versions of *Green Paintings*[41] show monochrome green surfaces in the corners while the remaining sections present images from the mass media. One of the *Green Paintings* that he selected for Peter Weibel's exhibition *Inklusion : Exklusion* of 1996, juxtaposes five photographs showing pools of blood on the street with a green surface in the corners, a reference to green as a holy color in Islam that is also the color of the flag of Pakistan. The strips of Urdu writing were taken from newspaper headlines referring to Nixon's visit to Pakistan and the house arrest of Benazir Bhutto.[42] The work addresses the imagination of people in Pakistan, but in fact it was exhibited in London where it had to be explained; in Pakistan, it would have been unfamiliar as a work of art. To quote John Roberts, "Araeen reworks elements of both his own culture and his 'adopted' one as a form of 'cross cultural mapping' in which the voice of the subaltern is shown as no less split across the spaces of representation than that of the 'Western subject'." Here we encounter the falsity of "the myth of Modernism's historical distance from traditional cultures [...]. By juxtaposing the conflicting ideological spaces of the 'primitive' [...] and the 'Modern' [...] Araeen destabilizes their respective orders of identification." And Araeen is quoted as stating that the two spaces are upside down or dialectical. "The 'primitive' periphery is cleared of all traces of expressionism (bloody ritual) which then is transferred to the central space (a cross/Ad Reinhardt). The Modernity of Minimalism is thus 'restored' to where it came from, Islamic culture, which remains fragmented (four parts) and occupies corners of the dominant culture."[43]

Araeen left the gallery space behind with twenty large billboards in the streets of London and one in Potsdam in 1993.[44] They were originally called *Golden Words* but he renamed them *Golden Verses* when he received a commission for them from "The Art Angel," a public art sponsoring agency in London, at the time of the controversy surrounding Salman Rushdie's *Satanic Verses*. The billboard shows an oriental carpet with three lines of an inscription in Urdu at the center. This work not only antagonized Western audiences, who were intrigued by the for them nonreadable writing and the symbol of oriental culture, but also managed to antagonize oriental audiences who could read the verses praising the white man and his civilization. The model for the carpet, which is today owned by The Textile Museum in Washington, D.C., is a work from Andalusia that was made at about the same time when, as Araeen remarks in a letter, Muslims and Jews were expelled from Spain.[45]

In the meantime Araeen concentrated on editing *Third Text*, which he had founded in 1987. As he explained in 2008, the journal was intended as "a conceptual art practice that proposes an entirely new way of using artistic expertise and imagination in reflecting and critically articulating the world."[46] He continues:

> "However, the idea of a collaborative art practice actually emerged much before *Third Text*. It began with my own development as an artist and at a time when I was still involved in producing art objects and events comprising art objects. I did not then see writing essential to this development. The emergence of writing, sometime later, as an integral part of my activity as an artist was due to a realization that art objects alone

41 **For more information see: Paul Overy**, "The New Works of Rasheed Araeen," in: Rasheed Araeen, exhib. cat. South London Gallery, 1994 and John Hansard Gallery, The University, Southampton, 1995, p. 17.

42 **As also the following quotes: John Roberts**, "Postmodernism and the Critique of Ethnicity: The Recent Work of Rasheed Araeen," in: *From Modernism to Postmodernism* 1988, n. p.

43 **Ibid.**, n. p.

44 **See: Rasheed Araeen 1994**, p. 32. The *Golden Verses* have also been shown in Potsdam, Germany in the context of the exhibition *Fontanelle* in 1993, see: *Kunstforum International*, 124, November/December 1993, p. 395.

45 **According to a letter from Rasheed Araeen** which he wrote to the editors in November 2005.

46 **As also the following quote: Araeen 2008**, p. 132.

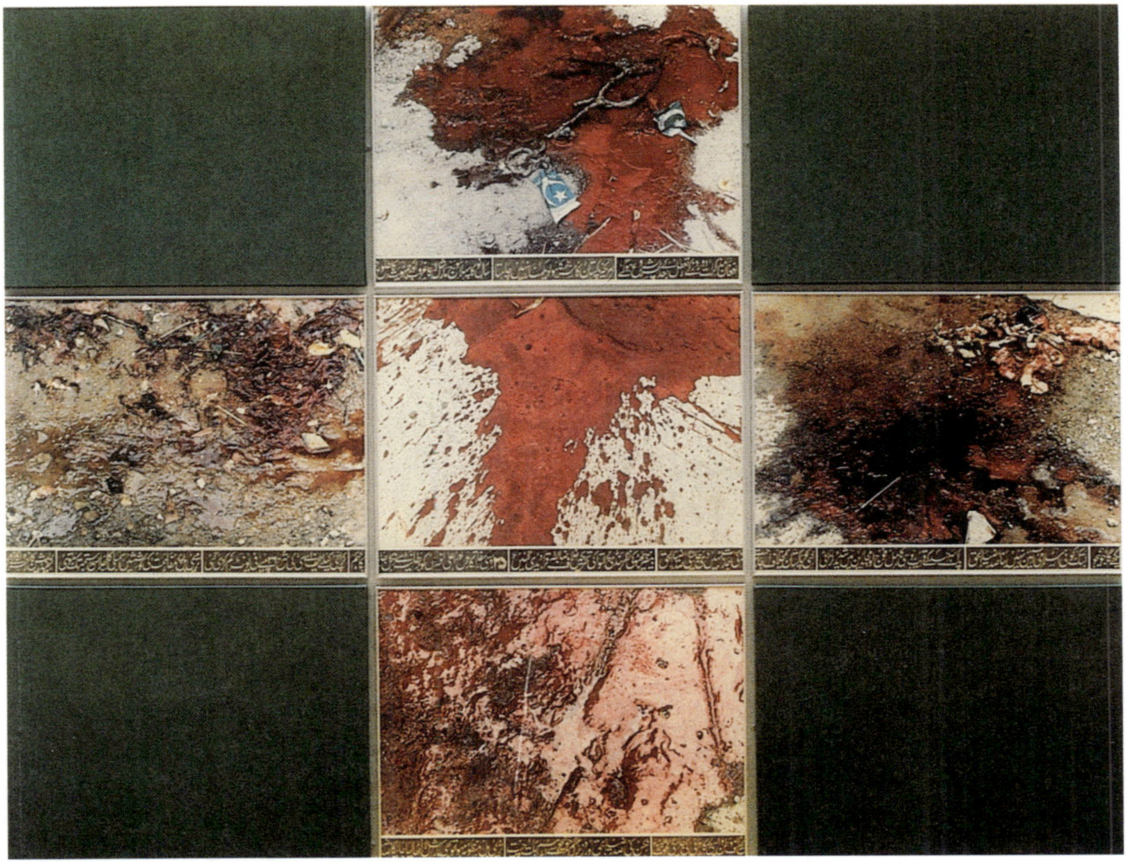

Rasheed Araeen, *Green Painting*, 1985–1986, mixed media, nine panels, 172.7 × 226 cm

could not adequately and critically reflect upon the world, let alone penetrate the system and question it."

Initially, *Third Text* was published with the subtitle *Third World Perspectives on Contemporary Art and Culture*. As the term "Third World" soon fell out of use after the end of the Cold War, while continuing its critical approach to the art world, the journal changed the subtitle in 1999 (issue 48) to *Critical Perspectives on Contemporary Art and Culture*. In its first phase *Third Text* was published by Kala Press, part of the organization Black Umbrella, initiated and established in 1983/1984 by Rasheed Araeen, and funded by Greater London Arts. Jean Fisher acted as the first longtime associate editor of *Third Text*: she was followed from 1999 by Ziauddin Sardar and others. Since 2002, *Third Text* is published by Routledge, Taylor & Francis Group. To date (December 2012) 119 issues have appeared. In 1989 the first two special issues were dedicated to the two 1989 landmark exhibitions *Magiciens de la terre* and *The Other Story: Afro-Asian Artists in Britain*. Special issues were later brought out also by invited guest editors and took up general topics, both in a geographic and a sociocultural sense. From 2003 onward Araeen extended the scope of the journal by initiating new *Third Text* editions in partnership: *Third Text Tercer Texto* came out in Spanish with a first print edition in 2003, followed by an online version in 2011. *Third Text Asia* had its first print edition in 2008, and *Third Text Africa* was launched as a quarterly online journal in 2010. These extensions seek to trigger cross-cultural dialog and discourse, and do not restrict their focus exclusively to their respective region. The new journals started with texts previously published in *Third Text*, but aimed also to include original articles and to establish their own editorial and advisory committees.[47]

In the first issue of *Third Text*, Araeen declared his principle that "considerations of art cannot be separated from questions of politics."[48] Cultural identity was neither available within the official system of Western modernism nor could it be recovered by a return to "nationalist/traditional art." Despite the progressive spirit of modernism, non-Western artists still experienced "an almost total exclusion from the history of modern art." At the time when the exhibition *Magiciens de la terre* was running in Paris, *Third Text* published

47 See for more information: http://www.thirdtext.com/, accessed 11/21/2012.

48 See also the following quotes: Rasheed Araeen, "Why Third Text?," in: *Third Text*, no. 1, Autumn 1987, p. 4.

most of the articles from the special issue of *Les Cahiers du Musée d'Art Moderne*, the journal of the Centre Pompidou, in English to inform its readers, but also to open a debate about this exhibition. Araeen contributed a text of his own with the ironic title "Our Bauhaus, Others' Mudhouse":

> "The central concern [of the curators in Paris] remains the same old-fashioned debate about the relationship between modernism and the tradition of others. It is not perhaps generally known that the 'other' has already entered into the citadel of modernism and has challenged it on its own ground."[49]

His main criticism concerned "the lack of any radical theoretical or conceptual framework that can justify the *togetherness* of works which represent different historical formations."[50] He finally asked the rhetorical question "Are we really breaking the distinctions or reinforcing the very same assumptions which divide the world into the West (modern/dynamic) and the 'Other' (traditional/static)?"[51] Though Araeen himself participated in *Magiciens*, his invitation did not prevent him from opening a fresh discussion about what such a global exhibition should be in the future.

In 2009 the editors of *Third Text*, at that time Rasheed Araeen and Richard Appignanesi, launched a call for papers for the special centenary issue scheduled for September 2009. The topic of the issue was announced as "Art: A Vision of the Future," in other words a vision of what art should be and what it should do in the twenty-first century when the context of art's production already demanded a radical departure "in the light of the changed and changing conditions of the world."[52] The issue gathered together 25 contributors who had followed the invitation to join the editors. In the call for papers Araeen affirmed that the journal was following its own tradition "as a collective work" that "must continue to move forward collectively." Some of the authors had been contributors to the journal from early on, and in the meantime they were major theoreticians after having made their entrance into the discourse of global matters as authors of *Third Text*. Issue no. 100 concluded with Araeen himself and his "Manifesto for the 21st Century" under the heading "Ecoaesthetics."[53] The text ends with the proposition that from now on artists "should focus their imagination on what is there in life, to enhance not only their own creative potential but also the collective life of Earth's inhabitants."[54] Thus, the radicality of his early writings still shines through although it addresses new questions which go beyond the art scene proper.

Revised and supplemented version of Andrea Buddensieg's essay "Visibility in the Art World: The Voice of Rasheed Araeen," first published in: Peter Weibel and Andrea Buddensieg (eds.), *Contemporary Art and the Museum. A Global Perspective*, Hatje Cantz, Ostfildern, 2007, pp. 50–65.

49 **Rasheed Araeen**, "Our Bauhaus Others' Mudhouse," in: *Third Text*, no. 6, Spring 1989, p. 3.

50 **Ibid.**, p. 7.

51 **Ibid.**, p. 11.

52 **Rasheed Araeen**, in: *Third Text*, vol. 23, no. 5, September 2009, pp. 501f.

53 **Rasheed Araeen**, "Ecoaesthetics: A Manifesto for the Twenty-First Century," in: *Third Text*, vol. 23, no. 5, September 2009, p. 679.

54 **Ibid.**, p. 689.

Room of Histories

Art's Globalization in Context

Documents
Art Spaces
The Reading Room
Mapping
Branding
trans_actions
Global News from *The Art Newspaper*

The following chronicle addresses art institutions, art exhibitions, and art markets in the last twenty years but is neither about art history nor about art theory. The documentation describes the rise of a plurality of art worlds which had either not existed before or had not found attention in the era that the West has called modernism. In the meantime, we take for granted the existence of other or alternative modernities. Contemporaneity has assumed a leading role, as will be evident in the different sections that together form the *Room of Histories*. The documentation aims to visualize the changing conditions and the expanding geography of art.

The biennials (more than 100 today against 10 to 15 twenty years ago), which have spread rapidly over the entire globe, contribute to a new mapping of art regions that are in competition with each other and aspire to developing a profile of their own. As a result, the new art practice can no longer be framed within the established patterns of modern art criticism. Other forms of narration are required in order to do justice to the geopolitical situation which is mirrored in art. Therefore, a plurality of narratives rather than a single history can best describe the current situation. The hegemonic role of a unitary art world is a thing of the past. (HB)

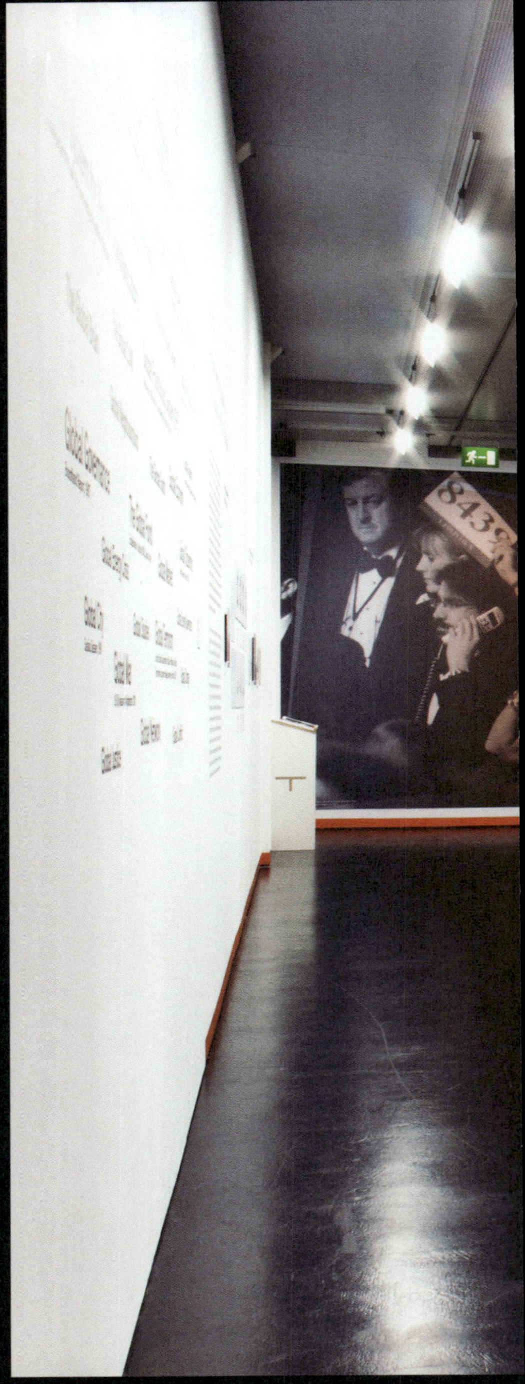

The Global Contemporary. Art Worlds after 1989, section: *Room of Histories*, exhibition view, ZKM | Karlsruhe, 2011–2012

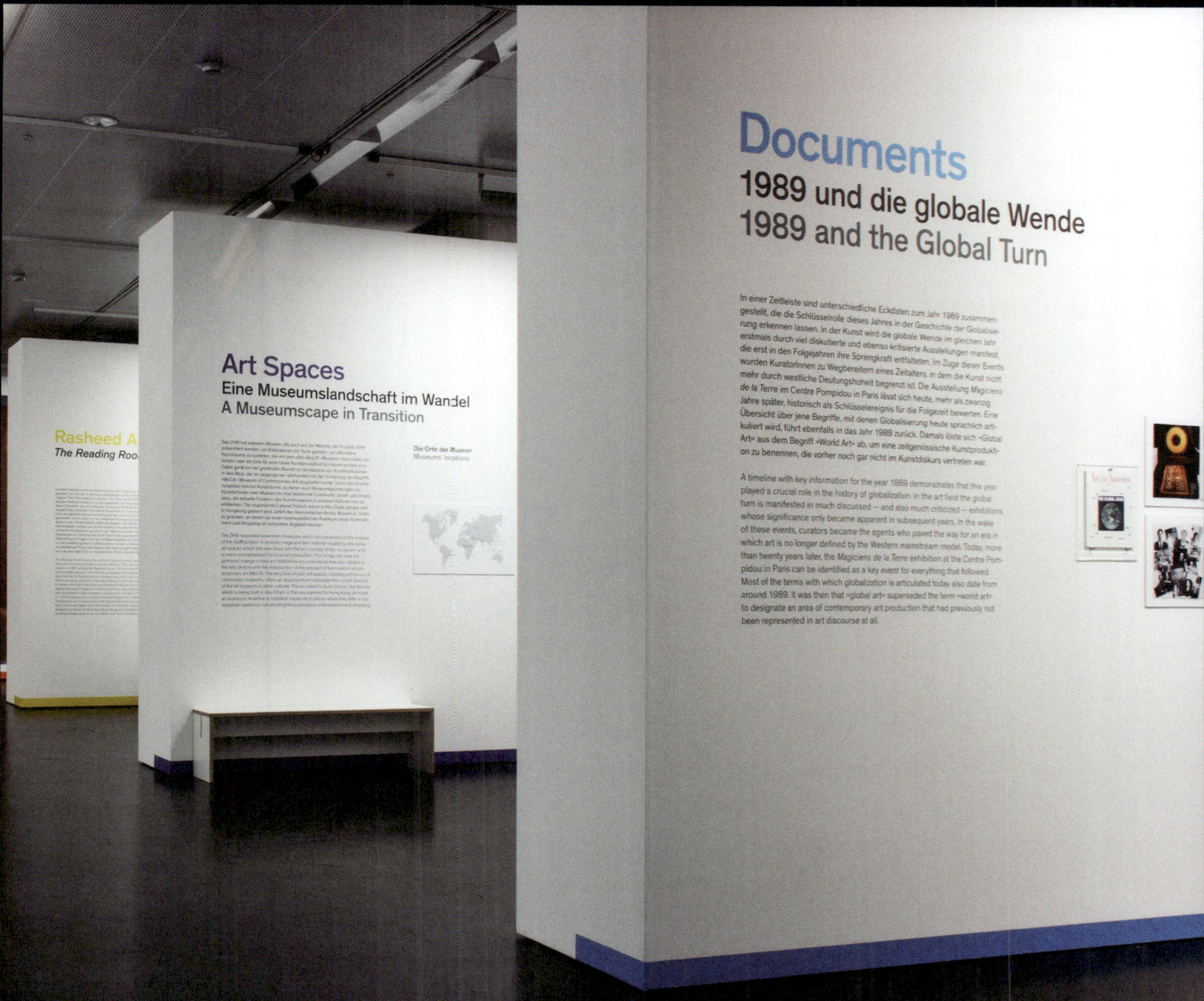
Documents
1989 und die globale Wende
1989 and the Global Turn
Art Spaces
Eine Museumslandschaft im Wandel
A Museumscape in Transition
Die Orte der Museen
Museums' locations
The Reading Roo

Global Vocabulary

Glob

Global (Communication) Network
J. C. R. Licklider, MIT, working paper *Man-Computer Symbiosis*, 1960.

Glob
"1989 in a Gl
Germany, 200
(eds.), *The Gl*
University Pre

Global Warming
Wallace Smith Broecker, "Climate Change: Are We on the Brink of a Pronounced Global Warming?," in: *Science*, New Series, vol. 189, no. 4201, August 8, 1975.

Global City
Saskia Sassen, *The Global City. New York, London, Toky*
Press, Princeton (NY), 1991.

Global Positioning System (GPS)
Developed in 1989 and first used during the Gulf War, 1990/1991.

Global Terrorism
United States Department of State, Patterns of Global Terrorism, report released every year since 1995.

Global
Alexander King and B
by the Council of the C

Global Art
The research program "Global Art and the Museum" was initiated by Hans Belting and Peter Weibel at the ZKM | Center for Art and Media Karlsruhe in 2006.

Global Financial Crisis
Referring to the 2008–2012 financial crisis.

Global Change
"Challenges of a Changing Earth: Global Change Open Science Conference," landmark conference held in Amsterdam, The Netherlands in 2001.

Global 1960s
Courses at the New York University in Abu Dhabi and at the Columbia University in New York; book: Samantha Christiansen and Zachary A. Sc
(eds.), *The Third World in the Global 1960s*, Northeastern University Bos
Berghahn Books, New York (NY), Oxford, 2012.

Global Surveillance

Global Economy

The Global Brain
Peter Russell, *The Global Brain*, Tarcher, Los Angeles (CA), 1983.

Global History
Conference on Global History at Bellagio (Italy), July 8–12, 1991. Launch of a new discipline of history by Bruce Mazlish, Ralph Buultjens, and Wolf Schäfer.

Global Governance
World Commission on Environment and Development (WCED), *Our Common Future*, also known as the Brundtland Report, Oxford University Press, Oxford, 1987.

Global Mark

Global English or
David Crystal, *English as a Global Language*, Cambridge U

uth

Global Village

Marshall McLuhan, *The Gutenberg Galaxy: The Making of Typographic Man*, University of Toronto Press, Toronto, 1962.

89

international conference held in Leipzig,
Lawson, Chris Armbruster, and Michael Cox
ity and Change in World Politics, Cambridge
010.

Global Energy Crisis

Jeremy Leggett, *Half Gone: Oil, Gas, Hot Air and the Global Energy Crisis*, Portobello Books Ltd, London, 2005.

Global Player

sity

Global Event

Jean Baudrillard, "L'esprit du terrorism," in: *Le Monde*, November 11, 2001.

lution

, *The First Global Revolution. A Report*
nt Longman, Andhra Pradesh, 1990.

Global Society

Global Society. Journal of Interdisciplinary International Relations, published by Routledge, London, on behalf of the University of Kent at Canterbury since 2005.

Global Citizenship

Barack Obama's speech in Berlin, 2008.

lobal War

bal War on Terror," US invasion of Afghanistan, 2001.

Global Politics

Global Capitalism

Robert J. S. Ross and Kent C. Trachte, *Global Capitalism: The New Leviathan*, State University of New York Press, Albany (NY), 1990.

Global Theater

Marshall McLuhan, "At the moment of Sputnik the planet became a global theater in which there are no spectators but only actors," 1973, published in: *Journal of Communication*, vol. 24, no. 1, March 1974.

Global Age

Martin Albrow, *The Global Age: State and Society Beyond Modernity*, Stanford University Press, Stanford (CA), 1997.

Global Studies

New Global Studies, periodical of De Gruyter since 2006. Founders/editors: Nayan Chanda (Yale University), Akira Iriye (Harvard University), Bruce Mazlish (MIT), and Saskia Sassen (Columbia University).

Global Justice Movement

Symbolical birth: Protests against the World Trade Organization, Seattle 1999.

The Global Fund

The Global Fund to Fight AIDS, Tuberculosis and Malaria, established in Geneva, Switzerland in 2002.

al Language

ambridge, 1997.

Global Vocabulary

The cloud of "global terminology" presented on the previous page is the result of Internet-based research, and as such, it represents an attempt at unpacking our everyday rhetoric and knowledge. By tracing back the origins and sources of familiar locutions such as "global warming" or "global village," we came across more specialist linguistic formations which range from historiography with "global history" or "the global 1989," to politics with "global governance," "global greens," or "global justice movement." What clearly emerges from the timeline of these formations is that the first references to a global – and not to a world, earth, or universal – model appeared in the field of communication studies with Marshall McLuhan theorizing the "global village" in 1962 and J. C. R. Licklider foreseeing a "Global (Communication) Network" in 1960. Both concepts hinted at the idea of a hyper-interconnected globe, which prophetically recalls the World Wide Web. Most of the terminology cited here, however, arose in the course of the 1990s and 2000s. The development of new communication technologies such as the "Global Positioning System," which was widely used by the Americans during the first Gulf War in 1990/1991, played a seminal role in establishing an unprecedented global condition based on satellite maps of the globe. The reactions to and consequences of the New World Order, and thus to globalization itself, led to a new take on existing disciplines and fields as exemplified by "global history," "global capitalism," or "global English." Many recent terms mirror neocapitalism, such as the current "global financial crisis," while others postdate recent political events. The 9/11 attack on the World Trade Center in New York has been defined by French philosopher Jean Baudrillard a "global event," and consequently led to the "global war on terror," coinciding with the U.S. invasion of Afghanistan. Certainly relevant to the discourse of globalization after 1989 was the expression used by Barack Obama in his Berlin speech during the 2008 presidential campaign. Referring to John F. Kennedy's famous "Ich bin ein Berliner" [I am a Berliner] (1963), Obama spoke this time of "global citizenship."

Economics, technology, politics, and science all offer a great number of new and specific linguistic formations referencing a global perspective; however, within the fields of art and culture there has been no comparable flowering of "global" linguistic formations – with the exception of the umbrella term "global art." (SG)

Museum as...

The collection of museum terminology on the following page seeks to sketch a semantic landscape of what an art museum could be, what it could represent today. Using the search terms "Museum as…" we explored different functions of the museum. Born in France with the Louvre, the establishment of the art museum coincided with the creation of the nation-state in the aftermath of the French Revolution. From the outset museums served as "guardians" of national art heritage or colonial collections. The preservation of its artifacts was always conceived of as a distinctive feature of an "educational institution" that creates audiences and shapes the sense of belonging – as the mission statement of The Museum of Modern Art in New York underlines. Through its permanent collections and display strategies, the museum is also a place where artistic production is selected, canonized, and classified. As a "way of seeing" it therefore creates paradigms and conditions of inclusion and exclusion. The idea of the art museum as a "temple" or "time capsule" has been questioned by James Clifford with his concept of "contact zone," defined as "the space of colonial encounters, the space in which peoples geographically and historically separated come into contact with each other […]" (Mary Louise Pratt quoted from: James Clifford, *Routes: Travel and Translation in the Late Twentieth Century*, Harvard University Press, Cambridge (MA), 1997, p. 192). The vision of a dialogic and more practice-oriented museum is echoed by many examples of its contemporary use, which treat the museum as a "platform," "distributed network," "arena," or "public sphere." The tendency to act against the burden of national representation in the age of globalization is a pivotal feature of the initiative "Museum as Hub," conceived by Gerardo Mosquera and inaugurated in 2006 by the founding partners Insa Art Space, Seoul; Museo Experimental El Eco, Mexico City; Museo Tamayo, Mexico City; New Museum, New York; Townhouse Gallery, Cairo; and the Van Abbemuseum, Eindhoven: "The museum as an international hub of artistic activities means a decentralized institution that will simultaneously conceive, curate, and participate in diverse projects in different places worldwide. [...] For the museum, as for many other things, the future will mean an increasingly global and decentralized activity" (Gerardo Mosquera, "Notes on the Museum-As-Hub," available online at: www.micromuseo.org.pe/lecturas/gmosquera.html, accessed 09/25/12). (SG)

Museum as...

Degenera

Travis English, "Hans Haacke,
Kritikos: An International and I
Cultural Sound, Text and Imag

Guardians

Arapata Hakiwai, "Museums as Guard ans of our Nation's Treasures," in: *Agmanz Journal*, vol. 19, issue 2, 1988.

Are

Christian Kr
Artists on In
lung Walthe

Public Sphere

"Performing the Museum as a public sphere: Gallery education as 'Differend'," conference at Lentos Kunstmuseum (Linz), April 18–19, 2008.

Hub

Gerardo Mosquera, "Seven Notes on the Museum-as-Hub," in: *Re-Shuffle: Notions of an Itinerant Museum*, Center for Curatorial Studies, Bard College, Annandale-on-Hudson (NY), 2006. "Museum as Hub," project initiated by the New Museum (New York), Insa Art Space (Seoul), Museo Tamayo Arte Contemporáneo (Mexico City), Town House Gallery of Contemporary Art (Cairo), and Van Abbemuseum (Eindhoven) in 2006.

Contact Zones

James Clifford, "Museums as Contact Zones," in: Clifford, *Routes: Travel and Translation in the Late Twentieth Century*, Harvard University Press, Cambridge (MA), 1997.

Heterotopia

Michel Foucault, "Of Other Spaces," in: *Diacritics*, vol. 16, no. 1, Spring 1986.

Ci

Mikhail
no. 3, A

Catalyst

Barbara Kirshenblatt-Gimblett, "The Museum as Catalyst," keynote address at the conference "Museums 2000: Confirmation or Challenge," organized by ICOM Sweden et al., September 29, 2000.

Resource

Susan K. Donley, "Cultural Diversity. The Museum as Resource," in: Beverly Sheppard (ed.), *Building Museum and School Partnerships*, American Association of Museums and Pennsylvania Federation of Museums and Historical Organizations, Washington D.C., 1993.

Learni

"Museums as learnin
group within the EU
2010–2013.

Educational Institution

Excerpt from the Mission Statement of MoMA, New York: "Founded in 1929 as an educational institution, The Museum of Modern Art is dedicated to being the foremost museum of modern art in the world.'

Medium

James Putnam, *Art and Artifact: The Museum as Mediu*
Thames & Hudson, London, 2001.

Method

Nicholas Thomas, "The Museum as Method," in: *Museum Anthropology*, vol. 33, issue 1, Spring 2010.

Muse

The Museum as Muse: Artist
March 14–June 1, 1999.

Dreamland

David R. Prince, "The Museum as Dreamland," in: *International Journal of* Museum Management and Curatorship, vol. 4, issue 3, September 1985.

opia

Degenerate Utopia," in:
urnal of Postmodern
07.

Forum

Duncan Cameron, "The Museum: a Temple or the Forum," in: *Journal of World History*, vol. 14, issue 1, March 1972.

Museum als Arena; The Museum as Arena.
e, Kunsthaus Bregenz, Verlag der Buchhand-
2001.

Social Enterprise

Stephen E. Weil, "New Words, Familiar Music: The Museum as Social Enterprise," in: Weil, *Making Museums Matter*, Smithsonian Institution Press, Washington D.C. 2002.

Process

Carol S. Jeffers, "Museum as Process," in: *The Journal of Aesthetic Education*, vol. 37, no. 1, Spring 2003.

Playground

Stefano Casciani, "Museum as Playground," in: *Domus* Magazine, no. 931, December 2009.

useum as City," in: *Hermitage Magazine*,

A Way of Seeing

Svetlana Alpers, "The Museum as a Way of Seeing," in: Ivan Karp and Steven D. Lavine, *Exhibiting Cultures: The Poetics and Politics of Museum Display*, Smithsonian Institution Press, Washington D.C., 1991.

l Site

vilizing Rituals: Inside Public Art Museums, Routledge,

Platform

"The Museum as Platform for Reflection and Thought," panel discussion during the conference "Thinking Latin America: Contemporary Cultural Constructions," MUSAC – Museo de Arte Contemporáneo de Castilla y León, November 6–7, 2010.

ace

ng spaces in museums," working
project *LEM – The Learning Museum*,

Distributed Network

Nancy Proctor, "The Museum as Distributed Network," in: *Museum Identity*, issue 5, 2010.

Classroom

Jessica Portner, "The Museum as Classroom: Q&A with Guest Scholar George Hein," blogs.getty.edu, May 2, 2011.

Time Capsule

"A Museum as Time Capsule – Studying a Mongolian Saddle as an Example," Secondary Lesson Plans, Asia Society, 2008.

on at MoMA, New York,

Temple

Duncan Cameron, "The Museum: a Temple or the Forum," in: *Journal of World History*, vol. 14, issue 1, March 1972.

Timeline 1989

The satellite television service Sky Television plc is launched in Europe. February 2

The last Soviet troops leave Kabul, ending nine years of military occupation. February 2

The National Art Museum of China, Beijing presents the exhibition China/Avant-garde. February 5–19

The USA puts the first of 24 satellites of the Global Positioning System (GPS) into orbit. February 14

The World Wide Web is invented by Tim Berners-Lee at CERN, Geneva. March

Free elections for the Congress of People's Deputies of the Soviet Union. March 26

The Centre Pompidou and the Grande halle de la Villette in Paris present the exhibition Magiciens de la terre. May 18–August 14

The Tiananmen Square massacre by the Chinese army in Beijing, commonly referred to as the "June Fourth Incident" in China. June 4

R. B. Kitaj publishes *First Diasporist Manifesto* with Thames & Hudson, London. June

Francis Fukuyama publishes the essay "The End of History?" in the neoconservative journal *The National Interest*. Summer

France celebrates the 200th anniversary of the French Revolution. July 14

Gallery Collegium Artisticum and Skenderija Olympic Center, Sarajevo, Bosnia and Herzegovina organize the Jugoslovenska dokumenta '89, the second and last edition of the Yugoslav version of Germany's documenta. July 1–August 1

Nintendo releases the handheld video game device Game Boy. July 31

Foundation of the ZKM | Center for Art and Media Karlsruhe, Germany. August

F. W. de Klerk is elected president of South Africa and introduces reforms that lead to the end of apartheid. September 6

The 2nd International Istanbul Biennial entitled Contemporary Art in Traditional Spaces takes place. September 29–October 31

The 3rd Havana Biennial entitled Tradition and Contemporaneity (Tradición y Contemporaneidad en las Artes Plasticas y el Ambiente del Tercer Mundo) takes place. October 27–December 31

The Asia-Pacific Economic Cooperation (APEC) forum is established. November 6

East Germany opens border crossing points in the Berlin Wall. November 9

Brazil holds its first free presidential election since 1960. November 12

The Gentle or Velvet Revolution advances the peaceful overthrow of the Czechoslovak communist regime. November 17–December 29

The Hayward Gallery, London presents the exhibition The Other Story. Afro-Asian Artists in Post-War Britain. November 29–February 4

Pierre Bourdieu responds to the fall of the Berlin Wall by founding *Liber*, a European literary review. December

In a meeting off the coast of Malta, George Bush and Mikhail Gorbachev release statements indicating that the Cold War between their nations may be coming to an end. December 3

Chile holds its first democratic presidential elections in sixteen years, ending Augusto Pinochet's dictatorship. December 14

Nicolae Ceaușescu is overthrown and then executed in Romania. December 22–25

Documents.

Exhibitions and the Global Turn

In the art context, the global turn is best documented in controversial but influential exhibitions whose significance to make history or mark history on their own only became apparent in the years that followed. In the wake of these events, curators as their agents paved the way for an era in which art is now no longer practiced in terms of the Western mainstream model alone. Today, more than twenty years later, the *Magiciens de la terre* exhibition at the Centre Pompidou in Paris (1989) is acknowledged as a turning point in the acceptance of global art production. It was hailed in Paris already at the time as the "first global (*mondiale*) exhibition of contemporary art," at least in the attention of the former West.

The timeline with key information for the year 1989 (pp. 58–59) demonstrates that this year probably played a crucial role in the Western encounter with global art production. But also in general terms, the ideas, which today play a role in the discourse of globalization, only became common currency in the late 1980s and early 1990s. It was at about the same time that the notion of global art came into use and replaced the term "world art" (in the sense of the art "of the others") for a practice of contemporary art that had previously played only a minor role in art criticism. (HB)

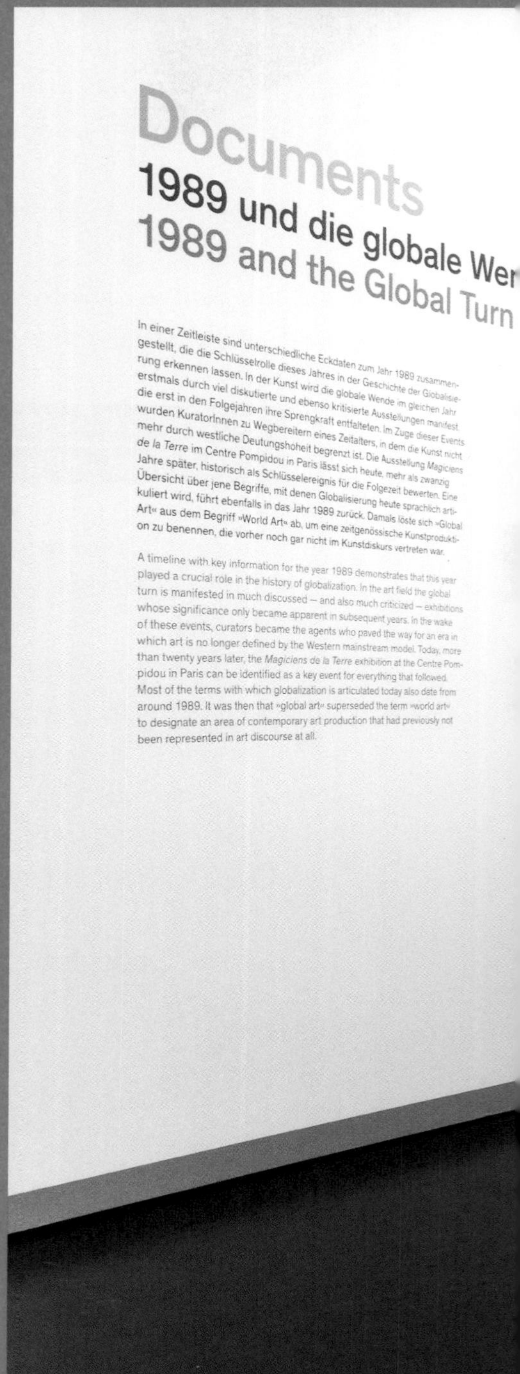

The Global Contemporary. Art Worlds after 1989, section: *Room of Histories*, exhibition view, ZKM | Karlsruhe, 2011–2012

Late Modernism

The Global Turn

Landmark Exhibitions:
1989 and After

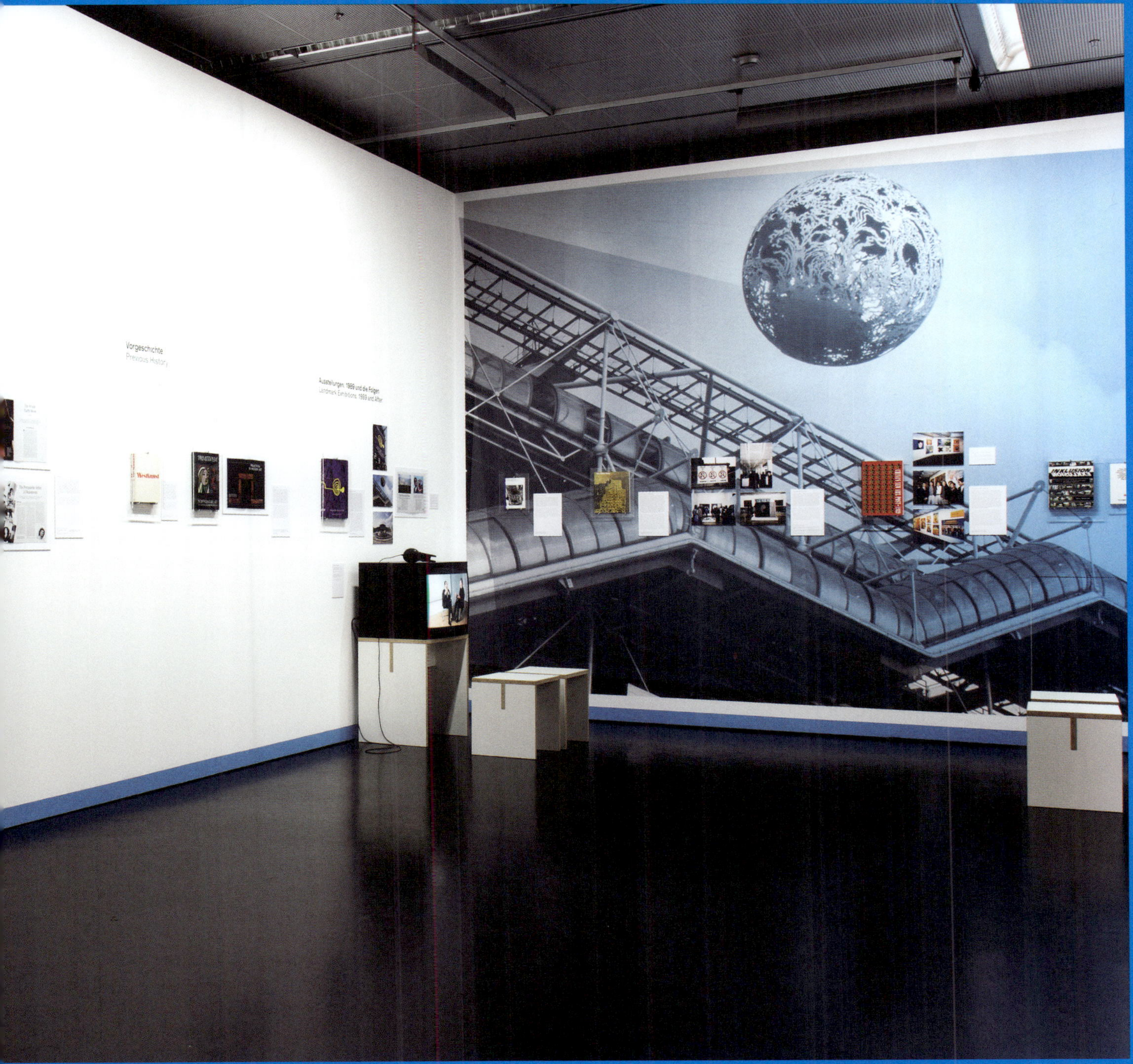

Late Modernism

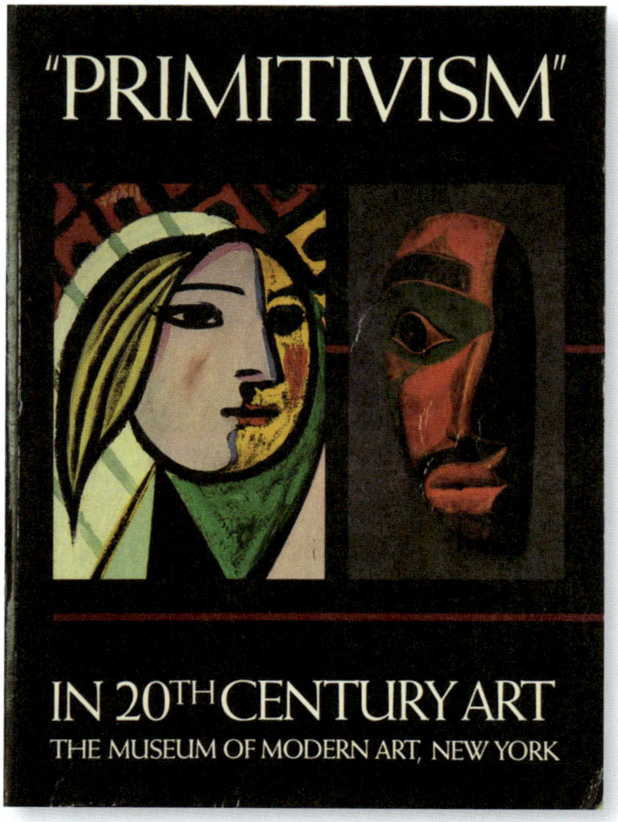

Primitivism and Modern Art

The concept of "primitivism" since Robert Goldwater (1938) refers to the appropriation of "primitive" African and Oceanic art in the first decade of the twentieth century. Driven by nostalgia for its origins, art became modern through the search for archetypes of "authentic expression." As a result masks were transformed into modern paintings and sculptures.

This "primitivism" was last celebrated in the exhibition *"Primitivism" in 20th Century Art* organized by William Rubin at The Museum of Modern Art, New York, in 1984. Once again, the colonial view of the "other" was downplayed as the "affinity" between modern and "tribal art." However, the time for repeating this credo of modernism was already over. The exhibition provoked counter models, such as *Magiciens de la terre* (Paris, 1989). In *Magiciens*, the anonymous "others" entered the stage as colleagues of Western artists possessed of a passport and a name. The idea of a common "contemporaneity" was leveled against the separation of modern and non-western art. (HB)

Above:
William Rubin (ed.), *"Primitivism" in 20th Century Art. Affinity of the Tribal and the Modern*, exhib. cat., The Museum of Modern Art, New York (NY), 1984

Art/Artifact. African Art in Anthropology Collections, 1988

In 1988, Susan Vogel, executive director of the Center for African Art in New York (today Museum for African Art), organized a sort of meta-exhibition on the way African Art was displayed in Western museums' collections. The friction between the semantics of the terms "art" and "artifact" in Western languages is mirrored in the oscillating and often arbitrary presence of African aesthetic objects in anthropological museums rather than art museums.

The exhibition was structured in four main settings showing how primitive art has been staged throughout history: "As souvenir in curiosity rooms; as educational information in natural history museums; for aesthetic pleasure in art museums; and as merchandise in commercial galleries" (William Wilson, "Primitive Art: Breaking New Ground: 'ART/artifact,' at UCLA, examines the degree of racism and the image of white superiority in past exhibitions of African objects," in: *Los Angeles Times*, April 1, 1990).

The accompanying catalog contained six essays, which engaged with the unsolved difficulties concerning the categorization of objects, whose acquisition derives from Western colonial enterprise, into Western paradigms. Unlike the 1984 *"Primitivism" in 20th Century Art* exhibition at The Museum of Modern Art, New York, which emphasized the universalism of modern art by embracing primitive formalism, *Art/Artifact. African Art in Anthropology Collections* represented more a pause for self-reflection. The issues surrounding the classification and display of non-Western art led Arthur C. Danto to speculate in his contribution on the philosophical foundations that define art itself. (SG)

Below:
Art/Artifact. African Art in Anthropology Collections, exhib. cat., Center for African Art, New York (NY), 1988

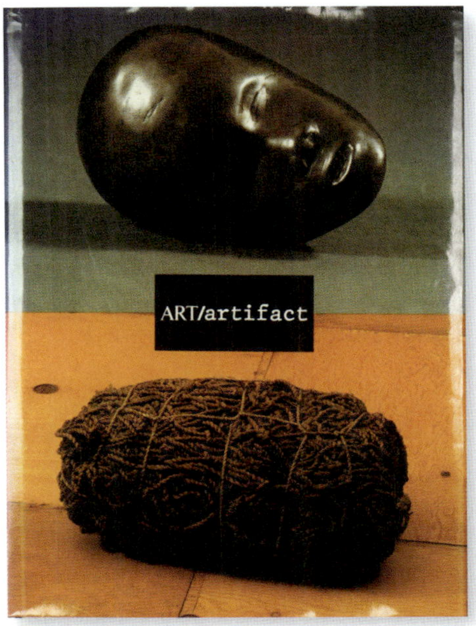

The Global Turn

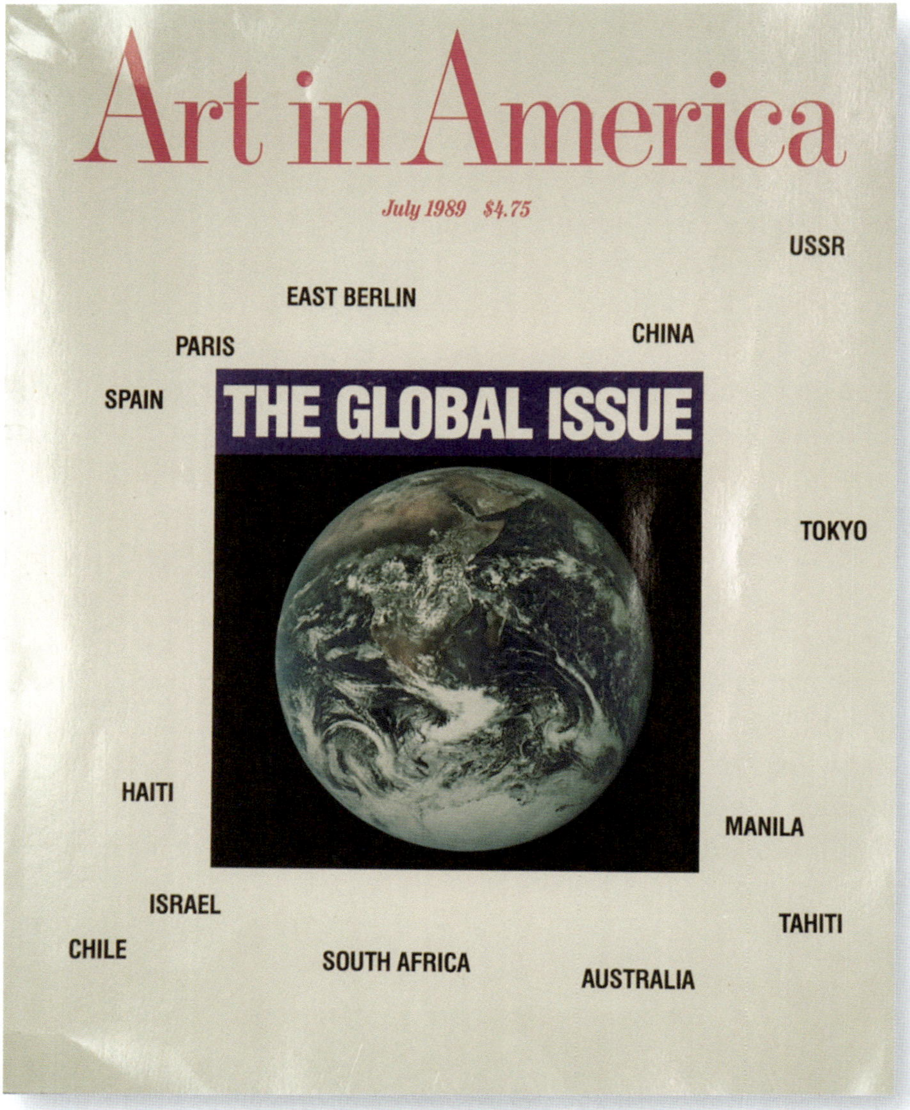

Art in America: “The Global Issue“

In July 1989, the periodical *Art in America* appeared with a NASA shot of the Earth on the front cover bearing the title “The Global Issue.” In order to justify what was a neologism in the art scene, the magazine presented six statements on globalism, among them a text by the artist Martha Rosler and one by anthropologist James Clifford. There was a general feeling about the danger of an unwelcome homogenization and consumer culture, caused by the euphoria of Theodore Levitt’s view of “the marketing imagination.” But Craig Owens (1950–1990), former senior editor of *Art in America*, nevertheless concluded: “Perhaps it is in this project of learning how to represent ourselves – how to speak to, rather than

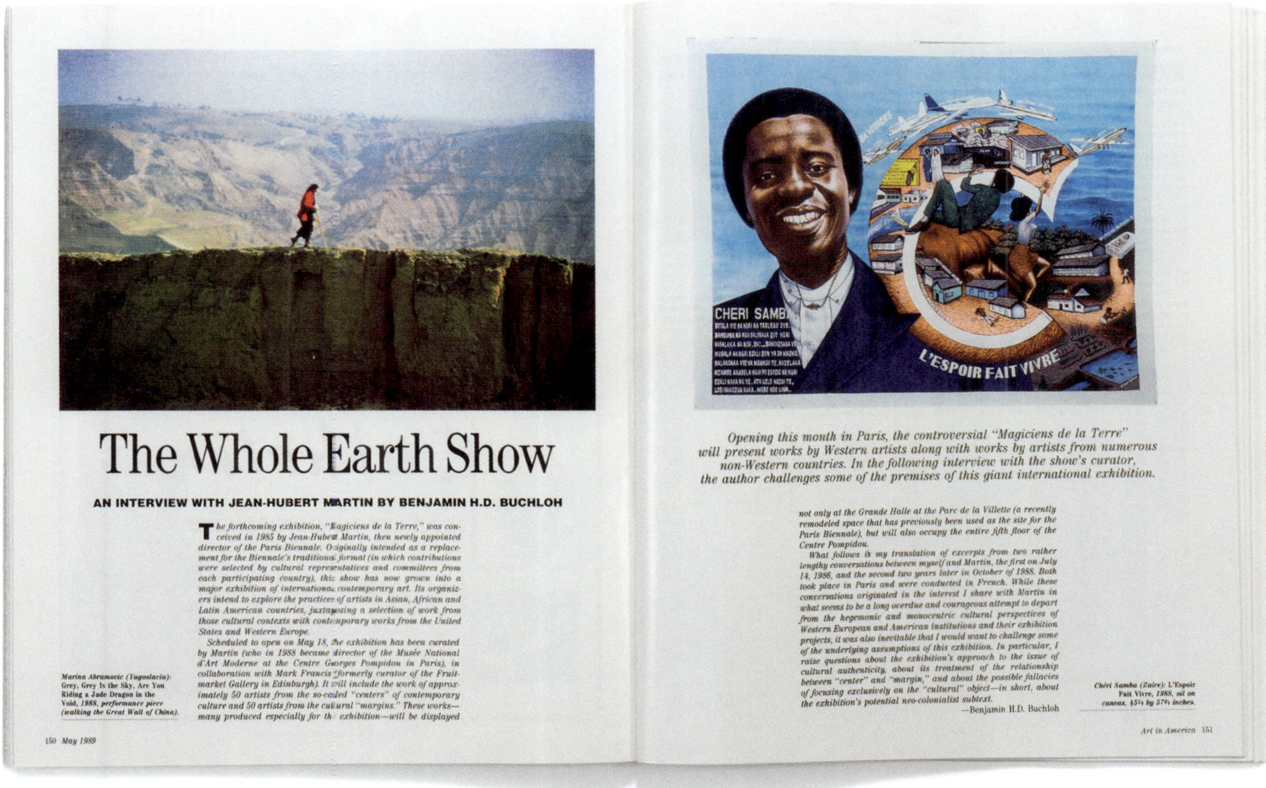

The Whole Earth Show

AN INTERVIEW WITH JEAN-HUBERT MARTIN BY BENJAMIN H.D. BUCHLOH

The forthcoming exhibition, "Magiciens de la Terre," was conceived in 1985 by Jean-Hubert Martin, then newly appointed director of the Paris Biennale. Originally intended as a replacement for the Biennale's traditional format (in which contributions were selected by cultural representatives and committees from each participating country), this show has now grown into a major exhibition of international contemporary art. Its organizers intend to explore the practices of artists in Asian, African and Latin American countries, juxtaposing a selection of work from those cultural contexts with contemporary works from the United States and Western Europe.

Scheduled to open on May 18, the exhibition has been curated by Martin (who in 1988 became director of the Musée National d'Art Moderne at the Centre Georges Pompidou in Paris), in collaboration with Mark Francis (formerly curator of the Fruitmarket Gallery in Edinburgh). It will include the work of approximately 50 artists from the so-called "centers" of contemporary culture and 50 artists from the cultural "margins." These works—many produced especially for the exhibition—will be displayed

Marina Abramovic (Yugoslavia): Grey, Grey Is the Sky, Are You Riding a Jade Dragon in the Void, *1988, performance piece (walking the Great Wall of China).*

150 *May 1989*

Opening this month in Paris, the controversial "Magiciens de la Terre" will present works by Western artists along with works by artists from numerous non-Western countries. In the following interview with the show's curator, the author challenges some of the premises of this giant international exhibition.

not only at the Grande Halle at the Parc de la Villette (a recently remodeled space that has previously been used as the site for the Paris Biennale), but will also occupy the entire fifth floor of the Centre Pompidou.

What follows is my translation of excerpts from two rather lengthy conversations between myself and Martin, the first on July 14, 1986, and the second two years later in October of 1988. Both took place in Paris and were conducted in French. While these conversations originated in the interest I share with Martin in what seems to be a long overdue and courageous attempt to depart from the hegemonic and monocentric cultural perspectives of Western European and American institutions and their exhibition projects, it was also inevitable that I would want to challenge some of the underlying assumptions of this exhibition. In particular, I raise questions about the exhibition's approach to the issue of cultural authenticity, about its treatment of the relationship between "center" and "margin," and about the possible fallacies of focusing exclusively on the "cultural" object—in short, about the exhibition's potential neo-colonialist subtext.

—Benjamin H.D. Buchloh

Chéri Samba (Zaire): L'Espoir Fait Vivre, *1988, oil on canvas, 45¼ by 57⅞ inches.*

Art in America 151

for or about, others – that the possibility of a global culture resides." Further, the fourteen "peripatetic artists," as they were labeled in the issue, confirmed in their interviews that a new global territory of art making was emerging. In the same edition a review of the exhibition *Magiciens de la terre* appeared under the heading "The Whole Earth Show." The exhibition, curated by Jean-Hubert Martin, was described as a "controversial worldwide survey of contemporary art." (HB)

Left page:
Art in America, July 1989
Above:
Benjamin H. D. Buchloh, "The Whole Earth Show: An Interview with Jean-Hubert Martin," in: *Art in America*, May 1989, pp. 150–151

Landmark Exhibitions: 1989 and After

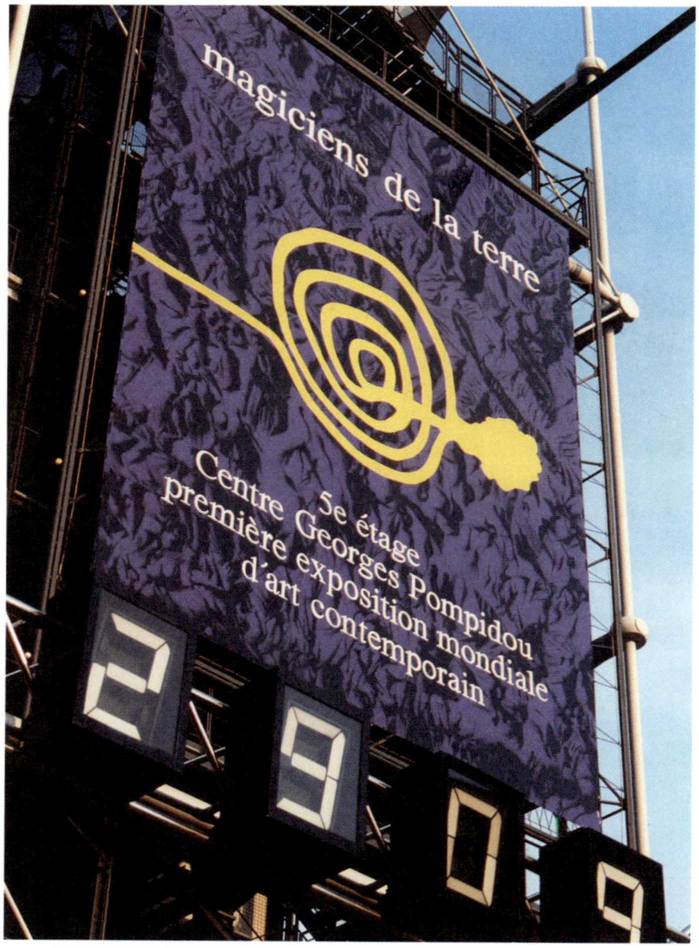

Magiciens de la terre, Paris, May 1989

The Paris exhibition that opened simultaneously in May 1989 at the Centre Pompidou and the Grande halle de la Villette, Paris with the controversial title *Magiciens de la terre* (Magicians of the Earth, instead of artists of the globe) was curated by Jean-Hubert Martin and understood itself as a debut for the collective appearance of 100 artists, of which exactly half had not been represented in the art system before. This program underscored *Magiciens'* diametrically opposed position to the exhibition *"Primitivism" in 20th Century Art* at The Museum of Modern Art, New York (1984) where, for the last time, the priority of modern art over "primitive" art of "indigenous peoples" was proclaimed as representative of the "authentic" art practice of a separate "world art." In Paris, by contrast, representatives of "authentic" art practice in the sense of old traditions were exhibited

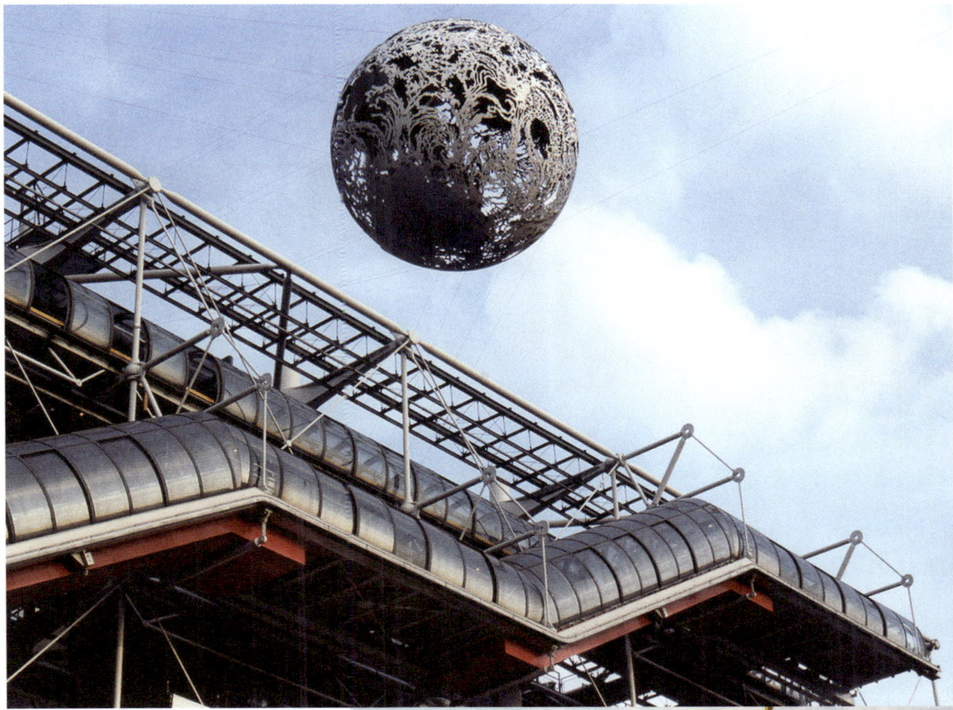

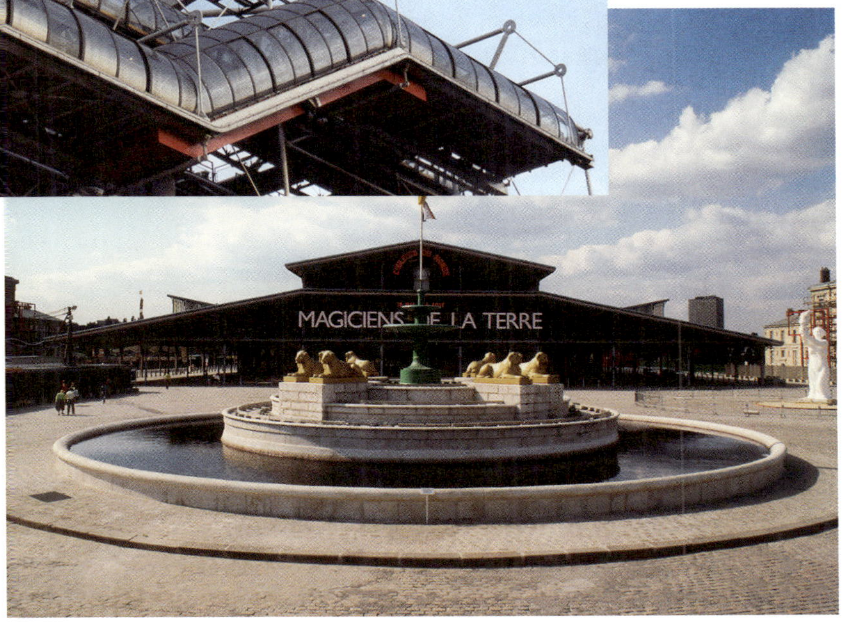

next to professional artists from Africa who worked with new media. The debate on Jean-Hubert Martin's concept of "worldwide" (*mondialisé*) art has substantially influenced the discourse in subsequent exhibitions and has spawned numerous counter models. For a number of artists, such as Chéri Samba, this was their first opportunity to participate in an international exhibition. Especially controversial was the juxtaposition of Richard Long's Minimalism with the earthwork of an Australian Aborigine group. (More information is available on the exhibition website http://magiciensdelaterre.fr) (HB)

Left page:
Magiciens de la terre, exhibition poster in front of the Centre Pompidou, 1989
Above, from right:
Neil Dawson, *Globe*, 1989, hanging in front of the Centre Pompidou for the exhibition *Magiciens de la terre Magiciens de la terre*
External view of the Grande halle de la Villette Paris, 1989

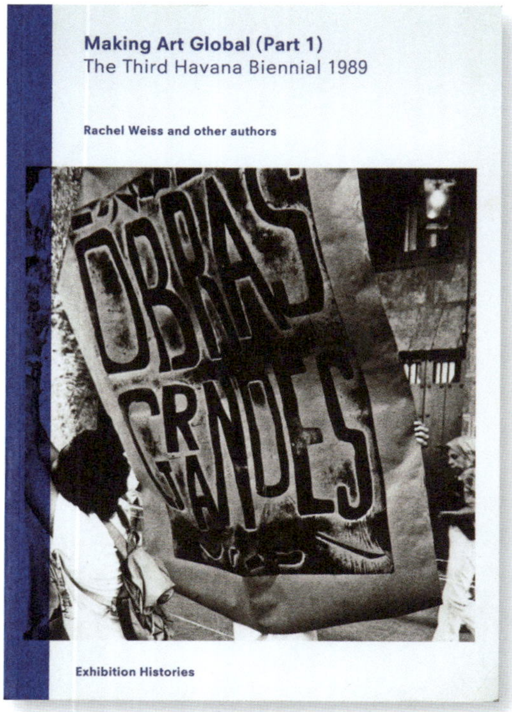

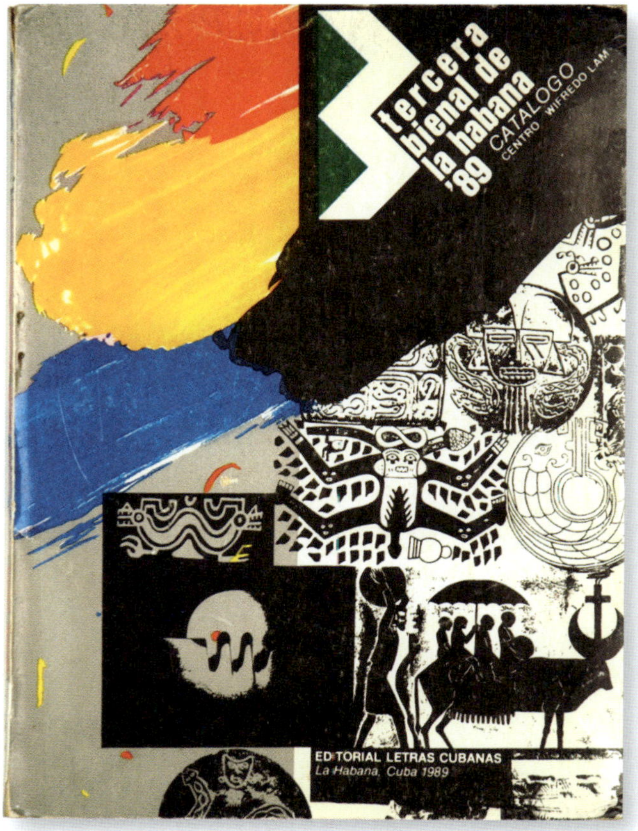

Bienal de La Habana, Havana, October 1989

At the time of its foundation in 1984, the Havana Biennial concentrated on Latin America and only extended its focus to the "Third World" in 1986. With the participation of 690 artists from 57 countries it was the "the first global contemporary art show ever made" (Gerardo Mosquera, 2011). The Third Havana Biennial, which was postponed from 1988 to 1989, for the first time had a theme, which was formulated in its title *Tradition and Contemporaneity in the Arts in the Environment of the Third World (Tradicion y Contemporaneidad en las Artes Plasticas y el Ambiente del Tercer Mundo)*. More than fifty countries participated. Thus, "a new space, acting as a gigantic *Salon des Refusés*" (Mosquera, 2011) was created. However, in Cuba itself the censorship, which critical art from its own country encountered, caused a wave of emigration. (HB)

Above, from left:
Rachel Weiss et al., *Making Art Global (Part 1): The Third Havana Biennial 1989: Exhibition Histories*, vol. 2, Afterall, London, 2011
Tercera Bienal de La Habana. Tradicion y Contemporaneidad en las Artes Plasticas y el Ambiente del Tercer Mundo, exhib. cat., Centro Wifredo Lam, Editorial Letras Cubanas, Havana, 1989

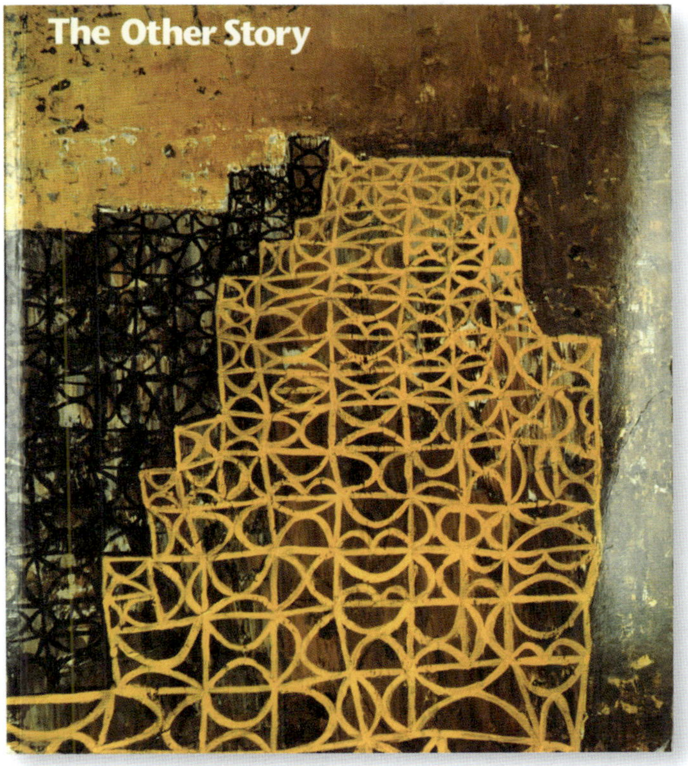

The Other Story, London, November 1989

The discussion of "forgotten" or "lost" avant-gardes currently serves to reconstruct the history of modernism. However, they were not forgotten; rather, they were dismissed in order to keep the picture of modernism clear. Rasheed Araeen began to reclaim a share in the history of modernism that for a long time was denied to artists with a different provenance. *The Other Story*, as Rasheed Araeen titled his London exhibition of "Afro-Asian artists in post-war Britain" at the Hayward Gallery in 1989, highlighted "the absence of non-European artists from the history of modern art." The recovery of neglected names was an appeal to rethink modernism. Their absence in a way had made the narrative of Western modernism possible. The recovery of missing chapters in modernism was the reason why Araeen launched the periodical *Third Text* in 1987. A special issue of *Third Text*, edited by Jean Fisher in Autumn/Winter 1989, was dedicated to *The Other Story*. Fisher wrote: "*The Other Story* is not an attempt to rewrite history but to present the simple fact that historiography has been an exclusive construct that has written out of British art history the contributions, and existence even, of its 'other' artists" ("The Other Story. Afro-Asian Artists in Post-war Britain," in: *Third Text Special Issue*, 1989, p. 4). (HB)

Above:
Rasheed Araeen (ed.), *The Other Story. Afro-Asian Artists in Post-war Britain*, exhib. cat., Hayward Gallery, London; Wolverhampton Art Gallery; Manchester City Art Gallery and Cornerhouse; Southbank Centre, London, 1989

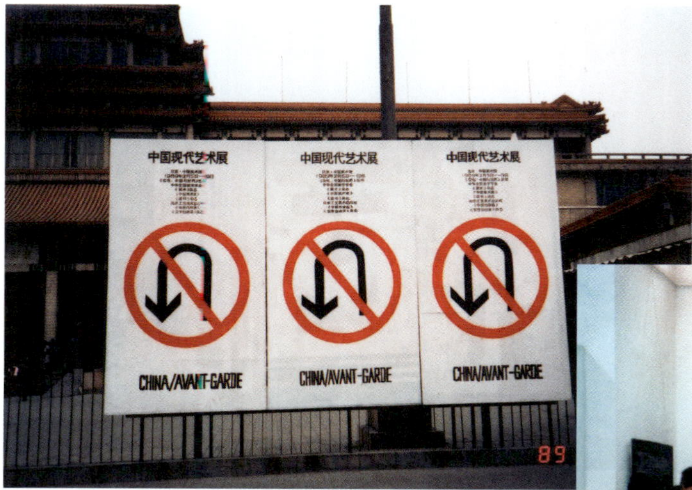

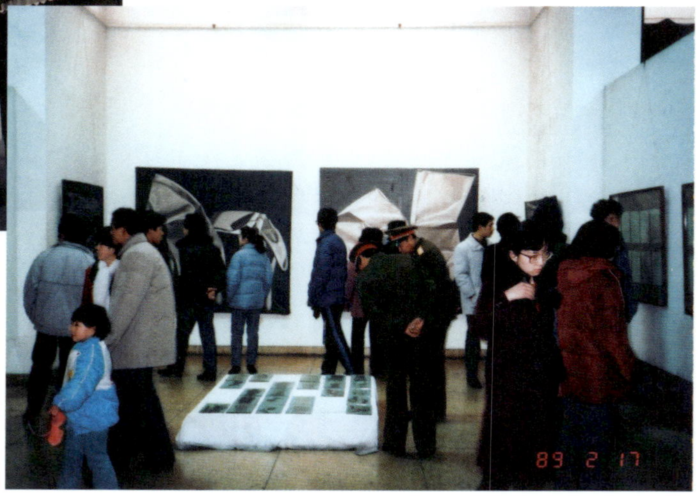

China/Avant-Garde, Beijing, February 1989

On February 5, 1989, the *China/Avant-Garde* exhibition opened (and soon closed again) at the National Art Museum of China, Beijing. Curated by Gao Ming Lu and others, it was the first large-scale contemporary art exhibition conceived by art critics as well as the first national avant-garde art exhibition in China. The show was meant to present the '85 New Wave Movement and therefore encountered a lot of resistance from the government, given the political implications of the art shown. The exhibition was also controversial because of the provocative performances staged by some artists during the opening reception. A total of thirty artists participated in the show. A catalog was never published. This momentous exhibition was later labeled as "the farewell ceremony of the '85 Movement," just a few months before the Tiananmen Square massacre. In 2007, the curator Fei Dawei and the Ullens Center for Contemporary Art in Beijing, staged an exhibition as a moderate commemoration of the movement with the subtitle *The Birth of Chinese Contemporary Art*. (HB)

Above, from left:
China/Avant-Garde, exhibition posters, National Art Museum of China, Beijing, 1989
Works by Zhang Peili at *China/Avant-Garde*, National Art Museum of China, Beijing, 1989

China's New Art, Post-1989, Hong Kong, 1993

A kind of follow-up to the *China/Avant-Garde* exhibition was the show *China's New Art, Post-1989* at the Hong Kong Arts Centre and Hong Kong City Hall. It was curated by Chang Tsong-zung (Johnson Chang), Li Xianting, and Oscar Ho. Afterwards, the exhibition traveled to Australia, Canada, and the USA. In Australia, it was given the title *Mao Goes Pop*. It is significant that the Hong Kong show took place outside of mainland China. The exhibition also reacted to the crisis of the avant-garde in China and dedicated one section to the topical Cynical realism, which in the meantime had become established in Chinese art. One of the contributions in the accompanying catalog dealt with "Artful Marketing from China, 1989 to 1993." Unlike the *China/Avant-Garde* exhibition, this time a monumental catalog documented the new importance and visibility of contemporary art from China at the moment when the global art worlds were taking notice of the new phenomenon. The year 1989 was utilized as a watershed. The show was first discussed with the Beijing critic Li Xianting in February 1989. Li Xianting coined the terms "Political Pop" and "Cynical realism" in 1991. Chang Tsong-zung, also as gallery owner, realized for the first time in 1993 "the idea of a contemporary art show from China." (HB)

Below:
Valerie C. Doran (ed.), *China's New Art, Post-1989*, exhib. cat., Hong Kong Arts Centre, Hong Kong City Hall, Hanart T Z Gallery, Hong Kong, 1993

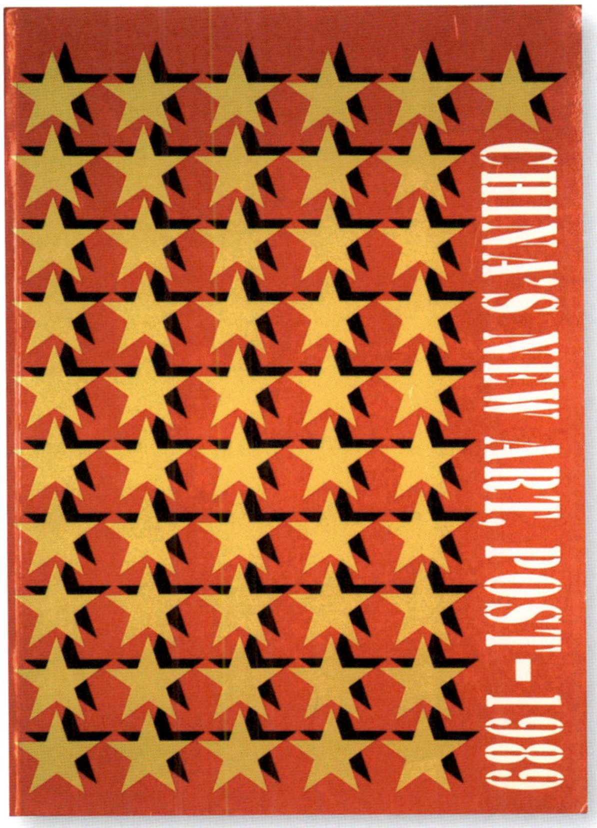

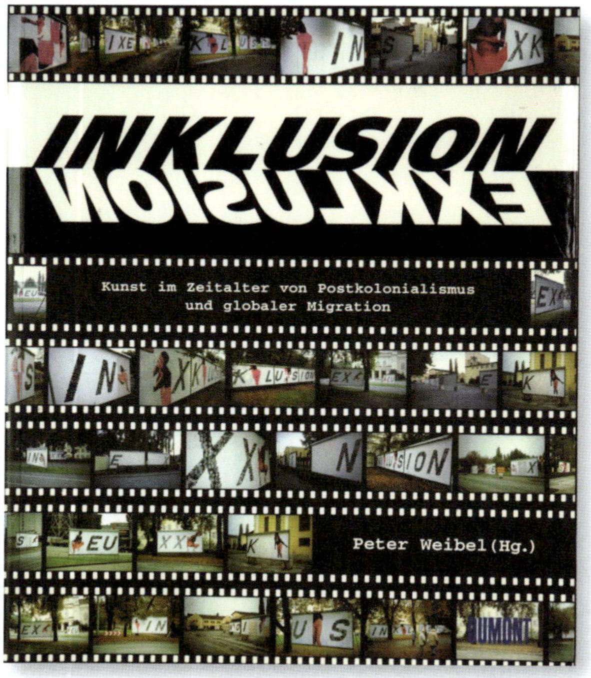

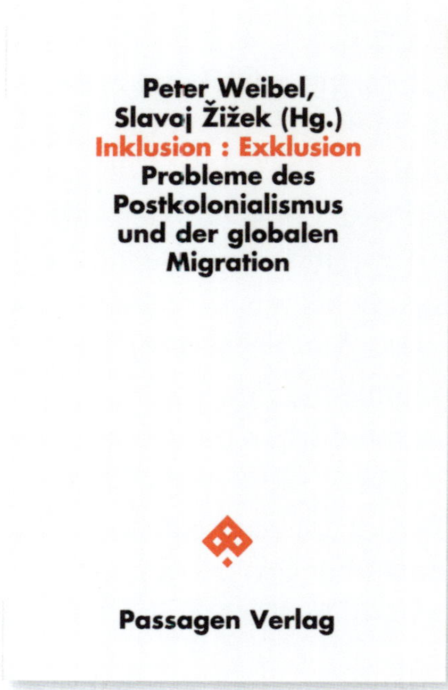

Inklusion : Exklusion, Graz, 1996

The exhibition *Inklusion : Exklusion – Kunst im Zeitalter von Postkolonialismus und globaler Migration* [Inclusion : Exclusion – Art in the Age of Postcolonialism and Global Migration] was curated by Peter Weibel in 1996 in the context of the steirischer herbst 96 festival in Graz, Austria. It was an attempt to draw up a new cartography of art in the age of postcolonialism and global migration, as the subtitle of the catalog announced. The exclusion of artists of non-Western origin had been a central problem of hegemonic modernism. Thus, the exhibition demanded that the colonial situation of the Third World be overcome and the imperial discourse of the binarism of center and periphery be ended. The map of culture must be decolonized in the sense of a veritable global culture (see: Peter Weibel (ed.), *Inklusion : Exklusion: Versuch einer neuen Kartografie der Kunst im Zeitalter von Postkolonialismus und globaler Migration*, exhib. cat., steirischer herbst, Graz, DuMont, Cologne, 1997, p. 11).

The exhibition, in which numerous artists took part, was grouped around thematic areas which built the basis for Weibel's conception (1996) under the overall title "Museum of Global Art" of the future Künstlerhaus Graz. A companion publication put together with Slavoj Žižek elaborated the concept of the exhibition. (HB)

Above, from left:
Peter Weibel (ed.), *Inklusion : Exklusion: Versuch einer neuen Kartografie der Kunst im Zeitalter von Postkolonialismus und globaler Migration*, exhib. cat., steirischer herbst, Graz, DuMont, Cologne, 1997
Peter Weibel, Slavoj Žižek (eds.), *Inklusion : Exklusion. Probleme des Postkolonialismus und der globalen Migration*, Passagen Verlag, Vienna, 1997

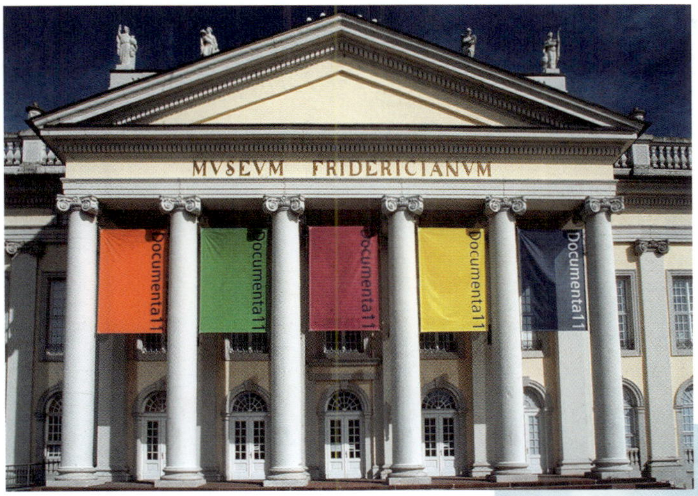

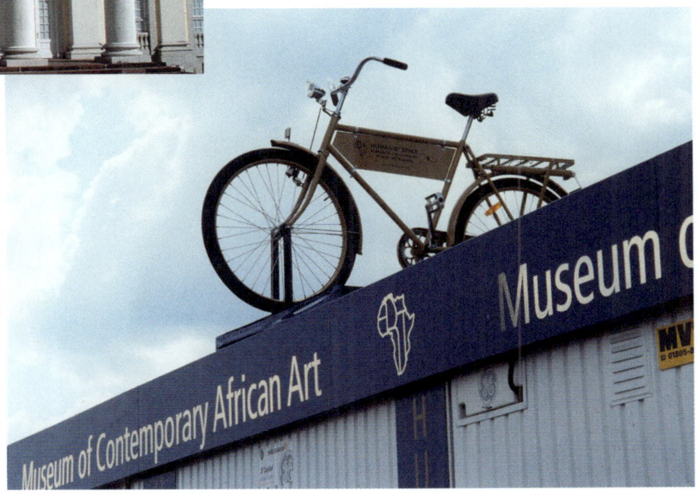

Documenta 11, Kassel, 2002

Documenta 11, which was curated by Okwui Enwezor, is regarded as a turning point in the long history of Germany's most important international exhibition of contemporary art for it appointed its first non-European artistic director. The show was prepared by four platforms in other parts of the world at which cultural and political subjects were discussed as the true issues in the global age.

The success of Documenta 11 was confirmed by two opposing criticisms; one complained that it was no longer Western enough, and the other maintained that it was still too Western. The truth is that the show abolished any firm dividing line between Western and non-Western art, exhibiting artists of any origin. Of the 118 artists, the Western proportion was no longer predominant for around 40 artists were non-Western. In the exhibition catalog Jean Fisher wrote an ironical text on "Globalization and Its Critics." (HB)

From left:
Exterior view of the Kunsthalle Fridericianum at Documenta 11, Kassel, 2002
Meschac Gaba, *Humanist Space*, 2002, exhibition view, Documenta 11, Kassel, 2002

Art Spaces.
A Museumscape in Transition

The ZKM | Center for Art and Media Karlsruhe requested seventeen museums, which are presented on the website of GAM – Global Art and the Museum, to provide image and text material visualizing alternative art spaces which link new ideas with the old concept of the "museum" and/or were conceptualized for local art production. This brings into view the profound change in how art institutions are understood that was initiated in the last century with the introduction of the concept of the museum of contemporary art ("MoCA"). The very look of such art spaces, including artists-run or community museums, offers an opportunity to rediscover the current function of the art museum in other cultures. The so-called "Cultural District," like the one which is being built in Abu Dhabi or the one planned for Hong Kong, provides an economic incentive to establish museums in places where they offer a cosmopolitan audience cultural attractions alongside entertainment and shopping. (HB)

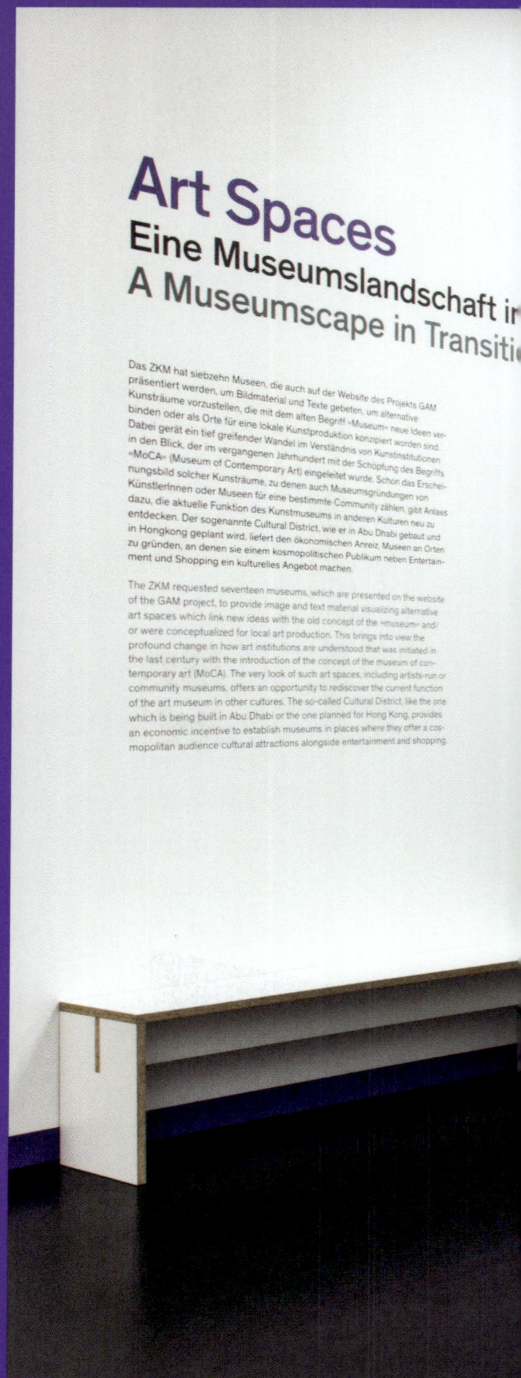

The Global Contemporary. Art Worlds after 1989, section: *Room of Histories*, exhibition view, ZKM | Karlsruhe, 2011–2012

Al-Ma'mal Foundation
BAC
Bandjoun Station
Cemeti Art House
Devi Art Foundation
Inhotim
MAC USP
MoBY
MSU
OCAT
PERMM
Sàn Art
santralistanbul
SMCA
Today Art Museum
Vargas Museum
Zinsou Foundation
The West Kowloon Cultural District
Saadiyat Cultural District

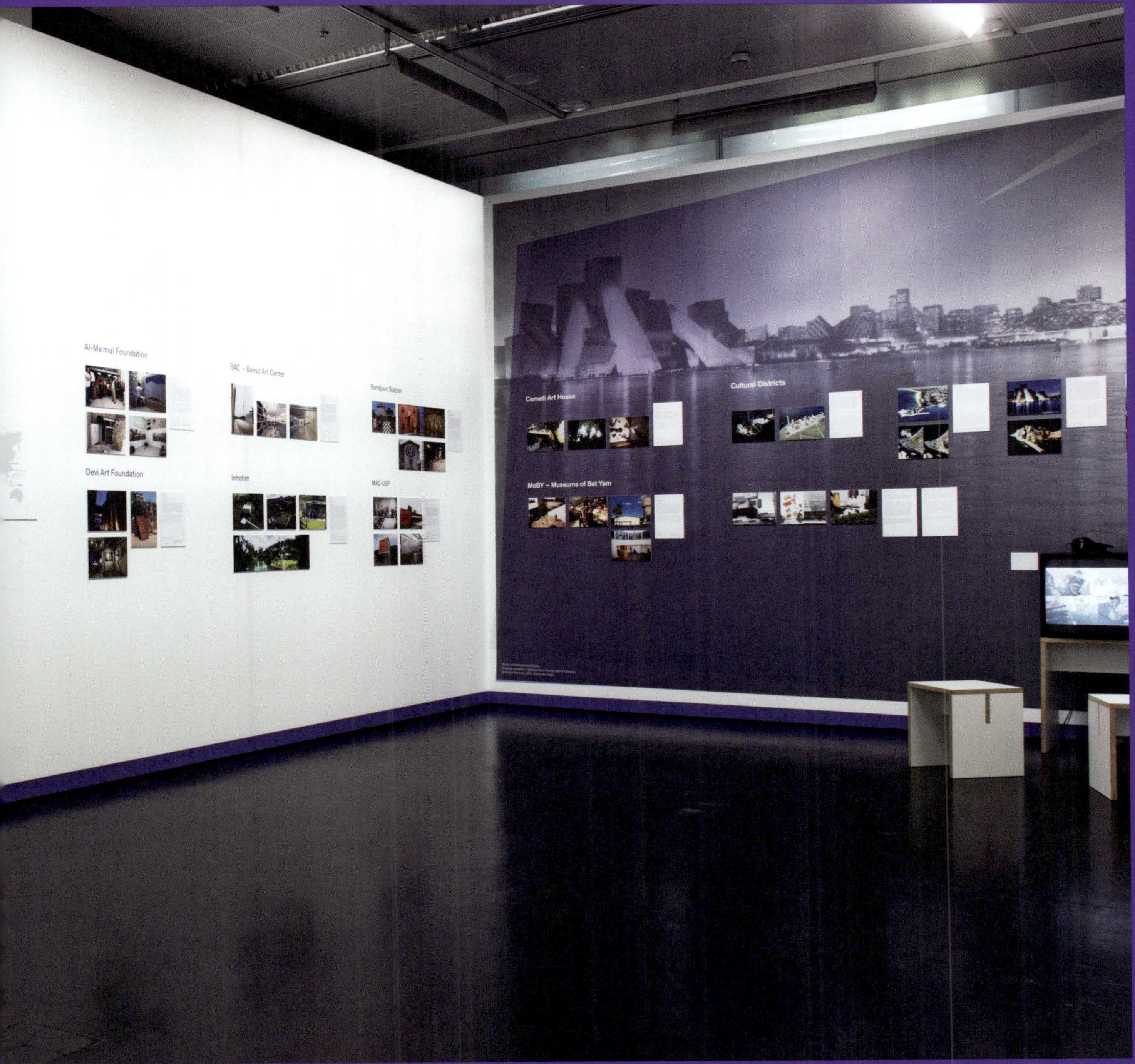

Art Spaces

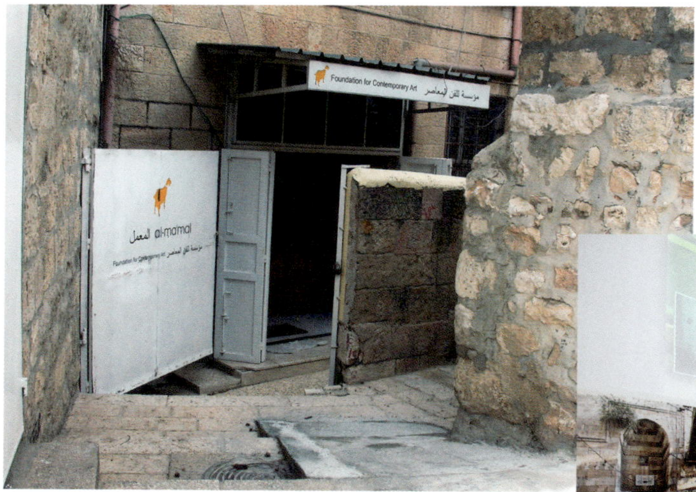

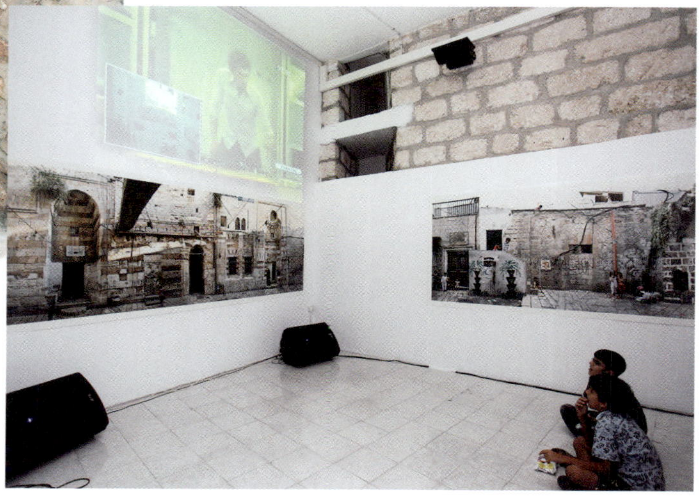

Al-Ma'mal Foundation for Contemporary Art, Jerusalem, Israel
Founding year: 1998
Type: Non-profit, private foundation
Founder: Jack Persekian

Mission

The Al-Ma'mal Foundation is committed to promoting visual literacy and the advancement of contemporary art, navigating through social and political oppression. Through the Foundation, the initiators strive to contribute towards the evolvement of the cultural fabric of Palestinian society. Since its outset Al-Ma'mal has provided Palestinian youth with creative programs and workshops and invited numerous local, national, and international artists to work and exhibit in Jerusalem. Always engaged with its community and aware of both the harsh realities and the sublime beauties of the city, Al-Ma'mal has been a pioneer and a catalyst for making the city of Jerusalem a center for contemporary art.

Above, from left:
Al-Ma'mal Foundation, exterior view
Tarek Atoui, *UnDrum Strategies of Surviving Noise*, performance, live projection from Amman, Jordan

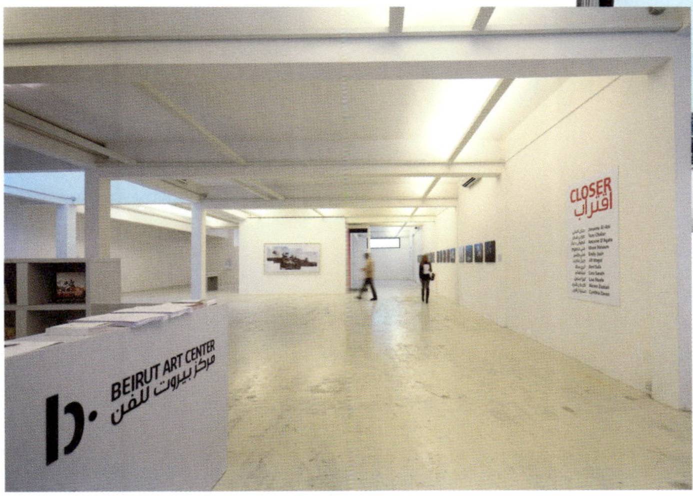

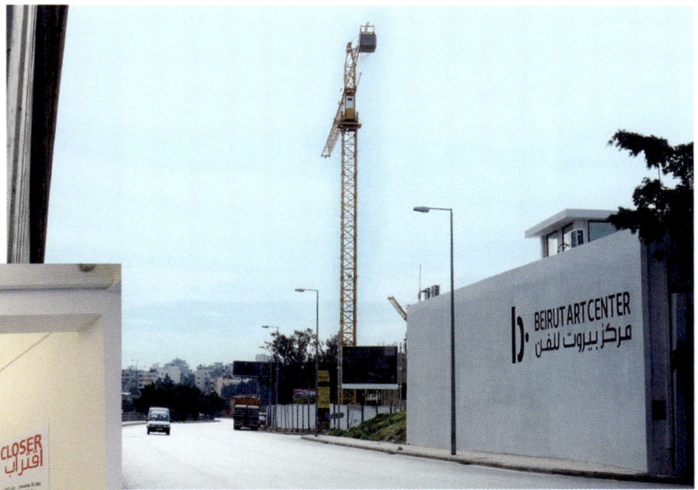

BAC – Beirut Art Center, Beirut, Lebanon

Founding year: 2009
Type: Non-profit association
Founding directors: Sandra Dagher and Lamia Joreige

Mission

Beirut Art Center aims to produce, present, and promote local as well as international contemporary art and cultural practice. Designed by architect Raed Abillama, BAC also has a screening and performance room, a mediatheque, and a bookshop, where lectures, concerts, performances, video projections, and workshops are regularly organized. The purpose of BAC is to serve as a catalyst for the realization of contemporary art projects and for the interaction of local and international cultural players. In particular, the center supports local and regional contemporary artists, who face great difficulties due to the lack of financial and institutional support in this field.

Above, from left:
Beirut Art Center (BAC), exhibition view *Closer*, January 16–April 2, 2009
Beirut Art Center (BAC), exterior view

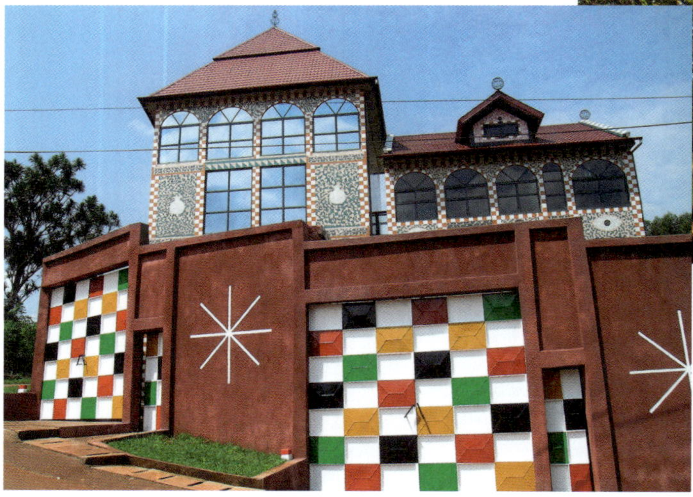

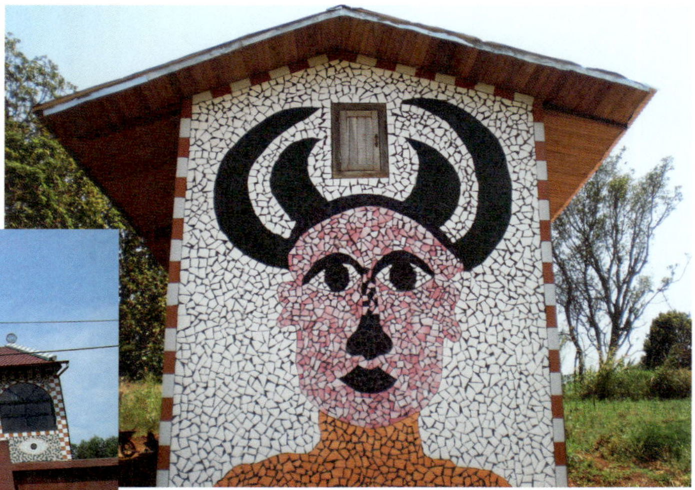

Bandjoun Station, Bandjoun, Cameroon

Founding year: 2008
Type: Non-profit, artist-run initiative
Founder and director: Barthélémy Toguo

Mission

"Our African countries must set up a large number of vibrant and innovative structures in order to stimulate creativity and the desire for culture, as well as to develop the practical side and bring projects to fruition" (Barthélémy Toguo). In order to achieve an independent space for the visual arts, Bandjoun Station has been conceived as a place for art production and exhibition. Its foremost objective is to design a creative workshop environment in order to gather and support fellow artists. Besides residency-programs and temporary exhibitions, Bandjoun Station's mission is to establish an intense dialog with the local community. To pursue such an objective, the center is engaged in a broad spectrum of activities, which range across agriculture, poetry evenings, screenings, concerts by local singers, and even wedding parties.

Above, from left:
Bandjoun Station, exterior views

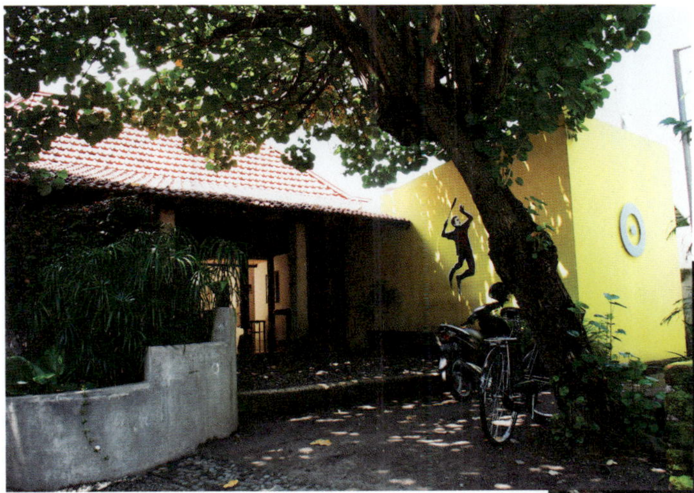

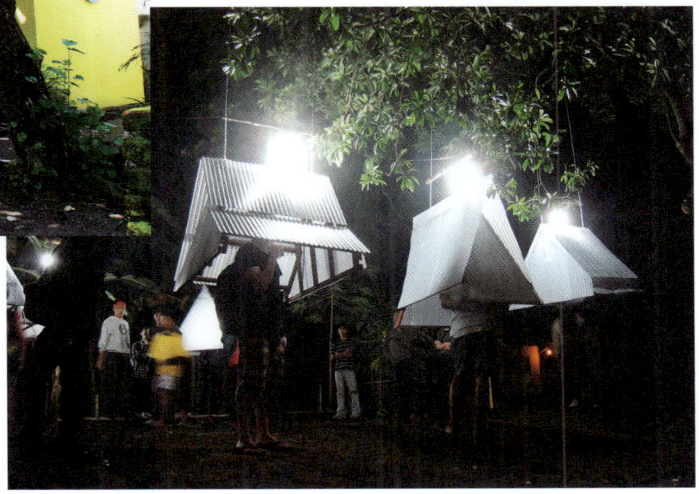

Cemeti Art House, Yogyakarta, Indonesia

Founding year: 1988
Type: Non-profit, artist-run cultural center
Founding directors: Nindityo Adipurnomo and Mella Jaarsma

Mission

The Cemeti Art House presents more than ten projects a year, ranging from site-specific, community-based exhibitions to performances involving local and foreign artists, writers, and curators. Since its foundation the Cemeti Art House has been actively promoting and stimulating practices in the contemporary Indonesian art scene and on a wider international platform, in order to establish, among others, important partnerships with Australian and Dutch institutions. The Cemeti Art House and its studio aim to function as a place for research and exchange where curators, writers, art critics, and artists meet each other in one of the several residency programs offered by the institution.

Above, from left:
Cemeti Art House, exterior view, 2007
Cilia Erens, *Soundspace Yogya*, installation view, presentation of *Landing Soon #10*, 2009

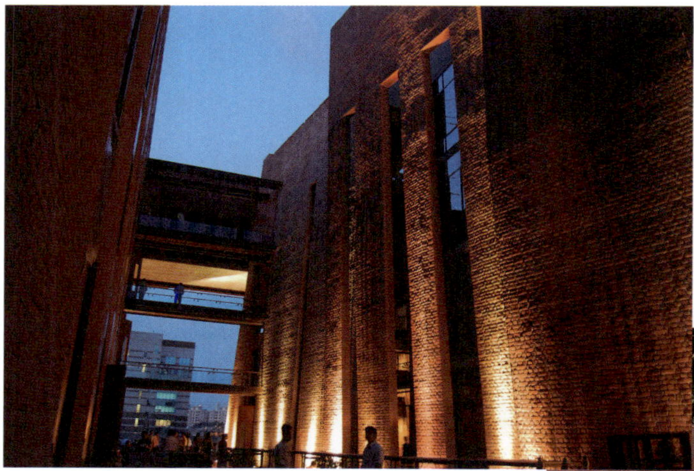

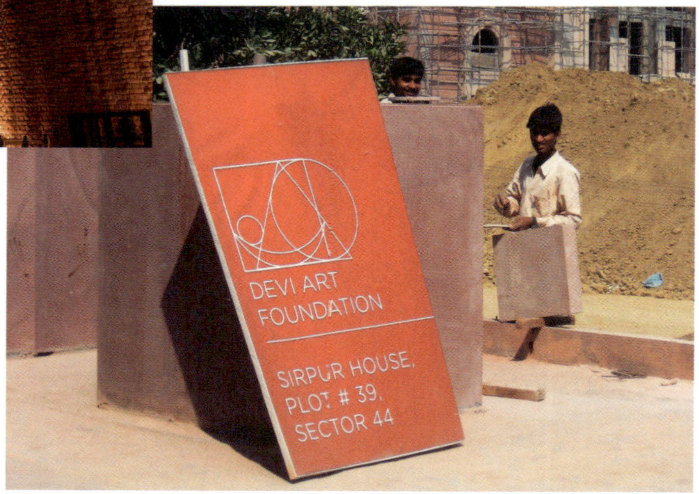

Devi Art Foundation, New Delhi, India

Founding year: 2008
Type: Non-profit institution, collector's museum
Founders: Collectors Lekha Poddar and Anupam Poddar

Mission

The Devi Art Foundation promotes artists from the region engaged in cutting-edge, experimental work. Along with providing a platform for contemporary artists, the Foundation closely interacts with and encourages young curators and critics. By undermining geopolitical divides, the objective of the Foundation is to foster a dialog from within the Indian Sub-continent amongst various art practitioners, comprehensively enhancing the understanding of a shared Indian history. A series of talks and lectures are designed to accompany the exhibitions in an attempt to bridge the gap between art production and a wider audience.

Above, from left:
Devi Art Foundation, exterior view
Devi Art Foundation, still under construction

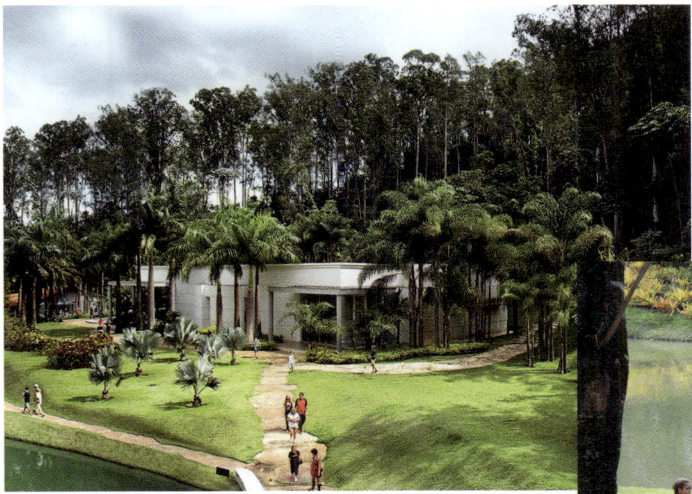

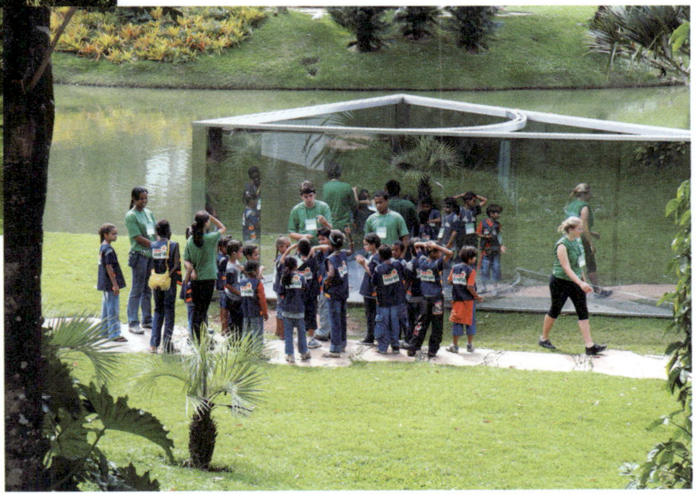

Inhotim, Brumadinho, Brasil

Founding year: 2002
Type: Non-profit, private institution
Founder: Bernardo Paz

Mission

Instituto Cultural Inhotim is a museum complex, formed by a nonlinear sequence of pavilions in the midst of a botanical garden, designed in collaboration with Brazilian artist Roberto Burle Marx. Inhotim holds a precious collection of contemporary art as well as a large number of botanical treasure s. There the environment lives in harmony with art, and both are the basis of wide-reaching educational initiatives of social nature. Inhotim actively contributes to the articulation and implementation of policies focused on improving the quality of life in the region both through their own activities and in partnership with the local authorities. The representative collection of contemporary art at Inhotim has been formed since the mid-1980s, focusing on works created from 1960 onwards. There are paintings, drawings, photographs, videos, and installations by Brazilian and international artists.

Above, from left:
Instituto Cultural Inhotim, view of Galeria Mata
Instituto Cultural Inhotim, schoolchildren during a monitored visit to Dan Graham's artwork

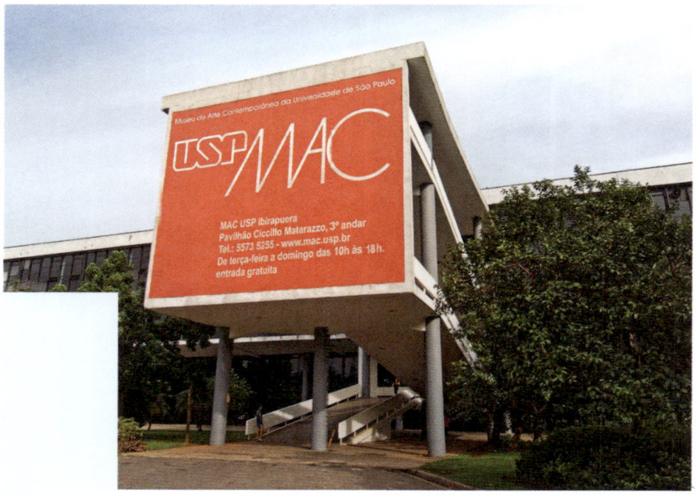

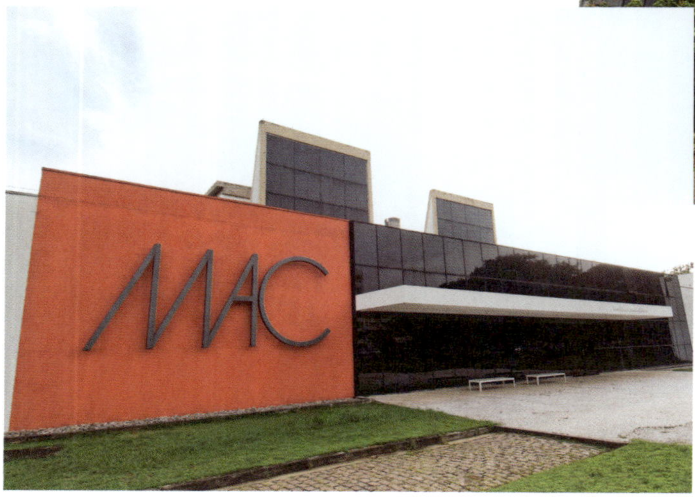

MAC USP – Museum of Contemporary Art of the University of São Paulo, São Paulo, Brazil

Founding year: 1963
Type: University museum
Founder: University of São Paulo

Mission

MAC was created in 1963, when the collection of the Museum of Modern Art of São Paulo (MAM) and the collection of its chairman, the Italian-Brazilian businessman Francisco Matarazzo Sobrinho, were donated to the University of São Paulo. With approximately 8,000 national and international works, the museum collections cover a period from the modernist avant-gardes of the early twentieth century to the present day. As a university museum, its main aim is to research and publicize its collections. The academic research is undertaken by professors who develop their work as scholars and curators by organizing exhibitions, lectures, conferences, and seminars.

Above:
MAC USP, exterior views

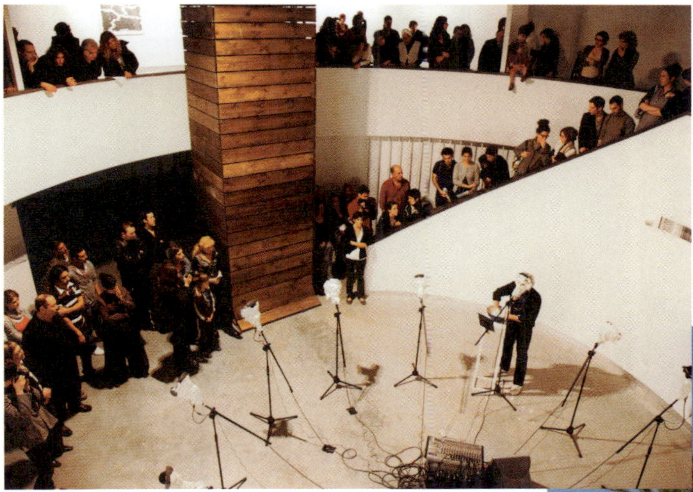

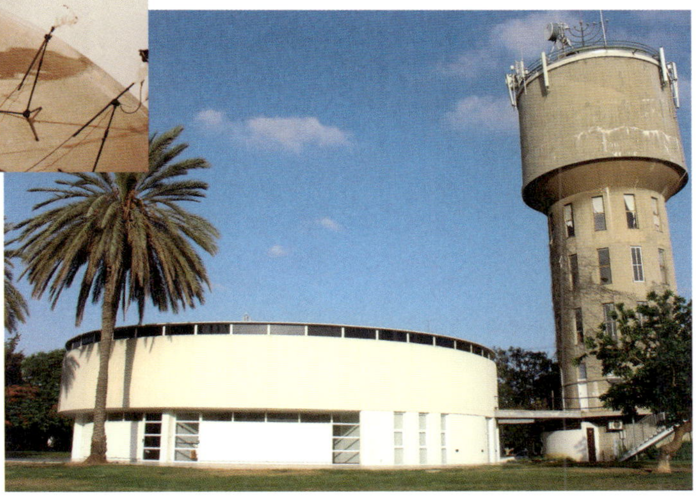

MoBY – Museums of Bat Yam, Bat Yam, Israel

Founding year: 2007
Type: Non-profit, private initiative
Founding director: Milana Gitzin Adiram

Mission

MoBY is a complex of three museums, offering a wide platform for cultural research, theory, and criticism. The museum hosts temporary exhibitions of international contemporary art and holds an ever growing permanent collection of contemporary and modern artworks. MoBY promotes experimental approaches to art, curatorial practice and education, initiates exchanges with peer institutions, and engages in ongoing dialog with various local communities. Over the past three years, the new managing staff has set up an agenda of international exhibitions, public programs, and academic conferences accompanied by catalogs and other publications.

Above, from left:
Opening night of the exhibition *Anticipation Time*, March 6–June 26, 2010
Ben Ari Museum of Contemporary Art, exterior

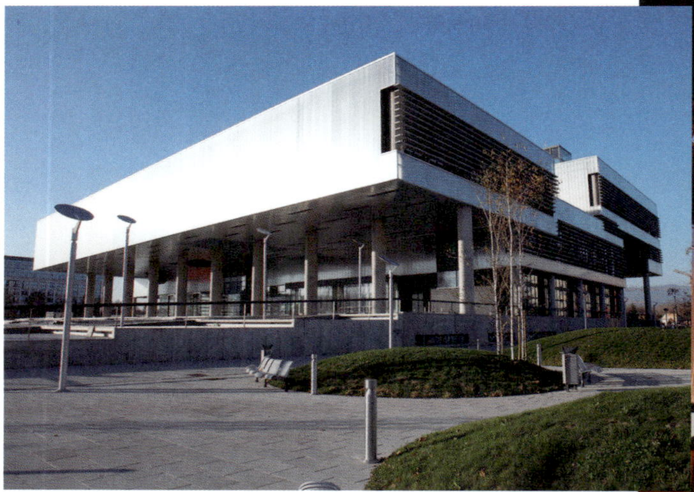

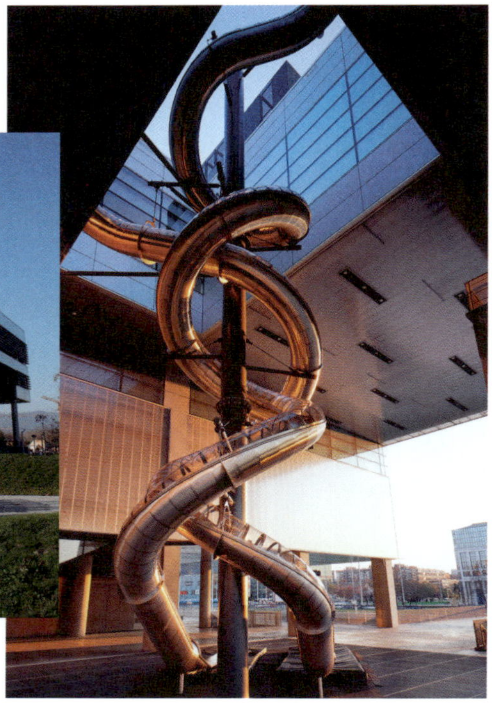

MSU – Museum of Contemporary Art, Zagreb, Croatia

Founding year: 1954
Type: National museum
Founder: National Council of the City of Zagreb

Mission

The mission of the museum is researching, documenting, and promoting events, styles, and phenomena in contemporary art. Since its very beginnings, the museum's goal has been to assemble a relevant collection and to operate in accordance with modern principles of museology. The new building, designed by Igor Franić and opened in December 2010, provides adequate exhibition space to display the museum's collection, which presently comprises around 5,000 artworks of modern and contemporary art. Furthermore, the building hosts several research and production departments, as well as a public library.

Above, from left:
MSU | Zagreb, exterior view
Carsten Höller, *Double Slide*, 2009

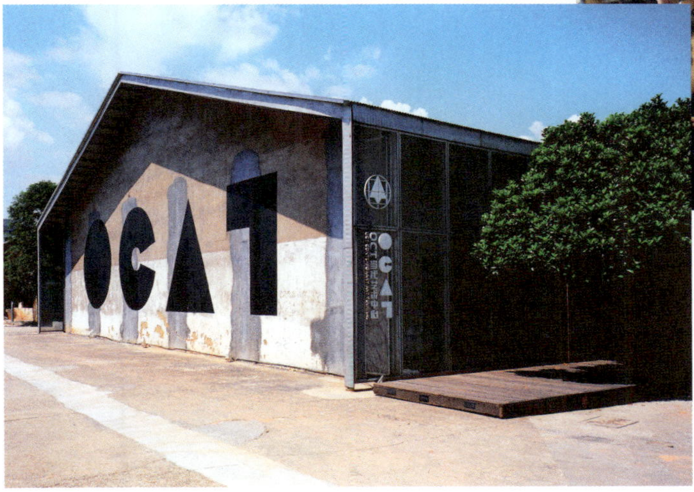

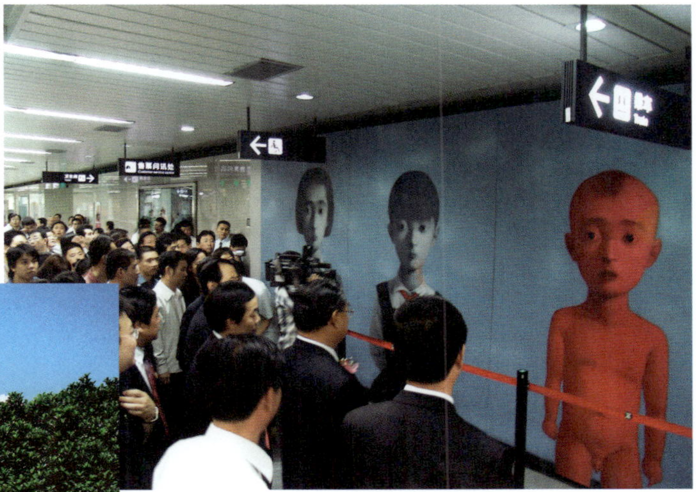

OCAT – Contemporary Art Terminal, Shenzhen, China

Founding year: 2005
Type: Non-profit, national institution
Founder: He Xiangning Art Museum

Mission

OCAT is a Chinese non-profit contemporary art organization formerly part of the national art museum He Xiangning in Shenzhen. In 2012 OCAT became an independent museum. It is named after the “Overseas Chinese Town,” a scenic spot in Shenzhen's Nanshan District in which it is located. Through exhibitions, forums, and artist-in-residence programs, OCAT aims to support Chinese art, while nevertheless maintaining an international vision. It is committed to functioning as a hub, a supply center, and a departure point for contemporary Chinese art, in other words an “international terminal” for contemporary Chinese art. OCAT's program is mainly based on visual art, but also includes performing arts, concerts, screenings, and multimedia presentations.

Above, from left:
OCAT, exterior view
Zhang Xiaogang, *Big Family – Subway*, 2006, part of the Shenzhen Overseas Chinese Town Subway Murals Project

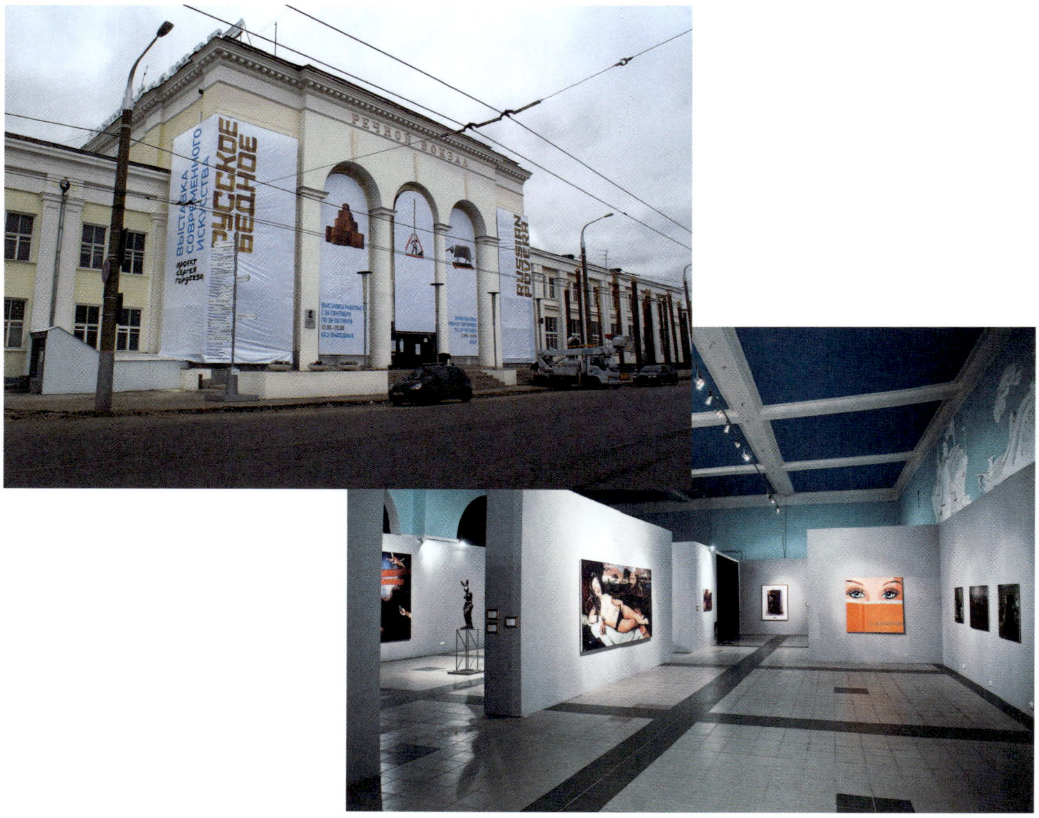

PERMM – Perm Museum of Contemporary Art, Perm, Russia
Founding year: 2009
Type: National museum
Founding Director: Marat Guelman

Mission

The museum program consists not only of exhibitions, but also of festivals, artist talks, lectures, workshops, concerts, and performances, serving as a cultural hub for the city. The museum aims to establish a new model for cultural institutions, becoming an important agent for the socioeconomic development of the Perm region. Offering an attractive cultural program in a new urban environment, the museum strives to facilitate the emergence of new artist generations as well as new cultural institutions. Furthermore, the museum's goal is to play a central role in the reshaping of the city's image as a new cultural destination, by cooperating with media, foreign museums, and creative industries.

Above, from left:
PERMM, exterior view
PERMM, *Night at the Museum*, December 24, 2009–February 28, 2010, exhibition view

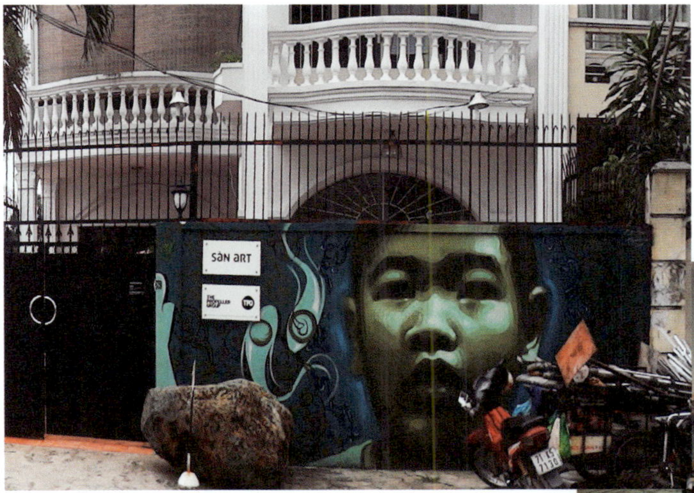

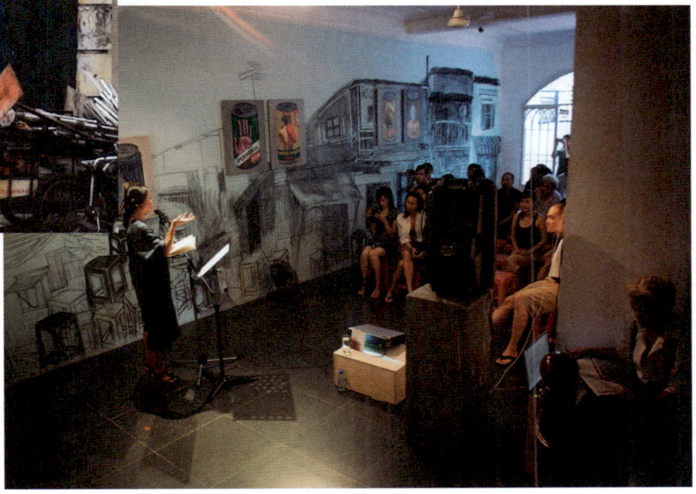

Sàn Art, Ho Chi Minh City, Vietnam
Founding year: 2007
Type: Artist-run, non-profit initiative
Founders: Dinh Q Le, Tuan Andrew Nguyen, Phù Nam Thúc Hà, and Tiffany Chung

Mission

Sàn Art is a production house, facilitator, collaborator, showcase venue, and meeting place. Its program addresses the great lack of access to resources and expertise in the areas of art history, exhibition making, curatorial practice, and criticism in the country. Sàn Art's mission is to empower established and emerging artists in Vietnam and the broader Southeast Asian region by nurturing talent, fostering innovation, and providing a forum for collaboration among local and international creative communities. Offering space and opportunity for artistic engagement by way of exhibition and education programs, Sàn Art operates as a hub that connects and facilitates discussion and projects between local and visiting artists, curators, writers, and researchers.

Above, from left:
Sàn Art, entrance
Reading by writer and poet Lê Thị Diễm Thúy, May 15, 2010

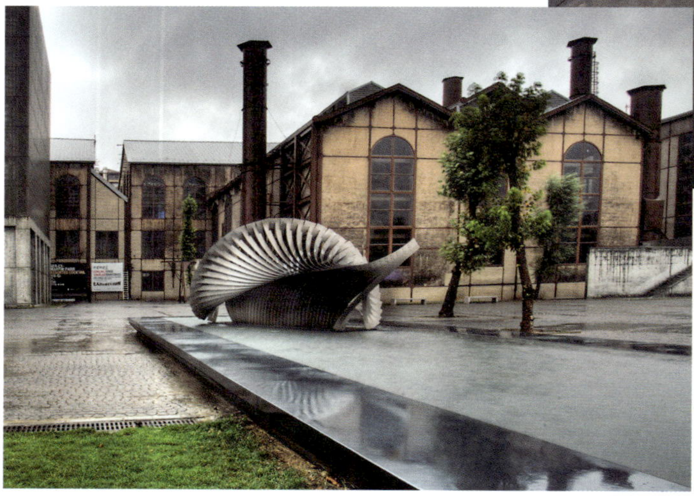

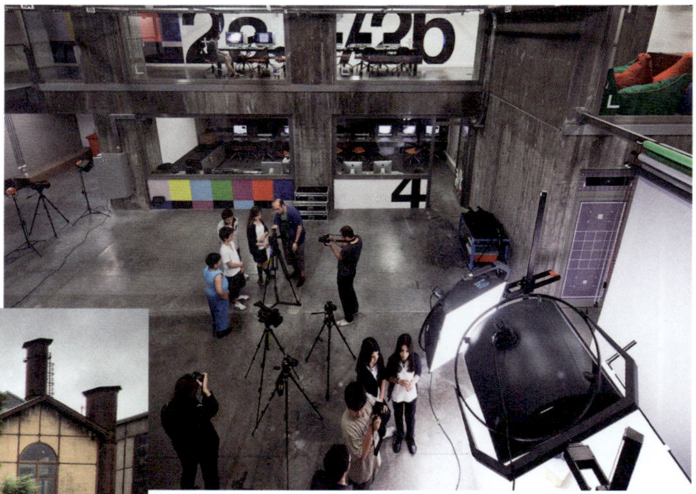

santralistanbul, Istanbul, Turkey

Founding year: 2007
Type: University museum
Founder: Istanbul Bilgi University

Mission

santralistanbul is part of the Istanbul Bilgi University campus and is situated on the site of an abandoned power plant built during the Ottoman Empire. Apart from the Main Gallery and the Museum of Energy, the colossal complex includes university classrooms and departments, a public library, a park, multiple cinemas, a dance hall, open-air performance spaces, a multipurpose tent, restaurants, a shopping street, and artists' residential facilities. santralistanbul aims at becoming an international platform for culture with the purpose of contributing to urban revival.

Above, from left:
santralistanbul, museum's square
Santralatölye (teenagers workshop), summer term 2010

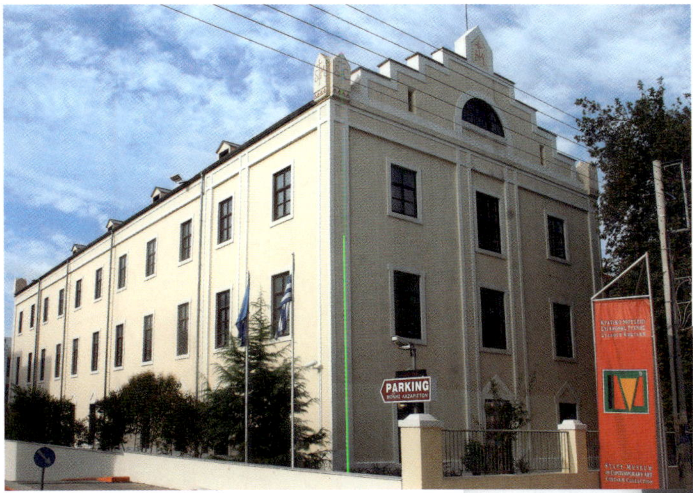

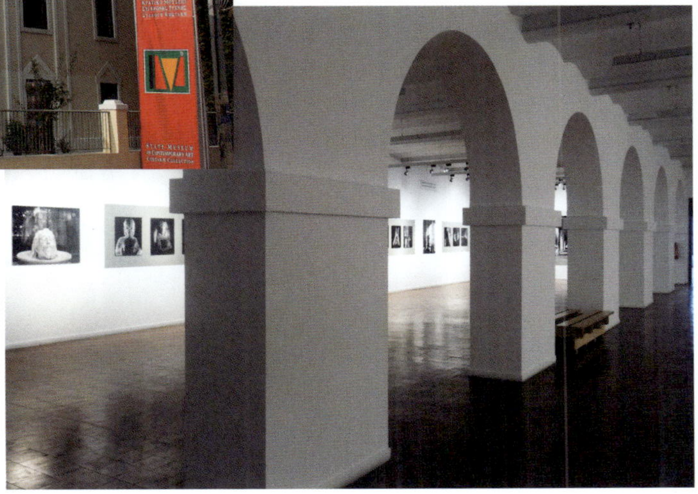

SMCA – State Museum of Contemporary Art, Thessaloniki, Greece
Founding year: 1997
Type: National museum
Founding Director: Miltiadis Papanikolaou

Mission

Since its founding, the SMCA has benefited from the donation of the Costakis Collection, the biggest collection of Russian avant-garde art outside Russia's borders. The museum also comprises the Center of Contemporary Art (CCA), an autonomous department located in the city's port. The CCA pays especial attention to social realities and stays abreast of international trends in contemporary art. In 2007, the SMCA and the CCA initiated the Thessaloniki Bienniale of Contemporary Art to strengthen the presence of Thessaloniki and Greece in the major contemporary art scene. The participation in Artisterium Tbilisi International Contemporary Art Exhibition and Art Events in Georgia and the Gyumri Biennial in Armenia reveals its particular interest in alternative sites for contemporary art.

Above, from left:
SMCA, exterior view
Ali Bramwell, installation view, Artisterium 3, 2010

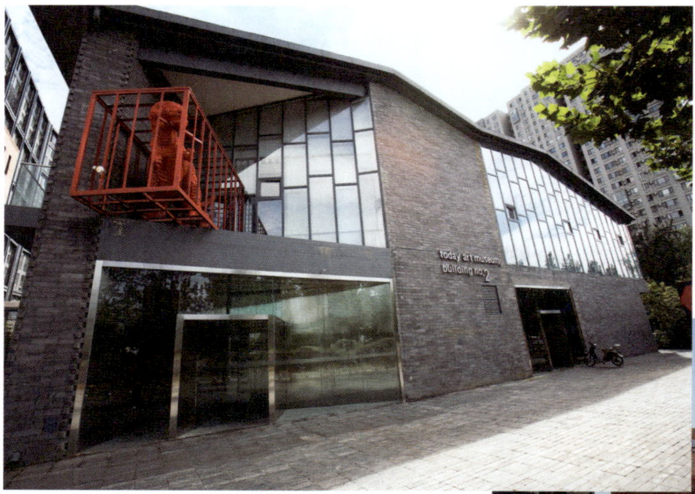

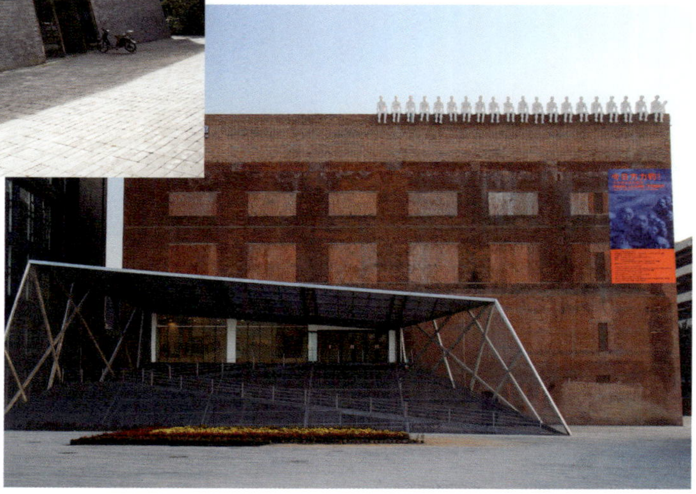

Today Art Museum, Beijing, China
Founding year: 2002
Type: Non-profit, private institution
Founder: Zhang Baoquan

Mission

The Today Art Museum's mission is to promote the advancement of Chinese contemporary art in its variety, movements, and genres. The museum is involved not only in showcasing established names but also in supporting emerging artists of the Chinese contemporary art scene. As a private and non-profit institution, the museum strives to negotiate between private and public, between art system and society, with the explicit intention to "enable people to feel, know, and accept today in today's art." Currently, the museum comprises the following departments: exhibition, academic research, education, collecting, editing and publishing, www.artnow.com.cn, public relations, an information center, video and photography center, bookstore, and other art programs, services, and facilities.

Above, from left:
Today Art Museum, building 2, exterior view
Today Art Museum, building 1, exterior view

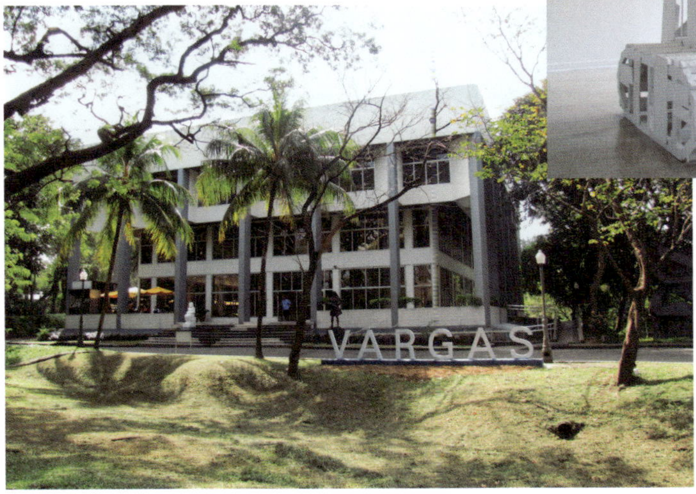

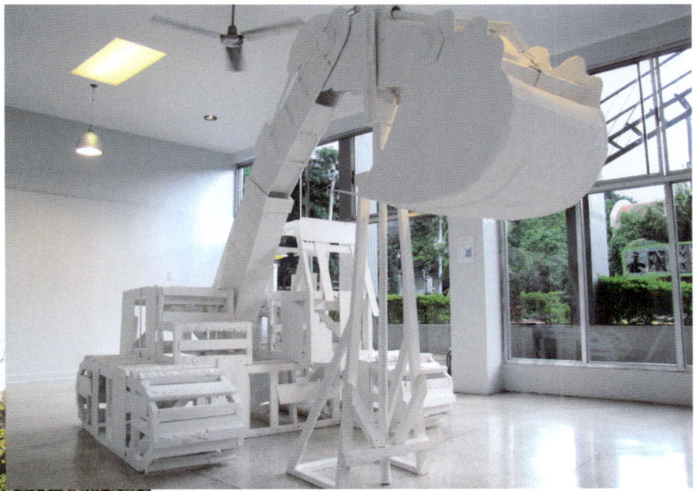

Jorge B. Vargas Museum and Filipiniana Research Center, Quezon City, Philippines

Founding year: 1987
Type: University museum
Founder: University of the Philippines

Mission

The Vargas Museum is the leading museum of the University of the Philippines and the largest in Quezon City, north of the capital Manila. The Museum was named after Jorge B. Vargas, the Philippines' first Executive Secretary and Mayor of Manila. As alumnus of the university, he donated his collection of art, stamps, coins, books, and archives to the institution in 1978. To date, the Vargas Museum is committed to exhibiting the benefactor's permanent collection in dialog with contemporary works to sustain conversations between past and present expressions.

Above, from left:
Vargas Museum, exterior view
Jose Tence Ruiz, *Diablo Ex-Machina*, exhibition view, *Bound*, June–December 2010, GF Lobby and West Wing Gallery

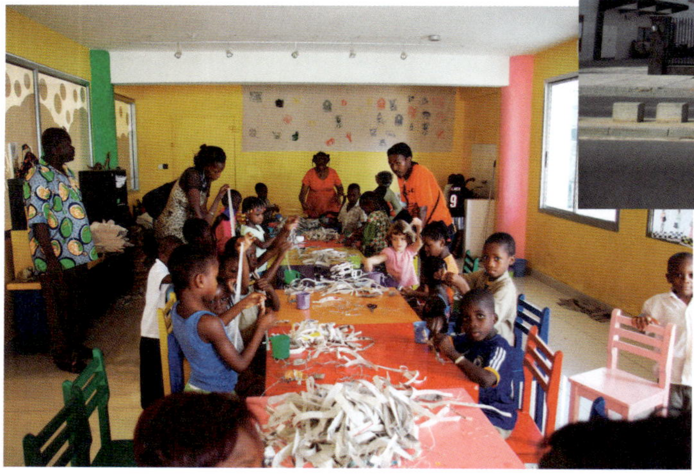

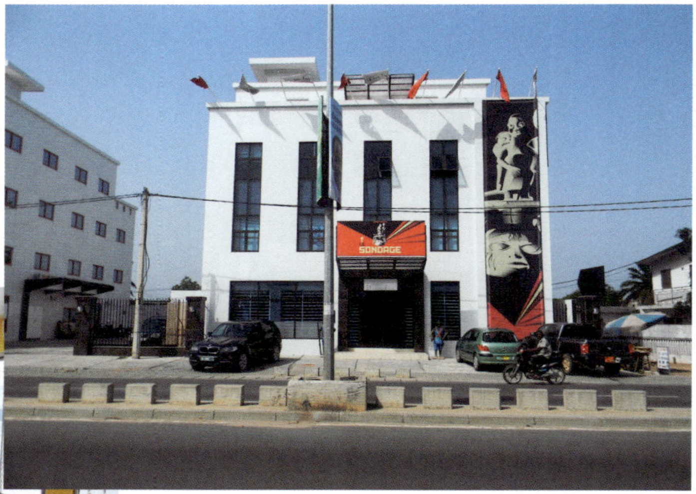

Zinsou Foundation, Cotonou, Benin

Founding year: 2005
Type: Non-profit, family-run foundation
Founders: The Zinsou family

Mission

Valorizing African contemporary art, promoting education, development, and reducing poverty are at the very core of the Zinsou Foundation. To reach a wide and differentiated audience, the Foundation has followed clear and basic principles from the outset: free admission, nonpolitical nature, multilingual communication, and involvement of several local institutions for development. In the beginning a platform for African artists, it has been very active in fields ranging from art to social commitment, always adhering to international standards. In 2009, the founders created an association, which includes French and European funding. Its mission rests on the Foundation's basic principles and mostly deals with fundraising and international relations.

Above, from left:
Children workshop
Zinsou Foundation, exterior view

The West Kowloon Cultural District, Hong Kong, China

The West Kowloon Cultural District (WKCD) is financed by the government of the Hong Kong Special Administrative Region, with a great diversity of stakeholders, to "provide quality culture, entertainment and tourism programs with a must-visit appeal to both local residents and visitors from around the world" (WKCD, www.wkcda.hk/en/about_wkcda/visionfunctionobjective/index.html#1). In an area of 40 hectares the WKCD will offer a rich program of performing art centers, a museum for contemporary visual culture (M+), exhibition spaces, and shopping areas. The master plan is the result of an international competition, in which the "City Park" plan of Foster + Partners (Sir Norman Foster) was selected out of the three entries; the others being by OMA (Rem Koolhaas) and Rocco Design Architects Limited (Rocco Yim).

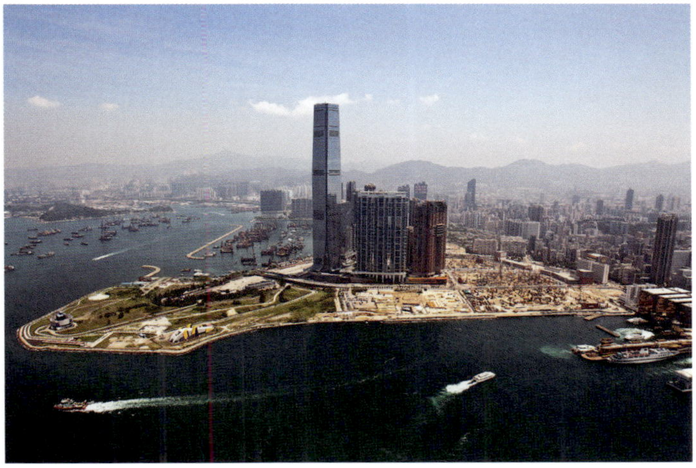

M+ Museum

The M+ is envisaged as a new type of cultural institution, which will focus on twentieth and twenty-first century visual culture. The Museum's Advisory Group has specified "four initial broad groupings," namely, design, moving image, popular culture, and visual art, including ink art (www.wkcda.hk/en/museum/index.html).

By concentrating on visual culture, the museum's collection will include various disciplines, art practices, and techniques from Hong Kong, China, Asia, and other regions of the world. Due to its wide field of interest, M+ has started operating before building is completed in 2016 as "M+ Mobile" – an itinerant hub for small exhibitions and discussion.

Above:
Aerial view of the The West Kowloon Cultural District, Hong Kong

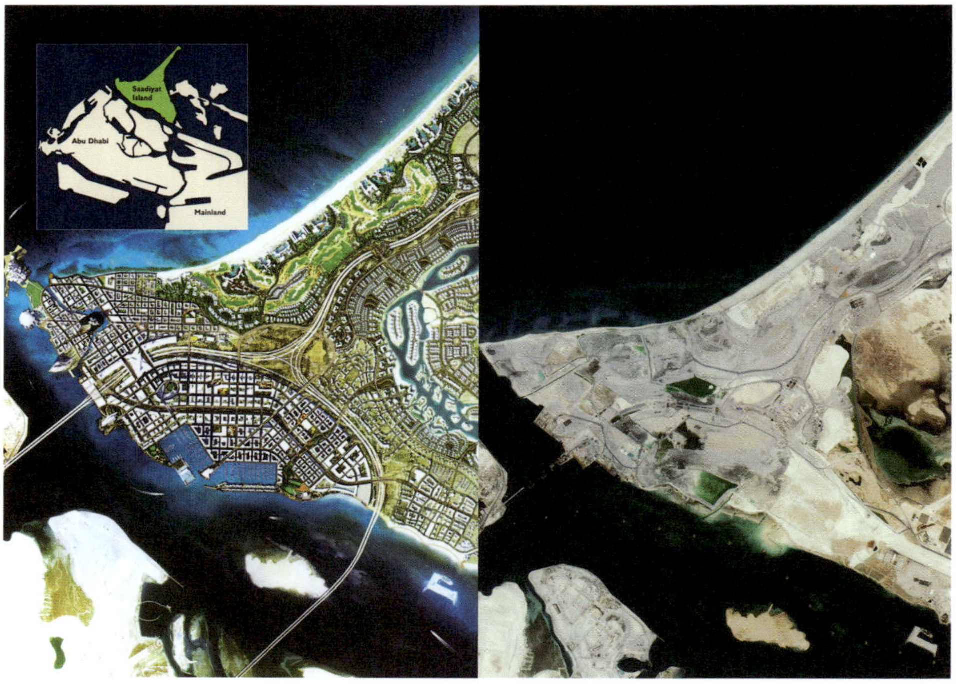

Saadiyat Cultural District, Abu Dhabi, United Arab Emirates
Zayed National Museum (Design: Foster + Partners)
Louvre Abu Dhabi (Design: Ateliers Jean Nouvel)
Guggenheim Abu Dhabi (Design: Gehry Partners, LLP)
The Performing Arts Centre (Design: Zaha Hadid Architects)
Maritime Museum (Design: Tadao Ando Architect & Associates)

Mission

The Saadiyat Cultural District is part of a major commercial, residential, and leisure project, which is currently under construction on Saadiyat Island, a low-lying island located 500 meters off the coast of Abu Dhabi. Expected to open in 2020, Saadiyat Island ("Happiness Island") "is set to redefine Abu Dhabi as an internationally renowned leisure and tourism destination" (TDIC, *Introduction to Saadiyat Cultural District*, Motivate Publishing, Abu Dhabi, 2008, p. 18). Planned and developed by the TDIC (Tourism Development & Investment Company), the project was initiated by Sheikh Zayed bin Sultan Al Nahyan (1918–2004), former President of the United Arab Emirates and Ruler of Abu Dhabi, and Sheikh Mohammed bin Zayed Al Nahyan, Crown Prince of Abu Dhabi and Deputy Supreme Commander of the UAE Armed Forces.

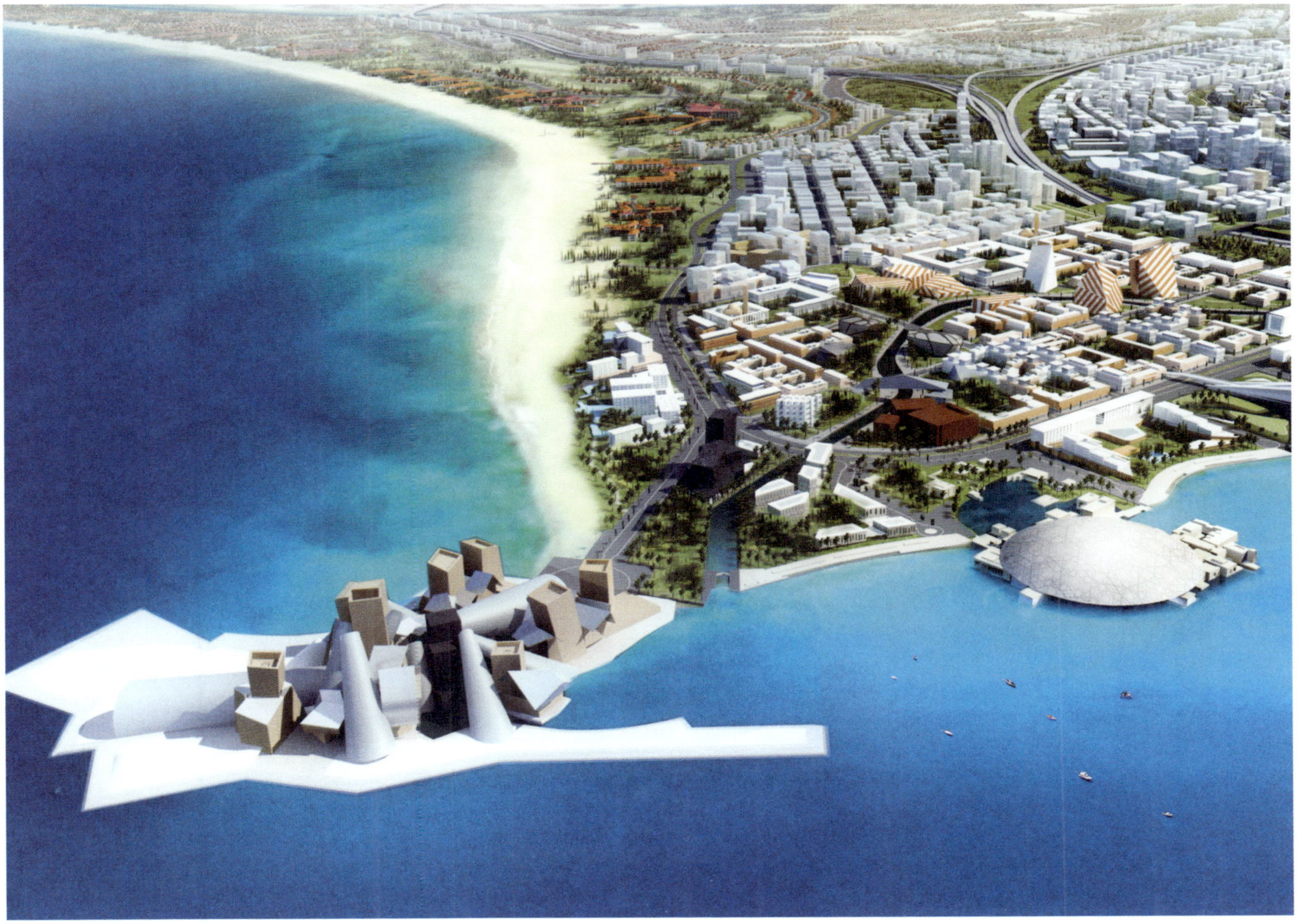

The Cultural District is seen as the most significant feature of the island, which aims to convert Abu Dhabi into an international venue for art and culture. With the "Bilbao Factor" as a model in mind and subscribing to a policy of cultural branding, it operates in partnership with established museums worldwide as well as with global "archistars" like Sir Norman Foster, Jean Nouvel, Frank Gehry, Zaha Hadid, and Tadao Ando.

Above, from left:
Saadiyat Island aerial view before and after development, in: *Saadiyat Island Cultural District Exhibition*, exhib. cat., Gallery One, Emirates Palace Abu Dhabi, 2010
Saadiyat Island Master Plan, in: *Saadiyat Island Cultural District Exhibition*, exhib. cat., Gallery One, Emirates Palace Abu Dhabi, 2010

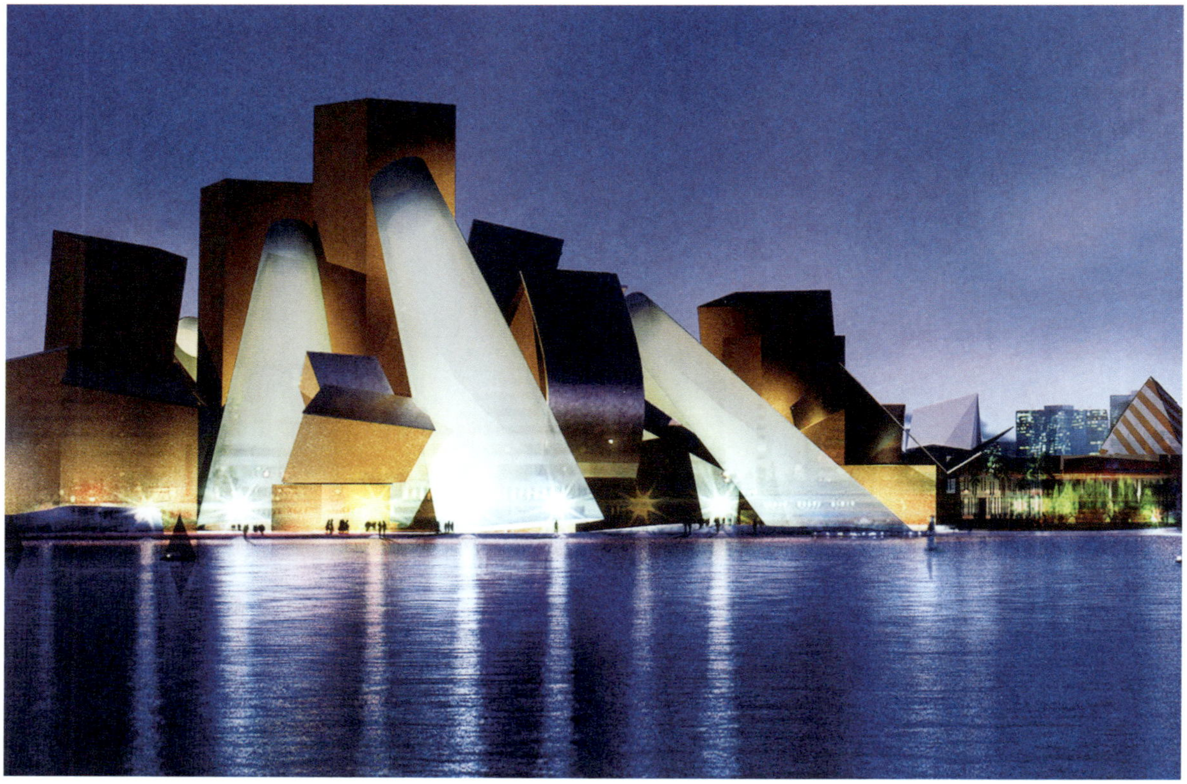

Guggenheim Abu Dhabi, Abu Dhabi, United Arab Emirates
With its 137,200 square meters, the Guggenheim Abu Dhabi will be the Guggenheim Foundation's largest facility. Its focus will be modern and contemporary art since World War II, and will include works from the Guggenheim collection. Scheduled to open in 2017, the museum "will have global art exhibitions and education programs with a particular focus on Middle Eastern contemporary art" (www.guggenheim.org/abu-dhabi). Originally conceived by Thomas Krens, who established the "Guggenheim global brand," the project is now supervised by Juan Ignacio Vidarte, deputy director and chief officer of the Guggenheim Foundation Global Strategies. Designed by Frank Gehry, the Guggenheim Abu Dhabi will show its permanent collection and special exhibitions, and feature a center for art and technology, a center for contemporary Arab, Islamic, and Middle Eastern culture, an education facility, a research center, and a conservation laboratory. "Dramatic conical forms, inspired by the local vernacular architecture, animate the building providing a series of transitional spaces. They function as entrance canopies, atria, and tempered spaces linking the museum's galleries" (TDIC, *Introduction to Saadiyat Cultural District*, Motivate Publishing, Abu Dhabi, 2008, p. 38).

Above:
Guggenheim Abu Dhabi, project rendering

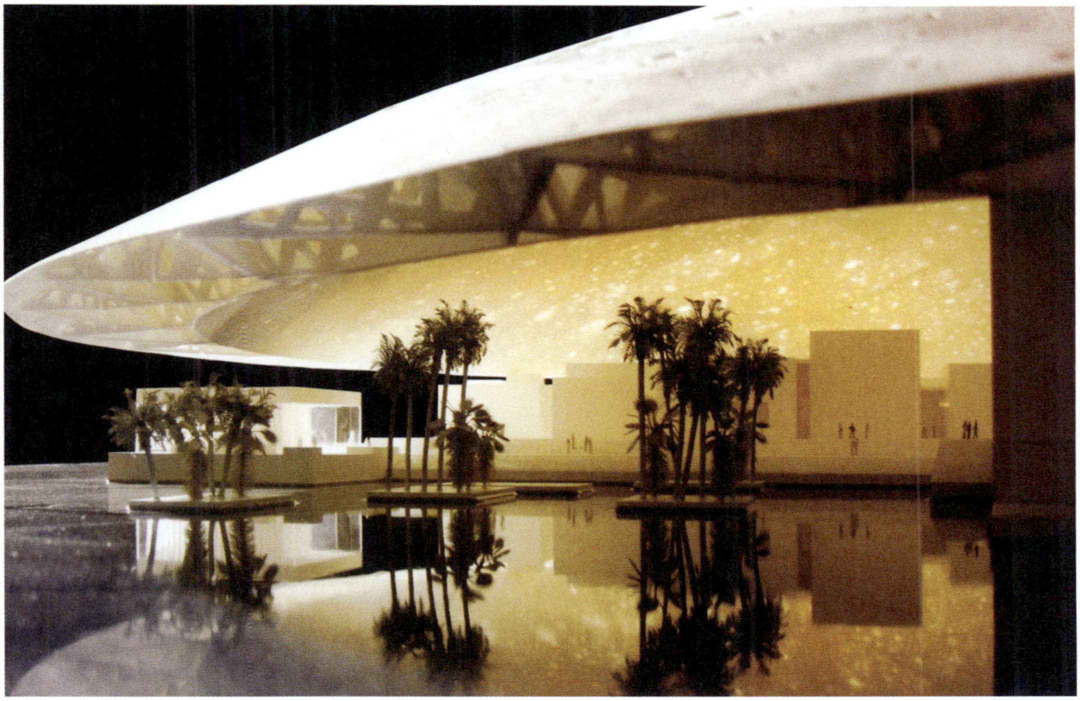

Louvre Abu Dhabi, Abu Dhabi, United Arab Emirates

On March 6, 2007, the French National Assembly signed an intergovernmental agreement with the United Arab Emirates to create the Louvre Abu Dhabi. For 400 million Euros, the Louvre has sold the rights to the Louvre name for thirty years, "while works from French museums will be loaned for a ten-year period beginning in 2015, when the museum is scheduled to open. French cultural institutions have undertaken the plan to organize exhibitions for the museum for a period of fifteen years" (Dominique de Font-Réaulx and Marie Coste, "Louvre Abu Dhabi," in: *The Louvre Magazine*, no. 18, September 2009).

Several major French museums participated in setting up an agency dedicated to advise and supervise the project. Topped by a dome reminiscent of the Arab Medina and covering 260,000 square meters, the Louvre Abu Dhabi by French architect Jean Nouvel is planned to become a universal museum. Its galleries will enable comparisons and contrasts between artworks of different historical periods and geographical areas: "In this connection, contemporary art, to which a minority of space may be allocated, shall be presented alongside with more historical works in order to [...] show how artworks from the past are shaped by contemporary perceptions" (TDIC, *Introduction to Saadiyat Cultural District*, Motivate Publishing, Abu Dhabi, 2008, p. 50).

Above:
Louvre Abu Dhabi, project rendering

The Reading Room. Rasheed Araeen's *Third Text*

The Reading Room in the exhibition *The Global Contemporary. Art Worlds after 1989* introduced exhibition visitors to the art magazine *Third Text*, which was founded in London in 1987 by the artist Rasheed Araeen. As the editor of this journal, which initially offered a "Third World" perspective (until 1999 the magazine's subtitle was *Third World Perspectives on Contemporary Art & Culture*), Araeen has had an enduring influence on the global discourse and has created a forum for writers who were previously excluded by the Western art scene. Over one hundred issues of *Third Text* have been published to date, and in its Special Issues the journal presents a rich spectrum of today's art world. With its "critical perspective," to which the subtitle used since 1999 refers (*Critical Perspectives on Contemporary Art & Culture*), the journal also puts questions about art's future tasks up for discussion. The exhibition space at the ZKM | Karlsruhe was designed by Araeen to show that taking charge of the intellectual practice of steering the discourse on art is in itself a new form of artistic practice. (AB)

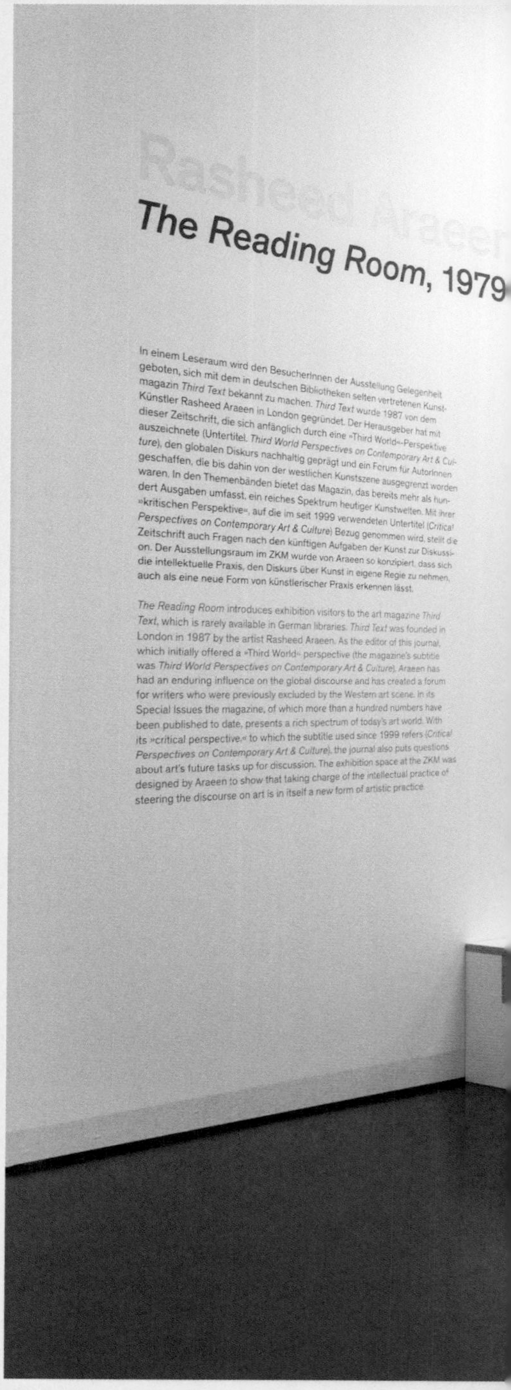

The Global Contemporary. Art Worlds after 1989, section: *Room of Histories*, exhibition view, ZKM | Karlsruhe, 2011–2012

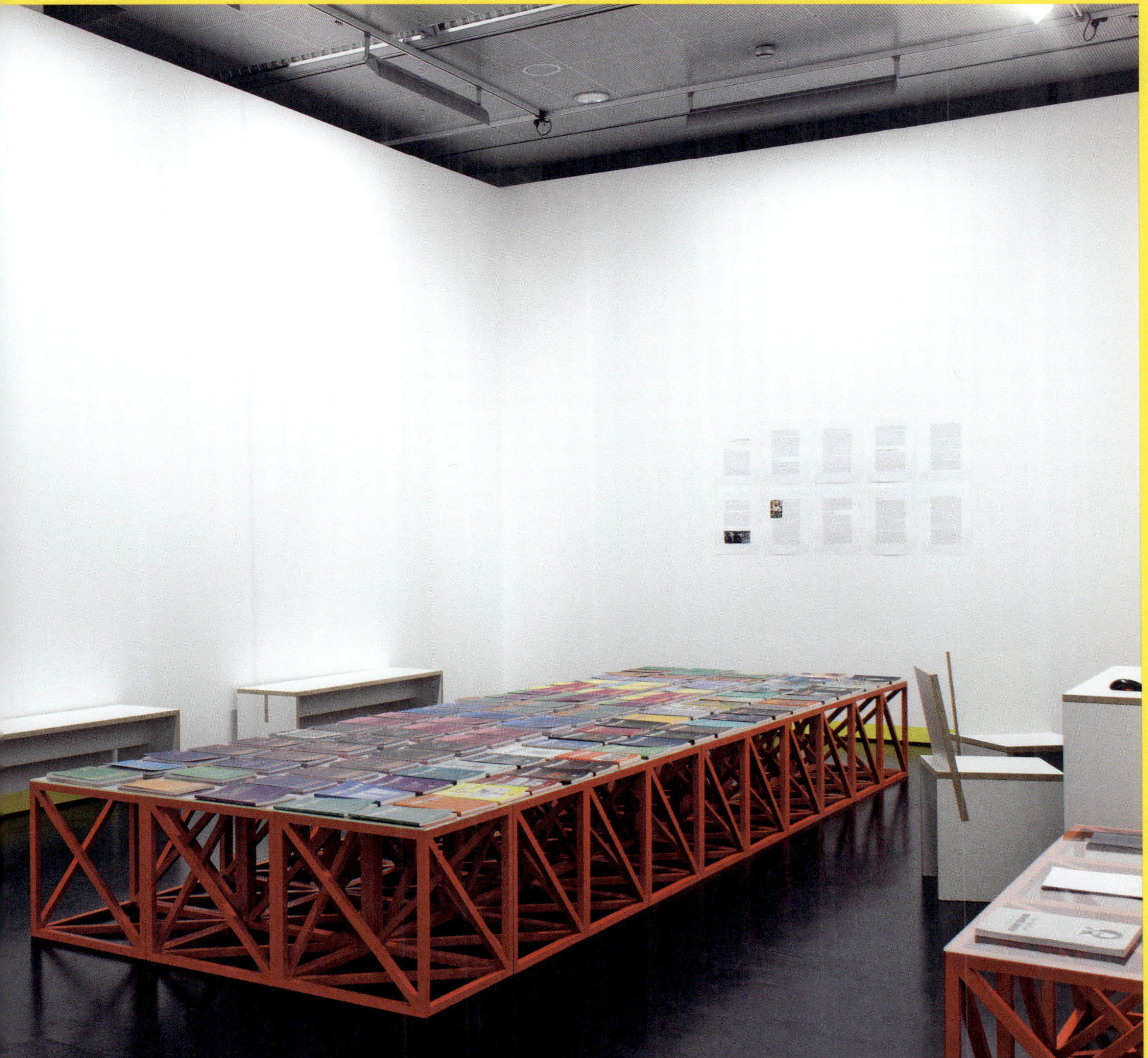

Mapping.
The Biennials and New Art Regions

Globalization has created a new world map of art, where the borders are still very much in flux. After the binary model of center ("Western Art") and periphery had been abandoned, the hectic "mapping" of a polycentric world articulated in supranational "art regions" followed. The biennials that have proliferated across the globe serve as the relay stations in a cartography unprecedented in the modern era. Contemporary art as geopolitical representation is expressed, for example, in the proclamation of "Asia-Pacific Art," an art region that reflects Australia's cultural reorientation, or in "Contemparabia," the cultural tour of biennials and museums in the Gulf region. The expansion of the biennial system has given rise to a network of institutions and curators who seek cultural identity in regional art in order to gain global recognition for it. (HB)

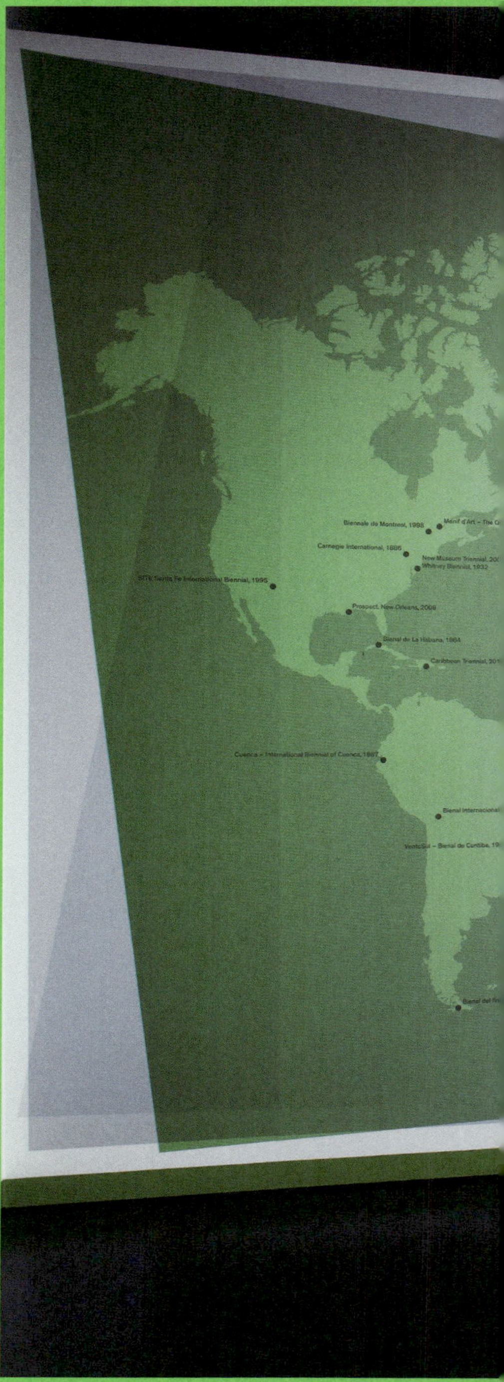

The Global Contemporary. Art Worlds after 1989, section: *Room of Histories*, exhibition view, ZKM | Karlsruhe, 2011–2012

The "Third World Perspective"

Asian Art

Asia-Pacific Art

Polycentric Europe

The Middle East

Art Geography in Africa

Aboriginal Australia. A Special Case

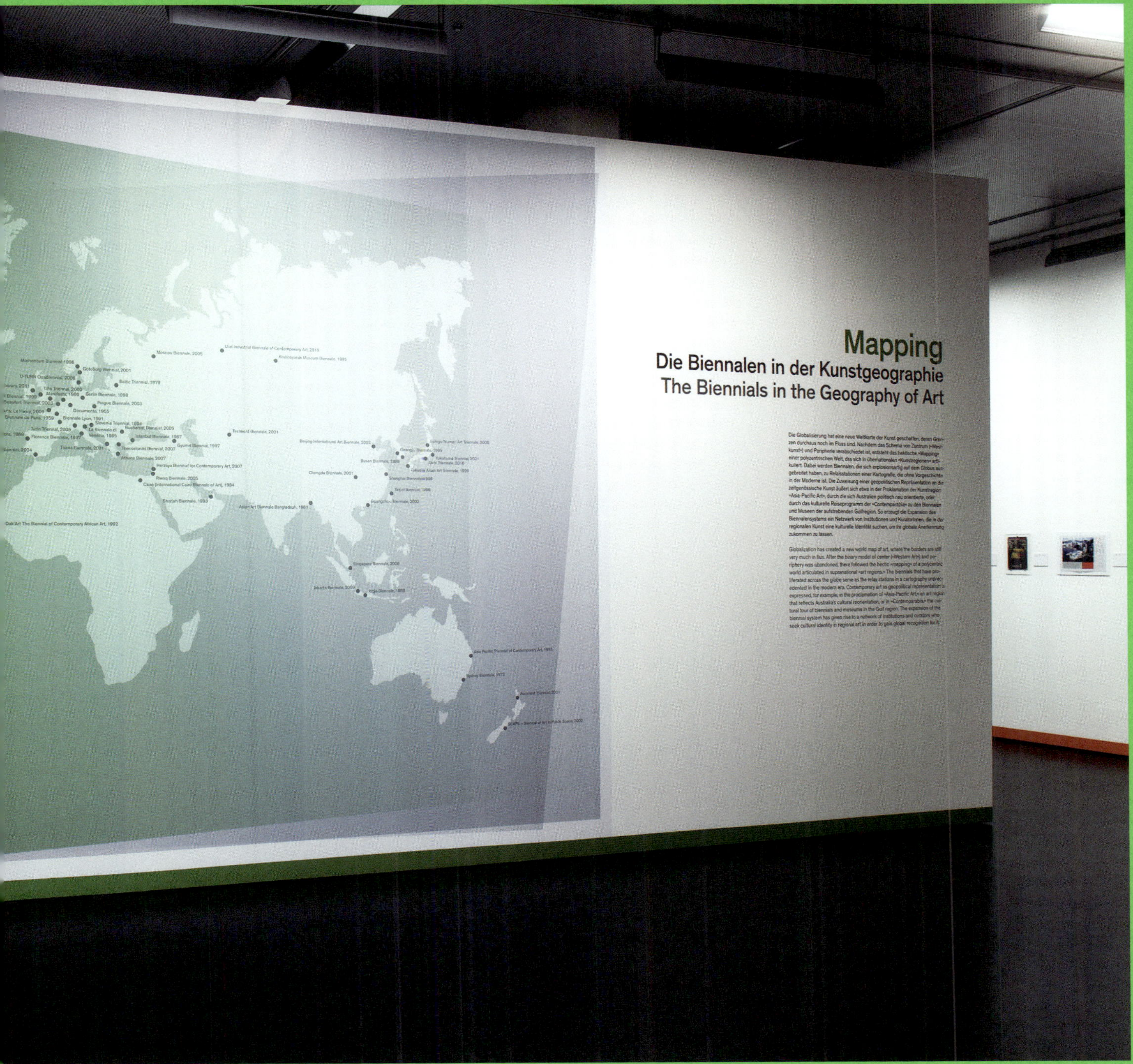

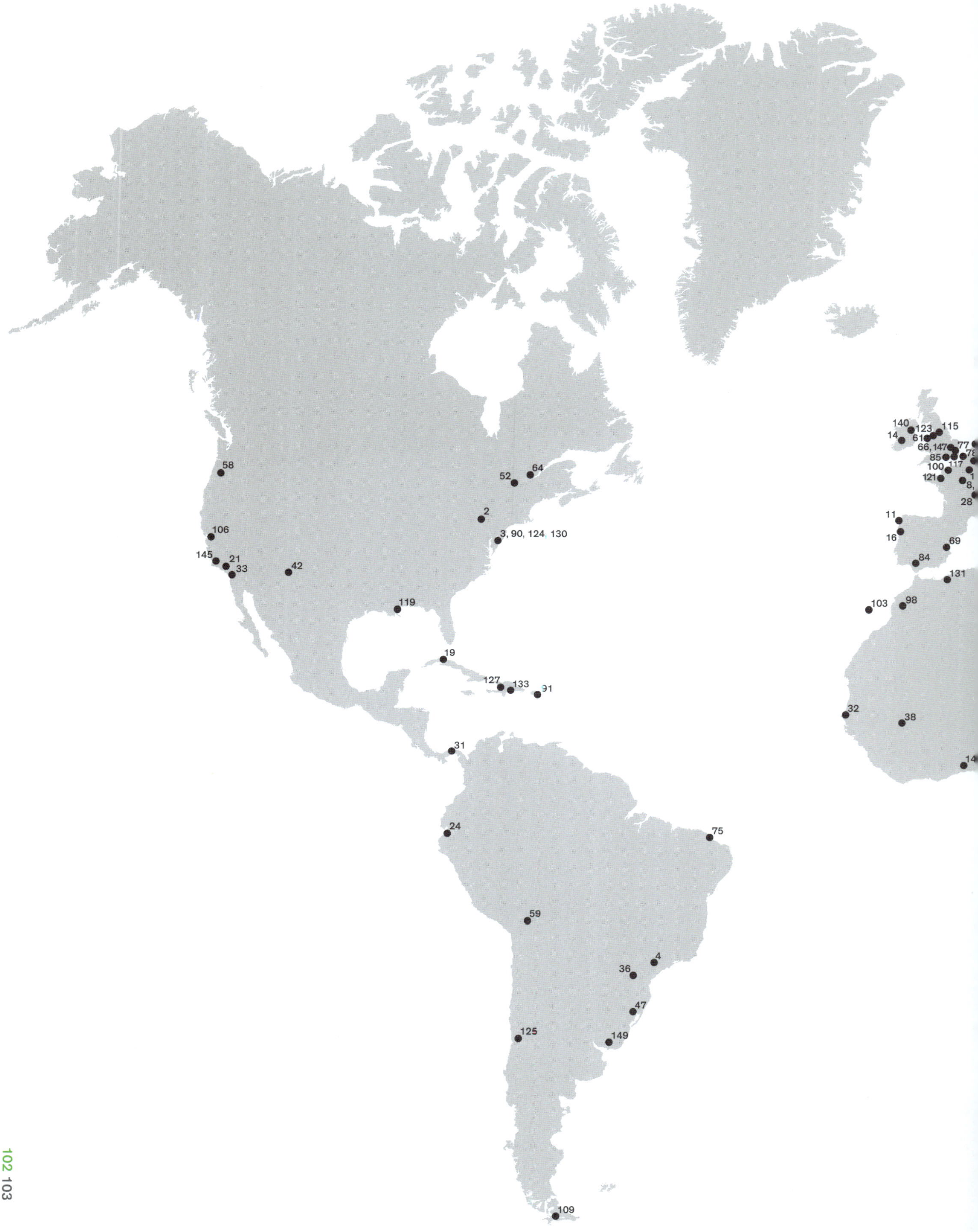
58
52
64
2
3, 90, 124, 130
106
145
21
33
42
119
19
127
133
91
31
24
75
59
4
36
47
125
149
109
140
123
115
14
61
66, 147
77
85
100
117
121
8
28
11
16
69
84
131
103
98
32
38

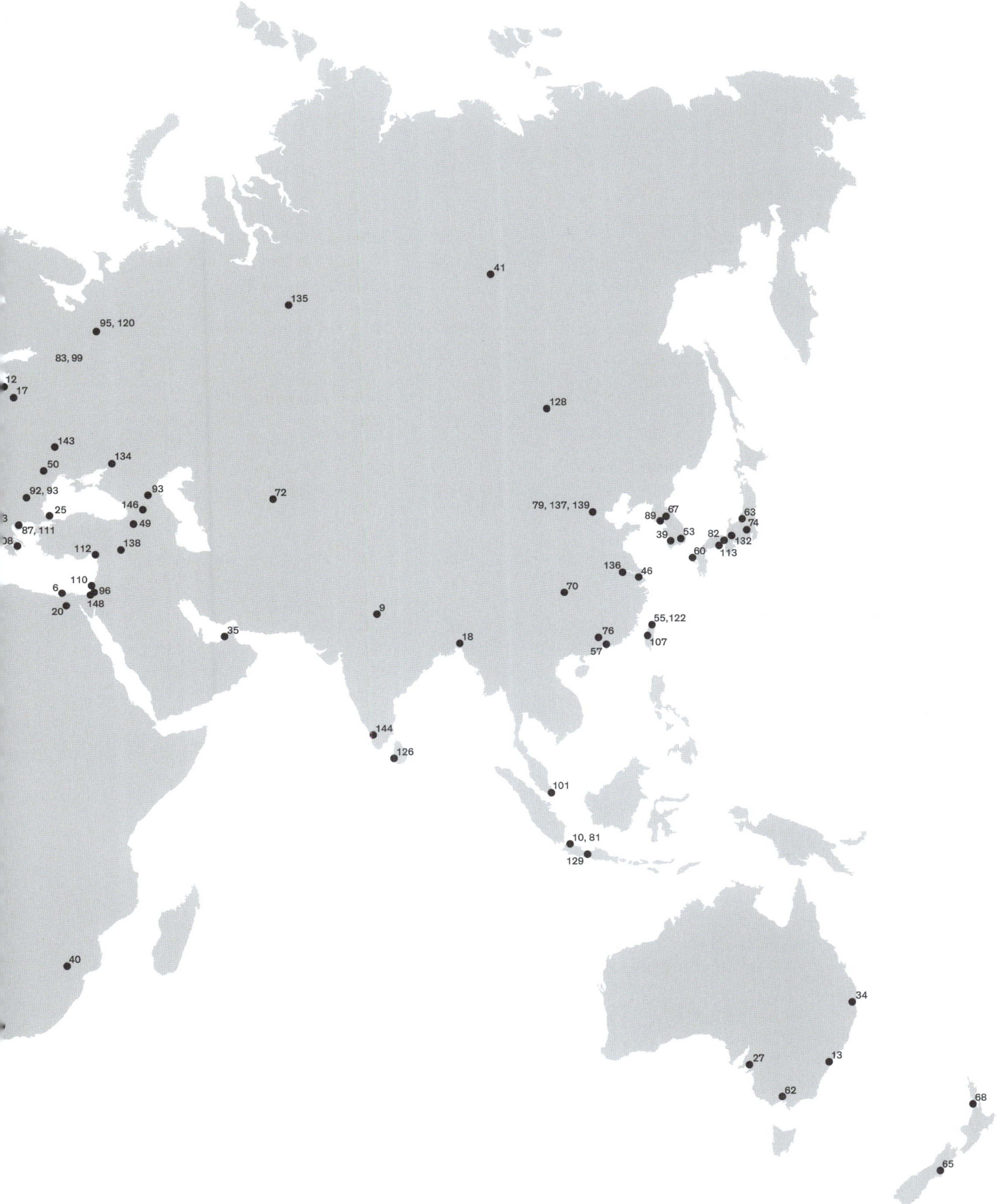
41
135
95, 120
83, 99
12
17
128
143
134
50
93
72
92, 93
146
79, 137, 139
89
67
63
25
49
74
87, 111
39
53
82
132
112
138
113
60
136
46
110
6
96
70
148
20
9
55,122
35
76
18
107
57
144
126
101
10, 81
129
40
34
27
13
62
68
65

	Name	First held	Last held	Location(s)	Nation
1	Venice Biennale	1895	2011	Venice	IT
2	Carnegie International	1896	2008	Pittsburgh	US
3	Whitney Biennial	1932	2012	New York	US
4	Bienal de São Paulo	1951	2012	São Paulo	BR
5	Documenta	1955	2012	Kassel	DE
6	Alexandria Bienniale for Mediterranean Countries	1955	2009/10	Alexandria	EG
7	International Sculpture Biennale of Carrara	1957	2010	Carrara	IT
8	Biennale de Paris	1959	2010/12	Paris (itinerant biennial)	FR
9	Triennale–India	1968	2005	New Delhi	IN
10	Jakarta Biennale	1968	2011	Jakarta	ID
11	Bienal de Arte de Pontevedra	1969	2010	Pontevedera	ES
12	Sculpture Quadrennial Riga	1972	2012	Riga	LV
13	Biennale of Sydney	1973	2012	Sydney	AU
14	eva International	1977	2012	Limerick	IE
15	Skulptur Projekte Münster	1977	2007	Münster	DE
16	Biennial of Cerveira	1978	2012	Cerveira	PT
17	Baltic Triennial of International Art	1979	2012	Vilnius	LT
18	Asian Art Biennale	1981	2012	Dhaka	BD
19	Bienal de La Habana	1984	2012	Havana	CU
20	Cairo Biennale	1984	2010/11	Cairo	EG
21	California Biennial	1984	2011	Newport Beach	US
22	Biennial of Young Artists from Europe and the Mediterranean	1984	2011	Turin	IT
23	Videonale Festival for Contemporary Video Art	1984	2011	Bonn	DE
24	International Biennial of Cuenca	1985	2011	Cuenca	EC
25	Istanbul Biennial	1987	2011	Istanbul	TR
26	WRO Media Art Biennale	1989	2011	Wroclaw	PL
27	Adelaide Biennial of Australian Art	1990	2012	Adelaide	AU
28	La Biennale de Lyon	1991	2011	Lyon	FR
29	Cetinje Biennial	1991	2004	Cetinje	ME
30	Ars Baltica Triennial of Photographic Art	1991	2008		DE
31	Bienal de Arte Panama	1992	2008	Ancón	PA
32	Dak'Art The Biennial of Contemporary African Art	1992	2012	Dakar	SN
33	InSite	1992		San Diego	US
34	Asia Pacific Triennial of Contemporary Art	1993	2012/13	Brisbane	AU
35	Sharjah Biennial	1993	2011	Sharjah	AE
36	VentoSul — Bienal de Curitiba	1993	2011	Curitiba	BR
37	Triennial of Contemporary Art in Slovenia	1994	2010	Ljubljana	SI
38	Rencontres de Bamako, Biennale Africaine de la Photographie	1994	2011	Bamako	ML
39	Gwangju Biennale	1995	2012	Kwangju	KR
40	Johannesburg Biennale	1995	1997	Johannesburg	ZA
41	Krasnoyarsk Museum Biennale	1995	2011	Krasnoyarsk	RU

	Name	First held	Last held	Location(s)	Nation
42	SITE Santa Fe International Biennial	1995	2010	Santa Fe	US
43	Ljubljana Biennial of Graphic Arts	1955	2011	Ljubljana	SI
44	São Tomé e Príncipe Biennial	1995	2011	Sao Tomé	ST
45	Manifesta — The European Biennal of Contemporary Art	1996	2012	Amsterdam	NL
46	Shanghai Biennale	1996	2012	Shanghai	CN
47	Bienal de Artes Visuais do Mercosul	1997	2011	Porto Alegre	BR
48	Florence Biennale	1997	2011	Florence	IT
49	Gyumri International Biennial of Contemporary Art	1997	2004	Gyumri	AM
50	Periferic Festival/Biennial	1997	2010	Iasi	RO
51	Berlin Biennale for Contemporary Art	1998	2012	Berlin	DE
52	La Biennale de Montréal	1998	2011	Montreal	CA
53	Busan Biennale	1998	2012	Busan	KR
54	Momentum — Nordic Biennial of Contemporary Art	1998	2011	Moss	NO
55	Taipei Biennial	1998	2012	Taipei	TW
56	Triennale zeitgenössischer Kunst Oberschwaben	1998	2008	Weingarten	DE
57	Shenzhen Sculpture Biennale	1998	2012	Shenzhen	CN
58	Vancouver Biennale	1998	2009	Vancouver	CA
59	Bienal Internacional de Arte — SIART Bolivia	1999	2011	La Paz	BO
60	Fukuoka Asian Art Triennale	1999	2009	Fukuoka-shi	JP
61	Liverpool Biennial	1999	2012	Liverpool	GB
62	Melbourne International Biennial	1999	1999	Melbourne	AU
63	Echigo-Tsumari Art Triennal	2000	2012	Tokamachi	JP
64	Manif d'art—The Québec City Biennial	2000	2012	Québec	CA
65	SCAPE — Biennial of Art in Public Space	2000	2011	Christchurch	NZ
66	Tate Triennial	2000	2009	London	GB
67	The Seoul International Media Art Biennale	2000	2012	Seoul	KR
68	Auckland Triennial	2001	2010	Auckland	NZ
69	Valencia Biennale	2001	2007	Valencia	ES
70	Chengdu Biennale	2001	2011	Chengdu	CN
71	GICBA – Göteborg International Biennial for Contemporary Art	2001	2011	Göteborg	SE
72	Tashkent International Biennale of Contemporary Art	2001	2011	Tashkent	UZ
73	T.I.C.A. – Tirana Institute of Contemporary Art	2001	2009	Tirana	AL
74	Yokohama Trienniale	2001	2011	Yokohama-shi	JP
75	Bienal Ceará América	2002/03	2002/03	Fortaleza	BR
76	Guangzhou Triennale	2002	2012	Guangzhou	CN
77	Whitstable Biennale	2002	2012	Whitstable	UK
78	Beaufort Trienniale	2003	2012	Oostende	BE
79	Beijing International Art Biennale	2003	2012	Beijing	CN
80	CAPE – Cape Africa Platform	2003	2003	Cape Town	ZA
81	CP Biennale	2003	2005	Jakarta	ID
82	Kyoto Biennale	2003	2003	Kyoto	JP
83	Prague Biennial	2003	2011	Prague	CZ

	Name	First held	Last held	Location(s)	Nation
84	BIACS – International Biennial of Contemporary Art of Seville	2004	2008/09	Seville	ES
85	Brighton Photo Biennial	2003	2012	Brighton	UK
86	Contour. Biennial of Moving Image	2003	2011	Mechelen	BE
87	Balkan Biennial	2004	2004	Thessaloniki	GR
88	Lodz Biennale	2004	2010	Lodz	PL
89	Incheon Women Artists' Biennale	2004	2011	Incheon	KR
90	Performa	2005	2011	New York	US
91	San Juan Poly/Graphic Triennal: Latin America and the Caribbean	2004	2012	San Juan	PR
92	Young Artists Biennial Bucharest	2004	2012	Bucharest	RO
93	Bucharest International Biennial for Contemporary Art	2005	2012	Bucharest	RO
94	Emergency Biennale	2005	2005	Paris/Grozny	FR/R
95	Moscow Biennale	2005	2011	Moscow	RU
96	Riwaq Biennale	2005	2012	Ramallah	PS
97	T – Turin Triennial Threemuseums	2005	2008	Turin	IT
98	AiM – Arts in Marrakech International Biennale	2005	2012	Marrakech	MA
99	ITCA – International Trienniale of Contemporary Art	2008	2008	Prague	CZ
100	Arts: Le Havre	2006	2012	Le Havre	FR
101	Singapore Biennale	2006	2011	Singapore	SG
102	Triennal de Wande	2006	2010	Luanda	AO
103	Architecture, Art & Landscape Biennial of the Canaries	2006	2011	Canary Islands	ES
104	La Triennale [2006, 2009: La force de l'art]	2006	2012	Paris	FR
105	U-Turn Quadrennial for Contemporary Art	2008	2011	Copenhagen	DK
106	ZERO1 Biennial	2006	2012	San Jose	US
107	Asian Art Biennial	2007	2011	Taichung	TW
108	Athens Biennale	2007	2011	Athens	GR
109	Bienal de Arte Contemporáneo del Fin del Mundo	2007	2011	Ushuaia	AR
110	Herzliya Biennial for Contemporary Art	2007	2011	Herzliya	IL
111	Thessaloniki Biennale of Contemporary Art	2007	2011	Thessaloniki	GR
112	Antakya Biennial	2007	2010	Antakya	TR
113	Kobe Biennale	2007	2011	Kobe	JP
114	SUD – Salon Urbain de Douala	2007	2010	Douala	CM
115	Asia Triennial Manchester	2008	2011	Manchester	GB
116	Brussels Biennial for Contemporary Art	2008	2008	Brussels	BE
117	Folkestone Triennial	2008	2011	Folkestone	GB
118	Mediations Biennale	2008	2012	Poznan	PL
119	Prospect New Orleans	2008	2011	New Orleans	US
120	Moscow International Biennale for Young Art	2008	2012	Moscow	RU
121	Ateliers de Rennes	2008	2012	Rennes	FR
122	Kuandu Biennale	2008	2012	Taipei	TW
123	Tatton Park Biennial	2008	2012	Knutsford	UK
124	New Museum Triennial	2009	2012	New York	US

	Name	First held	Last held	Location(s)	Nation
125	Chile Triennale	2009	2009	Santiago	CL
126	CAB – Colombo Art Biennale	2009	2012	Colombo	LK
127	Ghetto Biennale	2009	2011	Port-au-Prince	HT
128	Land Art Mongolia 360°	2010	2012	Ulaanbaatar	MN
129	Biennale Jogja	1988	2011	Yogyakarta	ID
130	Harlem Bienniale	2009	2011	New York	US
131	Biennale Méditerréenne d'Art Contemporain d'Oran	2010	2012	Oran	DZ
132	Aichi Triennale	2010	2010	Aichi	JP
133	International Triennial of the Caribbean (1992–2003: Carribean Biennial)	2010	2010	Santo Domingo	DO
134	South Russian Biennale of Contemporary Art	2010	2012[1]	Rostov-on-Don	RU
135	Ural Industrial Biennale of Contemporary Art	2010	2012	Yekaterinburg	RU
136	Nanjing Biennale	2010	2010	Nanjing	CN
137	Western China International Art Biennale	2010	2012	Beijing	CN
138	Mardin Biennial	2010	2012	Mardin	TR
139	CAFAM Biennale	2011	2011	Beijing	CN
140	Dublin Contemporary	2011	2011	Dublin	IE
141	Bienniale of Contemporary Art, D-O ARK Underground	2011	2011	Sarajevo	BA
142	Biennale Regard Benin	2012	2012	Cotonou, Ouidah, Abomey, Porto-Novo	BJ
143	ARSENALE	2012	2012	Kiev	UA
144	Kochi-Muziris Biennale	2012	2012	Fort Kochi	IN
145	Los Angeles Biennial	2012	2012	Los Angeles	US
146	Tbilisi Triennial	2012	2012	Tbilisii	GE
147	The London Open	2012	2012	London	UK
148	Qalandiya International	2012	2012	Jerusalem	PS
149	Montevideo Biennial	2012	2012	Montevideo	UY

[1] Cancelled to protest imprisonment of members of the band Pussy Riot.

This list was compiled in October 2012.

The "Third World Perspective"

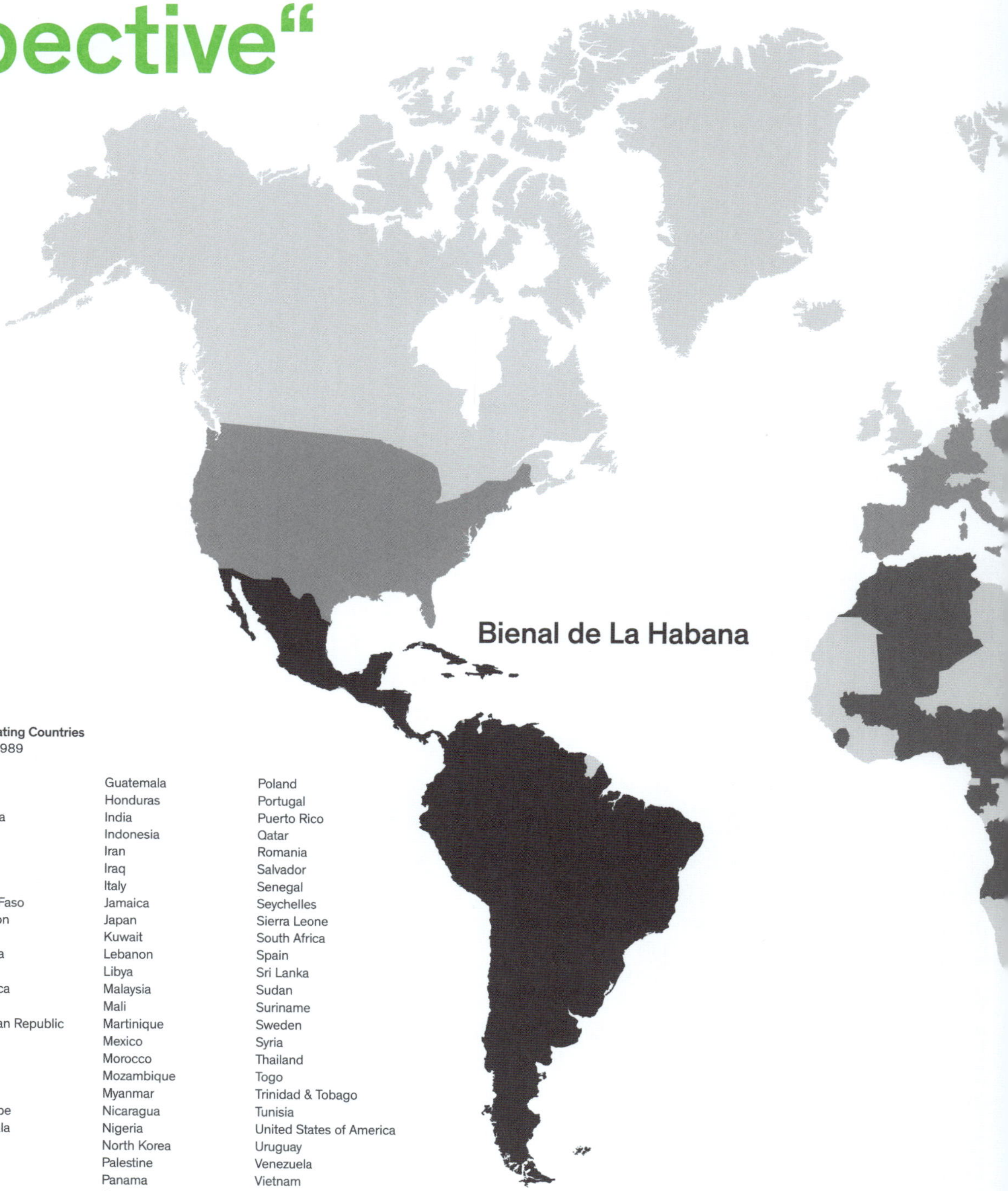

Participating Countries
1984–1989

Algeria
Angola
Argentina
Belize
Benin
Bolivia
Brazil
Burkina Faso
Cameroon
Chile
Columbia
Congo
Costa Rica
Cuba
Dominican Republic
Ecuador
Egypt
Ethiopia
Ghana
Guadalupe
Guatemala
Guinea
Guyana
Haiti
France
Germany
Guatemala
Honduras
India
Indonesia
Iran
Iraq
Italy
Jamaica
Japan
Kuwait
Lebanon
Libya
Malaysia
Mali
Martinique
Mexico
Morocco
Mozambique
Myanmar
Nicaragua
Nigeria
North Korea
Palestine
Panama
Peru
Philippines
Poland
Portugal
Puerto Rico
Qatar
Romania
Salvador
Senegal
Seychelles
Sierra Leone
South Africa
Spain
Sri Lanka
Sudan
Suriname
Sweden
Syria
Thailand
Togo
Trinidad & Tobago
Tunisia
United States of America
Uruguay
Venezuela
Vietnam
Zaire
Zimbabwe

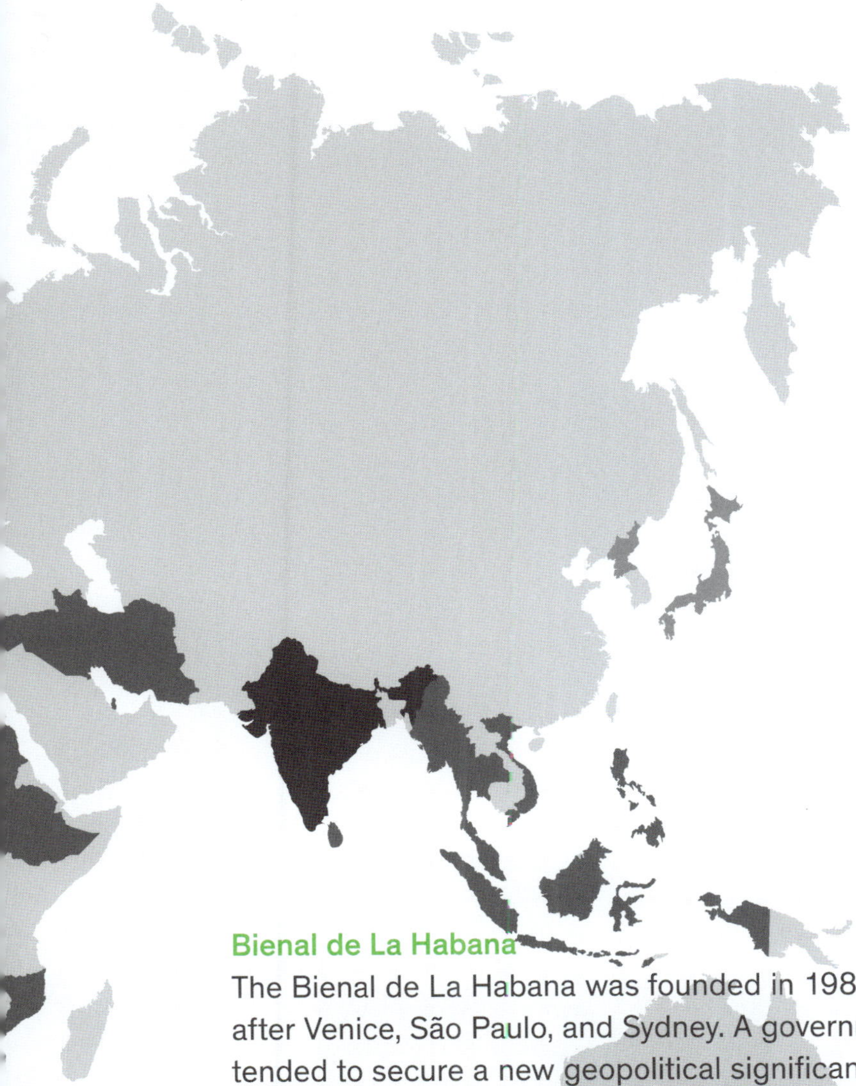

Bienal de La Habana

The Bienal de La Habana was founded in 1984 as the world's fourth biennial after Venice, São Paulo, and Sydney. A government project, the biennial was intended to secure a new geopolitical significance for Cuba within Latin America as well as the Eastern Bloc. In line with these objectives the second Havana Biennial (1986) was organized as a forum for art of the "Third World", with 690 artists from 57 countries. The third Havana Biennial (1989) made this focus its official theme in its title: *Tradition and Contemporaneity in the Arts in the Environment of the Third World*. Thus, the biennial was destined "to place Havana at the center of the Third World map" (Rachel Weiss, 2011). The program involved both opposition to the West, from whose art scenes these artists had been excluded as well as signifying a "vision towards internationalization of contemporary art" (Gerardo Mosquera, 2011). The organizers dispensed with nationality as a way of structuring the exhibition. However, one of the problems confronting this project was that the "Third World" could not be conceived of as a homogeneous art region. Additionally, the term "Third World" had become increasingly problematic after the end of the Cold War. (HB)

Asian Art

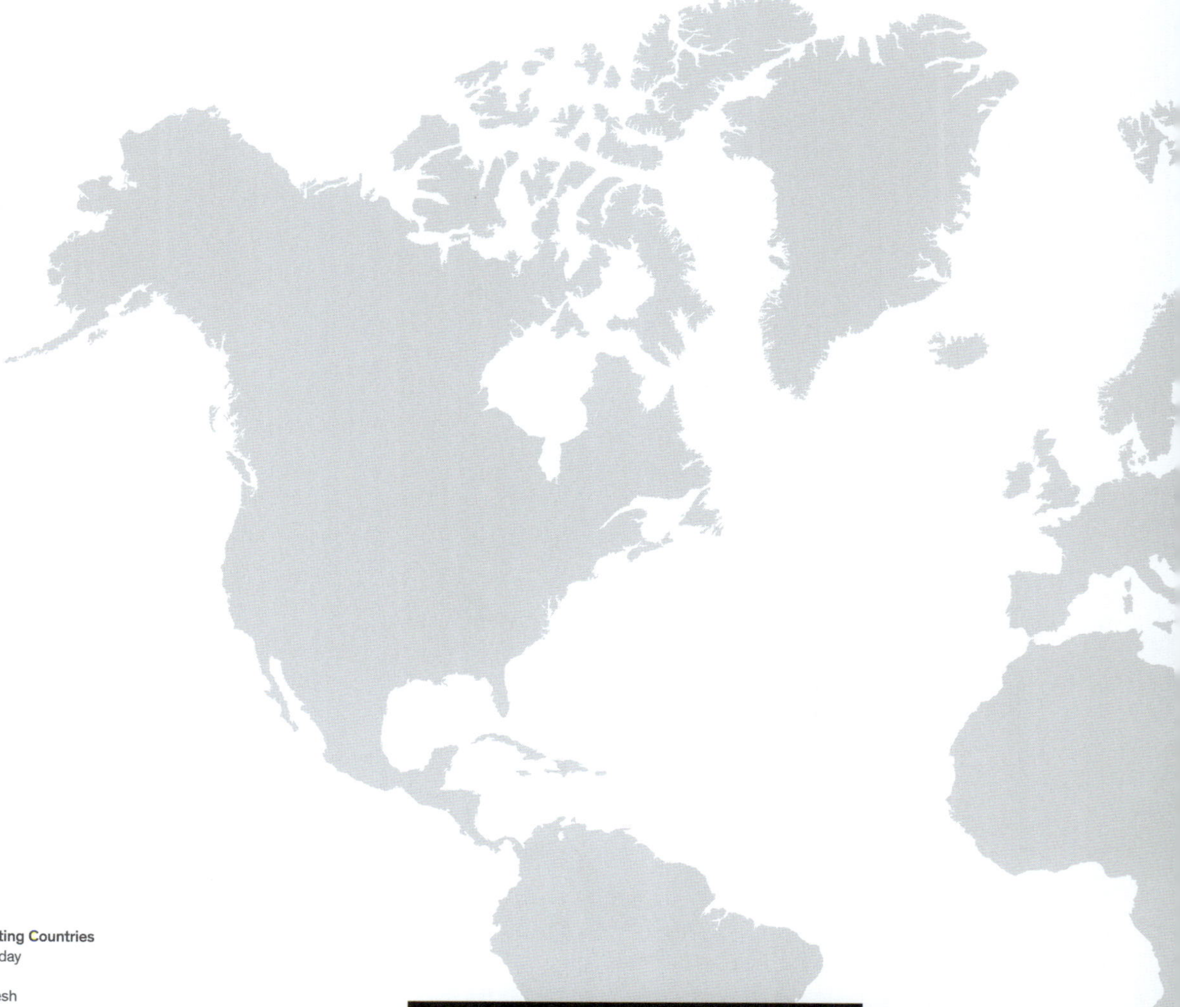

Participating Countries
1999–today

Bangladesh
Brunei Darussalam
Bhutan
Cambodia
China
India
Indonesia
Japan
Laos
Malaysia
Mongolia
Myanmar
Nepal
Pakistan
Philippines
Singapore
South Korea
Sri Lanka
Taiwan (China)
Thailand
Vietnam

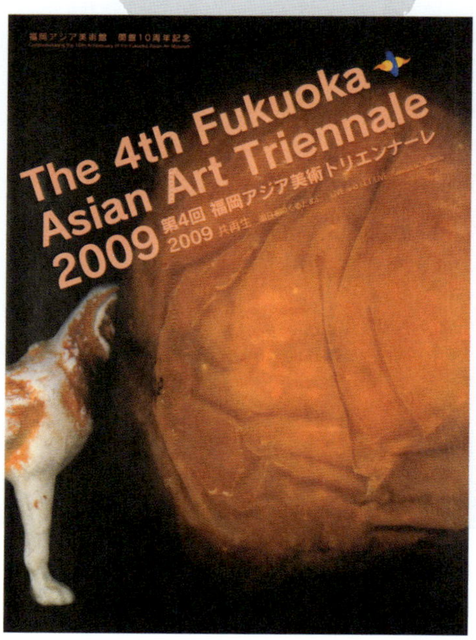

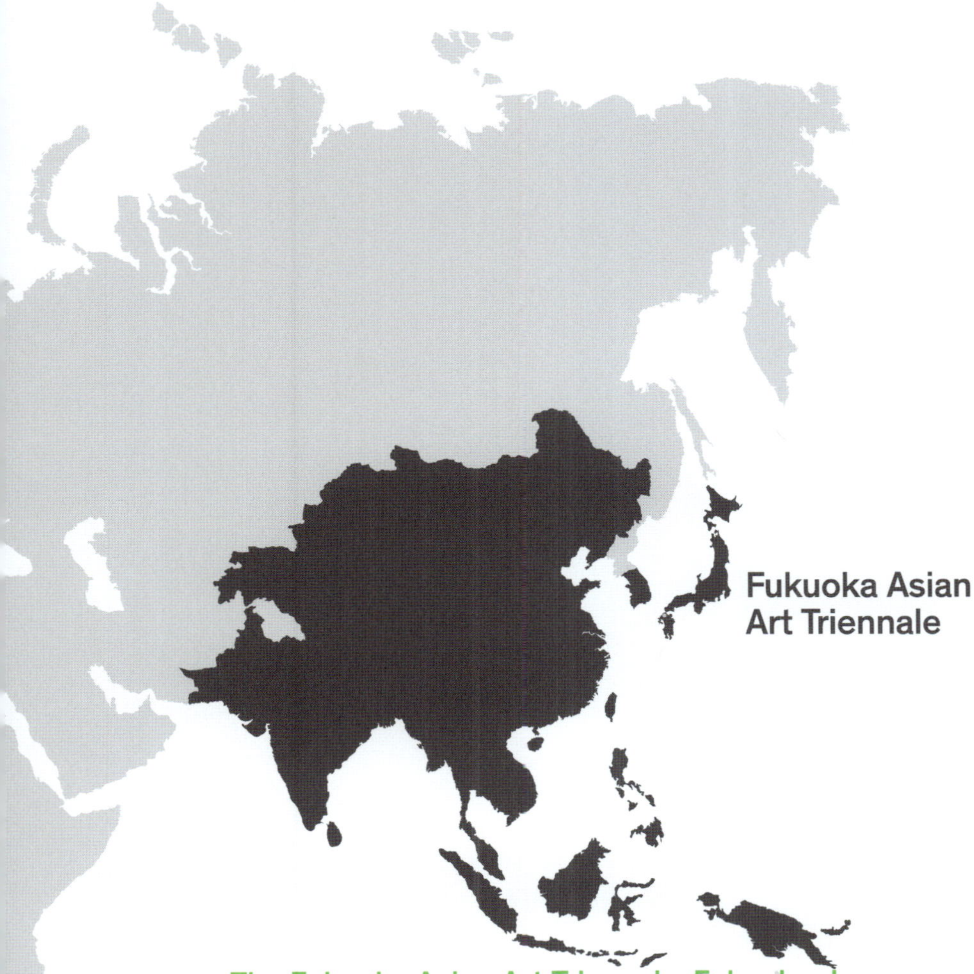

The Fukuoka Asian Art Triennale, Fukuoka, Japan

The Asian Art Museum in Fukuoka opened in 1999 with a triennial of contemporary Asian art, after the already existing Art Museum had hosted The Asian Art Show every five years since 1980. In this way, Japan also participated in decentralizing the art scene, but chose a new definition of Asia by excluding the Pacific region. The goal was to integrate Japanese art into the Asian region and to set different accents than the Asia Pacific Triennial of Contemporary Art in Brisbane, Australia. At the same time, the terms and conditions of artistic production were highlighted. Therefore, even the first triennial in which 55 artists from 21 countries participated was thematically oriented, as illustrated by the title *Communication: Channels for Hope*. An artist-in-residence program promoted cultural exchange, which was an important concern of the curators. Subsequent triennials set different priorities, and also selected "indigenous local material" in order to develop a counterpoint to the early modernization of Japanese art. (HB)

Left:
Fukuoka Asian Art Museum, Yamaki Yuko (eds.), *The 4th Fukuoka Asian Art Triennale 2009, Live and Let Live: Creators of Tomorrow*, exhib. cat., Fukuoka Asian Art Museum, Fukuoka City, 2009

Asia-Pacific Art

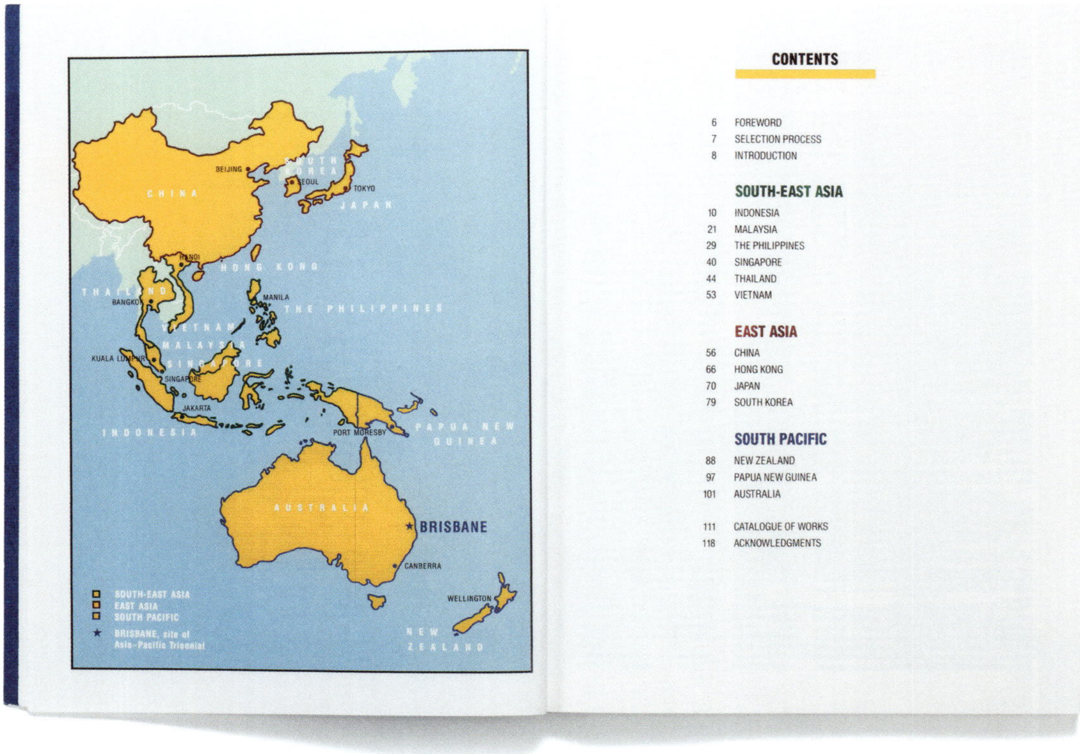

The Asia Pacific Triennial of Contemporary Art, Brisbane, Australia

The Asia Pacific Triennial that opened at Queensland Art Gallery in Brisbane in 1993, marked a shift in the contemporary art of Australia and the country's cultural reorientation, which saw its place in the Asian art region. In the accompanying publication, deputy director of the Queensland Art Gallery Caroline Turner, who adapted the title *Tradition and Change* from the third Havana Biennial and applied it to the contemporary art of Asia, marked this shift with terms such as "Extraregionalism" (Australia as outsider) and "Intraregionalism." 76 artists from twelve countries, for whom the map of this new region was drawn, took part. It was felt that the "Euro-Americentric perspectives" should be abandoned and new definition of Asian art be found. Asia did not have a common cultural identity but common regional themes. In the catalog of the 2nd Triennial (1996) co-curator Susan Cochrane demanded the liberation of the Asia-Pacific region from the dominance of Asia. Professor Jonathan Mane-Wheoki from New Zealand made a plea for a "re-centered world" in which "post-European" should be distinguished from "pro-indigenous" art. Artist Jim Supangakat from Indonesia initiated a debate about a distinctive discourse of contemporary art: "What, when, where."

Above:
Map of the countries represented in the 1st Asia Pacific Triennial, Janet Hogan (ed.), *The first Asia-Pacific Triennial of Contemporary Art*, exhib. cat., Queensland Art Gallery, Queensland Cultural Centre, Brisbane, 1993, p. 4

Australian Participation in The 1st Asia Pacific Triennial of Contemporary Art

The 1st Asia-Pacific Triennial of Contemporary Art offered a new map of Australia's art geography. For the first time, the locations of Aboriginal communities, such as Utopia, Alice Springs, and Mulga Bore, were added to the established art centers, such as Sydney and Melbourne, which were already on the map of modern and contemporary art production. The selection of nine artists from Australia to be shown in the triennial exhibition included three indigenous Australian women artists: Ada Bird Petyarre, Gloria Petyarre, and Kathleen Petyarre. The three artists, in fact sisters, had been working "with non-traditional media since the late 1970s," the result being "the exploration of contemporary materials and a new visual dialogue." Thus, the three artists, though starting in traditional forms, recently had "come to the fore as contemporary artists [...] This highlights the emergence of a new generation of contemporary Aboriginal artists" (all excerpts quoted from: Christopher Hodges and Rudolf Talmacs, "Adas Bird Petyarre, Gloria Petyarre, and Kathleen Petyarre," in: Janet Hogan (ed.), *The First Asia-Pacific Triennial of Contemporary Art*, exhib. cat., Queensland Art Gallery, Queensland Cultural Centre, Brisbane, 1993, pp. 106–107). (HB)

Below:
Portraits and map introducing the Australian participation to the 1st Asia Pacific Triennial, Janet Hogan (ed.), *The First Asia-Pacific Triennial of Contemporary Art*, exhib. cat., Queensland Art Gallery, Queensland Cultural Centre, Brisbane, 1993, pp. 101–102

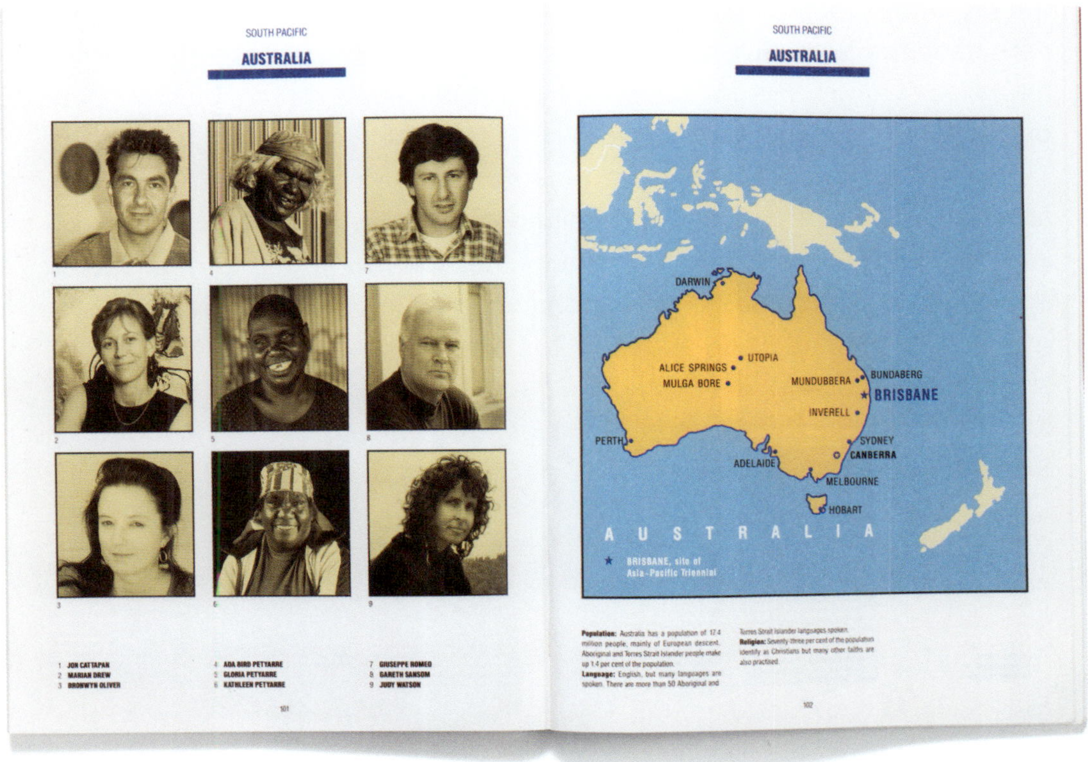

Polycentric Europe

After the fall of the Berlin Wall in 1989, and as a consequence of the continuous expansion of the European Union, the relationship between central and marginal areas for art production and exhibition practice in Europe started to move in the direction of a more polycentric order. Beginning in the 1990s, Europe witnessed a sustained growth of art biennials within its former periphery, and especially in former Soviet countries. Manifesta – The European Biennial of Contemporary Art – as well as the numerous biennials, triennials, and quadrennials located all over the continent aim to give a new centrality to local cultural scenes. Large-scale exhibitions facilitate depolarization of the art system and foster alternative artistic and curatorial solutions on a smaller scale. The new map reflects the multiplicity of artistic experiences and institutional systems in today's Europe, which are no longer dependent on capital cities or traditional centers, but span from Moscow to Seville and Tirana, passing by Vilnius, Prague, Bucharest, and Lyon.

Manifesta

Manifesta, the "only itinerant European biennial of contemporary art," (http://manifesta9.org/en/about-manifesta/) was founded in Amsterdam in 1996 as a critical response to the end of the Cold War and to the growth of the European Union. Since its first edition in Rotterdam, Manifesta has traveled to Luxembourg (1998), Ljubljana (2000), Frankfurt am Main (2002), San Sebastian (2004), Trentino/South Tyrol (2008), Murcia (2010/2011), and Genk (2012). Its nomadic character reflects the organizers' aim to keep a distance "from what are often seen as the dominant centers of artistic production; instead seeking fresh and fertile terrain for the mapping of a new cultural topography" (http://manifesta.org/biennials/about-the-biennials/).

Each edition of Manifesta promotes collective curatorship and presents artists, young professionals, and trainees from forty different countries. By paying special attention to minority groups and cultures within Europe, Manifesta also seeks to overcome cultural and economic barriers. Charles Esche sees the launch of Manifesta as an endeavor to bring "Western and Eastern Europe into closer cultural dialogue" (Charles Esche, "Making Art Global: A Good Place or a No Place?," in: Rachel Weiss et al., *Making Art Global (Part 1): The Third Havana Biennial 1989, Exhibition Histories*, vol. 2, Afterall, London, 2011, p. 10). (SG)

From left to right and from top to bottom:

Barbara Vanderlinden and Elena Filipovic (eds.), *The Manifesta Decade: Debates on Contemporary Art Exhibitions and Biennials in Post-Wall Europe*, The MIT Press, Cambridge (MA), 2005

Giancarlo Politi (ed.), *Tirana Biennale 1: Escape*, exhib. cat., Giancarlo Politi Editore, Milan, 2001

Prague Biennale 1: Peripheries Become the Center, exhib. cat., National Gallery, Prague, 2003

Tobias Berger, Virginija Januškevičiūtė (eds.), *Centre of Attraction: 8th Baltic Triennial of International Art*, exhib. cat., Contemporary Art Centre, Vilnius, 2003

Xenia Kalpaktsoglou, Poka-Yio, Augustine Zenakos, Theophilos Tramboulis (eds.), *Destroy Athens: 1st Athens Biennial 2007*, exhib. cat., Athens Biennale, Futura Publications, London, 2007

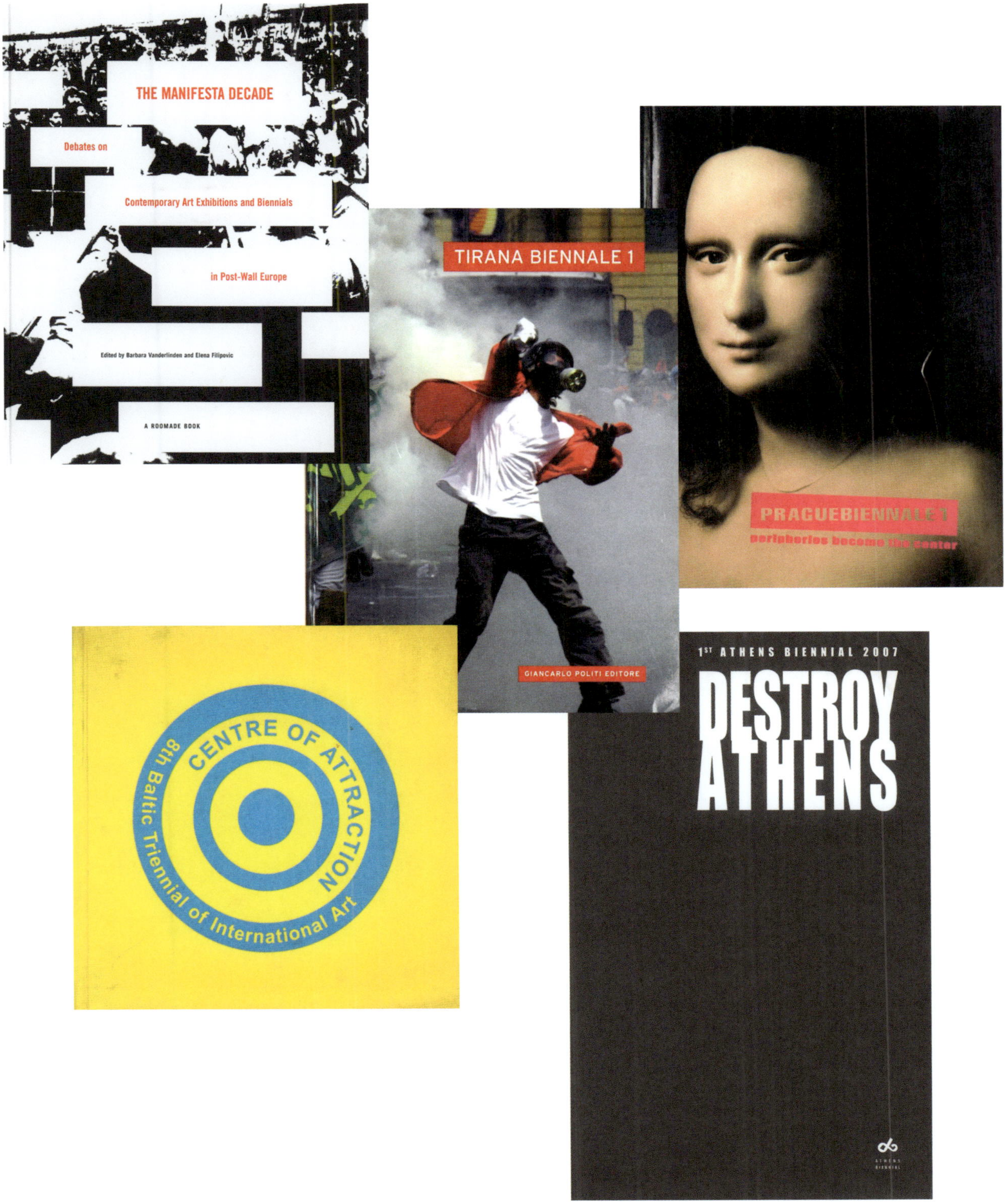
THE MANIFESTA DECADE
Debates on
Contemporary Art Exhibitions and Biennials
in Post-Wall Europe
Edited by Barbara Vanderlinden and Elena Filipovic
A ROOMADE BOOK
TIRANA BIENNALE 1
GIANCARLO POLITI EDITORE
PRAGUEBIENNALE 1
peripheries become the center
CENTRE OF ATTRACTION
8th Baltic Triennial of International Art
1ST ATHENS BIENNIAL 2007
DESTROY
ATHENS

The Middle East

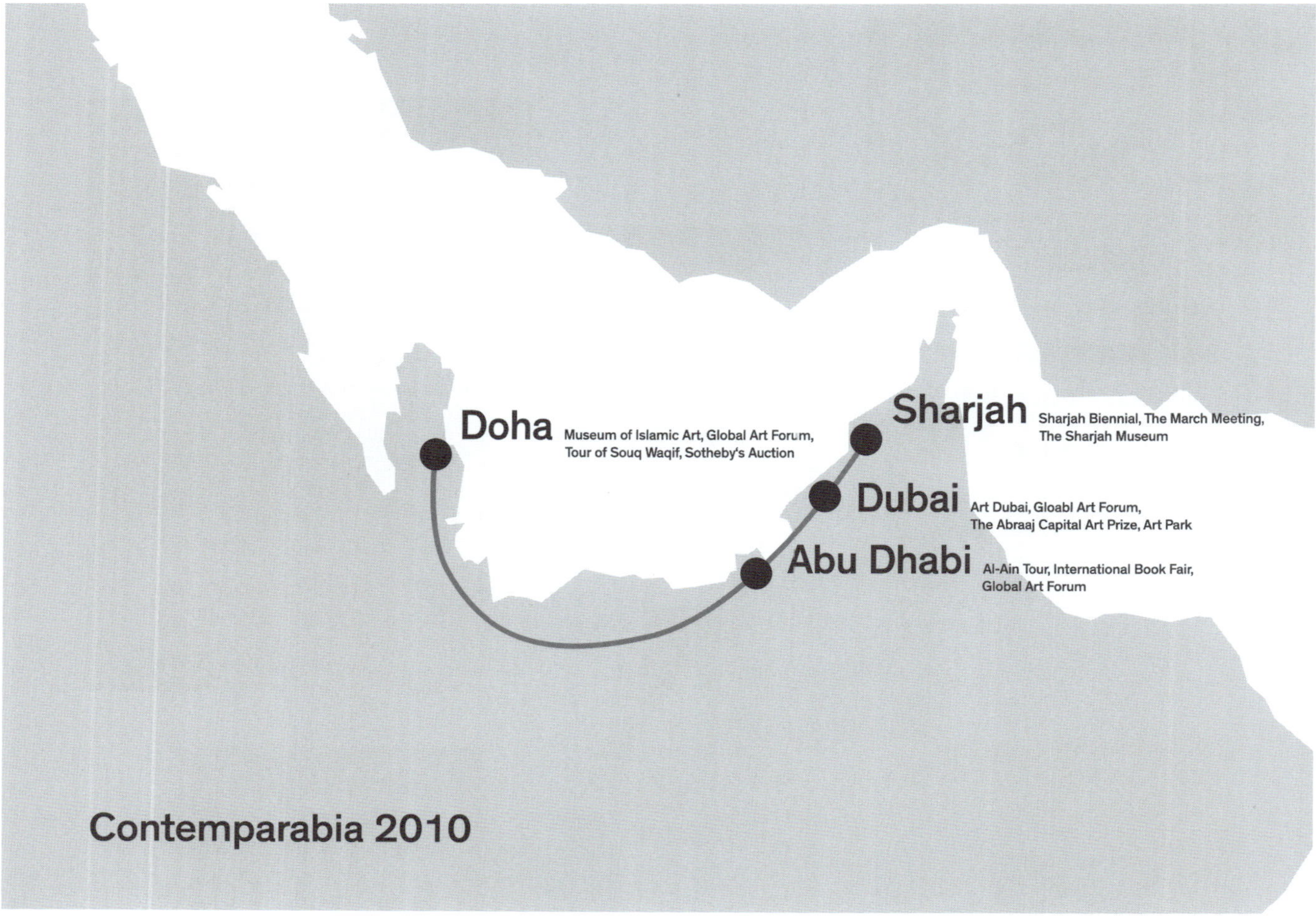

Contemparabia. A Grand Tour of the Persian Gulf

Contemparabia, a cultural travel program, is a collaborative enterprise of the Abu Dhabi Authority for Culture and Heritage (ADACH), Art Dubai, Sharjah Biennial, and the Qatar Museums Authority. Held for the first time in 2009, its itinerary is designed to span several events and institutions for contemporary art in the region, such as Art Dubai with its Global Art Forum and Sharjah Biennial. "Each featured city has a full program that incorporates artists' studio visits, visits to private collections, homes and showrooms, etc., as well as meeting key practitioners, art patrons and figures" (Contemparabia 2010 Press Release, see: www.contemparabia.com).

A clear reference to the Grand Tour of Europe of modern times, Contemparabia reflects the close relationship between the art market and exhibition practice. Particularly significant is that Sotheby's held its first auction in the region in Doha, Qatar, on March 15, 2009 as part of this "umbrella event" (Henry Howard-Sneyd, "Sotheby's in Doha," in: *Sotheby's Preview*, March/April 2009). (SG)

Sharjah Biennial

The Sharjah Biennial, relaunched by the Sharjah Art Foundation in 2003, is developing into a showcase for art produced in MENASA (Middle East North Africa South Asia), and illustrates the organizers' intention "to position Sharjah in the context of the Arab world, rather than simply in reference to the West" (Jack Persekian, "A History of Cultural Production," in: *Brownbook*, www.sharjahart.org/docs/BrownBook_1301471833.pdf). However, the Sharjah Biennial has to contend with certain constraints as a result of its location. During the tenth edition (2011), Mustapha Benfodil's installation *Maportaliche/Ecritures sauvages (It Has No Importance/Wild Writings)* (2011) was removed because it was considered anti-Islamic. As a consequence, the Biennial's artistic director Jack Persekian was dismissed by Sheikh Sultan bin Mohamed Al-Qasimi. For Jennifer Higgie this reveals "the contradiction that beats at the heart of Sharjah. It's the most religiously and politically conservative member of the United Arab Emirates [...] but also the most culturally active. Sheikh Al-Qasimi has singlehandedly funded not only the biennial but seventeen local museums, while his daughter, Sheikha Hoor Al-Qasimi, is the President of the Sharjah Art Foundation" (Jennifer Higgie, "Free Speech – Censorship and the Art World," in: *Frieze Magazine*, issue 140, June–August 2011). (SG)

Below:
Peter Lewis (ed.), *Sharjah International Biennial 6*, exhib. cat., Sharjah, 2003

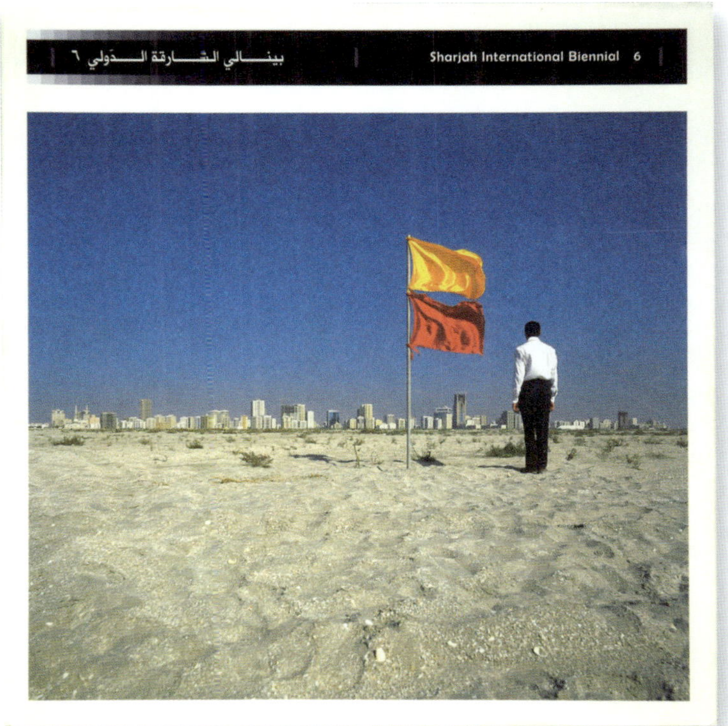

Art Dubai. The Global Art Forum

The Global Art Forum is an Art Dubai initiative and has been held in partnership with the *Financial Times* every year since 2007. Running alongside the Art Dubai fair and Sharjah Biennial, the Global Art Forum hosts the "world's leading artists, curators, museum directors, and art professionals to discuss issues that affect art today and will define its future" (Global Art Forum 2008, information brochure). Similar to the Sharjah Biennial, the various talks and round table discussions engage with art practices from the MENASA (Middle East, North Africa, South Asia) regions, with the aim of linking regional art scenes with an international network. The event evidences how the dividing line between critical discourse and market value are increasingly evaporating. The two aspects are now clearly interdependent and for the 2011 edition part of the Global Art Forum moved to Mathaf, the acclaimed new Arab Museum of Modern Art in Doha (Global Art Forum 2011, www.artdubai.ae). (SG)

Below, from left:
Global Art Forum 2 – Transcripts, Art Dubai, 2008
Global Art Forum, schedule, in: *Information brochure*, Global Art Forum 2008

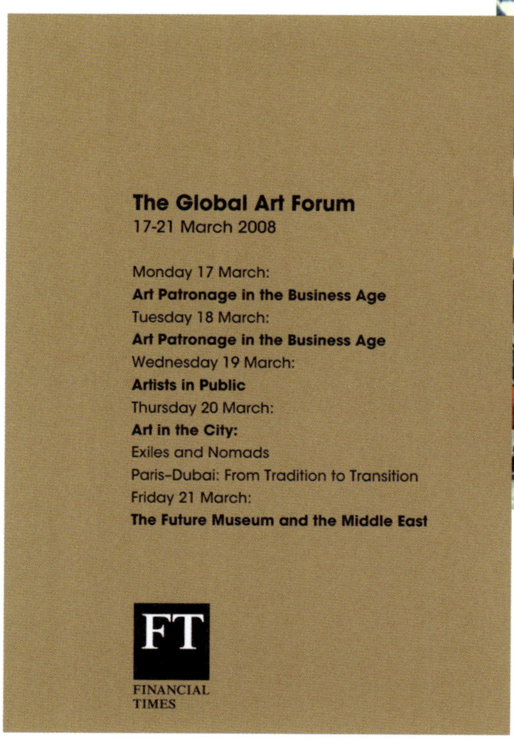

The Global Art Forum
17-21 March 2008

Monday 17 March:
Art Patronage in the Business Age
Tuesday 18 March:
Art Patronage in the Business Age
Wednesday 19 March:
Artists in Public
Thursday 20 March:
Art in the City:
Exiles and Nomads
Paris-Dubai: From Tradition to Transition
Friday 21 March:
The Future Museum and the Middle East

FT
FINANCIAL TIMES

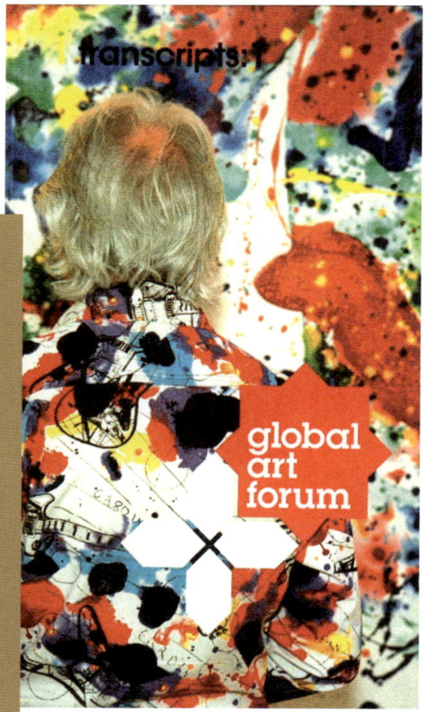

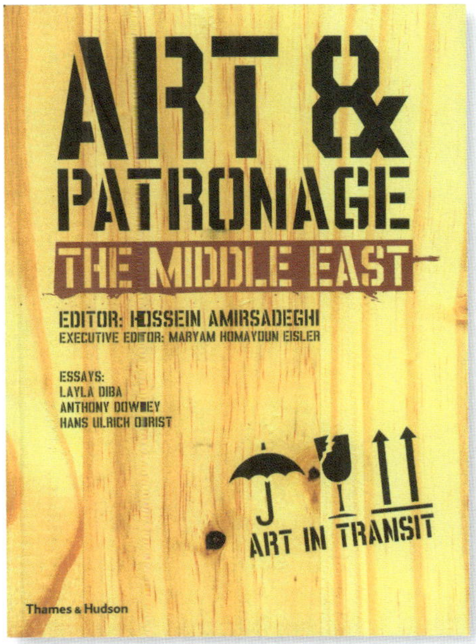

Art & Patronage

Edited by cultural entrepreneur Hossein Amirsadeghi, the publication *Art & Patronage: The Middle East* (2010) illustrates the role patronage plays in the Arab world, Iran, Turkey, and the Maghreb. The book profiles "important patrons, art collectors and institutional leaders within (and without) the region and among its diaspora" and also surveys different types of patronage: "the lavish government-backed Gulf model, the successful Turkish model of corporate and private patronage, the Iran diaspora model of patronage and support, the Egyptian NGO success story of Townhouse, and the Lebanese socioeconomic patronage model" (Hossein Amirsadeghi, *Art & Patronage*, p. 6).

With the aim of emphasizing how central patronage is "in the making of a progressive civil society"(Amirsadeghi, p. 6) in the region, the book contextualizes the various collectors' and foundations' profiles in a social and cultural discourse with three essays by Layla Diba, Anthony Downey, and Hans Ulrich Obrist.

The book later gave rise to a two-day "Art&Patronage Summit" held at the British Museum and Royal College of Art, London on January 12–13, 2012. The symposium was "an invitation-only event for top patrons, collectors, institutional leaders, curators, academics, artists, diplomats, and influential players involved in culture of and for the greater Middle East" (http://www.apsummit.com/) and led to the formation of the funding "A&P Project Mart" and "The Program for Cultural & Curatorial Practitioners." (SG)

Above:
Hossein Amirsadeghi (ed.), *Art & Patronage: The Middle East. Art in Transit*, Thames & Hudson, London, 2010

Art Geography in Africa

For historical and geographical reasons, it is nearly impossible to define and thus crystallize a coherent map of African art production. The monolithic identity and image we normally associate with Africa actually corresponds to a plural complex of practices, traditions, and systems. Instead of describing a homogeneous territory, cultural activities related to African art follow a centrifugal movement towards the valorization – as well as the questioning – of local, transnational, and diasporic paths.

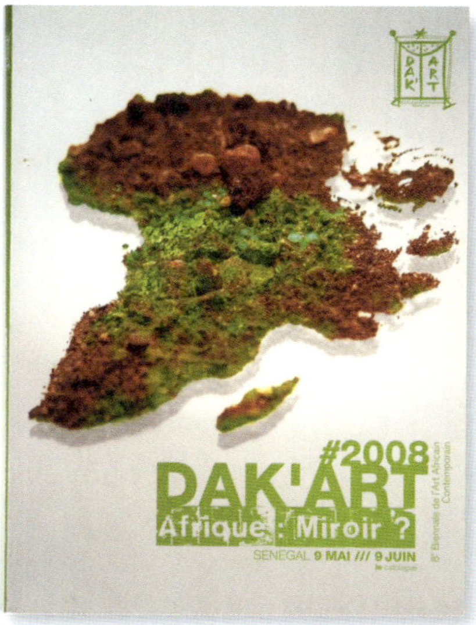

Dak'Art Biennial, Dakar, Senegal

Dak'Art is the first biennial that was founded in Africa. The idea reaches back to the period of Leopold Sédar Senghor, who – as the first elected president (1960–1980) of a newly independent Senegal– strongly promoted the fine arts and saw it as a program for the modernization of culture. However, the biennial was not founded until 1990, under the office of Senghor's successor Abdu Diouf, first as a forum for literature and then for fine arts in 1992. 102 artists were represented in the 1992 exhibition that was announced with the title *Arts et regards croisés sur l'Afrique*. From the beginning, the local École de Dakar was positioned in the framework of international art and was thus questioned in its aesthetic goals. In the following editions of the biennial, the question of diaspora artists and a pan-African sample show remained an unsolved problem that had left behind the definition of a contemporary African art (see: Elizabeth Harney, *In Senghor's Shadow: Art, Politics, and the Avant-garde in Senegal, 1960–1995*, Duke University Press, Durham (NC) and London, 2004; Yacouba Konaté, *La Biennale de Dakar: Pour une esthétique de la création africaine contemporaine tête à tête avec Adorno*, Harmattan, Paris, 2009). (SG)

Above:
Secrétariat Général de la Biennale de l'art africain contemporain de Dakar (ed.), *Dak'Art 2008, Afrique : Miroir?*, exhib. cat., 8th Biennial of African Contemporary Art, Dakar, 2008

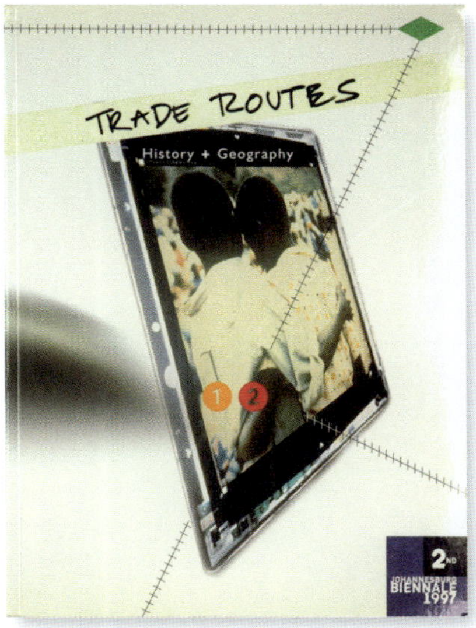

Johannesburg Biennale, Johannesburg, South Africa

The Johannesburg Biennale was launched in 1995 as part of the city's reconstruction and development program following the end of apartheid in 1994. With the establishment of an international biennial, the Greater Johannesburg Metropolitan Council wanted to demonstrate that Africa was "moving forward into the next millennium in unison with other continents of the world" (Victor Modise, in: Okwui Enwezor (ed.), *Trade Routes. History and Geography. 2nd Johannesburg Biennale 1997*, exhib. cat., Greater Johannesburg Metropolitan Council, Johannesburg, 1997, p. 4).

While the first biennial already gathered artists from 63 countries, the second one, curated by acclaimed Nigerian-born curator Okwui Enwezor, took one step further in the global art arena. The artistic director involved six internationally operating curators – namely Hou Hanru, Kellie Jones, Yu Yeon Kim, Gerardo Mosquera, Colin Richards, and Octavio Zaya – to question the notions of globalization and "placelessness." The six different exhibitions within the exhibition reflected the postnational nature characterizing 1997 South Africa at the end of the 1990s: "South Africa's population is equally hybrid, European, Asian and African. As such this country forms a microcosm of that critical address defined as globalisation" (Enwezor 1997, p. 8). Hinting at his own provenance and at the difficulties to define "Africa," Enwezor positioned the biennial "precariously between the disjunctive spaces of home and exile" (Enwezor 1997, p. 12). *Trade Routes* was the second and last Johannesburg Bienniale to date. The promoters' global ambitions encountered the reality of local financial problems so that the project unfortunately had to return to being a utopian idea. (SG)

Above:
Okwui Enwezor (ed.), *Trade Routes. History and Geography. 2nd Johannesburg Biennale 1997*, exhib. cat., Greater Johannesburg Metropolitan Council, Johannesburg, 1997

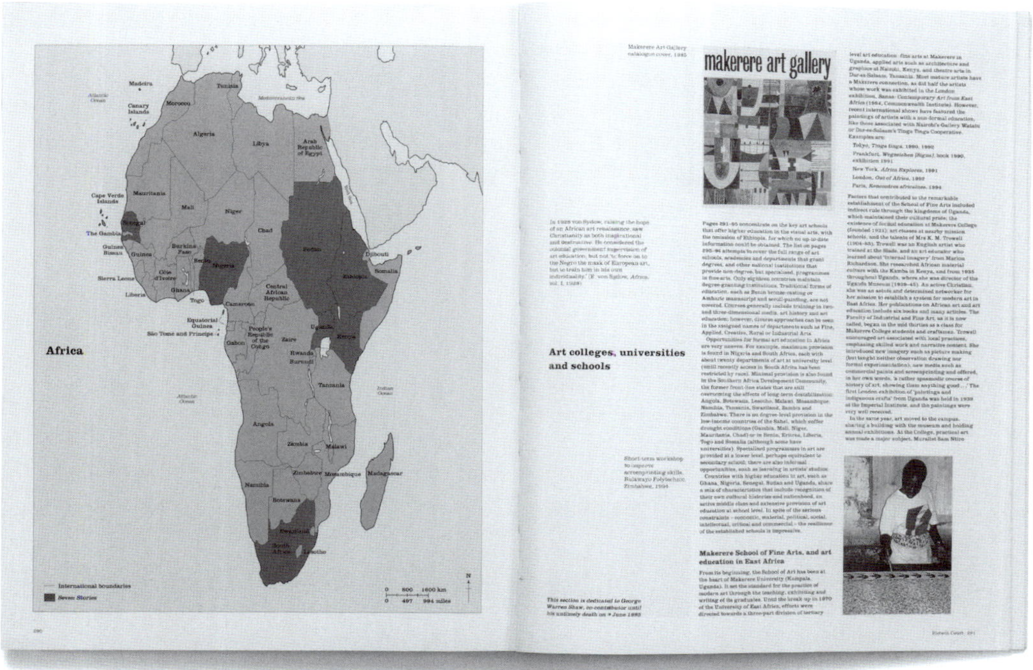

Seven Stories about Modern Art in Africa, London, United Kingdom

The exhibition *Seven Stories About Modern Art in Africa* that Clémentine Deliss organized at the Whitechapel Gallery in London in 1995 was an attempt to counteract, and improve, the usual presentation of artists from Africa by Western professionals. It was therefore decided to invite five personalities of African descent, among them two artists, to take over the responsibility of curating and to choose the narration of seven different art scenes distinguished, but not defined by the respective nations. This was also seen as an alternative discussion about Africa as a continent, which is usually the case in Western projection. The stories did not only narrate the respective history of an art scene in the modern sense in which the selected nations differed, but were also an allusion to the African tradition of storytelling. Chika Okeke-Agulu (Nigeria), El Hadji Sy (Senegal), Salah M. Hassan (Sudan and Ethiopia), David Koloane (South Africa), and Wanjiku Nyachae (Kenya and Uganda) acted as curators and chroniclers of their chosen field. The stories differed, but were all guided by the search for a forgotten history of African artists in the Western diaspora.

In the catalog, the seven African countries featured in the exhibition are represented in the so-called Gall-Peters projection, a very particular map that is unfamiliar to most of us. Our mental image of Africa has been distorted for centuries by the Mercator projection of 1569: the world map that is still most used and known but doesn't provide an accurate portrayal of landmasses. The most truthful representation of continent size remains the 1974 Gall-Peters projection, which is not Eurocentric and therefore reveals the actual main land areas. (HB/SG)

Clémentine Deliss (ed.), *Seven Stories about Modern Art in Africa*, exhib. cat., Whitechapel Gallery, London, Flammarion Paris, New York (NY), 1995, pp. 290–291

Marrakech Biennale, Marrakech, Morocco

Marrakech Biennale (in its first years called AiM – Art in Marrakech Festival/AiM – Art in Marrakech International Biennale) was founded in 2005 by British cultural entrepreneur Vanessa Branson, who had been active in the British and international art scene for the last three decades, together with the Vanessa Devereux Gallery in West London (1986–1991), The Portobello Arts Festival (1987–1989), and the establishment of The Wonderful Fund Collection, first shown in the frame of the first Marrakech Biennale (2005).

The Marrakech Biennale is "the first major trilingual (English, Arabic, and French) festival in North Africa focusing on cutting-edge contemporary art, literature and film" (www.marrakechbiennale.org/en/). Although strongly international, the biennial allows an international audience to taste morsels of the practice of local artists, writers, and intellectuals. Unlike many biennials which are set up by local or national administrations as operations of urban marketing – and thus with the aim to relaunch a given region through the appeal of contemporary art – the Marrakech Biennale can be looked at as an outsider touristic operation which somehow disturbs the conservatism of Morocco's royal family. Core of the festival is an international exhibition of contemporary art. Initially organized by Moroccan curators, such as Abdellah Karroum in 2007, the fourth edition of the Marrakech Biennale (2012) was curated by the young international curators Carson Chan and Nadim Samman. The exhibition *Higher Atlas* comprised entirely new site-specific installations by international artists and was accompanied by an exhibition reader, which creates a discourse on *The Marrakech Bienniale in Context.* (SG)

Below. from left:
Clémentine Deliss (ed.), *Seven Stories about Modern Art in Africa*, exhib. cat., Whitechapel Gallery, London, Flammarion Paris, New York (NY), 1995
Carson Chan and Nadim Samman (eds.), *Higher Atlas/Au-delà de l'Atlas. The Marrakech Biennale [4] in Context*, exhib. cat., Sternberg Press, Berlin, 2012

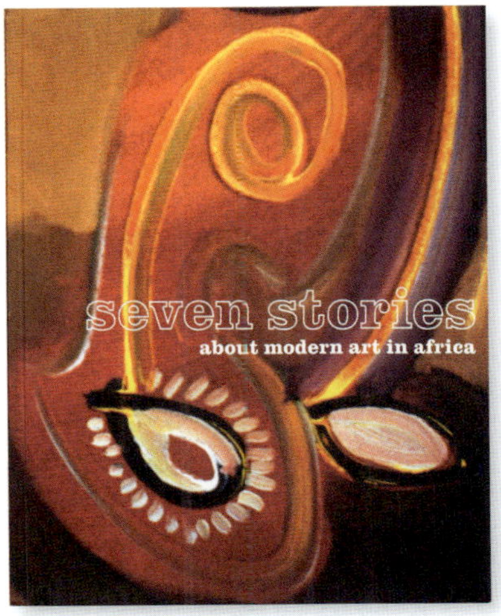

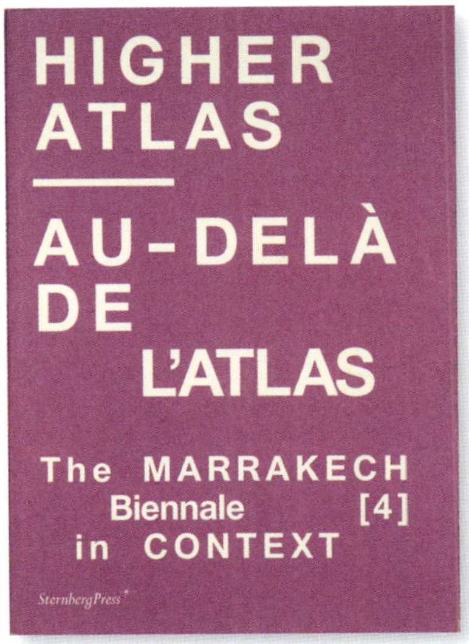

Aboriginal Australia. A Special Case

In their article "Aboriginal Art: Symptom or Success?" published in *Art in America*, July 1989, Tony Fry and Anne-Marie Willis discussed the recent success of Aboriginal art as both traditional and contemporary. Following on from, or coinciding with, the political controversy surrounding the Australian Bicentenary celebrating two centuries of permanent European settlement in 1988 – when Aboriginal Australians declined to participate in any celebrations of this event – exhibitions abroad began to show recent Aboriginal art.

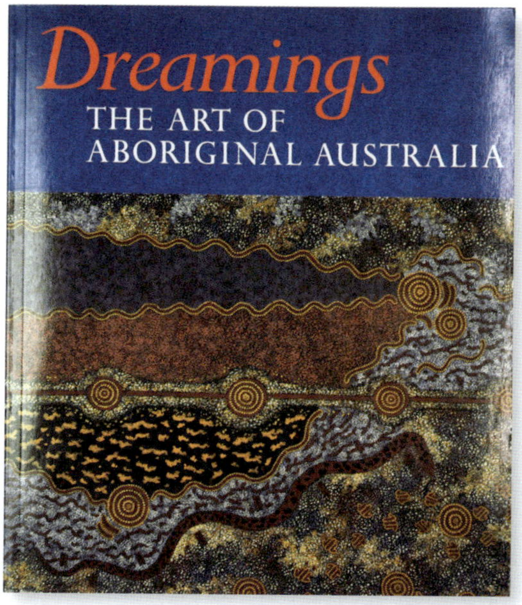

***Dreamings: The Art of Aboriginal Australia*, New York, Chicago, USA and Melbourne, Adelaide, Australia**

The traveling exhibition *Dreamings* was a collaboration between the Asia Society Galleries and the South Australian Museum, the latter holding the world's largest collection of Aboriginal art. The exhibition was first shown at the Asia Society Galleries in New York (1988) and then traveled to Chicago (1989), Melbourne (1989), and was finally shown in Adelaide (1990). Curated by the anthropologists Peter Sutton and Christopher Anderson, the exhibition attempted to integrate Aboriginal aesthetics "with the distinctive worldview and social values of Aboriginal tradition" (Peter Sutton (ed.), *Dreamings: The Art of Aboriginal Australia*, exhib. cat., The Asia Society Galleries, New York, George Braziller Publishers, New York, 1988, p. 2). Aboriginal languages have no distinct word for "art" (as we understand it in the West), but instead use terms that are equivalent to sign, design, and pattern. These meaningful marks, deriving both from nature and human activity, originate from the "Dreamings," intelligent beings that manifest their presence in the world through signs. This perspective allowed Sutton and Anderson to argue that "Aboriginal paintings, carvings, and other works are art, not 'by metamorphosis' and not merely because they are now in the global art market, but because they share with similar artifacts the act of representation and a particular potential for meaning" (Sutton 1988, p. 4). (HB/SG)

Left:
Peter Sutton (ed.), *Dreamings: The Art of Aboriginal Australia*, exhib. cat., The Asia Society Galleries, New York, George Braziller Publishers, New York (NY), 1988

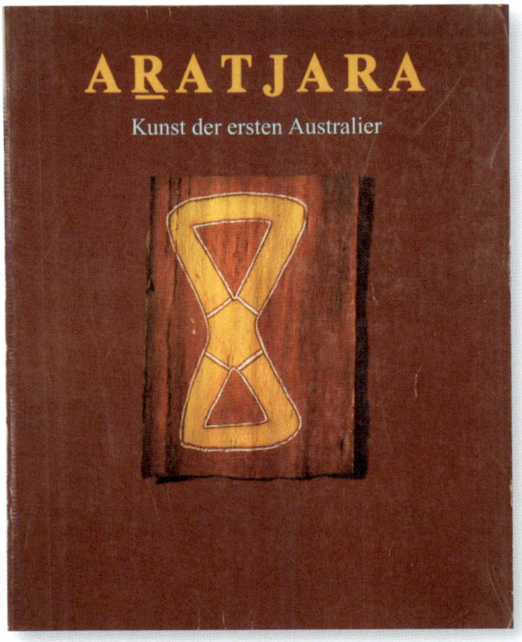

Aratjara. Art of the First Australians, Düsseldorf, Germany and Melbourne, Australia

After long years of preparation another exhibition opened in 1993 at the Kunstsammlung Nordrhein-Westfalen in Düsseldorf, Germany, titled *Aratjara. Art of the First Australians*. Curated by artist Bernhard Lüthi, this presentation later traveled to the National Gallery of Victoria in Melbourne. The exhibition documented the political significance of Aboriginal art production with two petitions consisting of bark and paper paintings, presented in 1963 and 1988, respectively, which sought to reclaim civil rights, land ownership, and the use of traditional names from the Australian government. (HB/SG)

Above:
Bernhard Lüthi (ed.), *Aratjara. Kunst der ersten Australier: traditionelle und zeitgenössische Werke der Aborigines und Torres Strait Islanders/Aratjara. Art of the First Australians: Traditional and Contemporary Works by Aboriginal and Torres Strait Islander Artists*, exhib. cat., Kunstsammlung Nordrhein-Westfalen, DuMont, Cologne, 1993

Before Time Today. Reinventing Tradition in Aurukun Aboriginal Art, Brisbane, Australia

The exhibition *Before Time Today. Reinventing Tradition in Aurukun Aboriginal Art*, curated by Sally Butler at the University of Queensland Art Museum in 2010, aimed to grant "Australian Aboriginal Art its proper place in the history of world art" (Sally Butler (ed.), *Before Time Today. Reinventing Tradition in Aurukun Aboriginal Art*, exhib. cat., University of Queensland Press, St. Lucia, 2010, p. 28).

For the first time traditional Wik and Kugu art from Aurukun in the far north of Queensland was reinterpreted in the light of recent developments and contemporary art production understood retrospectively. According to the curator, "[t]he concept of reinvention diminishes the allusion to repetitive cultural practices that persist within stereotypical ideas of a static, unchanging Aboriginal culture" (Butler 2010, p. 24). The accompanying catalog contained essays by leading authorities on Aurukun cultural history, aesthetics, and politics including Peter Sutton, curator of the 1988 traveling exhibition *Dreamings*, "one of the most significant survey exhibitions of Aboriginal art" (Butler 2010, p. 27). Alongside contributions by art critics, anthropologists, and sociologists, "the centrepiece of the book is a chapter where Indigenous artists themselves speak about their art and culture" (Butler 2010, p. 28). (HB/SG)

Below:
Sally Butler (ed.), *Before Time Today. Reinventing Tradition in Aurukun Aboriginal Art*, exhib. cat., University of Queensland Press, St. Lucia, 2010

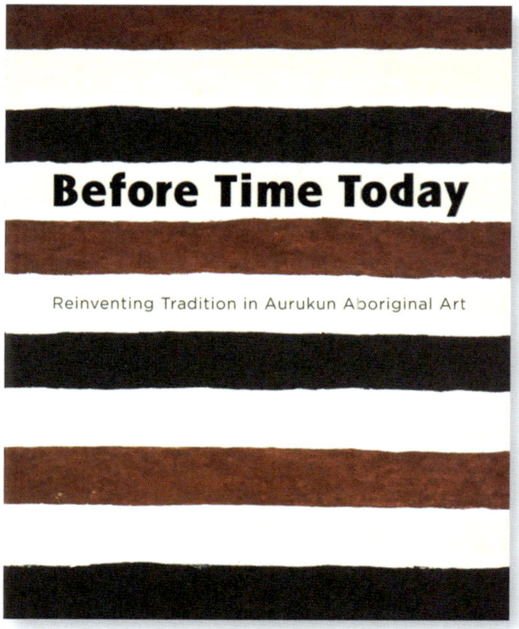

The National Gallery of Australia, Canberra, Australia

The National Gallery of Australia in Canberra, founded in 1982, ushered in a new era in September 2010 by opening eleven new galleries, which were designed for the exhibition of Aboriginal and Torres Strait Islander art. Over 600 works were selected from a collection of over 7,500 works of art, "the largest collection of Australian Indigenous art in the world." The Gallery's "first major purchase of Aboriginal art was made in 1972 and consisted of a series of eight bark paintings from Groote Eylandt." Franchesca Cubillo, senior curator, spoke of art "which has been created for over 40,000 years [and] continues to evolve and change." (NGA Media Release, September 30, 2010) A prominent place is held by *The Aboriginal Memorial*, consisting of 200 "painted wooden poles" commissioned by the National Gallery in 1988 for the Australian Bicentenary of European occupation of Australia. It was first shown at the 1988 Biennale of Sydney. In North-east Arnhemland, Aboriginal Australians hold the Hollow Log or Bone Coffin ceremony. Each hollowed log symbolically represents a bone coffin. Thus, in essence, the forest of wooden poles represents a large cemetery of deceased Indigenous Australians, a War Memorial to those Aboriginals who died defending their country. (HB)

Below:
Ramingining Artists, *The Aboriginal Memorial*, 1987–1988, installation of 200 hollow long bone coffins, courtesy of the National Gallery of Australia, Canberra

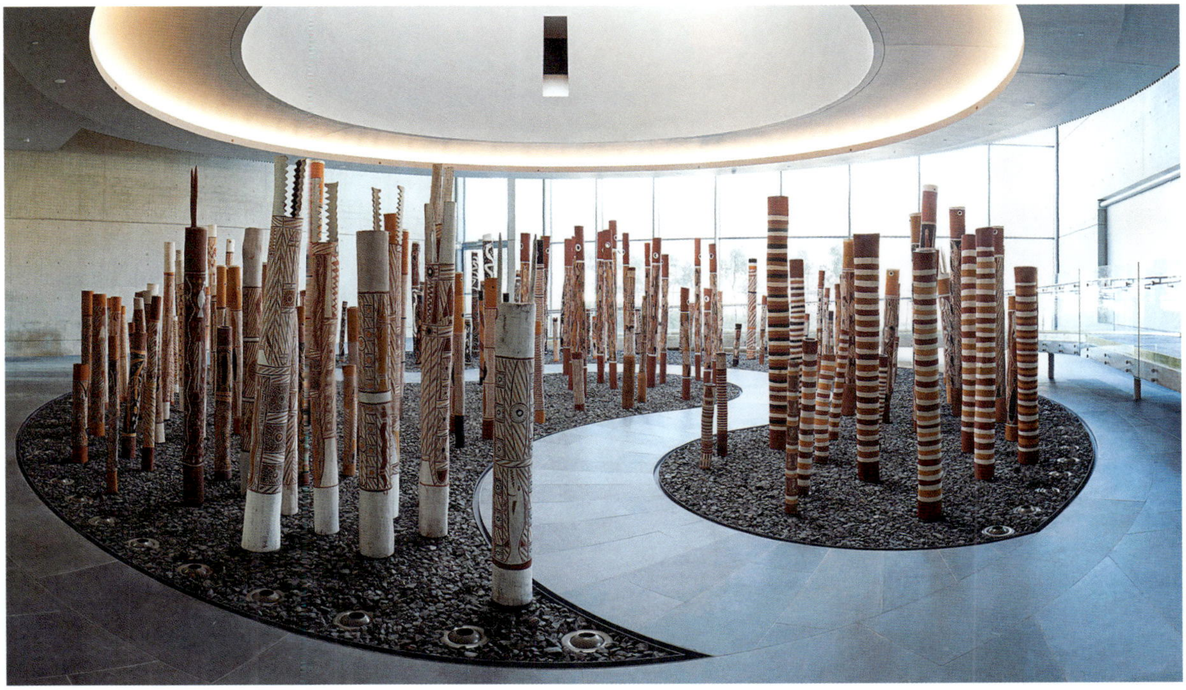

Branding.
New Art Markets and Their Strategies

The most powerful expression of the globalization of art is the strategy of large auction houses to promote contemporary art in geographic units (Chinese, Indian, Arab, and Iranian art) and thus succesfully address a clientele that previously did not buy art. In the meantime, the Chinese art market has increased enormously, exceeding the market share of most European countries, and with the sensational prices it commands has caught up with Western art's leading position. The interaction of the financial market with the art market demonstrates that art has been transformed into a speculative commodity for the luxury goods industry, which has also become the subject of a new branch of nonfiction literature. As not only art fairs but also biennials are now entering the network of the market, the cultural distance to a concept of art that is still regarded in any way as exclusive is growing rapidly. At the same time, however, the market plays a central role in the development of new art regions and in the public presence of artists from cultures remote from the art world. (HB)

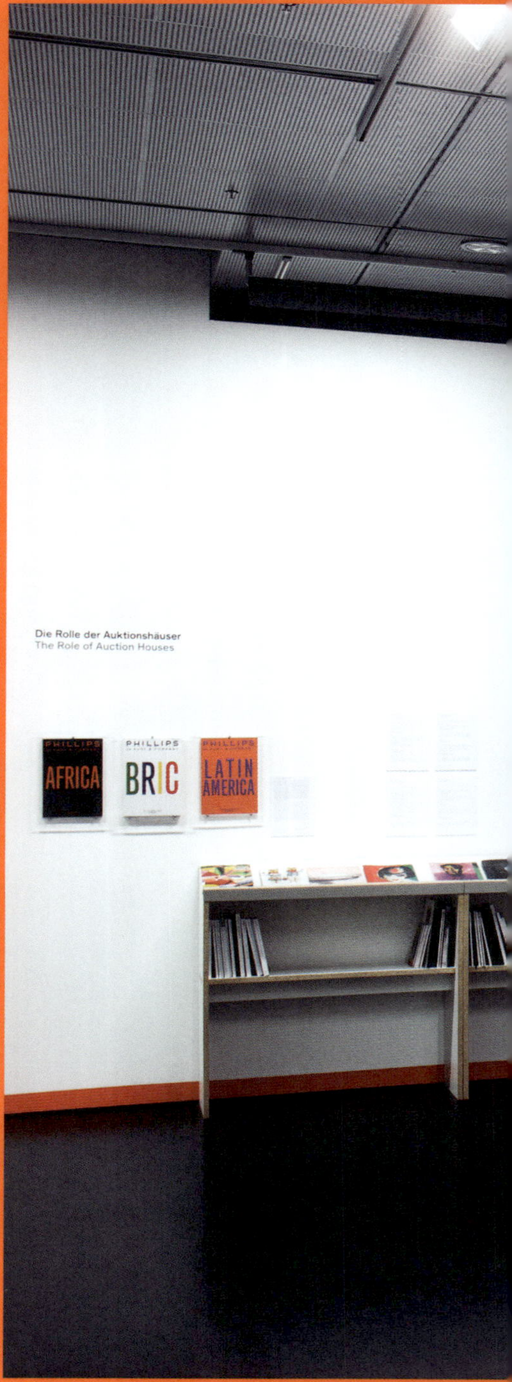

The Global Contemporary. Art Worlds after 1989, section: *Room of Histories*, exhibition view, ZKM | Karlsruhe, 2011–2012

Globalization Data

The Role of Auction Houses

Art and Market: Two Sides of the Same Coin

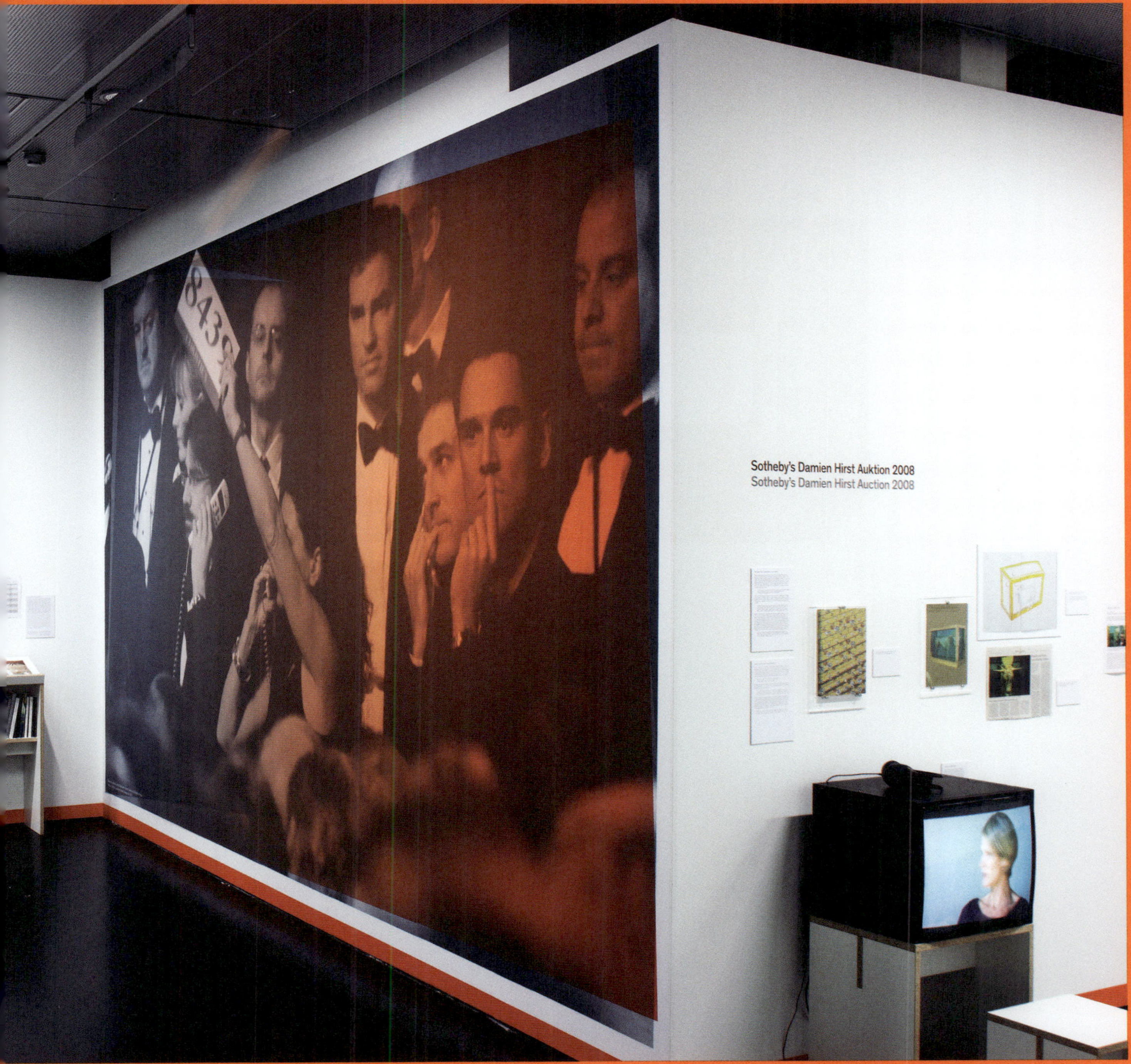

Globalization Data

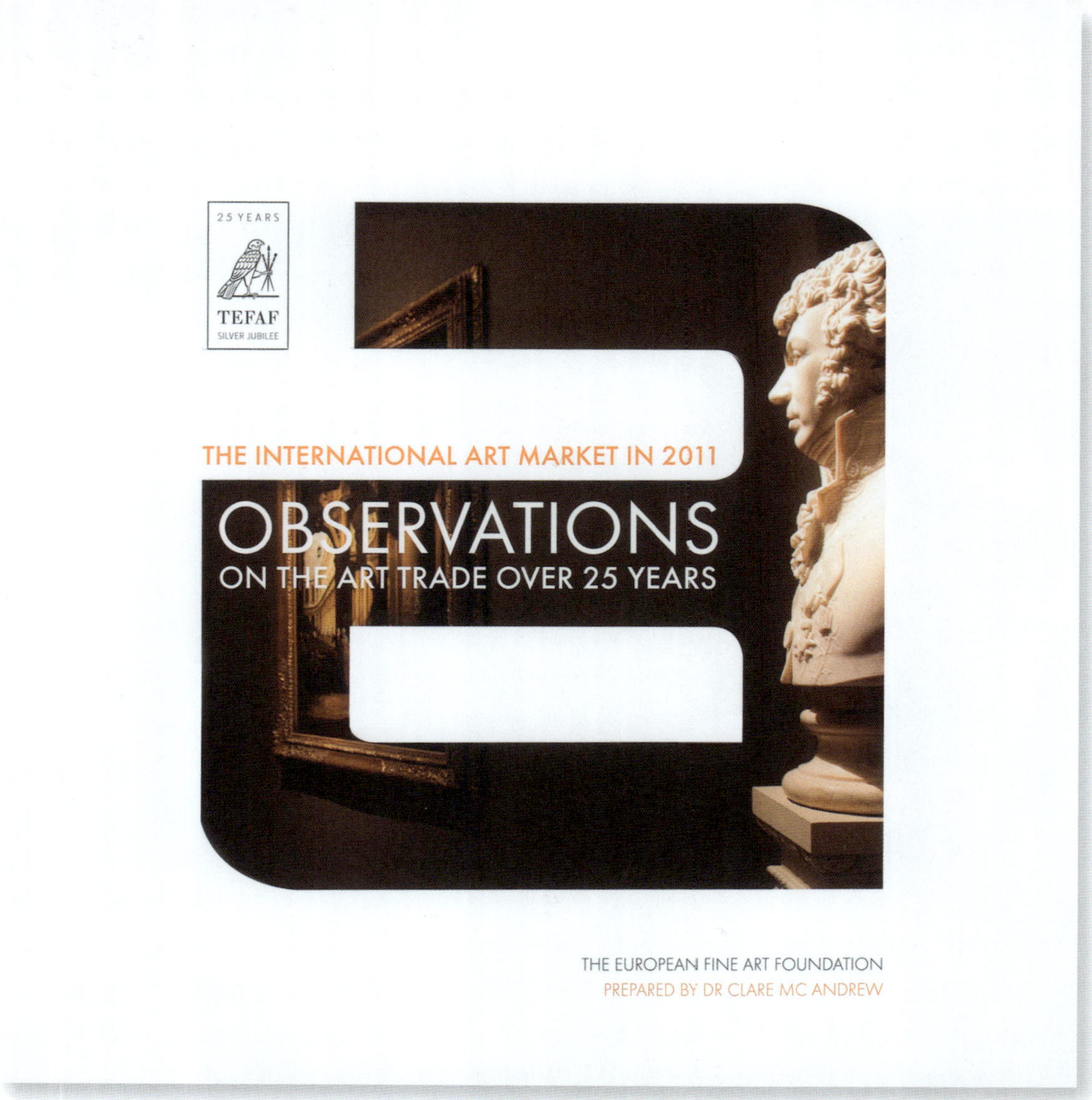

Texts, tables, and charts showing data taken from Clare McAndrew, *The International Art Market in 2011. Observations on the Art Trade Over 25 Years*, The European Fine Art Foundation (TEFAF), Helvoirt, 2012, pp. 19, 31, 32, 34, 43, 45–47, 63, 65, 69.

Above:
Clare McAndrew, *The International Market in 2011. Observations on the Art Trade Over 25 Years*, The European Fine Art Foundation (TEFAF), Helvoirt, 2012

The Global Art Market in 2011

The global art market continued to recover in 2011, with the market as a whole advancing 7% year-on-year to €46.1 billion, an increase of 63% from the market crisis of 2009. The volume of transactions in the global art market also increased in 2011 by 5% to 36.8 million. This is up 19% from its low point in 2009, but significantly less than the boom year of 2007, when nearly 50 million works were sold on global markets.

China overtook the U.S. to become the largest art and antiques market worldwide in 2011 for the first time, with a share of 30%, based on both auction and dealer sales.

The U.S.'s share dropped by 5 percentage points year-on-year to 29%, as the market showed low negative growth of –6%, reaching €13.6 billion in sales.

The EU achieved aggregate sales of €15.6 billion in 2011, down 2% on 2010 and representing 34% of the global art market.

Charts: Market Share of Fine Art Auction Market for Works Sold for More than €50,000

1. By Value of Sales

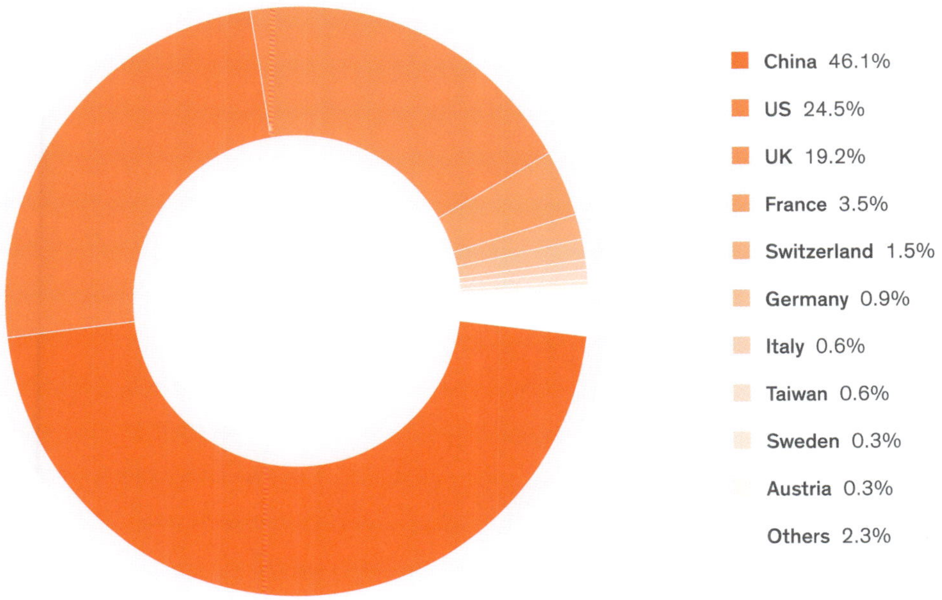

2. By Volume of Sales

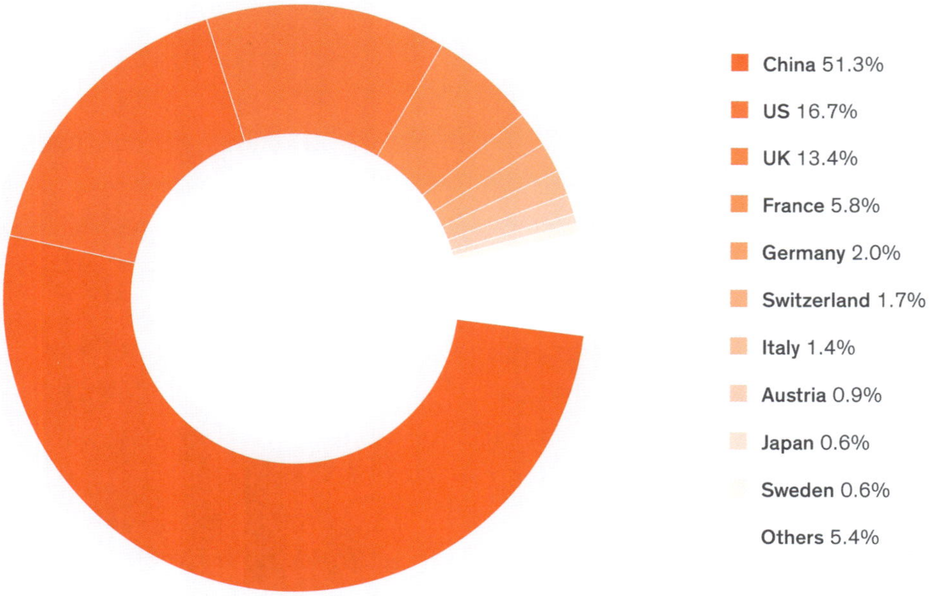

The Modern and Contemporary sectors combined to account for nearly 70% of the fine art market. Both sectors continued a strong recovery in 2011, leading them to levels in excess of the boom of 2007/2008.

Charts: Market Share by Sector of the Fine Art Auction Market in 2011

1. By Value of Sales

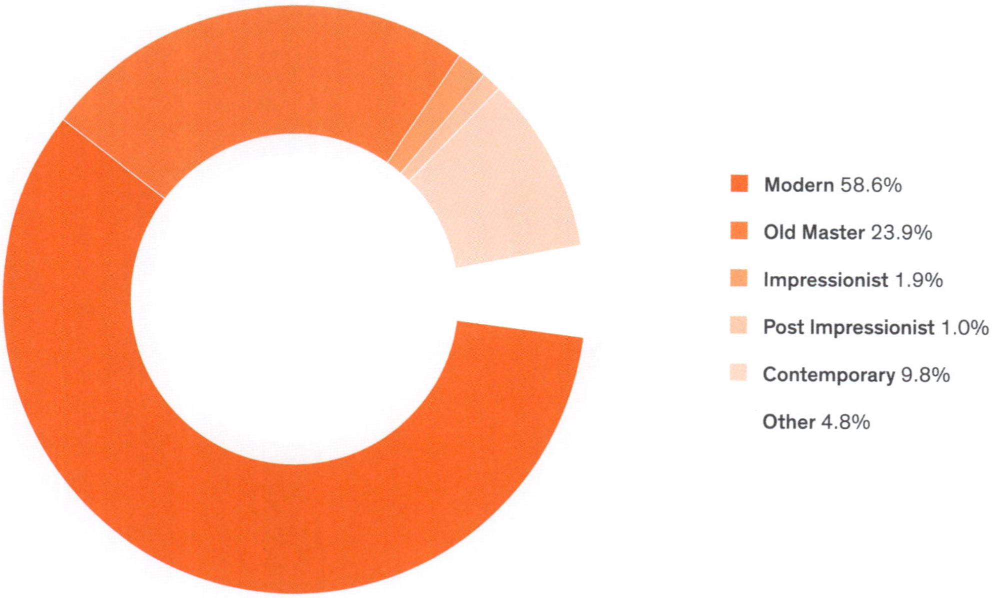

2. By Volume of Sales

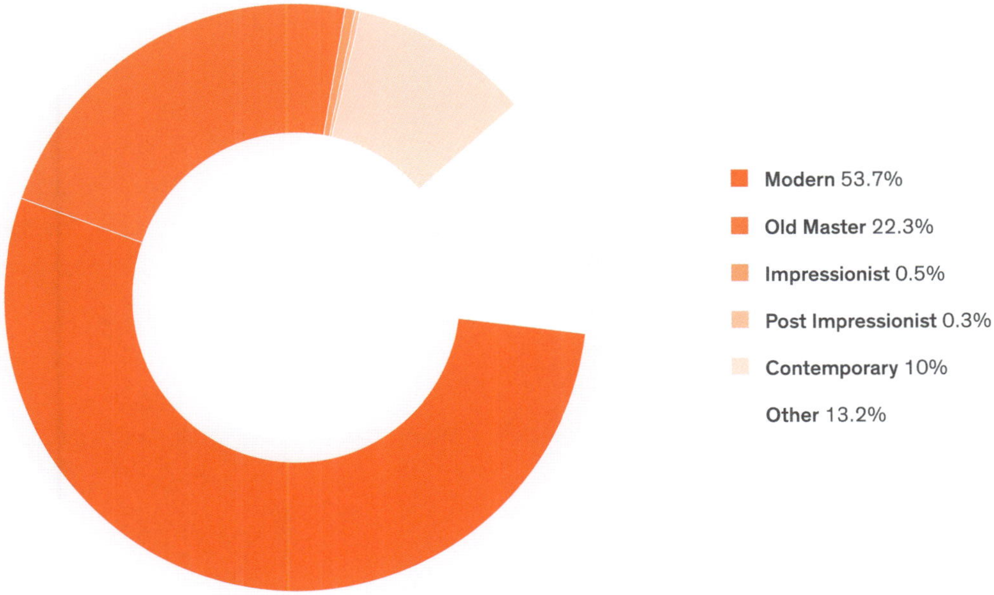

The Contemporary Art Market in 2011

The Contemporary art market reached a high of €955 million globally in 2011 with close to 35,180 transactions at auction. This represented a second year of recovery for the sector, with values increasing by 86% in 2010 and then 63% in 2011, after their sharp contraction of 66% in 2009.

Chart: The Contemporary Art Sector: 2002 to 2011

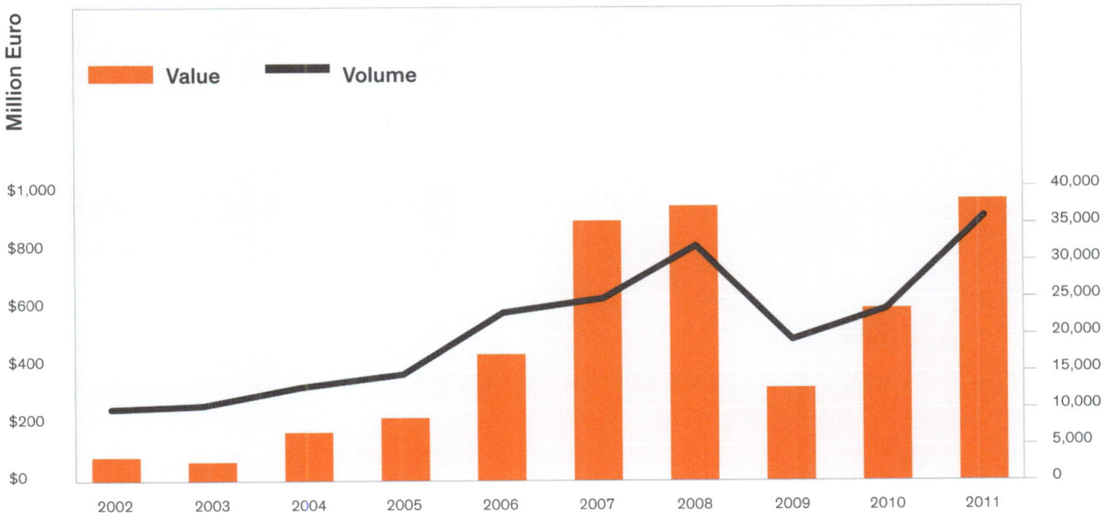

Strong auction and dealer sales in New York and London, particularly in the second half of the year, brought the market to its highest levels since the boom, while the Chinese Contemporary market has been on a rapid path of growth since 2009.

In 2011, the dominant markets for contemporary art were outside Europe, with China holding a leading share of 45% by value, up from 28% in 2010. China also accounted for the largest share of transactions at auction, at 23%. Average prices in the U.S. were still much higher than in China in 2011, but the U.S. median price was €2,875, which indicates that these were highly skewed by a few high value sales. While the median price in China at €9,575 does indicate a higher mid-point for this market.

Table: Market Share of Contemporary Art by Value and Volume and Average Prices in 2011

Country	By Value	By Volume	Average Prices
China	45.4%	22.6%	€44,763
US	24.7%	21.5%	€81,308
UK	19.2%	8.8%	€29,851
France	2.2%	8.3%	€13,418
Taiwan	1.8%	1.1%	€1,397
Italy	0.7%	7.9%	€8,497
Germany	0.6%	3.6%	€4,141
Sweden	0.5%	2.2%	€2,165
UAE	0.4%	0.5%	€438
Singapore	0.4%	0.7%	€578
Rest of World	4.1%	22.7%	€4,824
TOTAL	100.0%	100.0%	€26,858

A 25-Year Overview of the Art Market

The art market has more than doubled in size in 25 years and it grew over 575% from its lowest point in 1991 to its highest in 2007.

The recession of the 1990s took nearly a decade to recover from, whereas the contraction in 2009 has been relatively short lived. This is due in part to the increasingly global nature of the art market.

Chart: Sales in the Global Art Market 1990–2011 (U.S. Dollars)

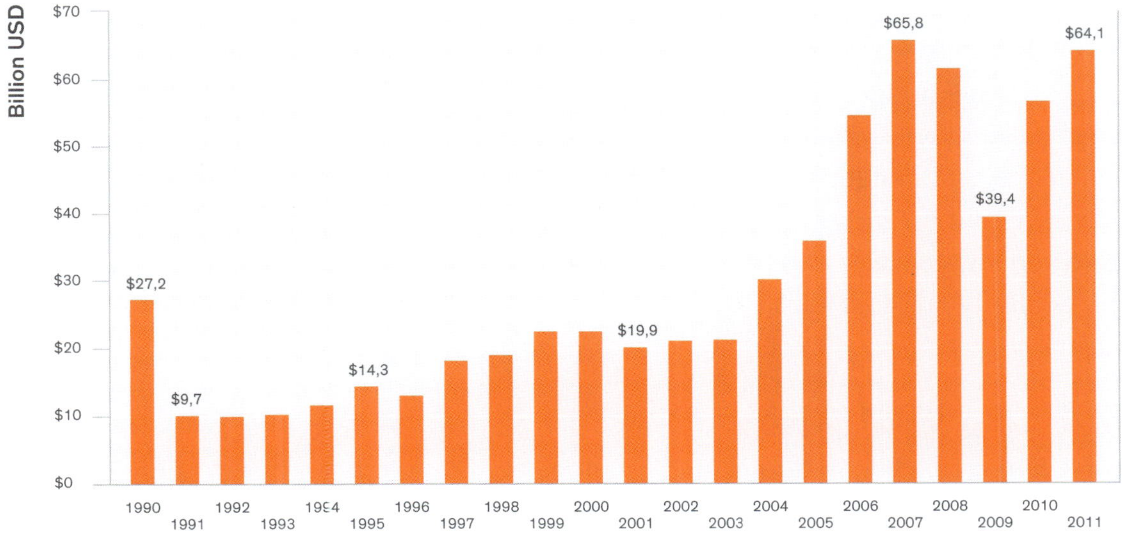

Globalization of the market, and in particular new buyers and markets in China and elsewhere, has been instrumental in driving growth.

The art market's expansion has been driven by the growth and wider global distribution of high net worth wealth around the world.

The art market has also been influenced by key macro-economic variables such as changes in GDP, GDP per capita, inflation, and interest rates. The geographical spread of major buyers has shifted, and most notably Chinese art buyers have become a dominant market force.

Table: Global Art Market Share 1990–2011

Country	France	Germany	Switzerland	Italy	UK	US	China	Rest of World
1990	17%	3%	2%	2%	23%	46%	‹0.4%	7%
1992	9%	2%	5%	3%	28%	42%	0.4%	12%
1995	6%	4%	2%	2%	26%	52%	0.8%	7%
1997	6%	3%	1%	1%	27%	57%	‹0.4%	5%
2000	6%	3%	2%	1%	26%	55%	0.4%	7%
2002	9%	3%	2%	3%	29%	43%	1%	10%
2006	6%	3%	2%	3%	27%	46%	5%	9%
2008	6%	2%	1%	3%	34%	35%	9%	10%
2009	10%	3%	2%	2%	23%	31%	18%	11%
2010	6%	2%	2%	1%	22%	34%	23%	10%
2011	6%	2%	3%	1%	22%	29%	30%	7%

The growth of the Internet and use of the online channel has changed the infrastructure of the market, dramatically altering the way business is conducted.

The traditional roles of dealer versus auction houses have blurred, with auction houses increasingly moving into the retail sector and expanding private sales.

Changing tastes have influenced the distribution of the art market. This has been particularly evident in the rise in popularity of contemporary art.

In recent decades there has been a noticeable growth in of the "cult of celebrity" in the art market. Celebrity collections and famous provenance have become an increasingly important factor driving sales and prices. Another aspect of the celebrity cult applies to artists. This can be called "the Warholian influence."

The Chinese Market in 2011

The Chinese art and antiques auction market continues to be the strongest growing market worldwide.

Chart: Chinese Auction Sales 2004–2011

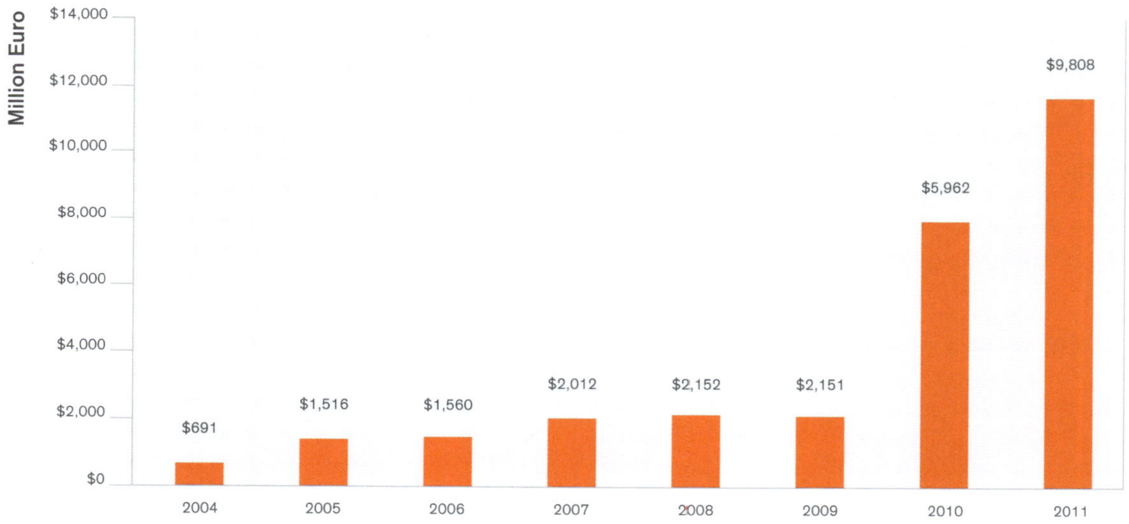

The rise of auction sales in mainland China has been particularly dramatic over 2010 and 2011. The two largest houses of China Guardian and Poly International had their strongest years to date in 2011

It is important to note that, at present, the Chinese art market, rather than becoming a principal international hub like London or New York, relies heavily on domestic buyers.

Despite its massive growth in recent years, there are several risk factors connected to the auction market that could threaten its future stability. The legal and regulatory framework of the market remains underdeveloped, and the problem of fakes and authenticity of works, particularly in smaller auction venues, is considerable.

Another key issue affecting the size of the auction market and its rate of growth over recent years is that, although the reported auction figures accurately reflect those items hammered down at auction, there are significant problems with nonpayment and late payment. Under regulations in China, full settlement for winning bids is supposed to be made within a six-month period.

The Role of Auction Houses

The Geographic Strategy of Phillips de Pury & Company

In September 2009 the auction house Phillips de Pury & Company started a series of thematic auctions of contemporary art that are held in London and New York. Through the programmatic themes the departments aim to strengthen their curatorial and research activity, suggesting interpretations on how to define and "where to find" contemporary art. BRIC (Brazil, Russia, India, and China) was the first thematic sale bearing a geographical label. The sale took place at Saatchi Gallery in London and was divided into five sections. On April 23, 2010 the evening sale comprised lots from all four countries, while on the following day, individual sales were held for artworks coming from each of them. The auction house also organized a cultural symposium in order to "promote an understanding of the contemporary cultural environments of Brazil, Russia, India and China, and to acknowledge the intellectual and commercial importance of the art and design coming out of these emerging power nations" (Phillips de Pury & Company, BRIC press release, 2010). Following the BRIC sale, Phillips de Pury & Company held "Africa" and "Latin America" sales in New York in May and September of the same year. (SG)

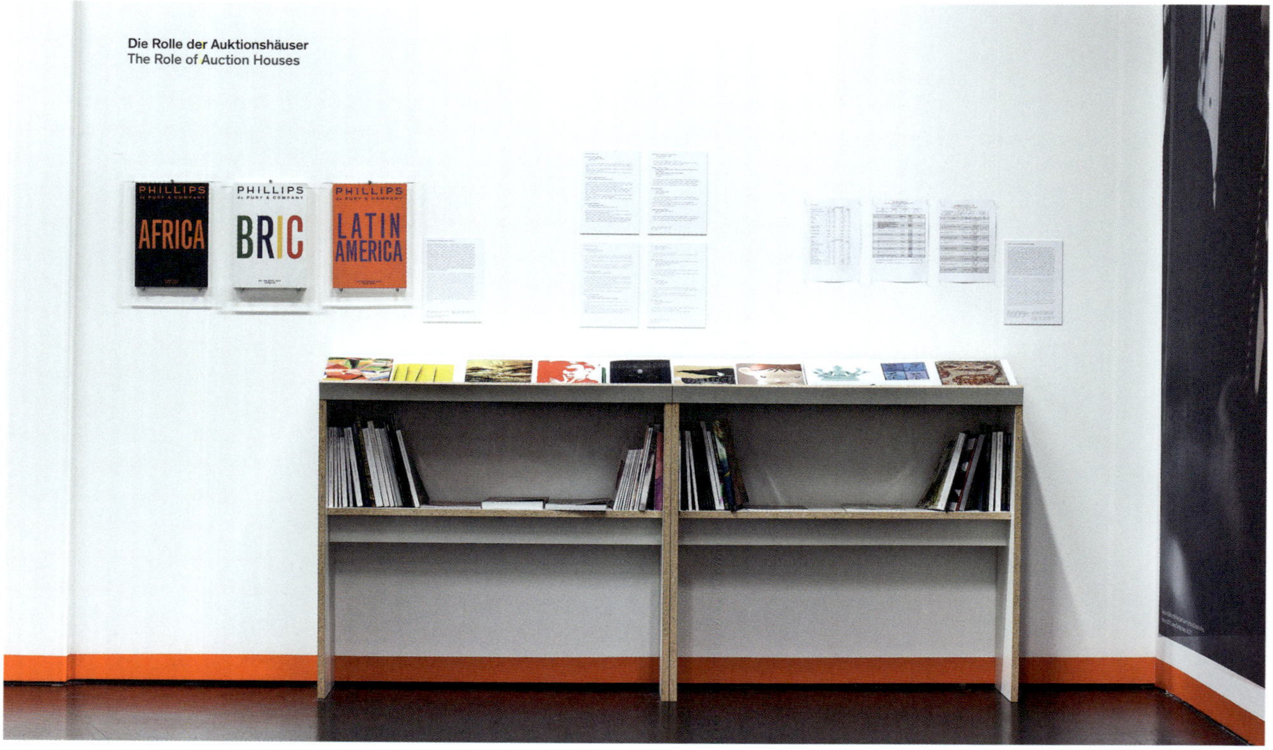

The Global Contemporary. Art Worlds after 1989, section: *Room of Histories*, exhibition view, ZKM | Karlsruhe, 2011–2012

Christie's Expansion in the Global Art Market

Founded in London in 1776 by James Christie, Christie's today has 53 offices and 10 salesrooms in 32 countries worldwide including London, New York, Paris, Geneva, Milan, Amsterdam, Zurich, Dubai, and Hong Kong. In light of recent developments of the global art market, the auction house has expanded its presence in emerging and new markets such as Russia, China, India, and the United Arab Emirates. Steven P. Murphy, Chief Executive Officer of Christie's International, sees the company's worldwide success as a result of "the firm's commitment to serve a global audience" (www.christies.com/presscenter/pdf/2011/Christies_Sales_Total_First_Half_2011.pdf, p. 2). Hong Kong and Dubai emerge as the key sale centers for China and the Middle East respectively, although records for Asian and Arab art were registered also in New York and London. Hong Kong sales in the "Asian Art" category, which are growing faster than anywhere else in the world, reach a 65% increase year after year "due to the strength of the economy in the region and Asian collectors' appetite for works of art" (www.christies.com/about/presscenter/releases/pressrelease.aspx?pressreleaseid=4940). (SG)

Sotheby's Worldwide

Founded in London in 1744 and now headquartered in New York, the multinational corporation of Sotheby's today has ninety offices in forty countries, with auction rooms in London, Geneva, Milan, Paris, Zurich, New York, Toronto, Hong Kong, and Doha.

According to the company's 2012 reports, 2011 was the best year in Sotheby's entire history: sales increased by 7% to US$831.8 million. William F. Ruprecht, Sotheby's President and Chief Executive Officer, said that "for the first time ever, Sotheby's consolidated sales in Asia reached $1 billion in 2011," and also reached "the point where the three geographic engines driving our auction business – the Americas, Europe, and Asia – are contributing to our success in roughly equal proportions."

The growing importance of sales outside of Europe and the Americas is the result of the company's recent global expansion into China and other "new" markets, such as the Middle East, with new Sotheby's premises opening in Hong Kong in 2012 (Sotheby's opened its first auction house in Hong Kong in 1973; in 2012 it opened new and larger premises) and a new office being established in Doha (2008). Another factor is the creation of geographically oriented thematic auctions, which are held at various locations worldwide, such as "20th Century Chinese Art," "Contemporary Asian Art," "Middle East & India," "Latin American Art," and "Russian Art," with the latter being one of the fastest expanding markets in 2011, together with Chinese contemporary art. (SG)

Sotheby's Damien Hirst Auction 2008

Damien Hirst's auction *Beautiful Inside My Head Forever* at Sotheby's London on September 15 and 16 comprised 223 new works, all specifically made for the auction, at a presale estimate value of US$122 to US$176 million. Bypassing his dealers, Jay Jopling and Larry Gagosian, Hirst shook the foundations of art business, declaring that the auction was a way to break free from the system. The sale on September 15, coincided with the day the global financial crisis exploded:

- American investment bank Lehman Brothers declared bankruptcy
- Merrill Lynch announced its sale to the rival Bank of America
- American International Group announced its failing.

Nevertheless, the gala evening sale realized US$127 million and the two-day total of US$201 million, with almost a quarter of the lots selling above US$1 million and three quarters above their high estimate:

> "The contrast between the tumultuous state of the global economy and the extravagances of the art world could not have been any sharper. (…) Sotheby's declared that one in three buyers was new, the majority of these coming from developing countries, such as the Middle East and Russia" (Noah Horowitz, *Art of the Deal. Contemporary Art in a Global Financial Market*, Princeton University Press, Princeton (NJ), 2011, p. XIV).

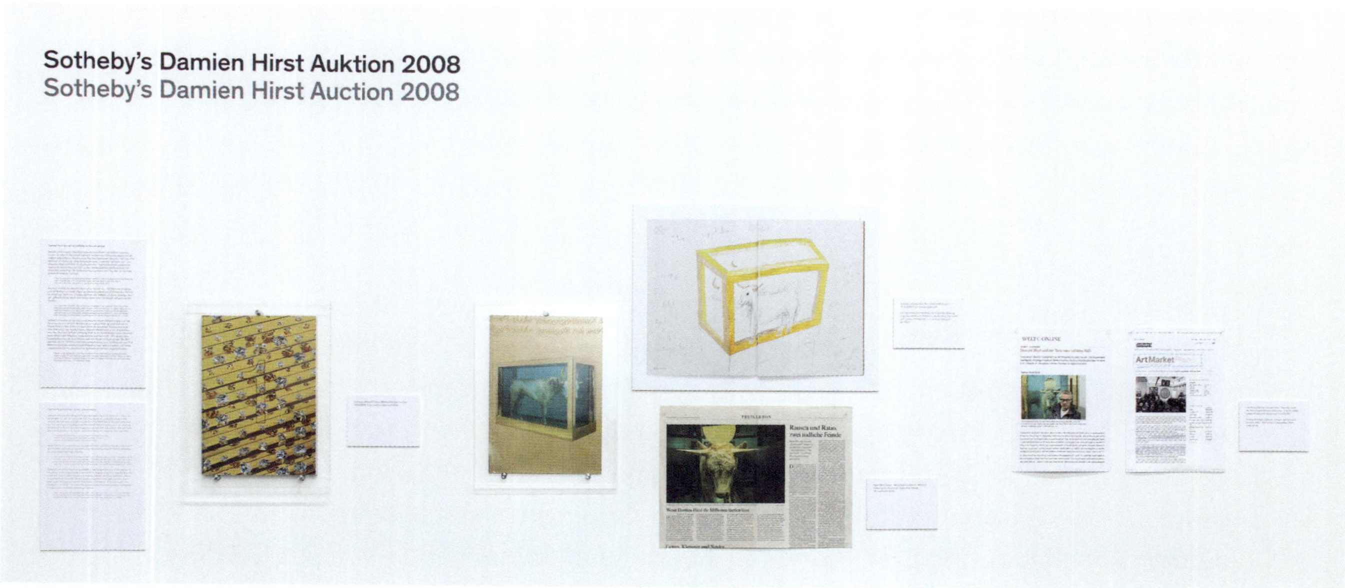

The Global Contemporary. Art Worlds after 1989, section: *Room of Histories*, exhibition view, ZKM | Karlsruhe, 2011–2012

Sotheby's interest in developing markets is also suggested by a small preview of fourteen pieces at the Oberoi Hotel in New Delhi in August 2008, the first exhibition the artist ever held in India. Despite the alliance between Hirst and Sotheby's, rumors suggested that the artist's dealers played a key role in the sale's success, especially in the two auction records: *The Golden Calf*, sold for US$19 million, and *The Kingdom*, sold for US$17.6 million. The protectionism of insider players' contributed in supporting prices and preventing a failure: "Were Jay Jopling and Larry Gagosian (Hirst's usual dealers) propping up prices to ensure the continuing value of their already extensive stocks?" (Rachel Campbell-Johnston, "No sign of a downturn at Sotheby's as buyers stage a bull run," in: *The Times*, September 17, 2008). (SG)

Beautiful Inside My Head Forever: Auction Results
Sotheby's, London, September 15&16, 2008

Sale total with Premium	$200,752,179
Total Lots	223
Lots Sold	218
Percentage Sold	97.80%
Average Lot Value	$920,882
Top Ten	$74,752,572
Top Ten as % of Total	39%

Top Ten

Title	Price w/Premium
The Golden Calf	$18,661,796
The Kingdom	$17,247,539
Fragments of Paradise	$9,368,104
Here Today, Gone Tomorrow	$5,327,368
The Black Sheep with Golden Horn	$4,721,257
Memories of/Moments with You	$4,721,257
The Dream	$4,197,934
Ascended	$4,097,353
The Abyss	$3,205,981
After the Flood	$3,205,981

The Estella Collection

Under Good Auspices

The Estella Collection was assembled by New York art dealer Michael Goedhuis, beginning in 2004. Over the course of three years, Goedhuis traveled throughout China, purchasing more than 200 works of art from galleries and artists' studios. The official aim was to create a major private collection of contemporary Chinese art to be featured in a book of "the highest scholarship" and eventually was to be donated to a museum.

Branding

The name Estella comes from Charles Dickens' *Great Expectations* (1861): "I felt it was a name the Chinese could pronounce," Goedhuis has said. "It's a pretty name" (Carol Vogel, "Contemporary Chinese on Sale in Hong Kong," in: *The New York Times*, March 28, 2008).

The Creation of Symbolic Value

From March 2007 to March 2008 the entire collection traveled to the Louisiana Museum of Modern Art in Denmark and the Israel Museum in Jerusalem. On both occasions an extensive scholarly catalog accompanied the exhibitions.

Sotheby's Announcements

During the exhibition *China Onward* in Denmark, Sotheby's announced the sale of the entire collection in two auctions in Hong Kong in April 2008 and New York in October 2008. It was also revealed that Goedhuis was not a private collector. He was representing a consortium of investors led by New York businessmen Ray Debbane and Sacha Lainovic (Weight Watchers International). The collection was auctioned in collaboration with New York Impressionism dealer William Acquavella, "with whom Sotheby's had actually acquired the entire body of work from the investors in August 2007" (Noah Horowitz, *Art of the Deal. Contemporary Art in a Global Financial Market*, Princeton University Press, Princeton (NJ), 2011, p. XVI).

The Sale

Auction Summary: US$15,227,214 (US$17,888,575 including premium), 26.7% (US$3,208,601) above high estimate.

Moral of the Story

The story of the Estella collection is "indicative of a global contemporary art economy in which boundaries between collecting and investing are increasingly blurred: a business strategy is identified (in New York); inventory is bought at a trade discount (in China); provenance, visibility and critical legitimacy are secured through museum exhibitions (in Denmark and Israel); the body of work, now a museum-quality collection, is sold at premium (to a New York dealer and a leading international auction house); and this collection is quickly sold at auction (in Hong Kong and New York)" (Horowitz 2011, p. XVII). (SG)

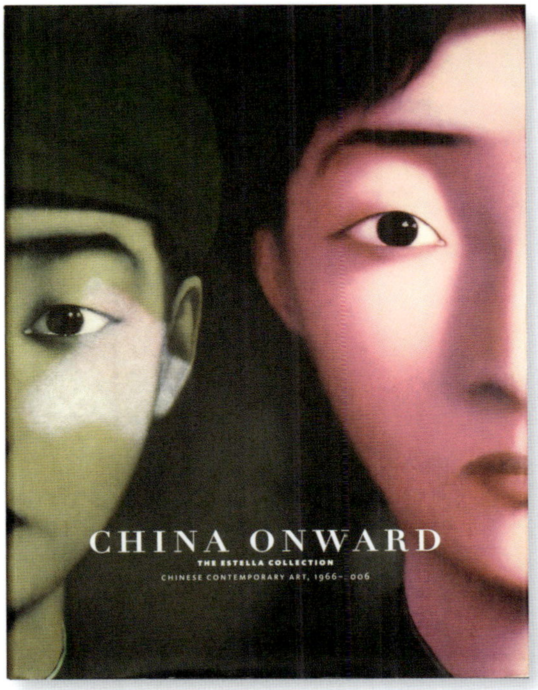

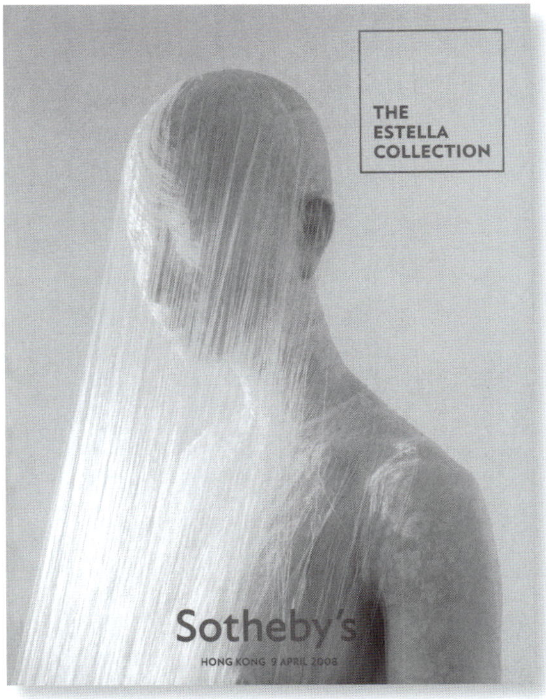

Above, from left:
Frances Bowles (ed.), *China Onward. The Estella Collection. Chinese Contemporary Art, 1966–2006*, exhib. cat., Louisiana Museum of Modern Art, Humlebæk, 2007
Sotheby's (ed.), *The Estella Collection*, auction catalog, Hong Kong, April 9, 2008

Art and Market: Two Sides of the Same Coin

Don Thompson, *The $12 Million Stuffed Shark*

The $12 Million Stuffed Shark. The Curious Economics of Contemporary Art is a book by economist Don Thompson. Thompson points out the branding strategies adopted by art dealers and auction houses – but also by museums and artists – in order to create and increase value in contemporary art. The peculiarity of this system is the almost complete alignment of agency and critical judgment between the market on the one hand and the critical or scholar milieu on the other hand, leading to the establishment of a market-driven contemporary art production. Focal point of the volume is Damien Hirst's stuffed shark *The Physical Impossibility of Death in the Mind of Someone Living* (1991) sold for US$12 Million by Charles Saatchi to Steve Cohen, an American hedge fund executive, in 2005. The sale represented a record for a work by a living artist and fueled discussions on what defines contemporary art and what actually rules its acknowledgment. (SG)

Below:
Don Thompson, *The $12 Million Stuffed Shark. The Curious Economics of Contemporary Art*, Palgrave Macmillan, New York (NY), 2008

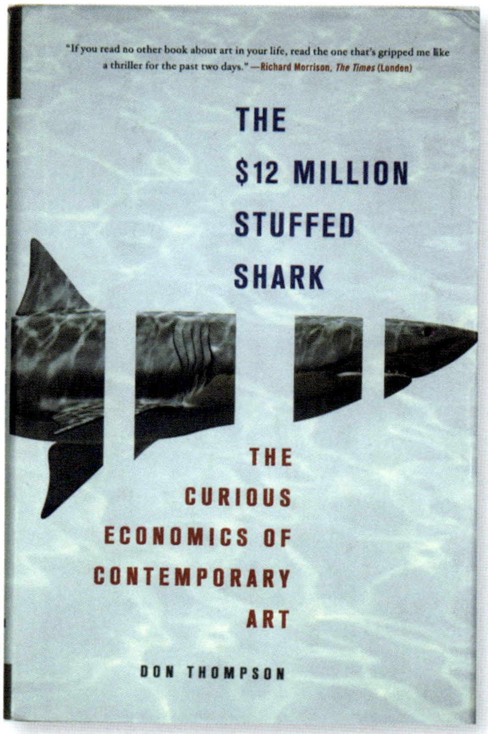

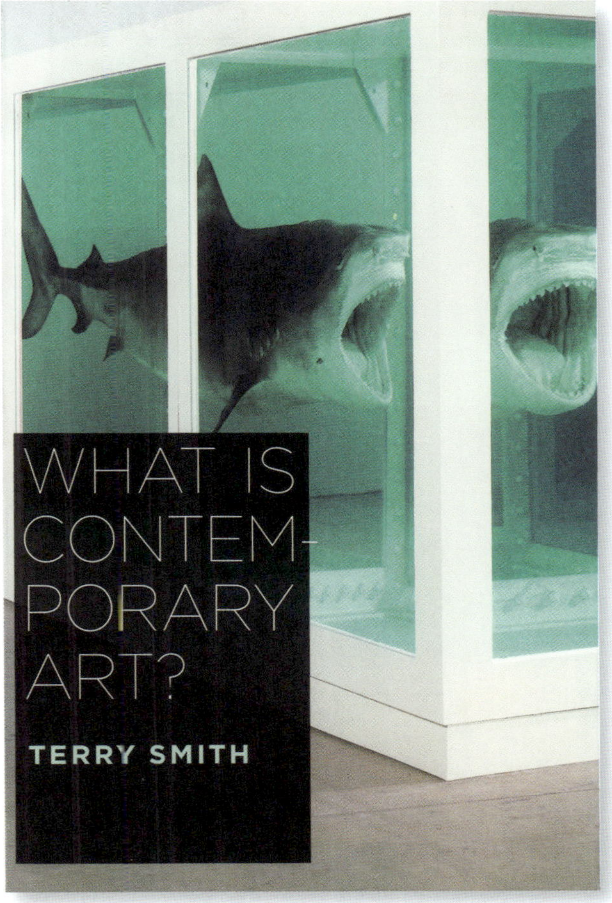

Terry Smith, *What Is Contemporary Art?*

In an attempt to outline the criteria behind the definition of contemporary art, art historian Terry Smith also speaks of the unprecedented merger of advertisement, marketing, and art production as a fundamental mark of contemporary art. In his journey through spectacular architecture, local and global markets, contemporary art museums, and the postcolonial turn, Smith positions advertising executive Charles Saatchi (Damien Hirst's patron) at the conjunction point of a series of global connections and transactions between luxury goods magnates, auction houses, artists, and institutions which at large shape the structure of contemporary art. Icon of the overlapping of art and capitalism is again *The Physical Impossibility of Death in the Mind of Someone Living*, portrayed on the book's cover. The presence of this work on both covers epitomizes the approach of two worlds and ironically the physical possibility of art as goods. (SG)

Above:
Terry Smith, *What is Contemporary Art?*, The University of Chicago Press, Chicago (IL) and London, 2009

trans_actions: The Accelerated Art World 1989–2011

Commissioned by the ZKM | Institute for Visual Media and the GAM project team, Stewart Smith, Robert Gerard Pietrusko, and Bernd Lintermann developed *trans_actions: The Accelerated Art World 1989–2011*, a work that depicts the temporal and spatial development of the biennial system and the global art market and was made for projection on the PanoramaScreen. These two sectors of the art system were selected because they impressively evidence the accelerated art world of the last twenty years. Statistical data was processed for animation as a panoramic data visualization. Clare McAndrew participated in this project along with a research group. The animated visualization of this data is an immersive experience and conveys an impression of the process of globalization. At the same time it presents a picture of the dense network that these newly established art worlds have spanned across the globe.

Trans_actions was created with Bronson, a data animation framework initially developed by Stewdio and Warning Office in 2008. In addition to creating visuals, Stewdio developed the *trans_actions* database structure and a content management system to interface with the database. The panoramic projection system was created by Bernd Lintermann. The ZKM | Institute for Music and Acoustics team led by director Ludger Brümmer contributed the audio compositions. (AB)

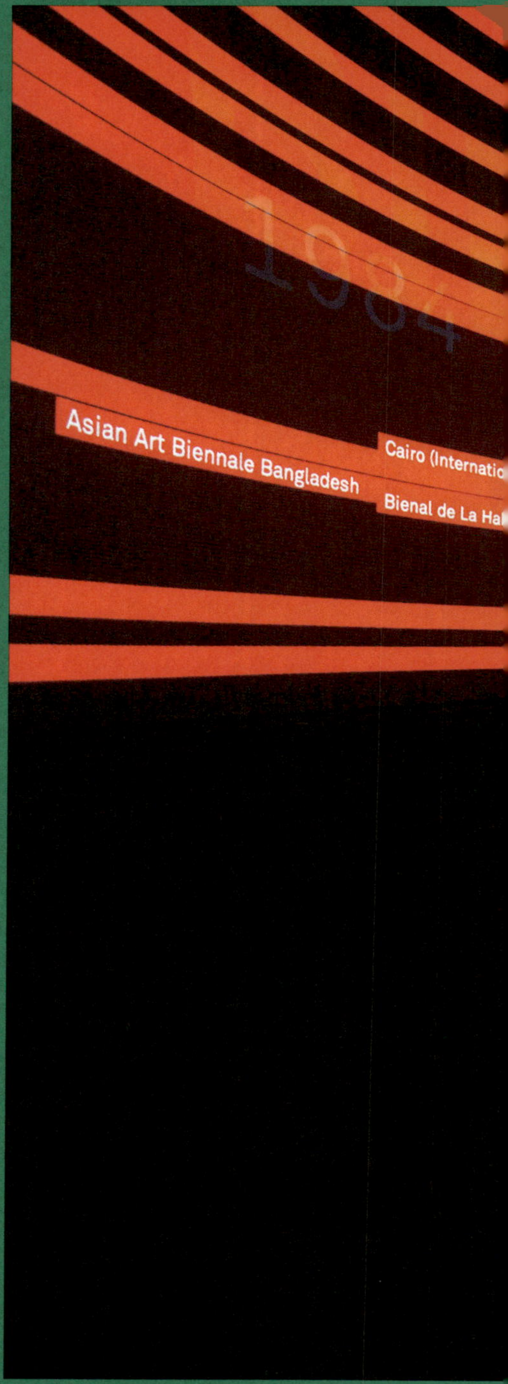

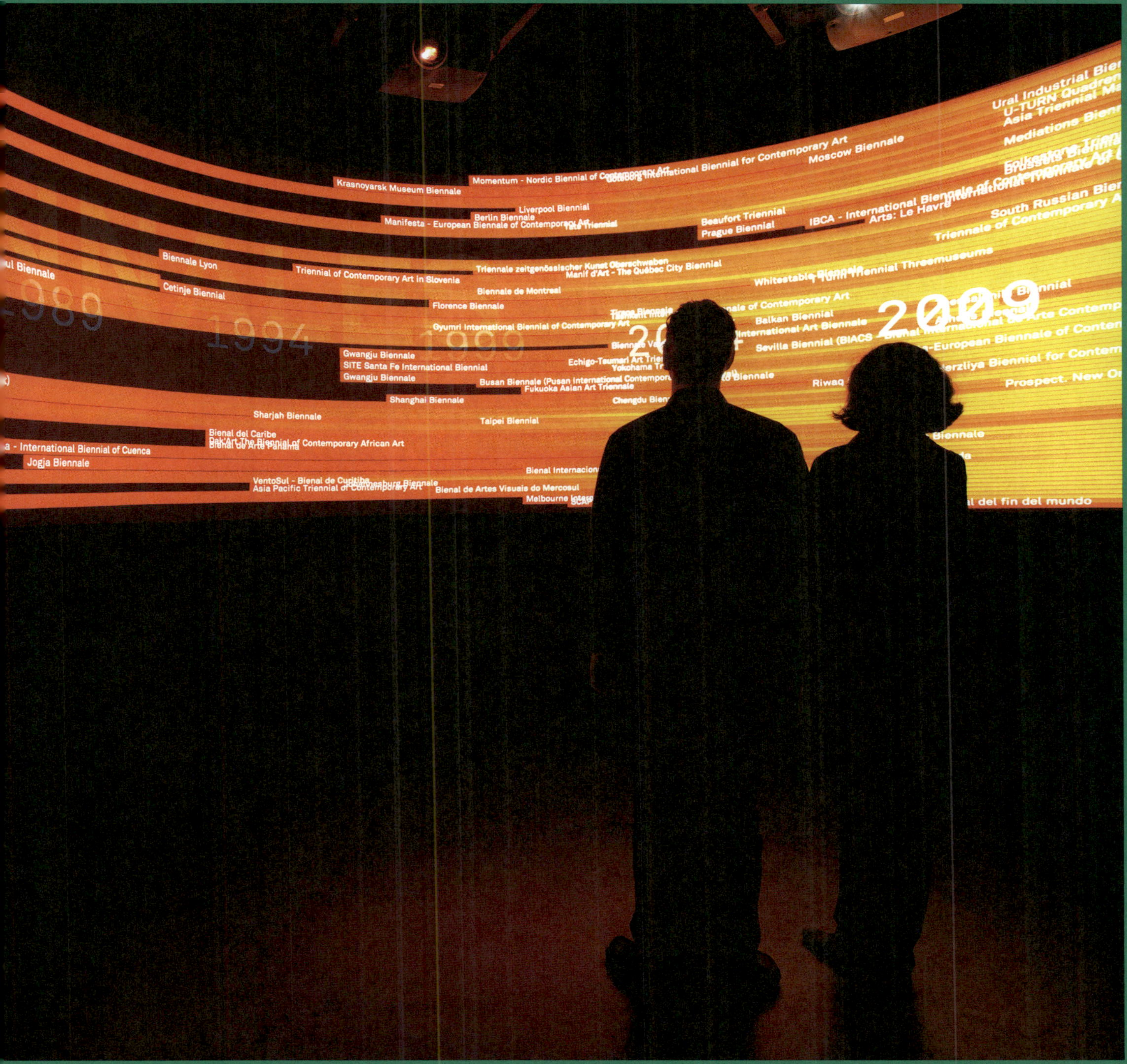
Krasnoyarsk Museum Biennale
Momentum - Nordic Biennial of Contemporary Art
Moscow Biennale
Liverpool Biennial
Berlin Biennale
Manifesta - European Biennale of Contemporary Art
Tate Triennial
Beaufort Triennial
Prague Biennial
Biennale Lyon
Triennial of Contemporary Art in Slovenia
Cetinje Biennial
Biennale de Montreal
Florence Biennale
1989
1994
1999
2009
Gwangju Biennale
SITE Santa Fe International Biennial
Gwangju Biennale
Shanghai Biennale
Fukuoka Asian Art Triennale
Sharjah Biennale
Taipei Biennial
Bienal del Caribe
Jogja Biennale
Bienal de Artes Visuais do Mercosul
Balkan Biennial
Whitestable Biennale
Riwaq

Timeline of Biennials

This section of *trans_actions* depicts the growth of recurring art exhibitions (biennials, triennials, etc.) since 1895, the year of the first biennial, namely the Venice Biennale. The timeline graphically portrays the increase of these major exhibitions on a global scale after the year 1989.

Before 1989 the world had approximately 25 biennials; after this date their number grew to the present figure of 159. Today biennials are organized in all corners of the globe, rejecting any residual cartography of center versus periphery. Starting from the mid to late 1990s, almost every year between five and nine new biennials were established; a trend that shows no signs of abating. *Trans_actions* also shows the peak of this development, located between 1998 and 2010. 1998 set the first record with the founding of eight biennials: Berlin (DE), Montreal (CA), Busan (KR), Moss (NO), Taipei (TW), Oberschwaben (DE), Shenzhen (CN), and Vancouver (CA). This was beaten in 2003 with nine new biennials: Beaufort (BE), Beijing (CN), Cape Town (ZA), Jakarta (ID), Kyoto (JP), Prague (CZ), Seville (ES), Brighton (UK), and Mechelen (BE).

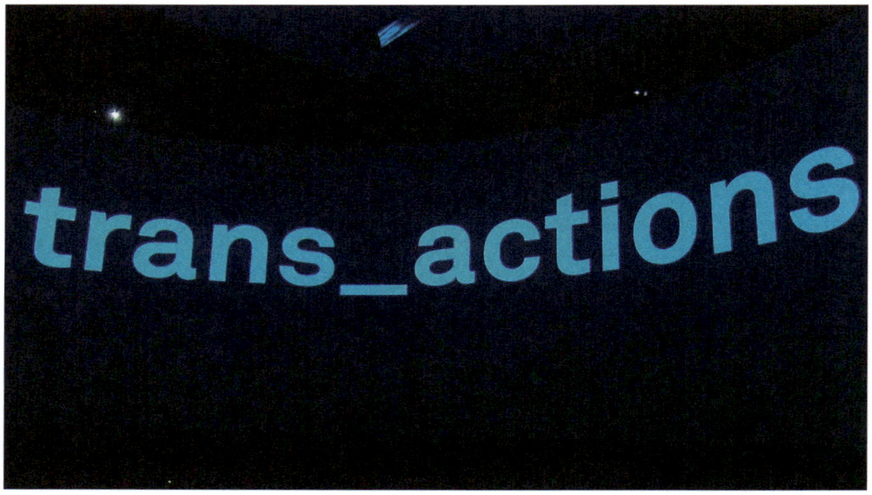

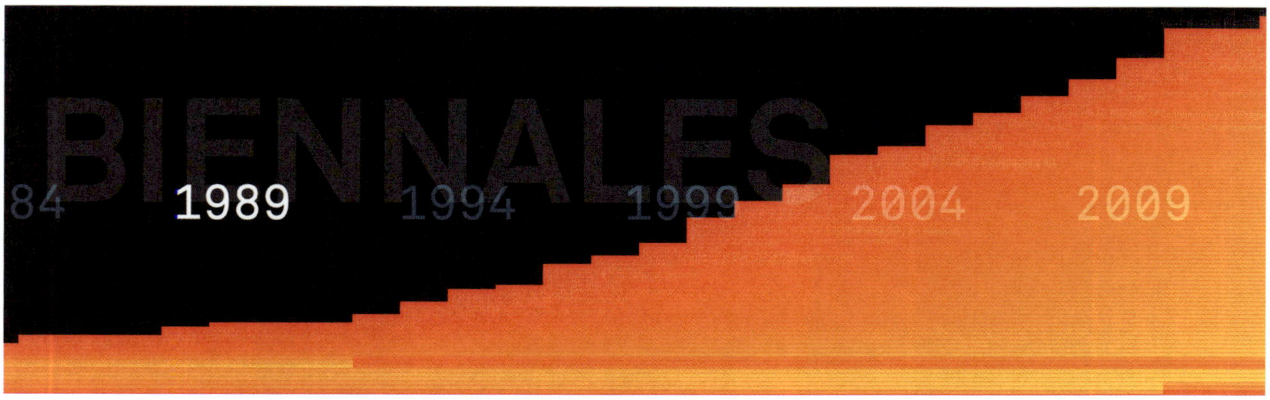

Traveling Artists

This section visualizes the intricate travels of artists from one biennial to another, thus highlighting the transnational, national, and regional dimensions of the events. In the form of animated "fire works," *trans_actions* gives a first portrait of the "traveling artist," a figure that emerged in the early 1990s and whose "at home" is a global journey consisting of multiple stations. Global refers not only to the dimension of the routes, but also to the provenances of the artists themselves. Outstanding traveling artists are, for example, Rikrit Tiravanija (*1961, TH), Pascale Marthine Tayou (*1967, CM), Jimmie Durham (*1940, US), Alfredo Jaar (*1956, CL), William Kentridge (*1955, ZA), Yang Fudong (*1971, CN), and Nedko Solakov (*1957, BG). Parallel to the traveling artist there is the traveling independent curator, who dedicates him or herself to a trans-national "biennial career." In addition, this section facilitates the identification of possible correspondences between the "traveling artists" and the artists who are most successful in the art market. (SG)

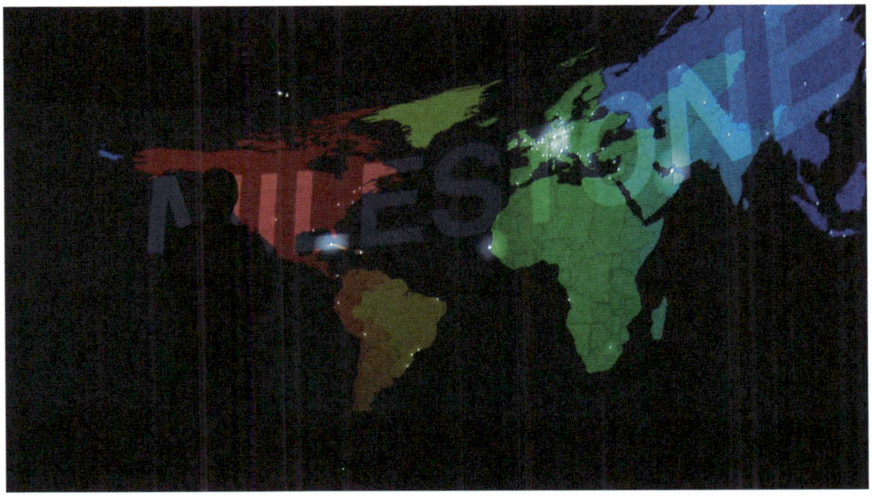

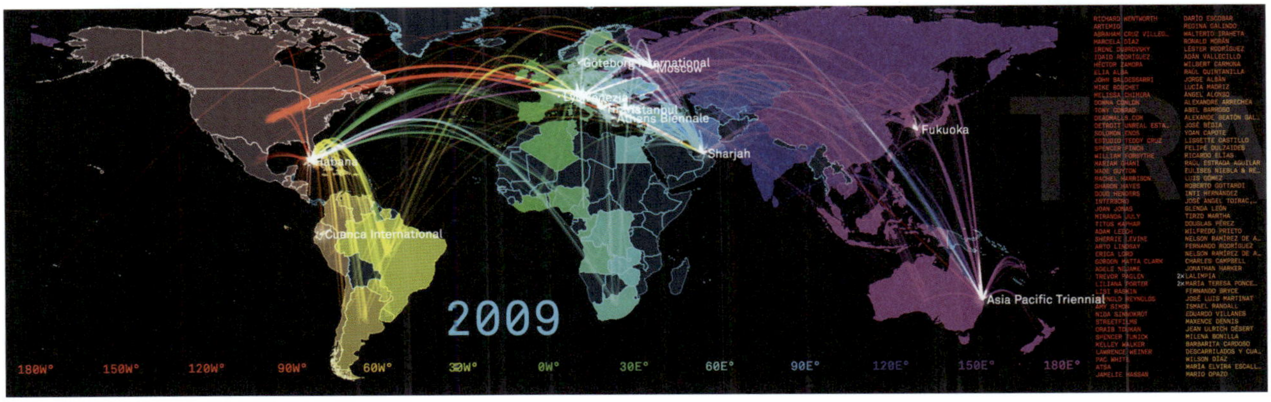

Art Fairs

Following the *trans_actions* chapter dedicated to the biennialization of the art world, the chapter of the art market begins by providing an overview of the expansion of art fairs in recent years.

The first art fair organized to increase galleries' sales of contemporary art was Art Cologne (DE) in 1967. Art Basel (CH) followed in 1969, TEFAF in Maastricht (NL) in 1975, Art Chicago (US) in 1980, and ARCO in Madrid (ES) in 1981. The first art fairs outside Europe and the USA were NICAF Tokyo (JP) in 1989 and Art Taipei (TW/CN) in 1992. Since the 1990s at least one to two art fairs per year have been established so that to date this market is divided into over 44 art fairs. *Trans_actions* visualizes the founding of new art fairs in space and time and shows the biennials existing in the various regions. This demonstrates the relationship between the two events whose organizers increasingly try to coordinate their opening dates in order to attract as many art lovers and art buyers as possible.

Economic Growth

The panoramic presentation of the *trans_actions* data visualizations shows the dramatic growth of the art market through a comparative overview of GPD, art imports, art exports, number of art fairs, and number of top auction houses in fourteen case studies of the countries with the largest share of the market: Brazil, France, Germany, Hong Kong, India, Italy, Netherlands, People's Republic of China, Russia, Singapore, South Africa, United Arab Emirates, United Kingdom, and USA.

Auction Houses

An indication of the growing importance of contemporary art sales all over the world is the foundation of auction houses and the opening of new departments

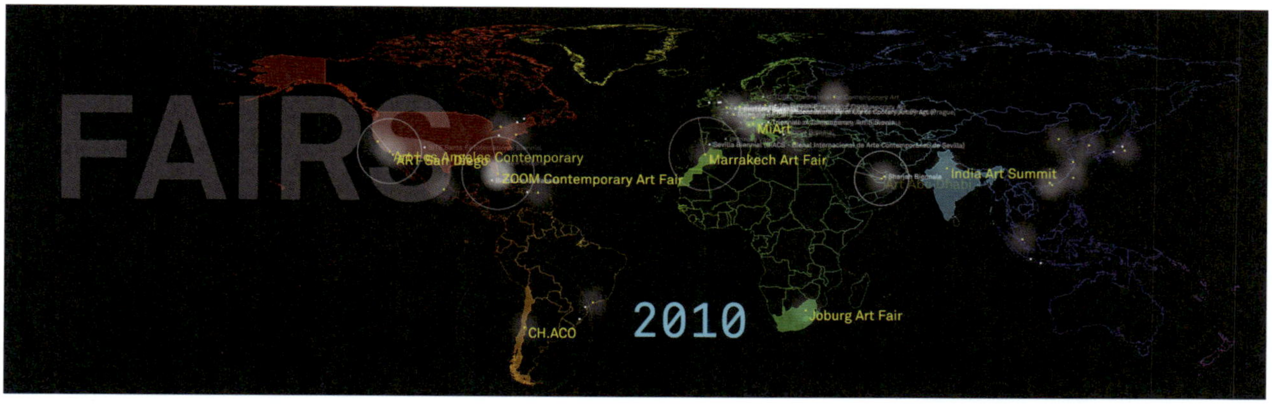

by the major auction houses Sotheby's and Christie's in countries outside the old West or the organization of special sales since the 1990s. It was only in 1993 that Christie's opened their Department of Latin American Art in New York. The Department of Chinese Contemporary Art in Hong Kong followed in 1996, the same year that Sotheby's established its Department of Southeast Asian Paintings and of Indian and Southeast Asian Art in Singapore. Christie's reacted to the growing hype of Indian contemporary art and opened their department in 1997 in London. After establishing departments in the Asian region in Singapore and Hong Kong, the next step was the opening of a Christie's department in Dubai for Middle Eastern and Turkish art in 2006 and a Sotheby's department of Turkish Contemporary Art in London in 2009. (AB)

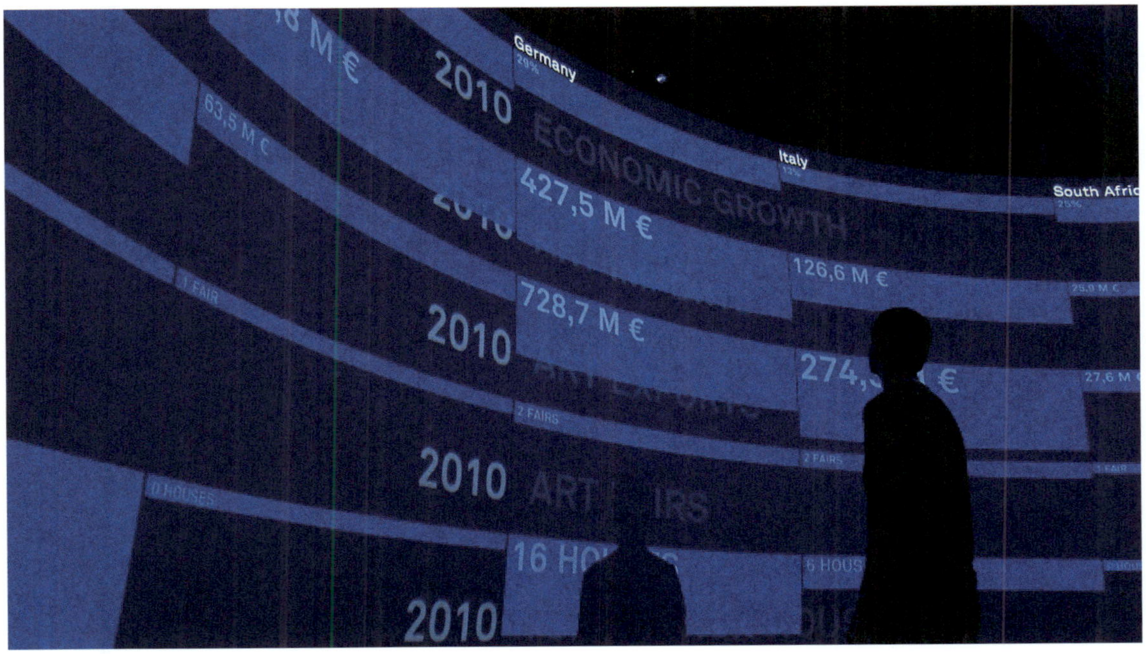

All images
Stewart Smith, Robert Gerard Pietrusko, Bernd Lintermann, *trans_actions*, 2011, intallation views *The Global Contemporary. Art Worlds after 1989*, section: *Room of Histories*, ZKM | Karlsruhe, 2011–2012

Global News from *The Art Newspaper* 2009–2011

The globalization of art does not follow a master plan that unfolds step by step. In fact, this process only happens in bits and pieces, which are far from spectacular when viewed individually. But viewed together, they indicate an overall pattern. We learn that everything is connected with everything else in a global network where the distance between the "here" and "there" is shrinking. The following compilation from *The Art Newspaper* was put together with the kind permission of the editorial board and reviewed by us over a period of two years, from August 2009 to May 2011. We kept this time frame also for the printed version since the materials selected prove their exemplary character. *The Art Newspaper* publishes eleven issues a year as an international edition. It includes sections on museums, the art market, exhibitions, and new books, but also contains general news or reviews and, above all, features which touch on most of what is topical in the art scene. The magazine offers facts and presents people who comment on what is happening in the realm of new and old art institutions. The selections thus document the ongoing process of globalization and can be read as a chronicle of what changes in art circles worldwide. Its news reaches us from many parts of the world, or highlights what is new and unprecedented in familiar institutions. The compilation is marked by several colors to indicate different topics which are also addressed by the *Room of Histories*: museums, art market, exhibitions, biennials. The sources are indicated at the end of each paragraph. (HB)

The Art Newspaper, front page, August/September 2011

INCLUDING WHAT'S ON

ISSN 0960-6556

INTERNATIONAL EDITION

THE ART NEWSPAPER™

UMBERTO ALLEMANDI & CO. PUBLISHING EVENTS, POLITICS AND ECONOMICS MONTHLY EST. 1983, VOL. XX, NO. 226, JULY/AUGUST 2011, UK £8.50/Europe €12.50/US US$16.99/ROW £10.50

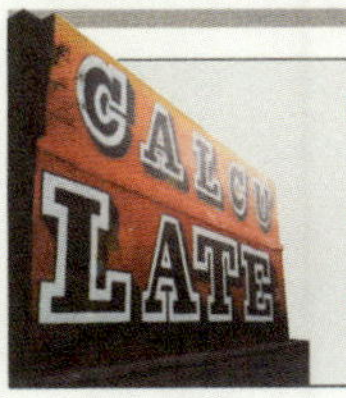

SPRAY CAN DO: HOW STREET ART WENT FROM THE SIDEWALK TO THE MUSEUM, P35

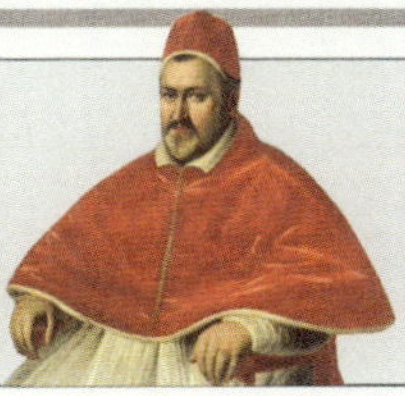

A CORNUCOPIA OF CARAVAGGIO BOOKS AND CATALOGUES REVIEWED, PP47-49

HEAVY METAL HERO: RICHARD SERRA ON BRANCUSI, ZEN AND WAITING FOR GIACOMETTI, P41

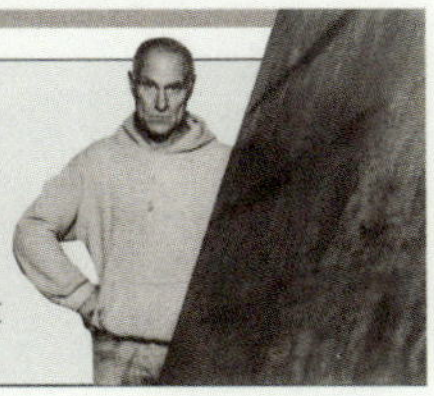

UK

Costs of the white horse run away

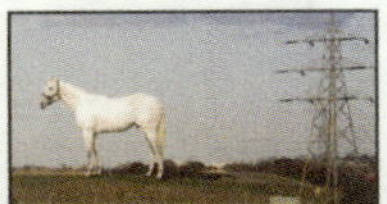

The ultimate equestrian statue?

LONDON. The costs of building a giant, 50-metre high white stallion by artist Mark Wallinger in Ebbsfleet, Kent, have ballooned to £12m. Wallinger won the competition to design a sculpture at the new Ebbsfleet International train station in February 2009. Costs were originally estimated at £2m.

Now that detailed plans have been completed, the sculpture has a more accurate price tag on it, said Ben Ruse, a spokesman for the project, who adds that the £12m includes maintenance such as graffiti removal for a period of 80 years. "We are not seeking any public funding for this," he added.

The organisers of the project—Eurostar, London and Continental Railways, and Land Securities—have provided seed funding but will not make any further contributions. Planning permission has been granted until April 2013, although when this expires, an application for renewal can be submitted. But Ruse said the project "can't last in fundraising mode forever. We'll have to take a view of where we are then." ■

Cristina Ruiz

The Gulf

Qatar revealed as the world's biggest contemporary art buyer

DOHA. The small but energy-rich Gulf state of Qatar is the world's biggest buyer in the art market—by value, at any rate—and is behind most of the major modern and contemporary art deals over the past six years, *The Art Newspaper* can reveal.

Working through a number of advisors, as well as buying directly from dealers and at auction, Qatar is reliably believed to be building up a top-class collection of modern and contemporary art. Last month, Sheikha Al Mayassa Bint Hamad Bin Khalifa Al-Thani—the 27-year-old daughter of the Emir of Qatar and a driving force behind the country's art buying—announced that Christie's chairman, Edward Dolman, will become executive director of her office. Dolman will also join the board of trustees of the Qatar Museums Authority (QMA), which oversees museums and cultural initiatives in the country and which the Sheikha chairs.

Sheikha Al Mayassa is not the only art collector in the family: her relative Sheikh Saud Bin Muhammad Bin Ali Al-Thani has always been a passionate art buyer, and was recently named as one of the world's top ten collectors by *Artnews*.

Dolman will be working on art acquisitions for the growing network of museums, which are directed by the art historian and former head of the Rhode Island School of Design, Roger Mandle. According to Dolman: "Qatar is looking to deliver a series of exciting cultural projects in time for the World Cup in 2022."

Because of the existence of confidentiality agreements, dealers and auctioneers are not prepared to go on the record about the deals that Qatar has made, but we have spoken to many well-placed sources in a position to know.

A key figure is the French agent Philippe Ségalot, whose partnership Giraud, Pissarro, Ségalot (GPS) is based in Paris and New York. Ségalot is believed to have negotiated many of the sales of modern art to Qatar. In the contemporary field, Qatar has already commissioned a major project from Richard Serra, is planning a Jeff Koons exhibition and funded the Takashi Murakami exhibition in Versailles last year, which is due to be shown in Doha in 2012. Mandle is understood to be responsible for commissioning contemporary works.

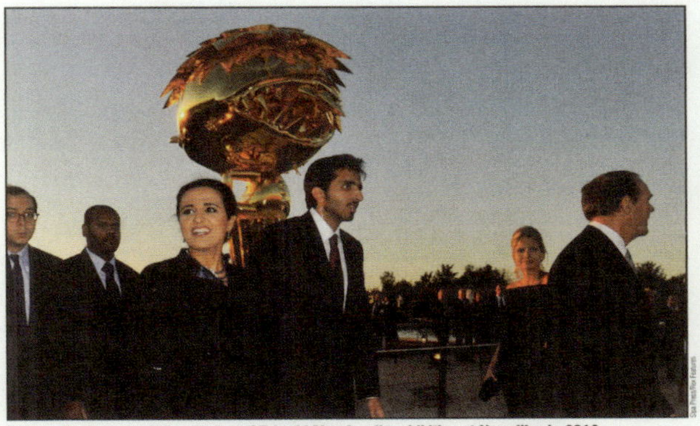

Sheikha Al Mayassa at the opening of Takashi Murakami's exhibition at Versailles in 2010

Among the purchases Qatar is believed to have made are:

❑ The "Merkin Rothkos": A $310m deal saw 11 Rothkos sold by court order to an "unidentified buyer" in 2009. They came from the collection of financier J. Ezra Merkin, who is being sued in New York over his role as provider of funds to convicted Ponzi-scheme fraudster Bernard Madoff; the collection was the largest private holding of Rothkos in the world. They were subsequently exhibited at the Garage Centre in Moscow, leading to rumours that they had been bought by the Russian oligarch Roman Abramovich, which was strenuously denied. Two very well placed sources maintain that they have gone to Qatar.

❑ The Sonnabend estate: $400m worth of art from the estate of the famous art dealer, comprising major works by Lichtenstein and Koons. The deal was negotiated privately in 2007-08, going to GPS; multiple sources identified its client as Qatar. Ségalot told us that "the group was sold to more than one client".

❑ The Claude Berri *dation*: A group of nine works by Ryman, Reinhardt, Morandi, Serra and Fontana was promised to the Pompidou Centre in Paris in lieu of tax. But the heirs of the film director finally sold them through Ségalot for about €50m to Qatar; he did not deny this but said "the reality was less exotic than the French press said at the time".

❑ Andy Warhol's *The Men in Her Life*, 1962, which sold for $63.4m at Phillips de Pury in New York in November 2010, in a sale orchestrated by Philippe Ségalot. He insists that the work was acquired by a US buyer. But a source who bought regularly from Ségalot said that sales often went through his US company, so while the buyer was technically

CONTINUED ON P4

Wanted: Met sponsors

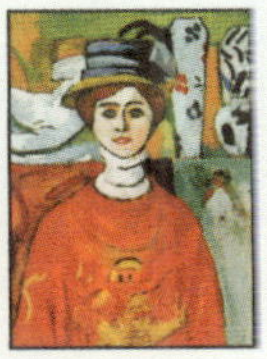

Museums are usually reluctant to say how much companies need to pay to sponsor their exhibitions, citing commercial sensitivity, which is why the Metropolitan Museum of Art's candour is refreshing. The New York museum now lists on its website future shows and their sponsorship price tag. "The Steins Collect" (including Matisse's *The Girl with Green Eyes*, 1908, right) is at the top end: $1m to be the exclusive sponsor of the show at the Met. Co-produced with the San Francisco Museum of Modern Art and the Réunion des Musées Nationaux, the show is due in New York in February 2012 following its San Francisco debut (until 6 September). For a sponsor with a limited budget wanting to add lustre to its name, "The Alfred Stieglitz Collection", October to January 2012, will cost $250,000. ■ J.P.

Gallery system is structurally weak

BRUSSELS. The traditional gallery model is in decline, according to a new report by the non-profit dealers' federation Cinoa (Confédération Internationale des Négociants en Oeuvres d'Art), which found that fair-led and online business is taking over as the main source of revenue.

Gallery visits are declining as the art market expands to new international centres served better by art fairs or electronic media.

"We do much more business at the fairs than at the gallery—no question," said Dominique Lévy, the co-director of L&M gallery.

András Szántó, consultant and contributing editor to *The Art Newspaper*, said: "The fairs have done very well in exploiting a structural weakness of the gallery system—it is inchoate and based on local markets." With the withdrawal of those markets during the downturn "the overall weight has shifted to clients who don't live where you work—so you service them through art fairs," said dealer David Zwirner.

According to a recent report from Capgemini, the Asia-Pacific region has overtaken the west in terms of the number of individuals with investable assets worth $1m or more. It is no coincidence that the Hong Kong art fair, Art HK, in which Art Basel bought a 60% stake in May, attracted such a stellar line-up of western dealers this year.

The growth of fairs brings with it huge pressures for dealers to fund travel, staff fairs and find enough material. Whether the traditional gallery model can

CONTINUED ON P7

Institutions
Art Market
Biennials
Exhibitions

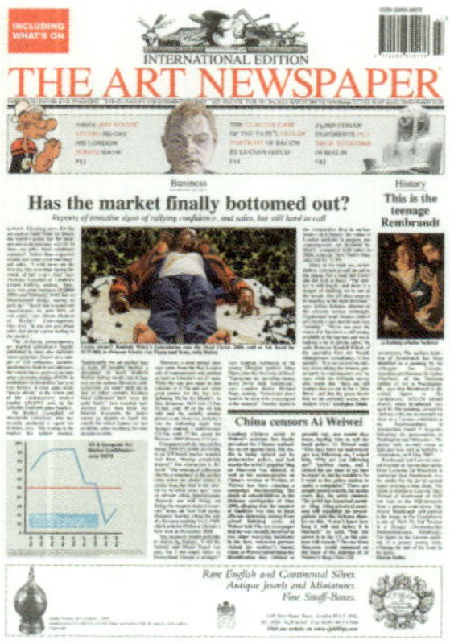
INTERNATIONAL EDITION
THE ART NEWSPAPER
Has the market finally bottomed out?
This is the teenage Rembrandt
China censors Ai Weiwei

Vol. XVIII, no. 204: July–August 2009

The Middle East, with its rapidly emerging art scene, stands out in the news. Sophie Flouquet gives a well-informed description of the projects for the Abu Dhabi Louvre. The laying of the foundation stone (May 26) was attended by Nicolas Sarkozy who was there "to inaugurate a French military basis." At the time, an exhibition *Talking Art* presented the first purchases by the emirate from a selection made by Agence France-Museums. The new Louvre branch will differ from its home base in Paris. The French minister of culture, Christine Albanel, announced a "completely new concept for a universal museum" from which, according to the terms of the contract, the French will withdraw only in 2040. (Sophie Flouquet, p. 16)

Thus, as is to be expected, the Middle Eastern Louvre will also collect modern and contemporary art, in order to compete with the Guggenheim branch nearby. At the same time, the authorities in Abu Dhabi "cancelled the contract with [...] Art Paris," a Gulf version of the French fair that was launched there only in 2007, as we are informed by Antonia Carver. The local administration is eager to get hold of this gallery scene. The Tourist and Development Investment Company (TDIC) at Abu Dhabi is determined to "capitalize on the last two years," with other words, on recent and preferably local contemporary art. "Now is the time to have a fair that is 100% our own." (Antonia Carver, p. 44)

But in the case of the Gulf states we may also ask with Anna Somers Cocks: "Are we colonialising Middle Eastern Art?" She insists in her editorial "it is still the Western art institutions [...] that give validation to contemporary art anywhere in the world." As an example, she points to the fact that, in London, "the Tate collects Western-style Chinese contemporary while Chinese-style contemporary is collected by the British Museum." In the case of Middle Eastern art, photography conceptual and video art "are being sought by the Tate, while calligraphic work will go into the British Museum." But "the market follows the lead of the Tate, not the British Museum." She therefore emphasizes the importance of a new initiative of the Victoria and Albert Museum that is supposed to "stimulate new Islamic design" instead of imposing a Western Fine Arts concept. The Jameel Prize, sponsored by a Saudi businessman, the patron being Zaha Hadid, at the same time favors an orientalist variant of contemporary market art. (Anna Somers Cocks, p. 26)

In Russia, other questions prevail in the midst of a flourishing art market. John Varoli gives a new report on the widening fundamentalist response to critical contemporary art in Russia. In a long lasting trial, two Moscow based curators, Andrei Erofeev and Yuri Samodurov, continue to be charged with having incited "hatred" for organizing an exhibition of "forbidden art" in March 2007. The exhibition had offended Orthodox groups but, according to A. Erofeev, "wasn't an attack on religion." It rather concerned "censorship and art in Russia." (John Varoli, p. 3)

The United States offers a most complex and contradictory picture of the old and the new art museum. Jason Edward Kaufman analyzes the precarious situation of the MOCA in Los Angeles which looks out for potential patrons, after the philanthropist collector Eli Broad, representative of a declining species in the US, can no longer guarantee the future of the museum and also cares more about his own collection. (Jason Edward Kaufman, p. 13)

Quite different are the problems in the planning of the Smithsonian National Museum of African American History and Culture in Washington. Kinshasha Holman Conwill, deputy director of the project, singles out the controversies around the collection of Afro-American art "in its past history and current practice," especially given the already existing holdings in the Museum of American Art and other institutions. Collecting is fine, but what happens “when one steps outside the vaunted and insular precincts of art”? “The vast territory of a larger society is less swayed by esoteric notions of the valorisations of art” and asks for participation and “the promise of change,” when even the White House in the era Obama has sent out signals that it will change its art collections. (Kinshasha Holman Conwill, p. 27)

A feature by Martha Lufkin, concerning a new pressure on “white” art in US Art Museums, deserves a closer look. “US minority groups will become the majority in a few decades. And art museums will have to diversify to survive.’ Arnold Lehman, director of the Brooklyn Museum, “considers diversity ‘a critical issue’ and therefore encourages programs for minorities. Such programs are sponsored by the Detroit Institute of Art (DIA), with the project ‘Community Connections’.” Graham Beal, director of the DIA, is reported to claim that “the community wants to see itself distinctly defined within the museum, but one problem is that the artists themselves often do not wish to be ‘segregated’ in this way.” In Houston, the Museum of Fine Arts “has tried to become ‘a place for all people’,” and its director approached the local minorities for sponsorship, since “our museum is the product of the people who live in Houston.” Houston’s schools are now 50% Latino. The same museum already has established the “International Center for the Arts of the Americas” in order to “make primary source material on Latin American art available in translation online.” The Los Angeles County Museum of Art has also launched a Latino Arts Initiative. Thus, “the status of single-ethnicity art museums may grow.” The Mexican Museum, in San Francisco, “has served as a catalyst for successful exhibitions of Latin American art at mainstream museums.” (Martha Lufkin, p. 29)

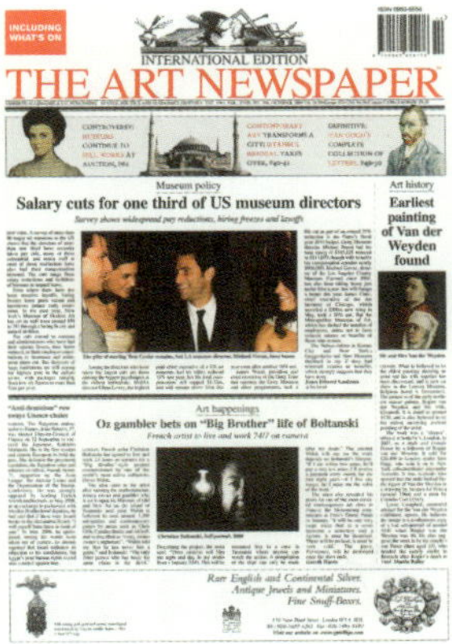
INTERNATIONAL EDITION
THE ART NEWSPAPER
Salary cuts for one third of US museum directors
Earliest painting of Van der Weyden found
Oz gambler bets on “Big Brother” life of Boltanski

Vol. XVIII, no. 206: October 2009

The Middle Eastern art scene remains an issue for top news. Anna Somers Cocks’ question whether the West is still colonizing Middle Eastern art (see: no. 204), is the target of a reply by Ali Khadra, publisher of Canvas, a magazine for art and culture from the Middle East and Arab World, in Dubai. He argues that patrons and artists who were not associated with Western institutions, acted as sponsors. He also defends Middle Eastern art as being not alienated by westernizing oriental clichés, but offers “a unique style born of an intricate mixture of rich history, deep-routed culture and on-going conflict.” Anna Somers Cocks replies that she was aware “of the power of major Western institutions to deform that identity, however unintentionally, to suit their own preconceptions of what art should be.” And she warned of the pitfalls of “clichéd subjects” such as the veil issue. (Ali Khadra and Anna Somers Cocks, p. 32)

It may be added that it becomes an open question who colonized whom. On the one side, the royal family of Qatar is cofounding an exhibition of Takashi Murakami at Versailles. (Roxana Azimi and Gareth Harris, p. 3) On the other side leading Western galleries will take part in the November Abu Dhabi Art fair. Fair organizers feel the need to upgrade the recently relaunched fair, which was before run by Art Paris. The fair, according to the press release, aims to create “an entirely new experience of modern and contemporary art” in the region. (Charlotte Burns, p. 62)

Today, the question is whether the Gulf is becoming a leading center for the art of the region or whether Istanbul with its geographic advantage and its closer relation to the European art scene, will take this role in the near future. The problem for

Istanbul is the lack of such governmental engagement, as is going on in the Gulf region. The Istanbul Biennial therefore in 2009 attempted to strengthen local sponsorship. The Koç family acted once again as the biennial's main sponsor. The 11th edition was curated by WHW, "four ex-Zagreb University curators: Ana Dević, Ivet Curlin, Sabina Sabolović and Nataša Ilić," thus following up Hou Hanru, the curator of the 2007 edition. One of the venues was a Greek school that was closed because of a shortage of pupils in 2002. The biennial was to recapitulate "the vast upheavals which have followed the collapse of the Soviet Union." Only 15 of 70 participating artists claimed a Western status. Sotheby's newly opened office in Istanbul staged an inaugural auction of Turkish contemporary art in March 2009. But Roger Bevan wonders: "Will the momentum be harnessed or will it be allowed to slip away?" (Roger Bevan, pp. 40–41)

Jason Edward Kaufman reviews the reopening of the Museo del Barrio in New York, on October 17, 2009. "The courtyard has been converted into an entry plaza," and the director Julián Zugazagoitia explains "we want to be transparent, open to the community so it is evident that it is a public building." The opening show carries the title *Nexus New York: Latin/American Artists in the Modern Metropolis*, "a 75-work loan show. The focus is on how Latinos working in New York contributed to modernity," as the director added. (Jason Edward Kaufman, p. 26)

Elizabeth Fortescue discusses a new installation in the Grand Courts of the Art Gallery of New South Wales, Australia. The main attraction is "a forest of 17 ceremonial ironwood poles, which are used as grave-markers by the indigenous people of the Tiwi Islands." The director of the gallery, Edmund Capon, explains that the poles (*tutini*) were created for the gallery in 1958. According to senior curator Barry Pearce "the *tutini* could no longer remain in Yiribana, the gallery's indigenous display area, because of their exposure to damaging light. He said the indigenous people were happy with the new location. Ironically, when the poles entered the gallery's collection in 1959, they were displayed in the Grand Courts" because there was no other place in the gallery. The *tutini* had been removed from their original display because people said "that stuff should be in a museum." (Elizabeth Fortescue, p. 22)

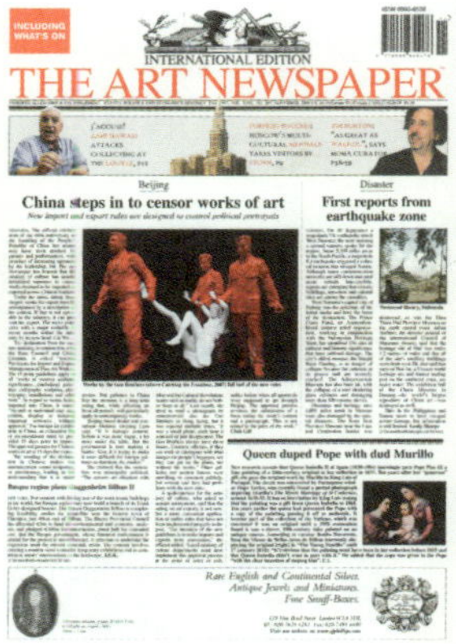
INTERNATIONAL EDITION
THE ART NEWSPAPER
China steps in to censor works of art
First reports from earthquake zone
Queen duped Pope with dud Murillo

Vol. XVIII, no. 207: November 2009

The November issue opens with an article about a new censorship of importing or exporting art across Chinese borders. As Chris Gill reports, the so-called "Interim Provisions for Import and Export Management of Fine Art Works," issued in August 2009, contained an 11-point guideline which for the future requests an ample documentation of the respective works and their destination. Whether this initiates a new policy or not, is not yet clear. Also the results cannot be estimated, since not enough time has passed for judging the application of the new guidelines. These regulations may represent a bureaucratic aim for control, but it is possible that in the long run the new rules will have an unwelcome impact on the vividly developing international art scene in the country. (Chris Gill, p. 1)

The same edition offers interesting insights into the present art scene in Russia. A full-page report describes the Third Moscow Biennale of Contemporary Art (see also: no. 204, p. 3), which was held in the Garage Centre for Contemporary Culture in September and October, whose founders are Roman Abramovich and Dasha Zhukova. The commissioner Joseph Backstein applauded the event as the first contemporary art exhibition on this scale in Russia. It would be an attempt of "Russia's reintegration into the international art scene." As John Varoli reports, the Biennale was a great success. The curator, Jean-Hubert Martin, explained his project as directed against exclusion, this time as a message for a Russian audience, which still favors a kind of cultural protectionism. "Increasing xenophobia and state censorship" have become a major concern for the art scene, especially with regard to "heavy pressure from nationalists." Martin emphasized that "in the age of globalization, Moscow needs to see works from Africa, South America, Asia, and the Pacific." From this follows that "the show is made for people in Moscow," to quote Martin again. Inspite of the "small foreign attendance" in the words of Valerie Hillings, the success of the event in Russia seems to be beyond doubt. (John Varoli, p. 9)

John Varoli also interviewed Irina Lebedeva, the newly appointed director of the State Tretyakov Gallery, Moscow. One of the issues was the situation of contemporary art for the museum. The former head of the related department, Andrei Erofeev, was dismissed in June 2008 and now is on trial for "inciting hatred" for organizing an exhibition of "forbidden art" (see: no. 204, p. 3). The director, whom John Varoli quotes, does not "understand the commotion over contemporary art at our museum, and why some think that the future is tied exclusively to Erofeev." As a result "of the enormous amount of emotion around this issue with Erofeev, we decided to wait before appointing a new head." (John Varoli, p. 22)

John Varoli also investigates the present crisis of the contemporary market in Russia. "The record attendance of the Biennale showed that there is a strong interest in contemporary art. But the dismal results at Russia's leading commercial contemporary art fair indicated that few are willing to buy, [...] and the Fair has failed to attract prominent international exhibitors and collectors." Though there are new clients, generally speaking "Russians are more likely to spend millions on a work by an artist who is in museums than spend $100,000 on a work by a little-known contemporary artist," as a dealer is quoted. (John Varoli, p. 62)

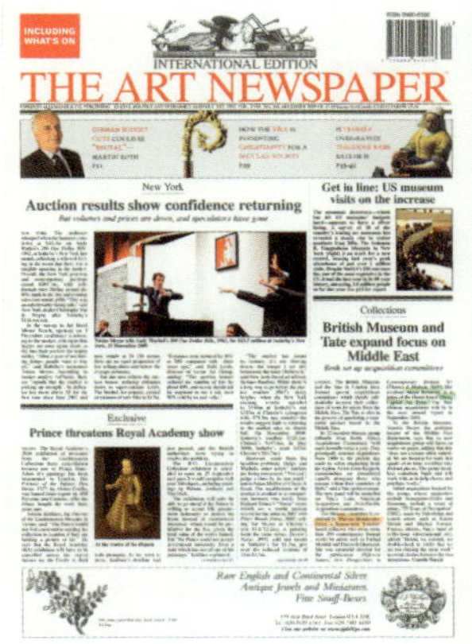
INTERNATIONAL EDITION
THE ART NEWSPAPER
Auction results show confidence returning
Get in line: US museum visits on the increase
British Museum and Tate expand focus on Middle East
Prince threatens Royal Academy show

Vol. XVIII, no. 208: December 2009

The December edition opens with a look on the acquisition policies of two London institutions, the British Museum and the Tate. Both institutions are directed towards collecting artists from the Middle East. The Tate's 22-member Menaac Group (Middle East North Africa Acquisitions Committee) is considering "acquisitions from 1960 to the present day made by artists originating from the region" including communities in the diaspora. "The new panel is modeled on Tate's Latin American Acquisition and Asia Pacific Acquisition Committees." The committee is co-chaired by Maryam Homayoun-Eisler, a Teheran-born London based collector who also edited the publication *Different Sames: New Perspectives in Contemporary Iranian Art* (Thames & Hudson 2009), and by Maya Rasamny, a juror of the Dubai-based Abraaj Capital Art Prize. At the British Museum, the Middle East department focuses on works on paper, including prints made by Palestinian and Israeli artists. Whereas the British Museum continues its ethnographic collections, the Tate worries about a possible overlapping of collections that risks clashes between the two institutions. (Gareth Harris, p. 1; see also: no. 204, p. 26)

Iain Millar, in his feature on Saatchi and the BBC2's recent reality TV show *School of Saatchi*, quotes Mathew Collings with the statement that "people probably don't understand the difference between contemporary art and art." Saatchi had asked him and his group to select six finalists "leading to one winner who will be included in the latter stages of Saatchi's *Newspeak: British Art Now* show at the Hermitage." The candidates, we learn, "are constantly being asked to explain why what they are doing is art." Collings intended the series to make "the audience in Britain notice there was such a thing as contemporary art." In the next selection phase, "the public had the opportunity to vote" and to decide "whether they disliked or liked the works." The show *School of Saatchi* on BBC2 "is a program with no populist pretensions," but is "a bauble for the cultured elite." In Millar's opinion the impact of the series will impede the creation of a program that takes contemporary art serious: "Saatchi remains the Kurtz at the dark heart of the art world jungle, too terrible for the gaze of ordinary folks." (Iain Millar, p. 37)

In the section "Art Market," Georgina Adam reports on Abu Dhabi Art, the new contemporary and modern art fair in the Palace Hotel. Since there is no art market in Abu Dhabi, "the fair was organized by the government of Abu Dhabi, which is determined to establish one *ex nihilo* in the tiny Gulf state to tie in with its ambitious multi-billion dollar museum-building projects on Saadiyat Island." The French project of Art Paris had failed after two editions. Thus the cultural authorities "brought in an array of art world luminaries, led by art world supremo François Pinault (flanked by the high command of Christie's which he owns)." The organizers pointed out "that the potential for museum purchases was immense. 'All the institutions exist already; even if these buildings aren't here yet,'" as a representative of The Tourism Development and Investment Company is quoted. The dealers complained the sparse attendance: "Abu Dhabi essentially only has two major collectors, the royal family and the government." Initial sales concentrated on Middle Eastern artists, but international art dominated in the end. "There were about thirty top class works of art in the fair," which dealers recommended "as an excellent nucleus for the new museums." (Georgina Adam, p. 52)

Chris Gill reviews the first edition of Fine Art Beijing that took place in November 2009: "The fair saw a relatively brisk trade. 'There are about 100 collectors now in Beijing. Many of them are new [and] low profile' according to Yan Bing, whose wife (Aye Gallery) was one of the thirty classic and modern dealers." "China has a longer history of collecting than the west – but, traditionally in China, collections are for private viewing," as he added. Fair director Dong Mengyang, who also runs Art Beijing, one of Beijing's two main contemporary art fairs, was aware that "it can take 20 years to develop a top art fair [...] We opened a super market to see who would come." The first edition's purpose was to create the market for traditional art. (Chris Gill, p. 52)

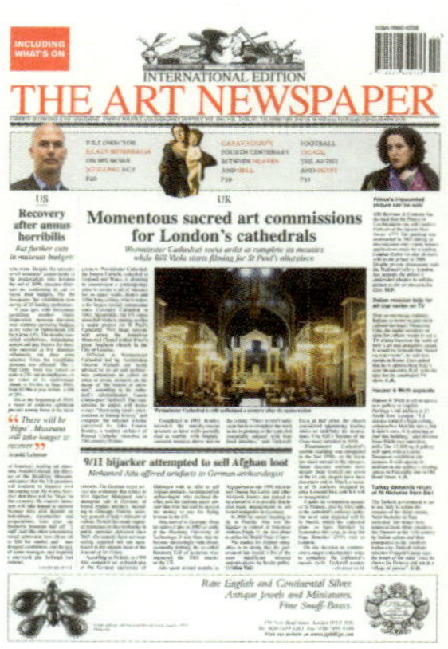
INTERNATIONAL EDITION
THE ART NEWSPAPER
Recovery after annus horribilis
Momentous sacred art commissions for London's cathedrals
9/11 hijacker attempted to sell Afghan loot

Vol. XVIV, no. 210: February 2010

One of the key issues this time is the appointment of the New York art dealer Jeffrey Deitch as director of the MoCA in Los Angeles. The argument was that Deitch "ran a business for a long time" and regards "finding money" as an important goal. Though he feels "obliged to sever all ties to the commercial art world," he does not rule out exchanges with his own art collection. (Lindsay Pollock, p. 18)

The same issue is taken up by Edward Winkleman who reminds the reader that it almost has become a rule that people take the opposite direction and change from non-profit institutions to the commercial sector. Though he has no objections against this appointment, he admits that the downturn in the art market may be a reason for dealers to change sides. He also admits the existence of Deitch's long-term relations to MoCA Trustee and super collector Eli Broad. (Edward Winkleman p. 27)

In the section on the art market, the appointment of François Curiel, Christie's president of France and Europe, to the position of president of Christie's Hong Kong deserves attention. Curiel argues that the Asian art market "is the only area to have seen growth of 2.4% last year." Besides "two series of sales in Hong Kong, Christie's has a deal with the Mainland Chinese auction house *Forever*" that may serve to improve the Chinese trade.

(Georgina Adam, p. 46). A small note on a Chinese art fund records that Shanghai Minsheng bank's "second art investment scheme for private investors sold out within days." The minimum investment for the fund was set at US$ 73.000. The fund does not serve to buy art but to profit from revenues of the fund. (Chris Gill, p. 46)

Amidst the debates on contemporary art's globalization, one often forgets that there is a second area with global aspirations. Thus, Neil MacGregor, director of the British Museum, is planning an exhibition on the Hajj, the Muslim pilgrimage to Mecca. The museum thus prepares the first museum exhibition "devoted to the Hajj from a global perspective." Venetia Porter, a member of the Middle East department, will curate the show in November. (Martin Bailey, p. 12)

Such projects reveal the ambition of the BM to tell the history of civilizations. This also applies to the museum's series for BBC radio 4 *A History of the World in 100 Objects*, which covers "two million years of human history interpreted through the museum's treasures, from Stone Age axes to 21st century credit cards." The BM's "global reach rebalances the story begun by Kenneth Clark, [...] director of the National Gallery in London," who did the landmark 1969 TV series *Civilization* through fine art and architecture. (Judith Bumpus, p. 36)

A full-page feature is dedicated to Abdulnasser Gharem. The Saudi Arabian artist who is having his first solo exhibition in Dubai suffered from religious or political censorship for a long time. He decided to stay in the Saudi Arabian army in order to remain "among the people" despite a military's limitations to being an artist. Furthermore being a colonel allows him to get "into places that would be off-limits to a civilian [...]. Once I'm in these places, I can make art." And he admitted that he had only become an artist due to the Internet, given the lack of art education in his country. On the occasion of the exhibition *Edge of Arabia* at London's School of African and Oriental Studies, he was forced to withdraw the work *The Paths*, because considered "religiously insensitive." But the visit of the Saudi Arabian deputy minister of culture to Venice changed his situation over night, since the minister liked a video based on *The Path*. Almost immediately, collectors of the region became attentive of his art. This incident proves that art collection in the region is full of uncertainty and surprises. (Henry Hemming, p. 32)

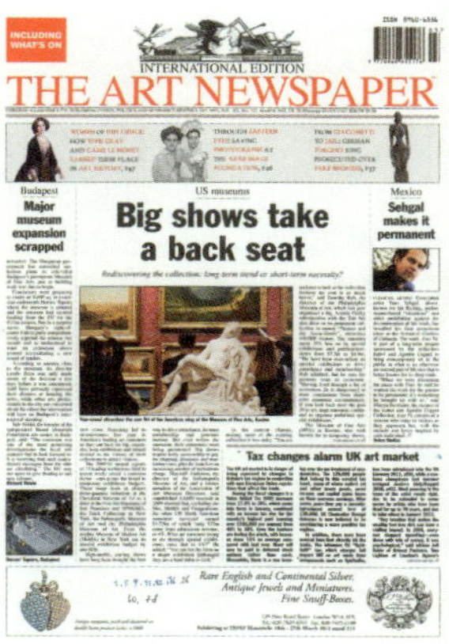
INTERNATIONAL EDITION

THE ART NEWSPAPER

Budapest
Major museum expansion scrapped

US museums
Big shows take a back seat

Mexico
Sehgal makes it permanent

Tax changes alarm UK art market

Vol. XVIII, no. 211: March 2010

This edition stands out by offering space for the debate about a crisis of the art concept in contemporary art that results from its commodification on the global art markets. There is first the case of the National Museum of XXI Century Arts in Rome (MAXXI) where Vittorio Sgarbi now acts as supervisor of acquisitions but is "known for his antipathy to contemporary art." He thus will "concentrate on the generation in its fifties," as a museum in Italy "should be different" from other museums in Europe. Even when "Sgarbi will not directly acquire works," his refusal to engage in experiments is obvious. It may be added that the new hype of art production worldwide may very well reopen the controversy with conservative critics. (Alessandro Martini and Gareth Harris, pp. 1, 3)

In the section *Features* we find Jean Clair's complaint about the decline of quality and of culture in today's world. "From cult to culture, from culture to the cultural [...] we have descended to the cultural: businesses, products, activities, cultural pastimes." "The techniques for promoting and selling a work termed 'contemporary art' are like those for selling anything at all. [...] Hedge funds and securitizations have illustrated how financial manipulation can make something out of nothing." Clair then touches upon the globalization issue when he writes, "the Louvre lends its name and hires out its collections to a country [Abu Dhabi] in which the workers are cruelly oppressed." (Jean Clair, pp. 30–31)

Robert Hewison, member of the think tank Demos, readily admits that "the art market is one of the least regulated forms of commodity exchange: greed, snobbery, and corruption are powerful forces at work." But he argues that the commodification of culture calls for a redefinition of cultural value for it only occurs "when the aesthetic and spiritual aspects already exist." The same kind of non-answer also applies to his conclusion that "culture constantly renews itself, and so must its presentation and interpretation." (Robert Hewison, p. 31)

The same edition then turns to China and the debate about its public museums. The controversy is caused by "The Art Museum Assessment Report," launched in December 2010 by the Chinese Ministry of Culture, and concerns also the state of contemporary art collections. The debate is about "museums' inadequate acquisition budgets, self-censorship and caution. Most museums, critics claim, have missed the boat on collecting China's biggest contemporary artists." Part of the problem is that the ministry has set a bar for annual acquisition budgets. The Swiss bank Sarasin, thus is needed to sponsor the Shanghai Biennale. At a forum held at the Minsheng Art Museum in Shanghai, owned by the bank of the same name, Chinese collector Guan Yi argued against "a perception that contemporary art is anti-government." Guan collected 800 contemporary works that he intends to make accessible to the Chinese audience. The Minsheng Art Museum is currently showing part of the British council's permanent collection. Director Zhou Tiehai hopes that the show "would be enlightening for the Chinese." (Chris Gill, p. 11) This picture markedly differs from our expectation of art's presence in today's China. The part of private collectors certainly helps in making art accessible but also leaves many open questions about the impact of their taste.

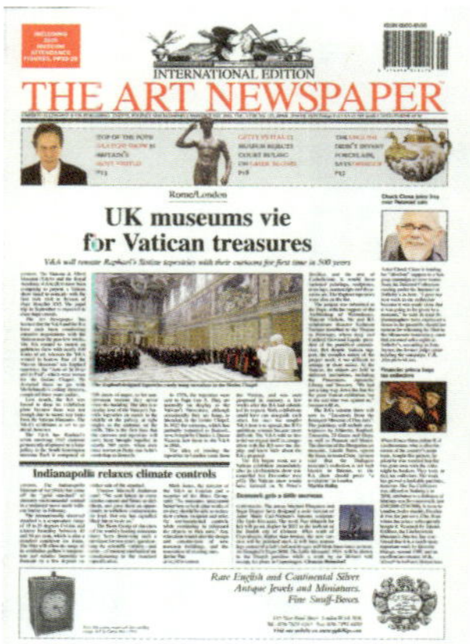
INTERNATIONAL EDITION

THE ART NEWSPAPER

Rome/London

UK museums vie for Vatican treasures

Indianapolis relaxes climate controls

Vol. XVIII, no. 212: April 2010

The section of the "Art Market" is of special interest again in the April edition. Of considerable importance is a report from China which reveals the prevalent taste of important Chinese collectors. According to Rupert Hoogewerf "Chinese collectors are becoming more interested in traditional Chinese art. For the rich it has become a dream to buy art – to become a noble." China's Hurun organization which he founded "has found a marked increase in sales of traditional Chinese art at auction at home and abroad in the last year." As a result, a top artist such as "Zhang Xiaogang fell from the first to the 13th place, while Zeng Fanzhi's 2009 sales totals were only a third of that of 2008." Top collectors are "people who are traveling abroad and seeing the effect of art museums on society." Traditional art seems to be gaining back its predominant position on the market in contrast to the international taste. (Chris Gill, p. 67)

In a review of international contemporary art fairs, we learn that the new director of Art Paris, Lorenzo Rudolf, former director of Art Basel from 1991–2000, plans to create "platforms with areas devoted to art from Africa, Indonesia, Finland, and the Ukraine." (Anna Sansom, p. 71)

The fourth edition of Art Dubai was held from March 17 to March 20. Georgina Adam sees "a radical transformation" in the choice of artists. Nevertheless, "Indian and Middle Eastern artists sold the best, while international names did not find many buyers." Last year, the fair faced a new challenge "when the Abu Dhabi government poured money" into the fair in part to cover acquisitions for the new museums. Thus, Art Dubai "has become a largely regional fair," although there was a hype around a group of Chinese artists. Renuka Sawhney calls the fair "a growth engine for the local area and local artists." The most expensive work on show was a tapestry by African artist El Anatsui. Sultan Sooud Al-Qassemi, a 32-year-old local collector, has built up a collection of some 200 works in the last three years, which focuses on the region. "The collection has been placed in a new foundation in Sharjah." After the financial crisis broke out, "there seems to be a new climate of conservatism in Dubai." Before the visit of the ruler, the cultural authorities removed a work by the Dubai-based, Iranian artist Ramin Haerizadeh. The same happened to a work by the Iranian artist Sara Rahbar, which was however sold to a collector from Kuwait. Additionally, the *Canvas* fair daily paper "was threatened with being withdrawn because it featured another Haerizadeh on the back cover." This confirms the precarious balance between freedom and censorship. (Georgina Adam, p. 71)

Yet, censorship is also an issue in other areas of the world. Thus, at the ARCO Madrid the Israeli embassy was upset about a sculpture of Eugenio Merino, whose work *Stairway to Heaven* showed a Muslim, a Christian, and a Jew, each at prayer, forming a human tower together. (Anna Sansom, p. 71)

Recent exhibitions curated by Jean-Jacques Aillagon at Versailles, former director of Pinault's Palazzo Grassi in Venice, have been accused of being connected with the art dealer Emmanuel Perrotin who, in turn, "lists Pinault as one of his most important clients." Controversies were "sparked by the decision to stage a Jeff Koons exhibition at Versailles," followed by artists Takashi Murakami and Maurizio Cattelan, who all are from "the stable of Paris dealer Perrotin." The latter argued "Pinault is among Versailles' most important donors." When the show opened, "the 20 biggest collectors in the world were all there – immensely wealthy people." (Claudia Barbieri, p. 65)

The business aspect also applies to the nomination of James Murdoch, chairman of a UK television network and director of News Corporation, for election as a director of Sotheby's. The auction house has "been losing ground to rival Christie's in online sales." And Sotheby's, therefore, counts on Murdoch's expertise in new media. (Charlotte Burns, p. 65)

Also the purchase of the Haunch Venison Gallery by Christie's in February 2007 has stirred a controversy. British artist Keith Tyson has now announced that he is to leave the gallery that "has changed beyond recognition. "As a subsidiary of an auction house, Haunch of Venison – which has branches in London, Berlin, New York and Zurich – is excluded from participating in the main contemporary art fairs." (Louisa Buck, p. 8)

Against the current interest of the local collectors of contemporary art and visiting dealers, Silvia Karman Cubiñá, the director of the Bass Museum in Miami Beach, believes that the collector's museum "has to ask questions about the past." In fact, the museum is inaugurating the first permanent gallery of Egyptian antiquities in Florida. She further argues that the "museum's voice is in this community." For that reason she is trying to create "a dialogue between the permanent collection and contemporary art," especially in the exhibition The *Endless Renaissance* (2009). And she concludes "all art is informed by art that came before it." (Cristina Ruiz, p. 20)

Laurie Taylor interviewed a defensive Damien Hirst on UK satellite channel Sky Arts 1. In the interview he argued, "money's a fantastic tool to get people to take you seriously. Walking down Bond Street after the (2008) auction, I'd get recognized by business men." On his work in general, he said: "I always try and say something and deny it at the same time [...] my responsibility is to hide from the viewer." (Iain Millar, p. 53)

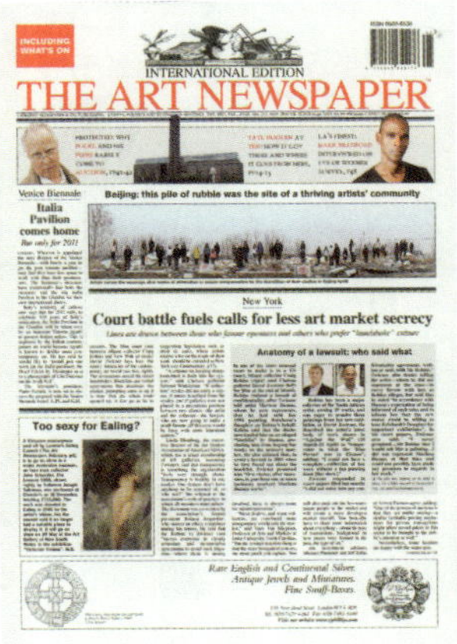
INCLUDING WHAT'S ON
INTERNATIONAL EDITION
THE ART NEWSPAPER
Venice Biennale
Italia Pavilion comes home
Beijing: this pile of rubble was the site of a thriving artists' community
New York
Court battle fuels calls for less art market secrecy
Anatomy of a lawsuit: who said what
Too sexy for Ealing?
Rare English and Continental Silver
Antique Jewels and Miniatures
Fine Snuff-Boxes

Vol. XVIII, no. 213: May 2010

The May 2010 edition clearly documents the

erosion of a single definition of art due to terms such as "elite art," a protective notion within the primary art market, "high art" or, conversely "outsider art." Thus Wendell Castle, the popular designer, thinks furniture to be "just high art, like sculpture." (Brook S. Mason, p. 49)

The reader wonders whether art becomes a mere market concern. This would also explain the general tendency to speak of art in a negative sense. Thus, in the midst of much confusion as to its true mission, Anna Matirolo, the director of MaXXi Arte, deplores "the huge lack of sensitivity towards the contemporary art world" in Italy. (Federico Castelli Gattinara, p. 13)

In her feature, Lindsay Pollock describes the ups and downs of the dealers' attempts to protect the primary market against the auction houses and thus to create something like "elite art." At the same time dealers are secretly cooperating with the auction sale, a sale well above their own price level. Their new concern is to what extent, and to whom, they make prestigious artists' works available. Thus, they look for a proper "context" for the work they want to sell, and be it a museum or "a collector considered to be a taste maker." "The art placing strategy" is reflected in the "complex mating rituals of art acquisition." (Lindsay Pollock, p. 42)

The art market continues to be frequented by bidders with a new provenance. In the 2010 Spring sale of modern and contemporary Turkish art at Sotheby's London, sixteen artists achieved record prices. "But the climax came with the sale of Fahrelnissa Zeid's overpowering *Untitled* canvas, 1954, [...] that slowly climbed to £ 657,250, the highest selling lot." Among the bidders was Aziz Karadeniz, managing partner of the Turkish auction house Beyaz Müzayede. The painting, consigned by a prince from Jordan, became "the first modern Turkish work to exceed the $1 million mark in an international auction." (Gareth Harris, p. 69)

The top news comes from the six-day sale at Sotheby's Hong Kong. "The main story was the dominance of Asian bidders including super-collector Wang Wei, who snapped up the top-lot, Liu Ye's *Bright Road*, 1995," for more than $2 million. According to Anders Petterson, from the market analyst Art Tactic, "up to 2008, speculative western buying fuelled the drive but now non-western houses are stepping up, and there is increased domestic buying." Thus, he predicts "a second cycle in the Chinese art market." (Charlotte Burns, p. 69)

The 17th Biennial of Sydney, which opened on May 12, in the words of its curator David Elliott, wants to acknowledge "the brutal history of Australia's colonization." The sites include the historic prison, on Cockatoo Island. The poetic title *The Beauty of Distance: Songs of Survival in a Precarious Age* indicates "the importance of traditional cultures in a global world" and that once again boundaries are an important issue. As if in self-defence, the curator insists on the need of recognizing quality despite its loss of meaning today, also beyond the accepted art scene. Among the 67 artists from Australia, 42 participants are from indigenous communities. (William Oliver, p. 75)

It is a strange coincidence that the University of Sydney is establishing a research program for "bringing the study of outsider art into the academy." (Elizabeth Fortescue, p. 10) Outsider art, once synonymous with *art brut* or Raw Art refers to almost any untrained artist or artist outside the realm of mainstream art. Thus, the question "Is it art?" is once more in the center of the show.

An exhibition of Islamic embroideries in Abu Dhabi was to force a revaluation of embroidery as an "important craft within the Muslim world." The local Tourism Development and Investment Company (TDIC) launched it with the intention to strengthen native aesthetics and cultural heritage. (Emily Sharpe, p. 81)

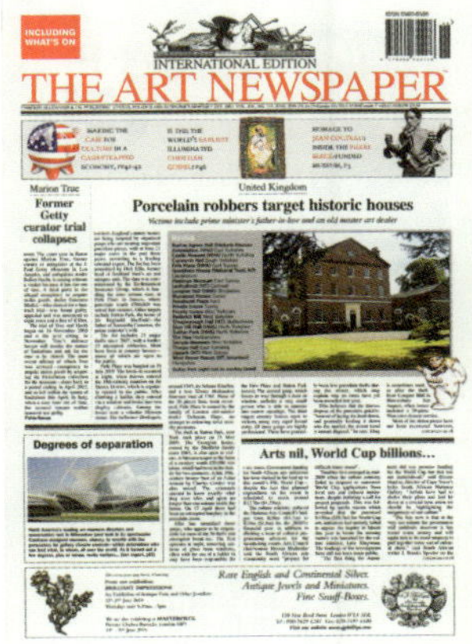
INTERNATIONAL EDITION
THE ART NEWSPAPER
Porcelain robbers target historic houses
Degrees of separation
Arts nil, World Cup billions...

Vol. XVIII, no. 214: June 2010

There are many exhibitions, which take pride in their choice of Middle Eastern or Indian art etc. But what about a museum collection, which was built up to represent art history? This issue came up when Tate Modern proudly announced the purchase of 13 works (not a very impressive figure to be sure) of artists with non-Western origin, thus indicating their intention "to broaden the collection." (R. S., p. 17)

Broaden yes, but in what direction and with which intention? This embarrassing topic was brought up when David Barrie, from the School of World Art Studies at Norwich, accused UK museums of "insularity" and suffering from a "heritage mind set." He criticized the Tate for selecting works that have a certain "'connectivity' with the existing collection of Western art." (Javier Pes, p. 17)

Barrie also wrote a feature in which he sees the Tate's initiative in relation to efforts of the British Museum and the Victoria and Albert Museum "to build a shared collection of Middle Eastern photography." However, such plans are still ahead of the current practice. "There are complex choices to be made in building the new collections – choices that have ethical and political as well as aesthetic dimensions. The issue of 'connectivity' may turn out to be crucial. Curators may feel more comfortable acquiring works that are connected stylistically or intellectually with our present, Eurocentric collections." And then Barrie adds: "Religious divisions and economic inequalities lie at the heart of many of the most serious challenges facing us. And yet the inexorable processes of globalization at the same time make this an increasingly inter-dependent world. If we are going to solve our problems, we must learn to work together." (David Barrie, p. 38)

Biennials have their own problems, according to their geographic situation and the cultural background they are linked with. Thus, indigenous art, despite or because of political correctness, is usually treated in a half-hearted manner. The Sydney Biennale, curated by David Elliott brings this to the fore. "Some of the biennale works by Australian artists dealing with history are disappointing in their simplicity and execution. The most beautiful Australian work here is the art produced by indigenous artists: a striking installation of intricately decorated burial poles by Yolngu artists from North East Arnhem Land at the MCA." It says much about prevailing hierarchies in the art world, when Elliott at the biennale press conference felt it necessary to justify the inclusion of the burial poles. "You can't help showing indigenous art in Australia," he said, adding: "It's good. It measures up." The poles, once an integral part of Aboriginal funerary rites, are now seen as sculptures; the examples on display at the biennale are on loan from the broadcasting billionaire Kerry Stokes in Perth." (Cristina Ruiz, p. 9)

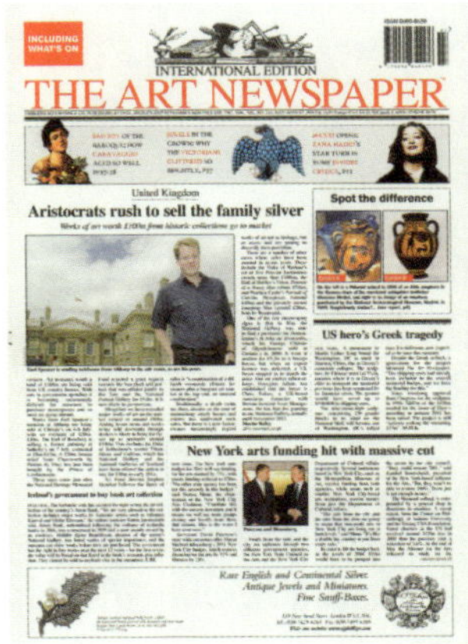
INTERNATIONAL EDITION
THE ART NEWSPAPER
Aristocrats rush to sell the family silver
Spot the difference
US hero's Greek tragedy
New York arts funding hit with massive cut

Vol. XVIII, no. 215: July–August 2010

Two pieces of news from Australia epitomize the contradictions and conflicts in the global art scene. There is, first, a report on the inconsistencies within the Aboriginal art scene. Recently, street sellers and local galleries are fighting each other in Alice Springs Town, Northern Territory, over the sale of art by indigenous artists. Michael Hollow from the Aboriginal Desert Art Gallery in Todd Mall complained to the City Council that he was "constantly losing business to street sellers. There are Aboriginal people selling art right outside my shopfront." Paul Sweeney, from the Aboriginal-owned Papunya Tula Artists gallery, however, would rather support the artists. Many of them create and sell their paintings on the lawn between the Mall and a nearby church whose minister argued, "the lawn artists provide a unique tourist experience and are gainfully self-employed." (Elizabeth Fortescue, p. 44)

The other news concerns the most unusual art museum of the world, which will open on the island of Tasmania, off the southern Australian coast. The owner, and collector David Walsh, mathematician, professional gambler, vineyard and brewery owner describes the "Museum of Old and New Art" (MONA) as both an "unmuseum" and a "subversive Disneyland." MONA has around 6,000 sqare meters exhibition space and is, among other things, very smelly as it will show Wim Delvoye's *Cloaca*, which creates excrements. Walsh will present first his antiquities, followed by Australian modernists and a collection of contemporary art of which Walsh owns some 300 works. MONA "will include four signature pieces from Charles Saatchi's 1997 *Sensation* show," among them Ofili's *Holy Virgin Mary*, "which caused a political storm when it was shown at the Brooklyn Museum." "Australia has never had a YBA show," says Mark Fraser. The article is worth reading for many reasons. The museum "overturns virtually every accepted notion of institutional practice" and represents not only the idiosyncrasies of the collector, but also a very relaxed, if not arbitrary handling of contemporary art. (Cristina Ruiz, p. 30f.)

We remain in the Saatchi shadow with the news about a wedding party in which art crossed the boundary line to entertainment. Simon de Pury, the auctioneer and some time DJ, celebrated his wedding with Michaela Neumeister, Philipps de Pury's head of art for German-speaking countries in the Saatchi Gallery. "The guests hurled champagne glasses over the balcony," and "the ensuing shower of glass" led to the "shattering of the showcase of Hirst's Shark." Another Saatchi-owned piece, Tracey Emin's *69 unmade beds* "filled the entire suite." (Louisa Buck, p. 35)

The same edition has a report on vandalism against the Berlin Biennale when activists accused it of "gentrification and eliticism. Galleries in the Künstlerhaus Bethanien were wrecked, art destroyed and 'Wanted' posters were put up around the neighbourhood with photos, e-mail addresses and mobile numbers of biennale organizers." Biennale spokesman Denhart von Harling defended the Biennale that it was political enough and therefore did not deserve such opposition. (Robert Rigney, p. 8)

Other news adds to the confusing mosaic of the international art world. In Italy Lamees Hamdan is awarded for "spearheading the campaign to bring the first United Arab Emirates Pavilion to the Venice Biennale in 2009. The Dubai-based skincare entrepreneur sits on the board of the Dubai Culture and Arts authority and is an avid collector of contemporary Middle Eastern art. Turkish writer and curator Vasif Kortun was recently selected to curate the UAE pavilion at the biennale 2011." (Emily Sharpe, p. 9)

In the section on the art market the two largest auction houses are reported to rethink the offer of "insurance for the difference between a work's guaranteed price and its actual sale price." But guarantee insurance could threaten the dealers of the secondary market. According to Louise Hallett of insurers Hallett Independent "many of them are already struggling to compete with the resources and global reach of auction houses." "During the boom years, both auction houses laid out hundreds of millions in guarantees they were offering themselves," mostly for modern and contemporary or impressionist art. "This all changed with the credit crise in 2008." At the time both auction houses looked "to third parties to provide guarantees." A representative of Christie's argued that "any discussions regarding insurance for our global business needs are confidential." (Cristina Ruiz, p. 44)

A new kind of book such as Iain Robertson's *The Art Business* (2007), and Don Thompson's *The $12 Million Stuffed Shark. The Curious Economics of Contemporary Art* (2008) tends to advise buyers on how to invest in art. There is also James Goodwin's *International Art Markets: the Essential Guide for Collectors and Investors* (2008). *The Art Newspaper* recommends the book *Fine Art and High Finance: Expert Advice on the Economics of Ownership*

(2010) edited by Clare McAndrew, GAM's adviser for the art market part in the documentation in the ZKM exhibition *The Global Contemporary*. The contributors to the book, in one section, deal with the "practice of art banking" and its dangers. One of them, the art lawyer Ralph Lerner of Withers, discusses "Art and Taxation in the United States." "McAndrews, more than her predecessors, makes a convincing case that art–while perhaps not a market in the conventional sense–is still an asset class worthy of economic analysis." (Melanie Gerlis, p. 38)

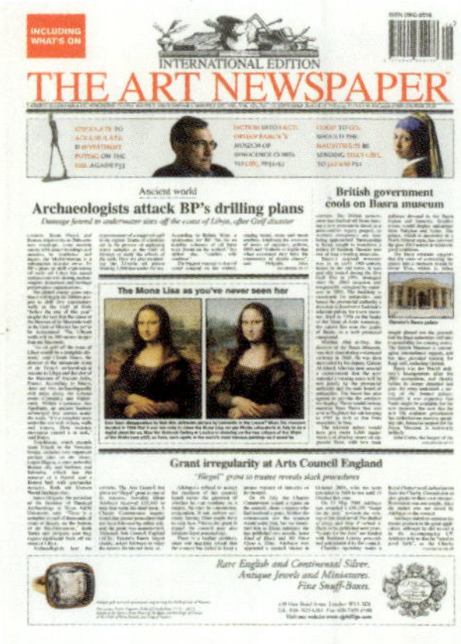
THE ART NEWSPAPER
INTERNATIONAL EDITION
Archaeologists attack BP's drilling plans
British government cools on Basra museum
The Mona Lisa as you've never seen her
Grant irregularity at Arts Council England

Vol. XIX, no. 216: September 2010

According to Capgemini SA and Merrill Lynch & Co "the number of global millionaires grew 17% last year, and, with financial markets in flux, art had emerged as the most popular category of *passion investment*." Richard Feigen explains that "because people are afraid of currency, they have been told that art is a place to park cash." Art, in the words of Todd Levin of the Levin Art Group, has become "a hedge against inflation." On the other hand, Michael Plummer of Artvest Partners calls collector behavior "the most unpredictable factor of all." The article points to Francesco Forte and Michela Mantovani's publication *Economics and Politics of Cultural Heritage*, which documents the real annual return on 20th century art between 1977 and 1996. (Charlotte Burns, p. 53)

The Abu Dhabi Art (ADA), which opened last year, is sponsored by the government-run Abu Dhabi Authority for Culture and Heritage (ADAH) and the Tourism Development and Investment Company (TDIC). The authorities insist on "the cultural aspects of the fair." Aoun Abdo stresses: "This is not an art fair, which is why the word 'fair' is missing from the title. This is much more of a community event to talk about art." "Six out of the 48 participating galleries come from neighbouring Dubai." Some of them complained that the international galleries "leave no mark on the local scene," but Pace Gallery president, Marc Glimcher, states that the fair is "associated with the Guggenheim. Their collection has to be in order if they are going to fill that new museum space." And Paris-based dealer Kamel Mennour adds: "There may be no collectors in Abu Dhabi, but there are museums being built. [...] And they all need art." (Marisa Mazria-Katz, p. 57)

In London, the idea of a new MoCA is causing a heated discussion, following Saatchi's announcement that he is "gifting over 200 works, and the Saatchi Gallery," albeit Saatchi does not mention that Phillips de Pury & Co., the auction house, "leases display place on the gallery's upper level." But the major problem is the question "which public body might administer MoCA." In discussion was also The Tate, "but there is no indication that it would want to run MoCA, which would be a smaller rival to Tate Modern." It will be interesting to see how the always-agitated London art scene will react. (Martin Bailey, p. 12)

The São Paulo Bienal also receives a lot of attention. Biennial director Ivo Mesquita had shocked the art world by the emptiness and discursive character of the 2008 Bienal. According to the new director, Moacir dos Anjos, the biennial "must differentiate itself from other institutions in the crowded, homogeneous biennial circuit" in that it mirrors the "ongoing geopolitical changes in the world in which Brazil and other countries increasingly move closer to the role of major players." "More than 50 Brazilian artists" will "reflect the South American slant of this year's Biennial." (Gareth Harris, p. 61)

The Gwangju Biennale has this time a European director, Massimiliano Gioni. He intends the show to tell "the story of people through the images they create and the images they leave behind," but also to follow "the lives of images themselves, tracing their endless metamorphoses, from funerary statue to commercial propaganda, from religious icon to scientific tool." The idea is to "transform the biennial into a temporary museum. That is why the show goes from 1901 until today." It is obvious that he wants to attract visitors from Korea and "to strengthen the Biennial routes across the region." (Marisa Mazria-Katz, p. 61)

Istanbul is the subject of a critical editorial by Necmi Sönmez, artistic director of the Contemporary Art Triennial, Port Izmir. "The breakthrough for contemporary Turkish art began in the 1990s with the first boom on the local art market. The second boom was the focusing of auction houses Beyaz, Antik and Portakal on contemporary art. The last boom was probably generated by the impact of the annual Contemporary Istanbul art fair, launched in 2006." Also international auction houses, such as Sotheby's, favor Turkish art. But there is another side to it. Turkish contemporary art that still depends on "the private, mainly bank-sponsored art spaces and museums," is labeled merely "as a national phenomenon." This is of course a key problem for most of the new art worlds, which rise in the global era. The critic Ahu Antmen complains about the "anachronism" in the reception of Turkish contemporary art as a national phenomenon. The "obsolescence of such stereotypes is [. . .] the key problem that faces young Turkish artists today." (Necmi Sönmez, p. 28)

But there is movement in the Turkish art scene. Gareth Harris introduces a new art center in Ankara, Cer Modern, which opened in April. Quoting its director Zihni Tümer, it is "the first private/public initiative in the cultural field" in Turkey and, "the institution will [. . .] host Turkey's first studio artist residency program." The government will also assist the Vehbi Koç Foundation to create "a campus museum and cultural center" in Istanbul, including the "first Turkish private art museum," launched in 1988. (Gareth Harris, p. 32)

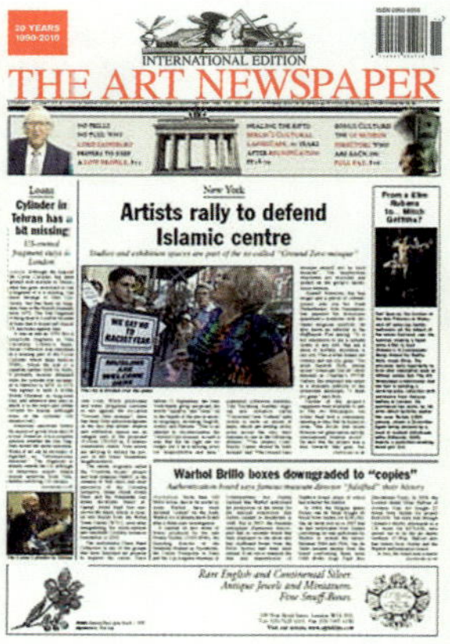
INTERNATIONAL EDITION
THE ART NEWSPAPER
New York
Artists rally to defend Islamic centre
Warhol Brillo boxes downgraded to "copies"

Vol. XIX, no. 217: October 2010

One of the most interesting parts of the October edition is an insert about the art fair Abu Dhabi Art (ADA). The fair also represents "the most comprehensive exhibition of Middle Eastern modern and contemporary art ever held, from private collections. [...] It stretches back a hundred years. [...] Now that Middle Eastern contemporary art has gained so much respect, people are looking back to what preceded it." We also learn that the cultural district of Saadyat Island in Abu Dhabi initially features an exhibition pavilion, called Manarat Al Saadiyat or "place that provides enlightment." One of its spaces was given to the Gagosian Gallery. Other spaces explain the forthcoming museums on the site, with an emphasis on the Zayed National Museum. The museum bears the name of Sheikh Zayed, the founder figure of the United Emirates, and will be developed together with the British Museum, which assists in topics such as "environment, heritage, unity, education, and humanitarism." Organized by local authorities and the fair itself, workshops will serve the training of local curators, since "art is not yet part of many people's life over here." "The word has been valued most highly" in former times. The goal is "building an audience for the museums," a local audience that is missing. In the public program section "Talking Art" the Guggenheim will introduce "a global perspective on contemporary art and culture" with the title *Representing History Now*. Since the Louvre claims to be "the first universal museum outside the western world and a major player in the global museum landscape of the 21st century," we see obviously a competition with the Guggenheim. (Insert "Abu Dhabi Art," pp. 1–7)

The Taipei biennial, curated by Hongjohn Lin and Tirdad Zolghadr, will explore "the global phenomenon of biennials." The explanation reads: "Instead of using art as a camera, we wanted to look at the camera itself." (Chris Gill, p. 10)

Massimiliano Gioni defends the under-representation of Asian artists at the Gwangju Biennale (see: no. 216, Marisa Mazria-Katz, p. 67): The biennial "is not the United Nations or the Olympics of art." The show includes "62 studio portraits taken between 1907 and 1968 of Chinese entrepreneur Ye Jinglu. Unearthed by journalist and collector Tong Bingxue, the archive tracks the history of Ye's life through the lense, while also unveiling gradual stylistic changes to photographic portraiture over the course of the 20th century." (Marisa-Mazria Katz, p. 10)

The section on the art market informs us that the Shanghai Contemporary "has changed drastically since its inception. Launched with the ambition of attracting big-name western galleries, it now features mainly those from the Asia-Pacific region. Many local galleries chose to focus on their own spaces." The fair "made extra efforts to engage with international collectors this year: organizers arranged complimentary hotel rooms for 230 collectors, according to director Colin Chinnery, who would not reveal further details except to say the collectors 'were not from China'." China is now the world's largest art market together with the US and the UK. (Chris Gill, p. 79)

But Paris is still the first place for the trade in African and Oceanic art. Marguerite de Sabran, from of the African and Oceanic department at Sotheby's Paris, confirms the city's position "as the hub of the tribal art market." "Major recent auctions [...] underscored Paris' pre-eminent role." Pierre Moos, the organizer of the fair "Parcours des Mondes," states "tribal art does not seem expensive compared with prices fetched by contemporary works of art." Sheikh Saud Al-Thani of Qatar "is a major collector with a special interest in the Mangbetus of Zaire and Polynesian artefacts." After "New York has been in decline over the past decade, Christie's only organizes sales in New York in order to dispose of an entire collection, [...] while individual items from US collections regularly appear in the two annual Paris auctions." (Roxana Azimi, p. 73)

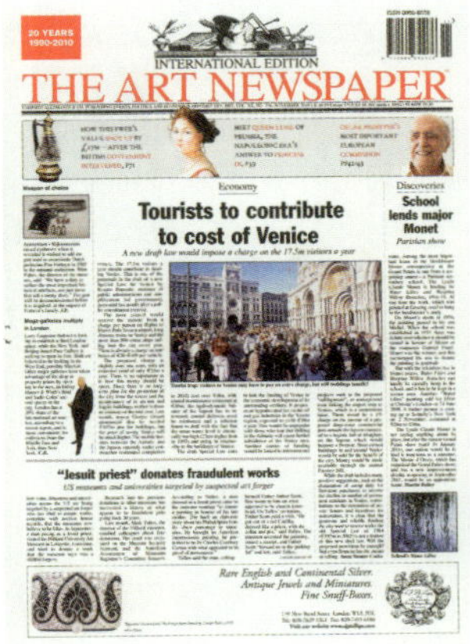
20 YEARS 1990-2010
INTERNATIONAL EDITION
THE ART NEWSPAPER
Tourists to contribute to cost of Venice
School lends major Monet
"Jesuit priest" donates fraudulent works

Vol. XIX, no. 218: November 2010

Aboriginal art as a disputed catalyst of Australia's cultural identity, has been given a new and official museum presence. The National Gallery of Australia (NGA) in Canberra, which owns 7,500 pieces of Aboriginal and Torres Strait Islander art, has just opened 11 new galleries with historical and contemporary art. It is, as director Ron Radford explains, the first extension of the exhibition space, since the museum opened in 1982. A prominent place is held by the so-called *Aboriginal Memorial*, consisting of 200, "painted wooden poles," and commissioned by the Sydney Bienniale of 1988 for the Bicentennial of white occupation in Australia. The collection also includes "watercolors from the Hermannsburg School (an art movement that began in the 1930s characterised by western-style landscapes)." The Gallery commissioned works such as a spherical aluminium sculpture, entitled *Eran* [River] that was created by Thanakupi, a tribal elder from Weipa in North Queensland. (Elizabeth Fortescue, in: "Museums," p. 26)

The museum's effort to parallel Western and Aboriginal art has a political message, given the prestigious site of the National Gallery of Australia. In the meantime indigenous artists also enter the theatre stage. Descendents of Albert Namatjira, a painter who died in 1959, are creating works on stage in a piece with the painter's name at the Belvoir st Theatre in the Sydney suburb of Surry Hills. "Part of the project is to assist indigenous artists in the Namatjira family to travel to their ancestral lands to create paintings." The hero of the piece "set up the first ever indigenous art centre in Hermannsburg, central Australia." According to creative director Scott Rankin, "the indigenous art centre movement is now the largest employer of Aboriginal people in Australia." (Elizabeth Fortescue, in: "News," p. 10)

In the Middle East, "a new museum dedicated to works made by Arab artists from the 1840s to the present is due to open in Qatar's capital Doha, in December." "Mathaf, which means museum in Arabic," owns the former collection of Sheikh Hassan bin Mohammed bin Ali Al Thani whose private villa was formerly home to his collection. The new museum, still located in a provisional building, plans to cooperate with Qatar's museum of Islamic Art, which opened in 2008 in a building designed by I.M. Pei. But Mathaf has a different mission. "The Arab world's modern period has been a little bit forgotten," as Wassan Al-Khudairi, the chief curator and acting director is quoted. (Marisa Mazria-Katz, in: "Museums," p. 26)

In this respect it is worth mentioning that the Centre Pompidou has signed a contract with a new Centre for World Culture in the Saudi Arabian city of Dharhan, where a museum will be built by 2013. The new center is funded by the national oil company Saudi Aramco. The collaboration will include joint acquisitions and the training of curators in Paris. (Gareth Harris, in: "Museums," p. 20)

Sotheby's third auction of Arab and Iranian contemporary art in London sold with 75.3% by lot and 90.2% by value. "The sale room was dominated by established Egyptian collectors and young Iranian buyers." Prominent among the buyers was Dubai-based collector Mohammed Afkhami (Gareth Harris, p. 87). At the same time, Sotheby's announced the first sale dedicated to calligraphy with "Islamic, Ottoman, modern and contemporary works" in Qatar. Sotheby's inaugural series of auctions took place in Doha in early 2009 (Gareth Harris, p. 87). In London, Sotheby's sold a "Princely collection" whose provenance was debated. But dealers brought in the name of David Khalili who already in 1981 sold a collection that represented "1400 Years of Islamic Art" (Georgina Adam, p. 87).

The unity of contemporary, modern, and traditional art does not correspond to western practice. It would be totally unacceptable in the west to exhibit and to sell contemporary together with, say, medieval art.

Marisa Mazria-Katz writes an exceptionally interesting feature on the Islamic Departments of major museums in the U.S. and in Europe. The sponsorship includes influential donors from the Middle East. The money aspect is as obvious as the political one. Thomas Campbell, the director of New York MET, celebrated the "understanding" of Islamic culture "at a time when the debate about Islam has 'become polarised' in the city" (see: no. 217, pp. 1, 4). The MET's main donor for the galleries with Ottoman art is the Turkish entrepreneur Rahmi Koç. The Museum of Fine Arts, Houston opens exhibition spaces for its Islamic art collection, which only began in 2007. The Louvre's new wing dedicated to the Arts of Islam and largely funded by Saudi Prince Al-Waleed bin Talal, will open in 2012. The Victoria and Albert Museum in London received a donation from the Saudi Arabian Jameel family. Such news is not irrelevant for the future of art museums in the West. The 2010 book by Hossein Amirsadeghi *Art & Patronage: The Middle East* takes up the subject. (Marisa Mazria-Katz, p. 16)

At the same time, Istanbul is emerging as a global art center with a new series of galleries including Arter, a big space owned by Omer Koç of the Koç Holding conglomerate. The Istanbul-born film director Kutluğ Ataman, who prepares his first solo show at Istanbul Modern, complains that despite his international success, he faces difficulties in Turkey. "The country was, until recently, dominated by a Soviet-style statist ideology and was closed to the world in many ways. Istanbul Modern (which opened in 2004) had to cater to the old guard at the start." But in the meanwhile, "art has democratised things." Ataman credits the Istanbul Biennial with transforming the country's contemporary art scene. (Gareth Harris, in: "What's On," p. 10)

As a nice epilogue to the issue of globalization, we would like to mention the exhibition *The*

Global Africa Project at the Museum of Arts and Design in New York. Lowery Stokes Sims, cocurator and former director of the Studio Museum in Harlem, speaks of "Cultural Fusion" as an important theme. A key figure in the show, Cameroon-born and Tokyo-based designer Serge Mouangue has created "Wafrica," a style of Japanese kimono made with "African" printed fabrics in the Netherlands. (Helen Stoilas, in: "What's On," p. 2) The domain of fashion makes "Cultural Fusion" explicable.

Vol. XIX, no. 219: December 2010

Among the "benchmarks for 2000–2010" which record *The Art Newspaper*'s second decade, a short column summarizes all that has changed the art scene in the last ten years. Top museums have appointed curators who are able to fill the gaps in the collection with non-Western art. Among the museums, which have opened across the globe, the MoCAs outnumber by far the others. The international trade in contemporary art is due to the global auction houses. "There hardly was a market for Middle Eastern art until Christie's held its first sale in Dubai 2006. Antedating such auctions [...] are the biennials all over the world from Gwangju in Korea, the first big one in Asia, to the influential one in Sharjah in the UAE." Finally, there are the new art fairs, at Abu Dhabi, Dubai, Singapore, Hong Kong, Shanghai, Istanbul, Moscow, and Melbourne, all "developing local markets and hoping to attract the big dealers who give credibility to their art scene." (N.N., p. 33). New is also the trend to create cultural districts with museums and galleries, a project well on the way in Abu Dhabi, but also long in discussion in Hong Kong. Such a district is also in preparation in St. Petersburg, where Roman Abramovich is funding "a commercial and cultural center" with a space of 103.000 square meters. (Cristina Ruiz, p. 1)

In London's East End, the Crossway Foundation is said to create "the first facility in the UK solely dedicated to Middle Eastern arts and education [...] The foundation will feature a gallery, studios, educational facilities" and also sponsor an artist-in-residence program. The project, cooperating with the Regeneration Trust of the Prince of Wales, "is born out of a friendship between British and Saudi-Arabian artists and aims to encourage grass-roots collaborations," as Fred Taggart, the project's director is quoted. (Marisa Mazria-Katz, p. 16)

At Abu Dhabi, the Louvre presented the French team for the new museum. It was explained that the museum will be "divided into 12 sections, showing art from the Neolithic period to the present day" and encompassing all the world religions. Emmanuel Coquery, curator of paintings, did not reveal any details. "We would like the opening of the museum to be a surprise." (Anna Somers Cocks, p. 22)

In Europe the Chinese government and the Italian Government contracted the opening of art spaces in Rome and in Beijing, collaboration respectively. The cooperation concerns art of every age including contemporary art. The Chinese government "will oversee a 600 sqm space at the Palazzo di Venezia for the next five years," whereas Italy, in return, will claim a wing in the National Museum of China. "Chinese press reports point out that [...] collection-sharing agreements make up for the lack of international art" in Chinese museums. (Gareth Harris, p. 13).

Globalization also touches the rediscovery of local modernities. Thus, "Pre-Revolutionary Iran" is a topic of a show in New York's Asia Society that in 2013 will introduce a four-year focus on modern Iranian art. Layla Diba, adviser to the exhibition, sees Iranian art between 1950 and 1980 as a "chapter of lost history." Kamran Diba, the founding director of the Tehran Museum of Contemporary Art (TMCA) complains that we "were not asked to act as advisers," though he calls the show a challenging project. But also another aspect has to be taken into consideration: funding by the Iranian-American community. Donors include Sharmin and Bijan Mossavar-Rahmani among others, who also made "a $10m donation to New York's Metropolitan Museum of Art [...] and have a gallery [there] named in their honor [N.N., no. 218, p. 16]." (Marisa Mazria-Katz, p. 18)

In the expanded section "What's On," the eight edition of the Shanghai Biennale, titled *Rehearsal*, is the subject of an overview. Gao Shiming, already curator of the 2004 edition, calls his new show "different," since it is "more low key." New is the emphasis on "off-site events and lectures, some of which are to be held as far afield as New York and Zagreb." "This biennale is about rehearsals, the backstage, so I'm not really worried about the audience," to quote the curator again. (Chris Gill, p. 76)

In the art market section, there is a feature by Michael Plummer and Jeff Rabin, principals of Artwest Partners. They describe "a sea change in investor perceptions of art as a store of value." "Chinese and other Asian buyers [who] are participating in western art auctions at a level not seen before [...] are much more cautious and discerning" and "bid aggressively on under-valued works." But also "the auction houses now play a more critical role than ever as the only transparent venue in an otherwise highly opaque market." The authors underline that the sensational Damien Hirst auction in 2008 "was a step too far," and subsequently the Hirst market has not performed very well. (Michael Plummer and Jeff Rabin, p. 28)

Interestingly, the Maastricht School of Economics and Business is creating an "International Institute for Art Finance." Rachel Campbell, who teaches at the school, explains the intention "to improve the transparency and professional standards of research and teaching in the area of both art and finance." But who is profiting from academic research? And do the markets allow transparency? (Georgina Adam, p. 58)

Georgina Adam, again, brilliantly analyzes the Chinese art market. "Based on sales by Sotheby's, Christie's, China Guardian and Hanhai, the global Chinese art market increased from $928m in 2008 to $1.21bn in 2009, a year-on-year increase of 41%. The strongest growth took place in the domestic market, with China Guardian and Hanhai reporting a 70% increase in volume from 2008 to 2009 (ArtTactic)." The author also points to the number of new auction houses in China such as Guardian, Poly, and Hanhai. "All this is taking place in a country that only authorized auction houses a couple of decades ago." But Wang Tao of the School of Oriental and African Studies in London warns that this market" is still unregulated" and without guarantees for the figures which are published. "If the mainland figures remain subject to caution, there is no doubt about the growth in Hong Kong, which in 2007 ousted France as the world's third biggest market." (Georgina Adam, p. 64)

Vol. XX, no. 220: January 2011

The next Venice Biennale grants permanent space in the Arsenale to countries other than the 32 countries with permanent pavilions in the Giardini. A concession of circa 20 years is made available "in return for funding the renovation works" in the Arsenale. Portugal and the United Arab Emirates are among the applicants along with Bahrain, China, and India. (Laura Traversi, p. 12)

There is a certain anachronism in the Venice event (with its background of world fairs in the colonial past), which also explains the hot debates about the election of a curator worthy to represent a nation. The nomination of Stella Kesaeva as commissioner of the Russian Pavilion is the first case when a private collector was chosen "rather than an employee of the state." Kesaeva, the wife of an oligarch, estabished the Stella Art Foundation and is now setting up a new contemporary art museum in Moscow that is in competition with the Garage art space of Roman Abramovich's partner Dasha Zhukova. In her words, the Venice pavilion will "show what was going on behind the Iron Curtain in the 1970s: specifically conceptual art," thus emphasizing a national concern rather than exhibiting the current art scene. (Claudia Barbieri, p. 34)

Hong Kong, the foremost Asian art market, had remained rather poor in public art institutions representing contemporary art. In the meantime, the situation will change due to the former Central Police Station (CPS), which the Hong Kong Jockey Club Charity Trust is transforming into the first major non-profit contemporary art space. David Elliott was commissioned to advise the club on governance, finance, and programming. The Asia Art Archive (AAA), the Hong Kong based contemporary art resource, was asked to develop a concept. Claire Hsu, founder of the AAA, speaks of "forming an arts cluster alongside a Whitechapel Gallery-type exhibition programme." The goal of the CPS, in her words, is to fill the gap "between small existing spaces and the future megamuseum in West Kowloon," the cultural district under construction. (Gareth Harris, p. 10)

As a place of art trade, Hong Kong offers a very different picture. Due to the favorable tax conditions and the new Mainland China clients, the city has reached a climax in the art trade. Sotheby's, in response to the rising number of Chinese collectors in London and New York, even launched a Hong Kong sale preview in Beijing. Art dealers in Hong Kong are profiting from the new hype. Currently, thirteen paintings by Picasso are on display at Ben Brown Fine Arts. "The paintings come from three different sources all in Europe," Ben Brown is quoted. The prices range from $2.9m to $6m, with "one extra painting currently reserved, at a higher price." (Chiara Zampetti, p. 66)

The next Hong Kong art fair, Art HK, will present 161 dealers; most of them were present at Art Basel Miami Beach in December. Western dealers explain that they "can't wait for Chinese collectors to come to us." Magnus Renfrew, director of the Art HK, is "committed to showcasing the very best work from the region," as defined by the art fair. (Melanie Gerlis, p. 66)

Gagosian's inaugural exhibition in central Hong Kong presents a new version of Damien Hirst's diamond skull, entitled *Forgotten Promises*. Gagosian's strategy is to promote his new space with a world premiere. (Charlotte Burns and H.S., p. 1)

However, the Hong Kong art market is not unchallenged. Viv Lawes gives an impressive picture of the rise of the Chinese domestic auction market. "There is no doubt that Chinese auction houses are doing amazing things–they're going to take over–and I know that Western dealers and collectors are increasingly consigning works to auction in China," as the London dealer Giuseppe Eskenazi is quoted. Since 2007, Beijing Poly has been holding preview exhibitions in Europe and America. It also deserves attention that Shanghai Hosane decided to auction European furniture and decorative arts. Hosene "was founded in the early 1990s to serve western buyers of Chinese art, opening a permanent office in Germany and then developing the domestic Chinese market a few years later." The recent trend for Chinese ink paintings and calligraphy outshadows Chinese contemporary art. "At Beijing Poly Chinese ink paintings–including classical, modern and contemporary–brought in £318m while Chinese contemporary made £41.5m. Top seller was an anonymous Song dynasty hand scroll." (Viv Lawes, p. 66)

Zhou Tiehai, artist and director of Shanghai's Minsheng Art Museum, which is supported by a bank with the same name (see: no. 211, p. 11), invited museum curators and politicians to discuss problems that Chinese museums suffer from. Zhou Tiehai on this occasion stated that they had "to create a system in Shanghai, from galleries to art fairs and now museums." The latter "slowly are involving into a local model." (Chris Gill, p. 22)

We come back to the art market with Sotheby's second auctions held in the Gulf state of Qatar. The first auctions in the spring of 2009, with Arabic, Iranian, and international contemporary art, went below expectation. The incoherent mixture of contemporary art and Islamic art had not worked out. By contrast, the second auctions in December 2010 went far better. The second sale, built on the popularity of the British Museum's *Word into Art* exhibition held in London (2006) and Dubai (2008), which included the use of calligraphy in modern and contemporary art "as a kind of nationalism, a language in which non-western artistic identity could be expressed." (Anna Somers Cocks, p. 65)

The Middle East remains the site of large-scale art projects and also the source of income for Western museums. Thus, a project with Oman will provide the London Tate with several million pounds due to a loan of pictures from Tate Britain for the

Sayyid Faisal bin Ali Museum in the capital Muscat. "Oman's major cultural project is a new National Museum, which is under construction in the old town of Muscat." (Martin Bailey, p. 13)

On November 26, 2010, the local authorities of Abu Dhabi offered further news about the Zayed National Museum, which will be the first to open on Saadiyat Island. Foster + Partners is building a structure of wind towers, which will be designed to evoke the end feathers of the falcon, the former Sheikh's passion. The forthcoming museum involves the British Museum for developing a program and also the training of local curators. (Anna Somers Cocks, p. 14)

The January edition offers unexpected news about the situation of the new hub of Aboriginal art. Hogarth Galleries, a Sydney institution founded in 1972, is reported to be selling off its collections. The owner, Clive Evatt, gave a critical comment on the present situation. The gallery "wasn't contributing anything to the Sydney art scene. Aboriginal art is in a state of over-supply and becoming very repetitive." Art adviser Jane Raffan "agreed that the quality of much Aboriginal art had dropped." As she said, "Aboriginal art centers in remote areas now tend to supply only those selected few dealers who they have decided are at the top end." (Elizabeth Fortescue, p. 65)

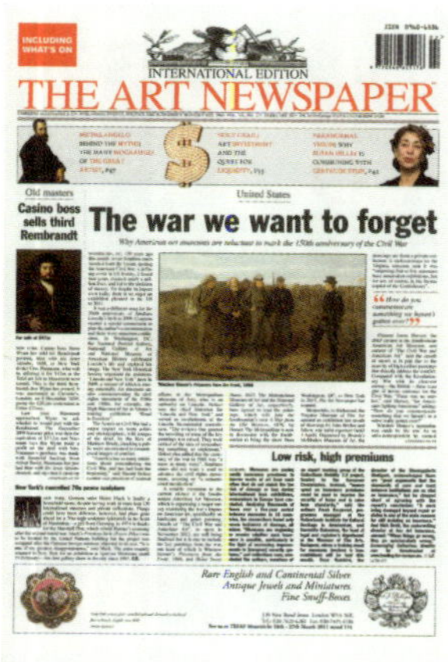
INTERNATIONAL EDITION

THE ART NEWSPAPER

Casino boss sells third Rembrandt

The war we want to forget

Low risk, high premiums

Vol. XX, no. 221: February 2011

The news from the Gulf States overshadows everything else. It is not always the newness but also the applied strategies, which need our attention. A case in point is the Museum of Modern Art in Doha, capital of Qatar, which opened last December, just two years after the Museum of Islamic Art (see: no. 218, Marisa Mazria-Katz, "Museums", p. 26). Sheikh Hassan bin Mohammed bin Ali of the ruling family who introduced the site as a temporary compromise, gave 6,000 works of his collection to the museum. In his opening address, he emphasized the "urgent need for modern art museums in the Middle East" as "an encyclopaedia of modern Arab art." The Doha museum will show art from the collapse of the Ottoman Empire to the present, though mostly from other parts of the Arab world, since the Gulf was not producing art for most of this period. According to Anna Somers Cocks, new interests maybe also come from an "art market driven from the region, ever since Christie's held its first sale in Dubai in 2006." (Anna Somers Cocks, p. 22)

There is an unexpected link to what Georgina Adam writes about the rumour that the Qatar Investment Authority will buy Christie's. "The Qataris are definitely shopping for luxury brands and are major art buyers [...], with an ambitious museum program and several potential institutions to fill. Christie's appointment of a new chief executive, Steven Pleshette Murphy, last September–who does not come from an art background–fuelled speculation that the company is being dressed up for sale." (Georgina Adam, p. 59)

Paradoxically enough, the recent financial crisis strengthened Dubai's cultural scene with the Dubai International Financial Center (DIFC) "focus on art institutions" after a sharp drop in rents across the capital. Hisham Samawi, director of Ayyam Gallery, "also hopes the additional location will broaden his collector base, particularly as the DIFC is a 'free zone'–a location that enables international organisations to open in Dubai without taking a local partner, as its customary for the rest of the city–and attracts visitors from around the world." (Marisa Mazria-Katz, p. 58)

In Georgina Adam's predictions, "2011 should be the year China's Poly and Guardian leapfrog (if they haven't already) into numbers three and four slots. According to Poly, it made £885m worth of sales in 2010, while China Guardian reported about £380m." The author explains the strength of the art market by an "intense competition between the very rich for trophy pieces; private museums remain the 'must-have' of billionaires, who compete for the best art to fill them; [....] India and China have increasing numbers of ultra high net worth individuals." Adam also expects that the leading art fairs continue to squeeze out most of the others. "This is the year that Hong Kong's May fair, ART HK 11, should reinforce its position as 'Asia's Art Basel' and become the world's fourth or even third most important modern and contemporary art fair." Finally, Mainland China continues to have the biggest growth in art sales. "Christie's is knocking at the Chinese door in the person of its key player, François Curiel, who has been moved to Hong Kong." (Georgina Adam, p. 59)

It comes as no surprise that the Asian market has shifted from Japan to China. Western auction houses avoid sales in Japan "because of high corporate tax rates on profits, and to this day, no Japanese house has grown large enough to compete with the Western houses in Hong Kong and Beijing." In 2007, the art market in Tokyo was only a tenth of the size of Beijing's even though Tokyo is a wealthier city. "It seems that Japanese buyers have been cautious since the bursting of the Japanese art bubble in the early 1990s." One reason, as Tokyo gallery owner Misa Shin is quoted, "is a young generation who purchase affordable art works to enjoy," to be found in small local art galleries. (Katharine Albritton, p. 62)

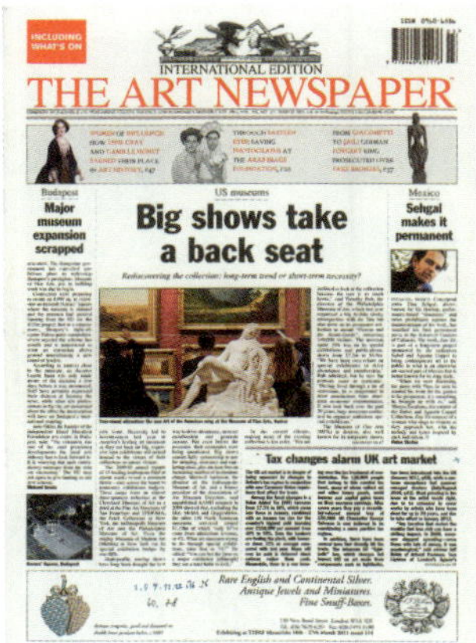
INTERNATIONAL EDITION
THE ART NEWSPAPER
Major museum expansion scrapped
Big shows take a back seat
Sehgal makes it permanent
Tax changes alarm UK art market

Vol. XXI, no. 222: March 2011

The Middle East offers a utopian perspective, which is still in the planning stage and therefore only surfaces here and there in museum projects, art fairs, and cooperation initiatives with the west. News from the Gulf States reveals the growing dimensions of contracts with major Western art museums. The latter export or loan their art treasures as part of an economic strategy from which both sides profit. The Rijksmuseum in Amsterdam is now joining other metropolitan museums and lends masterpieces to the new Museum of Islamic Art, Doha, as part of a long-term partnership with the Qatar museum authorities. (James Hall, p. 78)

It also is noteworthy that the new chief executive officer of Abu Dhabi's Tourism and Investment Company is the American James Pringle. "An international competition was run in 2008 for a director-general of museums, but this plan was shelved in favor of autonomy for each, with the creation of an overarching, museum-operating body." With the financial crisis, the Louvre project had been recast and the assignment of the contract was postponed. (Anna Somers Cocks, p. 11)

With respect to the Gulf States, the creation of a noncommercial art space in Dubai also deserves attention. Emaar, the biggest property developer in the Gulf, opened the 1,700 square meters. Pavilion in downtown Dubai, in its former sales office, in front of the tallest skyscraper in the world. Dubai doesn't have a contemporary art museum project, but Emaar is "working with Cultural and Engineering Dubai for cultural development planning and the training of cultural entrepreneurs." (Anna Somers Cocks, p. 9)

In the section "Art Market," a whole page is dedicated to India for the first time. The coverage begins with a report on a new private museum for modern and contemporary Indian art. The Kiran Nadar Museum of Art opened in New Delhi and houses the collection of Kiran Nadar, the wife of entrepreneur and philanthropist Shiv Nadar, who brought together works by the Progressive Artists' Group for some time. (Roxana Azimi, p. 60)

The third edition of New Delhi's India Art Summit in January, despite its successful earnings, was overshadowed by the controversy around the artist M. F. Husain, whose paintings of nude Hindu deities had caused a scandal. Husain gave up his Indian citizenship and is living in Qatar, "following threats from

Hindu extremists who have been campaigning against him since the mid-1990s." (Roxana Azimi, p. 60)

A new art fair was launched in Chennai, former Madras, by the Indian east coast. The "festival," called Art Chennai, was "financed by Tulsyan NEC Limited, a company in the Indian stock exchange and whose owners are collectors." "The idea is to galvanise the Southern market, which has a large share of IT billionaires who don't buy art," as Sharmistha Ray, the artistic consultant, is quoted. (Roxana Azimi, p. 60)

A general estimation of the art market confirms that India's own auction houses are still far behind their Chinese counterparts. Saffronart, Osian's (both launched in 2000), and Emami Chisel (2007) are all focusing primarily on modern and contemporary Indian art. Sotheby's and Christie's launched this art sector only in 1995. "The great leap came in 2005, and affected both the international and Indian auction houses. It was prompted by a change in the Indian government's policies" towards import duties on art and Indian currency leaving the country. In 2004, Sotheby's and Christie's made $6m and $3,6m, respectively, whereas in 2008 the peak had already reached $32m and $45m. Saffronart and Osian's experience "similar growth patterns." According to chief executive Dinesh Vazirani, the auctioneers also plan to extend their business via an online presence. (Viv Lawes, p. 60)

Vol. XX, no. 224: May 2011

The May 2011 edition has reshaped "The Art Market & Special Focus", part as a new "Section 2" under the heading "Hong Kong and Beijing" with a separate page numbering (1–30). This is a clear indication of the art market's key role in the realm of contemporary art. The contributions also bring to light the new problems in discussing art and economy as separate subjects. "The link between art and commerce is much stronger today," as a London-based lawyer is quoted, after even traditional buyers are "treating art as an investment." This development also plays its part in litigation cases that are involving law suits. (Georgina Adam, p. 7)

On April 5th, the first modern and contemporary Turkish art sale took place at Bonhams in London, followed by another one at Sotheby's London. There was a remarkable share of Turkish collectors who "buy and sell art quickly" (quoting the statement of a consultant for Bonhams). Even art dealers in Turkey consign works to auction houses in order to introduce their "artists to an international audience." "Within Turkey, the contemporary art scene is still mainly supported by a few wealthy families" mostly from Istanbul and owners of their own museums. But the tide is changing. (Chiara Zampetti, p. 7)

At Sotheby's April auction in Hong Kong, Filipino artist Ronald Ventura's *Grayground* (2011) "became the most expensive contemporary work of art in a Southeast Asian sale," mostly dominated by Indonesian art. (Patricia Chen, p. 12)

Art HK, Hong Kong's major art fair (May 26–29) is commented by Magnus Renfrew, the fair's director. He welcomed the competition with SH Contemporary (Shanghai), which started to create interest in the region. Part of Art HK's success is the tax situation, as there are no tariffs on export or import of art. As far as the new regulations are concerned, Renfrew confirmed for the section Art Future "that artists have to be 35 years old or younger. We originally said that galleries had to be five years and under, and assumed this might mean their artists were young too." He also confirmed the increasing application of international galleries and a future partnership with Art Basel. (Charlotte Burns, p. 16)

However, this is not the only story from Hong Kong. We also learn that Sotheby's auctioned 105 works from the Guy Ullens collection in Hong Kong, billed as "The Nascence of Avant-Garde China" and "marketed with a six-city tour, a hardback catalogue and a museum-style display at the Hong Kong preview." Twelve works went for over $1.3m. "While several Southeast Asian, Hong Kong and Taiwan collectors were bidding, no mainland buyer was credited for any of the top ten purchases." Among the overseas clients, Acquavella New York was identified as a buyer. "Ullens still has over 1000 pieces in his Chinese collection." Thus, a second auction at Sotheby's is expected to happen in the fall. "Beijing's Poly auction will sell 34 contemporary works from Ullens, edited for mainland tastes." (Alexandra Seno, p. 12)

Given the new prominence of the Chinese art market, possibly already number two, it is expected that major international galleries will settle in Mainland China and Hong Kong as well. But the different "systems" make market decisions for single galleries a precarious topic. The opportunities in Mainland China are obvious, as the region "almost doubled the number of billionaires in 2010 alone." But, still, the highest prices are paid for traditional art and artifacts. The Chinese auction houses have global ambitions and are looking also for Western art. Philip Dodd, chairman of the cultural consultancy "Made in China," sees new museums such as the Zendai Museum of Modern Art in Shanghai and Beijing's Today Art Museum, in search of a collection of their own including Western art. But regulations "hardly encourage free trade," given the taxes in import and export. And also censorship is unpredictable. Seen against this situation, Hong Kong is still "a magnet for the whole region." Christie's and Sotheby's held auctions last year which totalled $1.36bn. Auction houses from Indonesia, South Korea, Japan, and Taiwan also hold sales in Hong Kong. But "the cost of conducting business in Hong Kong is probably the most expensive in the world." And museum infrastructure is still weak. Thus, the future of Hong Kong and Beijing, in terms of their art trade, cannot be predicted with any certainty. (Georgina Adam, p. 19)

What seems certain, however, is the growth of Chinese buyers in the contemporary market. "Young people, with a more international outlook," now are the majority in Shanghai galleries. Buyers are increasingly attracted "by works that draw on imagery and aesthetics with a history of cultural meaning." The priority, however, is to look for a big brand artist. (Melanie Gerlis, p. 23)

The rich "Section 2" ends with an inside view of the art market, written by Zhao Li, professor in the Department of Art of the Chinese Central Academy of Fine Arts, Beijing. The recent financial crisis, he explains, mostly affected the area of Chinese contemporary art when speculative capital moved to classical Chinese art. The private collectors, as a rule, have made their money in the major growth industries. But there is an increasing presence of institutional investors, who are marginalizing individual buyers in auction sales. Art museums have so far a limited part in the art market, and private museum collections are still at an early stage of development. "The problem for those selling contemporary art is that very few collectors or institutions in China have a mature understanding in this field. Many collectors, particularly newer buyers, struggle to judge the artistic value of contemporary works. The fact is, against the backdrop of globalisation, that the creation of contemporary art is not only the expression of individual will or of a local reality, but reflects the collision, communication and integration of different cultures. As a result, to understand Chinese contemporary art, collectors need to be familiar with art in both the local and global context, and actively engage in broad cultural discussions without losing their individual perspectives. Of all the issues that face the Chinese art market, addressing this is the highest priority." (Zhao Li, p. 30)

Room of Histories

Art's Globalization in Context

Documents

Art Spaces

The Reading Room

Mapping

Branding

trans_actions

Global News from The Art Newspaper

Essays

From World Art to Global Art: View on a New Panorama

Hans Belting

Recent books with titles such as *World Art History* and *Global Art History* seem to suggest that the two terms can be used as synonyms. But, in fact, *world art* and *global art* today have very different meanings, ever since the notion *global art* came up around twenty years ago. *World art* is an old idea complementary to modernism, designating the art of the others because or although it was mostly to be found in Western museums. It continues to signify art from all ages, the heritage of mankind. In fact, *world art* included art of every possible provenance while at the same time excluding it from Western mainstream art - a colonial distinction between art museums and ethnographic museums. *World art* is officially codified in international laws for the protection of cultural heritage and monuments. *Global art*, on the other hand, is recognized as the sudden and worldwide production of art that did not exist or did not garner attention until the late 1980s. By its own definition *global art* is contemporary and in spirit postcolonial; thus it is guided by the intention to replace the center and periphery scheme of a hegemonic modernity, and also claims freedom from the privilege of history (for an overview of publications see: this volume, pp. 60-73).

This essay was written to prove how the notion of *world art* and its new companion term *global art* came into use, how the meaning of the terms changed, and what they reveal about the history of ideas and the inherent notions of art. I hope to make it clear how terminology provides a key to understanding the underlying intentions. However, one and the same notion, namely *world art*, also changed what it referenced, especially when the term *global art* came into use. This essay is divided into four parts, and begins with the concept of *world art* before turning to *global art*. A Paris exhibition in 1989 serves as a missing link, as it marked the time when *world art* split from *global art*. A fourth and final section deals with art history and its new challenges.

1.

World art was initially coined as a colonial notion that was in use for collecting the art of "the others" as a different kind of art, an art that was also found in different museums where anthropologists and not art critics had the say-so. The so-called *Atlas of World Art*, which John Onians edited in 2004, admittedly corrected this bias by including Western art in such an overview, the only remaining distinction being geographical difference. But up to this date the colonial connotation had been inherent in the conception of *world art*. It was central to the separation of *world art* from Western art by the abyss created by art history's narratives. The Vienna school of art history, a hundred years ago, favored the term *Weltkunst* in order to expand the discipline's field of competence. In this sense, Heinrich Glück, in the Festschrift for Josef Strzygowski, in 1934, wrote a study with the title *Hauptwerke der Weltkunst*. In Germany, the magazine *Die Kunstauktion*, founded in 1927, was relabeled *Weltkunst* in 1930 since world art had become attractive for collectors. For some people, *world art* nourished a feeling of nostalgia whenever they felt disillusioned with modern art and longed for a lost past.

This is not to say that a general study of art production across the world makes no sense; it depends on which purpose its description serves and whether it includes or excludes the one who is speaking. "World History," as initiated by William H. McNeill and others in the postwar period, proved to be a successful approach; however, it left no doubt that it included the West and that there was no longer a Eurocentric view of the "other" as a subject for writing history.[1] Ultimately, historians have the same problem with a terminology that distinguishes between world history and global history - despite the obvious need for such a distinction in the global age. History has less of a problem in the case of "world literature" as a comparative field of studies and in the sense that Goethe used the term when he recomposed the German translation of Arab poems in his *West-Eastern Divan*. After all, translation as a burden and challenge distinguishes literature from the field of art. Colonial trading and collecting of art and artifacts was always directed toward single objects or artifacts, which more often than not were deprived of their history and previous use when they arrived in Western collections. When we look back on colonialism the reader and the collector are two different roles.

The history of the *world art* discourse also distinguishes the background of two schools which have introduced education in *world art* into the academic curriculum. There is, on the one hand, the new School of World Art Studies at Leiden University, which was initiated as an interdisciplinary project by the art historian Kitty Zijlmans and the ethnographer Wilfried van Damme. At Leiden, the global production of today's art is seen against the presence of the colonial history of the Netherlands.[2] And, on the other hand, there is the Sainsbury Centre for Visual Arts at the University of East Anglia in Norwich whose Department of Art History was renamed in "Department of World Art Studies" in 1992. In this case, the Sainsbury Collection of art from Africa and Oceania was presented to the university as a gift, and John Onians, in his *Atlas of World Art*, paid tribute to the legacy of the Sainsbury collection in his own way.[3] The magazine *World Art*, which was launched by the Sainsbury Centre in March 2011, in its editorial pointed to "a major change in attitudes concerning what art is." "World art," the text continued, "has widely differing resonances," and is "centered on human creativity [...]. The consideration of ancient cultures around the globe must inform a broader rethinking of world art."

The Sainsbury collection was, however, guided by a Kantian value judgment as an aesthetic postulate. This justified art by what seemed to be its universal and timeless form, purified from whatever content and cultural context. Thus, so-called *world art* was regarded as evidence that art had always been modern and had always been nothing but form, whatever its cultural conditions may have been. This view served both ends and justified modern art as well as *world art*. The Sainsbury family enjoyed "primitive" art for the same reasons as modern art, collecting the one and the other side by side. The collector Sir Robert Sainsbury found general consent when he confessed, to quote from the mission statement of the museum, that he had brought together "work spanning 5000 years of human creativity." This confidence, however, only worked when the two parties were neatly separated: on the one hand the anonymous object, and on the other modern artists who by definition had to be Western and, preferably, British, like Francis Bacon whose work was collected in the 1950s by the Sainsbury family.

The Sainsbury Centre in the meantime acknowledges the fact that a watershed separates the traditional artisan, as he appeared in a colonial gaze, from a postcolonial artist who was born into the diversity and coevalness of "contemporary worlds," to borrow Marc Augé's felicitous term, and can no longer be represented by an ethnographic object.[4] He or she may work next door as an artist-in-residence. At the British Museum, the Department of Ethnography, with its rich collections also from the Sainsbury family, started an initiative to actively collect contemporary art and to collaborate with artists, mostly of African origin, as a wall text informed visitors to the collection in 2007.[5] But artists from the former colonies turned against such Western collections with their postcolonial critique, since these did not allow for the self-representation of their ancestors. Also Western curators of ethnographic museums face a crisis which makes the collection principles and exhibition practices a difficult problem. Sally Price points up the problem trenchantly in her book *Primitive Art in Civilized Places*, an acerbic account of the appropriation politics of foreign artifacts and religious art in Euramerica.[6]

World art - a kind of aesthetic appropriation of objects as pure "form" or as proof of individual creativity on a universal

1 **Bruce Mazlish**, "Comparing Global History to World History," in: *Journal of Interdisciplinary History*, vol. 28, no. 3, 1998, pp. 385–395.

2 **Kitty Zijlmans and Wilfried van Damme (eds.)**, *World Art Studies: Exploring Concepts and Approaches*, Valiz, Amsterdam, 2008.

3 **John Onians**, "A New Geography of Art Museums," in: Peter Weibel and Andrea Buddensieg (eds.), *Contemporary Art and the Museum. A Global Perspective*, Hatje Cantz, Ostfildern, 2007, pp. 124–138; John Onians (ed.), *Atlas of World Art*, Laurence King, London, 2004. The latter is a book with 68 contributors that intends to cover the whole history of human picture production.

4 **Marc Augé**, *An Anthropology for Contemporaneous Worlds*, Stanford University Press, Palo Alto (CA), 1999, pp. 89ff.

5 **See: Hans Belting**, "Contemporary Art as Global Art," in: Hans Belting and Andrea Buddensieg (eds.), *The Global Art World - Audiences, Markets, and Museums*, Hatje Cantz, Ostfildern, 2009, pp. 38–73, p. 56, fig. 8.

6 **Sally Price**, *Primitive Art in Civilized Places*, The University of Chicago Press, Chicago (IL), 1985.

scale – was best described in André Malraux's book *Le musée imaginaire*[7], first published in 1947, a book based on a universal aesthetics despite cultural and historical differences.[8] The author, a writer with personal experience of the French colonies in Asia, claimed to have overcome the traditional dualism between (Western) art and (ethnic) world art, which he identified as an outdated colonial attitude. Malraux also applied a Western art concept, the formalism of those days, without regard to the chronology and geography of art history, and compared medieval Western art and Buddhist sculpture or the art of Gandhāra. Paradoxically, he still worshipped the museum, even if he dreamed of an ideal museum without walls, a museum in the brain or, for that matter, in a book.

World art, in the meantime, matters for identity politics in cultures that had no previous share in colonial selecting and collecting. Their history, whether precolonial or colonial, was embedded in and embodied by objects as items of cultural practice, but usually this was lost with their entry into a Western museum. Neil MacGregor, the director of the British Museum, therefore turned the tables when he published his BBC series *A History of the World in 100 Objects* in 1996. He gave their history back to the objects and also included modern Western examples or objects with a colonial use among them. The change from the exhibition hall to the text of a book also made it possible for him to include specimens of mass culture from the modern age.

But *world art* nowadays also receives unwelcome attention due to the growing pressure of repatriation claims from the former colonies. Metropolitan museums of the West, often accused of being outposts of empire and colonialism, today have to rethink their arguments in order to defend their collections. The British Museum is among them, and Neil MacGregor, claimed his museum to be "not only a museum of the world but also a museum for the world."[9] Along these lines he opened a blockbuster show with the Chinese Terracotta Army that attracted large crowds in 2007,[10] thus ascertaining his claim not only to own, but also to promote *world art*. A bookshop on Great Russell Street I came across at the time, unintentionally offered a telling example for the need of our distinction. The owner of the shop presented two books on *world art* and one on *global art*, although all three books were about art from China, side by side in the same window display.[11] The catalog of the show at the British Museum across the street shared the window with a book that was dedicated to visits to the studios of living *Artists in China*, as the title stated, and therefore would not have been possible as recently as twenty years ago.

The relation of *world art* to modern art, as the very canon of Western art, was linked to the notion of so-called *Primitivism*, as Robert Goldwater called a certain current of modern avant-garde in his book *Primitivism in Modern Painting* of 1938, published a few years after the MoMA had launched the exhibition *African Negro Art* in 1935. Primitivism, one of the basic creeds of modernism, was represented, and representable, for the last time ever in William Rubin's Museum of Modern Art show of 1984 when its time already was over and the reviews concentrated almost unanimously on the ethnocentric bias of the concept. The show's subtitle "The Affinity of the Tribal and the Modern" was an attempt to explain, and to exculpate, the hegemonic appropriation of tribal artifacts by modern artists who borrowed "primitive" forms for their own work, thus translating them into an idiom of modern art. After the fact, the so-called affinity was celebrated as a proof of the universality and timeless formal value of the modernist canon. But James Clifford, in a review of the show, objected that one should "question the boundaries of art and the art world,"[12] and also opposed the distinction between modernist art and traditional craftsmanship in a colonial discourse.

A few years later, in 1988, Susan Vogel launched the exhibition *Art/Artifact* in the Center for African Art in New York as an attempt to reconsider the issues of the MoMA show. The debate about art and artifact had been lingering on for quite some time and had divided the exhibition practice of ethnographic museums. However, now the debate took a new turn. The shift happened at a moment when the Western concept of art had lost its clear profile in contemporary practice and had left the definition of art up in the air. A symposium linked to the 1988 show addressed the question "What makes something art?". Thomas McEvilley, one of the participants, stated that "the boundaries of what had been called art had been stretched to the point where it seemed silly even to bring it up," and he added that so-called primitive art "is the only context left, which brings up the question of what is art." As a result he proposed "anthropology as a cultural critique, not forcing objects from other cultures into our categories, but rather allowing those objects to raise questions about ours." The author concluded: "The fact that we designate something as art means that it is art for us, but says nothing about what it is in itself or for other people."[13]

7 **Hans Belting**, *Art History after Modernism*, The University of Chicago Press, Chicago (IL), 2003, pp. 153ff.

8 **Ibid.**

9 **See: Belting 2007**, p. 33.

10 ***The First Emperor**: China's Terracotta Army*, The British Museum, September 13, 2007 – April 6, 2008.

11 **See: Belting 2009**, p. 43, fig. 3.

12 **James Clifford**, *The Predicament of Culture: Twentieth-century Ethnography, Literature, and Art*, Harvard University Press, Cambridge (MA), 2002, p. 213.

13 **Thomas McEvilley**, *Art and Otherness: Crisis in Cultural Identity*, McPherson, Kingston (NY), 1992, pp. 164–165.

In the catalog of Susan Vogel's show, Arthur C. Danto not only challenged the modernist creed of universal art. He even turned the debate about the so-called primitives on its head and maintained "there is no art more advanced than theirs."[14] In other words, the notion of "art" had lost its clear agenda in late modernism and could no longer be applied to or turned against the ethnographic object. Rather, the debate centered after 1989 on the question of how to deal with the fact that modern international art had lost its geographical frontiers, or home base, and had now ended up in *global art*, as the new distinction from *world art* was called. The former dualism of art and artifact was put aside when contemporary art production in a professional sense had become general practice and was no longer the West's prerogative.

2.

A first step along this road was taken by the Havana Biennial, founded in 1984, at its two venues in 1986 and 1989. With 690 artists from 57 countries, the 1986 Biennial "created a new space, acting as a gigantic 'Salon des Refusés'," to quote Gerardo Mosquera.[15] The focus on Latin America was a critical response to mainstream art, although the notion of "Third World Art" was only included in the official title for the 1989 venue. The two Havana Biennials still insisted on otherness and proclaimed an alternative internationalism without the dictate of Eurocentrism. Already in 1987, Rasheed Araeen had founded the periodical *Third Text* as a critical forum "for Third World Perspectives on the visual arts." The concept of "Third World" went out of use with the end of the Cold War but it served as an interlude before *global art* emerged (see: this volume, pp. 41–48). The third Havana Biennial, in 1989, mixed high art with popular art in order to undermine the Western art system and to insist on local traditions other than art history's narratives.[16]

The MoMA exhibition of 1984 had still been a colonial project, although it took place in the postcolonial era. Jean-Hubert Martin was ready to go beyond this divided world by proclaiming division as a practice had to be abolished. *Magiciens de la terre*, as the participants were called to avoid any protests by Western art critics, was hailed as "the first really global exhibition of contemporary art" (*La première exposition reellement mondiale d'art contemporain)*, to quote the *Gazette des Arts* (see: this volume, pp. 66–67 and pp. 212–220). The huge discussion and dissent which his show provoked, was not only due to its location in a former center of colonial politics and modernist Western art. Of equal importance was the unprecedented confrontation of a number of renowned Western artists with an equal number of formerly excluded artists from what had been the colonies. Each artist was given equal treatment, two pages in the catalog, giving only his or her name, work title, and place of birth.

It was a bold step to leave the opposing worlds of *modern art* and *world art* behind and to arrive in a shared world of *global art*. But Martin was accused of continuing the colonial game of the authentic because of selecting so-called "native" artists as the counterparts of their Western colleagues, especially since postcolonial artists working with video and installation already replaced the former artisans. Martin also invited professional artist, for example, Chéri Samba, who presented his artistic self in the show with a self-portrait and a biography: the anonymous artisan from Africa had become a face with a name and a professional career. In the end the show succeeded in that both parties, even against their will, emerged as contemporaries with a name and a passport. The one no longer looked modern, and the other no longer ethnic in the old colonial sense.

A few years later, in 1995, Jean-Hubert Martin became the director of André Malraux's Musée des Arts d'Afrique et d'Océanie (founded 1962) in Paris. As participating curator of the first Johannesburg Biennale, *Africus*, in the same year, Martin analyzed what he hoped would be a new future for *world art*, as a contemporary practice, in the museum.[17] He distinguished between the ethnographic museum, where everything is explained, and the art museum where living artists, as representatives of human creativity, would honor "art's heroes and ancestors." But the boundaries, as he argued, were to become "increasingly unclear, and we have yet to create an art museum [...] where artists of all the world can meet [...] and compare themselves with historical works." His own museum in Paris, Martin hoped, would "become such a place" and also artists would be able to take over the former role of anthropologists.

At that time Martin did not know that his museum would soon be incorporated in the newly created Musée du Quai Branly in Paris, which opened its doors in 2006 and initially excluded professional contemporary artists from

14 **Arthur C. Danto**, "Artifact and Art," in: *Art/Artifact: African Art in Anthropology Collections*, exhib. cat., Center for African Art, New York, et al., The Center for African Art, New York (NY) and Prestel Verlag, Munich, 1988, pp. 18ff.

15 **Gerardo Mosquera**, "The Third Bienal de la Habana in its Global and Local Contexts," in: Rachel Weiss et al., *Making Art Global (Part 1): The Third Havana Biennial 1989*, Exhibition Histories, vol. 2, Afterall, London, 2011, pp. 70–79, p. 74.

16 **See: Luis Camnitzer**, "The Third Biennial of Havana," in: Rachel Weiss et al., *Making Art Global (Part 1): The Third Havana Biennial 1989*, Exhibition Histories, vol. 2, Afterall, London, 2011, pp. 206–214, p. 207.

17 **Jean-Hubert Martin**, "Art in a multi-ethnic society," in: *Africus: Johannesburg Biennale*, exhib. cat., Transnational Metropolitan Council, 1995, p. 49.

Africa and Oceania in order to celebrate once again the old myth of the *arts premiers*, a myth from colonial times. André Malraux had founded his museum as a place where ethnic art would be staged as an aesthetic experience, as was the creed of modernist times. In the meantime, however, such a colonial attitude was passé, and it was generally agreed that Malraux's project no longer represented the global age.[18]

3.

In 1990 Thomas McEvilley, who had previously contributed to the catalog, reviewed the *Magiciens* show under the heading "The Global Issue."[19] Despite all criticism, whether from the right or the left, he acknowledged that the show was a first attempt to curate art in a truly postcolonial way. This was also the general response in the July 1989 edition of the magazine *Art in America* where a review of the *Magiciens* exhibition appeared titled "The Whole Earth Show." The front cover of the same magazine featured a NASA shot of the Earth together with the title "The Global Issue" (see: this volume, pp. 64–65). For the first time the planetary view had been taken from an extraterrestrial position in space. In order to justify what was a neologism in the art scene, the magazine presented six statements on the global world, including a text by the artist Martha Rosler and one by the anthropologist James Clifford. There was a general feeling about the danger of an unwelcome homogenization and consumer culture, caused by the euphoria of Theodore Levitt's view of "the marketing imagination."[20] Nevertheless, Craig Owens concluded: "Perhaps it is in this project of learning how to represent *ourselves* – how to speak *to*, rather than for or about, others – that the possibility of a 'global' culture resides."[21] Further, the interviews with fourteen "peripatetic artists," as they were labeled in the same edition, confirmed that a global space for art was in the making.

History writing changed as well with the arrival of globalization. A "New Global History," as Bruce Mazlish called it, "focuses on the history of globalization" and views "processes that are best studied on a global rather than a local, national, or regional level."[22] After all, he continued, "globalization is a process now going on around us, while world history stretches in all directions. One speaks of globalization; one can hardly speak of *worldlization* as a movement operating today." It was a paradox to write a history not of the past, but of living together on the planet.

Globalization, indeed a road of no return, provided a place for artists who for a long time had been excluded with the label *world art*. Thus we can call the *Magiciens* show an intermezzo in which the cards were shuffled again. One could also call it a *rite de passage*, which marked a one-off transitory event that passed. The project would have been impossible before, and was no longer possible afterwards when globalization had opened up a new territory of art. Both terms, modern art and *world art*, suddenly looked old. The *Magiciens* project led into no man's land where we still are and where we navigate with the help of provisional terminology. The show happened at the same time the *post-history* debate reached its climax and the Cold War, with its confrontation of two systems, collapsed. It now seemed that *inter-national* art, an art between nations, though to be sure Western nations, had been an affair of the modern age and that the term no longer covered a polycentric map where cultures took over the former distinctions of nations.

With the Paris *Magiciens* show, *global art* made its entry into the art world. While *world art* remained synonymous with the art heritage of the "others," *global art* by contrast crossed the boundaries and demanded acceptance as a contemporary practice on an equal footing with Western art. As the term *global art* was not yet acceptable to everybody, in January 1992 the journal *Kunstforum International* returned to the term "Weltkunst," but linked it to an explanatory definition of "Globalkultur." The editor, Paolo Bianchi, reminded his readers that a *new kind of ethnicity* was transforming the visual arts.[23] Ethnicity had been a concern in the debate on *world art*, but never in modern art. Now it became an issue in aspirations to identity and difference even for those who presented themselves as *postethnic* (for example, as "artists from Africa" instead "African artists").[24] As a result, curators of biennials take over the former "fieldwork" of ethnographers to promote local artists and to create new "art regions" with a common transnational profile.

There was another notable episode in the terminology of the 1980s. Shortly before the term *global art* became

18 **Bernard Dupaigne**, *Le scandale des arts premiers: La veritable histoire du musée du quai Branly*, Mille et une nuit, Paris, 2006.

19 **McEvilley 1992**, p. 153.

20 **Theodore Levitt**, *The Marketing Imagination*, Free Press, New York (NY), 1983.

21 **"The Global Issue:** A Symposium. James Clifford, Boris Groys, Craig Owens, Martha Rosler, Robert Storr, Michele Wallace," in: *Art in America*, vol. 77, no. 7, July 1989, p. 89.

22 **Bruce Mazlish**, "The New Global History," available online at: www.newglobalhistory.com/docs/mazlich-the-new-global-history.pdf, p. 5, accessed 09/04/2012. See also: Bruce Mazlish, "On History Becoming History: World History and New Global History," available online at: www.newglobalhistory.com/docs/mazlish-on-history-becoming-history.pdf, accessed 09/04/2012. I thank Sara Giannini for this link.

23 **Paolo Bianchi**, "Vorwort," in: Bianchi (ed.), "Weltkunst – Globalkultur," in: *Kunstforum International*, vol. 118, 1992, pp. 72–291, p. 73.

24 **See: Hans Belting**, "Contemporary Art and the Museum in the Global Age," in: Peter Weibel and Andrea Buddensieg (eds.), *Contemporary Art and the Museum. A Global Perspective*, Hatje Cantz, Ostfildern, 2007, pp. 16–38, p. 34.

firmly established, the old term *world art* was given a new significance as a label for the emerging new geography of art production. Thus, Jean-Louis Pradel's book chose the title *World Art Trends. 1983–84* in order to include a few newcomers from non-Western countries among the international artists. This kind of confusion also reached the seventh Sydney Biennale of 1988 which was proclaimed as *A View of World Art 1940–1988* (see: this volume, pp. 60–73). It should be noted that a show in Cologne, seven years earlier, in 1981, with the same time period (1939 to 1981) marked the inclusion of American artists in what the curators called postwar "Western art" (*Westkunst*). However, this postwar position no longer represented the new frontiers. It was even attacked in retrospect when in 1989 Rasheed Araeen curated the exhibition *The Other Story* in London, emphasizing the other, neglected story of modern art.[25] The Sydney catalog explains the 1988 Biennale's purpose as "an exhibition in Australia of contemporary art both from here and overseas"[26] and as an "attempt to view key developments in *world art* since 1940 from an Australian perspective,"[27] as against the old center and periphery view from Paris or New York.

The year 1988 also marked the bicentennial of white settlement of Australia, a commemoration that caused a hot debate among the Aboriginal Australians about their participation at the Sydney Biennale. In order to cope with the controversy, the curatorial board commissioned 200 hollow log bone coffins to be created by twelve Aboriginal artists from the Ramingining Artists Community symbolizing 200 years of oppression (see: this volume, p. 127 and p. 167). But it could not be overlooked that the Biennale was otherwise restricted, as far as Australia's part was concerned, to twenty-six "European Australians," among them several pioneers of the modernist movement. Five years later, indigenous Australians entered the official ranks of the contemporary art scene. Three Aboriginal women artists were included among the nine participants from Australia. The Asia Pacific Triennial of Contemporary Art, launched in 1993 by the Queensland Gallery, Brisbane, was an ambitious attempt at remapping the former art world (see: this volume, pp. 112–113). Australia in the meantime opted for the Asia-Pacific region as its cultural background. The official acceptance of Aboriginal art as contemporary art had been heralded by the exhibition *Dreamings* in 1988, which left behind the ethnocentrism at the Sydney Biennale of the same year. Thus, Aboriginal art, as a branch of what had formerly been called *world art*, entered the territory of contemporary art under the auspices of what was now called *global art*.

25 **Rasheed Araeen (ed.)**, *The Other Story: Afro-Asian Artists in Post-war Britain*, exhib. cat., Hayward Gallery, London, 1989.

26 **Franco Belgiorno-Nettis**, "Chairman's Preface," in: *From the Southern Cross: A View of World Art c. 1940–1988*," exhib. cat., 1988 Australian Biennale, Biennale of Sydney, 1988, p. 7.

27 **Nick Waterlow**, "A View of World Art c. 1940 – 88," in: *From the Southern Cross: A View of World Art c. 1940–1988*," exhib. cat., 1988 Australian Biennale, Biennale of Sydney, 1988, p. 9, italics added.

4.

The global conditions of today's art production, to come to my final section, leaves art history with unexpected questions. Can art history become global at all? Who writes art history in the future, and does it need to be art history in the common sense and with a common concept not only of art but also of history? It was not a coincidence that the 2008 Congress of the International Committee of the History of Art (CIHA), which took place in Melbourne, Australia, did not by chance address these questions with such vigor. And because this was so, it changed the history of art history forever. Its title *Crossing Cultures*, understood as a move in every direction, indicated a shift of perspective that gave up the idea of a privileged viewing point and also the notion of cultures not already penetrated by other cultures. Understandably enough, though, there was still ambiguities in terminology as there were many participants. Conference sections with titles such as "Perspectives on Global Art History" and "The Idea of World Art History" raised the question whether the two notions mean the same at all.[28] If we are willing to use definition as *distinction*, rather than as *affirmation*, then the different history of the two terms cannot be overlooked. After the arrival of *global art*, also *world art* must be newly defined and, ultimately liberated from its colonial baggage.

The same CIHA congress had a section on *global art*, but labeled the latter as contemporary art in a new sense. "Writing the history of contemporary art,"[29] to quote the title of Terry Smith's essay, is a paradox for an art which, in many ways, comes after history and even turns against history. Alexander Alberro, in the same section, concluded that periodizing contemporary art is "subject to a battlefield of narratives and stories."[30] This conclusion is almost inevitable, since contemporary art is site specific and looks very different when we pass from one local perspective to another. The only consensus was that the term contemporary art no longer merely designates the most recent art, but distinguishes this art from modern art. The term *postmodern*,

28 **See: Jaynie Anderson (ed.)**, *Crossing Cultures: Conflict, Migration and Convergence. The Proceedings of the 32nd International Congress in the History of Art*, The Miegunyah Press, Carlton (Victoria), 2009.

29 **Alexander Alberro**, "Periodising Contemporary Art," in: ibid., p. 938

30 **Terry Smith**, "Writing the History of Contemporary Art," in: ibid., p. 918.

however, is not available, as it stood for something inside modernism. Terms like "multiple" or "alternative modernities" are only serviceable to those who want to reclaim a neglected or forgotten modernity of their own.[31] *Global art* is not only polycentric as a practice, but also demands a polyphonic discourse. Art history has divided the world, whereas the global age tends to restore its unity on another level. Not only is the game different: it is also open to new participants who speak in many tongues and who differ in how they conceive of art in a local perspective. We are watching a new mapping of art worlds in the plural (see: this volume, pp. 246-254), which claim geographic and cultural difference.

Art history, as I have insisted myself on various occasions, suddenly appears to have been a rather local game that worked best for art from the Renaissance onwards. I have called it a *post-Vasarian* narrative that does not even adequately describe medieval art and its religious images.[32] To speak of *Art History after Modernism*, as I did in the title of a book[33] which continues the arguments of *The End of Art History* with reference to the exodus of contemporary art from art history, means art history faces a new challenge after the end of modernism. *Global art* not only accelerates contemporary art's departure from the guidelines of a linear art history, it also flourishes in parts of the world where art history has never been practiced or where it only followed colonial models. The loss of a central place of art history in art theory and art display may also explain the new role of curatorial studies or visual studies that have replaced art history in the curriculum of art academies such as the Goldsmith College in London. The majority of today's art curators is trained in political, social, or cultural sciences rather than in art history, and thus tend to emphasize art's political or cultural agenda as against aesthetics.

However, we need not speak of art history's crisis unless we are thinking of a necessary crisis. The time has come to rewrite art history in the West as well in order to respond to a new audience that looks at Western art with other premises. I therefore do not share a current trend in US American art history that excludes the rest of the world either by writing "World Art History" on a universal scale and thus restoring an old privilege of the West[34] or by denying that art history can ever work outside the West.[35] Rather, I feel the need to encourage other, new narratives with a local perspective of art history that abandons obedience to the colonial gaze of former *world art* studies. *World art*, in the old sense, tended to support the mainstream art discourse via exclusion. Today, we need a new paradigm and a postcolonial discourse for *world art studies* that are based on comparative studies which are on equal footing. For example, we take for granted the study of Chinese language and history at Western institutions but shut our eyes to the news that the National University of Beijing has opened a Department of Western Classics (Greco-Roman) and supports a bilateral conference with Durham University. In short, world art history is only justified as a cross-cultural project that also admits looking at Western culture and art history from the outside. This is the challenge of the global age, in which we have to recover our narratives with new eyes.

Yet Western art history also faces a problem on its own territory. This is the noncontinuity of the story that connects premodern, modern, and current art. The linear story in the genealogy of modern art which Alfred H. Barr, Jr. devised for the MoMA in the 1930s, no longer continues to represent art since the 1960s even in the West, as an unsuccessful attempt to prolong this genealogy demonstrated at the Tate Modern in London.[36] And the methods of art history fail to explain the transition from the *artwork*, with its given place in history and its survival in a collection, to *art projects* that are ephemeral and badly documented, to give just one example from changing art practice. I am not complaining about this turn of events, but I do wonder whether art history needs to look back and discover its own past with fresh eyes. It appears that we have reached a watershed where the West is encountering the same situation as other cultures. Entry into the global age where art production has become general not only marks a beginning but also an end, the end of the old world map of art with its center and periphery scheme.

At the same time, when art production becomes a global condition, the diversity of visual cultures or art histories that appear behind today's art practice and art theories is something we all have in common. In other words, what at first sight looks like the new homogeneity of a "flat" world, a second glance reveals as a diversity of traditions that demand a similar diversity of local narratives, including that of Western art history. I ventured forth in this direction when, in a recent book, I tried to show that the invention of perspective in Florence in the end turns out to have been a local game and, furthermore, that it responded to an Arab

31 **See: Araeen's Magazine** *Third Text*; and books like Dilip Parameshwar Gaonkar (ed.), *Alternative Modernities*, Duke University Press, Durham (NC), 2001.

32 **Hans Belting**, *Likeness and Presence: A History of the Image Before the Era of Art*, The University of Chicago Press, Chicago (IL), 1994.

33 **Hans Belting**, *Art History after Modernism*, The University of Chicago Press, Chicago (IL), 2002.

34 **For critical reflections** on the problems implicated see: David Carrier, *A World Art History and its Objects*, Penn State University Press, University Park (PA), 2008.

35 **James Elkins (ed.)**, *Is Art History Global?*, Routledge, London et al., 2007.

36 **Belting**, 2009, p. 46.

theory of optical perception (called "perspective" in the Latin translation), that, however, represented a different visual culture. It needs a cross-cultural investigation to look at Western art in the new expanded space from the outside.[37]

Today art history faces a challenge of a different kind. The rise of new *art worlds* in many parts of the world demand a narrative that also takes into account the growing role of economics and the politics of art in describing art. The documentary part of the exhibition *The Global Contemporary* in 2011/2012, therefore, turned to descriptions that, in contradistinction to the paradigm of self-referential art history (art as a system apart), emphasized the need for geopolitical and institutional aspects beyond issues of style, innovation, and progress (see: this volume, pp. 50–59). It was the documentation's aim to create a space for different and even competing *histories* instead of a single art history. Art's complicity with contemporaneous social, religious, and cultural worlds was surely always given, but its complicity goes further since art today "has more to do with clarifying cultural identity than with aesthetic feeling," as Thomas McEvilley wrote in 1995.[38] Art is not only produced "in an atmosphere of global dialog," as he added, but serves the competition of conflicting politics of representation. The emergence of art spaces, which share the name but not the function of what we called a museum, is part of the game, as also is the spread of art markets to Asia. This new state of things, in retrospect, sharpens the view of what art has been in the past and demands the interaction of different art histories. In other words, the present world leaves most of us in a similar situation in the face of an unwritten history of *world art* as a joint enterprise.

Translated from the German by Elizabeth Volk.

37 **Hans Belting**, *Florence and Bagdad: Renaissance Art and Arab Science*, Harvard University Press, Cambridge (MA), 2011.

38 **Thomas McEvilley**, "Here comes everybody," in: *Africus: Johannesburg Biennale*, exhib. cat., Transnational Metropolitan Council, 1995, p. 57.

Contemporary Art: World Currents in Transition Beyond Globalization

Terry Smith

There is no doubt that contemporary artistic practice has been shaped above all by the forces of globalization that, from the 1980s until recently, predominated within international economic exchange, drove much of world politics, and disseminated spectacle as the theater of individual and collective imagination in the lives of people all over the world. Globalized perceptions of contemporary art have been heavily promoted by major museums in search of competitive edge as centers of attraction within spectacle culture. They are used by the international art market to push up prices of what became, around 2000, its most glamorous, risky, and, in principle, infinitely self-replenishing, sector. Contemporary art features prominently in the lifestyle agendas of the recently rich, prevails in popular media, and is used to anchor massive revitalization efforts or new real estate projects by cities and nations competing for tourist dollars. Acknowledging the broad outlines of these obvious connections between art and social change, a number of art critics, historians, curators, and theorists, along with certain students of visual culture, have pursued an interesting set of more specific questions.

Was the globalization of the art system prefigured in the internationalization of art during the 1960s? If so, was it expressed in aspects of the styles emergent at that time - Pop, Minimal, Conceptual, Process, Land art, etc. - or were these styles mainly manifestations of Cold War configurations? Did globalized art values spread from the modern cultural centers along with the inroads of multinational capital, intergovernmental agencies, and new technologies? Or did the globalization of contemporary art take hold in art producing centers around the world in ways distinctive to each of them? In considering these questions, should we include within the overall conception of "globalization" actions and attitudes such as antiglobalist resistance, defiant localism, critical cosmopolitanism, and evasive tangentiality? Should we see such reactions as in dialectical opposition to top-down globalization, as in continuity with previous countercurrents, or as emergent modes of living? Scholars of contemporary history wonder whether these developments can be periodized. For example, it is arguable that, in contrast to reaction to the events of 1989, the idea that globalization was the inevitable, hegemonic version of late capitalism, and therefore destined for world domination, came to seem less plausible during the fallout from 9/11. Since then, a number of unanticipated world-scale changes, notably the increasing disjunction between the leading economies - each with different models of economic organization, all prioritizing national objectives, and none seeking to universalize their model - has broken the hegemonic grip of globalization as a world phenomenon. In 2008 it seemed shaky indeed. Do we need other ideas to guide our thinking on these world-picturing levels? Perhaps we can no longer so conveniently substitute "globalization" for "modernity" and/or "postmodernity" when it comes to naming the overarching framework of present and future possibility?

The GAM - *Global Art and the Museum* project, led by the editors of this volume, has pursued these questions more thoroughly, and on a wider geographic scale, than most others. Among GAM's important precedents is the critical reaction to the Young British Artist phenomenon on the part of a few commentators who, rather than swallow the hype, placed these artists within a larger picture of contemporary art in the service of neoliberal capitalism and globalization: for example, the writings of John A. Walker, Julian Stallabrass, Peter Osborne, and Jonathan Harris.[1] In the US, by contrast, the contemporary art history academy and much of the art press has been, with few exceptions, complicit or quiescent in its response. Against such passivity, the aggressive public campaign against corporate art waged during the 1980s and up to his recent death by art critic Robert Hughes deserves our praise for its moral vigor if not for all of the terms in which it was put.[2] While I support strongly each of these enterprises, and regard them as the best accounts of the art of our times, it has become clear in recent years that certain assumptions underlying them no longer fully address the complexity of the most current situation.

Is it still the case that globalization remains the prevalent phase in the "natural" evolution of world economic order? In his 2012 essay "Making Modernity Work: The Reconciliation of Capitalism and Democracy," Gideon Rose, editor of the influential journal *Foreign Affairs*, pours scorn on those who would harbor such doubts: "The major battles about how to structure modern politics and economics were fought in the first half of the last century, and they ended with the emergence of the most successful system the world has ever seen [...] the postwar order of mutually supporting liberal democracies with mixed economies."[3] I have already hinted that this view, a version of what was called "the Washington consensus," is shaky, and will say more about it later. The second doubtful assumption is that, despite its vacuity and banality, one kind of art, the most globalized kind, just is the dominant form of contemporary art, and that the institutions sustaining it (especially the neoliberal markets and museums modeled on those in the West) will keep it that way. The authors cited in the preceding paragraph would agree that these are appalling presumptions. The problem is that, while many of these critics do favor instances of the really quite substantial amount of art being made today that does *not* fall subject to top-down globalization, none of them offers an alternative account of the structures that are in play. Negative description is not enough. We need an account that locates the forces of globalization as one set among others, and that identifies the relative strengths of each of the contending forces during recent decades and through the present.

From Modern to Contemporary Art

Let me outline such an account by offering a summary of the key ideas underlying my work on late modern and contemporary visual art.[4] These ideas take form as linked propositions about how contemporary art is made within, and how it contributes toward the making of, contemporary being-in-the-world. The propositions are, in turn, art historical, art critical, and ontological. Because my main purpose is to accurately describe, and to explicitly intervene within, the changing connectivities between world-picturing and placemaking in contemporary art and life, I will also have something to say about geopolitics, cultural formation, and aesthetics today.

The core *art historical* idea is the claim that a worldwide shift from modern to contemporary art was prefigured in the major movements in late modern art of the 1950s and 1960s in Euroamerica, and became explicit in artworld discourse there during the 1970s and 1980s. Postmodernist practice was an important signal of this change, postmodern and poststructuralist theory its first analysis. A market phenomenon in the major centers during the 1990s, contemporary art was at the same time expanded, but also divided, by art emergent from the rest of the world. Since then, contemporary art everywhere has engaged more and more with spectacle culture - with image-saturated commerce, globalized lifestyle, and social media - and with anxieties caused by political volatility and climate change. These developments flow through the present, thus shaping art's imaginable futures - in the short term at least.

Unlike the great art styles of the nineteenth and twentieth centuries, these changes from modern to contemporary art were not a monopolizing phenomenon that spread outwards from a predominant center. Rather, they occurred at different times and in distinctive ways in each cultural region and in each art-producing locality. I believe that the histories specific to each place should be acknowledged, valued, and carefully tracked alongside recognition of their

1 **Key texts** by these authors include: Rita Hatton and John Albert, *Supercollector: A Critique of Charles Saatchi*, Ellipsis, London, 2000; Julian Stallabrass, *Art Incorporated: The Story of Contemporary Art*, Oxford University Press, Oxford et al., 2004; and Jonathan Harris (ed.), *Globalization and Contemporary Art*, Wiley-Blackwell, London, 2011.

2 **See: Robert Hughes**, *Nothing If Not Critical: Selected Essays on Art and Artists*, Knopf, New York (NY), 1990.

3 **Gideon Rose**, "Making Modernity Work: The Reconciliation of Capitalism and Democracy," in: Gideon Rose and Jonathan Tepperman (eds.), *The Clash of Ideas: The Ideological Battles that Made the Modern World - And Will Shape the Future*, Foreign Affairs, New York (NY), 2012, p. 2.

4 **See: Terry Smith**, *What Is Contemporary Art?*, The University of Chicago Press, Chicago (IL), 2009; Terry Smith, *Contemporary Art: World Currents*, Laurence King, London, 2011.
Art historians interested in historiography and methodology might like to consult Terry Smith, "The State of Art History: Contemporary Art," in: *Art Bulletin*, vol. XCII, no. 4, December 2010, pp. 366-383.

interaction with other local and regional tendencies, and with the waxing and waning of more powerful regional and international art-producing centers. Applied retrospectively, under the banner of "alternative modernities," this approach has led to enriched histories of art throughout the world during the modern period.[5] Complexity within modernity itself laid the groundwork for the diversity that we now see flowing through the present.

Yet this diversity is not, as some claim, best understood as a "global art," a "world art," or a "geoaesthetics."[6] Certainly, each of these terms spotlights a key aspect of contemporary art. Nevertheless, however loosely defined or critically intended, each of them echoes the metropolitanprovincial models that held during the age of imperialisms and would-be empires, but are now fast becoming outdated. Worse, these terms mistakenly suggest an overarching coherence, an inclination toward hegemony that, while present within parts of them, is, I argue, residual within the whole ensemble. Rather, what is most striking now is the contemporaneousness of different kinds of contemporary art, each of which, if it has an "aesthetic," has its own, internally diversified one. From the multiscalar perspective of worlds-within-the-world, we can see that each is, at the same time but in distinctive ways and to specific degrees, local, regional, *and* international - that is to say, *worldy* - in character.[7] If, to this multiscalar layering of worlds, we add the intensified experience of the adjacency of difference now shared by peoples everywhere, and everyone's increased awareness of cotemporality, we come close to picturing the key elements of the *ontological* idea about contemporary being-in-the-world that is also at the core of my recent thinking. Together, these characteristics constitute our *contemporaneity* - a term that, for me, unlocks the present constellation more usefully than conceptions dependent upon ideas of modernity and postmodernity.[8]

5 **See**, for example: Kobena Mercer (ed.), *Cosmopolitan Modernisms*, Institute of International Visual Art, London and The MIT Press, Cambridge (MA), 2005.

6 **See**, for example: Charlotte Bydler, *Global Artworld Inc.: On the Globalization of Contemporary Art*, Uppsala University Library, Uppsala, 2004; Peter Weibel and Andrea Buddensieg (eds.), *Contemporary Art and the Museum. A Global Perspective*, Hatje Cantz, Ostfildern, 2007; Hans Belting and Andrea Buddensieg (eds.), *The Global Art World: Audiences, Markets and Museums*, Hatje Cantz, Ostfildern, 2009; Kitty Zijlmans and Wilfried van Damme (eds.), *World Art Studies: Exploring Concepts and Approaches*, Valiz, Amsterdam, 2008; as well as Amy J. Elias and Christian Moraru (eds.), *The Planetary Turn: Art, Dialogue and Geoaesthetics in the 21st Century*, Northwestern University Press, Evanston (IL), forthcoming 2013.

7 **Discussed** in more detail in: Terry Smith, "Currents of World-Making in Contemporary Art," in: *World Art*, vol. 1, no. 2, 2011, pp. 20-36. Valuable essays by Ian McLean and Marsha Meskimmon may also be found in this issue.

8 **On "contemporaneity"** as a world-picturing term, see: Terry Smith, Okwui Enwezor, and Nancy Condee (eds.), *Antinomies of Art and Culture: Modernity, Postmodernity, Contemporaneity*, Duke University Press, Durham (NC), 2008.

Contemporaneous Currents

What, then, are the different kinds of art that coexist in contemporary conditions? As a core *art critical* idea, I argue that three strong currents may be discerned within the extraordinary quantity and seemingly limitless diversity of art made since around 1989. *Remodernist, retro-sensationalist,* and *spectacularist* tendencies fuse into one current, which continues to predominate in Euroamerican and other modernizing art worlds and markets, with widespread effect both inside and outside those constituencies. Against these, art created according to nationalist, identarian, and critical priorities has emerged, especially from previously colonized cultures. It came into prominence on international circuits such as biennials and traveling temporary exhibitions: this is the art of *transnational transitionality*. For many of the artists, curators, and commentators involved, it has evolved through at least three discernable phases: a reactive, anti-imperialist search for national and localist imagery; then a rejection of simplistic identarianism and corrupted nationalism in favor of a naïve internationalism; followed by a broader search for an integrated cosmopolitanism, or worldliness, in the context of the permanent transition of all things and relations.[9] The third current cannot be named as a style, a period, or a tendency. It proliferates below the radar of generalization. It results from the great increase in the number of artists worldwide and the opportunities offered by new informational and communicative technologies to millions of users. These changes have led to the viral spread of small-scale, interactive, DIY art (and art-like output) that is concerned less with high art style or confrontational politics and more with tentative explorations of temporality, place, affiliation, and affect - the ever-more-uncertain conditions of living within contemporaneity on a fragile planet.

Each of the three currents disseminates itself (not entirely, but predominantly) through appropriate - indeed, matching - institutional formats. Remodernism, retro-sensationalist, and spectacularist art are usually found in major public or dedicated private museums, prominent commercial galleries, the auction rooms of the "great houses," and the celebrity collections, largely in or near the centers of economic power that drove modernity. Biennials, along with traveling exhibitions promoting the art of a country or region, have been an ideal venue for postcolonial critique. These have led

9 **The impact** of this current on the world as a whole has turned it into what Okwui Enwezor names "The Postcolonial Constellation," see: ibid., pp. 207-234.

to the emergence of a string of new, area-specific markets. The widespread art of contemporaneity appears rarely in such venues - although some of it doubtless will, as the institutions adapt for survival and certain artists make their accommodations - preferring alternative spaces, public temporary displays, the Net, zines and other do-it-yourself-with-friends networks. There is, of course, no exclusive matching of tendency and disseminative format. Just as crossovers between what I am discerning here as currents are frequent at the level of art practice, connections between the formats abound, and artists have come to use them as gateways, more or less according to their potential and convenience. The museum, many artists will say today, is just one event-site among the many that are now possible. But this mobility across institutional and quasi-institutional sites is recent, and has been hard won. While convergence certainly occurs, temporary alliance - the confluence of differences - is more common. In these conditions - where a multiplicity of languages coexists in close proximity - *translation* becomes the medium of necessity, of possibility, and of hope.

While these currents are contemporaneous now, how might we imagine them changing, in themselves, in relation to each other, in response to as yet unpredictable new currents and even less predictable changes to the whole flow of art in the world? The first of the currents I have discerned is dominant now, but is historically residual and may eventually fade; the second took shape due to local necessities but was also, everywhere, a reaction to the dominance of Euroamerican art. It has recently come to prominence and will prevail for some time. There is a dialectical antagonism in operation between these two currents, because both are products of modernity's inner historical logic, itself dialectical. But the third current is emergent and will increasingly set the terms of what will count in the future: these terms may be different in kind from those first formed during modern times.

The Planet to Override the Global

My argument about the currents within contemporary art can stand without dependence on the more general idea of contemporaneity, but genuinely historical hypotheses must encompass both the general and the particular. The emergent-dominant-residual paradigm that I just invoked is of course that of Raymond Williams: his 1970s, New Left revision of the relationships between the base and the superstructure in Marxist cultural theory.[10] Despite its recognition of volatility, this paradigm implies a continuation of the dialectical unfolding of human history, as a process of continuous resolution of oppositions. But there is, I believe, a larger, deeper, and more unsettling challenge facing us today. Big scale world pictures, and global forces and historical transformations, seem not only competitive but also incommensurable - indeed, they seem dangerous to the point of threatening historical extinction. This is how many in the West view terrorism from the Rest - a fear parodied by the Russian group ASE+F in their *Witness of the Future* series of postcards. More disturbing is the dawning realization that the evolution of the planet and the trajectory of human development may have diverged, fatally. As these larger trajectories contend and implode, the dark energy in dark matter comes to light. We see it everywhere today. Contemporaneity of difference, it seems, may be all that is left to us.

Introducing the essays that constitute his book *The Seeds of Time*, based on his Wellek Lectures given at the University of California, Irvine, in 1991, Fredric Jameson observed that:

> "[e]ven after the 'end of history,' there has seemed to persist some historical curiosity of a generally systemic - rather than merely anecdotal - kind: not merely to know what will happen next, but as a more general anxiety about the larger fate or destiny of our mode of production as such - about which individual experience (of a postmodern kind) tells us that it must be eternal, while our intelligence suggests this feeling to be most improbable indeed, without coming up with a plausible scenario as to its disintegration or replacement. It seems to be easier for us today to imagine the thoroughgoing deterioration of the Earth and of nature than the breakdown of late capitalism; perhaps this is due to some weakness in our imaginations." He goes on immediately to say: "I have come to think that the word *postmodern* ought to be reserved for thoughts of this kind."[11]

In 1991 Jameson's diagnosis of the sickness in the world picture was acute, and the concept of postmodernity as he deployed it was the most accurate analysis. I have come to think, however, that *now* - as the condition that Jameson diagnosed so well has become exacerbated beyond what even he might have predicted - the concept of contemporaneity offers us the best key to unlock an analytic toolkit

10 **See: Raymond Williams**, "Base and Superstructure in Marxist Cultural Theory," in: *New Left Review*, vol. 1, no. 8, November/December 1973, pp. 3-16; reprinted in: John Higgins (ed.), *The Raymond Williams Reader*, Blackwell, Oxford, 2001, pp. 158-178.

11 **Fredric Jameson**, *The Seeds of Time*, Columbia University Press, New York (NY), 2004, pp. xi-xii.

adequate to understanding our contemporary condition. It does not encompass all of this condition, yet is essential to unpacking its daunting complexity. We must to be able to imagine the deterioration of the Earth *and* the breakdown of late capitalism, along with many other world-shaping trajectories, less as constituting one, essentially conflicted but ultimately unified "mode of production," rather as unfolding through time contemporaneously, as a set of antinomies rather than eventually (or at least potentially) resolvable contradictions, these elements being in relationships of contingency rather than of necessary determination, and thus as generative of the paradoxes of the present - for example, the current coexistence of world capitalism and the Earth in a state of crisis, with the resultant paradox that a future containing both of them in a permanent state of crisis is all that most commentators seem able to imagine.

Is it possible to move our thinking about the contemporaneity of difference towards a framework that will encompass positive action in the face of impending disaster? In her *Death of a Discipline*, Gayatri Chakravorty Spivak urged students of writing to "cross borders under the auspices of a Comparative Literature supplemented by Area Studies"[12] by imagining themselves as "planetary rather than continental, global, or worldy." More explicitly, she stated:

> "I propose the planet to override the globe. Globalization is the imposition of the same system of exchange everywhere. In the gridwork of electronic capital, we achieve that abstract ball covered with latitudes and longitudes, cut by virtual lines, once the equator and the tropics and so on, now drawn by the requirements of Geographical Information Systems. To talk planet-talk by way of an unexamined environmentalism, referring to an undivided 'natural' space rather than a differentiated political space, can work in the interests of this globalization in the mode of the abstract as such [...] The globe is on our computers. No one lives there. It allows us to think that we can aim to control it. The planet is in the species of alterity, belonging to another system; and yet we inhabit it, on loan. It is not really amenable to a neat contrast with the globe. I cannot say 'the planet, on the other hand.' When I invoke the planet, I think of the effort required to figure the (im)possibility of this underived intuition."

There is much to be done to invest with substance Spivak's proposal that "the planet should override the globe" in our imaginative world-picturing. To that end, let us now shift gears up through the scale of the psychic, social, economic, and political worlds-within-the-world that - layered together and framed by the Earth within the universe - constitute our planetary sphere. The currents in the visual and other arts, I have been arguing, are manifestations of the great changes that have occurred since the mid-twentieth century in the distribution of power within and between these levels. On the political and economic levels, it is now a commonplace to observe that, while the era of the European and North American colonizers seems to be in decline, their enormous influence persists, and is taking new forms. Some, in the years after 1989, believed that the United States stood alone as the world's "last remaining superpower," as the only "hyperpower." However, its failures in international policy and national governance during the years since 2001 are clear evidence that no nation retains the kind or extent of geopolitical influence once wielded by the advanced countries of the modern period. The economic rise of China, India, Brazil, and others is everywhere acknowledged, but it remains to be seen whether their efforts at global and regional influence will be of the same kind.[13]

In the twenty-first century, nation-states no longer align themselves according to the four-tier system of First, Second, Third, and Fourth Worlds. Multinational corporations based in the Euroamerican centers no longer control the world's economy, just significant parts of it. New global corporations are located in South, East, and North Asia. Manufacturing, distribution, and services are themselves dispersed around the globe, and linked to delivery points by new technologies and old-fashioned labor. Some would argue that, with globalization, or, more broadly, within "the postwar order of mutually supporting liberal democracies with mixed economies," capitalism has achieved its pure form. Certainly, the living standard of millions has been lifted, but only at enormous cost to social cohesion, peaceful cohabitation, and natural resources. National and local governments, as well as many international agencies, seek to regulate this flow and assuage its worst side effects - so far without conspicuous success. The institutions that drove modernity seem, to date, incapable of dealing with the most important unexpected outcome of their efforts: the massive disruptions to natural ecosystems that now seem to threaten the survival of the Earth itself. Despite the

12 **Gayatri Chakravorty Spivak**, *Death of a Discipline*, Columbia University Press, New York (NY), 2003, p. 72. Also for the following quotes.

13 **The editor of** *Foreign Affairs* is in no doubt about the way things are going: "The much-ballyhooed 'rise of the rest' has involved not the discrediting of the postwar order of Western political economy but its reinforcement: the countries that have risen have done so by embracing global capitalism while keeping some of its destabilizing attributes in check, and have liberalized their polities and societies along the way (and will founder unless they continue to do so)." Gideon Rose, "Making Modernity Work: The Reconciliation of Capitalism and Democracy," p. 6.

efforts of vested interests to foreclose debate on these issues (notably the campaigns against climate change science), consciousness of our inescapably shared, mutually dependent existence on this fragile planet is growing.

Many artists working today imagine the physical conjunction of a number of different kinds of worlds: the intimate, personal sense of "my world"; the close neighborhood of the local; nearby worlds, then increasingly distant beyonds, until a sense of the world in general is reached. In between these, and traversing them, are transitory spaces, "no-places," passages of physical trafficking and virtual interconnection. This multiscalar picture also evokes both the geophysical adjacency of these worlds and their cultural cotemporality. It recognizes the differential rates of their movement through actual time, and the mobility of those whose lives weave between and through them. When it comes to individual and collective experience, antinomial friction is the most striking feature of relationships between people and their worlds, however persistent everydayness might be. Within contemporary experience, one also sees gestures of connection, of reconciliation, and of coexistence. Both friction and connection are essential components of the (im)possible figure of planetarity. To imagine this figure is the task that the present requires from artists of all kinds; indeed, from all workers in the realms of the imagination.

Curating Contemporaneous Worlds

The great, historic task of the biennial exhibition - to survey the art being made around the world today, and to position local art in relation to it - is retreating as its main goal. Instead, many large-scale exhibitions attempt to show crucial aspects of contemporary art's contemporaneity - that is, it's being-in-the-world, *this* world, as it is now, and as it might be.

To date, no single exhibition has attempted to exhibit the three currents that, in their differentiation and connectedness, constitute contemporary art's ways of world being - perhaps because this would be akin to mapping the world with a map that would be indistinguishable from the world itself. Some exhibitions, including *The Global Contemporary* and Documenta 13, offer carefully considered proposals about art's contemporaneity, that is, its current world situatedness. They explicitly question terms such as "global art," or "world art," in favor of art that is, in some strong sense, "worldy." To show such art, and at the same time show the worlds in which it is being made, has become *the* challenge facing ambitious exhibition-makers today. Certainly, it is the goal of those who would make an exhibition that aspires beyond local significance.

Everyone embarking on projects of this kind is acutely aware of controversial precedents, such as *"Primitivism" in 20th Century Art: Affinities of the Tribal and Modern* (1984), *Magiciens de la terre* (1989) and Documenta 11 (2002). Just as important has been the groundwork laid in exhibitions that have, since 1989, profiled the major changes in art in different parts of the world. These include (to name just one of a number from each continent, with a preference for an exhibition that traveled) *Cities on the Move: Contemporary Asian Art at the Turn of the 21st Century* (1997-1998), *After the Wall: Art and Culture in Post-Communist Europe* (1999), *Inverted Utopias: Avant-Garde Art in Latin America* (2004), and *Africa Remix: Contemporary Art of a Continent* (2005 and 2008). Each of these, along with many others, has asked: what is distinctive about the contemporary art of our region, how does it derive from, break away from, or stand at an angle to, art made during our modernity, and how does it relate to "international" (Western, then transnational) contemporary art? These are art critical, and then art historical, questions, to which these exhibitions give curatorial answers.[14]

The curators of *The Global Contemporary* insisted to highlight the importance of a global practice that has changed contemporary art radically. This is a powerful generalization about contemporary art. A number of contemporary artists explicitly state that achieving such a practice is their goal, and many, such as the Raqs Media Collective, are among its most articulate theorists.[15] Some have posed it as a generality, for example, Indian cultural theorist and curator Nancy Adajania draws on Enwezor's identification of a widespread "will to globality" on the part of peoples everywhere to characterize "globalism" as "the foundational premise" of her practice, one that is "not merely a reaction to globalisation, but as the audacious and positive reflection of a desire to release the cultural self towards others in a manner that bypasses dependency and embraces collaboration, thus making for a productive cosmopolitanism."[16]

The claim that the art exhibited at Karlsruhe demonstrates the emergence of a global practice that has changed

---

14 **I devoted** a chapter of *Thinking Contemporary Curating* to a survey of exhibitions that have tackled these questions, including the remarkable number that have tracked feminist contributions during the past four or five decades. See: Terry Smith, *Thinking Contemporary Curating*, Independent Curators International, New York (NY), 2012.

15 **See the link** "print" available online at: http://www.raqsmediacollective.net/print.aspx. For example, the January 2012 discussion, "Has the Moment of the Contemporary Come and Gone?"; accessed 11/19/2012.

16 **Nancy Adajania**, "Time to Restage the World: Theorising a New and Complicated Sense of Solidarity," in: Miranda Wallace (ed.), *21st Century: Art in the First Decade*, Queensland Art Gallery/Gallery of Modern Art, Brisbane, 2010, pp. 222-229.
For the internal quotation, see: Okwui Enwezor, "The Black Box," in: *Documenta 11: Platform 5*, exhib. cat., Hatje Cantz, Ostfildern, 2002, p. 42.

contemporary art radically is a curatorial, a critical, and a historical idea as important as any that have been proposed in the past two decades. It is identical to that I make about what I call the transnational transition: that, in the many art-producing centers in the rest of the world outside Euroamerica, a variety of local negotiations between indigeneity, tradition, modernity, and globalization led, first, to the forging of distinct kinds of modern art, and then, in artistic exchanges within nearby regions and with distant centers, the emergence of specific kinds of contemporary art. These developments have been underway since the 1950s in Africa, the 1960s in Latin America, the 1970s in the Central Desert of Australia, the 1980s in Central Europe and China, the 1990s in Southeast Asia, the 2000s in India and the Middle East, etc.[17] Taken together (their separate origins connecting into a world current) they amount to a substantial reorientation of the way art is made in the world: they claim value for the making visible of local issues and they have become an important way in which both local and global inequities are renegotiated toward respect for difference. In doing both, they are artists' contributions toward the coming-into-being of what has been called a "new internationalism" or a "cosmopolitan aesthetic."[18]

In more general terms, we can see that in recent years many survey, biennial, and mega-exhibitions have demonstrated that the second current is a major force in the world's art. Of course, there are many challenges facing artists and curators who are active in this current, not least is the seduction of easy exoticism, the invitation to fall for aesthetic tourism of the Other, or to simplify the local specificity of work - in other words, to become the stereotype that uncritical audiences in the West instinctively desire. Yet these exhibitions have helped us see the shape of its flow through the regions that they treated and in some of the nations that constitute each region. They alert us to the connections between regions and those that reach across to what were once the colonial centers. In some cases, these old centers remain important forums through which art must pass to have international purport. Yet new ones constantly emerge, driven first by art, with markets following on behind. (If the reverse occurs, as is happening in the Middle East at the moment, the market soon retreats.) Among the next steps to be taken by historians and curators is the researching, staging, and circulation of retrospectives of major artists from the decolonizing regions who have made breakthroughs of world-picturing relevance. For example, Emily Kame Kngwarrye and El Anatsui.[19]

Some remarks in conclusion. I have described what I believe to be the actual situation of contemporary art within contemporary conditions. I am not advocating this state as desirable or ideal - far from it. I believe that we must move from the present situation, in which a crisis contemporaneity of conflicted and mutually destructive incommensurabilities is the norm, to a state in which the planet and everyone and everything on it can imagine a constructive mutuality based on an inspired sharing of our differences. "Contemporaneity" and "planetarity" are the words I have come to think should be reserved for thoughts of this kind. They open us to the multiplicitous interactions through which we continuously make our worlds-with-the-world, a world still being globalized at the same time that it moves, quickly, beyond globalization.

17 I track them in the central chapters of *Contemporary Art: World Currents*.

18 INIVA (Institute for International Visual Arts) has argued the first since the 1990s; Marsha Meskimmon profiles the latter in her book *Contemporary Art and the Cosmopolitan Imagination*, Routledge, London, et al., 2010. See also: Nikos Papastergiadis, *Cosmopolitanism and Culture*, Polity Press, London, 2012.

19 See: *Utopia: The Genius of Emily Kame Kngwarreye*, National Art Center, Tokyo, 2008 and National Museum of Australia, Canberra, 2008; *El Anatsui: When I Last Wrote to You about Africa*, Royal Ontario Museum, Toronto, 2010. For my review of the latter, see: *Nka: Journal of African Art*, no. 28, Spring 2011, pp. 142-145. for an essay on Emily Kame Kngwarreye, see: "Kngwarreye Woman Abstract Painter," in: Jennifer Isaacs (ed.), *Emily Kame Kngwarreye*, Craftsman House, Sydney, 1998.

The Endogenous-Exogenous Interface in Globalism: The Case of China and Thailand

John Clark

Globalization in the domain of art can appear as a process of stylistic transmission and transformation. By the 1990s, however, globalization had become manifest as a series of exposures to cultural difference in which both endogenous and exogenous values were relativized. The very terms of endogenous discourse in cultural fields such as art were changed by the penetrability of the nation-state to new electronic media, access to international languages such as English, or the dispersed facility to translate from them, as well as increased motility of artists between non national cultural centers.[1]

Clearly the notion that postmodernity, and the privileging of global above local, was a step away from the modern whose teleological progress had completed. But the postmodern, according to this viewpoint, allowed the rediscovery of the modern, which now appeared as a kind of local transformation of the "premodern."

The authority of modernist narrative was no longer hegemonic: there were plural narratives with plural subjects to explicate these stories. This decomposition of authority under modernity later became part of the ideological structure of artistic modernism itself. It was a further kind of modernity in art that had become self-conscious of its own practices and values - with its simultaneity of non-contiguous times and spaces, multiple viewpoints and, for example, its increased flexibility to shift notional subjects between narrative contents, technical effects, and artistic intentions.

There could well arise "a delocalized trans-nation which retains special ideological links to a putative place of origin but is otherwise a thoroughly diasporic collectivity."[2] This may amount to saying, as did Wolfgang Welsch, that under certain conditions and for a specified group of actors - which included artists and their mediators - culture was always "transculture" and "transcultural identities comprehend a cosmopolitan side, but also a side of local affiliation. Transcultural people combine both."[3]

1 **I avoid** the alternative terms *particularistic* and *universalistic* because they are mired with ineluctable Euroamericanism. This does not mean that, from a Euroamerican view of globalism, they are without hermeneutic power. See: Roland Robertson, "Social Theory, Cultural Relativity and the Problem of Globality," and Immanuel Wallerstein, "The National and the Universal: Can There Be Such a Thing as World Culture?," in: Anthony D. King (ed.), *Culture, Globalization, and the World System: Contemporary Conditions for the Representation of Identity*, Department of Art and Art History, State University of New York at Binghamton (NY), Macmillan, Houndsmills, 1991. The conference on which these papers were based took place in 1989, serving as one indicator that the globalism debate has its origins in intellectual concerns of the mid-1980s, if not late 1970s. I see "globalism/globalization" as a discourse about the nature and extent of the continued pattern of world economic and cultural hegemony centered on the USA after the politico-military defeat in Vietnam in 1976, as much as taking place fifteen years later in 1991 after what might be called the peace of Berlin when "actually existing" communism fell.

2 **Arjun Appadurai**, *Modernity at Large: Cultural Dimensions of Globalization*, University of Minnesota Press, Minneapolis (MN), 1996, p. 172.

3 **Wolfgang Welsch**, "Transculturality: The Changing Form of Cultures Today," in: *Filozoski Vestnik*, vol. 22, no. 2, 2001, pp. 59-86. Welsch's informed studies of transculturality are linked to Wittgenstein's position that "culture is at hand wherever practices in life are shared. The basic task is not to be conceived as an understanding of foreign cultures, but as an interaction with foreignness."
See also: Wolfgang Welsch, "Rethinking Identity in the Age of Globalization: A Transcultural Perspective," in: *International Yearbook of Aesthetics*, vol. 8, 2004, pp. 167-176.

China

The double articulation of globalization has not often surfaced in debates about art. However, from the late 1990s there has been considerable debate about regional modernization against the center, and independent access to processes of globalization and their redistributive patterns from the regions of China, particularly from Sichuan. It surfaced most notably in the sometimes wild, sometimes regional, chauvinist writings of Wang Lin.[4] He complained publicly of the choices of art exhibited abroad as Western choices. He agreed with the interpretation of Chinese art of the 1990s in terms of political rebellion. For Wang Lin this was because of the contemporality of processes analyzed elsewhere as successive stages: "In the 1990s Chinese live in a cultural environment where premodernism, modernism, and postmodernism simultaneously exist."[5]

The Chinese revolution had been one solution to a problem bequeathed from the nineteenth century where the history of modern Europe appeared as the modern *per se*. However, in the 1990s the problem for Chinese art theorists was more complex than this view. They had both to recognize their debts to the revolution and at the same time grasp the pace of societal change, particularly after 1993. According to the art critic Yi Ying, "The speed of Chinese social development in the 1990s surpasses the speed of imitation of Western modern art in the 1980s."[6] The 1980s had seen artists experimenting with "Western modernist" art as a "demonstration of the ego,"[7] but this was problematic because Chinese society at that time did not provide the conditions for individual independence. It was by the late 1990s that social conditions made it possible for a person to "lead an individualized form of life, and for individualization to become a potential subject of art."[8] Thus secure establishment of a situation that allowed individuation was necessary rather than a situation necessitating a hybrid-like living between historical pasts-in-the-present. Yi Ying represented a Chinese opposition to that very hybridity and transculturality, which theorists as varied as Homi K. Bhabha and Welsch have seen as marking cosmopolitan life in the postmodernist West.

Yi Ying thought that Chinese artists had turned away from multiculturalism or Eurocentric ideas "because the methods suggested by the ideas are not compatible with the Chinese artists' life experience in Chinese society. Only in this moment can we feel the existence, or the forming, of the Chinese style of language."[9] The narrative of revolution had lost its social power, but not its moral legitimacy, so Chinese art theorists like Yi Ying in the 1990s were beginning to reinvestigate the conditions of modernity, the goal of that revolution. What was depressing in this exploration was how it tended to revert towards national closure by the subterfuge of inventing a parallel or alternative national modernity. Globalism was conceived merely as the flow of international tendencies to the national level, rather than as the transnational slippage between levels made possible by a local mediation of an already present heterogeneity.

The identity of Chinese artists during the 1990s was not articulated against multiple levels of different cultural affiliation. It was indicated by a set of endogenous problems: the still perceived clash between China and the West in the cultural field of modern art practice; the rendering irrelevant of China's past cultural values or their use merely as a subject for vulgar manipulation by mass culture; and the proper course for the dynamic of social development arising from the revolutionary past.

For many Chinese art theorists the main problem of new identity still lay in the paradox of cultural conflict between East and West, because of the very cultural multiple layering in the history of China's own modern art since the 1900s. Artists were reexamining their own tradition and searching for what was valuable in it "from its spirit and character instead of from the level of material and technique."[10]

Clearly Fan Di'an, curator and one of the directors of NAMOC (The National Art Museum of China), thought it was necessary for artists to insist on the cultural value and cultural idea of art. Characteristically, he linked this to the dynamic of social progress. Chinese life as a basis for universality legitimated work based on a particular cultural constitution (modernism at home), but it also opened up space for criticizing how Chinese the life was, how far from Chinese life the forms were, how changed the conditions for universality were as a result of more permeable cultural borders.[11] If life values were the basis of culture, when there

4 An indicative collection of essays in a small catalog, which anticipated some quasi-official exhibitions of Chinese and international art in the following five or so years, was Fan Di'an et al. (eds.), *'98 [Fuzhou] Yataidiqu Dangdai Yishu Yaoqingzhan Zuopinji*, Fuzhou, 1998 [Record of works at the *Invitation Exhibition of Contemporary Art of the Asia-Pacific Region*, Fuzhou, '98]. Texts have no pagination and translations in the catalog by Li Lin are adjusted by me. It includes the texts of Fan Di'an, who kindly gave me a copy of the catalog, and several of the writers subsequently mentioned here. Wang Lin's own writings are collected in *Dangdai Zhongguo de Meishu Zhuangtai*, Jiangsu Meishu Chubanshe, Nanjing, 1995.

5 '98 [Fuzhou] 1998, n. p.

6 Yi Ying in: '98 [Fuzhou] 1998, n. p.

7 '98 [Fuzhou] 1998, n. p.

8 Yi Ying in: '98 [Fuzhou] 1998, n. p.

9 Ibid.

10 Ibid.

11 See: Yin Jinan, *Duzi koumen: jinguan zhongguo dangdai shuliu yishu*, Sanlian Shudian, Beijing, 1993, pp. 32f; translated from the Chinese by the author.

was a presumption of a difference of forms with a cultural other, this was usually specified or implicitly understood as an undifferentiated West. Given that Chinese life had changed, should the procedure for evaluating art based in it also have changed? In other words, if there was a space of transnationality inside Chinese art, it could only exist because of a change in that space within Chinese life.

Those who have analyzed public culture in China have indicated changes in the permitted range of ideological discourse around the mid-1990s, such as the establishment of the International Society of Confucianism in 1994. One month earlier the Central Committee had issued *Guidelines for Implementing Patriotic Education*, in which Karl Marx was mentioned only once.[12]

Dai Jianhua saw other signs of this exploration of national discourse, such as the replacement in Intel advertisements of astronaut and ballerina figures by Beijing Opera characters in 1997.[13] He noticed omissions like the fact that *nouveau riches* or new urban youth hardly featured in 1990s advertisements,[14] even though it was precisely in this era that the class of new urban rich and adolescent consumers arose.

Such censorship out of other than a national discourse was not just a question of state interventions within endogenous discourses. It was also of a particular kind of endogenous-exogenous interface that resulted in the exogenous selection of artists concerned with so-called cynical pop mannerisms for the 1993 Venice Biennale. The art historian and critic Yin Shuangxi had noticed that "experimental art which made serious study of man's life and art's language was not given the attention it deserved because it lacked 'Chinese characteristics'."[15] Since 1994, in a view also shared by many international observers, no more overall art currents were to be found, and the enhancement of artistic personality in the cult of momentary celebrity had resulted in the elimination of a sense of authority and centrality from art. The foregrounding of the artist's personality as subject was perhaps an epiphenomenon of hybridization under conditions of global relation between endogenous and exogenous artistic discourses where the artist's personality itself functioned as a site of cultural mediation.

12 See: Dai Jianhua, "Behind Global Spectacle and National Image Making," in: *Positions*, vol. 9, no. 1, 2001, p. 173. Andreas Huyssen generally observes that: "Politically, many memory practices today counteract the triumphalism of modernization theory in its latest guise of 'globalization'. Culturally, they express the growing need for spatial and temporal anchoring in a world of increasing flux in ever denser networks of compressed time and space." See: Andreas Huyssen, "Present Pasts: Media, Politics, Amnesia," in: *Public Culture*, vol. 12, no. 1, 2000, p. 36.

13 See: Dai 2001, p. 168.

14 Ibid., p. 181.

15 '98 [Fuzhou], n. p.

Thailand

In the 1990s, contemporary Thai art presented a very different case from China in relation to issues of globalism, modernity/postmodernity, and identity. By the mid-1990s the Thai economy had become linked to the world economy via the use of foreign, chiefly Japanese, capital to turn Thailand into a major manufacturing base. Bangkok was a global megalopolis on a scale unlike many cities in China, and unlike most in Southeast Asia, even rich ones like Kuala Lumpur or Singapore. Thailand's art world had been linked to the world via the receptiveness of the late nineteenth-century Siamese court to chiefly European models of artistic practice and decoration. These could be transformed for local expression. Despite the absence of a historical painting tradition - there was no official academy discourse as such against which to react - it was relatively unproblematic for Thai artists to produce endogenous discourses by the 1970s, allowing for many types of modernist expression, which ranged from a kind of social realism to a vigorous expressionism.

Nineteenth-century Siam had not been colonized and the skill of the court, even after its theoretical loss of absolute power in adapting modern administration and forms of government, meant that Thailand had never suffered the cutting-off of legitimate authority which could be identified with a culture, a people, and a state. Thus Thai artists were unimpeded in accepting and devising endogenous extensions of whatever art style. The bifurcation of selves for artists, in bilingual or bicultural situations occasioned by forced overseas diaspora or a concealed endogenous rhetoric of passive resistance through internal exile, did not occur.[16]

A number of Thai artists have hardly been able to sell their artworks at home, and despite being appreciated by their students and peers, have only received major acclaim from overseas, like the late Montien Boonma. Artists of a younger generation, such as Chatchai Puipia or Kamin Lertchaiprasert, who exhibited overseas in the early and then later 1990s, received higher appraisal at home. These artists were able to circulate styles or art practices thought to be exogenous into endogenous subject matter and thereby achieve appraisal both at home and overseas. They situated their work where transfer and transformation processes overlapped in two directions: towards both the exogenous and endogenous at once.[17] If globalism allowed

16 The exception being the Marxist tendency from the 1950s underlying the *Sinlapha phua chiwit* [Art for Life] movement of the 1970s. Significantly, reconsideration of this movement has only recently begun to surface again.

17 The situation resembles the reception of the painter F. N. Souza as both a "modernist" in India and "a contemporary Indian painter" in London in the 1950s and 1960s.

for more authority and circulatory space at the global level to local narrative, this was because the exogenous metanarrative of globalism precisely required this incorporation of the endogenous.

It may be useful to look at one global Thai artist to see what globalism may indicate in the context of Thai art discourses. The son of a Thai diplomat, Rirkrit Tiravanija was born in Buenos Aires in 1961, and spent much or most of his early life outside Thailand. His 1995 curriculum vitae indicated no exhibition in Thailand before 1995.[18] Indeed, his entire art education was obtained in Canada and the USA between 1981 and 1986. His first solo exhibition was *Pad Thai* (Pad Thai is the name of a Thai noodle dish) in New York in 1990. His appearance at the Venice Biennale was in the exhibition *Aperto '93* in 1993 with curator Matthew Slotover and a food performance piece called *May Mee Kum Plakorp.* Ten years later, Tiravanija in 2003 had become a cocurator of the *Utopia Station* section of the Venice Biennale with Hans Ulrich Obrist and Molly Nesbit.

What accounts for this trajectory from cosmopolitan, overseas Thai artist to transnational biennial cocurator? It certainly cannot have been due to his prominence in Thailand, since Tiravanija did not exhibit there until his 1996 cooperation with Navin Rawanchaikul in the Chiang Mai Social Installation *Tuk-Tuk co-op.*[19] Nor can it have necessarily been due to anything Thai in his work.[20] Tiravanija's "works," processual events not physical objects, appeared to be spontaneous and perhaps haphazard but in fact depended on conceptual not formal precision.[21] These dicta indicated that Tiravanija was working a space dependent on the expectations of his audience who he then opened up to a redefinition of their relationship via an encounter with the artist's performance, or through a modularization of this in the space left by the artist for them to perform.[22] There were certain minimum conditions for interaction or participation. This could result in the temporary enculturation of the quotidian space of interaction itself, at least as a compact of communication between work, artist, and participants. Thus cultural reference or context was only a tag for the audience to latch onto in participant enaction of the performance, through references to one particular Thai culture, or to other cultural specifications, such as Western European consumer culture. There was great room for ironic deployment of *my*-cultural references, when the artists may not have felt that the *myness* was an identity to which they themselves subscribed, but which gave the participant audience a way out of their own closure in their own *my*-culture.

Tiravanija's coming to a curatorial role at Venice in 2003 must also have been because one characteristic of recent global art practice was to see the roles of artist and curator as relatively interchangeable, or at least for their boundaries to be seen as more ambiguous. Having artists serve as curators also privileged the curators to think they served in a way like an artist, or had become equal participants in the creation of an artwork with an audience aware of the new and open relationships made possible by the artwork.

Navin Rawanchaikul in a way represented this transition because he was first trained as a sculptor at Chiang Mai University under Montien Boonma in various modernist techniques. His early 1990s participation in group exhibitions in Bangkok, together with his conceptual pieces in 1994, indicated a real liking for objects in their placement. In 1995, he moved away from this towards an engagement with objects or tools, in 1996 including vehicles from everyday life in his exhibitions in a taxi, and then his *Tuk-Tuk* project for the Chiang Mai Social Installation, a cooperative that included the participation of Rirkrit Tiravanija.[23] Navin switched from an engagement with conceptualization of objects taken from everyday life, towards a rendering of interactions that blurred the difference between them. This was particularly true of the trashy, popular culture quality of the art exhibited in the *Tuk-Tuk* or the taxi,

18 **Available online at:** http://www.adaweb.com/context/artists/tiravanija/rtbio.html, accessed November 2003.

19 **According to Gridthiya Gaweewong**, "On Thai Artists and an Issue of Cultural Identity," a paper for a July 2001 conference in Brazil. Available online at: http://www.apexart.org/conference/Gaweewong.htm, accessed June 2008.

20 **Indeed**, Rirkrit Tiravanija was awarded the Smithsonian Museum's Lucelia Artist Award for "an *American* [author's emphasis] artist under the age of 50 who has produced a significant body of artwork that demonstrates exceptional creativity." See: Blake Gopnik in: *The Washington Post*, April 9, 2003. The same article noted (without a hint of irony) that "[t]his multicultural, international profile has made him a perfect fit for the globalizing, globe-trotting tendencies of today's art world." The jury, which included Cindy Sherman and Robert Storr, cited him, according to this report, for a "welcoming, generous and optimistic approach to art."

21 **See: Ami Barak**, "Conversation with Rirkrit Tiravanija," Montpellier, March, 1996, p. 2, available online at: http://web.mit.edu/allanmc/www/rirkrit.html, accessed July 2012.

22 **They resemble** Édouard Glissant's views of 1990 as summarized by Bainard Cowan in his "Introduction" to Bainard Cowan and Jefferson Humphries (eds.), *Poetics of the Americas, Race, Founding, and Textuality*, Louisiana State University Press, Baton Rouge (LA), 1997, pp. 4-5, that "The great form of action in cultures today is *Relation*, a meeting and melding that preserves difference but goes beyond it. In Relation, questions of filiation and legitimacy are superseded. The new form is rhizomatic and branching, but its particulars are unknown, and the quest for it, and with it an effective sense of destiny is part of the epic." Glissant thinks that "the self-consciousness of Western cultures passes from myth to epic to tragedy to history."

23 **Navin Rawanchaikul's** work can be found in the group catalogs *Melancholic Trance*, Visual Dhamma Gallery, Bangkok, May 23 - June 30, 1992, n. p.; and *Social Contract: New Art from Chiangmai*, Visual Dhamma Gallery, Bangkok, February 28 - March 31, 1993. For the Chao Phraya water piece, *Treated, Ozonated, and Bottled*, see: *Art Record*, vol. 1, no. 4, April 1994. Other illustrations are in the exhibition catalog by Navin Rawanchaikul and Kosit Juntaratip, *Substanceaboutnonsubstance*, Goethe-Institut, Bangkok, 1995.

including cartoon books for an ongoing series of taxi pieces in the language of the country where the taxi exhibition took place: "My intention is to entertain and draw people into a creative experience in a familiar environment about a familiar subject. [...] The gap between Thai people and art is so wide that they will never go to a gallery, so you must bring creative experiences to them in a taxi."[24]

This series of re-exhibitions in different contexts of basically the same work (Thailand, Vienna, London, Sydney, Fukuoka, New York, etc.) indicated the rapidity with which some Thai artists adjusted to the hectic pace of globalized art and the way in which its circulation between sites became both an integral component and a formal element in the work.

This meant the authority of an exogenous, fine art object narrative as within a formal discourse was challenged because there was no firm and permanently applicable set of interpretive codes by which to evaluate each instance of the work. The work was instantiated by its site. This position implied that the community of cosmopolitan or transnational artists and curators did not in itself constitute a body with authority to allocate interpretations. However, if we take a Habermasian position, the apparent opening within an endogenous site of discourses ostensibly excluded from art, did not thereby mean an opening or expansion of art discourse itself. That could only come if there had been sufficient instances of the application, the constitution of particular instances of relationality, for the artists to have served as their own curator and audience. The motility of art events, and through this the participation of previously non-art practitioners in the making of artworks, was valuable in itself.

Thai culture had already faced the issue of creating an identity between other cultural continua, particularly Chinese and Indian culture, before globalism in the 1990s. Some critics, like Gridthiya Gaweewong, even gave voice to another hybrid of being Thai: "Thai people are good in blending cultures and adapting them to our own version."[25] Many artists doing conceptual art or work events got around the problem of identity and international communicability by focusing on actions or physical states with which the participant audience could identify directly.

24 **The idea** of the taxi as an icon came to Navin Rawanchaikul in 1992 when stuck in a taxi in a traffic jam on the way to his own exhibition, which nobody attended because of the traffic. He then invented a fictional *Taximan* in 1999, a superhero who would save the world from evil Millenium Man, and had to tour the exhibition to eight cities to harness taxipower. See: Thomas Crampton, "Thai Artist Does Battle In 'Taximan'," in: *International Herald Tribune*, available online at: http://www.nytimes.com/2000/05/27/style/27iht-taxi.2.t.html, accessed July 2012.

25 **Gaweewong 2001**, p. 1.

China and Thailand Compared

Until the late 1990s there was always more foreign interest in Chinese nonofficial art than would appear to have ever been the case for radical art in Thailand. Foreign intervention in the endogenous discourse, by the direct purchase of preferred categories of work that were not in official taste, was a direct feature of the Chinese art world not found in Thailand.[26] In part this was to do with the global linkage of Chinese artists to a diaspora after the political caesura of the 1989 Tiananmen Beijing Massacre. In part it was also to do with a lack of local cultural capital prepared to support the so-called unofficial art, before enough time had elapsed and alternative structures for the art world could be organized that gave it support. The latter condition did not in large measure exist until the late 1990s when some entrepreneurs supported private art museums, and the silliness of the official art establishment's treatment of leading-edge art became clear, even to it. Besides, the information environment of Chinese art had changed radically during the 1990s, and even official and conservative Chinese artists *en mission* to various foundation-supported studios in Paris knew there was another art world beyond the official one, whose curators were in large measure more prestigious in Europe than the highly conservative mediators of the French official art world with whom they had contact.

By the early 1990s Thailand also had a quite large and functioning market for art, tied in many cases to personal relations with patrons, but nonetheless effectively larger than any foreign interest. Unlike foreign diplomats and businessmen in Beijing from the late 1980s to early 1990s, their counterparts in Bangkok did not feel constrained or morally advantaged enough to form a parallel salon of the conscientiously sympathetic. In any case, in Bangkok, the Goethe-Institut, Alliance Française, and British Council frequently held exhibitions and mediated overseas educational and exhibition opportunities to Thai artists in a way not subject to local constraint and widely accepted as legitimate cultural diplomacy. This was also part of such organizations' duties in Beijing, but often works would appear in their exhibitions that would not find official approval.

In China, the rise of a nonofficial cynical realism in the early 1990s, its international market and legitimation by exhibition at Venice in 1993, meant that this art was largely unexhibited in China until the late 1990s, and that any critical support for it could not avoid being politically tinged

26 **With the rare** overseas purchase of some work by Vasan Sitthikhet.

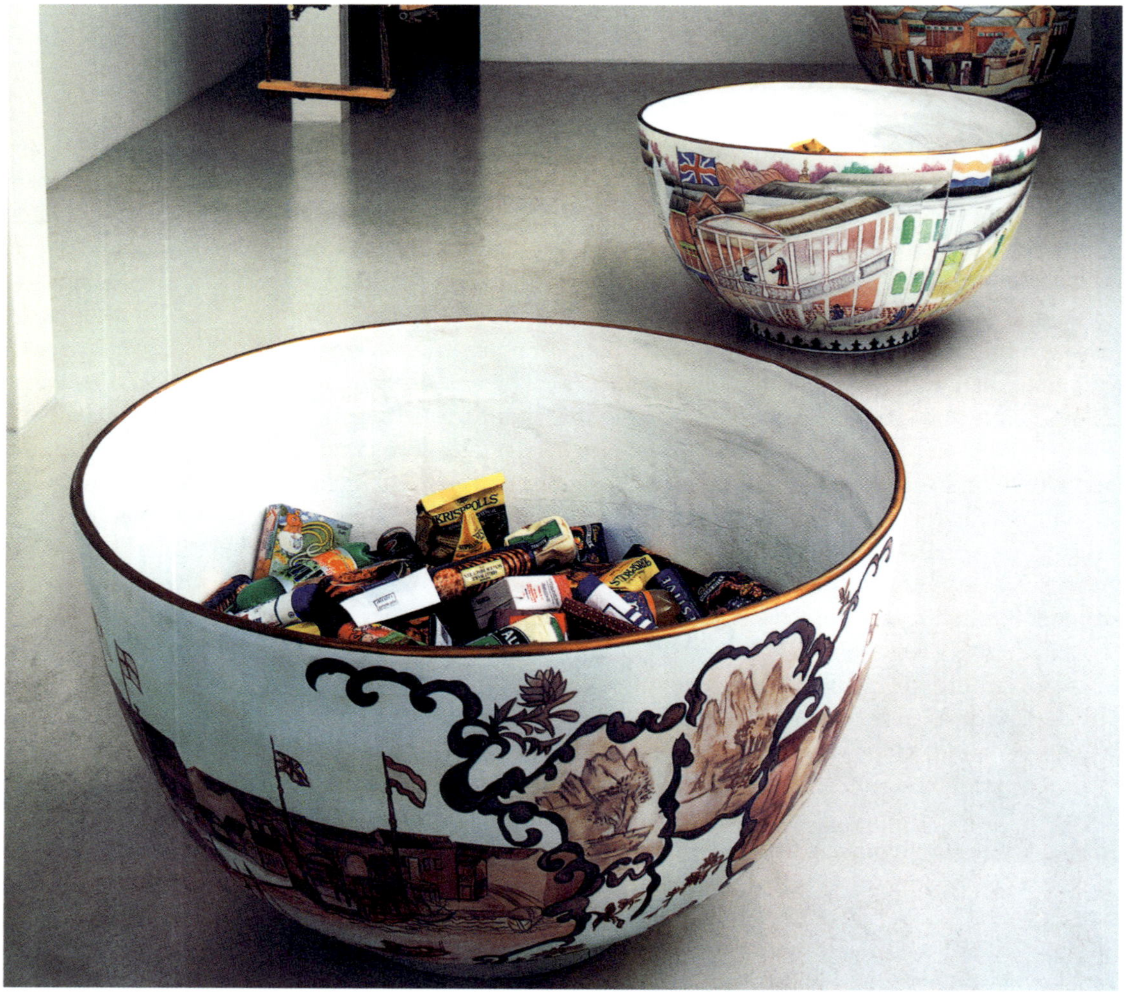

Fig. 1 Huang Yong Ping, *Da Xian - The Doomsday*, 1997, three fiberglass bowls and food stuffs with expiration date of July 1, 1997, each 80 × 150 × 150 cm

for being antiofficial.[27] The effective banning of public exhibition of performance and installation art at the China Art Gallery in Beijing after 1989 meant that when it reappeared with official approval it would do so fourteen years later in the shape of work by Lü Shengzhong, the friend and peer of Xu Bing, who had been widely exhibited abroad and largely lived as an art teacher and writer on ethnic arts. Lü was only given official selection for works that would have gone to Venice in 2003.[28] This situation was quite unlike that in Thailand where state intervention in art discourses was far less, and performance and installation art widely practiced from the early 1990s. Yet in 2001 in Thailand, there was still no adequate national gallery of modern art, nor any stable art magazine that published contemporary art criticism, unlike the eight to ten museums that exhibited contemporary art and the plethora of national and local art publishing in China. Thus the absence of state intervention/support in Thailand until the 1990s came at a negative price.

The major impact of globalism on Chinese and Thai artists came in their personal identities and the way they organized degrees of affiliation to the national in their daily lives. It did appear that the right to interpret correct degrees of national character was highly variable between these two state systems and broad cultural backgrounds. Many Chinese artists went abroad and stayed there, making their way as members of the local art community, sometimes ironically putting forward Chinese contents or references in their work, like Huang Yong Ping (fig. 1) or Xu Bing (fig. 2), and sometimes more explicitly presenting themselves and their work as "Chinese," like Cai Guo-Qiang (fig. 3). They

27 The background is from my interview with Francesca Dal Lago, June 12, 2003.

28 See the Beijing exhibition catalog for Lü's works originally intended for the Venice Biennale in 2003, Fan Di'an and Wang Yong (curators), *Zaojing / Synthi-Scapes*, China International Exhibition Agency Beijing, and Guangdong Museum of Art, Guangzhou, 2003. The exhibition was on view during the Beijing Biennale, Wangfujing Galleries of the Central Academy of Fine Arts, August 2003.

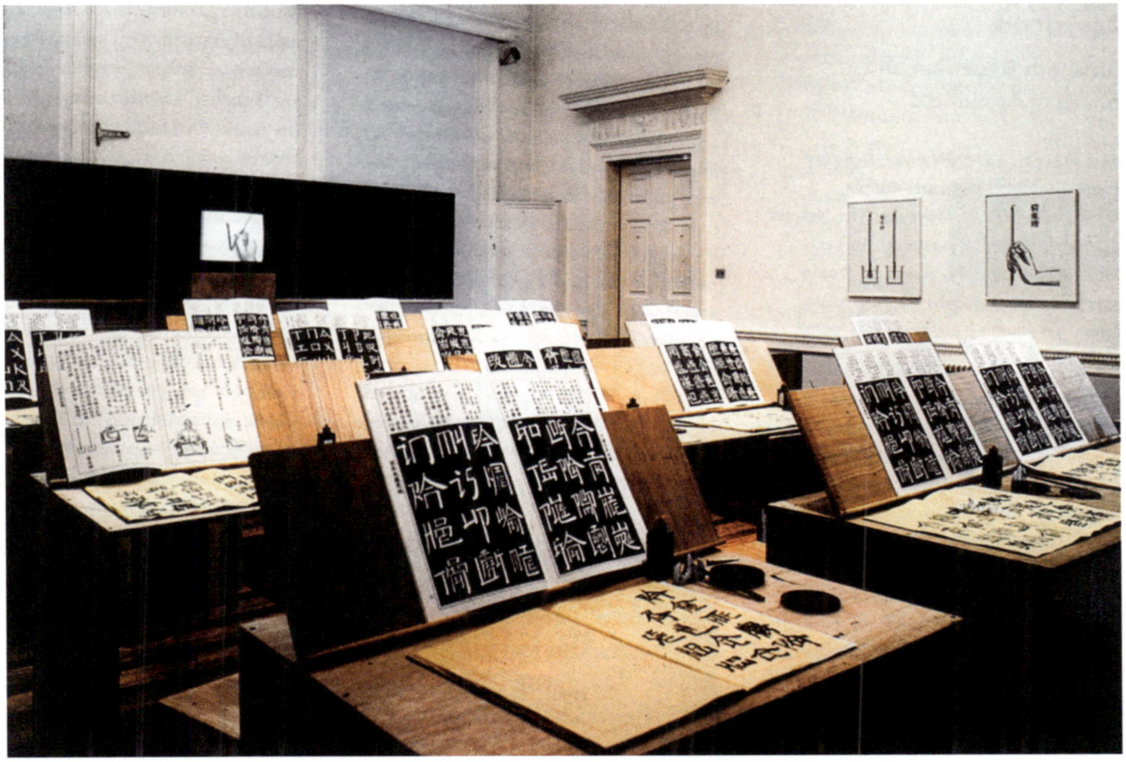

Fig. 2 Xu Bing, *Square Calligraphy Classroom*, 1994, mixed media installation, desk, chair sets, copy and tracing books, brushes, ink, video

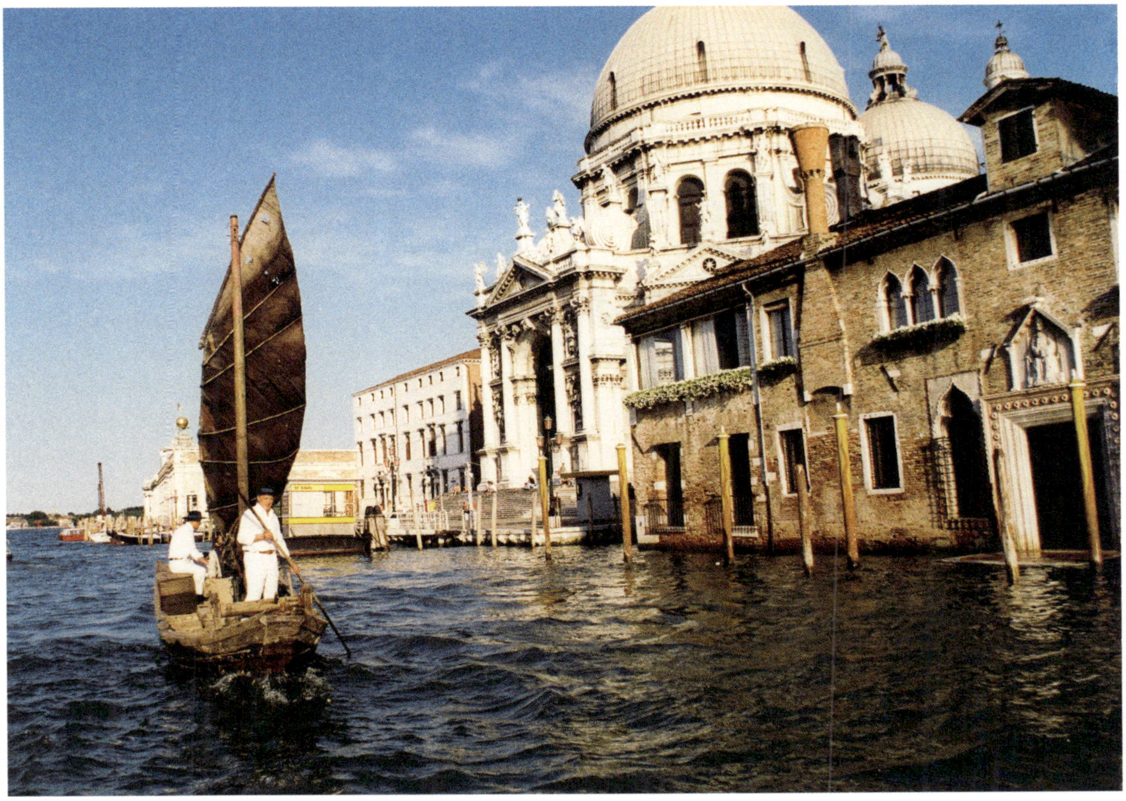

Fig. 3 Cai Guo-Qiang, *Bringing to Venice What Marco Polo Forgot*, 1995, installation incorporating wooden fishing boat from Quanzhou, Chinese herbs, ginseng (100 kg), boat: 700 × 950 × 180 cm

benefited from, and in many cases at the juncture of their early arrival were supported by local and previously settled Chinese communities. Except for rare examples this did not appear to be the case for Thai artists, who in most part lacked this local community of artists already partially assimilated to the art world who supported them when they were overseas. The large majority of Thai artists returned home, often in the end to institutional niches like those they had left.

Any argument about transnationalism, under conditions of vastly increased global flows of information, peoples, goods, and even cultural values, thus had to be highly specific to the particular cultures, or array of cultures, from which artists came. Chinese artists - like some Indian artists - were clearly better equipped and better supported than Thai ones in maintaining multiple selves in international environments so that they could cross barriers of state and cultural identity. Reasons for this may be sought in the inexplicit and often inarticulate attribution of Thai cultural values to particular attachments including those to art forms, to the lack of an explicit ideological or belief structure that can be negotiated or countered, and perhaps also to the very passive tolerance for difference so attractive to many outsiders in Thai society. It is a tolerance that has produced space for cultural difference but without the drive to change or dominate it.[29]

Implications for Hypotheses about Modernity in Art

Globalism is often presented in terms of an undifferentiated collapsing of boundaries and general intervention of the exogenous in the endogenous. As we have seen, the boundaries did not always collapse, and may even have been reinforced or relocated by globalism. The exogenous did not exercise all the hegemony presumed of it. In any case, the actual degree of its lack of hegemony over the endogenous was extremely difficult to perceive from an exogenous position. Globalism presents us with the illusion of the lost concrete, always everywhere around us and in which we live and now perceive ourselves as living. The semiotic hollowing out of the endogenous so often presumed of globalism may in fact have been replaced by a reinforcement of the kinds of superficialities, for example Thai ornamentalism, which globalism was presumed to have rendered relativized, even simulacrous.

Antiglobalist opposition to globalism's superficies is highly partialized to the presumed progenitor of the domination; there may be much complaint about McDonald's and Starbucks (American), but little about chain food outlets such as Délifrance (French) or Dôme (Australian). The worldwide conquest of multinational coffee brands like Nescafé, Illy, or Lavazza is almost impervious to criticism. This partiality of critique has confused in another way, like the notion of monolinguality, the intrinsic lack of an original language or discourse identified by Jacques Derrida. Globalism made prominent and available to everyday observation and understanding phenomena previously buried by efforts of the state. It tried to constitute units around a falsely presumed single culture, race, and economic structure. Modernity in art was also always likely to have been a plural phenomenon with different routes of access. The monolineal descent presumed of its Euroamerican avatar was always untrue in the world, however much it would appear to still remain the unacknowledged ideological frame of many Western art historians and critics. All globalism may have brought to the surface is that we always live in a multiverse of many histories, times, and worlds at once.[30]

Reperceived from this perspective, modernity would not appear as a single situation, but as a set of plural modernities, all of which were *other modernities* to each other. At the very least modernity has always remained with two faces, if not multifaced, with one face to the past and one to the future. Now seen under globalism, modernity has one face to the exogenous and one face to the endogenous. This new space for transnationality means that for inquiry into a comparison of different or other modernities, like China and Thailand, focus has to be on the liminality or boundary conditions for this otherness as much as on the exogenous or endogenous flows and structure that construct it.

Yet the most startling impact of globalism is one that is to date under-researched. Because the cycling of styles, artists, and information about them between exogenous and endogenous discourses has increased in speed and intensity, the role of overseas approbation in reinforcing appraisals of artists and works, and creating a new space for mediators and curators to move, has radically changed. It is now possible for an artist to live and work in one country without

29 **I do not** subscribe to the justly criticized *national cultural* or *ethological* school of comparative anthropology, and do not want to make these typifications too rigidly. Obviously, both broad and narrow cases can be made for these kinds of comparative difference, but here I would simply wish to bring these issues out into the open in a more explicit form for debate or counter-indication, rather than leave them as nonspecific essences or final causes.

30 **The concept** of a *multiverse* is that of Gulam Mohammed Sheikh. See: Gulam Mohammed Sheikh, "Among Several Cultures and Times," in: Carla M. Borden (ed.), *Contemporary Indian Tradition: Voices on Culture, Nature, and the Challenge of Change*, Smithsonian Institution Press, Washington, D.C., 1989.

being given particular prominence there. Yet at the same time they can be known very widely at an international level because of the circulation of their works and information about them. Many artists active at the international level as Chinese or Thai are actually products of a North American educational and appraisal system, and they work mostly from studios in New York.

Some thinkers on modernism like Rosalind E. Krauss have emphasized seriality as a feature of modernist practice.[31] Under globalism there is not the seriality in works so much as of the succession of sites provided to exhibit the same or highly cognate works. There is no circulation or repetition as a formal element in the work or its series, but there is circulation in the intersubstitutable places where the work is located, and to whose local conditions the work may adjust. This can be clearly seen in Navin Rawanchaikul's taxi series (fig. 4), but is also known in the display of different versions of works from the same series across many different sites, such as the circulation of cynical pop work from China through Hong Kong, Australia, Berlin, and Oxford in the *Mao Goes Pop* and *China Avantgarde* and related exhibitions of the early 1990s.

Such circulation may effectively have brought an end to the vertical notion of alternative modernities, with modernities existing in parallel at different sites with different endogenous structures. This is the level some curators refer to as that of an international art language.[32] But in the circulation of works and artists stacked up to a higher or international level by a vertical process, there is paradoxically room left for horizontal art circulation across actual national and cultural boundaries between artists.[33] This may be another and possibly far more benignly significant consequence of globalism.

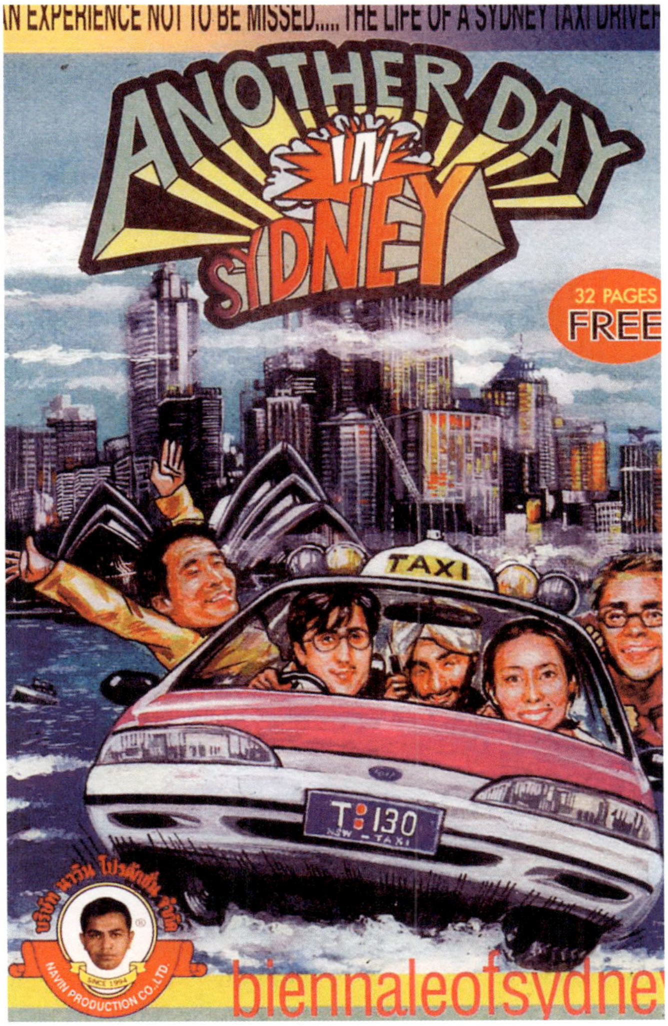

Fig. 4 Navin Rawanchaikul, *Another Day in Sydney*, 1998, comic, cover page

The text is a much abridged version of Chapter 7 "The Global" of John Clark's book, *Asian Modernities: Chinese and Thai Art, 1980s to 1990s*, Power Publications, Sydney, 2010, pp. 225–248. The arguments presented here are explored in depth in the book.

---

31 **See: Rosalind E. Krauss**, *The Originality of the Avant-Garde and Other Modernist Myths*, The MIT Press, Cambridge (MA), [1986] 1993.

32 **Such is** the overall tenor of essays in Philippe Vergne, Vasif Kortun, and Hou Hanru (eds.), *When Latitudes Become Forms: Art in a Global Age*, Walker Art Center, Minneapolis (MN), 2003.

33 **For example,** the camp of women artists for *Womanifesto III*, 2001, at Kantharalak near Sri Saket, Thailand. See: Brian Mertens, "Womanifesto 2001," in: *ArtAsiaPacific*, no. 36, 2002. Another example is the camp held in April 2003 that brought together artists from Australia and all over Southeast Asia in the Blue Mountains, Australia. A local municipality grant funded food and tent accommodation and all the artists found their own airfares.

Writing on Art after 1989

Piotr Piotrowski

The fall of communism in Europe in 1989 was one of the factors that supported rethinking art history, or - in general - writing on art, particularly on contemporary art, but not only. The year 1989 is a challenge to construct a horizontal cultural plane, which includes art history understood as a discourse on past and contemporary art practices. The fall of communism in Europe, which accompanied a series of much more profound historic shifts, functioned as a catalyst for this project. It is important to note that the events in Eastern Europe, namely the Polish Round Table Agreement signed on April 4, 1989, which led to the first democratic elections in Eastern Europe, the tearing down of the Berlin Wall, and collapse of the Soviet Union, coincided with the collapse of the apartheid regime in South Africa (instituted as a state policy in 1947, again coinciding with the introduction of Stalinist cultural policies in the countries of the Eastern Bloc) and a dramatic increase in interest in postcolonial studies. The year 1989 also witnessed the Tiananmen Square massacre and the shift in the "new" Chinese policies initiated in 1978, which did not, however, stop the development of Chinese contemporary art. On the contrary, its development became much more dynamic and its Western reception (including its energetic rise within the international art market) began to reach ever-wider audiences, and soon became a global phenomenon. However, this growth was not accompanied by a sustained art critical discourse within China. Rather, Chinese contemporary art attracted attention mainly in the West, but also in Eastern Europe.

If we add to the horizontal historic plane established by the date 1989 earlier events that culminated in the rejection of the totalitarian regimes by various South American countries (Argentina, Brazil, Chile), as well as discussions about the "former West" that began taking place on the eve of the new millennium, we could arrive at a conclusion that the collapse of the Eastern Bloc was a component of a much larger shift that impacted politics and culture on a global scale. Seeing it in this way it raises two basic questions: What has been the significance of the fall of communism not only for Central and Eastern Europe, but also for the world, and how is this event situated within the conditions of global contemporaneity? In her short text Susan Buck-Morss notes, for instance, that the postcommunist condition is not only affecting Eastern Europe. In other words, it does not have a spatial, but rather a temporal character and therefore describes a historic moment in which we are still situated. In other words, the postcommunist condition describes a historic and universal condition of contemporaneity.[1] Boris Groys, however, discusses the postcommunist condition from the perspective of universal categories, as a particular current vision and description of the world, its parameters and points of reference.[2] The historic process that shaped contemporaneity began with premodernism, and continued through modernism and postmodernism. In reality, this shift from the modernist uniformity (artificial-

1 See: **Susan Buck-Morss**, "The Post-Soviet Condition," in: IRWIN (eds.), *East Art Map Contemporary Art and Eastern Europe*, Afterall Books, London, 2006, p. 498.

2 **Boris Groys** has written extensively on this subject. See in particular: Boris Groys, *Art Power*, The MIT Press, Cambridge (MA), 2008, pp. 149–163 and pp. 165–172; as well as Groys, "Back from the Future," in: Zdenka Badovinac and Peter Weibel (eds.), *2000+ Art East Collection. The Art of Eastern Europe*, Folio Verlag, Vienna et al., 2001, pp. 9–14.

ity) to postmodern diversity constitutes a move towards the market. It is this postmodern market that generates purely aesthetic intensification of artificiality – difference sells.

In the communist era, the world was based on a binary order. Now, since 1989, such an order has apparently become useless as an instrument of description. Understanding politics and culture in terms of oppositions – us, dissidents, and them, communists – did not favor alternative ways of thinking, which was why cultural critique developed much more freely in the West. Still, when the ("former") Eastern Europe became free of Soviet/communist domination, the activists and artists of both sexes from that part of the continent also joined the emancipation movements. Hence, one could say that the deconstruction of gender in the last two decades of the twentieth century overlapped with the fall of communism and its consequences, which implies a general revision of the world perception.

Thus, the question of the global is one of the impacts of the post-1989 world. There is a great deal of literature on the issue of the global,[3] and one of the most important aspects is Hans Belting's view that contemporary art is global by definition because it touches on problems important all over the world;[4] that is, its critique targets the processes shaping the present time anywhere. What is more if it touches on locally specific questions concerning, for example, production, exploitation, labor, Internet control, migration, wars, rebels, it is in fact still addressing global issues, since what is local in the frame of the Empire (in terms of Michael Hardt and Antonio Negri) is global at the same time. Such a process accelerated in 1989, not only because of the end of communism in Europe, but also because of other social, political and – what is very important here – communication transformations. Alexander Alberro argues that 1989 marks the new period.[5] The most spectacular events in the arts in 1989 were three exhibitions with a global character: first Jean-Hubert Martin's *Magiciens de la terre* in Paris, Rasheed Araeen's *The Other Stories. Afro-Asian Artists in Post-war Britain* in London, and Gerardo Mosquera's third edition of the Havana Biennial. These mega exhibitions can be seen in a wider institutional and global context, such as biennials. Of course, there are many views about biennial art as a global phenomenon and one of them is its critical role. For example, Boris Groys writes that such initiatives can help to constitute something as a global "politeia," a global constitution of international democracy, which would be able to create mechanisms to defend the global society from globalization understood as the "Empire."[6] Comparable critical potential of the biennial exhibition network is stressed by Charles Esche, too.[7] Also Okwui Enwezor sees mega world exhibitions as a "'counter-hegemonic' or 'counter-normative'"[8] approach to the Western art system.

The other perspective I would like to mention here is the postcolonial condition and its relation to the postcommunist one. The work of authors such as Rasheed Araeen, Okwui Enwezor, or Partha Mitter, to mention but a few, has mainly focused on the colonial diasporas in Europe, and historic studies of the modernist culture of European colonies and postcolonial countries.[9] An example of this is an exchange published in *The Art Bulletin,* which consisted of responses to the important article by Partha Mitter "Decentering Modernism: Art History and Avant-garde Art from the Periphery."[10] Mitter's conclusions concern the so-called new art history, which was supposed to have heterogeneous character, break down of the monolith of Western modernism, reveal through art historical studies the resistance of the colonial world to the dominance of the metropolis. However, the author does not mention the tensions internal to the so-called metropolis, or the "Old World," which has

3 **Of the vast bibliography on this subject see especially: Jonathan Harris (ed.),** *Globalization and Contemporary Art*, Wiley-Blackwell, Chichester et al., 2011; Silvia von Bennigsen, Irene Gludowacz, and Susanne van Hagen (eds.), *Global Art*, Hatje Canz, Ostfildern, 2009; Charlotte Bydler, *Global ArtWorld Inc.: On the Globalization of Contemporary Art*, Uppsala University Press, Uppsala, 2004; and Julian Stallabrass, *Art Incorporated. The Story of Contemporary Art*, Oxford University Press, Oxford, 2004.

4 **See: Hans Belting**, "Contemporary Art and the Museum in the Global Age," in: Peter Weibel and Andrea Buddensieg (eds.), *Contemporary Art and the Museum. A Global Perspective*, Hatje Cantz, Ostfildern, 2007, pp. 16–38; and ibid., "Contemporary Art as Global Art: a Critical Estimate," in: Hans Belting and Andrea Buddensieg (eds.), *The Global Art World: Audiences, Markets, and Museums*, Hatje Cantz, Ostfildern, 2009, pp. 38–73. Hans Belting's concept of the museum as elaborated in these essays was the main inspiration for developing my strategy of the critical museum as director of the National Museum in Warsaw. See: Piotr Piotrowski, "Museum: From the Critique of Institution to a Critical Institution," in: Tone Hansen (ed.), *(Re)Staging the Art Museum*, Henie Onstad Kunstsenter, Høvikodden, Revolver Publishing, Berlin, 2011, pp. 77–90.

5 **See: Alexander Alberro**, "Periodising Contemporary Art," in: Jaynie Anderson (ed.), *Crossing Cultures. Conflict, Migration, and Convergence*, The Miegunyah Press, Carlton, Victoria, 2009, pp. 935–939.

6 **Boris Groys**, "From Medium to Message. The Art Exhibition as Model of a New World Order," in: *Open. Cahier on Art and the Public Domain*, no. 16, 2009, pp. 56–65.

7 **See: Charles Esche**, "Making Art Global: A Good Place or a No Place?," in: Rachel Weiss et al., *Making Art Global (Part 1). The Third Havana Biennial, 1989*, Afterall Books, London, 2011, pp. 8–13.

8 **Quoted from: Monica Juneja**, "Global Art History and the 'Burden of Representation'," in: Hans Belting, Jacob Birken, Andrea Buddensieg, and Peter Weibel (eds.), *Global Studies. Mapping Contemporary Art and Culture*, Hatje Cantz, Ostfildern, 2011, p. 293.

9 **See: Rasheed Araeen (ed.)**, *The Other Story: Afro-Asian Artists in Post-war Britain*, Hayward Publishing, London. 1989; Olu Oguibe and Okwui Enwezor (eds.), *Reading the Contemporary: African Art from Theory to the Marketplace*, The MIT Press, Cambridge (MA), 1999; Saloni Mathur, *India by Design: Colonial History and Cultural Display*, University of California Press, Berkeley (CA), 2007; Partha Mitter, *The Triumph of Modernism. India's Artists and the Avant-garde 1922–1947*, Reaktion Books, London, 2007.

10 **See: Partha Mitter**, "Interventions: Decentering Modernism: Art History and Avant-Garde Art from the Periphery," in: *The Art Bulletin*, vol. 90, no. 4, December 2008, pp. 543–548.

its own centers and peripheries, and where development of modernism should also be decentered. The respondents to Mitter's article did not mention them either, though they did make interesting observations concerning "provincializing modernity" (Rebecca M. Brown) and "comparative modernism" (Saloni Mathur),[11] which suggest their consistency with the conception of horizontal art history, as I have called it elsewhere.

The question is: how can postcolonial studies provide a common background for the politics of emancipation? To look at this issue closer we of course realize that the colonial experience of India is completely different than that of South America, even from a historical point of view. India gained its independence in 1947, and somehow that was the beginning of the postwar struggle for independence not only in Asia, but also in Africa. Yet at that time there were no European colonies any more in South America. Therefore: To what extent (ethnically, culturally) are South American societies, and even nations, postcolonial? How and on what level can we compare them with India? Furthermore, if we look at African countries and their struggle for independence with West European colonizers, how we can deal with South Africa, which was then already an independent country? Was apartheid in South Africa colonial within the same framework as the experience of the black Africans in Congo, or Arabs in Algeria in the 1950s and 1960s?

To go into details let's discuss vocabulary, or at least some basic concepts of the postcolonial scholars. The first notion that should be formulated more clearly and precisely is "Eurocentrism," or "a crisis of Eurocentrism," or even - simply - "Europe." Most of the scholars, whether they come from the Global South (or the former Third World), or from the West, completely neglect inner European tensions, especially East-West relations. To them Europe is simply a homogeneous continent. For us East Europeans, however, this issue is a crucial one. There is not one Europe; so-called postcolonial Europe is just a part of the continent, actually the Western part, or even merely a section of it. The other countries which are considered Western, such as Italy, had only little experience in such issues, as did the Scandinavian countries. The example of Greece (Western country?) is even more complicated: it was facing Asian colonization; that is, the Other was the colonizer, and the Self colonized. There are also countries like Germany and Austria - particularly important for us East Europeans - whose colonial experience is completely different to the imperial countries in the West (it should be also differentiated to each other). The difference lies in the fact that their main colonial strategies, with only a few overseas exceptions, were directed toward their neighbors, other Europeans. This is definitely a different colonization. We can say the same about Russia, and later the USSR. For Eastern Europe, or Central Eastern Europe to be precise, particularly in terms of the Cold War, this point is crucial.

Thus, what do we, Croats, Czechs, Hungarians, Poles, Serbs, and Slovaks, have in common with colonial history (talking of course about the post-1945 period)? Do our nations bear a sort of responsibility for so-called European colonialism, and finally, shall we share the postcolonial social and political experience? Were we ever in the center, or Euro-Center? What does "Eurocentrism" mean in such a situation? It simply means ignoring European history, geography, politics, and culture. This vocabulary has to be changed. Thus the problem is not a critique of Eurocentrism, but Westcentrism instead. We have to name those who are responsible for colonization.

The final questions in terms of the relation between post-communist and postcolonial studies are: Who was the colonizer, and who the colonized, when did colonization take place and in what ways? These questions are posed, of course, in terms of the post-World War II period, and not others, since we are talking about "postcommunist." A commonsensical answer seems clear: after 1945 East-Central Europe was colonized by the Soviet Union. But was this really the case? Beyond any doubt, one attempt at colonization was the introduction of Socialist realism as an obligatory artistic and ideological doctrine in most countries of Central and South-Eastern Europe, as well as in those Soviet republics which before World War II had been independent states, such as Lithuania, Latvia, and Estonia. Still, in some of the Eastern Bloc countries Socialist realism either did not appear at all (as in Yugoslavia), while in others it was merely an episode (Poland). In most of them it remained just an ideological facade. Modern art, which was definitely more important for East Europeans than Socialist realism, and which came from the West, not from the East, was developing independently of its tenets, determining the genuine cultural identity of Eastern Europe in the period 1945–1989. Finally, I presume that the word "occupation" would be better in this context than "colonization," and this is another major problem for the adaptation of postcolonial studies to the study of East European art.

Postcolonial studies developed out of an entirely different range of historical and geohistorical experiences. In general, postcolonial studies scholars' aim has been to critique the center from the position of a "far-off" Other, or to put it in different terms, to critique the cultural hegemony

11 See: **Rebecca M. Brown**, "Response: Provincializing Modernity: from Derivative to Foundational," in: *The Art Bulletin*, vol. 90, no. 4, December 2008, pp. 555–557; Saloni Mathur, "Response. Belonging to Modernism," in: *The Art Bulletin*, vol. 90, no. 4, December 2008, pp. 555–557.

of Europe. For Dipesh Chakrabarty, such a critique "provincializes Europe." He is not referring to a form of "postcolonial revenge" (shift of power from the center to a periphery), but rather to a "renewal" of European thought from a marginal position through its "translation." Chakrabarty writes that European thought (he focuses mainly on the analysis of two authors, Karl Marx and Martin Heidegger) is at once "necessary" and "insufficient" for the needs of the postcolonial world.[12] One could say that the fundamental difficulty in adapting postcolonial studies to the work on European margins has to do with the very different status of the not-European Other vis-à-vis the Eastern European Other. The former occupies the position of the "far-off" Other while the latter has that of the "close" Other; one is not European by definition, while the other is certainly European, but marginalized, which is not the same. What (East) European art history can learn from postcolonial studies, however, is its critical, decentralizing view in which he or she can see the West, as above mentioned Partha Mitter shows.

Instead of the postcolonial framework, discussed above, the still problematic, postapartheid and postauthoritarian conditions in South Africa and South America could perhaps provide more promising prospects for postcommunist studies. As I mentioned before, chronological coincidences are certainly intriguing. In South Africa, 1989 marked the fall of the apartheid system and the election of Nelson Mandela as the country's first black president. In South America, the first half of the 1980s witnessed the collapse of a series of military dictatorships and the return of democracy. In Argentina and Brazil the military gave up power in 1983. In Chile, a national referendum led to the departure of Augusto Pinochet in 1988, and a year later a return of democratic elections. In Paraguay, the long-lived military dictatorship was abolished in 1989. In Uruguay, the process of erosion of the dictatorship and return of democracy took place in the second half of the 1980s, and was finalized by the end of the decade.

It is true that such comparisons are not unproblematic, especially if we consider the art world. John Peffer observes in his wonderful book on the art of the apartheid period that the work produced under such conditions reacted to the politics of racial segregation, and continued to do so even after 1994, when such policies ceased to function legally and politically.[13] Of course in the case of South Africa, we are dealing with a single country and therefore with a much more homogeneous environment, even though South African society is far from homogeneous linguistically. In the case of Eastern Europe, we have to consider many different and distinct administrative and political systems, pursuing different, sometimes diametrically opposed cultural policies, even though until 1989 they were all officially embracing the ideology of Marxism-Leninism. We will also notice considerable differences if we consider art itself, its institutional apparatus, symbolism, and reception. There are significant differences, for instance, between Polish and Hungarian art. What matters is that in both instances, in South Africa and in Eastern Europe before 1989, artistic cultures functioned under conditions of confinement that limited their development, but also provided a challenge. Moreover, the fact that the societies of South Africa and Eastern Europe defeated totalitarian regimes at virtually the same time creates a possibility for a comparative perspective encompassing not only artistic production, but also, and primarily, culture released from the authoritarian straitjacket. Such analysis still awaits us, mainly because these processes have not yet been fully digested by art criticism.

The same could be said with regard to South America. The postdictatorial systems there are quite different from the postcommunist ones in Europe in terms of access to consumer culture, economic development, free market structures, art institutions, and so on. But, it is precisely those differences that are important. This type of comparative, interregional art history must aim to establish such diversity. What connects contemporary art produced in the regions emerging from the totalitarian systems with the postcolonial countries, such as India and Pakistan, is its marginalization vis-à-vis mainstream art culture, and its neglect within and omission from the Western art discourse in art historical narratives produced from the perspective of the center or the position of symbolic power. The centers and their power are still identified for many reasons (economic, political, cultural, etc.) with the West. That is why the new world art history, or global art history (and not universal art history) should not consist of the history of Western art appended with other art histories; it should be the history of both - the West and the Others, on equal terms, and the so-called West (some call it the "former West") should be seen as the Other, too. To borrow Dipesh Chakrabarty's term, such world art history should "provincialize" the West; it must identify it as one of its regions. By locating the West within a historic and cultural context as one of the regions of the art world, admittedly a very influential one, it will make it possible to analyze its influence from a historic perspective, to deconstruct it, and to approach it axiologically in the way that we have been approaching the art of South America, Asia, Africa, or

12 See: **Dipesh Chakrabarty**, *Provincializing Europe: Postcolonial Thought and Historical Difference*, Princeton University Press, Princeton (NJ), 2000.

13 See: **John Peffer**, *Art and the End of Apartheid*, University of Minnesota Press, Minneapolis (MN), 2009.

Eastern Europe. This horizontal approach will have the effect of provincializing the West. I am not arguing that we should deny or negate the existence of the West, since its continuity is assured on many levels as an artistic tradition, system of values, institutional infrastructure, art market, etc. What I am arguing for is a need to see Western culture not in terms of its hegemony, but its geographic specificity: as a culture of one of the regions of the world.

The great challenge coming from the perspective of provincializing the West as a result of the 1989 changes, would not necessarily be to write on contemporary art, but also to rewrite art history instead, at least (but not only) so-called recent art history; that is, postwar art history, along with the horizontal, comparative art studies. I particularly mean something called the transregional approach to art history (instead of transnational), where by comparing different regions such as Eastern Europe, Latin America, Asia, and Africa, would finally show the West as another province among the others. The problem of comparative, transregional art history, however, is the platform of mediation. If we talk about interregional relations, we should identify some fields where such relations would meet each other. I argue that such a level is global politics. After World War II and during the Cold War, obviously, politics was global, as I have mentioned before. East-West confrontation, and the emergence of the Third World in the light of such competition is the core of postwar history. Thus, we can find out some key dates of that history, and relate them to the art. It is not an issue of neglecting Western influences on art around the world; on the contrary - the issue here is to deconstruct them and reconstruct their meanings in particular, local contexts, and to compare them. Let me just mention two possible examples. The first date would be the end of the 1940s which is the beginning of cultural Stalinism in Eastern Europe dominated by the Soviets, at the same time the Yugoslavian breakout from the Soviet world, and the beginning of the nonaligned states movement. There is also a moment when India and Pakistan declared their independence (1947), apartheid was officially introduced in South Africa (1947), and Israel emerged as a new state in Palestine (1948), changing the map of the Middle East radically up till today. These are many dates like this in the West, East, North, and South. The general approach to the art world from this perspective, is a sort of dialectical bounds between Socialist realism, on the one hand, and modernism on the other; two myths of universalism created on either side of the "Iron Curtain." Both of them had a global dimension as competitive art and political strategies, and this is a crucial issue in terms of comparative global art history for that time. Another date, or a sort of horizontal cut, would be 1968. Many things were happening at that time, both in the West ("Euramerica," in John Clark's terms) and in the East, including the Prague Spring and Polish March. At the same time there was the Vietnam war, the Middle East conflict, harsh military regimes in South America, cultural revolution in China, and so on and so forth. In terms of art it was the time of a rigorous critique of modernism, on the one hand, and the appearance of critical and rebellious art (called sometimes neo-avant-garde), on the other.

To illustrate this method let me compare two experiences: East European and Latin American in terms of 1968, or more precisely: Polish and Argentine. Both countries started to "modernize" art in the mid-1950s, in similar geographically oriented points of origin, namely French, and at a somewhat comparable historical moment - the collapse of authoritarian systems: Peronism in Argentina and Stalinism (but not Communism) in Poland. Art modernization in Argentina after Juan Domingo Perón's removal from power resulted in reinforcing and reopening (1957) the Museo Nacional de Bellas Artes (MNBA) in Buenos Aires under new directorship, namely, under famous Jorge Romero Brest (appointed in 1956); founding the new museum of modern art, Museo de Arte Moderno (MAM) in 1956; and two years later the Instituto Torcuato Di Tella (ITDT). This represented a strong institutionalization and internationalization of modernism, as Andrea Giunta argues.[14] In Poland no museums were founded, but a similar institutionalization of modernism can be observed. For example, in 1957 there was the *Second Exhibition of Modern Art* at one of the most notable and prestigious art institutions in Poland, the Zachęta National Gallery in Warsaw, which was followed by a very important contribution of Polish modern art to the most important official exhibition of the art of socialist countries in Moscow in 1958/1959, where - as the only delegation - Polish curators decided to show modern (abstract) art, instead of socialist realism, as all other delegations did.[15] Of course, Peronism was not the same as Stalinism; nevertheless, the broad acceptance of modernism almost at the same time after the fall of authoritarian regimes as a reply to them, is quite striking. In both cases modernism (the French, not the American version) was perceived as the right attitude towards freedom and free and modern culture. What is more, contrary to the US conceptual art trend, art in both Argentina and Poland derived somehow from modernism, that is, Informel and especially geometric abstraction art,

14 See: **Andrea Giunta**, *Avant-garde, Internationalism, and Politics: Argentinian Art in the Sixties*, Duke University Press, Durham (NC), 2007.

15 See: **Susan E. Reid**, "The Exhibition 'Art of Socialist Countries,' Moscow 1958-1959, and the Contemporary Style of Painting," in: Susan E. Reid and David Crowley (eds.), *Style and Socialism. Modernity and Material Culture in Post-war Eastern Europe*, Berg Publishers, London et al., 2000, pp. 101-132.

rather than from Minimal art. In additional, object art, that is, art that operates with real things, developed a comparable historical dynamic at the beginning of the 1960s, and was submerged in existential issues, rather than in an ironic attitude to low culture, as in North America.

However, the Argentine artists of 1968 discredited the modernist mythology and abandoned it as a tool of power (at that time under the military regime after the coup in 1966), whereas their Polish counterparts still believed in that myth; to be frank, until the end of the 1970s. In both cases modernism was the mainstream of national culture. In Argentina, however, the artists rejected all of it and took the radical position of questioning art as such, and responded with direct, political action (the most striking example was a collective project called *Tucuman Is Burning*, Rosario and Buenos Aires, 1968). In East-Central Europe such radicalism was unknown. Even Hungarians, the most political artists in the entire Eastern Bloc, created their critical positions through metaphors rather than direct actions, and did not question the value of art. Although some of their events looked purely political (e. g., Tamas Szentjóby's *Sit Out*, 1972), they were recognized primary as art. In Poland the neo-avant-garde artists discarded modernist visuality (abstract painting), somehow the mainstream institution, but not the value system with autonomy of art and its self-referentiality at the top. Instead of political action, like that mentioned above, Polish artists were involved in analyzing art language and visual media. The grounds for this were, on the one hand, the persisting trauma of socialist realism understood as the only art doctrine accepted by the authorities in the public sphere during the first half of the 1950s and political confusion concerning global US politics, and on the other hand a kind of conformism. This conformism stemmed from the pseudoliberal cultural policy that granted artists the pseudofreedom to do anything he or she wanted to in art (abstract art, conceptual art, performance, body art etc.), quite unusual at that time in the Soviet Bloc, except political engagement. That was of course banned, and anything connected with critique of the political system was censored. It looks as though the artists did not want to lose such a "velvet prison," and it was the reason why the modernist value system was maintained so long. When these artists looked at the 1968 movements elsewhere, whether in Western Europe, the US, or South America they mostly depoliticized it, especially in Poland (Hungary was different), precisely because of the infamous and traumatic tradition of cultural Stalinization in the first half of the 1950s. Politics (once more: particularly in Poland) was more the negative point of departure of art at that time than the welcome message. This situation was just the opposite in Latin America, including Argentina, where politics and art went together, even though the first had priority.

As I mentioned above, *Tucuman Is Burning* was just the tip of the iceberg in the process of politicization of Argentine art in the 1960s. In Poland probably the only response to March '68 in terms of visual art was a ball in Zalesie near Warsaw titled "Farewell to Spring," in which many people from the art scene, especially connected with the Warsaw Foksal Gallery, participated, and had actually organized.[16] Seen from this perspective, the event was intended to function as a gesture of protest against politicization (*sic*) of intellectual life and the pressure to be political in the Polish reality of 1968, and not vice versa. I must say that at first glance this looks strange; however, if we consider the modernist background of the Polish neo-avant-garde, discussed above, it does have a sort of logic. Even in Czechoslovakia in the course of normalization after 1968, after suppression of the Prague Spring by Warsaw Pact troops where repression and persecution were definitely much stronger, the artists also responded in a comparable way: they just congregated in bars, drank beer, or organized outdoor trips, simply in order to spend some time together.

This essay is based on a lecture given on the occasion of receiving the Igor Zabel Award in Theory and Culture, Barcelona 2010, and an abbreviated version of a chapter in Piotr Pitrowski's book *Art and Democracy in Post-communist Europe*, Reaktion Books, London, 2012.

16 **See: Anka Ptaszkowska, Paweł Polit et al.**, "Remarks and Comments: Discussion on the Zalesie Ball and Participation," in: Claire Bishop and Marta Dziewańska (eds.), *1968–1989. Political Upheaval and Artistic Change*, Museum of Modern Art, Warsaw, 2009, pp. 106–111.

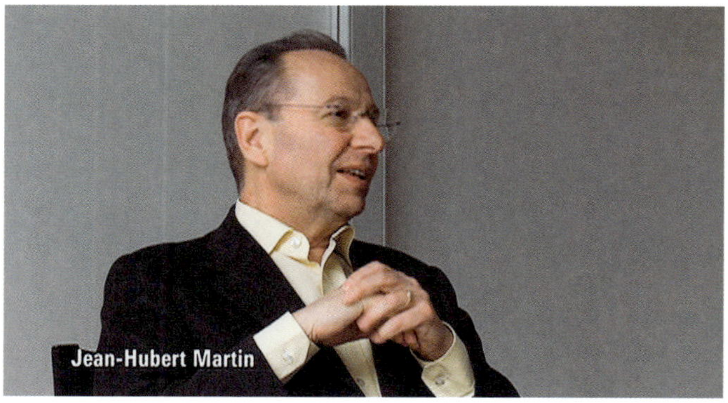

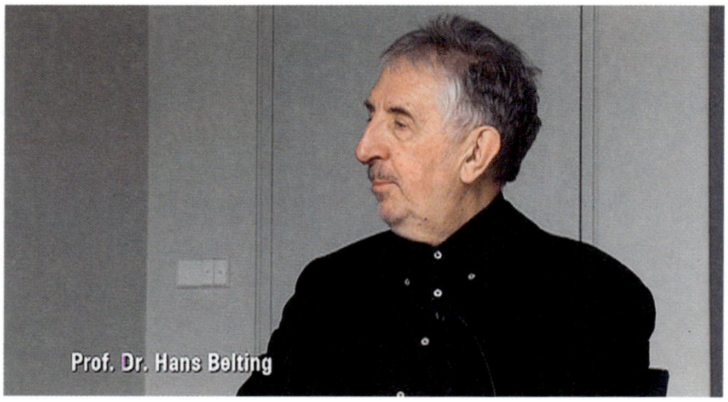

Magiciens de la terre

Hans Belting in Conversation with Jean-Hubert Martin

(February 20, 2011)

Hans Belting
Anyone who talks about the globalization of contemporary art always starts with your exhibition *Magiciens de la terre* of 1989. *Connaissance des Arts* wrote at the time: "La première exposition mondiale de l'art contemporain." Did that surprise you?

Jean-Hubert Martin
No, that didn't surprise me; that was the goal of the exhibition.

Belting
How did you come up with the name? It seems surprising at first that you did not speak not of "Artistes du globe" but rather of "Magiciens de la terre."

Martin
The title of the exhibitions has caused many misunderstandings. It is in fact a poetic title. We wanted to avoid the term "art," since it is once again a Western concept. But neither did I want to call the hundred artists who were represented in the exhibition "magicians". In the end, the division was very difficult: a first half of artists from the West juxtaposed with another half of artists who came, for example, from the former colonies.

Belting
At the time you said you wanted to bring to Paris artists with a name and a passport who in ethnological exhibitions had often been treated anonymously as producers of artifacts.

Martin
Precisely, that was very important to me. For example, old African art usually made it to us as anonymous works. But I wanted to meet the personalities, that is, the people who play a certain role in their own culture and who produce not just objects but also symbolic forms, which stand in a certain dialectical relationship to their own culture.

Belting
It was perceived as a provocation that you juxtaposed artists with a Eurocentric context with other artists whose names had yet to be introduced. You once said that traditional art has subject matter other than just art itself.

Martin
Exactly. I wanted to put these artists, as different as they were, on the same level, even if they came from a different context, for example, from cultures where there is no art history and no historical view of art. And I wanted to show

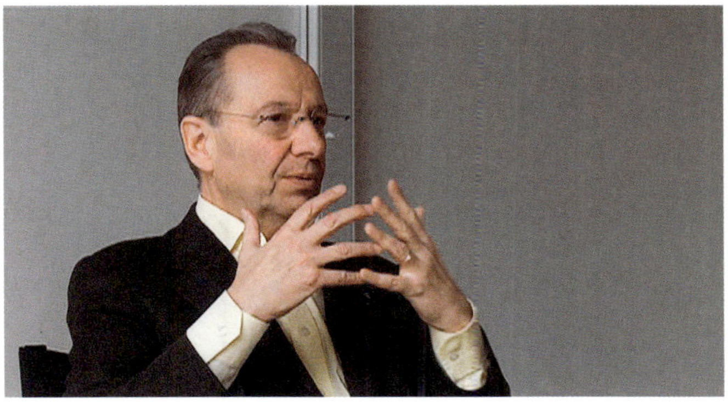

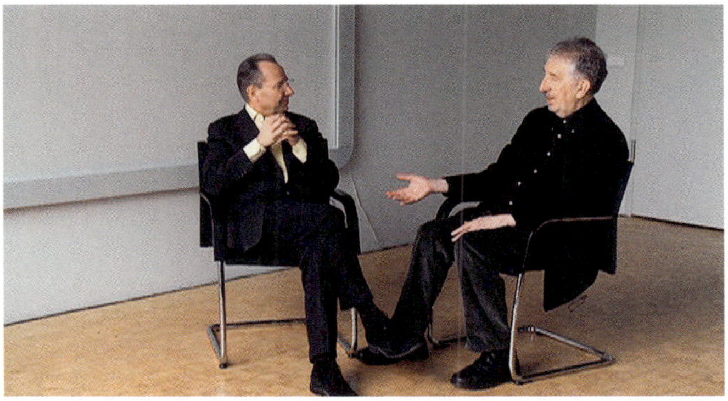

that our so-called modern or postmodern situation belongs to a tradition. So the idea was a "rencontre avec des personnes remarquables." Except that, unlike the ethnological museums, I did not want to explain the differences.

Belting
Naturally people recognized that you were transgressing old boundaries, but on the other hand there were polemics about the fact that you chose traditional artists and not those using the most modern techniques.

Martin
That criticism was made, of course, but I always put our modernism in context as a typical Western issue. How would it be possible to demonstrate all of Chinese culture by exhibiting Huang Yong Ping?

Belting
That was the first time we saw contemporary artists from China in the West. But you also showed relatively many Africans. How have they developed in globalization since? Have the Africans established themselves in the contemporary art scene in a way similar to the Chinese?

Martin
The Chinese have caught on and developed incredibly in the past fifteen years.

Belting
And it is striking that it is different with the Africans. They were in fact present in Paris quite early on, as a result of colonial ties between France and Africa, so that it is surprising that globalization has really followed a different course in Africa.

Martin
The fact that the colonial powers England and France formed art schools in the colonies was a problem for my exhibition, because in many countries in Africa there were artists who had studied at these schools. So I often saw the École de Paris being assimilated, for example. If I had shown such works in the exhibition, everyone would have said they were imitations of Western art of the 1950s, say. The trick was that I was looking for, and found, something quite different. But that sparked criticism on all sides. The Africans were not satisfied, and neither were the Europeans, because it did not correspond to their perception.

Belting
And yet in a curatorial credo Okwui Enwezor said that *Magiciens de la terre* was still the exhibition he struggled with most. In his view, you excluded the diaspora artists educated in the West in order to make the Africans primitive again, so to speak.

Martin
That was his critique. His opinion has, I believe, since become more complex. He has since come to understand the principle better. But certain artists also expressed the criticism of primitivism. But I still insist that twenty years ago, when I was organizing the exhibition, primitivism was not yet dead.

Belting
I believe that the exhibition *"Primitivism" in 20th Century Art*, which had been shown at MoMA in New York five years earlier, was an impetus for you to do it differently.

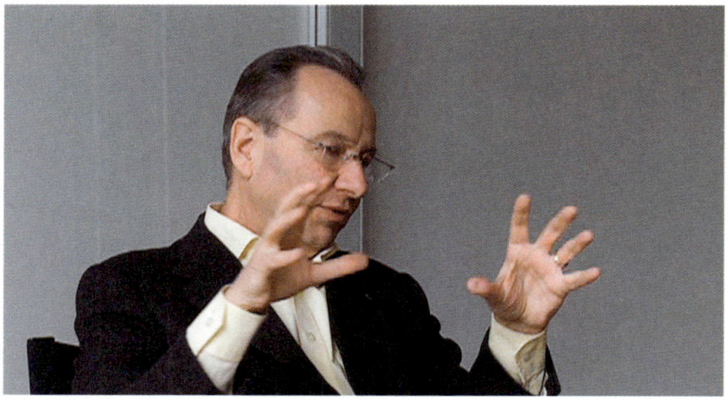

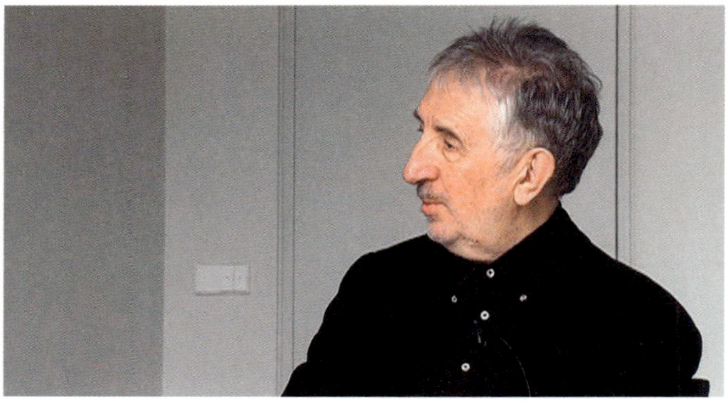

Martin
Yes. I found the exhibition interesting and yet open to criticism. I was quite shocked that the final section, the contemporary section, was so weak. And that encouraged me to continue to develop my exhibition, which was already being planned at the time.

Belting
People tell an anecdote about you that in 1977 when the Centre Pompidou was being opened you included artifacts from the Musée de l'Homme.

Martin
That's right.

Belting
Almost like a Trojan horse in that temple of modernism.

Martin
Yes and no. In collaboration with Pontus Hultén, the director at the time, we wanted to show African and Oceanic art to establish not so much their connection to Cubism and Surrealism, not primarily from the historical view that Cubism derives in part from these masks, but to demonstrate that there is living art in these regions of the world. At the time I wrote a brief text that was made available to visitors about this.

Belting
But the major criticism of modernism was that it universalized form. Many collectors exhibited modern art alongside African and Oceanic art to show that they look quite similar and that both are art. By contrast, critics lamented the loss of context in such a purely formal comparison. You are familiar with such criticism, of course.

Martin
Yes, of course. I would add that the criticism is justified if you look at many collections from the first half of the twentieth century. In nearly every case, so-called "Black art" is found alongside the avant-garde.

Belting
... or there are exhibition titles like *Five Thousand Years of Modern Art*.

Martin
Yes, but the collectors knew that these masks or so-called fetishes had a religious value and hence possessed a transcendent and spiritual message. By contrast, this art of the avant-garde was so new that it no longer permitted any spiritual values.

Belting
Then so-called primitive art served as more than just inspiration for form?

Martin
... precisely ...

Belting
... but also contributed to mythologizing of its own art forms.

Martin
Yes, this history of "Black art" and Cubism has been told formalistically. There are many more types of appropriation.

Belting
Surrealism too had a very different kind of appropriation.

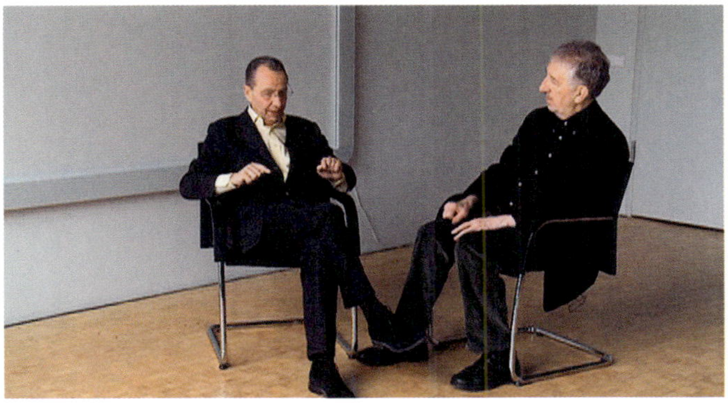

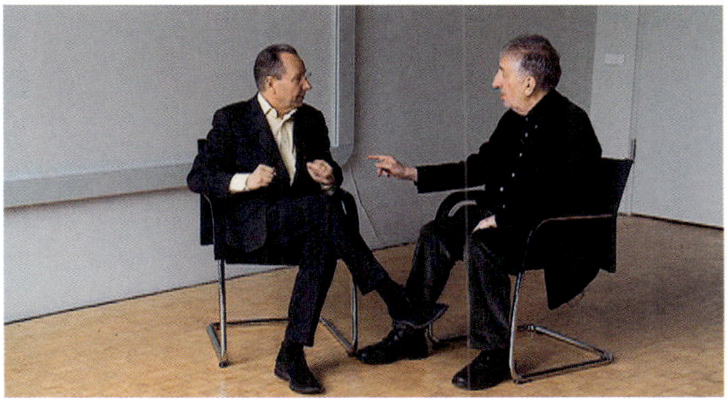

Martin
Yes, for Breton and the Surrealists, it was a different matter.

Belting
If you look back at the year 1989, the globalization of contemporary art was just developing out of origins you had already seen. What history has resulted from it? What course has globalization taken? You know more now than you did in 1989. How do you regard the situation today?

Martin
Magiciens de la terre sought to pose many questions, as well as to tell a new history of art that was just beginning. On the one hand, the exhibition was a success, because now every curator who organizes a group show has to include not only women but also Africans and Asians. On the other hand, we wanted to raise the very important question of the difference between the arts and the crafts. These decisions and the expertise about authenticity are still mostly relying on the West. That important question is never asked. Over the last twenty years we have seen many artists from these other continents appear on the international art scene who have been formed by the Western system of galleries and collections. What is totally ignored is what is happening outside this incestuous network: for instance religious art and art made in remote communities for their own sake. Can you believe that it is all craft?

Belting
If you were to do the exhibition again today, would you do it exactly the same way or would you conceive it differently?

Martin
No, definitely not; it would of course be a completely different exhibition. But I believe you can still be provocative.

Belting
I am convinced of that. It must be a nice feeling to know that you started a global era in art with an exhibition like *Magiciens de la terre*, even if many have debated whether it was the right kind of start. But no one denies that it was a start. So I am sincerely grateful to you for this interview and for coming to Karlsruhe.

Martin
Thank you very much.

Translated from the German by Steven Lindberg.

Itinerary of a Curator. *Magiciens de la terre* and After

Andrea Buddensieg

1.

Jean-Hubert Martin's Paris exhibition *Magiciens de la terre* which opened in May 1989 at the Centre Pompidou and also at La Grande Halle de la Villette was hailed as "a first really global exhibition of contemporary art."[1] No other exhibition of the last twenty years has received so much attention, and the discussion still continues. Many critics condemned it as the wrong start. However, such commentators focused only on the *Magiciens* exhibition, and neither considered nor mentioned Martin's activities as a curator before or after. It is therefore time to take an in-depth look at his other exhibitions in which he repeatedly questioned the mainstream art world that for so long denied visibility to outsiders. It is the context of Martin's other work that puts the *Magiciens* show into perspective. In 1989, in a year of momentous political changes, the art world too was ready for a change.

In July 1989, France celebrated the bicentenary of the French revolution and in that year Paris was Cultural Capital of Europe. These circumstances already go some way to explaining why the impact of *Magiciens* was on such an international scale. The French exhibition was even reviewed[2] in Hong Kong, Venezuela, Turkey, Mexico, and Japan, to mention but a few countries. Jean-Hubert Martin, who began to develop the overall idea in 1984, launched the show together with Mark Francis as cocurator and Aline Luque and André Magnin as assistant curators.[3] Martin set about deconstructing the mainstream institutional art definition. Instead of contributing to an overall discourse, he asked all participating artists to give their personal answer to the question "What is art?"[4]

Martin surprised everybody by his unprecedented step of confronting fifty renowned artists representing the mainstream art world with an equal number of artists and artisans who would formerly have been excluded from such an exhibition. The second group, with popular, traditional, folk, and native artists, represented the neglected side of art production. In an interview with Benjamin Buchloh, Martin described his ambition to display this art "in a manner that has never been used for objects from the Third World."[5] His most important concern was to present artists, who were formerly excluded or unknown, as individuals with a name and a passport. Martin referred to the members of both groups as *magiciens,* also to avoid the connotations of the word "artist." He deliberately did not base his selection

1 Denis Picard, "Liberté, Égalité, Magie," in: *Connaissance des Arts* 450, 1989, p. 57; translated from the French by the author.

2 A list of press reviews can be found at: http://magiciensdelaterre.fr/contexte.php?id=1#, accessed 06/07/2012. This website was launched in 2011 by Jean-Hubert Martin and offers texts, archival materials, and images relating to the show.

3 Jean-Hubert Martin et al. (eds.), *Magiciens de la terre*, exhib. cat., Centre Georges Pompidou and Grande Halle de la Villette, Paris, 1989. The catalog includes essays by the curators and texts by Pierre Gaudibert, Thomas McEvilley, Homi Bhabha, Jacques Soulillou, and Bernard Marcadé. Marcadé contributed "une fable visuelle et textuelle" on "L'Autre, ce grand alibi" (pp. 33–70).

4 It was Lawrence Weiner's idea to pose this question to the artists, see: Martin 1989, p. 71.

5 Benjamin H.D. Buchloh, "The Whole Earth Show: An Interview with Jean-Hubert Martin," in: *Art in America*, May 1989, p. 154.

of the participants on names put forward by national commissions or cultural functionaries; this had been the practice of the Paris Biennale and it had resulted in "a disaster of official and officious culture." Instead, Martin argued that

> "since we are dealing with objects of visual and sensual experience, let's really look at them from the perspective of our own culture. I want to play the role of someone who uses artistic intuition alone to select these objects which come from totally different cultures."[6]

In the same interview Martin stressed the importance of his collaboration with anthropologists, but said he could not embrace their suggestions entirely as for an exhibition he needed to put together works that "communicate sufficiently well in a visual-sensuous manner to a Western spectator."[7] The exhibited works, in all their diversity and new equality, were expected to speak for themselves and to offer a direct impression of immediacy. The advice of anthropologists did not resonate in the catalog where the introductory essays were written prior to the exhibition.

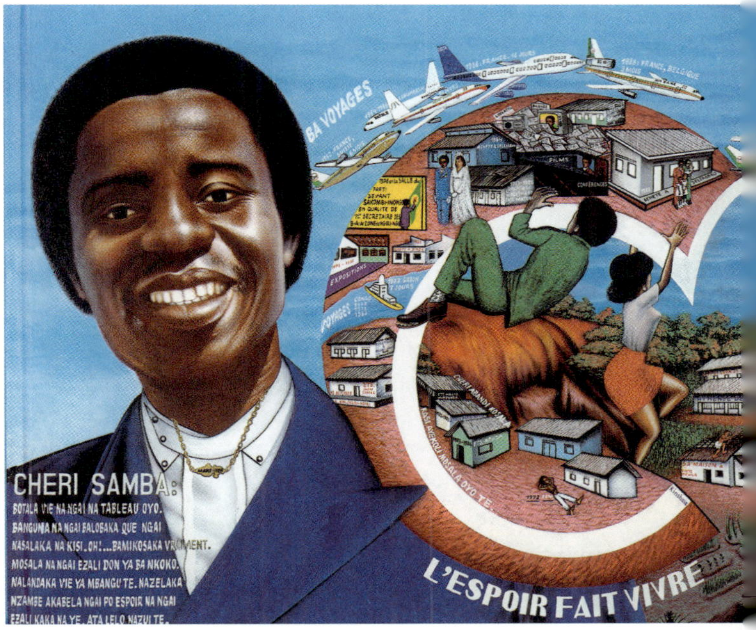

Chéri Samba, exhib. cat., Musée national des Arts d'Afrique et d'Océanie, Edition Hazan, Paris, 1997, book cover.

Martin's project was driven by outright rejection of the 1984 show *"Primitivism" in 20th Century Art* at MoMA, in which William Rubin had once again presented tribal art as a mere inspiration for modern art. In contradistinction to this concept, Martin aimed to reintroduce the "others" as contemporaries. Furthermore, he spoke of creation rather than art. Nevertheless, Martin was attacked both for undermining the safe profile of Western art and also for paying scant attention to diasporic artists. Yet the exhibition's two groups of artists were by no means divided by geography alone. Rather, one could have drawn a line between conceptual artists who questioned the notion of art and others who did not. The hostility that the exhibition encountered was largely the result of one ensemble in the exhibition where Martin had juxtaposed Richard Long's minimalist *Mud Circle* with tribal art - an Aboriginal sand painting on the floor by a group of Australian Yuendumu artists. Scandalized critics claimed this was an unheard-of transgression of art's boundaries. But this space, with its merely formal analogy, did not exemplify the exhibition as a whole. What remained an issue for Martin, was the reinterpretation of Aboriginal Australian artists and their political mission, which he addressed in further exhibitions.

The *Magiciens* show especially attracted controversy over contemporary art in Africa. This was partly due to André Magnin, who later built up Jean-Christophe Pigozzi's Contemporary African Art Collection (CAAC) and preferred self-taught or so-called traditional or popular artists like mask carvers, coffin makers, or sign painters to any academism.[8] The controversy also reached the discussion in the *Revue Noire,* which was first published as a forum for art criticism of the new African scene in 1991.[9] A special case was the self-styled popular painting of Chéri Samba from the Democratic Republic of Congo (former Zaire), who contributed a self-portrait, itself a novelty in the framework of a professional biography and created at the moment when he was ready to depart for France at the time of Martin's exhibition.[10]

At a conference in Berlin in 1995, Martin defended his *Magiciens* concept against almost unanimous rejection.[11] The idea had been to show "that there is creativity everywhere in the world, also today. Our aim was to break the existing taboo and to group exotic, religious and modern art together on an equal footing."[12] Thus, Martin insisted on recognizing "each artist as an individual and a creative personality"[13] in every culture. And for this reason it was so important to invite living artists from the former colonies

6 **Buchloh 1989**, p. 152f.
7 **Buchloh 1989**, p. 153.

8 **See: Thomas Fillitz**, *Zeitgenössische Kunst aus Afrika*, Böhlau, Vienna, 2002, pp. 277ff.
9 ***Revue Noire*** was founded in 1991 by Jean Loup Pivin, Pascal Martin Saint Lóon, Bruno Tilliette, and Simon Njami, 35 issues until 2001.
10 **See: Cesare Poppi**, "From the Suburbs to the Global Village," in: *Third Text*, Spring 1991, pp. 85ff.
11 **See: Jean-Hubert Martin**, "Das Marco-Polo-Syndrom," in: Gerhard Haupt and Bernd M. Scherer (eds.) in cooperation with Haus der Kulturen der Welt, *Das Marco Polo Syndrom, Neue Bildende Kunst*, no. 4/5, 1995, pp. 64–69.
12 **Martin 1995**, p. 67; translated from the German.
13 **Martin 1995**, p. 67.

in order to overcome "the old myth of collective creativity in other cultures."[14] The living artist had to replace the anonymous objects that for so long had been exhibited in ethnographic collections.

Thomas McEvilley initially criticized the *Magiciens* exhibition for supporting the romantic idea of the native artist. The curators, he remarked, spoke of "spirituality implying universals."[15] But he continued in a placatory tone: The exhibition attempted "a post-colonial way to exhibit the works of First and Third World artists together" and he concluded: "It was a major event in the social history of art, not in its esthetic history. *Magiciens* opened the door of the long insular and hermetic Western art world to artists."[16] Rasheed Araeen, who had participated in the *Magiciens* show, later objected that, with its binary system, it did not question the

> "assumptions that privilege the Western artist (modern, white and male) and exclude the non-Western artist (the 'other') from the domain of modern art." But his "main criticism concerns the lack of any radical theoretical or conceptual framework that can justify the togetherness of works which represent different historical formations."[17]

To underline his critique Araeen quoted from a 1986 statement in which Jean-Hubert Martin explained the sections of the exhibition: Whereas "African and Asian artists living in the West" were still identified by "their own cultural roots," "Western artists" were chosen because of their "concern for cultures other than their own."[18]

The African diaspora scene accused Martin of a so-called re-primitivization of African art. In 1991, Everlyn Nicodemus blamed Pigozzi for having sent Magnin "into the bush in Africa in search of the same kind of image makers" who deceive us with a "virgin 'purity' which never existed."[19] Olu Oguibe made a new "Western expansionism" responsible for "neo-primitivizing" African artists on the condition they were "other" and preferably "naïve."[20] Meschac Gaba recalled in an interview the arrival of Magnin in Benin in search of possible candidates for the Paris show.[21] Magnin

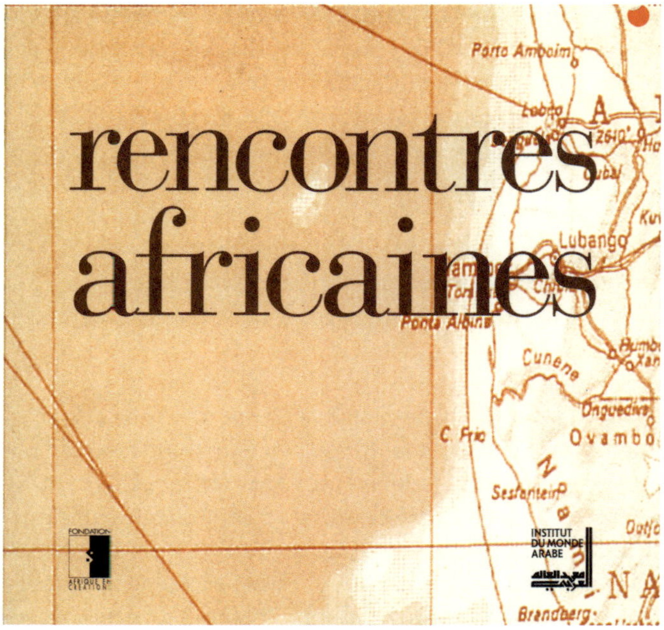

Rencontres Africaines: exposition d'art actuel, exhib. cat., Institut du Monde Arabe, Paris, 1994, book cover.

"had chosen the path of anthropology, the intercultural road." In Gaba's view, "painting was something that came with colonization" and he also considered the poster style a colonial legacy: "I regard the work of Chéri Samba as billboards. I have made billboards myself in Benin but for merchants, not for exhibitions." Magnin had visited "artists whom I had always regarded more as artisans." In Gaba's view the African artists had been chosen according to a colonial art concept because, against academism, Martin included "African artists" with so-called precolonial purity and religious or ritual connotations.

2.

It is necessary to consult the career of Martin as curator as a whole in order to understand better his concept for *Magiciens*, the idea of which he developed further in several subsequent projects. Martin began his career at the Musée National d'Art Moderne in Paris before he moved to the Centre Pompidou. Already in 1977, when the Centre Pompidou opened, he was keen to include several loans from the Musée de l'Homme in the inauguration show in order to "prove the existence of art and artistic expression beyond the Western world."[22] Thus, his life's project surfaced at a very early point in time.

14 **Ibid.**
15 **Thomas McEvilley**, "The Global Issue," in: Thomas McEvilley, *Art and Otherness*, McPherson & Company, Kingston (NY), 1992, p. 154.
16 **Ibid.**, p. 157.
17 **Rasheed Araeen**, "Our Bauhaus, 'Others' Mudhouse," in: *Third Text. Third World Perspectives on Contemporary Art and Culture*, no. 6, Spring 1989, p. 9.
18 **Ibid.**, p. 8.
19 **Everlyn Nicodemus**, "The Center of Otherness," in: Jean Fisher (ed.), *Global Visions: Towards a New Internationalism in the Visual Arts*, Kala Press, London, 1994, p. 102.
20 **Olu Oguibe**, "A Brief Note on Internationalism," in: Fisher 1994, pp. 56f.
21 **See: Bert Steevensz (ed.)**, *Museum of Contemporary Art*, exhib. cat., Artimo Foundation, Amsterdam, 2001, pp. 22f. See also for following quotes.

22 **Martin 1995**, p. 67; translated from the German by the author.

It should be noted that Martin, after he left the Centre Pompidou in 1990, built up a collection of contemporary art in the historic Château d'Oiron. Guided by the idea of a curiosity cabinet, he invited over seventy artists to create works in situ in the historic surroundings. The collection sought to demonstrate the symbiosis of "contemporary creation in an ancient patrimony," and was presented in 1993 under the title *Curios & Mirabilia*.[23] As Martin frequently mentioned, it was the legacy of the Surrealists that had inspired him to create unusual combinations of art and curiosity objects.

3.

One of the earliest projects after *Magiciens* was the exhibition *Rencontres Africaines*, which could be paraphrased as "Africa Meets Africa," in 1994.[24] It was held at the new Institute du Monde Arabe building, because at the time Martin had no exhibition venue in Paris. Nine artists figured in the show; five from the Maghreb countries plus Ethiopia and Egypt, and four from sub-Saharan Africa.[25] They represented an "encounter" between "white" and "black" Africa, which as the artists argued, had never taken note of each other in the field of art. Selection was in the hands of the artists Farid Belkahia from Morocco and Abdoulaye Konaté from Mali; there was no interference of French curators in order to allow two aesthetic creeds to meet each other and to discover their "affinities." The two artists were of different ages: Belkahia represented an older generation with exhibition practice going back to the 1970s; Konaté had first studied painting in Cuba, but in the meantime had turned to installation art. Both had positions in the developing art scene of their respective countries. Exchanges between Belkahia and Konaté (interviews and dialogs) were conducted in French, the lingua franca of the former colonial rulers, and thus represented Francophone Africa, which in the 1990s was soon challenged by the institutional power of Anglophone Africa (including its overseas links with the Afro-American scene). *Rencontres Africaines* also traveled to Johannesburg in South Africa, where it opened in 1995. A beautiful publication expanded on the message of the exhibition with artists' talks and a dialog between Martin and Abdelwahab Meddeb, the Paris-based writer from Tunisia.

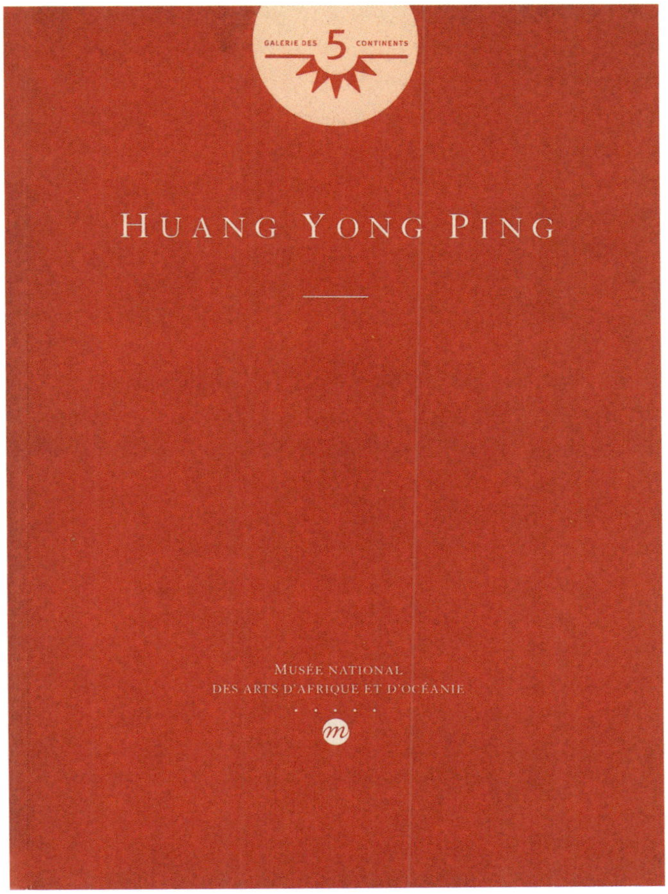

Galerie des 5 continents, *Huang Yong Ping*, exhib. cat., Musée National des Arts d'Afrique et d'Océanie, Paris, et al., Réunion des Musées Nationaux, 1995, book cover.

4.

In 1994, we find Jean-Hubert Martin, rather surprisingly, as director of the Musée National des Arts d'Afrique et d'Océanie (MAAO), in other words, in a straightforward ethnographic context. The museum had been founded by André Malraux in 1962 to give more weight to the display of art against the anthropological background. Martin explained the need to reinvent the museum at the first Biennale of Johannesburg.[26] He condemned the mutual exclusion of the ethnographic museum and the art museum as a signal failure which must be overcome. A reciprocal anthropology would integrate both traditions: "We have yet to create an art museum that excludes no geographical population, a place where artists of all the world can meet on equal

23 **See: http://magiciensdelaterre.fr**/pdf/Biographie_Jean_Hubert_Martin, accessed 05/26/2012.

24 **See: *Rencontres Africaines:*** *exposition d'art actuel*, exhib. cat., Institut du Monde Arabe, Paris, 1994.

25 **See: Brahim Alaoui and Jean-Hubert Martin**, "Introduction," in: *Rencontres Africaines*, 1994, pp. 8f. See also for the following quotes.

26 **Jean-Hubert Martin**, "Art in a Multi-Ethnic Society," in: *Africus: Johannesburg Biennale 1995*, exhib. cat., Transitional Metropolitan Council, Johannesburg, 1995, p. 49. See also for the following quotes.

ground." In this sense, the MAAO in Paris, in his vision, also would give artists "the opportunity to add (or to substitute) their own commentary or analysis to that of Western anthropologists." A new principle of classification "will correspond to the globalization of art."

As director of the MAAO, in September 1995 Martin inaugurated a cycle of solo exhibitions, some of which presented artists from *Magiciens* in a different manner. He named this program *Galerie des 5 continents*, although the title was not meant literally but signified a global space in which every artist had a different background.[27] For Bruly Bouabré, from Ivory Coast, and David Malangi, the indigenous Australian painter from Arnhem Land, Martin could draw on the resources in the MAAO collections. Each artist was invited "to show his work but also to choose a certain number of objects from his own culture and to comment on them,"[28] as Martin wrote in the preface of the small, carefully composed catalogs. In this way Martin linked contemporary art to a specific culture, which the invited artists represented themselves. They offered twofold evidence of a culture's continuity as a living tradition and in their own work.

Bruly Bouabré had close connections with the museum at Abidjan from which he chose some of the objects for comparison. The drawings of his project *Knowledge of the World*, which had been exhibited in *Magiciens*, were already in the museum's collection, which Bouabré praised as "un temple des monuments de l'art africain."[29] Aboriginal artist David Malangi, born in 1927, was asked to comment on the works of fellow painters, which had been collected by the MAAO. Some of Malangi's own works had also been acquired by Karel Kupka for the MAAO as early as 1962 when they were still classed as specimens of traditional art.[30] Huang Yong Ping, another *Magiciens* artist, chose old Chinese animal figures from the Musée Cernuschi in Paris as reference points for his works such as *Le Théatre du Monde*.[31] Huang accepted Martin's idea of a dialog with one's own culture, but objected that "comprehension of one's own culture could not be left to personal opinion."[32]

The situation of the two French artists Bertrand Lavier and Laurent Joubert was different. They were not supposed to link to their own culture, but as part of Martin's contribution to the first Johannesburg Biennale in 1995, they cooperated there with local artists. Lavier exhibited items from everyday culture together with drawings by Esther Mahlangu in which she had rephrased the same type of object in an aesthetic of her own. Joubert organized an installation with street signs that were created by South African women painters, mostly specialized in house painting like Esther Mahlangu.

5.

In 1997, Martin invited Chéri Samba, who had been a great success at the *Magiciens* exhibition, to put on a solo show of 38 works at the MAAO. Museum visitors had first to pass through the exhibition *Arts du Nigeria* with 276 pieces from archaeological sites before they reached the show of Samba's work.[33] Chéri Samba fascinated the French audience with his photorealism, which he linked with pseudo-naivety to a kind of painted cartoon. In the text in his pictures, he uses colonial French and the local language side by side. It was important for his reception in France that his sharp anticolonial slants went hand-in-hand with a relentless critique of the art world. Like anthropologist Bogumil Jewsiewicki, Martin saw Chéri Samba as a Gauguin in an inverse sense.[34]

6.

It should be remembered that Martin had been involved in the Paris Biennale des Jeunes whose 1985 edition, planned on a huge scale, went bankrupt and was eventually moved to Lyon. In 2000, when curating the fifth edition of the Lyon Biennale of Contemporary Art, Martin "continued where *Magiciens de la terre* left off in 1989."[35] The title *Sharing Exoticisms* (*Partages d'exotisme*) confirmed the curator's "radical position toward art with regard to modernity as a neocolonial enterprise, as well as to the opening up of the artistic value criteria."[36] The focus, according to Martin, was the intention to encourage the "sharing of reciprocal

27 **For each** of the exhibitions an individual small catalog was published: *Joe Ben Junior [1]; Huang Yong Ping [2]; Fréderic Bruly Bouabré [3]; David Malangi [4]; Bertrand Lavier [5]*, series Galerie des 5 continents, exhib. cats, Musée National des Arts d'Afrique et d'Océanie, Paris, et al., Réunion des Musées Nationaux, 1995.

28 **Jean-Hubert Martin**, Introduction to the first four catalogs, *Galerie des 5 continents*, pp. 6f.

29 ***Fréderic Bruly Bouabré***, p. 11.

30 ***David Malangi***, p. 11.

31 ***Huang Yong Ping***, p. 45.

32 **See: "Interview with Philippe Garcia de la Rosa,"** in: *Galerie des 5 continents. Huang Yong Ping*, p. 17.

33 **See: Edith Paillat**, in: *Le Journal des Arts*, no. 36, 04/18/1997, (http://www.lejournaldesarts.fr/jda/archives/docs_article/68958/splendeurs-du-nigeria.php, accessed 05/26/2012). The exhibition *Arts du Nigeria*, 04/23–08/18/1997 was curated by Ekpo Eyo and Frank Willett.

34 **See: Jean-Hubert Martin**, "Le non-dit de l'art paint par Chéri Samba," in: *Chéri Samba*, exhib. cat., Musée national des Arts d'Afrique et d'Océanie, Edition Hazan, Paris, 1997, p. 7.

35 **Charlotte Bydler**, *The Global Art World Inc.: On the Globalization of Contemporary Art*, Figura Nova Series 32, Uppsala University Library, Uppsala, 2004, p. 280.

36 **Ibid.**, p. 280.

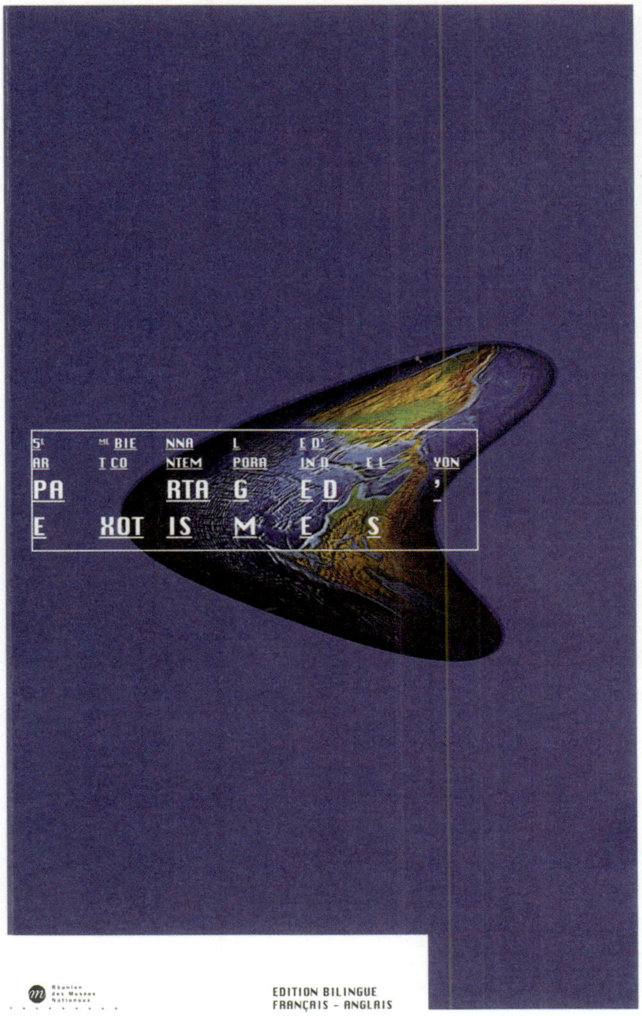

Partage d'Exotismes: 5e Biennale d'art contemporain de Lyon, vol. 2, exhib. cat., Halle Tony Garnier, Lyon, Paris Editions de la Réunion des musées nationaux, Lyon, 2000, book cover.

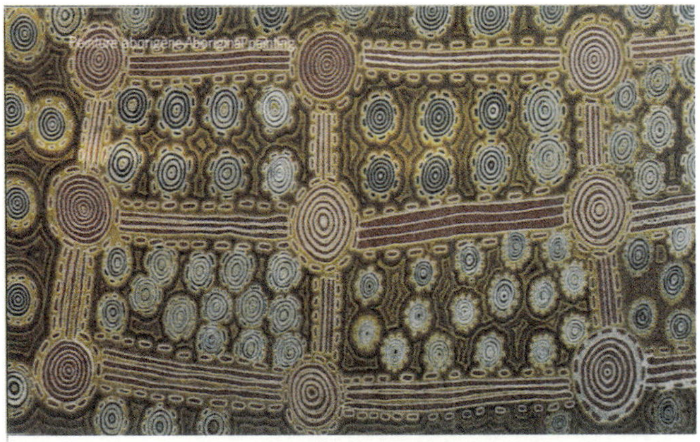

Aboriginal painting: a political art form

One of the essential components of Aboriginal culture is the attachment of the different cla are connected up by "dream lines" stretching over hundreds of kilometres. The member virtue of their filiation, have rights and duties relating to these sites, which are called reference to the "dream time", the primordial age when the mythical ancestors trave continent, shaping the landscape, setting up social rules and putting in place the spirits c be born. They inherited the prerogatives of ceremonies, and the rites associated with t those of representing them in sand drawings and paintings. Thus the owner of a drawi owner of the territory that it showed, and the right to create, or re-create, the former im moral and spiritual authority over the site. In the 1960s, when the Aborigines began their r policy of assimilation, which rejected in principle any idea of Aboriginal culture, their prima official recognition of their rights over ancestral territories. Given that the rules governi land in Aboriginal society were closely connected to those governing the ownership of concerted territorial claims were predicated on the validity of traditional paintings as "title 1963, the people of the Arnhem territory (a tropical region in the north of the country), submissions to the governmental commission for the examination of property rights, pre on bark to substantiate the legitimacy of their claims. (As it happened, they had to wait 1

Aboriginal painting, in: *Partage d'Exotismes: 5e Biennale d'art contemporain de Lyon*, vol. 2, exhib. cat., Halle Tony Garnier, Lyon, Paris Editions de la Réunion des musées nationaux, Lyon, 2000, detail, p. 110.

exoticisms."[37] He was convinced that "if the imposition of an exclusively Western interpretation is to be avoided, an appeal must be made to anthropology."[38] The theoretical framework was delivered by anthropologists like Marc Augé and Carlo Severi. The 22 sections, which were proposed by the anthropologists, represented a novelty with regard to *Magiciens* and "were based on basic human functions […] such as 'to inhabit,' 'to eat' or 'to die'."[39] As he had already done with *Magiciens*, Martin relied completely on the visual: "Each section is introduced not by a title but by an object - in general one that does not belong to the field of contemporary art - which gives the thematic atmosphere and orientation."[40]

The sections were divided by blue curtains whose "insubstantiality suggested that the boundaries were not […] permanent"[41] but could be crossed Some of the more than 100 artists had already participated in the *Magiciens* exhibition. In his review Andrew Budge admitted:

> "[T]he structure did something to mitigate the previously thorny issue of binary polarisation. In fact, the selection of work went further by seeming to embrace a degree of hybridity that contrasted strongly with the 1989 exhibition's search for purity and spirituality."[42]

37 **Jean-Hubert Martin**, "Introduction," in: *Partage d'Exotismes: 5e Biennale d'art contemporain de Lyon*, vol. 1, exhib. cat., Halle Tony Garnier, Lyon, Paris Editions de la Réunion des musées nationaux, Lyon, 2000, p. 51. The catalog comprises two volumes.
The first includes essays by the editors and the curator as well as by the advisory anthropologists (Marc Augé, Alban Bensa, Jacques Leenhardt, Philippe Peltier, and Carlo Severi). The second introduces the artists as well as the 22 sections of the exhibition.

38 **Ibid.**, p. 51.

39 **Andrew Budge**, "*Partage d'Exotismes*: Do 'Magicians' Grow Wise or Just Old?," in: *Third Text*, vol. 16, issue 1, 2002, pp. 87f.

40 **Martin 2000**, vol. 1, p. 51.

41 **Budge 2002**, p. 87.

42 **Ibid.**, p. 89.

7.

The Museum Kunstpalast (until 2011 known as museum kunst palast) in Düsseldorf, of which Jean-Hubert Martin became founding director in 2000, was inaugurated in September 2001 with the exhibition *Altäre: Kunst zum Niederknien* [Altars: Art for Kneeling Down],[43] which immediately triggered a heated discussion in the German media. Already for *Magiciens* Martin had considered including a section "dedicated to the sacred arts and the visual forms of devotion," as he recalled in the Düsseldorf catalog,[44] but this section had now become the theme of an entire exhibition. It was certainly a risk to transgress the well-protected borderline between art and religion but, in questioning this distinction and the prejudices of the modern art system, Martin was pursuing one of his quintessential interests: to rethink the relation of art and ritual in other cultures. He insisted that one had to be prepared for *shared exoticisms* (the title he chose for the Lyon Biennale) now that aesthetics had become "pluralistic" in the global age and the "exotic" was no longer a reason for exclusion. Already at the time of *Rencontres Africaines* he had "dreamed of an exhibition of altars of different religions and cultures including the Catholics."[45] He introduced the Düsseldorf show with the statement that "altars are comparable with contemporary art installations [...] the difference lies in the freedom of the artist and the group of recipients."[46] The only parallel he was prepared to allow was the voodoo exhibition *Face of the Gods* which Robert Farris Thompson had shown 1993 in New York's Museum for African Arts.[47]

8.

The next occasion for bringing together mainstream art and tribal art was the show *Dialog: Richard Long Jivya S. Mashe*, which Martin curated together with Hervé Perdriolle in 2003 in Düsseldorf. Richard Long was juxtaposed with Jivya Soma Mashe.[48] Mashe belonged to the Warli tribe in the state Maharashtra in India, a tribe with animistic beliefs and a special cult of the Earth. Already in 1976 Mashe

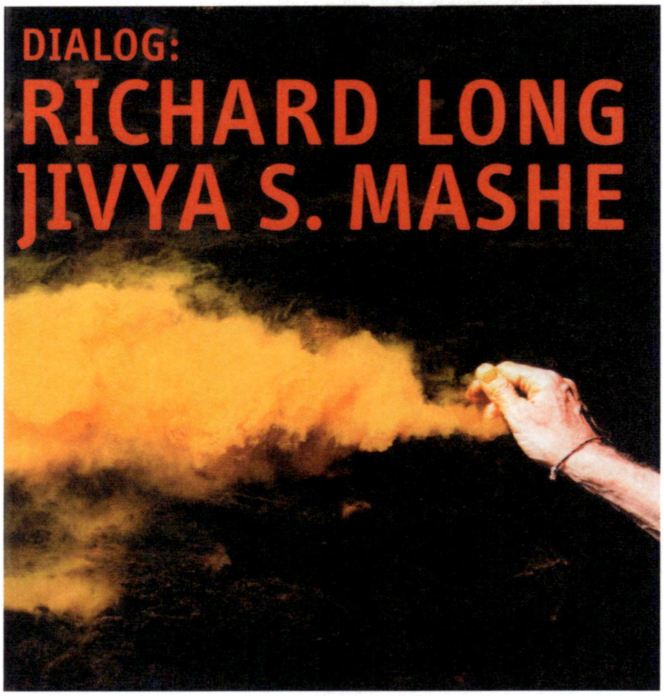

Hervé Perdriolle and Jean-Hubert Martin, *Dialog: Richard Long, Jivya Soma Mashe*, museum kunst palast, Düsseldorf, 2003, book cover.

had received an international award from the Indian government. Perdriolle also had recommended him for the *Magiciens* exhibition but Mashe declined to participate because of obligations in India. The Düsseldorf exhibition documented an encounter of Richard Long and Mashe in the Indian artist's village, which Perdriolle had moderated. The curator wrote in the catalog:

> "Indian tribal art is a more or less unknown quantity for us [in the West]. [...] the proliferation of sacred Buddhist, Jain, Hindu, and Muslim arts has as good as eclipsed the tribal art of this subcontinent. [...] In the 1970s [...] the Indian government came to the rescue of all its different ethnic communities." It "provided these artists [...] with paper and canvas. [...] these new materials [...] helped to introduce [...] ancestral art [...] beyond their geography boundaries."[49]

In the Düsseldorf show, the old situation of Western exhibition art and tribal art, in a way, was turned upside down. Richard Long was presented with photographs from his projects in the tribal landscape of India, while Jivya Soma Mashe contributed his paintings, executed on canvas and framed, for the exhibition space.

43 **See:** ***Altäre - Kunst zum Niederknien***, exhib. cat., museum kunst palast, Düsseldorf, Hatje Cantz, Ostfildern, 2001.

44 **See: Martin 2001**, p. 14.

45 **Martin 1995**, pp. 70f.

46 **Martin 2001**, p. 13.

47 **See: Ibid.**, p. 10.

48 **See: Hervé Perdriolle and Jean-Hubert Martin**, *Dialog: Richard Long, Jivya Soma Mashe*, museum kunst palast, Düsseldorf, 2003.

49 **Hervé Perdriolle**, "Jivya Soma Mashe. Warli Tribe," in: Perdriolle and Martin 2003, p. 36.

9.

In 2004, Jean-Hubert Martin and David Elliott presented a new view on African art when they engaged Simon Njami as curator of the traveling exhibition *Africa Remix* with 86 artists, which started in Düsseldorf.[50] The choice of a curator from Africa was not by chance but was intended to change the perspective on African art. Simon Njami from Cameroon had been editor of the *Revue Noire* from 1991 on. In a way the show was an answer to Enwezor's Documenta 11 exhibition (2002) in which only five artists from Africa had participated. In the catalog for the 3rd Moscow Biennale of Contemporary Art (2009), Martin recalled that the show *Africa Remix* had produced "a vibrant interest in African cultures and their contemporary conditions."[51] In the Düsseldorf catalog he argued that globalization no longer allows any purity of style nor for following the familiar patterns of art history. The new mobility, in his view, had removed the old frontiers.[52] It is again the issue of exclusion that Martin was seeking to overcome. When traveling with friends in the late 1970s in Nigeria he had discovered a type of colorful funeral art. One of the artists, Mike Chukwukelu, he had therefore included in his *Magiciens* show. It is significant that Martin, at great length, again justified a lifelong project which began with *Magiciens*. And it was the implied criticism of Western modernism which led him to challenge the mainstream art exhibitions with their tendency to exclude any participant who would not be acceptable to Western taxonomy.

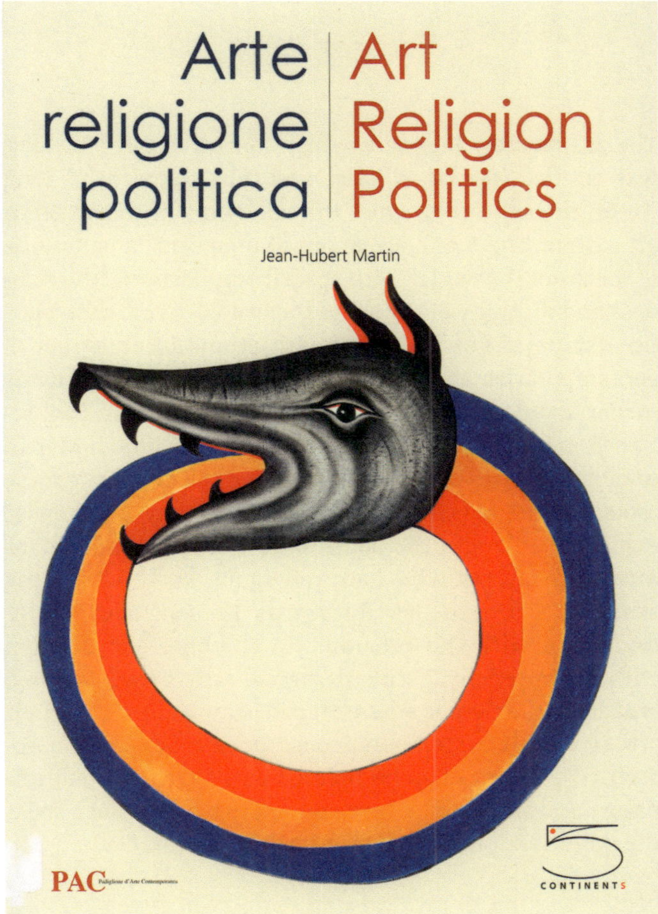

Jean-Hubert Martin (ed.), *Art, Religion, Politics*, exhib. cat., Padiglione d'Arte Contemporanea, Milan, 2005, book cover.

10.

In 2005, Martin curated *Art, Religion, Politics* at the Padiglione d'Arte Contemporanea (PAC) in Milan as an occasion to reintroduce his concern for the neglected part of religion.[53] There were again Aboriginal artists and artists like Bruly Bouabré or José Bedia from Cuba. Their counterparts were six avant-garde modernists such as Joseph Beuys and Lucio Fontana who represented in Martin's view "the Christian tradition [...] in the trajectory of modernity."[54] "The difference between the resurgence of Christian symbols in contemporary Western art and works deriving from traditional beliefs pertains to the distinction between the sacred and the religious."[55] The sacred, as he argues, belongs to all religions, whereas religion "requires a community sharing a faith." Today's intercultural relations demand new questions as to the "role that religious forms are likely to take in artistic creation." The Western artists were also chosen for their engagement with matters of religion.

50 **See: *Afrika Remix., Zeitgenössische Kunst eines Kontinents*,** exhib. cat., museum kunst palast, Düsseldorf, et al., Hatje Cantz, Ostfildern, 2004. Apart from the German edition abridged editions were published in English and French. The exhibition also traveled to Stockholm and Johannesburg.

51 **Jean-Hubert Martin,** "Against Exclusion," in: *3rd Moscow Biennale of Contemporary Art 2009: Against Exclusion*, exhib. cat., The Garage Center for Contemporary Culture, Moscow, Artchronika, Moscow, 2009, p. 30.

52 **See: Jean-Hubert Martin,** "Die Rezeption zeitgenössischer afrikanischer Kunst und ihre Entwicklung," in: *Afrika Remix*, pp. 33f.

53 **See: Jean-Hubert Martin (ed.),** *Art, Religion, Politics*, exhib. cat., Padiglione d'Arte Contemporanea, Milan, 2005.

54 **Martin 2005**, p. 20.

55 **Ibid.**, p. 21. Also for the following quotes.

11.

The 3rd Moscow Biennale, which Martin curated in 2009, was entitled *Against Exclusion* and thus signaled his long commitment to counteract the taxonomy of the Western art system. The Biennale set out to represent "a panorama of the art of the world" with special emphasis on "the richness and diversity of the art of the world."[56] This time Martin juxtaposed Russian artists with a transcultural group of contemporaries. Again in this exhibition he returned to his earlier activities and reintroduced works such as *The Theatre of the World – Bridge* of Huang Yong Ping, which Martin understood as an acknowledgement of the artist's Chinese roots. For the benefit of the Russian visitors, he likewise explained at length the political nature of the indigenous Australian artists who had undergone such a "striking evolution"[57] over the last forty years. He concluded his introduction with the program "to combine globalization with heterogeneity."[58] The Aboriginal artists were featured broadly in the catalog where Martin again argued that their art is certainly contemporaneous. "Critics of Australian Aboriginal paintings," as he pointed out, negate its political nature and all too often "pretend not to notice what a striking evolution it has made over the last 40 years."[59]

Conclusion

In summary, the professional record of Jean-Hubert Martin clearly reveals personal motives for breaking with the routine art exhibitions of the period when his career began. He endeavored to overcome the sterile dualism of art museums and ethnographic museums, which he rejected as a legacy from colonial times. It was not coincidental that, in an interval of only a few years, he was director of the Centre Georges Pompidou and of the Musée des Arts d'Afrique et d'Océanie, in that order. Yet the resonance, which his *Magiciens* project had worldwide, cannot be explained solely in terms of his personal concept. It happened at a moment when everybody was looking for a change in the exhausted modernist routine. Thus, the hostile reactions are easily explainable as thwarted expectations, when people were waiting for quite a different start into the global age.

The *Magiciens* show, as a result, attracted controversies which continue to the present day. To explain its historical role requires a fresh look at the context in which it was conceived. This context also included the Frenchman's attention to the colonial past. Martin was often accused of exoticizing the "others" in the art world, but in fact, his primary concern was to liberate them from the ethnographic prison in which he had found them already back in the 1970s. However, the longing for native art's innocence was threatened by the new dominance of market art which today reaches every part of the globe. The "others" have easily segued into professional artists who look impure with regard to Martin's ideals. Although he attacked William Rubin's outdated '*Primitivism*' show, he was still susceptible to a certain nostalgia for the authentic in ritual and religious art.

It must be added that Martin did not try to recover other modernities or to discover forgotten artists. Instead, his real concern was a new contemporary stage where artists of every kind and provenance would be able to represent the world of today in all its facets. As a result he did not seek to introduce history, but addressed his whole energy to creating a vision of a global world to come. "When I organised *Magiciens de la terre*, many people criticized me for not including artists of the raw art tendency. [...] it would have been exactly opposed to my intention: to put the marginals and the excluded together."[60]

By way of an epilog it must be said that Martin's show did not only act as a catalyst for art in the global age. Its second importance was that it opened a Pandora's box in ethnographic museums which could no longer ignore the emergence of contemporary art outside their colonial collections. Thus, the debate on art from Africa or African art from today similarly became a major issue after the 1989 exhibition.[61] In 1991, Susan Vogel reacted to the *Magiciens* exhibition with the show *Africa Explores* in New York. From the outset she rejected Martin's idea of universal art and divided African art into five different categories (traditional art, new functional art, urban art, international art, and extinct art); categories, however, which were not long-lived. Instead, it soon became clear that such problems are not confined to Africa. Ethnographic departments reluctantly open their doors to the Trojan horse of contemporary art, which releases living artists with a name, a passport, and a sudden success on the market. Generally speaking, from 1989 onwards the impact of globalization on the ethnographic field is no less marked than in the field of biennial art.

56 **Martin 2009**, p. 27.
57 **Ibid.**, p. 30.
58 **Ibid.**, p. 27.
59 **Ibid.**, p. 30.

60 **Martin 2001**, vol. 1, p. 49.
61 **See: Yukya Kagawuchi**, "The Possibility of a Narrative," in: Kenji Yoshida and John Mack (eds.), *Images of Other Cultures*, exhib. cat. The National Museum of Ethnology, Osaka, 1997, p. 272.

Global Art and Anthropology: The Situated Gaze and Local Art Worlds in Africa

Thomas Fillitz

Introduction

Following the reflexive period in anthropology after the "Writing Culture" debate of the mid-1980s, in the late 1980s and early 1990s the program of anthropology shifted massively towards processes of globalization. New concepts were elaborated and discussed, such as Arjun Appadurai's "global cultural economy," Ulf Hannerz' "global culture," and shortly afterwards scholars like Nina Glick-Schiller introduced studies on "transnationalism".[1]

Research fields became pluralized, in the sense of a greater consideration of cultural flows and scalar cultural interconnections. What had been for a long time an unspoken given - the link of culture, territory, and people - became destabilized. Specifically, it was the Indian-American anthropologist Akhil Gupta's and the American anthropologist James Ferguson's achievement to have transferred the old conception of cultural difference and cultural subjugation, as a matter of disconnected cultures and the advent of colonial domination, to conceiving difference as a consequence of the specificity of spatial connections, characterized by power relations.

> "For if one begins with the premise that spaces have *always* been hierarchically interconnected, instead of naturally disconnected, then cultural and social change becomes not a matter of cultural contact and articulation, but one of rethinking difference *through* connection."[2]

With these overall thematic changes in general anthropology, and the attendant methodological reformulations of ethnographic field research, new concepts were introduced. Anthropology nowadays rather engages with diversity as the uneven, power-related distribution of cultural difference, with disjunctive global cultural flows, with alternative (multiple) modernities, and with situated gazes on social, economic, political, and cultural phenomena - from the viewpoints of the societies concerned.[3]

The anthropology of art, as a subdiscipline of anthropology, also operates with these concepts to understand how the flow of images and works of art is affected. It is from such a vantage point that the following reflections are formulated. In the first part, I deal with the shifts in research and introduce several concepts, which scholars have elaborated to cope with present global art phenomena from an anthropological perspective. In the second section, I present

1 **Arjun Appadurai**, "Disjuncture and Difference in the Global Cultural Economy," in: Mike Featherstone (ed.), *Global Culture. Nationalism, Globalization, Modernity*, Sage Publications, London, 1990, pp. 295-310; Ulf Hannerz, "Cosmopolitans and Locals in World Culture," in: Featherstone 1990, pp. 237-252; Nina Glick-Schiller and Georges Fouron, "Terrains of Blood and Nation: Haitian Transnational Social Fields," in: *Ethnic and Racial Studies*, vol. 22, no.2, 1999, pp. 340-366.

2 **Akhil Gupta and James Ferguson (eds.)**, *Culture, Power, Place. Explorations in Critical Anthropology*, Duke University Press, Durham (NC), 1997, p. 35.

3 **The notion** of "situated knowledge" was introduced by Donna Haraway. See: Donna Haraway, "Situated Knowledges; The Science Question in Feminism and the Privilege of Partial Perspectives," in: *Feminist Studies*, 1988, pp. 575-599.

scholarly attempts to produce periods of art and schemas of ordering the modern and contemporary art of Africa. These artworks are important, as it is obvious that neither looking at these works with categories drawn from Western imaginations of African societies, nor using notions and categories of the European-North American art world[4] can apprehend what were the real activities and strategies enacted by artists from Africa. Finally, I propose in the third part, from an anthropological vantage point, an approach that takes as its starting point the local art world, the conditions under which art is created. It is an approach that challenges us to consider closely what "global interactions" mean, and to conceive global discourses as regionally scalar in their spatial outreach. The other main idea presented in this section concerns the analysis of particular works of art. If a multiplicity of artistic trajectories is acknowledged, and if we look at these from the specific art worlds, then we might unravel the complex matrix of combinations of styles, concepts, themes, or political situations, which are compressed within the artistic expression.

Repositioning the Anthropology of Art

Until well into the 1980s, the anthropology of art was solely concerned with art created according to "traditional" stylistic canons in small-scale societies, focusing according to different concepts on the "value of art," the work of art in relation to everyday and noneveryday social phenomena, that is, the cultural values and qualities.[5]

The shift towards studies of processes of globalization in anthropology furthered the quest to reposition the anthropology of art within the overall discipline. In the US, George E. Marcus and Fred R. Myers advocated a new "critical anthropology of art."[6] They located their argument in the close relationship between anthropology and the contemporary Western art world. Instead of "translating" artworks for audiences in Europe and North America, they proposed to analyze the flow of art objects into the European-North American art world. Marcus and Myers suggested that the critical anthropological approach would consist in unraveling the broader contexts of practices involved in the production of images in other cultures. According to Marcus and Myers, art is a central field where difference, identity, and cultural values are produced and negotiated, and it is anthropology's task to clarify and criticize the production and articulation of cultural difference as practiced in the global art world.

The consequences of this approach are: there is not only one and essential meaning of artworks that we anthropologists have to grasp. Rather, we should strive to explain how, during such cultural flows, meanings are transformed, and how hegemonic power strategies are enacted for the European-North American art world to keep control of these flows. Contrary to evaluating artworks from wherever according to unitary standards, anthropologists are well equipped to consider the complexity of artworks from regional art worlds, with either no connection to Western art history, or with multiple connections to artistic expressions from different local, regional, and global cultural contexts.

Another theoretical approach focusing on art from wherever was Alfred Gell's *Art and Agency*.[7] Gell seeks to embed the anthropology of art well within the overall discipline of social anthropology. He radically advocates that art is about doing; therefore, an anthropology of art must be connected to theories of agency. Alfred Gell thus formulates two major concepts: efficacious agency and distributed mind. First, art objects may take a mediating role in the social process: seeing the splendor of an artwork incites the beholder to agency. The warrior, for instance, who is confronted with the artistic beauty of the Asmat shield, may see in its carvings the product of nonhuman forces (spirits), which are allies of his enemy. Second, relying on fractal concepts developed by Marilyn Strathern in Melanesian cultures, Gell transformed Strathern's concept of the "distributed person"[8] into one of the "distributed mind." This aids analysis (a posteriori) of the œuvre of an artist through understanding different periods of the artist's creativity as spatial connections with various concepts, ideas, or sociopolitical phenomena. In a similar way, the concept may be applied to connect a singular work to the artworks of the art world.[9]

All these concepts of an anthropology of art have one feature in common: the study of the phenomenon of art

4 **The notion of art world** is used in the sense used by Becker. See: Howard Becker, *Art Worlds*, University of California Press, Berkeley (CA), 1982. For anthropological studies see, e. g.: Deborah Ericson, *In the Stockholm Art World*, Stockholm Studies in Social Anthropology, University of Stockholm, 1988; Fred R. Myers, *Painting Culture. The Making of an Aboriginal High Art*, Duke University Press, Durham (NC), 2002.

5 **This approach** was introduced in 1925 by Raymond Firth against former evolutionist and diffusionist forms of understanding. See: Raymond Firth, "The Maori Carver," in: *Journal of the Polynesian Society*, vol. 34, no. 136, 1925, pp. 277–291.

6 **George E. Marcus and Fred R. Myers**, "Introduction: The Traffic in Culture," in: George E. Marcus and Fred R. Myers (eds.), *The Traffic in Culture. Refiguring Art and Anthropology*, University of California Press, Berkeley (CA), 1995, pp. 1–51.

7 **See: Alfred Gell**, *Art and Agency. An Anthropological Theory*, Clarendon Press, Oxford, 1998.

8 **See: Marilyn Strathern**, *The Gender of the Gift. Problems with Women and Problems with Society in Melanesia*, Studies in Melanesian Anthropology 6, University of California Press, Berkeley (CA), 1988.

9 **This approach** corresponds in some way to Arthur C. Danto's notion of the Art World. See: Arthur C. Danto, "The Artworld," in: *Journal of Philosophy*, vol. 61, no. 19, 1964, pp. 571–584.

on the basis of anthropology's most prominent empirical methodological tool: ethnographic field research. This has important implications, insofar as the primary framework of scrutiny is constituted by a regionally specific art world, whether the focus is on global or transnational flows, or on the specific production of works of art.

Any question related to the global art world, such as global art, will therefore be approached from the situated gaze of the interconnections between a particular, local, or regional art world and the global. In this context, Nicholas Thomas and Diane Losche have developed the notion of "double vision."[10] This draws our attention to the complex entanglements between global processes and the particular regional trajectories of art creation. "Double vision" encourages scholars and artists to consider the global art world as a disjunctive order, to look at the production of contemporary art from the perspective of dislocated centers, and to acknowledge specific historical trajectories of conjuncture and disjuncture between local art worlds and the global art world.

Periodization and Structuration of Modern and Contemporary Art of Africa

From the above, it appears obvious that for a long time the anthropology of art did not deal with the changes in the arts of African cultures which followed colonial conquest and dominance. With few exceptions, anthropological studies contributed to those debates mainly by focusing on various local forms of popular art within assumed, bounded local art worlds, and possibly extended these considerations to a few other modern art expressions in local art worlds before the 1990s. The centrality of the methodology of ethnographic fieldwork also favors a focus on local forms of art, and since the mid-1980s, as I outlined in the introduction, anthropology has refrained from grand narratives in any respect.

With these remarks in mind, the following examples of periodization and structuration of modern and contemporary art of Africa are dealt with less against the horizon of tending to develop such a grand narrative of the periods and structures of these arts, and more to support study of the diversity of contemporary art of Africa through debates about global art. There are various difficulties in such grand attempts at ordering. Local art worlds in Africa were long considered as disconnected and confined to the new states' territories. The first art schools, however, institutionalized before and immediately after the independence of African states mainly created training programs that had connections to old European art traditions. At that time artists who had trained in Europe and returned were also dealt with only within these political and cultural boundaries. The workshop schools, founded by expatriates in the period from the 1940s to the 1960s, were considered as production of art by creating close interconnections with old regional African art traditions, and the phenomenon of popular art, although even locally quite diverse, was viewed only as specifically local. Finally, in the early twentieth century, and even more in the time around states gaining their independence (broadly speaking from 1950 to 1960), the already existing multiplicity of cultural spaces in Africa became even more pluralized, and so did the artistic production.

Dealing with the development of modern art of Africa from the early 1900s until the 1970s, Kojo Fosu adopted a historical periodization divided into five parts. "Transition" covers the period in which artist carvers developed a neotraditionalist style as well as new stylistic expressions which were inspired by early twentieth-century interactions with European colonial powers and Christian missions. "New directions" comprises artists who introduced new forms of artistic expression, in particular Aina Onabolu, who became famous for the introduction of portrait painting in African art. "Experimentations (1960s–1970s)" corresponds to the period of the independent nations. Fosu deals with what he designates as folk art, souvenir art, the workshop schools, but also with movements of former art students, like the so-called "Zaria rebels" (the Zaria Art Society). "Independent experimentalists (1960s–1970s)" is substructured under the criterion of the "Sculptural Idiom," which is artistically articulated either as "stylized elongations" (e.g., Kobina Bucknor), or as "magnificent elongations" (e.g., Vincent Kofi). This section also contains the subcategory "Structural assemblage" - the combination of different materials (e.g., Christian Lattier), and ends with the "Makerere direction," artists trained at and influenced by the Makerere Art School (Kampala). The periodization ends with "Challenges since the 1970s," and deals with a variety of artists from West Africa (mostly Nigeria and Ghana) and East Africa.[11]

Marshall Mount's account of the development of modern art of Africa from 1920 to the early 1970s is structured in two main parts. One part deals with different art genres ("survival of traditional styles," "mission-inspired style," and "souvenir art"), and the other, the "emergence of a new art," is subdivided mainly according to European-style art

10 See: **Nicholas Thomas and Diane Losche (eds.)**, *Double Vision. Art Histories and Colonial Histories in the Pacific*, Cambridge University Press, Cambridge (MA), 1999.

11 See: **Kojo Fosu**, *20th Century Art of Africa*, Artist Alliance, Accra, 1993.

schools either in Anglophone or Francophone East, Central, and West Africa.[12]

Jean Kennedy focuses on the years after independence. She structures her history, first, according to regions, and second, differentiates within them using categories that seem close to imaginations of some African cultural cores. The principal chapters are "responding to the challenge" (Nigeria and the West African Coast), "crescent in the hand" (Senegal and Sudan), "wax and gold" (Ethiopia), "creators of myth" (artists from Tanzania, Kenya, Uganda, Mozambique, and Zimbabwe), and "testament" (South Africa).[13]

In the context of a major exhibition on the twentieth-century art of Africa, Susan Vogel aims at another structure. She distinguishes, for instance, between "traditional art: elastic continuum," "new functional art: future traditions," "urban art: art of the here and now," and "international art: the official story."[14] Her structure is based on form and content; she considers these chapters as "five loosely defined strains" which are based not on one overall criterion, but on "clusters of traits."[15]

Before dealing with three other, more promising attempts at structuration, some remarks regarding these first examples seem appropriate. First, given the plurality of modern and contemporary art creations of Africa, it is obvious that a narration according to a few criteria is quite unsatisfactory. Kojo Fosu, for instance, shifts in his historically based discourse between ordering according to sociopolitical events (the periods of independencies) and others, which pretend to be more connected to art discourses. Moreover, the differentiation between "experimentations" and "independent experimentalists" is not very convincing, particularly considering that "experimentations" is comprised of such fundamentally different art genres as folk art, souvenir art, and the workshop schools - and even includes such highly challenging art movements as the Nigerian "Zaria rebels."

In the case of Kennedy's and Vogel's periodizing structures, things are different insofar as a Western gaze is obvious. Kennedy quite clearly relates her categories to some ideas of African cultural cores - myths, symbols, ancestors, and spirits. Vogel's main categories, "new functional art," "urban art," and "international art," are more than vague.

Although Susan Vogel acknowledged from the beginning "that the whole exercise is typical of late twentieth-century Western scholarship,"[16] it is worthwhile restating the underlying structure of these categories; namely, Western-construed ones into which artworks of Africa have to fit, as John Picton criticizes.[17] Then, the consequence is that under "international art," academically trained artists and local workshop schools trained artists - by expatriate Europeans - are mentioned side by side. This was the case with the Senegalese artist Iba N'Diaye, who was fiercely opposed to workshop schools and considered himself in the tradition of modern art *tout court*.

The three structurations of modern and contemporary art of Africa presented in the following, are different. They distinguish artistic production in relationship to the multiple cultural spaces, as well as the sociopolitical configurations that have been shaping present African States, and which influence the life worlds of the artists.

Valentin Mudimbe proposes two sets of criteria, internal and external, in order to distinguish between three main currents in contemporary African art. Internal criteria deal with style, motif, theme, and content, whereas the external criteria concern contexts - of the artwork's creation, of the cultural history, the sociological milieu, and the artist's intention. On this basis, he identifies a "tradition-inspired trend, a modernist trend, and a popular art"[18]:

> "In short, where modernist and tradition-inspired art reflect the highest cultural values as defined and, supposedly, lived out in the inner circles of acculturated African society, popular art, made at the periphery of the same society, scans, interprets, and occasionally defies such values by diffusing their explicitness, challenging their discursivity, and bringing into circulation new readings of founding events, mythologies, and social injustice, as well as popular representations of a history of alienation ...".[19]

Finally, Mudimbe considers that the tradition-inspired and modernist trends constitute a single trend as they have three traits in common: first, the sociocultural context of the artistic creativity (ateliers or art schools); second, a philosophical trait, a spiritual and intellectual "revolution" in a creolized social milieu; and third, an aesthetic trait, the artistic activities of symbolizing. Popular art is strongly connected to local or regional histories, and is quite diverse in its forms of expression.

12 See: **Marshall W. Mount**, *African Art. The Years since 1920*, Da Capo Press, New York (NY), 1989.

13 See: **Jean Kennedy**, *New Currents, Ancient Rivers. Contemporary African Artists in a Generation of Change*, Smithsonian Institution Press, Washington, D.C., 1992.

14 See: **Susan Vogel**, *Africa Explores. 20th Century African Art*, The Center for African Art, Prestel, Munich, 1991.

15 **Ibid.**, p.10.

16 **Ibid.**

17 See: **John Picton**, "In Vogue, or the Flavour of the Month: The New Way to Wear Black," in: *Third Text* 23, 1993, p. 95.

18 See: **Valentin Y. Mudimbe**, "Reprendre," in: Valentin Y. Mudimbe, *The Idea of Africa*, Indiana University Press, Bloomington (IN), et al., 1994, p. 161.

19 **Ibid.**, p. 162.

André Magnin and Jacques Soulillou selected a spatial concept for ordering. Their purpose, however, is less a focus on modern and contemporary art of Africa in general, and more a close view on the works of the "Contemporary African Art Collection" (CAAC), that is, from artists, who were not trained in European or North American art schools, whose artistic expression is so to speak "100% African."[20] Magnin and Soulillou speak of an "imaginary map" which is divided into three regions, "territory," "frontier," and "world":

> "Our investigations have led us to draw a map which we have creased twice to define three areas: Territory, Frontier, and World. These categories are not meant to create a new stylistic taxonomy, like the terms 'traditional,' 'urban,' 'international,'... To begin with, we do not consider these categories hard and fast ...
> While Territory is congruent with an area of *forces,* World is congruent with an area of *signs.* Frontier is the grey area between forces and signs."[21]

The last approach is that of Okwui Enwezor and Chika Okeke-Agulu, which they developed for contemporary art of Africa since the 1980s.[22] The authors acknowledge the complexity and multiplicity of cultural spaces that shape the sociocultural, political, and economic landscape of Africa today. A discourse about contemporary art of Africa requires a fundamental difference to the narrative of modern (Occidental) art history. They therefore contextualize the art production in reference to the geopolitical changes, and deal with artistic strategies, theories, and themes, or artistic reflections about the body, gender, and sexuality. In doing so, Enwezor and Okeke-Agulu avoid any narration following a periodization according to style, because artists develop strategies for working with media that are at hand in the present to cope with societies in a permanent flux:

> "Hence, within the aesthetic structures and formal methods of contemporary African art, artistic concepts and their discourses are deployed in a panoply of ways. Here local and nonlocal, international and global, academic and neotraditional strategies intermingle, creating the aesthetic glue that binds new artistic languages to contemporary perceptions of art."[23]

These three last approaches differ from the former ones because they aim at developing the system of ordering the artistic productions from a more local or regional perspective. Although Mudimbe's categories still seem quite informed by the project of Susan Vogel, he nevertheless formulates them within the framework of his concept of *reprendre* which he considers to be an "image of the contemporary activity of African art."[24]

Magnin and Soulillou, as well as Enwezor and Okeke-Agulu, go further with their respective approaches. Magnin and Soulillou refer to "intensities" which constitute fluid connections to territory, frontier, and world. Enwezor and Okeke-Agulu distinguish as contexts political constellations, artistic strategies, and themes. Moreover, they include creations of works of art from Northern and South Africa, whereas in most of the other narratives presented, these regions are not dealt with.

Multiple Spaces and Entanglements of Contemporary Art of Africa

The consequences of the difficulties of the debate sketched above are, first, that no exclusionism and no exclusivism should be applied to considerations of the contemporary art production of Africa; that is, that there is not one encompassing contemporary artistic expression, and the notion of the contemporary applies to the multiple art forms existing at present in Africa. Second, a close study of regional art worlds is required, as for a long time they received only very light flows of information or knowledge of what was going on at a global scale, whereas the global art world assumes and asserts intensified global flows and interconnections.[25] Third, as both Magnin and Soulillou as well as Enwezor and Okeke-Agulu suggest, an approach with a more varied set of frameworks, or contexts, has to be reflected upon, which takes into consideration the spatial "spreading out" for the specific imagination of the concrete artistic production.

Regarding the notion of "contemporary," Soulillou challenges and even rejects the European-North American notion for art of Africa. According to him, "contemporary" in the European-North American art world defines the horizon of artistic expressions so far created, as it is taught in

20 **This was the title** of an exhibition of artworks of the CAAC at the Guggenheim Museum, Bilbao, October 2006 - February 2007.

21 **André Magnin and Jacques Soulillou**, "Introduction," in: André Magnin, Jacques Soulillou (eds.), *Contemporary Art of Africa*, Abrams, New York (NY), 1996, p. 11.

22 **See: Okwui Enwezor and Chika Okeke-Agulu**, *Contemporary African Art since the 1980s*, Damiani, Bologna, 2009.

23 **Ibid.**, p. 6.

24 **Mudimbe 1994**, p. 154. The notion of *reprendre* nevertheless applies to artistic practices before and after independencies; it is no longer an issue for the younger generations of artists.

25 **In the meantime**, however, institutions like Dak'Art, the art biennial of Dakar, have aimed at reducing this problem to some extent, although artists at the 2010 venue still mentioned the existing barriers to mobility and flows of knowledge.

art schools, and how this education is combined with the training of going beyond and finding new forms of representation. For Soulillou, such preconditions are missing in African contexts. There, "contemporary" refers to a continuum between activation and transposition of visual traditions of ethnic groups, as in the documentary paper drawings of Frédéric Bruly Bouabré, and the reference to contemporary social reality, as in the visionary city models of Bodys Isek Kingelez.[26]

Enwezor and Okeke-Agulu place their reflections on the "contemporary" in a wider horizon, and take into consideration the panoply of artistic backgrounds, strategies, and scalar interconnections. For them, "to be contemporary [...] means having the conceptual capacity to deploy a response to the present through self-reflexive reanimations of methods of creative inquiry."[27] This conception of "contemporary" allows to better discriminate among the actual diversity of artistic expressions by consideration of the self-reflexive processes.

Much has been postulated about the encompassing global flows and interconnections, their intensities, and their speed. Empirical gazes on local art worlds, nevertheless, unravel a different image, and rather suggest huge structural differences, as my research in Abidjan's and Dakar's art world prove. In Dakar, the school of fine arts, École des Arts du Sénégal, was founded in 1957, and the Manufacture des Tapisseries in 1966 in Thiès, some 70 km east of Dakar, which is identified with the work of Papa Ibra Tall. The original *village des artistes* in Colobane, old colonial buildings of a former military camp that had been reoccupied by artists, was cleared by the police in 1983, a new one was installed in the late 1980s by the Senegalese government with some sixty studios near the town's main football stadium.

The main space for interaction and exchange of knowledge is the art biennial Dak'Art, founded in 1992, and which is dedicated since 1996 to contemporary art of Africa. The first museum for modern art in sub-Saharan Africa, the Musée Dynamique (founded in 1966), was closed by the mid-1970s, and today there is only one private museum for contemporary Black arts, the Musée Boribana (founded in 1990). The Galerie Nationale (founded in 1983) has no exhibition program, but can be hired for specific art events. Within the space of the Musée de l'IFAN is another exhibition space, the Musée Théodore Monod, which is rented, for example, by the Dak'Art secretariat to host the official venues of the biennial. Other exhibition spaces are the former factory Biscuiterie de Médina, privately owned, and others provided by the cultural institutions of foreign states like the "Institut Français," particularly its Galerie Le Manège, the German Goethe-Institut, and the British Council. There are several galleries, and their number is growing, but they do not correspond to galleries in the meaning of the European-North American art world. These venues allow artists to exhibit, and gallery dealers are, as some artists said, dealers of artworks, which they sell in addition to handicraft commodities (furniture, textiles, etc.). Additionally, there is a growing number of collectors, both private and institutions, the most important one being Eiffage-Sénégal, curated by artist Mauro Petroni. There are some art critics, art historians, and a few curators.

What this local art world lacks is specialized shops for artistic materials, and, above all art media: journals, magazines, catalogs, or radio and TV broadcasts. Questioned about the local situation of their creative processes, artists in Dakar mostly mention the missing connections and exchanges, be they with their homologues in other African states, or with the contemporary global art world, although most of them nowadays rely on the new technologies of the Internet. Such characteristics of this art world have profound repercussions on artistic practices, and inform self-reflexive activities. A consideration of the local art world, therefore, raises the question of what is possible at a given time in a given environment, and of the actual quality of what is called "global."

Reflections on global art also imply consideration of the notion of the "art world" as developed by Arthur C. Danto, in particular in the context of its reconsideration. In the context of a pluralistic art world, the contemporary is now characterized by the style of the bricolage of different forms of style.[28] In the following I shall not include power relations within the global art world, or the power of exhibition. Here, my focus is the various connections artists rely upon in their creative endeavor, or what Gerardo Mosquera calls art "from here."[29] Although I prefer to speak of spatial trajectories that the artists produce, my considerations relate to Gell's concept of the "distributed mind" and Thomas' and Losche's "double vision."

To the section "Rétrospectives" of Dak'Art 2010, Viyé Diba, winner of the prize of the President of the State in 1998, contributed the installation *mémoire économique* (2008). The main part of the work consisted of questionnaires in transparent sheet protectors hanging on nylon strips from the

26 See: **Jacques Soulillou**, "Für eine Phänomenologie der afrikanischen Kunst," in: Alfons Hug (ed.), *Neue Kunst aus Afrika*, Haus der Kulturen der Welt Berlin, Edition Braus, Heidelberg, 1996, pp. 77, 80.

27 **Enwezor and Okeke-Agulu 2009**, p. 21.

28 See: **Arthur C. Danto**, *Das Fortleben der Kunst*, Wilhelm Fink Verlag, Munich, 2000, p. 32, (original: *After the End of Art*, Princeton, 1997).

29 See: **Gerardo Mosquera**, "The Global Sphere. Art, Cultural Contexts and Internationalization," available online at: http://www.globalartmuseum.de/site/guest_author/304, accessed 06/26/2012.

ceiling. The topic of the installation was the nondocumented emigration of young Senegalese on fishing boats over the Atlantic Ocean, an acute topic in Senegalese society, and Diba had conducted questionnaire interviews among the local population.

From the beginning of his work as an artist, Diba has been interested in the relationship of humankind and environment.[30] From a local perspective, this interest may be related to the experience of traditional art, insofar as this art always has been connected to concrete social contexts. Regarding the material used in the installation - pieces of textiles and cloth on the floor, small bits in the sheet protectors - a trajectory may be traced to his early use of recycled material in his paintings, a strategy employed by many artists in Senegal; a central element of the Moustapha Dimé's works, for example, was driftwood. This strategy relates to the École de Dakar, but there are also other strategies which have been quite dispersed in West Africa from the 1970s onwards. Another possible trajectory links up with the laboratory Agit-Art, which was most active in the 1970s, and objected strongly to the state-art of *Négritude*.[31] Specifically, Diba's form of representation may be connected to Joe Ouakam's installations in the middle of his courtyard in the center of Dakar; however, it must be made clear that Ouakam's intentions are different to those of Viyé Diba.

Further, it must be borne in mind that the artist has traveled widely outside of Africa, and this installation must also be viewed from the perspective of its connections to the European-North American art world. At this point I would like to mention the importance of the questionnaire interviews and the collected textiles and pieces of cloth which bring Diba into the framework of what Hal Foster designated "the artist as ethnographer."[32] Additionally, the type of social intervention Viyé Diba chose for *mémoire économique* can also be embedded within Nicolas Bourriaud's concept of "relational aesthetics," which he developed for artistic strategies in the global art world that focus on intensive interaction between artist and local populations and audiences.[33]

This brief example should suffice to show how important it is to analyze works of art created in particular art worlds from the viewpoint of "double vision," and to elaborate, from an anthropological perspective, the various trajectories found compressed (or articulated) within the individual work of art.

If the *mémoire économique* installation is considered solely in terms of its relationship to "the artist as ethnographer," all other trajectories would be neglected. Viyé Diba's work *mémoire économique* would be experienced only within the appropriative epistemology of the European-North American art world, and other major entanglements erased. Dominant styles of expression may be disseminated in the global art world, nevertheless, it is vital to elucidate the multiple trajectories elaborated in respect to Viyé Diba's installation, and therefore to unravel the complex aesthetic matrix that such a work of art represents.

Conclusion

In this essay, I have reflected on the relationship between the anthropology of art and discourses on global art. Embedded within the methodology of ethnographic fieldwork, the framework of the anthropology of art is constituted by notions such as diversity and multiplicity of cultural spaces, of disjunctive global flows, and the constitution of difference through connection. I have focused thematically on one aspect, emphasizing the situated gaze; namely, achieving knowledge of the artistic creative processes from the vantage point of a local art world.

Becker's notion of the art world enables, first, to approach the multiple forms of contemporary art within a place, and second, and more importantly, it helps to understand the specificity of such an art world. Instead of postulating a vague or fuzzy global cultural circulation of images, such a gaze provides a concrete idea of the global in a specific place, insight into the constraints artists face, the availability of interactions, exchanges and debates, which forms of knowledge may be appropriated, that is, the possibilities of artistic creative practices.

The shift to Danto's notion of the art world, in his reformulation of the 1990s, is of interest for anthropological inquiry, as it allows consideration of the work of art, or the œuvre of an artist, within its spatial spreading out - the concrete spatial connections artists produce, for example, in relation to the medium, the material used, the styles, the concepts, also to certain historical, economical, or political situations. The situated gaze, therefore, is mandatory for approaching the artistic work and acknowledging its complex cultural matrix, instead of considering it solely from the hegemonic conceptual gaze of the global art world.

30 **See: Elizabeth Harney**, *In Senghor's Shadow. Art, Politics, and the Avant-Garde in Senegal, 1960–1995*, Duke University Press, Durham (NC), 2004, p. 192.

31 **Ibid.**, pp. 106–141; see also: Ima Ebong, "Negritude: Between Mask and Flag. Senegalese Cultural Ideology and the 'Ecole de Dakar'," in: Vogel 1991, pp. 206–209.

32 **See: Hal Foster**, *The Return of the Real*, The MIT Press, Cambridge (MA), 1996, pp. 171–204. The topic of the artist as ethnographer, but focusing on the artistic representation as a new form of representation for accounts of anthropologists, is dealt with by Arnd Schneider and Christopher Wright (eds.), *Contemporary Art and Anthropology*, Berg, Oxford et al., 2006.

33 **Nicolas Bourriaud**, *Relational Aesthetics*, Les Presses du Réel, Dijon-Quetigny, 2002, [Original: *Esthétique relationnelle*, 1998].

An Anthropologist in the Exhibition

The Global Contemporary

For and with Britta Heinrich

Thomas Hauschild

Preliminaries

"Social anthropology" and "cultural anthropology" constitute a conglomerate of academic disciplines, which up until decolonization in the 1950s were able to develop great consistency. The common denominator of all anthropological or (in France and Germany) "ethnological" activity was the experience of doing fieldwork in "other cultures," in non-Western societies. If one dates the beginning of this discipline approximately from early nineteenth and twentieth-century's evolutionary and anti-evolutionary anthropology (e.g., James Frazer, Edward Tylor, Adolf Bastian, Wilhelm Wundt, Émile Durkheim, Arnold van Gennep), then it falls into two halves. The discipline matured in the 1920s and 1930s into a field-oriented, empirical discipline of comparison between cultures and societies. From the 1950s to the 1980s the self-critical, deconstructive turn brought anthropological thought worldwide success - in a world that had been recently decolonized. Half of the discipline's history was very consistent and the other half self-critical. But throughout both phases of its development, the term "anthropology" signaled research on non-European and non North American, non-white societies. From the outset, however, there had been also demands that at least the primitive origins of European peoples and the Mediterranean area should be included. Other opponents of mainstream primitivism tended to incorporate written sources, which led to the founding of specialized branches of philology like tibetology or the study of African languages. In the end, anthropology matured into the microsociology of all living human cultures which it is today.

Parallel to this expansion of the area of expertise a tendency became established whereby only topics were acceptable that were directly based on first-hand field research. This methodological concept could be upheld even after the advent of decolonization. Nowadays most nations, former colonial nations as well as formerly colonized nations, finance their own regional brand of anthropological research or micro-sociology, which conducts detailed and self-reflective research on societies, communities, and networks of humans of every regional and "cultural" origin. Even art and literature criticism benefit from the worldwide rise of a scientific endeavor that literally "traces" human micro-behavior.

This vigorously growing field of knowledge - which protests flawed state and imperial plans and fights forms of racism - continues to live in the shells of colonial and precolonial specialist terms, institutions, and specialist journals. Today the discipline appears to fill those forms entirely, indeed, to be too much for them. But the representatives of the anthropological disciplines themselves often seem to overlook the extent to which in the course of these developments the objects of their research - and thus the results of their research - have become removed from themes which were once the focal point of the subject: rituals and relationships, exchange networks and so-called "primitive" medicine, technology, clothing, food, - and art. Today the production of "primitive art" is regarded as virtually at an end. Today there is hardly anything self-made and autochthonous produced, hardly any art beyond the hegemonic traditions of Europe and North America, if one disregards the numerous subcultures of the global world which grow and grow inside its cosmos. Therefore, the new themes of anthropological research are hybridity (but the question of what these new cultural fusions were created from is no longer asked), migration (but the question of where the migrants came from is not asked), citizenship and branding in the imperial world (but no questions are asked as regards traditional origins and counter-concepts).

From both branches of anthropological activity, the "old school" as well as the self-reflexive postmodern one, an enormous body of data has been generated, data that come from research in "traditional societies" as well as from microsociological research in Western societies and their global offshoots. These data float freely around in museums and libraries, indigenous NGOs, and far-flung niches of the Old World. Increasingly artifacts are emerging from this perspective which were produced in the nineteenth and twentieth centuries, for example, by African tribes, and which close ranks with the heritage of rural cultures and other peripheral phenomena of the industrial centers of those eras. For a long time this "popular art" heritage was administrated by a discipline all of its own - folklore research or in Europe ethnology - whose heirs, like the anthropologists, attach little importance to the "old material." The same applies to ethnomusicology, ethnomedicine, and medical anthropology, ancient legal ethnology and other subdisciplines of ethnology and anthropology.

The "older" forms of this type of arts and knowledge, their material, written and photographic, phonographic and cinematic evidence are only poorly integrated in the contemporary Western discipline of history. Mostly they continue to survive in the archives of academic institutions of anthropology and of anthropological museums. At the same time, however, all forms of the material heritage of "ancient," "primitive" societies are reaching the market for art and craftwork, the media, and many other areas of public interest. This entails rising prices, in particular where "art" is concerned - in case this "art" parallels with Western canons of art in some way - big statues sell high, small decorations, as subtle and elaborate as they may be, sell low. This discrepancy between decreasing academic interest and a certain hype of the art market is understandable in view of the fact that the development of originary forms of primitive and popular art is largely complete, and that its distance to industrial production is still increasing. Today the globalized economy is probably facing two different paths: stagnation or collapse on the one hand or the development of new forms of energy on the other, together with the amalgamation of the natural world by the global "system." A similar duplication is indicated in the body of "primitive" things as forms of art and knowledge. One possibility is that new knowledge about the mode of production of "primitive objects" will mature and make the term "primitive" - nowadays considered to be objectionable - wholly acceptable some day. In the event of no extraterrestrial civilization visiting the Earth, this "primitive" culture will be the only "other" or "alien" that the civilization of the future will have at its disposal (if we think of it as being combined with the knowledge about prehistoric and historical humans up to the founding of the capitalist world economy). Nor can the permanent mise-en-scène of youth as the ever-new alien element in the capitalist world of commodities change this in any way, as it is precisely the young people who catch hold of the knowledge of "others" and "primitives," for example, in the form of heresy. The other possibility is that knowledge of the "Old World" will fuse into a source of comfort and advice with regard to survival techniques, in a Middle Ages of humanity that continues forever. This, then, is precious knowledge.

The Visit

My visit to the *The Global Contemporary* exhibition in the very first minutes made me aware of just how deep anthropology's current crisis is. Before my eyes, anthropological knowledge broke into two parts: on the one hand knowledge about traditional societies and the alternatives that opposed them, and on the other a critical micro-sociology, which conducts field research on current social behavior and cultural productivity in a globalized world. But continuing my visit, the longer I stayed in the exhibition, the more I rediscovered both - the self-exploration of postmodern worlds as well as the "world of old," the "primitive." Both are displayed in works by artists from non-European societies. This exhibition, one of truly global significance, is self-reflective. It does without any vague postmodern motto and portrays the market in which its objects are found. In the rooms of the ZKM | Center for Art and Media the micro-sociologist (myself) soon tracks down an attendant, who confirms to me the avant-garde status of the project. When, as is the long-standing habit of anthropologists, I question him, the layman, aged around 60 and who has no idea about art, confirms my and his prejudgment: "Only insiders ever come here [...] everyone else just goes away again [...] the man in the street I mean [...]." The micro-sociologist in me is happy with that. Yet just a few steps further on the anthropologist in me awakens.

I am standing in front of boots, belts, saddles, holsters, military musical instruments, and oriental military

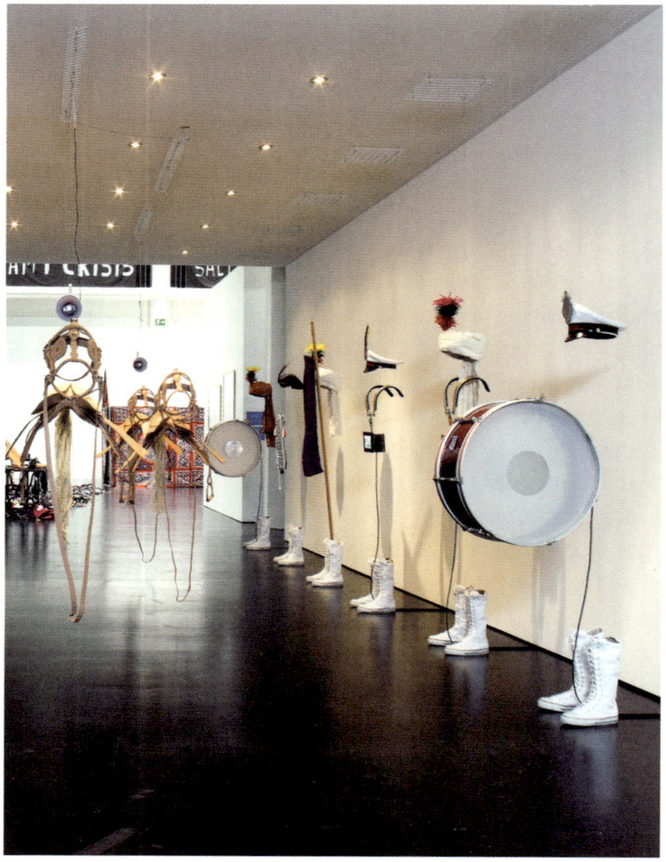

Jompet, *Cortege of the Third Realm*, 2010, installation view *The Global Contemporary. Art Worlds after 1989*, ZKM | Karlsruhe, 2011–2012

turbans, suspended freely in the air, as if their human wearers had evaporated. They "stand" in front of me, I stand behind them. They are neatly arranged in rows. Each small assemblage creates a person, who only becomes visible in the equipment, for the wearer remains invisible. "Parade of a phantom army" reads the brochure for *Cortege of the Third Realm* (2010) by the Indonesian artist Jompet (see: this volume, p. 354). This procession of the costumes constitutes an Encounter of the Third Kind. And I remember where I encountered this before: ancient Roman bodies corporate and their European legal successors, as well as various tribal societies in Africa, Asia, Australia, and South America created assemblages such as these to indicate an ancestral group, a "company" in the truest sense of the word. The individual wearers of the equipment are secondary, the parade weapons and totems are all that count. Jean Rouch, one of the great anthropological filmmakers of the twentieth century, described the spectral aspect of every parade. In his much-discussed 1955 film *Les maîtres fous* [*The Mad Masters*], he confronted the military parodies of a colonial workers' spirit possession cult with the British colonial military ceremony "Trooping the Colour." The proximity to death and violence, like the obsession of the imitation, transforms the bearers of military holsters and instruments into spirits. In the colonial parody *Cortege of the Third Realm* the old Javanese and Dutch costumes become a counter-world for the dead and a forum, which I would certainly not refer to as "anti-colonial," but rather "counter-colonial."

I came across something similar in the installation *Musée de l'Art et de la Vie* by Meschac Gaba, an artist from Cotonou in Benin. Crucifixes, colonial headgear, (see: this volume, pp. 348–349) and reminders of great Western intellectuals become motifs for African masks. The faces of the invisible mask wearers have fringes hanging down in front of them. Some masks reveal syncretic symbols like a crucifix or a dollar symbol; others allude to Joan of Arc or the legendary King Guézo von Dahomey. Gaba's masks resemble a form of costume, which has been around in West Africa from Mali to Nigeria for centuries and today can still be seen in traditional processions. Powerful, cross-tribal secret societies often used these masks, as well as traditional market wardens, who literally achieved control of the forum. Like European policemen and military personnel with their tall helmets, they embodied authority and in emergencies exercised force to protect the free markets and other hot spots in the indigenous cultural conflicts between the old African cultures. In Meschac Gaba's case the exaggerated masks become a parade of "exalted" symbols and ideals of the Western world as well. To all the players in the postcolonial world, including the donors and recipients of development aid and disaster relief, the artist makes an offer to disappear behind the mask.

The Response

The Karlsruhe world exhibition gave rise to "forum"-like structures (shops, parades, markets, tents) of every sort and thus was a clear reminder of the fact that markets existed everywhere long before the Western hegemony of the markets and financial world. Contemporary artists are turning classic quantitative power relationships into qualitative stimuli and dialogs. In the work of Pieter Hugo from Johannesburg, which uses the genre of portrait photography (see: this volume, pp. 350–351), in a portrait reminiscent of *Querelle of Brest*, a female role appears out of a German sailor's uniform, or voodoo Baron Samedi, with whom we are familiar from the James Bond film *Live and Let Die* (1973), poses with an axe in his hand in a car park like a serial.

The "forum" structures of the Karlsruhe exhibition, the serving trolleys, tents, and market stands ingeniously declared to be assemblages, invitations to a form of participa-

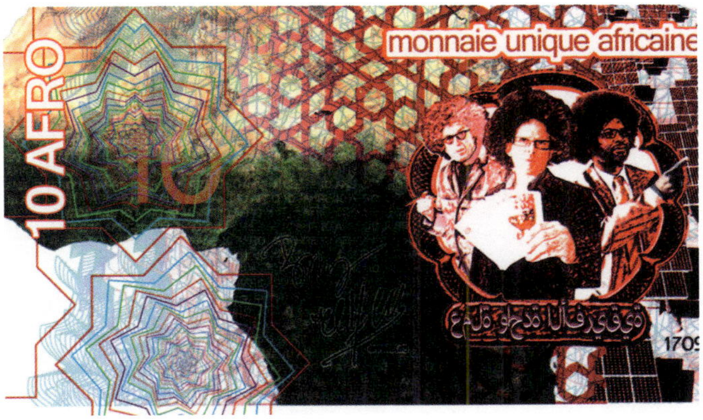

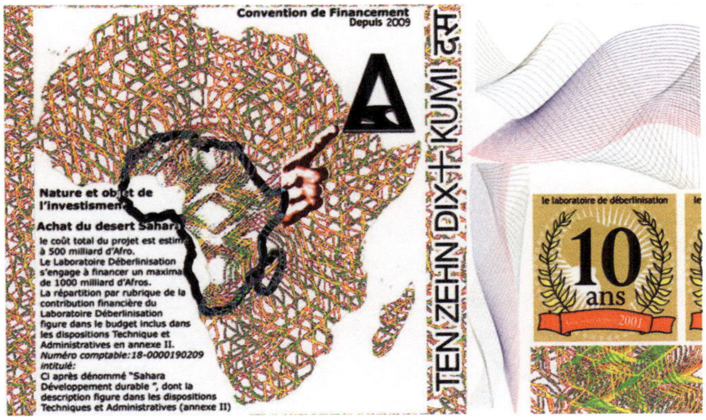

Le Laboratoire de Déberlinisation, *Mobile Exchange Office* (detail), "10 Afrobill", 2008.

tion from which a politically correct audience in the West steps back in horror. In Fritz W. Kramer's classic study of possession and mask cults in Africa[1] one finds the anthropological background to this: "non-European" societies" had and of course still have their "aliens." Spirits and members of neighboring societies, whites and Arabs, natural forces and technical objects of indigenous and exogenous origin were, and indeed still are, transferred by means of rituals, markets, and channeled forces to a world of their own, as can be seen in the ZKM exhibition. The answer to colonialism and its ethnological exhibitions of the subjugated becomes the anthropology of the world in the shape of possession and a mimesis of masquerade. In this case racism is sometimes a productive variant. This was recognized early on by the Surrealists of 1920s Paris. The naked realism of trauma, masks, and the spirits is being offered now to a global audience through new art forms. "The whites" only need to see, to hear, or just to buy, to experience the spectral nature of their existence.

The "spirit" stands opposite to money and this meant that it goes with money. In the *Mobile Exchange Office* the so-called "Afro" currency is worth € 316.644 (see: this volume, p. 402). There is a plan to buy the Sahara for 500 billion Euros and industrialize it; a real gain in knowledge is beginning to emerge. It seems that *Le Laboratoire de Déberlinisation* discovered Berlin's central role in the international financial crisis earlier than the Germans. Parallel to the artists' virtual *laboratoire* the "real" Europeans' project, the harnessing of the Sahara's solar energy through photovoltaics and the exploitation of its water supplies hidden deep down, is taking shape. And Chéri Samba depicts his life as an international artist in the form of a wave of success, which comprises network relationships in Europe and Africa.

The display cabinets in Liu Ding's *Store* offer eastern and western junk for sale (see: this volume, pp. 422–423) and in Tsuyoshi Ozawa's *Museum of Soy Sauce Art* the sauce, used here to produce art, is suspiciously reminiscent of blood (see: this volume, p. 384). The store and the museum also represent forums of the anticolonial and real "others." Here Aby Warburg's "thought space" is again of relevance, enabling as it does the "Greifmensch" (the person who grasps) to take a step back. A highly differentiated theory from the turn of the nineteenth to the twentieth century is today wrongly suspected of disseminating colonial ideology.[2]

"Be sure to reckon with Venezuela" trumpets Hugo Chávez in Tirzo Martha's video animation *The Invasion of the Netherlands supported by Chávez ...* (see: this volume, p. 446). "Get the air force airborne." When this happens virtually, the planes look like carpet patterns in the grainy digital version of an old videotape, and militarily they are not worth much either. The criticism of South American military dictatorships is transformed into liberating laughter about the apparent rationalism and linguistic pomp of Western military figures. In their work *Oasis* the AES Group presents islamic tents from Russia (see: this volume, p. 327) that show images of a London that has become Muslim, which would be neither more or less attractive than the center of the capital, which today is financially out of the reach of most of its inhabitants. Everywhere innovation spills out and appears in this global exhibition. It will only be noticed later. Nor can the subtlest of Western assaults deter these voices of anticolonization; in the Ghanaian film and art project *Elmina* Doug Fishbone plays a white farmer who mediates in the conflict between black farmers and bureaucrats about the resources that are needed for micro-research (see: this volume, p. 346). After a short space of time one feels just like

1 **See: Fritz W. Kramer**, *The Red Fez. Art and Spirit Possession in Africa*, Verso, London, 1993.

2 **Aby Warburg**, "A Lecture on Serpent Ritual," in: *Journal of the Warburg Institute*, vol. 2, 1939, pp. 277–292.

one does in a good ethnographic film.[3] One no longer sees the color of the skin, only faces that can be met with in people's everyday lives all over the world: the kind-hearted guy, the villain, the sensible person, the loud-mouth, etc., like a medieval or Renaissance book of human types in multicultural Central Europe.

Classics, like NSK from Slovenia with its post-Socialist art state (see: this volume, p. 401), lead further and further into the fairy tales of the "projects"; perhaps we will be soon be finding "real" major projects of global significance such as construction of a bridge from Calabria to Sicily, the tower in Abu Dhabi, the reconstruction of the "Stadtschloss" palace in Berlin, and the USA's missile defense shield as new fairy tale motifs. We stay with realities: tortured Chinese people, just about bearable in painted distortion; a naïve-ethnographic stand with Chinese money for the spirits, which is burnt at funeral ceremonies; a giant pile of waste textiles, which I perceive as a non-European comment on Edoardo Nesi's[4] swan song to the Italian textile industry in the age of globalization.

The exhibition represents equally the mobilization of reserves from the past and the recognition of today's everyday worlds beyond the mainstream. This goes directly against the still prevalent stream of discourse typical for Western societies when it comes to the "other societies or cultures": Despite the basic fact that all human groups have the same mental and intellectual potential, in the ranking of nations and production methods they are labeled either "weak" and "inferior" or "victorious" and "strong" (militarily or economically). I state this as a member of a society that has twice attacked the rest of Europe. It also reintroduced slavery on a large scale in Europe, where for a century this bad habit had been regarded as obsolete. In the course of my life Germany has developed from two "weak" post-war societies, in the West and in the East. Both had produced strict rituals of self-contempt and religious or political forms of collectivism and, in their own way, after 1989 assimilated the globalized, seemingly egalitarian world to become the "strong" Germany of today. Artistic products from other societies seem to me to be in transformation process similar to the process German post-war societies and their predecessors had to undergo. This is why as a German in the Karlsruhe exhibition you could encounter all this again, the critique of capitalism and nationalist or fundamentalist self-deception; fascist boasting and cynical, critical intelligence; romanticism and trauma. The exhibition at ZKM first divided me, and then restituted me, similar to what happens in ancient rites of initiation which lead from the performance of accepted social roles to liminal behavior - and back.

At some point I run out of steam during my visit. I get my breath back in front of a Chinese computer-Michelangelo (*The Last Judgement in Cyberspace - Where Will I Go*) (see this volume, p. 382). And I calm down in front of Gabriele di Matteo's installation *China Made in Italy* (see: this volume, p. 426). He commissioned copies of Chinese paintings from Neapolitan workshops, which makes me think he may be a former Maoist comrade. When di Matteo and I were born, in the mid-1950s, Jean Rouch was making his avant-garde film about possessed Ghanaians and British military personnel. That today all this is being turned into a lot of money in an explosive art market was unavoidable, as is portrayed by a documentation in the exhibition, which attempts a differentiated synopsis of avant-garde art theory, art production in non-Western countries, and the global art market of the last decades. Anticolonization forums become propitious "traps,"[5] which seduce and subdue me, thereby inducing a greater sense of reality. In any tried and tested masquerade, as, incidentally in the spirit possession cults, works of art allow the unimaginable to become imaginable: there are European totemists and animists, African financial geniuses, and Venezuelan world strategists. Again they all represent human beings and their bodies, their wealth, their reserves (here understood as the mechanisms of control of and knowledge about resources) ... and their relatives, friends, medics, psychotherapists, drug dealers, anthropologists, and art dealers. The anthropologist, the micro-sociologist, indeed even the macro-sociologist get their money's worth in the exhibition in Karlsruhe, not to mention the youthful Maoist from way back. I leave this major exhibition a changed man. I'm finished with postcolonial negative self-adulation, with the anti-anti-anti-relativism of mainstream North Americans and Western Europeans. Western knowledge and economics are neither superior nor inferior to the capacities and reserves of the rest of the world. The fact that this or that "culture" ends up in a geographic zone with a certain potential for wealth or in poor zones is probably down to pure chance.[6] If we fail to use the reserves (aesthetic, economic, social, and most recently psychological) and everything we possess that the world provides us with, then all the dead who lived before us passed on their knowledge and their arts to us in vain.

Translated from the German by Jeremy Gaines.

3 **For example**, the film *Them and Me* by Stéphane Breton, 2001 which shows talkative mediation and performance of local intrigue between - New Guinean highlanders and the French anthropologist and filmmaker.

4 **Edoardo Nesi**, *Storia dell mia gente*, Bompiani, Rome, 2011.

5 **Alfred Gell**, "Vogel's Net: Traps as Artworks and Artworks as Traps," in: *Journal of Material Culture*, vol. 1, no. 1, 1996, pp. 15–38.

6 **Jared Diamond**, *Guns, Germs and Steel. The Fates of Human Societies*, Cape, London, 1997.

Beyond Anthropophagy: Art, Internationalization, and Cultural Dynamics

Gerardo Mosquera

In 1976 Juan Downey took this photo of a Yanomami filming him - and by extension us, the viewers of the photo - with a video camera in the Amazon. The image represents a shift of the gaze taken on by the "primitive," the "peripheral" - the usual object of anthropology - who instead has become an active subject. Nevertheless, we only know this picture taken by the artist, not the picture of Downey - of us - taken by the anonymous Yanomami. The "other" filming us is still a representation from the central self: it does not imply a plural circulation of gazes and representations. The problem is not only cultural but also of access and power. Can't the subaltern speak, as Gayatri Spivak would say? Is instrumentalization always present?

This paper is based on my own practical experience as a freelance international curator. It will analyze problems of art and cultures in the context of contemporary globalized art circuits, delving into the tensions between homogenization, co-optation, contexts, cosmopolitism, appropriation, and the agency of multiple new cultural subjects on a global scale. Following this situation, it will discuss new epistemological grounds for the cultural dynamics of artistic discourses in an expanding international arena. The relationships between contemporary art, culture, and internationalization have been silently yet dramatically transformed in the last fifteen years. We have left behind the times of art trends and manifestos, as well as those of centralized establishments. The key issue for contemporary art today is the tremendous expansion of its regional and global circulation, and the implications that this expansion has in cultural and social terms. There are approximately two hundred biennials and other "perennials" (periodic large-scale artistic events) in the world, to mention only one aspect in the growth of art circuits. This explosion involves a vast multiplicity of new cultural and artistic actors circulating internationally, who either did not exist before or were confined to local environments.[1] For example, some Asia-Pacific countries have virtually skipped modernism and passed directly from traditional culture and socialist realism to contemporary art. In some cases they "learned" contemporary art through the Internet.

This change has initiated very dynamic cultural negotiations between artistic practices, contexts, traditions, international circuits, markets, audiences, and other agents. It seems set to continue in a twofold way. On the one hand, it contributes to the development of ever-increasingly globalized art scenes as a result of the growth of international art networks, events, communications, and global public spheres, together with the activity of emerging artistic and cultural subjects from all over the world. On the other hand, it stimulates the new energy that is producing new contemporary art locally in areas where it didn't exist before. Most of this activity is "local" in the sense that it is the result of artists' personal and subjective reactions to their contexts, or because it seeks to create a cultural, social, or even political impact in the artists' milieus. But these artists are frequently well informed about other contexts, about mainstream art, and are also looking for an international audience. Sometimes they move in and out between local, regional, and global spaces. Usually their

1 **To get an idea** about the diversity of the international art circuits today, see: http://universes-in-universe.de.

art is neither bound to nationalistic modernism nor to traditional languages, even when it is based on vernacular cultures or specific backgrounds. Contexts themselves are becoming more global through their interconnection to the world. These processes do not exclude frictions, compromises, and inequalities; they still respond to remaining colonial configurations and segregations, and to economic and structural disproportions that determine the power to legitimate art. The term "glocal" blurs these contradictions, since it connotes a fluid and universal connection between the two terms that it mixes together.

The art world has changed a lot since 1986, when the Second Havana Biennial held the first truly international exhibition of contemporary art, gathering 690 artists from 57 countries[2] and pioneering the extraordinary internationalization of art that we witness today.[3] Because of the silent mutation that has taken place, the multiculturalist discourses and practices of the 1990s, which involved policies of correctness, quotas, and neo-exoticism, are no longer relevant to our times, to the extreme of connoting a simplistic programmatism. Until recently, a balanced national pluralism was sought after at shows and events. Now the problem is the opposite: curators and institutions have to respond to contemporary global vastness. The challenge is to be able to stay up to date in the face of the appearance of new cultural subjects, energies, and information bursting forth from all sides. It is no longer possible for a curator to work today just following the New York - London - Germany axis (as used to be the case not long ago), and to look down from that highbrow view. Now curators are forced to move around with open eyes, ears, and minds. This is a task that proves difficult to accomplish, since our eyes, ears, and minds have been programmed by specific canons and positions.

At the same time, the mystification of the processes of globalization and the spread of communications lead us to imagine a planet interconnected by a grid-like network that extends in all directions. In reality, globalization is not as global as it appears. Or, to paraphrase George Orwell, it is far more global for some than for others. There is no doubt that the world is now much more global in terms of economics, culture, and communication. For as Manray Hsu has indicated, in some way or another and to a greater or lesser extent, we all are cosmopolitans today, because "there is no more world out there"; the "being-in-the-world" of Heidegger has become coextensive with "being-on-the-globe".[4] However, what we in fact have on a planetary scale is a radial system extending from diverse centers of power, of varying sizes, into multiple and highly diversified economic areas. Such a structure implies the existence of large zones of silence, barely connected to one another or connected only indirectly, via self-decentered centers.[5] This axial structure motivates intense migratory movements in search of connection. On the other hand, national, ethnic, and religious separatisms tend to "balkanize" the globalized world, while regionalism, nationalism, ethnocentrism, frontiers, migration, and fanaticism continue to be issues which are as significant as they are polyhedral.

The times of globalization are also those of movement, migrations, and accelerated urbanization. We are living in an era of "roadrunners" that has broken down the idea of fixed identities and generated postnational subjects who find themselves in constant physical and cultural movement. Immigrants use their feet, but also other parts of their bodies: a Hispanic baby is born every thirty seconds in the United States - a time bomb that has unleashed apocalyptic fears in the minds of Samuel P. Huntington[6] and others. Cities grow vertiginously and chaotically as a result of massive exoduses that take place from the countryside in Africa, Asia, and Latin America, while brand new cities bloom in China and other emerging countries. At the beginning of the twentieth century, only 10 percent of the planet's population lived in cities.[7] Now, half of the globe inhabits urban environments. From 1975 to 2000 the world's city dwellers duplicated, and they will double again in 2015. The chief aspect in this vertigo is that two-thirds of the urban population will live in poor countries.

Obviously, cities are not prepared to afford such demographic shock. Thus, one hundred million people do not have permanent lodging - a majority of them are children. Many millions more inhabit improvised, precarious slums that proliferate in today's cities, with the attendant contamination, insalubrity, and violence. The situation seems untenable but, as Carlos Monsiváis put it, "the city is built upon its systematic destruction."[8] The cultural implications of this spontaneous ecology are obvious. A most im-

2 **See: Catalog of the Second Havana Biennial:** *Segunda Bienal de La Habana'86*, Ministerio de Cultura and Wifredo Lam Center, Havana, 1986.

3 **See: Elena Filipovic, Mieke van Hal, and Solveig Øvstebø (eds.):** *The Biennial Reader. An Anthology on Large-Scale Perennial Exhibitions of Contemporary Art*, Bergen Kunsthall and Hatje Cantz, Ostfildern, 2010.

4 **Manray Hsu**, "Network Cosmopolitanism. On Cultural Exchange and International Exhibition," in: Nicholas Tsoutas (ed.), *Knowledge+Dialogue+Exchange: Remapping Cultural Globalisms from the South*, Artspace Visual Arts Centre, Sydney, 2005, p. 80.

5 **Gerardo Mosquera**, "Notes on Globalisation, Art and Cultural Difference," in: Edith Rijnja (ed.), *Silent Zones. On Globalisation and Cultural Interaction*, Rijksakademie van beeldende kunsten, Amsterdam, 2001, p. 32.

6 **Samuel P. Huntington**, *Who Are We?: The Challenges to America's National Identity*, Simon & Schuster, New York (NY), 2004.

7 **All statistics are taken from:** *The UNESCO Courier*, vol. 52, no. 6, June 1999, as well as from Helmut K. Anheier and Willem Henri Lucas, "Indicator Suites," in: Helmut K. Anheier and Yudhishthir Raj Isar (eds.), *Conflicts and Tensions*, The Cultures and Globalization Series, vol. 1, Sage, Los Angeles (CA), 2007.

8 **Carlos Monsiváis**, "Arquitecture and the City," in: Gerardo Mosquera and Adrienne Samos (eds.): Ciudad Multiple City. Urban Art and Global Cities: An Experiment in Context, KIT Publishers, Amsterdam, 2005, p. 270.

portant one is the complex, metamorphic, and multilateral process that entails the substitution of the traditional rural environment by the urban situation, a clash that involves a massive amount of very diverse people.

These processes interact with external migrations that are redrawing the ethno-social maps within receiving countries, unraveling heterogeneous cultural dynamics. All these displacements entail acute problems such as xenophobia (whether practiced by skinheads or by ex-victims of apartheid in South Africa), racism, nationalism, tribalism, and fundamentalism based on "purities" of different kinds, growing anti-immigration barriers (which even prohibit internal displacements within a country, as happens in China and Cuba), and the odysseys of boat people, asylum seekers, and refugees. Much more than ever before, cities are today complex laboratories that produce heterodox urban culture, neologisms, and "border culture." The connection between art and the city has not evolved very far yet, but will probably indicate a main course of action for artistic practice in the near future.

Nor has there been much progress in "South-South" and "South-East" linkage (so to speak, now that the "East" is beginning to leave the "South"), other than economic recessions. Globalization has improved communications to an extraordinary extent, just as it has dynamized and pluralized cultural circulation while providing a more pluralist consciousness. Yet it has done so by following the very channels delineated by the economy, thus reproducing the structures of power in good measure, while maintaining a deficit in "horizontal" interactions. Although the situation has improved, the development of "horizontal" circuits and spaces continues to be of major importance in order to "fill in," on the global level, the grid of the "vertical," "North-South" radial circulation schemes traced from power centers - which are inherent to the globalization of cultural exchange - extending and democratizing these circuits and spaces, while also connecting the "zones of silence." And even more importantly: "horizontal" networks subvert the control axes typical of the radial scheme by including a variety of new centers on a smaller scale. This whole process will contribute to pluralizing and enriching culture, internationalizing it in the real sense, legitimizing it according to different criteria and to the criteria of difference fostered by the diversification of circuits, constructing new epistemes, and unfolding alternative actions. Only a multidirectional web of interactions will pluralize our definitions of "international art," "international art language," "international art scene," and even what we call "contemporary."[9]

In the early twentieth century, Brazilian modernists created the metaphor of anthropophagy in order to legitimate their critical, selective, and metabolizing appropriation of European artistic tendencies. This notion has been used extensively to characterize the paradoxical anticolonial resistance of Latin American culture through its inclination to copy (only the Japanese beat us in this), as well as to allude to its relation to the hegemonic West. The metaphor goes beyond Latin America to point to a procedure characteristic of postcolonial art in general. It was coined by the poet Oswald de Andrade in 1928; not as a theoretical notion, but as a provocative poetic manifesto.[10] Its emphasis in the subaltern subject's aggressiveness is extraordinary, as well as its bold negation of a conservative, lethargic idea of identity. Andrade even dared to affirm: "I am interested only in what is not mine,"[11] reversing the fundamentalist politics of authenticity.

"Anthropophagy" has been developed by Latin American critics as a key notion for the continent's cultural dynamics. It has not only survived the pugnacious modernism of its origins, but it has been impelled by poststructuralist and postmodern ideas about appropriation, resignifying, and the validation of the copy. "Anthropophagy" has been a very influential paradigm in Latin America, and even the subject of the memorable 24th São Paulo Biennial curated by Paulo Herkenhoff in 1998. Contrary to Homi K. Bhabha's notion of "mimicry" - which outlines how colonialism imposes upon the subordinate subjects an alien mask from which they negotiate their resistance amid ambivalence - "anthropophagy" supposes an attack: to swallow voluntarily the dominant culture for one's own benefit. It is important to underline that anthropophagy and transculturation articulate their discourses from their position in early neocolonial modernity and their indirect foundations on anthropology, diverging with similar notions in classic postcolonial theory, which departed from literary criticism and the colonial situation.

Although the notion refers to a "critical swallowing," we must be alert to the difficulties of such a pre-postmodern program, since it does not take place in a neutral territory, but is subjected to a praxis which tacitly assumes the contradictions of dependency. As Heloísa Buarque de Hollanda has warned, anthropophagy can stereotype a problematic concept of a carnivalizing identity that always processes beneficially everything that "is not its

9 **See: Gerardo Mosquera**, "Alien-Own / Own-Alien. Notes on Globalisation and Cultural Difference," in: Nikos Papastergiadis (ed.), *Complex Entanglements: Art, Globalisation and Cultural Difference*, Rivers Oram Press, London, 2003, pp. 22-23.

10 **Oswald de Andrade**, Manifesto Antropófago, São Paulo, 1928, reprinted in English as "The Cannibalist Manifesto," in: *Third Text*, vol. 14, no. 46, Spring 1999, pp. 92-95.

11 **Ibid.**, p. 92.

own."[12] It is necessary also to examine whether the transformations that "cannibals" experience when incorporating the dominant culture do not subsume them into it. Also, viewed from the other side, appropriation satisfies the desire of the dominant culture for a reformed, recognizable other who possesses a difference in the likeness - which, in the case of Latin America, departs from its cultural kinship with Western metaculture, creating perhaps its perfect alterity - facilitating the relation of domain without completely breaking the difference that allows it to construct the hegemonic identity by its contrast with an "inferior" other. Yet this quasi other acts at the same time as a mirror that fractures the dominant subject's identity, rearticulating the subaltern presence in terms of its rejected otherness.[13]

If the tension of "who swallows whom?"[14] is more or less present in any intercultural relationship, then it is also true that "frequently one plagiarizes what one is ready to invent," as Ferguson has said.[15] Cultural appropriation is not a passive phenomenon: the receivers always remodel the elements they appropriate according to their own cultural patterns.[16] Moreover, subordinate receivers also transform and resignify the models imposed on them by dominant cultures. Often, these appropriations are not "correct." Receivers are usually interested in the productivity of the element seized for their own ends, not in the reproduction of its use in its original context. Such "in-corrections" are commonly situated at the base of the cultural efficacy of appropriation, and frequently constitute a process of originality in the sense of a new creation of meaning.

The peripheries, due to their location on the maps of symbolic power, have developed a "culture of resignification"[17] out of the repertoires imposed from the centers. Nevertheless, cultural appropriation must be qualified to break with connotations that may prove too affirmative. Even though it has been a path to resistance and affirmation of the subaltern, co-optation is a menace to all cultural action based on syncretism. Today, in the global and postcolonial era, the syncretistic processes are defined as a basic negotiation of difference and cultural power.[18] But those processes are turbulent: they cannot be comfortably assumed as though they presented a harmonious solution to postcolonial contradictions. They need to maintain their critical edge. Beyond all these interpretations of cultural processes, a more arduous problem persists: the flux of culture still continues to circulate following to a considerable extent the same North-South direction dictated by the power structure, its circuits of diffusion, and the accommodation to them. No matter how plausible the appropriating and transcultural strategies are, they imply a rebound effect that reproduces the same hegemonic structure, even if they contest it. The current must also be reversed, not to create a "repetition in rupture," as Spivak would say, but to contribute to a true pluralization and enrichment of international cultural circulation.

Anyway, "anthropophagy" and the prevalent cultural strategies of appropriation and syncretism typical of postcolonial and "peripheral" art are increasingly being replaced by a new perspective that we could call the "from here" paradigm. Rather than appropriating and critically refunctionalizing the imposed international culture, transforming it to suit their own needs - as artists in postcolonial situations had done until recently - now artists are actively involved in the first-hand creation of that metaculture. They do so unfettered: from their own imaginaries and positions and on a planetary scale. This epistemological transformation consists in changing from an operation of creative incorporation to one of direct international construction from a variety of subjects, experiences, and cultures.

The work of many contemporary artists, rather than naming, describing, analyzing, expressing, or building contexts, is made from their personal, historical, cultural, and social contexts in international terms. The context thus ceases to be a "closed" locus related to a reductive concept in order to project itself as a space from which international culture is built naturally. This culture is not articulated in the manner of a mosaic of explicit differences engaging in a dialog within a framework that both gathers and projects them. It works, largely, as a specific mode of recreating a hegemonic set of codes and methodologies established in the form of a global metaculture. In other words, cultural globalization tends to configure an international code multilaterally, instead of appearing as a multifaceted structure of differentiated cells. This codification acts as a defective lingua franca that allows communication and that is forced,

12 **Heloísa Buarque de Hollanda**, "Feminism: Constructing Identity and the Cultural Condition," in: Noreen Tomassi, Mary Jane Jacob, and Ivo Mesquita (eds.), *American Visions. Artistic and Cultural Identity in the Western Hemisphere*, ACA Books, New York (NY), 1994, p. 129.

13 **See: Homi K. Bhabha**, "Of Mimicry and Men: The Ambivalence of Colonial Discourse," in: *October*, vol. 28, Spring 1984, p. 85.

14 **See: Zita Nunes**, "Os males do Brasil: Antropofagia e a questão da raça," in: *Papéis Avulsos*, no. 22, CIEC/UFRJ, Rio de Janeiro, 1990.

15 **Quoted from: Paul Mercier**, *Historia de la Antropología*, Península, Barcelona, 1969, p. 170; translated from the Spanish by the author.

16 **See: R. H. Lowie**, *An Introduction to Cultural Anthropology*, Rinehart, New York (NY), 1940.

17 **Nelly Richard**, *La Estratificación de los Márgenes*, Zegers, Santiago de Chile, 1989, p. 55; translated from the Spanish by the author.

18 **See: Marcos Becquer and José Gatti**, "Elements of Vogue," in: *Third Text*, vol. 5, no. 16/17, Autumn/Winter 1991, pp. 65-81. For a thorough discussion on the idea of syncretism regarding Brazilian religions and culture, see: Sérgio Figueiredo Ferretti, *Repensando O Sincretismo*, EDUSP, São Paulo, 1995.

knocked about, and reinvented by a diversity of new subjects who are gaining access to international networks undergoing outright expansion. In a near sense, Charles Esche has also mentioned a combination of sameness and non-self-conscious singularity in art today.[19] As Gilles Deleuze and Félix Guattari have argued of "minor literature," many artists work by "finding [their] own point of underdevelopment, [their] own patois, [their] own third world, [their] own desert"[20] within the "major" language.

Difference is increasingly constructed through specific plural modes of creating artistic texts within a set of international idioms and practices that are transformed in the process, and not by means of representing cultural or historical elements characteristic of particular contexts. Difference lies in action more than in representation. This inclination opens a different perspective that opposes the cliché of "universal" art in the centers, derivative expressions in the "peripheries," and the multiple "authentic" realms of "otherness" in traditional culture.

Artists are less and less interested in showing their passports. Moreover, if they were, their gallery owners would probably prevent them from stating local references that might jeopardize their global potentials. As Kobena Mercer puts it, "diversity is more visible than ever before, but the unspoken rule is that you do not make an issue of it."[21] Cultural components act more within the discourse of works than in relation to their strict visuality, even in cases in which these have been based upon the vernacular. This is not to say that one cannot point to certain identifying traits of particular countries or areas. The crucial fact is that these diverse identities have begun to show themselves more through their features as artistic practices than through their use of identifying elements taken from folklore, religion, the physical environment, or history. Thus, their specific art practices are identifiable more by the manner in which they refer to ways of making their artistic texts than by outward projections of their contexts.

This procedure seems a plausible strategy in the globalized, postcolonial, post-Cold War, and pre-China-centric world of today. Naturally, it is not a path without obstacles, and many challenges and contradictions remain. Although art has much to gain from the rise of artists from all over the world who circulate internationally and exert influence, on the other hand this development simplifies art, since artists have to express themselves in an "English" of art that has been hegemonically constructed and established. It makes intercontextual communication possible, but at the same time indirectly consolidates established structures, while incorporating the authority of the histories, values, poetics, methodologies, and codes that constituted the language. The active, diversified construction and reinvention of contemporary art and its international language by a multitude of subjects who operate from their differences, supposes not only an appropriation of that language, but also its transformation from divergences in the convergence itself. Hence, art language pluralizes itself, despite having been broadly instituted by mainstream orientations. This is crucial, because to control language and representation also entails the power to control meaning.[22] Of course, this dynamic takes place within a porous strain between renovation and establishment, in which the hegemonic structures show their weight.

Another difficulty is that the use and legitimation by artists worldwide of an international language set up by the Western mainstream, even when transforming this language, implies the discrimination of other languages and poetics. Consequently, artistic manifestations that do not speak the prevalent codes are excluded beyond their individual contexts, marginalized in ghetto circuits and markets. This exclusion is even more radical if we consider that the international language of art has seized for itself control of the right to be contemporary and to act as a vehicle for artistic contemporaneity.

The old paradigms based on appropriation reproduced the situation of domain, as they depended on an imposed culture: cannibals are only cannibals if they have somebody to devour. Although the "from here" paradigm does not indicate a rebellion or an emancipation, and while it confirms the hegemonic authority, it has simultaneously mutated the ping-pong of oppositions and appropriations and the alienation of the subaltern subject, thus creating a new artistic-cultural biology where this subject is inside of central production from the outside.

What about museums, Kunsthallen, alternative spaces, and other institutions that deal with contemporary art? It seems as though these institutions are having difficulties answering the new problems brought about by the expansive cultural dynamics of these changing times. Perhaps the new situation suggests the prospect of a major shift in

19 **Charles Esche**, "Making Sameness," in: Arjan van Helmond and Stani Michiels, *Jakarta Megalopolis. Horizontal and Vertical Observations*, Valiz, Amsterdam, 2006, p. 27.

20 **Gilles Deleuze and Félix Guattari**, "What Is a Minor Literature?," in: Russell Ferguson, Martha Gever, Trinh T. Minh-ha, and Cornel West (eds.), *Out There. Marginalization and Contemporary Cultures*, Documentary Sources in Contemporary Art, vol. 4, The New Museum of Contemporary Art New York and The MIT Press, Cambridge (MA), 1990, p. 61.

21 **Kobena Mercer**, "Intermezzo Worlds," in: *Art Journal*, vol. 57, no. 4, Winter 1998, p. 43.

22 **See: Jean Fisher and Gerardo Mosquera**, "Introduction," in: Fisher and Mosquera, *Over Here: International Perspectives on Art and Culture*, Documentary Sources in Contemporary Art, vol. 6, New Museum of Contemporary Art New York, The MIT Press, Cambridge (MA), 2004, p. 5.

their practice, one that will lead them from the prevalent space-centered routine to another, more dynamic endeavor, in which the institution will be a moving activity spread all over the globe. This is what I call the museum-as-hub.[23] If museums have brought the world into their space, perhaps the moment has arrived to launch museums into the world. The museum as an international hub of artistic activities entails a decentralized institution that would conceive, curate, and/or participate simultaneously in a diversity of projects in different places worldwide. Its level of involvement in these projects (exhibitions, events, ephemeral urban art, workshops, gatherings, etc.) should be very flexible. Projects would be organized mainly as joint ventures and collaborations with other institutions, informal groups or individuals, with varying degrees of commitment. The results could have full or partial manifestations in the museum's space, or have none. In fact, the space would tend to disappear, since the museum would function more as international network of exchanges and activities, participating in a flux of information, projects, and actions in several ways and directions. The museum-as-hub would be an attempt to match the new developments in a changing world, with the museum participating directly at the very spot where art practices take place. For the museum, as for many other things, the future will mean an increasingly global and decentralized activity.

Upon arrival in America, the Spaniards were obsessed for years with knowing whether they had arrived at an island or mainland. A historian of the nineteenth century, a priest from the Cuban village of Los Palacios, told us that when Columbus asked the indigenous people of Cuba whether that place was an island or a continent, they answered him saying that it was "an infinite land of which no one had seen the end, although it was an island."[24] James Clifford has pointed out that perhaps "we are all Caribbean now in our urban archipelagoes."[25] Are we living today on a globe of infinite islands?

---

23 **See: Gerardo Mosquera**, "Seven Notes on the Museum-as-Hub," in: *Re-Shuffle/Notions of an Itinerant Museum*, exhib. cat., Center for Curatorial Studies, Bard College, New York (NY), 2006.

24 **Andrés Bernaldes**, "Historia de los Reyes Católicos," in: *Memorias de la Real Sociedad Patriótica de La Habana*, vol. 3, no. 128, Havana, 1837, quoted from: Cinto Vitier and Fina García Marruz, *Flor Oculta de poesía Cubana*, Editorial Arte y Literatura, Havana, 1978, p. 6; translated from the Spanish by the author.

25 **James Clifford**, *The Predicament of Culture: Twentieth-century Ethnography, Literature and Art*, Harvard University Press, Cambridge (MA), 1988, p. 173.

"J'est un autre:" Notes on Cannibalism and Contemporary Art

Sara Giannini

A major phenomenon is manifesting itself in the landscape of global contemporary art, namely, the definitive disappearance of the boundaries defining the category of art as a coherent whole. Contemporary exhibitions not only disperse art outside the institutional space of the museum, but also embrace the most diverse practices, disciplines, and objects. This essay constitutes an attempt[1] to analyze the dynamics of global contemporary art through the symbolic structure of cannibalism. The space I am stepping into engages with the "participative opposition" between global contemporary art and the heritage of Western modernity, in other words how a global contemporary exhibition, understood as a "cannibal system of relations," can rearticulate the "modern system of classification."

Cannibalism as a Participative Opposition

In order to employ cannibalism as a semiotic and analytical category, I shall focus on and emphasize the symbolic substrate of cannibalism as a "cultural system."[2]

A constant belief in ritual cannibalism is that by eating another human being (either enemy or relative), one could absorb and assimilate his or her knowledge and skills. The act of consuming human flesh in ritual practices discloses a nondialectical merging of two otherwise separated individuals into a dynamic and multiple subjectivity. As anthropologist Eduardo Viveiros de Castro reported in his studies on the Tupi-Guarani populations of Brazil, where cannibalism represented a social bonding agent, anthropophagy lies on mutual movements of interiorization of the external and exteriorization of the internal. The Tupi-Guarani societies were characterized by an immanent relation to alterity, where the embodiment of the "other" depended on going out from oneself.[3]

From this viewpoint, the cannibal's desire of the other perturbs the binary "same vs. other" opposition, which justifies the formation of identity in Western modern culture. The distinction from the other implies the emergence of self-consciousness but also its protection from any external threat that might possibly transform and eventually erase it. Within this mechanism, cannibalism figuratively represents the other to be definitively rejected. In Western anthropology as well as common opinion, the practice of cannibalism is in fact the evidence that symbolizes those non-cultures otherwise referred to as barbarian, uncivilized, and primitive:

> "In modern Western culture, cannibalism enjoys a virtually unparalleled hold on the popular imagination as an act of primal social violence. It is frequently held up

1 **The essay is part of** the ongoing PhD project *Re-Articulating Differences. Cannibalism and Contemporary Art* that I am writing under the supervision of Prof. Kitty Zijlmans at the Leiden University Centre for Art in Society.

2 **Anthropologist Peggy Reeves Sanday** defines a cultural system as "a system of symbols and ritual acts that provides models of and for behavior," in: P.R. Sanday, *Divine Hunger. Cannibalism as a Cultural System*, Cambridge University Press, Cambridge, 1986, p. 31.

3 **See: Eduardo Viveiros de Castro,** *A inconstância da alma selvagem*, Cosac & Naify, São Paulo, 2002.

> as an almost unthinkable transgression of the social and moral codes which make us who we are."[4]

The aim of my text is to resemanticize this widespread social taboo, which mainly arose during the Western colonization of the Caribbean and since then has been holding an almost mythical position in the Western compendium of bias. Even the word cannibalism comes from the Spanish mispronunciation of "Caribs," a term indicating natives from the Caribbean islands, widely believed by Europeans to have been anthropophagites. As literary theorist Claude Rawson (1999) states, cannibalism, differently from anthropophagy, "is a geographical and ethnic term. It points a finger at a particular people, and it dates from 1492."[5] In a paper on cannibalism as an "unspeakable rite," he also underlines that the creation of the man-eating barbarian mixed in Europe with the discussions around the sacrament of the Eucharist between Catholicism and Protestantism, and eventually led to the metaphors of the "body" and the "blood." According to the author, the shift of cannibalism into the semiotic realm epitomizes that Europeans can't face the idea of cannibalism straight but only in a diffused metaphorical form. We can observe a similar form of denial in other social taboos among which the sexual sphere, certainly the most investigated, can provide useful elements for our analysis.

Sexual intercourse in fact implies exceeding one's own body's borders in order and fuse with another individual. Georges Bataille stated that eroticism, thus the desire for reproduction in human beings, is strictly connected to the death of the individual understood as a monolith. He writes:

> "Reproduction implies the existence of discontinuous beings. [...] Between one being and another, there is a gulf, a discontinuity. [...] It is my intention to suggest that for us, discontinuous beings that we are, death means continuity of being. Reproduction [...] brings into play continuity; that is to say, it is intimately linked with death."[6]

As sexual activity suspends the definition of the single being for the creation of a third presence, which beholds similarities and differences, cannibalism, with its paradigms of incorporation and becoming, represents the radical other that threatens the Western modern self.

In his book *We Have Never Been Modern* Bruno Latour defines modernism as a state of mind guided by the principles of purification, rupture, and critical partition of the relational continuum that actually forms human societies.[7] The recurrences of conceptual couples, such as "continuity and discontinuity" or "partition and unification," suggest that modernism and cannibalism imply and belong to each other. What we still have to clarify though is the kind of relationship they entertain. Not a binary opposition, which would instead respond to the modern logic of exclusion, but a participative opposition: something that is opposed to a part of itself. Cannibalism opposes modernism, which it nevertheless has already incorporated within the movements of interioration and exteriorization that characterize it. A maybe clearer example for a participative opposition is the one between man and woman in most European languages. "Man" is the extensive element of language referring to humankind, which however already contains a part of itself, namely, the intensive "man" in terms of gender.

The idea of a disjunctive synthesis prompted by cannibalism challenges and incorporates that of Western dualism which had been forming exclusive and opposite couples such as "barbarian vs. civilized," "nature vs. culture," "self vs. other," "exotic vs. familiar," and therefore excluded a whole spectrum of exchange, modulations, and contaminations. Cannibalism symbolizes an instable, unpredictable rearticulation of difference and subjectivity,[8] a noun that is preferable to identity, which instead refuses transformation and implies a static coherence: staying identical. In its rearticulating endeavor cannibalism always lives the moment of becoming, as Gilles Deleuze and Félix Guattari beautifully explained:

> "The orchid deterritorializes by forming an image of a wasp; but the wasp reterritorializes on that image. The wasp is nevertheless derritorialized, becoming a piece in the orchid's reproductive apparatus. But it reterritorializes the orchid by transporting its pollen. [...] A veritable becoming, a becoming-wasp of the orchid and a becoming-orchid of the wasp."[9]

4 **Carlos Rojas**, "Cannibalism and the Chinese Body Politic: Hermeneutics and Violence in Cross-cultural Perception," in: *Postmodern Culture*, vol. 12, no. 3, The Johns Hopkins University Press, Baltimore (MD), 2002. Available online at: http://pmc.iath.virginia.edu/text-only/issue.502/12.3rojas.txt, accessed June 2012.

5 **Claude Rawson**, "Unspeakable Rites: Cultural Reticence and the Cannibal Question," in: *Social Research*, vol. 66, no. 1, Spring 1999, p. 167.

6 **Georges Bataille**, *Eroticism*, Marion Boyars, London, 1987, p. 13.

7 **See: Bruno Latour**, *We Have Never Been Modern*, Harvard University Press, Cambridge (MA), 1993, p.7

8 **Brazilian psychoanalyst** and cultural critic Suely Rolnik speaks of an "anthropophagic subjectivity."

9 **Gilles Deleuze and Félix Guattari**, *A Thousand Plateaus: Capitalism and Schizophrenia*, University of Minnesota Press, Minneapolis (MN), 1987, p. 11.

Brazilian Cultural Cannibalism

The fundamental shift from cannibalism as social practice to cultural cannibalism as cultural tactic[10] is to be found in the Brazilian Anthropophagous Movement of the 1920s.

Among the exponents of Brazilian modernism, poet and intellectual Oswald de Andrade divulged his *Manifesto Antropófago* in 1928, suggesting cultural cannibalism to be Brazil's idiosyncratic way to modernism and meanwhile an antidote against the hegemony of modern Europe. Through an anthropophagic rereading of Brazil's multicultural history, De Andrade formalized a new national artistic practice based on the appropriation of forms, imaginaries, and styles of the (dominant) other. He lucidly proposed cannibalism as a sort of "nomadic war machine" against Europe, hence a becoming force "which lies outside dualities of terms."[11] The artists and intellectuals who gathered around De Andrade overturned the reception and assimilation of the outside into a creative enunciation, whose production could be read as an anthropophagic body where the barriers between external and internal become evanescent. De Andrade's theory emancipated the act of assimilation: the relationship between enunciator and recipient was overturned. The anthropophagic movement proposed a recursive and cyclic temporality, which tends to merge individuals, cultures, histories, and traditions.

The Cannibal Exhibition

The historical - or ideological - age we are living and discussing presents two main lines of hybridization and encounter: the "contemporary," as a conjunction of times (from Latin *cum-tempora*), and the "globality," as the emergence of a supranational, yet internally differentiating culture. The global contemporary allows differences to cohabit in a unique tense and in a unique world. The question is whether the lens of (cultural) cannibalism legitimates the reading of contemporary cultural practices and objects as decolonizing forces, which neutralize the authority of modernism and colonialism by reprocessing categories, master narratives, and geographical or national belongings.

Whereas modern museums' collections are ruled by principles of classification and non-Western art is conceived of and shown as an ethnic symbol of primitive and authentic cultures, the (con)temporary exhibition rearranges new contextual frames for art, objects, and practices from all corners of the globe and all historical periods. Both artists (as curators) and curators (as artists) perform a shift from the value of a single work of art to that of a disjunctive synthesis. Through selection and combination, he or she incorporates singularities in a more complex and heterogeneous unity. Within the exhibition's physical and conceptual borders, meanings arise in the theoretical and phenomenological relation *between* the objects displayed. This perspective makes the exhibition an internally differentiated body where the semantic bound between formalism and content of each single work is completed by the external links the artworks generate reciprocally.

Unlike modern and ethnological collections where artworks or artifacts are assembled in the name of historical and geographical continuity and discontinuity, today's curatorial and artistic practice adopts a temporary modulation of artworks, common objects, documents, and ethnologic pieces from different backgrounds, in terms of both space and time.

The 2012 edition of La Triennale - the triennial art exhibition in Paris formerly known as La force de l'art - was entitled *Intense Proximity* and provides us with a first good example. Artistic director Okwui Enwezor and his associate curators built up an exhibition "in which the artwork and the cultural object converge [...], where the thoughts that govern the relationship between concepts and forms, materials and mediums, gestures and actions, and all the activities that sum up the work of art and the cultural object, are given absolute primacy."[12] The creation of a space of relations and of disciplinary trespassing is well exemplified by the combination of photos of Brazilian natives taken by Claude Levi-Strauss in 1937 and installations by contemporary artists in the giant space of the Palais de Tokyo. The juxtaposition makes the historical chronologies and disciplinary canons collapse within the discursive space of the exhibition. What do these cultural objects tell the visitor once they are related to one another?

The contemporary art exhibition represents a form of temporary recycling of the symbolical forms stored in the museums, where instead they are classified in atemporal categories. If the archive is comparable to the museum and its collections, whose establishment dates back to the modern era, the exhibition is the ephemeral process during which cannibalistic appetites reawake static paradigms.

10 **For tactic see: Michel De Certeau**, *The Practice of Every Day Life*, trans. Steven Rendall, University of California Press, Berkeley (CA) [1980], 1984.

11 **Deleuze and Guattari** 1987, p. 388.

12 **Okwui Enwezor (ed.)**, *Intense Proximity*, Triennale de Paris, exhibition reader, 2012, p. 15.

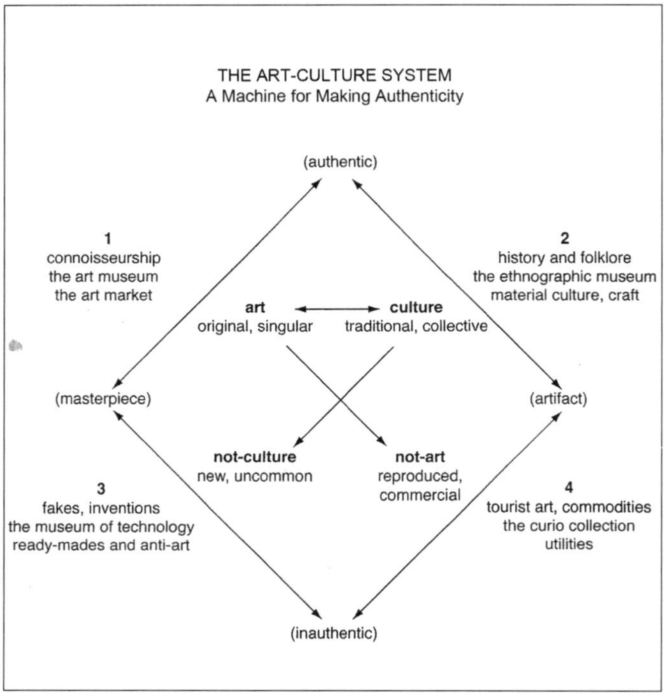

James Clifford, *The Art-Culture System*, 1988

The cannibal exhibition unpacks the archives of modernity and can be thus read as a possible decolonization and decanonization (as well as recolonization and recanonization) of art and cultural history. It does so through a process of appropriation, reinterpretation, and reformulation of the historical and cultural categories established during modernism and colonialism and first attacked by Marcel Duchamp with the concept of the ready-made at the beginning of the twentieth century.

"The Art-Culture System" elaborated by James Clifford in 1988 visualizes the logic structure, which in the first place the ready-made and later the contemporary cannibal exhibition have been undermining, stretching the domain of art to a radical overflow.

Clifford argued that the positions and the relative values assigned to art and cultural objects have and will be continuously switching over time and on converging disposals inside and outside the aesthetic field. Western modernity, through the appropriation and exhibition of exotic artifacts, has materialized the primitivist prejudice of a presumed originality of other cultures' products. Tribal artworks, generally collocated in an undefined and durable past, are extracted from their temporal frame and recontextualized in the ethnological museum-container. A first crisis of this system could be singled out in the subversion operated by Marcel Duchamp. Duchamp's ready-made has begun to threaten the meaning and the status of art, complicating the semantic of the four square's positions. Considering that the main goal of inclusion/exclusion strategies in collecting is to describe regions of authenticity, fake, and aesthetic value, the placement of a urinal in the artistic sphere opened up new horizons for all possible kinds of cultural texts and objects.

Contemporary curatorial and artistic practice reiterates the ready-made selection, and thus enables the renewal of archival and sleeping forms. There is a contiguous cannibal and transformative approach between a mixed-media installation by an artist, where non-art objects are presented as a work of art, and a mixed-media exhibition, where non-art objects are presented alongside works of art to shape an art exhibition. The dynamics of becoming belongs to both and unveils an instable aesthetic value that exists only on conditions of coexistence in a world of provisional connections. The single elements in the relation can elsewhere and otherwise convey different meanings and carry other values.

Vincent Vulsma's self-curated exhibition *A Sign of Autumn* (2011) at the Stedelijk Museum Bureau Amsterdam (SMBA)[13] stretched the roles of artist and curator, as well as the categories of art and artifacts, to a radical overlapping. The exhibition focused on a Baoulé mask loaned from the Tropenmuseum in Amsterdam. The mask carries the traces of a long journey through the history of European and American primitivism: bought by a German ethnographer, it was later purchased by art dealer Charles Ratton and was eventually staged in the MoMA exhibition *African Negro Art* in 1935.

The MoMA exhibition included Kuba textiles, which inspired Vulsma's new series of large-scale Jacquard-woven reproductions shown in the SMBA. Furthermore the artist realized a series of assemblages, "combining stools made in the Congo (probably around the 1930s) with a set of Ray Eames' Walnut Stools, which were designed in 1960 and which are still industrially produced and commercially distributed today."[14] Vulsma's practice of cannibal combining heralds the tendency of interrogating the cultural canons and the institutional and conceptual spaces, which we received from the modern era and, normally, defines that which they contain.

Another attempt at cannibalizing the walls of modern categories comes from the Weltkulturen Museum in Frankfurt am Main. Under the direction of Clémentine Deliss, the museum has undertaken an epistemological rethinking of its collection and activities towards a *postethnographic museum*. Deliss writes:

13 **The exhibition** is part of the SMBA's ongoing research and exhibition program "1975" on Dutch postcolonialism.

14 **Kerstin Winking**, "Vincent Vulsma - A Sign of Autumn," exhibition press release, 2011, available online at: http://www.smba.nl/en/exhibitions/vincent-vulsma-a-sign-of-autumn/, accessed Juli 2012.

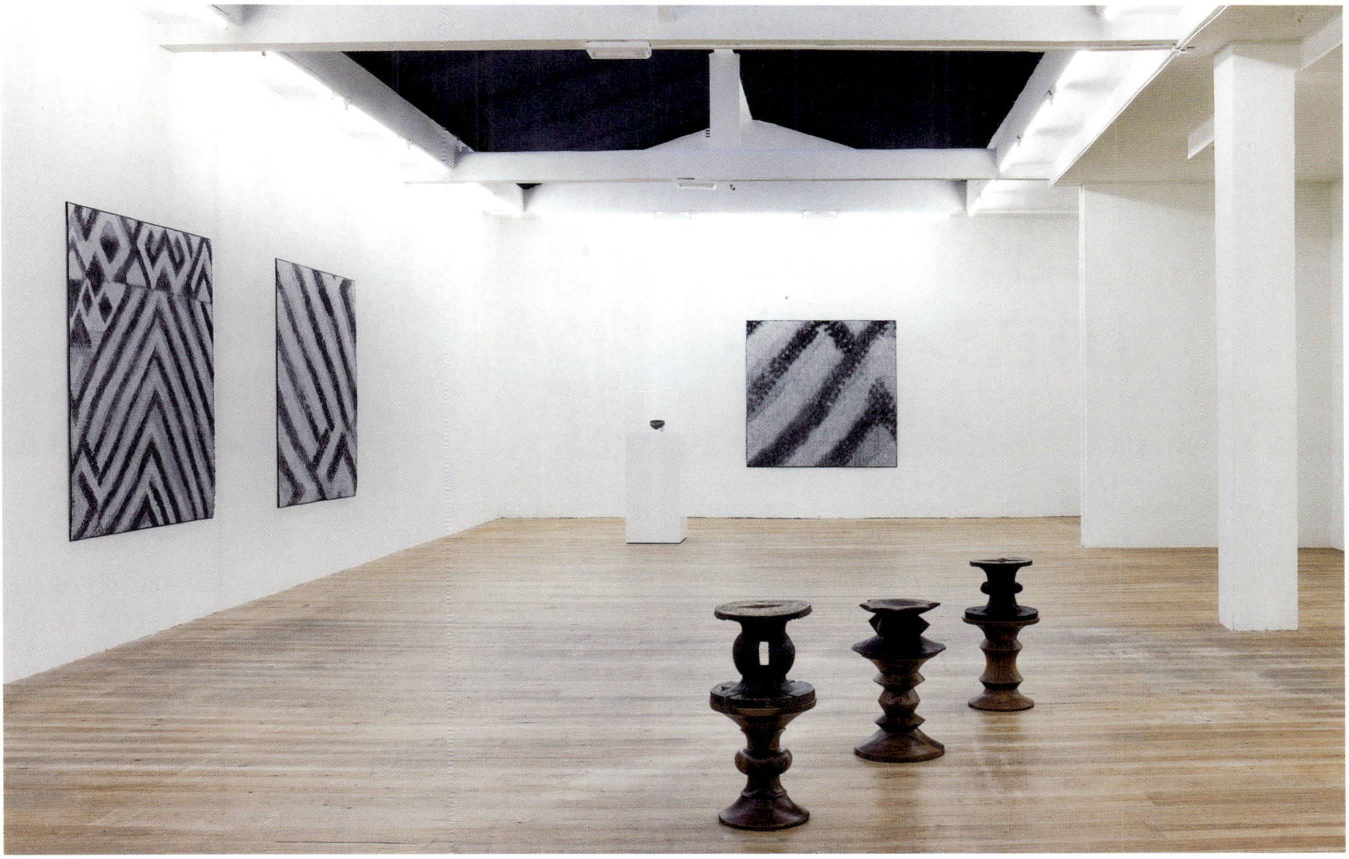

A Sign of Autumn - Vincent Vulsma, installation view, Stedelijk Museum Bureau Amsterdam, 2011

> "The philosophy behind the Weltkulturen Museum holds that in 2011 each individual artefact in the collection is a prototype and therefore a trigger for future concepts. To reference the American artist Allan Kaprow, the objects in the collection contain stored code. To decipher them requires a productive, engineered confusion between histories, roles and disciplines."[15]

The idea of remediating the ethnographic collection finds a place in the "Weltkulturen Labor" [research lab] program, where artists, scholars, and curators from all over the world are granted a residency at the museum in order to research on and formulate new interpretations of the collection. The residency prepares the ground for temporary exhibitions, of which *Object Atlas. Field Research in the Museum* (2012) is the first outcome. The exhibition draws together the work of the artists, who undertook field research at the Weltkulturen Museum in 2011, and the collection pieces whose new

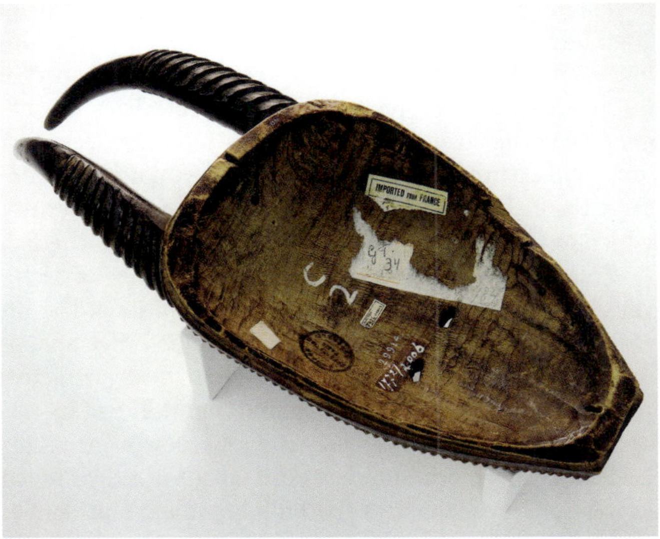

Vincent Vulsma, *No. 124*, detail, antelope mask, Baoulé, Ivory Coast, before 1933, on loan from Tropenmuseum, Amsterdam, custom-made wooden pedestal with Plexiglas display case, Stedelijk Museum Bureau Amsterdam, 2011

15 **Clémentine Deliss**, "Remediating Collections in a Post-ethnographic Museum," in: *Vincent Vulsma - A Sign Of Autumn*, SMBA Newsletter no. 124, 2011.

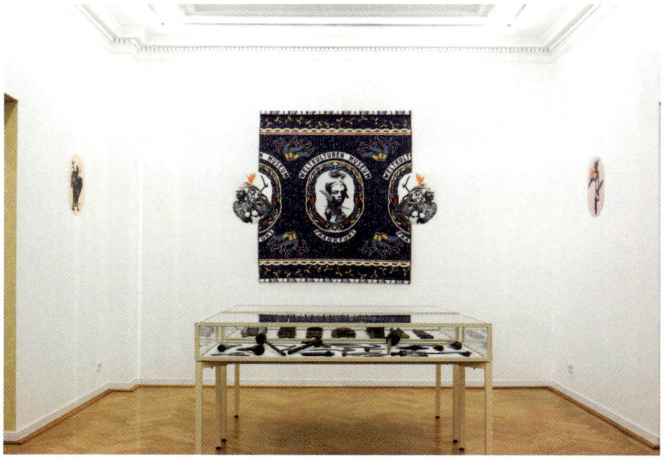

Objekt Atlas - Feldforschung im Musuem, exhibition view, Weltkulturen Museum, Frankfurt am Main, 2011/2012

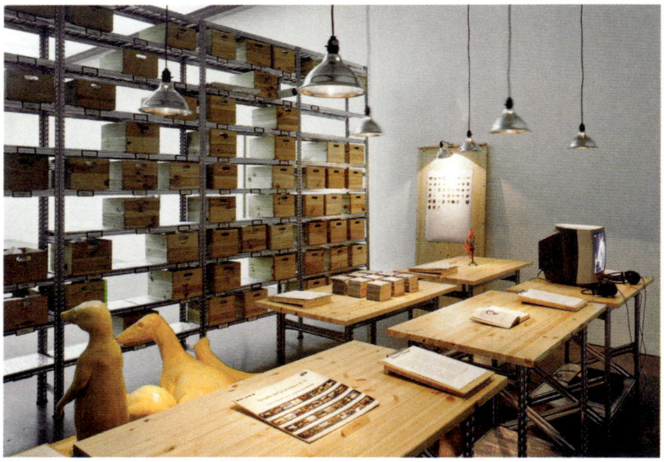

Agency, Assembly (Animism), installation view *Animismus. Moderne hinter den Spiegeln*, Generali Foundation, Vienna, 2011

works constitute a sort of commentary. Without dwelling upon aesthetic or conceptual achievement, the show is a sign of the unprecedented merging of the cultural categories and their respective physical spaces represented by the art museum on the one hand and the ethnological museum on the other hand, two faces of the same coin. Like the cannibal subsumes an alterity for the creation of a third complex subjectivity, which is no longer the one nor the other but simultaneously both, an exhibition like *Atlas* represents an incubation for a third art, no longer art nor artifact, but simultaneously both.

The shared space of the cannibal exhibition does not let itself be trapped in a definition but stays open to a modulation of judgments. Through the relations established in its heterogeneous corpus, however, it neutralizes the hegemony of the former paradigms in favor of an inconstant processing. Through the texture of the exhibition we observe the global contemporary incorporation of modernity, which nevertheless doesn't melt in a definitive synthesis.

This is particularly visible in the large usage of archival documents in contemporary art exhibitions. The archive is the result of modernity's scientific order and, as we learned from Michel Foucault, constitutes an active system of enunciation.[16] The apparent neutrality of its categories in fact hides an ideology and a discursive formation. Like the modern museum born in France with the French Revolution, it emphasizes the Enlightenment's principles of collection, classification, and neutralization of cultural objects, by means of an almost anatomic partition. Rather than an objective rhetoric that hides behind the apparent immediacy of its objects and seeks to eliminate any trace of its intervention, the cannibal exhibition operates a declared process that opens and unfolds the system. The presence of archives' components in contemporary art exhibitions follows a consolidated artistic attitude, but has recently abandoned the realm of artistic creation to embark on a wider critical operation.

The long-term exhibition and publication project *Animism* (2010–2012), which has been shown in Antwerp, Vienna, Berlin, and New York, perhaps ideally exemplifies how global contemporary art is changing through devouring the modern mindset and its archaeology.

The show gathered new commissioned artworks, already existing artworks, and an extensive selection of archival materials, from documents and photographs to books and documentaries. The rich body of works was brought together to investigate the premodern concept and practice of animism against the big divide between nature and culture in modern science. In order to affirm the validity of animism as an alternative way of thinking and living, the exhibition's head curator Anselm Franke had to enter the paradigms of Western modernity (animism's other), to appropriate with their cells and finally to combine them within a new body of relations.[17] Also the small exhibition *Tropicomania: The Social Life of Plants*, one of the several venues of La Triennale at the Bétonsalon, comprised "artworks, scientific illustrations, archive documents, literary accounts and films produced in a variety of contexts," to address "the interrelation between science, exoticism

16 **Michel Foucault**, *The Archaeology of Knowledge*, Routledge, London, et al., 2002.

17 **See: Anselm Franke (ed.)**, *Animism Vol. 1*, Sternberg Press Berlin, Extracity Kunsthal Antwerp, and M HKA - Museum of Contemporary Art, Antwerp, 2010; Anselm Franke and Sabine Folie (eds.), *Animismus: Moderne hinter den Spiegeln; Animism: Modernity Through the Looking Glass*, Generali Foundation, Vienna and Verlag der Buchhandlung Walther König, Cologne, 2011.

and commerce, and the power relations engendered by this very alliance."[18] Once again the exhibition space of interrelations becomes an input for reflection and speculation on topics other than art, topics that reverberate in the curatorial practice itself.

By remediating collections, canons, and heritages, the cannibal exhibition is shedding new light on the objects of her intervention, because they are caught in a new set of connections. But at the same time, by breaking the boundaries of pertinences and belongings, it is renegotiating the space and the value of art. What contradistinguishes "global contemporary art" goes beyond the mixing of cultures in a new, imploded cartography to include different historical times, social realities, disciplines, knowledge, and expertise. Documenta 13, directed by American-born curator Carolyn Christov-Bakargiev, happened simultaneously in Kassel, Kabul-Bamiyan, Alexandria-Cairo, and Banff from June to September 2012, thus nourishing herself by diverse localities and shaping an unusual geography. Like other shows by the same curator,[19] Documenta 13 connected art works from very different historical periods, thus doubting the validity of one art history. Not only delocalized onto the globe, the artworks were also sprawled throughout the city. The selected buildings formed together a spatial and transhistorical narrative that pushes the meaning of art to be mirrored and investigated through nonartistic questions. The exhibition comprised also a residency for writers, scientific installations as well as placed artistic installations in museums dedicated to science. In the curator's words, documenta works on "terrains where politics are inseparable from a sensual, energetic, and worldly alliance between current research in various scientific and artistic fields and other knowledges, both ancient and contemporary."[20] The convergence of realms of knowledge and disciplines through the dialectic of interiorization and exteriorization was condensed by the Rotunda in the Fridericianum, refered to as "The Brain."

The curator employed an organic, bodily image, which clearly suggests heterogenic connectivity in place of sectorial compartments, as a gesture to communicate the whole documenta project. Artworks, objects, and documents were subtracted from an original elsewhere to be gathered into an associative space that recalls the cannibal body assimilating the energy, the spirit, and the knowledge of the other. Modern certainties are eaten up, decomposed, and rethought, while at the same time liberating "the contemporary global self" from the barricade of distinction and identity. The status of compenetration and unpredictability obscures any teleological chronology and makes the fear of disappearance an actual possibility: "I am not sure that the field of art will continue to exist in the 21st century."[21]

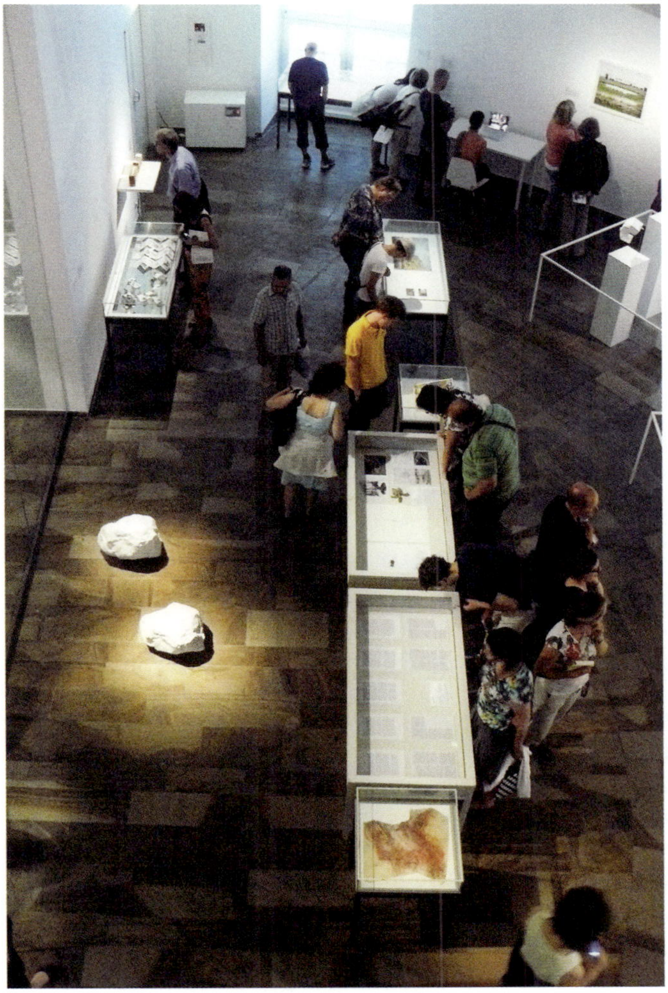

The Brain, installation view, Documenta 13, Kassel, 2012

No clear shape, no clear future awaiting, but a contemporary incertitude which, however, loudly states: "J'est un autre."[22]

18 See: **Bétonsalon – Centre for art and research**, *Tropicmania: The social Life of Plants*, press release, p. 2, available online at: http://betonsalon.net/PDF/DP_betonsalon_tropicomania%20_triennale-BR-light.pdf, accessed 08/20/2012.

19 **See**, e.g.: 16th Sydney Biennale, *Revolutions – Forms that Turn*, 2008.

20 **See: http://www3.documenta.de/#welcome/**, accessed 08/20/2012.

21 **Carolyn Christov-Bakargiev** as quoted by art critic Jerry Saltz in: "A Glimpse of Art's Future at Documenta," available online at: *Vulture Magazine*, www.vulture.com/2012/06/documenta-13-review.html, accessed 08/20/2012.

22 **Arthur Rimbaud** wrote "J'est un autre" ["I is an other"] in a letter dated May 15, 1871 addressed to his friend Paul Demeny. See: Wyatt Mason (ed.), *I Promise to Be Good: The Letters of Arthur Rimbaud*, Modern Library, New York (NY), 2004.

The Plurality of Art Worlds and the New Museum

Hans Belting

1.

As we reach the global age, art museums no longer represent a master narrative of art, as was the case in modernity. On the one hand, contemporary art production is expanding across the globe; on the other, this practice no longer follows a single mainstream notion of art, for which the museum was invented. It is true that the museum was also a place of competition and conflict, though this was restricted to the western art world. In general, the museum was the official address of a shared idea of art even in cases where it was expected to defend art's history against non-believers and avant-garde activists. This profile of the art museum is obviously not applicable to every part of the world, but it is apt to change in such cultures where museums may respond to other demands. And, finally, new art spaces (whether they are called museums or not) function in the age of accelerated art traffic even as places for the production of contemporary art, and thus, no longer resemble the museums that collected art of the past (including that of modernity).

In many parts of the world, art museums either lack any history or are suffering from the history of colonization. It is therefore likely that alternative art spaces will change or replace the profile that developed over in the Western history of museums. Such spaces are expected to respond to the complexity of the given society they are built for, since migration and the intervention of minorities have become a prominent feature everywhere. The Community Museum, as an example, was first developed in the US but is spreading quickly to places where the growing social dynamism of minorities demands a flexible idea of art's role.

"Art" was for a long time undisputed as a shared concept, whose ethnocentrism excluded any other notion of art as an expression of "Otherness." This disparity was the reason why, beginning in the 1950s, conceptualism was welcomed by artists from the former periphery who started to question an art concept imposed on them from the outside. Thus, conceptual art, in such cases, was not one of several currents like in the Western art scene, but a critical response to the art concept as such. For the same reasons, the self-referential aesthetics of art's autonomy became controversial whenever a local audience demanded that artists play a political role. Thus, in the 1990s the only two biennials in South Africa, after apartheid ended, triggered, "an ongoing debate about the *autonomy* of art vis-à-vis the social and political worlds in which it is embedded."[1] Colin Richards reminds us that, as soon as contemporary art had gained momentum, art's claims for protection and autonomy seemed to weaken its public presence and political role. He therefore asked the rhetorical question: "What remains distinctive and beguiling about art?"

1 **Colin Richards**, "The wounds of discovery," in: Antonio Pinto Ribeiro (ed.), *The state of the world*, Carcanet Press, Manchester, 2007, pp. 18ff.

2.

The last remaining stronghold of the Western art concept was the notion of an art world in the singular which survives even today as the belief in a "global art world," again in the singular. In other words, what was once a prerequisite of the West is believed today to survive in global expansion. This resistance to (or fear of) giving up the belief in a single art world, with an official authority even on a global scale, may be explained in part by the history of the term, and by its theory in recent Western philosophy and sociology. Art worlds, in the plural, were only acceptable when they designated different arts including literature, music, and dance, but they did not apply to the visual arts alone. The editors of the second book of the GAM-Global Art and the Museum series in 2009 initially used the common notion "The Global Art World" in the singular as a title as well, but even back then we linked it to the subtitle "Audiences, Markets, and Museums" in the plural.

As a matter of fact, today we are experiencing the rise of a plurality of art practices that recommends the plural usage also for the art world. The mapping of art regions with a transnational character is clear proof of the intention to organize art worlds in parts of the world that felt marginalized by the center and periphery map as we know it from modern times. In the following, art museums will provide a case study to elaborate on this concept. Museums are no longer defined by a single art world but testify to the rise of independent art worlds that are all contemporary and yet differ among themselves, both in a horizontal way (geography) and in a vertical way (audiences, markets, and museums). Thus it appears that the former art world in the singular, as it culminated in the modern age, ceases to offer a single-line genealogy for new museums to follow. It can be argued that the markets act against the new regional mapping and strive to preserve art's ubiquity in sales and trade, which means branding the artwork as an easily replaceable object of speculation. However, the market status of a work of art, a fiction in itself, is equally linked to the diversity and the specificity of new art worlds, which carry their own cultural codes and art practices.

The newly emerged class of curators seems to level the different art worlds in that they apply similar concepts with respect to an international clientele, in biennials and art fairs across the globe. But their audience is nevertheless local, since it is divided by a different experience, or no experience, of art. It is true that art practice has become a global condition but that does not mean that the single work or project acquires a global sameness in significance and acceptance. Even one and the same artwork may change meaning when it travels from one place to the next. Likewise, art in general neither simply *owns* one single meaning nor can it lay claim to universal significance. In other words, it needs an audience who identifies with cultural and social premises that make an art world.

With respect to the *plurality of worlds*, as a *contemporary* condition, the recent anthropology of the contemporary, which Paul Rabinov has placed under the title *Marking Time*,[2] is developing a pertinent model. Marc Augé describes the new fieldwork as *An Anthropology for Contemporary Worlds* when he writes: "The world's inhabitants have at last become truly contemporaneous, and yet the world's diversity is recomposed every moment: this is the paradox of our day. We must speak, therefore, of worlds in the plural" in order to cope "with the coexistence of the singular entity implied by the word contemporaneous and the multiplicity of worlds it qualifies [...] Every society is made up of several worlds."[3]

The contemporary, in a symbolic and even ideological way, has been recognized as the all-defining feature of today's art production. But at the same time, it "is made up of several worlds" (Marc Augé). In other words, the global is no longer synonymous with the totalizing term *world*. It denotes the space of a "multiplicity of worlds" in societies and cultures at large. This also applies to a multiplicity of art worlds in place of one independent and unitary "art world" as we know it from modern times. This is due partly to the fact that *art production* is presently turning into *culture production*, especially in regions where "art" was still a new experience and sought its cultural roots in order to reach a local audience.

The one and only art world created by modernism was defined with the help of a distinction between art and the real world. Yet even then, this distinction was simplifying the case. The Western art world was never as unified as the theory suggested. We only need to recall the debate about the prewar art world in Europe and the postwar art world in America, which have been presented in contrast with each other at the Museum of Modern Art in New York up to now. Today, the coexistence of several art worlds has not found an appropriate discourse, but is either taken for granted or is covered up by the retrospective look at the former unity of a single art world. The "multiplicity of worlds" in fact seems to contradict the essence of art as a world of its own. But if art nowadays is slowly giving up the distance (as defined by aesthetics) to the social world, and if the latter consists

2 **Paul Rabinow**, *Marking time: On the Anthropology of the Contemporary* Princeton University Press, Princeton (NJ), 2008.

3 **Marc Augé**, *An Anthropology for Contemporaneous Worlds*, Stanford University Press, Stanford (CA), 1999, pp. 89ff. See also: Francis Affergan, *La pluralité des mondes. Vers une autre anthropologie*, Albin Michel, Paris, 1997.

of several worlds (contemporary and traditional), then it is equally as "multiple" as the world it addresses explicitly or implicitly.

Therefore, it may be useful to quote Marc Augé once more when he distinguishes "the world of the image" from the real world. "The problem of how images are received, cannot be resolved merely by analyzing [their] [...] institutions, since the image also functions as memory, reference point, imaginative creation and/or re-creation." In a similar way, art also cannot be defined only by its institutions and markets, but acts via "memory" and imagination as a symbolical representation of "contemporary worlds."

The *picture worlds*, in the sense of visual cultures, as they were distinguished from *real worlds* in the ZKM exhibition (see: this volume, pp. 338–357), differ from art worlds in the same way, ever since art turned against mass media. But today's art increasingly appropriates images of the mass media, such as Nollywood clichés in Africa, and thus is no longer the exhibition art of the white cube as discussed by theoreticians in modern times. Of the threefold composition, that makes up an "art world," namely "audiences, markets, and museums," we will pursue here the part of the museum.

3.

Before turning to the museum, it may be useful to recapitulate the discourse of "the art world," as begun by Arthur C. Danto in 1964.[4] His famous text was written in the capital of modern art, New York, where Danto was surprised by the encounter with Pop art. His point was the distinction of the *Brillo Box*, which Andy Warhol exhibited in an art gallery, from the Brillo Box in a supermarket, when the one and the other looked alike. As a result, they could only be distinguished by the authority of what Danto identified as the art world. The art world, as he would later defend his functional theory against George Dickie's institutional view, is not just another word for its institutions, but "is the discourse of reasons institutionalized."[5] He argues that the role of the philosopher would come after "traditional art" had reached the end of its previous history and was no longer based on evolution and novelty of form. It is no mere coincidence, that five years later, in 1969, the Hungarian-born conceptual artist Joseph Kosuth, also living in New York, turned the tables and published his essay "Art after Philosophy" in which he insisted that art would take over what had been the part of "traditional philosophy"[6].

The cultural bias of such a debate was the belief in one art world that went equally uncontested as the belief in one philosophy. The American sociologist Howard S. Becker, in 1976, distinguished "art worlds and social types" that were "coexisting at one time," whether "in conflict or in some sort of symbiotic or cooperate relation." However, he was thinking of various arts of which each formed an art world of its own.[7] He therefore distinguished the artists, as "integrated professionals," from "naïve artists" and "folk artists" in terms of their art. As a result, an art world in its contradictions would "mirror society at large." In a later essay, Becker considered the art world as "a network of cooperative activity," whose conditions changed with the arrival of the communication technologies of the Internet.[8] But Becker still lacked the experience of globalization that decentralized the former art world. Pierre Bourdieu, too, based his theory of the "art system" on the Western art scene, which he chose as his one and only "field" of study.

James Clifford, in the meantime, introduced a new argument into the discourse of the art world. An anthropologist by profession, he was confronted with a binary situation that in fact contradicted the belief in a single art world. There was on the one hand the "culture collecting" as a colonial practice, and on the other, the "art collecting" in the mainstream art world. Two types of museums and of art, "tribal art" and "modern art," had for a long time not only excluded but also mutually defined each other. Clifford, in retrospect, could therefore speak of *the modern art-culture system* "in which culture ideas and art ideas" were supplementing each other and "through which exotic objects had been contextualized in the West."[9] It had become apparent that this dual type of collecting was "a local story," which had come to an end when art and culture ceased to be understood as opposition and new claims of ethnicity began to surface in the global practice of contemporary art. Cultural issues, in the sense of an artist's cultural background, for the first time began to matter in what had been an ethnocentric art world. The time was gone when the one and only art world had protected itself against the participation of other cultures with the universalism of mainstream art.

4 **Arthur C. Danto**, "The Artworld," in: *Journal of Philosophy*, vol. 61, no. 19, 1964, pp. 571–584. See also: Danto, "The Art World Revisited. Comedies of Similarity," in: Danto, *Beyond the Brillo Box. The Visual Arts in Post-historical Perspective*, Farrar, Straus and Giroux, New York (NY), 1992, pp. 33–53.

5 **Danto 1992**, p. 46.

6 **Joseph Kosuth**, "Art after Philosophy," in: *Studio International*, no. 915, October 1969, pp. 134ff. (Reprinted in: Kosuth, *Art after Philosophy and After: Collected Writings, 1966–1990*, MIT Press, Cambridge (MA), 1991, pp. 15ff.)

7 **Howard S. Becker**, "Art Worlds and Social Types," in: *American Behavioral Scientist*, vol. 19, no.6, July 1976, pp. 703–718.

8 **Howard S. Becker**, *A New Art Form*, available online at: http://www.uv.es/~fores/programa/becker_hypertextfiction.html, accessed 09/06/2012.

9 **James Clifford**, *The Predicament of Culture: Twentieth-Century Ethnography, Literature, and Art*, Harvard University Press, Cambridge (MA), 1988, pp. 215ff.

Since the 1990s, art's new outposts, called biennials, have reached the most unlikely places. As recurring events, they serve not only the recovery of "alternative modernities," but also the emergence of new art worlds, that had been marginalized during modernism. Their agents, a class of multinational curators, bring international and local artists together and thus change the rules, which had supported the authority of a single art world. Thus, they take over the traditional role of art critics and museums. In 1989, Yves Michaud published a pamphlet with the title "The artist and the curators" (*L'artiste et les commissaries*) in which he attacked curators as the new players "who have replaced the artists in making art."[10] The usual criticism sees, rightly or wrongly, curators in complicity with art fairs. The markets certainly play a dominating part in art's globalization. It is a matter of debate whether the emerging art worlds will end up in the grip of the markets or will gain their freedom from the mechanisms of the global art trade and sales.

The global art production certainly leaves behind the earlier theories of one mainstream art world. It is only a matter of debate whether one should speak of a "global art world" in the singular or whether such an all-encompassing entity, with its loss of any distinction, is a contradiction in itself. Some, however, even ridicule the term "art world" and offer an ironical insider view, like Paul Werner in a pamphlet about the Guggenheim Museum with the title: *Museum, Inc.: Inside the Global Art World.*[11] Charlotte Bydler, in her book *The Global Art World Inc.* discusses the role of biennials as vectors of a progressive "culturalization" that is breaking up the modern art concept.[12] For Pascal Gielen "the worldwide art system is in fact a meshwork of countless international sub-networks."[13] The present concern is the "mapping" of new art regions, like that of the Asia Pacific Triennial (see: this volume, pp. 112–113) or that of the Gulf Region rushing to replace the former art world with a new art geography. Peter Weibel's 1996 Graz show *Inklusion : Exklusion – Kunst im Zeitalter von Postkolonialismus und globaler Migration* likewise sought to draw "a new map" in order to cope with the artists' "global migration."[14]

Rasheed Araeen, in 1987, introduced his London magazine *Third Text* with "the aim of providing a critical forum for third-world perspectives on the visual arts."[15] The notion "Third World," which collapsed with the end of the Cold War, is sometimes replaced by "Global South,"[16] but the issue is still the same. *Third Text* was to represent "a historical shift away from the center of the dominant culture to its periphery." In its first decade, *Third Text* was "devoted to revealing the institutional closures of the art world." In its second decade, its aim was to examine "the assimilation of the exotic Other into the new world art," as Sean Cubitt reminds us.[17] A new type of "art-institutional racism," as he remarks, forced the "assimilation of newcomers" by the art world. "Others have abandoned the concept of art altogether" and look for "alternative modes of cultural practice."

Jean-Hubert Martin with his exhibition *Magiciens de la terre* (1989), seemed to deprive the existing art world of its privileges when he opened up its frontiers for newcomers who had for a long time been labeled as "native," "traditional," or "indigenous."[18] He thus juxtaposed the minimalist Richard Long, a star of the art world, with a group of Aboriginal Australians who did their "earth painting" on the floor before his installation (see: this volume, pp. 66–67). The French curator, then still director of the Centre Pompidou, even chose an equal number of "integrated professionals" of the art world and former outsiders with name and provenance. The designation as "magicians" stood for "artists" in a metaphorical sense, who, almost with Malraux's words, allowed "une enquête sur la création dans le monde d'aujourdhui," [an inquiry into creation in today's world].[19] Martin's exhibition would not have been possible earlier, at a time when the art world was still in command, and it lost its momentum soon afterwards, when the art world surrendered its right of exclusive power.

4.

Museums were of central importance for the formation of the modern art world. The Museum of Modern Art in New York, the first of its kind in the world, is a case in point. "The

10 **Yves Michaud**, *L'artiste et les commissaires. Quatre essais non pas sur l'art contemporain mais sur ceux qui s'en occupent*, Editions Jacqueline Chambon, Paris, 1989, p. 210.

11 **Paul Werner**, *Museum, Inc.: Inside the Global Art World*, Prickly Paradigm Press, Chicago (IL), 2010.

12 **Charlotte Bydler**, *The Global Art World, Inc. On the Globalization of Contemporary Art*, PhD diss., Uppsala University, Uppsala, 2004, esp. p. 242.

13 **Pascal Gielen**, *The Murmuring of the Artistic Multitude. Global Art, Memory and Post-Fordism*, Valiz, Amsterdam, 2010, pp. 192ff.

14 **Peter Weibel (ed.)**, *Inklusion : Exklusion: Versuch einer neuen Kartografie der Kunst im Zeitalter von Postkolonialismus und Globaler Migration*, exhib. cat., steirischer herbst 96, Graz, Dumont, Cologne, 1997.

15 **Rasheed Araeen, Sean Cubitt, and Ziauddin Sardar (eds.)**, *The Third Text Reader on Art, Culture and Theory*, Continuum, London, New York (NY), 2002, pp. 3ff.

16 **Beral Madra**, "Reflections on the Global South," in: Peter Weibel and Andrea Buddensieg (eds.), *Contemporary Art and the Museum. A Global Perspective*, Hatje Cantz, Ostfildern, 2007, pp. 110–122.

17 **Sean Cubitt**, "Prologue – In the Beginning: *Third Text and the Politics of Art*," in: Araeen, Cubitt, Sardar 2002, pp. 1–8, p. 3.

18 **See: Thomas McEvilley**, "Ouverture du piège: l'exposition postmoderne et 'Magiciens de la terre'," in: Jean-Hubert Martin (ed.), *Magiciens de la terre*, exhib. cat., Centre Pompidou, Paris, Grande Halle la Villette, Paris, 1989, Editions Centre Pompidou, Paris, 1989, pp. 20–23; Homi K. Bhabha, "Hybridité, hetérogénéité et culture contemporaine," in: ibid., pp. 24–27.

19 **Jean-Hubert Martin**, "Préface," in: ibid., pp. 8–11, p. 8.

MoMA made us modern," to quote Arthur C. Danto who epitomized the importance of the institution for a new canon of art and aesthetics. It was due to two MoMA exhibitions of the 1930s that modernism became a myth early on.[20] The Americans, who had felt culturally colonized by European modernism, soon began to colonize Europe with the help of the same museum. The MoMA thus opted for the double canon it had created itself, when it reopened its galleries in 2004. One floor was reserved for European prewar modernism while the other floor, with a few exceptions, presented American postwar modernism. It became abundantly clear that the museum officials had decided to represent the museum's own history as a solid myth. But a MoMA conference which followed the reopening in April 2005, discussed the question "When was Modern Art?" It was, as the subtitle added, a "contemporary question" which could not have been asked when modern art was still in power.

Ten years before, William Rubin had again staged the modernist myth, again with two complementary exhibitions both defending modernism as a living past; for the last time. After the Picasso show, which opened in 1980, six years after the artist's death, the exhibition *"Primitivism" in 20th Century Art* that followed in 1984, could just as well have been called "Picasso and Primitive Art"[21] (see: this volume, p. 62). Its aim was to tell again the story of the avant-garde once more, but, in fact, it again reiterated the colonial perspective that reduced the masks and fetishes to a mere "inspiration" for Western artists. Today ethnic arts and crafts, which had been the favorite child of colonial teachers and collectors, no longer continue as a living tradition even if they survive as a commodity for global tourism. "The death of authentic primitive art," to quote the title of a book by Shelly Errington, opens a space that contemporary art invades with its double character: as *posthistorical*, with respect to the West, and as *postethnic*, with respect to colonial history.[22]

It appears that the history of art has become a burden for Western artists similar to the ethnic tradition for "non-Western" artists (also this latter term loses its distinction). The global experience, in retrospect, allows "multiple" or "alternative modernities" to come into view.[23] Thus, to be "modern" has become a historical notion that in the West might even appear as a local past, in the way that other cultures are viewing their past. "Modern art" becomes a source of memory and identity at MoMA when its audience wants to see what it loves. Even the name MoMA, with its nostalgic charm, has been generally replaced by the brand name MoCA (Museum of Contemporary Art) in many parts of the world where contemporary production is celebrated as an art without geographic borders and without "history" in Western terms. The art market followed the MoCA when Christie's and Sotheby's replaced the trademark "Modern" with new labels such as "Contemporary" and "Postwar Art."

How do museums cope with the rise of new art worlds? It may be useful to consult the recent history of the Guggenheim Museum, which has opted for quite some time to be what Karsten Schubert called "a global museum."[24] When Thomas Krens joined the staff in 1988, he soon developed "the idea of global expansion" through the creation of "a network of semi-satellite institutions." However, the "global branding of mass-produced goods" proved to be a difficult model. Only the Bilbao museum, due to Frank Gehry's spectacular building, has fulfilled the expectations so far but this branch, too, is handicapped by its financial dependence on the New York home base.

It remains to be seen whether Guggenheim's Abu Dhabi branch, its building also a project by Frank Gehry, will mark a successful entrance into a new art world or suffer from neocolonial politics of the old art world, such as pretending to be, like the Louvre branch, a "universal museum." The local audience is the crux in Abu Dhabi. But what is a local audience in the Gulf States beyond the ruling class? The global rhetoric hardly conceals the political and economic interests of the Western and Arab partners in planning a "Cultural District" (comparable with the West Kowloon District in Hong Kong with its plans for a "Museum Plus," see: this volume, p. 93). Western star architects, as a rule, make such a site prestigious. Also, the international and local markets (galleries, auction houses, and art fairs) are heavily involved in the two museum projects, since they strive to make their profits with instant museum acquisitions and steer the institutions toward displays of sensational exhibits with a global or Arab link-up. Pace Gallery President, Marc Glimcher, states that the Abu Dhabi Art fair is "associated with the Guggenheim. Their collection has to be in order if they are going to fill that new museum space." And Paris-based dealer Kamel Mennour adds: "There may

20 **See: John Elderfield (ed.),** *Imagining the Future of the Museum of Modern Art*, Studies in Modern Art 7, The Museum of Modern Art, New York (NY), 1998.

21 **See: William Rubin,** "Picasso," in: Rubin (ed.), *"Primitivism" in 20th Century Art: Affinity of the Tribal and the Modern*, vol. 1, exhib. cat., Museum of Modern Art New York, Detroit Institute of Arts, Dallas Museum of Art, 1984/1985, pp. 241–340.

22 **Shelly Errington,** *The Death of Authentic Primitive Art and Other Tales of Progress*, University of California Press, Berkeley (CA), 1998. See also: Sally Price, *Primitive art in Civilized Places*, University of Chicago Press, Chicago (IL), 1989; Raymond Corbey, *Tribal Art Traffic: A Chronicle of Taste, Trade and Desire in Colonial and Post-colonial Times*, KIT Publishers, Amsterdam, 2000.

23 **See: Dilip Parameshwar Gaonkar (ed.),** *Alternative Modernities*, Duke University Press, Durham (NC), London, 2001; Santosh Gupta, Prafulla C. Kar, and Parul Dave Mukherji (eds.), *Rethinking Modernity*, Pencraft International, New Delhi, 2003.

24 **Karsten Schubert,** *The Curator's Egg: The Evolution of the Museum Concept from the French Revolution to the Present Day*, One-Off Press, London, 2002, pp. 113ff.

be no collectors in Abu Dhabi, but there are museums being built. And they all need art."[25]

In the meantime, the Guggenheim has announced a new venture for expanding its collection. On April 12, 2012, the Guggenheim Foundation and the Swiss bank UBS contracted the project "Guggenheim UBS Map" in which the bank supports the Guggenheim officials in building up a global art collection at their home base in New York. The new parts of the collection that go abroad, which are each related to a specific area of the globe, will be shown at two venues. But what is a "global art collection"? Is it at all possible to simply globalize *a posteriori* an existing museum collection without depriving it of its history and profile? Shouldn't such metropolitan museums finally accept to remain what they have always been, institutions with a Western profile that, however, need redefining in the face in the global era?

5.

The issue is not whether these museums qualify as models for "a global museum" anywhere in the world. The question is rather whether in the global age the art museum will survive at all as an institution with a single purpose and a common appearance. In many ways, the educational part will be its strong side, and this also applies to the need for a public forum where a community looks to art as a social practice rather than at art for exhibition. Western dominance, accompanied by corporate funding and missionary zeal, will not suffice where institutions search for a dynamic role and an individual profile. Museums today are called to inform a local audience, but are in turn informed by their public. They need to familiarize new audiences with art. Contemporary art, which starts together with its audience, lacks the kind of history that art collections used to live from. It is often hailed as liberation from modernism's baggage and from art history, with its Western-based narrative. Avant-garde, originally a military term, acted as history's spearhead in the guise of *art history* whose narrative, in turn, needed *art museums* to be displayed in.[26] Since there was no art history in most parts of the world, however, its narrative cannot be appropriated like a ready-made.

The quest for new art worlds will provide museums with a new and critical role. The mapping drive which aims to develop interacting art worlds in geographic (but not in national) terms, calls for places on the map that symbolize an art world in the making. But such places do not require the same kind of institution. As a result, museums will vary from one place to the next and from one institution to another, as it is the participation of a public that matters here. Art museums have inherited a notion of art (sometimes as colonial baggage) that, presently, does not divide one society from another, but instead separates the economic elite from the majority in *any* given culture. The global art market is a distorting mirror, as it is a market for global players, whereas museums await a local audience, providing that they keep their independence as nonprofit places with an educational mission.

Museums of contemporary art in many parts of the world are expected to represent an expanding global experience using the mirror of local art. Their boom does not mean that they all subscribe to the Western idea of an art museum. Rather, they differ more in what they consider to be art than they do in their architecture, which is better transferable from one place to another. In this sense, museums increasingly turn into an ephemeral stage for living art that, as site-specific and installation art, they often create, and even commission. A museum collection has always been based on the need of selection for the public's memory and excluded what did not deserve memory. However, there are no longer general (global) rules for what is to be excluded and included in art. By implication, also Western museums may suddenly look "local" when they continue to exclude what remains outside their collecting tradition.

Art museums once used to be regarded as extraterritorial, in the terminology of Michel Foucault, a *heterotopia,* that is a site different from real sites or, in other words, an enclave with a time and reality of its own in the midst of any given society.[27] In such a capacity, they served to transform the *presence* of the world into art and thus into a symbolic *representation* of that presence. Today, it is installation art, that creates its own place (a place for the here and now) and thus continues the heterotopic tradition. For museums, on the other hand, the term "contact zones" that James Clifford coined, meets with more approval as a description of their role. Such zones not only offer contact with art but contact between one group and another in a given society. They represent, in Clifford's words, "the different agendas - aesthetic, historical, and political - that diverse *publics* bring to contexts of display."[28]

25 **Marisa Mazria Katz**, "Dealers Shy of Abu Dhabi Return. Over a Third of Last Year's Galleries will Stay Away," in: *The Art Newspaper*, no. 216, September 2010, p. 57.

26 **See: Hans Belting**, *Art History after Modernism*, University of Chicago Press, Chicago (IL), 2003.

27 **See: Michel Foucault**, "Of Other Spaces," in: *Diacritics. A Review of Contemporary Criticism*, vol. 16, no.1, Spring 1986, pp. 22ff.

28 **James Clifford**, *Routes: Travel and Translation in the Late Twentieth Century*, Harvard University Press, Cambridge (MA), 1997; James Clifford, *On the Edges of Anthropology*, Prickly Paradigm Press, Chicago (IL), 2003, pp. 36ff.

Clifford, to be sure, was primarily speaking of ethnographic museums on the Pacific Northwest coast, but Masaaki Morishita appropriated the same term for art museums in Japan that, like the Tochigi Prefectoral Museum of Fine arts, "attempt to negotiate different cultures in the local artistic field."[29] He describes the struggle of local artists to conquer the "empty museum" - to use his term - for their own work as a kind of "salon." But in the end, the artists accepted the idea that a museum has to serve the community as a whole and thus be available as a public stage for themes of common interest. Such controversies are also going on in other parts of the world where artists demand a museum for their own interests, but will have to admit that a museum is not a rentable art space. By contrast, Clifford sees "the museum - that most stodgy and Eurocentric of institutions - as a dynamic, disseminating institution which could take a diversity of forms in particular local/global conjunctures."

6.

There is, as yet, no typology in sight for museums of contemporary art that represents their new diversity. But the international GAM conference (2007), which addressed "the global challenge of art museums," discussed several museum types that specialized on a single audience. A new type of university museum, focusing on the survival of a local culture in a global world, is a case in point. One example is the Vargas Museum, a museum at the University of the Philippines (1978), based on a private collection and acting as a forum to link the local tradition with the present state of the country.[30] There is additionally the santralistanbul (2008) in the precinct of a private university on the Golden Horn, and the Museo Universitario Arte Contemporaneo (2008) in Mexico City, which addresses the students of the National Autonomous University with an ambitious program of contemporary art and culture.[31] The educational role, in all such cases, is the condition for the museum's activity and art practice, since the audience is a given.

Another case is the community-based museum, which also has a given audience or is demanded by such an audience. This type has been introduced, against much resistance, in São Paulo where the Museo Afro Brasil is run by its founder, the artist Emanoel Araújo.[32] In the US, "minority groups will become the majority in a few decades, and art museums will have to diversify to survive," as Martha Lufkin wrote in *The Art Newspaper* in 2009 (vol. XVIII, no. 204, July-August 2009, p. 16, see: this volume, p. 155). Arnold Lehman, director of the Brooklyn Museum, considered diversity "a critical issue," and Graham Beal, director of the Detroit Institute of Art (DIA), stated that "the community wants to see itself distinctly defined within the museum" as a place for all people (vol. XVIII, no. 205, September 2009, Martha Lufkin, p. 29, see: this volume, p. 155. The future Museum for Afro-American Art will not be the last link in the chain of community museums on the Mall in Washington, D.C.[33]

Collector-run museums reveal the invasion of the art markets into museum territory with the trade in "museum quality" works. Some museums in Asia are built like airports awaiting the arrival of international art. Collectors with a market competence (a kind of VIP in the art world) build their own museums and unduly gain prominence in places where there is no balance with a "free" art scene to speak of. Today corporate-funded museums are on the move. Japanese department stores began to attract their clients with museums on their premises in the 1980s. The Mori Art Museum in Tokyo (2003) is situated on the 53rd floor of a skyscraper close to shopping areas, and restaurants, with a sky view. Thus, we are in a period of transition where art museums exist under strong pressure from the outside. This situation explains the contradiction that exists between boom and crisis (the boom of museum buildings and the crisis of their purpose).

Meanwhile, the Asian museum boom attracts institutional criticism from within. Kao Chien-hui from the Taipei Museum of Contemporary Art launched the exhibition *Trading Place* as a "commentary exhibition" in which she wanted to address the vicissitudes of the art scene.[34] The artists in this show dealt with topics such as "stealing, exchanging, trading, re-presenting, and misappropriating" art and mounted a "replica exhibition arena" in order to challenge the art concept and mobilize the local audience. In China, the museum boom has just begun, but it is a building boom and suffers from a controversy over the meaning of contemporary art for the Chinese audience. Abroad, contemporary Chinese artists rank prominently on the art markets. At home, the interest of the general public is still

29 **Masaaki Morishita**, "Museums as Contact Zones: Struggles Between Curators and Local Artists in Japan," in: Hans Belting and Andrea Buddensieg (eds.), *The Global Art World. Audiences, Markets, and Museums*, Hatje Cantz, Ostfildern, 2009, pp. 316ff.

30 **See: http://www.globalartmuseum.de/site/moca_of_the_month/174**, accessed 10/23/2012.

31 **See: Rafael Sámano Roo**, "A New Setting for the Contemporary: A University Museum In Mexico City," in: Belting, Buddensieg 2009, pp. 348-357; Karen Cordero Reiman, "Addendum: The MuAC and Its Initial Encounter with Its Publics, in: ibid., pp. 358-367.

32 **Emanoel Araújo**, "The Museum Afro Brasil in São Paulo," in: ibid., pp. 180-188.

33 **See: Paul De Bruyne and Pascal Gielen (eds.)**, *Community Art. The Politics of Trespassing*, Valiz, Amsterdam, 2011.

34 **See: www.aaa.org.hk/Collection/Details/13570**, accessed 10/24/2012.

very low. Fan Di'an, head of the National Gallery in Beijing, made collectors responsible, since collecting had become a "business rather than a service for the community."[35] In Beijing's District 798, the Ullens Center for Contemporary Art, owned by the Belgian collectors Guy and Myriam Ullens, still holds a key position, but the founders are retreating from their sponsoring.[36] The World Art Museum, a public institution at the China Millennium Monument in Beijing (2000), presents invited shows of Western art from Europe, such as nineteenth-century French painting. The newly emerging discipline of "world art history" in China reverts the perspective of "Museums of World Cultures" in the West.

In the Middle East, the museum situation is both spectacular and uncertain. There was no proper museum tradition in the Gulf States when the foreign museum projects in Abu Dhabi started to make the global news. Among local museum foundations, the Art Museum in Sharjah, together with the related Biennial, was the first project of its kind. The Museum of Modern Arab Art in Qatar that collects "works from the wider Middle East, from North Africa all the way across to Iran,"[37] is presently under construction. The United Arab Emirates, beyond their narrow confines, are attracting collections of art with a common religious and cultural background that exemplify a newly emerging art world. In 2008, the Art Dubai, in conjunction with *The Financial Times*, organized a Global Art Forum with several panels on topics like "Branding of Museums" or "The New Museum Think Tank - Cultural Institutions in the Middle East." Key issues of the latter were the education of the audience and the training of professional local curators. Some of the participating artists protested against the power of prestigious museum collections that would not serve their interests, but instead prevent the community from a first-hand encounter with living art. Lamia Joreige, an artist from Beirut, wondered whether such institutions might not be "a danger for artistic production," if they promoted "national or institutionalized artists" only.[38]

The African museum scene still suffers from the colonial past and lacks the backing of a trained audience. In postcolonial times, African artists were early on the global art map, but they encountered drawbacks due to continuing colonial interference and the lacking infrastructure of art institutions. However, this is going to change. A recent exhibition in Brussels with the title *Geographics: A Map of Art Practices in Africa, Past and Present* listed a number of new "art centers" across the continent that are increasingly supported by private collectors and public funds.[39] The role of traditional art (with the colonial bias of its ethnographic history), however, remains a problem and, in addition, the powerful diaspora scene, with its overseas institutions, has no such equivalent in Africa.

7.

The concept of a single art world reached a turning point at the time when Arthur C. Danto, who had once coined the term, wrote an essay for the Venice Biennale of 1993. Curator Achille Bonito Oliva had asked him to comment on the Biennale's topic "compass points of art" (*punti dell'arte*), which was meant to guide people through the unity of the art world, against the diversity displayed in the same Biennale's national pavilions. This was still the old idea, but it was already seriously challenged when Danto received an invitation to contribute to the first Johannesburg Biennale whose curators had taken the decision to "put that city on the map [...] of art."[40] The author realized that the new concept stood against the Venetian one, but he could not figure out what the difference would be in the end. To be sure, the artists in South Africa had claimed "a place on the map of international art. That is, because that map is of a single world, the internation of art." But what would the new map be like? Danto was aware that "when Africanism strengthens, Internationalism will belong more and more to the past." He wondered whether "national centers of national art" would take its place.

But the days of the national idea in promoting art were already passing. In fact, Australia had taken a transnational turn when the Queensland Art Gallery in Brisbane, with strong government support, launched a Triennial in the same year, 1993, when the former West still seemed to be unchallenged in Venice. The idea was to create the region of "Asia-Pacific art" whose twelve countries plus Hong Kong had discovered their cultural affinities via contemporary art. Caroline Turner, as curator, insisted on the priority of internal relations that connected the new region ("intra-regionalism"), as opposed to the external view of Australia's position on the periphery of art ("extraregionalism"). "While there have been exhibitions of South-East Asian Art

35 **Chris Gill**, "China. Beijing Plans Major Museum Exclusive Interview with the Head of the National Gallery," in: *The Art Newspaper*, no. 196, November 2008, p. 22.

36 **See: www.globalartmuseum.de/site/moca_of_the_month/61**, accessed 10/23/2012.

37 **"The New Museum Think Tank.** Cultural Institutions and the Middle East", in: *Global Art Forum 2 -Transcripts*, Art Dubai, 2008, p. 257.

38 **Ibid.**, p. 263.

39 **The exhibition** was organized by the Centre for Fine Arts, Brussels, in the fall of 2010.

40 **Arthur C. Danto**, "Mapping the Art World," in: *Africus: Johannesburg Biennale*, exhib. cat., 1995, pp. 24ff.

and East Asian art within Asia," the Asia Pacific Triennial of Contemporary Art was "the first exhibition of this scale to focus on the Asia-Pacific region."[41] Australia had political reasons for reconsidering "its place in the world" by embracing the visual cultures of Asia.[42] Interestingly enough, it was an art museum, the Queensland Art Gallery, which took the lead in the creation of a new "art region."

Today Australia can also be considered an "art world" on its own. This is evident from the museum scene whose distinct features are not to be found elsewhere. Gerard Vaughan has described the emergence of what he calls "the cross-cultural museum" in the sense that Asian and especially Aboriginal art has become an integral part of both the collection and the exhibition policy of public art museums. "When Sydney's new Museum of Contemporary Art was constituted in 1989 (the Gallery opened to the public in 1991), it [...] developed a strong curatorial policy to support [...] contemporary Indigenous art" with an emphasis on "city-based Indigenous artists."[43] The Australian National Gallery in Canberra (renamed the National Gallery of Australia in 1993) as well considers "Indigenous art [...] as part of the contemporary Australian main stream." In the first Asia Pacific Triennial, the curators invited three Aboriginal women artists among the nine participants from Australia and drew a map of Australia on which the places of Aboriginal art production were marked. Such museum strategies demonstrate Australia's claims to be recognized as an independent "art world."

The art museum is closely connected with the rise of competing "art worlds" whose mapping indicates the tendency to break down the global panorama down into smaller units with a geographical or cultural profile of their own. The same decentralization undermines the art concept whose universal claims are contested today. Also in this respect, museums are called upon to serve the politics of representation in the name of a local community or the society at large. Traditionally, the significance of museums was based on their role to relate a master narrative that was shared by their audience. This narrative no longer allows for the universal claims of modern times. There exist today competing histories (religious, ethnic, or postcolonial) that deconstruct an exclusive significance of "art." Nevertheless, museums still qualify as outposts of what is considered to be art. Today, they have been "transformed from a temple of beauty into a kind of cultural fair."[44] As such, they are expected to offer more immediate contact with people than the traditional art museum normally provides.

Translated from the German by Elizabeth Volk.

41 **Caroline Turner**, "Introduction. From Extraregionalism to Intraregionalism?," in: Janet Hogan (ed.), *The First Asia-Pacific Triennial of Contemporary Art*, exhib. cat., Queensland Art Gallery, Brisbane, Australia, 1993, pp. 8–9, p. 8.

42 **Gerard Vaughan**, "The cross-cultural art museum in Australia," in: Jaynie Anderson (ed.), *The Cambridge Companion to Australian Art*, Cambridge University Press, Cambridge (MA), 2011, p. 288.

43 **Ibid.**, p. 271.

44 **Arthur C. Danto 1992**, pp. 11ff.

Bridging the World. The Role of Art Criticism Today

Sabine B. Vogel

The Situation Today

"China has overtaken the United States as the world's biggest market for art and antiques ending decades of American domination."[1]

Global Art Market

This sensational announcement was published in March 2012 by the organizers of the European Fine Art Fair (TEFAF), the world's most important fair for art and antiques. It was the result of Clare McAndrew's analysis of the art market in 2011. Two decades earlier, in 1990, China's share in the international art trade was just 0.4 percent, while that of the United States was 46 percent. France accounted for 17 percent of the sales at that time, but only 6 percent in 2011. By contrast, already in 2010 China accounted for 23 percent and a year later 30 percent of the international trade in art and antiques. China thus pushed the United States (29 percent) into second place and the United Kingdom (22 percent) remained in third place.[2]

Aside from the fact that there was a lack of transparency in the basic data -the highest bidder is not always a customer, and not every work that is auctioned is also paid for - the highest prices distort the results. McAndrew wrote that 20 percent of the works generate 80 percent of the sales value: in 2011 just 0.2 percent of the global art auctions accounted for 28 percent of the sales value of works over two million Euros.[3] To cite another statistic: According to McAndrew's analysis, the art market has grown an incredible 575 percent from its lowest point in 1991 to its highest in 2007.[4] In 2011, the record volume of sales was 46.1 billion Euros, 23.1 billion Euros of which was sold by auction houses. For contemporary art, McAndrew calculated that China accounted for 22.6 percent of the international trade; the US for 21.5 percent, the United Kingdom for 8.8 percent; Germany for 3.6 percent; Singapore for 0.7 percent, and the United Arab Emirates for 0.5 percent (see: this volume, p. 134).[5]

In addition to the economic potential of art, these figures reflect two significant changes: the sheer quantity of art sold and the number of artists, buyers, and sellers has increased enormously. Just a few years ago, the art world was still a small, elite, largely closed community living primarily in the geopolitical West and consisting of artists, directors of institutions, gallery owners, and critics. Collectors were welcome but did not play a leading role. Those days are clearly over; collectors and art buyers have become the drivers in a new community known as the "art industry."

1 **Announcement of Clare McAndrew's publication**, *The International Art Market in 2011: Observations on the Art Trade over 25 Years: TEFAF Art Market Report*, The European Fine Art Foundation, 2012. Available online at: http://www.tefaf.com/DesktopDefault.aspx?tabid=78, accessed 07/20/2012.

2 **Ibid.**, p. 69.

3 **Ibid.**, p. 40.

4 **Ibid.**, p. 15.

5 **Ibid.**, p. 47.

Art Industry

This term is used to denote a recent phenomenon that has arisen since the turn of the millennium: an ever closer relationship between culture and business.[6] Distinct from the employees of "cultural institutions," this new group includes representatives of the so-called "cultural industries": from auction houses, investment firms, art insurance companies, and art consultant companies. Professional activities in the field of art are no longer understood idealistically as a calling, but rather as the basis for profit-oriented enterprise, and this is true not only of the consultants etc., but also of artists such as Jeff Koons, Damien Hirst, and Takashi Murakami. Their studios supply the market with large quantities of editions and merchandising objects - everything labeled with their signatures - which are more brand products than works of art: originality, meaning, and stylistic questions are secondary to the factors of recognizability and marketability.

In the art industry, art is quantified: in order to turn art into an investment, market research reports are produced according to industrial standards, and statistics on sales and buyers, rates of return and rankings, replace art historical criteria. Algorithms determine value.

The Borders of the Art World

The second fact we can read from these numbers concerns the boundaries of the art world: in 2011 0.5 percent of the sales were generated in the Emirates, and 0.7 percent in Singapore; compared to the size of these states, their art traditions, and the still very recent infrastructure for art, that is an enormous amount. These numbers indicate nothing less than a new order in the art world: the notion of a small community is finished; the hegemony of the West has ended, and, as far as the art industries are concerned, idealism and the search for meaning have also been deposed.

Art Criticism and the Market

These numbers are indicative of a third change: they provide me with a lead-in to an essay on art criticism. Since when has art criticism been interested in sales statistics? Art critics are trained art historians, and unlike journalists it is not their remit to report on record figures and the art market but rather to interpret works and theorize about art.

That too has changed significantly. Today art and the art market can no longer be separated. We can no longer ignore the art market. On the contrary, this field represents a new, exciting challenge for us. McAndrew reads the statistics with an eye to investment in art. Art critics can, by contrast, analyze this data and develop a counterweight to the art industry. Thus art critics face a new task: we are no longer challenged only to analyze and evaluate works of art as in traditional art history. We have to analyze the changes.

A Retrospective

First, let us look back briefly: The origins of art criticism can be dated to the beginning of the Renaissance. At the time, such texts served to differentiate between the fine arts and the applied arts. Usually they were written by artists, and they did not write critically but rather descriptively, often biographically and larded with anecdotes.

Even into the eighteenth century, art criticism was expected to be convincing as a literary performance, not as a critical one. For example, Novalis (1772–1801) declared the critic to be a poet, the artist's coauthor.

Central Developments

At the end of the eighteenth century, the basic prerequisites for art criticism were altered by three developments that can be summed up by three keywords: first, bourgeoisie; second, infrastructure, and, third, metropolitan art.

Bourgeoisie: The emergence of a bourgeois and increasingly enlightened public led to a new audience for art.

Infrastructure: Art was no longer produced on a commission basis for the aristocracy and the church but instead addressed an anonymous audience at salon exhibitions. Soon newspapers began to report on this very new form of presenting art to the public, which led to a new form of art criticism.

Metropolitan art, or cultural centers: Whether in Paris, London, or Berlin, or later in New York, art exhibitions were metropolitan phenomena. Capital cities in the geopolitically Western world, mind you, thus the art world was a geographically and culturally delimited region.

Art Critics as Judges

Governed by these three preconditions, during the nineteenth century the function of the critic evolved into that of a judge. One of the most prominent representatives of this genre was Charles Baudelaire (1821–1867). In his short essay "What Is the Good of Criticism?" of 1846, he wrote that criticism has to be "partial, passionate and political," that is, "written from one exclusive point of view."[7] This "exclusive point of view" should not be a formal aspect such as

6 **Press release for the Viennafair**, April 24, 2012.

7 **Charles Baudelaire**, *Art in Paris, 1845–1862: Salons and Other Exhibitions*, ed. and trans. by Jonathan Mayne, Carl Hanser, Munich, 1977, pp 44–45.

the line or color but rather assess the "temperament," as Baudelaire called it. In his view, art criticism must, on the one hand, review artistic innovation and imagination and, on the other hand, observe the emotions triggered in the observer. In the modern era, that meant above all not giving in to any aversion to changes in art but rather examining art in terms of its potential to innovate. For precisely what was not understood initially would later be classed as groundbreaking.

This kind of criticism required a thorough knowledge of art history, because art reacts to art, and through innovative forms, materials, and styles declares existing traditions outmoded. Radical innovations were rarely understood by a wider audience, for the "isms" that dramatized breaks with earlier styles and aesthetic parameters were too provocative; one only has to think of Cubism, Expressionism, or Dadaism.

In 1915 Albert Dresdner published *Die Entstehung der Kunstkritik im Zusammenhang der Geschichte des europäischen Kunstlebens* [The Emergence of Art Criticism in the Context of European Art History].[8] Dresdner argued that the art critic should take sides, for the few, against the many; should decisively codetermine the canons of all the arts that are important; and should be an opinion maker. Art criticism serves, as Dresdner put it, as a "Schaltstelle" [control center] and mediator between the work of art and the audience, between the avant-garde and the art market that follows it.

Art Criticism as Art Theory

This role as a control center expanded again in the middle of the twentieth century. In no small measure thanks to emigrants from Europe, New York became a new center for artistic innovation. Young art critics soon established themselves as something more than judges and mediators. Art critics became art theorists, filling the gap between retrospectively oriented art history and the contemporary art market. Their best-known representative was Clement Greenberg, who wrote his famous essay "Avant-garde and Kitsch" for the literary quarterly *The Partisan Review* in 1939. His texts on Abstract Expressionism, Jackson Pollock, and Barnett Newman contributed significantly to the success of those artists.

It was not coincidental that Greenberg published his essay in a journal. At the time there was no demand either in universities or on the book market for theoretical writings or catalogs on contemporary art. Retrospective works on Old Masters in art history were nearly all that was published. Catalogs in today's sense were not even common practice at the Venice Biennale. Even in the 1960s, the catalogs of the Bienal de São Paulo showed only the works exhibited without any explanatory texts. The most important media of art theory into the 1980s were therefore art journals: the journal *Artforum* was founded in the United States in 1962 and *Kunstforum* was founded in Germany in 1973. Nowhere else could one find such detailed information about current art. Nowhere else could one get informative analyses with information about the art historical background. Nowhere else was art criticism possible.

The functions of art criticism we have identified thus far were summed up by Stefan Lüddemann in 2003 in his dissertation *Kunstkritik als Kommunikation* [Art criticism as communication] with the catchy phrase "admission control." Because the gap between the avant-garde and the audience grew constantly in the modern era, art critics took on the role of unconditional supporters, of the "propaganda of the new."[9]

Globalized Art World

Do these attributes still apply today? Is art criticism still an "admission control" that decides everything? And deciding for what: for the market, for the art world? Art criticism, like art history, is a discipline of the geopolitical West. Let's recall briefly the market analysis cited above: the expansion of the art world and the new marketplaces suggest that there are no fixed borders today; hence, there can no longer be a universally valid order for admission, either. Where would it be stationed? The geopolitical West is no longer dominant and art journals have not retained their leading position as shapers of opinion. For issues of stylistic innovation and unfamiliar terrain can no longer - or could never be - answered identically all over the world.

Developments Today

Let's also recall briefly the three elements underlying the evolution of early art criticism: the emergence of a new bourgeoisie, a new infrastructure, and metropolises as centers of the production and consumption of art. What significance do these factors still have in the early twenty-first century? And how do they influence art criticism?

8 **Albert Dresdner** (1866–1934) was a German historian, art critic, and art historian, who wrote one of the first systematic presentations of the origins of art history: *Die Kunstkritik, ihre Geschichte und Theorie*, vol. 1, *Die Entstehung der Kunstkritik im Zusammenhang der Geschichte des europäischen Kunstlebens*, Bruckmann, Munich, 1915; reprinted in 1968 and 2001)

9 **Stefan Lüddemann**, *Kunstkritik als Kommunikation: Vom Richteramt zur Evaluatiuonsagentur*, PhD diss., FernUni Hagen, 2003, Deutscher Universitätsverlag, Wiesbaden, 2004, p. 35.

The Bourgeoisie

We can observe a worldwide expansion of the bourgeoisie in the sense of a wealthy and culturally interested middle class. As a consequence, there are more and more people interested in art or in buying art, not only in the United States and Europe but also in the Arab world and in the Middle East, North Africa, South Asia (MENASA), Southeast Asia, Russia, Latin America, and China. This new social stratum is not associated with art through family tradition but is increasingly interested in art as an investment. "Buying art is no longer elitist but mass consumption; no longer just for some fifty thousand buyers but probably for half a million of them," says the Russian art investment consultant Sergey Skaterschikov.[10]

Infrastructure

Whereas in the nineteenth century it was the salons that contributed to the expansion of the art world, today it is the auction houses, art fairs, and biennials. Whereas in those days it was journals that reflected growing interest, and since the end of the twentieth century the art catalog, today the Internet serves as the new medium for information.

The evolution of biennials reflects this change: until the 1950s, there were around five of these events that took place every other year and attracted wide attention because of their international orientation: the biennials of Venice, São Paulo, and Tokyo along with the Documenta and Sonsbeek. The Whitney Biennial is not included here because it is a national event. By the end of the 1980s, that number had grown to thirty, although of the more recent biennials only those of Sydney and Paris have become better known. As a result of newly founded biennials and the internationalization of existing ones they are now too numerous to follow. Every biennial creates new artists. The sheer number of artists represents an enormous challenge to art criticism as do their contexts. How can art critics live up to their universal claim to understanding and qualitative criteria if every new art scene brings with it new historical and intellectual referential networks? Who knows enough about the main philosophical and religious traditions, texts, and the iconography of China, India, and Latin America to judge the works at biennials intelligently?

It is not only the number of biennials but also the number of galleries that is constantly increasing; new centers for galleries are emerging as well, in Jeddah, Saudi Arabia, and Lahore, Pakistan; in Singapore; in Bangalore and in Mumbai, India, and in Berlin, Germany. New art fairs have successfully established themselves: Zona Maco, México Arte Contemporáneo (since 2004), Art Dubai in the Emirates (since 2006), sp-arte São Paulo in Brazil (since 2005), Art Hong Kong in China (since 2008), Art Stage in Singapore (since 2011). The number of visitors to fairs is increasing in parallel; none of these fairs is attended by fewer than twenty-five thousand interested visitors. The leader is Art Basel, which had 65,000 visitors in 2012. In contrast to Art Cologne, which had nearly 60,000 visitors, the audience at Art Basel consists almost exclusively of art buyers.

All this expansion creates need for information, which has led to conspicuous changes in the market for art journals. In addition to the classic journals like *Artforum*, *Art in America*, *Parkett*, and *Kunstforum*, which carry analyses of works and interviews, there are more and more "art newspapers" and "annual reports" from art investment companies. Every important art fair brings out a newspaper each day that summarizes the latest sales and background information in a reader-friendly way. And the goal of this new form of reporting on art is no longer to study, evaluate, and influence art; it is to study, evaluate, and influence the market for art. Most of these new formats are available on the Internet, which is accessible to all as a main source of information. Information about artists, the art market, and art history have long since ceased to be reserved for an academically educated elite.

Metropolises

This decentralization brought about by the Internet corresponds to the decentralization of the art world. Like the print media of elite specialists, the metropolises of the modern era have also expanded. Paris and New York have lost their positions as centers of artistic innovation. New hubs have emerged; for artists it is Berlin, while the art trade has followed the financial markets to Dubai, Hong Kong, and Singapore.

So what do the developments summed up by the three keywords bourgeoisie, infrastructure, and metropolises still mean for art criticism? Does the "partial, passionate and political" interest that Baudelaire called for still suffice to maintain relevance in this new art world? Do we critics still have the power to define quality? How much interest do the new participants from the art industry have in a theoretical, art historical approach to art, that is to say, to the classic task of art criticism? Who still buys and reads art journals that consist mainly of analyses of works?

10 **Interview with Sergey Skaterschikov** by Sabine B. Vogel, available online at www.artnet.de/magazine/interview-mit-viennafairinvestor-sergey-skaterschikov, accessed May 10, 2012.

Art Criticism Today

The influence of art criticism is indeed disappearing. That is evident from the decline in opportunities to publish. Especially in the new markets, artists deliver direct to auction houses; on the one hand, because often there is little or no local gallery scene and, on the other hand, because it is the shortest path to opening up new markets. Catalog texts and monographic essays in art journals are no longer necessary for market introductions and increasing prices. Basic information is read in the auction catalog or gathered on the Internet. Reporting on art is increasingly found in lifestyle magazines such as, most recently *Harper's Bazaar Art*, and is not critical but entertaining, for the art world is presented more and more as an event-driven world.

New Tasks

Nevertheless, art criticism still exists - and it has new functions. The most striking characteristic of art criticism today is that we write in intelligible language. For we are no longer addressing a small circle of the initiated but an ever larger, anonymous audience.

So what are our tasks? First and foremost, today we write critiques that are supported by knowledge but formulated in ways that can be widely understood. Daily newspapers are allotting ever more space for reporting on art. We do not want to leave that space to journalists. Talking about art means talking about society, about values, about connections, about the most recent and future developments. Art is neither an occasion for journalistic stories nor material for profitable business - both lead to trivializing it, to transforming it into an arbitrary event, an arbitrary commodity.

Art criticism today cannot establish new positions or trends in the art market - and neither can it prevent them, as the success of artists from the art industry such as Damien Hirst and Jeff Koons has shown. Nor can we change developments on the art market. However, we can analyze the situation and counter the move toward commodities and entertainment through critical examination of local exhibitions, through informative reports on global developments in art, and especially through an unbiased, open view.

From this derives our second task: analysis. Art criticism today does not so much analyze individual works as global developments. The key questions are: How does art relate to social processes? This concerns the Arab spring, liberalization in India and China, but also sustainability, understanding science, and commodification. What role does art play in these developments? Why, for example, are facts promoted in such a way that China is in the headlines as now the largest art market in the world? What is the significance of the new ranking, in which the United States and Europe have lost their top spots, even though the commodity being sold is still primarily Western, since hardly any Chinese artists make it into the lists of artworks over two million Euros? What economic and what political developments can be read from that?

Conversely, with regard to the art industry we must also ask what market developments mean for art: For example, can art withdraw from the market, for example, by means of the increasing number of documentary or docu-fictional works, or is noncompliance impossible? Are political and critical positions increasingly restricted to biennials, so that two parallel spheres, art and the art industry, are evolving?

At this point it becomes necessary to analyze and work on terminology: central tasks for art criticism today! Further, the enormous changes at museums and national galleries must be accompanied by art theory rather than art history: What does the increasing number of private collectors' museums signify for the idea of the museum?[11] Are we seeing a development comparable to the Renaissance, or is it not the case that the sheer numbers - the number of museums, the amount of art shown, the high prices of the works - make for striking differences? Unlike Western museums, today's private museums are not restricted to national art but are usually global in scope. Does that reflect a new understanding of the world?

Discussions about quality are also enormously relevant in this context, if collections are not to be undervalued as examples of diverse idiosyncrasies. What criteria can endure in a global perspective without overvaluing the highlights of a single culture? Discussions about substance are indicated here. "No-nonsense discussion" was the term one art investment consultant used for his profit-oriented arguments for the decision to buy art. Can the art industry really dispense with the "nonsense" discussions inherent in art?

Such questions are more important to art critics than monographic analyses, which we can leave to art historians. Art criticism seeks to determine the context of contemporary art. As art critics, we have the necessary knowledge to do that, for we look disinterestedly at an enormous quantity

11 **During Art Hongkong 2012** there was a forum for owners of private museums with forty participants, most of them from Asia, including Li Bing, owner of the Bejing He Jing Yuan Art Museum; Dr. Oei Hong Dijn, owner of the OHD Museum, Mangelang; Budi Tek, owner of the Yuz Museum in Jakarta; Wang Wie, owner of the Dragon Art Museum, Shanghai. There are also important new private museums in India (Kiran Nadar Museum of Art, New Delhi, 2009), the United Arab Emirates (Salsali Private Museum, Dubai, 2011), and Qatar (Mathaf, Doha, 2010).

of local and global works, and at exhibitions in highly diverse contexts.

The third task is to make people aware of connections. On all my journeys to international biennials and art fairs, time and again I am struck by how intensely artists work to establish connections. Unlike the modernist avant-gardes, they do not create a tabula rasa situation or orchestrate breaks with traditions. Instead, they build bridges between traditions, cultures, and historical eras. Artists create images that emphasize the contemporary relevance in the historical. This looking back is constructive in order to speak openly about the present and the future. Art is less and less elitist, and instead cobbles together patchwork-like connections - I regard communicating this fact as the most urgent task of art criticism today.

Conclusion

Art and the art market are inseparable. But the art market without any content or substance is also inconceivable. Reporting on records and statistics cannot replace analytical observations. We have to engage with these developments, think about the possible division into two parts, and follow the consequences attentively.

Art criticism is no longer "admission control," because the doors to the art world are always wide open. Our task is to contribute to building bridges. Today we no longer write for artists and connoisseurs, but for readers, for visitors, for students, and even for buyers. We do not focus on a specific work or œuvre but on connections. Art is no longer avant-garde; with its materials, themes, and media it has arrived in society. Art criticism reacts to this situation not by asking about style but about social relevance.

Art criticism today no longer explains innovations that establish a style but rather analyzes stereotypes and clichés in art, looking at art, and perceiving the world. We no longer concentrate on the art world but on the world in Kant's sense: as the embodiment of all phenomena, as the result of our ideas.

Art criticism today no longer takes place against a national horizon but rather against a transcultural one. The old world order of the West's hegemonic power, clear boundaries, and unambiguous classifications is over. Baudelaire's motto - "partial, passionate and political" - still applies, but in a new context: we have to work to integrate rather than demarcate; we have to build partial, passionate, and political bridges.

This text is a revised version of the original German text "Global Player: Wem gehört die Kunstwelt?" [Global players: To whom does the art world belong?], presented at the UBS Arts Forum, April 2012, Wolfsberg, Switzerland, available online at: http://www.wolfsberg.com/documents/Statement_Sabine_Vogel.pdf.

Translated from the German by Steven Lindberg.

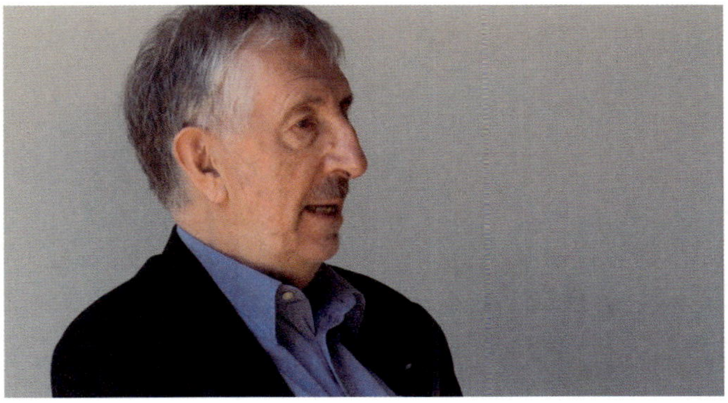

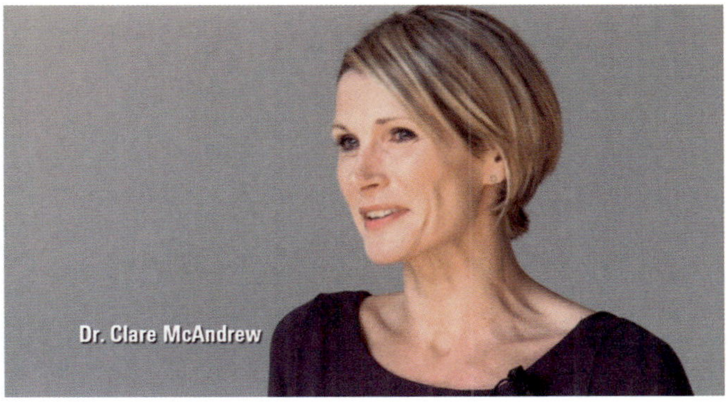

The Art Market

Hans Belting in Conversation with Clare McAndrew

(February 20, 2011)

Hans Belting
Clare, what was your original idea or motive when you started your project?

Clare McAndrew
It began with my interest in the art market. I started out as an academic economist, and I think a lot of the pioneering research in the financial studies of the art market had started in some form of academia. But I looked at how the international trade in art differs from the way other markets and other industries trade. And I started to look at the differences in how people buy and sell, and I found that the art market had a lot of unique features. So I began to look in a more academic perspective and then worked as an economist in the U.S. for a number of years for a small specialized firm that just worked in the art market, and came back to Europe in 2005 and started my own company, focussing on fine and decorative art research. So I've been looking at the market for about fifteen years, but always from the point of view of an economist looking in from the outside. It's always a kind of outsider's view, but a different perspective, maybe, than others.

Belting
You mentioned the unique features of the art market. What are those unique features?

McAndrew
One of the key things about art versus, for example, trade in commodities is that artworks are unique. Each work has no substitute. So even works by the same artist or a series of prints, they are not necessarily substitutable, so it's a very heterogenous market. And art trades on a very thin and illiquid market, thus the turnover in the art market is very slow compared to other markets. And these features make it more difficult for us financial people to apply very standard, black box quantitative models to it - they throw up a lot of difficulties in valuation. But we've come up with methods to get around that. So it's a different marketplace, but we're getting our arms around how it is valued and how it functions. But it does have these unique features, and they are based on the fact that each good that's thrown up on the market is quite unique. I did some research a few years ago, and it takes about thirty years on average for a piece of art to reappear on the art market after being sold. So, for example, if you sell a piece it probably won't resell for another thirty years. That was the average we've found, and in fact some pieces never resell. So it's a slow-moving, unique marketplace that makes it very different from other financial markets.

Belting
It is a recent phenomenon that a lot of economists have

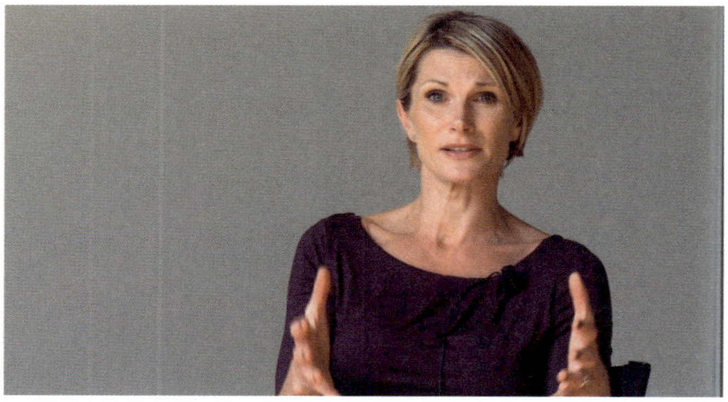

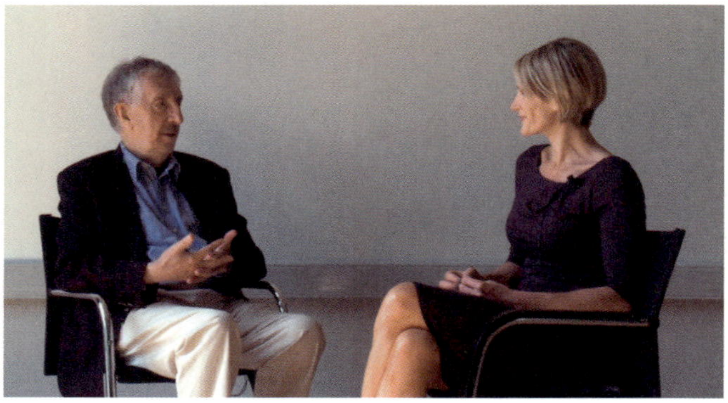

addressed the art market who in former years did not pay very much attention to it. Is there a special reason why there is this sudden new interest in the art market?

McAndrew
I think definitely there is; you just have to look at the numbers. Last year, in 2011, the art trade turned over 64 billion dollars in sales. So it's very easy to see why it has attracted the interest of the mainstream investment community: it's big business. And it's also a very global business. There are literally art sales happening all over the world. It's been very geographically dominated by New York and London until the last few years where it has become a lot more global and diversified marketplace. So it's a big global business, and this is why it really sparked the interest of economists like myself and the mainstream investment community.

Belting
You mentioned several times the difference between trade and sales. Could you perhaps explain this a little bit?

McAndrew
Sure. There are a lot of trading centers in the art market. It's made up of global hubs where much of the trade takes place, and then it's made up of a lot of domestic marketplaces. So when we talk about sales we talk about what's happening on the ground in a particular country or city, whereas trade is the flow in and out, the imports and exports of art. So these are two related but not identical events. Some markets might be what we call *entrepôt* markets where they have a lot of trade flows in and out, and buyers and sellers often come from a completely different place than the hosting city... So you have big global *entrepôts* and then you also have large domestic markets. And the biggest example of that in recent years is China, which is now the largest art market in the world. It came from virtually not being on the map at all ten years ago. If you look back to the end of Chairman Mao's reign in the late 1970s, it was actually illegal to own or inherit or trade a piece of art in China. So it was completely closed off against the rest of the world, and now it's the largest art market in the world with 30 percent of all sales. But that's a very good example of a very domestic marketplace. Mainland China doesn't trade a lot; it doesn't do a lot of importing and exporting with the rest of the world, but it has huge sales in cities such as Beijing and Shanghai. So that's a very good example of that concept. If you look at the more traditional, older markets of New York and London, they do both: they have a lot of sales and they trade a lot. Or a very interesting market may be Switzerland, which has a lot of imports and exports but not many sales on the ground. So that's another case in point. There's a difference between flows and actual sales on the ground.

Belting
You published recently the book *Globalisation and the Art Market*. Now for us this is a very clear example of how and in what sense to speak of the globalization of art, especially of contemporary art. So could we perhaps talk a little bit about the features which come from globalization and such features which single out contemporary art as a unit of its own?

McAndrew
I think when I was looking back at the first decade of this twenty-first century the key things that are really going to stand out about contemporary art are firstly, the huge increase in the size of the market. The market increased nearly tenfold from around 2002 to its peak in 2007/2008.

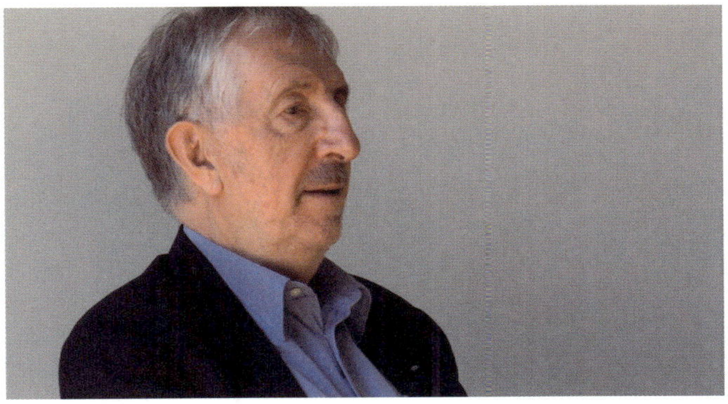

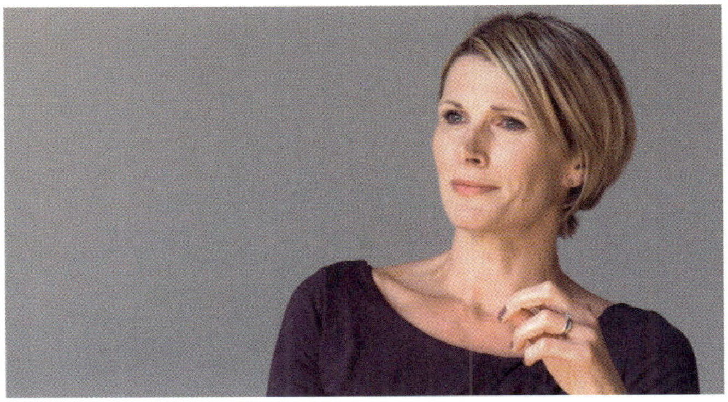

So it was a period of astonishing growth - the contemporary sector amplified what was going on in the market as a whole. Contemporary art was that much more volatile up and down. It went through a particularly rough patch in 2009, the market contracted by around 70 percent, but it has recovered very strongly again. So it's been an extremely volatile marketplace. It's seen some highs and lows, but over all it's been a period of growth relative to any other periods. And although 2009 saw probably the worst recession since the recession of the early 1990s, it's still at a much higher level than it's ever been, and in 2011, it surprised us once again and is at a higher level than the peak of 2007.

Besides that growth, I think one of the key features about the art market now is that it's a very global trading. And the most important markets for contemporary art are now definitely outside Europe. In 2010 the U.S. was still the largest contemporary market, but China overtook the U.K. to be the second largest. In 2011, China is by far the largest - based on auction sales it had a 45 percent share versus the U.S. at 25 percent. And China has come from virtually 1 percent or 2 percent in 2002. So it's been an astonishing rise, and it's these markets outside Europe that have really helped the art market as a whole and contemporary art especially to come out of the hole it was in 2009. The fact that the contemporary art is now much more globally diverse has helped protect it from the downside risk that it would have been subjected to had it only been reliant on buyers and sellers from the U.S. and Europe. So that has helped it to recover stronger and has protected its downside a lot more than would have been the case had it been that very New York-London-polar market that it once was.

Belting
Is this also maybe the reason for the quick recovery?

McAndrew
Yes, definitely. The recovery, especially in contemporary art, has been driven by the U.S. and China. So it's been a recovery in the U.S., but another year of continued boom in China. China has seen a massive increase in sales. The Chinese market as a whole is now generating sales of over 15 billion dollars with dealer and auction sales and all the different categories. While other markets have tried to recover from a couple of very poor years, it's just been another year of boom in China. While the U.S. and China had growth figures of over 100 percent in 2010, Europe was positive on the whole, but sluggish compared to the rest of the world. So the most important markets for contemporary art are now definitely firmly outside of Europe. But I think in the future what we'll see is that there'll be many centers all around the world; there won't be this idea of the art market as New York and London. There will be maybe six, seven or eight or more centers all over the world. Definitely a couple in Asia, something in Europe, something in the U.S., maybe something in the Middle East. It will be a more globally diversified picture in the future.

Belting
Is it also relevant for the type of clients who are acting in these newly developing centers?

McAndrew
Absolutely. Considering the Asian boom first, these trends are supply-driven to some extent especially in China, which has a great wealth of art to sell, but they are also very much demand-driven. The global shift in wealth is dominating what's happening in the art market, so the fact that China is now the fourth highest base for high-net-worth individuals has really driven sales there as well. But I think what's very interesting if you look at China, India, Brazil,

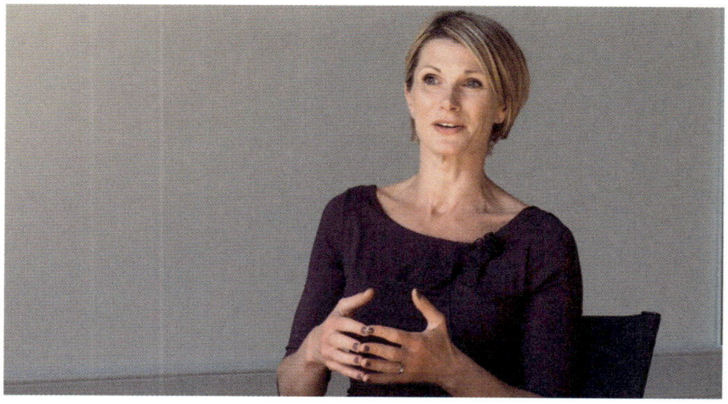

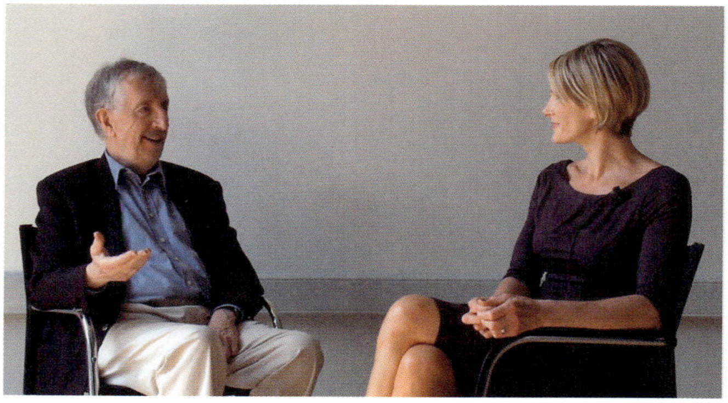

all these countries, their average incomes have increased by maybe 200 percent on average over the last ten years. So they've come from very poor average incomes, and in some cases they literally increased ten or more fold. But despite this, they're still much lower than incomes here in Europe or in the U.S. What's happening in all these countries still is that art is being bought by a very small handful of people, if you look at China, Brazil, India, or any of these new emerging markets. So it's a very strong indicator for the future, because average incomes are expected to keep on rising at a fairly rapid pace. In countries such as China and India, the middle class hasn't even come on stream yet. For example, in China the average income now is about 5,000 dollars a year, and they expect that by 2020 it'll reach about 10,000 dollars. And this is when they expect a middle class will have formed within China, and these people are not even buying art yet, so it's a very strong indicator for the potential future expansion of the market - the growth trajectory is very strong. It's interesting to think how it'll look in the future if these trends keep going. But it has been wealth-driven in many respects. Art does tend to follow where the money is to some extent.

Belting
Could you say a few words about the key role of big auction houses versus privateers?

McAndrew
Sure. I think probably from the 1980s auction houses have wrested quite a lot of power from dealers. I think a lot of dealers had a very strong position in the postwar period, but from about the 1980s onwards, auction houses began actively to take private clients from dealers. So the shift in the auction-dealer divide has moved a little bit further towards auction houses since the 1980s and 1990s when they began to look actively for retail clients whereas they used to be wholesalers in the market. But sales are still around 50:50 between them worldwide. In some new markets the auction sector tends to be the first that's more developed, for example, in the Emirates, which is one of the countries where dealer sales would only be 10 percent of the market. However, if you look at a very well-established market like France, for example, dealer sales are about 70 percent of the market. It's the same in China; the dealer infrastructure is not as developed, and only accounts for about 30 percent of sales. But I think what's happening more than anything is that the traditional divide between these two sectors of the market is becoming outdated to some extent. If you look at auction sales now, auction houses are doing a lot more private sales, and dealers are behaving a lot more like auction houses in their models. So the idea of being a collector-dealer is not one many dealers can afford any more. A lot of them are working more on commission as an agent. I think, although there's a lot of competition between them, the boundaries are blurring between these two sectors. That's something that's going to continue in the future; there will be a lot of different ways to buy art.

Belting
Is it also a different psychology for clients to go to an open auction instead of into a gallery?

McAndrew
Yes. I think a lot of the newer buyers from emerging markets are tending to buy from auction first, because it is the kind of concept that you don't need to know so much, whereas there's an impression (which is not necessarily correct) that you need to know a little bit more about art when you buy from a dealer. But I think it's a more obvious channel for buyers to use first. So novice buyers tend to buy

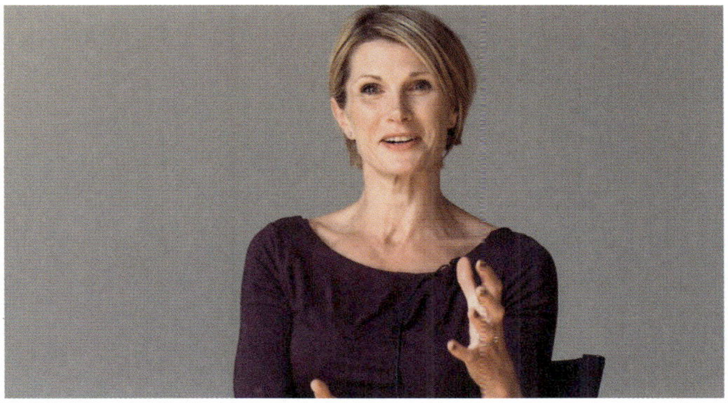

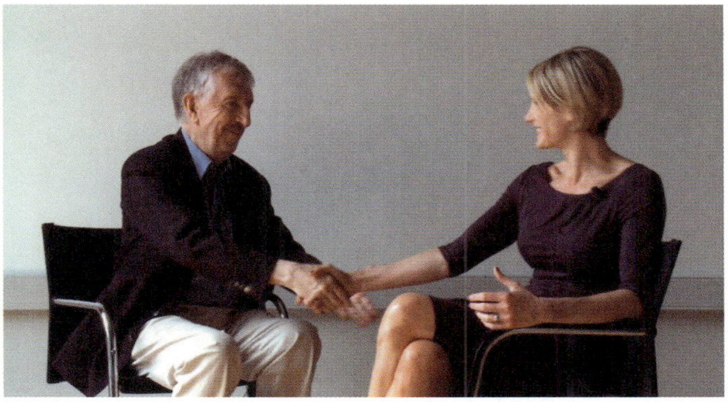

first at auctions, and when they become established collectors in particular sectors they'll hook on to dealers and use them more. That tends to be the path they take.

Belting

In art circles the subject of art speculation or speculation in investing in art is still a bit looked down upon. If you are consulting people to choose art, what are the advantages? I mean you are an economist, you are free from these prejudices which we have that it is just commerce and lacks the feeling for art. You look at it from another side.

McAndrew

Sure. But I think art is definitely accepted now as an asset class. And collectors that I speak to might even say they're not interested in this financial value, but I think there is probably a spectrum that exists between the icon of pure collectors and pure investors, and neither end of that spectrum is a very good position to be in. If you're a pure collector and you don't care about the value - you are in danger of ignoring a lot of responsibility that goes with owning art at a high level for the next generation and for art itself. And if you're a pure speculator - you're in the wrong market! I would not advise people to speculate in the art market at all. I think it is a long-term investment, and I think there's often an over-focus on how much the price is going to increase on returns in the art market. I think the most attractive investment perspective that art has is its risk properties, so the fact is that art often moves on a very different level than a lot of other financial and other asset indices. So it can be a very good tool for risk diversification in your total wealth portfolio. Adding art into a diversified portfolio, or the risk dimensions of art as an asset, are by far its most attractive feature. And there's obviously no such thing as the art market as a whole. There are hundreds of independently moving markets within the art market all operating at their own level and on their own different growth path. So you cannot only use art as a tool for risk diversification within a portfolio of wealth, but your art portfolio itself can also be held in such a way to reduce risk. You can hold art as a diversified collection if you can build a kind of an eclectic collection of art, which a lot of people are increasingly trying to do. You can actually be internally diversified within the art collection itself. So I would always advise not to over-focus on returns, I would advise not to speculate. But I think the risk dimension is one that is going to be the thing people focus on. People have got very badly burned in trying to speculate not just in art but in other sectors of the financial markets, and I think what they are looking for now is long-term secure assets with tangible value. And I think this is why art probably fared a lot better during the recession than a lot of other asset classes. It had that idea that it was a real, physical asset, it had enduring value and this value tended to increase over time. It's a buy-and-hold strategy for art investing, and also a very useful and often tax-efficient way to transfer wealth through generations.

Belting

We have learned a lot about globalization from these crystal-clear analyses of the art market. And there is very good reason for art experts to engage with the art market; certainly to a greater extent than has hitherto been the case. It is a new world that opens before us, and you have given us a very good introduction to the globalization of the art market. Thank you very much indeed, Clare.

McAndrew

Thank you.

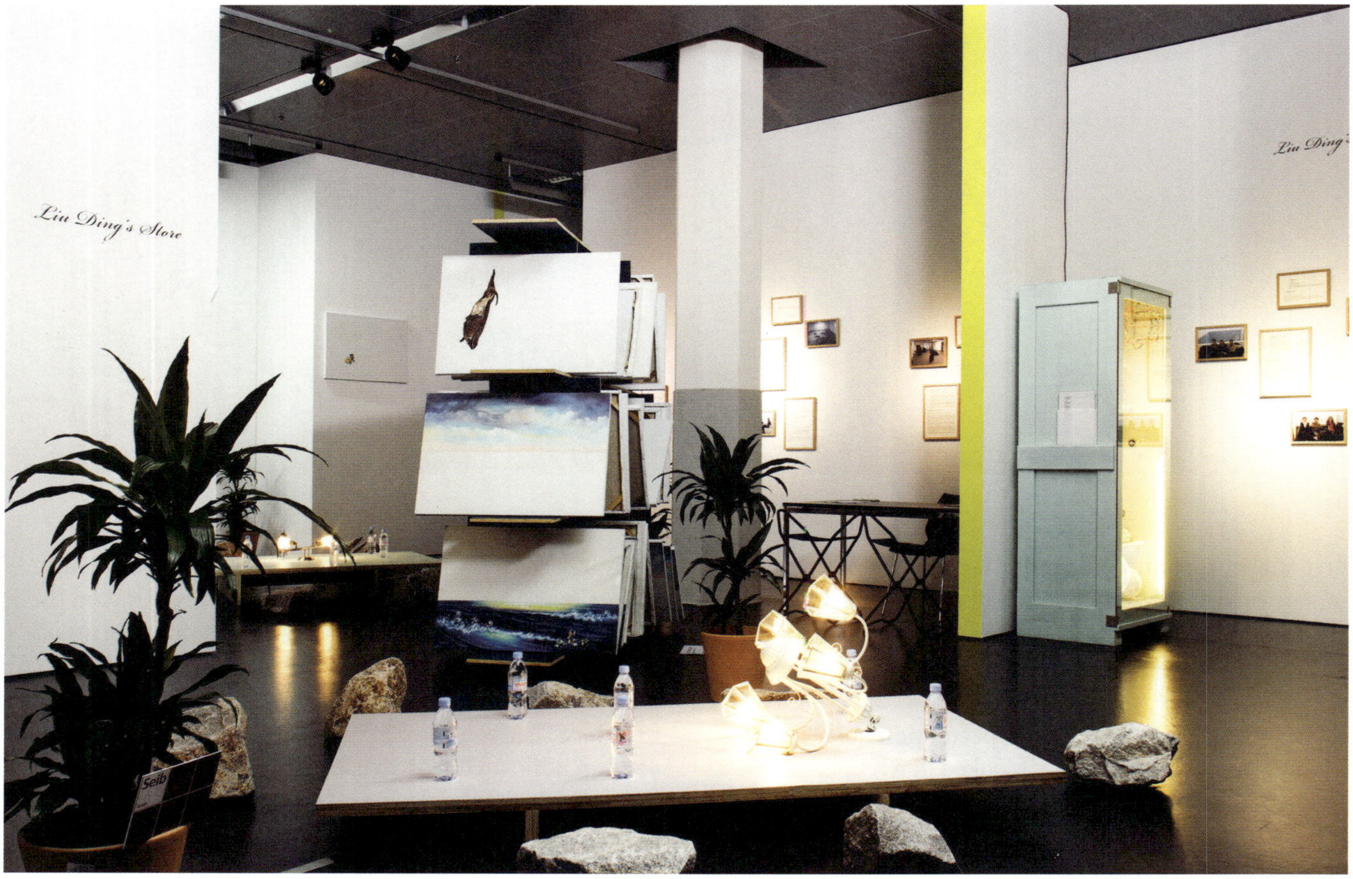

Liu Ding, *Liu Ding's Store*, installation view *The Global Contemporary. Art Worlds after 1989*, ZKM | Karlsruhe, 2011–2012

Priceless Images, Heartless Paintings: The Critical Complicity of Liu Ding

David Spalding

"If the soul of the commodity which Marx occasionally mentions in jest existed, it would be the most empathetic ever encountered in the realm of souls, for it would have to see in everyone the buyer in whose hand and house it wants to nestle [...] The commodity whispers to a poor wretch who passes a shop window containing beautiful and expensive things. These objects are not interested in this person; they do not empathize with him."

Walter Benjamin, *Charles Baudelaire: A Lyric Poet in the Era of High Capitalism*, 1938, p. 63.

"[...] a Manhattan collector who has been buying Chinese contemporary art since 1990 said that yesterday she watched her holdings appreciate by 10,000 percent. 'And it's just going to keep going,' she added."

Carol Vogel, "China: The New Contemporary-Art Frontier," in: *New York Times*, April 1, 2006.

Liu Ding is an archaeologist of the present. The artist excavates everyday objects, embellishing and arranging them in ways that amplify the cultural desires they embody and foster. Liu's interdisciplinary exploration began in 2005 with the multipart series *Samples from the Transition*, followed by the interactive installation *Take Home and Make Real the Priceless in Your Heart*[1] (2008); it continues today with newer iterations of *Liu Ding's Store*, including *The Utopian Future of Art, Our Reality* (2008-ongoing). Taken together, this cycle of related works offers a kaleidoscopic look at the blurred line between artwork and commodity. Through strategies that include appropriation, performance, and site-sensitivity, these projects question the various signs and structures that are used to confer value onto artworks. These include pricing schemes, the artist's signature, production methods and materials, notions of originality, and sites and modes of display.

The critique waged by Liu Ding's artwork can only be characterized as viral. By continually mutating, it endures in nearly any context, threatening to infect all it touches. In the process, it jeopardizes the fixed status of the artist, his artwork, the workers who fabricate it, the galleries and museums that show his work, the collectors who buy it, and the critics who privilege or deny certain meanings produced by the work. Throughout his practice, Liu demonstrates the ambivalent space that art occupies in discussions of our commodity culture, fashioning an endlessly twisting Möbius strip of critique and complicity that refuses easy resolution.

Samples from the Transition began by confronting viewers with artifacts that point to the absurd contradictions produced by China's booming capitalism. For his 2005 installment of the series, *Fantasies of Small Potatoes*, Liu used items associated with power - including a gun, a globe, a banknote, and a notebook computer - completely covering them with one of his then-signature materials: glittering, artificial gemstones. Displayed in spot-lit vitrines that evoke department store display cases, the tacky opulence of *Fantasies* is unnerving, precisely because it is so seductive. Ultimately, the installation yields narratives of violence, greed, and domination, but the sparkling jewels assure that these visions are rendered with the amorality of a child's cartoon. As if, under the spell of these things - and the agency they promise - the pain of others would seem inconsequential. One only has to pick up a newspaper to see such scenarios realized outside the gallery's walls. If, as Liu's projects suggest, the Chinese economy is characterized by a Vesuvian explosion, it has buried its residents in

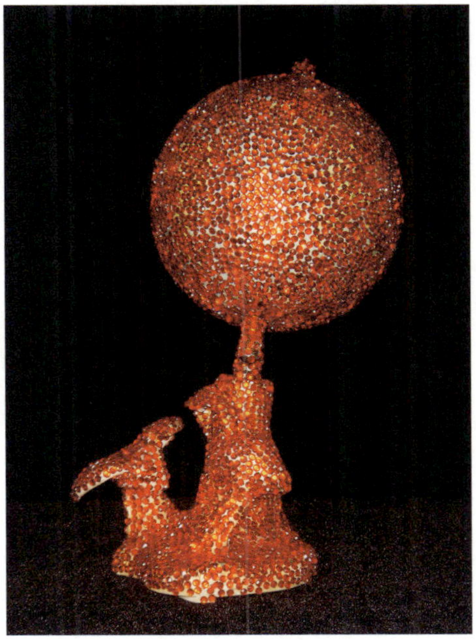

Liu Ding, *Samples from the Transition: Fantasies of Small Potatoes* (detail), "Globe," 2005, mixed-media installation, found objects, artificial gemstones, display case, Second Guangzhou Triennial, Guangdong Museum of Art, Guangzhou

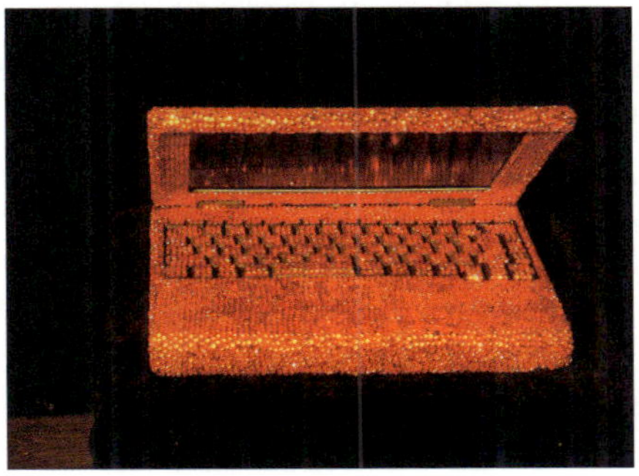

Liu Ding, *Samples from the Transition: Fantasies of Small Potatoes* (detail), "Notebook," 2005, mixed-media installation, found objects, artificial gemstones, display case, Second Guangzhou Triennial, Guangdong Museum of Art, Guangzhou

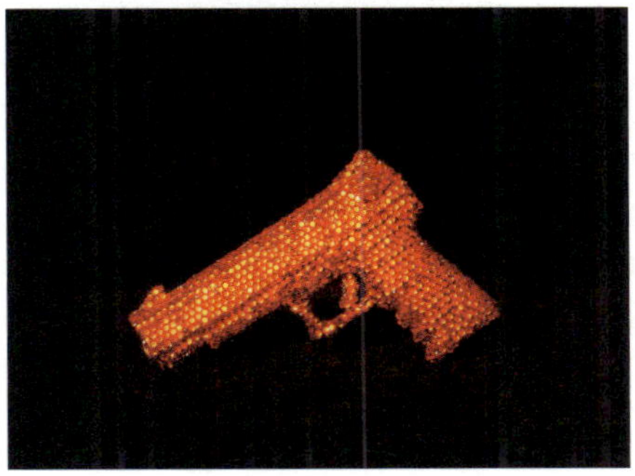

Liu Ding, *Samples from the Transition: Fantasies of Small Potatoes* (detail), "Gun," 2005, mixed-media installation, found objects, artificial gemstones, display case, Second Guangzhou Triennial, Guangdong Museum of Art, Guangzhou

1 **First presented** in the exhibition *Far West* on view at Arnolfini, Bristol (UK) from June 28 - August 31, 2008.

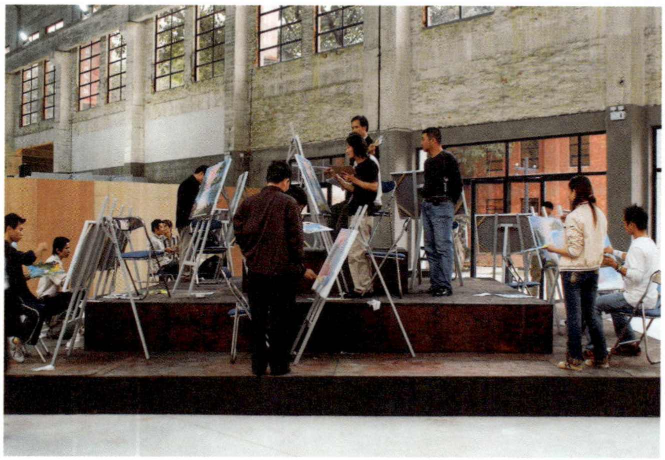

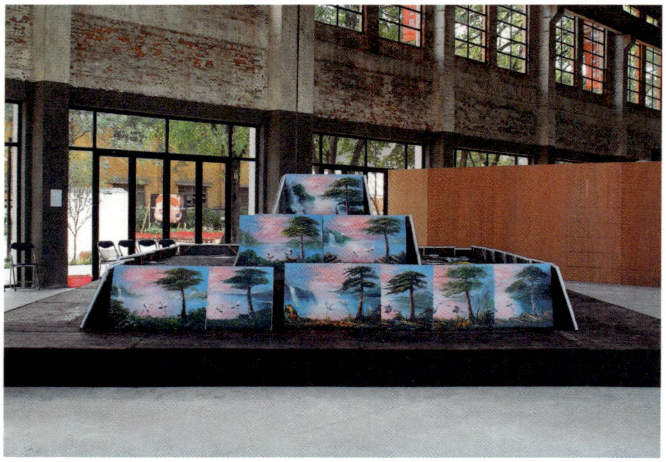

Liu Ding, *Samples from the Transition: Products*, 2005, performance and installation, Second Guangzhou Triennial, Guangdong Museum of Art, Guangzhou

the ashen spectacle of consumer culture. Through his artworks, Liu Ding is not just offering evidence of this "transition." He is trying to dig us out.

For *Products* (commissioned for the Second Guangzhou Triennial in 2005), another iteration of the *Samples* series, Liu enlisted the participation of thirteen professional artists from the southern city of Dafen, China's "painting factory" village, where workers produce thousands of paintings daily to fuel a giant export business. Under Liu's direction, the artists performed their assembly-line painting process during the opening of what was then China's most important international art exhibition. Working in an ancillary site temporarily annexed by the Guangdong Museum of Art, the painters were positioned on a pyramid of platforms, where they moved from canvas to canvas as they added their contributions (one artists paints only a tree, another a stork, and so on) to forty nearly identical landscape paintings. The artists were paid their standard factory wage for their four hours of work. The resulting paintings remained on view for the duration of the exhibition - not hung, but poised on easels in their original configuration.

Site is central to *Products'* various entanglements. Integral to the work's staging in Guangzhou is the Guangdong Museum of Art's location in the Pearl River Delta, or PRD: a cluster of southern Chinese cities, including Shenzhen and Guangzhou, that has experienced a surreal growth spurt since the 1970s, when the area began to mushroom into a network of urban sprawl and factory zones that beckons with opportunity and repulses with an underbelly of decadence. As such, Guangzhou is a nadir (or zenith) of advanced capitalism, a perfect site for Liu's ongoing explorations.

Regardless of curatorial attempts to create a platform for ongoing exchange, the Second Guangzhou Triennial, like many of the triennials and biennials that continuously operate worldwide, is also another node in the art market, a temporary site where the status and value of artworks is affirmed and heightened through their selection (presumably by a team of well-known experts) and presentation within the exhibition. In addition, the catalog and related press coverage are just two of many related affirmations that can elevate the careers of participating artists. Through his staging of *Products,* Liu called into question the authority of the Triennial to confer merit upon artists, and the ability of the art market to bestow value on works of art. After all, the quality and value of the artworks made in Dafen is anything but arbitrary: quality control agents approve paintings that accurately resemble their models; those that do not are revised or destroyed. The value of the works is equally clear-cut, as one company, called Eager Art, explains to potential customers on their website: "The price of paintings is decided [by] whether they are easy or hard to paint."[2] Visitors were left to consider how the paintings made in the Dafen factories differ from the other works on view in the Triennial, and why.

> "Everything has value only in so far as it can be exchanged, not in so far as it is something in itself. For consumers, the use value of art, its essence, is a fetish, and the fetish - the social valuation which they mistake for the merit of works of art - becomes its only use value, the only quality they enjoy."
>
> Theodor W. Adorno and Max Horkheimer, *Dialectic of Enlightenment*, [1947], 2002, p. 128.

Continuing his exploration of how context can shift our perception of art and its value, the following year at Frank-

2 http://www.eager-art.com, accessed 03/06/09.

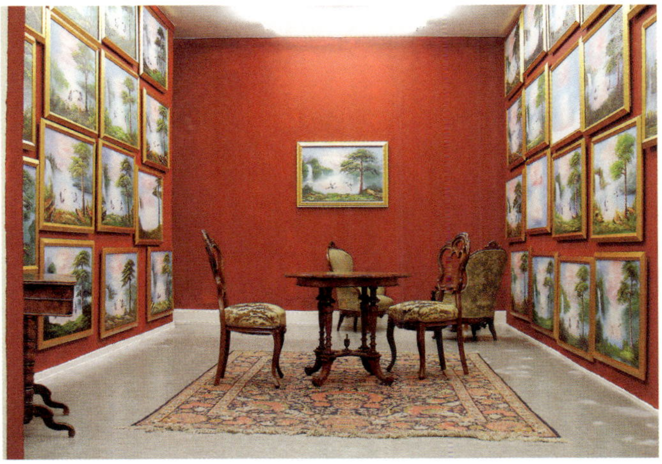

Liu Ding, *Samples from the Transition: Products*, 2006, mixed-media installation, 40 paintings in gold frames, home furnishings, L. A. Galerie, Frankfurt am Main

furt's L.A. Galerie, Liu Ding presented the Dafen paintings in gold frames, hung salon-style in a staged sitting room, complete with red damask wallpaper and a suite of Chippendale chairs and carved wooden tables.[3] In their gilded frames, surrounded by symbols of "European" luxury, the paintings were clearly adept at social climbing, given their humble origins. Even though many were in a state of partial completion, these *Products* were both comical yet plausible markers of wealth and taste.

Just as Guangzhou and the surrounding Pearl River Delta has spawned one of today's most extreme forms of capitalism - and its Triennial has served as a locus for the christening of artworks with a stamp of art world currency - *Products'* second incarnation in Frankfurt proved an ideal place to activate another aspect of the installation's reflexive criticality. It was first at Frankfurt's Institut für Sozialforschung during the late 1920s and early 1930s that theorists such as Max Horkheimer, Theodor W. Adorno, Herbert Marcuse, Leo Löwenthal, and Erich Fromm - in dialog with Walter Benjamin - formulated a sophisticated, interdisciplinary set of tools for the analysis of what they dubbed "the cultural industry." The neo-Marxist approach of the Frankfurt School of critical theory saw capitalist ideology as the generator behind mass-mediated cultural forms (from soap operas and radio broadcasts to popular art and visual culture). They attempted to awaken readers and alter their paths toward the consumption of these poisoned pleasures. As Douglas Kellner has pointed out, "[m]ass culture for the Frankfurt School produced desires, dreams, hopes, fears, and longings, as well as unending desire for consumer products."[4]

If Liu Ding has taken "samples" of material culture and used them to diagnose the bizarre contradictions and collective fantasies arising from China's warp-speed economic growth, it was the Frankfurt School that first developed a methodology that Liu's projects draw from. To realize *Take Home and Make Real the Priceless in Your Heart*, which extends ideas raised by the *Samples* series and serves as a bridge to *Liu Ding's Store*, the artist designed ten banal paintings of the type one encounters in hotel rooms - those anonymous creations that promise to soothe viewers into pharmaceutical sleep but with a few important differences. Again, Liu returned to Dafen to have the works produced, but rather than having a team of artists collaborate on a single painting in the usual fashion, these new works were deemed complete after each artist painted his singular element on an otherwise empty canvas. Thus, the paintings appear to be unfinished, each offering up only an iconic, isolated image floating in a field of white. Everything else looks as if it has been erased, so that in one work, a gilded sunset hovers over emptiness, while in another, a saccharine waterfall seems to float in space as it curls around invisible rocks. Thus the fantasy of the perfect landscape is denaturalized and estranged, and with it, our desire for pacifying clichés of nature (the exception, an image of a manor in the American colonial style, is an equally empty gesture). Of course, according to the logic of Dafencun, the paintings produced there do not reflect the contents of their makers' hearts. Quite the opposite: they are only understood as commodities, to be produced as quickly and exactingly as possible, assembly-line style, according to templates.

The paintings that comprise *Take Home* have been signed by Liu Ding, and are available (in editions of ten) to purchase for a mere 100 pounds each. Thus, the project's title can be read as both a command and an invitation, extended to audiences who are asked to weigh their desires against one another. Thus buyers are presented with a choice: to either take home the paintings and complete them (looking to those "priceless images" in their hearts for inspiration) or to hang onto the work in hopes that Liu's signature and growing reputation will ensure that their value will steadily increase. The speculative art market has never been hotter, as more and more buyers see art as an investment with the potential for tremendous returns. And Liu's works are certainly tempting. After all, given the current skyrocketing auction results, which contemporary Chinese artist's work can you presently collect for less than the cost of good meal? One can either add to the canvas, eroding its value and undermining is authorship, or one can recognize the purchase as an investment and leave it unaltered. Whether or not the possibility of profit surpasses the desire for personal expression, the buyer is implicated either way.

3 **Liu Ding's exhibition** *Samples of the Transition* was on view at the L.A. Galerie, Frankfurt (DE) from June 29 - July 22, 2006.

4 **Douglas Kellner**, "The Frankfurt School," available on ine at: http://pages.gseis.ucla.edu/faculty/kellner/papers/fs.htm, accessed 04/19/2012.

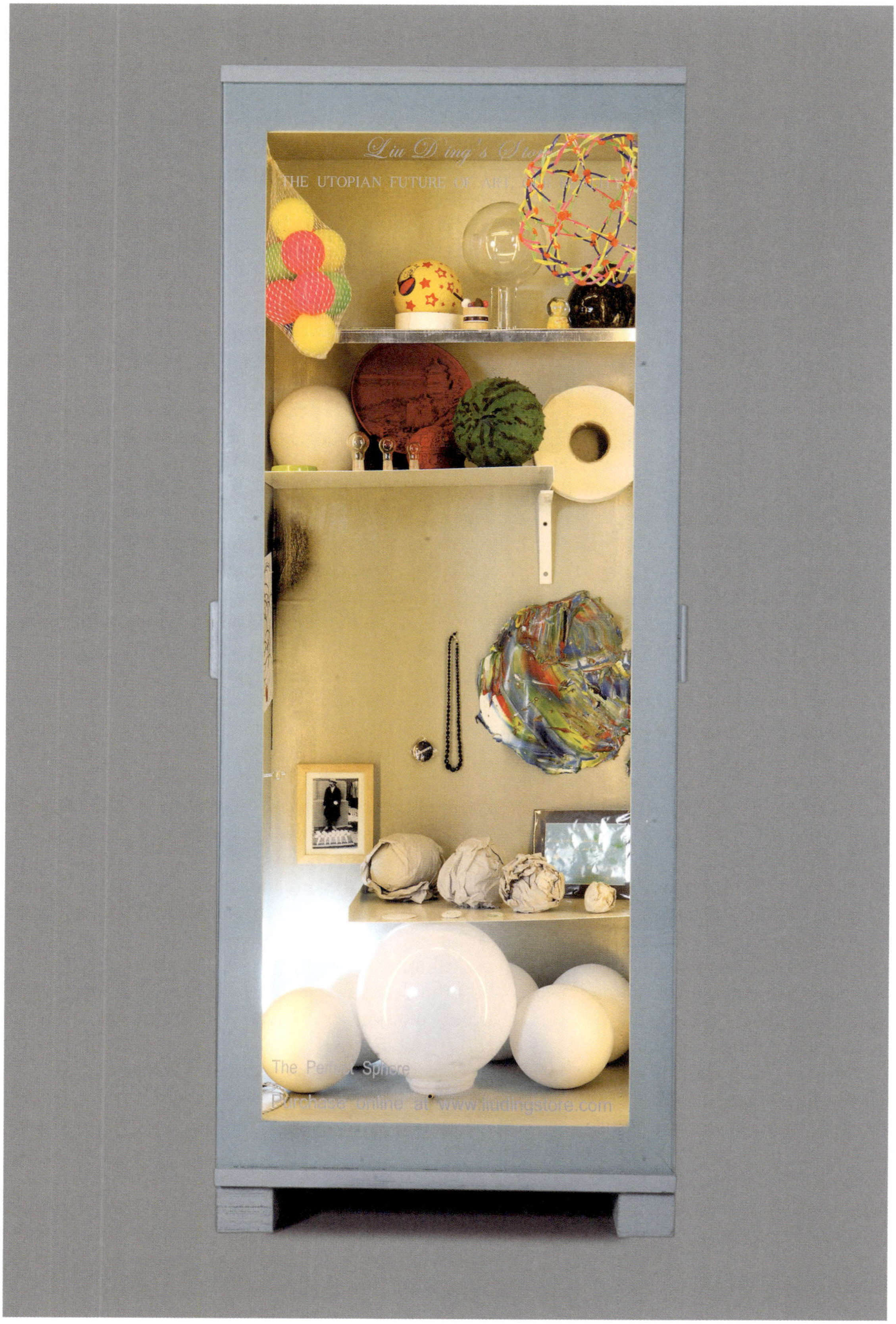

Liu Ding, *Liu Ding's Store*, detail

Liu's *Take Home* and the related works in the *Sample* series are linked to a number of important art historical precedents. During the 1980s, American artists working on both coasts drew from the Frankfurt School to produce art that worked both against and within an increasingly hyperbolic art market, making their efficacy difficult to gauge.[5] In a strange series of dialogical turns, artworks produced with an air of self-criticality were often subsumed back into the very market they attempted to censure. Some of these works, such as the early sculptures of Jeff Koons (*Wet/Dry Double Decker,* from 1981, remains emblematic), substituted commodities - in this case, vacuum cleaners - for art objects, suggesting an interchangeability between the two. This may seem to parallel Liu's presentation of *Products* in a Triennial setting - a gesture that immediately calls into question the status of all of the works in the show. Yet in the gallery, encased in custom Plexiglas vitrines and ensconced in a nimbus of Flavinesque fluorescence, Koons' vacuums assumed the aura of an art object - its critical stance reduced to a knowing smirk. Others' works, like Allan McCollum's *Surrogates* (1982) and *Perfect Vehicles* (1986), deployed the forms of paintings and sculpture (respectively) to create forms that were only signs for artworks, pure commodities deliberately void of any "content" or meaning. Chosen by Liu for their banality, the images in the partially painted canvases of *Take Home,* as well as the paintings reproduced in Guangzhou and presented again in Frankfurt and elsewhere are also ciphers. In Liu's installations, the paintings are transformed into a series of ready-mades, and while the artist is indebted to these earlier practices of commodity critique, he takes things further.

In *Products,* the paintings' status as a commodity is both laid bare and undone by Liu's insistence that the labor (indeed, the laborers) required for their production are visible. Further, his sensitivity to site ensures that even while the paintings are empty referents, they illuminate cultural and historical conditions in the locations where they are created and displayed. With *Take Home,* the cycle of exhibitions reached its natural conclusion by asking the viewers to choose sides in the impossible battle between art and commerce.

Liu Ding's Store: The Utopian Future of Art, Our Reality, which debuted in the Chinese Pavilion at the 53. Biennale di Venezia and is still evolving, continues the artist's ongoing challenge to our received notions of value. Returning to the language of retail display (large, rectangular glass-fronted cases lit from within), Liu carefully curates a surprising assortments of items - from cheap household goods to signed works of art - setting up interrelationships between them that deliberately suspend hierarchy in favor of visual pleasure. The catch is that everything in these commercial *Wunderkammers* is for sale for the exact same price - an average cost calculated using the total value of all the objects in each case. In *The Perfect Sphere,* for example, the price of child's rubber ball emblazoned with a cartoon cat (7,026.8 Yuan or 881.11 Euro) is the same as a brightly colored sculptural work by artist Lu Zhengyuan. Creating a suspended state of equality, Liu's cases also invite us to linger over objects we might otherwise overlook; a white, spherical light bulb cover made of plastic takes on an alluring, even Platonic dimension, rhyming nicely with the snowballs seen in the framed photograph of David Hammond's topical 1983 performance *Blizzard Ball Sale.* Smashing again at the conventions of assigned worth, these more recent projects invite us to reconsider how we monetize and privilege some objects over others for reasons that appear contextual and arbitrary within the framework established by Liu's *Store.*

Taken together, Liu Ding's works are reminiscent of the artificial gemstones he sometimes uses: magnetic and multifaceted, they reflect and critique the status of the art object from a dizzying array of angles. From the *Samples of the Transition* series (including *Fantasies of Small Potatoes* and *Products*) to *Take Home* and other works that comprise the more recent *Liu Ding's Store* series, the artist's projects are much more than material evidence of a culture in flux. As they begin to coalesce, these artworks promise to compromise the very foundations that form the basis for their own display, circulation, and value. In doing so, Liu Ding's works are suggesting new possibilities for artists to simultaneously resist and participate in the culture they are helping to create.

Revised and expanded version of David Spalding's essay, "Priceless Images, Heartless Paintings: The Critical Complicity of Liu Ding," in: Nav Haq and Liu Ding (eds.), *Liu Ding PRODUCTS,* exhib. cat., Arnolfini, Bristol, 2008, pp. 31-37.

5 **For more information**, see Hal Foster's excellent essay "The Art of Cynical Reason" in: ibid., *The Return of the Real: The Avant-garde at the End of the Century,* The MIT Press, Cambridge (MA), 1996.

Actually Existing: Aesthetic Effect and Effective Relations in Southeast Asia

Patrick D. Flores

In the late 1960s and early 1970s, David Medalla, a Philippine artist who emigrated to Europe, began a series of what he called "participation-production-propulsion." One of these forays asked members of the public to sew all sorts of things onto a cloth in what would be known as *Stitch in Time*. According to Medalla, who later gained prominence in the West for his pioneering kinetic sculpture, the gesture was about creating a physical and psychological space as well as sharing it with others.[1] For his part, in 1985 the Indonesian artist Moelyono presented his thesis for a degree in fine arts at the Fine Arts Academy of Indonesia in Yogyakarta titled *KUD* or *Kesenian Unit Desa* [Art in the Village Units] in reference to the government's Kooperasi Unit Desa [Village Unit Cooperatives]. Laid out on a badminton court that likewise served as parking area and public road were 22 woven mats of around 2×1 m. On each mat was a traditional banana-leaf plate containing a handful of soil with seeds of cassava, corn, and water spinach. This work resulted from his experience of living in the small village of Waung in East Java, and was inspired by what he thought was expected of him as a student who had wanted to concretize his responsibility in the form of "instruction, research, and the socialization of knowledge."[2] The thesis was not accepted; the school officials deemed it not art, at least not sculpture or painting.

These cases demonstrate a response to a need for space and reciprocity in the context of what Medalla called "nerve-wracking fragmentation" under an authoritarian government. What Medalla and Moelyono might represent in Southeast Asian practice in the long term is the coming together of the potentialities of avant-garde and activism. These tendencies transcend the pressure for art to profess to an "autonomy," and finally make it accept its "precarity." In a postcolonial setting in Southeast Asia, the telos of autonomy is always precarious because it came by way of conquest, wrought by the conversion of the "great traditions" through a wide range of techniques, from Indianization to Westernization, Islamization to Hispanization, all of which index the imperiousness of China, India, Europe, and America. To insist on the autonomy of art is to deny this history and this pedagogical moment of lasting consequences. On the other hand, to reduce this kind of art to mere diffusion from the center is to negate its force as a condition of possibility and the production of distinctive form. The contexts of the avant-garde and of activism, therefore, overcome the impasse that confounds Western modernity because the relationality inherent in them recognizes the materiality of the condition of transfer, or the fact that the condition is material in the act of transfer, that it is vital and that it is sensibly distributed.[3] It is difficult to grasp this experience in the tenor of normative art history, but the words of the philosopher of the Baroque José Lezama Lima come close: "errant in form but firmly rooted in its essences."[4] Errant in

1 **Guy Brett**, *Exploding Galaxies: The Art of David Medalla*, Kala Press, London, 1995.

2 **Sumartono**, "The Role of Power in Contemporary Yogyakartan Art," in: *Outlet: Yogyakarta within the Contemporary Indonesian Art Scene*, Cemeti Art Foundation, Yogyakarta, 2001, p. 29.

3 **I am indebted to John Clark** for his concept of "transfer". John Clark, "The Transfer," in: Clark, *Modern Asian Art*, Craftsman House, Sydney, 1998.

4 **José Lezama Lima**, "Baroque Curiosity," in: Lois Parkinson Zamora and Monika Kaup (eds.), *Baroque New Worlds: Representation, Transculturation, Counterconquest*, Duke University Press, Durham (NC), 2010, p. 213.

the sense that it is contingent, inclined against norms; and essential because it is necessary, elemental, and worldly.

Medalla's and Moelyono's avant-garde and activism, terms used with circumspection and ultimately under erasure, are strongly placed as aesthetic and ethical propositions. After all, Moelyono's disruption of the expectations of the academy and its roots in the colonial transmission of knowledge of art through the art school, and Medalla's provocative sorties via impromptu performances (from rice fields to the opening of Imelda Marcos's Cultural Center of the Philippines in 1969) and the convening of people in organizations like Signals London, Exploding Galaxy, and Artists for Democracy, converse with the aspirations drawn to the avant-garde and activism. This said, the antinomy governing activism may have to be rethought altogether under the broader rubric of relationality.

Such convergence had been heralded by the seminal modernists of their respective art histories who reflected deeply on the question of "reality" in the early part of the twentieth century. The Indonesian Sudjojono thought about reality and how art must realize it as truth: "If an artist creates a work of art, then in actuality the piece is no other than the artist's visible soul."[5] This philosophical reflection led him to a concept of realism: "Draw a spoon as a spoon, a bamboo bench as a bamboo bench."[6] Sudjojono's peer in the Philippines, Victorio Edades, shared this sentiment and remarked that art "should be an intrinsic element of our buildings, homes, streets, roads, parks, and ports; in our household furniture - chairs, tables, utensils; in our manners and in all that we touch, see, and hear in our everyday life."[7] Both artists were responding to the untruth of the idealization of reality via the picturesque, as mediated by the idiom of the exotic and the academic, and sought the potency of the immediate and the intimate, which constitute Medalla's and Moelyono's avant-garde and activism.

Pertinent here is how the nation-state had fragmented social life, giving rise to the lost object of relationality. It foisted a mythology of national identity on its citizens, and thus repressed their various subjectivities as well as differences, alienated people from each other so that the impression or artifice of commonality under the New Society of Ferdinand Marcos and the New Order of Suharto could be conjured and prosper as spectacle and fetish.[8] That Moelyono would refer to the program of the government, which is similar to Marcos's own, takes us to how the state had tried to address the dire needs of its citizens through development programs, to infringe and co-opt their interior, with the village supposedly being the cell of social life. This idea of development is intricately related to art and culture. In fact, an articulation of experimental art in Manila in the same period was called "developmental art," which argued for an art that was innovative, quick, fast-tracked, and accelerated. Such a notion of the "developmental" had an internationalist dimension, not unrelated to the overall designs of modernization and industrialization in the particular context of a "developing" country and under a government which wanted to get things done with alacrity, like the building of roads and the dissemination of information on population control. Such a coordination of state-led "cultural development" was in tune with the inculcation of a "Filipino identity" as well. The artist-curator Raymundo Albano says that the gesture was aimed at "stimulating public minds and at the same time allowing the artists to question and investigate with their work [...] It made one relatively aware of an environment suddenly turning visible."[9] Finally, a very important point is that both Moelyono and Medalla manifested in their work the desire to go inward into the village as well as outward into exile. This sense of locality and migrancy is salient in mapping out relationality because it configures a wide, maybe transnational, community of sensing within which their practices found their audience and public.

It is in such a context that this essay endeavors to sketch out certain modes of relationality in Southeast Asia that may prove useful in understanding notions such as community, collaboration, dialog, participation, and so on. We can propose, therefore, that the history of art and the discipline of art history from a global purview be informed and animated by a history of relationality and not of the excessive aspirations to autonomy.

First is the workshop or the cohort of likeminded peers who worked together and were engaged in various struggles within the social world of art. This formation was exemplified by the sanggar in Indonesia, the nucleus of art making that became the site of peer-to-peer interaction, apprenticeship and mentorship, and ideological discussion. The sanggar system is linked up with the role of collectives in the early years of Southeast Asian modernism like the Persagi (Union of Painters) in Indonesia (1938) and the Thirteen Moderns (c. 1941) and Neorealists (c. 1949) in the Philippines from the late 1930s to the late 1940s.

Second is the manifesto that was drafted and circulated by artists in the 1970s as declarations of their belief in what

5 **Amir Sidharta**, "S. Sudjojono: The Artist, *Realiteit,* and Truth," in: *Strategies Towards the Real: S. Sudjojono and Contemporary Indonesian Art*, National University of Singapore Press, Singapore, 2008, p. 43.

6 **Ibid.**

7 **Victorio Edades**, unpublished manuscript.

8 **For fuller theoretical elaboration** of this process, see: Achille Mbembe, *On the Postcolony*, University of California Press, Berkeley (CA), 2001.

9 **Raymundo Albano**, "Developmental Art of the Philippines," in: *Philippine Art Supplement* 2, no. 4, 1981, p. 15.

art could effect in society. The most influential of these were the manifestos by the Indonesian New Art Movement in 1974, 1979, and 1987; the Malaysian artists Redza Piyadasa and Sulaiman Esa by way of the catalog-manifesto *Towards a Mystical Reality* in 1974; the Artists' Front of Thailand in 1975; and the Kaisahan (Solidarity) in the Philippines in 1976.[10] These texts are texts of alterity: they move beyond the self and relate to others in a collective deed and address an encompassing community. This mode of relationality could be framed ideologically within, for instance, socialism and could be spiritually within, let us say, Buddhism. The Thai artists, to cite an instance, were keen on both Mao Zedong's lectures at Yenan Forum and traditional Thai values, which are informed by Buddhist thought. Thus, in their formulation of "art for life," "life" pertains to these sources of transformation: the inclusive being and the extensive self.

Third is the space, which like the sanggar, is initiated, organized, and sustained by the artists themselves, a channel transgressing the traditional circuits of validation like the museum, the market, academe, and the established curatorium and at times cooperating with them at varying levels of stamina.[11] The Ruangrupa artists' initiative, established in Jakarta in 2000, may well be emblematic in the way that it has flourished all this time through initiating activities with diverse local and global communities in which the artist becomes a "collaborator" or "mediator." What might be a constructive reference to the Ruangrupa platform or model is its relationship with RAIN, which is a network of (visual) artists' initiatives from countries in Africa, Asia, and Latin America, set up by artists who are former participants of the Rijksakademie van beeldende kunsten in Amsterdam, the Netherlands. Its aim is to activate "pluriform internationalization" and explore emergent, transpositional socialities within and across levels of totalities from the national to the global. The interdisciplinary space Reyum Institute of Art and Culture in Phnom Penh, for its part, integrates art with heritage, a discourse usually instrumentalized by the state for its national imaginary, but which might actually be a conjuncture in which art comes to belong to a wider sphere of culture and the history of that culture or the formation of the cultural.

In Thailand, Rirkrit Tiravanija's and Kamin Lertchaiprasert's *The Land* is worth noting as an instance in which artists carved out a piece of land away from the city to propose an alternative locality. Rirkrit, clearly, is well-known in circles conversant with "relational aesthetics." Claire Bishop, who considers Thailand as the spiritual home of Relational art and one of the most oft-cited examples of a socially engaged "Relational project" by curators like Hans Ulrich Obrist and Daniel Birnbaum, has written about its quaint failure:

> "Tobias Rehberger's pavilion was made with Swedish wood for a show at the Moderna Museet, and is now rotting in the tropical climate. Philippe Parreno's *Battery House*, which is supposed to generate its own electricity through an 'elephant plug,' has never worked. The building was supposed to fulfill Kamin's request for a meditation hall, but the concrete floor is curved, and punctuated by many struts, and cannot be used for this purpose. The ratio of water to land on the farm is organized according to the principles of a Buddhist agriculturalist, Chaloui Kaewkong, but this too isn't really working: the water is stagnant rather than flowing. Ironically, all these 'failures' really endeared the project to me."[12]

After her visit, she felt that the project was falling into a state of entropy, which she curiously found endearing. A similar sentiment of wonder verging on the exotic came from Charles Esche, who after going around the villages north of Jogjakarta in 2004, was moved to speak of a terrain "largely unconceptualized by Western contemporary art," and in his estimation the workshop *Fixing the Bridge* which he attended may have created the "germ of a rural proposition."[13] The scholar Janet Kraynak, however, links up this problematic of the "rural land" with the sensitivity to sustainability. It is this trope of the "sustainable" that may surmount the aporias and reifications of what she calls "critical negation" or even activist art.[14] What might be contemplated here is an "open space" of sustainable technologies and economies and communities of bricoleurs in which the appropriation of "land" as a location recedes in the words of Rirkrit into "another condition," a nomadic, archipelagic flux within an aesthetic of reassembly elsewhere/everywhere.

Fourth is the event or performance that creates the zone of contact with the world beyond art. The *Chiang Mai Social Installation* may lead us to the ways in which artists organize activities that confront those considered strangers to

10 **See: Patrick D. Flores**, "First Person Plural: Manifestos of the 1970s in Southeast Asia," in: Hans Belting, Jacob Birken, Andrea Buddensieg, and Peter Weibel (eds.), *Global Studies: Mapping Contemporary Art and Culture*, ZKM | Karlsruhe, Hatje Cantz, Ostfildern, 2011.

11 **See: Publication series** of the Japan Foundation based in Tokyo on artist-initiated spaces in Asia.

12 **Jennifer Roche**, "Socially Engaged Art, Critics and Discontents: An Interview with Claire Bishop," Community Art Network, 2006, available online at: *doublesession.net/indexhibitv070e/files/bishopinterview.doc*, accessed 08/28/12.

13 **Charles Esche**, "Agonism and Bilaterality," in: *Fixing the Bridge*, Cemeti Art Foundation, Yogyakarta, 2004, p. 9.

14 **Janet Kraynak**, "The Land and the Economics of Sustainability," in: *Art Journal*, vol. 69, no. 4, 2010.

art and face the risks of this exposure to a society at large. Beginning in 1992, artists organized the project to realize the possibility of figuring reality as socially installative and cooperative in the everyday life of the city and its people. In 1996, they wrote in their statement "Seven Collective Principles from Friends":

> "Chiang Mai Social Installation is an annual Cultural festival open for all disciplines in society that wants to 'rouse' an atmosphere and stimulate activities on a Contemporary Cultural level. The capitalist market economy does not encourage such activity, but rather promotes egotistical greed, competition, exploitation and commercial entertainment."[15]

Within this orbit, it might be instructive to assess performance art festivals in Asia and Southeast Asia and the networks arising from these instigations; in this regard, the efforts of artists from Burma/Myanmar to sustain activities around performance art amid intense surveillance and prior restraint through *Beyond Pressure*, which started in 2008, are remarkable. As a corollary, recent initiatives indicate that the locus of the event is at the intersection of the street and new media, as can be seen in the work of Pilipinas Street Plan, Neo-Angono, and TutoK in the Philippines and the House of Natural Fiber in Indonesia, which find precursors in Taring Padi and Apotik Komik in Indonesia.

Fifth, the institutional critique, which directly challenges the authority of art, may also be considered a modality of relationality. The Philippine artist Judy Freya Sibayan's Scapular Nomad Gallery presents a cogent elaboration of what this critique might entail in Southeast Asia.[16] Tangentially, we could situate the critique of institutions in light of a certain character of state and society. It is at this node that the claim to the public becomes contentious, which may be cast broadly as the "people" and therefore reference the popular, the mass, the national, and the democratic. And here it might be useful to revisit concepts of strong and weak publics, as well as strong societies and weak states, and the possibility of replacing activism with civic imagination, of the formation not of opposing enemies but of worthy adversaries. This mode of institutional critique via the artist-curator traces its lineage to four exemplary figures in the 1970s and 1980s, namely, Redza Piyadasa from Malaysia, Jim Supangkat from Indonesia, Apinan Poshyananda from Thailand, and Raymundo Albano from the Philippines.[17]

This provisional map of relationalities in Southeast Asia attempts to configure a "network" paradigm. A network, among other things, is about alignments. That said, it might be interesting to begin a reflection on the "network paradigm" in Southeast Asia with a gathering that is premised on nonalignment. In 1955, the Asian-African Conference took place in Bandung, Indonesia, attended by 29 countries, which represented a fourth of the Earth's make-up, around 1.5 billion people, and newly independent and developing states in the postcolonial sphere. The delegates talked about the possible ways to cooperate and coordinate efforts to resist neocolonialism and challenge the dominant logic of the bipolar agenda of the Cold War under the aegis of the United States and the Soviet Union. In its final communiqué, it declared that "colonialism in all its manifestations is an evil which should be brought to an end."[18] The meeting animated the Non-Aligned Movement, comprising forces that Indonesia's first President Sukarno described as "newly emergent." The conference committed itself to human rights and sovereignty in a common declaration of principles; at its heart was the project of decolonization over which America was vexed because of the potential "anti-Western" fallout and the fact that its French, Dutch, and British allies were still in Southeast Asia as colonial overlords. Still confounding America were developments in its homeland, marked by the pivotal 1954 Brown vs. Board of Education judgment that declared segregation in schools unconstitutional. Such specters of civil rights in America and universal human rights in Bandung clarified the basis of freedom on which expressions of the political and the aesthetic rested. We might ask what kind of network of art-making in our own time would have a future outside this fundamental tension of postcolonial belonging. Further, what kind of network would survive without this historical consciousness of struggling for justice and liberation through what may be broadly characterized as "decolonization" as premised in a fraught reification of the colony and the non- or anti- or post-colony, as though the latter terms were not constitutive of the colonial and its afterlife altogether, through and through.[19]

Bandung in 1955 throws into sharp relief the ethical premises of gathering a reciprocity of interests against a

15 **Ray Langenbach**, "Through the Keyhole," in: *ArtAsiaPacific*, vol. 3, no. 3, 1996, p. 88.

16 **For fuller elaboration** of Sibayan's ideas see: "Paradise Lost, Paradise Gained: Boredon and the Business of Making Things Visible in Art," in: *Locus: Interventions in Art Practice*, Lopez Memorial Museum and Pananaw ng Sining Bayan, Manila, 2005.

17 **See: Patrick D. Flores**, "Turns in Tropics: Artist-Curator," in: Nora Taylor and Boreth Ly (eds.), *Modern and Contemporary Art in Southeast Asia: An Anthology*, Cornell University Press, Ithaca (NY), 2012.

18 **Carlos P. Romulo**, *The Meaning of Bandung*, The University of North Carolina Press, Chapel Hill (NC), 1956, p. 98.

19 **For further insights**, see: Christopher Lee (ed.), *Making a World After Empire: The Bandung Movement and Its Political Afterlives*, Ohio University Press, Athens (OH), 2010.

certain habit of governing. The network in Southeast Asia is enlivened by this history of convergence and generosity, alternating between the critique of social and art world institutions, which were colonial in origin, and the desire to build institutions, to participate in the discourse of modernity, and possibly to mediate it. At the outset, this network slips away from boundaries expected in more regimented and specialized art worlds and mingles multiple tendencies or modalities of intervention. This is not to say, however, that such a network is perpetually protean and promiscuous; it is better to grasp it as tactically emergent, responsive to contingencies that always flare up in places that, first, had not consummated the fantasy of the autonomy of art and, second, tend to the precarity of art as a site of semblance; that is, a likeness of the norm somewhere else that must be aspired to even if the necessary economy to underwrite it proves to be prohibitive.

The work, or better still, the network of David Medalla and Moelyono had paved the way for a particular mode to make sense of relationality in Southeast Asia, a region in the world that has had alternating histories of colonialism and military authoritiarianism and, in the case of the Philippines, is still witnessing an actually existing armed revolution. Deepening this trajectory are the inflections of a woman, the Philippine artist Lani Maestro, acting as the go-between of the public and political prisoners in an early project and coordinating situations of dwelling or hospitality through the scaffold of a native hut in Sydney (*Pulse*, 1998) or the fabricated benches in a deconsecrated church in Caen in Normandy (*je suis toi*, 2006). Like the work of Medalla in Documenta 5 in 1972 in the People's Participation Pavilion, her art is about a coming together, a critical sensing, intimations of a gathering and reciprocities. While studying feminist theory and the history of craft and its "disappearance" through modernity, and so facing the processes of facture and memory, she did *Correspondences* in 1983 in Canada in which two of the works tried to touch the fragile fringes of the activist "self" and the incarcerated "other." *Manila Envelopes* was her first installation, which was motivated by the "need to share... to 'organize'... to bring... activist work to 'school.'" This was how

> "the participation aspect of opening the letters came into being. One became complicit in the sharing of the contents of the envelopes in the work... the table and the chair was an expansion of the image of 'interrogation,' but this time one took that choice...and so perhaps this led to an interrogation of oneself."[20]

20 **Lani Maestro**, e-mail interview with the author, September 3, 2011.

The other work *Correspondence* was, according to Lani Maestro, the nexus to the community as activist work. She describes:

> "a tiny box with a photograph of a political prisoner held a stack of small envelopes. Each one had a name of a political prisoner and an address where they could be written. And people took an envelope and wrote... I remember reports ... that people received mail... I think the fact that someone outside of prison, in another country, knew their situation helped the prisoners in many ways... for me it is the act of human kindness that was political,"[21]

a self-consciousness of an act which might be rendered needless in the end according to her. Perhaps it is Maestro's being irreducibly but unreductively "woman" that renders her aesthetic more compassionate, or prone to "suffering together" or "being together with passion;" an intimacy that is humbled by the "commonality of finitude" and devoted not only to homeliness in a time of global households but also to a shelter of bare possession - like the pliant armature of a native hut surrounded by the sound of agitated birds and public-transport motorcycles waking to the same first light that is open to the presence and rights of others.

This essay was prepared for the 7th Asian Museum Curators' Conference in September 2011 at the Japan Foundation in Tokyo with additions from notes for a brief text for the Asian Art Council meeting convened by the Guggenheim Museum in New York in September 2011.

21 **Ibid.**

Reflections on Indonesia in the Realm of Global Art

Jim Supangkat

In 1990, Klaus Schwab, founder of the World Economic Forum, foresaw that globalization would emerge following the end of global armed conflict - in fact, the Cold War (since 1945) had ended just the year before. He was not just questioning global economy. Klaus Schwab stated that the impact of globalization would only be recognized once cultural signs appeared. Schwab's prediction became meaningful in its verity because no one had expected how globalization in economy would also lead to the global art market.

In 2000, global art became indisputably notable. Contemporary art, which has developed since the 1980s, is now known as global contemporary art following its rise to become a global art market staple since the turn of the twenty-first century.[1] Can this notability of global art be seen as one of the cultural signs predicted by Schwab?

The global contemporary art market is close to globality: a new global reality where everyone, from everywhere, competes for everything. Companies have no center. The idea of foreignness is foreign. Commerce swirls and market dominance shifts. Western business orthodoxy entwines with eastern business philosophy to create a whole new mindset that embraces profit and competition as well as sustainability and collaboration.[2] Global contemporary art is a business phenomenon, not a cultural one.

1 **As noted** in *The Economist* (Nov./Dec. 2008), modernist works in the global art market stagnated at an increase of around 5% per year since 2000. Meanwhile, the increase in contemporary artworks in the global art market has been around 10-13% each year since 2000.

2 **Harold L. Sirkin**, James W. Hemerling, and Arindam K. Bhattacharya, *Globality: Competing With Everyone From Everywhere for Everything*, Business Plus, New York, Boston, 2008 pp. 1-2.

Predicating Global Art

In my view the predication process of global art started around 2005 with the discussions on the differences between global art and world art. These differences are not just circumstances that arise as the result of globalization (after the end of the Cold War). They serve to distinguish world art and global art from the emergence of a critical view towards the incorrect conceptions of world art. Globalization acts to further highlight this incorrectness. Globalization has led to the repositioning of various centers of world power in the post-Cold War era - the developments occurring in Asia, the ongoing conflicts in the Middle East, as well as realities in Eastern Europe.

The predication process places emphasis upon the awareness of a number of different, and as-yet-neglected, realities within the conception of world art. These realities are those found in the "dark corners" that exist outside our estimates. These realities are confusing, incomprehensible, even unrecognizable due to their inherent differences (they feel odd, nonsensical, like some foolish imitations, or unframeable within art history discourses).

I believe that the predication process of global art is not an attempt to redefine world art based on new observations that take into account previously unaccountable realities. This process tends to permit the forces behind these "dark corners" to (autonomously) explain their own realities, which are not understood widely due to the differences they have. As such, I foresee the occurrence of various negotiations and renegotiations (of perceptions, understandings, conventions, and agreements) within the predication process of global art. In other words, global art is a new deal in picturing world art. It stems from an awareness that past conceptions of world art actually began with a deformed picture of the world. In actuality, it is a process through which "global contemporary art" is scrutinized. As I read it, the exhibition *The Global Contemporary. Art Worlds After 1989* can be seen as an example of that scrutiny. The reference *"After 1989"* in the exhibition title inevitably connects us to the end of the Cold War and its attendant signs of transformation. In addition, this exhibition follows the rationalization of *Les Magiciens de la terre*, a landmark and sensational exhibition of 1989 presented at the Centre Georges Pompidou in Paris.

Les Magiciens de la terre, as revisited in *The Global Contemporary. Art Worlds After 1989*, brought together contemporary art with non-Western traditional art, which then led to controversy. The exhibition curator, Jean-Hubert Martin, was inundated with criticism, and this issue stayed away from the contemporary art stage for two decades. It left an idiosyncratic circumstance: the participants of that exhibition were members of the same generation, and were similarly positioned in their own culture's current developments.

In my view, *The Global Contemporary. Art Worlds After 1989* highlights this hidden issue within global contemporary art. It questions the connection between "contemporaneity" - which is behind the term contemporary art - with global art. Is the definition of "contemporaneity" (quality of belonging to the same period of time, quality of being current or of the present) adequate in predicating global art? In his book *What Is Contemporary Art?*, Terry Smith answered this question:

> "Within contemporaneity, it seems to me, at least three sets of forces contend, turning each other incessantly. The first is globalization itself, above all, its thirsts for hegemony in the face of increasing cultural differentiation (the multeity that was released by decolonization), for control of time in the face of the proliferation of asynchronous temporalities, and for continuing exploitation of natural and (to a degree not yet seen) visual resources against the increasing evidence of the inability of those resources to sustain this exploitation. Secondly, the inequity among peoples, classes, and individuals is now so accelerated that it threatens both the desires for dominations entertained by states, ideologies, and religions and the persistent dreams of liberation that continue to inspire individuals and peoples. Thirdly, we are all willy-nilly immersed in a infoscope - or better, a spectacle, an image economy or a regime of representations - capable of the instant and thoroughly mediated communication of all information and any image anywhere."[3]

James Elkins, editor of the volume *Is Art History Global?*, examines in depth the possibility of using art history to bridge the aforementioned differences (or multeity). In his travels to many parts of the world, James Elkins has discovered that although art history is known worldwide, it is understood, applied, and taught differently. However, "art history might be considered to compromise several different practices, which vary from one place to another; and [...] can be considered as a single, fairly cohesive enterprise - not one that is homogenous certainly, and not one that is distributed evenly around the world, but a field that shares some basic concepts and purposes."[4]

Then, James Elkins is faced with the question of how to make art history into a global discipline or a global enterprise, to unearth diverse art histories. I am in agreement with the premise that art history may be used to bridge these differences. However, similar perceptions about art history must first be established. On one hand, there is a need to modify (current) understandings of art history, to finally enable us to record local art histories, something we have failed to do so far. On the other hand, these modifications should not greatly alter the current understandings of art history. In the end we hope that distinct and diverse recordings of art history can position themselves as materials for negotiations and renegotiations in the predication process of global art.

Recording (local) art histories outside Europe and the United States has faced these complications for a long time, and has always failed in many ways. On the one hand, attempts to record these histories must deal with art history canons that appear odd and too unwieldy to be implemented properly. On the other hand, any attempt to examine the past will face roadblocks presented by the incommensurability thesis within the scope of anthropology, ethnography, and archaeology in examining non-Western cultures; this thesis still has a strong influence even now. Thus, in seeking similar perceptions of art history, we must immediately be aware that art history recording outside Europe and the United States cannot be done using methods that are traditionally restricted to the discipline of (Western) art history.

In my observation, the kind of art history currently known and applied in various studies outside Europe and the United States are art histories that have been reduced.

3 **Terry Smith**, *What Is Contemporary Art?*, University of Chicago Press, Chicago (IL), 2009, pp. 5-6.

4 **James Elkins**, "Art History as Global Discipline," in: James Elkins (ed.), *Is Art History Global?*, Routledge, New York (NY), 2007, pp. 3-22, p. 4.

Their art histories are related only to a piece of art development since the beginning of the twentieth century (modern art history), which they felt as relevant enough to be applied outside of Europe and the USA. This particular piece of art history is closely related to the development of (local) modern art anywhere in the world. I believe that this is the sort of understanding encountered by James Elkins during his tours to various countries outside Europe and the USA. I reckon that this kind of reduced art history can be used as the framework to record local art history. When (all) art histories are compared through this reduced art history, the differences are not as "sharply divisive" as those between art-making and ethnic arts, better known as the core of differences in art. Further local art history recording requires interdisciplinary approaches, such as those that have been developing in the last fifteen years. Such interdisciplinary approaches - linking with national history, anthropology, ethnography, philosophy of art, cultural theories, etc. - are needed to determine works that are thought to be historically significant. Through interdisciplinary approaches we will be able to discover possibilities to understand the differences between art-making and ethnic arts by analyzing the influences of ethnic arts in today's art development.

Similarities

To date, modern art and the emergence of a modern civilization have been heavily associated with the chronological development of discourses about the modern world in the realm of ideas: this is what we know as modernism. In strengthening frameworks used to record local art history, I tend to look at the emergence of a modern world based on social changes in reality (not in the realm of ideas). Seen from this point of view, we can identify some similarities in the emergence of modern societies around the world. Even in Europe, real social changes occurred only at the beginning of the twentieth century. The historical narrations I use as the basis of my views are commonly known narrations, despite them being seldom considered when one looks at the modern world. Drawing a line to the past, I would like to return to early ideas related to these social changes. In 1689, John Locke incorporated Ancient Greek Stoic philosophical doctrines regarding the natural rights of people with dignity - isogoria and isonomia - into the English Bill of Rights. This line of thinking (in Europe it evolved into the doctrine of "equality before God") was intended as a way to stop the exploitation of the lower classes by the educated nobilities, which had occurred in Europe since the Middle Ages.

Doctrines by these Stoic philosophers carry universal characteristics. As such, they did not end with just Europe. In 1776, thirteen American states incorporated this idea into the Declaration of Independence. In 1789, it was further elaborated in the U.S. constitution. By the nineteenth century, this idea of social change had spread to the colonies. In Indonesia, for instance, it inspired a number of educated aristocrats to scrutinize colonial politics critically. It was at the beginning of the nineteenth century, within the third wave of colonialism that practiced imperialism. Amongst them were Raden Saleh (1807-1880), the romantic painter who once resided in Dresden, Germany (1839-1844) and France (1844-1848); the philosopher-poet Ronggowarsito (1802-1873), who conceived modern Javanese literature and is considered by many the primary source of Javanology; also the self-taught female thinker, R.A. Kartini (1879-1904) who championed education for the indigenous people; and a Dutch intellectualist and writer residing in Indonesia, Edward Douwes Dekker (1820-1887), who wrote *Max Havelaar* in 1860 under his Indonesian pseudonym Multatuli criticizing the colonial system.[5]

The First World War (1914-1918) showed that the fate of the European lower classes stayed largely unchanged at the beginning of the twentieth century. World War I. which implicated great European empires, only served to demonstrate that the Industrial Revolution had only shifted poverty from peasants to laborers and workers. The Industrial Revolution actually led to imperialism, which in turn led to World War I. Every European country involved in that war deployed millions upon millions of soldiers in their infantries - drawn from peasants, industrial laborers, and mine workers. Ten million lives perished in that war, in part due to their nonprofessional soldiering. Famine quickly spread amongst the lower classes across Europe. Their suffering ushered in change. In the middle of war, a social revolution emerged in Russia, in 1917. The Bolsheviks, with support from the military (especially deserters made up of soldiers from peasant or working-class backgrounds) overthrew the monarchy, seized nobility-held lands and wealth, and established a socialist government in Russia. Later, concerns that this social revolution would spread and cut a swathe through Europe forced other European states to embark upon styles of governance that paid more attention to the lower classes.

However, imperialism was far from over, in both mainland Europe and the colonies (results of the third wave of

5 **See: Harry A. Poeze,** *Di Negeri Penjajah: Orang Indonesia di Negeri Belanda 1600-1950*, KITLV - Royal Netherlands Institute of Southeast Asian and Caribbean Studies, Jakarta, Kepustakaan Populer Gramedia, Jakarta, 2008. In English the title reads: *In the Land of the Colonists: Indonesians in the Netherlands 1600-1950.*

colonization). Imperialism culminated with the World War II, before it was finally extinguished. At the end of World War II, social change emerged to mark the end of worldwide human exploitation by fellow man signalized by a wave of decolonization around the world, post-World War II.

It is not difficult to see similarities in the emergence of modern societies around the world - hinging upon the same foundation and occurring in the same time frame (early twentieth century). The development of art in 1930s Europe, later known as the beginning of modern art development, celebrated this social change. New Realism as initiated by Fernand Léger, and Walter Benjamin's views on the requirements for artists and intellectuals to become producers to sustain proletariat solidarity, for instance, were examples that celebrated the rise of the lower classes as a new part of a new society. Meanwhile, constructivism, cubism, and functionalism - introduced by the Bauhaus design and architecture movement - are widely discussed as oppositions of the Hellenistic style that reflects aristocratic tastes. Artists who cultivated the ideas and fostered these movements, are widely known as socialist artists.

A similar development happened in the colonies. In Indonesia, for example, Sindhu Soedjojono, a socialist painter, conceived modern Indonesian art in the 1930s, by going against the tastes of colonial society. He especially cast aspersions on landscape painting that had developed for a century in Indonesia. Soedjojono not only criticized this mannerist tendency, he mocked the functions of these paintings - as attempts to record the natural beauty of Indonesia - which usually ended up as souvenirs bought by Dutch visitors and taken back to their country.

Soedjojono was a nationalist as well. As such, he and his disciples were heavily involved in the political tensions surrounding the Indonesian decolonization process between 1945 and 1949. It was a difficult process - protracted negotiations with the Dutch colonial government seemed to yield very little results, and armed conflicts were widespread and devastating. Due to his nationalist views, Soedjojono "severed" the ties that bind art-making in modern Indonesian art to the intricate Indonesian traditional art forms, mostly known through ethnographic and archaeological studies. These studies had been some of the Dutch colonial government's main concerns and were intensivelypursued throughout the colonial period.[6] In the 1930s, a number of Dutch critics had attempted to draw a connection between modern Indonesian art and Indonesian ethnic arts, but they faced Soedjojono's heavy opposition.

Once again, it is not too difficult to see similarities in the emergence of modern art worldwide. This is the basis of world art. By understanding this basis, there remains no doubt in viewing modern art, which appeared worldwide at the beginning of the twentieth century, as part of world art that also appeared during that time (early twentieth century). Through this understanding, the development and history of art-making in Europe and the USA - connected to the emergence of modern art - can be used as a frame of reference, or as a reference point, to identify the differences within attempts to record local art history.

Differences

Unlike modernist world art trapped within uniformity, attempts at picturing world art in predicating global art actually aim to seek differences that are hidden thus far. The search for these differences follow the common belief in current art discourses that art-making is part of culture. An understanding of these differences is needed to establish canonic norms in recording local art histories. The kind of significant differences that I would like to offer are the differences in how art and art-making are perceived. To question these differences, I must especially highlight development of art in Indonesia. Apparently, perceptions of art and art-making in Indonesia are different from the sort of perceptions that underlie almost all influential art discourses at work today. First, I shall discuss what I meant by "perceptions underlying art discourses today."

Although the beginning of modern art development was colored by a rejection of Hellenism, modern art and subsequent art developments cannot avoid the continuing oculocentric civilization founded upon Ancient Greek culture that predated even Plato. An oculocentric civilization emphasizes the eyes (ocular) as the source of human knowledge of reality. When Giorgio Vasari introduced art history in the year 1550, he made observations on the lives of many painters, sculptors, and architects. Vasari viewed their works (paintings, sculptures, and buildings) as standards of excellence; as the canonic norms by which he measured other art. This perception was further cemented by Immanuel Kant through the concept of "fine art," which would lead to the conception of "art" in the English language - oftentimes regarded as *raison d'etre* of art-making. Almost all art discourses throughout history, up to today, hinge upon this perception.

6 In 1815, the Kingdom of the Netherlands established the *Zaken van Kusnten en Wetenschappen* [Royal Commission for the Affairs of Arts and Sciences] - also known as the Reinwardt Commission - under the direction of Dutch scientist C.G.C. Reinwardt to conduct anthropological and archaeological excavations in Indonesia, following the model set by France's Egypt expedition. Dutch painters brought in to assist the Reinwardt Commission (including the well-known Belgian painter A.A.J. Payen) were tasked to create drawings or paintings as tools or auxiliaries for research - not as art.

Perceptions on art and art-making in Indonesia do not place materiality and visuality as their main focus. Parallel to the conception of art perceptions in Europe, this different perception appeared during the colonial period through a process of cultural translation in the nineteenth century. In an old text by Ronggowarsito (on whom I have written briefly above), we may find a contemplation that refers to the idea underlying this perception. Basing his treatise on the philosophy known as the *Widyatama*, Ronggowarsito made the observation that art-making is related to the search for the true sense, through the sharpness of intuition (*rasa*) and the ability to experience beauty. From this examination, we may conclude that the understanding, which appeared in Indonesia during the nineteenth century, seems to be an adaptation of (or something close to) a philosophy of aesthetics, rather than a fine art concept. Philosophy of aesthetics emerged in the eighteenth century and entered discourses on art history through the views of Johann Winckelmann (1755), who also pioneered art criticism. However, in reality, philosophy of aesthetics had to make way for the development of world art. Almost all art discourses from the early twentieth century onwards - believed as fundamentals of art-making - hinged upon the development of cognition stemming from Kant's treatise.

Perceptions on art and art-making, which are influenced by the aforementioned philosophy of aesthetics, endure in Indonesia even today. This is largely due to the consideration that, compared to fine art concepts, the philosophy of aesthetics is more suitable for Indonesian ethnic art. This awareness, conceived during the nineteenth century, can be found in the Indonesian term *seni*, which can be defined as "art" in the English language: this understanding of *seni* can be seen as Indonesian art-making's *raison d'etre.* In upholding an understanding that dates back to the nineteenth century, *seni* can be emphasized upon as an ontological symptom within metaphysics, whose understanding is not based on empirical examination. *Seni* is formless; it only gains its form after it becomes "artwork." In the Indonesian language, *seni* (the subject, the head) is further emphasized on the formation of terms that are derivatives of word *seni:* such as *seni rupa* (visual art), *seni tari* (dance art), *seni musik* (music art), and so on. These words: *rupa, musik, sastra, teater*, etc., are modifiers. They are adverbs (noun, verb, adjective) that describe the word *seni* (a noun). Further, the words *musik* (music), *sastra* (literature), *teater* (theatre) are nouns, meanwhile *tari* (to dance), *lukis* (to paint), *pahat* (to carve) are verbs, whereas *rupa* (visual/form) is an adjective. From all the adverbs that refer to the products of art, only the word *rupa* is an adjective. In a linguistic point of view, it is specially known as an attribute-based modifier, unlike other adverbs (nouns or verbs) seen as adverbial modifiers. In the English language, the adjective "visual", as an attribute-based adverb, is distinct from the main group of adverbs. As such, the English adjective "visual" occupies a special position. This special provision led to the term "visual art" or "art," which is differentiated from the adverbial arts, that is, the arts that refer to music, theater, and dance.

However, the derivatives of *seni* found in the Indonesian lexicon do not specifically differentiate adjectives from the wider group of adverbs; in other words, all art forms are adverbial. This is why the term *seni* can be connected to terms that point out ethnic art forms as well as to terms denoting the most recent art forms. This linguistic trait shows that the extra-ordinary standards of art are not determined by the type of artworks produced, but by the potential of the *seni* - a metaphysical phenomenon - that can appear in all art forms. Thus it is clear that visual art is not the canonic norm to measure other art (this shows how art is perceived in Indonesia).

Within the totality of a great work of art, there will always be presentations of definite aesthetic features, which demonstrate metaphysical force within the transcendent sphere as the capacity to present aesthetic experiences to the audience. Transmission occurs after the aesthetic properties in artworks undergo interaction with the viewer's mental properties that derive from their life experiences.

Asia Exhibited in Korea.

Image Conflicts in the Making of Asian Contemporary Art

Birgit Mersmann

Since the beginning of the 1990s, a veritable museum wave began to roll over Asia. This particular boom (in both size and quantity) of new art museums was first preceded, and later paralleled by the mushrooming of art biennials all over Asia. Forming the avant-garde, these international art exhibitions opened the floodgates for contemporary art, its institutions of production, intermediation and marketing, and thus sparked Asia's interest in becoming a global player within the world market of art.

In the following, I will look at a special case on the national level of how Asia has been exhibited in South Korea in the last decade since the art exhibition boom of the mid-1990s. Drawing upon theories about the function of exhibitionary places and practices as agencies of cultural representation and translation, this analysis will focus on the South Korean contribution to the making of Asian (especially Korean) contemporary art in the conflict zone between global, international, and local art definitions and market interests. Since South Korea has been at the forefront of the Asian art biennial wave - the 1st Kwangju* Biennale took place in 1995, directly followed by the 1st Shanghai and Taipei Biennial in 1996 - and has meanwhile built a substantial contemporary Asian (and international) art scene, it allows for first hypotheses about how the establishment of the art biennial has contributed to form, representation and promotion of the image of Asian contemporary art and thus led to a re- and transformation of the museumscape. Particular attention will be directed to the different functions of exhibitionary formats, models, and strategies to showcase Asian art and culture, varying from curatorial concepts to the museum's architecture. My analysis primarily centers on a comparison between two formats: 1. the biennial as temporary international, national, or local art event, and 2. the art museum as a local establishment of permanence and built entity. It will examine the various, differing and converging roles these two exhibition formats play in shaping contemporary Asian and Korean art and identity. For reasons of self-limitation, I will focus on the two most representative art exhibitionary institutions: the Gwangju Biennale as the first biennial event in Asia, and the Leeum, the Samsung Museum of Art as a new type of corporate art museum for the display, representation, and promotion of Korean, Asian, and international contemporary art.

Globality and Locality on Display: Identity Construction in the Image of the Leeum

In his article "Contemporary Art as Global Art. A Critical Estimate," Hans Belting discusses two types of art museums as representative museum institutions for the "global contemporary": 1. the MoCA (Museum of Contemporary Art Los Angeles) succeeding the MoMA (Museum of Modern Art New York), and 2. the Collector's and Corporate Museum. He states that the MoCA "is by implication global, as it

* **Kwangju written with the initial letter "K" follows the English transliteration of the Korean word**, before the revision of the Romanization of Korean became operative in July 2000. From the 2002 Biennale onwards, Gwangju is transliterated with the letter "G." Whenever the paper refers to the Gwangju Biennale as general event, it follows the transliteration rules of the new Romanization form.

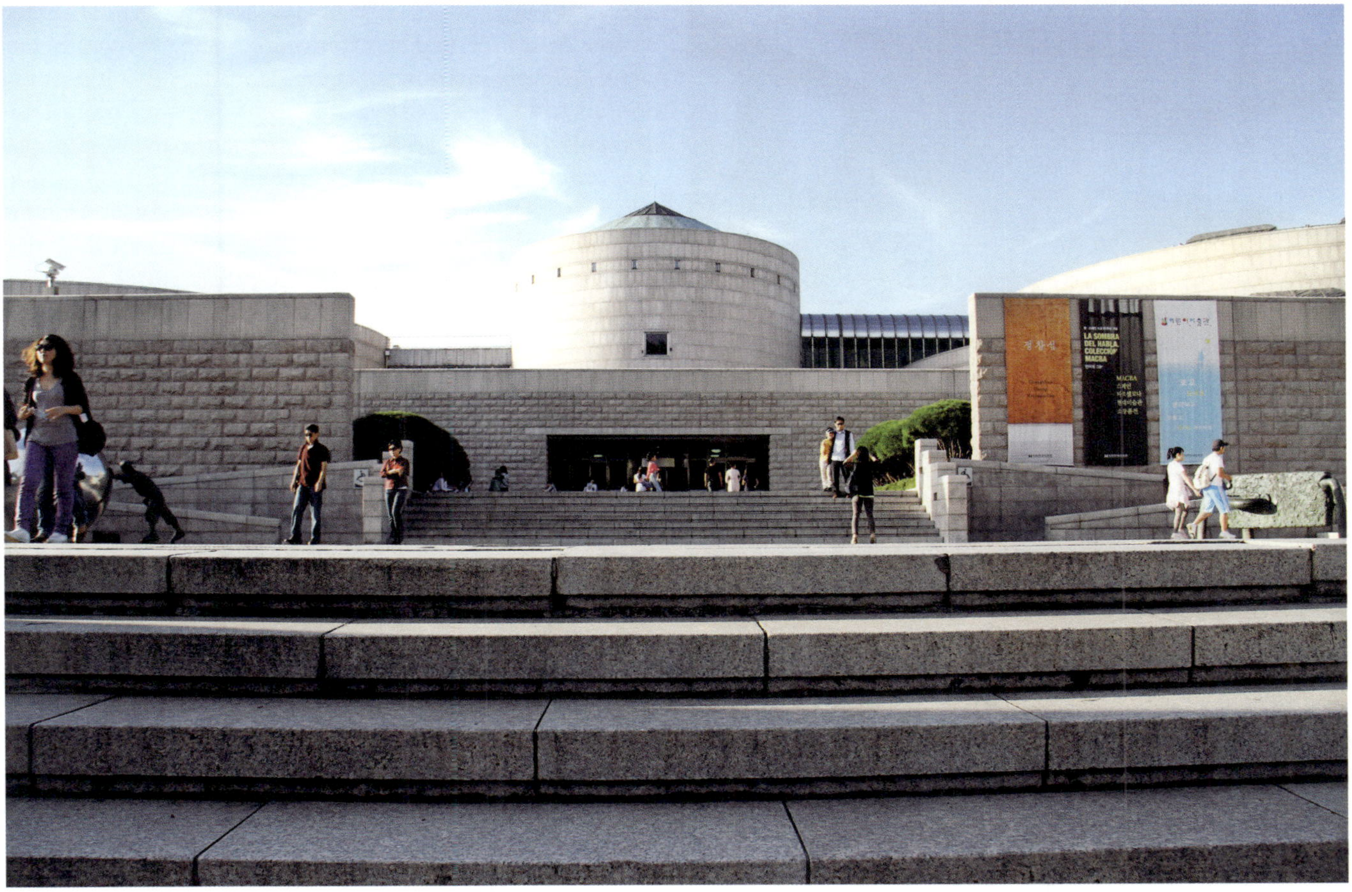

The National Museum of Contemporary Art in Seoul, designed by Tai Soo Kim Partners

celebrates contemporary production as an art without geographic borders, and without history in terms of Western modernism."[1] The museumscape in South Korea halfway fits this definition. It embraces the two before-mentioned museum types, the Museum of Contemporary Art and the Collector's and corporate museum. However, the MoCA is identified as National Museum of Contemporary Art, and the Leeum, Samsung Museum of Art as a corporate museum. The architectural rebuilding of the National Museum of Korea (finished in 2005) seems to have functioned as a link between the national- and individual-bound celebration of visual art and culture through museums. The national anchorage of the newly built Museum of Contemporary Art is better understood when it is taken into consideration that the museum was established in the year 1986. It was built in anticipation of the 1988 Olympics in Seoul, allowing "Korea's arts to be showcased to the world." According to its date of origin, the mission of the museum meets the classical standards "to survey and research contemporary art, collect and preserve works of art, and plan and host various exhibitions, both domestically and internationally."[2] Based on this definition, it obeys the dialectical logics of the "national-international" museum of contemporary art and thus proves to be either postmodernist or preglobal or both. The national endeavor and identification of the MoCA is also expressed by the museum's architecture. The museum was designed by Korean architects, the Tai Soo Kim Partners. Korean traditional form was fused with contemporary tastes and functions. The museum's architecture reflects the traditional Korean architectural style of fortress walls and a beacon mound. The design of the exterior space borrows elements of the traditional Korean garden. Even the building material, a light pink granite, stems from Korean soil. Following its mission statement, the museum incorporates a "traditional image that blends with the surrounding landscape. Fully equipped with modern facilities, scientific

1 **Hans Belting**, "Contemporary Art as Global Art: A Critical Estimate," in: Hans Belting and Andrea Buddensieg (eds.), *The Global Art World. Audiences, Markets, and Museums*, Hatje Cantz, Osterfildern, 2009, pp. 48–49.

2 **See: Homepage** of the National Museum of Contemporary Art in Seoul, available online at: http://www.moca.go.kr/eng/engGenInfo.do?_method=welcome, accessed 08/20/2012.

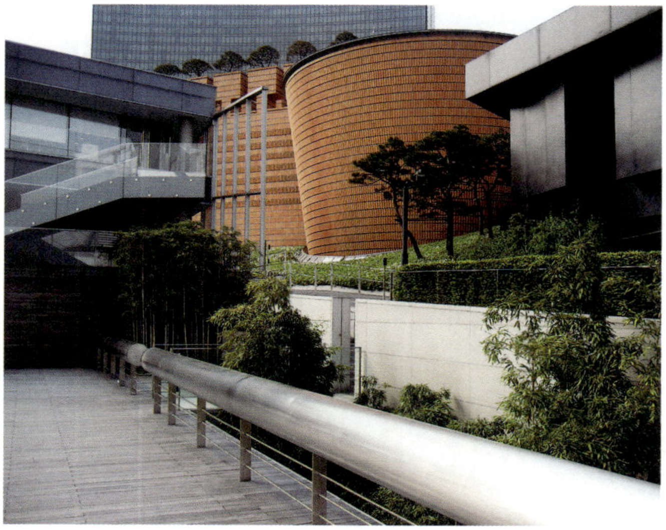

The Leeum, Samsung Museum of Art. General view with the buildings of Rem Koolhaas, Mario Botta, and Jean Nouvel (from left to right)

equipment and various installations, the museum is more than equal to the task of being the only national contemporary art museum in Korea."[3]

In the conceptual structure and composition of the Leeum, some aspects of the architectural design of the National MoCA, in particular the reference to traditional Korean fortifications, can be reencountered. Despite these borrowings from tradition, the Leeum, opened in 2004 on the slope of the Namsan Mountain, the highest elevation in Seoul City, represents a new "global" museum type, countering, transforming, and superseding the agenda of the former MoCA format as based on a national-international bias. In my view, the Leeum is affected by the global-local exhibitionary logics evolving from the Asian biennial boom and translates it into a new meta-museum structure that powerfully embraces and synthesizes a variety of different museum formats and functions in a sort of multi/ple or "mixed" museum.

It ambitiously seeks to integrate different museum types that, in the course of museum history, have emerged due to chronological and geographical, time and space-oriented specializations in art, culture, and knowledge production. It incorporates the National Museum of Art, the Museum of Modern Art, and the Museum of Contemporary Art, and combines these three classical museum types with a Cultural and Educational Center that is thought to serve the purpose of a museum for future generations. With this act of mega-merging, it builds in itself a new museum corporation, thereby also structurally reflecting its core definition and mission as a Samsung corporate museum. To summarize, the Leeum comprises two museums and an education facility: Museum 1 housing traditional Korean art, Museum 2 containing modern and contemporary Korean and international art, and the Samsung Child Education & Culture Center. The first and most prominent museum, the museum for traditional Korean art that also architectonically stands out on the hillside embracing the two other museum buildings, has adopted the function of the National Museum preserving and showcasing the Korean cultural heritage. It is dedicated to the exhibition of traditional Korean artwork, including 36 pieces designated as National Treasures. On display in the permanent ancient art collection is Korean ceramics from Goryeo celadon to Joseon bunchong and white porcelain, Buddhist art from the Goryeo dynasty, metal work as well as Joseon painting and calligraphy.

The national cultural orientation of this museum is also marked by its site-specific location. Its function as a nexus of national culture is stressed by its local connection to two other Korean cultural institutions nearby, the National Museum in Yongsan whose new museum building was completed in 2005, and the National Theater on Namsan Mountain. In showcasing modern and contemporary artworks by Korean and "foreign" artists (this is the category used on the official museum website) in permanent and temporary exhibitions, the second museum integrates two already well-established formats of the twentieth and twenty-first century's art museums' history, the MoMA and the MoCA. By opening these two formats for a mutual art-historical dialog between both the modern and the contemporary, and the Korean national and the international, a new global-local perspective is implemented.

This is reflected in the overall concept of the Leeum designed to "accommodate the past, present, and future of art and culture,"[4] connecting the Korean artistic heritage with national and international contemporary art practices. The "liaison between Korean and international art" shall provide "an open forum that allows audiences to access information, and create cultural environment for a diverse public, from artists and scholars to those who wish to cultivate aesthetic sensibilities."[5] The third museum, the Samsung Child Education & Culture Center (CECC) was included for the purpose of cultivating a new aesthetic sense and cultural competence in order to comprehend the high complexity of global art and culture. The global-local orientation of the

3 See: http://www.moca.go.kr/eng/engGenInfo.do?_method=mBuilding, accessed 08/20/2012.

4 See: Homepage of the Leeum, available online at: http://leeum.samsungfoundation.org/eng/aboutleeum/message.asp, accessed 08/20/2012.

5 See: Mission Statement of the Leeum, available online at: http://leeum.samsungfoundation.org/eng/aboutleeum/vision.asp, accessed 08/20/2012.

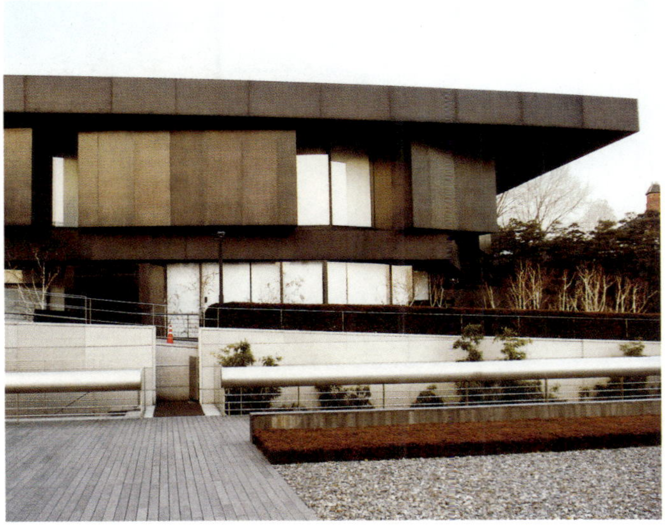

The Leeum, Samsung Museum of Art. Museum 2, designed by Jean Nouvel

Leeum as a comprehensive museum model and metastructure for linkages is also mirrored in the definition of its core functions and activities.

The Leeum supports the collection, preservation, investigation, exhibition of and education about Korean art from past to present and contemporary art from all over the world, thus harmonizing tradition and future, conservation and transformation. As a key concept, the crossbreeding of genealogies and geographies constitutes the corporate identity of the Leeum as the Samsung Museum of Art in its entirety. The latter is evidenced on all levels of design, from the museum logo to the museum architecture. According to the museum identity, designer Margot Perman, the logo symbolizes the "convergence of time and space." The convergence of time alone relates to the conjoining of past, present, and future. The museum logo "features the alphabetical character for Leeum with a timeline cutting through the character. Inspired by a typographical character borrowed from ancient Roman engravings, the logo has been designed to be both old and new, linked to heritage yet perpetually contemporary."[6] The uniquely Korean specificity and identity of the logo is represented by the use of six colors that are prototypical for traditional Korean painting. However, stressed in the Museum Identity statement is the universal accessibility and understanding of the logo in spite of its unique Koreanness. The museum's architecture is equally designed to meet the Leeum's desire to conjoin the past, present, and future of art and culture. Three distinct and internationally reputed architects, Mario Botta, Jean Nouvel, and Rem Koolhaas, were selected to express the idea of convergence of time and space by three separate, but interconnected museum units which build the overall structure of the Leeum. The first museum, housing the Korean traditional art collection, was designed by the Swiss architect Mario Botta. By shaping it like a fortress made of solid forms and using terracotta tiles, he turned it into a representation of the past, including reminiscences of Korean traditional architecture and ceramic art. In order to accentuate that the past of Korean national art has to be protected against the rush of modernization and globalization, the architect has placed trees on top of the building to look like flags on a fortress. The second museum, integrating collections of modern and contemporary Korean and international art, was designed by the French architect Jean Nouvel. Its architecture is positioned at the intersection of technological innovation and contemporary aesthetic practice, thus expressing the contemporaneity of present time as an ongoing transformation and innovation process. The newly developed material for the building, rusted stainless steel, reflects this idea of technological innovation as a cornerstone for modernization and transformation. Since Museum 2 was required to function not only as a place for collection and exhibition, but also as a space for interactive interrelations and translations between different time periods and regions of art production (modern and contemporary, Korean and international art), Nouvel decided to construct it as a fluid and transformable space. By eliminating columns as far as possible and enabling deductions and additions in the exhibition space, he maximized the flexibility and movability within the open space. For the interior of the exhibition space, he introduced not only a large number of movable walls to allow spatial transformability with regard to the exhibitionary requirements, but he also placed exhibition boxes of different sizes and orientations between the huge front windows of the museum building, thus creating mixed volumes and contrasting light effects. By the unsteady arrangement of these exhibition boxes, he set the static white cube aesthetics of the modern art museum in motion, creating a new migratory concept of the exhibition space that meets the needs of contemporary art and art practices as rooted in the temporarity of transition. The third museum building, the Samsung Child Education & Culture Center housing facilities of culture-related education programs and activities for children, was designed by the Dutch architect Rem Koolhaas. With its construction as a highly abstract space, it becomes a symbolic site not only for the future and futuristic visions of art and culture, but also a metaphor for the (rather questionable and uncertain) future of the museum itself. The building is designed explicitly to be featureless in order to completely harmonize with

6 See: **Museum Identity (MI) statement**, available on ine at: http://leeum.samsungfoundation.org/eng/aboutleeum/museum.asp, accessed 08/20/2012.

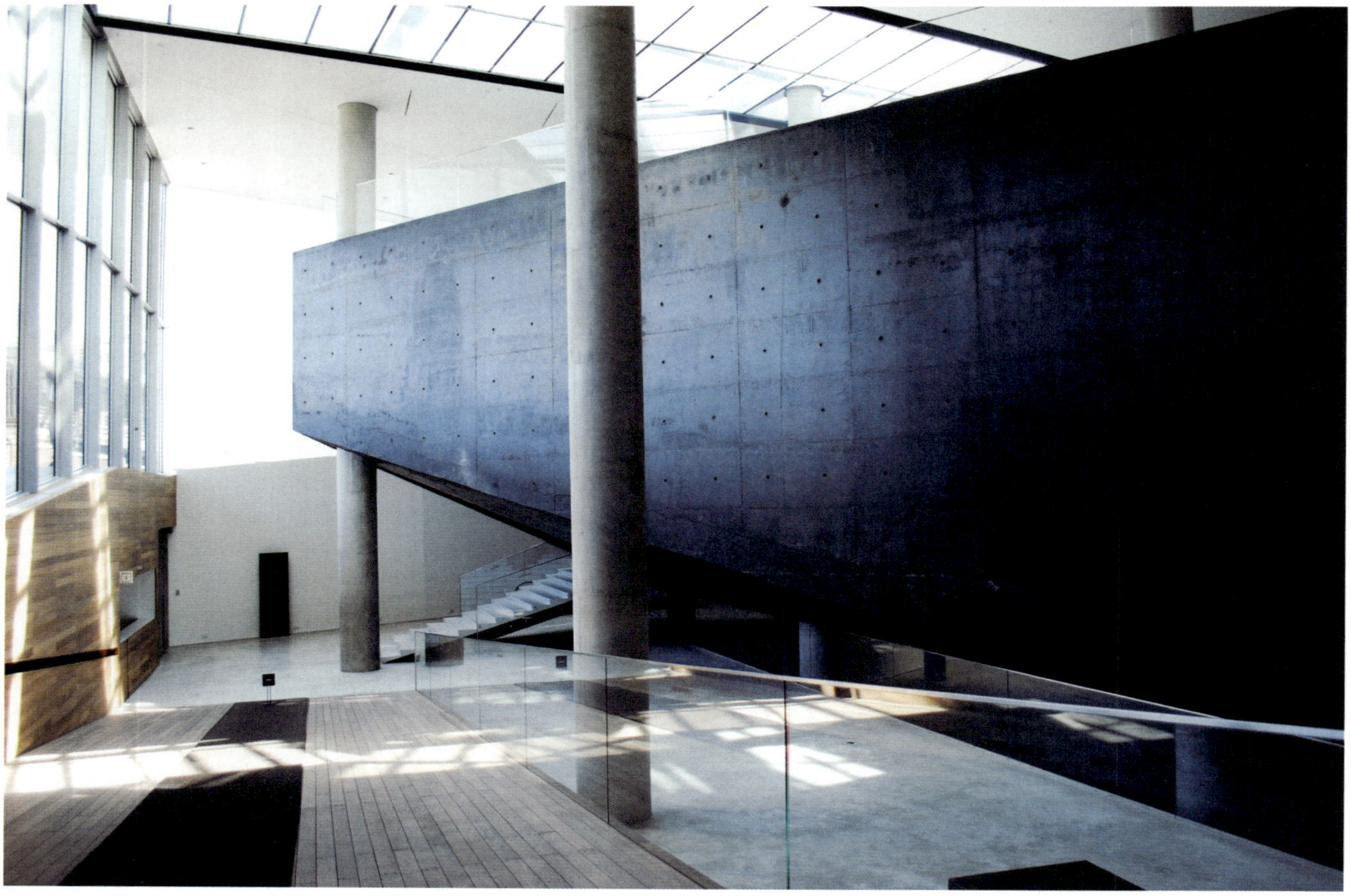

The Leeum, Samsung Child Education & Culture Center, designed by Rem Koolhaas

its existing context and natural surroundings, making its presence almost undistinguishable. Moreover, by flowing alongside the topographical surface and organically linking the two other museums, it emphasizes its contextual architectural function as a transitional museum building. Also in this respect, it defies the existence and definition of a museum as a fixed entity and institution in its own rights. For the multipurpose functions of the CECC as a new museum format of the future, Koolhaas created a huge, walled black box, over eight meters in height, that is completely independent of the outside mass of the robust horizontal building. The black box is a separate body made of black concrete, a new material that futuristically interacts with the aluminum floors and galvanized plate ceilings of the surrounding space. It forms a space within the space of the outer building, seemingly floating freely and thus transcending the gravity and inertia of the black concrete cube.

According to Koolhaas, it "blocks all light, enables manual operation and control. [...] All form of cultural event is possible in this space. Through the use of the black box, the Samsung Child Education & Culture Center not only has an experimental space that is different from the conventional, but also presents a model for future exhibition space that can hold a wide variety of cultural phenomena."[7] With this multifunctional conceptualization of museum-independent space, Koolhaas' architecture performs a transition from the museum as singular unit and autonomous body to the cultural complex, in which the museum plays the rather subordinated role of providing the infrastructural frame for staging art and cultural events. The Leeum presents itself as a hallmark of both the museum's history and its future. Under its umbrella, different museum functions as embodied by the three different museum buildings are unified. The closeness, fortification, and protectiveness of the architectural design of Museum 1 for traditional Korean art alludes to the traditional role of the museum to preserve uniquely outstanding material objects as cultural heritage. The openness and flexibility of Museum 2 for modern and contemporary art as well as its building's structure illustrates the opening of the museum, as is indicative of the modern and contemporary art museum, for border-crossing

7 See: Seong Tae Park (ed.), *Leeum. Samsung Museum of Art*, Leeum Samsung Museum of Art, Seoul, 2005, p. 111.

visual encounters and interactions between diverse media and cultures. The featural a-presence of the third museum building becomes a metaphor for the possible future dissolution of the museum, and its transition into a cultural forum and popular cult place for events. The museum boom in general, as well as the multiplication and potentialization of the museum on a single site in order to built a culture complex might signal the beginning of the deconstruction of the museum - or at least of the classical museum functions as they were formed in Western culture. Probably the most striking point about the Leeum is that its corporate identity as a Korean museum institution of global outreach was - in its full corporate design from the museum logo to the museum architecture - constructed and shaped by Western architects and designers of high international reputation with a strong global working portfolio; and that this was planned as such intentionally from its inception. At first sight, this may seem contradictory or concessive to the powerful past and present of Western museum architecture and culture. At second sight, it might demonstrate how the stardom of Western world architecture is instrumentalized, and then respectively subordinated in order to build a new Korean corporate identity as a powerful part of a representation of the New Asia. In this way, it is the West that stands in the image of the New Asia.

The Gwangju Biennale. Image Negotiations between Korean Regional and National, Asian, and Global Identity

What has been largely overlooked according to John Clark with respect to Asian biennials is that they did not merely function as mediators of international art to local Asian audiences, but also as attractors for contemporary art from other Asian countries, thus enhancing the processes of inter-Asian art circulation, comparison, and competition.[8] The Gwangju Biennale, one of the first Asian biennials, is a good case in point to prove this observation. By looking at its specific evolvement, in particular its development over the last decade, the Gwangju Biennale's transformation from a regional (or provincial), Gwangju-related exhibition event to foster the national-international art and culture relations to a truly Asian biennial exhibiting the "global-contemporary" becomes manifest. This internal Asian, or more precisely inter-Asian "biennial turn" can best be exemplified by two Gwangju biennials which, by comparison, mark the aforementioned paradigm shift: the millennium biennial of 2000 and the mid-decade biennial of 2006. I selected these two biennials for two reasons: 1. Both of them have been directed by Korean art scholars and curators in a collaborative teamwork with international curators, and 2. They chose an Asia-centered topic as their main theme: the 2000 Biennale relates to the (revived) Oriental discourse, and the 2006 Biennale enfolds the glocal Asian/isms debate. The main theme of the millennium Biennale, *Man + Space*, was thought to directly address Orientalism, or, in other words, Oriental values such as harmonious human interaction and integration as a counter-concept to Westernism. By using the Chinese characters for representing the biennial title, the desire to differentiate itself from Western definitions and ideas was accentuated. The Chinese characters contain more specific and at the same time more comprehensive meanings than the English translation *Man + Space*, namely in that it indicates 1. the relationship between a human being and the environment, 2. the human condition, and 3. a human being and his/her circumstance. It expresses Oriental values by denoting a relationship between human beings and space, that is, as Cha Bum-suk, chairperson of the Kwangju Biennale 2000, describes it, "not a relationship which human beings and space overcome or push each other, rather it is a relationship in which they embrace and give meaning to one another."[9] The value system of integration is also referred to as a new spiritual revolution that is said to be necessary for the New Millennium. The statement of the artistic director is very clear-cut and optimistically determined to achieve this revival of the integrative and spiritual power of Orientalism to finally transgress the long-standing, history-ridden cultural oppositions and power imbalances between East and West:

> "How can the East and West overcome those inevitable differences? [...] I think, though it may not be easy in the West, that it certainly is possible in the East. [...] My belief is that the East should set diversified values on the arts and serve as a critical flow as to the past monolithic ways of art. [...] The West-centralized view of contemporary art is still disillusioned with the idea that the West still rules the world. It should be restructured in various alternatives. A truly globalized culture

8 **John Clark**, "Histories of the Asian 'New': Biennales and Contemporary Asian Art," in: Vishakha N. Desai (ed.), *Asian Art History in the Twenty-First Century*, Sterling and Francine Clark Art Institute, Williamstown (MA), 2007, pp. 229-249.

9 **Cha Bum-suk**, "A Window on the Future," in: Kwangju Biennale Foundation (ed.), *Man + Space. Kwangju Biennale 2000 - The Special Exhibition*, exhib. cat., Kwangju Biennale Press, Gwangju, 2000, p. 13.

will be born as innumerous visions are presented and integrated in such ways as to incorporate the whole in an active and critical structure."[10]

In this Oriental context, Korea is praised as having the ideal prerequisites to strive for this integration of the two different cultures, as exemplified as the techno-scientific West and spiritual East - and, in fact, the argument is that it has already successfully harmonized East and West into a single culture. The conservative, if not reactionary Orientalist ideology that dominates the overall conceptualization and interpretation of the Biennale theme is complemented (or should we say countered?) by a strong regionalism, ranging from city marketing and cultural policy to art definitions and curatorial concepts. This can be seen first in the way in which the Gwangju Biennale is used to promote Gwangju as a city of art and human rights: "The reason why (this international festival) is held in Kwangju and not some other place is due to the specific image that the region has. Such an image is believed to contribute to the formation of the characteristics of the Kwangju Biennale."[11] Those characteristic regional features hint at Gwangju as cultural center of Korea and "the village of arts" since ancient times, as well as to Gwangju as a "village of justice" and holy birth place for democracy in Korea. This regional differentiation of Gwangju has not only been the chief motivation for the founding of the Gwangju Biennale, but it has also proven worthwhile to be integrated into the "world's major artistic art flow."[12] The curatorial concept of the *Man + Space* Biennale likewise follows a strict regionalism - but in this case, a world regionalism. For setting up the Biennale, the world map was divided into five regions, not representing continents, but inter-regions or intercontinental regions, and for each of these regions a commissioner was appointed. The pairings appear sometimes bizarre, if not arbitrary, only bound by a new regionalism of geographic neighboring. There were regional sub-exhibitions on 1. Europe-Africa (curated by René Block), 2. North America (Thomas Finkelpearl), 3. South America (You-yeon Kim), 4. Asia (Tani Arata), and 5. Korea-Oceania (Kim Hong-hee). Of significance is the split between Asia and Korea, and the coupling of Korea and Oceania; it highlights both the importance of uniquely defining and promoting Korean art and image identity on a national level as well as the interest in new interregional art and culture orientations. This double tendency is reinforced by the addition of a special exhibition on *The Facet of Korean & Japanese Art* dedicated to present - for the first time in the history of Korean and Japanese art exhibitions - the encounter between Korean Dansaekhwa and Japanese Mono-ho, two minimalist art tendencies in painting and sculpture that dominated the 1970s and 1980s. On one hand, the millennium biennial is still caught in the logics and rhetoric of Orientalism nurtured by the tradition-bound East-West dualism. On the other, it searches for a way out of Orientalism as a West-referencing, biased concept and thus proposes a new regionalism that enables the escape from the predominant Western perspective on cultural production and understanding. This idea for a new regionalism is not to "follow the far-right desires of distorted nationalism, the discriminative self-interest of local regionalism, nor the colonialistic concepts of primitivism or exoticism. Instead, a dynamic regionalism, consistent with international universality, is required to be able to create new traditions, contemporary cultures, and lively regional identities."[13] The desire to become a truly Asian biennial of international importance and global scope is enclosed in this claim for a dynamic regionalism: "It is our prerequisite [...] that the Kwangju Biennale be a distinctively Asian international event, substantializing the identity of Asia."[14] Whereas the millennium Kwangju Biennale seems to conceptually oscillate between an international, inter- and intraregional exhibition, and a revived Orientalism and new Asianism, thereby signaling a kind of transitional stage, the 2006 Gwangju Biennale titled *Fever Variations* presents itself as the first decisively Asian biennial with a regional-global exhibition focus. This is foremost reflected by the fact that Asia, respectively the formation of a new Asian identity, has been chosen as the overall theme. The focus of the Gwangju Biennale is thus shifted from an internationally oriented, but still provincial exhibition event in Asia, as such competing with other well established international biennials all over the world, to an Asian international biennial, searching to build a contemporary art and biennial network within the region of Asia. What stands on the cultural-political agenda is Gwangju's geographical and functional role in Asia. In order to build Gwangju as "A Cultural Hub City of Asia," the Gwangju Biennale is oriented towards the promotion of Asian discourses and aesthetics, thereby "connecting Gwangju, Korea, Asia and the world."[15] The strategy for the Gwangju Biennale to develop from a regional event to a

10 **Statement by Oh Kwang-Su**, the artistic director of the Kwangju Biennale, *Man + Space. Kwangju Biennale 2000*, exhib. cat., Kwangju Biennale Press, Gwangju, 2000, p. 27.

11 **Ibid.**, p. 14.

12 **Ko Jae-yu**, "The 21st Century and the 2000 Kwangju Biennale," in: *Man + Space. Kwangju Biennale 2000 - The Special Exhibition*, p. 11.

13 **Statement by Kim Hong-hee**, curator of the Korea-Oceania section of the 2000 Kwangju Biennale, in: *Man + Space. Kwangju Biennale 2000*, p. 254.

14 **Statment by Oh Kwang-Su**, artistic director of the Kwangju Biennale 2000, ibid., p. 19.

15 **Kim Hong-hee**, "The 6th Gwangju Biennale 2006 'Fever Variations,' in: Gwangju Biennale Foundation (ed.), *Gwangju Biennale 2006 - Fever Variations I*, exhib. cat., Designhouse, Seoul, 2006, p. 11.

truly world-class biennial is strongly localist and regionalist: due to its locally-bound unique identity and dynamics, "Gwangju aspires to be a geospatial metaphor for the development and transformation of Asia."[16] The usage of the term "metaphor" is more than meaningful in this context, since it hints at the explicitly nonessentialist search for a new Asian identity. Asia is defined as an abstract space and purely traveling concept that refuses to be bound to geographical borders and fixed identities, which the following quote from the artistic director exemplifies:

> "We can build a new image of Asia where transformation and migration become the reality, and the dynamics of fluidity rule the region. [...] Asian fantasy advocating migration, fluidity, transformation and dynamism manifests itself in Asian identities and the order of regional community in the face of world-wide globalization."[17]

The new image of Asia lies in the imagination of Asia. This is evidenced by the strong desire to create new urban spaces, the obsession to build a new (modern and global) Asia - which also includes, as demonstrated, the unlimited visionary projection of museum buildings as places to exhibit the new Asia. The exhibition structure of the Gwangju Biennale *Fever Variations* expresses this constructive, imaginative character of modern Asianness. It shows the two faces of Asia: the local and the cosmopolitan. The first exhibition chapter titled *Trace Root: Unfolding Asian Stories* looks at the roots of Asian identity in contemporary art. In a diachronic approach, it tracks the processes of Asian modernization and globalization and attempts to deconstruct the East-West dichotomy. The second exhibition chapter is homophonely titled *Trace Route*, but refers to the new ways of "Remapping Global Cities." Contrary to the first exhibition chapter, it adopts a synchronic approach of visualizing the Asia of continuous construction and migration, and examining the construction of new cities, urban cultures, and intercity networks. Especially with regard to the last point (the building of intercity-networks), the curators took an active role in geospatial and geocultural remapping by commissioning collaborative city networking projects all over the globe. The constructed networks entail 1. a European network connecting Berlin, Paris, Amsterdam, Rotterdam, Copenhagen, and Vilnius, 2. a network of East Asia, West Asia, central Balkan, and North America, linking Seoul, Gwangju, Shanghai, Tokyo, Manila, Belgrade, Beirut, New York, and Asia, and 3. a Latin American network connecting Buenos Aires, El Alto, La Paz, and Caracas. All of these world-wide (or should we say world-wild?) remappings of cultural routes between old and new, well-established and upcoming city centers of global cultural influence take place "in the image of Asia" as, once again, is a metaphor or traveling concept for the reconstruction and dynamic transformation of urban spaces, cultural places, and cityscapes. In its curatorial conceptualization, the first exhibition part, namely the show *Trace Root: Unfolding Asian Stories*, is of particular relevance to the topic of how Asia is exhibited in Korea and in which ways this affects the formation of Asian contemporary art and art history. Its chief curator Wu Hung eagerly put the most exigent and challenging questions on the exhibition agenda: "Is 'contemporary Asian art' a meaningful concept in art history and criticism? If so, then in what way(s) is this art both regional and contemporary? How is it related to global art at large?"[18] However, what Wu Hung is quite sure of is that contemporary Asian art is truly global art. For him, this identification is based on the fact that contemporary Asian art is "no longer confined to a single geographical sphere, nor is it defined by the artist's ethnicity."[19] It is exactly through de-territorializiation and de-essentialization that contemporary Asian art has become global. From that follows the fact that diasporic contemporary Asian art as well as conceptually "Asian" contemporary art produced by non-Asian artists that centrally deal with Asian themes, including philosophical traditions, religious ideas, and art practices, can be subsumed under the rubric "Asian contemporary art." But what Wu Hung is rather skeptical about is whether or not contemporary Asian art can (or should) prominently figure as meaningful concept in art history. Being aware of the fact that art history is a concept and discipline of Western coinage, he curatorially tries to circumvent it by suggesting a diachronic approach in presenting contemporary Asian art. In his view, this approach "differs fundamentally from the 'evolutionary approach' of art forms and styles, which characterizes the conventional master narrative of contemporary art based on a western model," in that it "deliberately abandon[s] the 'standard' structure and elements of the this narrative, such as chronology, stylistic evolution, and genealogy of artists and schools."[20] "Instead of producing a 'counter narrative' of the prevailing chronicle of modern and contemporary art," the new Asian diachronics is thought to "open up new spaces of historical imagination."[21] This is reflected in the

16 **Ibid.**
17 **Ibid.**, p. 12.

18 **Wu Hung**, "Contemporary Asian Art as Global Art: A 'Diachronic Approach,' in: Presenting Contemporary Art," in: Gwangju Biennale Foundation 2006, p. 21.
19 **Ibid.**
20 **Ibid.**
21 **Ibid.**, p. 27.

four themes of the subsections that make up the tracing of Asian roots of contemporary art: 1. Myth and Fantasy, 2. Nature and Body, 3. Trace of Mind, 4. Past in Present. Since Asian contemporary art cannot be "inserted into the existing history of modern and contemporary" art due to its specific context and timing, the idea of a consistent Asian art history is replaced by the bricolage of Asian art stories, fostering a fictionalization and imagination-based presentation of Asian art that produces Asianism in art. In my view, this resistance towards an art-historical metanarrative is not only characteristic for the representation of Asian contemporary art, as is suggested by Wu Hung. Does the seeming impossibility and impracticality to integrate Asian contemporary art into the existing history of modern and contemporary art not hold true in general for all contemporary art as global art?

Is it not exactly this aspect and category of global contemporaneity that obviates art history as historical narrative and chrono-logical historiography? In this respect, postmodernity with its declaration of the end of all metanarratives can be seen as a prelude of globality tantamount to contemporaneousness. The actual discussions on whether the traditional concept of art history is still applicable to the new conditions of global contemporary art together with new space-oriented approaches to analyze and represent visual art in a global perspective indicate that also in the West, art history is to be found in a legitimation crisis. What then would make the specificity of Asian contemporary art? Asian concepts and paradigms? The fictional and futuristic projection of Asia? If the Asian art discourse, as led primarily by curators and critics, is driven towards Asianization as a countermodel to Westernization, the thereby produced new Asianism apparently comes dangerously close to Orientalism. To avoid this, a new inter-Asian discourse on art is needed, more carefully analyzing the regional differences in Asian art. For stressing this perspective, I would like to close with a statement by Kim Hong-hee, the artistic director of the 6th Gwangju Biennale: "[G]lobalism must start from an exploration of roots in order to gain greater authenticity. However, lest the return to roots end up as mere exoticism and colonial Orientalism, a new discourse that analyzes the differences among Asian states with the concept of ambivalence is required."[22] As globalism grows strong from localism, so should the investigation of contemporary Asian art as global art start from regional studies of art and culture. This orientation would considerably contribute to grounding the often high-flying image of Asia not only in materialized museum architecture.

A first version of the essay was presented at the conference "In the Image of Asia: Moving across and between locations," in Canberra, Australia, hosted by the Humanities Research Centre, the Research School of Humanities and the Arts (RSHA), and the Australian National University, April 13–15, 2010.

22 **Ibid.**, p. 17.

Performing Identities in the Arena of the Global Art World: Nástio Mosquito

Antonia Marten

In the course of the relatively recent phase of economic and cultural globalization, the map of the international art world has also been fundamentally redrawn in the past few years. Whereas in the 1980s the white cube was still considered a Western derivative and a synonym for exclusion,[1] today the decentralization and pluralization of the global art world seem to have almost completely dissolved the old hegemonic claim of the Western center vis-à-vis the former colonial peripheries - and by extension an asymmetrical relationship between curating and curated cultures.[2] In the meantime, numerous protagonists, platforms, and institutions from all corners of the globe have taken the international art stage and help to define the latest artistic trends, academic discourse, and markets, which for their part have also pluralized and changed. The Internet-induced democratization of communication and associated global networking of players have also contributed to this development.

Despite the worldwide dissemination of biennials, institutions, and markets that relate the local to the global and focus the gaze of a potentially multivoiced and polycentric (art) world on formerly peripheral locations, our attention is repeatedly drawn to the "ultra-stability of center-periphery models in the field of art."[3] Thus artists from the former peripheral areas are still facing obstacles in the form of strict visa regulations, inadequate institutional infrastructure, restrictive political regimes, or economic stagnation, all of which hamper their entering the art world. For artists from African countries in particular, an education in the USA or Europe and life in the diaspora remain decisive factors in actual participation and artistic success. By contrast, having a professional international career based in the African continent today still seems to be bound up with major difficulties. The critical discourse such as is to be found in cultural und postcolonial studies has long since found its way into the art context. Yet the question arises as to whether and to what extent strategies of inclusion and exclusion,[4] or rather discourses on cultural identity and difference in the presentation and reception of "global art"[5] today are actually completely undermined. With regard to the relationship between the dominant culture of the Western metropolis and its postcolonial minorities, artist and art scholar Olu Oguibe spoke back at the dawn of the new millennium of a "culture game," which the postcolonial artist has to play to pass the "test of difference" before being "officially" accepted by the art world.[6] Although today, in times of global networking and the worldwide availability of images,

1 **See: Peter Weibel**, "Jenseits des weißen Würfels - Kunst zwischen Kolonialismus und Kosmopolitismus," in: Peter Weibel (ed.), *Inklusion/Exklusion: Versuch einer neuen Kartografie der Kunst im Zeitalter von Postkolonialismus und globaler Migration*, exhib. cat., steirischer herbst, Graz, DuMont, Cologne, 1997, p. 11.

2 **See: Gerardo Mosquera**, "Some Problems in Transcultural Curating," in: Jean Fisher, *Global Visions: Towards a New Internationalism in the Visual Arts*, Kala Press, London, 1994, pp. 133ff.

3 **Ulf Wuggenig**, "Fictions, Myths and Realities. Centers, Peripheries, and Art," in: Fernando Alvim, Heike Munder, and Ulf Wuggenig (eds.), *Next Flag. The African Sniper Reader*, jrp ringier, Zurich, 2005, p. 41.

4 **See: Weibel 1997**, p. 11.

5 **See: Hans Belting**, "Contemporary Art as Global Art: A Critical Estimate," in: Hans Belting and Andrea Buddensieg (eds.), *The Global Art World. Audiences, Markets, and Museums*, Hatje Cantz, Ostfildern, 2009, pp. 38-73. (For a definition see Belting, note [12].)

6 **See: Olu Oguibe**, "'Double Dutch' and the Culture Game," in: Olu Oguibe, *The Culture Game*, University of Minnesota Press, Minneapolis (MN), 2004, p. 34.

information, and new technologies, it is highly likely that traditional forms of expression are no longer expected of these artists in terms of their cultural localizability, certain thematic and contextual approaches (which allow a definite attribution of their work), are no doubt advantageous as regards acceptance within the art world. Victor Tupitsyn identifies in this context an adoption and therefore de-radicalization of postcolonial ideas by discourse: "The reason why postcolonial discourse has lost its radicalism is because it has been recolonized by the academic milieu. In the West, in addition to the orientalism of admirers of art, the orientalism of curators for whom non-European culture and non-Western art are distinguished only through an ethnographic lens, [...] academic consciousness is no less clichéd than mass consciousness."[7]

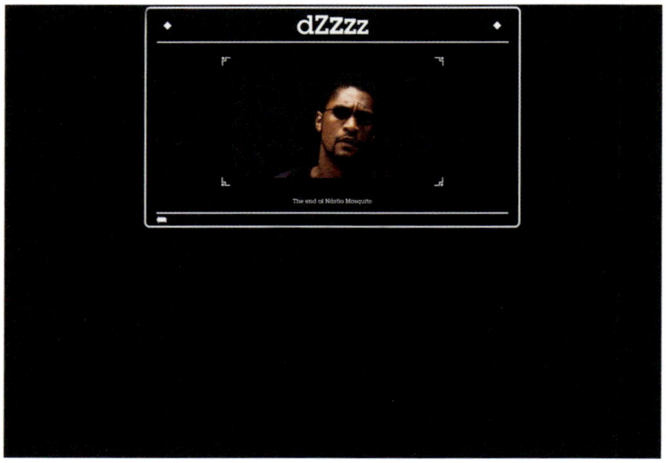

Nástio Mosquito, *The End of Nástio Mosquito*, video still

The stubbornness of cultural clichés and the perception of "non-Western" art through an ethnographic lens are reflected in international exhibition practices to this day. In the past decade, for instance, among other things contemporary art from Africa was frequently still bundled together in extensive "group highlights" and presented under catchy titles in the form of regional or continental case studies. In this context the first African pavilion (the only continental pavilion) at the 52nd Venice Biennale (2007) gave rise to much discussion and criticism as a homogenizing spectacle. Entitled *Check List - Luanda Pop*, it presented contemporary positions from a single collection.[8] Given the homogenizing method of presenting "African art" as practiced here and its preferred reception through political channels or discourses on cultural theory and identity politics, Anthony Downey calls for an expanded perception of these works, particularly on an aesthetic level: "[...] whilst the West can afford the luxury of contingent identities, African artists are compelled to wear, if not the fixity, then the fixture of their national, political, social, and artistic identities on their sleeves. [...] rather than reading African Art through the prism of the political, we [...] need to appeal to an expanded sense of the aesthetics in these works, one that is ultimately responsive - but neither reducible nor answerable - to sociopolitical, historical, and cultural concerns."[9]

Today people on all sides are highlighting the urgent need to acknowledge producers of art from the aforementioned regions as true contemporaries within the international art world and thus renounce the simplifying categorizations people still fall back on when classifying these positions: "People must begin to show confidence in the ability of individual African artists to stand shoulder to shoulder with their peers on the global stage."[10]

And indeed, a new, globally networked generation of artists is proclaiming "[...] 'contemporaneity' as an ambition, albeit a utopian one, to oppose every form of exclusion and to demand copresence in a worldwide *koine* of current art that has long been refused them."[11] Unlike modern art, which was shaped by belief in progress and a Western feeling of superiority, Hans Belting says of global art that "it is by definition contemporary, not just in a chronological but also [...] in a symbolic or even ideological sense."[12]

It is increasingly the case today that contemporary art takes the conditions of its own production and reception as its main theme. For many artists who contribute to the international exhibition circus as global players, their first concern is to analyze precisely this complex web of interrelationships between the protagonists, platforms, and institutions of the globally networked art world as well as the contexts and dynamics of the globalized world in general. Particularly for artists who enter this arena from the former peripheries, the question arises as to which strategies they can conceive given the external expectations placed on their geographical, political, or cultural provenance, and

7 **Victor Tupitsyn**, "Notes on Globalization. The Work of Art in the Age of Shoe-Throwing," in: *Third Text*, 100, vol. 23, no. 5, September 2009, p. 523.

8 **The Sindika Dokolo African Collection of Contemporary Art** was founded in 2004 by Congolese businessman Sindika Dokolo and Angolan artist Fernando Alvim in Luanda, Angola. The collection includes the collection of art collector and shoe manufacturer Hans Bogatzke, which Sindika Dokolo bought in 2005. See also: www.fondation-sindikadokolo.com, accessed 07/12/2012.

9 **Anthony Downey**, "Belatedness All Over Again. The African Pavilion at the 52nd Venice Biennial," in: *Third Text*, 89, vol. 21, no. 6, November 2007, p. 782.

10 **Martin Herbert**, "Olu Oguibe in conversation with Martin Herbert," available online at: www.camwood.org/oguibe_venice.html, accessed 07/12/2012.

11 **Hans Belting and Andrea Buddensieg**, "Introduction," in: *The Global Contemporary. Art Worlds after 1989*, exhib. brochure, ZKM | Center for Art and Media Karlsruhe, 2011, p. 7.

12 **Belting**, "Contemporary Art," p. 39.

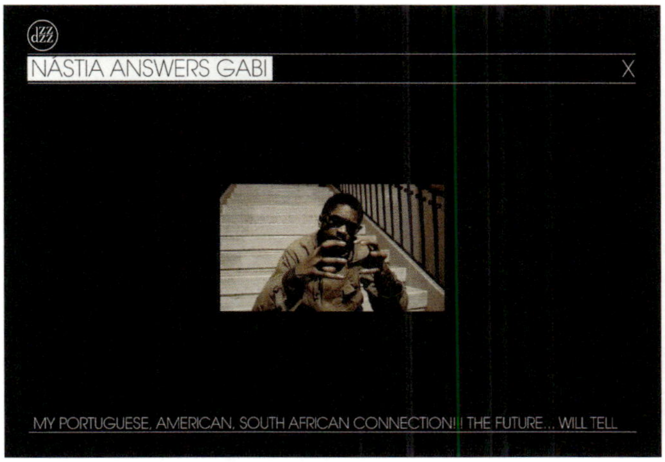

Nástio Mosquito, *Nástia Answers Gabi*, video still

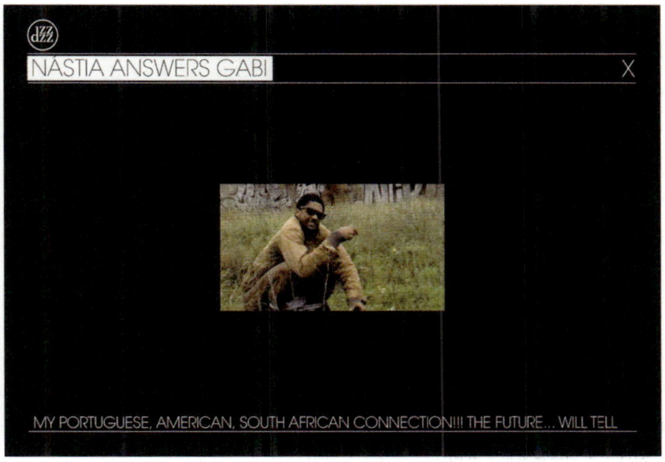

Nástio Mosquito, *Nástia Answers Gabi*, video still

which role(s) they can assume within this complex structure to exist in it and be acknowledged as a truly global player. How, as contemporaries and world citizens, do they approach the field of tension between cultural ascriptions and the universalistic discourses of global capitalism? How can they work in a contextual framework (be it geographical, political, or cultural) and at the same time lay claim to global contemporaneity?

"Hello, I'm here to tell you that Nástio Mosquito is dead."[13] These are the words the Angolan artist Nástio Mosquito puts in the mouth of his alter ego Nástia as he steps onto the stage in the video work *The End of Nástio Mosquito* (2008): Nástia, speaking with an exaggerated Russian accent, announces the passing of the artist, from whose "outdated" position he deliberately distances himself. While he finds Nástio's work lacking in aesthetic openness and too "ugly" and "African" despite the quality of its content, Nástia presents himself as an ironic, hypocritical and enthusiastic representative of a globalized media culture:

> "It is time to embrace good equipment, to look good [...], to emerge from the underground. I want to be mainstream!"[14]

With his multimedia approach, Nástio Mosquito works in the fields of music, performance, the spoken word, photography, film, television, and video. Blending entertainment and performance, the artist, who was born in 1981 in Huambo (Angola) and works in Luanda, Barcelona, and Lisbon, comments on the current globalized life. He especially focuses on questions of identity, the effects of imperialism, postcolonialism, war (particularly the Cold War), and migration. Moreover, he repeatedly examines the international art world with its inherent codes and dependencies and in particular its relationship to artists and cultural practitioners from the former peripheries. Mosquito always takes the stage himself in his video works and performances and by means of his own physical presence - his voice, body, and language as well as the precise use of sound and images - incessantly seeks to directly address and confront the audience. By using numerous pseudonyms for his work as an artist and musician (dZzzz, Gavião, Fly, The Night Fly, Saco, Nasty-O, Cucumber Slice, Zura, Zurara, Dzzzzura) and repeatedly assuming different, contradictory, and provocative roles on the narrative level of his videos too, Mosquito elicits in the observer a profound uncertainty as to which/whose perspective the artist is actually talking from.

In the video work *Nástia Answers Gabi* (2009) Mosquito uses a format that is currently highly widespread in the art context, the "artist talk." However, this is not a recording of a real meeting between two people. Rather, it shows Nástia alone in various places in Luanda; the questions of South African curator Gabi Ngcobo are simply faded in on a black background like title cards in a silent movie. The physical absence of the curator creates a confusing situation from the start - Nástia's "counterpart," located in the undefined off-screen space of a globalized art world, remains intangible.

With her questions, Gabi routinely probes Nástia's position on topics such as justice, territory, the Angolan/African context, post- and neocolonialism, development, and the relationship between artist and curator. Nástia answers at times with steely cynicism, at others in all seriousness - although the serious tone is constantly disrupted by confusing visual or plot elements. The highlight in this context

13 **Nástio Mosquito**, *The End of Nástio Mosquito*, 2008, video, 6:54 min, courtesy Nástio Mosquito and We Are Here! Films. Available online at: www.dzzzz.info/dzzzz/, accessed 07/24/2012.

14 **Ibid.**

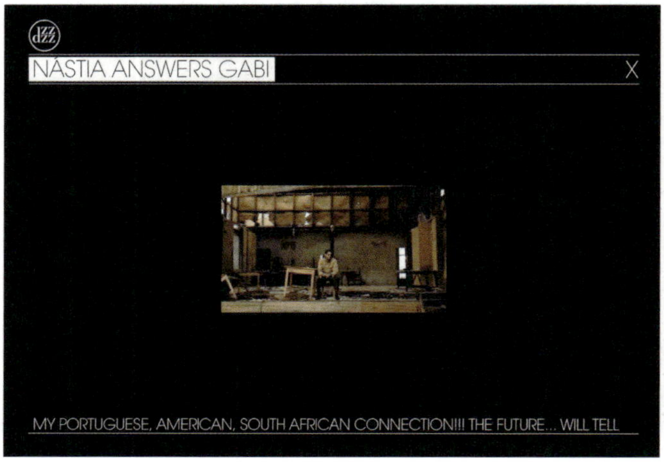

Nástio Mosquito, *Nástia Answers Gabi*, video still

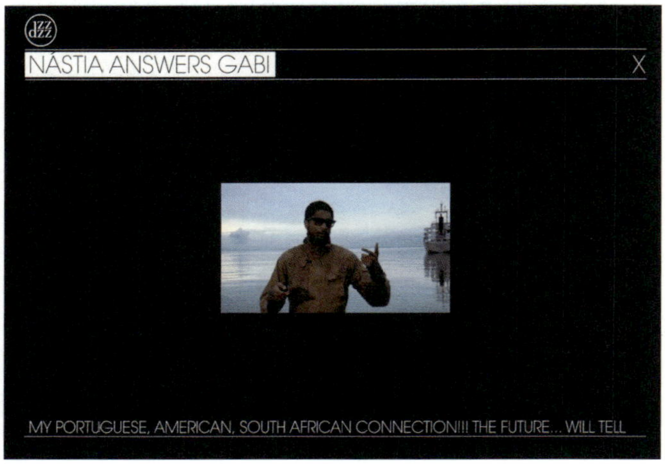

Nástio Mosquito, *Nástia Answers Gabi*, video still

is presumably the sequence in which Nástia talks about justice while squatting and defecating under a freeway bridge and then asks for toilet paper.

Nástia also makes contradictory statements regarding context (Luanda/Angola/Africa). On the one hand he appears to completely reject cultural classifications ("fuck context," "fuck Africa"). On the other, he admits that it is virtually impossible to distance yourself entirely from national or territorial categories. This determinacy is also evident on the visual level of the video, with Nástia appearing in profane and yet characteristic locations and as such being associated, as it were, with Angola's past and present - be it in a destroyed school building, under a freeway bridge, in a secluded part of the Luanda docks, or behind the wheel of a polished Volkswagen sedan. The chosen scenarios are certainly not purely arbitrary backdrops; rather, as placeholders for the current and historical social background, they reference the condition of Angola today which, traumatized by wars and under the influence of neocolonialism and failed international development aid policies, is caught between structural chaos, hopeful rebirth, and economic upswing.

Nástia's "ironic and hypocritical"[15] attitude can also be interpreted in the context of the more recent history of a country where the War of Independence (1961-1974/75) was followed by a long civil war (1975-2002) in which the various sides entered into shifting alliances with the rival superpowers on both sides of the Iron Curtain. Despite the subsequent establishment of a presidential republic, the wars left marks on Angola that are still felt today. The deep distrust felt by Mosquito's generation towards revolutionary or ideologically tinged rhetoric must also be seen in this

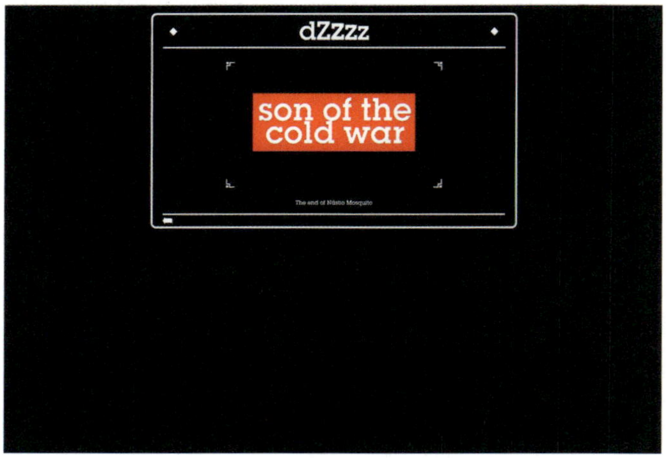

Nástio Mosquito, *The End of Nástio Mosquito*, video still

historical and political context. In contrast, a pragmatic and flexible approach to various substantive positions and identities seems to be a recommendable strategy for many in order to hold their own in the present.

By describing himself as "a son of the Cold War,"[16] Nástio Mosquito alias Nástia positions himself in the middle of his country's history, yet without fostering the prevailing, one-sided and prefabricated perspectives on the African continent. At all times Nástia shows his indifference or even snideness towards all too sentimental "African" sensibilities - he feels part of Africa just as much as Russia or global capitalism - and as such reveals himself to be truly contemporary.

Yet precisely in those moments when Nástia's hard-nosed superficiality seems to have reached its zenith, Mos-

15 **Nástio Mosquito**, *Nástia's Manifesto*, 2008-2009, video, 4:10 min, courtesy Nástio Mosquito and We Are Here! Films. Available online at: www.dzzzz.info/dzzzz/, accessed 07/24/2012.

16 **Nástio Mosquito**, *Nástia Answers Gabi*, 2009, video, 19:50 min, courtesy Nástio Mosquito and We Are Here! Films. Available online at: www.dzzzz.info/nastio.swf/, accessed 07/24/2012.

quito breaks through the ironic stance of his alter ego and the latter's distanced attitude to substantive concerns by taking a stand. His messages regarding overcoming one-sided dependencies and perspectives still dominated by the West on a backward-looking, crisis-ridden Africa and the need to look forward are directed both externally and internally:

> "I am very sorry that people in Africa have suffered and we had terrible wars and all that but fuck you it's time to go to work. I'm sorry, there's no other kind of solution. Go to work!"[17]

In the video work *My African Mind* (2010), for example, Mosquito makes use of all kinds of archive materials from African history to confront the biased perspective of the colonial powers with his own. By critically observing history and its one-dimensional narrative, the artist refers to the necessity of another kind of storytelling beyond the hegemonic strategies of the modern West and to the urgent need to develop autonomous perspectives.

He calls on contemporary African artists in particular (again in the role of Nástia) to renounce their safe retreat into theory and show more commitment in terms of actually developing their own, independent positions:

> "I'm sick of artists developing concepts, talking about concepts. Fuck concepts! I would like to see a bit more of life. I would like to see a little bit more forward perspective, especially from African artists, because they are close to me."[18]

In many of his projects Mosquito also addresses the complicated relationship between the "non-Western" artist and the international art world. Likewise in the video *Nástia Answers Gabi*, he explores in the role of Nástia the stereotypical ideas and clichés he perceives to still, and repeatedly, face as a cultural practitioner from Angola despite the increasing opening up of the art system into the global field:

> "People like you are very difficult to deal with because you try to encapsulate myself in a specific territory you know, be it physical or ideological or intellectual or philosophical or all this bullshit. I do not know, I am just doing my thing, improving at getting better and better and better at what I do. I need money actually."[19]

Nástia's demonstrative snideness as he answers the questions and the confusing distance resulting from the breaks between content and form overlay Mosquito's stubborn refusal to be labeled as an "African" or "African artist" and categorized in terms of discourses on identity politics, postcolonialism, or other (curatorial) topics. Other of his works attest to his deep distrust of theory and claims to knowledge, which in the colonial past all too often led to one-sided historical narratives. Moreover, he remains skeptical of the neocolonial continuation of old discourses in the guise of postcolonialism.

Thus one element of the artist's performance work is a continual exploration and renegotiation of how to work as a contemporary Angolan/African/global artist within the art world, and how to create an independent position for oneself without falling into the identity trap or being suspected of universalism:

> "I'm an Angolan artist, the only thing is that I don't produce Angolan art – I produce art. That is all. I think it is a big mistake to try to define Angola in a way. I am not interested in defining identity. I am interested in asking questions."[20]

In the role of Nástia he puts the dependencies within the art system in a nutshell as follows:

> "I love to fuck curators. I mean, I would like to fuck curators. And not really to get somewhere with my shitty work. I would just like to know how to do it."[21]

Finally with his piece *Nástia's Manifesto* (2008-2009) Mosquito presents a set of "guidelines," formulated by Nástia as his artistic manifesto and which promises success in the art world:

> "[...] 3. Outcome. Enjoy the process but you better deliver. 4. Love your experiments, specially if you get paid. Need a fucking drawing? [...] 10. Don't be cool, be relevant. Yeap! And if you can be relevantly cool, that is very good for you. 11. Collaborate. Not because you have to share the bill but because you'll grow taller with it. 12. Repeat yourself. Advice. Shut the fuck up... 13. Fuck original, be genuine. [...] 16. Get paid big money (even if you suck). Fuck winning, love earning. [...]"[22]

---

17 **Nástio Mosquito**, *dZzzz*, script for the eponymous audiovisual performance, courtesy Nástio Mosquito and We Are Here! Films, 2009, p. 12.

18 **Mosquito**, *The End of Nástio Mosquito*.

19 **Mosquito**, *Nástia Answers Gabi*.

20 **"Angola – The Moment of Truth,"** in: *CNBC Business*, Sept. 2011, available online at: www.cnbcmagazine.com/story/angola-the-moment-of-truth/1515/6/, accessed 07/12/2012.

21 **Mosquito**, *Nástia Answers Gabi*.

22 **Mosquito**, *Nástia's Manifesto*.

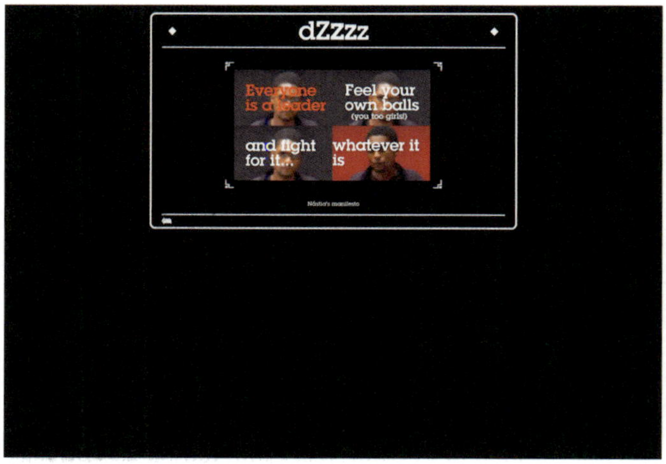

Nástio Mosquito, *Nastia's Manifesto*, video still

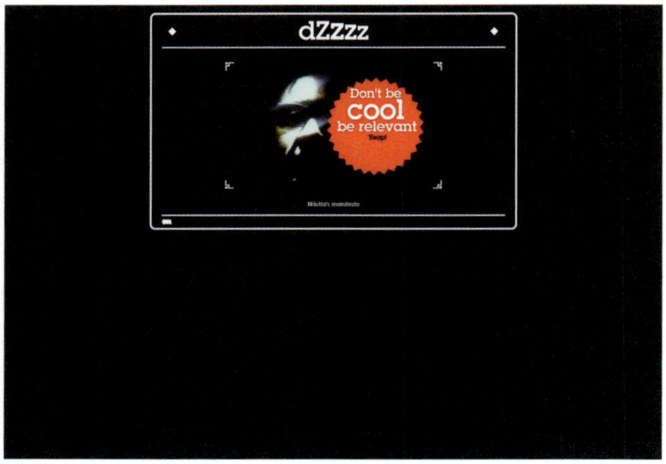

Nástio Mosquito, *Nastia's Manifesto*, video still

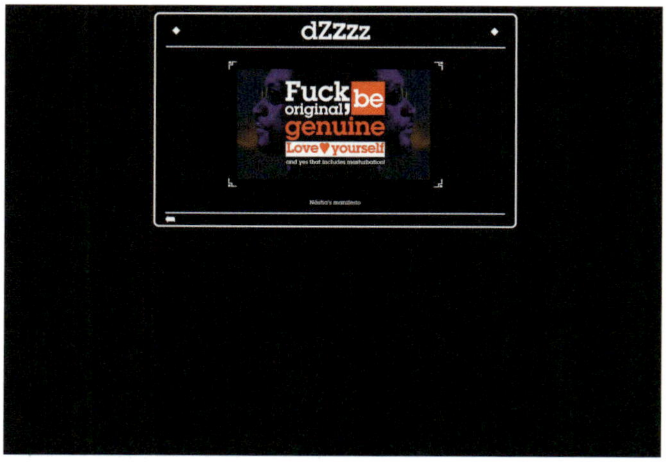

Nástio Mosquito, *Nastia's Manifesto*, video still

This piece again attests to a thoroughly realistic approximation of the sometimes harsh conditions on the international art market; Nástia takes a pragmatic approach to the contradictions, ambiguities, and ironies of the business. And yet on another level the manifesto also contains Mosquito's artistic strategies and principles. We see that, among other things, authenticity, criticism, relevance of content, artistic productivity, collaboration with various (international) partners, networking, transdisciplinarity, and openness towards new technologies are fundamental parameters of his artistic work. Yet the artist by no means closes himself off to the requirements and strategies of a (commercial) globalized media culture. On the contrary, in the past few years Mosquito has created with his collaborator Vic Pereiró an operating system based on "i" culture and new media that he successfully uses to disseminate his artistic "products" around the globe.

By establishing, among other things, various contradictory figures and clichéd roles (e.g., the African, the Angolan diaspora artist, the political activist, the migrant, the free individual and world citizen, the international real-estate shark, the representative of globalized capitalism, the superficial technology fetishist, the aid worker, etc.) the artist ensures himself the freedom to adopt seemingly irreconcilable positions. As such, a critical stance towards the continuation of (neo)colonial strategies under the mantle of postcolonialism and globalization no longer excludes the use of globalized media technologies and the potentially accompanying commercial success. Michael Hardt and Antonio Negri also argue with regard to their concept of "empire" that nothing exists any longer outside the world market. As such, resistance and criticism can only occur when the means of the empire itself are directed against it.[23] Nonetheless Mosquito repeatedly deliberately violates the technical perfectionism he propagates especially through the figure of Nástia by, for instance, playing with the specific use of visual and acoustic disturbance, seemingly amateur camerawork or a supposedly "low-fi" method of production.

In view of a current art world that likes to (primarily superficially) practise postcolonial discourse and at the same time in large part functions according to the laws of the market, artists from the former peripheral regions still seem to be reliant on conscious strategies concerning their own positioning within this arena. Delinda Collier analyzes Mosquito's use of artistic identities as follows: "Nástio and Nástia are the bookends of what Mosquito presents as the range of possibilities for the contemporary African artist within the art market: the earnest fantasy image of the 'real' African or the cynical hyperrealist image of a virtual

23 See: Michael Hardt and Antonio Negri, *Empire*, Harvard University Press Cambridge (MA), 2000, p. 190.

African. To operate in a space that is so incongruous, even just on the level of the visual, is to become a split subject."[24]

If Homi K. Bhabha defines personal identity as a continuously effective, unconscious process containing internal differences,[25] it follows that every fixed, uniform identity takes on something fantasized, imaginary. It is owing to internal differences that the "split" personality is able to feature in diverse contradictory spaces and discourses. Precisely by formulating his roles and artistic identities as contradictory extremes based on (cultural) clichés and decals, Mosquito repeatedly succeeds in evading definitive discursive pigeonholing.

By means of introducing his alter ego, who fundamentally questions his own artistic agenda, as well as Nástio's stubborn refusal to actually die (for despite multiple announcements of his death the artist tirelessly reappears: "[...] unfortunately I am inside this body and that's a relationship you cannot run away from [...]") Mosquito creates an ambivalent distance from which he questions and reinvents his (artistic) subjectivity time and again. This is where Gabi Ngcobo sees the artist positioned, in an intermediate space that enables him to assume a number of contradictory roles and positions, from whose perspective he interprets the complex, globalized present: "The performance of his own 'murder' places him in a precarious zone of being and non-being, unfixed yet fixed, a zone that highlights his practice as operating within an intermediate position. Within this position he plays both victim and perpetrator by applying metaphors, narratives, and other interpretive linguistic modes, using them to help us make sense of the world around us."[26]

When he elevates the development of his figures and artistic subjectivities to the agenda of his work as a whole, the dividing line between Mosquito as a person and his work also turns out to be confusingly permeable. And indeed, at no time does the artist actually seem to be where we presume him to be. While his audience and critics are still busy following and categorizing Nástia's statements, Mosquito uses this "lead" to strike out once again as a razor-sharp analyst and commentator of the globalized present. By incessantly "throwing out" bait in the form of (cultural) stereotypes, which are immediately broken down again and disintegrate, Mosquito proves at all times to be a brilliant player of the "culture game" and as such a contemporary through and through. In the same breath he puts his counterpart in the uncomfortable situation of having to fundamentally question his own knowledge, his own position which he thought to be safe, and ultimately give both of them up: "I am here to question the information you have. [...] What are you going to do with your education?"[27]

Translated from the German by Jeremy Gaines.

24 **Delinda Collier**, "'All I am is a Son of the Cold War': Nástio Mosquito's Embedded Videos," in: *Art South Africa*, Fall 2011, pp. 32–33.

25 **See: Homi K. Bhabha**, *The Location of Culture*, Routledge, London, New York (NY), 1999, pp. 40–65.

26 **Gabi Ngcobo**, "Nástio Mosquito. DZzzz and Other Related Projects - Part I," in: Angelika Burtscher and Judith Wielander (eds.), *Visible. Where Art Leaves Its own Field and Becomes Visible as Part of Something Else*, Sternberg Press, Berlin, 2010, p. 74.

27 **Mosquito**, *Nástia Answers Gabi*.

Capture the Flag.
Contemporaneity as an Artistic Project

Jacob Birken

"The long list of participants that appears at the end of a film, as the viewers gradually begin to leave their seats and make their way to the exit, manifests the fate of authorship in our age, something the art system cannot escape."
Boris Groys, "Multiple Authorship"

"[We] will host a Simultaneous World Dance Party, transmitted to everyone in the world at the same time. It will be fun. You are invited."
Decentralized Dance Party Manifesto

To Whom It May Concern

If artistic movements were predicated on syntactic models then contemporary art would presumably orient itself on the subject lines of e-mail headers; on statements prefaced by abbreviations such as "RE" and "FWD" which make it perfectly clear that they are not only a direct reference to another statement, but as messages they are seeking an addressee. In many respects contemporary art is an art of "RE," of "Regarding..." and "In reference to...". Concepts that were relevant to Romanticism and modernism like authenticity and autonomy are only interesting to the extent that as socially constructed categories they may themselves become an issue, but when it comes to defining the term "art" itself they are becoming less and less useful. Wolfgang Ullrich writes that given the dwindling legitimacy of art for art's sake, "a fundamental criterion of art will be if a discussion centering on a work can develop in which the issue of whether the work constitutes art or not plays no role at all."[1] Obviously, rejecting art (and authorship) that legitimates itself as an autopoietic creation or genealogically from the history of art, and instead embracing artistic projects as a starting point for possible discussions lend this a new sociopolitical dimension: the work relates to something, which relates to *us* - or at least might do if we commit to exploring it.

It follows that art understood in this way leads to specific strategies and a system that supports them. Today, art theories like Relational aesthetics which refer explicitly to the social context, are accompanied by very pragmatic practices of networking through international fellowship programs and workshops. Furthermore they correspond to questions affecting the whole of society: the economic and political imbroglios of authorship concepts, knowledge as property, and collective practices. It is hardly surprising that forms of contemporary art have been quick to emerge in which the creation of a circle of "persons affected" has become paramount and thus a *formal* technique. Probably the most well-known example of this is Rirkrit Tiravanija's cooking-as-art events in the 1990s, which were intended to transform the exhibition space into an explicitly *social* space by catering to the guests. This emphasis on interpersonal relationships in space and time constituted both the form and the goal of the project. Admittedly, the social effect was rather homeopathic since, as Claire Bishop remarked,

1 **Wolfgang Ullrich**, *Gesucht: Kunst! Phantombild eines Jokers*, Wagenbach, Berlin, 2007, p. 64; translated from the German by the author.

the art audience that came together did not have any grave social differences that needed to be overcome by eating together. The harmonious dialog of those present was already a given: "[T]he structure of [Tiravanija's] work circumscribes the outcome in advance, and relies on its presence within a gallery to differentiate it from entertainment."[2]

And in point of fact, a project like *Decentralized Dance Party* (DDP) by the Canadian duo Tom and Gary raises more questions about performative inclusion and harmonious formation of community, given that it involves everyone becoming part of a constantly expanding mobile disco who tune into the right shortwave frequency on a cassette radio player they have brought along. The DJ, who offers his mix here via a similarly mobile transmitter, may still be the choreograph and author in the broadest sense because he selects the music; however, he relies on the "guests" being there, for without them he would not only not be *heard*, but would de facto not be *audible*. True, the DDP does not take place in connection with one of the art biennials or in the white cube, but these are the only factors that distinguish it, structurally at least, from Relational aesthetics projects.

Although such practices - whether they are within or outside the established art system - have their own justification in that they at least form a transient community, which is at the same time an aesthetic project, this hardly exhausts discussion of art that *affects*. *Being affected* as a concern or being exposed to something reveals a network of relationships that is not so much a harmonious system as one showing *solidarity*. This needs to be discussed against the background of a contemporary art whose contemporary nature is not only understood as constituting an epoch, but also as political.

> "'Contemporaneity' for us means that in the contemporary moment there is a certain number of shared issues and urgencies, a certain critical currency but perhaps most importantly a performative enablement [...] 'Contemporaneity' means that there is a conjunction of problems, insights, methods and materials or practices, which meet momentarily and then fall away again."[3]

Irit Rogoff's definition describes very well the range of contemporaneity, which is expressed both in the *focus* on common issues and in an *increasing openness* regarding the methods used to address these issues. Put simply, contemporaneity means the insight that we are all joined together in a moment and for that moment need to find the right way to approach this insight. The most important knowledge to come out of this (and it is also the knowledge that *ex negativo* leads to the formation of this community in the first place) is that the underlying insight of being contemporary is not shared by everyone, that certain players withdraw from joint responsibility and exclude their functions in the community from dialectic access. In this sense, a fundamental practice within contemporary art is that of attacking its own structures which restrict its contemporaneity - for example, authorship as a power position. In his essay "Multiple Authorship" Boris Groys notes that art today can hardly be ascribed to singular authorship anymore. Complex projects such as installations or videos involve the creativity of numerous persons and are also influenced by external factors that impact on the circumstances of their production - in other words the venue, its architecture, and so on.[4] Moreover, the transient structure of many projects makes it necessary for them to be lent an enduring quality by being documented; producing this documentation again multiplies the number of people involved, as does every subsequent exhibition of this documentation - and its documentation in the guise of catalogs, archives, and reviews. This chain of persons involved in the art project, which can potentially be continued ad infinitum, corresponds to a deconstructivist model of justice under which no *single* person can be held responsible, and *everyone* must at least to a certain extent accept responsibility. In other words "authorship" no longer means empowerment, but rather the potential of being addressed - so to speak the prospect of supplying the *response* as implied in the term responsibility. The spread of multiple authorship can itself become an artistic practice, which then poses the question as to responsibility within a project - and by extension the question as to contemporaneity per se, even if this is only relevant for the duration of the art project.

Knitting as Entanglement

Besides paradigmatic practices, large-scale historical projects (and we want to see contemporary art as such, albeit historical in terms of aspiration and not of closure) also present their own language games; in some cases both aspects can be derived from each other. Several e-mails - to return to our initial metaphor - produce a thread, and we

2 **See: Claire Bishop**, "Antagonism and Relational Aesthetics," in: *OCTOBER*, no. 110, Fall 2004, pp. 51-79.

3 **Irit Rogoff**, "Academy as Potentiality," in: Angelika Nollert, Irit Rogoff, et al. (eds.), *A.C.A.D.E.M.Y*, Revolver, Frankfurt am Main, 2006.

4 **See: Boris Groys**, "Multiple Authorship," in: Barbara Vanderlinden and Elena Filipovic (eds.), *The Manifesta Decade: Debates on Contemporary Exhibitions and Biennials*, The MIT Press, Cambridge (MA), 2006, pp. 93-99.

shall now follow it. In fact, for some time now it appears that textiles make an ideal key material. Fabrics are ubiquitous in art today as a manufacturing process and trope, whether as a photorealistic wall hanging in Kassel and Kabul, or a 55m-long woolen rabbit installed on a hill in Piedmont; finally, Rosemarie Trockel and Yinka Shonibare mark two of the most relevant emancipatory or postcolonially motivated positions, and one of the more original trends in the new millennium's street art is Yarn bombing, subversive urban knitting enveloping objects - masts, trees, trash cans - in the public space. In the course of the "material turn" this subcategory of the material both as a historical topos and a field of metaphors has also entered academic debate; in recent years we find a number of specialist art and cultural conferences with titles such as "Beziehungsreiche Gewebe" [Fabric rich in associations] (Gießen/Cologne, 2006), "Meta-textile" (Lausanne, 2009), "Intelligente Verbindungen" [Smart connections] (Krefeld, 2009), or "ArchiTextile" (Zurich, 2011), seeking to undertake a further historical and political contextualization of textile production.

Naturally, there is a certain amount of novelty involved; knitting and crocheting do not *currently* belong to the canon of cultural production techniques, meaning their transfer to the sacred space of the (counter)culture from the profane realm of darning socks can first and foremost be understood as a strategy for deriving more value: a continual cycle in which the renewal of the canon can be effected most efficiently by something that least corresponds with the canon itself - in other words by something lacking value, something alien, something that was previously deliberately ignored.[5] As in the case of Yarn bombing, this must not by any means happen in the museum - here the "street" is the prevailing institution as the place of subversive creativity, the place whose formal, topical, and technical canon is being addressed. Seen in purely structural terms, the relationship between a tree branch covered in colored yarn and a sprayer tag is like that between Trockel's knitted picture and an oil painting by a "master." Craftsmanship as a nonartistic practice or trash as material have already advanced so far in their canonization that they have in many cases, at least on a representational level, not only lost their novelty but also often their emancipatory gesture.[6] As such the project *12 Ballads for Huguenot House* (2012) by U.S. artist and urban planner Theaster Gates, in which an old dilapidated house in Kassel was restored for Documenta 13 as a collaborative project, probably comes across as an orchestration of what a middle-class audience today would probably consider a "nonconformist creative scene." When a visitor urges her companion to take a look at the "crazy lamp" in the next room, the aesthetic border between visiting a socially committed art project and strolling through a furniture store has finally been removed - despite the different economic and social functions of the two locations.

Although this derivation of artistic practices from the rise and fall of short-lived trends is indispensable as a critical method, the diverse craft (and/or artistic) techniques and materials nonetheless point to social associations, which for their part are most certainly to be understood as power relations and possibly exploitation and suppression - and thus are a problem for contemporary art, which must address them. In other words, when Rosemarie Trockel focuses on patterns of female roles in the art system in her knitted pictures, or Yinka Shonibare clothes figures from (colonial) European history and science fiction in "Africanized" textiles, then it is only superficially about producing a textile object, and the meaning of the statement "to produce a textile object" itself is of equal or even greater importance. As such, the production process itself becomes a reference to the sociopolitical and geopolitical circumstances connected with the object, and an occasion for discussing them. By resorting to a do-it-yourself practice even Yarn bombing expresses criticism of industrial society and its urban spaces that are felt to be unwelcoming even though, seen ideologically, this is only a slightly more radical version of traditional middle-class criticism of consumerism.

Performing an action, therefore, is at the same time a portrayal of the overall context, and as Nicolas Bourriaud rightly observes when discussing operational realism: "[w]hen Alighiero Boetti gets 500 weavers in Peshawar, Pakistan, working for him, he represents the work process of multinational companies much more effectively than if he merely portrayed them and described how they work."[7] Also very apt, however, is the abovementioned criticism that Claire Bishop makes of Bourriaud's entire theory; namely, that the Relational art he advocates, which arises from the entirety of human relationships in a certain situation - produced as an art project - fails to show antagonisms. Indeed, only through the latter can it ultimately develop true emancipatory potential and amount to more than just events to pamper members of the art scene.[8] Boetti's series of rugs (which admittedly Bourriaud does not explicitly describe as Relational art) only becomes relevant as a *con-*

5 See here: Boris Groys, *Über das Neue. Versuch einer Kulturökonomie*, Hanser, Munich, Vienna, 1992.

6 See: Ullrich 2007, pp. 19-46.

7 Nicolas Bourriaud, *Relational Aesthetics*, Les Presses du Réel, Dijon, 2002, p. 68.

8 See: Bishop 2004.

temporary project today when we consider it together with a series of photos that Randi Malkin Steinberger took of the women employed by Boetti, anonymous in the work context and hidden away from the men (including Boetti himself), and together with the laconic inquiries by Mexican artist Mario García Torres, who sought to investigate in a work series the whereabouts of Boetti's "One Hotel" in Kabul and was confronted by the question of what the artist - whether Boetti or his contemporary "doppelgänger" - was doing in Afghanistan:

> "Even contemplating the trip, though, forced me to ask myself whether art has to have any immediate consequences - whether it could have an impact in a place at war, like Afghanistan, and if so, what the artist's role could be in such a situation."[9]

Uncertain Ground

Contemporary art does not lend itself to promises of salvation; nonetheless, such operational realism in an art project can most certainly satisfy the sociopolitical aspiration of the contemporary. In the text from which the above definition of contemporaneity was taken, Irit Rogoff also talks about the genealogy of critical practice:

> "[...] we have moved from criticism, which is a form of finding fault and of exercising judgment according to a consensus of values, to critique, which is examining the underlying assumptions that might allow something to appear as a convincing logic, to criticality, which is operating from an uncertain ground of actual embededness [sic]."[10]

Being "embedded" is the representative and ontological status of all contemporaries. Initially borrowed from the sociology of work, in the age of "embedded journalism" (when journalists join active military units) the term has taken on a harzardous metaphoric meaning, which naturally entails acting from "uncertain ground." In a conception of the world in which at least from a certain distance we are all connected with everything and everyone (be it the hole in the ozone layer, the Afghanistan conflict, or Documenta 13) every critical statement we express will also affect our own position at some point or another. Institutional critique in the twentieth century still assumed a clear division between itself and the object of its criticism; as in Appropriation art, which is at least related to it as regards the critical stance, it would be possible here to talk of an overbidding strategy of the authorship of a certain situation (the exhibition room, the display, the reproduction). As such, the institutional, commercial art system only needed to formally recognize the artists' claim to authorship in order to swallow them; today, Richard Prince works for the fashion label Louis Vuitton and Jeff Koons recently felt his copyright had been violated by the distributer of book stands shaped like balloon dogs.[11] What is ultimately not a very fruitful division between "critical art" and its object is today prevented by the realization of always being at least to a certain extent caught up in the problematic structures - whether the objective is to emerge out of them or to become immersed in them in order to understand or disrupt their inner workings.

It is obvious that entanglement has itself become an artistic practice, and the artistic project an attempt, if you will, to bring people onto the uncertain ground of contemporaneity. A final example from the textile industry: in *Invisible Threads* (2008) Jeff Crouse and Stephanie Rothenberg transferred a sweatshop for making jeans to Second Life, the online 3-D world that promises us "infinite possibilities" and "a life without boundaries."[12] As in the neoliberal promise of an unlimited globalism, it is naturally not explicitly ruled out that exploitation is also one of the "endless possibilities," and the virtual "global village" of the World Wide Web really does morph here into a periphery in which the population slaves away for low local wages in the "Linden dollars" of this virtual world so that a small elite can buy the finished product fresh from the plotter for real dollars. Anyone who only sees this as a frivolous allegory of what actually goes on in the fashion industry should realize that in the meantime the internal economy of the online worlds is transferable to the real financial world in a manner not to be underestimated. In 2009 total proceeds from virtual labor was estimated at three billion dollars, and has already sparked ideas for utilizing this labor market as a development aid measure.[13] Apparently in Chinese labor camps, too, prisoners have already been forced to earn money virtually for their overseers: "There were 300

9 **Tom McDonough**, "Mario García Torres Talks about *Tea*," in: *Artforum*, summer 2012, available online at: http://www.artforum.com/inprint/issue=201206&id=31098&pagenum=2, accessed 07/12/2012.

10 **Rogoff 2006.**

11 **See: Sam Whiting**, "Jeff Koons' Balloon-Dog Claim Ends with a Whimper," in: *The San Francisco Chronicle*, February 4, 2011, available online at: http://www.sfgate.com/entertainment/article/Jeff-Koons-balloon-dog-claim-ends-with-a-whimper-2461103.php, accessed: 10/04/2012.

12 **http://secondlife.com**/whatis/?lang=en-US, accessed: 10/04/2012.

13 **See: "Converting** the Virtual Economy into Development Potential," summary of an 2011 infoDev study, available online at: http://www.infodev.org/en/Article.696.html, accessed: 10/04/2012.

prisoners forced to play games. We worked 12-hour shifts in the camp. [...] The computers were never turned off."[14]

Whereas it is the primary topic in this example, play as a cultural technique within contemporary art is an important strategy. Masks, dressing up, and fakes are references to reality and at least have a symbolic impact, but they also refer to the distance *already existing* – for all its international networking – between the milieu of the art scene and the conditions of existence experienced by the global population as a whole. It is play as a mode of representation that makes operational realism viable by liberating it from the denial of its own representativeness. The *NSK State in Time*, a project by artist group IRWIN and the band Laibach, is based on the paradox of a world citizenship, which organizes itself as a national state – and for whose fictional passport several thousand "citizens" have registered for a wide variety of reasons (and also with varying degrees of understanding as to its "reality"). *NSK State* is both a parody of the traditional nation-state model and the hope for a world community; given the current geopolitical circumstances "uncertain ground" in both regards, which – although it may not be able to grant asylum to anyone – gains with every new citizen a further potential case study for the inadequacy of the prevailing geopolitical system. "NSK confers the status of a state not to territory but to mind, whose borders are in a state of flux, in accordance with the movements and changes of its symbolic and physical collective body"[15]: a form of statehood derived from contemporaneity. In this sense even the supremacist-totalitarian aesthetics of NSK, as its "folk art," must submit to the paraphrases and parodies, which the people who voluntarily joined the NSK consider to be representative of the state.

Just like the *Xijing Olympics*, the games of the Xijing Men (Chen Shaoxiong, Gimhongsok and Tsuyoshi Ozawa) this is mainly humorous and provocative and occasionally silly. With "Xijing," the "Western capital" intended to complement the capitals of the artists' three native countries, namely China, South Korea, and Japan, a utopian place is to come into existence that will have the potential to transcend the hardened political fronts between these three East Asian nations. This is an important objective, which already succeeds through the collaboration of the three artists; naturally, this has as little to do with a real political project as the escapades of rather unsporty-looking Xijing Men have to do with the Olympic Games.

Finally, Thierry Geoffroy, who as *Biennialist* takes on the roles of a Columbo-like detective and a "naïve UN peacekeeper" to investigate to what extent the political ambitions of large art shows are actually realized, has established that the embarrassing aspect of insisting on the relevance of social issues is a quality of artistic practice. In his *Emergency Room Dictionary* we read the following definition of "embarrassing": "[...] ready to look like an old gaffer playing guitar for / the benefit of The Salvation Army in front of the Department Stores / at Christmas / to collect coins for the homeless."[16]

Presumably art will appear somewhat ridiculous if it continues to insist on getting embroiled in world events in order to preserve its critical integrity – its contemporaneity. It is significant that by choosing the figure of Columbo as an "investigator," Geoffroy takes a person who, thanks to his persistent questioning, always achieves his goal. The extravagant proliferation of authorship issues and the endless entanglement in ever new responsibilities raise fears of a postmodern age in which every decision has to be suspended because its repercussions cannot be calculated. But perhaps we can see this, as an strategy and the hope that those people who preserve or tacitly accept unjust systems, inequalities of power and exploitation inside and outside the art system, who in other words close themselves off to dialectics and dialog, will accordingly run out of steam all the sooner when confronted.

Translated from the German by Jeremy Gaines.

14 **Danny Vincent**, "China Used Prisoners in Lucrative Internet Gaming Work," in: *The Guardian*, May 25, 2011, available online at: http://www.guardian.co.uk/world/2011/may/25/china-prisoners-internet-gaming-scam, accessed: 10/04/2012.

15 **Eda Čufer & Irwin**, "NSK STATE IN TIME," available online at: irwin.si/texts/nsk-state-in-time/, accessed: 10/04/2012.

16 **Thierry Geoffroy/Colonel**, *Emergency Room Dictionary*, online available at: http://www.emergencyrooms.org/dictionary/words/EMBARASSING.html, accessed: 10/04/2012.

In Search of Art

Oscar Ho Hing Kay

In 1992 I received a grant to undertake a curatorial research project in New York. During the visit, there was a brutal incident of family violence that aroused much media attention and discussions. Public outcries against domestic violence were overwhelming. Soon after that incident, many exhibitions addressing the issue of domestic violence were popping up in New York. The phenomenon fascinated me. An imaginary scenario came into my mind: inside a luxurious room a group of artists sit and wait. The door bangs open, in comes a curator screaming with enthusiasm, pointing in a direction leading outside the room, "Hey everybody! There is meaning over there!" Whereupon all the artists immediately rush over in the direction where meaning is located.

When I first got in touch with Chinese contemporary art in the late 1980s and Southeast Asian contemporary art in the early 1990s,[1] what impressed if not overwhelmed me was the urgency-laden sense in the artworks I encountered. At that time, the art scene within the region was still young enough to be fairly different from the largely market-led art scene of today's Asia. Art was made out of necessities.

For many Asian artists issues such as suppression, social injustice, corruption, and seeking the right and the channels for personal expression were all urgently demanding active responses. In the eyes of these cultural practitioners, they had concrete issues to deal with. When viewing a painting that exposed the continuation of slavery on sugar cane farms in the Philippines, it was not the artistic skills or the stylistic uniqueness or its significance within the history of art that made the artwork powerful. The power derived from the issue that was tabled, and the meaningfulness of the artwork when located within a specific location.

Art gains its extraordinary power when it is expanded to a context that is closely linked with a social, political, and emotional context. It makes art and the experience of looking a profound and emotionally engaging experience. It is precisely responses to necessities that give art power, especially when it is done with a sense of urgency and compassion. These necessities may stem from social and political needs, or from a much smaller, intimate context of human experience. When this comes together, it can bring forth an engagement from the viewers that is more profound than just being artistic.

Curating in Asia

Like many Asian cities in the late 1970s and the early 1980s, the economic growth in Hong Kong led to the speedy formation of a cultural infrastructure with many institutions being established within a short time. Most of these institutions, whether arts center, theater, museum, or gallery, were designed and operated following models of the West, and were monitored, if not run directly by civil servants. The lack of trained professionals to meet the sudden

1 **The definition** of contemporary art here refers to the art that adopts the language and format strongly influenced by the West and commonly employed in the global art scene.

growth resulted in the employment of nonprofessionals, or people from remotely related fields, usually civil servants transferred from other governmental departments. There arose a huge conservative, bureaucratic structure.

Within such a structure, artistic direction was dictated by boards or advisory committees of senior members of the community with "cultural taste," frequently people in socially prestigious positions such as businessmen, collectors, academics, lawyers, and doctors. Art remained esoteric and distanced from the public. In Hong Kong, during the 1980s, the Hong Kong Museum of Art mainly showed traditional Chinese literati ink paintings and antiques, with occasional exhibitions of works of major Western artists like Henry Moore. Photography was not formally recognized as an art form until the mid-1990s.

The debate about the translation of the word "curator" in the mid-1980s typified the dichotomy in the understanding of the function and role of a curator within the art community. The official Chinese translation of "curator" used by all government museums was "head of museum" (館長). It highlighted the bureaucratic hierarchy (head) and the institutional nature (museum). With such a translation, it would be awkward to have a guest curator (guest head of museum) or an independent curator (independent head of museum). The concepts of "guest curator" and "independent curator" did not exist within official thinking. After lengthy debates, the arts community adopted the Taiwanese translation that gave a practical, non-institutional title of "exhibition planner" (策展人), while the government museums, until today, continue to translate "curator" as "head of museum."

During the 1980s in Hong Kong, as in other parts of Asia, curatorial work outside of the government museum system was rare and lonely. The cultural ecology was just too underdeveloped and imbalanced for undertaking curatorial projects. On the other hand, because of its underdevelopment, there were plenty of possibilities. The lack of audiences and resources generated a positive dynamic. In order to earn support and to invite engagement among a disinterested public, one was forced to work hard and stay sensitive to the cultural needs of the community. Most of all, the situation forced one to constantly review one's curatorial perspective and its meaningfulness in the eyes of the public. Ironically, the lack of established vocabularies for curating offered unbounded freedom to experiment and to provoke, especially for someone who had no formal training in exhibition presentation.

Art and Curation

I received my formal education in studio art and had no previous training in curation. The occasions when I got closest to curation were when I organized my own exhibitions. I did my graduate studies in studio art at the University of California, Davis (UC Davis) in the early 1980s. At that time the art school was known as the camp of Californian Funk art, with representative figures such as Robert Arneson and Wayne Thiebauld teaching there. Uncomfortable with the East Coast intellectualism and the self-aggrandizement of artists, they mocked the elitism of art and sought inspiration from the ordinary, the popular, and the vulgar. Much of their inspiration came from pop and folk cultures. Art is no big deal, Bob Arneson liked to say. In any neighborhood, John plays basketball, Jimmy collects cards, and Mary paints. Art is a common, natural human act, that's all.

Stylistically my works did not fall into the Funk art tradition, but I appreciated their views, especially the dismantling of the elitist hierarchy, the light-heartedness in dealing with art, and the attempt to liberate art from its sacredness and make it something naturally human. Years later, these experiences at UC Davis had a lot of impact on my curatorial work. For a long time I was not even aware of this.

Four years after returning to Hong Kong, in 1988 I was offered the job of exhibition director of the Hong Kong Arts Centre (the Arts Centre), the only independent, nonprofit-making cultural institution in Hong Kong with a sizable, professionally equipped art gallery, along with two theaters and one cinema. Until then, the exhibition department of the Arts Centre had an all-embracing program and did not appear to have any particular area of emphasis. When I was recruited, I was not given any programming direction either. I was free to plan my program. A full time curatorial job outside the government system with large degree of independence was rare in this region, it was an extreme luxury. It was also a challenging task as Hong Kong, like China, was in one of the most turbulent periods in its history.

1989

The late 1980s was an unusual period for Hong Kong and for China. In China, it was a period of unprecedented zeal. Artists and critics were seeking new languages to soothe the wounds left by the Cultural Revolution and to explore new visions and solutions to bring China out of its century-long poverty and backwardness.

In addition to adopting art languages from the West, such as the Xiamen Dada, there were also movements that looked inside China: going back to the raw and the basic, from which one sought the resources and energies for the revival of a nation. The barren landscape of northwestern China in Ding Fang's (丁方) paintings and Chen Kai Ge's (陳凱歌) ground-breaking movie *Yellow Earth* of the 1980s were typical examples of the attempt to seek strength and inspiration from one of the poorest and roughest districts of China. These enthusiastic calls for rebirth and reform reached their peak in January 1989 with the controversial opening of the *China Avant-garde* exhibition at the Beijing Museum of Art. It was a historic exhibition that summarized the passion and the innocent desire for reform among the Chinese cultural communities of the 1980s. It was also a sad omen, a prelude to the inevitable tragedy of the Tiananmen Students Movement and the subsequent massacre on June 4, 1989. 1989 marked a turning point in Chinese art from a modernist zeal to a cynical breakdown of belief, which then further developed into a market-driven export of Orientalism.[2]

In Hong Kong, the restlessness took on a different and less noticeable form. The Sino-British agreement of returning Hong Kong to China in 1997 not only generated much fear and anxiety, but also led to a call for democracy as a way to secure protection from possible totalitarian suppression. The recognition of citizen's rights, including cultural rights, and the demand for democracy began to spread rapidly. The British colonial government encouraged this, as there were only a few years before their departure. The Tiananmen massacre intensified the fear, and led to massive migration among the rich and the middle class. It also heightened the quest for democracy among those who could not go or wanted to stay. Increasingly, the differences between those who had the financial capability to emigrate and those who had not, the rich and the poor, became socially divisive in the face of an uncertain future. It was in this social and political situation that I began my curatorial career.

Living with Art 1988

The first exhibition I handled at the Arts Centre was *Living with Art*, an open exhibition prearranged by my predecessor.

The exhibition was an imitation of the annual *Summer Art Show* of the Royal Academy in London. Intended as an annual review of the Hong Kong art scene, the public were invited to submit their artworks for public viewing. An adjudication panel would then select outstanding works to show the finest artistic achievements of Hong Kong artists.

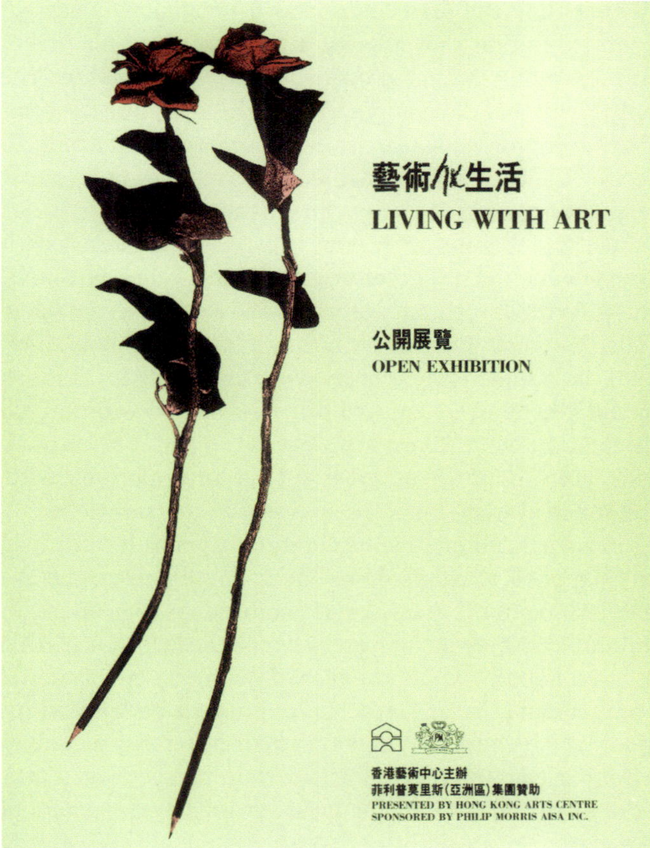

Exhibition poster *Living With Art*, Hong Kong Arts Centre, 1988

The education I received from UC Davis had implanted in me a cynicism about the snobbishness of the art establishment. I had always been suspicious of adjudicators and curators. My cynicism got stronger in a colonized community like Hong Kong where the art world was the game of a small group of powerful people, mutually coronated as "cultured" persons. The idea that some people could possess the exclusive power to make decisions about the quality of art and even the definition of art bothered me.

"Must we adjudicate?" - I decided to cancel the adjudication procedure. After much persuasion, the organizing committee agreed to make the exhibition a truly open one. Whoever submitted a work would go straight into exhibition without any selection. Other than the discomfort with the adjudication system, there was another reason for adopting a non-selective format, for it allowed me to look at Hong Kong art from a sociological and ethnological perspective, to look at art as a social activity in which everybody engaged.

2 **From 1991 to 1993** I cocurated the exhibition *Post 1989: New Art from China* with Li Shen Ting and Johnson Chang. During this period, the changeover from a trend to making art for the market became fairly noticeable.

At that time the Arts Centre was a prestigious place. An open exhibition that allowed anyone to show his or her work naturally attracted overwhelming participation. The only group that did not join in the exhibition was the community of professional artists, who were troubled by the direction the new exhibition director was taking and found it degrading to exhibit along with amateurs.

On the opening night, the galleries were packed with people who had never before entered our galleries. Grandma and grandpa, parents, brothers and sisters all came. Joyfully they took pictures with their family members to record the proud moment of showing their artistic creations at the Arts Centre. I enjoyed this festival like a communal celebration of art. *Living with Art* was an act of democracy, of defying an infrastructure that I felt uncomfortable with. But it had also put me in a self-contradictory position.

If such an all-embracing curatorial approach continued to be applied, what would the next, and the next, and the exhibition after that be like? If exhibition means taking in anything that comes along why would the Arts Centre need a curator at all? Would the idea of giving up all curatorial engagement in fact be an act of copping out, both artistically and intellectually? Was there anything wrong in holding a point of view, in processing a certain perspective in arts, or in anything else? Maybe I was terrified by the potential power and responsibilities that I had suddenly been given.

During a chat with my superior at the Hong Kong Arts Centre over my thoughts on this issue, he indicated that the Arts Centre employed me because they wanted my point of view, and believed that there were people out there that also wanted to learn about my way of looking. One should not feel guilty for expressing one's views. It dawned on me that my discomfort over having the power to define and select art in fact came from a response to a system that reinforced cultural domination. Because of governmental domination, the Arts Centre became the only alternative voice outside the government system. Fundamentally, the problem came from an imbalanced power structure that did not provide adequate platforms for expression of a broad range of views. There was no need to apologize for having one's personal interpretation and preferences.

Ultimately, the issue was not artistic or curatorial but political. The infrastructure needed to be changed. I ended up getting involved in politics and social action. Along with other activists from the arts community, in 1993 we successfully lobbied the government to set up an independent Arts Development Council.

It was obvious that one had to go beyond art, for there were many things that art could not do. But there were also many good things art could do, and I was determined to let the public know about that.

Mobile Art Show 1988

Visiting a museum or art gallery was not and is not part of the cultural experience in Hong Kong. One might go for dim sum or play mahjong on Sunday, but going to see an exhibition is definitely not a normal Sunday activity. The fundamental task of a curator in Hong Kong and in most parts of Asia is not to attract audience, but to create an audience, especially an audience for contemporary art. Making art more accessible and approachable has been an urgent curatorial task.

The *Mobile Art Show,* organized in 1988 soon after I took up my position, was an attempt to bring art closer to the community, instead of asking the public to come to the institution. After a long and painful process, we got all the licenses to organize an art exhibition plus performance at a recreation area in Mongkok, a densely populated working-class neighborhood. The day we moved in was a warm and sunny winter day, perfect for outdoor art activities. As our team walked into the recreation area and prepared to clear the area for our set-up, a group of teenagers were happily playing basketball. Before asking for the venue to be cleared, a question popped out: "What makes art more important than playing basketball that these young men have to give way to art?" If within a neighborhood, John plays basketball, Jimmy collects cards, and Mary paints, why should art be given such privilege? Feeling bad about our intrusion, in the end we found a corner to install the exhibition and give some art performances. The residents looked at the invading art presentation with indifference or mild curiosity. One may say that the exhibition failed. It was only a group of people using other people's space to celebrate what they had been doing, despite their sincere desire to communicate. It was a dislocation, and the task of curating in Hong Kong also appeared to be a dislocation. We were speaking in a totally different language.

Contemporary Hong Kong Columnist Cartoon 1989

The idea of dismantling the elitist hierarchy of art had been one of my obsessions during my early curatorial work. Hong Kong has one of the richest and most interesting cultures in Asia and it had been totally ignored by the official infrastructure. Ever since my return to Hong Kong, the description of Hong Kong as a "cultural wasteland" was heard frequently. It bothered me for it was a superficial com-

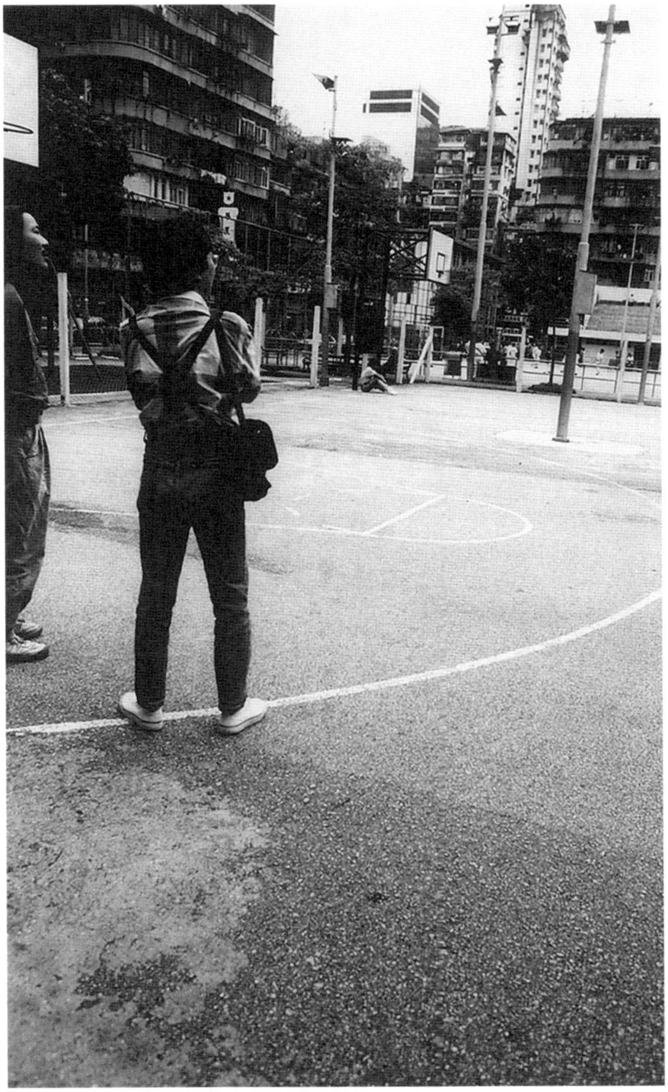

Mobile Art Show, basketball ground, Mongkok, Honk Kong, 1988.

ment based on a narrowly defined concept of culture, and it contradicted my everyday experience of living in Hong Kong. As soon as I picked up my curator job, one direction I turned to was the popular culture of Hong Kong. I wanted to defy the downgrading self-image of cultural wasteland by showing some of the outstanding Hong Kong cultures which had been ousted from the official definition of art.

Curatorially being the only sizable institution outside of the government system, planning the exhibition programming for the Arts Centre was a significant battlefield for challenging the domination of official conservativism. On the one hand we actively promoted the contemporary art of a generation of young artists, and on the other hand moved toward popular culture that would democratize art and echo the cultural experience of the people. Among the various popular art forms, cartoons were one of the most outstanding achievements of the city, not only because of its long and rich history, but also because of the increased popularity of political cartoons during the pre-1997 period. In 1989, a large-scale exhibition entitled *Contemporary Hong Kong Columnist Cartoon* was held and it marked the first attempt to branch out into popular culture, which continued for years in the exhibition program of the Arts Centre. The move into popular culture also marked the introduction of a programming strategy for constructing cultural identity in Hong Kong.

One thing I learnt from the *Mobile Art Show* was the necessity for a cultural institution to be humble. There was an arrogant assumption that if the public did not come to exhibitions, it was because of their ignorance and thus they needed to be educated. Not for a second would the curators ask, at least not in Hong Kong, whether the disinterest was a result of the failure of the institution in responding to the cultural experience and needs of the community, or if the curator could simply not understand the meaning of art among the public.

In Search of Art 1990

In 1989 I cocurated an exhibition entitled *In Search of Art* with David Clarke. The exhibition was based on the idea that everybody's home is a personal museum. We wanted to find out what made a visual object so meaningful that people would keep it as a personal collection. The exhibition invited the public to submit objects that no longer served any practical function but which people still kept simply to look at. Along with their submissions, the participants, sometimes with the help of our staff, had to write short notes explaining the reasons why they collected and continued to display these objects.

In order to get a broader communal representation, we needed to ensure that the participants would not be limited to the small group of the regular audience of the Arts Centre, who were mainly from the educated middle and upper class communities. The original plan was to focus on the Wanchai district in Hong Kong island, and to cut a vertical section of district from the top of the hill all the way down to the bottom. Hong Kong is a typical city where the rich live on the top of the hill, the middle class in the middle, and the poor at the bottom. Unfortunately, the lack of adequate sponsorship funding did not allow us to undertake such a large-scale, complicated survey as we would have wished. An alternative plan was to take an aggressive and personal campaign to collect exhibits from the public, with special efforts made to invite those who normally did not

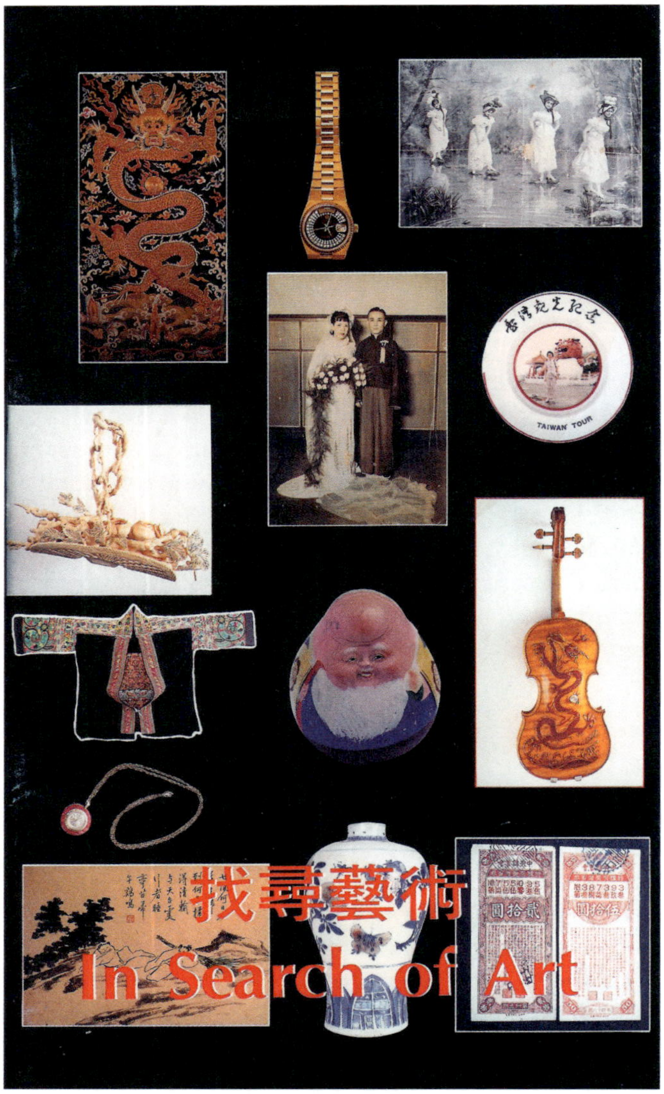

Exhibition poster *In Search of Art*, Hong Kong Arts Centre, 1990

engage in this type of cultural activity. Once again we went into the community, including distributing leaflets at the open air food markets of the working-class neighborhood, giving talks at community and social service centers, including the senior citizen centers and the Society for the Blind. On some occasions, the word "art" was replaced by "objects of visual interest" to encourage participation and avoid common assumptions that might alienate our targeted participants. Responses were more enthusiastic than we expected.

As the submissions started coming in, the objects collected fascinated us. A boy sent in a candle made in the shape of a clown. It was an ordinary, slightly discolored candle. The boy stated that the candle was the first prize he had ever won in a Christmas party lucky draw. He could still remember the moment of excitement when he learnt that he had won the prize. A young girl brought in a wooden comb, which was given to her before her grandmother died. A woman submitted a beautiful black-and-white photograph of herself. When she showed up at the opening, she was an older, slightly overweight lady. It was a picture recording her glorious past. A blind man sent in a Rolex watch. He lost his eyesight a few years ago, but could still remember well what a beautiful watch he had.

There were objects that did not carry any strong emotional attachment. These were just mundane, bits and pieces of intimate memories: family pictures printed on ceramic plate when traveling to Taiwan, a gift from a boyfriend, a copy of a Van Gogh painting by a relative, and a bamboo painting given by a friend, whose business in bamboo paintings had since failed.

An old lady in her seventies sent in a drawing that she did soon after the Japanese occupation of Hong Kong during World War II. She lost her sister at that time and had kept the drawing she did that described her lost sister. She wanted to participate in the exhibition so that her drawing could be seen publicly, with the hope that she might get lucky and through the publicity of exhibition she could find her sister. We arranged a television interview for her to tell her story. Up to the end of the exhibition, she had still not found her sister. However, she appreciated the opportunity and we appreciated the idea that art exhibitions can serve other purposes.

A taxi driver submitted a pineapple made out of Renminbi (Chinese currency) one-cent paper banknotes. The pineapple, which was made out of over a hundred paper banknotes, was delicately assembled with great effort and patience. He had made it for his girlfriend, whom he later married. When she heard about the exhibition, his wife insisted in sending in the pineapple as the most beautiful object in the world.

Interestingly, similar to *Living with Art*, participation was low among the regular art audience of the Arts Center. Only a few submissions sent in were in the category of "art" as commonly defined, and very few objects submitted were visually spectacular. Most of them were small, aged, somewhat tedious objects. The exhibition, however, was amazingly warm and engaging. It was full of intimate stories that made the viewing a distinctly humane experience. What made an object visually meaningful to people was the intimately warm association one had with the objects and the stories behind them, not the form, style, historical significance, or other sorts of cultural or intellectual significance. If one had only measured these works with formalistic or other commonly adopted artistic/academic approaches, these seemingly mundane objects would apparently have had no "artistic" value.

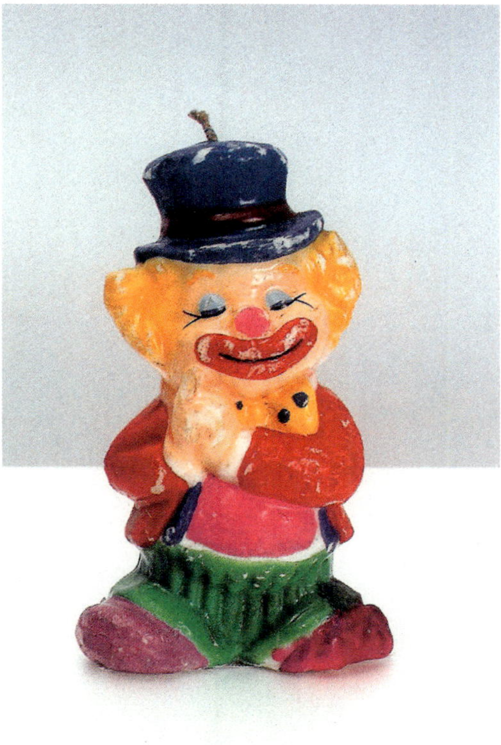

"Candle Clown," *In Search of Art*, Hong Kong Arts Centre, 1990

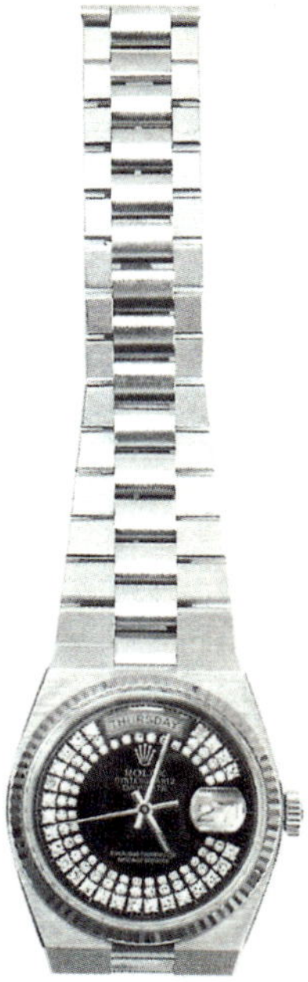

"Rolex," *In Search of Art*, Hong Kong Arts Centre, 1990

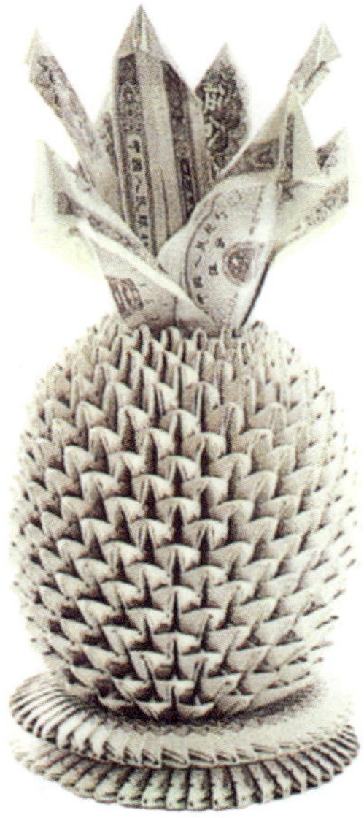

"Renminbi Pineapple," *In Search of Art*, Hong Kong Arts Centre, 1990

Often the stories associated with these objects were not easily accessible to outsiders. Viewers who did not know the stories could only retreat into constructing responses based on available methodologies and vocabularies to articulate their own interpretations. Unfortunately, these people who do not know the stories, namely the curator and the critic, are the ones that make the authoritative interpretations. *In Search of Art* was an attempt to get a glimpse of the other side of the objects that these critics and curators could not see. It was about the differences and limitations in interpretation, and it also showed the class division in the understanding of "art," or "objects of visual significance."

The exhibition intended to show the art of the humble and the ordinary, and the intimacy in looking. Whether these objects were recognized as art or not was of no importance. In fact, the exhibition revealed another dimension of visual experience that had been much ignored: the moment of joy of getting the prize of a lucky draw, the receiving of a gift from grandma before she died, the faded beauty preserved in photography, and the memories of a labor of love, etc. All of these bit and pieces made these objects meaningful and beautiful to look at, for they made us human.

My unprofessional beginning as a curator and unguided practice was a humbling experience from which I learnt about the disabilities of a curator, and the unjustified arrogance of cultural institutions. It also reminded me to be responsive to the cultural necessities of the art within a specific social and political context, which led me into more cultural battles during the transitional period of the 1990s.

Accidental Message: Art is Not a System, Not a World

Liu Ding and Carol Yinghua Lu

The proposition of *Accidental Message: Art is Not a System, Not a World* came from our long-term work and self-observation. It is a line of thought that starts from the perspectives of practitioners and creators while also setting them as the objects of our dialog. In the various practices we engage with, including our practices as artists and as writers, we have never been willing to bring our own work into the value systems, reference systems, or organizational methods that have already gained effectiveness and affirmation within reality. This mindset is the foundation of our work and the core of what our work attempts to transmit.

At this point it is necessary to look back over the practices and ideas we here concerned ourselves with in the past in order to present the inevitability and internality of this proposal in our work. Actually, in our work we often see different ideas and plans intermingle, connect, and influence each other.

In 2008, we began two projects that are very important to us. The first is the *Liu Ding's Store* project that Liu Ding began as an artist. This conceptual art project established a platform that is personal yet public, a shop that oscillates between a website and an exhibition, selling artistic creations to initate and participate in a discussion of the formation and essence of value. This store uses virtual methods to operate and recreate the various mechanisms in the art system to endow and create value and establish connectivity. The artist always places himself within this project, both the subject and object of description. This project experiments with outlining the shape of the system from within while also attempting to erect an independent system predicated on individual experience and spirit. The second project is one that Carol Yinghua Lu engaged with in her work as a writer of art criticism together with Su Wei, another writer. It entails the publication of each chapter of German art historian Hans Belting's book *Art History After Modernism* in the magazine *Contemporary Art and Investment*, accompanied by a series of critical essays. Belting's rethinking of the universal experience of art history as a carrier of academic authority and power, begun in the 1980s, has provided the discussion in this discipline with a breath of fresh air. Our in-depth readings and comprehension of these texts have opened up a new field of vision for our observation of art. With a gift for presenting profound ideas with simplicity, Belting effortlessly yet convincingly disintegrates the superstitious belief in certain existing systems. This superstitious belief and the spiritual sense of dependence on reference still shrouds the practices, thoughts, and value judgments of most practitioners in China, forming an intangible and insurmountable obstacle.

In November 2011, we visited German philosopher, art historian, and New York University Professor Boris Groys in New York. He had just taken part in a symposium at the Guangdong Museum of Art. When we asked him what he had learned through his interaction with members of the same field in China, he said that what he found most difficult to understand was that the critics he had encountered in China were all mentioning such European and American artists as Joseph Beuys and Andy Warhol as their points of reference. What are China's own references? As a European scholar who had carefully researched the cultural history of Russia and the Slavic countries, and who had taken part in the nonofficial art activities of Russia in the 1970s, Groys feels that the Asian countries are excessively tending towards treating the cultural systems of the West, especially those of Europe and America, as models for them to imitate and attempt to approach, while being far from gazing directly into the abyss, trajectories, and so-called fragments of their own culture and art. We often aspire to the storied art system of Europe and America. This system, through various historical phases of refinement, has grown solid and increasingly effective, possessing a kind of inherent advanced nature. We are even less hesitant about projecting our imaginings about a so-called perfected art system onto the art history and art system of Europe and America. Our curiosity and interest about the artistic trends in Europe and America far surpass our interest in and concern for ourselves, including our understanding of the art trends in neighboring Asian countries. As Groys sees it, this is a form of "repressed socialist modernity," where our aspirations for a more complete order and effective mechanisms lead us to overlook how our own society and ideology shape us. We have forgotten to survey the mine that lies beneath our feet - which may not be very rich - as we busy ourselves with exploring and excavating all of the mines around us. The progression of modernization in the Asian countries is not only different from that of Europe and America, there are also many differences in the level and paths of modernization between each Asian country, which has led to today's state of vast discrepancies in social form, cultural situations and ideology between these countries. China's modernization process cannot escape the close interaction it once had with the Soviet Union. If we don't amply release the uniqueness and concreteness in our own modernization process, and analyze the socialist ideology within it, then we will have difficulty truly recognizing our position today. This is the fundamental reason that we have trouble fully importing or following the European and American field of vision when engaging in self-observation.

In the second half of 2009, following the research topic *Little Movements: Self-Practices in Contemporary Art*, and after over a year of fieldwork of research, especially through roundtable discussions with practitioners, we presented seventeen cultural and artistic practices from China, America, and a few European countries at the OCT Contemporary Art Terminal in Shenzhen in an exhibition that combined documents and artistic creations. In this exhibition, we clearly emphasized art system organizational methods that are rooted in creative practices and thinking, and setting aside recognition methods based on time, region, the art system division of labor, and the allocation of authority, we proposed a historical view and set of art system organizational methods consisting of points and planes. We gave a public talk on this project in February 2012 at the Extra City Kunsthal in Antwerp, Belgium. As we introduced the project, one questioner raised a very critical issue: By placing Chinese artistic practices from various periods together with European and American art practices with no regard for temporal or regional boundaries, is it not your real aim to use this parallel presentation to provide a form of global legitimacy for Chinese art practices?

This question led us to look at our proposed pursuits from a different perspective. We hope to unearth the foundation for equality from art's interior in the belief that these self-practices, internal sources of momentum and instinctual creativity have the potential for transcending universal order. This is a starting point rooted in the local. We did not first affirm the advanced nature or effectiveness of a certain condition or highlight the superiority of any particular system, hoping instead to describe the internal connectivity between different practices and the organic nature of the relationship between practices and the contexts they produce. We began with the awareness that in the process of globalization, the most pressing problem is how to recognize the self, to determine which backgrounds and factors are closely linked to us, and which experiences we can view from a distance and not necessarily follow. Recognizing ourselves is more pressing even than any form of participation. Self-recognition includes recognizing which forms of experiences and conditions are more attractive to us, and which deficiencies and projections this attraction is constructed upon.

As the first phase of our work on *Little Movements: Self-Practices in Contemporary Art* came to a close, we realized that a lot of questions it touched on still lingered with us, such as the "anxiety of self-definition." This describes the spiritual crises that are produced through the connections and interactions that have arisen as the world's various boundaries began to loosen due to the high level of economic flows under globalization and free trade. It involves the reevaluation of preexisting value judgments and reference systems and the rethinking of self-cultural standpoints in a consideration of how to recognize and sift through one's own traditions of culture and thought in order to develop a self-awareness that is marked by individuality and subjectivity yet doesn't lack an all-encompassing perspective. In this discussion, we often returned to Hans Belting's research project, GAM - Global Art and the Museum at ZKM | Center for Art and Media Karlsruhe. This multi-year project set 1989 as the starting point for its discussion, especially the milestone *Magiciens de la terre* exhibition. *Magiciens de la terre* was the first exhibition in continental Europe to consciously present the works of non-Western artists together with those from artists working in Europe and America. This exhibition "was both hailed as 'the first global exhibition of contemporary art' and criticized as a false start in that it was tempted 'to exoticize Third World artists.'"[1] Belting's proposal of "global art" broke through the research method that treated artists as the foundation for the composition of art history, while also consciously breaking through the European perspective that alienated artistic creations from the Third World, bringing different facets of the art system and the artistic mechanisms and phenomena produced in different parts of the world into the arena of discussion. It also presented them in the form of documents and creations at ZKM in a large exhibition entitled *The Global Contemporary: Art Worlds After 1989*. As we see it, the core of *The Global Contemporary* was not the art from around the world which occupied most of the exhibition space, in which we saw hints of the suspect selection modes from the *Magiciens de la terre* exhibition; the real star of the exhibition was the exhibition of documentations, which was in a separate space off to the side of the exhibition site, appearing as a mere footnote. It was this display, entitled *Room of Histories*, which placed the depth, breadth, and openness of Belting's research on full display. It brought together exhibition documents from Europe since 1989, especially from France and England, that sought to rethink the existing order of art history, as well as videos of Belting's discussions with the curators. Here, the rise of the auction houses, the Chinese art market, the Asian biennial trend, and the rise of art institutions in the Middle East were all equally viewed as material for the description of art history. It also included a red structuralist sculpture by Pakistani artist Rasheed Araeen, a longtime London resident. These cubes presented the art magazine *Third Text*, which Rasheed founded, edited, and distributed from 1987. Interestingly, Araeen was one of the artists at the 1989 *Magiciens de la terre* exhibition. After the *Global Contemporary* exhibition, Belting held a discussion with three curators who had worked as consultants for the exhibition; two from Asia and one African living in France. As the discussion drew to a close, Araeen, although he had lost much expressive capability and was using a walker after a recent stroke, suddenly stood up in the audience and challenged Belting's approach, saying that though Belting repeatedly emphasized that "the German standpoint is still a local standpoint" and tried to dilute a certain Eurocentric sense of superiority, his very identity and foundation for expression seemed to conflict and counteract his approach.

In the epilog to the 2002 anthology *Third Text Reader*, entitled *A New Beginning: Beyond Postcolonial Cultural Theory and Identity Politics*, Rasheed Araeen looks back at his reasons for founding *Third Text* in 1987. At that time, as a person of color living and working in England, he had already foreseen the necessity of creating a channel for expression and space for creation for his own cultural identity and ideas within the British art system and ideology. By the time *Third Text Reader* was published in 2002, the journal had already published fifty volumes. It had provided an important platform for practitioners from the Third World working in Europe to voice their ideas, but in Araeen's eyes, true change had yet to take place. The basis for creating *Third Text* was the necessity to maintain a critical stance towards one's own cultural viewpoints. In contrast to the situation in 1987, by 2002 multiculturalism was one of the self-defined orientations of art organizations in Europe, especially in England, and creators from the Third World, including professionals, had gradually entered the exhibition projects and working teams of European art organizations; however these changes were only superficial. Araeen points out that the emergence and operation of multiculturalism in the art system merely covered up the exclusion and suppression of creations and ideas of nonwhite artists in the system we are trying to explore, while root structural change had yet to take place.

> "The main issue was not just the exclusion of the artists from the art scene, but the ignorance and suppression of the whole history of their contribution to the mainstream developments. This issue also had an international dimension: many Third World critics and art historians also questioned the way the history of modern art has been perceived and written, including only white artists from Europe and North America."[2]

Although Araeen has been highly successful in the European context, with the world-famous Tate Gallery holding a retrospective on his work in 2007 and *Third Text* shaping the critical discourse in Europe regarding art from the Third World, Araeen is profoundly aware that these doors may open occasionally for him to embody their multicultural nature, but for the most part they are shut tight. Araeen's predicament and insights are quite disheartening. No matter how proactively we work, we seem hard pressed to gain true discursive rights and sustained possibilities for participation. The condition here, however, is that we actually hope to gain the right to speak in the European and American context; it seems we are still unconcerned

1 **Denis Picard**, "Liberté, Égalité, Magie," in: *Connaissance des Arts*, no. 450, 1989, p. 57, translated from the French.

2 **Rasheed Araeen**, "A New Beginning. Beyond Postcolonial Cultural Theory and Identity Politics," in: Rasheed Araeen, Ziauddin Saradar, and Sean Cubitt, *The Third Text Reader on Art, Culture and Theory*, Continuum, London, New York (NY), 2002, p. 333.

with the space for expression we can gain within our own cultural contexts. We appear unable to appreciate the art mechanisms that grow in our own soil like we affirm the art mechanisms and standards of Europe and America. Our perennial mindset that we are the weak party leads us to engage unthinkingly in self-negation, but such sentiments, just like excessive self-isolation and magnification of the completeness of our own worlds, is a useless obstruction to creation and practice. According to Araeen, the problem in Asia is that we have not begun to write our own art history; what we use and discuss is still the art history and methods of thinking that have been written and handed down from Europe. In that case, how do we gain our own subjectivity?

In the 1997 essay, "Three Great Issues in Chinese Art Criticism of the 1990s," critic and Guangzhou Academy of Fine Art associate professor Huang Zhuan introduced three main theoretical issues that Chinese contemporary art criticism touched on from 1993 to 1996. One such issue is the issue of international identity in art criticism. We can see that the phenomenon of certain types of contemporary Chinese artistic creations entering into the European and American exhibition system and media coverage left many domestic critics unsettled and anxious. Most of their perplexity focused on how these creations, which represented a superficial and partial sampling of Chinese contemporary art, had gained "international recognition." On the one hand, their lack of understanding about the so-called international system led to an amplification of the "recognition mechanism" it possessed, but the influence of this secular recognition mechanism was so powerful that afterwards, these "composed and summarized," "presented," "recognized," and "widely disseminated" types of artworks and so-called "schools" would be repeated again and again as historical facts in future historical expositions. On the other hand, Chinese critics began to explore how to erect a critical discourse, and in what manner, to discuss and define the creativity and artistic practice taking place within China. This pursuit, including the question of recognizing the object of discussion in the work of Chinese practitioners, has lingered with us to this day, suspended and undecided.

As artistic practitioners, we cannot submit to certain narrative structures that have been standardized by authority and market value. We maintain the belief that the center of our discussion is each individual practitioner; we also believe that possibly the best starting point for self-recognition is a return to a past that relates to us. At the Lithuanian Pavilion of the 2011 Venice Biennale, Lithuanian artist Darius Mikšys used the exhibition and catalog forms to present the artworks that have been created under the sponsorship of the Lithuanian Ministry of Culture over the past twenty years (from 1992-2010). In the exhibition press release, the artist described his creative motivation as follows:

> "The Lithuanian state selects artists for a symbolic exhibition by allocating prizes and grants to further the practice of Lithuanian artists. It could be seen as a targeted programming of cultural products. In this way, the state acts as a curator, whose exhibition hall does not have walls, and whose exhibition is on show for decades. Is it possible to see such an exhibition? How does one visit it?"[3]

Over three hundred artists have been recipients of these grants, and 173 of them accepted Mikšys' invitation to participate in this national pavilion project. Each artist recommended an artwork they had created under the state grants for the catalog, and the audience was given the opportunity to select the artworks they liked. The selected works were then taken from behind a white curtain and placed on the stage. This extremely political work gave us immeasurable inspiration: what is our history? History is not a standardized discourse, let alone a rigid set of coordinates and order. It is a process of constantly looking back and recognizing anew.

The '85 Zhuhai Conference, a seven-day conference with presentations of slides of artworks and discussion, organized in 1986 by artists Wang Guangyi and Shu Qun, brought artists and groups who work collectively scattered across the country together for the first time. Participants described to each other their artistic ideals and creative content. The significance of this event, however, was that these collectivized self-introductions led many introspective artists to recognize the importance of returning to individual practice and individual shaping of values. Though collective voices and collective practices can gain more attention during a certain phase, the group art movement that took place from the mid to late 1990s turned much of the discussion about creation, released in the form of manifestos, into simplified releases and expressions of certain emotions. Art and creativity, however, must return to the individual. By discarding the illusion of collective revolution and shifting to individual practice, many artists' careers entered in the 1990s into an important period for creation, development and gradual maturity. They began seeking ways to break through and face themselves in their creations, seeking reference systems that belonged to them, and using creative thinking and cultural foundations to

3 www.cac.lt/en/exhibitions/past/11/4535, accessed 11/24/2012.

replace their excessive, even total reliance on modern European humanist ideas. They strove to analyze and reexamine latent experiences and awareness in the search for a crux to support the individual spirit.

Meanwhile, feedback from the level of reality, especially the selection and recognition of certain types of creations from certain European and American art mechanisms in the early 1990s, such as the Venice Biennale, as well as the embryonic domestic market, made the self-doubt and reconsideration that was internal to art appear not so prescient or pressing, and placed these fragmented, hesitative, chaotic, difficult, sincere, and personal thoughts from within creation temporarily on the sidelines, as if shrouded by a layer of fog. Conversely, the question of how to establish a systematism and rapid recognizability between criticisms and descriptions of creations became a key universal pursuit.

Reading through essays on artists and creations since the 1990s, one discovers that most of the commentary attempts to establish connectivity in artistic creations on the level of reality. Such explanations of art gained effectiveness on the level of reality, with the simplified explanations of artworks especially resonating with some of the European and American critics' projections about Chinese contemporary art. In turn, practitioners in the Chinese art industry, including artists and critics, also had their own projections of the Western art practices that disseminated into China. For instance, the practices of Pop art were widely understood to be a criticism of consumerism, and this critical component was magnified in Chinese Pop creations, turning such creations into a practice in the expression of socially critical meanings and attitudes. Such expositions and interpretations seemed to bestow these creations with standing in art history (Western art history), while establishing connectedness with the Chinese social reality.

On one hand, artists continued to engage in work according to their bodily and artistic instincts; on the other hand, some art criticism continued to seek out the basis for creations on the levels of psychology, sociology, and philosophy while continuing to overlook commentary on art itself. One could say that creation encountered the fate of transitional projection, while the artistic nature of creation, that is the recognition of art itself, had yet to be established. This gave artists a lot of confusion and even anxiety. For them, the entire discipline of art lacked recognition of the interiority of art and discourse on art. It seemed that artists always had to provide some legitimacy in reality for their creations, a false contextual relationship, but this wasn't necessarily where their interests lay, and it forced some artists to take a resistant stance. The widely disseminated "political Pop" and "Cynical realism" of the 1990s were one such result of the collusion between art criticism and artistic creation. They truly suited the needs of social psychology and the rapid dissemination and consumption of the market, but such a summation and definition served to mislead the recognition of creation itself, especially that of artists towards their own practices. Political directedness and social themes often became the media and languages for the artists' creations, and they were the sole channel for art criticism to enter into artistic creation. Artistic creation was symbolized and simplified. This confusion continues to the present day.

The various adornments, disseminations, and misreadings that extend out from creation have, on the material level, been expanded into a kind of perfect knowledge, particularly after entering into certain historicized narratives and when stripped of their original colors, as the organicness and randomness of artistic creation has been consciously and unconsciously ignored. Certain of art's clumsy and initial states, certain unclassifiable, primal, spontaneous, private, serendipitous, and individual elements in artistic creation and thought have been diluted, forgotten, and ignored in the process of the industrialization, universalization, and calibration of art.

To raise serendipity and the individual spirit of art again to important factors in the creation of art appears untimely. It seems to go against the standardization and concept of effectiveness in modernization, while at the same time diametrically opposing our widespread aspirations to effectiveness. If art is irreproducible, if there is no model for artistic creation, if the references for art are not clearly delineated, then how do we go forward? But there is a pressing need to raise the independence and internalization of art. If there is any belief worth turning to in creation, then it certainly does not stem from the advancement of any particular region or the effectiveness of the rules in any particular industry. It surely must come from the rule breakers, those who willingly and endlessly roam outside of the system and the unitary views of the world; people who are always prepared to throw out the rules and establish their own order.

Accidental Message: Art is Not a System, Not a World comprises the most sincere insights and understandings of creators; it is a basic pursuit and attitude that we propose towards our context. It is directed at the trends in creation and thought that are multiplying within the art system. The various mechanisms of the art system – for example the formation of the curator's role, the patronage mechanism for supporting artists, the rise of art museums and art centers, and the development of the art market – were initially produced out of the needs of art production. With the increasing industrialization of art, the progressive division of labor, and the incessant compartmentalization of artistic practices, we are now forced to confront a pressing issue: whether or not the experience we have accumulated, our established value judgments and our working methods are increasingly obstructing and ignoring the organic, agile, mobile, and serendipitous aspects of artistic creation and practice. We enjoy certain conveniences and securities provided by the art system, but we must remind ourselves that art has always been impossible to domesticate, beyond the reach of any person to control or rule, and exists entirely free of any laws. It does not exist to enter into a system or to gain any kind of affirmation or praise. Whether or not the art system exists, the work and ideas of artists will continue to exist, even if only in the artist's brain, notebook, or even under the bed. Like uncontrollable emotions and impulses, it is a fire that can never be extinguished.

When faced with a succession of crises, the problems that are exposed in various social organization methods lead people to rethink the various forces of systemization that we once believed in as universal experience and perfect knowledge - for instance, our faith in liberal economics. We must reappraise the social order on which we rely and the foundations of our existence. When one doctrine, order, and organizational method becomes powerful to the point of singularity, it inevitably conceals many crises. When art and economic life simultaneously march towards a model of standardized production and allocation, we must return to individual stories, individual situations, individual needs, and individual order. Factors from outside of the universal order are often defined as serendipitous factors, but serendipitous factors can sometimes become definitive factors because they cannot be classified, recognized, and digested by the universal system, but they cannot be avoided either. It is not always the universal order that impacts the state of affairs; differences and coexistence among individual affairs cannot be ignored by the rationalized existence of any organizational form. We are thus ready to place ourselves within such a set of coordinates: it is certainly not linear, nor two dimensional, or flat. It is a set of scattered points on multiple levels, existing simultaneously in different times and spaces, with no distinctions of sequential order or superiority. The glue that binds it comes from the secret language and mental bonds that exist between creative practitioners. In the end, it involves a deep one-on-one dialog, through unexpected encounters, chance glances, open hearts, and respect for individuals, rather than mere mutual imaginings.

This text is a shortened version of the curatorial text for the 7th Shenzhen Sculpture Biennale at OCAT in 2012.

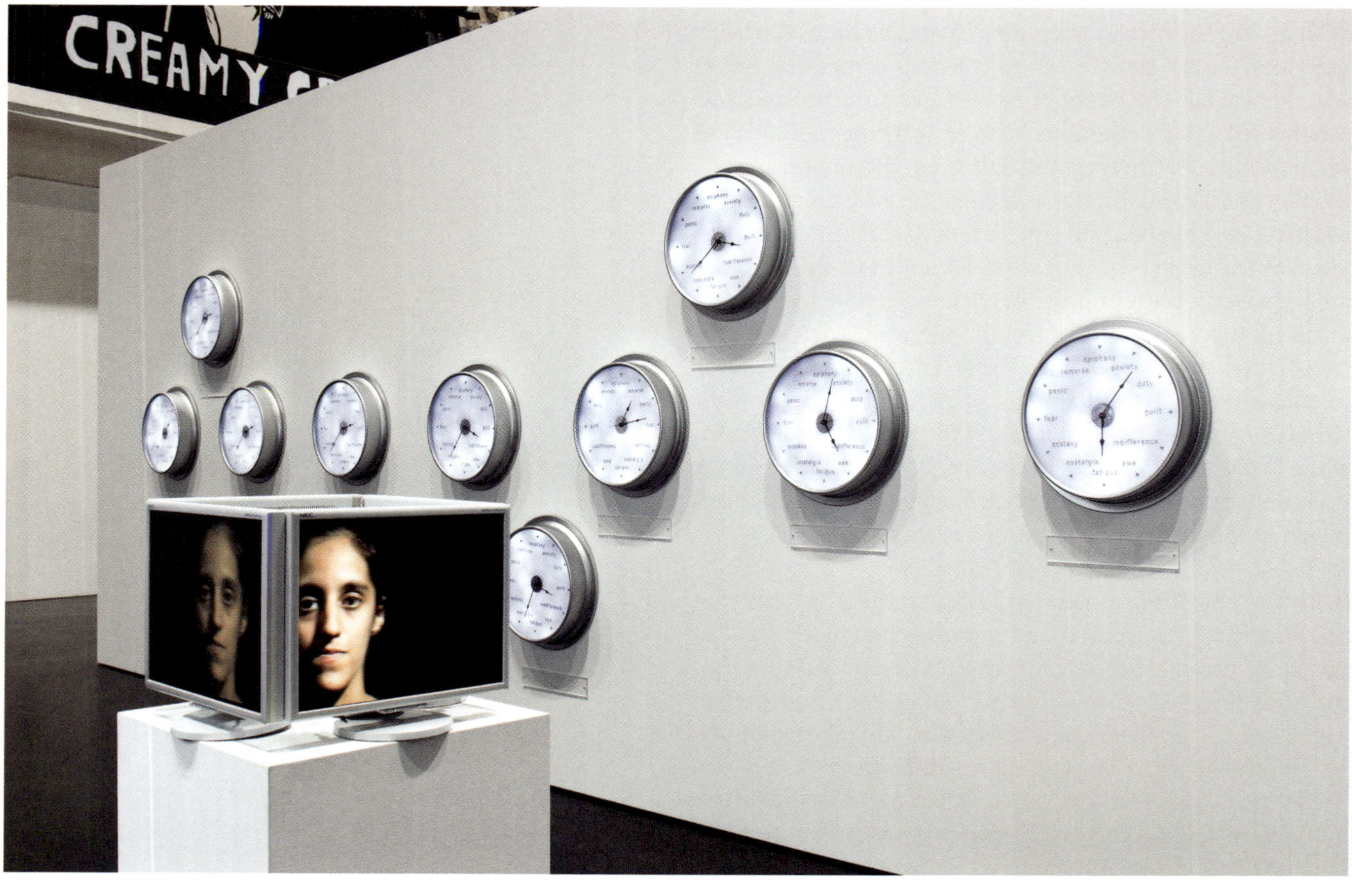

Raqs Media Collective, *Escapment*, 2009, installation view *The Global Contemporary. Art Worlds After 1989*, ZKM | Karlsruhe, 2011–2012

Now and Elsewhere

Raqs Media Collective

The Problem and the Provocation

We would like to begin by taking a sentence from the formulation of the problem that set the ball rolling for this lecture series. In speaking of the "hesitation in developing any kind of comprehensive strategy" for understanding precisely what it is that we call contemporary art today (in the wake of the last twenty years of contemporary art activity), the introduction to the series speaks of its having "assumed a fully mature form – and yet it still somehow refuses to be historicized as such."[1] Simultaneously an assertion and a reticence to name one's place in time, it is this equivocation that we would really like to discuss.

The Old Man and the Wind: Joris Ivens' Film

At the beginning of Joris Ivens and Marceline Loridan's film *A Tale of the Wind* (1988), we see a frail Joris Ivens sitting in a chair on a sand dune in the Gobi Desert, on the border between China and Mongolia, waiting for the arrival of a sandstorm. Elsewhere in the film, an old woman – a wind shaman – talks about waiting for the wind. Buffeted as we are by winds that blow from so many directions with such intensity, this image of an old man in a chair waiting for a storm is a metaphor for a possible response to the question "What is contemporaneity?"

1 **Julieta Aranda**, Brian Kuan Wood, and Anton Vidokle, "What Is Contemporary Art? Issue One," in: *e-flux journal*, no. 11, December 2009. Availabe online at: www.e-flux.com/journal/what-is-contemporary-art-issue-one, accessed 10/12/2012.

It takes stubbornness, obstinacy, to face a storm, and yet also a desire not to be blown away by it. If Paul Klee's *Angelus Novus,* celebrated in Benjamin's evocation of the angel of history, with its head caught in turning between the storm of the future and the debris of the present, were ever in need of a more recent annotation, then old man Ivens in his chair, waiting for the wind, would do very nicely. It is tempting to think of this dual obstinacy – to face the storm and not be blown away – as an acute reticence that is at the same time a refusal to either run away from or be carried away by the strong winds of history, of time itself.

We could see this "reticence," this "refusal to historicize," as a form of escape from the tyranny of the clock and the calendar – instruments to measure time, and to measure our ability to keep time, to keep to the demands of the time allotted to us by history, our contemporaneity. Any reflection on contemporaneity cannot avoid simultaneously being a consideration of time, and of our relation to it.

On Time

Time girds the Earth tight. Day after day, astride minutes and seconds, the hours ride as they must, relentlessly. In the struggle to keep pace with clocks, we are now always and everywhere in a state of jet lag, always catching up with ourselves and with others, slightly short of breath, slightly short of time.

The soft insidious panic of time ticking away in our heads is syncopated by accelerated heartbeat of our everyday lives. Circadian rhythms (times to rise and times to sleep, times for work and times for leisure, times for sunlight and times for stars) get muddled as millions of faces find themselves lit by timeless fluorescence that trades night for day. Sleep is besieged by wakefulness, hunger is fed by stimulation, and moments of dreaming and lucid alertness are eroded with the knowledge of intimate terrors and distant wars. When possible, escape is up a hatch and down a corridor between and occasionally beyond longitudes, to places where the hours chime epiphanies. *Escape* is a resonant word in the vocabulary of clock-making. It gives us another word – *escapement.*

Escapement[2]

Escapement is a horological or clock-making term. It denotes the mechanism in mechanical watches and clocks that governs the regular motion of the hands through a "catch and release" device that both releases and restrains the levers that move the hands for hours, minutes, and seconds. Like the catch and release of the valves of the heart that allow blood to flow between its chambers, setting the basic rhythm of life, the escapement of a watch regulates our sense of the flow of time. The continued pulsation of our hearts and the ticking of clocks denote our freedom from an eternal present. Each heartbeat, each passing second marks the here and now, promises the future, and recalls the resonance of the last heartbeat. Our heart tells us that we live in time.

The history of clock-making saw a definite turn when devices for understanding time shifted away from the fluid principles of ancient Chinese water and incense clocks – for which time was a continuum, thus making it more difficult to surgically separate past and present, then and now – to clocks whose ticking seconds rendered a conceptual barricade between each unit, its predecessor and its follower. This is what makes *now* seem so alien to *then.* Paradoxically, it opens out another zone of discomfort. Different places share the same time because of the accident of longitude. Thus clocks in London and Lagos (with adjustments made for daylight savings) show the same time. And yet, the experience of "now" in London and Lagos may not feel the same at all.

An escape from – or, one might say, a full-on willingness to confront – this vexation might be found by taking a stance in which one is comfortable with the fact that we exist at the intersection of different latitudes and longitudes, and that being located on this grid, we are in some sense phatically in touch with other times, other places. In a syncopated sort of way, we are "contemporaneous" with other times and spaces.

My Name is Chin Chin Choo

In *Howrah Bridge,* a Hindi film noir thriller from 1958 set in a cosmopolitan Calcutta (which, in its shadowy grandeur resembled the Shanghai of the jazz age), a young dancer, the half-Burmese, half-Baghdadi-Jewish star and vamp of vintage Hindi film, Helen, plays a Chinese bar dancer. And in the song *My Name is Chin Chin Choo,* a big band jazz, kitsch orientalist, and sailor-costumed musical extravaganza, she expresses a contemporaneity that is as hard to pin down as it is to avoid being seduced by.

The lyrics weave in the Arabian Nights, Aladdin, and Sinbad; the singer invokes the bustle of Singapore and the arch trendiness of Shanghai; the music blasts a Chicago big band sound; the sailor-suited male backup dancers suddenly break into Cossack knee-bends. Times and spaces, cities and entire cultural histories – real or imagined – collide and whirl in heady counterpoint. Yesterday's dance of contemporaneity has us all caught up in its Shanghai-Calcutta-Delhi-Bombay-Singapore turbulence. We are all called Chin Chin Choo. Hello, mister, how do you do?

2 See: **Raqs Media Collective**, *Escapement*, installation at Frith Street Gallery, London, July 8, 2009–September 30, 2009. See also this volume, pp. 334–335.

Contemporaneity

Contemporaneity, the sensation of being in a time together, is an ancient enigma of a feeling.

It is the tug we feel when our time pulls at us. But sometimes one has the sense of a paradoxically asynchronous contemporaneity - the strange tug of more than one time and place - as if an accumulation or thickening of our attachments to different times and spaces were manifesting itself in the form of some unique geological oddity, a richly striated cross section of a rock, sometimes sharp, sometimes blurred, marked by the passage of many epochs.

Now and Elsewhere

The problem of determining the question of contemporaneity hinges on how we orient ourselves in relation to a cluster of occasionally cascading, sometimes overlapping, partly concentric, and often conflictual temporal parameters - on how urgent, how leisurely, or even how lethargic we are prepared to be in response to a spectrum of possible answers.

Consider the experience of being continually surprised by the surface and texture of the night sky when looking through telescopes of widely differing magnifications. Thinking about "which contemporaneity" to probe is not very different from making decisions about how deep into the universe we would like to cast the line of our query. A telescope powerful enough to aid us in discerning the shapes and extent of craters on the moon will reveal a very different image of the universe than one that unravels the rings of Saturn, or one that can bring us the light of a distant star. The universe looks different, depending on the questions we ask of the stars.

Contemporaneity, too, looks different depending on the queries we put to time. If, as Zhou Enlai famously remarked, it is still too early to tell what impact the French Revolution has had on human history, then our sense of contemporaneity distends to embrace everything from 1789 onwards. If, on the other hand, we are more interested in sensing how things have changed since the Internet came into our lives, then even 1990 can seem a long way away. So can it seem as if it were only recently that the printing press and movable type made mechanical reproduction of words and images possible on a mass scale. One could argue that time changed once and for all when the universal regime of Greenwich Mean Time imposed a sense of an arbitrarily encoded universal time for the first time in human history, enabling everyone to calculate for themselves "when," as in how many hours ahead or behind they were in relation to everyone at every other longitude. This birthed a new time, a new sense of being together in one accounting of time. One could also argue that, after Hiroshima made it possible to imagine that humanity as we know it could auto-destruct, every successive year began to feel as long as a hundred years, or as an epoch, since it could perhaps be our last. This means that, contrary to our commonplace understanding of our "time" as being "sped up," we could actually think of our time as being caught in the long "winding down," the "long decline." It all depends, really, on what question we are asking.

And so Marcel Duchamp can still seem surprisingly contemporary, and net.art oddly dated. The moon landing, whose fortieth anniversary we have recently seen, brought a future of space travel hurtlingly close to the realities of 1969. Today, the excitement surrounding men on the moon has already acquired the patina of nostalgia, and the future it held out as a promise seems as well oddly dated. Then again, this could change suddenly if China and India were to embark in earnest on a second-wave Cold War space race to the moon. Our realities advance into and recede from contemporaneity like the tides, throwing strange flotsam and jetsam onto the shore to be found by beachcombers with a fetish for signs from different times. The question then becomes not one of "periodizing" contemporaneity, or of erecting a neat white picket fence around it; rather, it becomes one of finding shortcuts, trapdoors, antechambers, and secret passages between now and elsewhere, or perhaps elsewhen. Time folds, and it doesn't fold neatly - our sense of "when" we are is a function of which fold we are sliding into, or climbing out of.

A keen awareness of contemporaneity cannot but dissolve the illusion that some things, people, places, and practices are more "now" than others. Seen this way, contemporaneity provokes a sense of the simultaneity of different modes of living and doing things without a prior commitment to any one as being necessarily more true to our times. Any attempt to design structures, whether permanent or provisional, that might express or contain contemporaneity would be incomplete if it were not (also) attentive to realities that are either not explicit or manifest or that linger as specters. An openness and generosity toward realities that may be, or seem to be, in hibernation, dormant, or still in formation, can only help such structures to be more pertinent and reflective. A contemporaneity that is not curious about how it might be surprised is not worth our time.

Tagore in China

In a strange and serendipitous echo from the past, we find Rabindranath Tagore, the Bengali poet and artist who in some sense epitomized the writing of different Asian modernities in the twentieth century, saying something quite similar exactly eighty-five years ago in Shanghai, at the beginning of what was to prove to be a highly contested and controversial tour of China.

The poet's mission (and here, all we need to do is to substitute "artist" for "poet") is to attract the voice which is yet inaudible in the air; to inspire faith in a dream which is unfulfilled; to bring the earliest tidings of the unborn flower to a skeptic world.[3]

Tagore's plea operates in three distinct temporal registers: the "as yet inaudible" in the future, the "unfulfilled dream" in the past, and the fragility of the unborn flower in the skeptic world of the present. In each of these, the artist's work, for Tagore, is to safeguard and to take custody of - and responsibility for - that which is out of joint with its time, indeed with all time.

We could extend this reading to say that it is to rescue from the dead weight of tradition the things that were excluded from the canon, to make room for that to which the future may turn a deaf ear, and to protect the fragility of contemporary practice from present skepticism. Tagore's argument for a polyvocal response to the question of how to be "contemporary" was misinterpreted, in some senses willfully, by two factions of Chinese intellectuals. One faction celebrated him as an uncritical champion of tradition (which he was not), while the other campaigned against him as a conservative and "otherworldly" critic of modernity (which he refused to be). Between them, these partisans of tradition and modernity in 1920s China missed an opportunity to engage with a sense of the inhabitation of time that refused to construct arbitrary - and, indeed, uncritical - hierarchies in either direction: between past and present, east and west, then and now.

On Forgetting

As time passes and we grow more into the contemporary, the reasons for remembering other times grow, while the ability to recall them weakens. Memory straddles this paradox. We could say that the ethics of memory have something to do with the urgent negotiation between having to remember (which sometimes includes the obligation to mourn), and the requirement to move on (which sometimes includes the need to forget). Both are necessary, and each is notionally contingent on the abdication of the other, but life is not led by the easy rhythm of regularly alternating episodes of memory and forgetting, canceling each other out in a neat equation that resolves itself and attains equilibrium.

Forgetting: the true vanity of contemporaneity. Amnesia: a state of forgetfulness unaware of both itself and its own deficiency. True amnesia includes forgetting that one has forgotten all that has been forgotten. It is possible to assume that one remembers everything and still be an amnesiac. This is because aspects of the forgotten may no longer occupy even the verge of memory. They may leave no lingering aftertaste or hovering anticipation of something naggingly amiss. The amnesiac is in solitary confinement, guarded by his own clones, yet secluded especially from himself.

Typically, forms of belonging and solidarity that rely on the categorical exclusion of a notional other to cement their constitutive bonds are instances of amnesia. They are premised on the forgetting of the many contrarian striations running against the grain of the moment and its privileged solidarity. On particularly bad days, which may or may not have to do with lunar cycles, as one looks into a mirror and is unable to recognize one's own image, the hatred of the other rises like a tidal bore. Those unfaithful patches of self are then rendered as so much negative space, like holes in a mirror. Instead of being full to the brim with traces of the other, each of them is seen as a void, a wound in the self.

This void where the self-authenticated self lies shadowed and unable to recognize itself is attributed to the contagious corrosiveness of the other. The forgetting of the emptying-out of the self by its own rage forms the ground from which amnesia assaults the world. In trying to assert who we are, we forget, most of all, who we are. And then we forget the forgetting.

Kowloon Walled City and Its Memory

> "Nowhere, unless perhaps in dreams, can the phenomenon of the boundary be experienced in a more originary way than in cities."[4]

A few months ago we spent some time in Hong Kong, learning what it means to live in a city that distills its contemporaneity into a refined amnesia. We were interested in particular by what happened to the walled city of Kowloon and its memory.

Kowloon Walled City and its disappearance from the urban fabric of Hong Kong can be read as a parable of contemporary amnesia. The Walled City was once a diplomatic anomaly between China and the British Empire that functioned as a longstanding autonomous zone, a site of temporary near-permanence, an exclave within an enclave. The Walled City is not just a border in space; it also marks a border in time - a temporary suspension of linear time by

3 **Rabindranath Tagore**, "First Talk at Shanghai," in: *Talks in China* (Calcutta: Visva-Bharati, 1925), quoted in: Sisir Kumar Das, "The Controversial Guest: Tagore in China," in: Tan Chung (ed.) *Across the Himalayan Gap: An Indian Quest for Understanding China*, Indira Gandhi National Centre for the Arts, Delhi, 1998.

4 **Walter Benjamin**, *The Arcades Project*, The Belknap Press of Harvard University Press, Cambridge (MA), 1999, p. 88.

which the visitor agrees to the terms of a compact laid out by the current shape of the territory, a walled compound where a delicate game between memory and amnesia can be played out, apparently till eternity. This is the frontier where reality begins to cross over into an image.

Visiting the "Memorial Park" that stands on the former site of the Kowloon Walled City today is an uncanny experience. As with all "theme parks," walking in this enclosure is like walking in a picture postcard spread over hectares rather than inches. The constructed, spacious serenity of the park, its careful gestures to the tumult of the walled city by means of models, oral-history capsules, artifacts, replicas, and remains intend to provoke in the visitor some of the frisson in the fact that he or she is standing at what was once both condemned as an urban dystopia of crime, vice, and insanitation, and hailed as an anarchist Utopia. The neighborhood itself may have disappeared, but its footprint in popular culture can be discerned in the simulacral sites of action sequences in cyberpunk science fiction, gangster and horror films, manga, and multiuser computer games.

The walled city had approximately thirty-thousand people living in one-hundredth of a square mile, which amounts roughly to an average population-per-unit-area density ratio of 3.3 million people to a square mile. This makes it the densest inhabited unit of space in world history. If we think of this space as a repository of memories, it would be the most haunted place on Earth.

Why do such spaces - sometimes crowded, sometimes empty (but apparently crowded with ghosts) - appear in a manner that is almost viral, such that the trope of empty but haunted streets, set in the near future of global cities, begins to show the first signs of a cinematic epidemic of our times? Will we remember the cinema of the early twenty-first century as the first intimation of the global collapse of urban space under its own weight? Or is this imaginary appearance of a haunting, suicidal metropolis more of an inoculation than a symptom, an early shoring-up of the defenses of citizens against their own obsolescence? How can we remember, or even represent, an inoculation that could be an obituary just as much as it could be a premonition or a warning?

The surrealist poet Louis Aragon, speaking of the disappearing neighborhoods of Paris as the city morphed into twentieth-century modernity, once wrote that "it is only today, when the pickaxe menaces them, that they have at last become the true sanctuaries of the cult of the ephemeral... Places that were incomprehensible yesterday, and that tomorrow will never know."[5]

What happens when someone from within these spaces that were "incomprehensible yesterday and that tomorrow will never know" decides to make themselves known? How does their account of the space square with its more legendary reportage?

> "I recall the Walled City as one big playground, especially the rooftops, where me and my friends would run and jump from one building to the next, developing strong calf muscles, a high tolerance of pain, and control of our fear, and our feet. The rooftops were our domain, shared only with the jets that passed overhead almost within reach of our outstretched arms as they roared down the final approach to Kai Tak Airport. Among the tangle of TV antennae we hid our kid-valuable things, toys and things we didn't want our parents to know about because, well, most of them were stolen or bought with money we earned putting together stuff in the little one-room 'factories' that were all over the Walled City - if our parents knew we had money, they'd have taken it. We were good at hiding things, and ourselves."[6]

Disappearance and Representation: Haunting the Record

What does disappearance do to the telling of that which has disappeared? How do we speak to, of, and for the presence of absences in our lives, our cities? Ackbar Abbas, in his book *Hong Kong: Culture and the Politics of Disappearance,* meditates at length on disappearance, cities, and images:

> "A space of disappearance challenges historical representation in a special way, in that it is difficult to describe precisely because it can adapt so easily to any description. It is a space that engenders images so quickly that it becomes *nondescript*... we can think about a nondescript space as that strange thing: an ordinary, everyday space that has somehow lost its usual system of interconnectedness, a deregulated space. Such a space defeats description not because it is illegible and none of the categories fit, but because it is hyperlegible and all the categories seem to fit, whether they are the categories of social sciences, cultural criticism, or of fiction. Any description then that tries to capture the features of the city will have to be, to some extent at least, stretched between fact and fiction... If this is the case, then there can be no single-minded pursuit of the signs that finishes with

5 **Louis Aragon**, "Paris Peasant," in: Charles Harrison and Paul Wood (eds.), *Art in Theory, 1900-1990. An Anthology of Changing Ideas*, Blackwell, Oxford, 1993, p. 456.

6 **Chiu Kin Fung**, "Children of the Walled City," in: *Asia Literary Review*, vol. 10, Winter 2008, pp. 72-73.

> a systematic reading of the city, only a compendium of *indices of disappearance* (like the nondescript) that takes into account the city's errancy and that addresses the city through its heterogeneity and parapraxis."[7]

A parapraxis is a kind of Freudian slip, an involuntary disclosure of something that would ordinarily be repressed. It could be a joke, an anomaly, a revealing slip-up, a haunting. What does it mean to "haunt the record"? When does a presence or a trace become so deeply etched into a surface that it merits a claim to durability simply for being so difficult to repress, resolve, deal with, and put away? The endurance of multiple claims to land and other scarce material resources often rests on the apparent impossibility of arranging a palimpsest of signatures and other inscriptions rendered illegible by accumulation over a long time, and across many generations. In a sense, this is why the contingent and temporary character of the Kowloon Walled City endured for as long as it did. There is of course the delicate irony of the fact that the protection offered by its juridical anomaly with regard to sovereignty - a constitutional Freudian slip with consequences - was erased the moment Hong Kong reverted to China. The autonomy of being a wedge of China in the middle of Hong Kong became moot the moment Hong Kong was restored to Chinese sovereignty. Resolving the question of Hong Kong's status automatically resolved all doubts and ambivalences with regard to claims over the custody and inhabitation of Kowloon Walled City.

A Chinese Sense of Time: Neither Permanence nor Impermanence

It is appropriate to end with a quotation from a Chinese text from the fourth century of the Common Era, a Madhyamika Mahayana Buddhist text, *The Treatise of Sengchao.* When the sutras say that things pass, they say so with a measure of reservation, for they wish to contradict people's belief in permanence. (And here we would gesture in the direction of the assumption that this contemporaneity is destined to be permanent; after all, this too shall pass). And when the sutras say that things are lost, they say so with a mental reservation in order to express disapproval of what people understand by "passing." (And here we would gesture in the direction of the assumption that this contemporaneity is destined to oblivion; after all, something from this too shall remain).

Their wording may be contradictory, but not their aim. It follows that with the sages: permanence has not the meaning of the staying behind, while the wheel of time, or Karma, moves on. Impermanence has not the meaning of outpassing the wheel. People who seek in vain ancient events in our time conclude that things are impermanent. We, who seek in vain present events in ancient times, see that things are permanent. Therefore, Buddha, Liberation, He, it, appears at the proper moment, but has no fixed place in time.[8]

What more can we say of contemporaneity? It appears at the proper moment, but has no fixed place in time. In that spirit, let us not arrogate solely to ourselves the pleasures and the perils of all that is to be gained and lost in living and working, as we do, in these interesting times.

This text was first publish in: *e-flux journal*, no. 12, January 2010, pp. 40-57.

7 **M. Ackbar Abbas**, *Hong Kong: Culture and the Politics of Disappearance*, University of Minnesota Press, Minneapolis (MN), 1997, pp. 73-74.

8 **See: Chao Lun**, *The Treatise of Sengchao*, Hong Kong University Press, Hong Kong, 1968.

Eight Views fro

Bani Abidi / AES Group
Michael Bielicky & Kamila B. Richter
Roberto Cabot / Matthias Gommel
Rafael Lozano-Hemmer
Ni Haifeng / Adrian Paci
Raqs Media Collective / Ho-Yeol Ryu
Hito Steyerl

n an Exhibition

World Time: The World as Transit Zone

The first section addresses living in a planetary world that finds an apt metaphor in the airport. The transit zone is a place in between, where one does not arrive or remain, but merely awaits a new departure. World time has mapped and compressed global space but we experience a different time that escapes the 24 time zones on the clock when our bodies move in space. The installation of the Raqs Media Collective, which the artists called *Escapement* (the mechanism in a clock or watch responsible for the never resting movement of the hands on its face) seems to recall the clocks in the entrance hall of a hotel where a global clientele checks the different local times in those places they will be heading to. The hours on the phalanx of the 27 clocks (indicating the time of 24 real cities and three imaginary ones) are linked to diverse mental states, such as anxiety, nostalgia, and fatigue. In a commentary, the artists referred to themselves as "contemporaries of different times and spaces." "Contemporaneity harbors the simultaneity of very different ways of life," is a statement corroborated by many artists which were presented in the exhibition *The Global Contemporary.* In the center of the installation, a young woman with a dreamy expression on her face seems to be immersed in her own imagination, far away from the time competition among the surrounding clocks.

Several times in the same section the airport serves as a metaphor for the experience of a global condition that is familiar to every passenger as a paradox of freedom and enclosure. Security measures, at every airport, stand in the way of our free movement and raise highly visible borders between us and the departure gate. In Matthias Gommel's installation *Untitled (Passage)*, such queue management also forces visitors to the exhibition into a controled movement. A text on the bands of the security barriers cites the old naval song "A Life on the Ocean Wave" that bears the memory of uncertain duration and arrival when traveling in times past. The security barriers turn up again in Bani Abidi's work where they serve as allegories of state violence and strategies of demarcation in her hometown of Karachi. They adopt the most diverse forms in the views on the digital prints. Thus, although we think we see aesthetic objects, their designated titles reveal their actual functions as emblems of authority that regulate everyday life in this former part of British India.

Two other works bring to attention the contrast between the freedom of global traffic and the exclusion of many people, for instance, refugees. There is, on the one hand, Ho-Yeol Ryu's digital photograph *Flughafen* [Airport] where a dense "swarm" of starting airplanes, each of them sporting the emblem of a different airline, seems to take off simultaneously at the airport in Hannover, Germany, a place selected at random. In this view, the globally competitive airlines symbolize departure as a self-fulfilling promise. But whose departure is this? There is, by contrast, Adrian Paci's photograph *Centro di Permanenza Temporanea* [Center of Temporary Duration] which, together with the corresponding video, has become an unforgettable metaphor for the destiny of those who wait in vain for an escape from where they are. In fact, the gangway stairs upon which they are crowded, leads nowhere. It seems that in this deserted area the airplane has left forever.

Hito Steyerl's video *In Free Fall* introduces us to an airplane junkyard, a true cemetery of airplanes whose story has ended in a Californian desert. Various inserted constellations recover the real or imaginary story of a Boeing, which has been junked as a "ruin" among other remains of air traffic. There is even a simulated plane crash that alludes to the title of the video. In a related paper written by the artist, Steyerl says that *In Free Fall* represents "a thought experiment on vertical perspective." The horizon, which for so long served as orientation is no longer there; now, unstable ground replaces the former vanishing point. Air traffic is about leaving and reaching safe ground. But is there a ground to speak of in contemporary societies? In Steyerl's (and Shakespeare's) words: "Time is out of joint, and we no longer know whether we are objects or subjects as we spiral down in an imperceptible free fall."

Artists not only concurrently pursue their projects in several places, on-line as well as in various studios, but also, as Ni Haifeng's installation *Para-Production* demonstrates, they produce their projects in different regions of the world. This practice testifies to a new state of affairs that characterizes the art trade in the global era. (AB)

Bani Abidi

* 1971 in Karachi (PK), lives and works in Karachi and New Delhi (IN)

Security Barriers A–L, 2008

12 ink-jet prints, 28 × 44 cm each, framed

The artist Bani Abidi is a nomad of two cultures. Born and brought up in Karachi, Pakistan, she lives and works today in New Delhi, India. These biographical details run through her humorous works that depict the cultural and political differences and similarities between the two countries and their conflict-ridden border. In her work *Security Barriers A–L*, Abidi employs temporary architectural elements for an analysis of political manifestations of state violence, the maintenance of state power, and national strategies of demarcation.

In twelve prints, the artist catalogs the various models of security barriers in her hometown of Karachi, which she first photographed on-site, before going on to digitally rework them. She found the various constructions in front of embassies, consulates, at airports, and intersections. Arranged in rows of three, the brightly colored, clear, and sharply contoured vector drawings against a white background are like objects featured in a glossy catalog. One almost feels tempted to order one of these beautiful objects for the front yard, even though their design idiom is unambiguously that of a barrier. Only the attached titles establish the link to their original context and the related strategies of isolation and demarcation: type H stands out among the drawings with its all too vigorous expression of political superiority, while the flower-bedecked barrier in front of the British Deputy High Commission of the former colony almost seems smarmy. (KB)

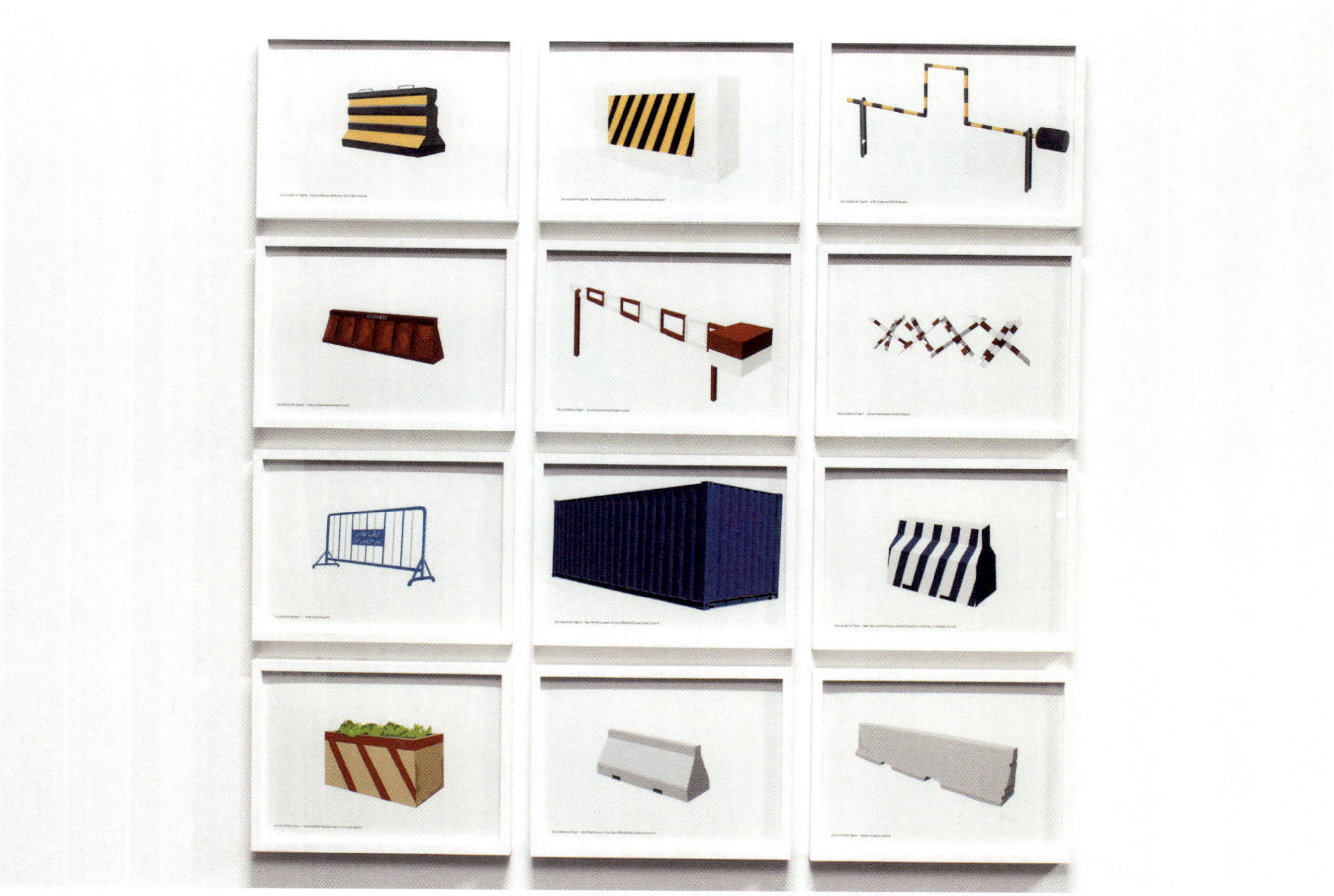

AES Group

Founded in 1987 in Moscow (RU)
Tatiana Arzamasova,* 1955 in Moscow; Lev Evzovich, * 1958 in Moscow;
Evgeny Svyatsky,* 1957 in Moscow; live and work in Moscow

Oasis, 2000

Mixed-media installation, dimensions variable

The work *Oasis* integrates some ideas of the *Islamic Project* launched by AES Group in 1996. In the interior of a Bedouin tent, traditional handmade carpets of oriental design are combined with digital prints on silk representing a dystopian world in the wake of a fictive Islamic invasion (as predicted for 2006). The prints are visible and provocative evidence of the decline of Western domination and the Islamic rewriting of Western history. This "documentation" of the future consists of well-known views of Western capitals surrealistically invaded by the Other in the form of Islamic symbolism, domes of mosques, minarets, tents, oriental markets, etc.

Originally conceived as an ironic parody of globalization and global tourism, the project reflects the tendency of mass media to exploit the mass phobia of the Western world. The visible "clash of civilizations" (Samuel P. Huntington) in the form of a worst-case scenario reveals the populism of political propaganda, showing the mechanisms for constructing "new" realities under the influence of mass media.

Over the course of time, and especially after 9/11, life itself transformed the project into a museum art object. Today, this paradoxical work documents "the future of the past." (DM)

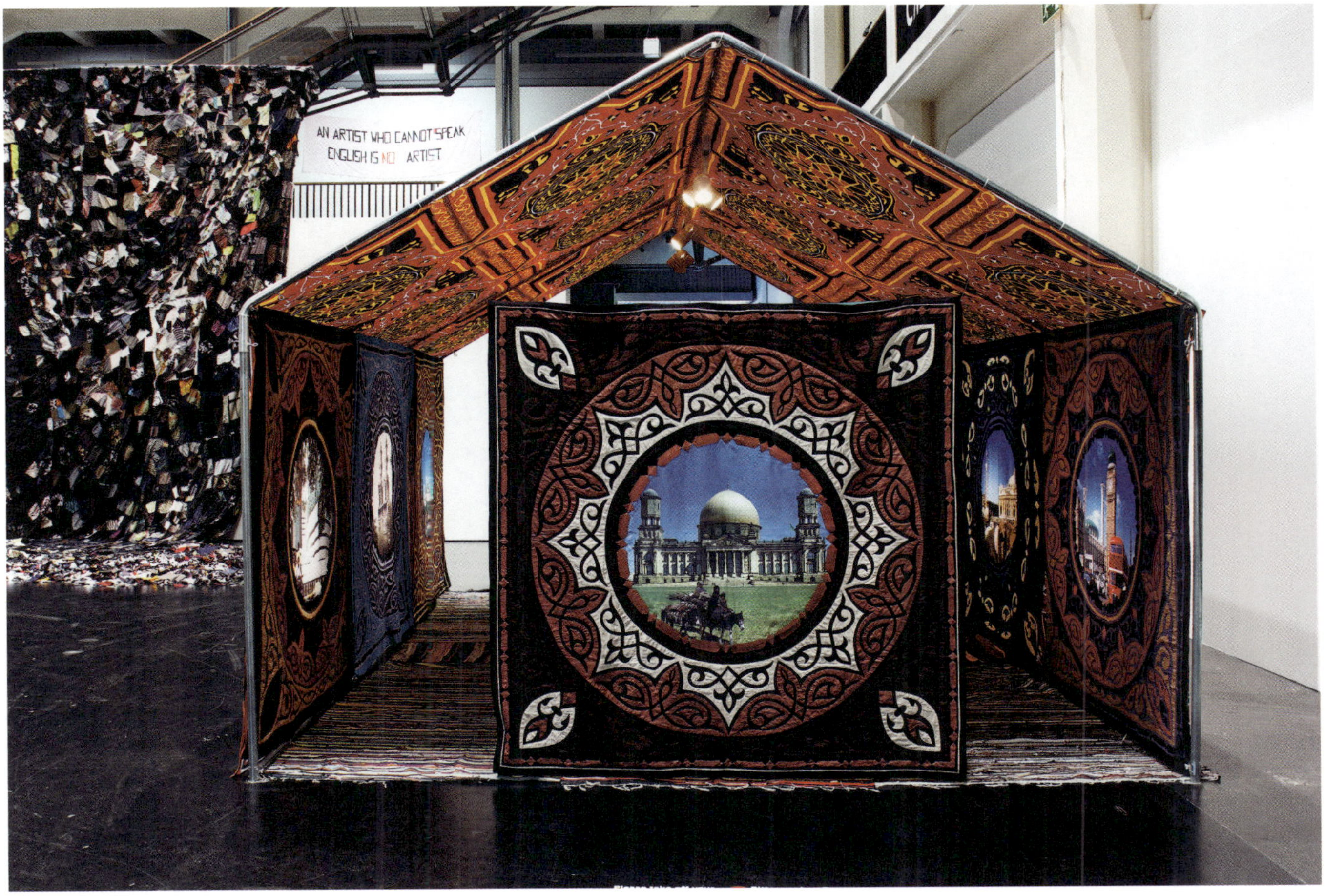

Michael Bielicky & Kamila B. Richter

Michael Bielicky, * 1954 in Prague (CZ); Kamila B. Richter, * 1976 in Olomouc (CZ); live and work in Karlsruhe and Düsseldorf (DE)

The Garden of Error and Decay, 2010/2011

Web-based installation, computer graphic

In their works Michael Bielicky and Kamila B. Richter examine the relationship between reality and simulation, perception and experience, and experiment with data visualization technologies in the spirit of "information art." In their installations they reduce the content of the news industry to recurrent headlines and tags, which they translate into a dynamic pictogram language in order to identify the patterns of information that today seemingly connect us with reality.

The network installation *The Garden of Error and Decay* narrates the ongoing story of today's global disasters. In keeping with our contemporary experience of digitally networked media, Twitter users and financial news feed the stories. Each time a topic relating to disasters is sent and discussed on Twitter, the installation translates it in real time into an animated pictogram. Using a gun as an interface, the users have the option to either eliminate or reinforce the disaster. But it is not within the users' power to change things. As in real life, it is the dynamics of the stock market and the headlines that dictate events. The moving-image format here acts as a data-fed narrative in real time, and is neither film, game, nor a nonlinear interactive story. In the installation and on their own computers via the Internet (www.gardenoferroranddecay.net), users are seemingly able to interact with the story. *The Garden of Error and Decay* reflects the networked media reality of the twenty-first century, which is increasingly affecting our perception of the world. (AB)

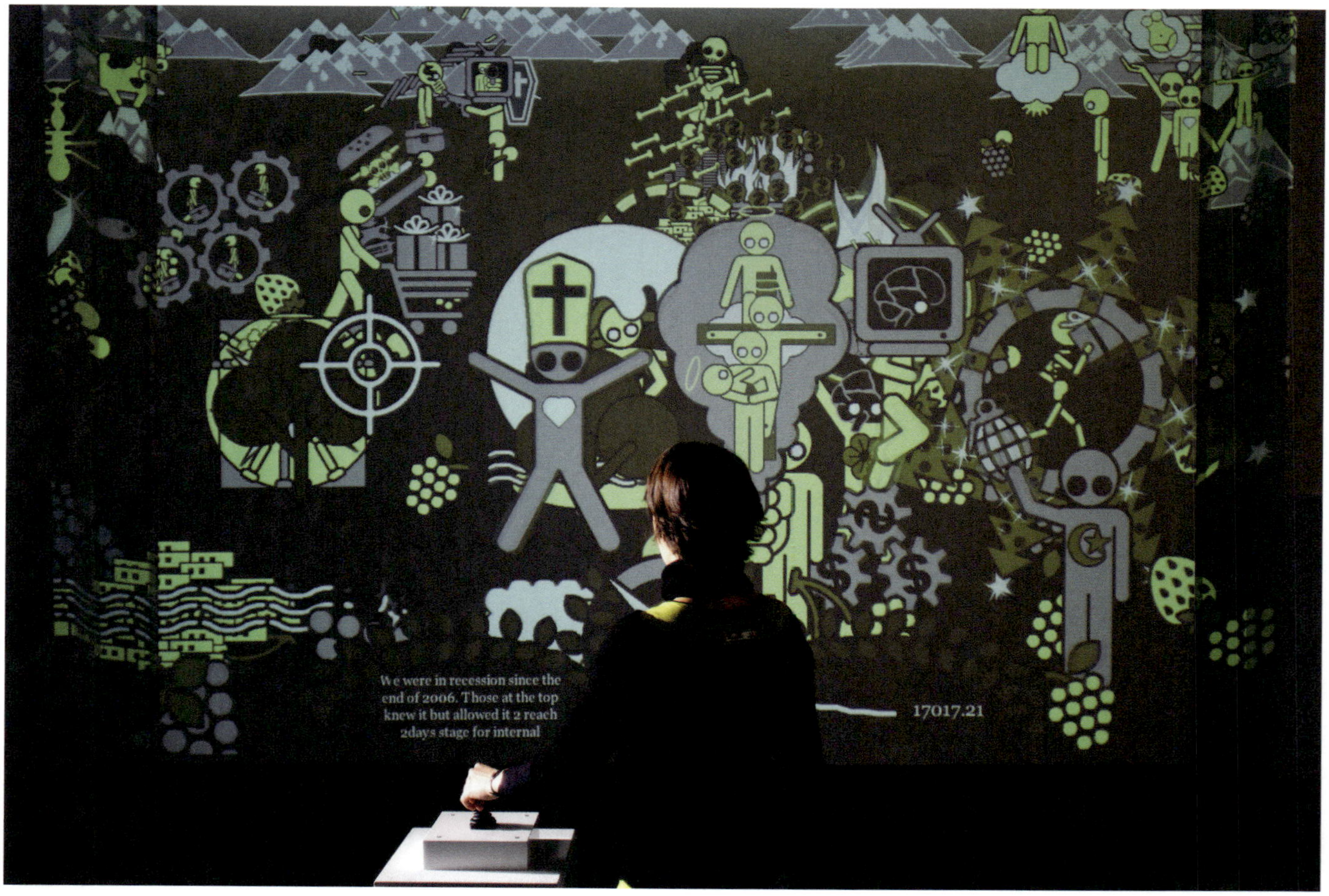

Roberto Cabot

* 1963 in Rio de Janeiro (BR), lives and works in Rio de Janeiro

Favela Chic, 2008

The UNO building in NY with Sugar Loaf reflected, 2008

Photographs from the series *E-Scapes*,
100 × 133.3 cm and
133.3 × 100 cm, framed, ed. of 6

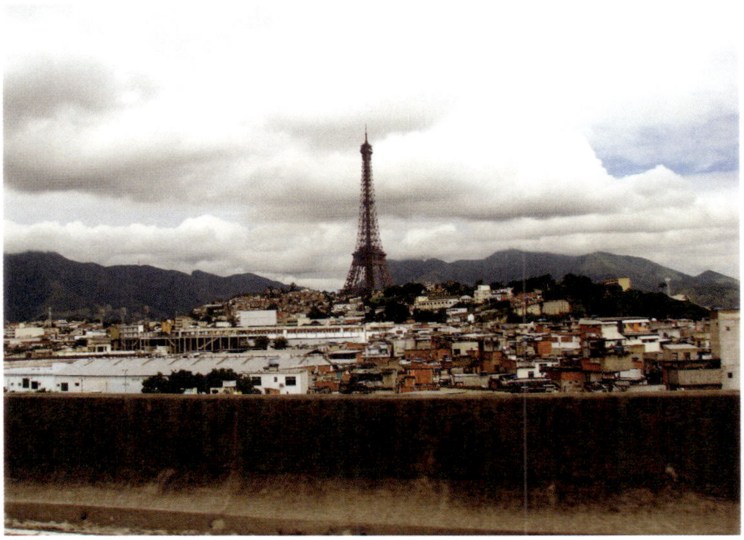

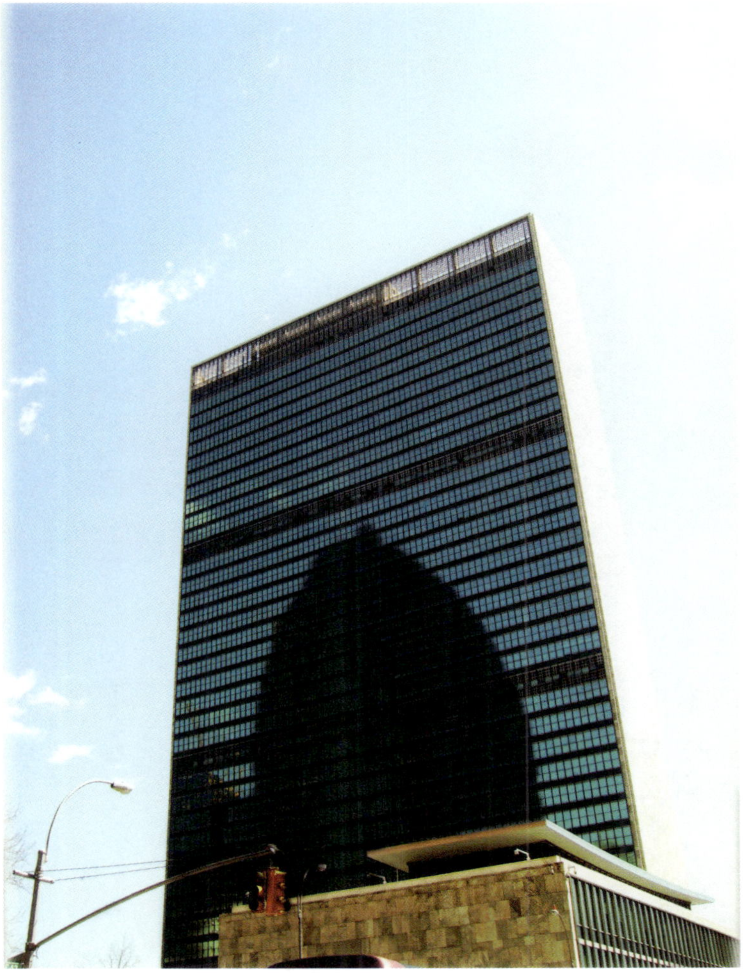

There is something wrong about the digital prints from the series *E-Scapes* by Roberto Cabot. In *Favela Chic* and *The UNO building in NY with Sugar Loaf reflected* the media artist has assembled absurd city views: the Eiffel Tower, symbol of the European belief in progress of nineteenth-century industrialization, clashes with the favelas of Rio de Janeiro, which are structures of random growth built of boards from wooden boxes, metal canisters, palm tree branches, and similar stuff. In the facade of the UN headquarters in New York, an architectonic landmark for the attempt by hegemonic powers to create a political institution after World War II that would assure world peace, the 394-meter high Sugarloaf Mountain of Rio de Janeiro is mirrored.

Through global circulation of images - for example, postcards or holiday snapshots - all motifs have become landmarks for the place where they are located and the worldview connected with it. Thus, it is not tourist landmarks that clash, but rather insignia of different world models and the methods to appropriate and explain them. By drawing them together in photomontages, Cabot makes their synchronicity visible. Neither the one image motif nor the other can claim prerogative of interpretation. The Eiffel Tower and the favelas, the UN building and the Sugarloaf Mountain are perspectives that refer to each other, which, like in the UN headquarters, continually mirror each other. (KB)

Matthias Gommel

* 1970 in Leonberg (DE), lives and works in Karlsruhe (DE)

Untitled (Passage), 2011

Mixed-media installation, Tensabarrier posts, printed barrier tape, sound, dimensions variable
Produced in collaboration with ZKM | Karlsruhe

In public places, structures are sometimes set up that define the approaches and paths to which people are obliged to conform. Barriers and checkpoints drastically restrict freedom of movement, but are supposed to ensure that people can move about in an orderly fashion and that everyone can reach his or her destination. Matthias Gommel's work *Untitled (Passage)* addresses an example of such order: the queue management system, a familiar sight at airports and museums. In practical terms, these management systems are a nuisance. They constitute a barrier, a distance between us and our destination, whether artwork or airplane. At the same time, they point to something special lying beyond: once the labyrinth of ordering cordons has been passed, the world behind them seems to open up.

This ambiguity of promising obstacles could be interpreted as symptomatic of contemporary life forever in transit between new places and lifestyles. In this way, the nonplace of the guidance system becomes a metaphor for the eternal journey, and the uniform play of the cordons like the play of ocean waves, through which the journey takes place. As in the old song "A Life on the Ocean Wave", which can be read and heard in the installation, the necessity of an arrival or a destination fades into the background of a life in transit. Such a life remains a romantic vision, yet one that bears within itself a certain tragedy; for departing to different shores is still today often a flight from inhuman living conditions, followed by an endless state of transition amidst bureaucracy and illegality. Even contemporary art, which looks upon myths of faraway places skeptically, is caught between the romantic and the tragic. Referring to the song mentioned above, the Dutch artist Bas Jan Ader named a small boat "Ocean Wave" in which he sailed out into the Atlantic in 1975 for the performance *In Search of the Miraculous*; he was never heard of again. (AM)

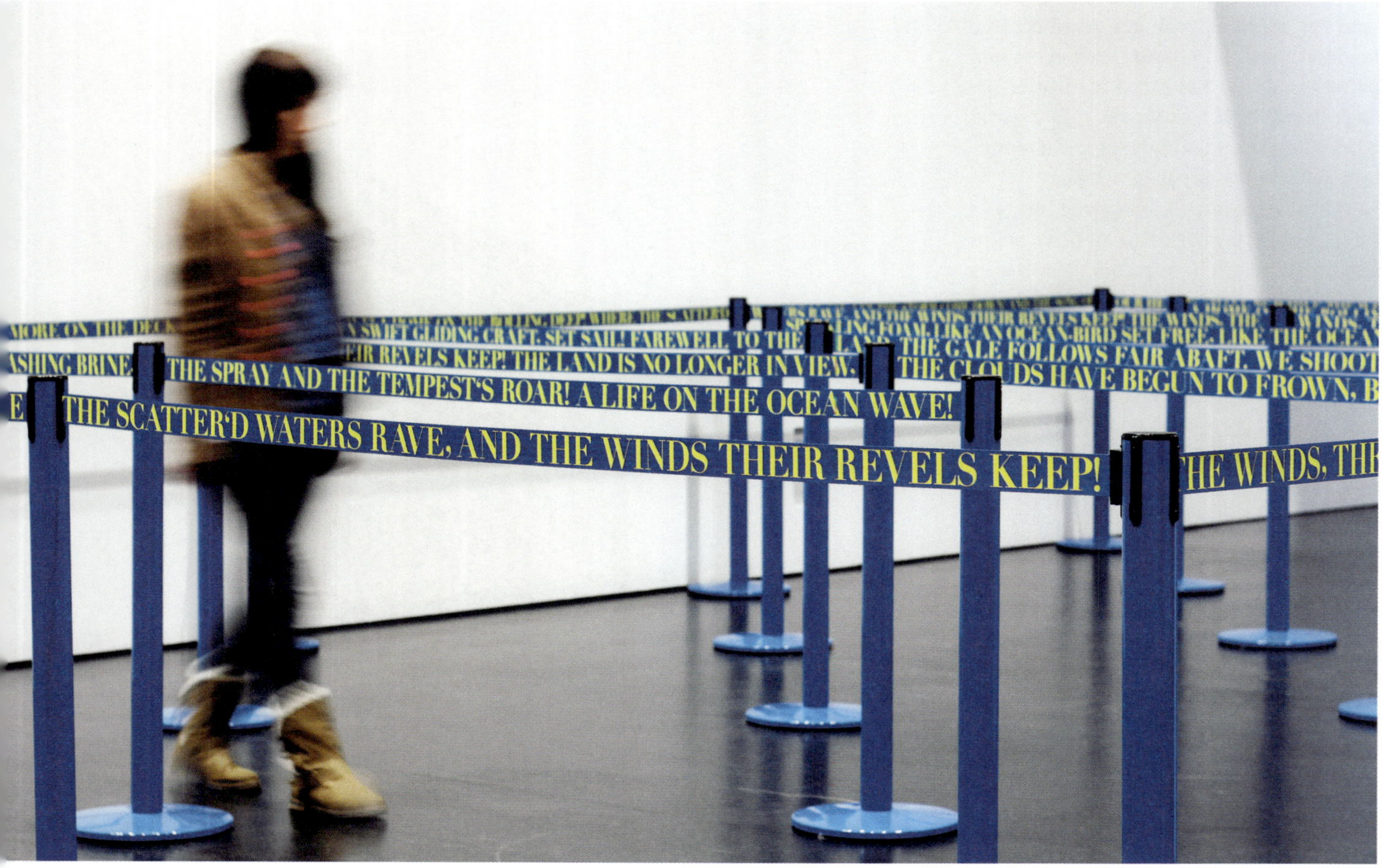

Rafael Lozano-Hemmer

* 1967 in Mexico City (MX), lives and works in Montreal (CA) and Madrid (ES)

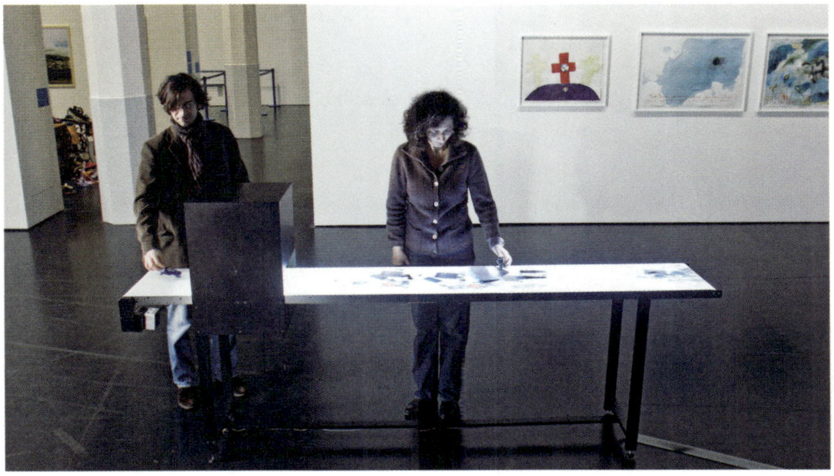

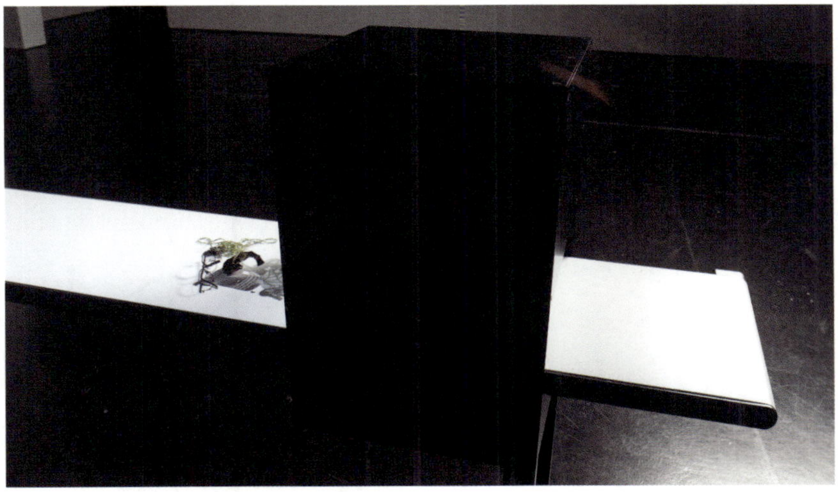

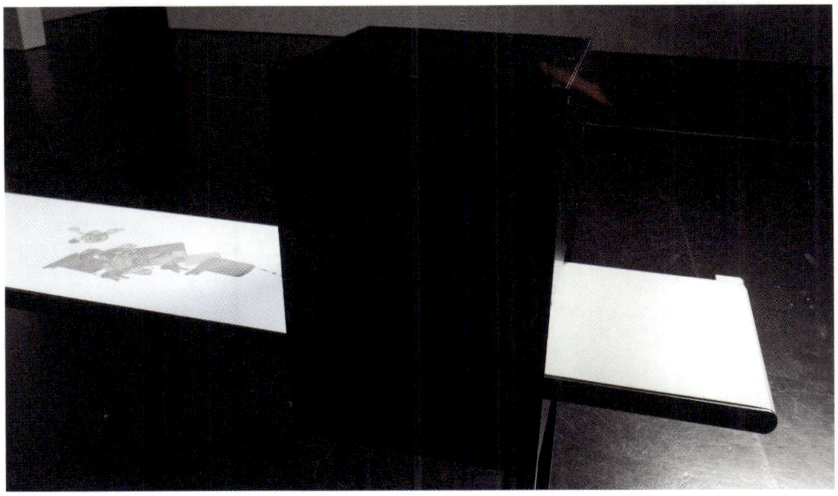

Please Empty Your Pockets, 2010

Interactive installation (conveyor belt, computer, HD projectors, HD camera), 273 × 42 × 124 cm dimensions variable)

Rafael Lozano-Hemmer is best known for his interactive installations, whether situated in an urban public space (as in the case of his *Relational Architecture* series) or in a gallery. In his artworks the artist makes use of a wide range of new media and devices such as sensors, biometric scanners, surveillance cameras, tracking systems, and microphones.

The installation *Please Empty Your Pockets* consists of a computer-controlled scanner and a conveyor belt. Anyone can participate in the creation of a new piece of interactive art by placing a small item of their choice on the conveyor belt. The installation's structure is reminiscent of an airport security scanner, the only difference being that in this case participation is optional. Scanned images of the objects appear at the other end of the conveyor belt. New items reemerge together with others scanned earlier and objects retrieved from a database of 600,000 items that were scanned and collected by the installation. With the aid of augmented reality techniques, the installation combines real objects with the traces they leave, and thus functions as a collective memory of the processed objects. (DM)

Ni Haifeng

* 1964 in Zhoushan (CN), lives and works in Amsterdam (NL) and Beijing (CN)

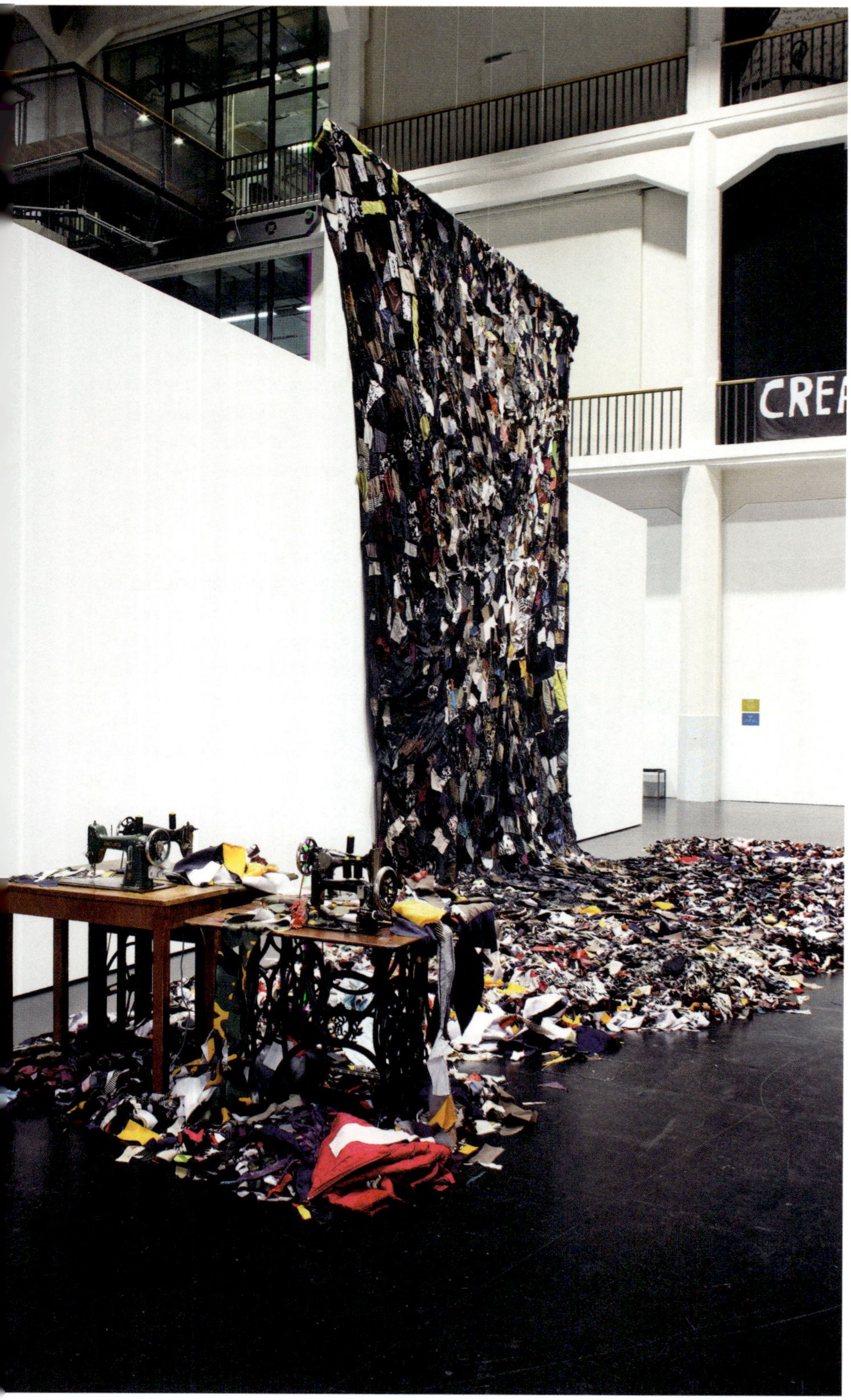

Para-Production, 2008

Mixed-media installation,
textile shreds, 4-5 sewing machines,
dimensions variable

In his works Ni Haifeng undertakes a critical examination of "Made in China" mass production and its effects on contemporary humans. *Para-Production* refers to the cyclical principles of capitalist commodity production - manufacturing process, labor, and capital gains - and turns them around conceptually. For reasons of cost efficiency, industrial nations often outsource the production of goods to Asia, whereas the final products are then transported back to the West for consumption. In Ni Haifeng's installation, waste products from Chinese mass manufacturing instead of finished products were brought to Europe, where people engaging in unpaid, collective labor make these into a huge tapestry. Exhibition visitors are invited to take part in this process.

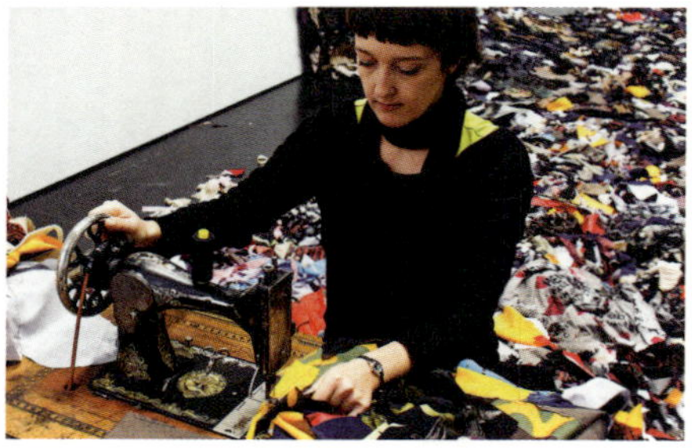

The result of the work is not economically useful - the goal is not the highest possible financial gain - but a socially valuable product, since it promotes the collective interaction of individuals. In contrast to the alienation of work and product, an alternative method of production so to speak emerges in the exhibition space. This temporary paraproduction (*para-*: Greek for alongside, next to, beyond) takes up the issue of the mass consumption of commercial goods and their reprocessing while at the same time proposing a redefinition of labor as social interaction. (EA)

Adrian Paci

* 1969 in Shkodra (AL), lives and works in Milan (IT)

Centro di Permanenza Temporanea, 2007

C-print on aluminum Dibond,
98 × 180 cm

The Albanian artist Adrian Paci works in various media (video, installation, painting, and sculpture) and with a thematic focus on sociopolitical content. His works comprise reflections on the existential moments of human existence and condense the consequences of conflict and social upheaval. Paci is an artist who has taken up the cluster of issues connected with migration, globalization, and cultural identity, impressively articulating his experience of these in images.

Paci's photograph *Centro di Permanenza Temporanea* [Center of Temporary Duration] formed part of the eponymous video work created in 2007. It shows a series of dark-skinned and Hispanic people on a gangway apparently leading to nowhere. The viewer never learns whether this group is to be deported or whether it is about to embark on a journey to some other, unspecified destination. And yet this human phalanx, which probably no airplane will ever collect, is the epitome of disappointed hope. One may detect irony or even self-irony running through this work, but perhaps it is also the expression of a historical awareness of the mutability of states and identities. (AE)

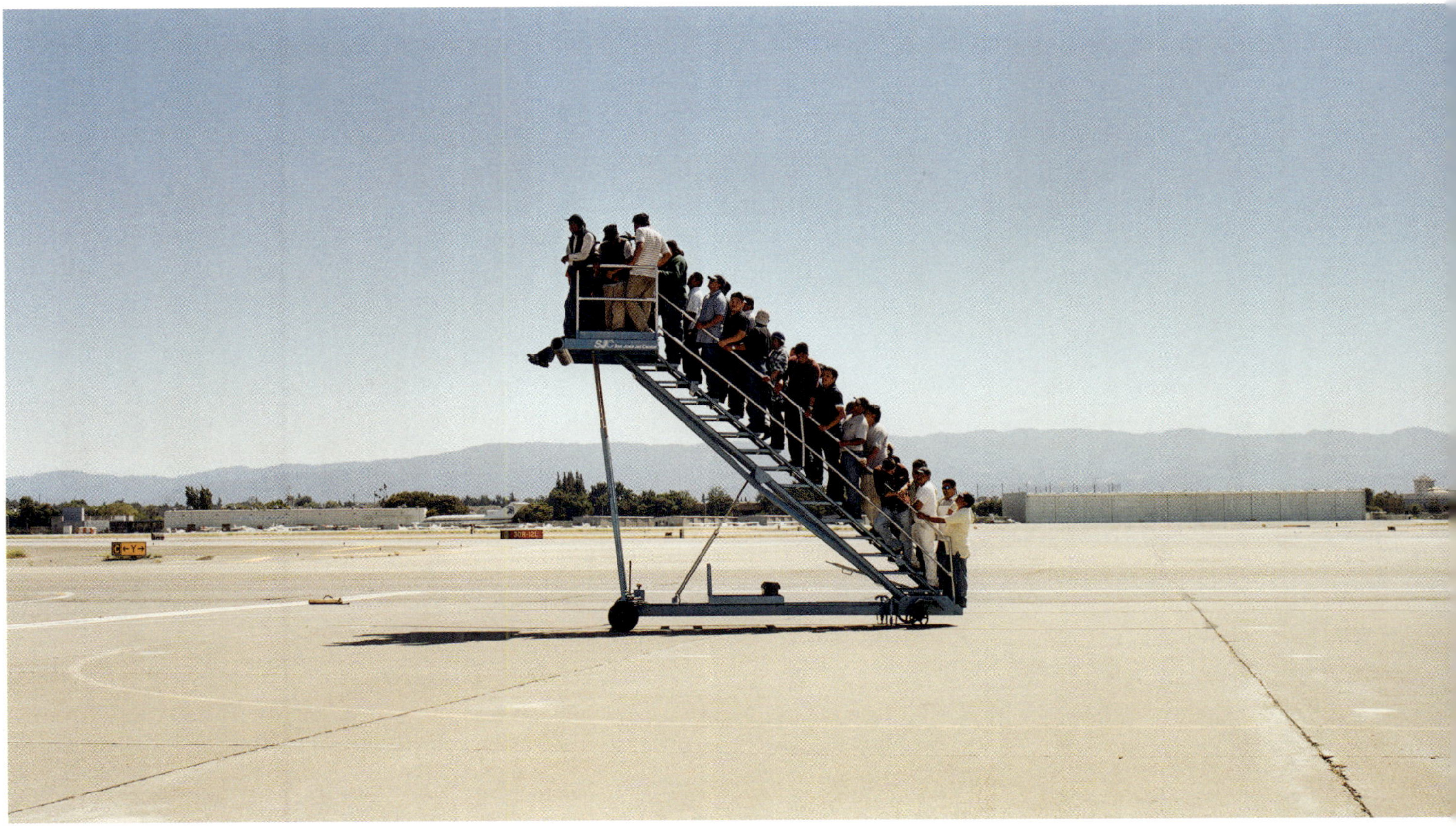

Raqs Media Collective

Jeebesh Bagchi, *1965; Monica Narula, *1969; Shuddhabrata Sengupta, *1968; live and work in New Delhi (IN)

Escapement, 2009

Mixed-media installation,
27 clocks, high gloss aluminum with LED lights,
4 flat screen monitors, video and audio in loop,
dimensions variable,
edition of 2

The artist group Raqs Media Collective has been based in New Delhi since 1992. The collective cofounded the research platform Sarai in 2001. A subject the artists treat in many of their works is the impact on the perception of time and contemporaneity made by information technologies in the digital age, whereby time and space apparently converge.

The installation *Escapement* consists of 27 clocks representing cities in different time zones, thus creating a map of the world. Three of the clocks signify fictitional or ancient cities, like Macondo or Babel. Instead of indicating the usual numbers, the clocks' hands point to words such as anxiety, guilt, fatigue, fear - words referring to complex emotional states of being that are the same for all regardless of geographic or temporal location. The installation's effect is reinforced by the sound of heartbeats, familiar noises of everyday communication, and a video of the expressionless face of a young man. An escapement is the mechanism in a clock that controls the hands and thus marks passage of time. The word connotes both the "escaping" or fleeting movement of time and refers to time's measurement. The invention of the clock has intensified the interval between "now" and "before." At the same time, we live within a grid comprising different degrees of longitude and latitude according to which world time is measured. But even though the clocks show the same time merely because they are located at the same longitude, as are London and Lagos, this does not mean that people in these cities have the same sense of time. On the contrary, we are "contemporaries of different times and spaces." Therefore, "we are also in a state of permanent jetlag, which makes us slightly out of breath and fall out of time. Contemporaneity harbors the simultaneity of very different ways of life." (AMB)

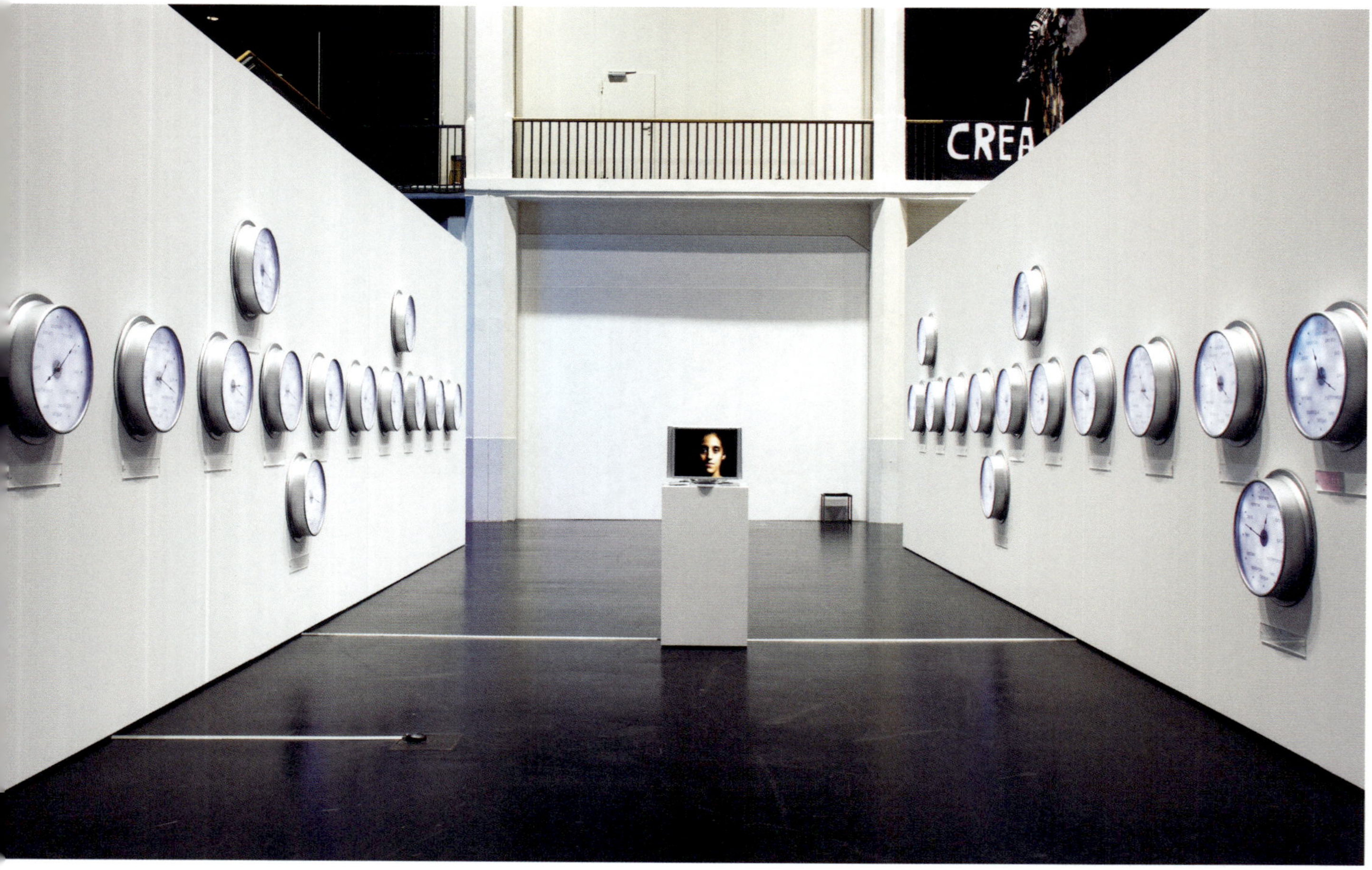

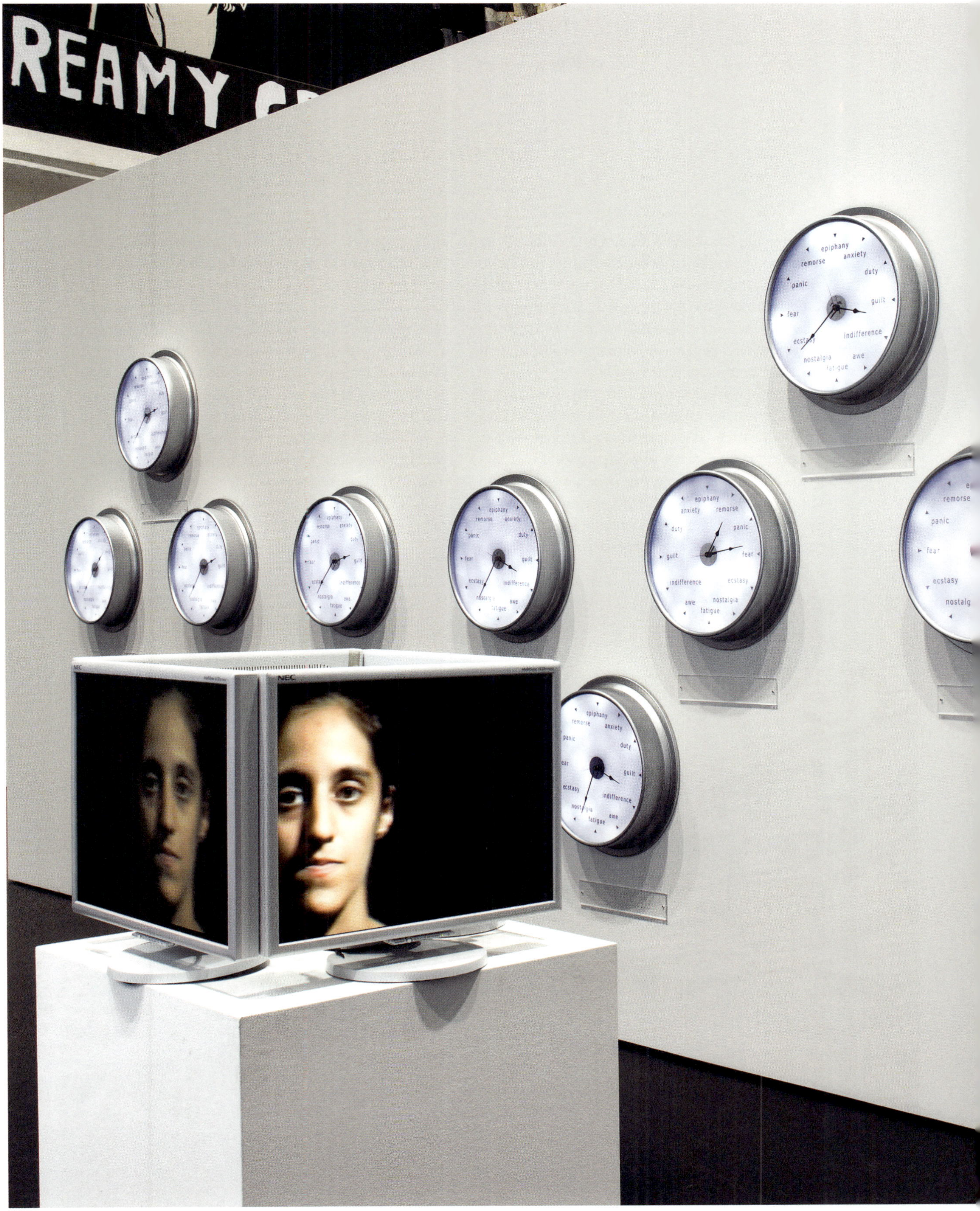
REAMY
epiphany
remorse
anxiety
duty
panic
guilt
fear
indifference
ecstasy
nostalgia
awe
fatigue
NEC

Ho-Yeol Ryu

* 1971 in Seoul (KR), lives and works in Seoul

Flughafen, 2005

Digital print, 100 × 150 cm

The photographic work of Korean artist Ho-Yeol Ryu renders the boundaries between reality and fiction permeable, and challenges the viewer's perception. Taking familiar everyday scenes as a starting point, Ryu uses the resources of digital editing to create miniature worlds that pose questions about reality and illusion in the medium of photography.

In Ryu's work *Flughafen* [Airport] (2005), which consists of various layered shots of airplanes taking off, different time levels overlap. In a globalized society airports are of decisive importance for it is at these transit sites, or non-places, that questions concerning migration and identity become apparent and borders are ostensibly renegotiated on a daily basis, such as at passport control. In his work, Ryu develops portraits of almost surreal, everyday events in a globalized world in which time and space are compressed. Overlapping different temporal levels distills the contraction of time and space - already operated by the airplane itself - into one unique moment. Although the image is obviously the result of postproduction, for the viewer it calls to mind a familiar and common experience. Who hasn't stared at the constant and apparently endless rhythm of departures and landing while waiting to board a plane? Who hasn't felt reassured and at home while looking at and participating in this dance that is truly shaping our lives? (AE)

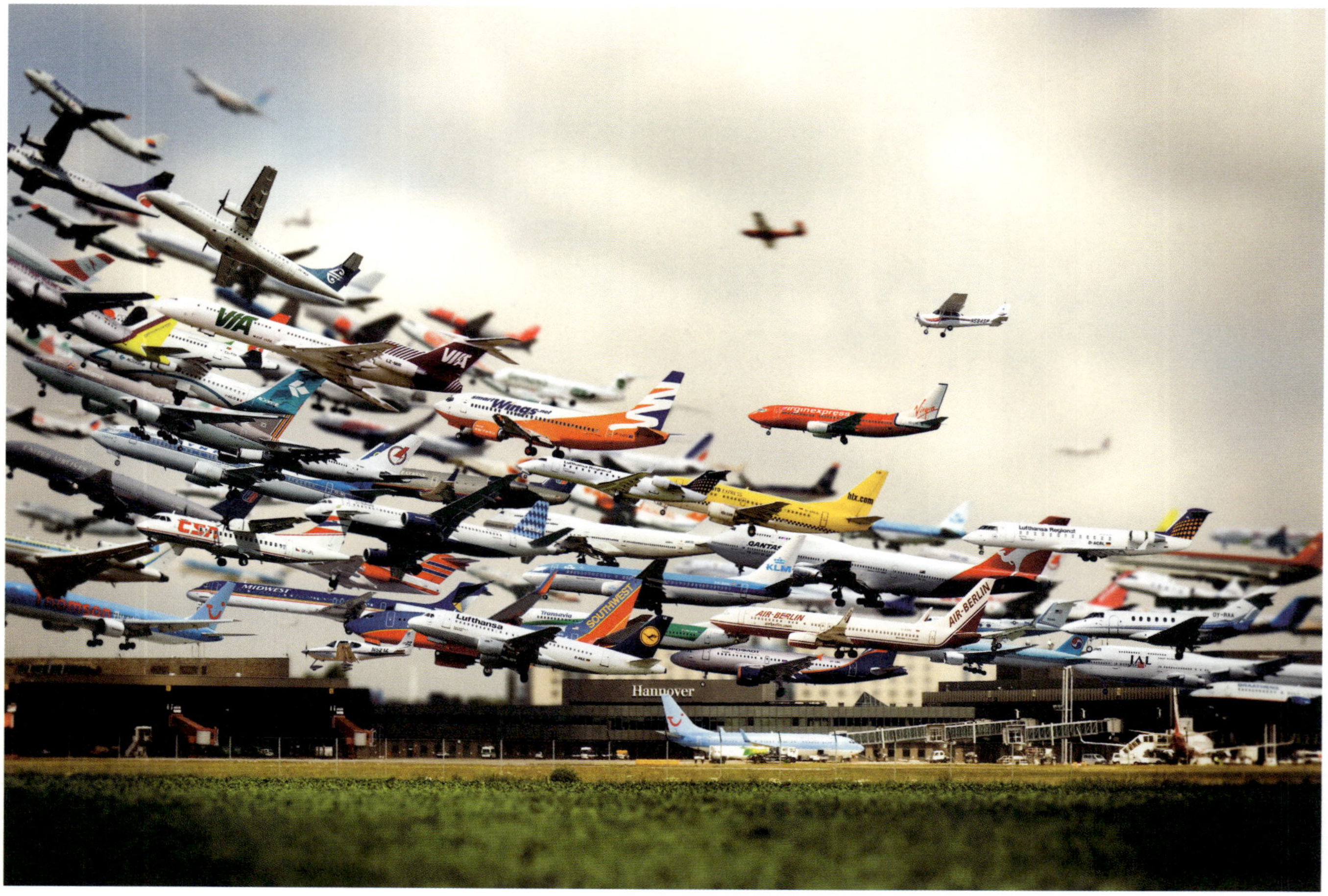

Hito Steyerl

* 1966 in Munich (DE), lives and works in Berlin (DE)

In Free Fall, 2010

HD video, color, sound, 32 min

As an artist, theoretician, and filmmaker Hito Steyerl examines the circulation of images in contemporary visual culture, as well as the dynamics of global capitalism. Her approach to contemporary art explores the interface of politics and aesthetics, and in so doing draws our attention to the close interplay of rhetorical device, historical narration, and the introduction of an increasing number of new visual norms.

Combining various segments and techniques, ranging from interviews to computer animations and archival footage, the video *In Free Fall* narrates the serviceable life of a Boeing 707-700 4X-JYI. Set in an aeroplane junkyard in California's Mojave Desert, the jet's service history is recounted chronologically by various characters, both fictional and real, and accompanied by a miscellany of videos displayed on a laptop screen resting among various pieces of scrap metal and disused airplanes. While the Boeing's story traverses the fine line between reality and fantasy, this multilayered orchestration by Hito Steyerl invites the viewer to reflect on the value of life in the age of global financial free fall: "[...] if there is no stable ground available for our social lives and philosophical aspirations, the consequence must be a permanent [...] state of free fall for subjects and objects alike."[1] (SG)

1 Hito Steyerl, "In Free Fall: A Thought Experiment on Vertical Perspective," in: *e-flux journal*, 24, April 2011.

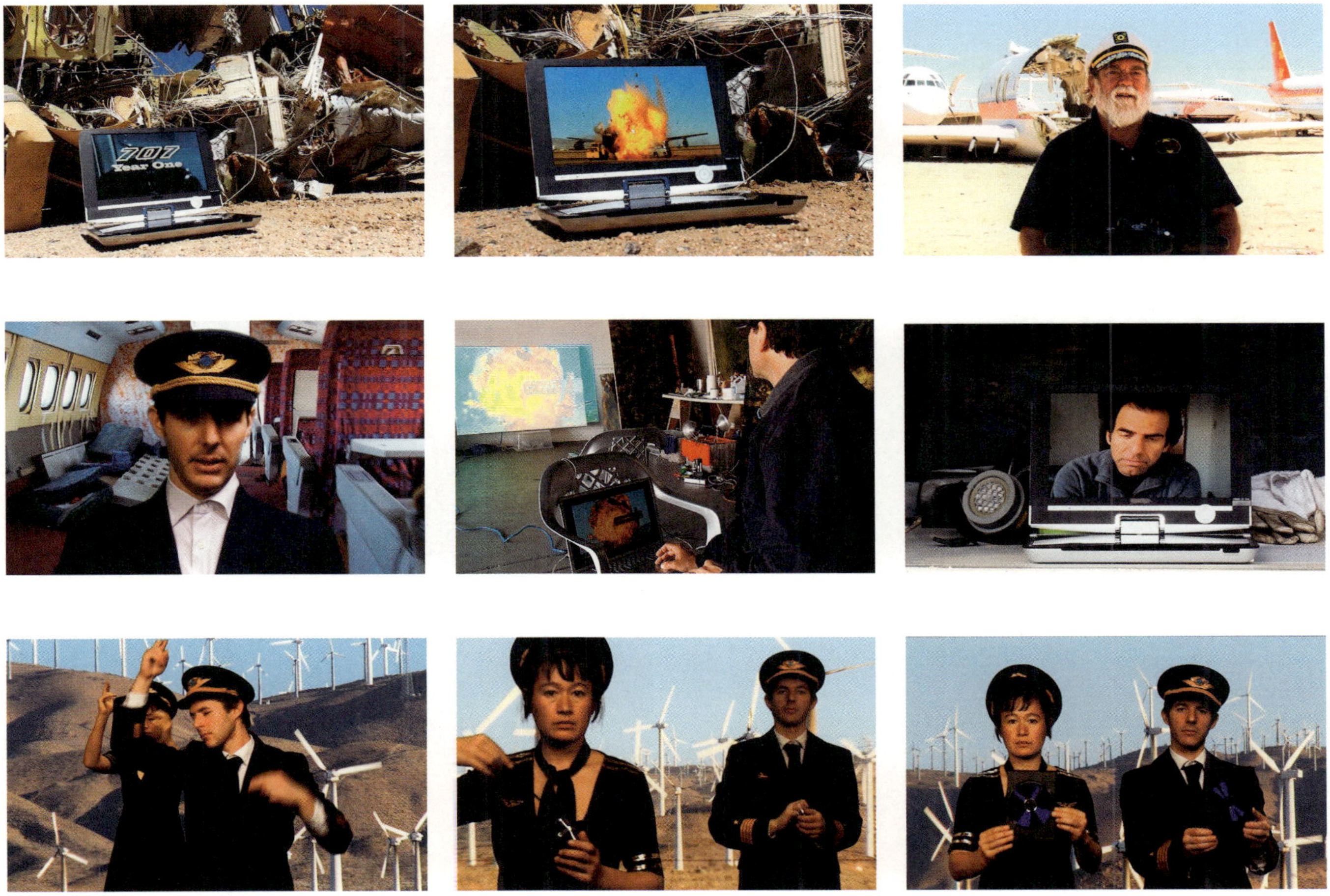

Bani Abidi / Halil Altindere
Rasheed Araeen / Kader Attia
Doug Fishbone / Meschac Gaba
Khosrow Hassanzadeh
Pieter Hugo / Anna Jermolaewa
Jin Shi / Jompet / Agung Kurniawan
Pavel Pepperstein
Elodie Pong

Real Worlds and Picture Worlds

In the global age, mass media such as TV and film have contributed to an unprecedented circulation of picture worlds that cross the borders of real worlds and spread the visual consumption of popular culture everywhere. Cinematic fashions such as Hollywood, Nollywood, and Bollywood reach local audiences while at the same time drawing on a repertoire of clichés that circulate globally. The new picture worlds connect different cultures with one another and often succeed simply by altering ethnic types or adopting local narrations in their storyboards. This ongoing process of rewriting a limited set of pictures has become the target of some of the artists represented in this section. In Bani Abidi's video, a young woman speaking the Urdu language of Pakistan recounts the plot of 26 Bollywood films, which the artist has concocted to a single, absurd story that reveals the clichés inherent to the genre. In Doug Fishbone's video, the American artist plays a role in a Ghanaian film of the Apea brothers which reverts to the part of the white colonizer when addressing a local audience but, in the end, raises the question as to whether Fishbone's intervention is convincing enough to create an art genre of its own.

Pieter Hugo has created a series of 43 photographs taken at Enugu, one of the three major sets of Nollywood, the Nigerian film industry, which is the third largest in the world, reaching an audience across the African continent. The pictures, staged with professional actors, in part reenact film scenes using Nollywood stereotypes such as bloodsucking vampires that had initially stepped out of the shadow of imported soap operas. Other pictures represent popular mythologies that often subvert the former colonial identity. A third part of the same series presents an independent grouping of prototypes, which as a mise-en-scène in the manner of a "tableau vivant," stands for the Nollywood picture repertoire as a whole, thus balancing between reproduction and ironic commentary. In one of the photographs, the artist stages himself half naked with a machete in his hands and surrounded by the bones of slaughtered animals – as a white man in the role of death personified with the famous Poussin slogan of "death existing even in Arcadia" emblazoned upon his chest. Pieter Hugo's Nollywood series can claim to have successfully translated the film episodes into a realm of photography with a highly symbolic visual language of its own.

Rasheed Araeen took another road when he identified the art world as an alternative place for playing the mass media game by confronting Andy Warhol's idol Marilyn Monroe four times as the *Golden Calf* with the bloody reality of the Iran-Iraq war of the 1980s that surfaces both on the battlefield and in the midst of mourning widows at public ceremonies. The high-priced glamour world of Western picture production contrasts sharply with the atrocities of the real world that can be traced back to the same Western roots as the art market. Marilyn, this time even more clearly a stereotype from the art world, also figures in a photograph by Halil Altindere, which shows the artist's Turkish grandmother leafing through an art book without paying attention to its character as a book on American Pop art. She likes, as the title suggests, the bright colors in the book as much as she likes the even brighter colors spread on the textile patterns of her furniture. It calls for a trained audience to discover the art world's message beyond the realm of popular picture worlds as these constitute two different worlds that float independently across global space, occasionally causing the local and the global to clash.

Anna Jermolaewa's *Kremlin Doppelgänger* series proves that even the real world, or the world of real places, can be subverted to fiction and turned into a picture world that offers a stage plot for global tourism. She has taken documentary photographs of what looks like the real Kremlin but is in fact a replica built for a vacation spot frequented by Russian tourists in Turkey. In Jompet's installation *Cortege of the Third Realm* uniforms and class symbols from Java's three-tiered society march on their own in military apparel for carnival, without being embodied by living representatives of their class. Thus, they stage a local picture world whose political claims they manifest in annual parades. Every shift to a new context changes the interaction of the picture world and the real world, which are mutually dependent. The imagination transforms the real worlds into worlds of collective pictures or "collective imaginaries," to quote Édouard Glissant.

A special place in this section is held by the large format photo series in which the Iranian Khosrow Hassanzadeh portrayed himself and some members of his family as "terrorists." This mise-en-scène, the hero staring at us in the midst of an inventory of his family's Muslim relics and photographs, openly addresses a cliché imposed on him from the outside, with the expectation of his willing response. On the other hand, his series takes up the stereotypes of Iranian government propaganda from the Revolution years when the war martyrs were celebrated as national heroes. Thus, the artist places himself at the intersection of two picture worlds, both of which he rejects as a framework for maintaining his identity.

Against this personal voice, the installation by Meschac Gaba conjures a public parade of global symbols, understood as easily accessible conventional signs, such as The Red Cross, and carried as wigs on the heads of living performers. The "masks" come only to life when they are embodied by living actors, and therefore the artist organized a street procession both in his native town of Cotonou, Benin, where they performed a walking museum, and in Karlsruhe. The picture world, it so happens, also turns out to be the network of symbols with a global reach that serves communication in the real world. (HB)

Bani Abidi

* 1971 in Karachi (PK), lives and works in Karachi and New Delhi (IN)

...so he starts singing, 2000

Video, color, sound, 3:30 min, loop

In *...so he starts singing*, one of Bani Abidi's early works, a young woman enthusiastically recounts the plots of twenty-six Bollywood films. From all these plots narrated over the course of an interview project with her very cinephile roommate, Abidi edited a single, absurd story which was related in all of three and half minutes. This quick run-through better summarizes Bollywood as a phenomenon than do any of the many classificatory attempts by film theory: its formulaic character - angry parents oppose a pair of lovers, a ménage à trois delays involvement, villains impede the happiness of the parties concerned - allows the creation of a clearly formulated and globally intelligible world of images. Reduced to a single narrative, the stereotypical schema stands out all the more.

The work's narrator is representative - not least by way of her sharply defined dialect and interjections in the Urdu language (the national language of Pakistan) - of the local cinema audience which becomes sucked into the undertow of images, and which internalizes the Bollywood stories and their pictures of everyday life, fashion, and love, before situating them in their own lives. At the same time, the simple, melodramatic narrative strategy levels cross-cultural hurdles and creates points of reference for an international audience that draws its ideas about life, morals, and culture from the Indian subcontinent. Abidi thus develops an ironic commentary on the one-dimensionality of globally circulating images, which still remain firmly attached to stereotypes. (KB)

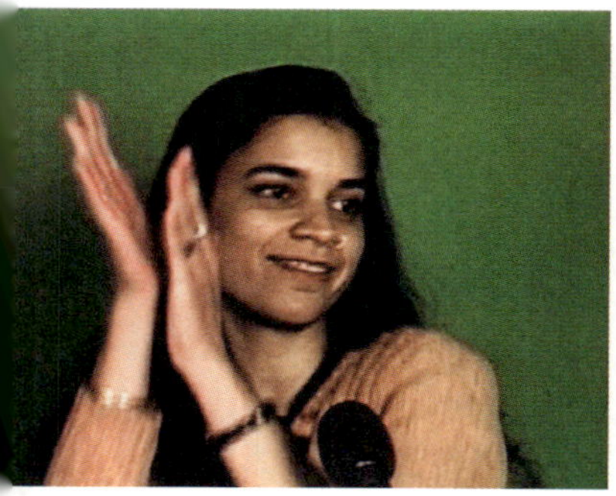

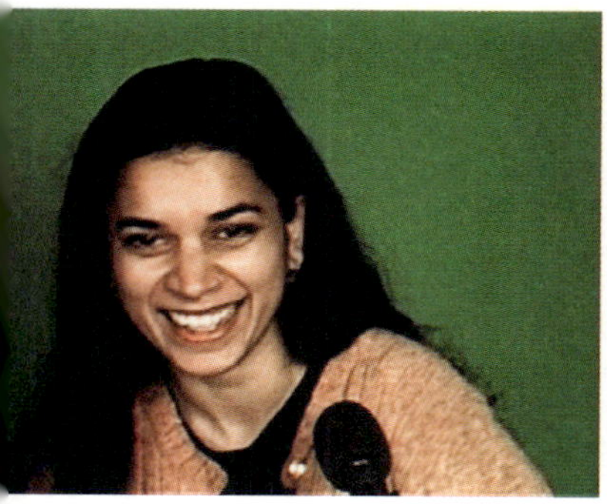

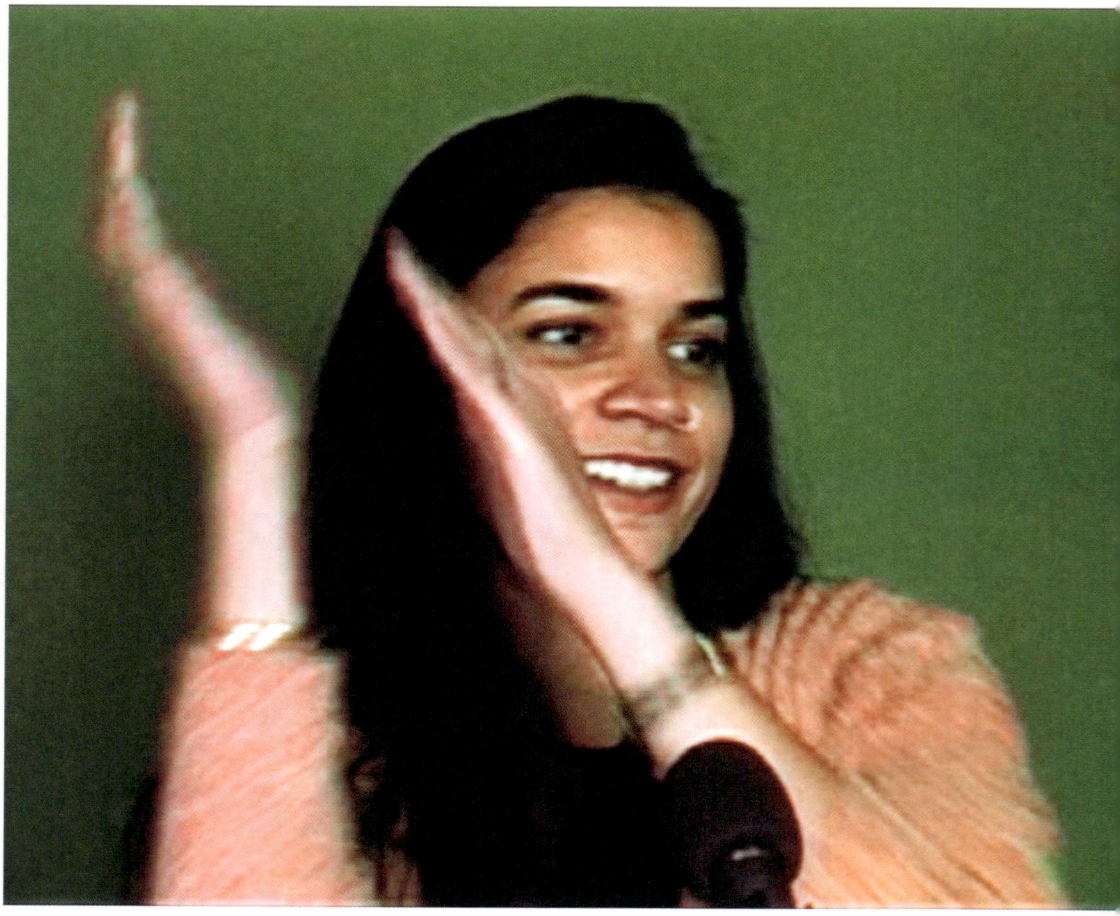

Halil Altindere

* 1971 in Mardin (TR), lives and works in Istanbul (TR)

My Mother Likes Pop Art Because Pop Art Is Colorful, 1998

C-print on aluminum Dibond, 100 × 150 cm

My Mother Likes Pop Art Because Pop Art Is Colorful is one of Halil Altindere's early works to have achieved cult status, albeit not comparable to Andy Warhol's *Marilyn* (1964), that celebrated epitome of Pop art adorning the cover of the book resting in the lap of the woman featured in Altindere's photograph. The work is symbolic of contemporary Turkish art and its balancing act between tradition and modernity, Orient and Occident, as well as Altindere's attempt to come to terms with Western art and its influence on his own artistic work.

Disguised as a brightly colored, innocuous-looking photograph, the picture delivers an ironic statement about the reception and perception of the West in Turkey and vice versa. Altindere simply reverses the relationship between "us" and "the others": the history of Pop art is a large-format glossy catalog in an unfamiliar context - a context that seems very traditional and, moreover, private - at least to the viewer who has grown up with contemporary Western art. Much in the same way that the term Orient has frequently come to betoken the Other in the Western world, and is thus the object of numerous projections, so also has Warhol's famous silk screen now become emblematic of the exotic ethos surrounding the term foreign. Both perceptions turn out to be stereotypes. Altindere's photograph points to an image now become cliché, while drawing attention at the same time to the potential simultaneity of tradition and modernity; something which makes visual migration at all possible and renders permeable apparently rigid boundaries. (KB)

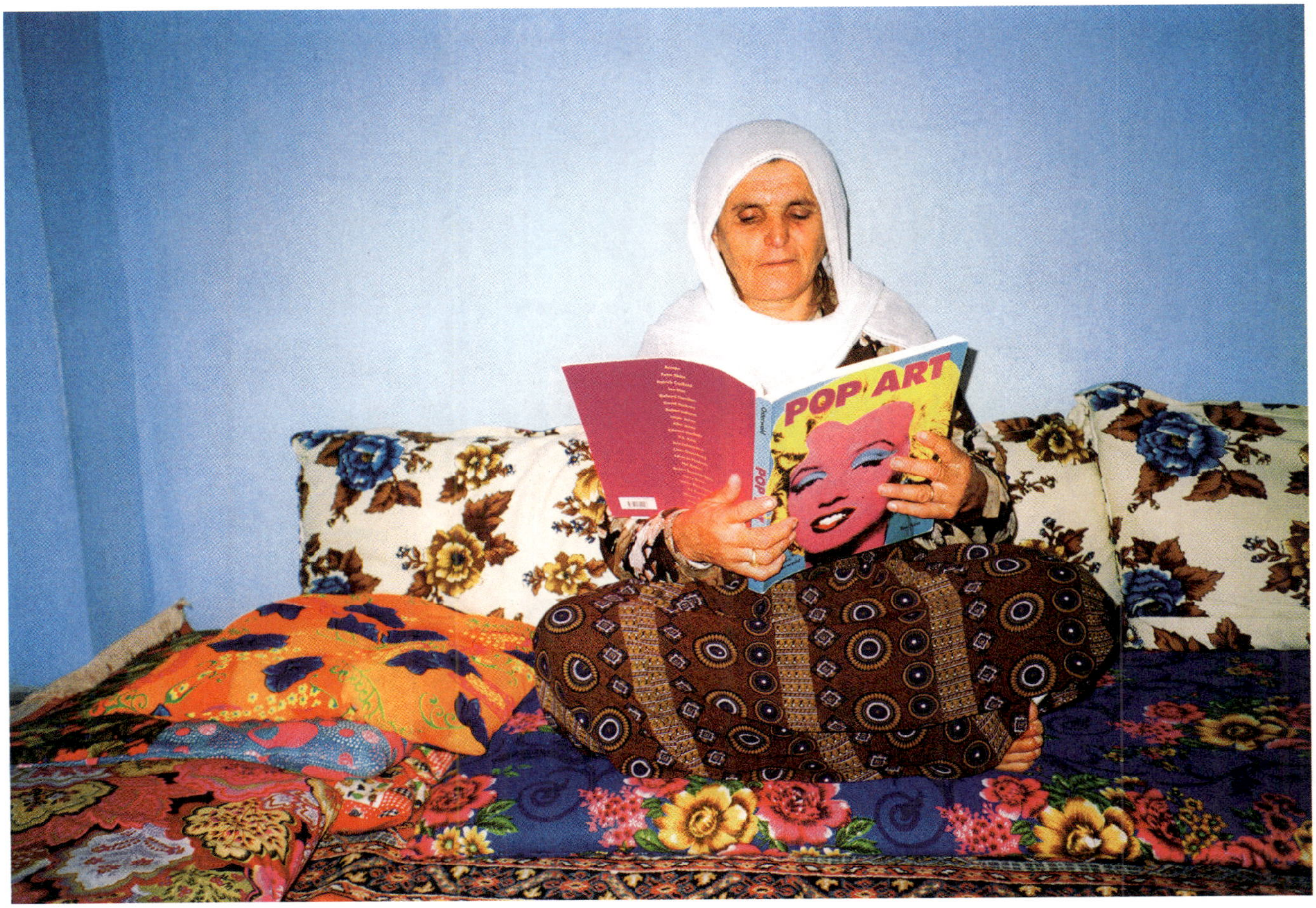

Rasheed Araeen

* 1935 in Karachi (PK), lives and works in London (UK)

Golden Calf, 1987

Mixed media, 9 panels, 152 × 179 cm

After his pioneering role in British Minimal art, Rasheed Araeen has continued the practice of integrating the serial arrangement of panels into his work. *Golden Calf*, an early example from 1987, is an arrangement of four Andy Warhol portraits of Marilyn Monroe and panels of silk-screen photographs depicting what appears to be a crowd of mourning women in the four corner sections. The Marilyn panels are arranged around and face the center of the nine-panel piece. This dramatically highlights the center panel taken up entirely by a single photograph of a fallen Iranian soldier. The close-up shows him lying in a pool of his own blood. The photograph is a document of the Iran-Iraq war, which raged throughout the 1980s. Originally published in conjunction with an Iranian newspaper article lambasting Iraq, Iran's erstwhile enemy, it was also a critique of the American imperialistic involvement in global politics.

Placing an image of Marilyn Monroe - icon of American mass media and celebrity culture - against the backdrop of the dark realities of a political warzone might initially seem to imply an indifference of the art world towards such treacherous political realities. The Monroe portraits, however, also represent one of Warhol's recurring leitmotifs, death. Here, Western art fetishes are contrasted with the stark realities of the contemporary world. Araeen's serial repetition of images, whereby each additional image adds a new layer of meaning, culminates in the image of the fallen soldier. The West's idolization and worship of dead movie stars is contrasted with the veneration of fallen Iranian war heroes by masses of mourning women. Both of the chief subjects represented become posthumous idols. (AMB)

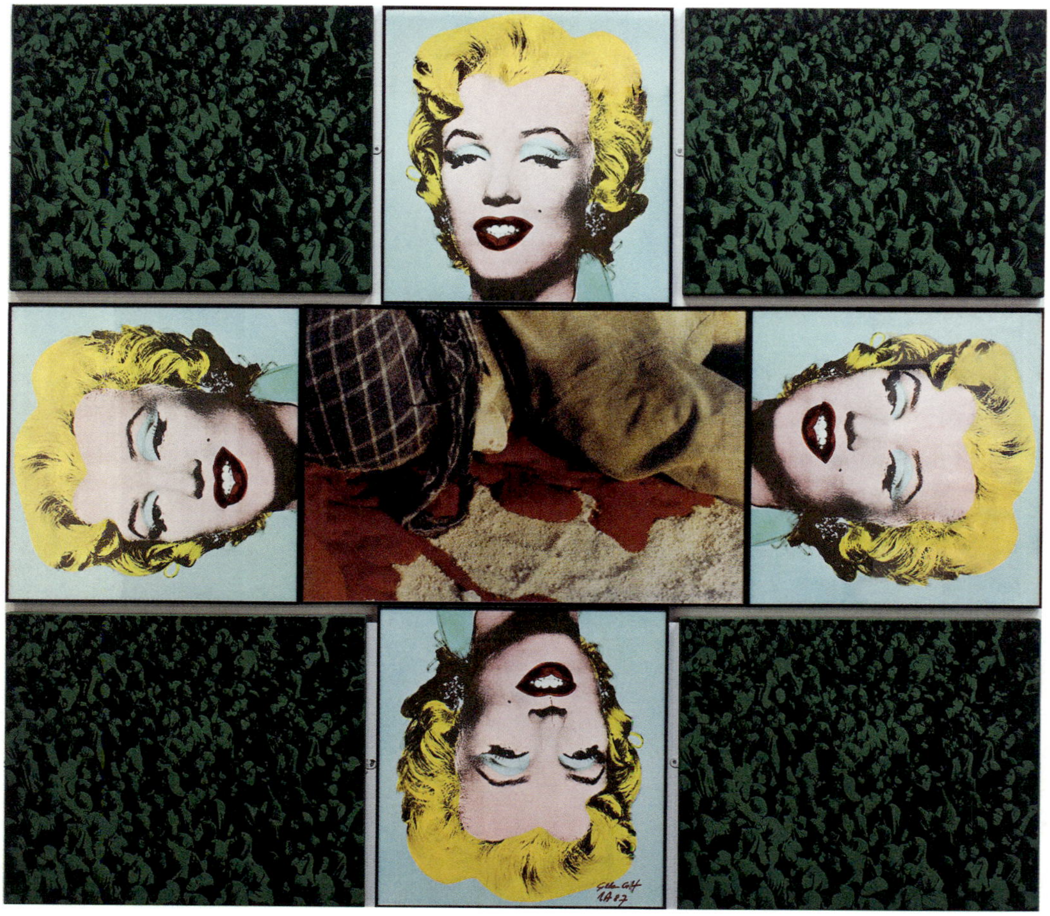

Kader Attia

* 1970 in Dugny (FR), lives and works in Berlin (DE)

Untitled (Plastic Bags), 2008–2011

Sculpture, empty plastic bags, dimensions variable

In Kader Attia's work *Untitled (Plastic Bags)* the plastic bag becomes the material that dreams are made of. For decades, this piece of polyethylene has been left over at the end of each shopping trip. Although the triumphal march of the plastic bag has meanwhile slowed down somewhat for ecological reasons, it still retains something of its erstwhile promise of being able to have, that is, buy everything – one simply goes to the shop next door. Linked to the image of the colored bag, however, are associations with smoldering suburban conflicts connected with migrants.

In *Untitled (Plastic Bags)* Attia presents nine colored copies of this machine of (dis-) illusion, which he collected in the Middle East, Africa, the Americas, and Europe. Before plastic became art in the form of sculpture, it was a receptacle for raw materials or basic foodstuffs: bottles of oil, bags of rice or flour, cartons of milk, etc. Once removed, the imprint of what it contained remains for a certain time although it begins to fade, and finally collapsed during the course of the exhibition. With a pronounced sense of irony, Attia develops his position towards globalization and its all too frequently ignored downside, which includes the exploitation of raw materials as well as the presentation of the cultural preeminence of the West as opposed to the "Other." Only as imprint, as empty form, does rice, for example, leave traces of its identity on the global, everyday material of the plastic bag, per se a symbol of the capitalist world order. (KB)

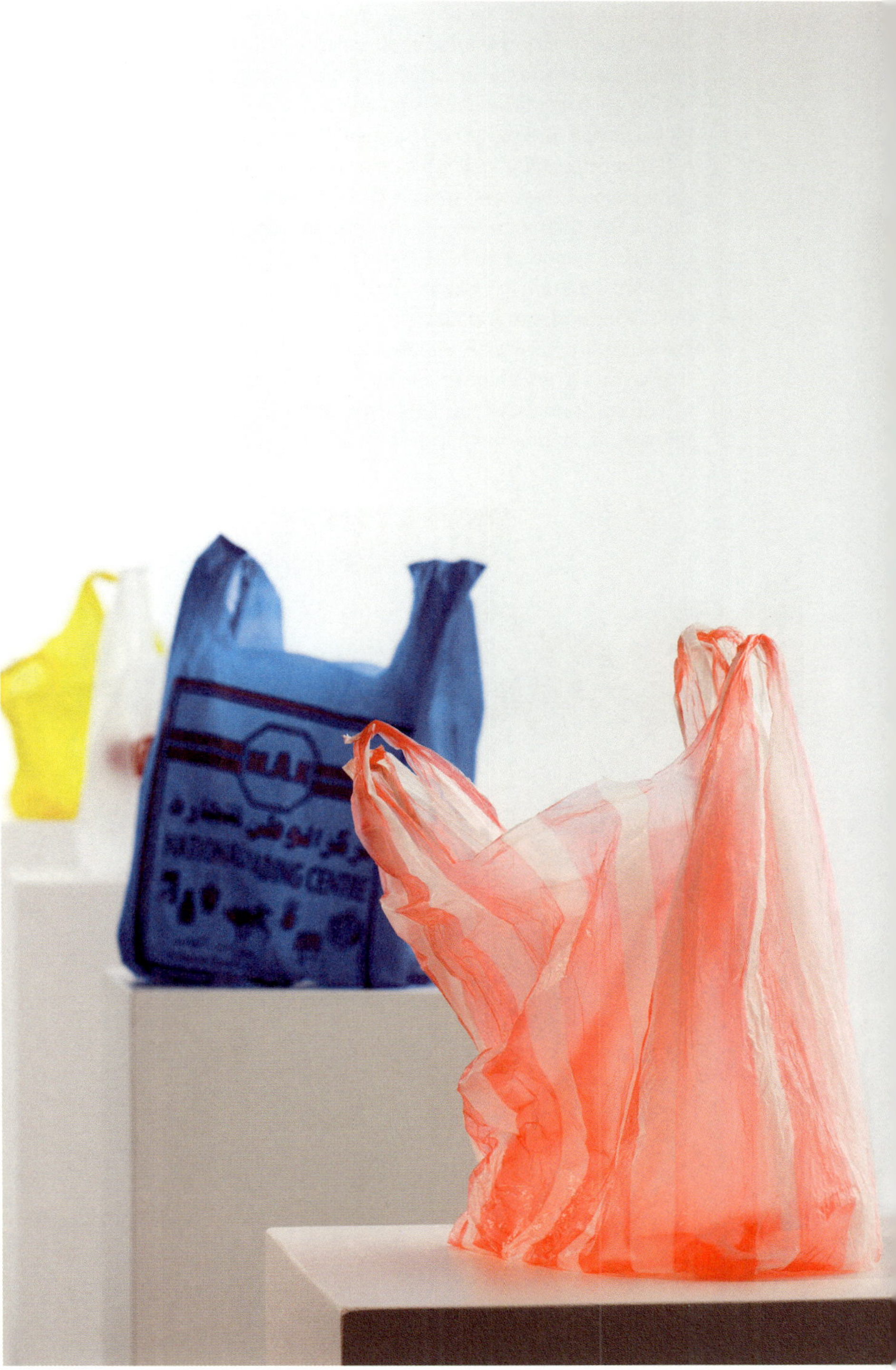

Doug Fishbone

* 1969 in New York, NY (US), lives and works in London (UK)

Elmina, 2010

Video, color, sound, 90 min

For the art world, globalization is an issue that manifests itself in the discourse about access to local and global forums and the necessity of social engagement; for a large part of the world's population, processes of globalization directly affect the possibility of leading a self-determined life. In *Elmina*, Doug Fishbone initiates a collision of these two perspectives at several levels. *Elmina* is a Ghanaian film by the brothers Emmanuel and John Apea that addresses the West African audience with a dramatic tale of exploitation and power; but *Elmina* is also one of Fishbone's art projects, which the artist financed with money acquired from the art market and in which he himself plays the leading role.

In the dramatized conflict between the farmer Ato Blankson and the corrupt rulers of the city, terms such as "progress" and "development" are merely pretexts for enrichment and the preservation of privileges, of conditions which culminate in most of the protagonists losing their moral integrity and, in some cases, losing their lives. Less drastic, but still conspicuous, are the conflicts broached by *Elmina* that touch on the system of globalized art: Is it legitimate to present, unquestioned, a white American in the role of a Ghanaian farmer? Does an appropriation take place here on the part of the artist, who transfers the commercial film product into the context of an exhibition, or rather by the Ghanaian filmmakers, who use the financial help of the art system to entertain their local audience? (JB)

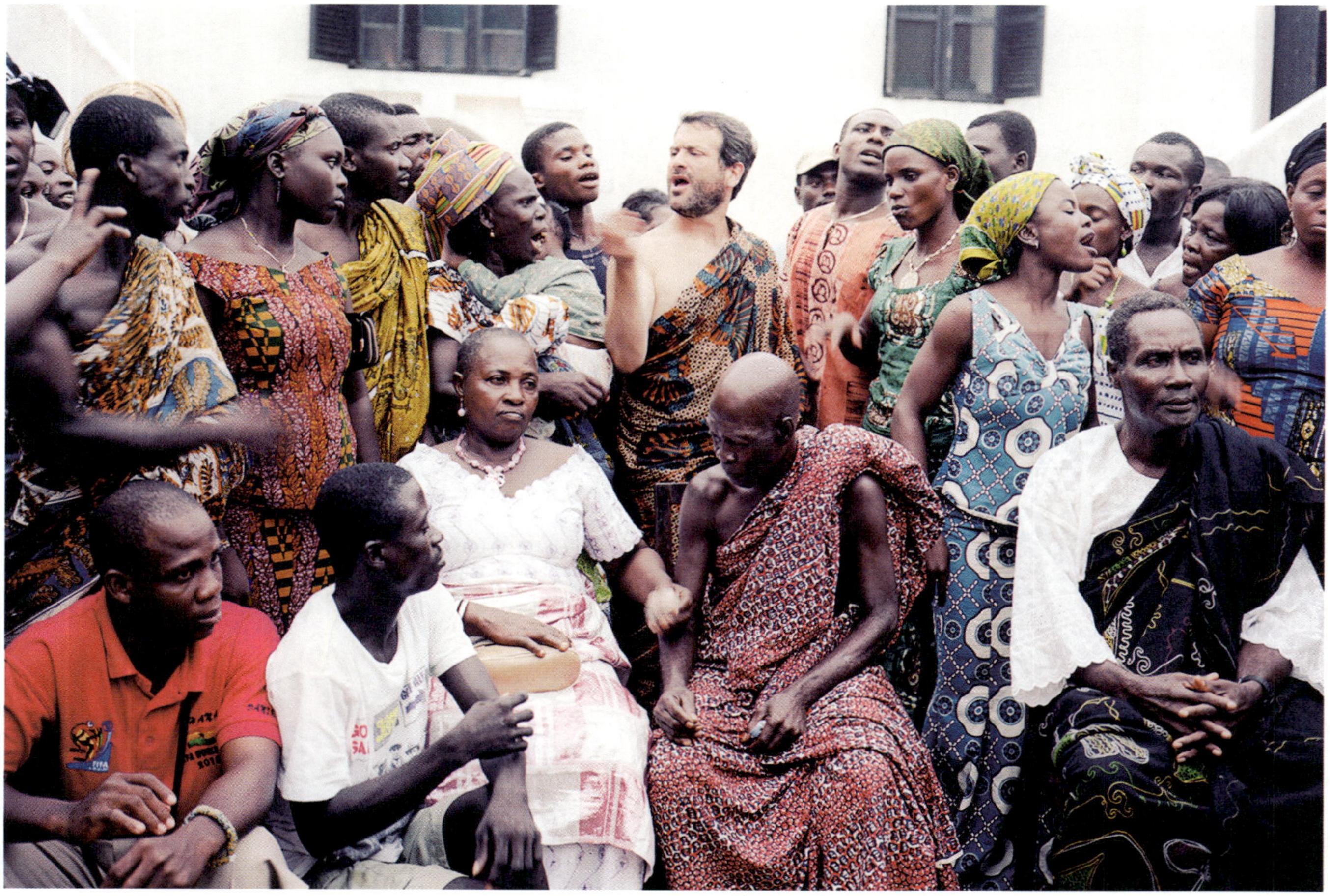

Khosrow Hassanzadeh

* 1963 in Tehran (IR), lives and works in Tehran and London (UK)

Terrorist Series: Nadjibeh, Azimeh, Khosrow, 2004

Selection of 3 silk screens, 200 × 320 cm each

Khosrow Hassanzadeh is an internationally active Iranian painter. Starting out as an artist in Tehran in the mid-1980s, he achieved international recognition with the exhibition of his *War Series* at the London Diorama Arts Centre in 1999. These paintings, based on the artist's firsthand experience of the Iran-Iraq war, have been intentionally rendered for an outsider, namely Western, perspective. The same gaze-oriented approach to artistic work was to characterize Hassanzadeh's future career: a tight-knit tapestry of issues of central importance for cultural imaginaries and depictions of conflicts between Western and Arab worlds in the aftermath of 9/11.

In the *Terrorist Series*, Hassanzadeh portrayed himself and some members of his family as "terrorists." These portraits are accompanied by images and signs indicating their nationality, belief, and history. The latter work reflects the artist's commitment to detect and then depict traditional Islamic characteristics so as to question the Western prejudice claiming that terrorism is intrinsically rooted in Islamic culture and religion: "What is a terrorist? [...] The West, with its personal definition of terrorism, gives itself the right to take over a country, while in the Middle East the West is clearly accused of being a full-fledged terrorist. In exploring these questions, I portrayed the people in whom I have the most faith: my mother and sisters."[1] (SG)

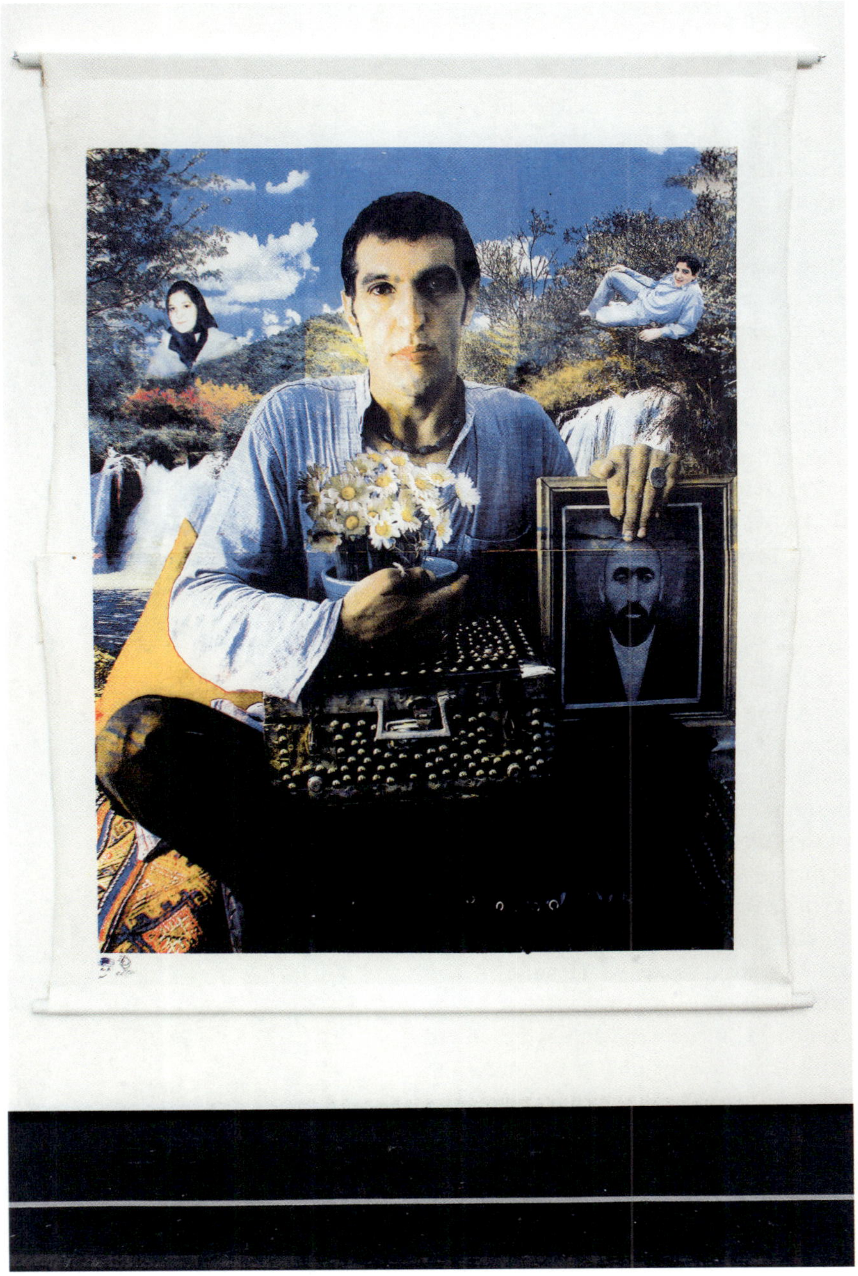

1 Khosrow Hassanzadeh, as quoted from: Mirjam Shatanawi, "The Disquieting Art of Khosrow Hassanzadeh," in: *ISIM Review*, 18, Autumn 2006, Leiden University.

Meschac Gaba

* 1970 in Dugny (FR), lives and works in Berlin (DE)

Musée de l'Art de la Vie Active, 2010/2011

Performance and mixed-media installation, 30 wigs (braided synthetic hair and wire supports), 2 videos (performances in Cotonou and Karlsruhe)
Produced with Laboratorio Art Contemporain, Galleria Continua in cooperation with ZKM | Karlsruhe

Meschac Gaba is known above all for his *Museum of Contemporary African Art* (1996-2002). In this work, which was realized in several stages, the artist examined the art world's mechanisms of exclusion and inclusion with respect to African art. In his new production *Musée de l'Art de la Vie Active* for the exhibition *The Global Contemporary*, the artist builds on his previous *Tresses* series. For the performance he created thirty wigs of synthetic hair which cite figures of global history through the use of universally intelligible symbols, including Martin Luther King, Kwame Nkrumah, Jeanne d'Arc, Fela Kuti, Pierre and Marie Curie, and King Guézo of Dahomey. By placing Western icons alongside important figures of African history, Gaba points to the need for a truly global history.

At the same time, the artist investigates the reasons why there is no tradition of museums in Africa (analogous to the museum tradition established and defined in the West). By declaring Cotonou, one of Benin's cities, a museum, and by traversing it with his idiosyncratic parade, Gaba foregrounds the urban space and its inhabitants' creative strategies of survival and improvisation. In so doing, Gaba is asking about other models and endeavors, as well as local interpretations of the museum: "The micro-macro economy represents the survival of the inhabitants of this city day after day. They need to create to be able to survive. In the city of Cotonou, you can see installations everywhere - it is like an open-air museum." (AM)

For the opening of the exhibition, Meshac Gaba organized a two-hour performance through the center of Karlsruhe, in which the procession previously staged in Cotonou was reenacted in a European context.

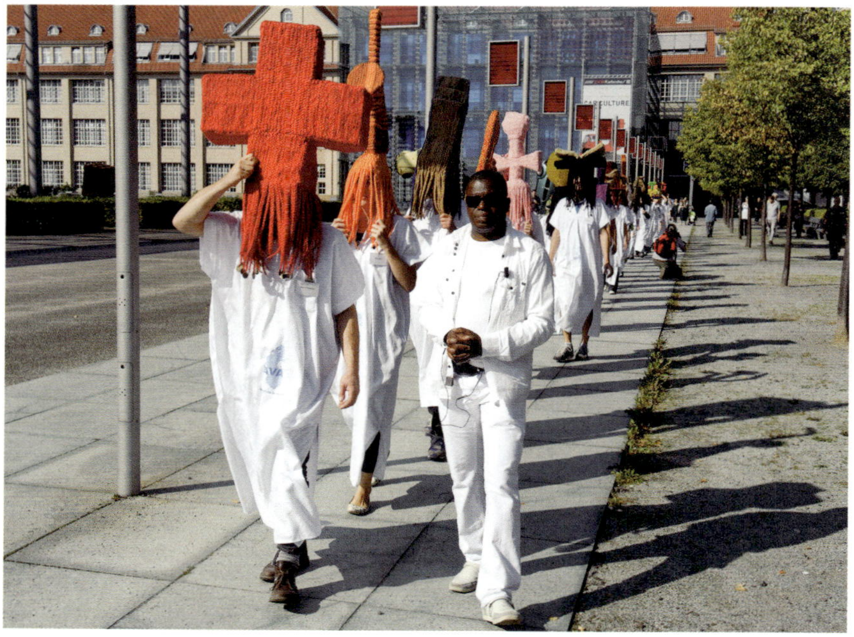

Procession through Karlsruhe, Germany

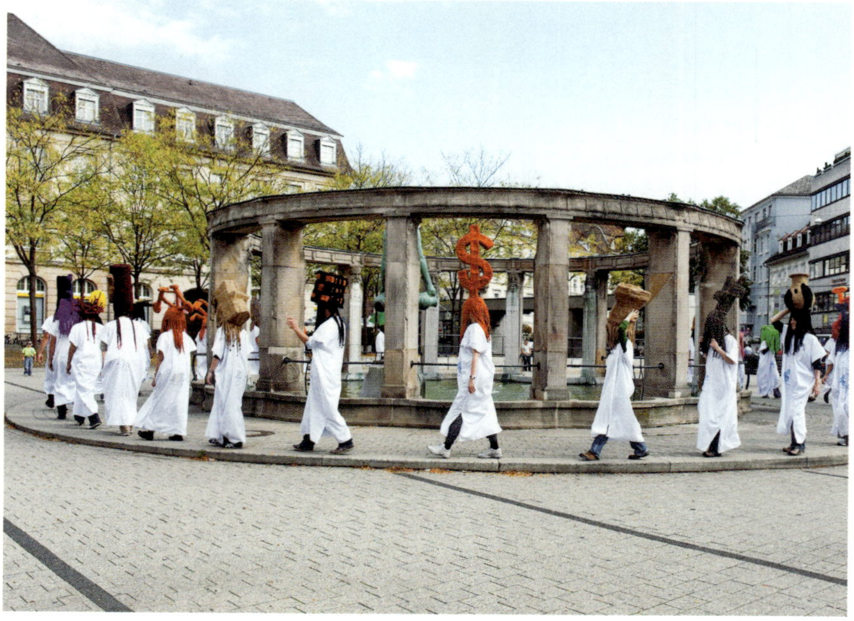

Procession through Karlsruhe, Germany

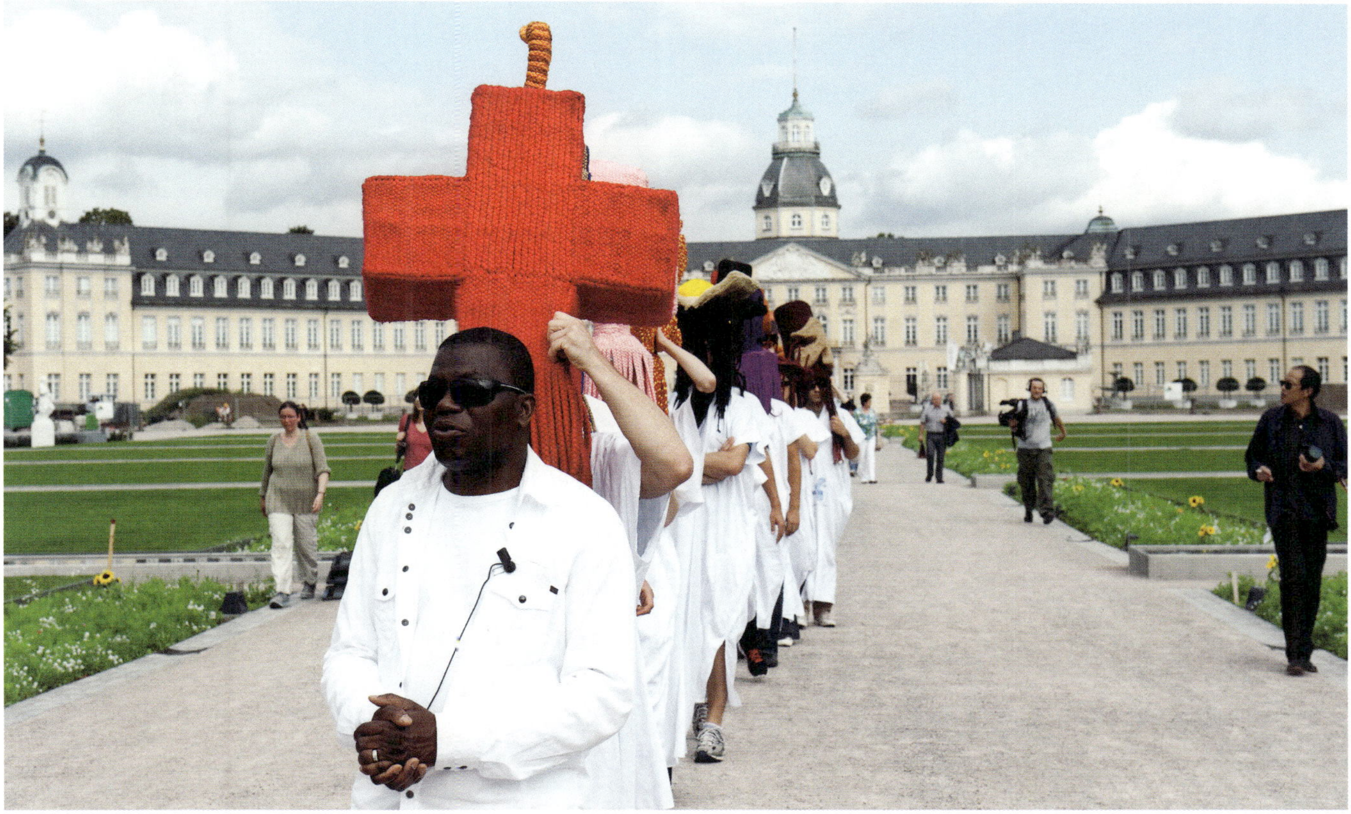

Procession through Karlsruhe, Germany

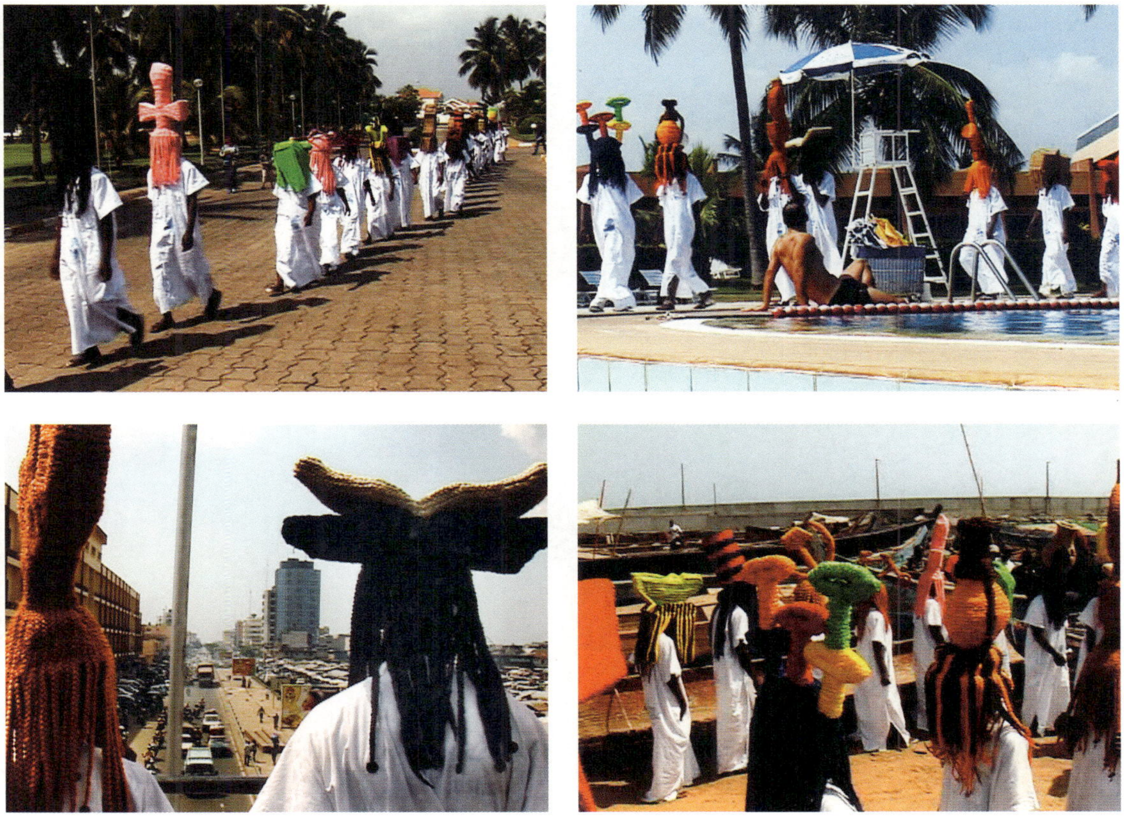

Procession through Cotonou, Benin, video stills

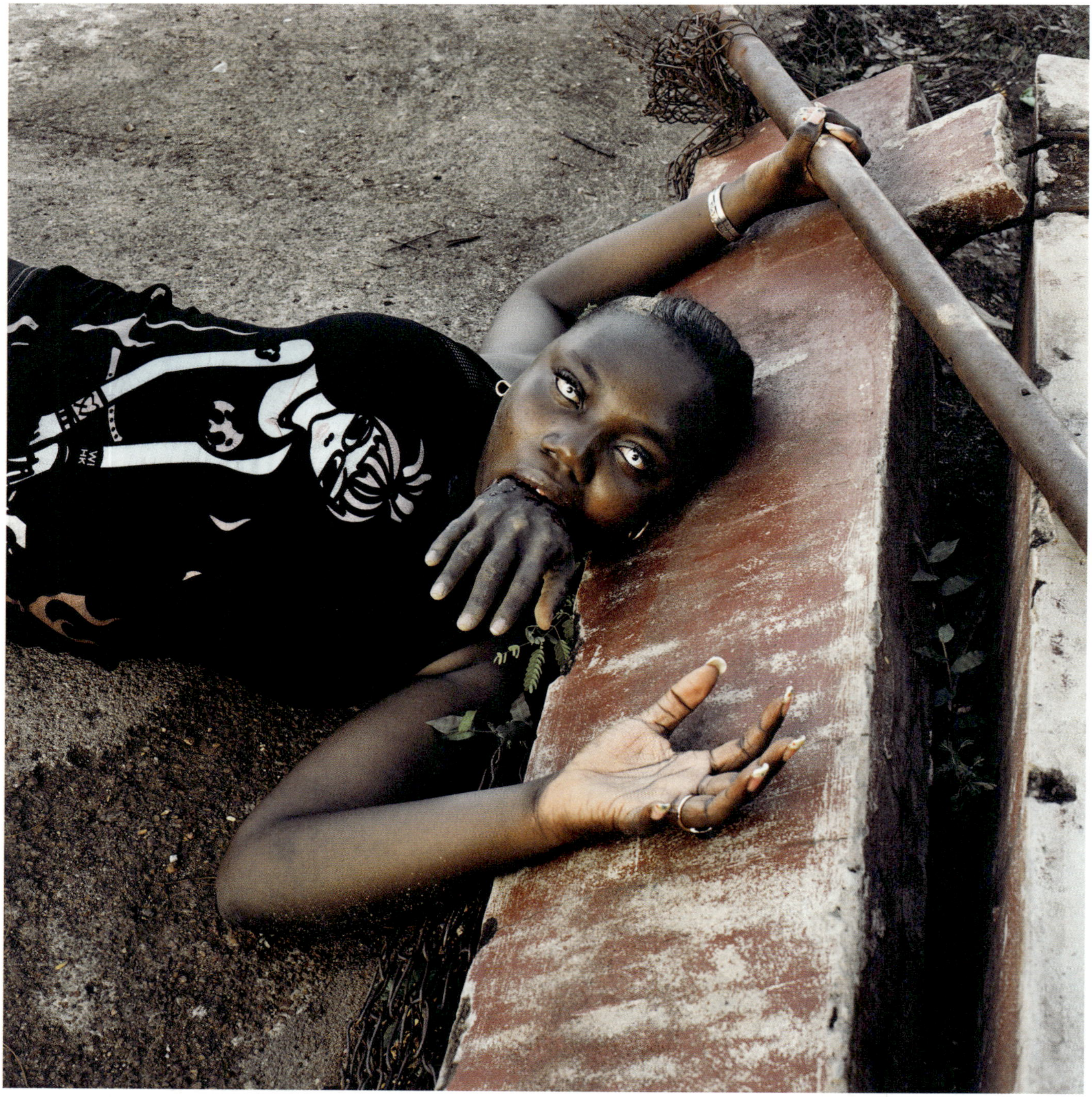

Princess Adaobi

Pieter Hugo

* 1976 in Johannesburg (ZA), lives and works in Cape Town (ZA)

Nollywood, 2008

Photo series, selection of 8 C-prints, 102 × 102 cm each (110 × 110 cm framed)

Individual titles:
Escort Kama, Enugu, Nigeria, 2008
Chris Nkulo and Patience Umeh, Enugu, Nigeria, 2008
Emeka Onu, Enugu, Nigeria, 2008
Obechukwu Nwoye, Enugu, Nigeria, 2008
Pieter Hugo, Enugu, Nigeria, 2009
Princess Adaobi, Enugu, Nigeria, 2008
Fidelis Elenwa, Enugu, Nigeria, 2009
Mr. Enblo, Enugu, Nigeria, 2008

For his predominantly documentary, sometimes staged photo series, South African photographer Pieter Hugo often draws on his subjects from the margins of African society. In the photo series *Nollywood*, he deals with a rare instance of African self-representation in the medium of film.

After Bollywood and Hollywood, Nollywood is the third biggest film industry in the world; under the most rudimentary technical conditions, such as the use of DV camcorders, and with minimal budgets and production times, up to 2,000 films are produced for Africans by Africans annually. In formats such as VHS, VCD, and DVD, these films are distributed mainly in Nigeria and West Africa, and play a central role in the everyday life of these countries. Rooted in local imagery, with their "trashy" shrill splatter aesthetics, and realistic yet dramatically overdone and excessive plots about love, religion, violence, civil war, prostitution, politics, corruption, and postcolonial conflicts, they enjoy consistent popularity across social milieus.

After Hugo's initial attempts to take pictures during shooting sessions on film sets failed because of the chaotic bustle of everyday production, he began to reenact typical Nollywood sets and themes in a quasi documentary manner with actors. Thus, there arose vivid portraits of intense theatrical moments in a process of collective imagination, in which cinematic fiction was scarcely distinguishable from social reality. At the same time, Hugo ironizes the common African stereotypes and their photographic representations - letting the people he portrays look back, unruffled, at the viewer. (AM)

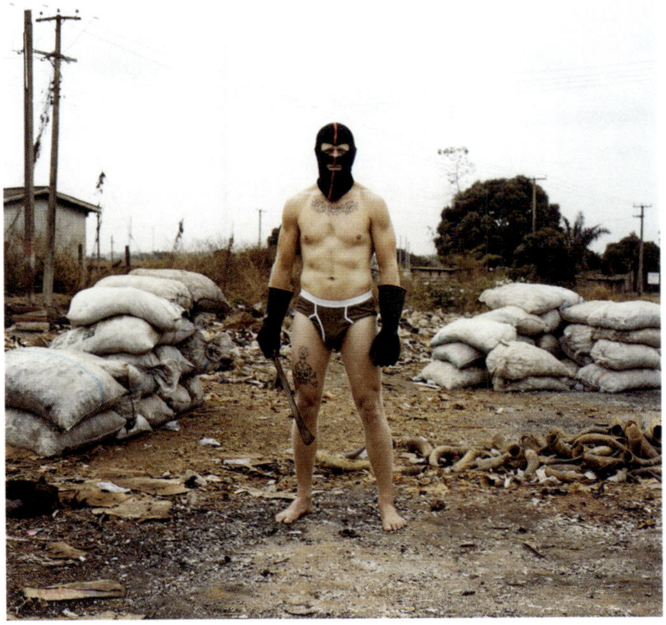

Pieter Hugo

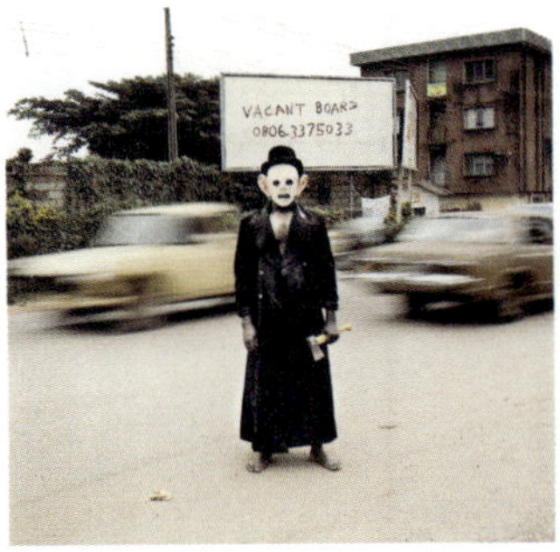

Escort Kama

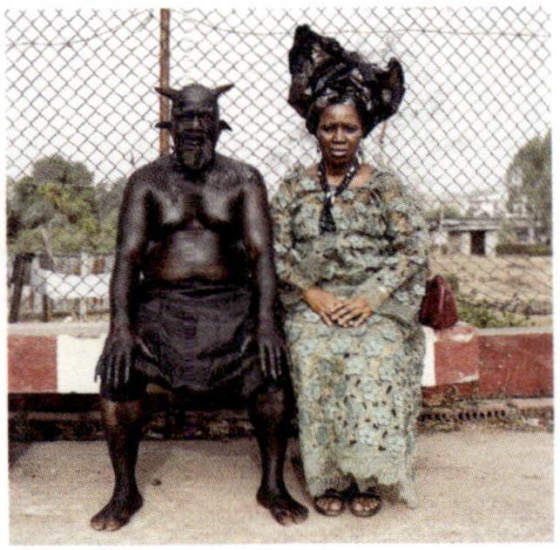

Chris Nkulo and Patience Umeh

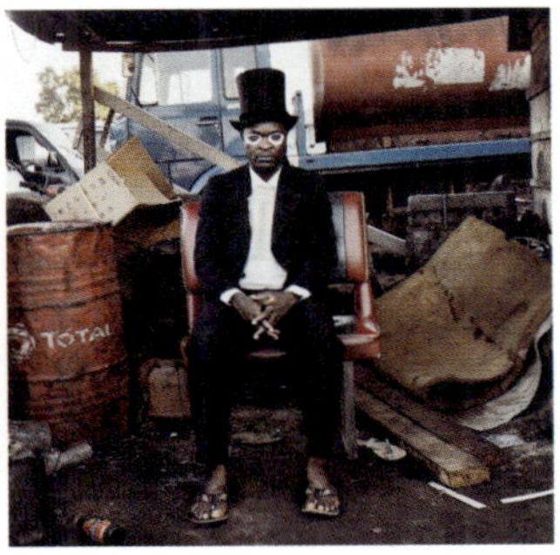

Emeka Onu

Anna Jermolaewa

* 1970 in Saint Petersburg (RU), lives and works in Vienna (AT)

Kremlin Doppelgänger, 2008/2009

Photo series (selection), 50 × 35 cm each, framed

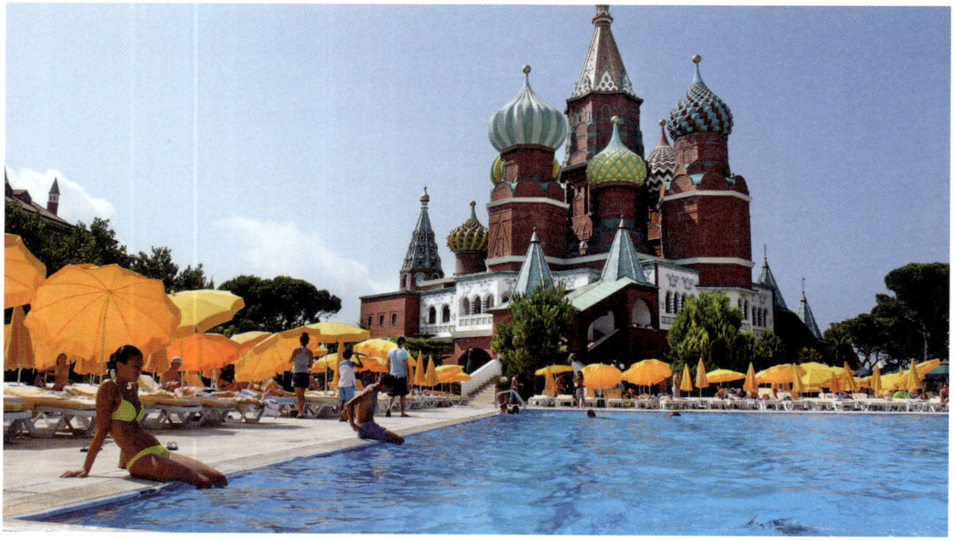

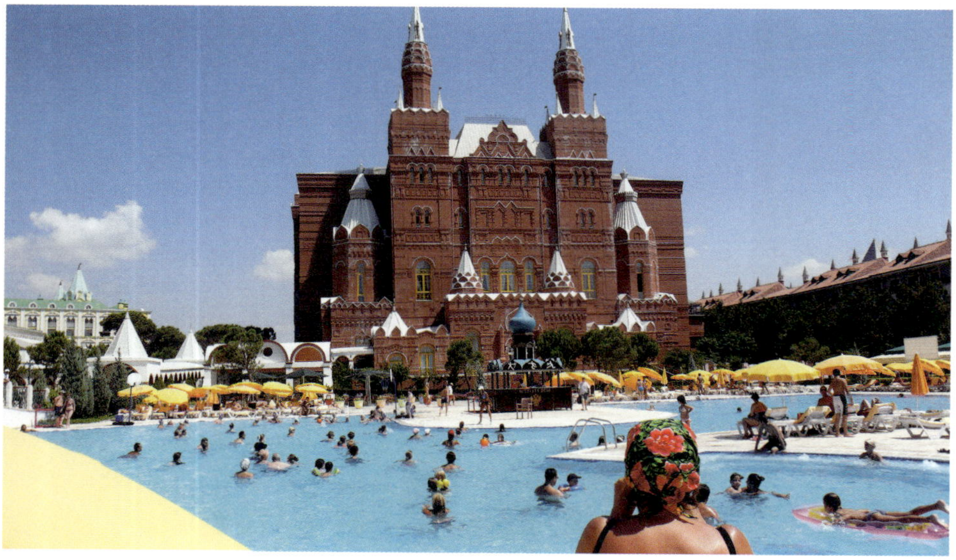

Anna Jermolaewa was brought up in Petrograd (present-day St. Petersburg, Russia). She suffered persecution in 1989 due to her editorial work for the magazine *Democratic Opposition*. She subsequently left Russia and has since been living and working in Vienna. Her video works, predominantly designed as documentaries, reflect the everyday, allegedly stable dimensions of our reality, and uncover its ambivalent, absurd, and bizarre aspects by employing a variety of filmic devices.

In the photographic work *Kremlin Doppelgänger*, Jermolaewa focuses on *the* symbol of Russian state power, present all over the world in the press in the form of pompous military parades. The artist shows a copy of history-drenched Red Square in Moscow, namely, the Kremlin Palace Hotel in Antalya, Turkey, which is especially popular among Russian holidaymakers. Here, in nostalgic surroundings, visitors play in the water, sunbathe, enjoy a meal, or shop. In the video of the same name, Mikhail Gorbachev's doppelgänger appears at the poolside and talks about his life in politics - each morning, the retired engineer stencils his birthmark on his forehead.

Jermolaewa initiates a dialog between reality and fiction, between the historic monument and its reproduction full of different content and values. She thus draws attention to the mobility, reinterpretation, and exchangeability of cultural or national ideas and their icons in the age of globalization, and the general fictitiousness of history. Which of the two phenomena is the more ominous, the original symbolic site or its copy, remains a matter of debate. (AM)

Jin Shi

* 1976, lives and works in Beijing (CN)

Retail Business: Karaoke, 2009

Mixed-media installation,
180 × 290 × 82 cm

Karaoke is a very contemporary leisure activity; it evokes the uniqueness and creativity of the stars combined with a friendly invitation to participate; a participation however, that has no consequences. Singing in karaoke bars or in front of gaming consoles we become united in "universal leisure time" amidst a postmaterialistic utopia, in which pure consumption is expanded to include a sense of participation and involvement. Viewed critically, karaoke, which was developed in Japan during the 1970s, anticipated what casting shows have now carried to extremes all-over the globe: the promise to escape everyday life and suddenly become the center of attention. In his series *Retail Business*, Jin Shi focuses on this tragic/hopeful aspect of leisure society: billiards, wellness centers, or the aforementioned karaoke are shrunk to dimensions transportable by bicycle so as to swell the stock of tawdry goods touted by market vendors and itinerant hawkers. Here, the culture of participation encounters the necessity of improvising with whatever is momentarily at one's disposal, and urban glamour meets the desire of the poor in megacities to forget their worries for a time. (JB)

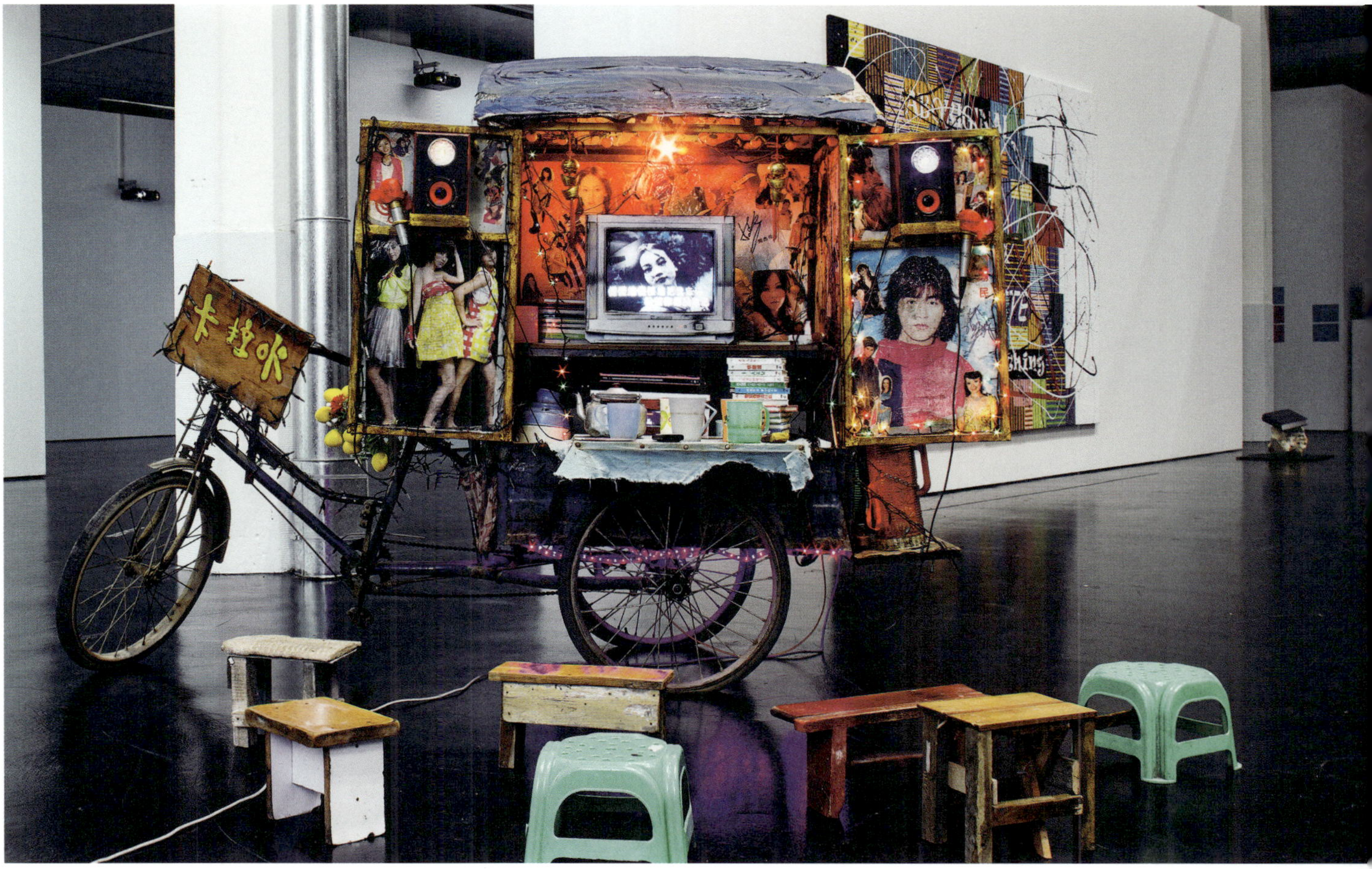

Jompet

* 1976 in Yogyakarta (ID), lives and works in Yogyakarta

Cortege of the Third Realm, 2010

24 life-size figures, electronics, video and sound installation, dimensions variable

The parade of a phantom army: in *Cortege of the Third Realm* Indonesian artist Jompet has created a complex multimedia installation in which the spectator initially hears only rhythmic drum beats. In accord with this immaterial announcement (sounds are transmitted by acoustic noise) gaiter-clad shoes suspended in midair then appear along with drums and headgear all vaguely reminiscent of Javanese military uniforms. Bodies are indicated only by the remaining empty spaces. The technical effort to conjure up these phantoms, however, is openly displayed. Cables are laid on the floor and small switchboxes power the spectral parade.

In this installation, Jompet, whose work has focused intensely on his own, Javanese, culture and cultural history, responds to the split between tradition and modernity, religious diversity, and syncretism in Java. The uniforms of the eighteen figures allude to military styles associated with various religious and cultural content. Reminders of Islamic, Western, and local traditions, they make reference to the intermediate cultural position Java has always occupied. In Java a syncretism purporting to sustain a continuity of the most diverse influences has been elaborated to perfection. Controlled externally by technical means, the figures are rooted in tradition while at the same time apparently subject to the unstoppable march of modernity. Do Jompet's soldiers march in support of cultural diversity and against the steady homogenization currently underway in the name of progress – or are they parading their commitment to this latter? (KB)

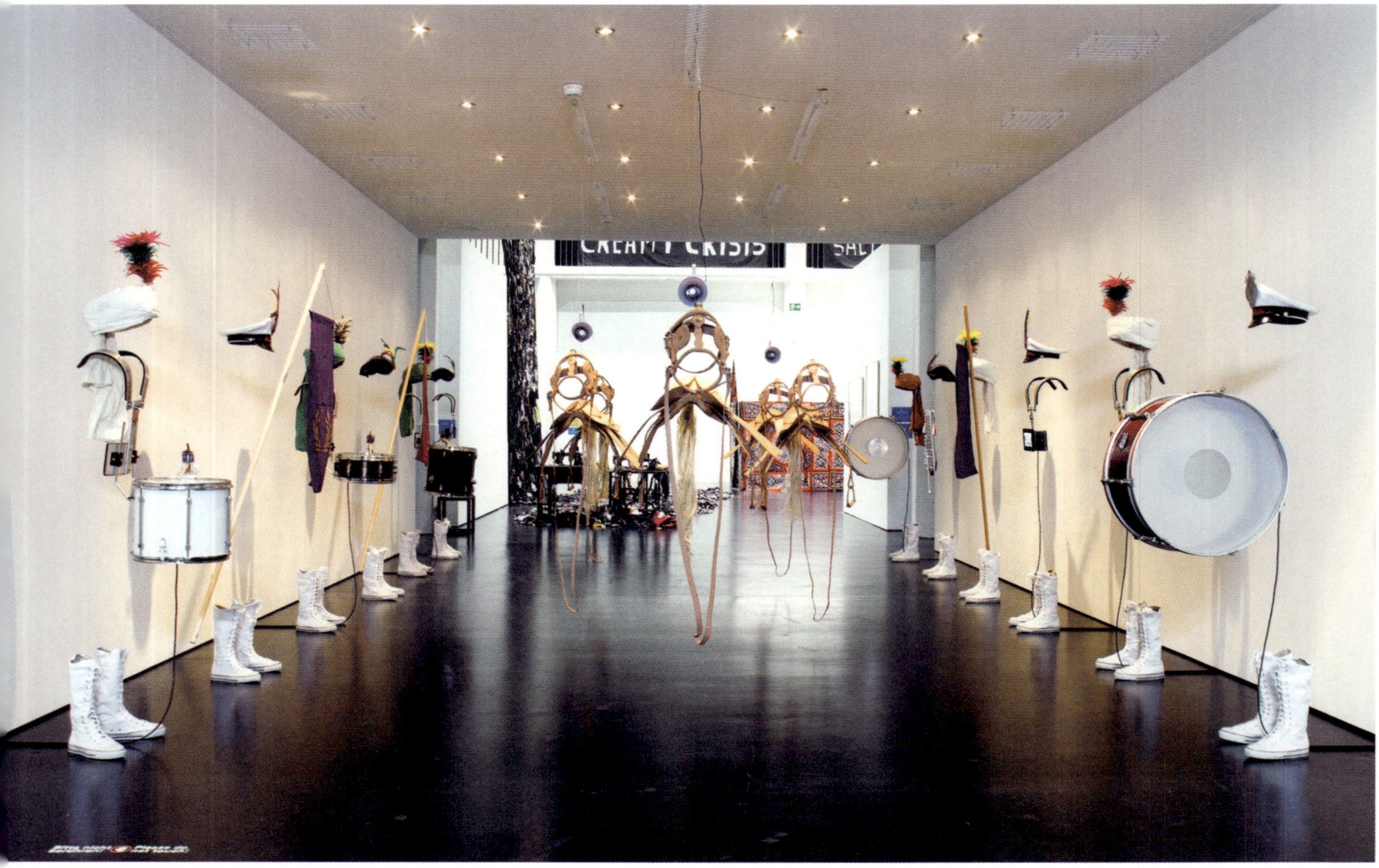

Agung Kurniawan

* 1968 in Jember, East Java (ID), lives and works in Yogyakarta (ID)

Souvenirs from the Third World, 1997–1999

5 objects of fiberglass, wood, aluminum,
70 × 35 × 35 cm each

During the 1990s, Agung Kurniawan's works primarily addressed social and political issues, subtly criticizing the violence of the fascist Suharto regime in Indonesia. Following the introduction of democracy in 1998, Indonesian artists increasingly devoted themselves to political themes, while Kurniawan began to turn away from them. For him, the advent of democracy had divested political art of its significance as a medium of criticism and resistance. At this time the art boom in countries such as India and China was spilling over into Indonesia. Art dedicated to political issues commanded high prices on the international market.

Souvenirs from the Third World criticizes this development, something which, in Kurniawan's view, has led to the commercial exploitation of the political past by artists and the art market. The colorfully painted figures of the installation stand on Indonesian street vendors' carts, and represent military or mythical beings as well as contemporary artists, jurors, and curators as Pinocchios, clowns, and rats - all of them prepared to sell out. The artist has become a vendor; art has become a commodity - a product that meets quality standards and can safely be put on display. Kurniawan shows up the hypocrisy of the international art world and criticizes a market that presents and sells art from developing countries as souvenirs. (EA)

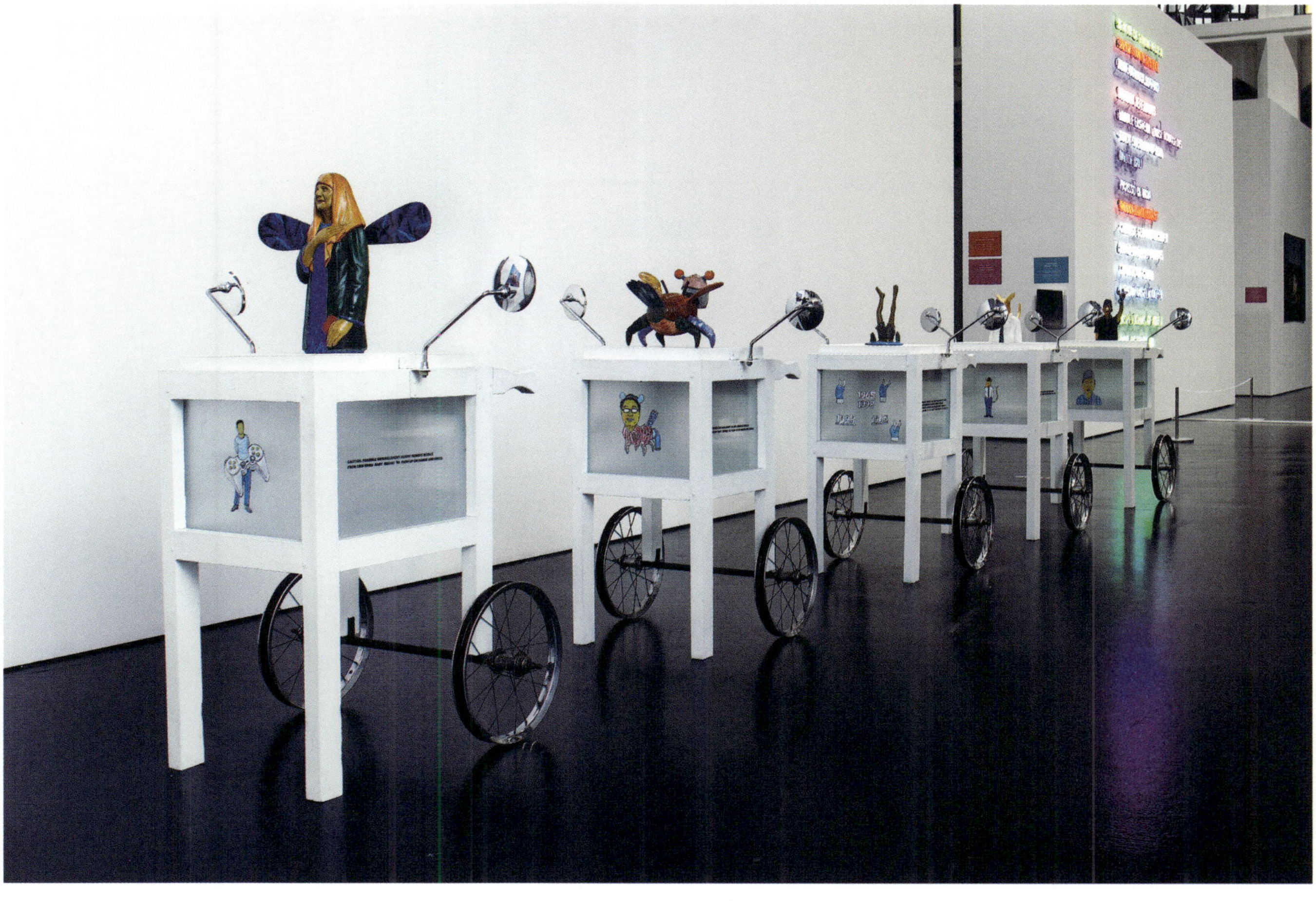

Pavel Pepperstein

* 1966 in Moscow (RU), lives and works in Moscow

The Gulf of Mexico Oil Spill Disaster, 2011

Watercolor on paper, 4 drawings, 66 × 101 cm each, framed

Pavel Pepperstein is one of the most acclaimed Moscow-based artists of the new generation. He is known as a writer and theorist, and as one of the founders of the artists' collective Inspection Medical Hermeneutics, established in 1987. Watercolors and drawings with a written commentary are among Pepperstein's favorite forms of artistic creation. He is thus affiliated to the tradition of Moscow Conceptualism, a movement headed by Ilya Kabakov and Viktor Pivovarov, Pepperstein's father, both of whom started out as graphic designers and illustrators of children's books and magazines.

In the *The Gulf of Mexico Oil Spill Disaster* series Pavel Pepperstein introduces Suprematist forms and ideological symbols into the depiction of a contemporary event that has global ramifications. This series makes reference to the accident on the BP oil platform in spring 2010. The oil spills on the ocean's surface assume the shapes of Malevich's Black Square, a swastika, a little mythological fawn, and a "sleeping face." These symbols make up the central themes in Pepperstein's recent creative work, while at the same time he seeks to establish them as a universal visual language for the depiction of everyday reality. Similarly, oil is an important universal source of market value in capitalist economics. Visual quotations, the appropriation of signs and symbols, and their surrealist reenactment are the main features of Pepperstein's "psychedelic realism." (DM)

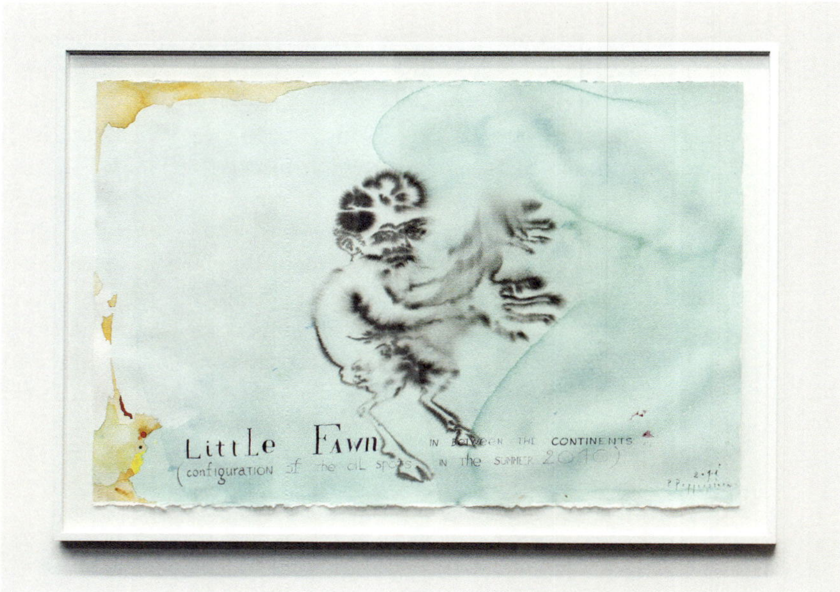

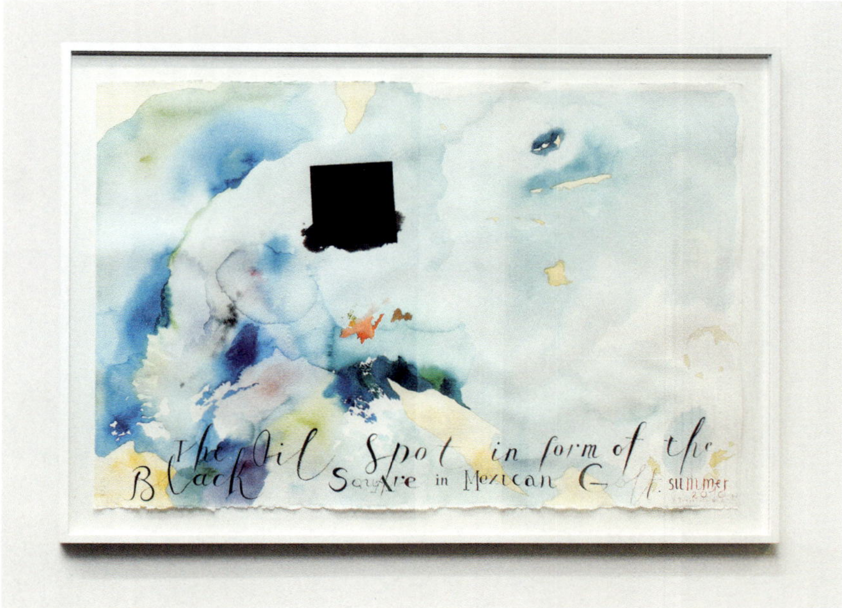

Elodie Pong

* 1966 in Boston, MA (US), lives and works in Zurich (CH)

After the Empire, 2008

HD video, color, sound, 13:50 min

In her experimental performances, installations, and video works, Elodie Pong examines the interplay of globalization and popular culture. Time and again she returns to analyzing the influence of cultural codes, their translocation, and the current state of cultural, political, and sexual identity.

In her video work *After the Empire*, Elodie Pong has icons from popular culture and political history collide with each other in absurd scenarios: Marilyn Monroe woos Karl Marx, a Japanese version of Minnie Mouse pores over sex ads and dances by herself, while a bored Elvis recites the lyrics of his songs, a young woman, alias Martin Luther King, meets Pong's grandmother from the Zurich Oberland, and a very shy Robin assures himself of Batman's affections in Swiss German. Against the backdrop of a post-apocalyptic industrial landscape, the actors embody the symbolic longings and utopias of the characters - but they seem to be trapped in their plagiarized existence, isolated and unable to realize their dreams or even to establish relationships to each other. (AM)

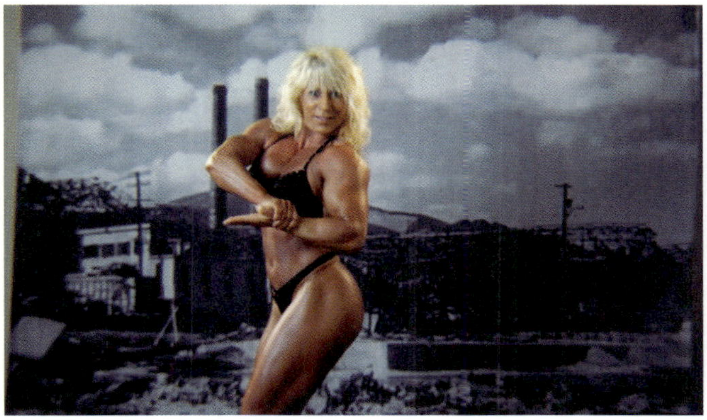

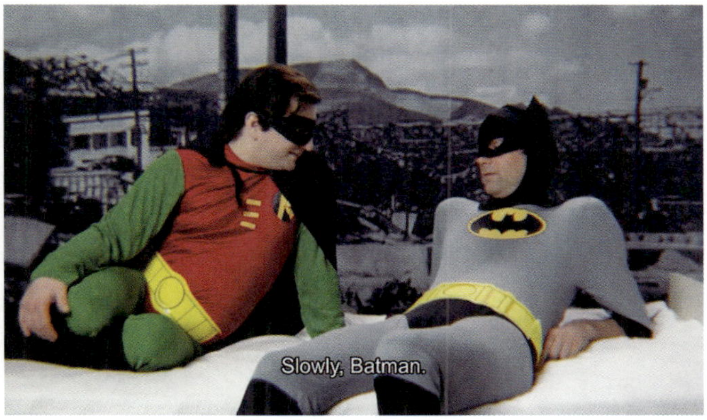

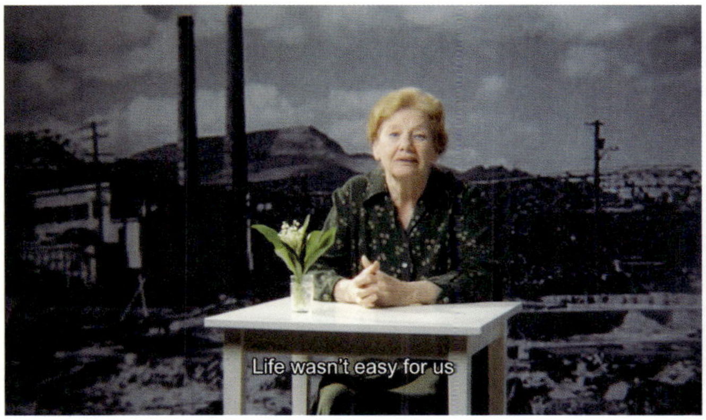

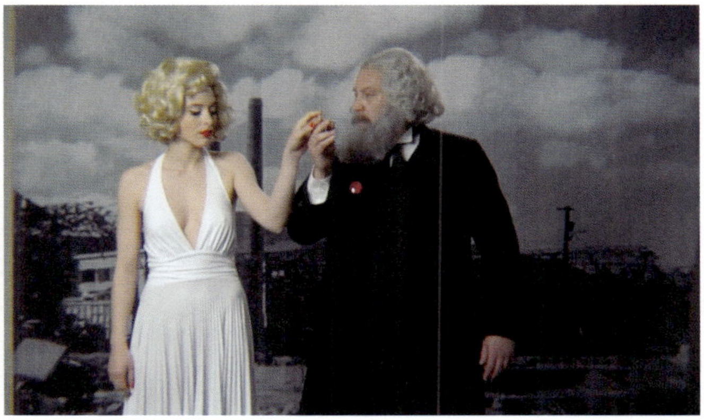

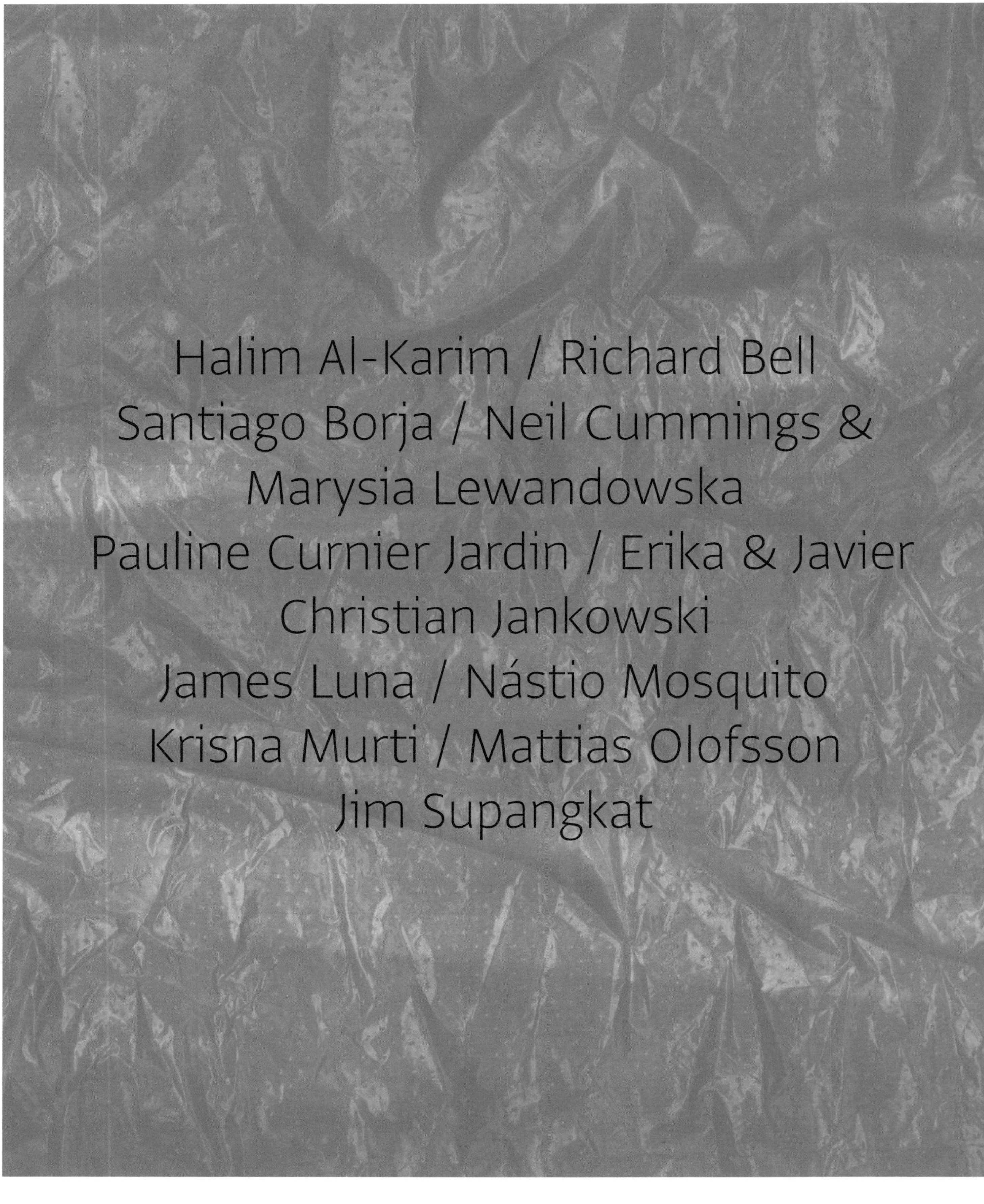

Halim Al-Karim / Richard Bell
Santiago Borja / Neil Cummings &
Marysia Lewandowska
Pauline Curnier Jardin / Erika & Javier
Christian Jankowski
James Luna / Nástio Mosquito
Krisna Murti / Mattias Olofsson
Jim Supangkat

World Art: The Curiosity Cabinet in Postcolonial Times

The collecting of exotic objects had its origin in the Renaissance-born *Cabinet des Curiosités* where one saw marvels created by nature placed alongside artifacts mostly produced in foreign cultures. In modern times, the ethnographic museum and the museum of natural history continued such collecting habits, though each had a different scientific profile. The ethnographic museum became a colonial institution devoted to "world art," an art produced by "the Others," and thus excluded from such mainstream art of the kind found in the Euramerican art museum. In the postcolonial era, in which this tradition is crumbling and contemporary art production is taking place in what were the former colonies, such collections all of a sudden resemble the curiosity cabinets from past ages. They are stamped by their colonial past and evoke the criticism of artists who do not feel represented by this type of ethnic collection where their ancestors became exoticized.

James Luna, a Native American artist who lives on a reservation, drew a drastic conclusion from his encounter with a local type of museum in that he himself performed as an *Artifact Piece*. He is seen lying outstretched, his body covered merely with a loincloth, in a coffin-like showcase where he is surrounded by personal documents and his name, the only legible item, as witness of his identity. He seems to have staged the memory of a nearly extinct group that nevertheless remains alive in his person. At the same time, he called into question the pretensions of museum displays to replace their producers and to reduce their selves to exotic objects. The two Paraguay-based artists Erika & Javier take another position along the same lines with an oversized photograph of a half-naked woman from the Guarani tribe. She carries "The Weight of Memory" (*El Peso de la Memoria*) in the guise of six memory sticks with programs against poverty in Latin America around her neck. Her large exposed body, symbolizing the traditional way of keeping memory alive, sharply contrasts with the digital tools of saving cultural memories that are no longer represented by the peoples themselves.

In his photographs, Krisna Murti introduces the artist's ambiguous role between tradition and present-day Indonesia. He simultaneously acts out roles staged as a group of dancing characters from *wayang kulit*, the Java-born Shadow Puppets Theatre. The stories of these plays were drawn from Hindu epics and thus originated in the religious sphere, but later they were adapted to become theatrical plays with living actors; today, they only survive as an outdated and already musealized genre. The fabrication of such puppets with a skin (*kulit*) of leather was, for centuries, one of the main activities of artists in Java who devoted all their skill to the figures' exceptional appearance. Murti, with his face make up and costume, performs these characters as multiple and contrasting self-portraits that, in historical disguise, populate an alienating environment of the global age. In a large-sized work entitled *The Last Photograph* he embodies a group of *wayang* characters, seen from various distances ranging from close-up to full-length figure, on a construction site that reveals the damage of capitalist exploitation to the original landscape.

The museum experience enters photographs taken by the Iraq-born Halim Al-Karim in the Louvre and the British Museum. The triptych *Hidden Prisoner* represents the faces of Sumerian full-length figure sculptures that are "exiled" in Western museums and, long before Greco-Roman antiquity, were produced on the soil of what is today Iraq. The artist seems to project his personal prison memories and his own hiding away during the first Gulf War to these museum pieces which, for him, are not merely alienated specimens of "world art" but rather become uncertain relatives. Their blurred features obscure the distance of time and the difference of stone in order to serve an almost tragic appropriation.

Contemporary art can play a questionable role in the museum, as is shown in a large painting by Richard Bell who accuses Aboriginal art of being a "white thing," written in white letters across the picture. Winner of a "National Aboriginal and Torres Strait Islanders Art Award" and author of a pamphlet against the commodification of what Australian museums today call "Contemporary Indigenous Art," Bell addresses the inherent problems that cover up political messages, as he wrote them black in black around the painted "triangle of discomfort," behind the innocent surface of aestheticism and a "national" branch of painterly abstraction. (HB)

Halim Al-Karim

* 1963 in Najaf (IQ), lives and works in Denver, CO (US) and in Dubai (AE)

Hidden Prisoner, 1993

Lambda print,
158 × 369 cm (triptych)

Hidden Prisoner is part of the *Hidden* picture series, in which Halim Al-Karim works through his personal experiences during the first Gulf War. He hid in a hole in the ground in the desert for almost three years to avoid being drafted into the Iraqi military. The photographic series documents artistically the impact that hiding as a means of survival made on Al-Karim. In the triptych *Hidden Prisoner*, the artist shows artifacts from ancient Sumer - the first civilization in human history which flourished in what is today Iraq. He photographed the objects far away from his home, locked behind glass in the Louvre and the British Museum: for the artist a painful reminder of visiting friends and family members in Abu Ghraib prison under the Saddam Hussein regime. In his work Al-Karim reveals things that are hidden from general view - for example, the appropriation of foreign cultural objects - and at the same time protects these millennia-old artifacts by withdrawing them from the viewer's gaze by depicting them as blurred. *Hidden Prisoner* contrasts the language and ideas of proximity and distance, home and exile, transience and eternity, war and humanism, and in this way invites viewers to think about the issues he raises. (EA)

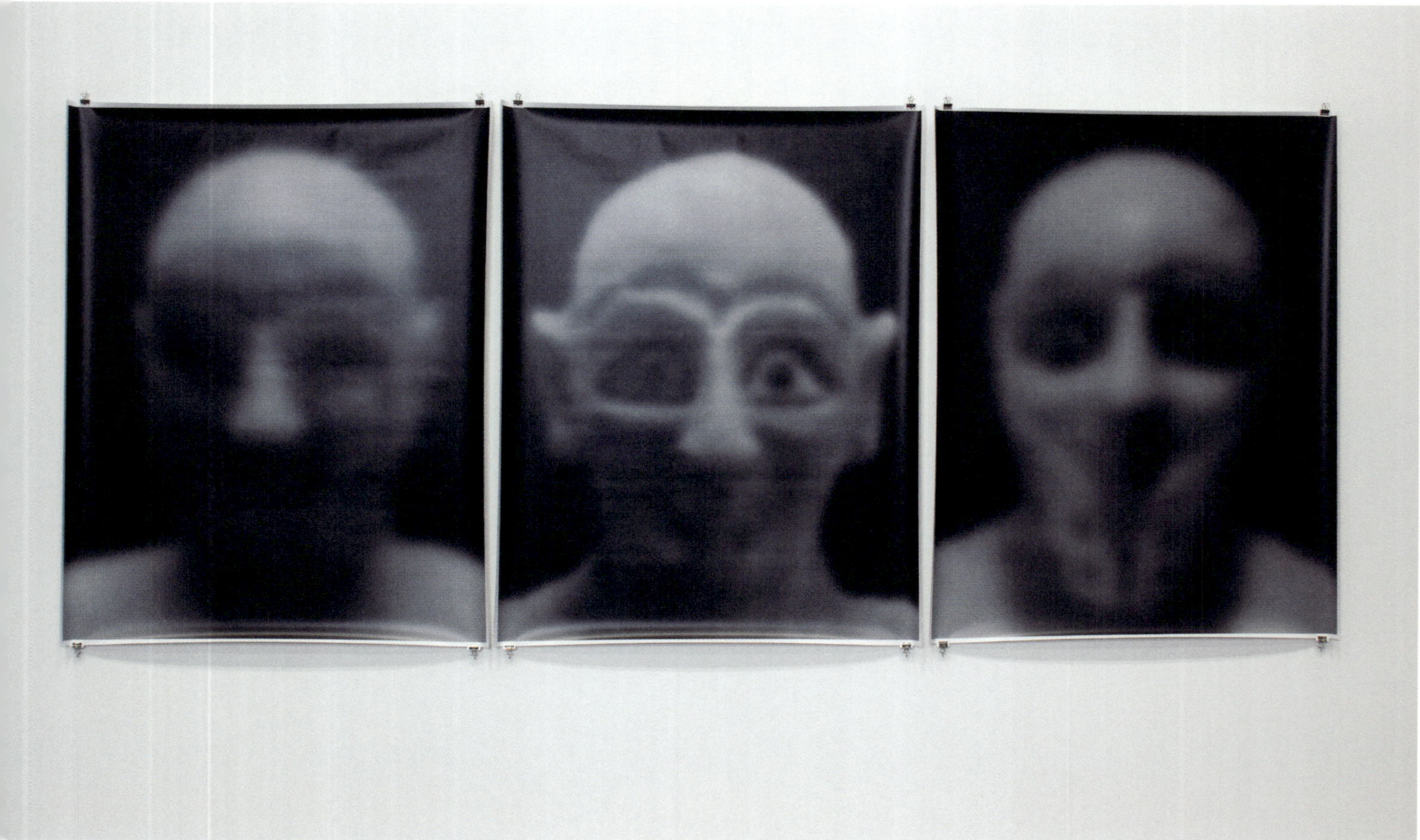

Richard Bell

* 1953 in Charleville, Queensland (AU), into the Kamilaroi tribe, lives and works in Brisbane (AU)

Scientia E Metaphysica (Bell's Theorem), 2003

Synthetic polymer paint on canvas,
240 × 360 cm (6 panels, 240 × 60 cm each)

The art of Australian artist and political activist Richard Bell is a response to crucial issues in Australian social history and politics, such as discrimination and racism, as well as to the functioning of the art system and market.

In his opposition to the usurpation of Aboriginal imagery and its commercial use in advertising campaigns, tourism promotion, etc. Bell appropriates styles and forms of Western Modernism, its painterly expression and iconography. The colorful, gridded patterns of *Scientia E Metaphysica (Bell's Theorem)* are reminiscent both of Pop art and the styles evolved by indigenous artists. They are inscribed with a text in the spirit of conceptualism that underscores a political message: "Aboriginal art - it's a white thing." Black and white drip and fields of the same colors on both sides of the painting bring into a concise visual formula the problems running through the sociopolitical history of black and white relations in Australia. The red "abstract" triangle refers to the existing "triangle of discomfort" from the critical text "Bell's Theorem"[1] expressing the extent of exploitation of Aboriginal artists at the hands of unscrupulous dealers and middlemen.

The painting's statement is directed against the commodification of Aboriginal art and against the control of Aboriginal culture by the non-Aboriginal Western art market. Bell's adamant concern is with the struggle against the marketing strategy of the industry that lobbies for Aboriginal art by selling typical "Aboriginal spirituality" and ghettoizing Aboriginal artists as "noble savages." (DM)

1 Richard Bell, "Bell's Theorem: ABORIGINAL ART - It's a White Thing!," available online at: www.kooriweb.org/bell/theorum.html, November 2002, accessed 07/15/2011.

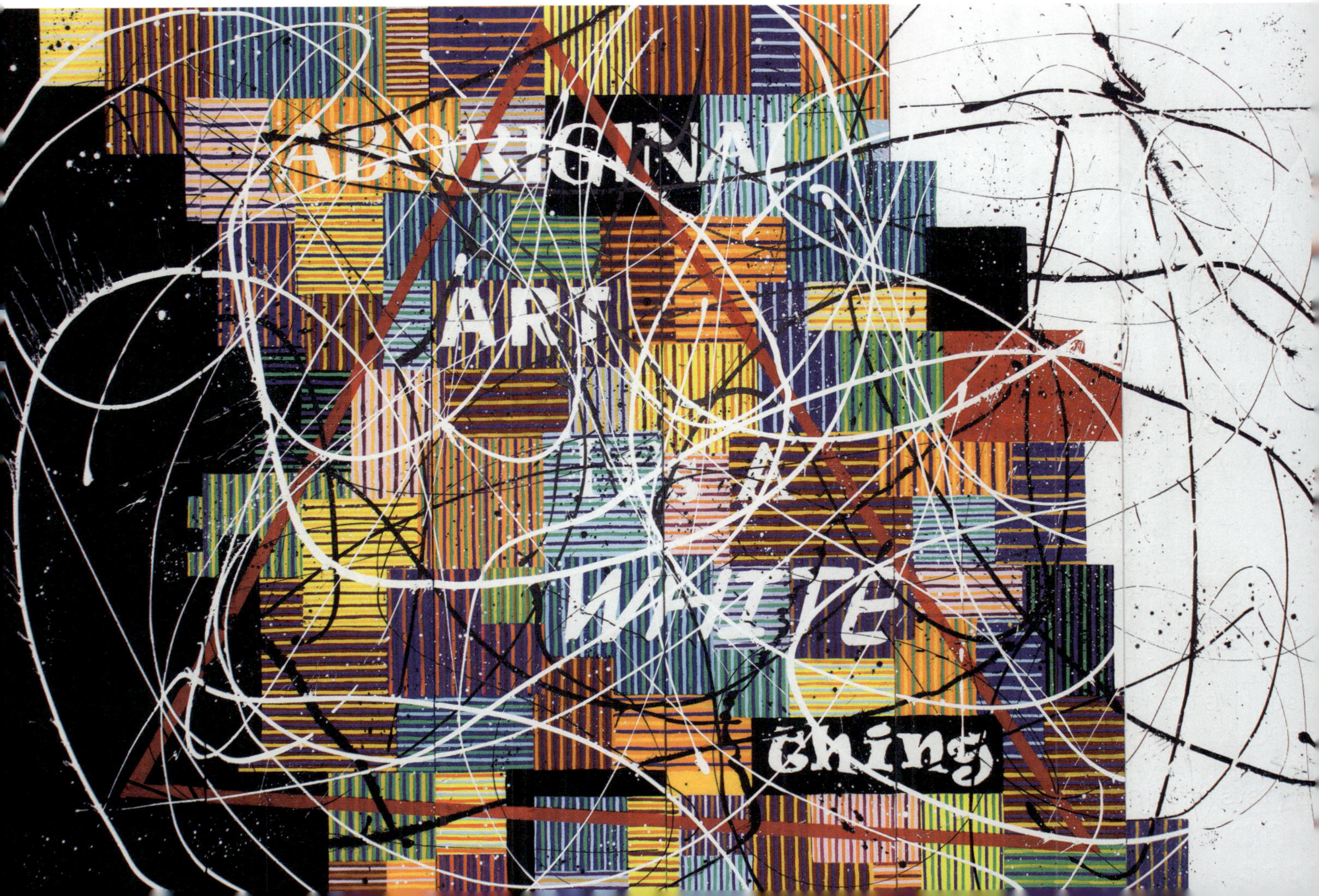

Santiago Borja

* 1970 in Mexico City (MX), lives and works in Mexico City

***Freud UXA-Aguila*, 2010**

Piezo print, carbon ink on cotton paper, 29 × 21 cm

***Diván*, 2010**

Digital print on cotton paper, 80 × 120 cm, framed

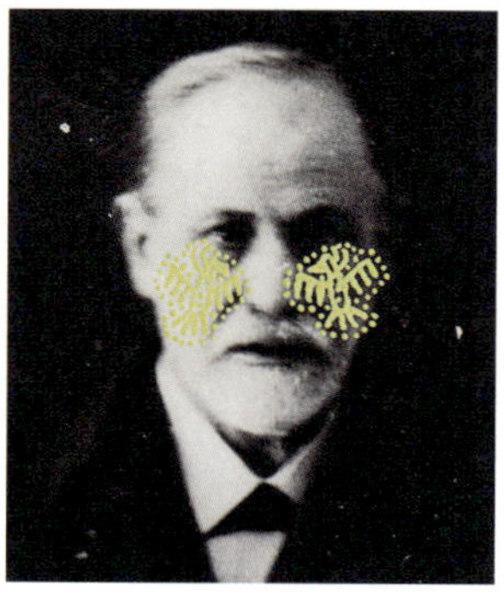

In the works *Diván* and *Freud UXA-Aguila*, Santiago Borja approaches one of the fathers of the Western theory of psychoanalysis: Sigmund Freud. In his search for universally meaningful values of human civilization, Freud surrounded himself with ancient objects of Egyptian, Greek, Roman, and Middle Eastern cultural heritage, which, in the nineteenth century, signified the origins of Western European culture. His famous couch draped with Persian carpets is indicative of this interest. The divan has become the symbol of psychoanalysis par excellence. Borja inserted a new element in his *Diván*. He asked members of the Huichol, an indigenous Mexican people, to make new covers and pillows for the couch. They have the same exotic effect on today's audience that the Persian carpets on Freud's couch had on people in the late nineteenth and early twentieth century. Thus, the idea of the birth of culture in classical antiquity becomes a cultural collage Borja uses to thematize the many possible origins of contemporary culture. Like *Diván*, the portrait *Freud UXA-Aguila*, decorated with patterns, is to be understood as a commentary on the founding myths of Western culture which, in Borja's photographs, confronts its own limits. (KB)

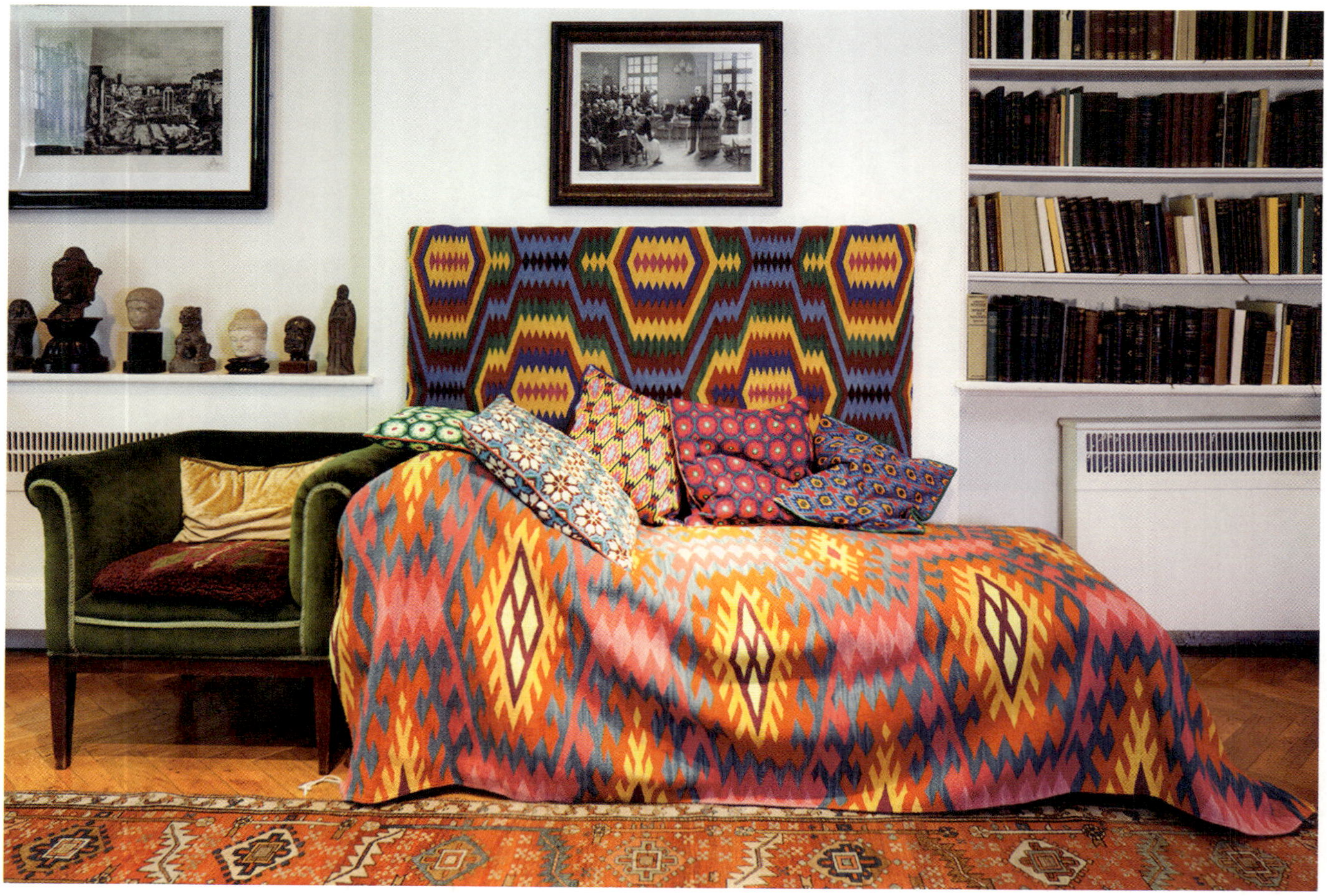

Neil Cummings & Marysia Lewandowska

Neil Cummings, * 1947 in Aberdare (UK), Marysia Lewandowska, * 1955 in Szczecin (PL); live and work in London (UK)

Museum Futures: Distributed, 2008

Video, color, sound, 32 min

The museum per se is a controversial place. The techniques of storing, arranging, and presenting carry with them the legacy of hegemonic violence, and for decades have been subjected to repeated criticism, deconstruction, and various cures by artists and scientists. The call for participation and transparency, for the liquidation of museal institutions in favor of platforms where art is no longer collected and exhibited as an item or artifact, but develops as a social process, is now *en vogue*. As with all revolutions, though, here too the question arises as to what will happen when these forces of change themselves become institutionalized.

Marysia Lewandowska and Neil Cummings offer us a possible answer in the form of a future vision of the museum presented as a retrospective interview on the history of the Moderna Museet - or, to be precise, of the Moderna v3.0 in the year 2058. In a discussion between the director and an archivist, an evolution is elaborated, which following the collapse of the art market as trade in commodities, led to open, cooperative practices. Were it not for a slight sense of the uncanny this would have been an utopian global art world: the emancipatory concepts of free content and participation have been reduced to mere technocratic newspeak, and behind social and ecological commitment lurks the will to administration. Thus, it is not surprising that the director of Moderna v3.0 responds in trepidation at the mere mention of artists involved in institutional critique such as Hans Haacke. (JB)

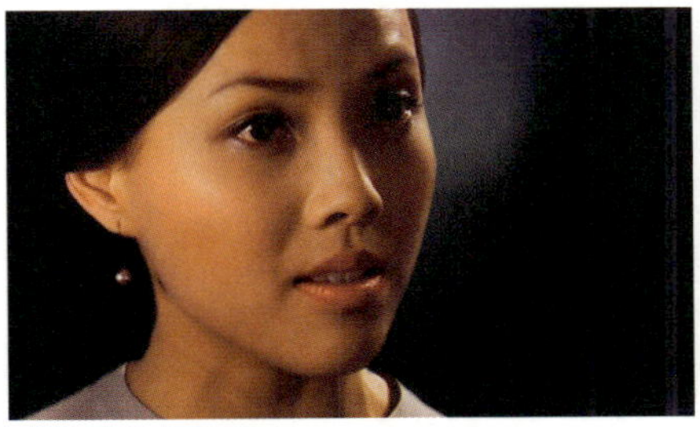
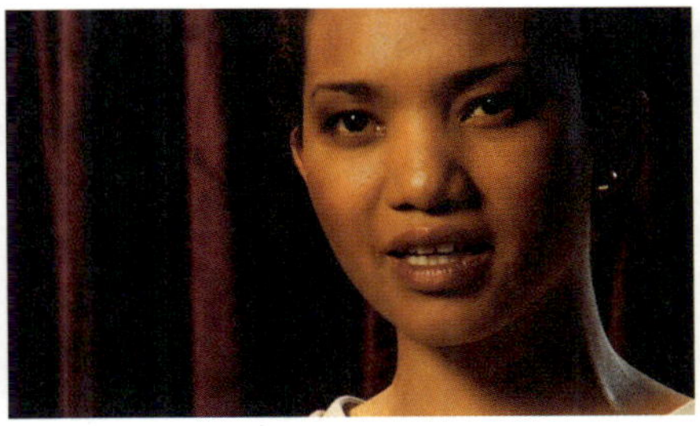
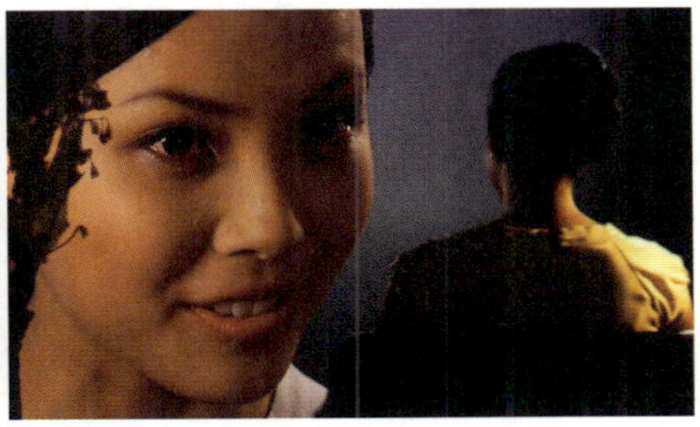
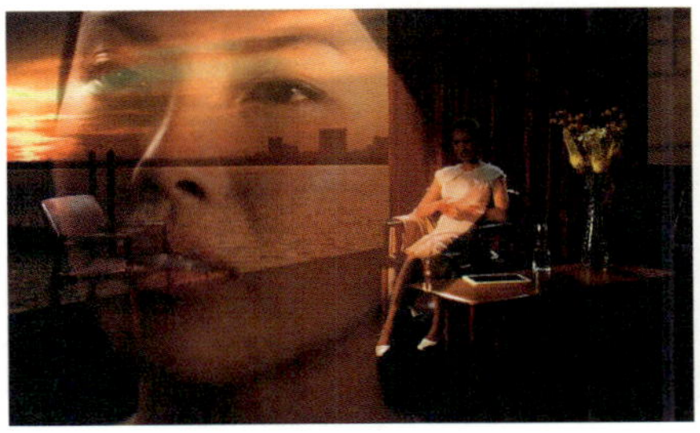
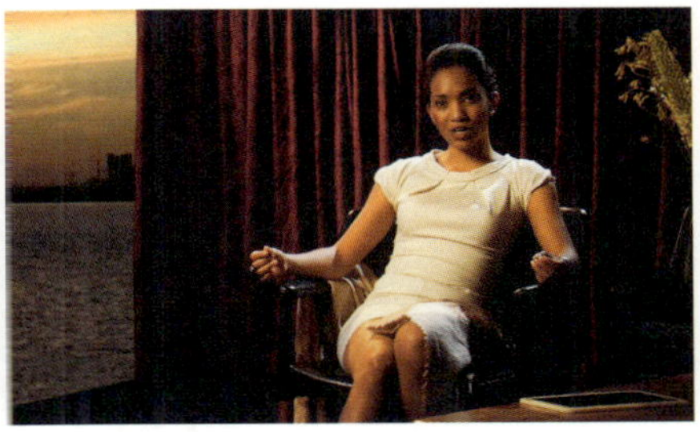
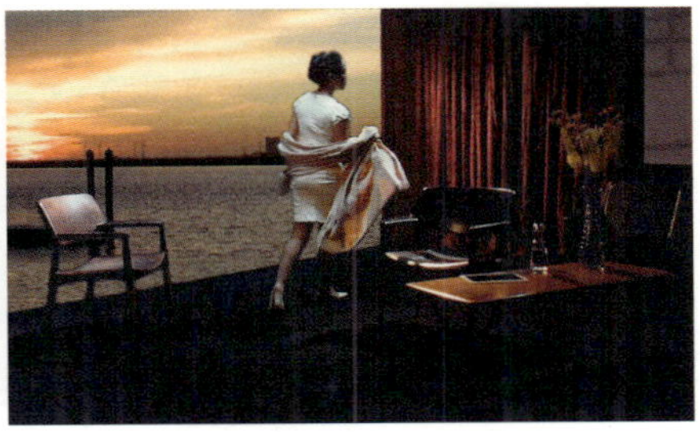

Pauline Curnier Jardin

* 1980 in Marseille (FR), lives and works in Paris (FR) and Berlin (DE)

Ami, 2009

Video installation, color, sound, 7 min

Pauline Curnier Jardin is a multimedia artist in the genres of graphics, performance, music, installation, and video. The common thread running through her artistic productions is an idiosyncratic sense of storytelling intimately connected to the hidden performative potential of images, found objects, and art pieces. Curnier Jardin's "patchwork narrations" create adventures and universes out of ready-made elements, which are then granted new imaginative vitality.

In her video installation *Ami* [Friend], the artist shows her own photographic collection of artworks and artifacts from art, ethnological, and natural hisory museums. Considered as lifelong friends, these objects are presented one after the other: a "love collage." Now set in a new constellation, these otherwise motionless objects are reactivated and rediscovered as characters in an erotic story line. The viewer's gaze is captured by the sexual detail in the sculptures while a ghostly piano motif recalls the nostalgic atmosphere of museums as archives of human production. By alternating images of internationally renowned works of art with so-called ethnic crafts, Curnier Jardin also hints at the controversial and unsolved question of artistic legitimation. (SG)

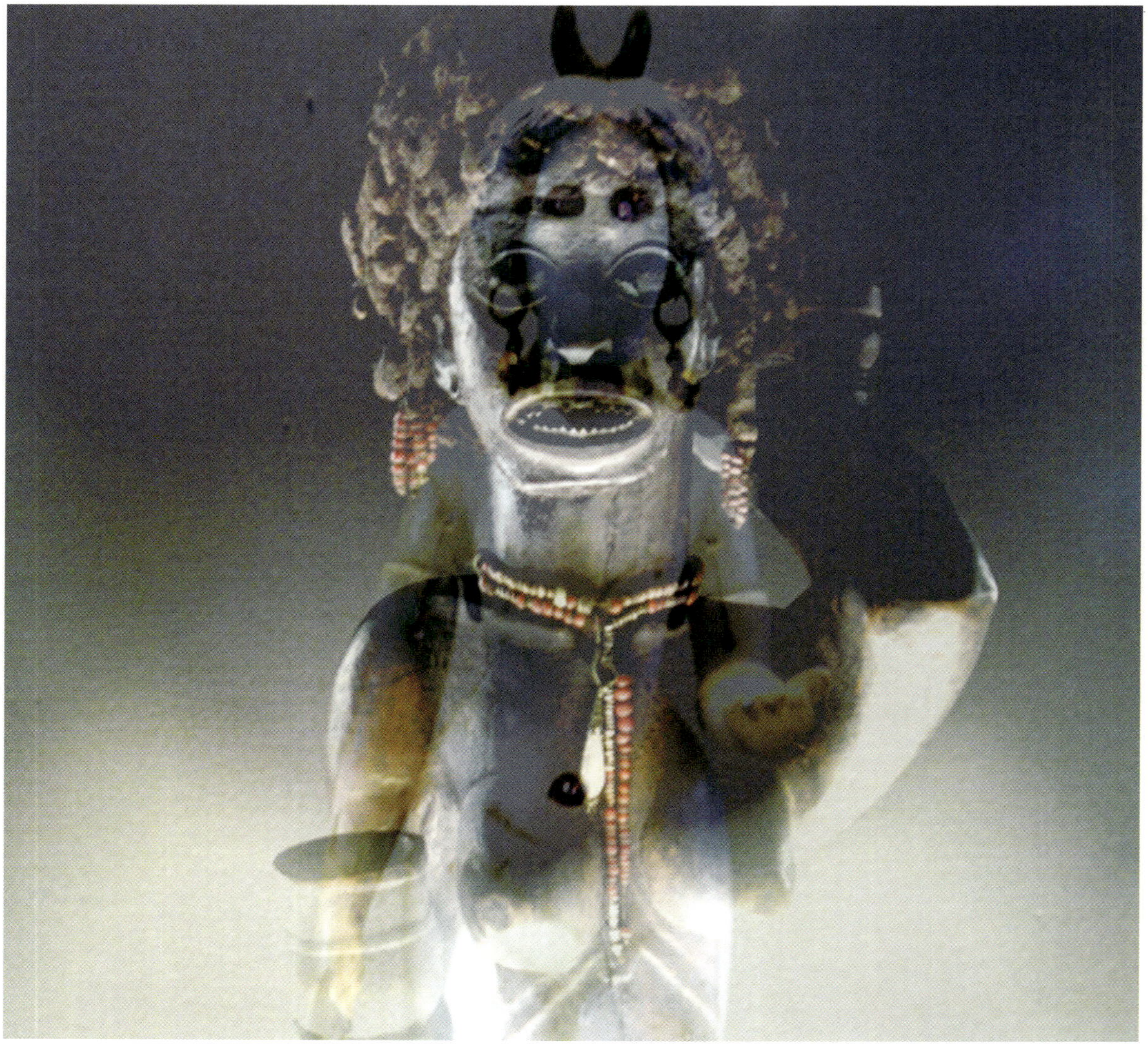

Erika & Javier

live and work in Asunción (PY)

El Peso de la Memoria (The Weight of Memory), 2007

Digital print on vinyl, 315 × 210 cm

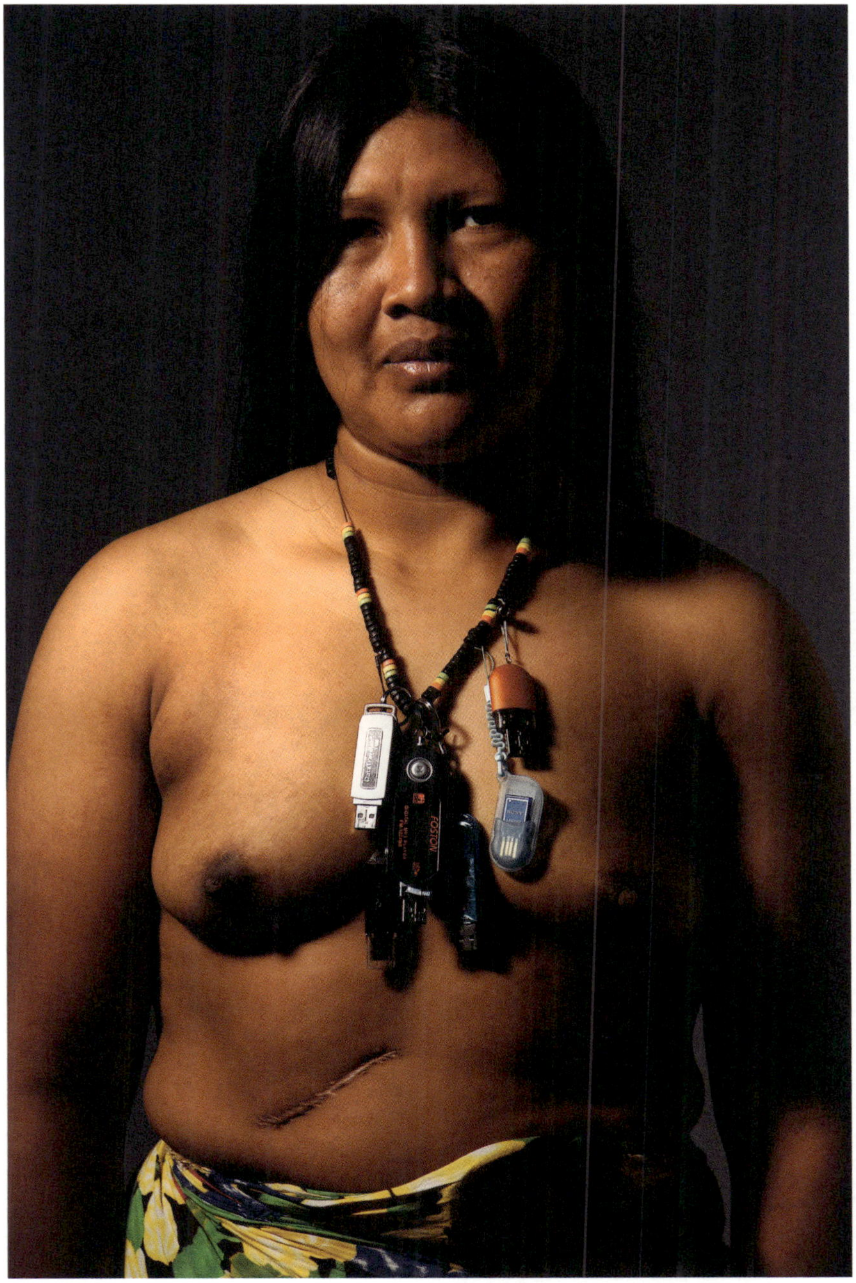

El Peso de la Memoria (The Weight of Memory) is a giant print by Paraguay-based artists Erika & Javier. The photograph displays a semi-naked Native American woman from the Guaraní tribe wearing what, at first glance, seems to be a traditional ornamental necklace. Yet, instead of charms, the Maka ethnic collar is decorated with six USB flash drives storing twelve gigabyte of information about international programs against poverty in Latin America. By featuring a technological device, the artists introduce a strong perturbation element into the institutional system of representation of the Latin American indigenous population. The artwork questions the legacy of clichés about supposed ethnic authenticities, thereby opening up a more complex horizon including issues of cultural encounter and appropriation.

The Guaraní people are one of the more widespread indigenous groups in South America, with settlements in Paraguay, Argentina, Uruguay, Bolivia, and southern Brazil. Reduced to slavery during the Spanish colonial period, they long have been targets of persecution, especially in Paraguay. If a society's collective memory is part of what shapes its present identity, Erika & Javier remind us of the obsolete nature of "the Other" as an anthropological category. Culture is certainly not a realm of essential and permanent properties, but rather a battlefield where values, identities, and heritage are endlessly being argued and negotiated. (SG)

Christian Jankowski

* 1968 in Göttingen (DE), lives and works in Berlin (DE) and New York, NY (US)

The China Painters, 2007/2008

Oil and acrylic on canvas
(selection of 10 paintings from the series)

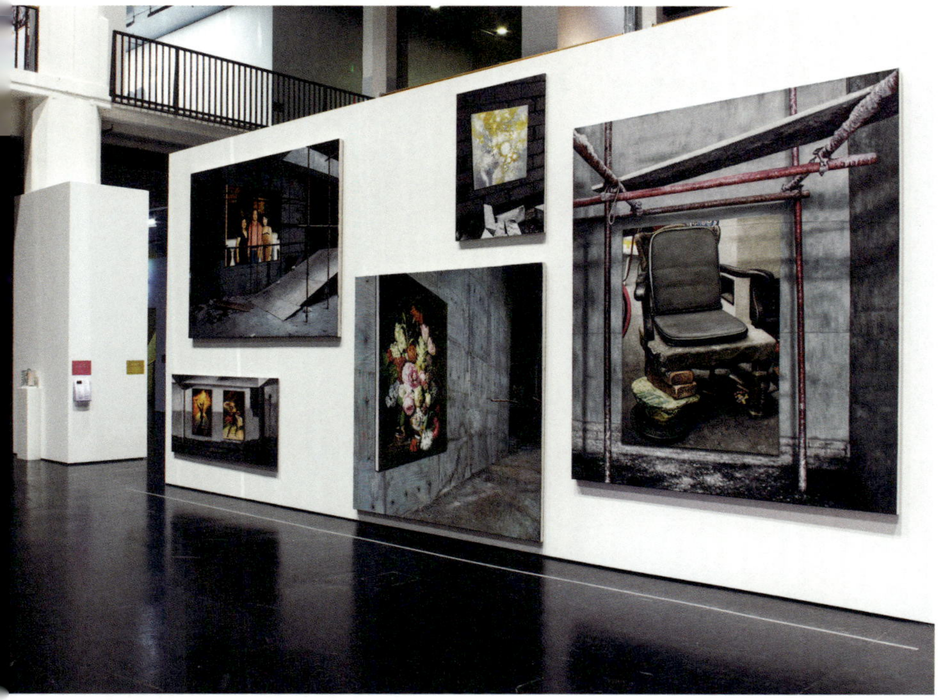

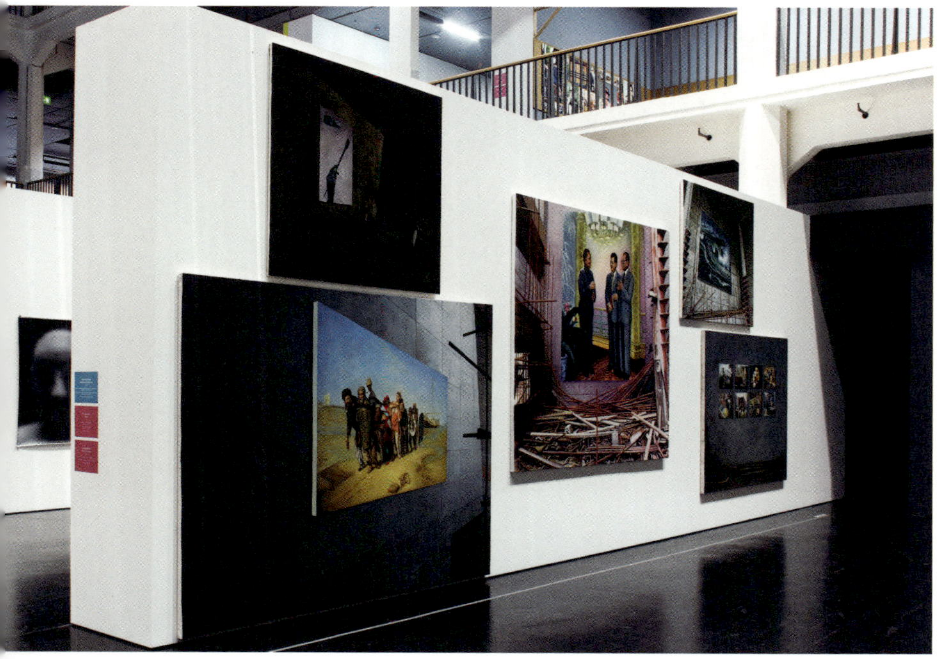

In the Chinese "village" of Dafen, copying paintings has become an industry. With an output of paintings running into the millions, Dafen is believed to be the largest producer of oil paintings in the world, although they hang in private living rooms and are not found at biennials or on the art market at the major auction houses. A place that is entirely dedicated to art certainly needs a museum, and one of these has been built in Dafen - but none of the copied works by Raphael and Wang Guangyi, which can be purchased in the town's shops, are displayed on its walls.

For his project *The China Painters*, Christian Jankowski made use of this bizarre situation of a space dedicated to collecting in a place dedicated to copying. Instead of commissioning the usual artworks from the art studios of Dafen, he ordered copies of photographs, which showed the as yet empty rooms of the unfinished museum. Further, he asked the artists to adorn the walls with works that, in their opinion, should legitimately hang there. In the imaginary museum that resulted, family photographs and socialist-realist propaganda works meet historic European painting, which was part of the canon that the artists studied in their predominantly classical training. Between raw concrete and scaffolding the imaginary museum demonstrates that the question as to what belongs in a museum can only be answered by means of a permanent building site. (JB)

James Luna

* 1950 in Orange, CA (US), lives and works in La Jolla Reservation, San Diego, CA (US)

The Artifact Piece, 1987/1990

C-print on aluminum Dibond,
180 × 116.5 cm

In his performances and installations, for the last three decades James Luna has engaged in a provocative and humorous way with the problems and issues facing contemporary Native Americans. Luna draws on personal observations and experiences for his artistic work. The artist has been living and working in La Jolla Reservation since 1975.

For the performance *The Artifact Piece*, clad in a loincloth Luna lay inside a glass showcase filled with sand. Around him were testimonials of his life: his diploma, his divorce papers, as well as personal objects and various mementos from his schooldays. Signs positioned within the showcase indicate his name, and comment on the scars on his body. The installation's arrangement is reminiscent of dioramas typically used in ethnological museums for visualizing the life of extinct societies. By presenting himself as an artifact, as a lifeless object, Luna unmasks in a satirical way the one-sided and stereotypical presentation of Native Americans as these are presented in museums. When confronted by the artist, the objectivizing viewpoint - which locates Native American culture firmly in the past, trivializing and romanticizing it as an extinct form of living - is revealed as an act of marginalization that persists to this day. (EA)

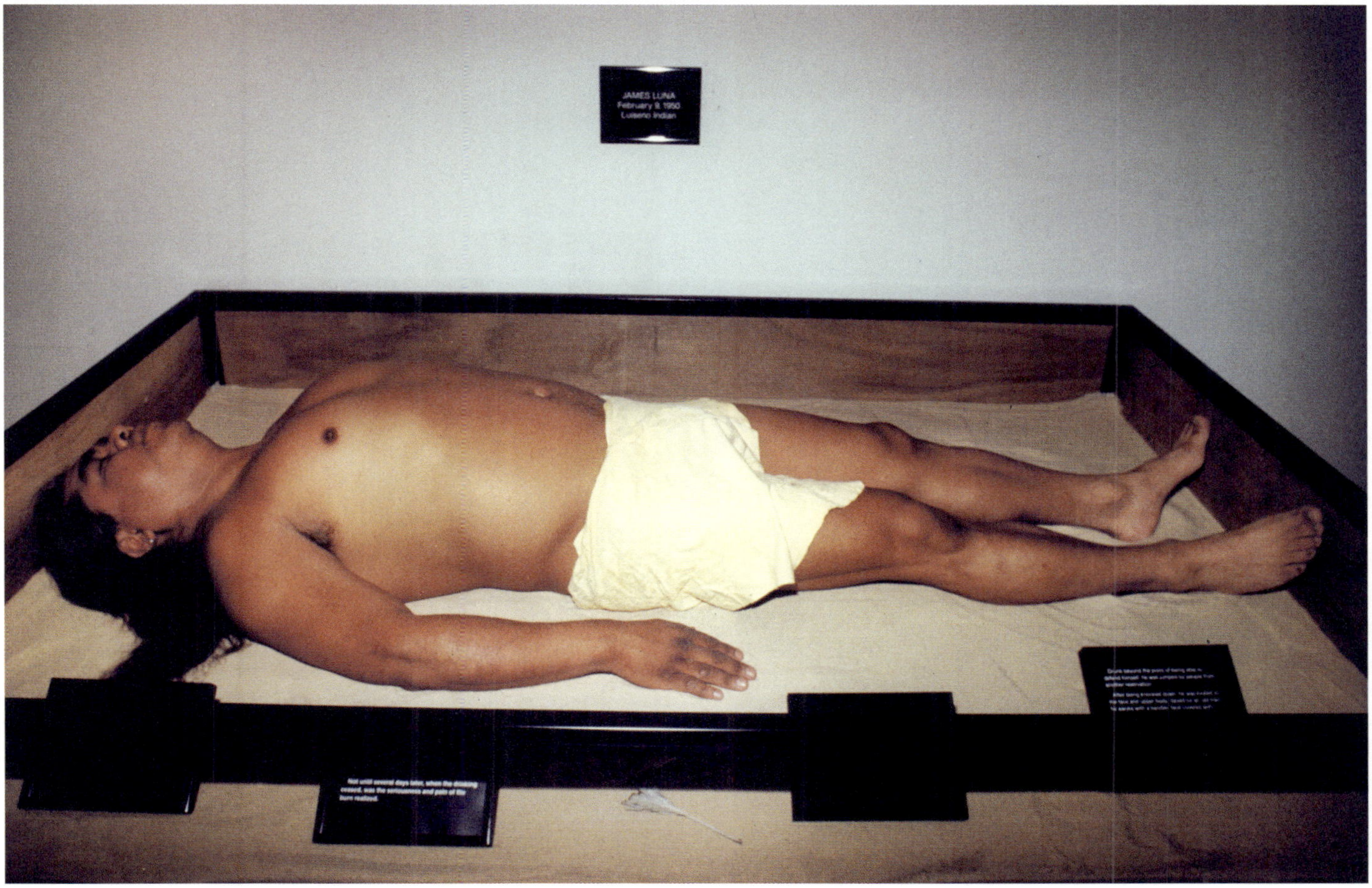

Nástio Mosquito

* 1981 in Haumbo (AO), lives and works in Luanda (AO)

***Africa*, 2010**

Video, color, sound, 1 min

***America*, 2010**

Video, color, sound, 6:30 min

***Europe*, 2010**

Video, color, sound, 3:30 min

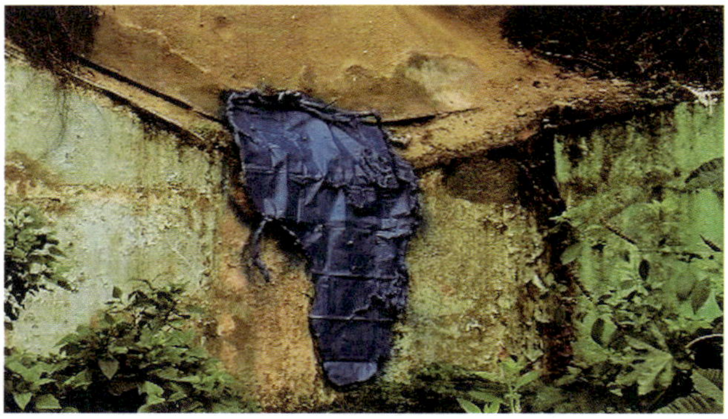

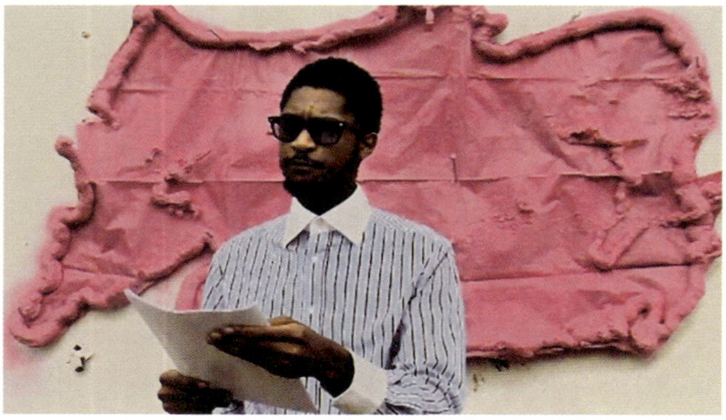

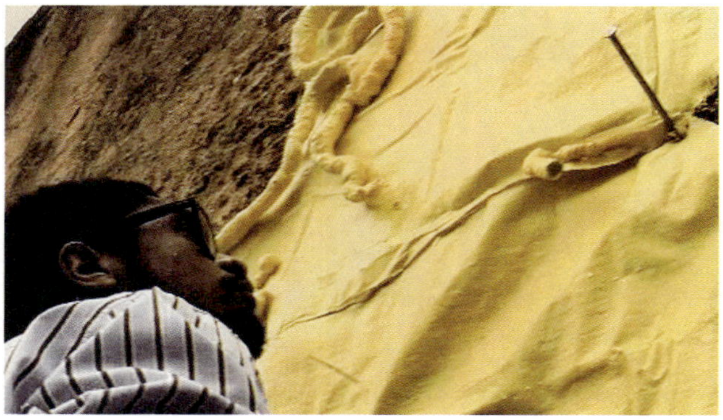

Nástio Mosquito is a multimedia artist and slam poet whose works include music, performance, the spoken word, photography, film, television, and video. Combining entertainment and performance, he comments on the globalized present and analyzes questions of identity and the effects of imperialism, postcolonialism, the Cold War, war as such, and migration. Acting from different perspectives - as an African, a diaspora artist from Luanda, a political activist, a migrant, a free individual and world citizen, or as his alter ego Nástia - with strong sense of irony and satire together with a precise use of language and vision, Mosquito confronts viewers with difficult issues and uncomfortable facts and associations.

In the video works *Africa*, *America*, *Europe*, Mosquito addresses topics of postcolonialism and the global dominance of Western capitalism by pointing back at their originator: "I bought Europe. Your pride of a Europe that no longer belongs to you." In the role of an African businessman, he showcases strategies of both cultural and territorial (re-) appropriation while at the same time confronting the Old World with its continuing imperialistic posture, ignorance, and isolationist policies. (AM)

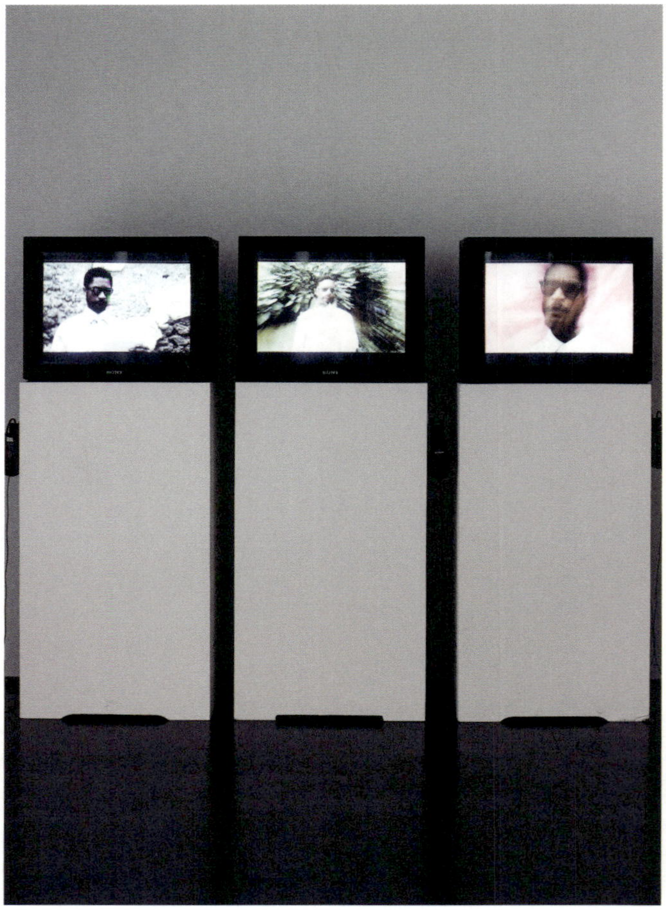

Krisna Murti

* 1957 in Kupang (ID), lives and works in Jakarta (ID)

For Odd For Ever, 2010

Digital print on board, 57 × 90 cm

Shop Theater #3, 2010

Digital print on board, 57 × 90 cm

Street Theater, 2010

Digital print on board, 57 × 90 cm

The Last Photograph, 2010

Digital print on canvas, 66 × 200 cm

The Old and the Beauty, 2010

Digital print on board, 57 × 90 cm

Krisna Murti's series of photographs shows the artist dressed in costumes of *wayang* characters from Javanese shadow theater. In *Street Theater* or *The Old and the Beauty*, the characters are placed in commercial urban settings. With their colorful costumes and *wayang* dance poses, they not only seem out of place but also completely disconnected from the area and pedestrians around them. They stand singly or in groups in front of large billboard advertisements as in *For Odd For Ever*, or before boutique windows, as in *Shop Theater #3*. The contrast of larger-than-life super models on the billboards and the colorful liveliness of the dancers raises questions about the representation of reality and fiction. This dynamic is accentuated in *The Last Photograph*, in which a group of ten *wayang* characters are placed in front of a vast stretch of land directly facing the camera. What, at first glance, appears as a romantic setting in the Indonesian countryside is revealed as a construction site, with bulldozers in the background plowing their way through the landscape.

The photographs rallude to the push and pull between the eagerness for economic development and the wish to conserve traditional customs and values. The medium of photography is not only employed here as a commentary on the consequences of consumer culture, but also as a means of documenting and preserving traditional forms that are slowly vanishing due to increased tourism and urban development, and an ensuing global, visual language of gentrification. (AMB)

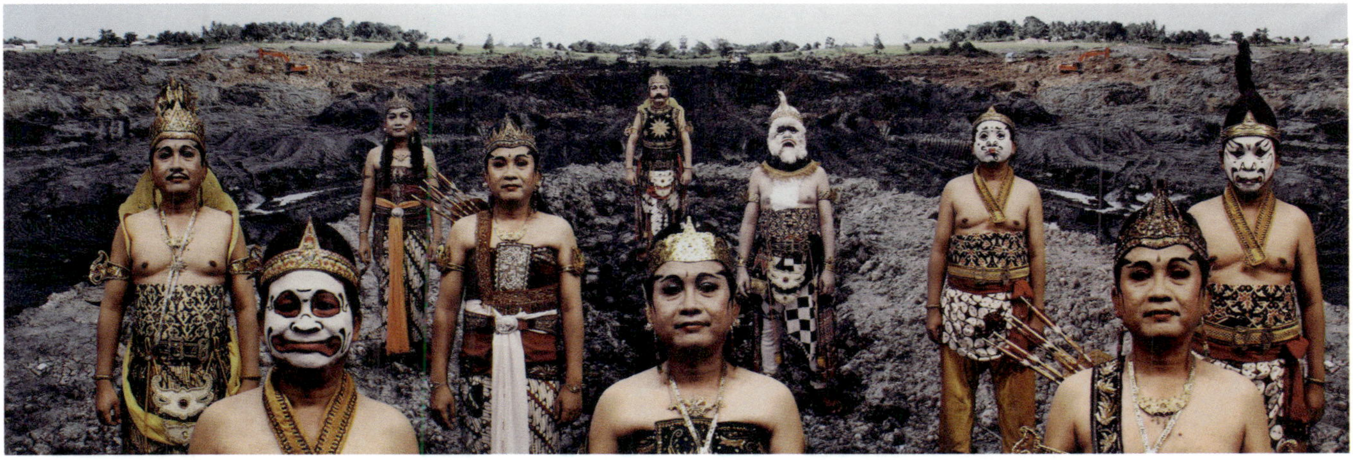

The Last Photograph

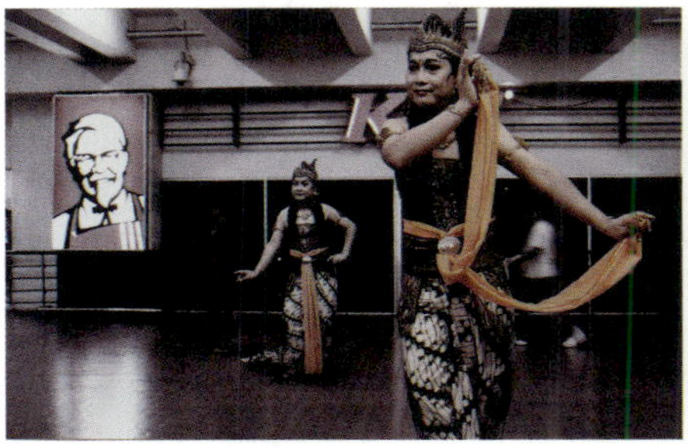

The Old and the Beauty

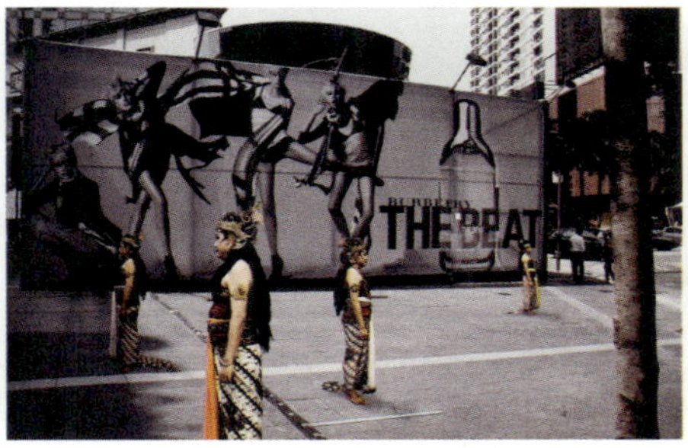

Street Theater

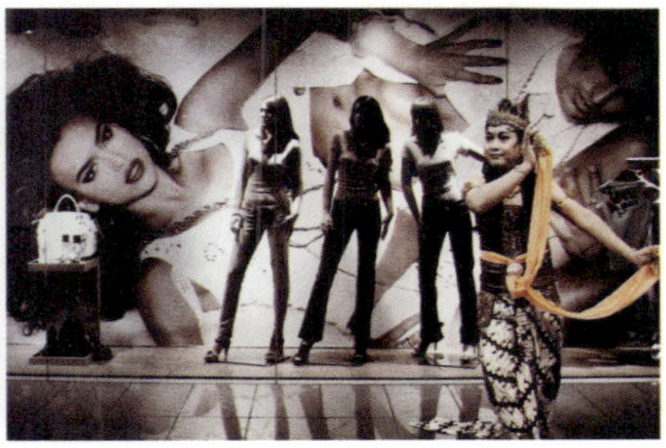

Shop Theater #3

Mattias Olofsson

* 1973 in Skellefteå (SE), lives and works in Umeå (SE)

Culture Constructing Nature, 2004

3 C-prints, 70 × 100 cm each, framed

In modern societies exoticism is a means of presenting people as "different": the fascination of something foreign merges with the desire to maintain a barrier between one's own society and that which is foreign. The motifs depicted on picture postcards from abroad are exotic as are the animals and things from distant places exhibited behind bars or glass - the alien and possibly dangerous is tamed, something which in this context not only satisfies our curiosity, but also demonstrates the power our institutions exert over it.

The "faraway" characteristic of the exotic does not necessarily pertain to the distance between continents. In his series *Culture Constructing Nature*, Mattias Olofsson refers to a famous young woman from Lapland known as Stor-Stina (Big Stina), who during the nineteenth century was exhibited at fairs as a sensation due to her size. Dressed in Stina's traditional costume of Sami origin, and presented in museum showcases, Olofsson demonstrates how artificial such exhibitions of the exotic are. At the same time he shows that no less for our society, the construction and exclusion of the Other - whether owing to appearance, culture, or sexuality - is neither museal nor historical. (JB)

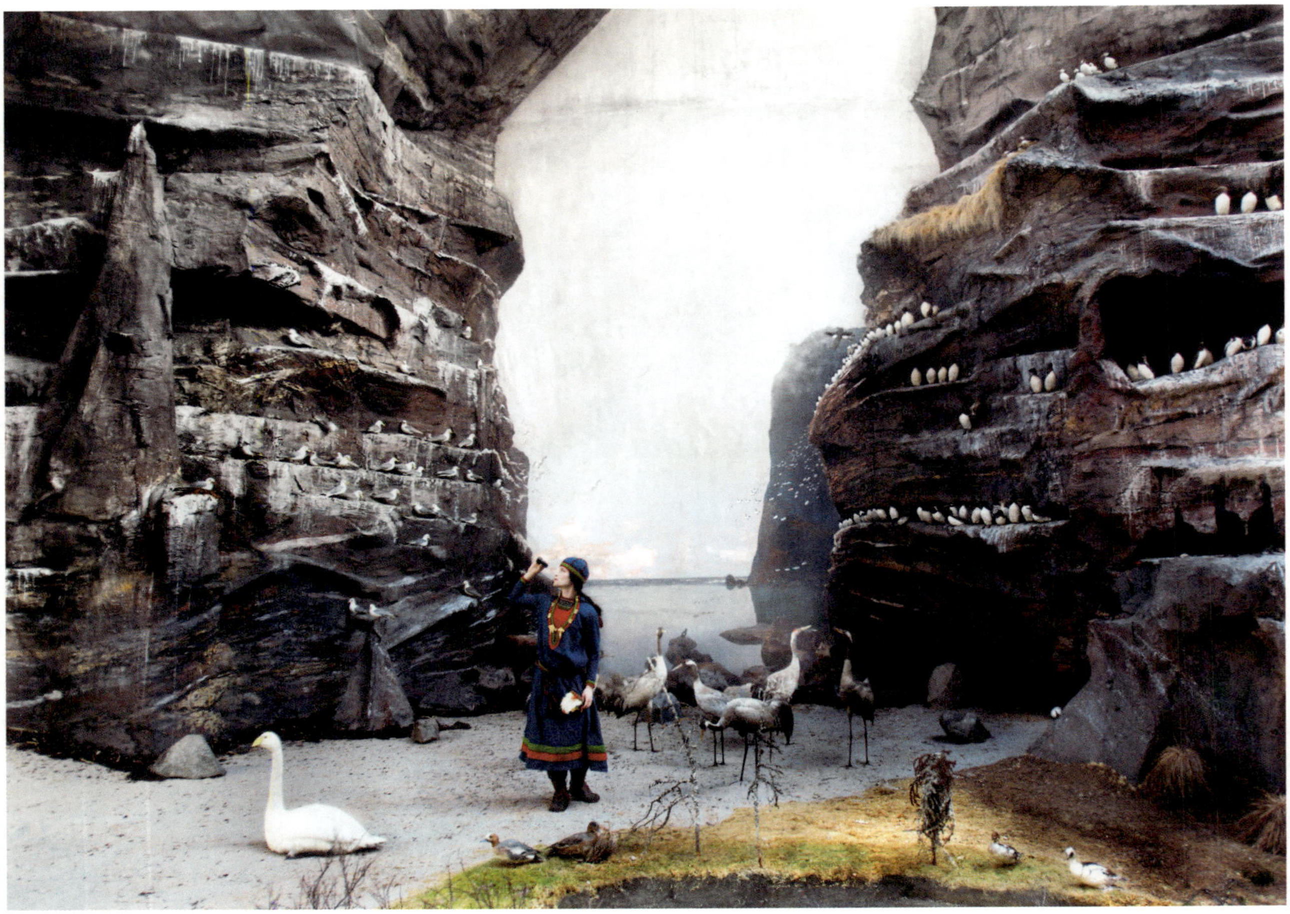

Jim Supangkat

* 1948 in Makassar (ID), lives and works in Jakarta (ID)

Kamar Ibu Dan Anak (Bedroom of a Woman and her Child), 1975 (reconstruction 2006, 2011)

Mixed-media installation (wooden furniture), 3 × 3 m (bed 190 × 70 × 75 cm, closet 60 × 40 × 100 cm, chair 50 × 45 × 90 cm, table 100 × 45 × 157 cm, child's bed 80 × 40 × 100 cm)

With his installation *Kamar Ibu Dan Anak (Bedroom of a Woman and her Child)*, Jim Supangkat takes us back to the Indonesia of the 1970s, a time when life was determined by a rigid, paternalistic regime – a circumstance that had fatal consequences for women and children. Supangkat presents a chair, a cupboard, a bed, a makeup table, and a child's bed made of heavy wood riddled with metal elements. Metal bars close off the bed; a pair of female legs, hanging on chains, are locked up in a cupboard with a metal door on one side and a glass front. Women and children are the prisoners of a dictatorship extending even into the most intimate space, the place where people sleep. And while the fatal effects on development and lives, especially on that of the children, remain unspoken and are barely imaginable, the repression and violence in such a social climate become physically tangible to viewers of the installation.

For over thirty years, the artist, curator, and art critic Jim Supangkat has significantly influenced current discourse on art in his homeland. In 1975, he founded Gerakan Seni Rupa Baru (Indonesia New Art Movement), an artist's group dedicated to redefining art and its possibilities of making an impact on social and cultural issues. He also founded several regional art forums in South East Asia. Since 2003, Supangkat curates the CP Biennale, an event committed to global representation that accounts for both non-Western and Western art. (EA)

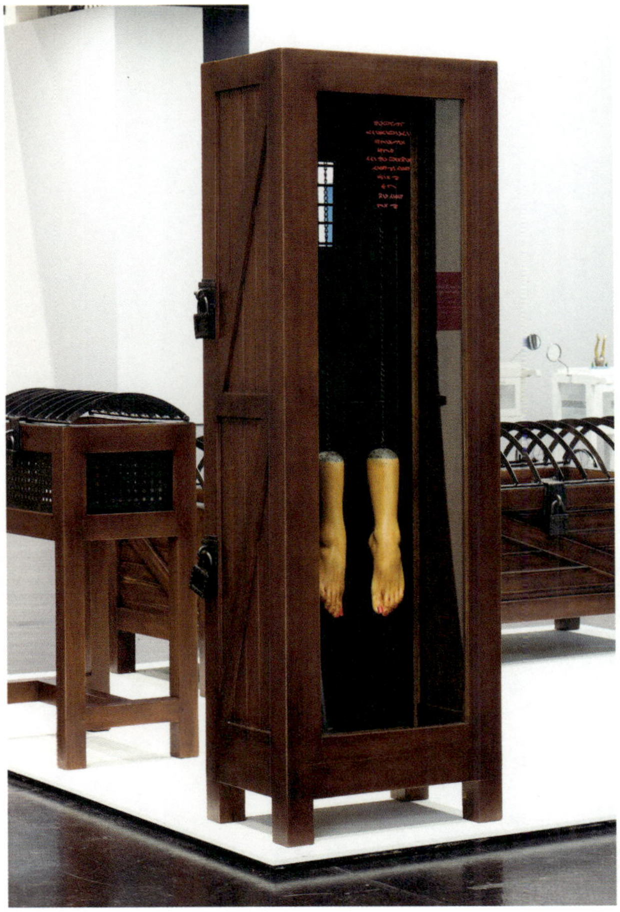

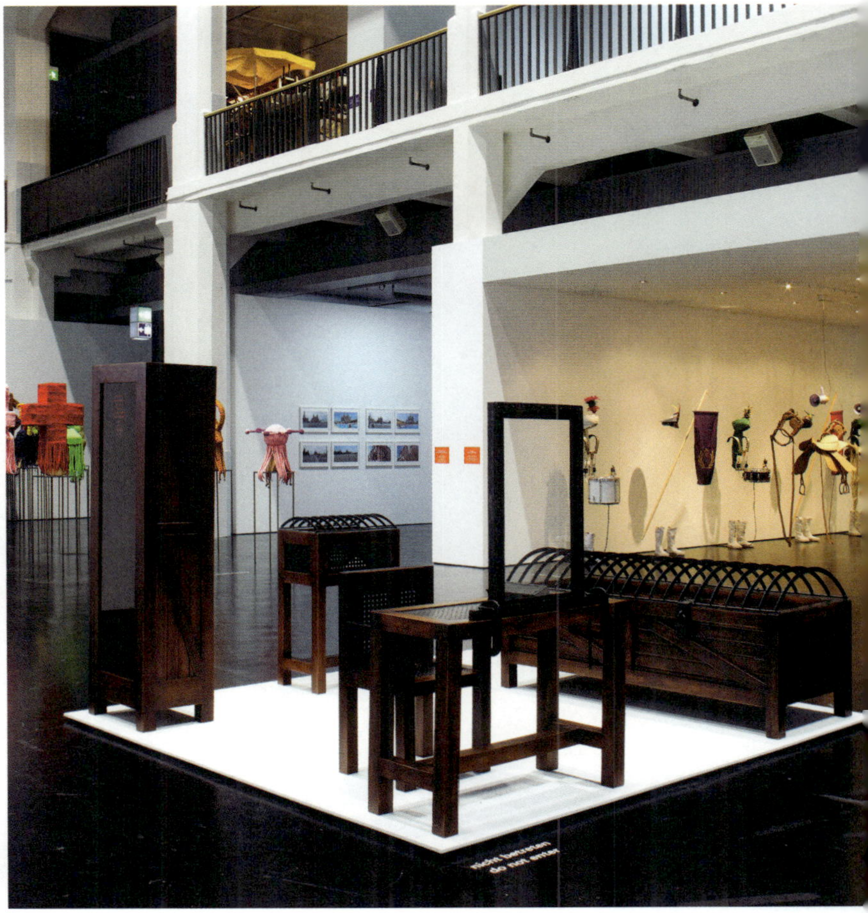

Zander Blom
Cai Yuan and Jian Jun Xi
Hong Hao / Liu Ding
Miao Xiaochun
Jun Nguyen-Hatsushiba
Tsuyoshi Ozawa / Leila Pazooki
Nusra Latif Qureshi
Araya Rasdjarmrearnsook
Sean Snyder

Boundary Matters: The Practice of Art After Modernity

"Boundary matters" can be read in a double sense. In the sense of "boundary is important," it recalls the self-evident claim of modern art to exclude other modernities or any art practices other than its own like an impenetrable wall. In the sense of "boundary issues," however, it serves to indicate the shifting boundaries of art production that are no longer protected by a single art concept. In fact, the idea of art is today subject to conflicting viewpoints when applied, for example, to exhibition or traditional art. The various art practices even penetrate the new, competing art markets where they are flattened out as equal commodities without becoming equal, without actually being equal per se. New boundaries also divide different audiences who do not share the same art education or (unlike the global clientele of the markets) are unfamiliar with "art" in the first place. As a result, the art concept, introduced as a mere fiction, has become the target for some of the artists who figure in this section. They play freely with art's "boundaries" (be it for aesthetic or political reasons) and also tend to expose art history as a foreign narrative that is not translatable to every audience within art's globally expanded confines.

A central piece in this section is the frieze-like portrait cycle by Nusra Latif Qureshi, which confronts the viewer with the ironic question *Did you come here to find history?* or rather, "Did you only come here to find me in history?" The answer is left in the air, as she has superimposed her own passport photograph upon Mughal paintings and Renaissance portraits such as Giorgione's *Laura*, the allegorical "portrait" of the art of poetry. As a result, this morphing of faces casts doubts on the possibility for representing one's own identity in light of cultural stereotypes and through the filter of art history. The artist was initially trained in Mughal miniature painting, the trademark of her Pakistan background. But she created this work, with its blending of modern photography and famous Venetian prototypes, for the 53rd Venice Biennale where she played with the celebrities of the local art memory and exchanged roles that had served the politics of representation in the past. She seems to have called up such multi layered fragments of history and presence with the intention to stage herself as a contemporary figure with multiple identities in today's biennial circuit where the audience will encounter her work with uncertain expectations.

The question of the audience takes an unexpected turn in a highly humorous video by Thai artist Araya Rasdjarmrearnsook. It shows a group of villagers sitting together in a rural Thailand location where they are asked to comment on reproductions of famous French paintings such as Manet's *Déjeuner sur l'herbe*, in which they see another group in the countryside. The comments which the whole group contributes reflect a perception that is not mediated by the cultural pedigree of the works shown. The video, in turn, also challenges a Western audience to reconsider what it expects to see in works that have originated in and are destined for another visual culture. The argument is taken up by Sean Snyder's work *Exhibition* where a Ukrainian peasant audience, mirrored in a Soviet audience of the 1960s, is instructed to understand the political message of Mexican Art. One of the participants asks the disarmingly basic question: "What is the most important thing in art?"

In her installation *Moments of Glory* Iranian-born Leila Pazooki plays with the idea of discovering new celebrities such as the "Indian Damien Hirst" or the "Chinese Gerhard Richter" outside the Western art world. But Damien Hirst or Gerhard Richter are not merely brand names of the art market; because they were born within a certain art system that, contrary to all claims of universality, has been a local, Euramerican story, they cannot simply be copied in other visual cultures. There is, at the other end of the possible spectrum, the case of Liu Ding's installation *Omission* that offers an ironic metaphor of the Chinese preoccupation with the history of contemporary art as a dubious construct. A voluminous book, it seems, carries the fictitious title: *A History of Chinese*

Contemporary Art 19XX to 2050. The date 19XX plays with the controversy over the origin (and end?) of Chinese avant-garde art in the 1980s, and the arbitrary date 2050 reveals the paradox of writing the history of an art that claims to be nothing but contemporary over any length of time. The book rests on what is the equivalent of the "Scholar's Rock," a symbol of Chinese literati culture. The old Chinese art history which the rock recalls, or rather its connection with contemporary art, is questioned in the epigram "Omission is the beginning of history writing." And finally, there is Zander Blom, the artist from Johannesburg, who used reproductions in art books, his only link to Western art, as models for three-dimensional installations, which he then documented in photographs again, thus exposing their double genealogy. (HB)

Zander Blom

* 1982 in Pretoria (ZA), lives and works in Johannesburg (ZA)

The Drain of Progress, 2007

Photo series (selection), ultrachrome ink on cotton,
45 x 60 cm each (framed)

Zander Blom grew up in Pretoria, South Africa, and today lives in the part of Johannesburg called Brixton, where he creates his processual, experimental interventions. His workshop and domicile is both pivot and fulcrum of temporary installations that Blom pieces together, as for example, for the photo series *The Drain of Progress*, from various materials including wood, cardboard, paper, paint, tape, and everyday utility objects. Before he changes or deconstructs them so as to rearrange them, Blom creates a photographic documentation of the works. This, after the adding of a diary-like note about place and time of creation, is what remains for exhibition.

Zander Blom's artistic practice is closely connected with his approach to Western (history of) art, through art historical publications and their reproduction of works of the classic modern period. The photographic depictions of works by Kazimir Malevich, Piet Mondrian, Jackson Pollock, Kurt Schwitters, and Vladimir Tatlin, with their specific mise-en-scène of light, color scheme, picture detail, and choice of paper, interest him as much as the originals. With his playful and ironic re-creations of modern Western classics, Blom puts their formal, utopian, and substantive concerns center stage and, at the same time, uses them for a very serious and personal analysis and determination of his own position in relation to art history. (AM)

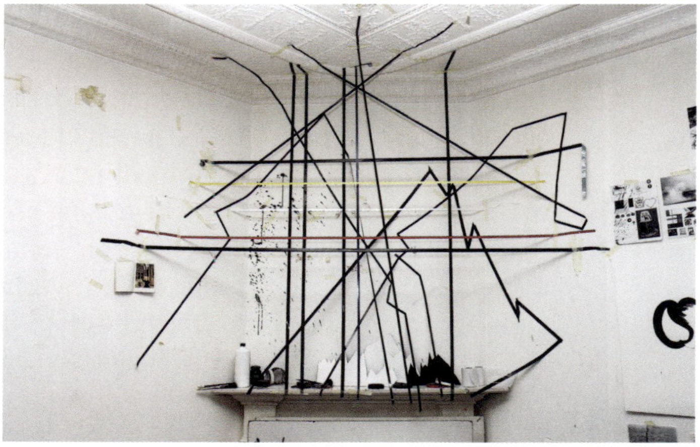

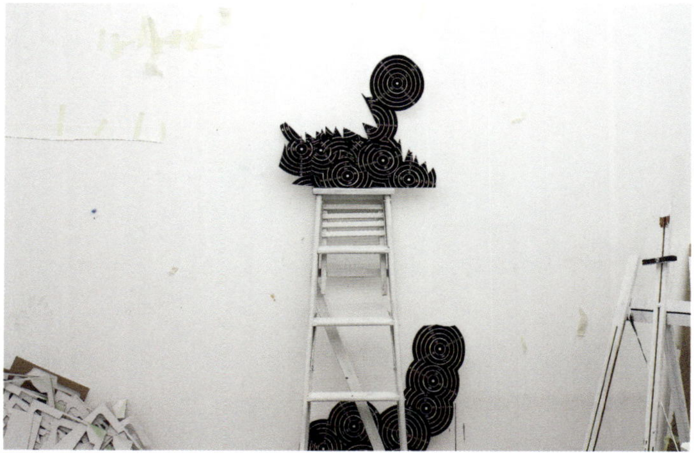

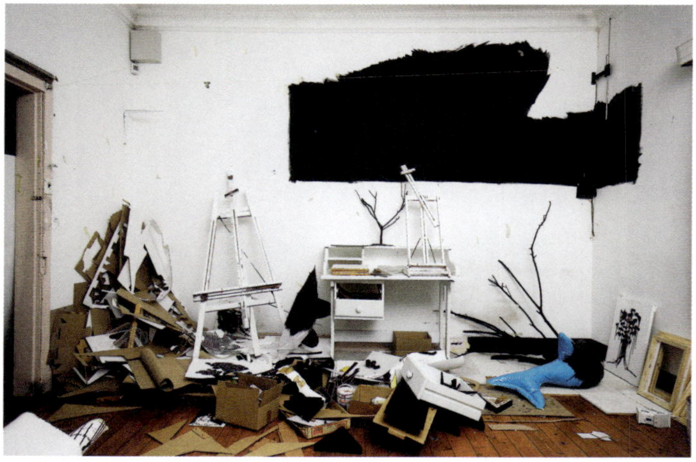

Cai Yuan and Jian Jun Xi

* 1962/1956 in China, live and work in the UK

Two Artists Piss on Duchamp's Urinal, 2000

Performance, Tate Modern, London, filmed by Eamon Lee, video, color, sound, 1:35 min

The gesture of iconoclasm is often misunderstood and dismissed as ignorance or vandalism directed against image-making itself. Yet attacks against images spring necessarily from a belief in their power, and the act of destruction itself produces not merely rubble but also new images. This is captured by the video, which shows the artist duo Cai Yuan and JJ Xi urinating on Marcel Duchamp's *Fountain* at the Tate Modern in London: like religious iconoclasts, the artists appear to have no respect for the venerable cultural tradition of European modernism. That both of them have lived outside China since the 1980s and were educated at prestigious London art schools does not prevent us from seeing here an image of "foreigners," who because of incomprehension or disbelief indecently assault "our" canon. And, in fact, Cai Yuan and JJ Xi seem to want to sideline the artistic achievement of modernism: the title of their work already calls the object a "urinal," simply ignoring Duchamp's act of translating an object of utility into the context of art.

Of course this is not a naïve rejection of modern art, but rather a humorous continuation of Duchamp's game with the concept of art, which Cai Yuan and JJ Xi extend through the postmodern mystification of cultural contexts. We should see the performance as, in their own words, a "celebration of the spirit of contemporary art," and the act itself as a release of *qi*, entirely in keeping with Chinese tradition. (JB)

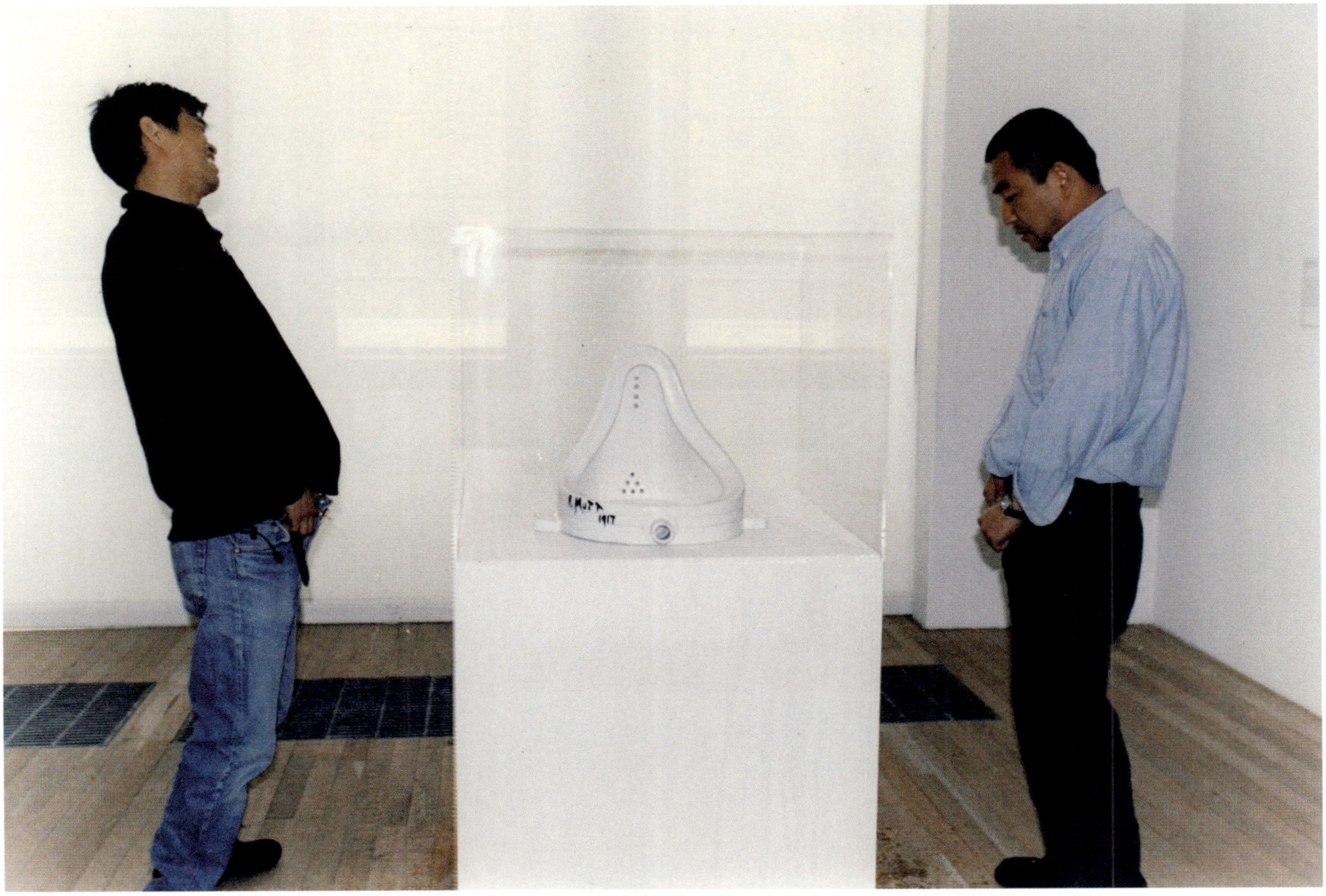

Hong Hao

* 1965 in Beijing (CN), lives and works in Beijing

Kassel City Defense Vertical View, 1997

Mixed media, silkscreen, 56 × 76 cm

At exhibitions of contemporary art the question of why works of certain artists should be shown is often overwritten afterwards by the question as to why others were *not* shown – and whether this exclusion was merely due to negligence or rather political interests. When the Documenta X was being organized in Kassel in 1997, this question was particularly relevant for the Chinese art world: Why, among the 120 artists exhibited, was there only one from China? This surely implied that current Chinese art was either not contemporary or had been excluded for some other reason.

The artists Hong Hao and Yan Lei used this as an opportunity for a sarcastic intervention. Using an appropriate letterhead and writing in semiofficial German, they distributed a bogus invitation from the Documenta organizers to take part in a special exhibition of contemporary Chinese art in Kassel as, in the words of the letter, “a sign of recognition” of its special position in the art world. The artists’ barb hit everyone involved: the organizers of Documenta X and their image of the art world that in fact shows only a corner of it, as well as the Chinese art scene, which was all too happy to embrace the false hope of worldwide recognition. In the exhibition the letter is placed against the backdrop of a fictional battle plan for the Documenta locations: the restricted access to venues of representation will not be achieved by peaceful negotiations, but must be fought for again and again. (JB)

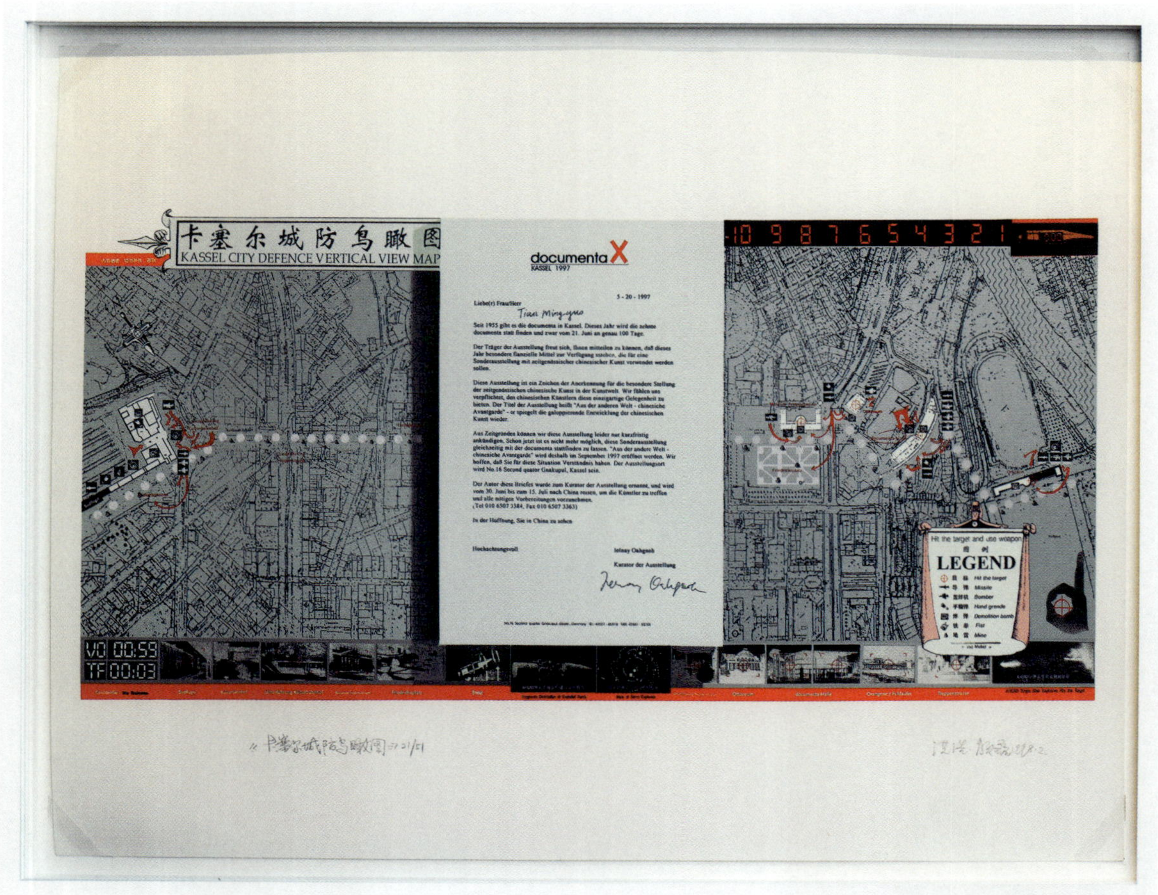

Liu Ding

* 1976 in Changzhou, Jiangsu (CN), lives and works in Beijing (CN)

Omission, 2009

Stone, book, marker, 34 × 34 × 30 cm

Liu Ding's work as an artist and curator investigates the various mechanisms and rules of the art system. *Omission* questions the framing of history. It consists of a marble rock bearing the inscription "Omission is the beginning of history writing," that carries a non existing book of art history (*A History of Chinese Contemporary Art: 19XX to 2050*).

The juxtaposition of the rock, alluding to the long history of the Scholar's Rock in China, and the bulky fake book about the short history of Chinese contemporary art, with its uncertain beginnings and apparently already planned future, shows us two different systems of history writing, which exist simultaneously and are both based on exclusions. (CL)

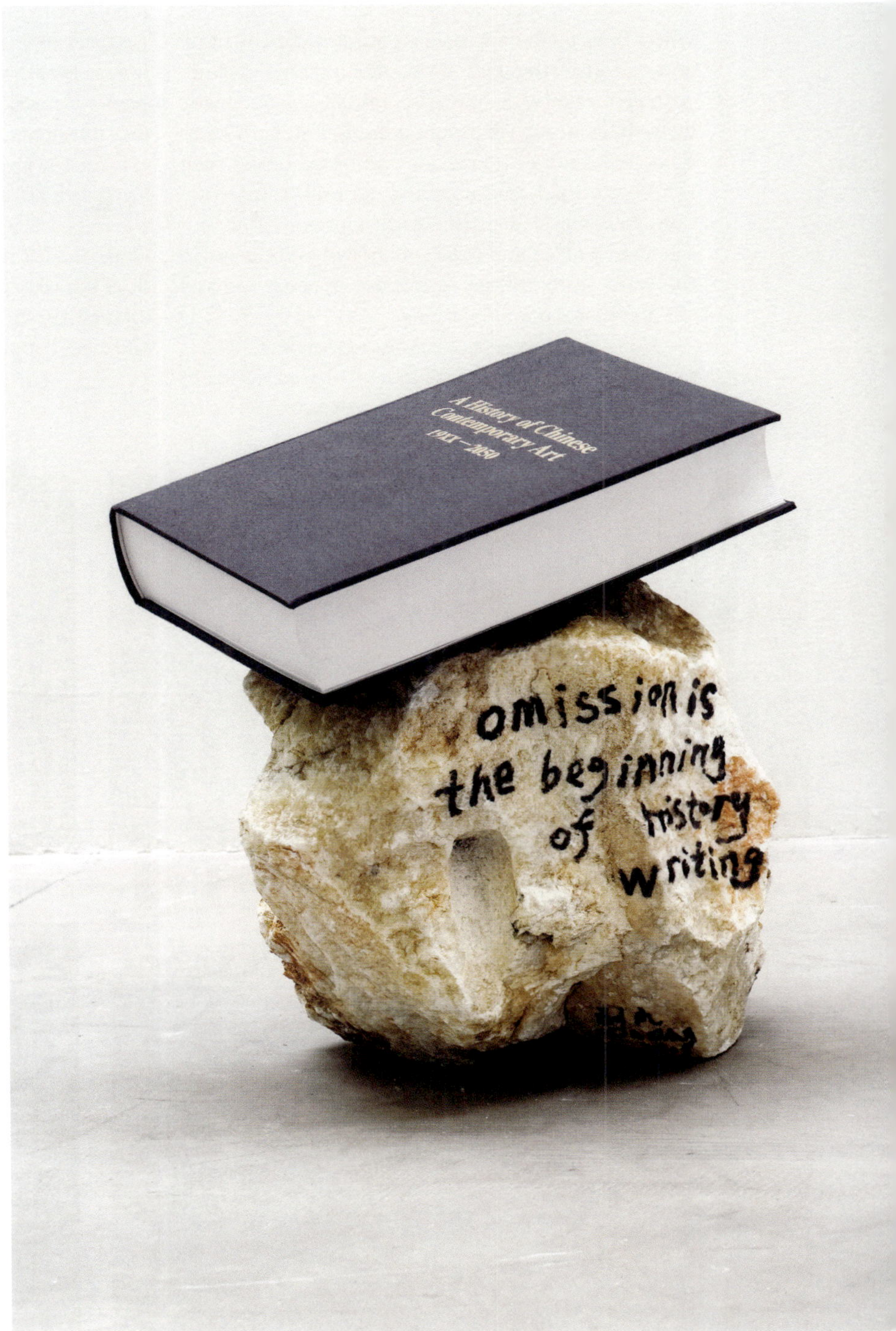

Miao Xiaochun

* 1964 in Wuxi, Jiangsu (CN), lives and works in Beijing (CN)

The Last Judgment in Cyberspace – Where Will I Go?, 2006

3-D computer animation, b/w, sound, 7:15 min

Miao Xiaochun is a photographer and new media artist whose intermedia approach combines documentary and narrative strategies in the photographic medium with performative, painterly, sculptural, and cinematic techniques in a 3-D virtual environment. Both technologies serve to explore interconnected topics such as China's rapid economic and cultural transformation, questions of identity and self-representation, and the history of art and media, all of which intersect in the overarching themes of cultural globalization and shifts of global power relations.

The Last Judgment in Cyberspace – Where Will I Go?, is a sequel to Miao Xiaochun's first 3-D-based work, *The Last Judgment in Cyberspace* (2006), constituting a virtual replica of Michelangelo's late Renaissance fresco *The Last Judgment* (1533-1541). Miao recreated Michelangelo's masterpiece by transposing the original painting's scenic elements into virtual space, and replacing its four hundred male and female figures with an ethnically distinct virtual clone modeled after himself, the layered views of which were subsequently captured in a series of black-and-white digital photographs. The video's added narrative amplifies the themes of artistic admiration and transgression while also imagining interactive strategies in the emergence of new cultural and visual interspaces. (IS)

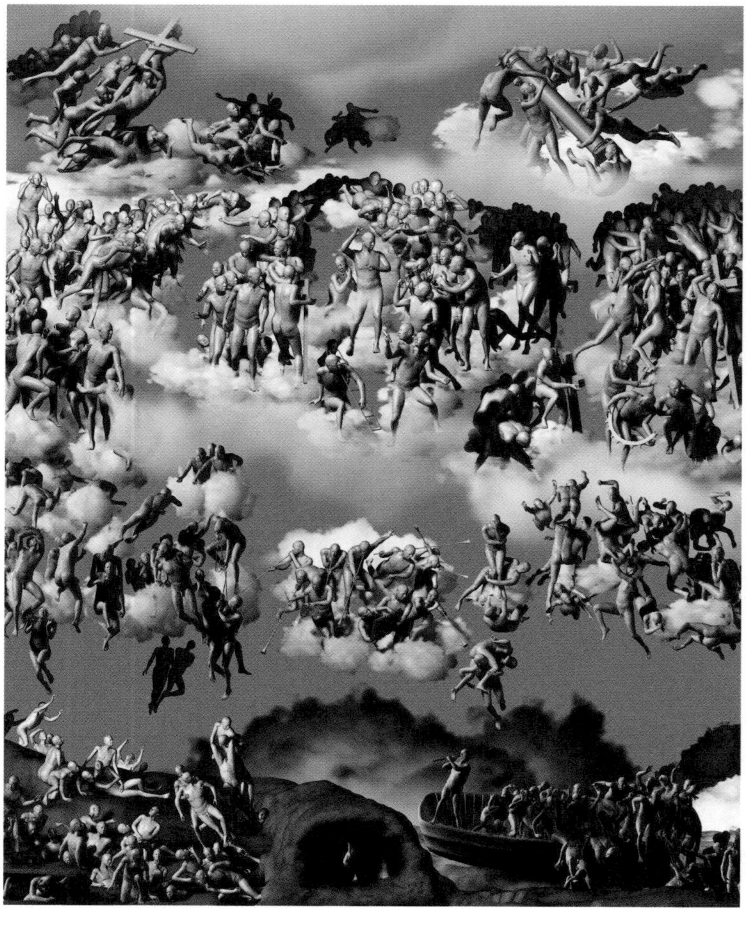

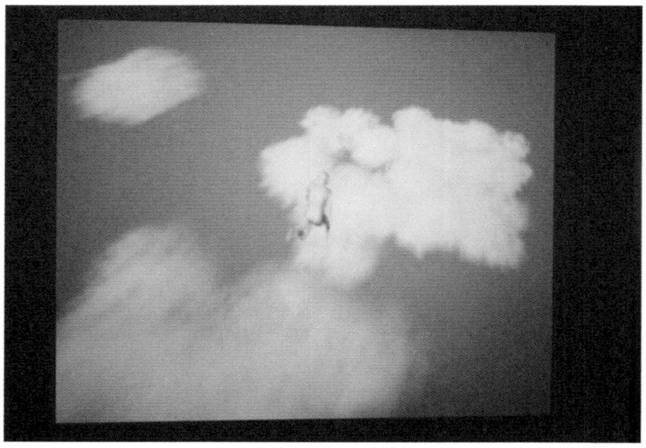

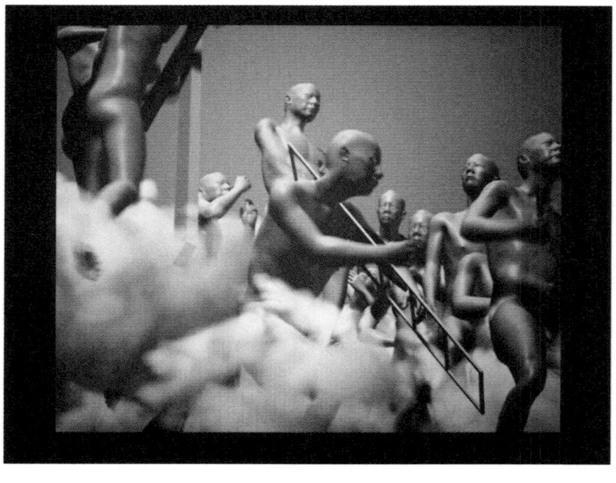

Jun Nguyen-Hatsushiba

* 1968 in Tokyo (JP), lives and works in Ho Chi Minh City (VN), Tokyo, and New York, NY (US)

The Ground, the Root, and the Air: The Passing of the Bodhi Tree, 2007

1-channel video installation, HD, 14:30 min

The work of Jun Nguyen-Hatsushiba mainly focuses on the sociocultural changes brought about by globalization. His video *The Ground, the Root, and the Air: The Passing of the Bodhi Tree* was realized in collaboration with fifty students of the Luang Prabang School of Fine Arts in Laos. In wooden motor boats and accompanied by Buddhist chants, the students slowly travel down the 4,000 kilometers-long Mekong, one of the longest rivers in Asia. They sit at easels and try to capture the beauty of the river landscape. As they approach a sacred Bodhi tree, some of the students suddenly jump into the water and swim towards it. Nguyen-Hatsushiba's video is an effective contrast of two different cultural practices. On the one hand, he presents the Western art practice of easel painting, which proceeds from a fixed observational point of view from which the artist views the world according to perspective. On the other hand, he shows the traditional Buddhist practice of worshipping the Bodhi tree, which in contrast to static observation represents a more active sensory experience. In this way Nguyen-Hatsushiba poetically illustrates that in today's Laos globalized and traditional ways of life exist simultaneously and equally alongside one another. (AB)

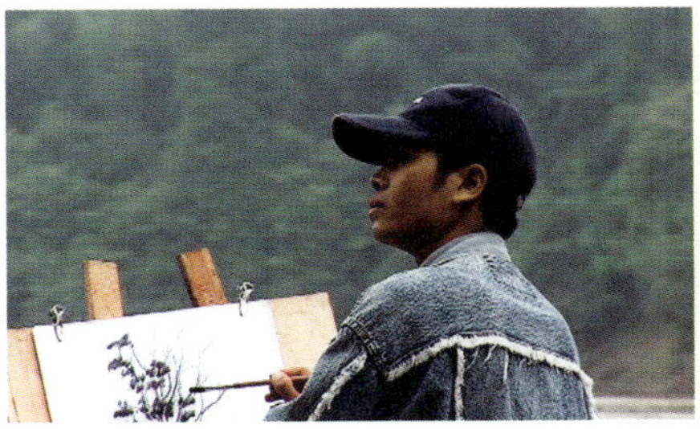
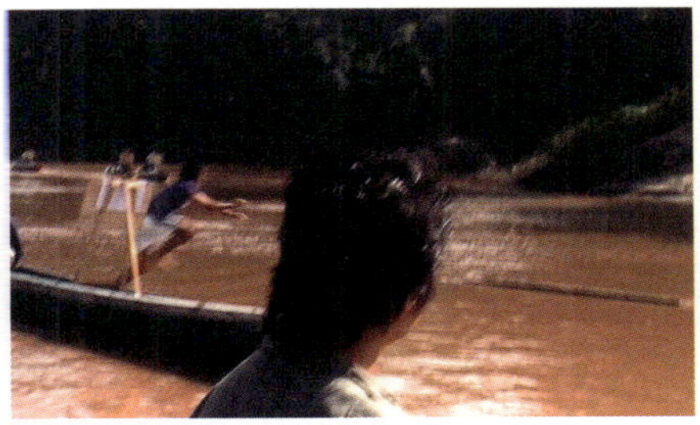
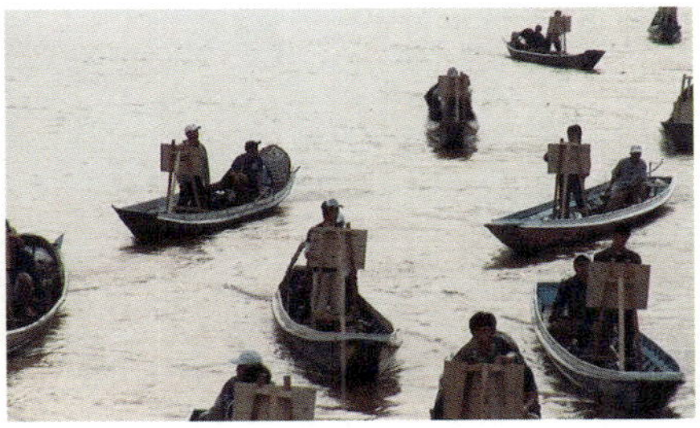
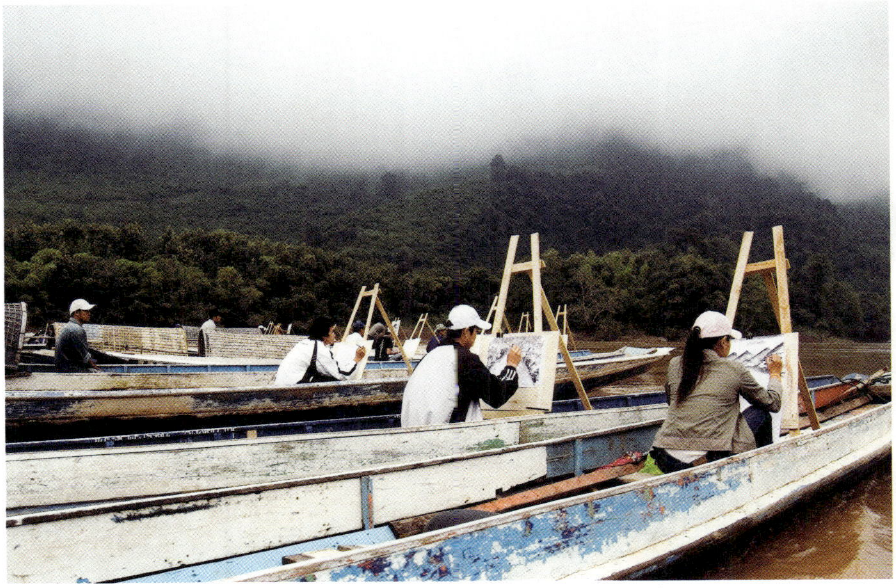
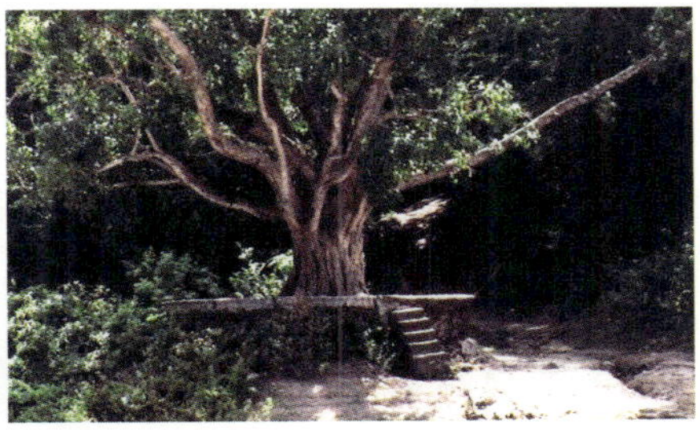
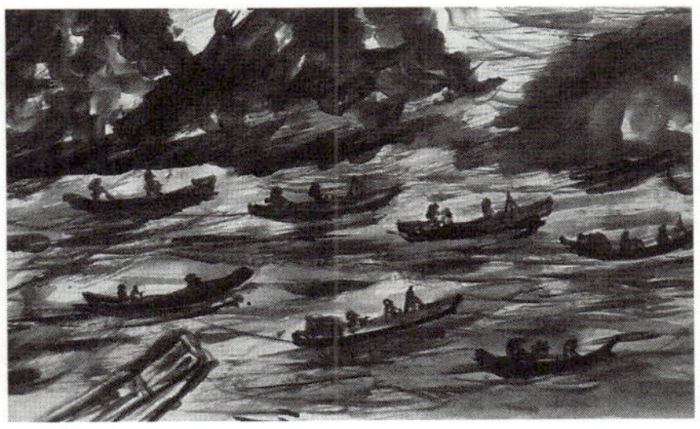

Tsuyoshi Ozawa

* 1965 in Tokyo (JP), lives and works in Tokyo

Museum of Soy Sauce Art, 1998–2000

Mixed-media installation, 2.50 × 9.25 × 1.85 m

The invention of the museum is intimately connected with the concept of tradition. The objects that a museum gathers together are supposed to represent an era or the cultural identity of a region – they result in a picture of history, which appears immovable, exclusive, and valuable. Therefore, one could say that the museum itself is a place where tradition is not only kept, but is also constructed – therefore invented – as a self-contained and consistent story.

In his work *Museum of Soy Sauce Art*, Tsuyoshi Ozawa plays with the museum as a factory of the fictitious. In several small rooms, sorted by epochs and genres, products of art and culture are presented, which follow the obscure tradition of soy sauce painting – from its archaic beginnings up to the present. As the director of this "museum," Tsuyoshi Ozawa sees it as his responsibility to preserve and communicate this often "forgotten" genre of art: both as an explicitly Japanese cultural artifact and as a part of Asian history and world culture in general. The *Museum of Soy Sauce Art* takes a humorous look at the often naïve and sometimes grim determination of museums to assign cultural products a rightful place in the art historical canon. Ozawa's work confronts us with the question as to the ways in which we recognize paintings and other things as historical objects – and why we let museums tell us stories and history. (JB)

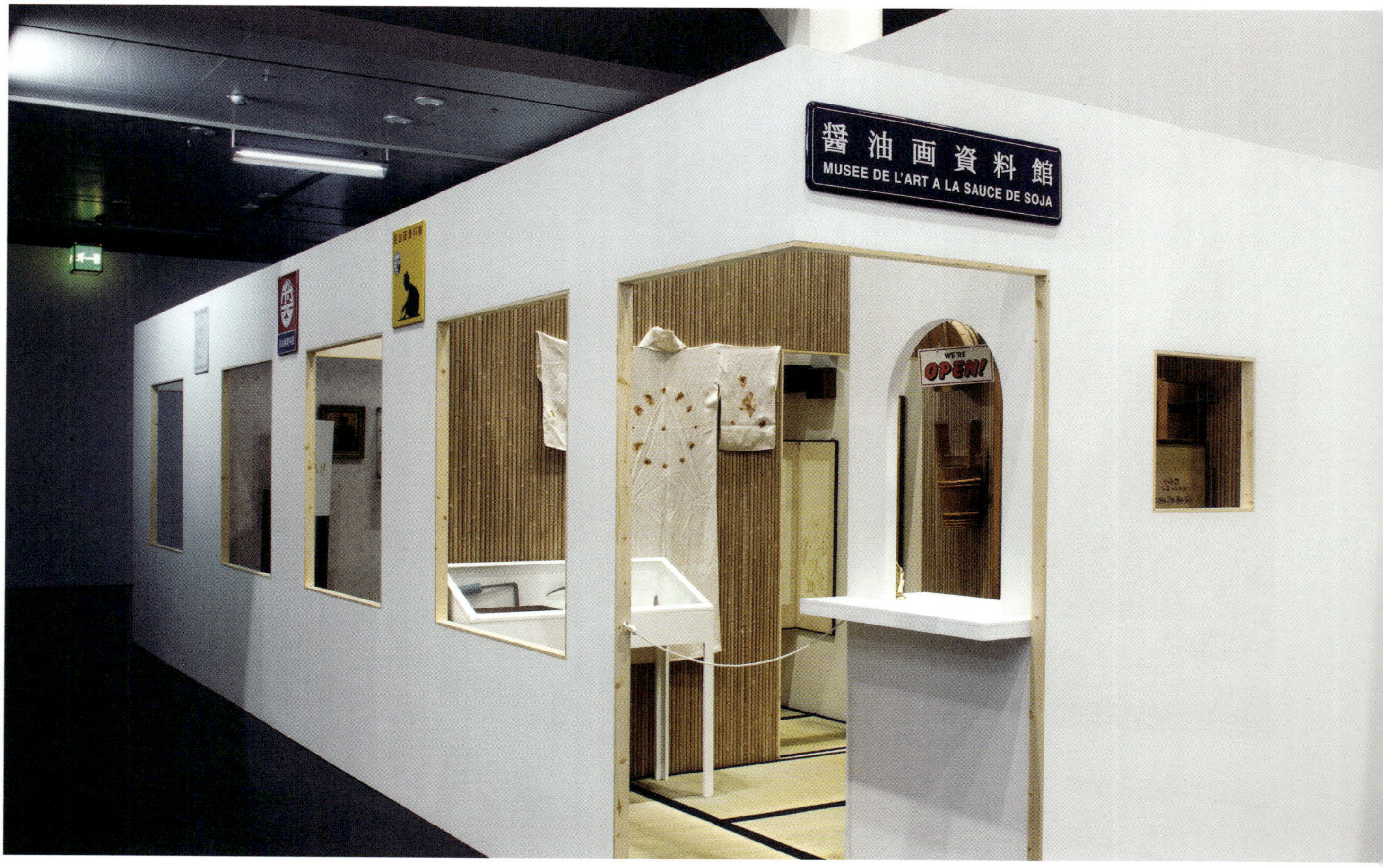

Leila Pazooki

* 1977 in Tehran (IR), lives and works in Berlin (DE)

Moments of Glory, 2010

Neon tubes, transformers, 15 parts, length between 65 and 200 cm

Is Leila Pazooki the Iranian Tracey Emin, Jenny Holzer, or a Bruce Nauman? She has created an installation of words and light that immediately conjures up associations with works by these artists, at least if one is a regular visitor to museums of contemporary art in Europe, the USA, or Canada. And who is the Indian Damien Hirst or the Asian counterpart to Cindy Sherman? The ironic work by Pazooki demonstratively does not answer such questions. Her installation is a bold reaction to such all too easily drawn parallels found in the press. The deliberate proliferation of comparisons of artists from Asia, Africa, or the Middle East with heavyweights of Western art historiography, such as Louise Bourgeois, Auguste Renoir, Andy Warhol, Salvador Dalí, Pablo Picasso, Francisco de Goya, and others, demonstrates that such analogies say more about those who make them than about the artists to whom they supposedly refer.

The function of such categorizations is that they allow people to integrate artists in their own system of norms and values and, by so doing, they assert their cultural superiority over entire continents while at the same time protecting themselves against what is "alien." After all, it is a lot easier to measure art against the standards that have been established in Western art historiography than to consider such works against the backdrop of the specific cultural context in which they were created, an approach that might lead to an entirely different view. What if, as Ashley Rawlings has facetiously suggested (*ArtAsiaPacific*), a reverse comparison were drawn and Marcel Duchamp was declared the Ai Weiwei of France? (KB)

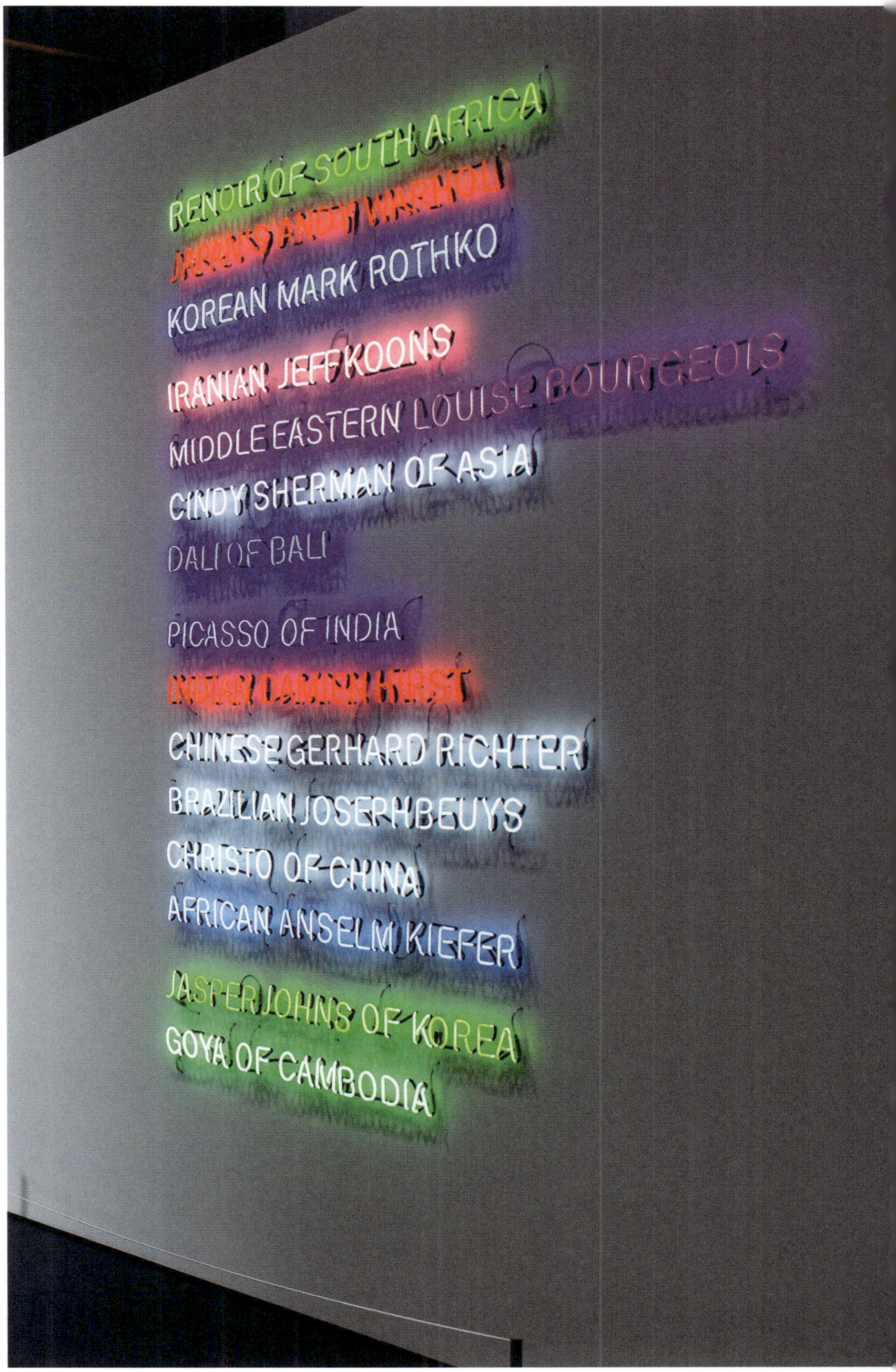

Nusra Latif Qureshi

* 1973 in Lahore (PK), lives and works in Melbourne (AU)

Did you come here to find history?, 2009

20 digital prints on transparent film,
70 × 870 cm

In her work, Nusra Latif Qureshi uses mainly traditional (painting) techniques, develops them, and puts them into new contexts as to articulate contemporary issues. After studying at the National College of Arts Lahore in Pakistan, where she had learned the traditional art of Mughal miniature painting, she emigrated to Melbourne in 2001.

In *Did you come here to find history?* the Pakistani artist poses the question about the constitution of cultural history and identity. Ostensibly, traditional Mughal miniature portraits, early colonial photographs, and portraits created by Venetian painters are here merely strung together horizontally. The first impression created by this "ancestral gallery" is fractured by the photographic self-portrait of the artist that shines through it. Her passport photograph, the epitome of official regulation of identity, mixes with the depictions of illustrious Persian kings and nobles, commoners, and the nameless. In this way, Qureshi pictorially suspends the linear structure and forming of history, and, in Walter Benjamin's sense, lets a (momentary) anachronism, the intertwining and interpenetration of present and past, become visible. Ultimately, Qureshi leaves the question about historical identity unanswered and instead, invites the viewer to engage with it. (EA)

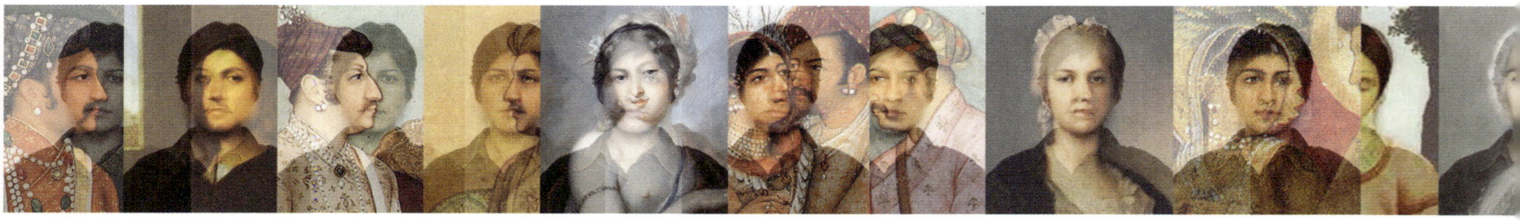

DID YOU COME HERE TO FIND HISTORY?
Digital print on clear film
70 x 900cm
2009

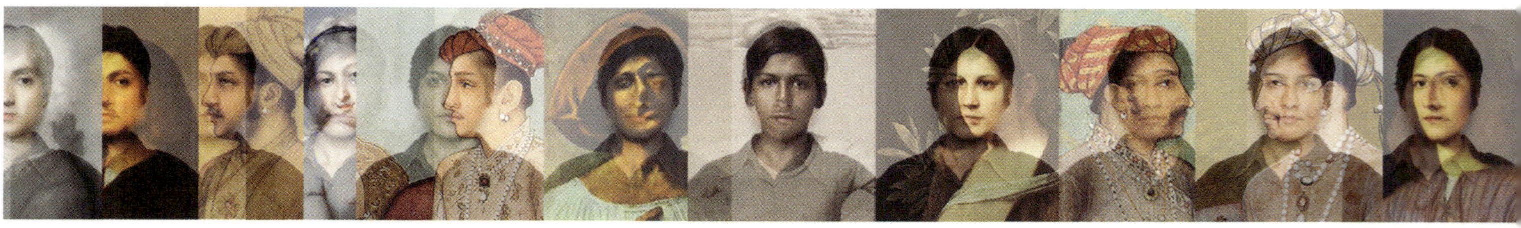

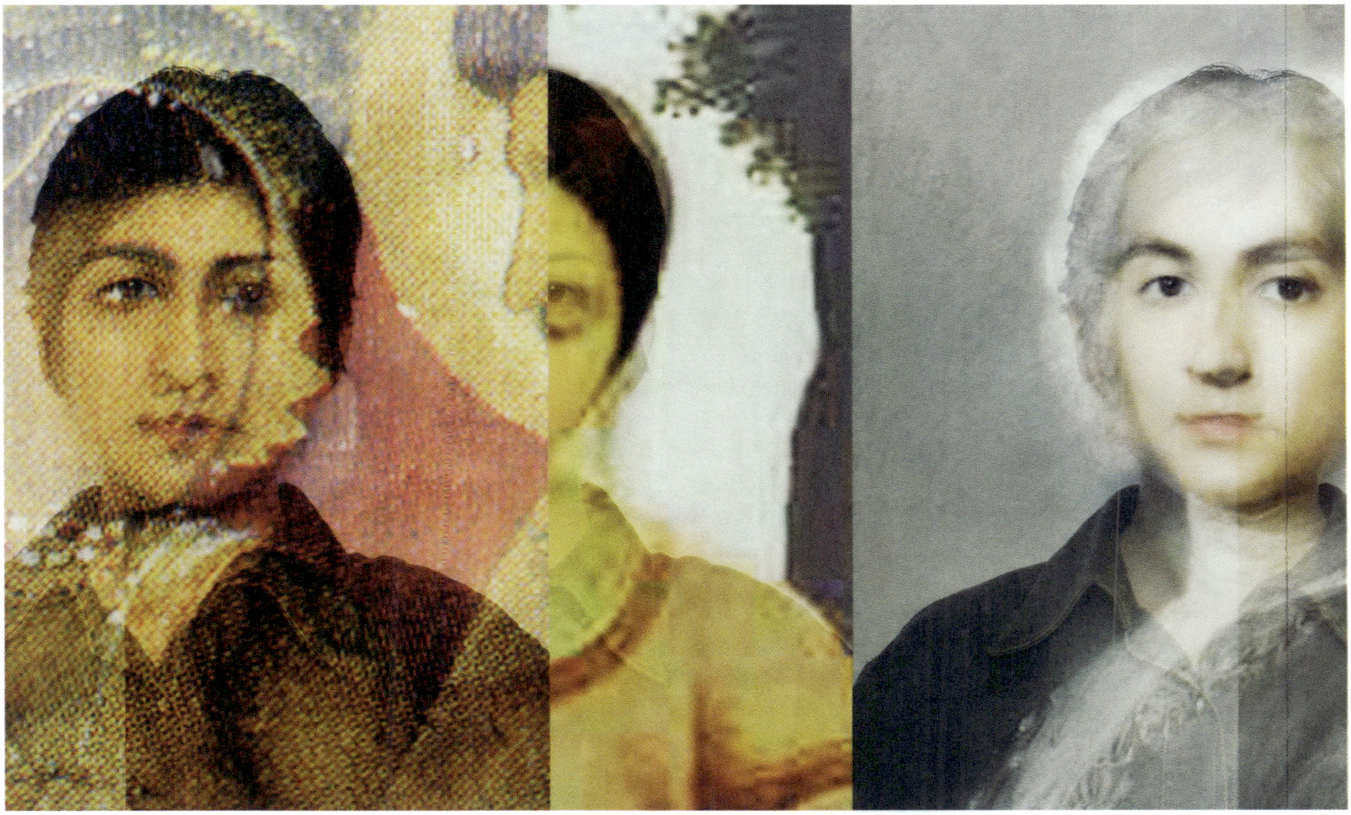

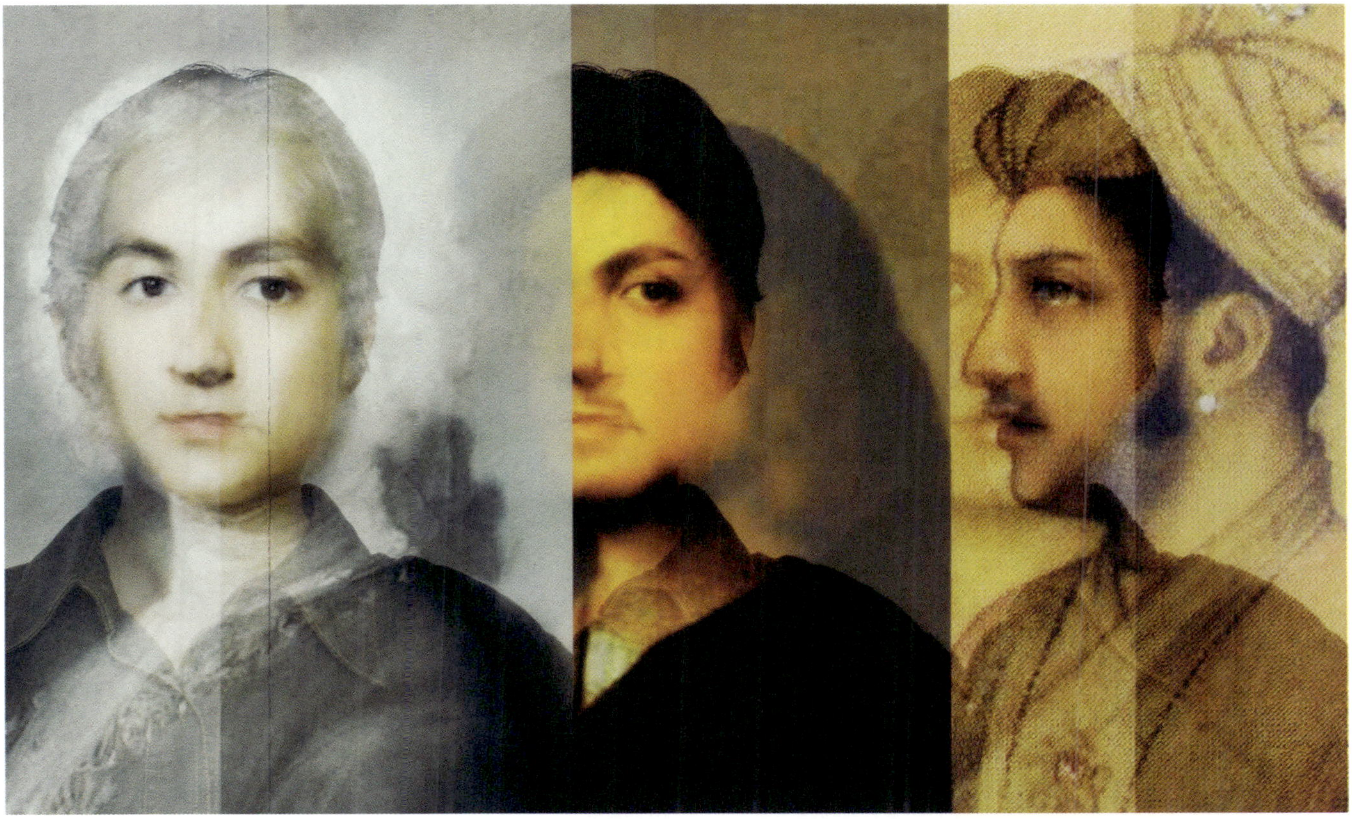

Araya Rasdjarmrearnsook

* 1957 in Trad (TH), lives and works in Chiang Mai (TH)

Dow Song Duang (The Two Planets Series), 2008

Video, color, sound, 18:30 min

In four short sequences, Araya Rasdjarmrearnsook's film *Dow Song Duang (The Two Planets Series)* depicts a group of villagers set against the backdrop of various rural locations in Thailand. Canonical European masterpieces of the nineteenth-century landscape genre by Jean-Francois Millet, Édouard Manet, and Vincent van Gogh have been placed before them for critical assessment. They huddle together and, based on their own experience and points of reference, humorously ponder the relationships between the persons represented, consider the nature of the depicted activities, and contemplate the vast, beautiful landscapes that surround the subjects. Rasdjarmrearnsook, in turn, frames the villagers in the breathtaking scenery of rural Thailand.

In the film, the artist juxtaposes the European academic approach to art analysis to analysis by the unschooled eye, showing how the meaning of an artwork depends upon its sociocultural context. Rasdjarmrearnsook, who has herself moved from the countryside to the city, wants to show the collision of two worlds within Thailand: the academic world of urban cosmopolitism and the simple rural life of farmers. The work reflects on the translation of visual culture, the influence of European artifacts and discourses, and what happens to forms, theories, and contents when they are considered outside the Euro-American academic tradition. (AMB)

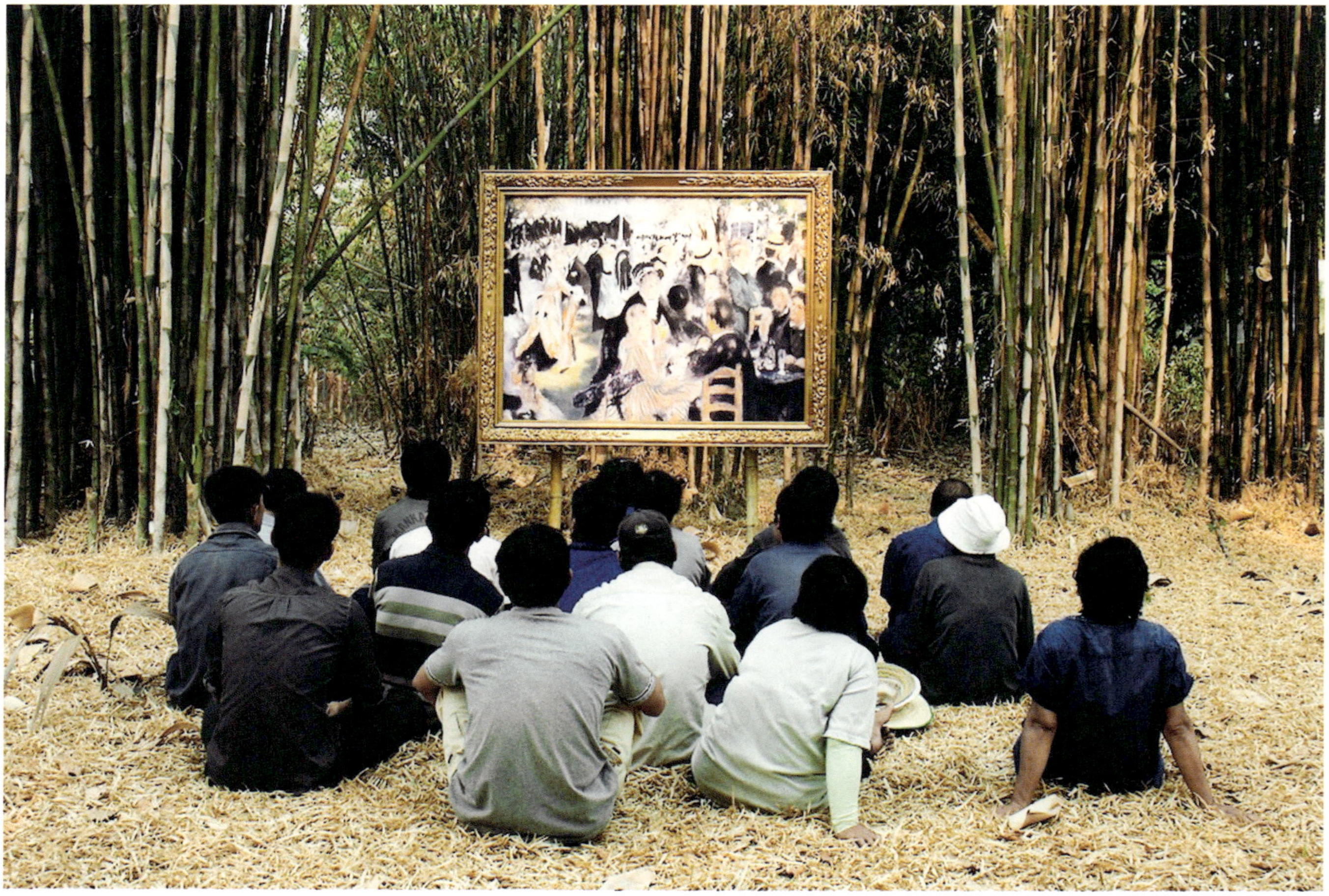

Sean Snyder

* 1972 in Virginia Beach, VA (US), lives and works in Kiev (UA) and Tokyo (JP)

Exhibition, 2008

Film transferred to DVD, 7 min

Sean Snyder's video works and installations are instruments of analysis, used to investigate globally circulating images as tools of political propaganda, as well as to produce and preserve knowledge contexts. Based on a Soviet "documentary" of 1965, which was screened under the title *Noble Impulses of Soul* (director: Israel Goldstein), *Exhibition* explores the role of ideology in exhibitions as educational institutions. He reedited the original video about the organization of an exhibition of contemporary Mexican art in a Ukrainian museum, including the communication methods employed: guided tours, opening speeches, art history seminars. He rearranged the chronology, and the voice-over is now only partially heard, complemented by intertitles that repeat part of what is said.

The result of this rearrangement is a film, that lays bare the ideological structure of the original film, thus demonstrating the impossibility of delivering on its promise of documentary objectivity. At the same time *Exhibition* is a work that through systematic pauses in the telling of its story makes it clear that any and every museum order is an expression of an ideological substrate; it may mask itself as universally valid, but inevitably remains the expression of a history of art with only limited validity. (KB)

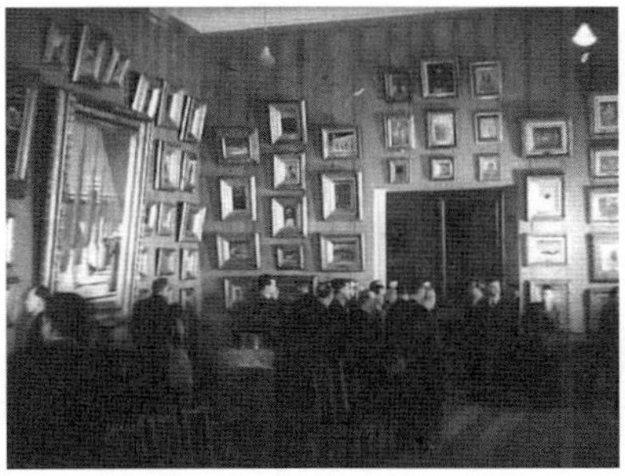
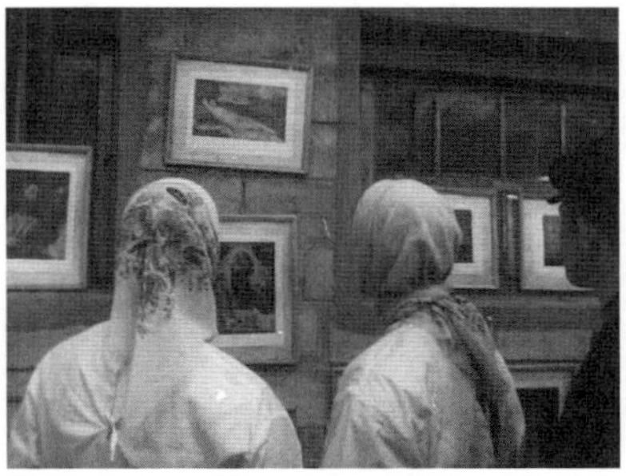
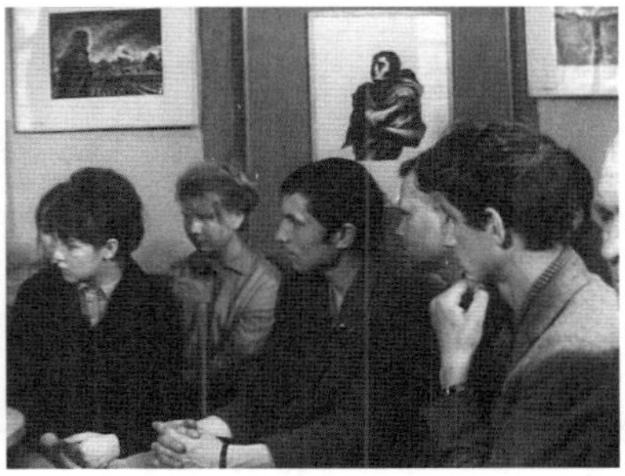
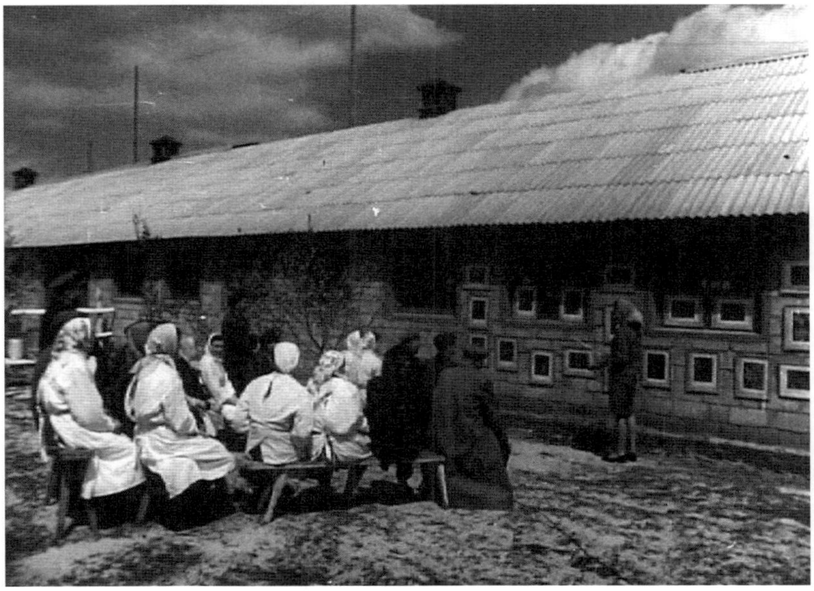
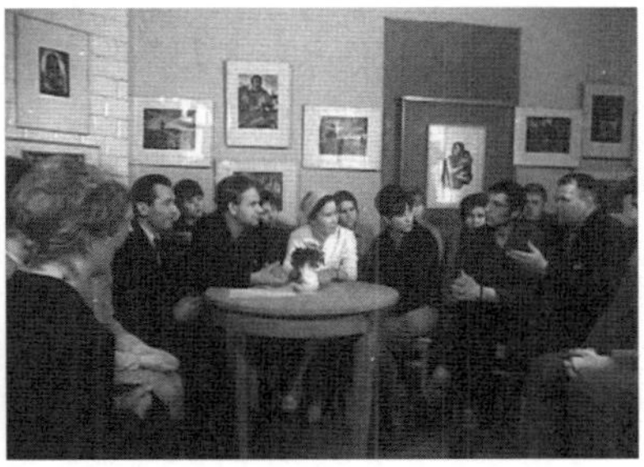
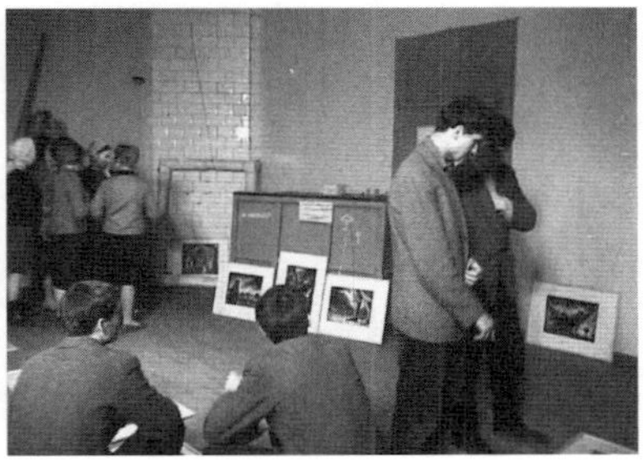

Yto Barrada
Ursula Biemann / Chto delat?
Com&Com / Ghana ThinkTank
Anawana Haloba / Ashley Hunt
IRWIN and NSKState.com
Le Laboratoire de Déberlinisation
Pinky Show / Tadej Pogačar / RYBN.ORG
Michael Stevenson / Jens M. Stober
The Xijing Men

Networks and Systems: Globalization as Subject

In this section, networks of collaborating artists of different nationalities engage with systems that have established new power structures in the globalized world.

The French art collective RYBN, together with the ZKM | Institute for Visual Media, has developed a trading bot, which actually invests and speculates on the stock market, to expose the arbitrariness of the financial market; a placeless and nameless entity that regulates our daily life. The program's activities were shown in a "trading bot performance" on a panorama screen for the duration of the exhibition. The "dark side of globalization" is also confronted by the group Pinky Show in their comics and videos which are populated by hand-drawn cats. The dialogs between the cute cats, whose look is a nod to the digital Pop culture of memes, sharply critique the global play of forces. Utilizing a similar defamiliarization effect, in *The Greater G8 Advertising Market Stand* the artist Anawana Haloba invites viewers to participate in an installation which parodies the fashion for fairly traded commodities in the G8 countries.

The interaction between the viewer and the artwork is a feature of other artworks that share the same ironic and denunciatory attitude and, furthermore, assign a critical value to interaction. Tadej Pogačar's cynical game *MonApoly, A Human Trade Game* turns the viewer into a player in an abstract planning game on the subject of human trafficking. By establishing think tank groups in so-called developing countries to solve the problems of the developed world, the artists' group Ghana ThinkTank exposes the absurdity of the solutions demanded as part of Western aid to developing countries.

The fluxes and trading that go on beneath the surface of an apparently homogeneous global world are targeted by many works in this section. Ashley Hunt's *A World Map: In Which We See...* clearly demonstrates the need for collective investigation of these mechanisms. Through a series of workshops held in various cities, the artist is compiling a world map that, instead of showing continents and states, displays the otherwise invisible interconnections, the "machinery of globalization" (Ashley Hunt) through diagrams and conceptual graphics.

A parallel issue to the emergence of an opaque multinational system is the question of national borders and their role within the unequal distribution of power and privileges. With her photographic series *Bus*, Yto Barrada addresses the issue of emigration from Morocco towards the coast of Spain, and thus points the finger at the postcolonial relationship existing between Africa and Europe, while in *Tectonic*, a world map where continents can move towards one another, she visualizes a utopia of the world becoming truly global. Ursula Biemann's hybrid filmic montage of fiction and fact addresses the uncertain status of Palestinian refugees, who are without political representation in a system of nation-states.

The paradoxical and sometimes phantasmagoric role of the nation is mirrored by a group of works that introduce imaginary states. The three artists of The Xijing Men collective proclaim a fictional artists' state with Olympic flags in their work *Xijing Olympics*. By contrast, artists' collectives IRWIN and NSK (New Slovenian Art) founded a spiritual und virtual state – the NSK State. Though NSK State issues passports and proudly presents its regalia of national power and identity in the installation *NSK Folk Art*, the objective is not to provide a new homeland for artists of former Soviet states, but to criticize the very notion of national identity.

Linked to African postcolonial discourse is *Le Laboratoire de Debérlinisation*, an artistic and political project that investigates the possibility of a "Panafrican State" by issuing a currency, the "Afro," the Global Pass, and AFRO Express Card.

In such projects, the artists use similar subversive methods to analyze the system, frequently using the metaphor of a nonlinear, noncanonical narrative as the medium. The urgency of penetrating the facade of the global contemporary in fact requires a new way of writing history that must abandon the logic of a single teleological path, which is built on the discriminatory concept of a dualist world, and instead embraces a plurality of possibilities.

Jens M. Stober's computer game *1378 (km),* in itself a medium for alternative storytelling, challenges two players to deal with the history of the Cold War and the Berlin Wall in particular, a symbol of the binary order that globalization has discarded forever. The refugee and the border guard can decide in each situation which history will unfold.

Art productions such as these are global to the extent that this is their theme. Across the borders of today's systems, artists feel challenged as contemporaries to react critically to the growing problems of globalization. (SG)

Yto Barrada

* 1971 in Paris (FR), lives and works in Tangier (MA)

Tectonic, 2004/2010

Wooden model with movable continents,
122 × 200 cm

Bus, Tanger, 2004

4 C-prints, framed, 88 × 88 cm each

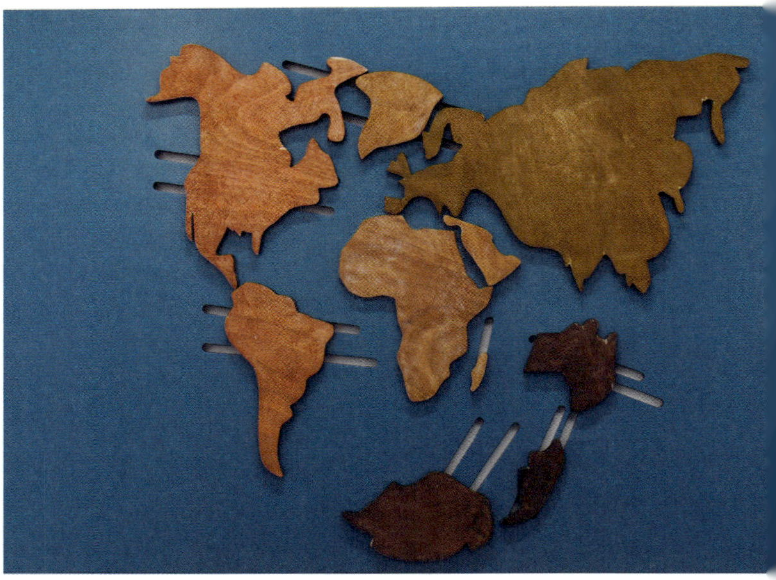

Yto Barrada addresses contemporary life in her Moroccan home city Tangier, which is heavily influenced by its geographical location almost directly on the border to Europe. Every day in Tangier, people from various African countries try to cross the merely fourteen-kilometers-wide Strait of Gibraltar to reach the Spanish mainland. Not only adults, but also very many children and teenagers embark on this dangerous journey, hoping their age will save them from being extradited.

As unwanted guests, they often hide under the chassis of tourist buses and in this way try to cross the Strait undetected. With detail shots of the logos of bus companies, the photographic series *Bus* makes reference to this emigration of children and teenagers from Morocco and other African countries, who are able to read the logos on the buses as direction signs for their destinations. In parallel, through their selection of image excerpts, the photographs forge a bridge to classic modern art with its purportedly universal language of abstraction, throwing up questions about the enmeshment of art, (neo)colonialism, and current geopolitical conflicts.

Tectonic also illustrates the desire to produce images different from the widespread depictions of migration in the mass media. For her world map made of wood in which the continents can move towards each other, Barrada takes as her motif the geological phenomenon of continental drift. Continents moving closer together can be read as visualizing a blueprint for a future in which borders slowly dissolve and free, borderless and non-life-threatening migration becomes possible. (HP)

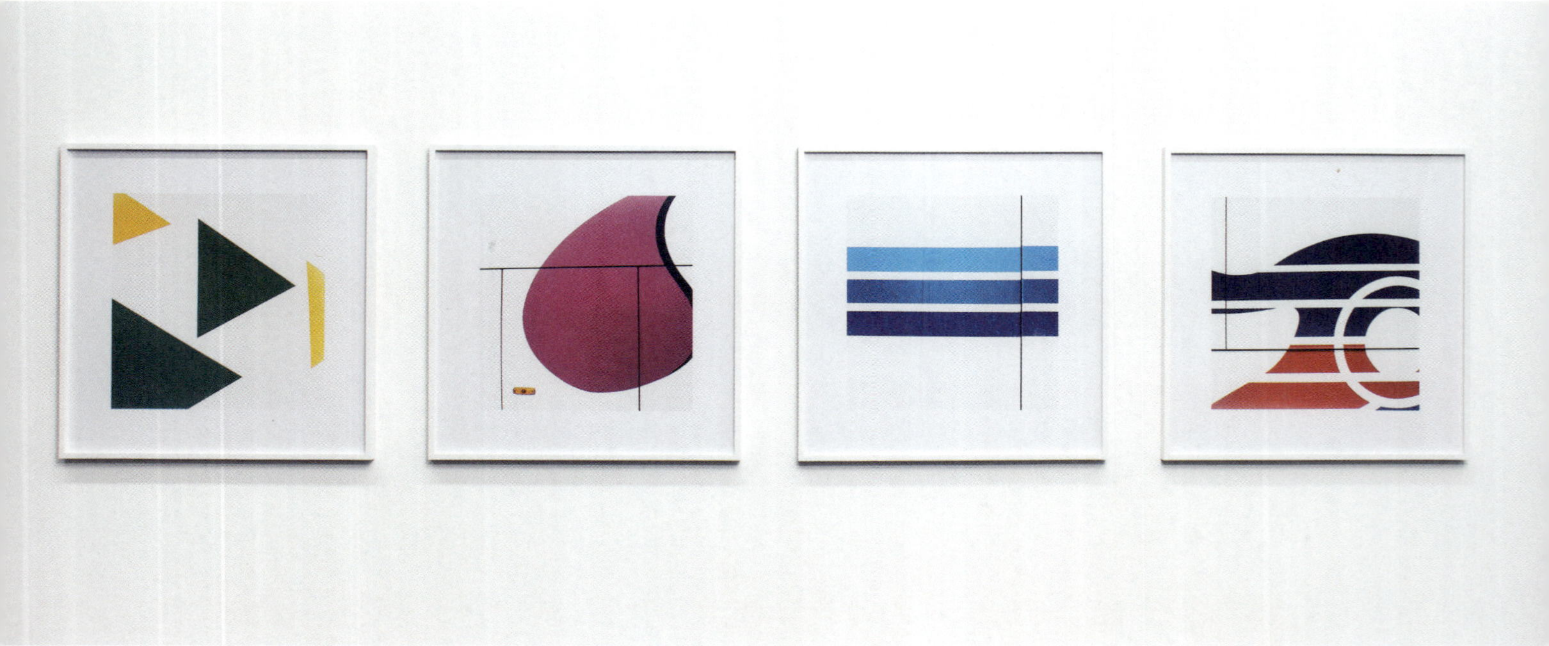

Ursula Biemann

* 1955 in Zurich (CH), lives and works in Zurich

X-Mission, 2008

Video, color, sound, 40 min

The Swiss artist Ursula Biemann occupies a position within the canon of contemporary artists whose approach lies in an intermediate region comprising documentation, theory, political practice, and aesthetic reflection. In her video works she attempts to find a method for artistic knowledge to explore cultural contexts. She repeatedly engages with issues that are closely bound up with current debates that are critical about globalization.

In her video essay *X-Mission* Biemann describes the possibilities of a cultural and political representation of Palestinian refugees and thereby ventures upon highly controversial political terrain. In five chapters and a prolog, she develops a picture of the diverse discourses in which the status of Palestinian refugees is negotiated: the refugee as a legal person, as a symbolic figure in a state of crisis, as a myth, and as a refugee in postnational space. Biemann chooses to work at the borderline between fact and fiction: she links short interview sequences with images shot on the spot, found footage, war games, and excerpts from news broadcasts, and shows them in different combinations. The result is that seeming certainties become questionable, and new possibilities for rethinking the figure of the refugee are revealed. (KB)

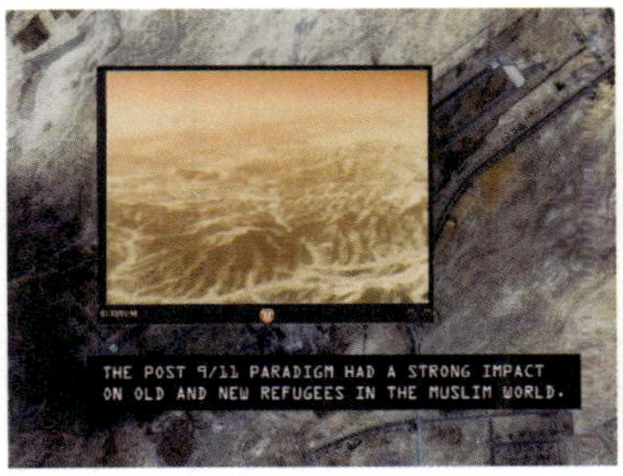

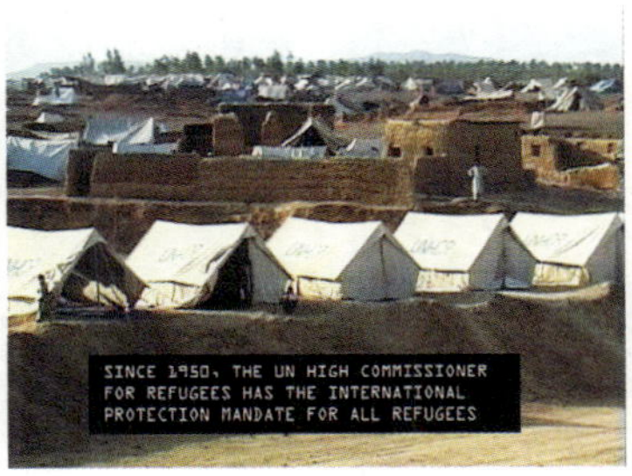

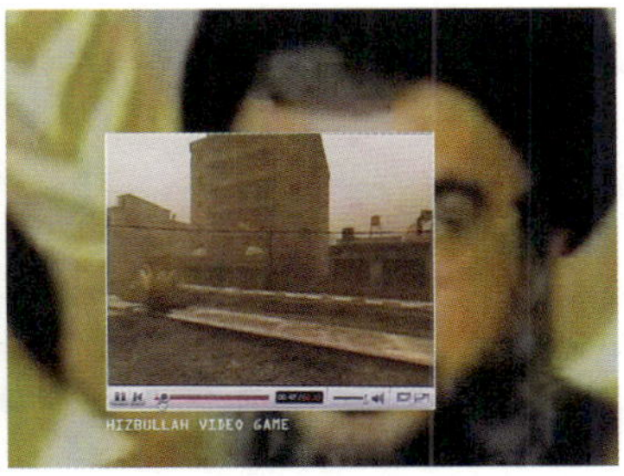

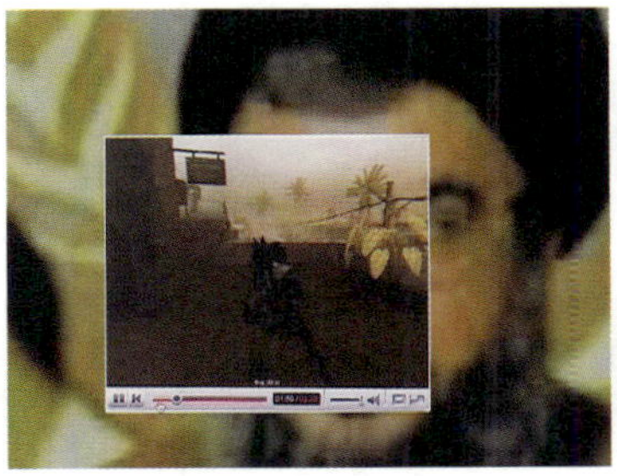

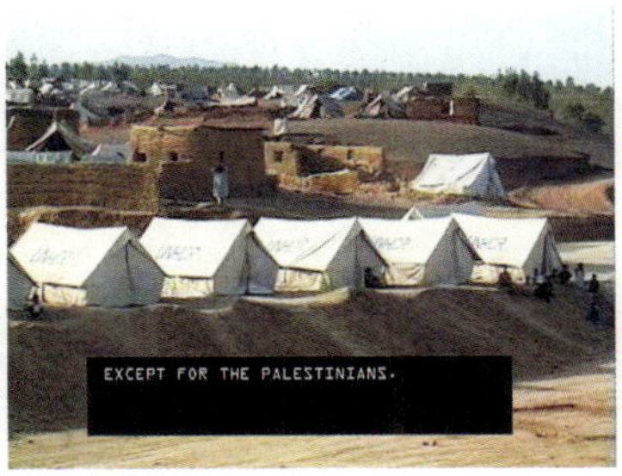

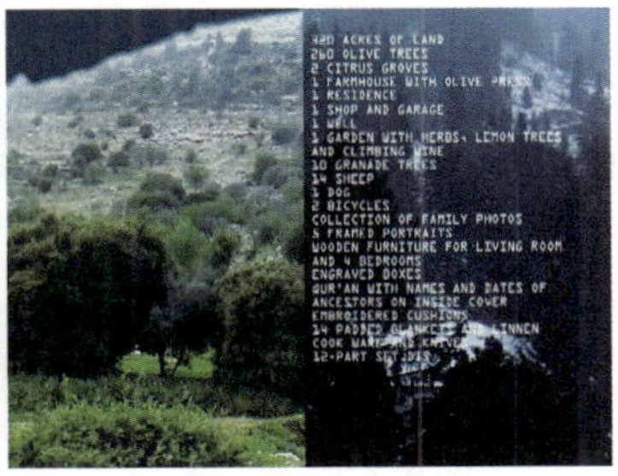

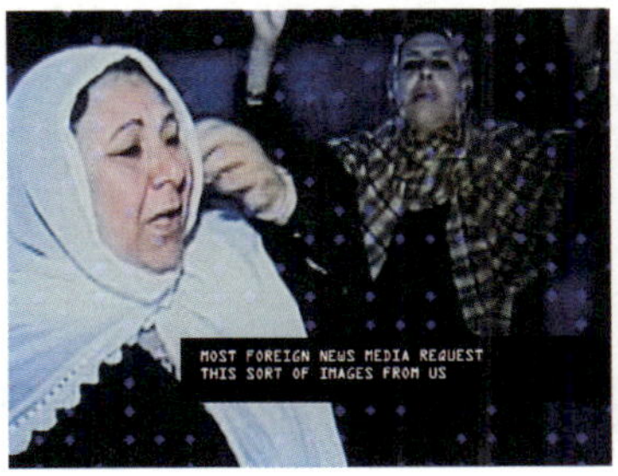

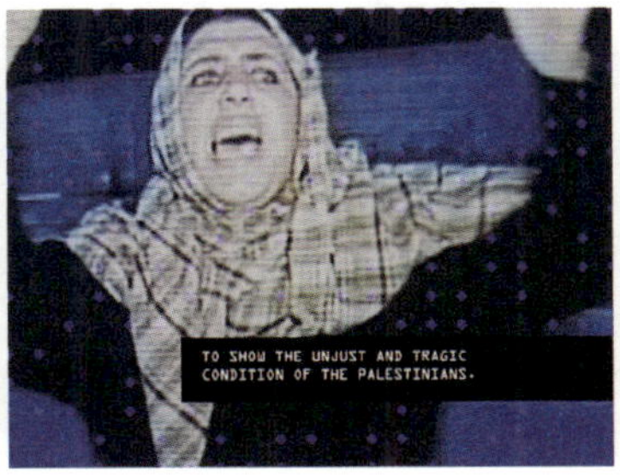

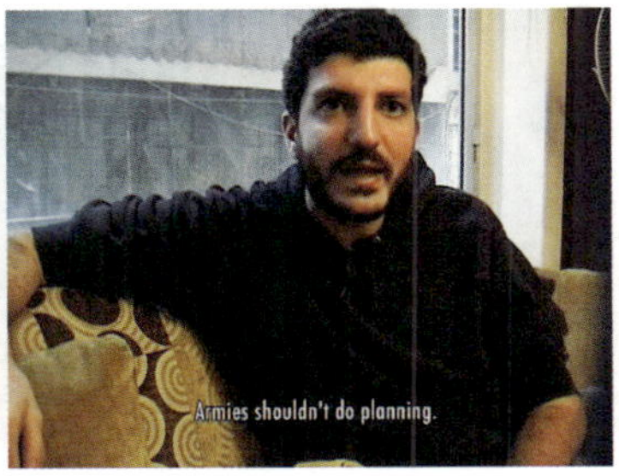

Chto delat?

Founded 2003 in Saint Petersburg (RU). The platform unites artists, activists, philosophers, critics, and writers from different regions of Russia.

The Tower: A Songspiel, 2010

HD video, color, sound, 36 min

Chto delat? [What is to be done?] sees itself as a platform that seeks the synthesis of political theory, art, and activism. The group's name refers to the novel of the same title by Nikolai Chernyshevsky (1863), which became a source of inspiration for revolutionary groups and leftist intelligentsia in Russia. Like Chernyshevsky, Chto delat? rejects "art for art's sake" and the commodification of art, and sees the goal of art in the transformation of reality itself.

The Tower: A Songspiel is the final part of a trilogy of socially committed musicals. It is a reflection on a real conflict over the construction of the Okhta Center in Saint Petersburg, a 403 meters high skyscraper, where Gazprom planned to house its headquarters. The new structure would have changed the appearance of the city forever, introducing a new dominant point in the skyline - a symbol of a new modernized Russia.

The film is staged as a confrontation of different social and age groups with the "power lobby" over the issue of constructing a corporate tower. The power of the lobby group as well as the autonomy of the community turn out to be fictitious, since in the end the lobby is dismissed and the chorus strangled by the tentacles of the authorities.

The action develops through direct appeals by the representatives of power to the community-chorus and the viewer. The enactment follows the principles of Brechtian epic theater and aims at provoking rational self-reflection and developing a critical perspective in the viewer so that he or she comes to recognize social injustice and manipulation. (DM)

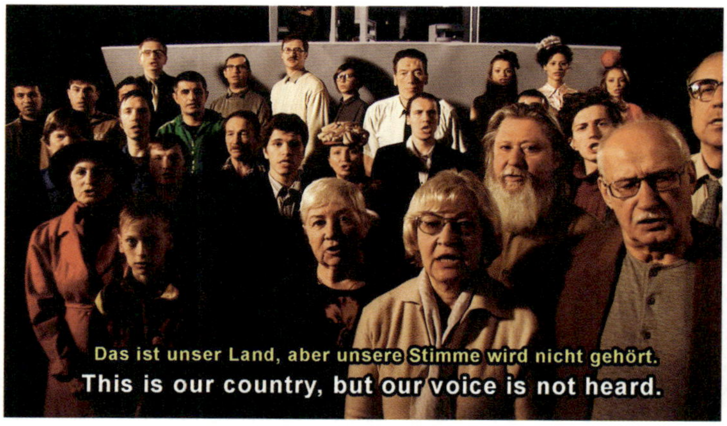

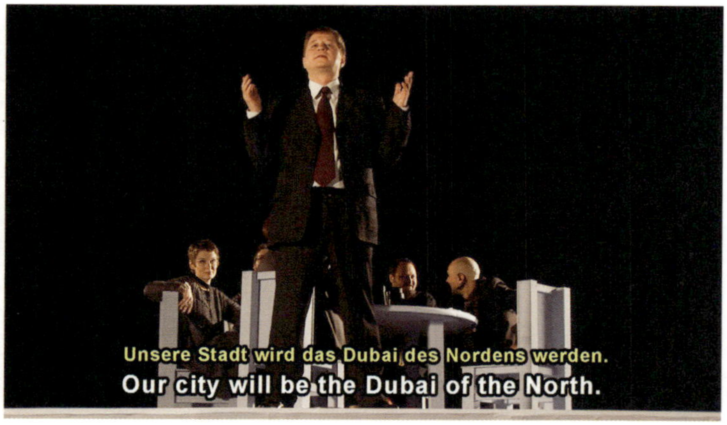

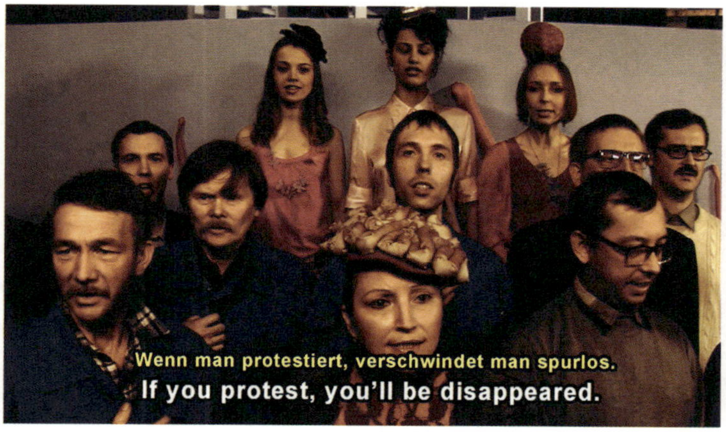

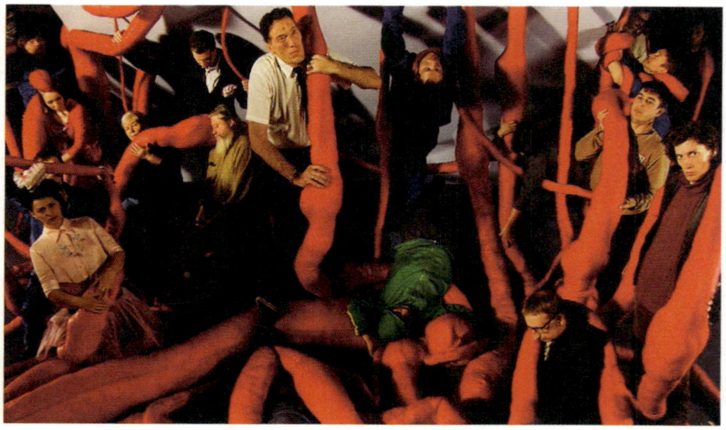

Com&Com

Founded in 1997 by Marcus Gossolt, * 1969 in St Gallen (CH); Johannes M. Hedinger, * 1971 in St Gallen; live and work in St. Gallen and Zurich (CH)

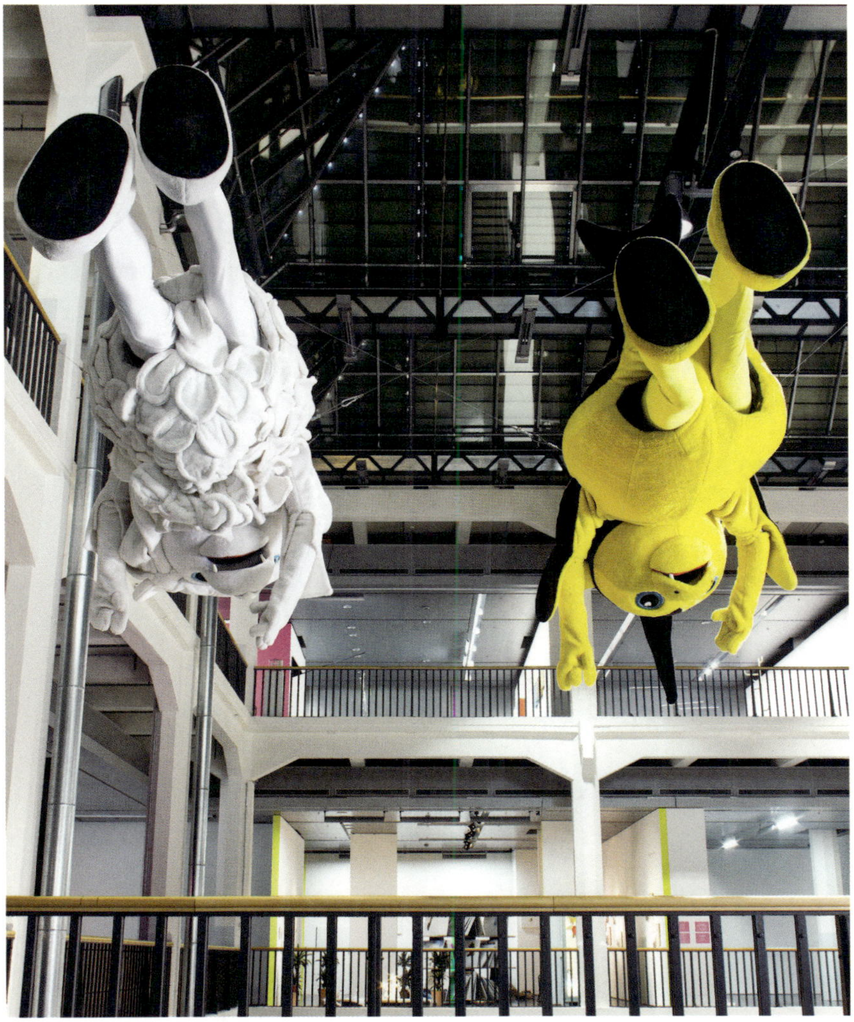

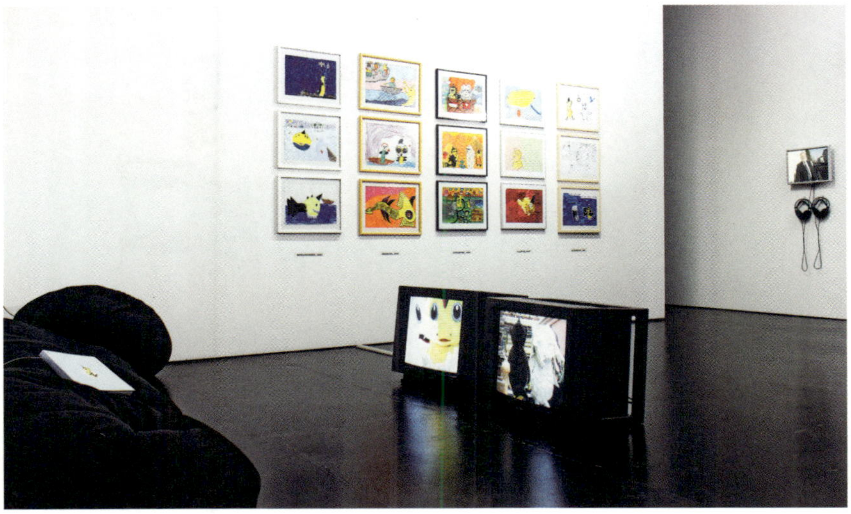

Mocmoc & Mermer

2006–2011,

Mixed-media installation,
(2 mascots, 15 drawings,
30 × 35 cm each (framed), 3 videos,
1 publication),
dimensions variable

In a globalized world, which emphasizes mobility and networking, there is no room for rigid and distinct identities; the question of membership has become a game of forms and relations that are constantly being overwritten and redefined. Conversely, in populist forums, mourning the loss of regional or national identities alternates with the fear of "foreigners" forming a cultural unit. Here questions of belonging sometimes become deadly serious.

The artist duo Com&Com have made both the seriousness and the playfulness of identity formation the core of the project *Mocmoc & Mermer*. For a competition held by the town Romanshorn on Lake Constance, they developed the fictional character Mocmoc, who along with a fake "local" legend was implanted in the cultural memory of the place and represented by a stately statue. The pop aesthetics of the sculpture stirred up controversy; while a citizen's initiative was founded for the "disposal" of the statue, younger people in particular supported the in the meantime cherished monument. In *Mocmoc & Mermer* Com&Com found a suitable companion for Mocmoc in Merlion, a figure developed by the Singapore Tourist Authority in the 1960s. In their naïve artificiality, the figures illustrate that identity today can be understood only with an awareness of its fictional nature - and may well arise out of shared laughter (at oneself). (JB)

Ghana ThinkTank

John Ewing, * 1964 in Ithaca, New York, NY (US), lives and works in Boston, MA (US);
Maria del Carmen Montoya, * 1974 in Houston, TX (US), lives and works in Providence, RI (US);
Christopher Robbins, *1973 in Atlanta, GA (US), lives and works in New York, NY

Ghana ThinkTank in Karlsruhe, 2011

Mixed-media installation, dimensions variable
Produced in cooperation with ZKM | Karlsruhe

Ghana ThinkTank was originally formed in 2006 by the artists Christopher Robbins, John Ewing, and Matey Odonkor in response to their experiences gained through working in developmental aid organizations across the globe. In contrast to the usual mission of NGOs, the aim of their collective is to create problem-solving strategies for the so-called developed world. Since then, experts from their network have formed think tanks in countries such as Ghana, El Salvador, and Serbia to formulate solutions at a distance to problems in cities where Ghana ThinkTank becomes active. These solutions are implemented directly on location even if they seem ridiculously unsuitable for the local situation. While some solutions turn out to be helpful, others have merely created awkward situations that show how difficult it is to grasp the sociocultural context of another country and how absurd it is to impose off-the-rack solutions on a community from the outside, without taking local conditions and habits into account. The long-term project not only draws attention to inefficiencies of current practices in international aid organizations, but also emphasizes the importance of large institutions reevaluating solutions after they have been executed. This step is also often neglected in other sectors of society. (AMB)

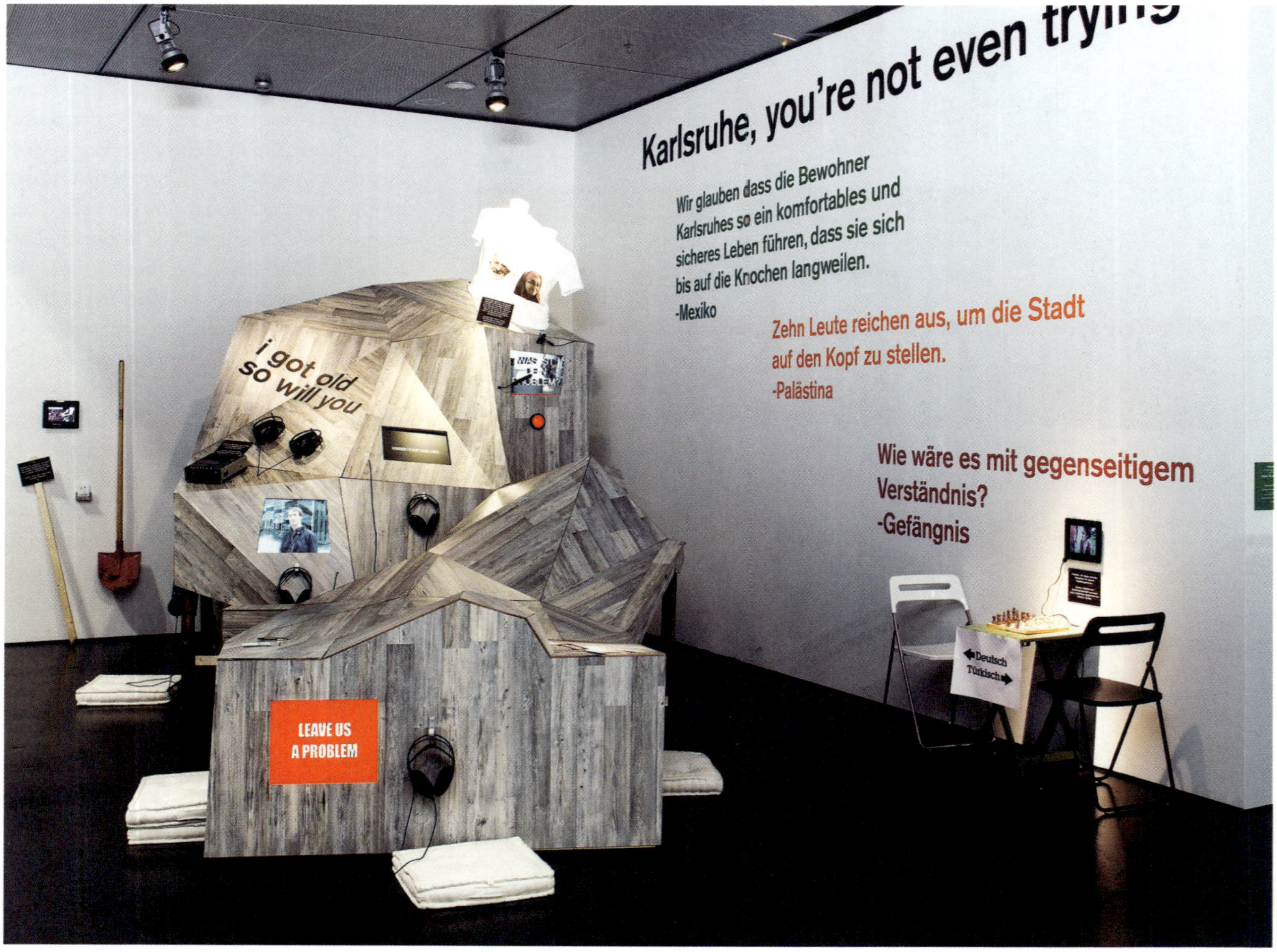

Anawana Haloba

* 1978 in Livingstone (ZM), lives and works in Oslo (NO)

The Greater G8 Advertising Market Stand, 2007–2009

Interactive sound installation,
dimensions variable

Zambian-born artist Anawana Haloba trained at both the Norwegian National Academy of Fine Arts in Oslo and at the Rijksakademie van beeldende kunsten in Amsterdam. Spanning different media, from video to interactive installations, Haloba's work comes to grips with the constant redefinition of cultures as well as with individual and collective memory in the global fluxes of symbolic and economic values.

The Greater G8 Advertising Market Stand, originally realized at the Rijksakademie in Amsterdam and then on show at the 53rd Venice Biennale (2009), parodies the possibility of fair and enlarged "free trade." This interactive installation consists of a typical-looking roadside vendor selling organic and eco-friendly products from Moldova, Iraq, Sudan, Colombia, Bolivia, Malawi, the Philippines, and Somalia. While the goods are advertised as "Bolivian Organic Soybeans" or "Vigobe Corn Flakes: A Malawian product not genetically modified," their substance betrays their promises. When visitors open the different boxes, they actually find only Western industrial candies. In a kind of semiotic short-circuit between expression and content, the artist denounces the hollowness of political slogans announcing a better world. (SG)

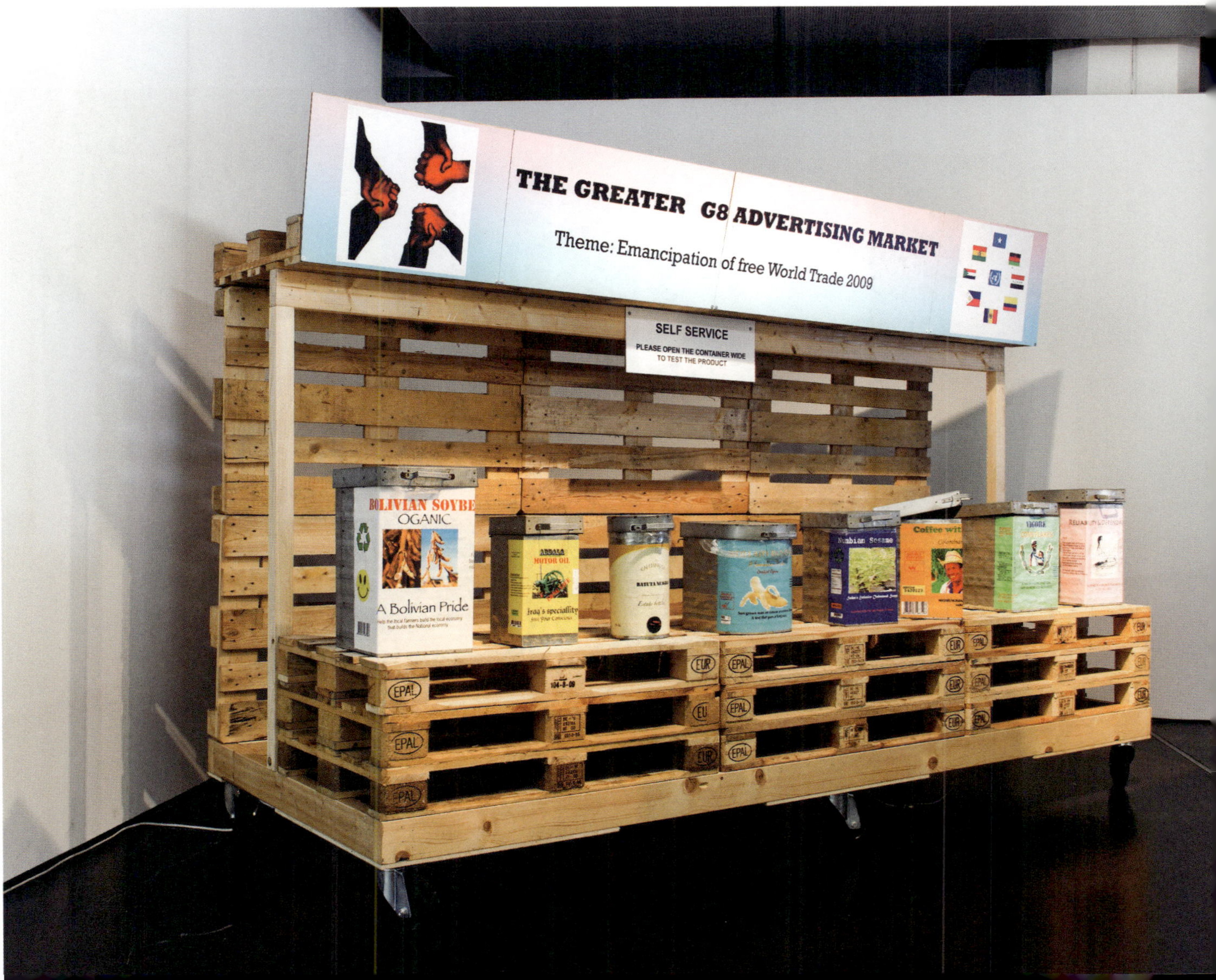

Ashley Hunt

* 1970 in Los Angeles, CA (US), lives and works in Los Angeles

A World Map: In Which We See..., 2004 (ongoing)

Mixed-media installation, 16 plates, ca. 60 × 100 cm each

Ashley Hunt uses video, photography, maps, and texts to draw attention to social processes and conditions that have no visibility in the media. A perennial subject of his artistic investigations is the theme of power and its disproportionate distribution, both with regard to the individual and to commercial enterprises and countries.

A Worldmap: In Which We See... is part of Hunt's depiction of the interconnections of power and representational strategies: taking globalization processes as its basis, *Worldmap* visualizes the interrelations between states and individuals, laws, borders, and historiographies, and highlights whether they are visible or nonvisible. Besides geographic aspects, the issues of citizenship and statelessness, as well as social mechanisms of inclusion and exclusion, are of central importance. Hunt produced the world map of globalization as a collaborative work in 2010 at Stuttgart's ifa-Gallery. He invited activists, students, and anyone who was interested to produce the map with him as a collaborative public project. The map again became a topic of discussion, including among artists, in the run up to *The Global Contemporary* exhibition. This resulted in a metaphor being found for contemporary existence - unwieldy but profit-oriented: a pinball machine, which gave rise to various interpretations as well as rules for a "game" of globalization. As a local interpretation of his *Worldmap*, this collaborative piece was shown in the exhibition next to Hunt's original work. (HP)

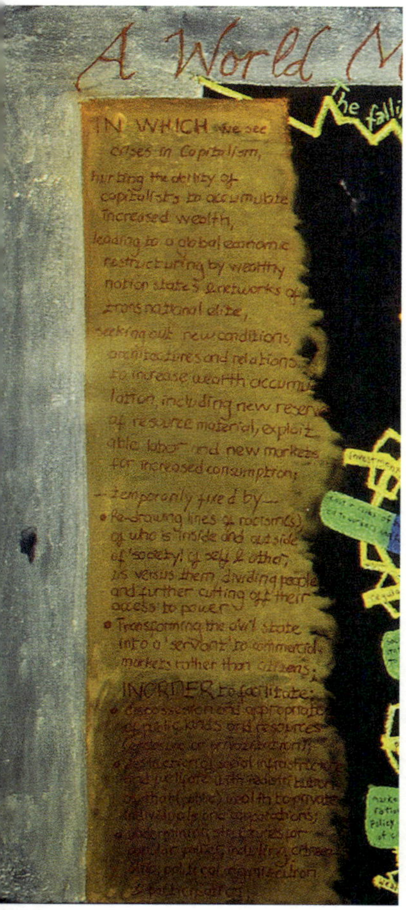

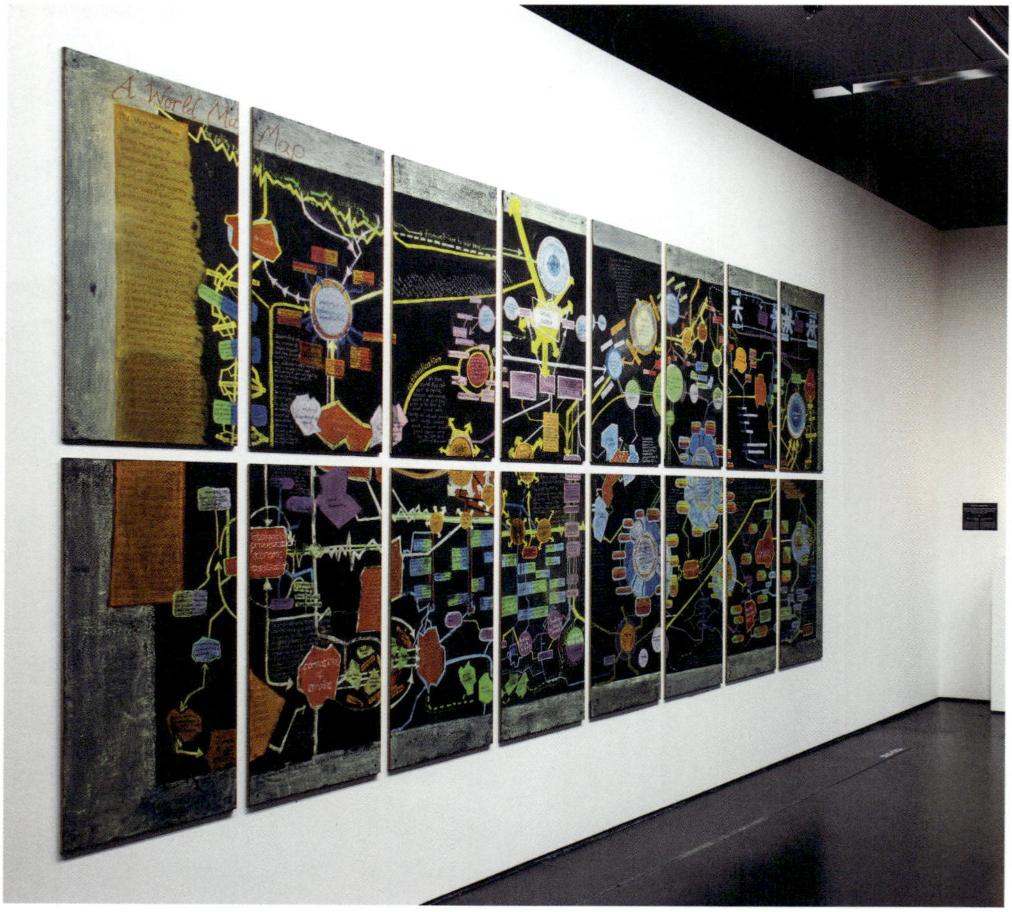

IRWIN and NSKSTATE.COM

IRWIN is an artists' collective established in 1983 in Ljubljana (SI).
Along with the music group Laibach and Scipion Našice Sisters Theater, IRWIN is an original founding member of NSK (New Slovenian Art) that was formed in 1984.

NSK Folk Art, 2008 (ongoing)

Mixed-media installation, dimensions variable

All three core groups of NSK explore similar areas in various media. Their main interests are the relationship between art and ideology, the functioning of ideology and totalitarianism, in which the idea of the state plays a key role. The point of departure for all NSK's activities is a reflection on the experience of Slovenian history.

In 1991, NSK declared itself a "State in Time," without territory or national borders. The NSK State is a "spiritual, virtual state" that issues real original passports in accordance with international standards. Anybody can obtain a passport of the "first global state of the universe" and thus acquire the status of one of its citizens. The passports are documents "of subversive nature and unique value" and take NSK reprocessing of state motifs to the extreme. They bear witness to the artistic appropriation of state power. NSK has opened embassies and consular offices throughout the world. The organization of congresses and meetings are further examples of their activities.

The fundamentals of NSK "statist aesthetics" is a sort of retrospective manipulation and "recycling" of the images and symbols of the avant-garde, "Nazi Art," and Socialist Realism. The NSK insignia, the emblem of the "retro-avant-garde," is typical of the eclectic visual language of the organization. The NSK State currently includes several thousand citizens from all over the world. In collaboration with NSKSTATE.COM, IRWIN has collected a number of artworks created by NSK citizens that reflect on different aspects of the NSK project and are executed in its style. (DM)

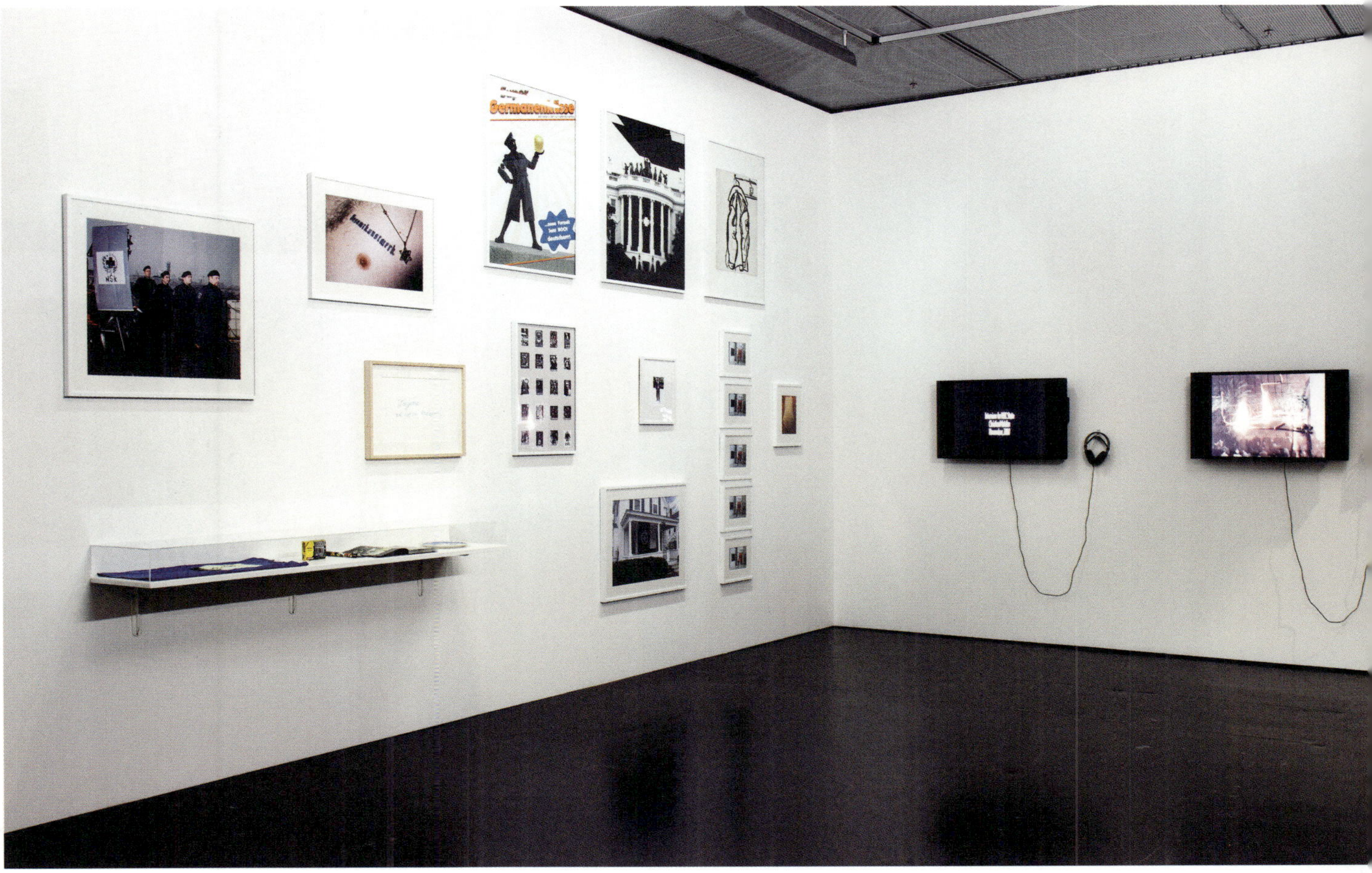

Le Laboratoire de Déberlinisation

Mansour Ciss Kanakassy, * 1957 in Dakar (SN), lives and works in Berlin (DE) and Dakar;
Baruch Gottlieb, * 1966 in Montreal (CA), lives and works in Berlin and Seoul (KR);
Christian Hanussek, * 1953 in Frankfurt am Main (DE), lives and works in Berlin

Mobile Exchange Office, 2011

Mixed-media installation, (wooden exchange office, computer, 2 videos, color, sound, digital prints), dimensions variable

Le Laboratoire de Déberlinisation is an artistic project that was founded in Berlin by Mansour Ciss Kanakassy together with Baruch Gottlieb, and Christian Hanussek in 2001. Le Laboratoire de Déberlinisation aims to spark debate on Africa's postcolonial conditions, while its name resonates and challenges the Berlin Conference of 1884–1885, at which the European colonial powers regulated European colonization and trade in Africa. By diverting financial and political issues into art concepts and works, Le Laboratoire de Déberlinisation operates on the line between art and social activism, "where the idealism of the arts meets the realism of geopolitics and economics."

For the exhibition *The Global Contemporary*, Le Laboratoire de Déberlinisation realized the *Mobile Exchange Office*. Both a public performance at the Karlsruhe Main Station and an installation in the exhibition's space, the work spread the Afro project among the local community and the exhibition's audience. The Afro was first launched at the 2002 Dak'Art Biennial in Dakar, Senegal, and is the collective's prototype for a truly pan-African currency, recently joined by the AFRO Express Card and the Global Pass. With video screens displaying Afro exchange rates and slogans such as "Exchange your money with the money of the future," this project seeks to invite reflection on the populations' right to financial and political self-determination and as well on the value of contemporary art. In the middle of the European financial crises, random travelers that happened to be at Karlsruhe Main Station on September 17 collided with the hitherto utopian proposal of exchanging their Euros for Afros – for some certainly a safer investment! (SG)

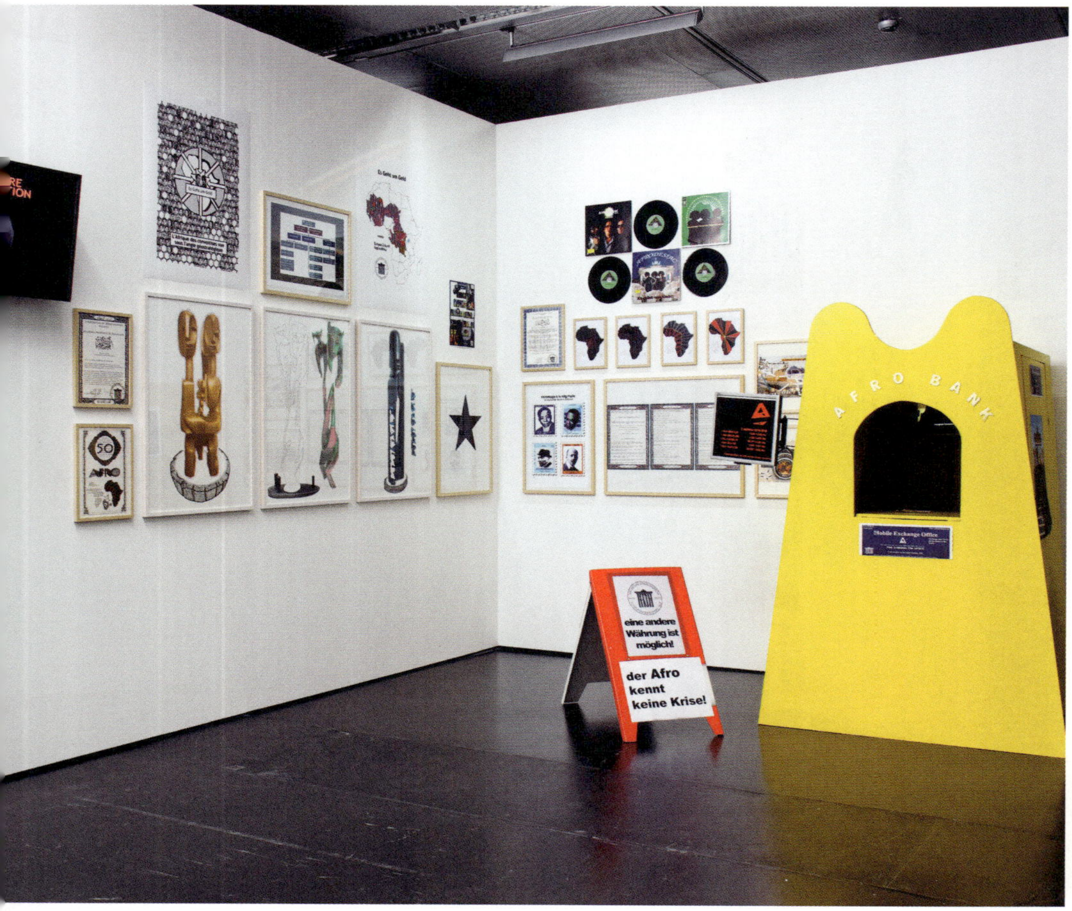

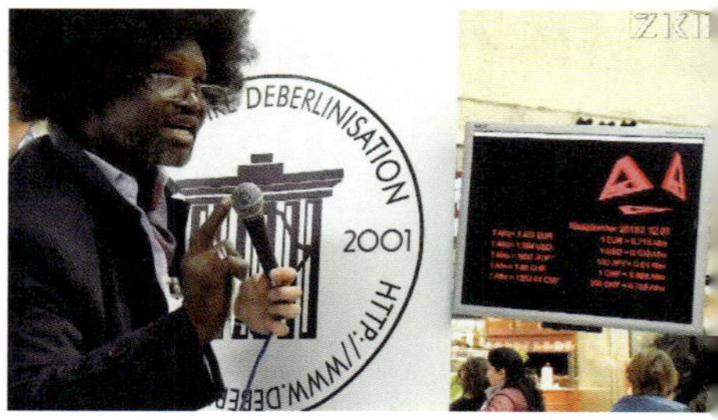

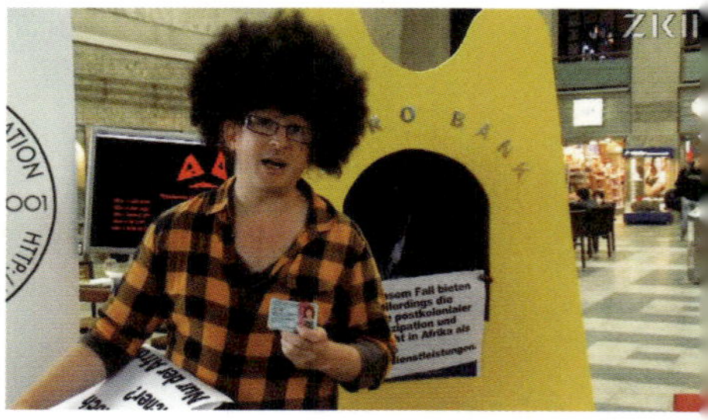

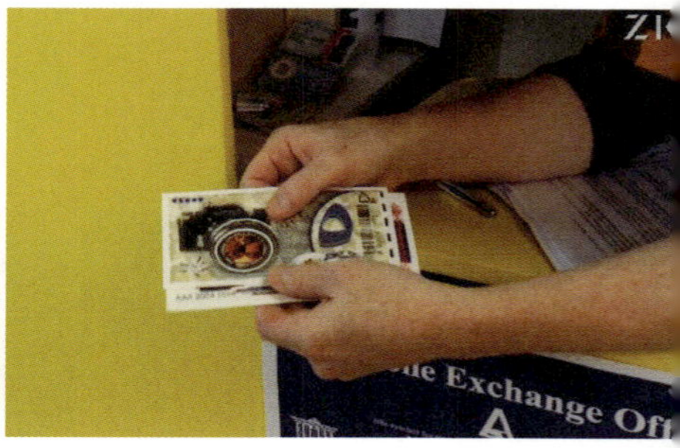

Pinky Show

Live and work in the desert (US)

Banked Into Submission (The Globalizationist's Guide to Developing Poverty), 2007

Comic and video, color, sound, 3:14 min

Defending Globalization... A Mission for the Educated and Enlightened, 2007

Comic and video, color, sound, 3:02 min

Globalization (and the Metaphysics of Control in a Free Market World), 2007

Comic and video, color, sound, 3:02 min

For the last five years Pinky Show has been working on reprocessing and disseminating knowledge that is misrepresented, ignored, or in some other way banished from current discussions in the mass media and in schools. As a nonprofit organization, the artists' collective analyzes and presents contemporary social and political problems as scandalous, for example, the construction of the "Other," the effects of colonialism that persist to this day, and mechanisms of exclusion that operate in public institutions, such as museums. The themes are depicted and distributed via the Internet in the form of comics and videos, in which animated hand-drawn cat characters talk about relationships between historiography, ideologies, and power in simple and informal language. In the Pinky Show's globalization comics, the cat called Bunny explains the complex effects of globalization and above all reveals the various interests, which are behind the processes of globalization. (HP)

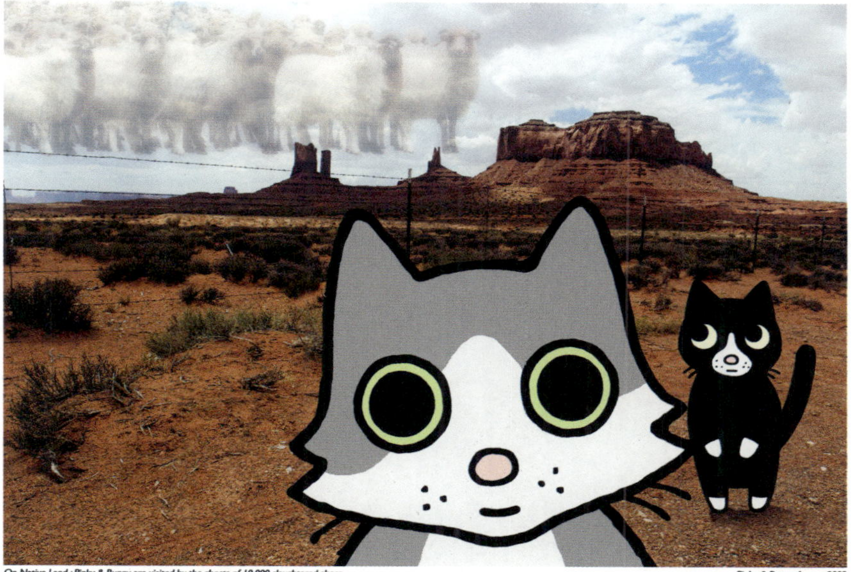

On Native Land : Pinky & Bunny are visited by the ghosts of 10,000 slaughtered sheep Pinky & Bunny, August 2009

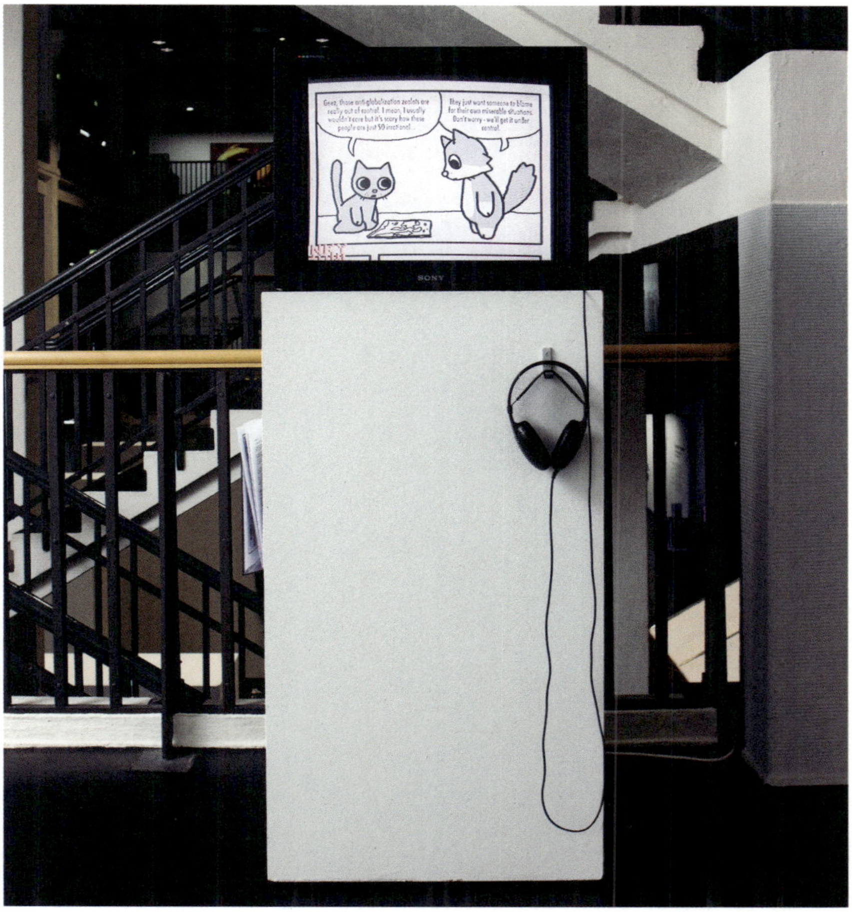

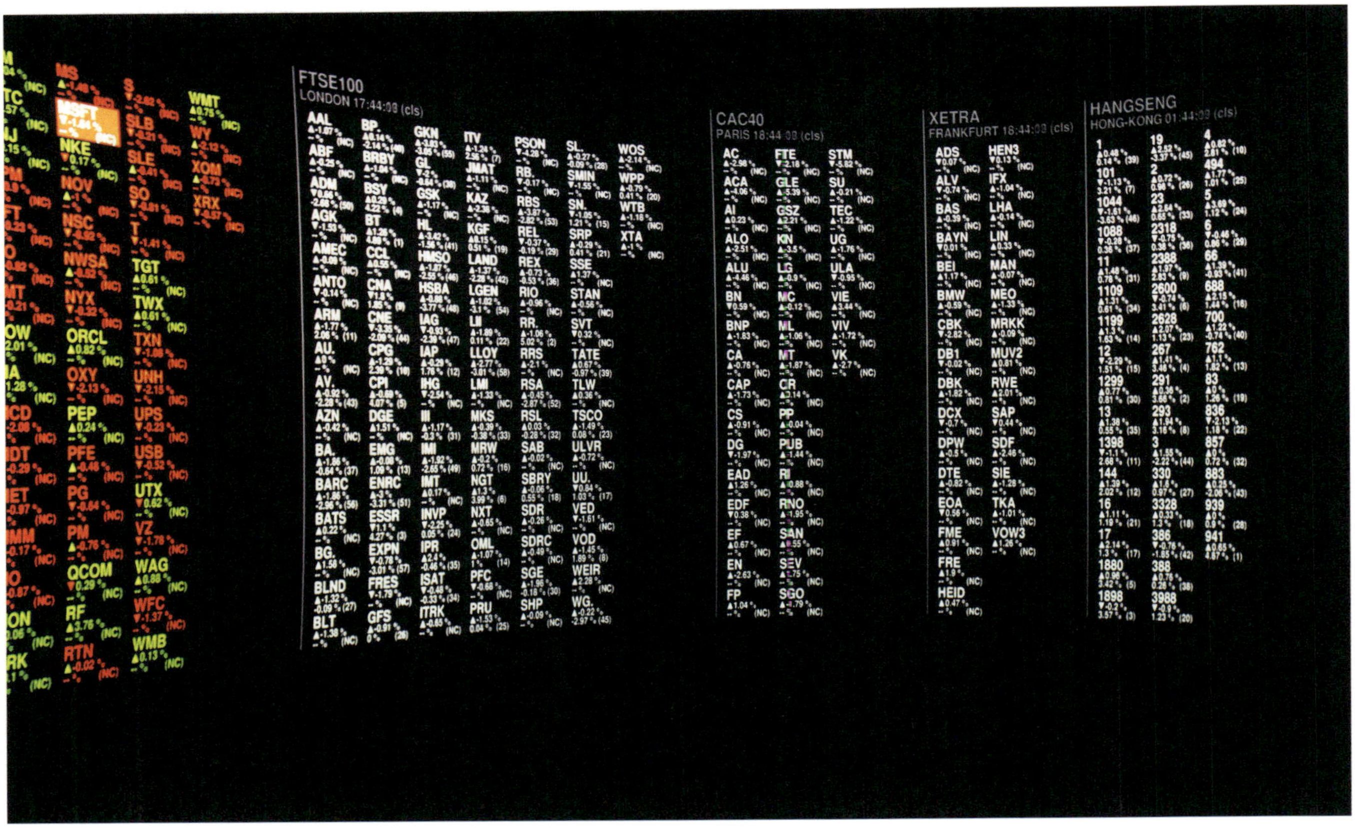
FTSE100
LONDON 17:44:09 (cls)
CAC40
PARIS 18:44:08 (cls)
XETRA
FRANKFURT 18:44:08 (cls)
HANGSENG
HONG-KONG 01:44:09 (cls)

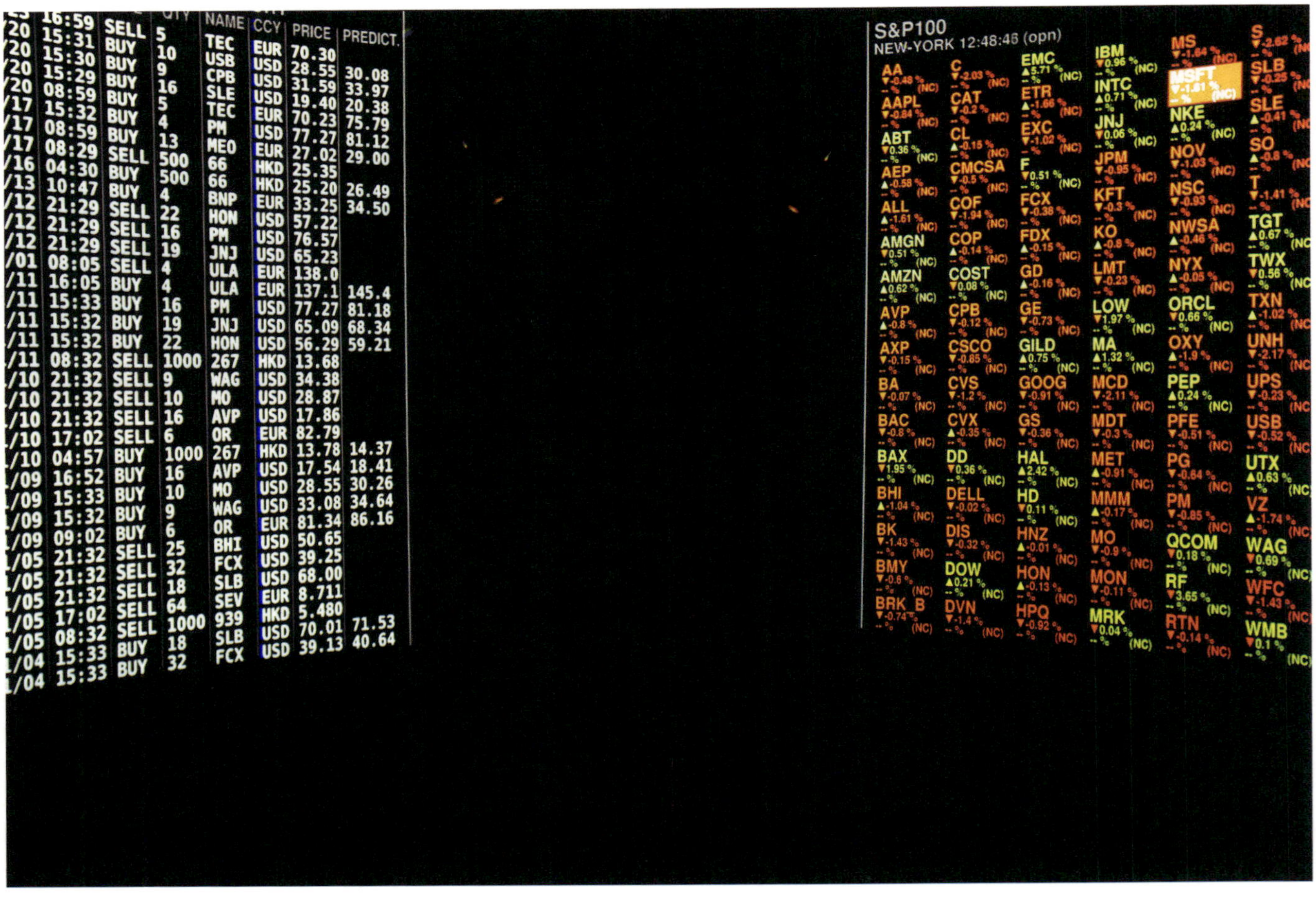
NAME
CCY
PRICE
PREDICT.
S&P100
NEW-YORK 12:48:46 (opn)

RYBN.ORG

* 1966 in Munich (DE), lives and works in Berlin (DE)

ADM VIII, 2011

Trading bot performance, panoramic installation
Realized in collaboration with ZKM | Institute for Visual Media

On May 6, 2010, around 2:40 p.m., the Dow Jones index fell about 900 points in less than twenty minutes. The loss was estimated at one trillion dollars. Following this event, all transactions made that day between 2:40 and 3 p.m. were canceled. This instantaneous stock market crash, now referred to as the "Flash Crash," was caused by miscalculations carried out by high-frequency trading robots operating on the markets. Despite its virtuality, this crash sheds light upon the actual architecture of finance; its particular temporality and scale reaches far beyond human physical capabilities and perceptions, where robots trigger thousands of orders each second and flood the market with millions of fake data to hide their true investments, a process which is called "quote stuffing."

Engaging finance in its most recent and complex developments, RYBN.ORG has undertaken the construction of its own trading bot, designed to invest and speculate on the financial markets. Using an online broker service to directly access the markets, this autonomous program can trigger orders as well as buy and sell stocks. Its decisions are taken with the help of an internal algorithmic intelligence system, and can be influenced by a wide range of external, arbitrary parameters. The whole decision system allows the program to foresee the next moves in the markets, while it tries to identify and anticipate the relevant and effective patterns within the chaotic financial oscillations. The robot's activity, along with its computations and performance, is monitored, recorded, and visualized within a dynamic cartography. A panopticon of information unfolds that is formally similar to the control rooms of the stock exchanges' back offices. (RYBN)

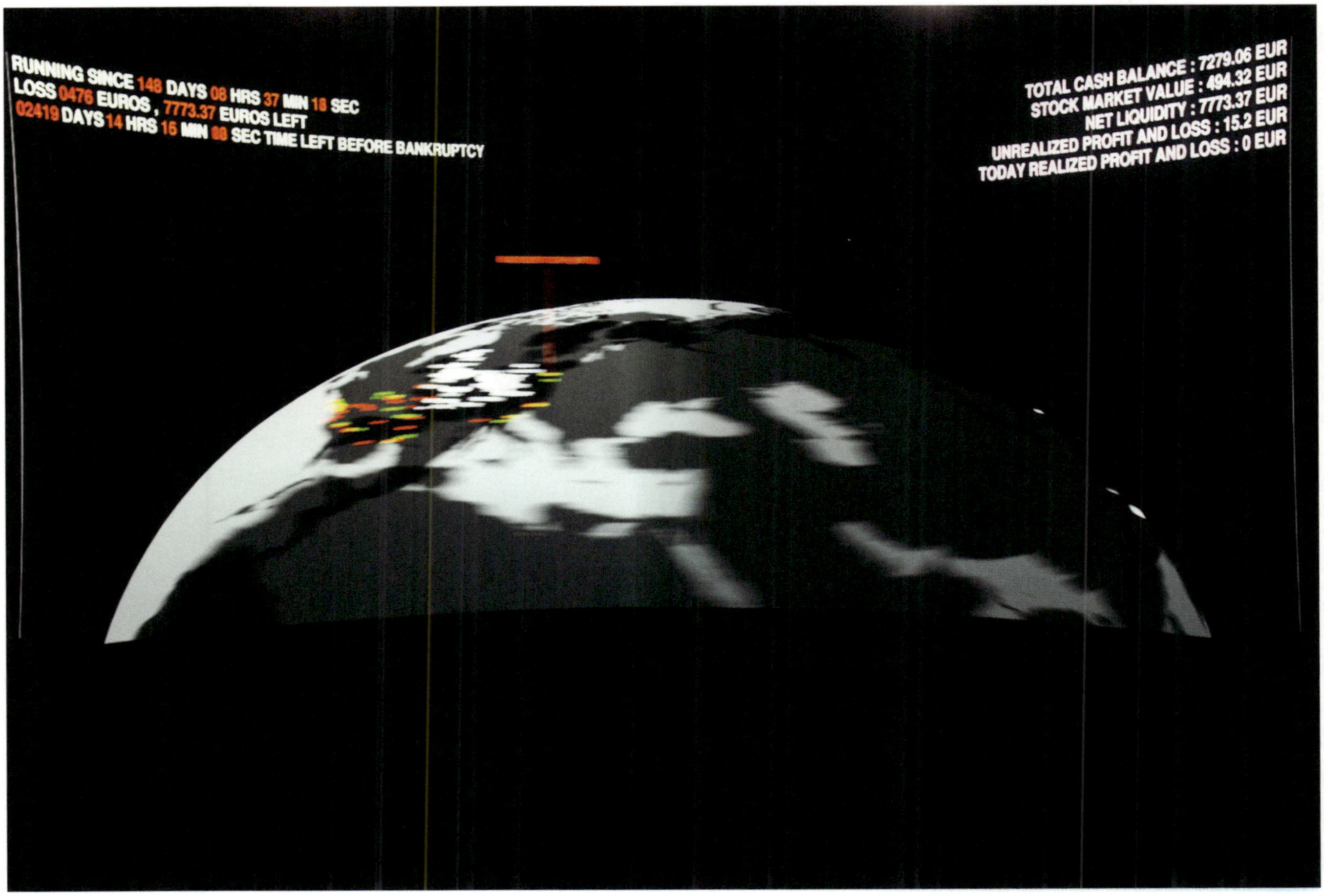

Tadej Pogačar

* 1960 in Ljubljana (SI), lives and works in Ljubljana

MonApoly, A Human Trade Game, 2004

Mixed-media installation, board game (edition: 50), inkjet print on vinyl (249 × 249 cm), 3 *MonApoly* games

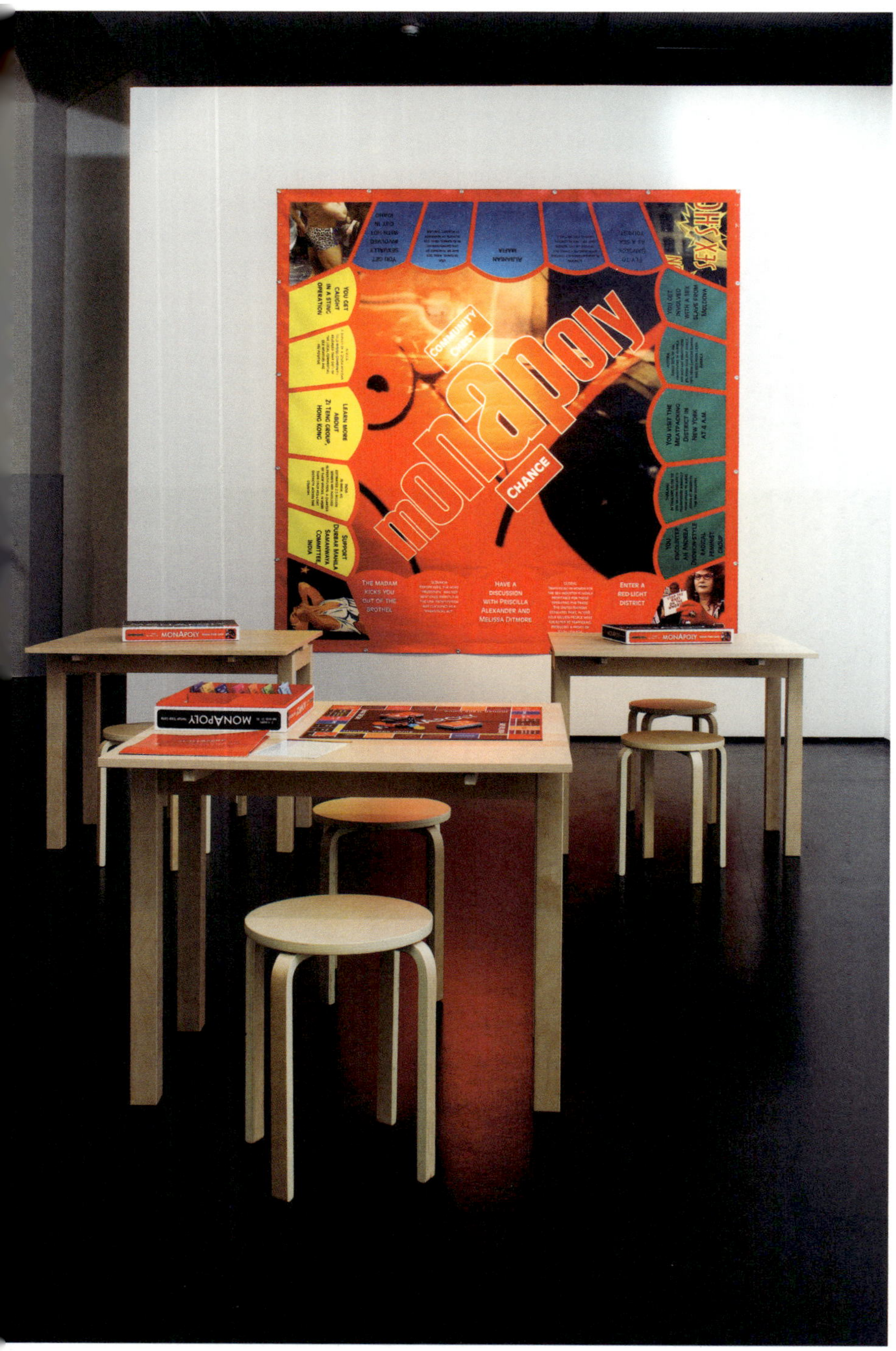

Tadej Pogačar is the artist, curator, and founder of the virtual critical platform, *The P.A.R.A.S.I.T.E. Museum of Contemporary Art* (1990). From this platform, he developed a new theory and method for creating an alternative culture and social activities, which he calls "New Parasitism." Pogačar's projects are based on the use of various media and focus on urban interventions and collaborations with social minorities. Pogačar investigates different systems and produces transregional levels of reference.

The game *MonApoly* is a new and critical version of the popular board game *Monopoly* and is a result of Pogačar's long-standing engagement with the situation of sex workers worldwide. The players receive information about global sex working, important places, committed organizations, gangs that control the trade, and so forth. During the course of the game, it is possible to finance the construction of a safe house, support the activities of groups who fight for the rights of sex workers, or get a sex slave from the Republic of Moldova freed.

MonApoly enables a new cartography of human trafficking. Instead of amassing capital like in *Monopoly*, the artist explains to the players the geopolitics of sex working in the era of late capitalism and globalization. Tadej Pogačar analyzes the parallel markets that are created as a reaction to existing markets, and the sociopolitical and social developments, that are characterized by illegality, ensuring survival, fear, and expulsion. (AE)

Michael Stevenson

* 1964 in Inglewood (NZ), lives and works in Berlin (DE)

The Fountain of Prosperity, 2006

Plexiglas, steel, brass, aluminum, rubber, cork, string, concrete, dyed water, pumps, and fluorescent lamps, 2.5 × 1.6 × 1 m

When in 1949 the New Zealand economist Bill Phillips designed "MONIAC," a hydraulic device to illustrate national economic processes, globalization in its present form was unimaginable. Thus MONIAC only illustrated export and import by having water drained from or fed into the hydraulic system. Yet, in its day MONIAC was a success; by means of water levels in the individual tanks, it directly visualized the relations and effects of investment, taxes, and welfare on the economic system - and very quickly a dozen such devices stood in educational institutions around the world. Legend has it that in 1953 the Central Bank of Guatemala acquired a model. The artist Michael Stevenson took research about the whereabouts of this model as the occasion to address its mixed metaphors by building a replica of MONIAC. Left by itself in the exhibition space and abandoned to possible dereliction, the old-fashioned machine illustrates the gap between the abstractions of economics and their reality - and the moments in which the economy subordinates reality to itself. When in 1954 the CIA overthrew the democratically elected president of Guatemala and degraded the country to the status of a "banana republic" for decades, this was done largely at the urging of the American United Fruit Company corporation, which saw its business threatened by the impending land reforms. (JB)

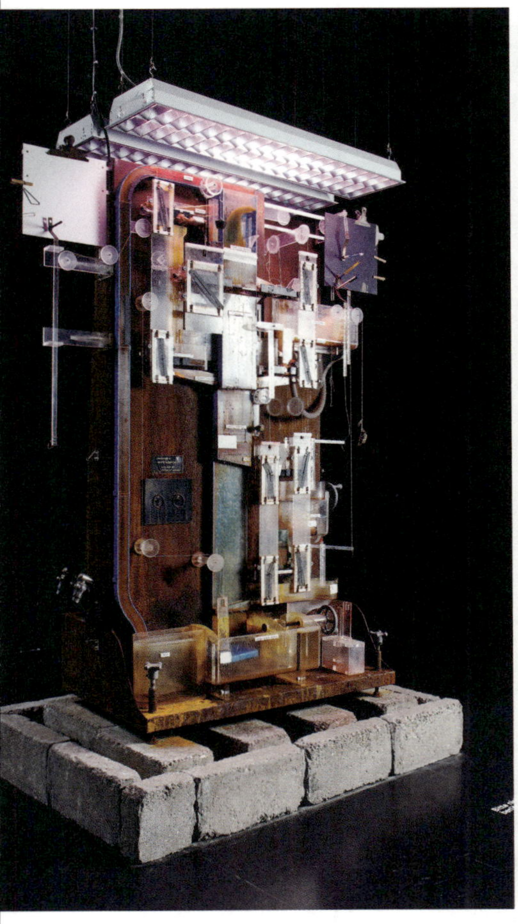

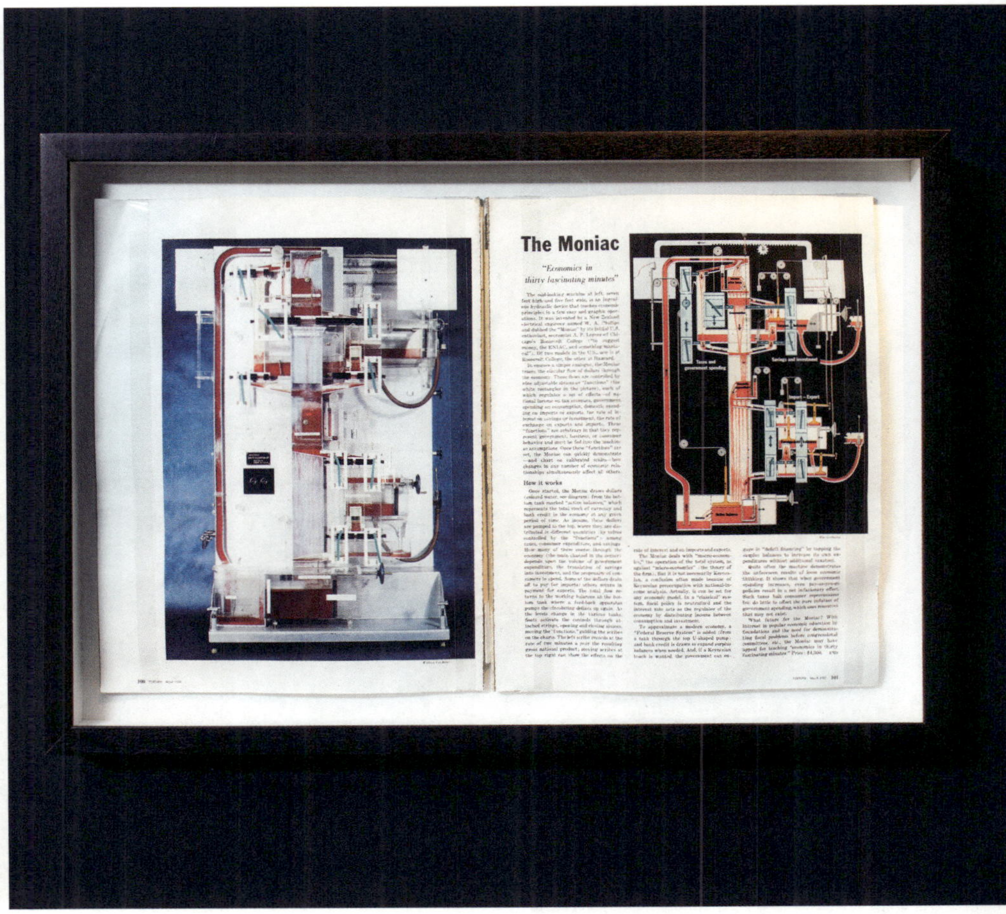

Jens M. Stober

* 1986 in Karlsruhe (DE), lives and works in Karlsruhe

1378 (km), 2010

Computer game installation for two players

If the ideologists of globalization had had their way, then the end of the Cold War around 1989 would have also been the end of historical narratives. The triumphal march of democracy and the free enterprise economy would have cleared up all political and economic conflicts and, therefore, also the necessity to put these down in words, pictures, and stories. A never-ending series of wars, terrorism, and catastrophes has so far not confirmed this assumption. At the same time, the introduction of digital media and the Internet have had consequences for historiography and storytelling in general, the scale of which is still difficult to foresee. Over recent years, video games have become a mass medium that offers very specific techniques of storytelling.

The possibility of subjective participation in the gaming action, which, however, is orientated on a predetermined aesthetic and contextual framework, renders it possible to make questions about subjectivity and the freedom to decide an immediately experienceable part of the story.

It is against this background that Jens M. Stober's "serious game" *1378 (km)* is situated. As gamers we are confronted with the choice of taking over the role of a refugee or that of a border guard at the former border between the two Germanies. As the latter we have the choice of following the GDR regime's order to shoot, to refuse, or to try to escape across the border ourselves - whoever shoots, is taken to court in the game after a narrative time leap into the year 2000. That the populist media tried to brand *1378 (km)* as a violent shoot-'em-up game merely shows that they did not even take the possibility of free choice into account; this matches exactly the kind of logic that uncritical obedience within any political system follows. (JB)

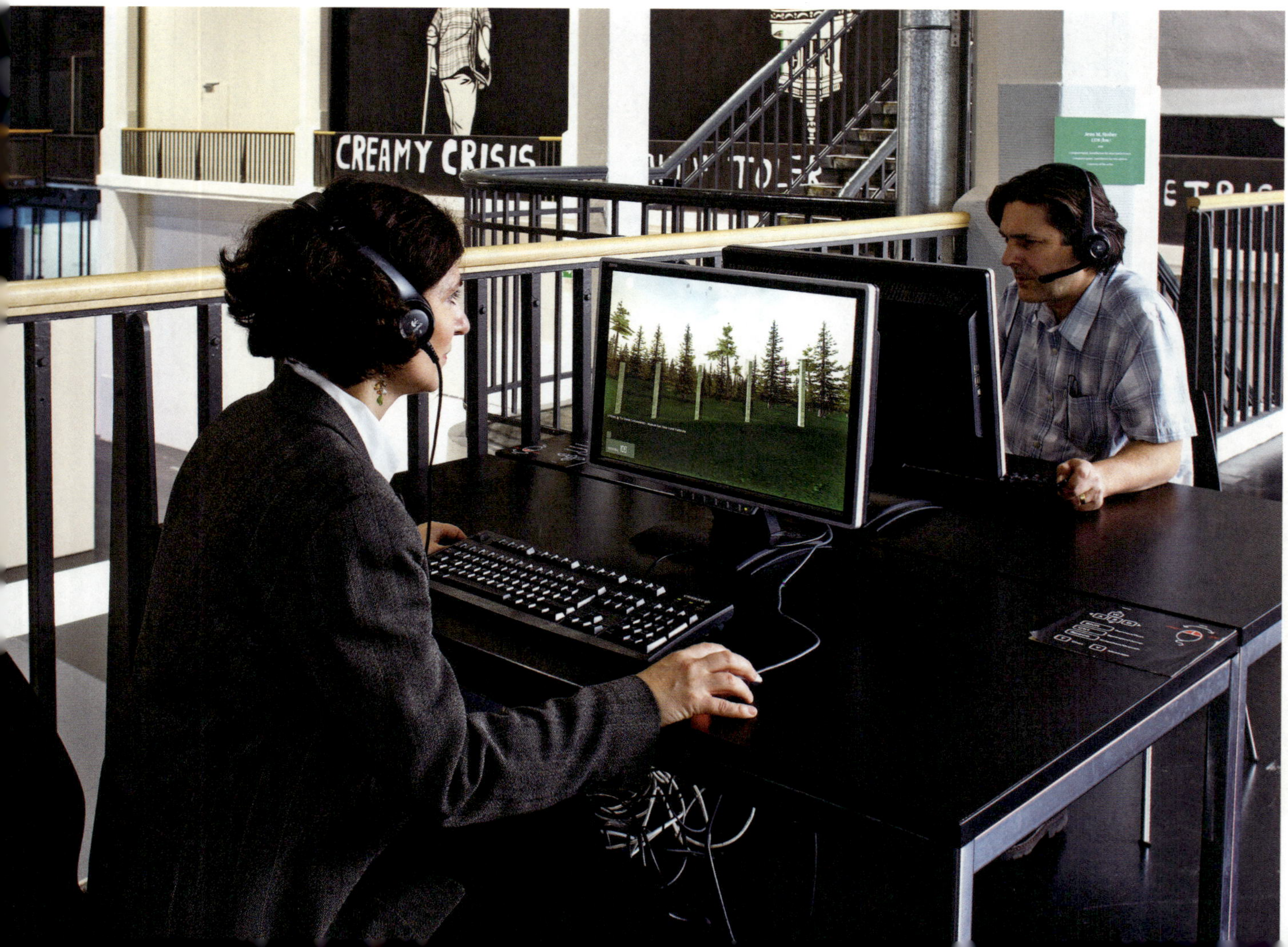

The Xijing Men

Chen Shaoxiong, * 1962 in Shantou, Guangdong (CN), lives and works in Guangzhou (CN); Gimhongsok, * 1964 in Seoul (KR), lives and works in Seoul; Tsuyoshi Ozawa, * 1965 in Tokyo (JP), lives and works in Tokyo

Welcome to Xijing – Xijing Olympics, 2008

Video, color, sound, 35 min, 2 flags, dimensions variable

In the age of globalism the nation-state plays a rather questionable role; it only appears to stand in the way of the ideology of open and free traffic of data and commodities, although for the time being it is still retained for administrative purposes. As for culture, the nations are supposed to guarantee a peaceful coexistence of plural identities which find their expression in the colorful diversity of customs and idioms. The potential for conflict, which is inherent in dividing the world up into nations and peoples, is accordingly defused through amicable competition, such as sporting events as harmless spectacles.

Chen Shaoxiong, Gimhongsok, and Tsuyoshi Ozawa take this peaceful and fanciful picture of regional identity in the *post-histoire* period and drive it to extremes; as The Xijing Men they are the representatives of the fictitious city Xijing – the legendary "Western capital" of equivalent standing to Beijing in the North, Nanjing in the South, and Tokyo in the East. In view of the conflict-ridden history of relations between China, Korea, and Japan the quest to find this city, or actually to found it, is a lovely utopia. The slapstick sequences of *Xijing Olympics* that the three artists stage demonstrate the absurdity of state pomp and ceremony, and the only identity that is defended in this competition, using brushes, melons, and dumbbells made of bottle caps, is that of the artists, who play the part of subtle humorists. (JB)

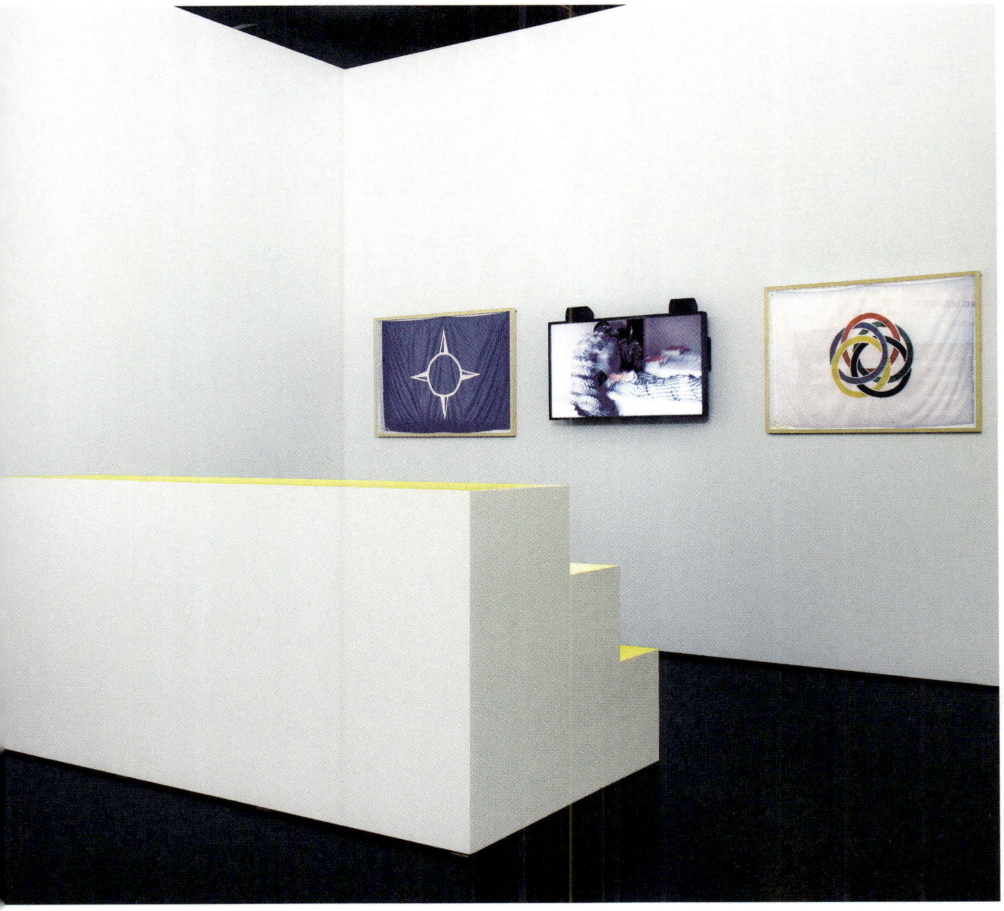

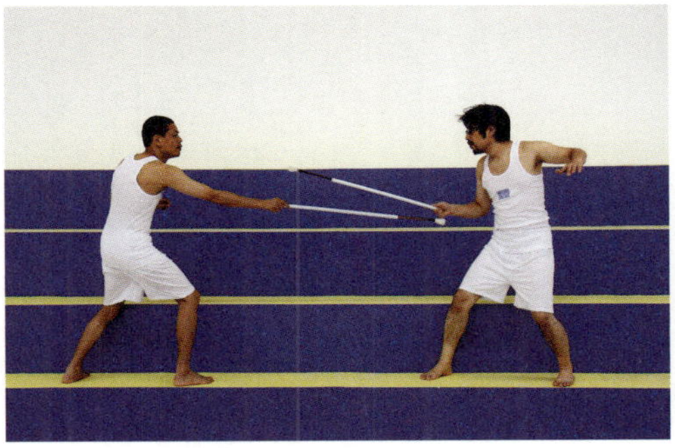

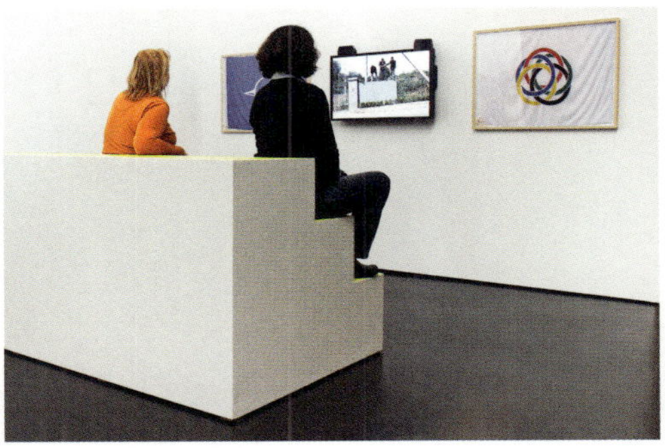

Luchezar Boyadjiev
Ondrej Brody & Kristofer Paetau
Elmgreen & Dragset / Antonia Hirsch
David Jablonowski / Melanie Jackson
Christian Jankowski / Surasi Kusolwong
Liu Ding / Navin Rawanchaikul
Gabriele di Matteo / Christa Sommerer
& Laurent Mignonneau / SOSka group
SUPERFLEX / Stephanie Syjuco
Zhou Tiehai

Art as Commodity: The New Economy and the Art Markets

Nowhere is globalization so glaringly evident as in the new worldwide art markets. Not only does the art trade cross geographic borders that had formerly protected the art world. The new economy has also produced a global clientele of billionaires who, as collectors, no longer go for a specific art taste and no longer represent a specific social class. The majority of them collect contemporary art because they regard it as a global symbol of their lifestyle. In the meantime, Hong Kong is competing with New York and London on the ranking list of trade centers. As a result, it has become a common prejudice to accuse today's art of being produced entirely in the service of the market. But, as many works in this section demonstrate, the same market has become the target of a new type of criticism which, in the hands of the artists, is unmasking the fiction inherent to the market mechanisms and especially the exaggerated prices that overshadow the works in question and are important in themselves as welcome news for market speculation. The artists respond by openly questioning creativity, after it has become a marketable commodity, with the brand of the all-important artist's name.

But the oddities of the market are sometimes also targeted in general, as is the case with a photograph by the duo Elmgreen & Dragset, entitled *Prada Marfa*, which represents an isolated, sealed-up Prada store in the unlikely place of Marfa, Donald Judd's foundation in the Texas desert. With the installation the photograph reproduces the artists chose commodity culture as their target, but linked it to art as a commodity. The Prada shop, at this lonely location, is nothing but fiction and reveals window-shopping as a gallery experience intended to attract potential collectors. Art, in a way, is easily turning into a mere brand, similar to the way Prada products are a global brand for consuming luxury goods.

Christa Sommerer and Laurent Mignonneau approached market criticism as market fiction from another angle in that they confronted the visitors with an arbitrary nineteenth-century seascape ("storming sea") that was connected with a sensor registering the time length of their stay in front of the painting. Some visitors did not even notice that, before their feet, a printout emerging from a machine listed the alleged value increase of every second they remained facing the work. Thus, the artists playfully argued that value increase is measurable as a result of interest. With *GastARTbeiter*, Luchezar Boyadjiev touches upon another critical aspect, which has arisen in the economics of international artist funding and sponsoring as an important prerequisite of personal art marketing. As his target, Boyadjiev has chosen the relation of art and economy in the international system of fellowships and the worldwide expanding artist-in-residence programs. As a case study, he meticulously listed the amount of money and institutional help that was invested in him personally over a period of ten years.

The fictionalization of the art trade is taken up by an installation plus video and photographs that the Ukrainian SOSka group contributed to this section entitled *Barter*. The argument they bring forward concerns the value of art when relocated in a social context where art is deprived of any surplus value in the sense of symbolic value or connoisseurship. In a small village in the middle of nowhere, a young man tries to trade art works in exchange for farm products, thus in the primitive style of barter trading. The works of art in question are print reproductions of famous originals, which are unknown to the clients and therefore only have any interest for them when they believe they have discovered a figure who resembles a relative of theirs.

Liu Ding's Store was the only place in the exhibition *The Global Contemporary* where art was actually sold. He offered paintings of one and the same size for sale, which he had commissioned from copyists, with a fictional price that contradicted the rules of the art trade. The "unfinished paintings," mostly with a detail of a seascape or landscape, had been merely signed by the artist. The installation thus invited the audience to discuss the value system that is today represented by the art trade.

Navin Rawanchaikul and Gabriele di Matteo address the China hype on the art market in an ironic, pseudo-propagandistic way. In a giant-sized painting in the billboard style for Bollywood cinema entitled *SUPER CHINA!*, Rawanchaikul stages top market personae like collectors, curators, and artists side by side with figures known from contemporary Chinese painting like a big puzzle of a new art world. It seems that the star cult of the cinematic world is merging with the protagonists of the art market. In a humorous postscript the market is introduced as "survival art corp." In his installation *China Made in Italy* Gabriele di Matteo responds to the same market by commissioning actual copies of expensive Chinese masterpieces of today, copied in a flattening uniform black-and-white style and produced in Naples, the former center for copying oil paintings worldwide before the Chinese took over. The space with the installation in the exhibition offered the illusion of being a shop in the Chinese copyist village of Dafen. The inherent market critique substitutes the masterpiece with a brand, which can also be recognized in the copy. (AB)

Luchezar Boyadjiev

* 1957 in Sofia (BG), lives and works in Sofia

GastARTbeiter, 2000–2007

Digital print on vinyl, 210 × 510 cm

Luchezar Boyadjiev is an artist of international standing and an active representative of the contemporary Eastern European art scene in the so-called Western world. In his work he reflects on the radical changes in the way of life and economic system that began with the end of the socialist societies.

In his wall piece *GastARTbeiter*, Boyadjiev traces his artistic career during the 1990s. Unlike the usual artist's biography, this one is not presented in terms of prizes, grants, exhibitions, and solo shows, but through the financial resources he received. In addition to hotel bills, restaurant receipts, contracts, exhibition budgets, and other documents, the work contains photos, reminiscences, and commentaries by Boyadjiev, and is thus a kind of personal chronicle.

Since his participation in a guest artist program in Stuttgart, and because of his grievances with the institutional art market system, he began calculating how much money Western foundations and funding programs had been prepared to invest in his career over a ten-year period.

Boyadjiev examines the relation of art, economy, and everyday life, and takes up an equally ironic and critical position with regard to the social and political contexts of art. Furthermore, he questions the capitalist operating system of art itself. (AE)

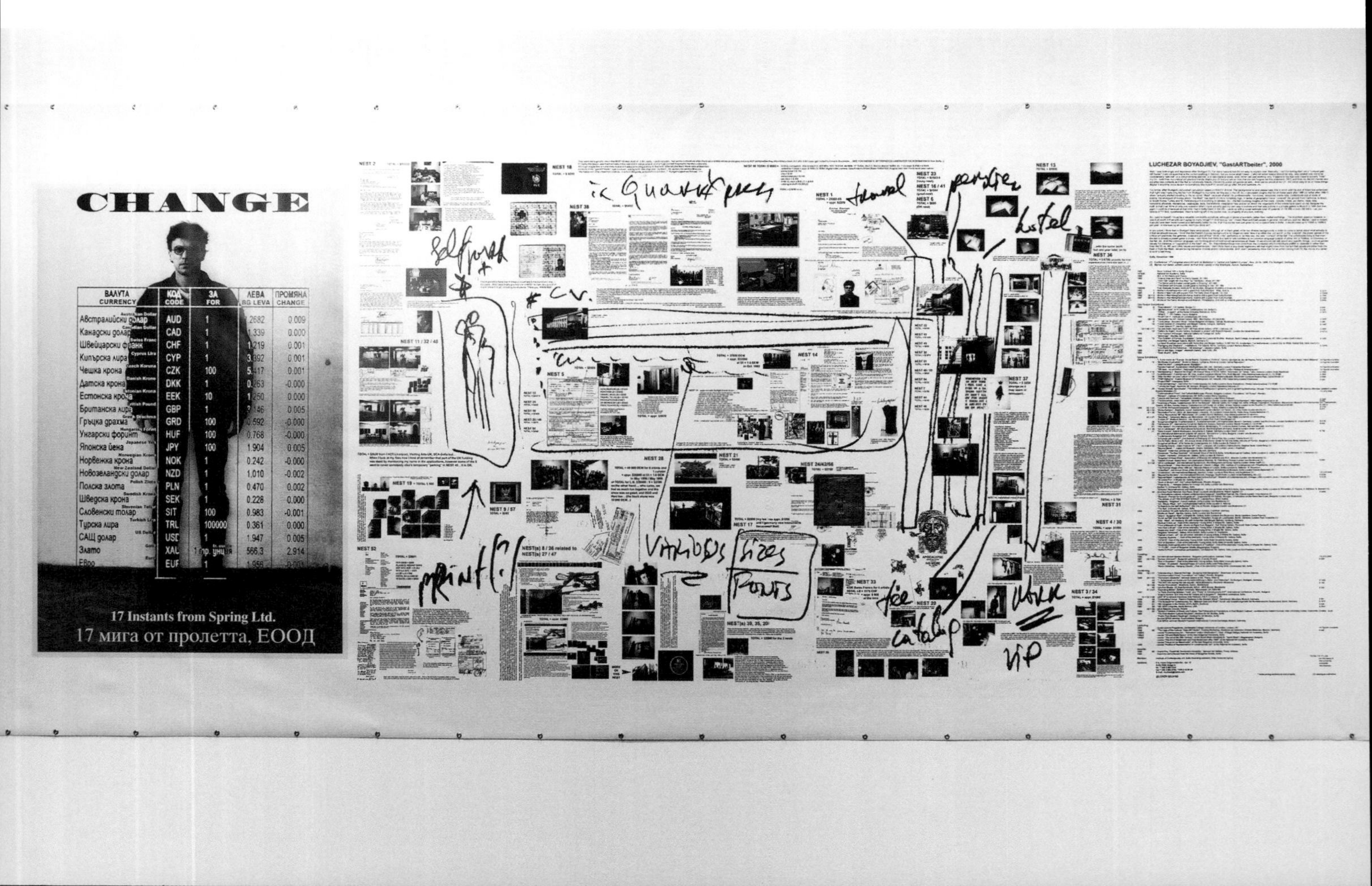

Ondrej Brody & Kristofer Paetau

Ondrej Brody, * 1980 in Prague (CZ), lives and works in Prague;
Kristofer Paetau, * 1972 in Borg (FI), lives and works in Rio de Janeiro (BR)

Wang Bin Torture in Commercial Quality, High Quality and Museum Quality, 2010

3 paintings, oil on canvas, 110 × 160 cm each

In our perception we usually distinguish between images from the mass media and artistic images. If we experience the former only as carriers of information or feelings that are for rapid consumption, the latter possess a value in themselves, which is generated by a particular artistic intention or a complex process of production. Since the advent of modernity, this supposedly clear-cut order of images has itself become a subject of art. When, for example, the transient images of the mass media are suddenly reproduced with techniques that we find appropriate only in art - that is, framed and hung on a wall in a museum - this order begins to totter and, with it, the standards according to which we judge images as relevant, unique, or beautiful.

With this in mind, the artist duo Ondrej Brody and Kristofer Paetau commissioned a Chinese painter by e-mail to reproduce a photo of the corpse of Wang Bin - a member of Falun Gong, who allegedly died while under arrest - in the different degrees of "commercial," "high," and "museum" quality. Juxtaposed, the pictures illustrate the arbitrariness with which the craftsman's production becomes the measure of value. They also illustrate the power relations inherent in images and art: between censorship and voyeurism, between art as a means of enlightenment and as a market commodity, between showing and being shown. (JB)

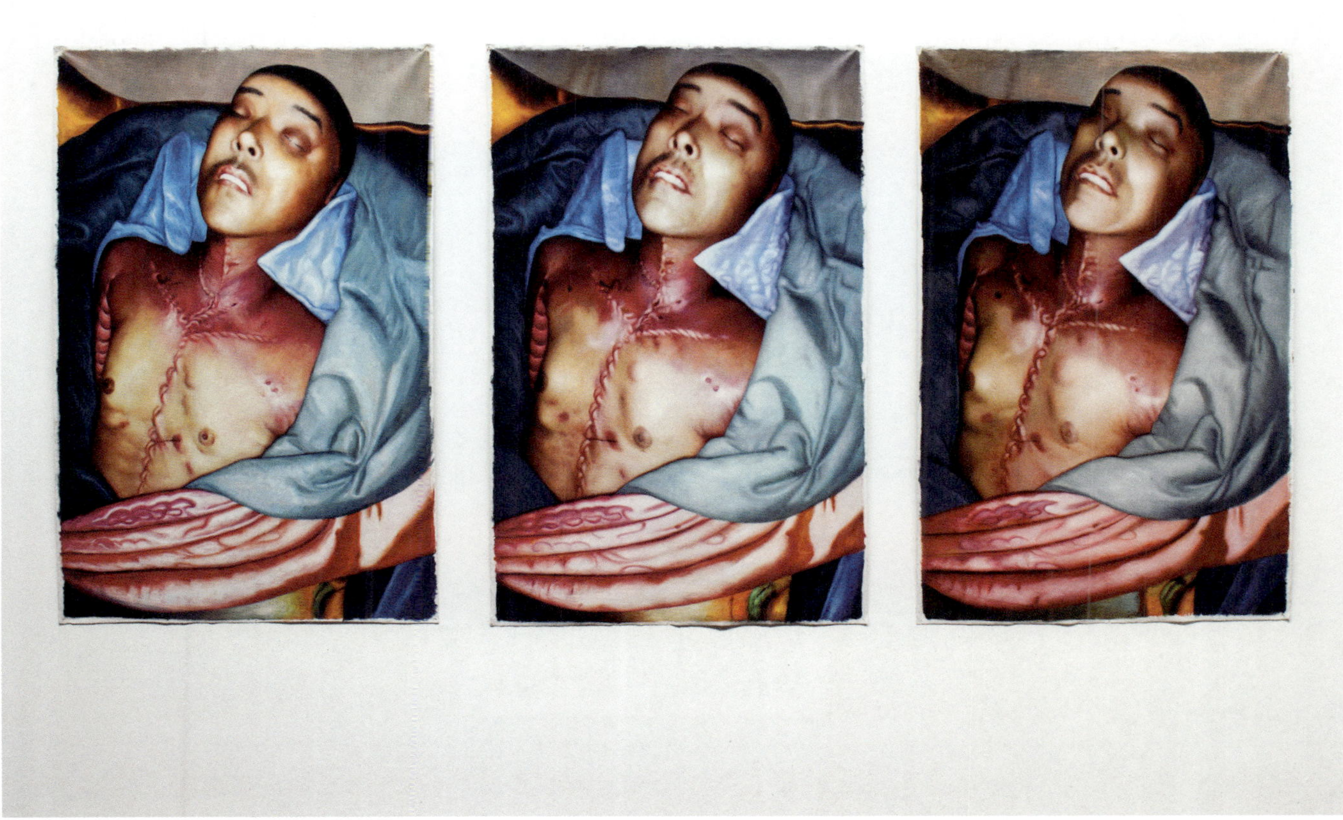

Elmgreen & Dragset

Michael Elmgreen, * 1961 in Copenhagen (DK);
Ingar Dragset, * 1969 in Trondheim (NO); live and work in Berlin (DE)

Prada Marfa, 2005

C-print, 160 × 204 cm

The artist duo Elmgreen & Dragset gained international fame for their monumental and sensational installations in public and art spaces. Their interventions take critical pokes at everyday notions of socioeconomic realities and aesthetic canons. By setting up hyperrealistic scenes, the artists surround the spectator with surreal, yet likely environments, that interrogate the ambivalent interface of art and life, narration and reality. This could be observed in *The Collectors*, their contribution to the 53rd Venice Biennale, and also in their solo exhibition *Celebrity – The One & the Many* (ZKM, 2010/2011) in which they presented a residential tower block, juxtaposed with an aristocratic ballroom, and thus drew attention to the disparities existing between the masses and the elites in present day society.

Prada Marfa is a white Prada store located in the middle of the Texas desert. Although the entrance is nonfunctional, shoes and bags from Prada's 2005 fall collection are on display in the boutique's windows. To achieve a perfect replica, Miuccia Prada provided the goods, the right to reproduce the brand logo and even gave design instructions. *Prada Marfa* addresses today's commodity culture and also plays with contemporary American art history. As a lonely, permanent luxury store in Texas' desolate landscape, it encompasses traditional avant-garde features and can thus be considered a true example of global contemporary Pop-Land art. (SG)

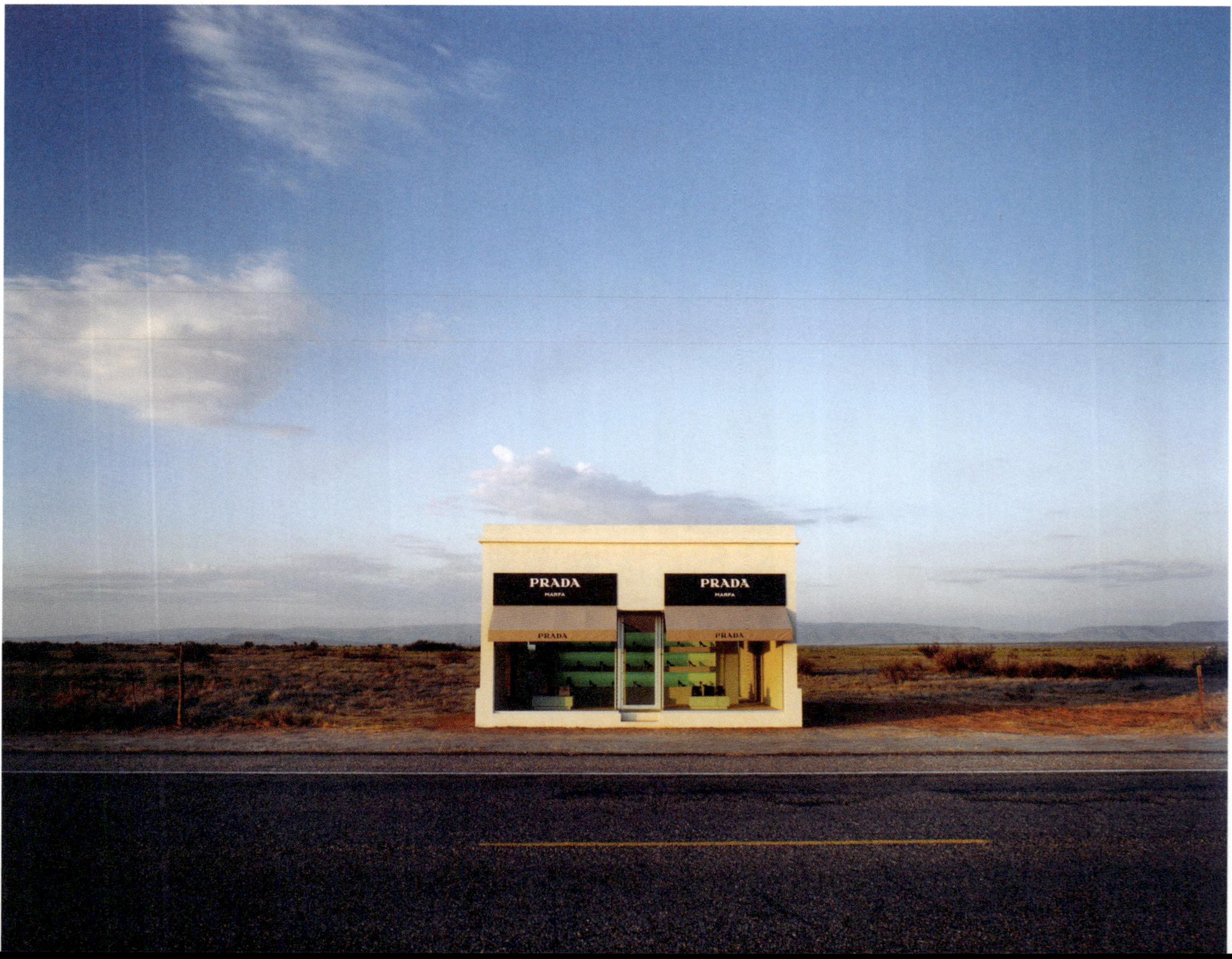

Antonia Hirsch

* 1968 in Frankfurt am Main (DE), lives in Vancouver (CA) and Berlin (DE)

ARTnews Top 200, 2004

23 carat gold on paper, 102 × 67 cm

Historically, the map of the world plays an ambivalent role; it is used both to inform and to exercise power. On its surface, regions coalesce into a unity, and without it, international exchange - whether of ideas or commodities - would be impossible. In parallel, a world map confirms the world order that conforms to the ideas of the cartographers who made it: borders are drawn, regions are named and set in relation to each other, both symbolically and in terms of power politics.

In her series *World Map Project*, Antonia Hirsch addresses the map as an often random graphic abstraction of the world, which at the same time controls economic and social realities. For her artwork *ARTnews Top 200*, she used a list of the most important art collectors compiled by the U.S. journal *ARTnews* and made the size of the countries on the map proportional to the number of art collectors living in them, but mirrored and made of 23 carat gold leaf. The map thus created only depicts the world fragmentarily and distorted, although as an image of the commercially determined art market, it probably contains more truth than a map that depicts the world as an unfractured whole existing untouched by any political borders and differences between rich and poor. (JB)

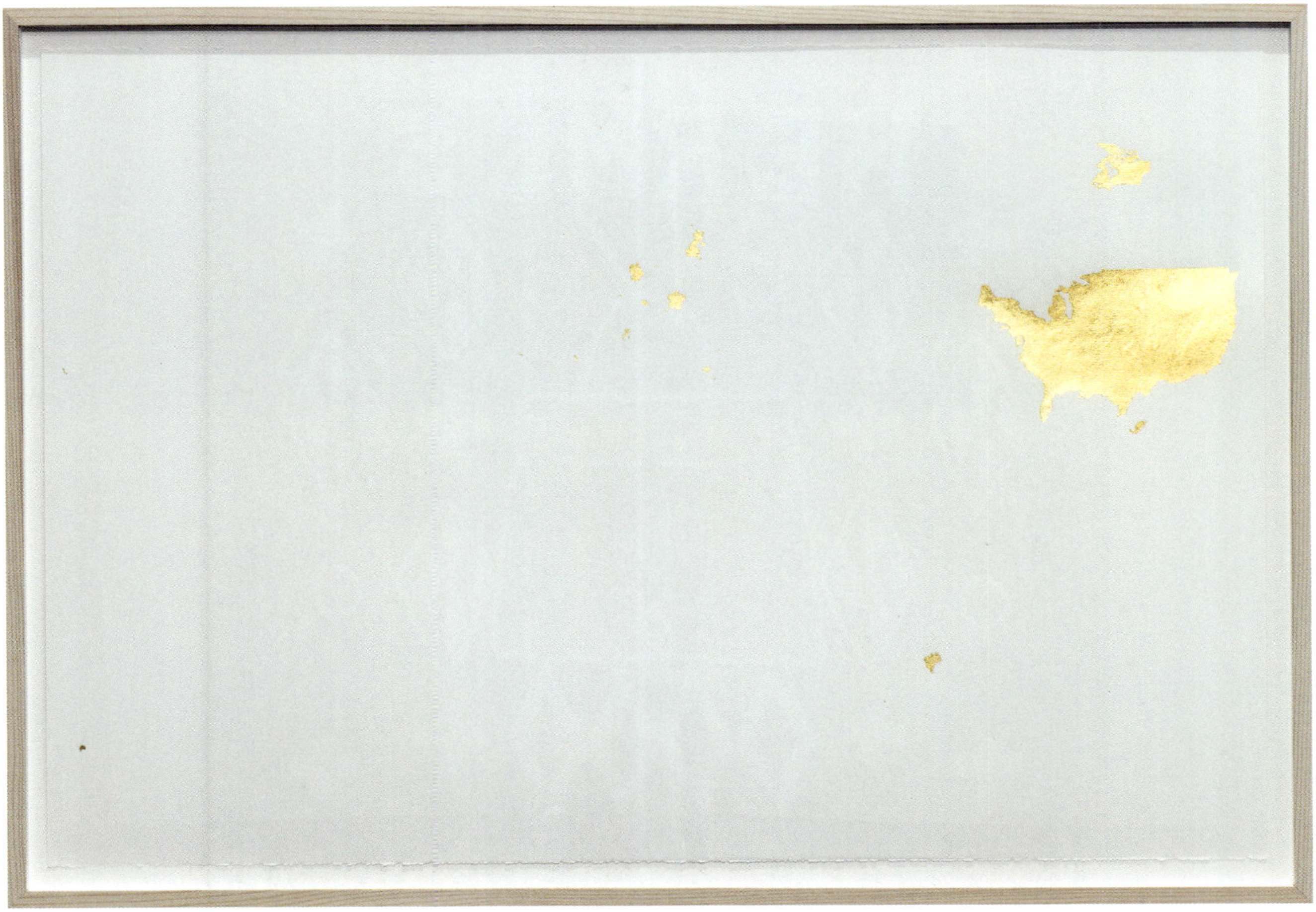

David Jablonowski

* 1982 in Bochum (DE), lives and works in Amsterdam (NL)

Kelly en Perles (3D) in Coop. With Cameroonian Artist, 2011

Hermès scarf, sound system (iPod, loudspeaker), aluminum, 64 × 68 × 3 cm

Through sculptural arrangements and film David Jablonowski analyzes the mechanisms of communication and language in contemporary visual culture. *Kelly en Perles (3D) in coop. with Cameroonian Artist*, presents a fashion icon, a silk scarf by the old established French haute couture house Hermès, stretched over an aluminum plate and accompanied by sound. In 1997, Hermès chose "Africa" for its fashion and other products, it used this handmade beadwork embroidery design by a Cameroonian artist which features the motif of the iconic Kelly Bag. The design was printed with a 3-D effect on silk scarves for the Hermès winter collection. With slogans like "Africa. Earth and Mother," "Africa. Cradle of Humankind," and "Hommage à l'Afrique," accompanied by traditional "African drum music," Hermès' website marketed stylized notions of authenticity and ethnicity. Jablonowski reflects one of today's basic dialectics: the naive and bigoted longing of the Western world for the pure, natural, and authentic (and their commercial exploitation) versus the desire for luxury Western goods in developing countries, evidenced by practices like product piracy and the black market. With the title of his work Jablonowski underlines what the status of the "African artist" is: despite the global success of their products they remain anonymous, and seemingly limited to traditional handicrafts. (AM)

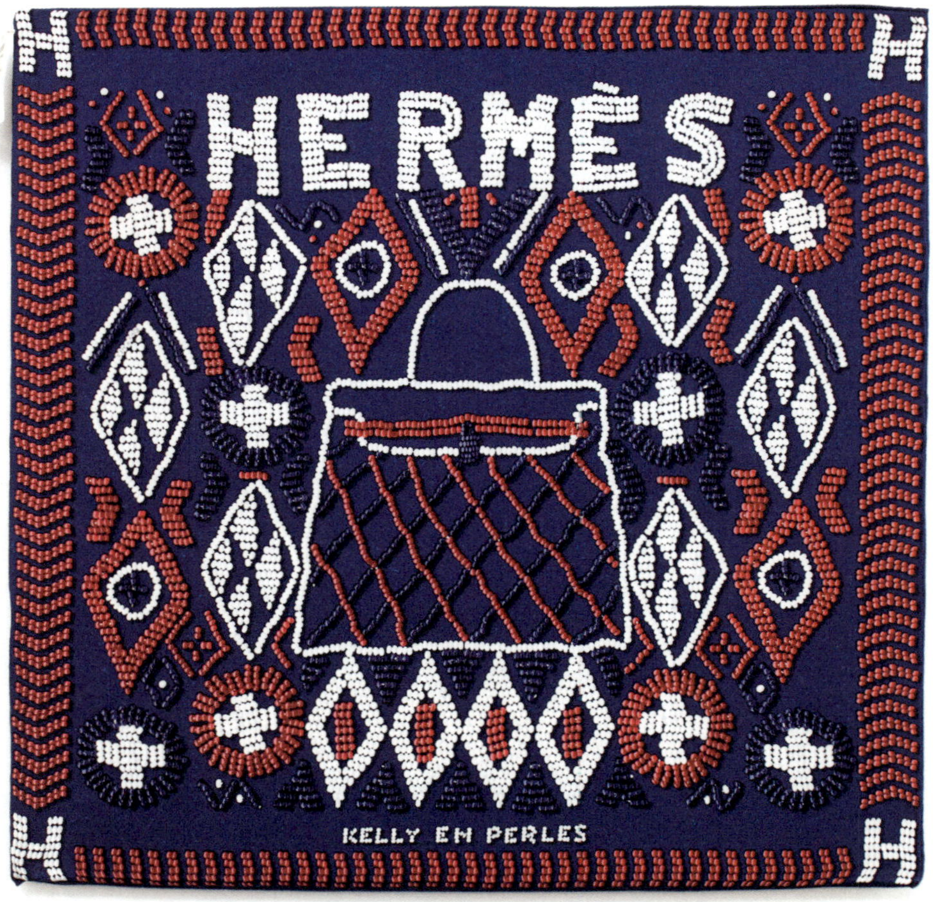

Melanie Jackson

* 1968 in Hollywood (UK), lives and works in London (UK)

From the Bank of Hell, 2008

Mixed-media installation, dimensions variable

The custom of burning paper replicas of valuable items during festivals as offerings for ancestors stems from traditional Chinese beliefs. Some of the imitations are industrially made and some by hand; the product range mirrors that of today's consumer society - from branded electronic goods to household items, but also banknotes with outrageous face values. These banknotes are commonly known as "Hell Bank Notes." The name's origin is attributed to a chain of mistranslations between Christian missionaries and Chinese people. Yet what would it mean in the age of global capitalism if there actually were a bank on the spiritual "other side" of our world with which we would have to reckon up our property at least symbolically? For her installation *From the Bank of Hell*, Melanie Jackson imported a vast quantity of paper objects, as would be stocked by a shop selling Chinese prayer articles. The symbolic religious value of the "faux" products merges with our clichéd idea of Asia as a cultural region of copies and forgeries, as well as with the cult status that is constructed around "genuine" luxury goods. For ultimately their value does not derive from their practical use value, but from the societal fictions that are woven around them. (JB)

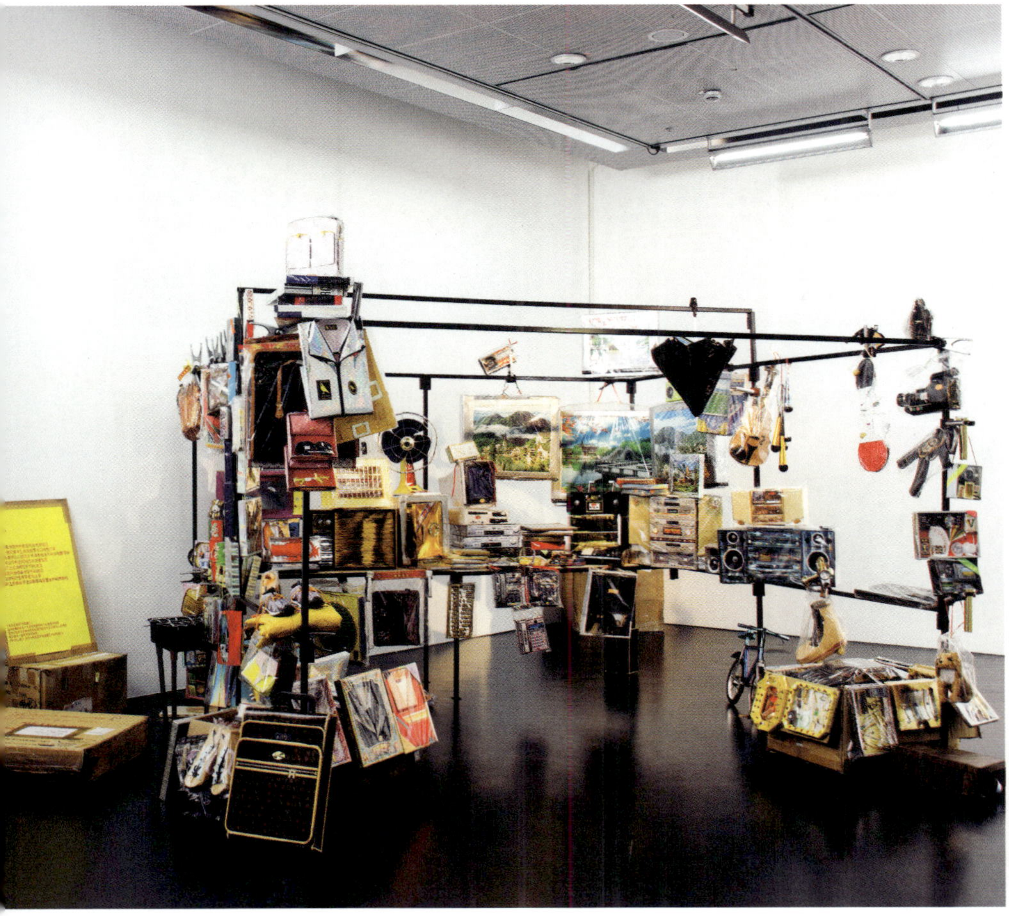

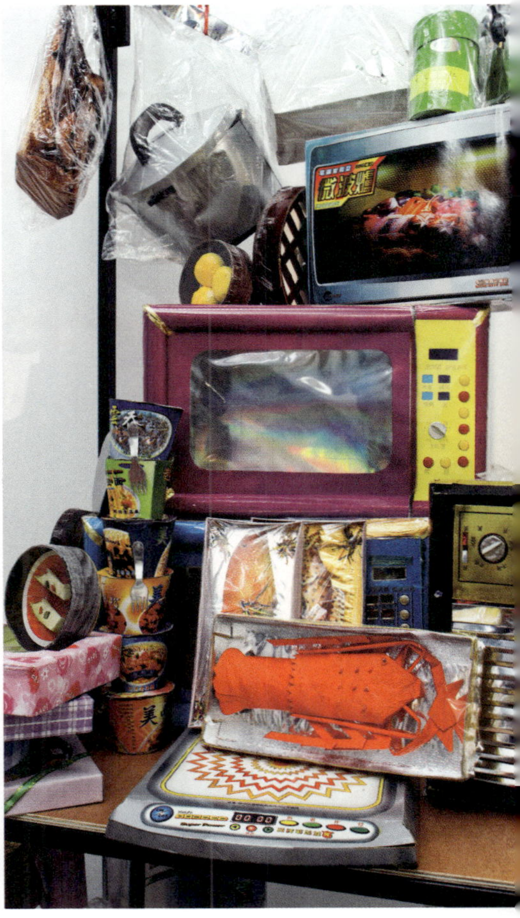

Christian Jankowski

* 1968 in Göttingen (DE), lives and works in Berlin, Hamburg (DE), and New York, NY (US)

Kunstmarkt TV, 2008

Video, color, sound, 45 min

In capitalism, everything is simultaneously a product and a myth: everything must be translatable into monetary value, but has to offer something else in addition that appeals directly to our feelings like the promise of happiness, security, or success. This internal conflict - having to be at the same time both (ex-)changeable and unique - is exceptionally dramatic in contemporary art. Artworks have ideational meanings, which only develop within a web of aesthetic, political, and art historical references. However, artworks also possess a market value, which is assigned to them by means of fashions and personae that are just as fleeting.

The ideational and the market value of art thus appear to belong to two different worlds between which the work of art switches sides like a double agent. In Christian Jankowski's *Kunstmarkt TV* [Art Market TV] the absurdity of this system is brought to light: For the Art Cologne fair in 2008, the artist hired professional salespersons to sell art live to the paying (TV) audience. At first the relocation of trading in art to the "low-brow" format of a home shopping channel seems amusing; however, when John Dahlke and Khadra Sufi randomly use material values, artist biographies, or their own feelings as their sales pitch when looking at art, it seems that only their rhetoric differs from those who operate in the "genuine" art system. Further, the work leaves behind it the uncomfortable question, whether the "special" feature of an art object as a trading commodity actually differs very much from the "special" feature of a vacuum cleaner or an attachment for cordless screwdrivers. (JB)

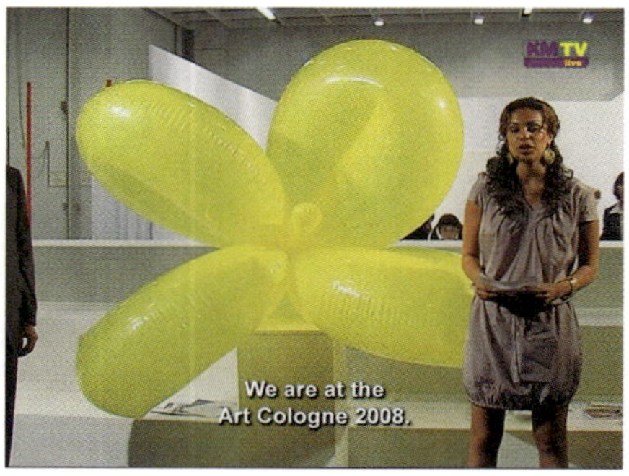

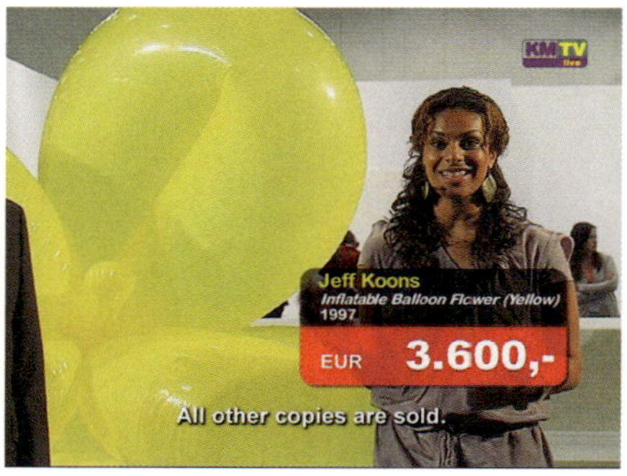

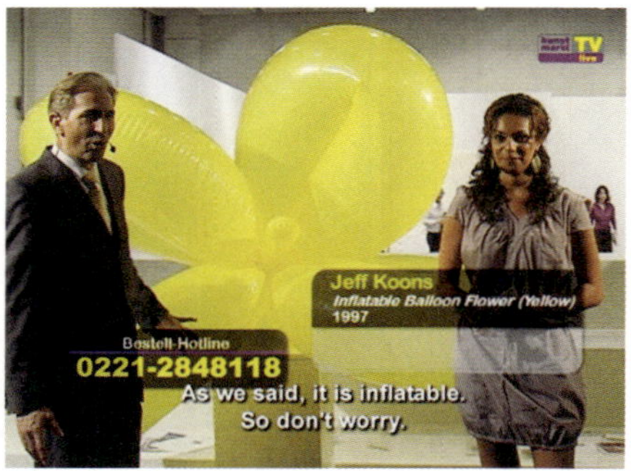

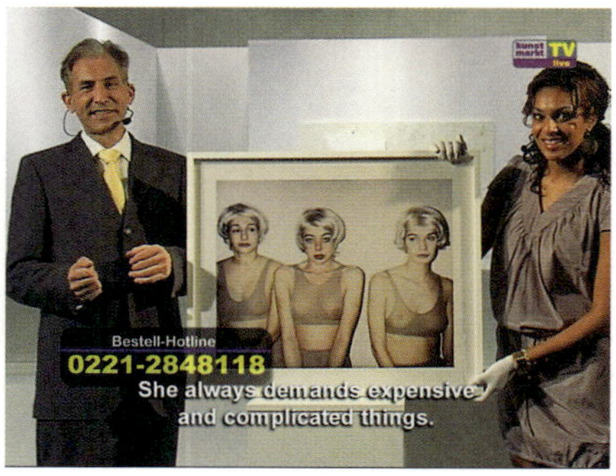

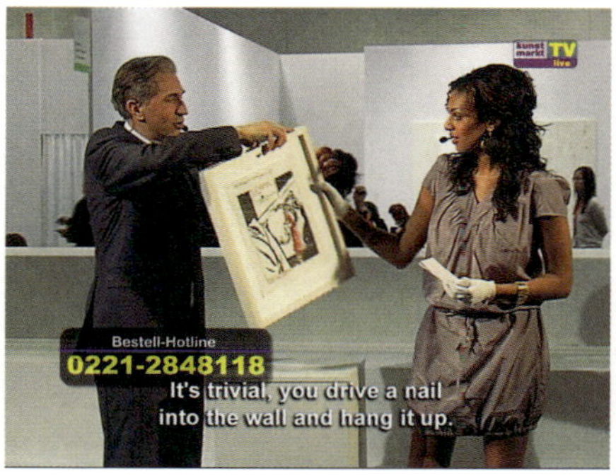

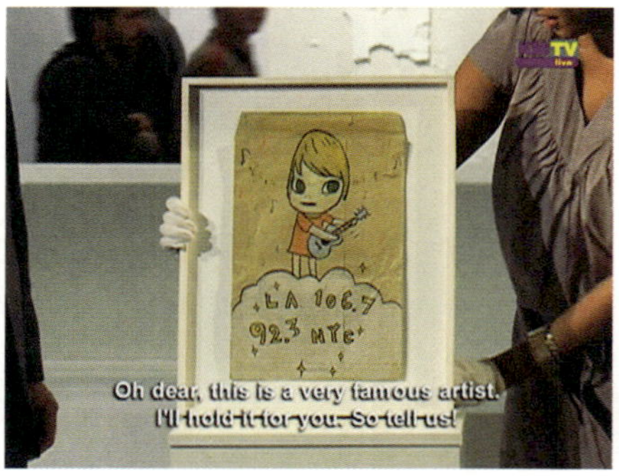

Surasi Kusolwong

* 1965 in Ayutthaya (TH), lives and works in Bangkok (TH)

50% OFF BOOKS (Never Mind Kapital = Never Mind Kunst), 2011

Performance

One Pound Turbo Market (You'll have a good time), 2006

Video, color, sound, 15:04 min,
billboard, wall color, dimensions variable

There has been much discussion about art as a strategy to transform something worthless into something valuable; this statement is one of the most common accusations leveled at modern and contemporary art. That there are creative aspirations involved in creating a social situation in which goods and values are exchanged, is often overlooked. In recent years, Surasi Kusolwong has organized markets at various locations, where the event of buying and selling becomes a public performance. The cynical interpretation that contemporary art is only ever thought about in terms of economics, is countered by Kusolwong's performance which foregrounds the market as a spectacle in which the artist - as DJ and animateur - sells the tawdry goods at one price. The act of exchange is greater than the sum of the parts that we take home from the market, and the participation of the audience, so often demanded by contemporary art, becomes ironically ambiguous. Whether Kusolwong's markets point up the culture of globalized capitalism, which also turns museums into places for bargain hunting, or whether they rather celebrate the social event and its specific aesthetics, is a question that remains unanswered. Equally, it is not possible to ascertain whether the beautiful arrangement of the objects follows the logic of shop displays or an artistic installation.

In addition to a documentation of the *One Pound Turbo Market (You'll have a good time)* at the Tate Modern, Kusolwong showed the performance *50% OFF BOOKS (Never Mind Kapital = Never Mind Kunst)* in the exhibition. At the opening he sold catalogs by artists important for his own work at a discount price. (JB)

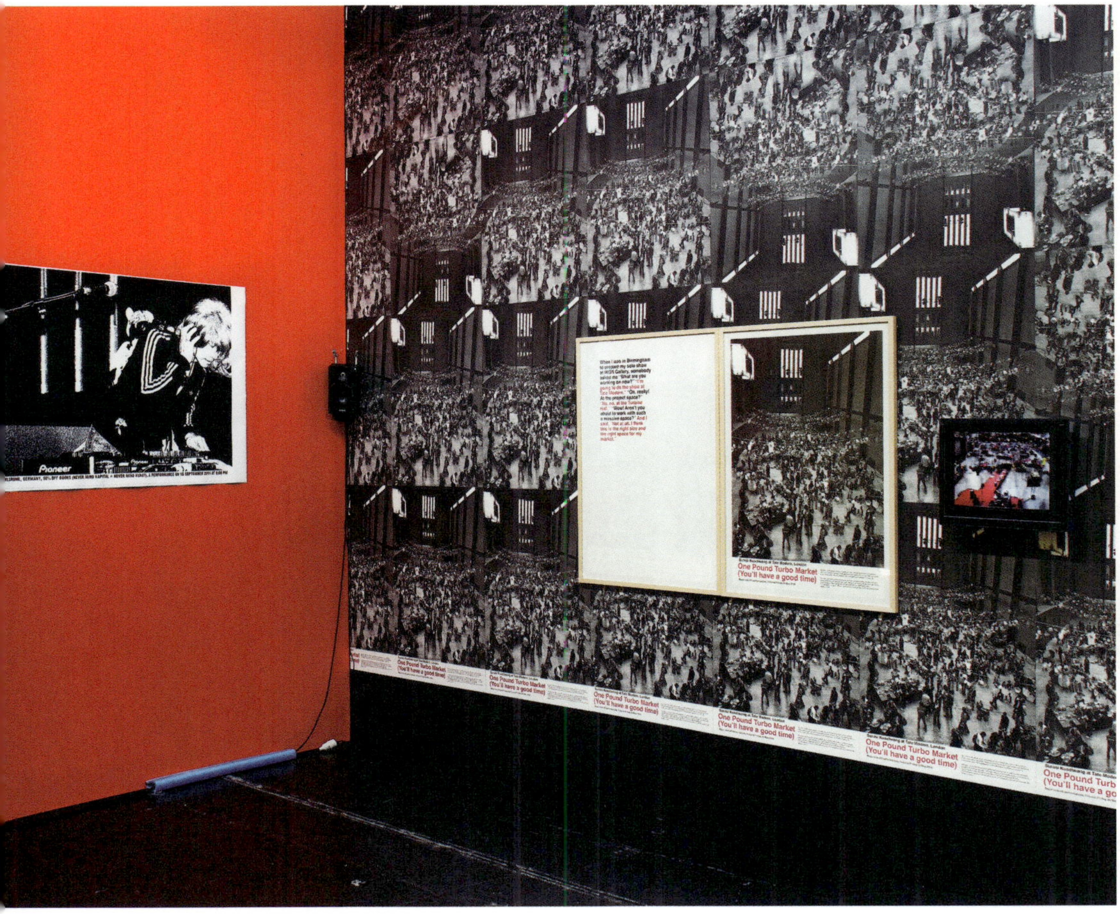

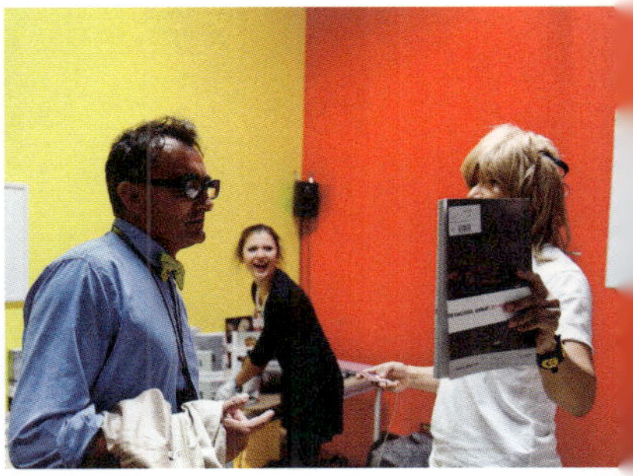

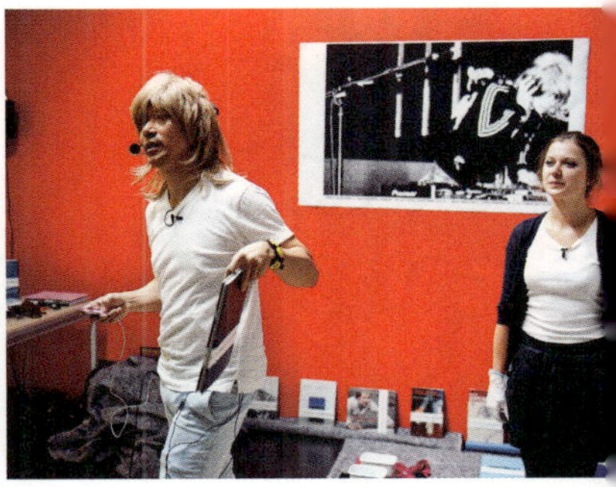

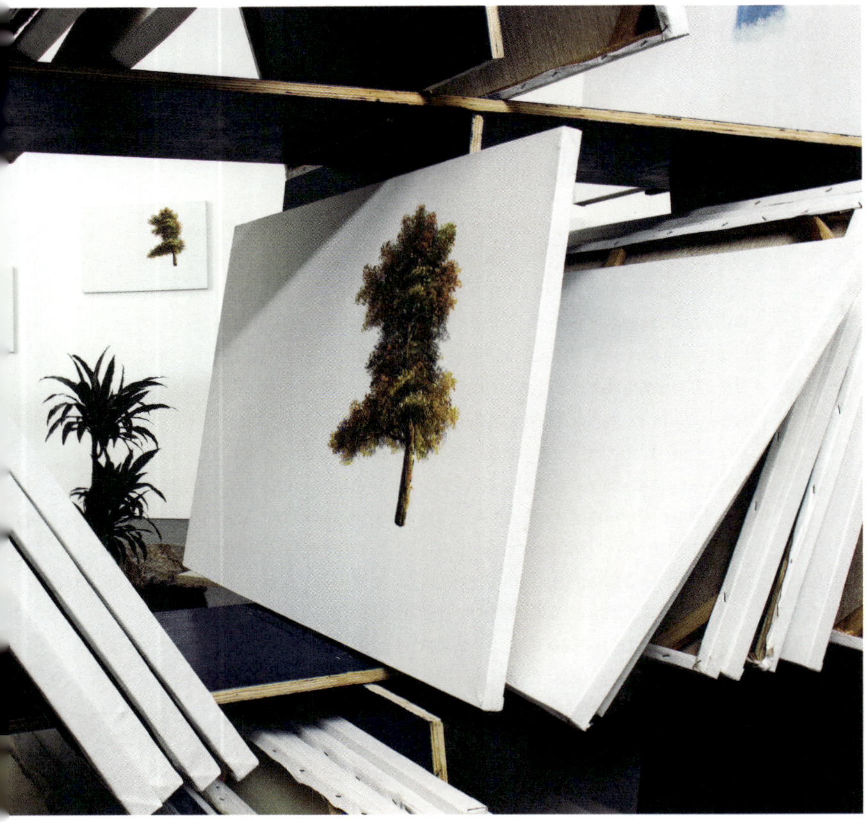

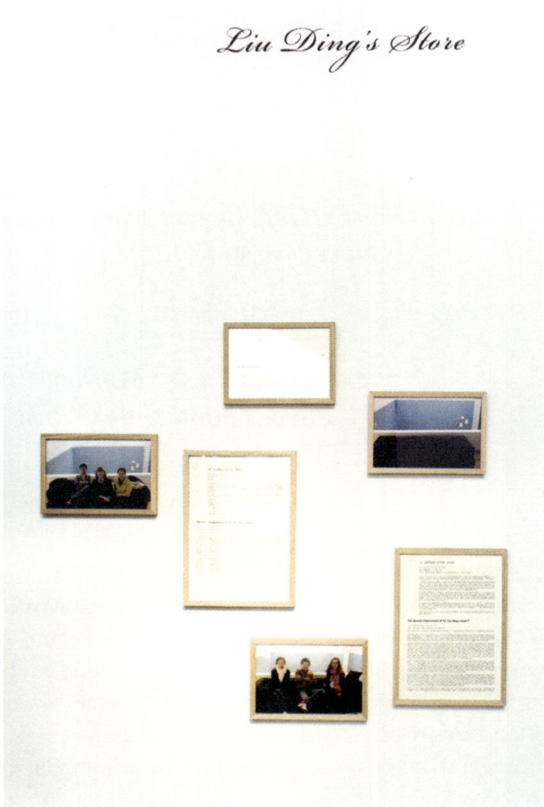
Liu Ding's Store

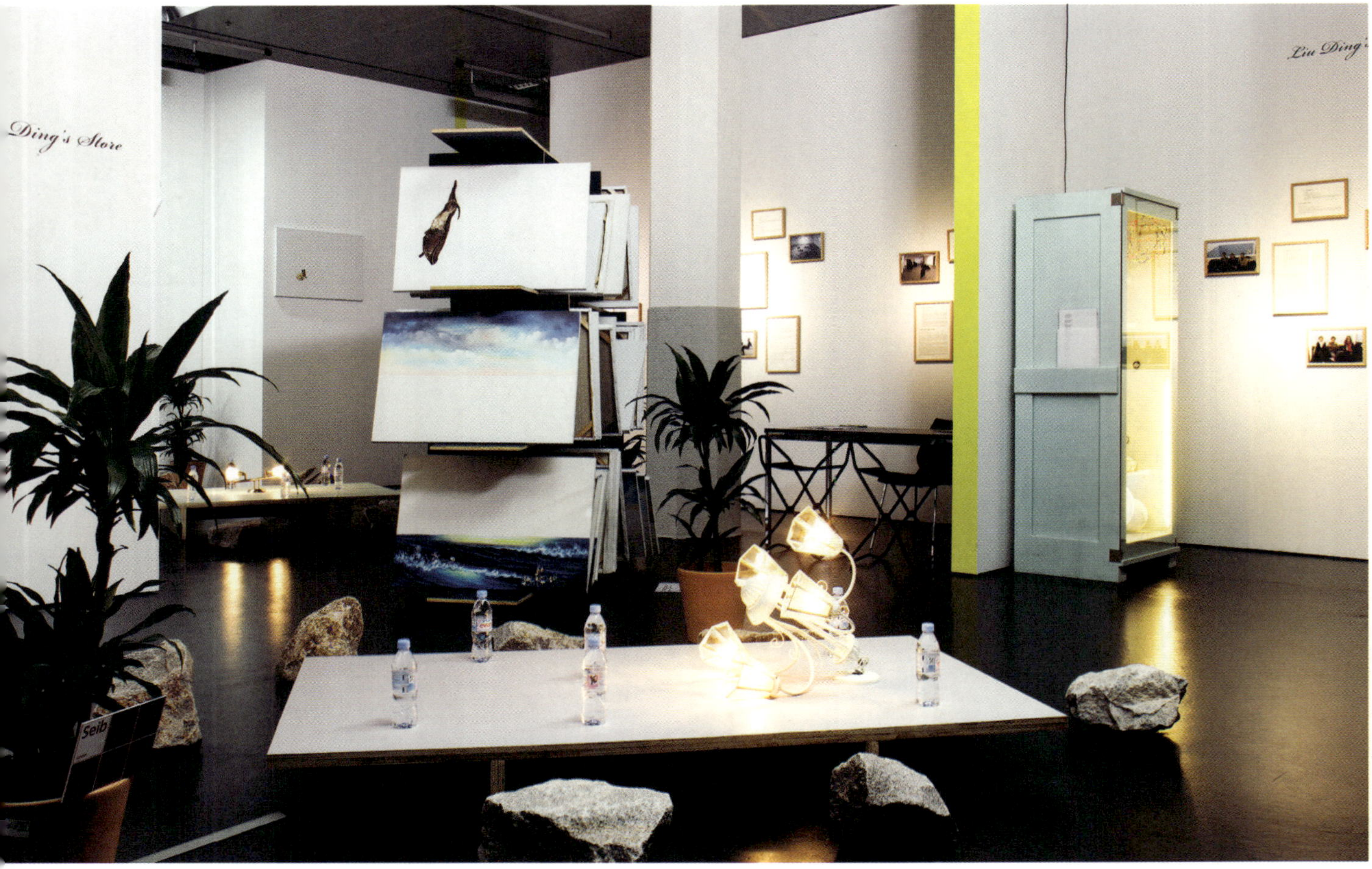
Ding's Store

Liu Ding

* 1976 in Changzhou, Jiangsu (CN), lives and works in Beijing (CN)

Liu Ding's Store comprises 4 projects:

Take Home and Make Real the Priceless in Your Heart, 2010/2011
Mixed media (wooden shelf, 52 paintings, oil on canvas),
215 × 40 × 244 cm (shelf),
60 × 90 cm (paintings)

Conversations, 2010/2011
C-print, paper, frames,
dimensions variable

Friendship, 2010
a) *No. 2*, 2010
Wood, paint, stones, plant, terracotta pot, lamp,
dimensions variable (wooden table 23.6 × 200 × 110 cm)
b) *No. 4*, 2010
Wood, paint, stones, plant, terracotta pot, lamp,
dimensions variable (wooden table 15.6 × 200 × 110 cm)

The Utopian Future of Art, Our Reality, 2009
a) *A Container of Experience*, 2009
Mixed media,
200 × 80 × 60 cm (cabinet)
b) *The Perfect Sphere*, 2009
Mixed media,
200 × 80 × 60 cm (cabinet)

Liu Ding's Store, 2008 (ongoing)

Mixed-media installation

Liu Ding's work as an artist and curator investigates the various mechanisms and rules of the art system. *Liu Ding's Store* was launched in 2008 as an ongoing project developing new lines of work. In addition to selling works online (www.liudingstore.com) it employs a functional economic model - a shop - to establish a platform for thoughts and discussions about the creation of value. *Liu Ding's Store* frequently makes appearances and sales in a variety of contexts and situations, from social and cultural events to art exhibitions. Artifact, production, pricing, presentation, marketing, trade, circulation, and the human relationships resulting from such processes comprise the basic components of this shop. At the same time, each of these elements is the platform on which the artist projects his sense of value, along with his reflections on and discussion about this phenomenon. *Liu Ding's Store* began by posing questions about the role of the artist and the production and circulation of artworks. He then went on to consider the relationship between artworks and various other types of objects, before extending its scope to understanding the full range of production relationships in the art system, as well as cultivating a sense of value in spiritual and intellectual space. To date, *Liu Ding's Store* has developed four product lines: *Take Home and Make Real the Priceless in Your Heart*, *The Utopian Future of Art, Our Reality*, *Conversations*, and *Friendship*. (CL)

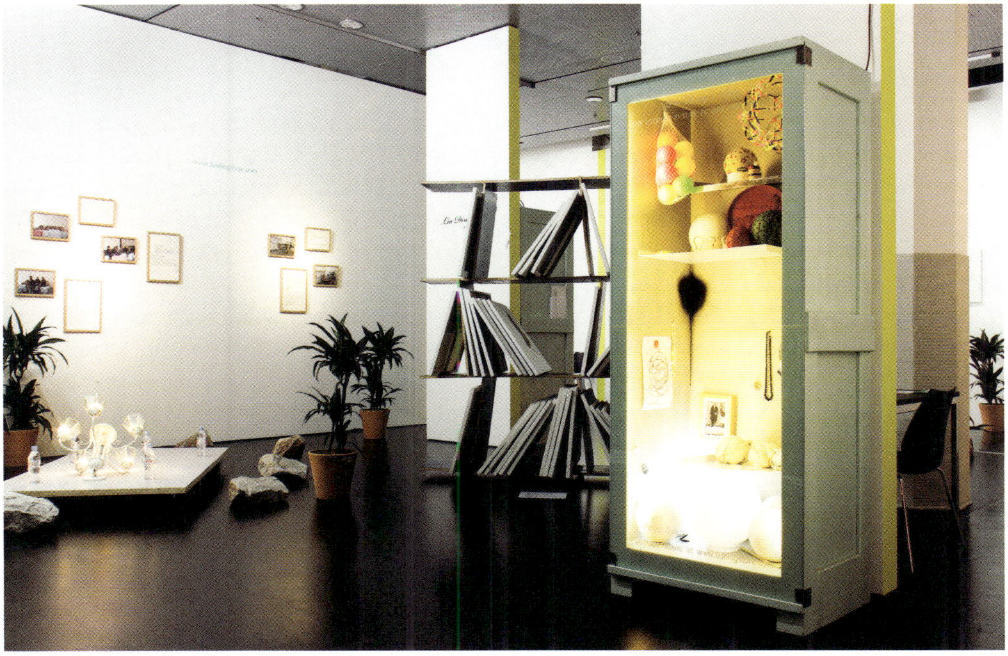

Navin Rawanchaikul

* 1971 in Chiang Mai (TH), lives and works in Fukuoka (JP) and Chiang Mai

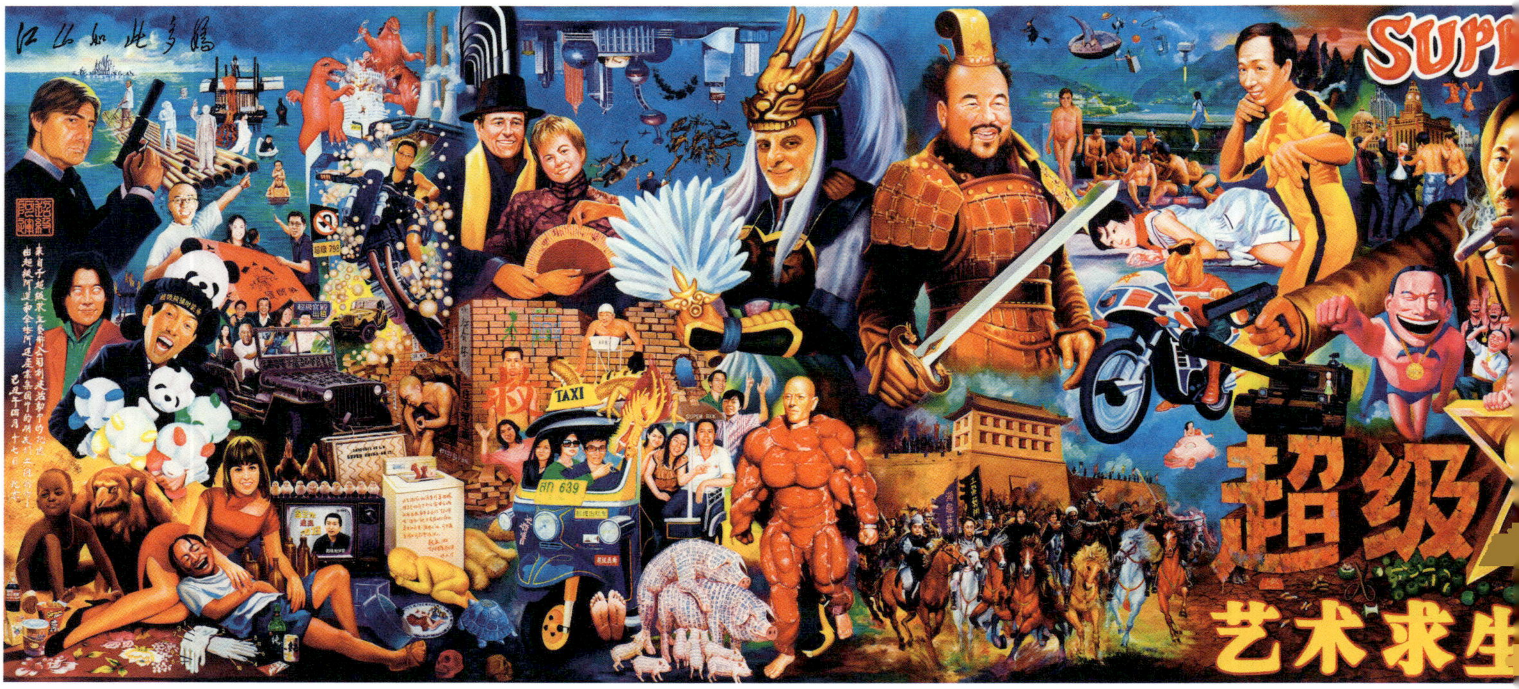

***SUPER CHINA!*, 2009**

Acrylic on canvas, 2.7 × 12.6 m

***Curator Man and Navin*, 2002**

Painted fiberglass, 60 × 45 × 175 cm (Curator Man),
75 × 70 × 158 cm (Old Navin)

With his dynamic and site-specific interventions and displays, Navin Rawanchaikul, who calls himself a "lonely son of diaspora and product of a globalized world," humorously interrogates a range of topics like cultural and national identity as well as their significance in today's internationalized art world. Developed under his company's label Navin Productions, Rawanchaikul's projects are conceived from the outset as joint collaborations in the interplay between everyday culture and the context of art, as well as between local conditions and the various influences of globalization.

With the large-format painting *SUPER CHINA!*, cast in the style typical of Bollywood billboards, Rawanchaikul portrays the power players of the Chinese art scene at a point in time when its meteoric ascendency is already in decline, and the dealers have long since been in the red. The humorous, exaggerated, almost propagandistic depiction of the actors in the Chinese art scene as heroes and superstars refers to a unique phenomenon often criticized in the West because of the connections between and reciprocal influence of art producers and the market. At the same time, this boom also includes an important emancipatory moment, since now, for the first time, a market for contemporary art independent of the Western art system has been established under the national label "China."

In *Curator Man and Navin*, Rawanchaikul presents the international art world as a construct of social relationships and a "networking community," where rivalries and dependencies rule, and various roles are fulfilled. While the curator who with hand luggage and mobile phone jets from one biennial to the next seems to have become the superstar of the "brave new (art) world," in this future scenario the slightly graying artist appears to have assumed a rather insignificant supporting role. Somewhat awkwardly, he nevertheless attempts to force his card onto this very busy person. Art now seems to have almost disappeared behind its marketing, dissemination, classification, and interpretation. (AM)

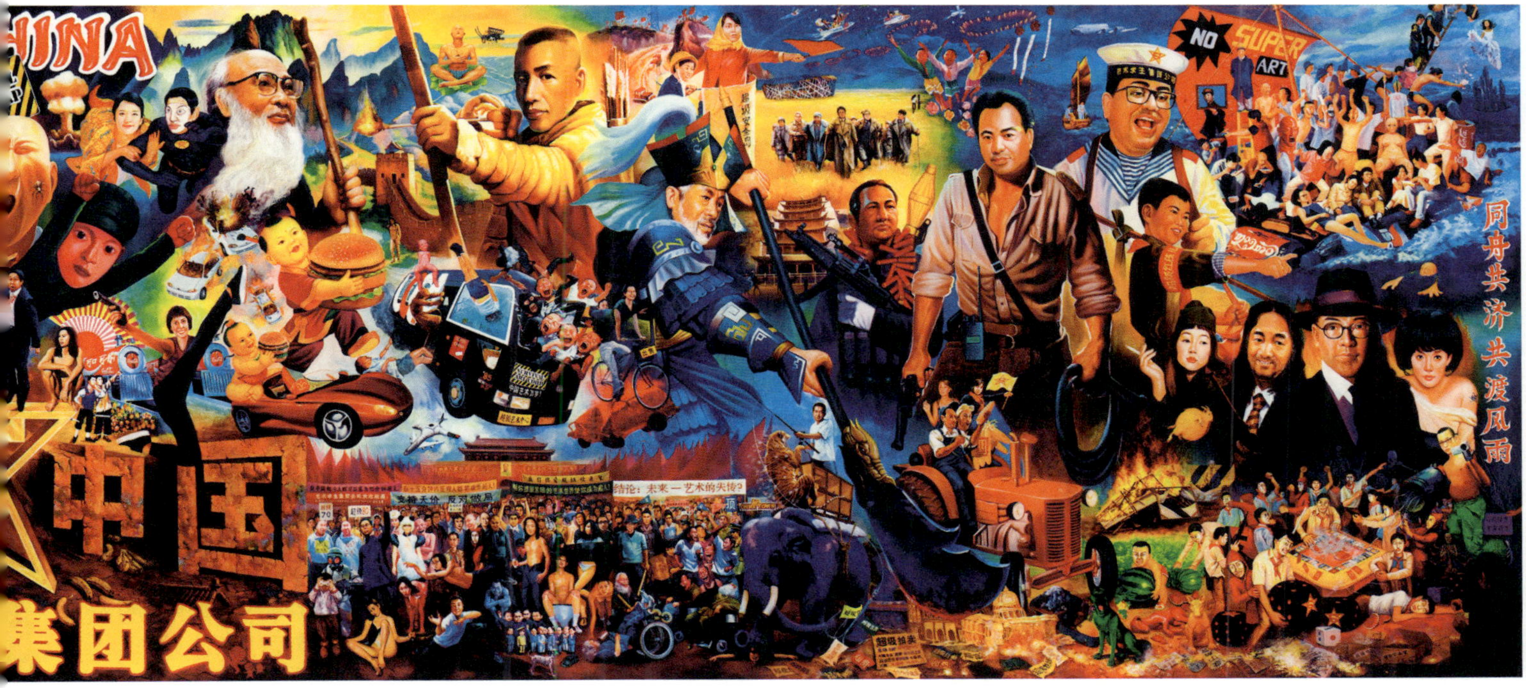
NO
SUPER
ART
同舟共济共渡风雨
中国
集团公司

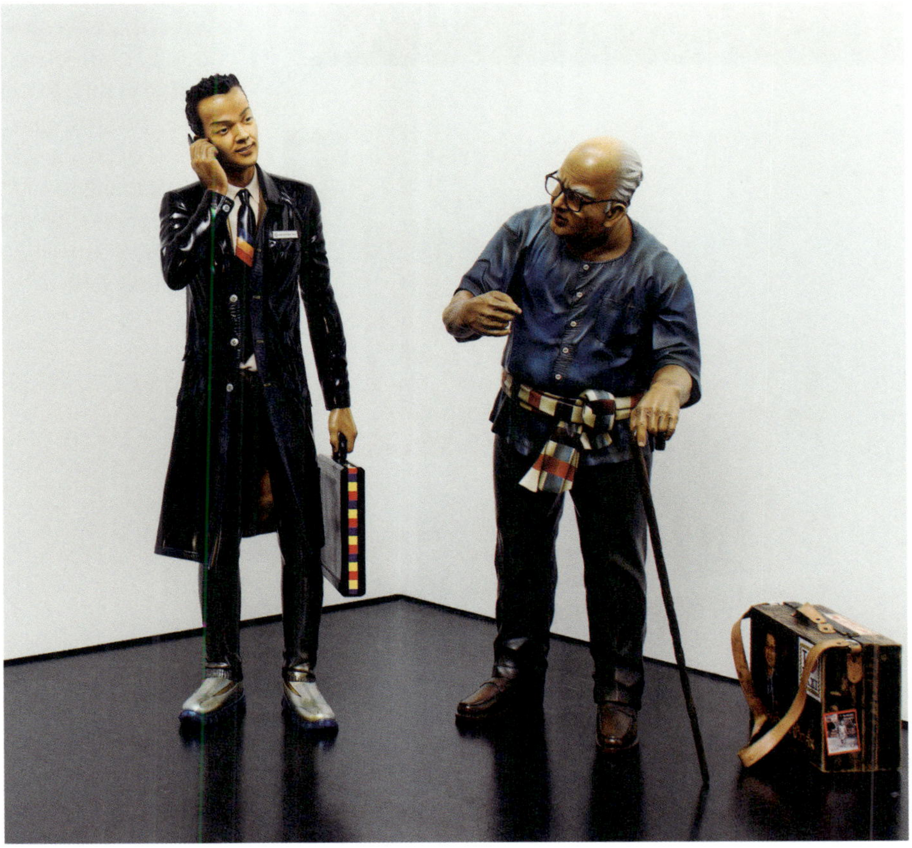

Gabriele di Matteo

* 1957 in Naples (IT), lives and works in Milan (IT)

China Made in Italy, 2008

Installation, 34 paintings, dimensions variable

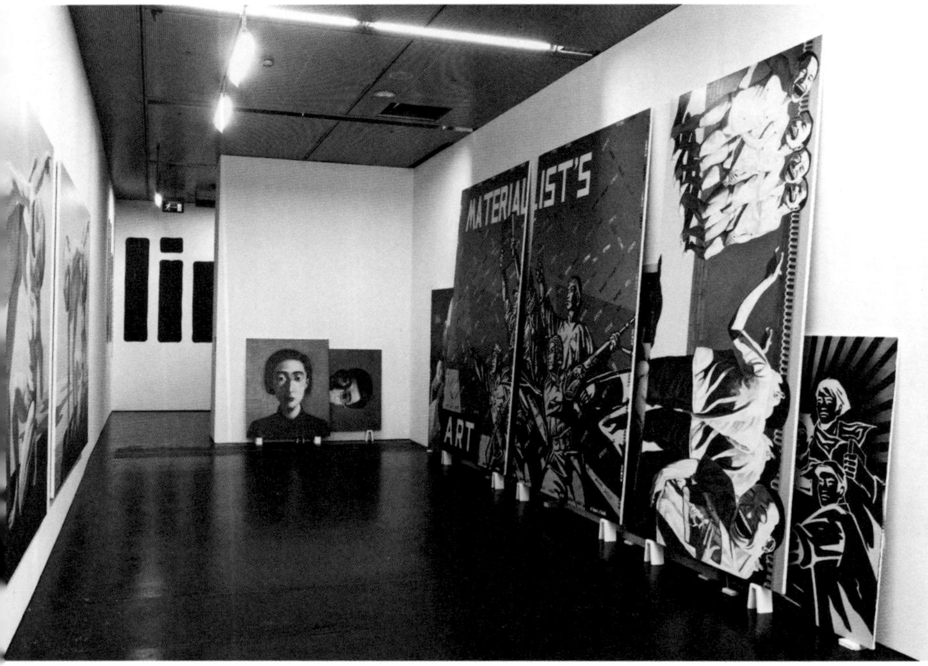

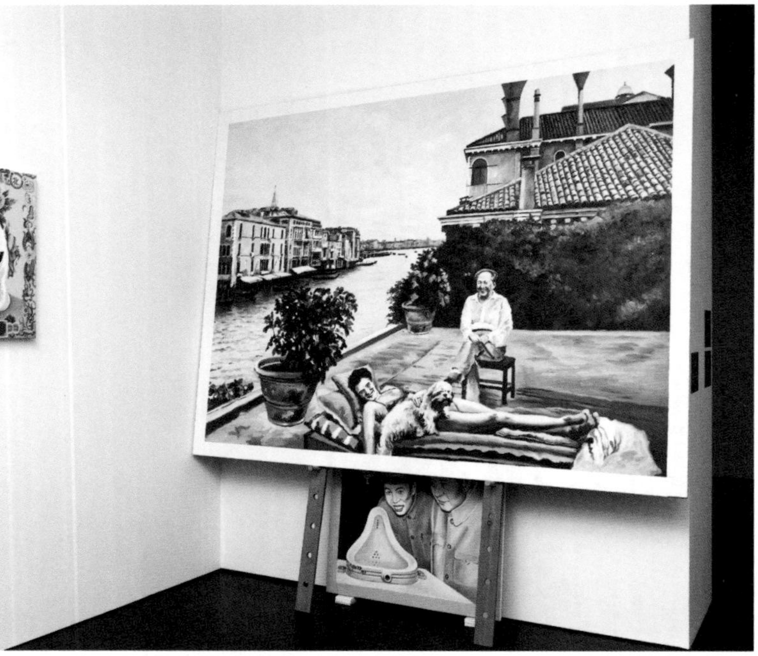

Gabriele di Matteo's work as a painter highlights the tensions between copy and original, as well as the notion of the author in contemporary art. His series of paintings consistently redefine the shift from conceptual creation to material execution. In *Quadro di Famiglia* [Family Portrait] (2011), the artist commissioned expert copyists from Naples to reproduce twenty commercial copies of Velázquez's masterpiece *Las Meninas*, while in the series *Jackson Pollock, Une vie, éléments et documents* (2009) he transformed several photographs depicting Pollock's private life into paintings.

Besides exploring art history in his objects, subjects, and strategies, di Matteo's *China Made in Italy* addresses the issue of (re)production from a global and political perspective. This series of paintings consists of black-and-white copies of paintings by Chinese superstar artists currently valued at millions, but in this case executed by Italian artisans. Gabriele di Matteo's works shake up our common conceptions of originality, branding, and luxury, while at the same time point out the accelerated dynamics currently reshaping the global art world. (SG)

Christa Sommerer & Laurent Mignonneau

Christa Sommerer, * 1964 in Gmunden (AT);
Laurent Mignonneau, * 1967 in Angoulême (FR); live and work in Linz (AT)

The Value of Art (Unruhige See), 2010

Media installation, Painting, 92 × 85 cm

Christa Sommerer & Laurent Mignonneau produce innovative interactive works of art, which establish "connections between artificial life and genetic art." Initial international recognition came with the installation *Interactive Plant Growing* (1992), a milestone in the newly emerging media art, now part of the ZKM_Collection. The installation places the audience within a dark environment, where digital plants grow in response to how much the visitor caresses their physical counterparts.

The Value of Art (Unruhige See) marks the beginning of a new project that investigates the relationship between the exhibition and the market value of a work of art. For the realization of the work the artists purchased a painting at an auction house in Vienna for 450 Euro and subsequently transformed it into an interactive installation. Sensors installed within the painting measure the amount of time a viewer stands in front of it and, through this, estimate the amount of attention and appreciation the artwork receives. At the same time, an integrated printer produces a bill indicating the painting's current price based on purchase and production costs and the continually increasing exhibition value. The artists see the new series as "anthropophagic works where we buy art work at auction houses as ready-mades, cannibalize them and equip them with our sensor technology and price calculation unit, so as to transparently recalculate their monetary values based on the artists' and audiences' time and attention." (SG)

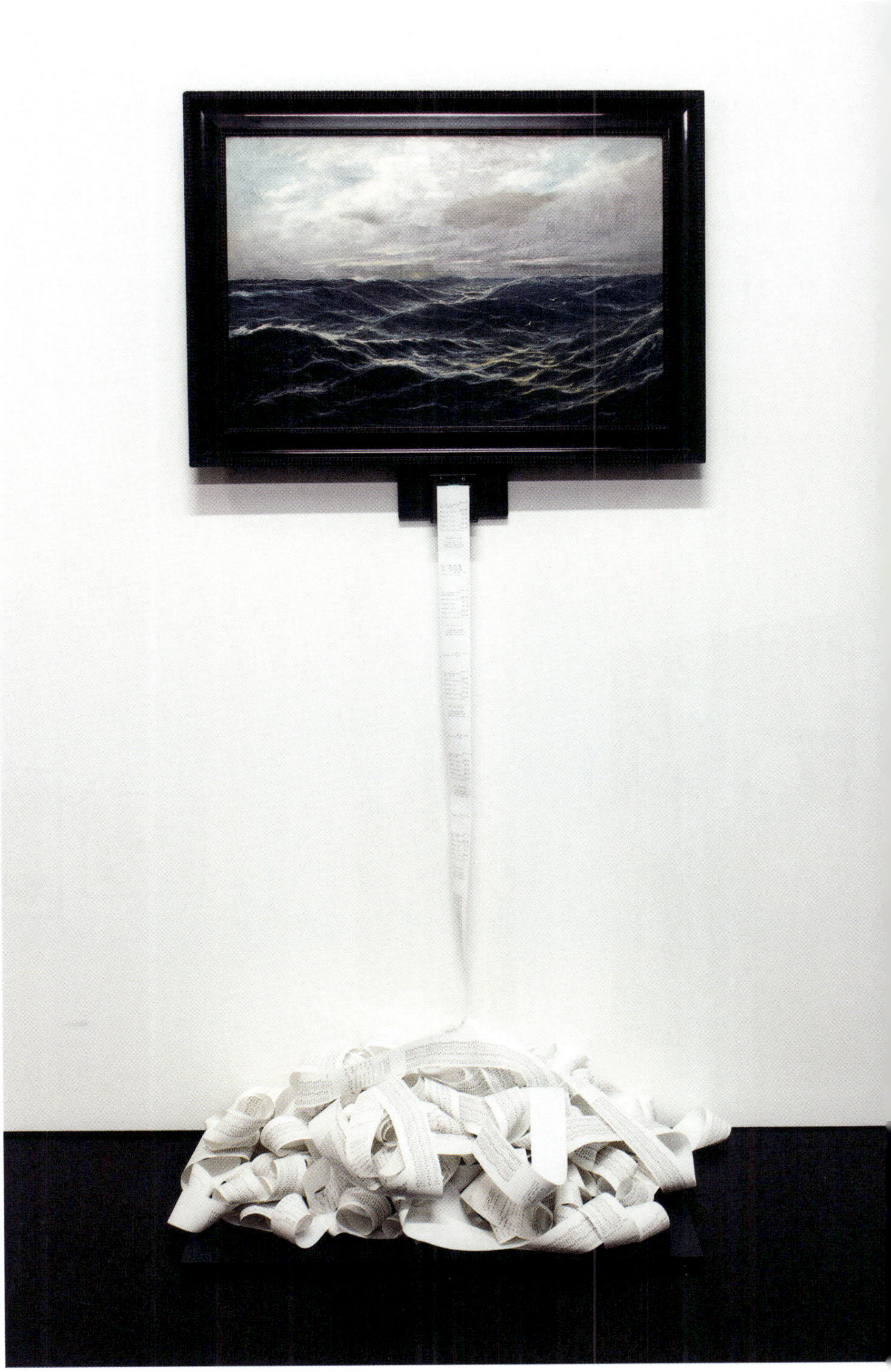

SOSka group

Founded in 2005 by Mykola Ridnyi, * 1985 in Kharkov (UA);
Ganna Kriventsova, * 1985 in Evpatoria (UA);
Serhiy Popov, * 1978 in Komsomolsk (UA); live and work in Kharkov

Barter, 2007

3 C-prints, 100 × 150 cm each (on aluminum Dibond), 4 C-prints,
50 × 70 cm each (framed), video, color, sound, 6:50 min

In a farmer's yard, a young man puts together a small gallery of artwork prints by famous artists – amongst them darlings of the art scene such as Neo Rauch, Roy Lichtenstein, Andy Warhol, Cindy Sherman, Komar and Melamid, and Chuck Close – and attempts to trade them with the villagers for various products. Judging by the video images, the location of these events is in a rural area. To be precise, this takes place in a small village in the Ukraine, in Prokhody.

Barter, the title of the video work means to exchange goods or services for other goods or services without using money. Whereas globally the prices for modern and contemporary art appear to skyrocket – the financial crisis of 2007 only briefly slowed this price development – a work by Cindy Sherman here is worth as much as a chicken. A Close and a Lichtenstein blonde are auctioned off together for three dozen eggs simply because the artist's self-portrait reminds the buyer of her deceased husband and the blonde looks a bit like her granddaughter. Warhol's famous *Campbell's Soup Cans* arouse no interest at all. With great humor the video shows works of art, which actually command the highest prices on the art market, in a rural setting where art is not important and the works are "only pictures" and, therefore, simple trading goods. The trade on the farm points on the one hand to the basic mechanisms of the art market, under whose auspices the art system produces stars and determines the value of the art. On the other, *Barter* also shows the limitations of the historiography of art, which (not only in Prokhody) can scarcely uphold any claim to universal validity. (KB)

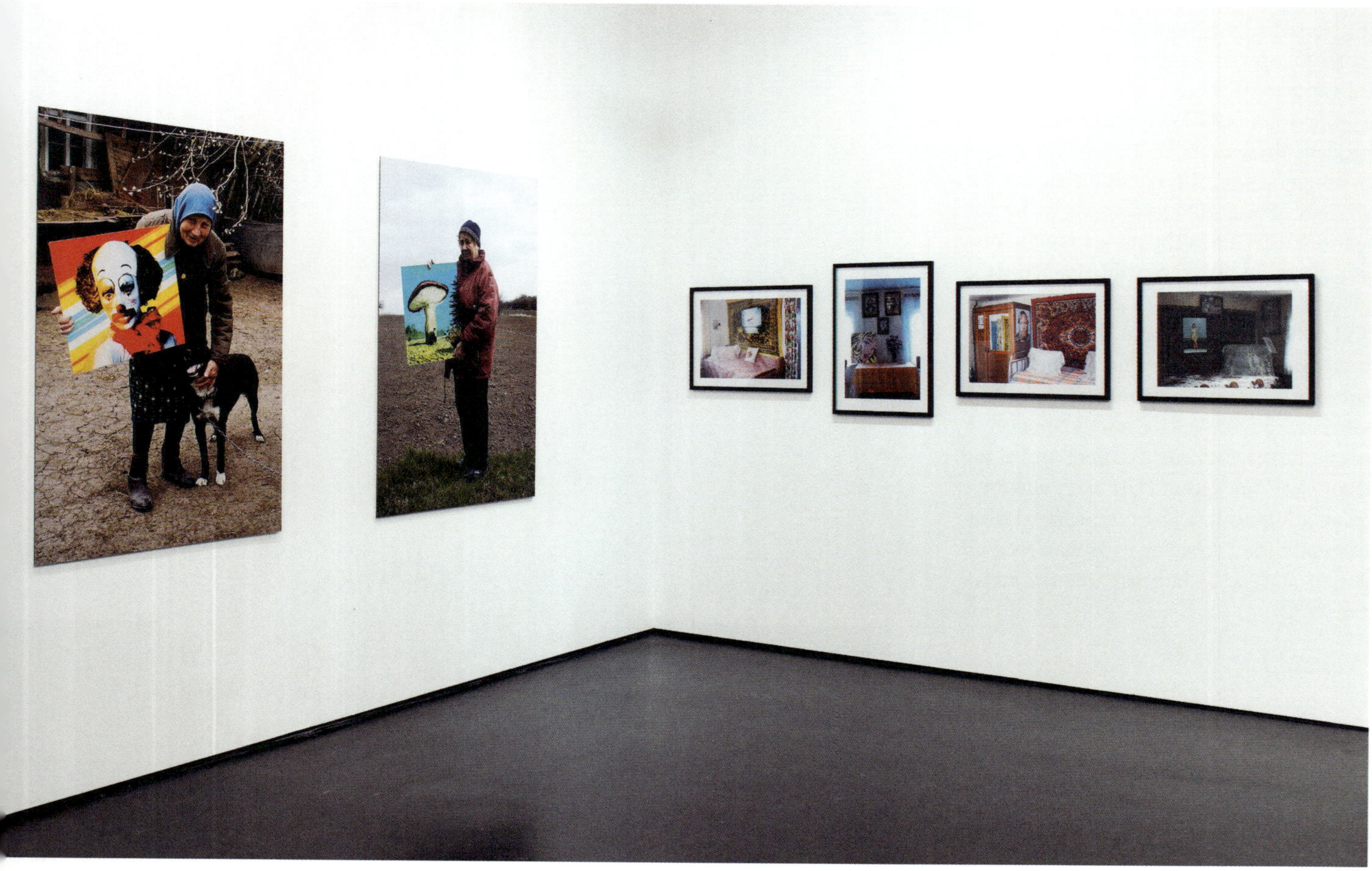

SUPERFLEX

Bjørnstjerne Christiansen, * 1969 in Copenhagen (DK); Jakob Fenger, * 1968 in Copenhagen;
Rasmus Nielsen, * 1969 in Copenhagen; live and work in Copenhagen

Free Beer & Counter-Game Strategies / Art World Machine, 2007

Interactive installation for two or more players, dimensions variable,
(part of the series *Counter-Game Strategies*)

The interactive installation *Free Beer & Counter-Game Strategies / Art World Machine* is a skill-based game, which is a parody of the art market. One of the players (the "artist") puts handmade masterpieces (represented by potatoes) into a pipe. The other players (the "collectors") try to purchase these works symbolically by smashing the potatoes with a hammer. Playfully, SUPERFLEX act out relationships of power and principles of the art world. The cultural product (the potato) becomes the property of the collectors, and is at the same time destroyed. Disregarded, the pieces of potato spread out all over the room rot. The work is part of the *Counter-Game Strategies*, a series of seven installations, which question and thematically vary the market principles of cultural production, preservation, and perception.

The Danish artist collective SUPERFLEX, which was founded in 1993 in Copenhagen, describes its projects as tools, which are designed to contribute actively to changing the prevailing economic methods of production. To this end, the tools they have developed can be used and modified by other groups or people. They call their artistic strategy "social-economic integration": art as cultural intervention with the goal of supporting alternative economies as well as democratic conditions of production and self-organization. Amongst other things, SUPERFLEX have developed an alternative production method for power generation (*Supergas*, 1997), an internet TV channel (*Superchannel*, 1999), and also fairly produced and license-free products (*Guarana Power*, 2003; *Free Beer*, 2004). (EA)

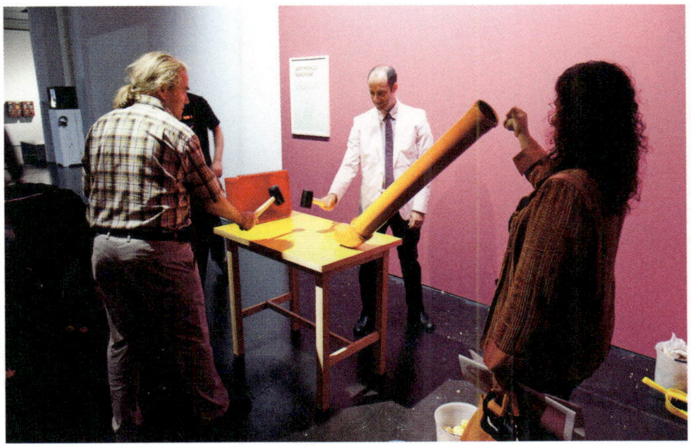

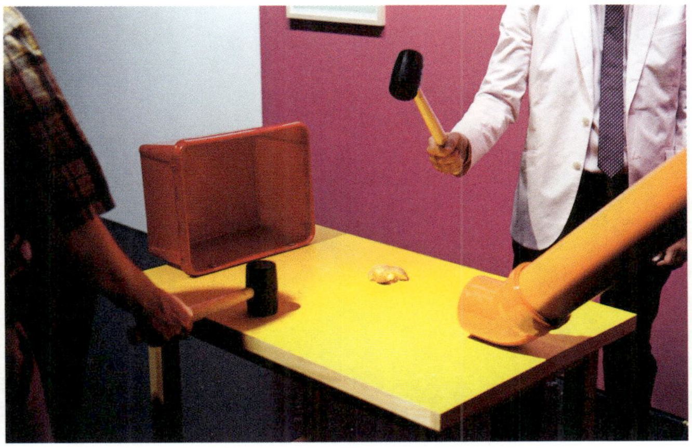

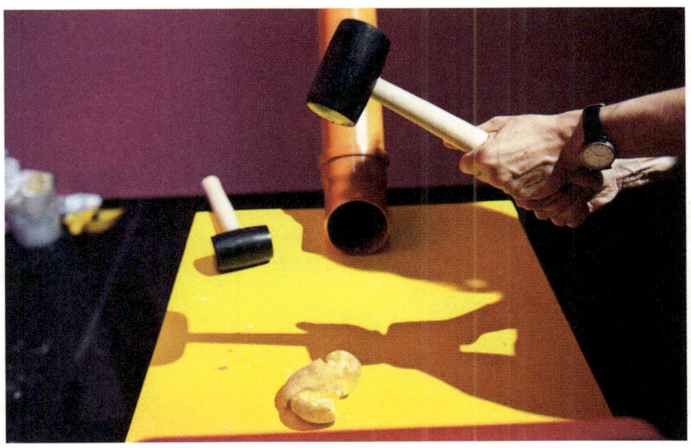

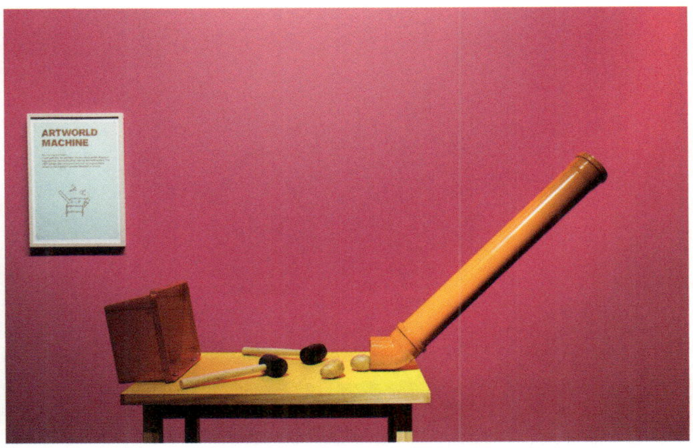

Stephanie Syjuco

* 1974 in Manila (PH), lives and works in San Francisco, CA (US)

The Counterfeit Crochet Project (Critique of a Political Economy), 2008

Mixed-media installation, dimensions variable

In her installation and Internet platform of the same name, *The Counterfeit Crochet Project*, Stephanie Syjuco invites anyone who is interested to crochet their own designer handbags after models by Gucci, Louis Vuitton, or Fendi, for example. Modeled on the pictures in glossy magazines, unique crocheted objects are created that look like mutations of the originals and thus represent a counter-design to the expensive designer originals. In calling on collaborators to produce "counterfeits" of luxury goods with their own handiwork, *The Counterfeit Crochet Project* is an ironic commentary on the globalized world's obsession with brands, the outsourcing of production of consumer goods to low-wage countries, and the practices of product piracy and the black market. Stephanie Syjuco's installation not only subverts regular market mechanisms by the strategy of handmade copies. When she presents her installation at an exhibition the artist borrows the crocheted handbags made by her global collaborators to underline the fact that she is not the sole creator and owner of the objects; this, of course, makes it impossible to sell the installation and thus runs counter to the commercial logic of the art market.

In the educational program accompanying *The Global Contemporary* Stephanie Syjuco offered workshops on themes such as the black market, strategies of piracy and work, and, together with participants, crocheted copies of designer goods which were then displayed in the exhibition. (HP)

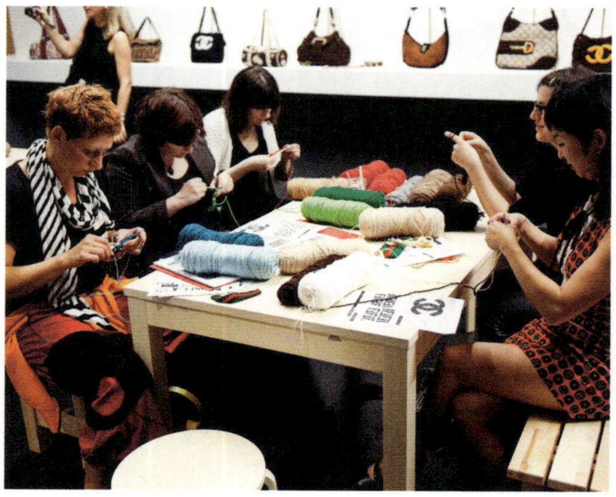

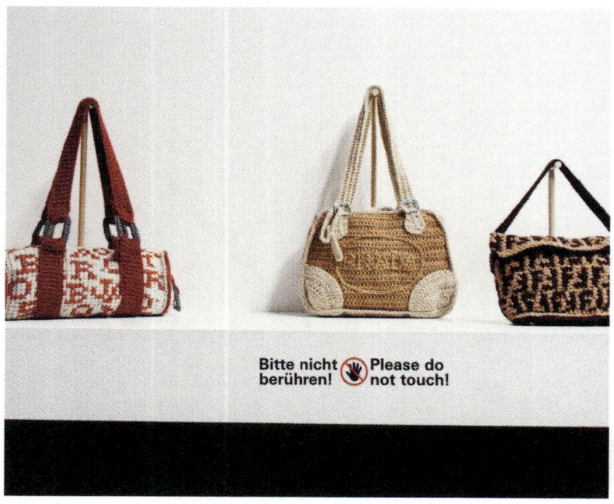

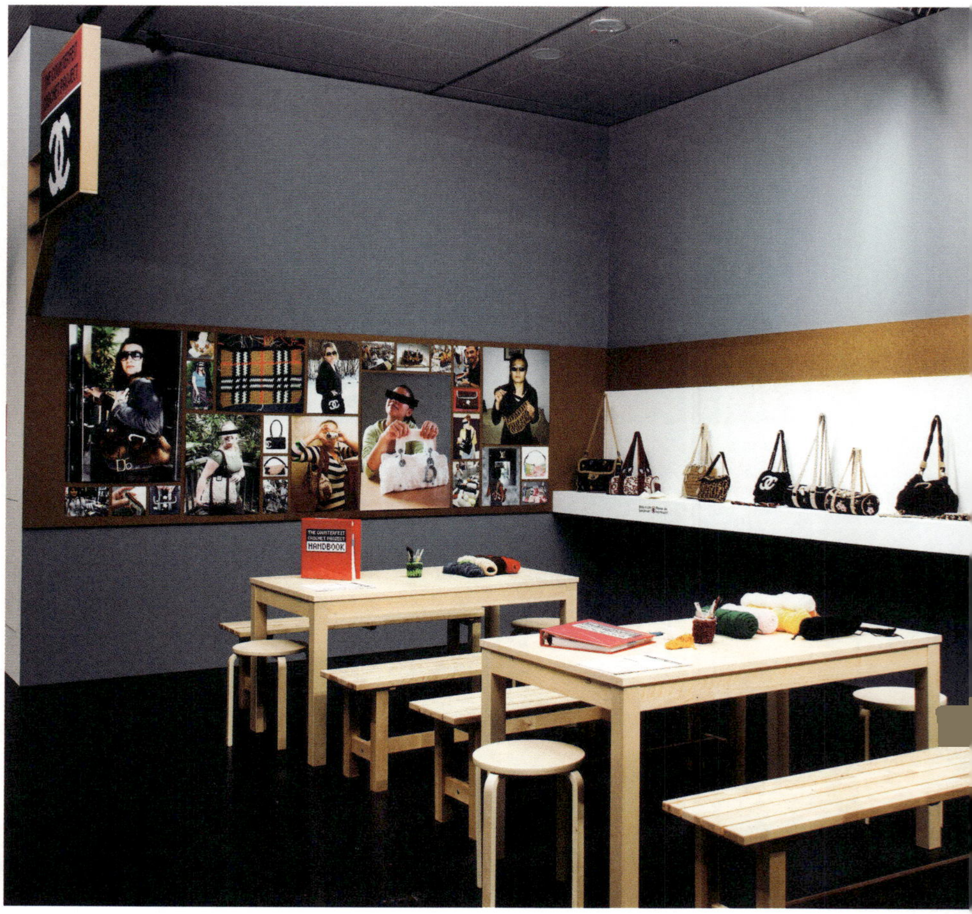

Zhou Tiehai

* 1966 in Shanghai (CN), lives and works in Shanghai

Press Conference, 1997

Photograph, digital print, 55 × 102 cm

Since the turn of the century contemporary art from China has become a sought-after commodity and a popular exhibition object. Thanks to their stylish or provocative aesthetics the works were easy to grasp and testified to a critical awareness, which was readily accepted by the international art scene as an example of art that was both very topical and at the same time "different." However, the market and the opportunities to exhibit internationally were controlled, also for Chinese artists, by power structures that were by no means characterized by equality and transparency. "The relations in the art world are the same as the relations between states in the post-Cold War era," proclaimed Zhou Tiehai in 1997 in front of flags from countries all over the world while on a graph and in a press statement the value fluctuations of "Zhou Tiehai shares" were presented; after the initial and short-lived enthusiasm of European investors the price had stabilized and will remain a good investment in the future. With a later series in which he implanted "Joe Camel," the advertising mascot of the Camel cigarette brand, in classic European paintings, Zhou Tiehai actually was represented at most of the international exhibitions of Chinese art and in corresponding collections. In *Press Conference* Zhou Tiehai demonstrates how the global art scene, in spite of its emancipatory ideology, is determined by the strategies - and the vagaries - of the art market. (JB)

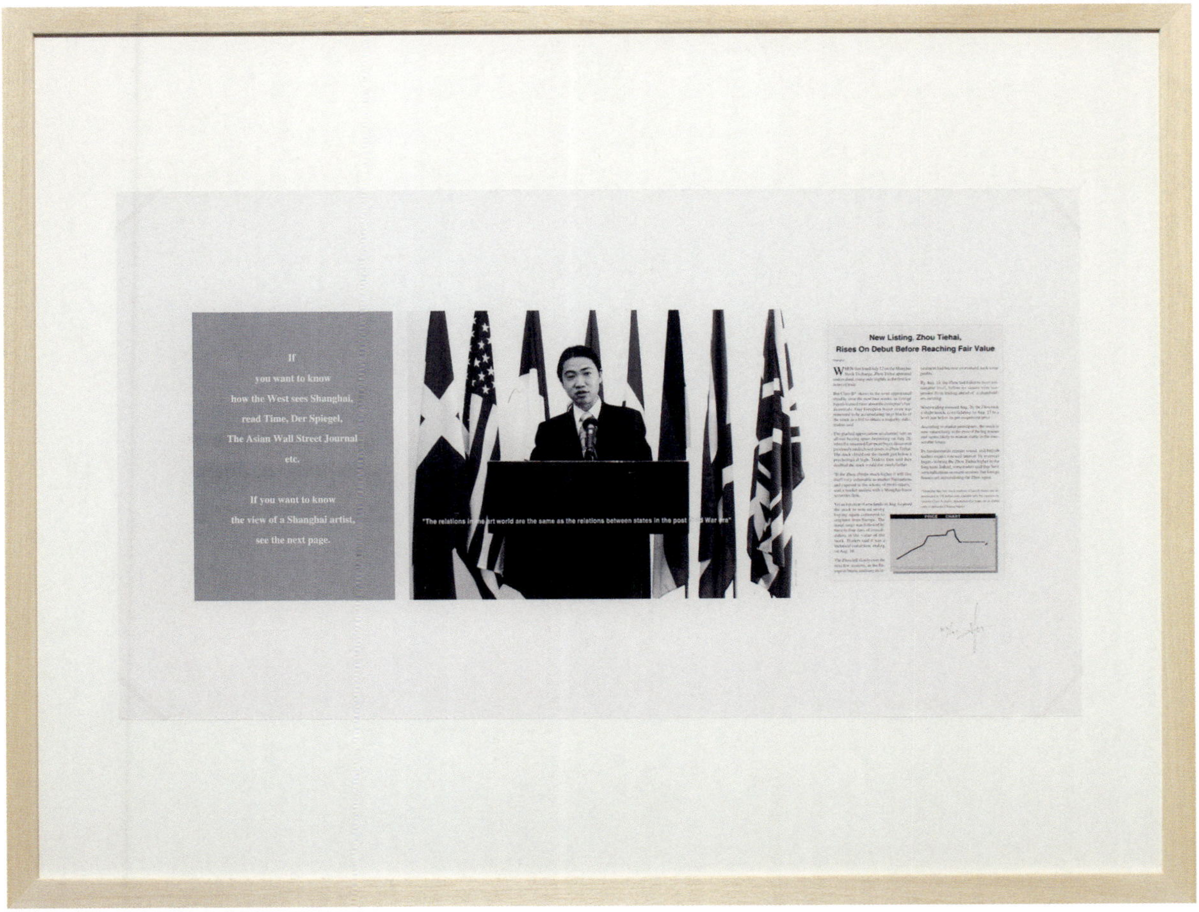

Francis Alÿs / Guy Ben-Ner
Tamy Ben-Tor / Erik Bünger
Nezaket Ekici
Thierry Geoffroy/Colonel
Josh Greene with Yangzi
Mona Hatoum / Martin Kippenberger
Moshekwa Langa
Tirzo Martha / Chéri Samba
John Smith / Mladen Stilinović
Xu Bing / Zhou Tiehai

Lost in Translation: New Artists' Biographies

The artists in this section articulate their own interests by recounting their life stories, or by giving expression to the artistic self that has made them nomads in various art worlds.

The nomad status of the contemporary artist who travels from one residency to the next can be read as transposing the flexible and precarious rules of the labor market onto the domain of art. In exchange for their services and products, institutions worldwide provide artists with accommodation and a studio. When the production of site-specific works of art emerged in the 1960s, artists were striving to undermine the exchange value of art. The question is whether residencies, as a new form of site-specific production, may themselves become a form of art market. Artists find themselves trapped in a translation mode that has to combine international expectations, the construction of a globally recognizable identity, and contextual conditions.

The parachuting of the "visiting artist" into different human and social contexts finds an echo in the photograph *Turista, Catedral Metropolitana* by Francis Alÿs. In this photographic documentation of a performance, Alÿs staged himself among several job seekers waiting in a central square in Mexico City. Curiously, he carries a label that says "turista," as if to underline the paradoxical role of the contemporary artist traveling in order to work, or rather working in order to travel.

The human need to put down provisional roots reinforces the tendency to adopt fictional identities. Self-representation is no longer a portrait in the former sense of the term, but rather the performance of roles played for a specific audience in every new context in which artists become artists, as is the case with international artist-in-residence programs.

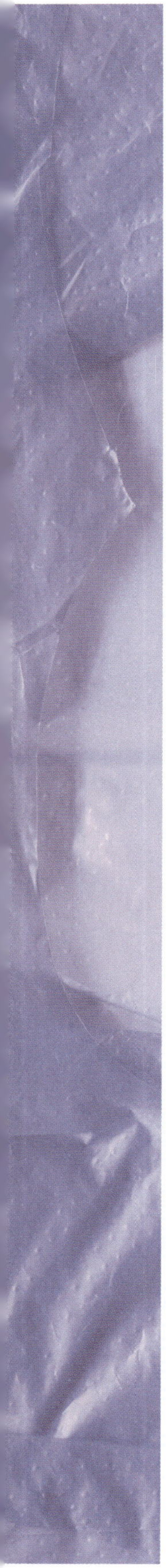

In her film *Artist in Residence* Tamy Ben-Tor plays an uninspired artist who declares her lack of ideas with regard to a residency program in Baden-Baden, but these nevertheless have to be concretized in a new production. The same critical tone is found in another video piece by Ben-Tor, namely, *The End of Art*. In this clip the artist plays another artist and an art critic, cynically and hilariously parodying recognizable facets of the art system and its representatives, who, for the sake of self-justification, proclaim mediocre and easy expedients as valuable works of art. The two films introduce a multilayered dimension, which collapses in the meta-identity of the artist, who is at once enunciator, actor, and subject of the discourse.

The splitting and consistent overlapping of subjectivities are tackled in *Drop the Monkey* by Guy Ben-Ner. In this video we see the artist talking to his other self on the telephone. One time in Berlin, one time in Tel Aviv – he actually flew between the two cities to make the video – Ben-Ner communicates to us a sense of his feelings of displacement and melancholy.

In a two-day performance at the opening of *The Global Contemporary* exhibition, Nezaket Ekici reenacted *Work in Progress – Personal Map*. The work consists of an oral and gestural narration of the artist's travels during the last ten years. While recounting her experiences, she marks each place with a nail on the smooth white stage, and then connects them with a red thread according to anecdotes and particular connections. The result is an individual cartography that visualizes points of intensities and trajectories which opens up a kind of temporal dimension. Each point of the map represents an encounter of personal and collective histories, negotiated through processes of translation.

The parallel between spatiotemporal and cultural or psychological distancing is poetically addressed by Mona Hatoum's *Measures of Distance*. In this video piece the artist recalls the time of her first separation from her family and country in the 1970s. The artist reads aloud, in English, the letters her mother wrote during those years and which we can see running on a screen in Arabic. The separation is rendered by an overlapping of written and spoken words that nevertheless shift. The viewer only gets a partial meaning because voice and text do not complete each other. Translations can never capture the full meaning of the original, they are doomed to be a fragment. *Measures of Distance* illustrates that a translated life always contains both: that which is left behind and lost, and that which is newly gained.

The question of (un)translatability, however, not only affects the individual artist who has to communicate to different audiences and convince the representatives of cultural institutions, but first and foremost the artwork itself. With the advent of a global yet multiple art world, art travels through the most diverse cultural spheres and its value and meaning follow the same unstable dynamics. The "clash of cultures" conceals a most complicated web of encounters and communication tactics.

The American conceptual artist Josh Greene investigated the issue of "artistic export" from West to East. For the *The Global Contemporary* exhibition, Greene commissioned the Chinese artist Yangzi to reproduce a series of ephemeral and conceptual artworks that he had realized over the past ten years. A rich archive of letters, contracts, images, including Yangzi's video diary, showed the exhibition's visitors the impossibility of any simple relocation and aseptic reproduction of art. The dialog between the two artists actually revealed a second author - not a mere executor of alien ideas, but an active player in the conception of an entirely new artwork.

The polyphony of the global art circuit is reminiscent in Chéri Samba's *L'espoir fait vivre no. 2*. The painting shows a self-portrait of the artist, surrounded by icons symbolizing his professional career in the international art world and alluding to the entry of once-excluded artists into the contemporary art arena.

This section reveals a status of the artist that is characterized by floating and incertitude, and it leaves us with a long list of open questions. The laconic title of Mladen Stilinović's *An artist who cannot speak English is no artist* offers a last sarcastic commentary. (SG)

Francis Alÿs

* 1959 in Antwerp (BE), lives and works in Mexico City (MX)

Turista, Catedral Metropolitana, 1994

Color photograph,
29.8 × 23.6 cm, framed

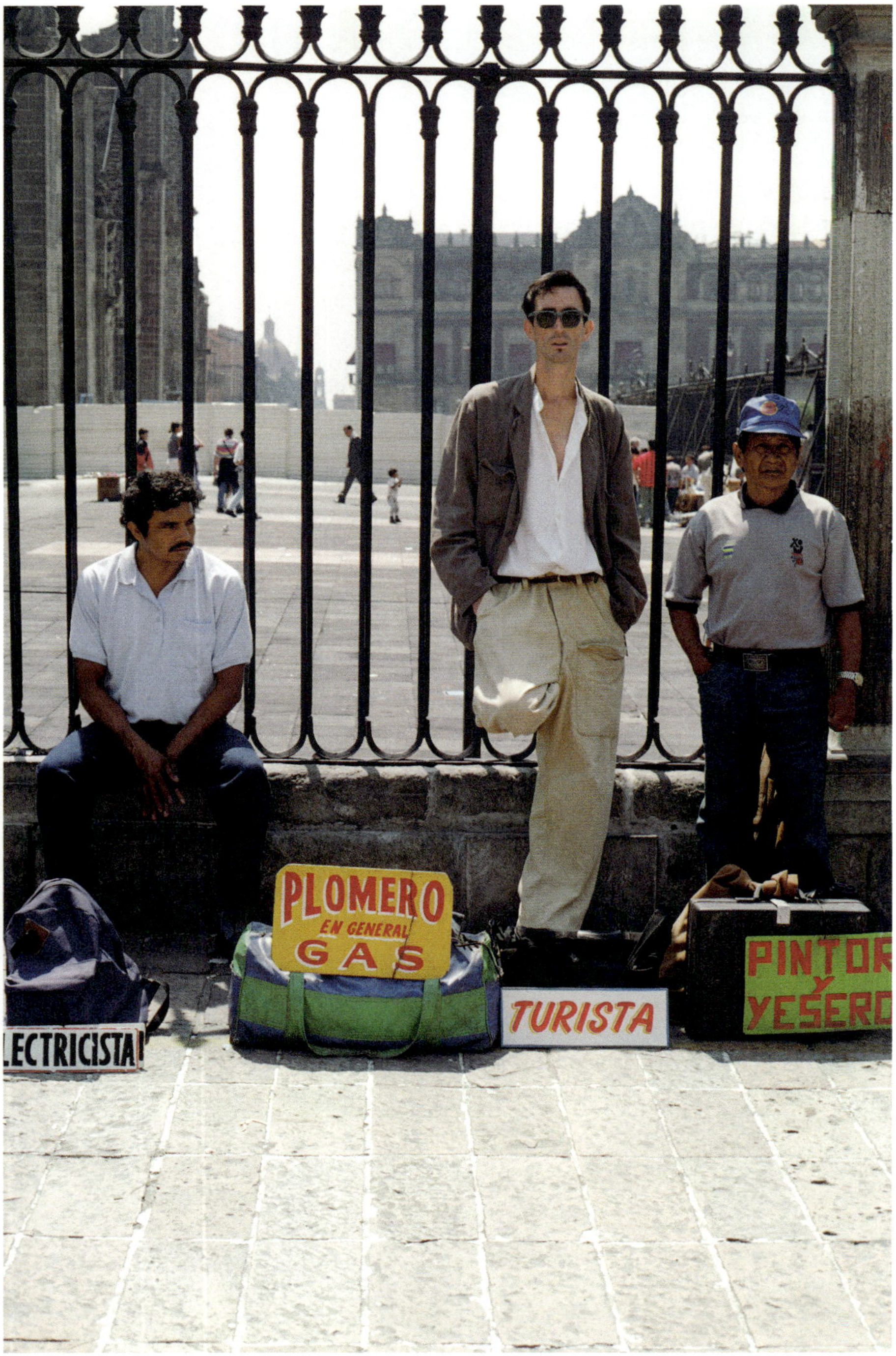

For the last twenty years the public spaces in and around Mexico City have been the primary sphere of the Belgian artist Francis Alÿs' activity, who untiringly traverses the megalopolis staging his ephemeral walks, actions, and performances. Alÿs uses the temporary marks he sets down in the urban space to indicate the poetic, as well as political dimensions of everyday survival strategies which many people develop - sometimes with an effort, sometimes playfully - when confronted by a society that oscillates between the extremes of innovation and tradition, between progress, failure, and stagnation.

In the photographic documentary of the performance *Turista, Catedral Metropolitana*, the artist joins the queue at Zócalo, a central square in Mexico City, where painters, electricians, plumbers, and other day laborers wait for work. By showing himself as part of the "authentic" background with a cardboard sign that identifies him as a tourist, Alÿs turns the gaze of the staring, photographing, or filming tourist back on its perpetrator. Yet at the same time the work can be understood as precise and ironic commentary on the dialectical mechanisms of a globalized art world, which is defined as much by a facile international jet-setting class as it is by a precarious labor market. And Alÿs scrutinizes his own role as a artist who is both a global as well as a local actor. Although he integrates himself into the local setting, the laborers around him are pursuing a common goal whereas the artist remains an external observer and singular commentator of society. (AM)

Guy Ben-Ner

* 1969 in Ramat Gan (IL), lives and works in Tel Aviv (IL)

Drop the Monkey, 2009

Video with German subtitles,
color, sound, 8:30 min

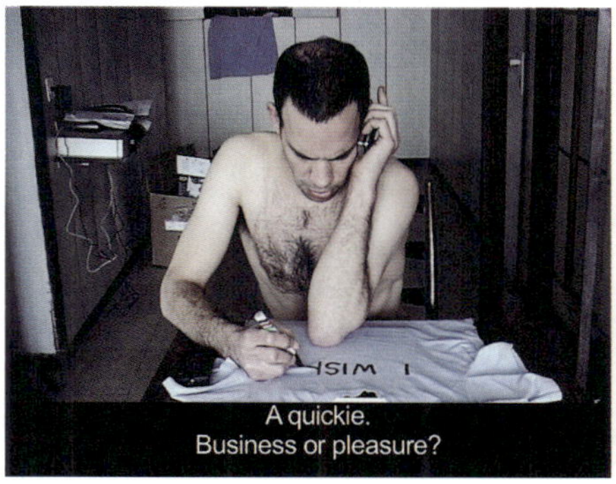

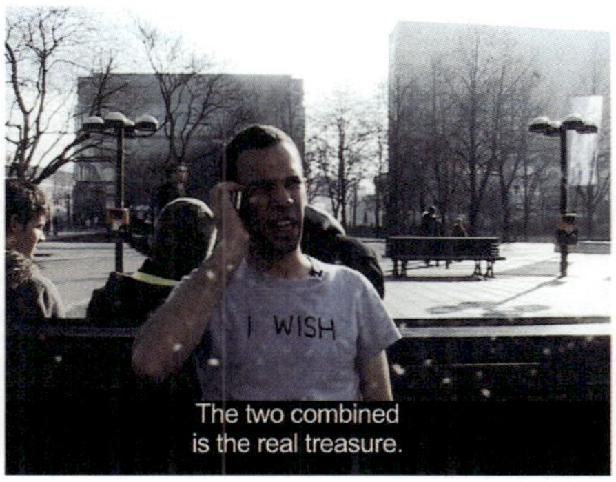

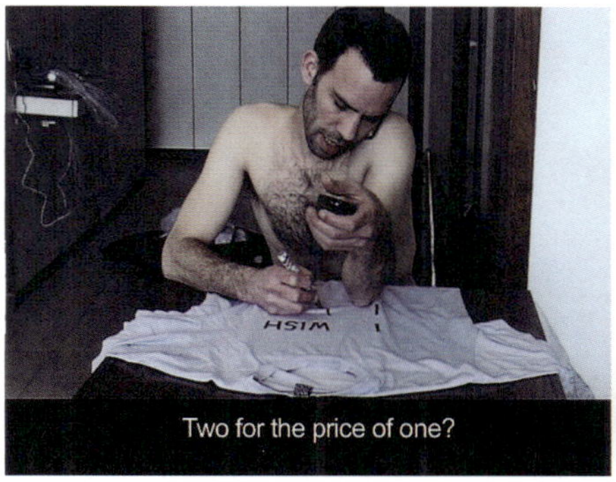

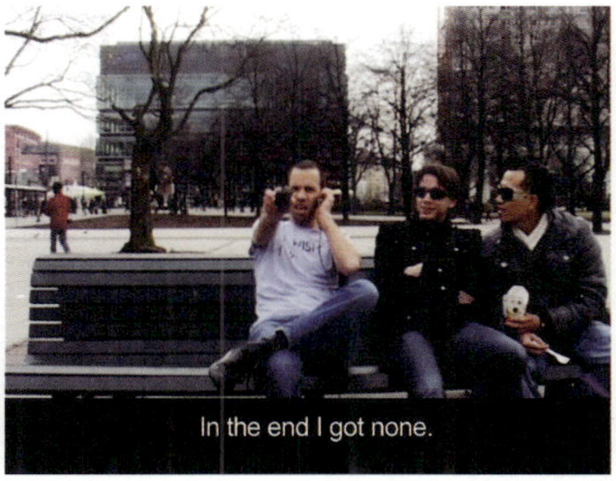

In his earlier video works Guy Ben-Ner mainly performed in front of the camera along with the rest of his family thematizing the boundaries between public and private spheres and staging his own modest means of production inventively, his more recent works deal with his hectic life in the international art context, as well as the artist's ambivalent relationship to the fruits of his success.

In his video *Drop the Monkey*, the artist holds a dialog with himself on the geographic distance between Berlin and Tel Aviv. The conversation is arranged as a telephone call, and since the material was all cut live on camera, Ben-Ner actually had to travel between the two cities by airplane. While he makes the conditions and the process involved in the production of the work itself the central theme of the piece, as well as arguments for the pros and cons of the mixing of art and life, Ben-Ner equally draws our attention to the present-day state of (artists') diasporic identity which is marked by inner conflict and melancholy: "I Wish I Was Somewhere Else." (AM)

Tamy Ben-Tor

* 1975 in Jerusalem (IL), lives and works in New York, NY (US)

***Normal*, 2006**

Video, color, sound, 4:20 min

***The End of Art*, 2006**

Video, color, sound, 7 min

***Artist in Residence*, 2005**

Video, color, sound, 3:55 min

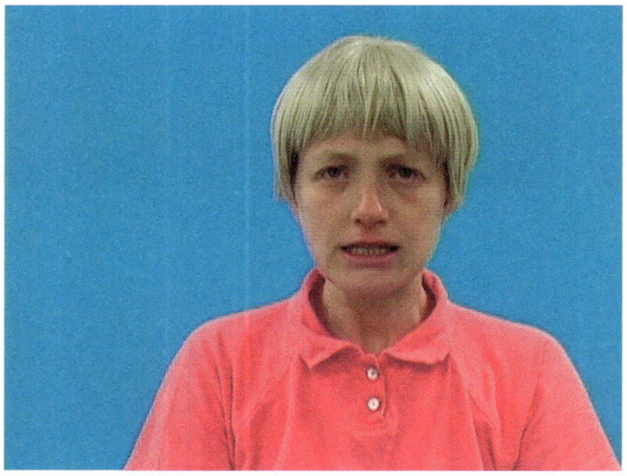

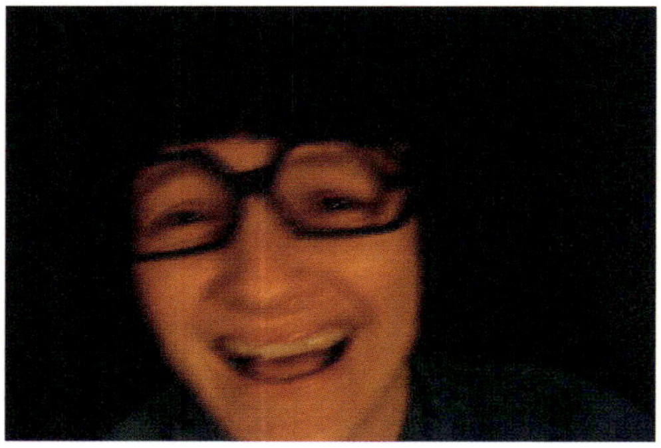

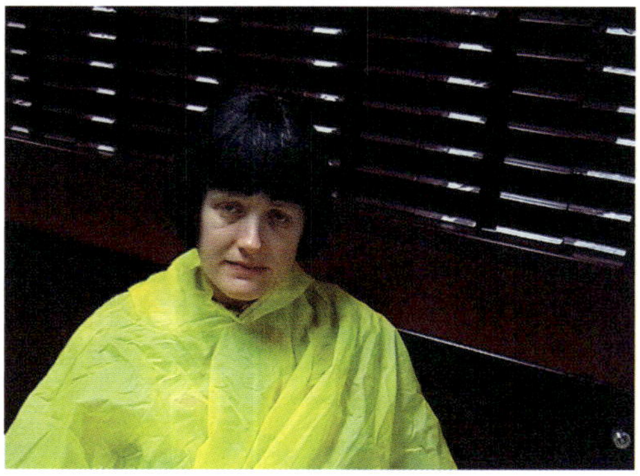

The Israeli-American artist Tamy Ben-Tor began her career in experimental theater. In her solo performances and video works, she stages cultural stereotypes and taboos, which she parodies with a virtuosity that is almost painful. Whereas all of Ben-Tor's multiple characters possess idiotic features and mumble, slur, stammer, or yell their multilingual texts, they still frequently contrive to bring astonishing truths to light.

With her works exhibited here, Tamy Ben-Tor is revealed to be as an acute observer of the international art world and its protagonists. Thus, in *The End of Art*, a Thai artist and typical American critic speak contrasting monologues on the amenities and absurdities of the art business. While this "outsider artist" with a heavy accent (the allusion to Rirkrit Tiravanija is impossible to miss) is visibly amused when her "culinary art" is praised as social sculptures, and that these have even made her wealthy, the art historian (clearly a reference to Francis Fukuyama, author of *The End of History and the Last Man*) readily admits with pursed lips and grand gestures that she neither values nor, for that matter, has any especial love of art. But she enjoys all the more being one step ahead of her generation in anticipating new trends and being able to shift something to the center of attention with just one word. With this video, Ben-Tor exposes the potency of cultural clichés in the sphere of art, as well as the mechanisms of liberalism, the market, and criticism.

The video work *Artist in Residence* features a far more humble figure - a not-so-young anymore artist-in-residence clad in a yellow rain cape. In an entirely uninspiring manner, she reports on her archival projects in Baden-Baden: "We didn't have any ideas. So I found something and we decided to make an archive of this." A scathing commentary on the system of publicly sponsored grant programs and on the concept of nonprofit art locations which, not infrequently, become platforms for mediocre art production while at the same time providing a livelihood for less aspiring artists.

In her video *Normal* Tamy Ben-Tor accelerates the communicative spiral of magniloquent e-mail chains to the point of being intolerable. Visibly overchallenged, both from her own demands on herself as well as by those of her environment, and exhausted by uninterrupted multitasking, the protagonist personifies the everyday madness of a hectic culture of communication, which appears to have become an end in itself. (AM)

Erik Bünger

* 1976 in Växjö (SE), lives and works in Berlin (DE)

The Allens, 2004

Video, color, sound, 28 min

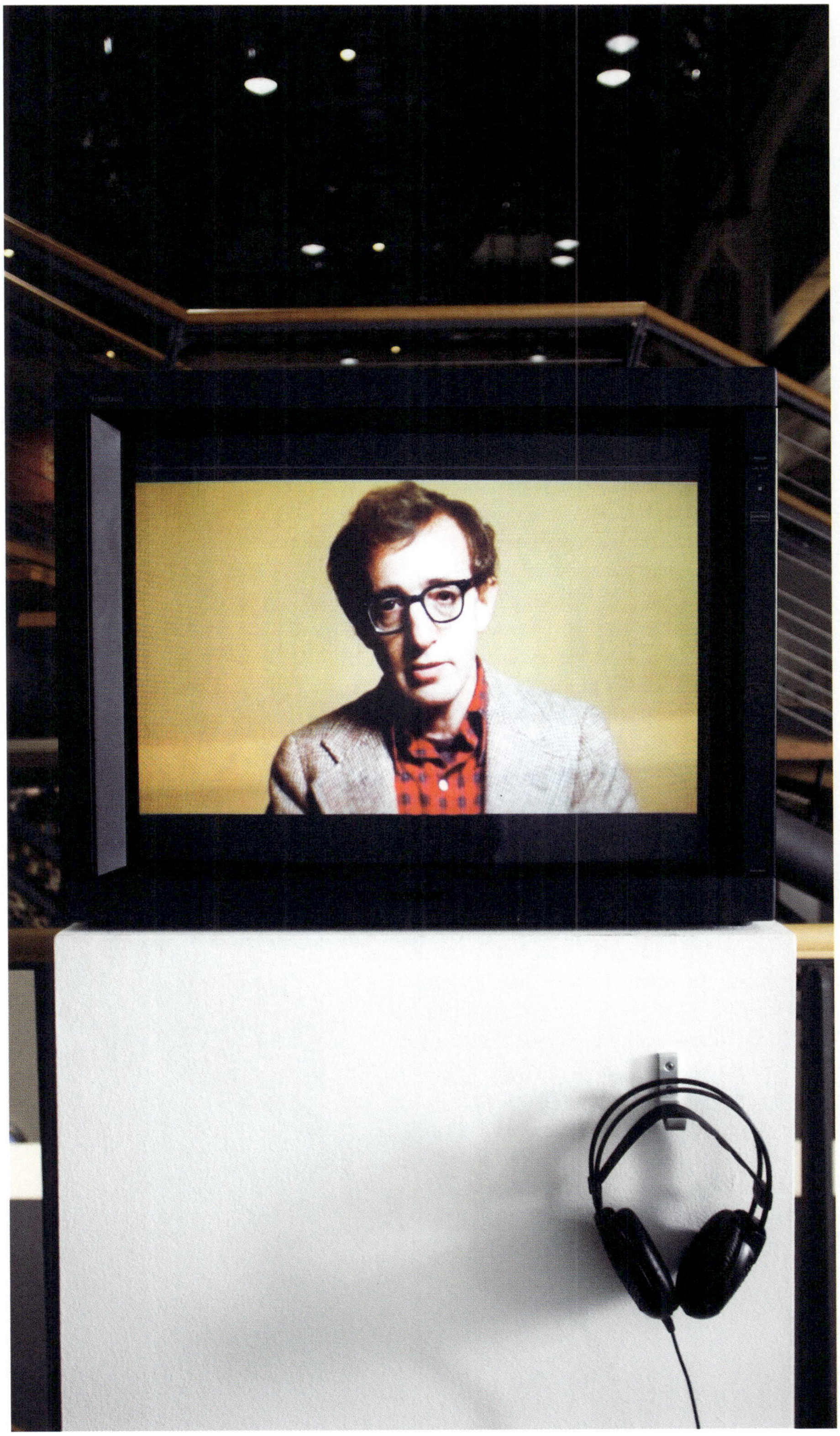

In his lecture performances, videos, and installations, Swedish artist Erik Bünger examines the use of music and language in sound and image productions of popular culture, and makes their manipulating and myth-building mechanisms visible by recontextualizing and commenting on found footage from diverse sources.

With the video work *The Allens*, Bünger also engages with the interaction of language, speaking, and voice in film, as well as its influence on figures and narratives. When Bünger saw a dubbed film for the first time, in Germany, he was slightly perturbed by the strangely inapposite voices, which, for him, completely altered the contents of the film. "To my unaccustomed ears this gave a ghostly kind of sensation, as if Robert De Niro had been possessed by a German spirit. And I started to wonder about these guys who sell their voices for money." It seemed to him as if, through this technology, not only was the specific quality of the language, and thus the cultural location of the films lost, but that the characters shrunk as a result.

Using the example of Woody Allen, whose character is defined especially through his specific use of language, Bünger lays bare the inner tension of the character that results from his various speaker personalities in different languages. At the same time, Bünger creates an incisive picture of the current schizophrenic state of culture - something which becomes especially perceptible in the international context of art, where a flexible approach to mutually contradictory cultural realities, as well as to a playful adaption of the most diverse roles, is something especially sought after. (AM)

Nezaket Ekici

* 1970 in Kırşehir (TR), lives and works in Berlin and Stuttgart (DE)

Work in progress – Personal Map, 2008 (ongoing)

Performance,
mixed-media installation, ca. 4 × 3 m

As part of a two-day performance at ZKM for the opening of *The Global Contemporary* the artist Nezaket Ekici created a new vision of her work entitled *Work in progress – Personal Map,* in which she represents the various stages of her work as an artist over the last ten years. Starting with her earliest performance, Ekici reports – with the use of language and bodily gesture – on her video, performance, and works in installation art, and the respective exhibition contexts in which these were presented. Her anecdotal narratives about herself and her art are among the personal encounters as are the everyday experiences when traveling through the various countries she visited. She marks each place she visited by a nail on a white platform and connects it by a red thread with the stages to which it relates. In this way Ekici turns her work-related stays in over eighty cities, twenty-five countries, and three continents into an object of her artistic reflection.

Further, the interlacing of art and her personal, everyday experience also finds expression at a second level: In her performances, Ekici directly integrates the public into the production of her "map" and in discussions with the visitors, she establishes links between her own and their experiences. *Work in progress – Personal Map* thus becomes a travelogue, a personal map in which the boundaries between the professional and the private, between the artistic and the everyday, between the past and the present become fluid. (HP)

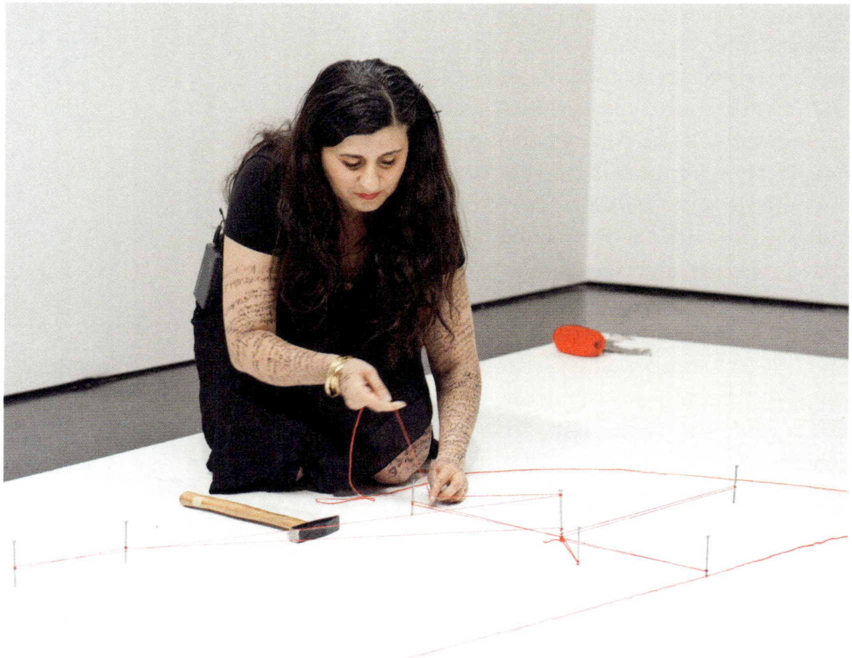

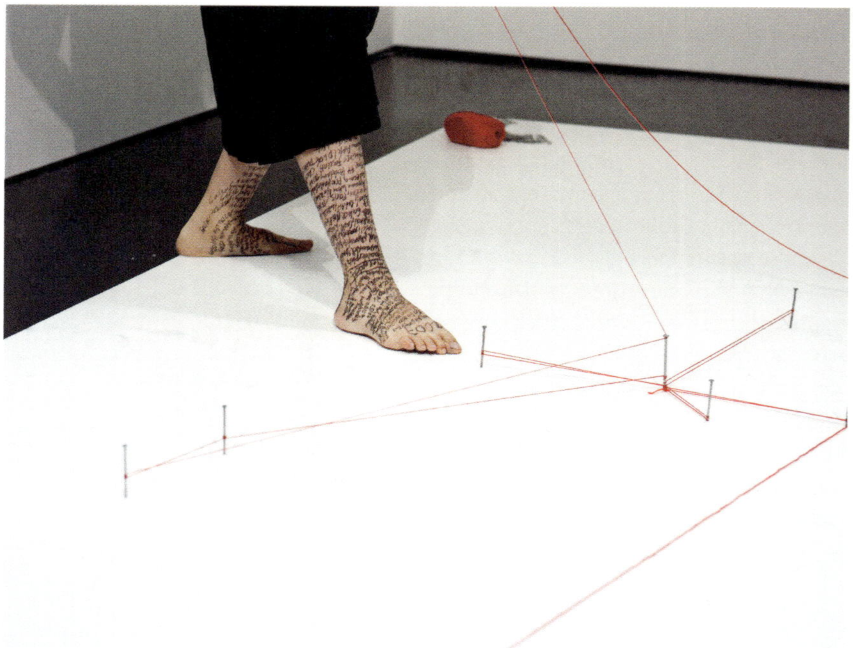

Thierry Geoffroy/Colonel

* 1961 in Nancy (FR), lives and works in Copenhagen (DK)

Biennalist Mini Retrospective, 1989 (ongoing)

Mixed-media installation with video, photograph, and photo prints, dimensions variable

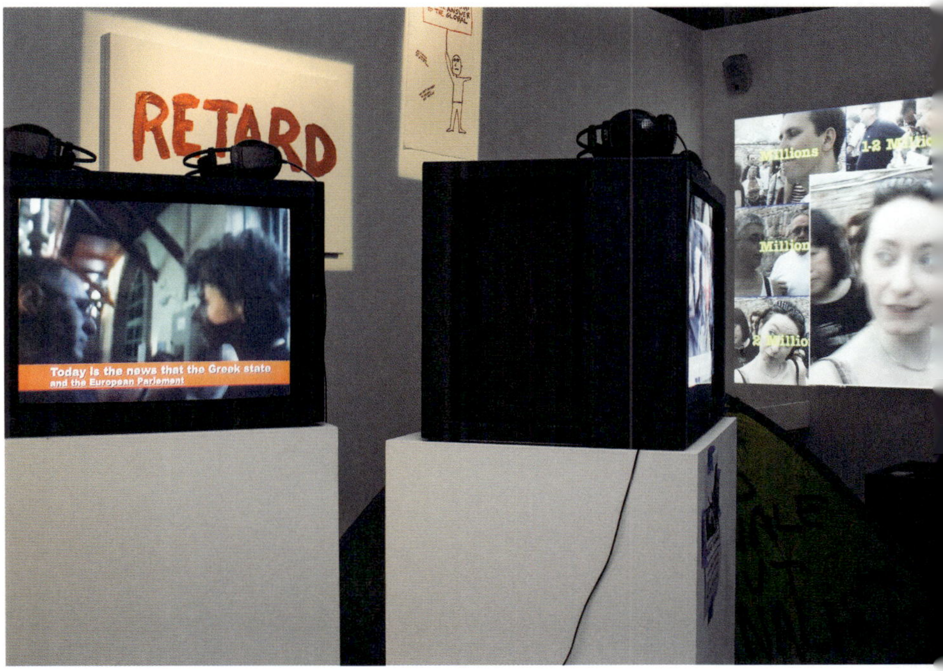

Thierry Geoffroy takes biennials seriously. When a big international exhibition opens under a discursive-poetic title that is supposed to convey its relation to politics and life, this is only rarely to be seen as a guideline and only sometimes as a correct description of the exhibited art. The "Biennalist," however, refuses to take these empty words with the appropriate ironic distance: with only the seeming naivety of an Inspector Columbo, he prefers to ask time and again what really lies behind this or that claim, the one or the other decision of a curator. For just as ambitious titles and press releases often conceal conceptual weaknesses or half-heartedness with regards to the content of an exhibition, behind the exhibition itself stand financial or political interests that are hardly compatible with the critical claims of the artistic actors.

Taking biennials seriously leads inevitably to an alienation effect that can just as well debouch in slapstick as in satire. For his actions at biennials, Geoffroy has developed various humorous and critical formats that include both the public and those participating in the exhibitions. *The Global Contemporary* presented previous projects of the "Biennalist" in the form of a retrospective. In autumn 2011 Geoffroy produced a new session of the *Biennalist* at the Athens Biennale 2011 in collaboration with ZKM, which also reverberated in the exhibition. (JB)

Biennalist, 2011 (ongoing)

Performance and mixed-media installation, dimensions variable,
Produced in cooperation with ZKM | Karlsruhe

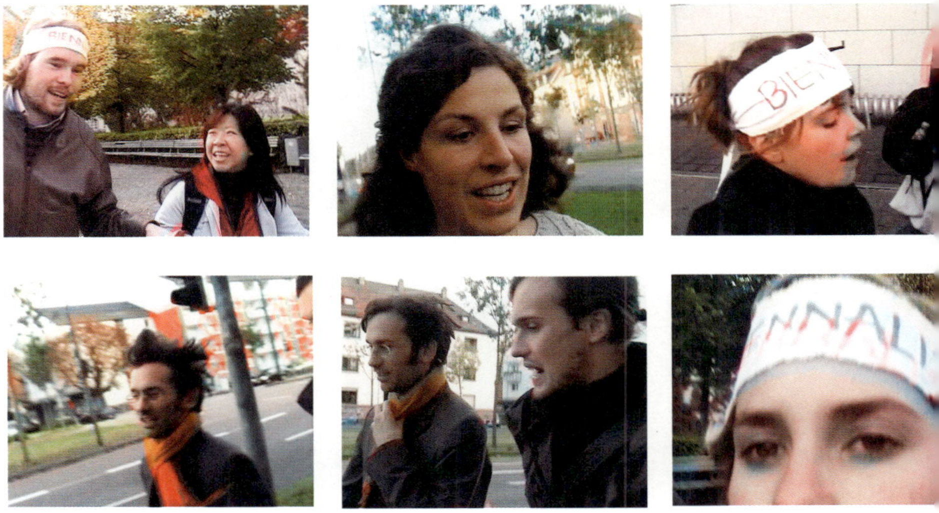

Josh Greene with Yangzi

Josh Greene, * 1971 in Santa Monica, CA (US), lives and works in San Francisco, CA (US)
Yangzi, * 1971 in Anshan, Liaoning Province (CN), lives and works in Beijing (CN)

Red/Greene, 2011

Mixed-media installation, dimensions variable, produced in cooperation with ZKM | Karlsruhe

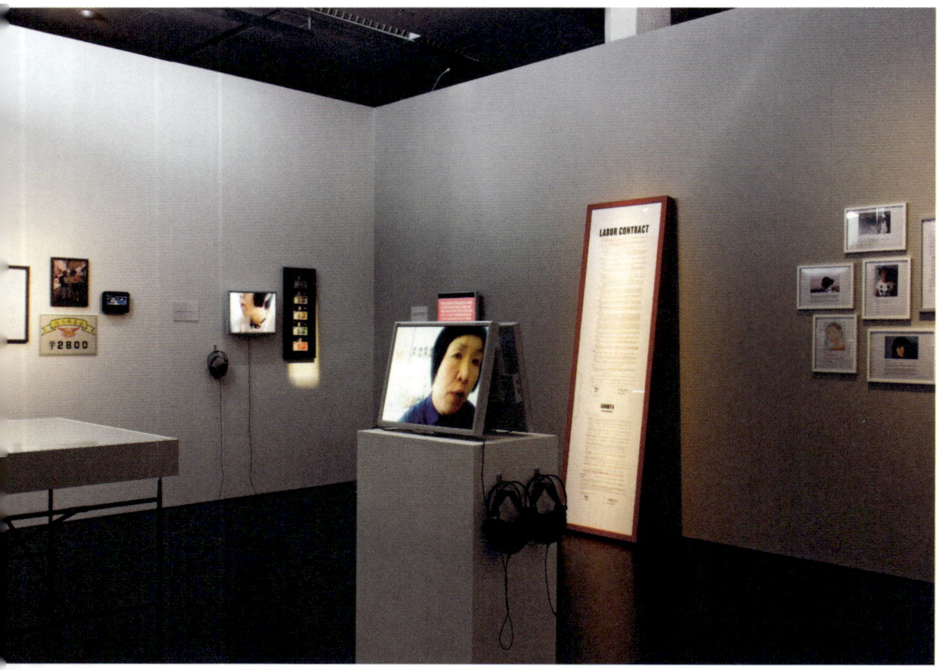

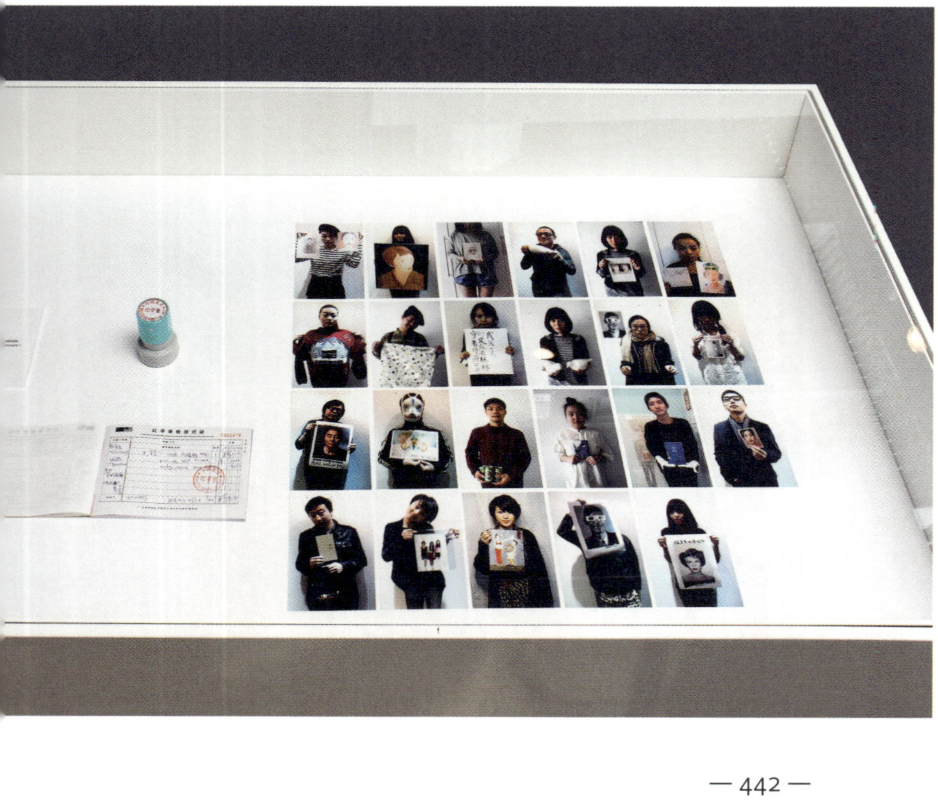

In his conceptual work, Josh Greene focuses on topics ranging from service, psychology and economics, the boundaries between the private and the public, the context of art and its habitual modes of perception, to the conditions of artistic production. It is rare that his projects are object-based; they contain various dynamic parameters and manifest themselves mostly in the interaction with other persons. Thus, during a vernissage in his apartment he offers his private property for sale *(Greene)*, presents himself on the Internet as well as in the art space as an amateur therapist *(Unlicensed Therapist)*, sells money below its current value *(Less Than Face Value)*, or, on request, spends a lovesick phase in Sophie Calle's bed *(Sophie Calle's Bed)*.

For *The Global Contemporary*, Greene commissioned the Chinese artist Yangzi to reproduce a selection of his works of the past ten years in Beijing. Here, the artist drew attention to the common practice of conceptual development in the West and cheap (mass) production and manufacture in Asia. Due to the impossibility of directly reproducing and transferring projects based on the communication and relations of a different personal, political, and cultural context, questions begin to emerge regarding authorship, cultural transfer, the interplay of politics, freedom, and art, as well as the translatability of ideas. Through Yangzi's accompanying video diary, the perspective of the "second author" is directly reflected back onto the project. (AM)

Mona Hatoum

* 1952 in Beirut (LB), lives and works in London (UK) and Berlin (DE)

Measures of Distance, 1988

Video, color, sound, 15 min

Considered to be one of the most important Palestinian-British artists of her generation, Mona Hatoum's wide-ranging works are permeated by a poignant, critical, and ironic interpretation of gender and political issues. Born in Beirut to a Palestinian family, Mona Hatoum travelled to London in 1975 where she was forced to remain following the outbreak of the Lebanese civil war. Educated at the Byam Shaw School of Art and the Slade School of Fine Art, she began her artistic career with interactive performance pieces, which, by pursuing Michel Foucault's concept of bio power, highlighted the political nature of the human and particularly female body. In the late 1980s Hatoum ceased her performances in favor of installations and objects which, in a more subtle manner, preserved the same alienating attitude.

The video *Measures of Distance* is an explicit reference to her years of exile in London. The screen is criss-crossed by a succession of sentences in Arabic, which disturb a female figure showering in the background. Listening to the artist's voiceover reading the text aloud in English, we realize its content: Hatoum makes public her mother's letters, which conveys feelings of separation and displacement. By presenting a woman naked, the work is driven by a strong critique of the stereotyped representation of Arab women as passive and non sexual beings. (SG)

— —

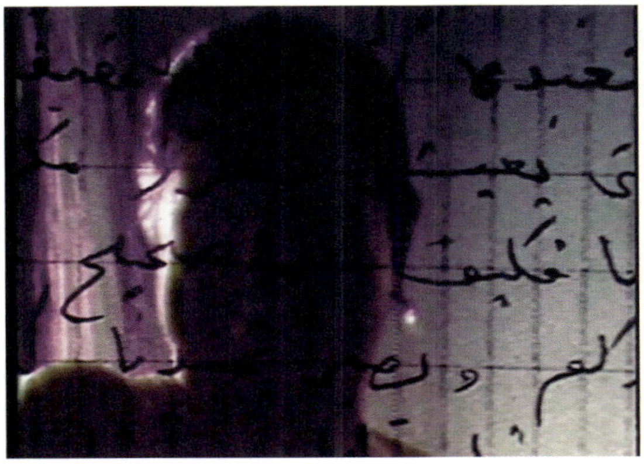

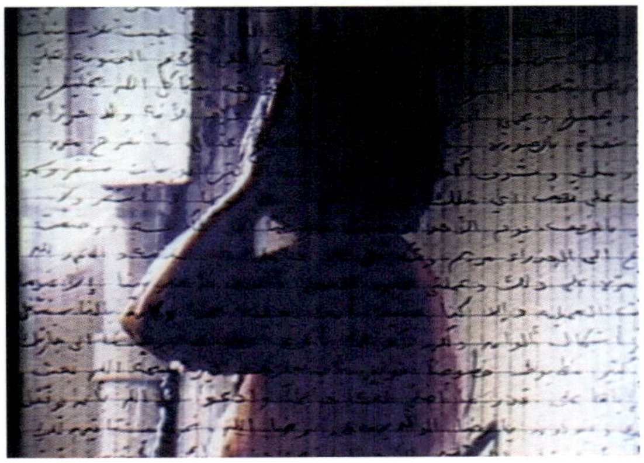

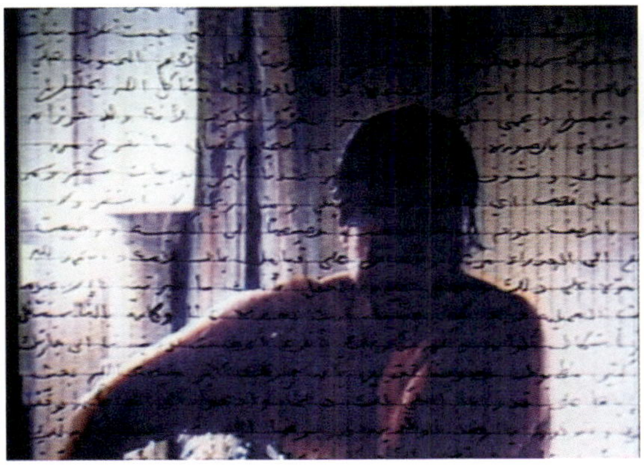

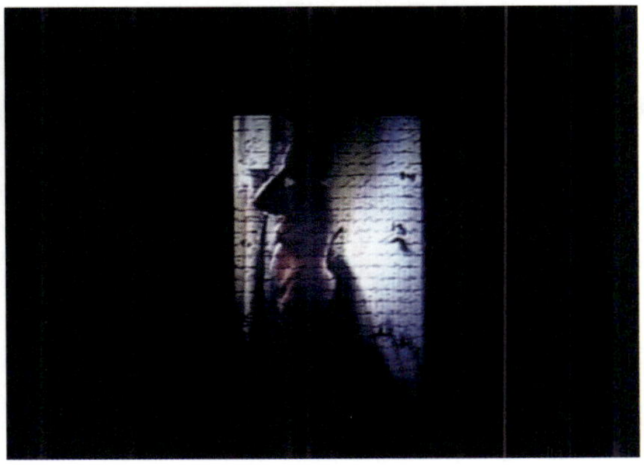

Martin Kippenberger

* 1953 in Dortmund (DE), † 1997 in Vienna (AT)

Ohne Titel, 1990

10 drawings (selection), mixed media on hotel stationary, with printer's imprint, 37.5 × 48.5 cm each

Regarded as one of the most outstanding figures in the history of German contemporary art, Martin Kippenberger, who died in his forties, always shocked his audiences through his provocative, humoristic, and sarcastic works of art. His infamous and eccentric lifestyle, coupled with unpredictable and multimedia artistic productions, propelled him to legendary status, a status, moreover, which continues to evolve.

This untitled series, better known as the "Hotel Drawings", consists of hundreds of drawings made on hotel stationary over the last ten years of the artist's life. Although Kippenberger often spent several months in the same hotel, he never used notepaper from the hotels in which he resided, but rather used notepads picked up at various locations. The series as a whole comprises sketches and studies for projects that highlight the transitory and paradoxical value of art. Furthermore, considering the paper not just as a blank page, nor as a neutral base for art, Kippenberger converted a rough material into a proper artistic medium. As reinterpreted forms of ready-mades, the "Hotel Drawings" could be perceived as an ironic, but also biographical commentary on the contemporary art system, where the artist is both subject and object. (SG)

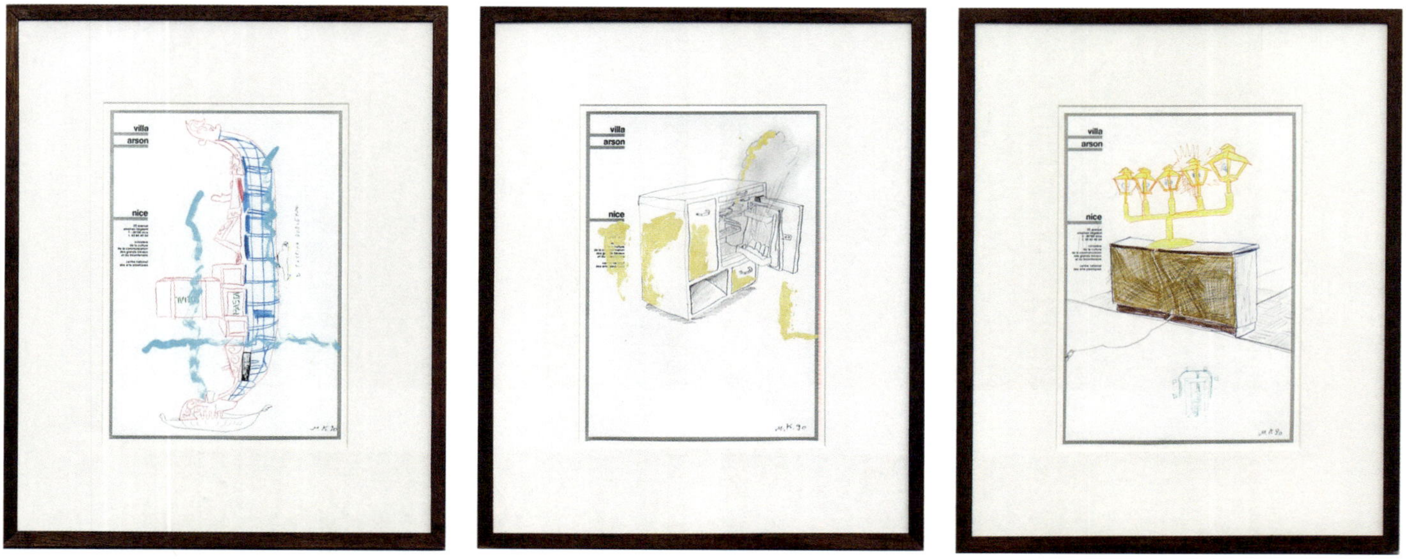

Moshekwa Langa

* 1975 in Bakenberg, Potgietersrus (ZA), lives and works in Amsterdam (NL)

Untitled, 2003

2 × ink on paper, 140 × 100 cm each,
1 × pastel crayon on paper, 122 × 86 cm

Moshekwa Langa, who characterizes himself as an artist who works in a documentary way, focuses first and foremost on topics such as identity and social affiliation as well as on religious rituals. For Langa, art production also includes a therapeutic and ritual dimension. He resists, furthermore, the classification of his art as South African or Black, while defining himself as an individual outsider who doesn't belong anywhere.

Langa observes life and creates "maps" of his geographic, social, and psychological history. Here, the process involved in their production is just as important as the result itself. With ink or pastel crayon, Langa writes or jots down on paper the names of people or places, maxims, quotes, or stories. His sketches do not result in a linear, logical semantic narrative but are rather a kind of artistic diary, a subjective cartography extending beyond space and time. The artist envisages each peace as a particle within an "open-ended continuum" which is developing over time. The idea of a work in continuation recalls Umberto Eco's theory of avant-garde art as being structurally open to interpretation and consequently to the passing of time. Langa points at the fluidity of an "open artwork" also when he says: "These things don't have titles because titles tend to fix things." (AE)

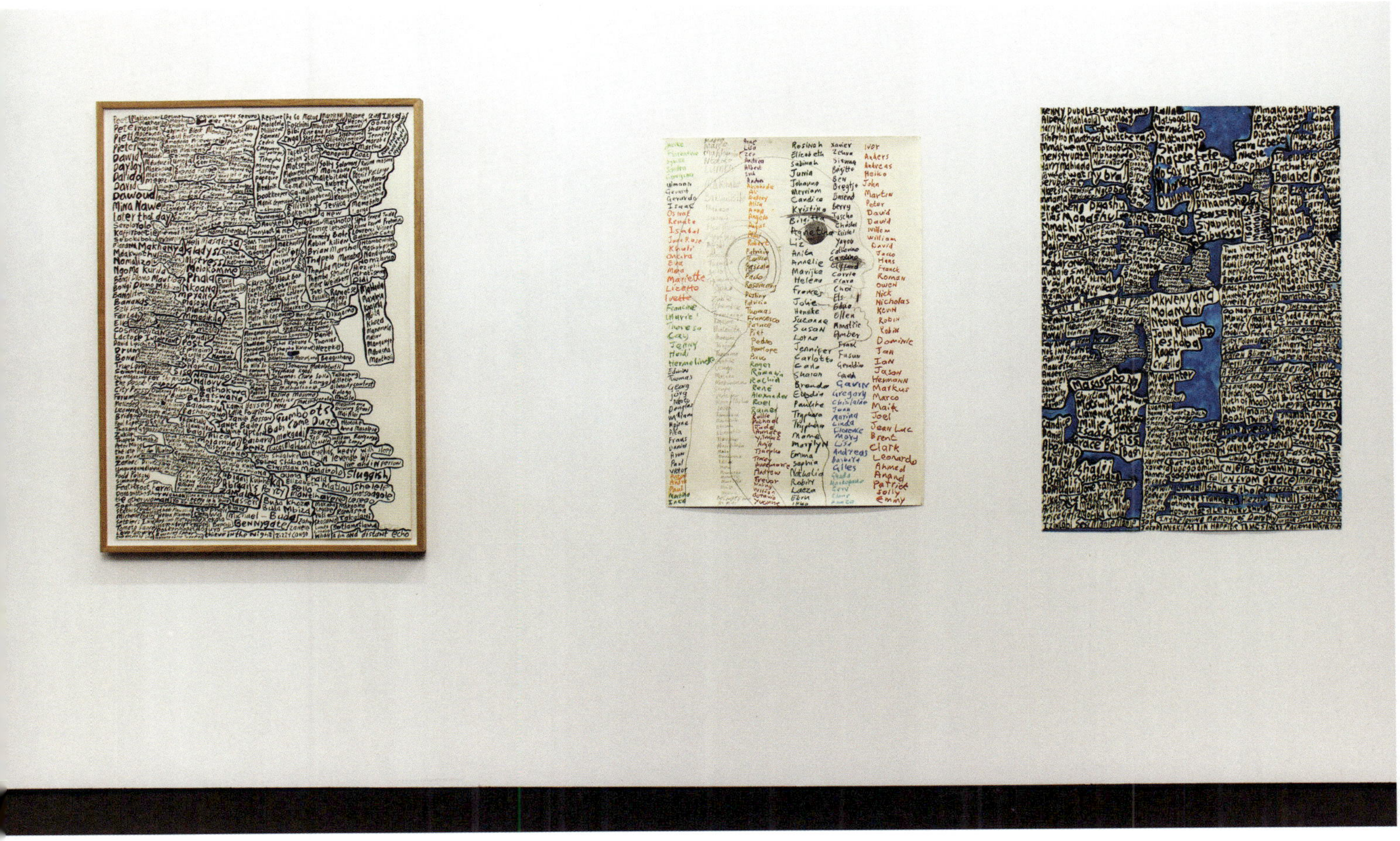

Tirzo Martha

* 1965 in Curaçao (AN/NL), lives and works in Curaçao

The Invasion of The Netherlands supported by Chavez (Chavez had to stop at IKEA in Spain to buy himself a new presidential chair), 2008

Mixed-media installation,
dimensions variable

The installations and performances of Caribbean artist Tirzo Martha hold up an ironic mirror to the sociopolitical state of Caribbean societies. With his multimedia, open works, Martha undertakes social analysis and thus treads the fine line between fiction and reality.

The Invasion of the Netherlands supported by Chavez (Chavez had to stop at IKEA in Spain to buy himself a new presidential chair) is a remarkable collection of everyday objects - a construction comprising used furniture, crockery, and various other domestic material. Reminiscent of improvised street barricades in the context of political protest and social unrest or of patchwork altars, amongst other things, the artwork consists of IKEA furniture collected as talismans of Western culture, of Caribbean souvenir articles, or small replicas of gaudy Catholic symbols.

Martha's ironic and sarcastic reflections focus on the present-day state of postcolonial Caribbean societies, marked by poverty and dependency on international tourism and other, more recent forms of slavery, and show the peoples' disappointments, anger, and daily fight for survival. At the same time, he makes reference to their dreams and the vitality of a new Creole identity and culture, which positions itself confidently in the area of the "in-between." In addition, Martha confronts the audience with the cliché of a colorful and naive Caribbean art, or a corresponding attitude of expectation. (AE)

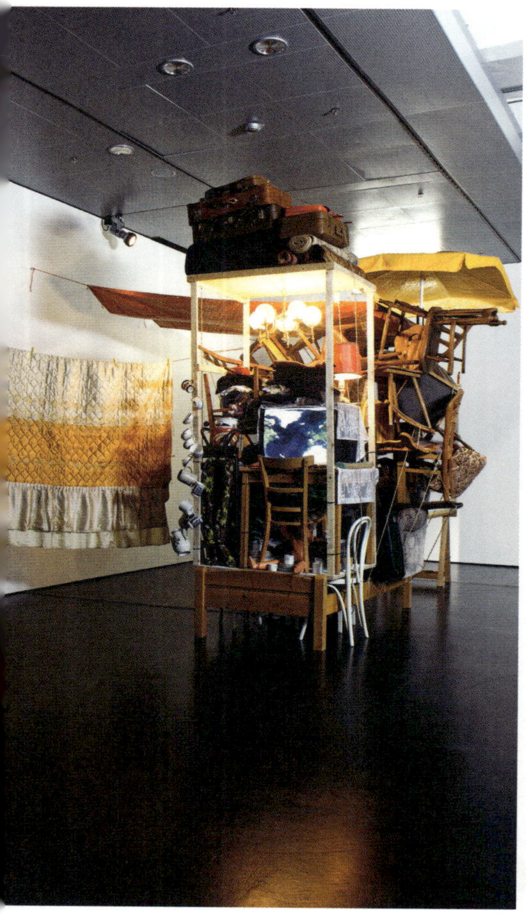

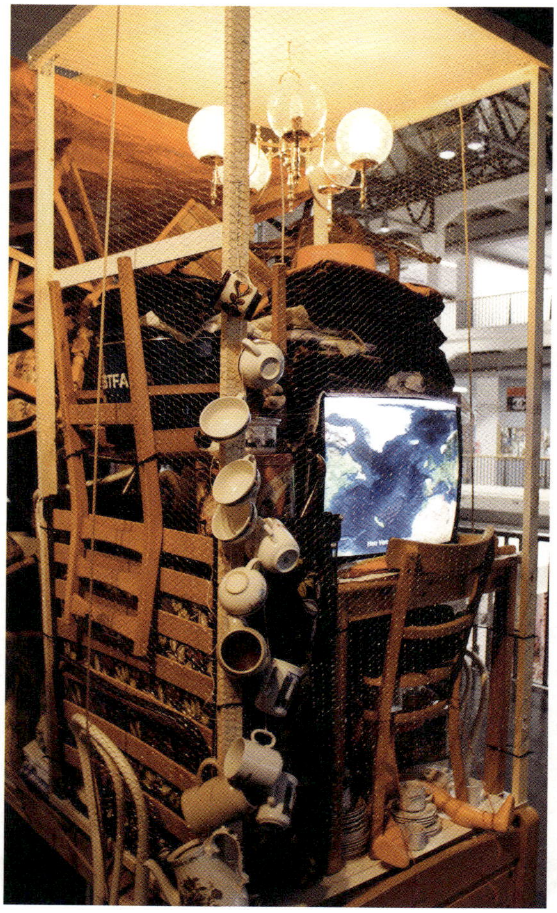

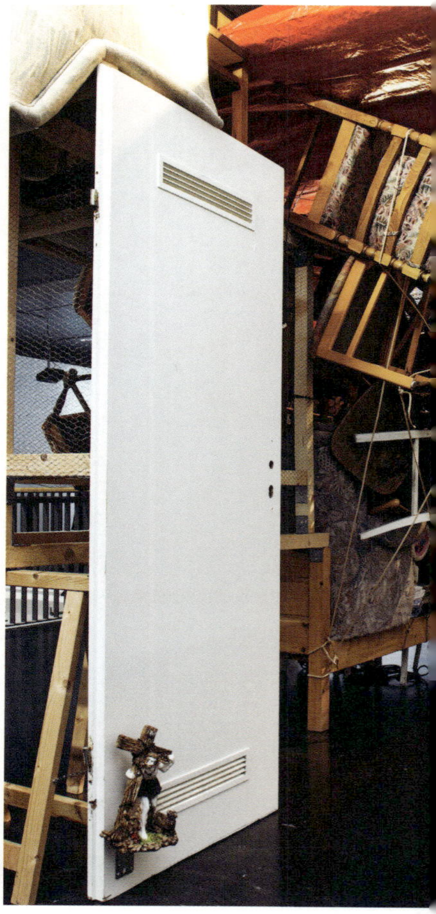

Chéri Samba

* 1956 in Kinto-M'Vuila (CD), lives and works in Kinshasa (CD)

L'espoir fait vivre no. 2, 1997

Acrylic, sequins, photographs,
glue on canvas, 130 × 194 cm

Chéri Samba is an autodidact and began his career as an advertising artist and sign painter for advertising agencies in Kinshasa, where in 1975, he opened his own studio. His participation in the exhibition *Magiciens de la terre* (1989) in Paris brought Samba international recognition.

Samba contributed the first version of his self-portrait to the exhibition which was titled *L'espoir fait vivre* [Hope Permits Us to Live] and narrates his life story up to his departure for Paris. The artist "clings to the 'C' in the presence of his first advisor," which refers to his first name, "Chéri," and illustrates "various stages in his biography as an artist," as he wrote in a commentary; the "S," as in "Samba," however, tells of his life "during childhood." In the same year, 1997, in which there was a solo exhibition of his work at the Musée national des Arts d'Afrique et d'Océanie in Paris, Chéri Samba painted a new version of his self-portrait, exhibited at *The Global Contemporary*, in which he extended his biography and recorded how he looked in 1997, rather like a protocol. His self-portrait of 1989 was based on a concept. It challenged the viewer to take a fresh look at an artist from Africa, an artist, moreover, with a name and a biography - just like one is accustomed to in Western art. (AB)

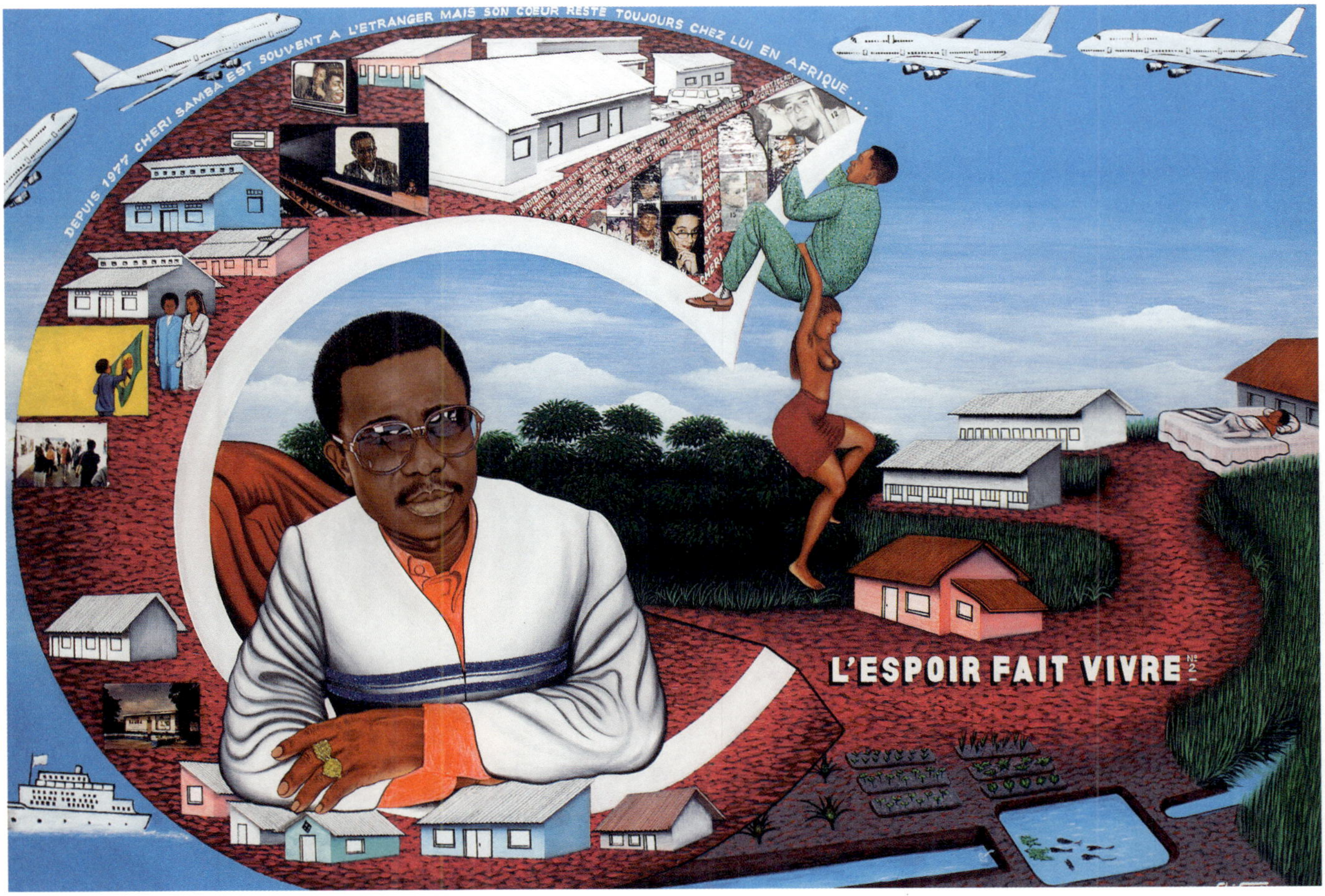

John Smith

* 1952 in London (UK), lives and works in London

Hotel Diaries, 2001–2007

Video, color, sound, 82 min

Individual titles:
Frozen War, Ireland, October 8th 2001, 11 min
Museum Piece, Germany, October 14th 2004, 12 min
Throwing Stones, Switzerland, November 13th 2004, 11 min
B & B, UK, November 26th 2005, 6 min
Pyramids/Skunk, Netherlands, January 29th 2006/
January 29th 2007, 16 min
Dirty Pictures, Palestine, April 15th/16th 2007, 14 min
Six Years Later, Ireland, October 20th 2007, 9 min

British filmmaker and video artist John Smith has been a presence in the film, television, and the art context since the beginning of the 1970s. While influenced from the outset by the formal ideas of 1960s structural filmmaking, Smith is also interested in the potential of narrative and language. Using the images found in his everyday life, the artist explores the limits of documentary and fiction, hence playfully exposing the language and manipulative power of cinema.

The multipart video work *Hotel Diaries* is a kind of travel diary the artist recorded over a period of six years always at night in hotel rooms in different places around the world. While the camera wanders around the furniture in anonymous hotel rooms, Smith speaks in a drowsy voice about crises in contemporary world politics, particularly the Israeli-Palestinian conflict. Here, banal objects form a bridge between personal experiences and primarily media-transmitted political reality through which the artist makes astonishing connections. (AM)

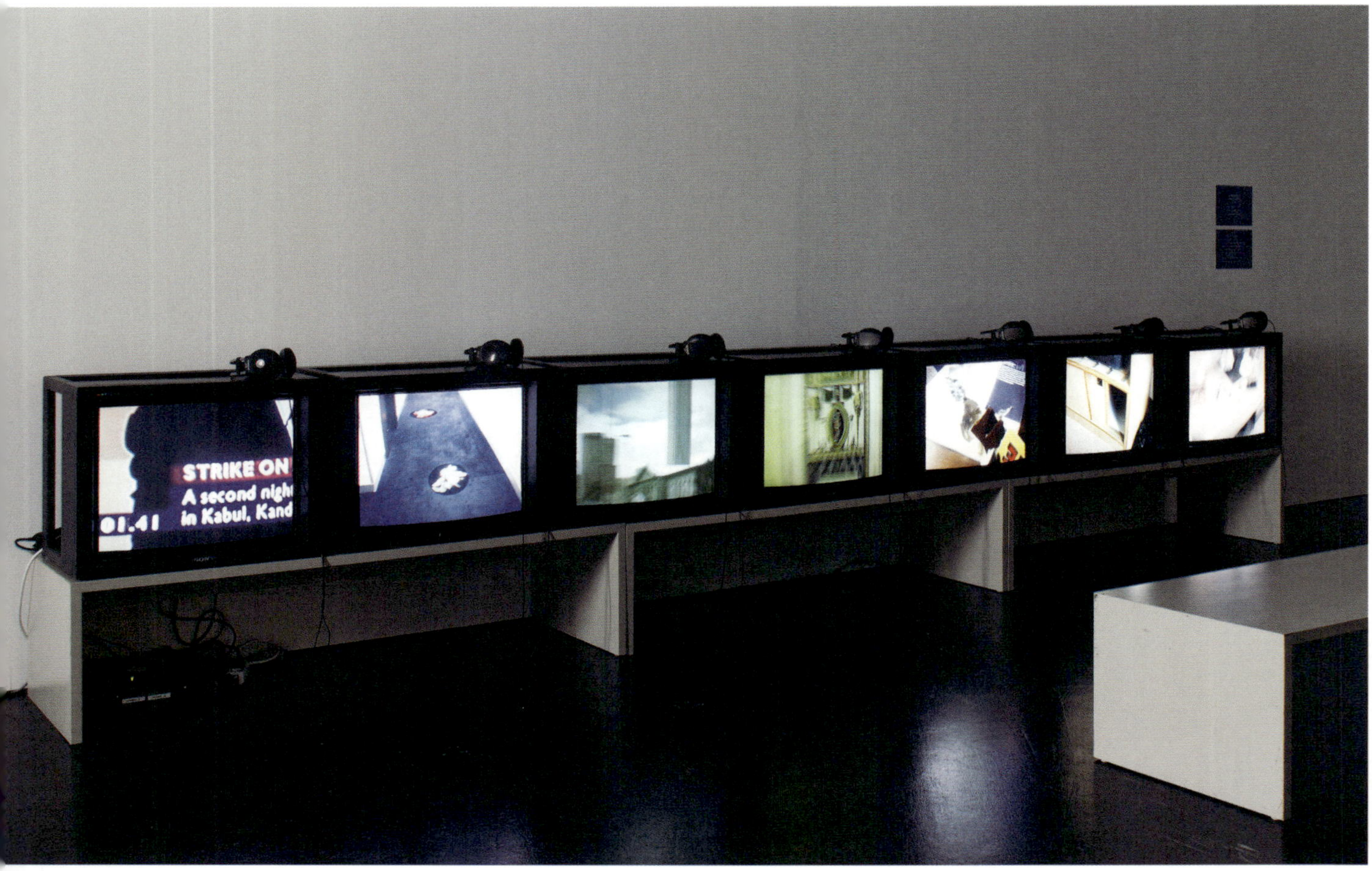

Mladen Stilinović

* 1947 in Belgrade (HR), lives and works in Belgrade

An artist who cannot speak English is no artist, 1994

Acrylic on artificial silk, 410 × 160 cm

It is difficult to conceive of contemporary art and the new channels of communication as being separate from one another: the Internet and mass media facilitate unlimited access to news and to knowledge, something which is essential for critical and engaged art; only through this can complex transnational projects be organized and mediated. However, the necessary technologies and languages have to be mastered to these ends, and anyone who refuses to do so or has no opportunity to learn will be barred entry into the utopian "global village." With the statement "an artist who cannot speak English is no artist" Mladen Stilinović makes a caustic comment about an ostensibly global art world. The words are sewed onto a banner like a slogan; however, it remains open as to whether it is a demand, a protest, or an expression of resignation - after all, the statement is only "intelligible to all" because it is in English.

Since the 1960s, Stilinović has been working in Croatia in an art scene which was no less active or relevant - no less "artistic" - than that of Western Europe. The issue of a world language of art thus remains unresolved: prior to 1989, English was the language of the part of the capitalist world which laid claim to the "grand narrative" of art and thus to the definition of who should be considered an artist; in the present era, English enables worldwide exchange. Does this mean that those who are unable or do not wish to use this language are not contemporary artists? (JB)

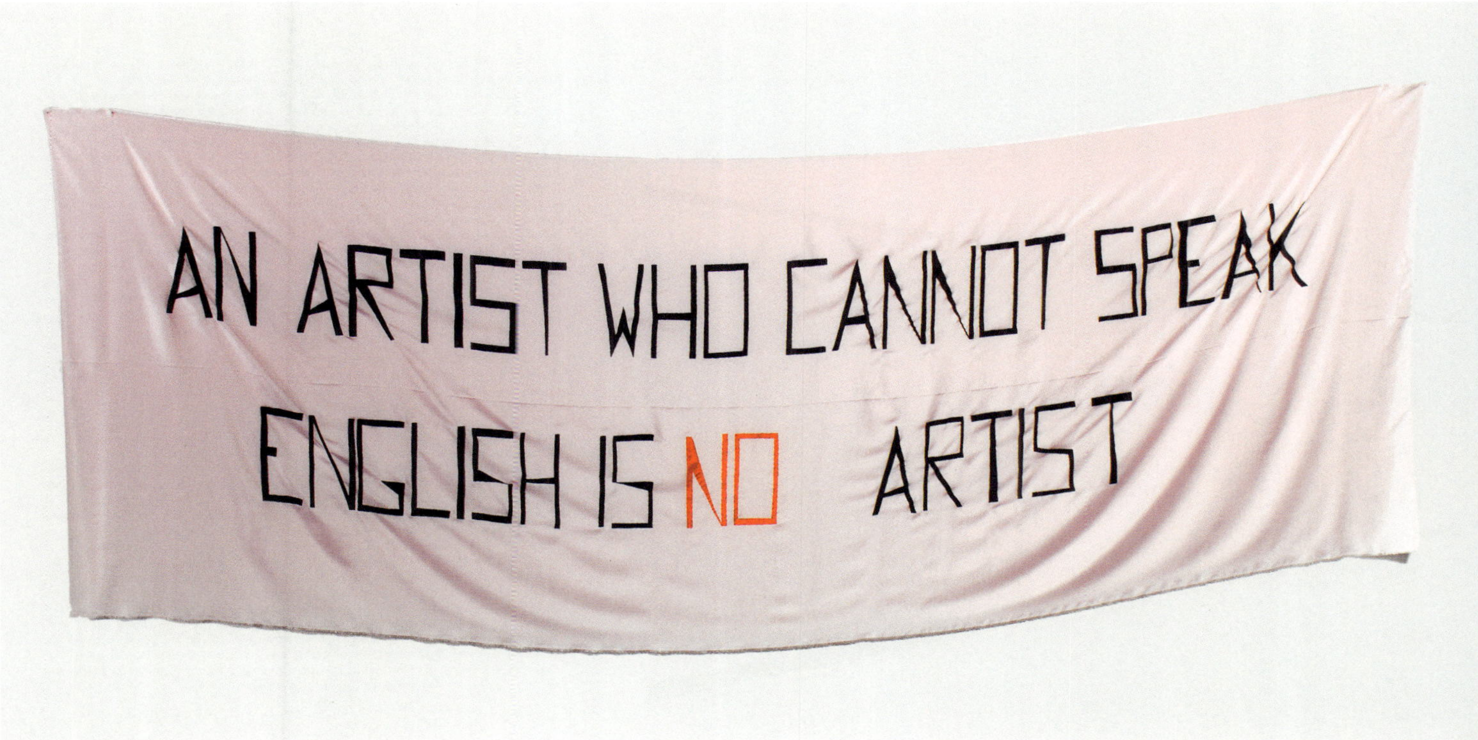

Xu Bing

* 1955 in Chongqing (CN), lives and works in New York, NY (US) and Beijing (CN)

Telephone, 1996–2006

Translation project,
10 written pages (paper), framed

The principle of Xu Bing's work is as simple as it is humorous and clever. In the game "Telephone" short messages are relayed by whisper from one person to another - often until such point that the original message has been grotesquely distorted. In *Telephone* there is long distance between two Chinese texts: Xu has an original text - taken from a study of the literary scholar Lydia Liu - translated into English; from English into French; from the French into Russian, German, Spanish, Japanese, and Thai before then being translated back into Chinese and into English. In this experiment, the impossibility of a translation retaining its original meaning is also formally shown on the subject of language: the English version includes correction notes; in the French, single passages - perhaps only those difficult to translate - are highlighted. Each text is also signed by the translators, together with the date. The individual sheets thus become a signed unicum, a work of art.

As a wanderer between cultures, with the work *Telephone*, Xu Bing not only poses the question about the limits of language and inevitable misunderstanding. The artist wants us to consider that art also has its limits, even if it is open in some points for different interpretations. Perhaps Xu's work will therefore be shown also in the context of Chinese traditions, as well as in connection with Western-influenced, contemporary conceptual art. (KB)

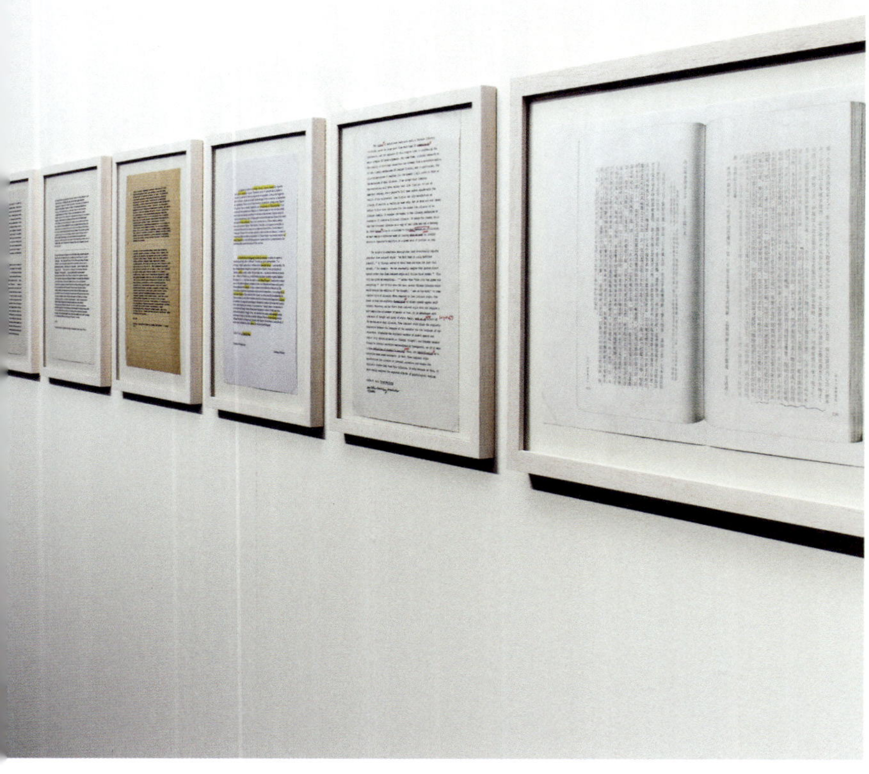

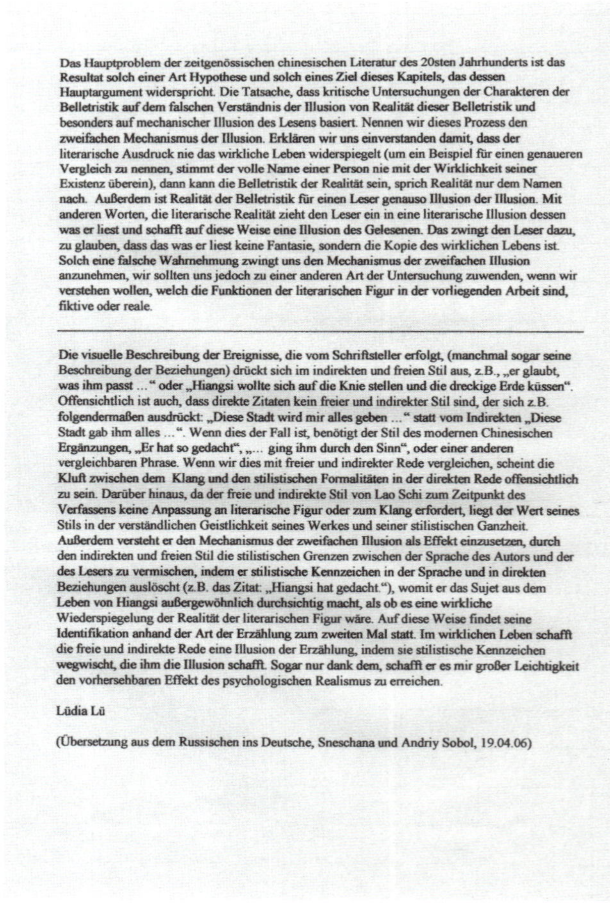

Das Hauptproblem der zeitgenössischen chinesischen Literatur des 20sten Jahrhunderts ist das Resultat solch einer Art Hypothese und solch eines Ziel dieses Kapitels, das dessen Hauptargument widerspricht. Die Tatsache, dass kritische Untersuchungen der Charakteren der Belletristik auf dem falschen Verständnis der Illusion von Realität dieser Belletristik und besonders auf mechanischer Illusion des Lesens basiert. Nennen wir dieses Prozess den zweifachen Mechanismus der Illusion. Erklären wir uns einverstanden damit, dass der literarische Ausdruck nie das wirkliche Leben widerspiegelt (um ein Beispiel für einen genaueren Vergleich zu nennen, stimmt der volle Name einer Person nie mit der Wirklichkeit seiner Existenz überein), dann kann die Belletristik der Realität sein, sprich Realität nur dem Namen nach. Außerdem ist Realität der Belletristik für einen Leser genauso Illusion der Illusion. Mit anderen Worten, die literarische Realität zieht den Leser ein in eine literarische Illusion dessen was er liest und schafft auf diese Weise eine Illusion des Gelesenen. Das zwingt den Leser dazu, zu glauben, dass das was er liest keine Fantasie, sondern die Kopie des wirklichen Lebens ist. Solch eine falsche Wahrnehmung zwingt uns den Mechanismus der zweifachen Illusion anzunehmen, wir sollten uns jedoch zu einer anderen Art der Untersuchung zuwenden, wenn wir verstehen wollen, welch die Funktionen der literarischen Figur in der vorliegenden Arbeit sind, fiktive oder reale.

Die visuelle Beschreibung der Ereignisse, die vom Schriftsteller erfolgt, (manchmal sogar seine Beschreibung der Beziehungen) drückt sich im indirekten und freien Stil aus, z.B., „er glaubt, was ihm passt … " oder „Hiangsi wollte sich auf die Knie stellen und die dreckige Erde küssen". Offensichtlich ist auch, dass direkte Zitaten kein freier und indirekter Stil sind, der sich z.B. folgendermaßen ausdrückt: „Diese Stadt wird mir alles geben … " statt vom Indirekten „Diese Stadt gab ihm alles … ". Wenn dies der Fall ist, benötigt der Stil des modernen Chinesischen Ergänzungen, „Er hat so gedacht", „… ging ihm durch den Sinn", oder einer anderen vergleichbaren Phrase. Wenn wir dies mit freier und indirekter Rede vergleichen, scheint die Kluft zwischen dem Klang und den stilistischen Formalitäten in der direkten Rede offensichtlich zu sein. Darüber hinaus, da der freie und indirekte Stil von Lao Schi zum Zeitpunkt des Verfassens keine Anpassung an literarische Figur oder zum Klang erfordert, liegt der Wert seines Stils in der verständlichen Geistlichkeit seines Werkes und seiner stilistischen Ganzheit. Außerdem versteht er den Mechanismus der zweifachen Illusion als Effekt einzusetzen, durch den indirekten und freien Stil die stilistischen Grenzen zwischen der Sprache des Autors und der des Lesers zu vermischen, indem er stilistische Kennzeichen in der Sprache und in direkten Beziehungen auslöscht (z.B. das Zitat: „Hiangsi hat gedacht."), womit er das Sujet aus dem Leben von Hiangsi außergewöhnlich durchsichtig macht, als ob es eine wirkliche Wiederspiegelung der Realität der literarischen Figur wäre. Auf diese Weise findet seine Identifikation anhand der Art der Erzählung zum zweiten Mal statt. Im wirklichen Leben schafft die freie und indirekte Rede eine Illusion der Erzählung, indem sie stilistische Kennzeichen wegwischt, die ihm die Illusion schafft. Sogar nur dank dem, schafft er es mir großer Leichtigkeit den vorhersehbaren Effekt des psychologischen Realismus zu erreichen.

Lūdia Lū

(Übersetzung aus dem Russischen ins Deutsche, Sneschana und Andriy Sobol, 19.04.06)

Zhou Tiehai

* 1956 in Shanghai (CN), lives and works in Shanghai

Will / We Must, 1996

35 mm film, transferred to DVD,
b/w, silent, 9:17 min

There are many stories about art and life; the artist's ego (for the most part, male) in the struggle for recognition and authentic expression has provided the dramatic material for numerous novels and films. In contemporary art, which places the analysis of its own conditions and its social significance in the foreground, such clichés rarely play a role. However, this by no means suggests that conflicts only take place on the level of discourse. In his video *Will / We Must*, Zhou Tiehai shows episodes from the contemporary art world in which things occur quite emotionally and in terms of destiny. However, the short scenes have nothing to do with a naive reproduction of sensitivities; a break emerges simply by the fact that Zhou Tiehai presents the episodes with the stylistic devices of a black-and-white silent movie: the travails of the film characters to survive with their art in their surroundings, their city, and also in the ominous world beyond the Chinese borders, make the episodes seem like narratives from a past epoch to which we now look back with a sense of ironic distance or nostalgia. But the scenes themselves are precise observations of the contemporary art system: if Zhou Tiehai stages the artistic happening as a military crisis or pens a melodramatic one-liner – "I'll take part in any exhibition you have!" – he finds an appropriate allegory for art and life between strategy and the everyday. (JB)

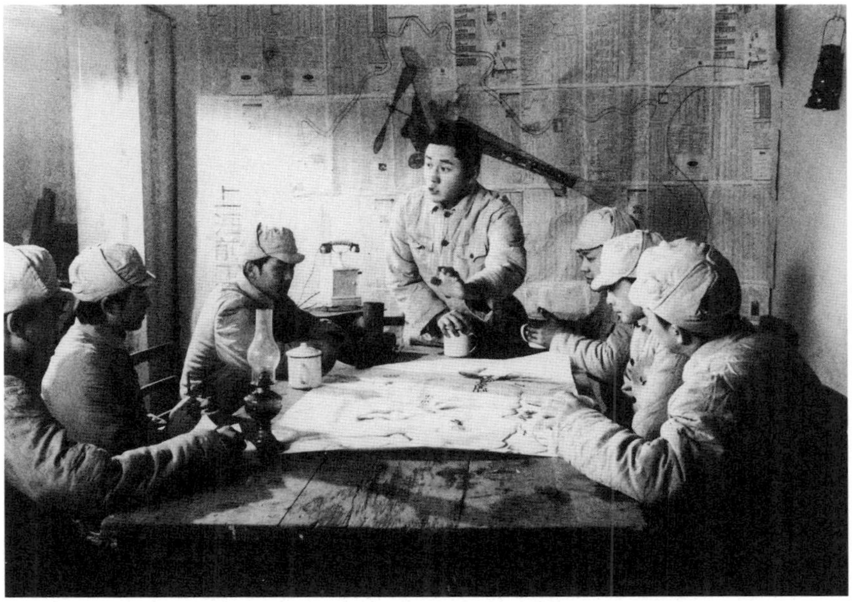

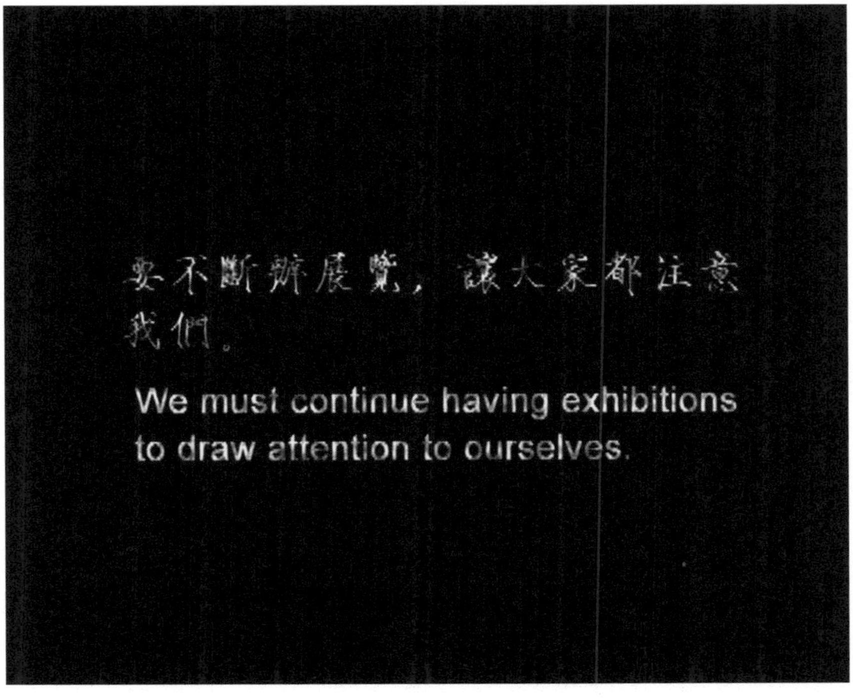

Anetta Mona Chişa & Lucia Tkáčová
Minerva Cuevas / Ala Ebtekar
Yara El-Sherbini / Brendan Fernandes
Will Kwan / Pooneh Maghazehe
Karen Mirza & Brad Butler
Eko Nugroho / Ruth Sacks
Tintin Wulia

Artist-in-Residence Program

A central aim of the *The Global Contemporary* exhibition was to investigate the international art world through scholarly and experimental studies. To this end, an artist-in-residence program was launched and eleven international artists and artist groups were invited to explore the issues addressed and the concepts presented by the exhibition (which was already up and running), and to analyze these critically during their six-week stay in Karlsruhe. The concept did not restrict the artists to focusing on subject matter; they were explicitly requested to participate in curatorial processes or revisit the curatorial concept. The artists invited – Anetta Mona Chişa & Lucia Tkáčová (RO/CZ and SK/CZ), Minerva Cuevas (MX), Ala Ebtekar (US), Yara El-Sherbini (UK), Brendan Fernandes (KE/CA/US), Will Kwan (CN/CA), Pooneh Maghazehe (US), Karen Mirza and Brad Butler (UK), Eko Nugroho (ID), Ruth Sacks (ZA), and Tintin Wulia (ID/AU) – have in their previous work not only investigated subject-specific issues, but also made conscious use of performative or participative strategies in the context of alternative platforms. The resulting artistic projects from the program were subsequently included in the exhibition, and imbued it with the special quality of a laboratory or a construction site.

Ever since their inception in the early twentieth century artist-in-residence programs have existed to provide artists with the opportunity of being creative away from their usual cultural environment through limited stays at other institutions. In addition to biennials, museums, and art markets in the wake of globalization these programs have emerged as an essential component of the international art scene and have helped foster the global network of artworld players, who have now become "global" within the art system. Especially for young artists, who have not yet broken into the art market, the myriad of differently themed residency programs offer new platforms where they can produce and present their projects.

The artist-in-residence program was one of the centerpieces of *The Global Contemporary* and specially conceived for it. There were several different layers, which were interesting to us as curators, that were addressed and explored during the course of the project. First, the practices of international artist-in-residence programs were implemented while at the same time drawing attention to them. Second, new joint projects and networks were fostered between participating artists of different cultural origins and from various geographic backgrounds. Third, the artistic (and if necessary location-specific) process had to directly involve or address the local audience. Fourth, the artistic projects were required to relate to the themes of the exhibition, and fifth, the artists were invited to reflect on the curatorial concept and/or the exhibition and offer their critical appraisal. The decision to conceive and treat the project as a dynamic process was based on the idea that an exhibition with a focus on international art production under global conditions will never be able to paint a coherent and complete picture; instead, it must be understood as an experimental laboratory or indeed a "construction site." With regard to the exhibition's architecture the residency artists' projects suggested a different approach to the exhibition. In this way, the projects undermine or subvert the original thrust of the exhibition's themes. (AM & JB)

Anetta Mona Chişa & Lucia Tkáčová

Anetta Mona Chişa, *1975 in Nădlac (RO), lives and works in Prague (CZ)
Lucia Tkáčová, *1977 in Banská Štiavnica (SK), lives and works in Prague and Bratislava (SK)

The Importance of Doing Nothing (and Discussing Everything), 2011–2012

Theater play written on 5 euro banknotes
Produced in cooperation with ZKM | Karlsruhe

In the language of contemporary art, "participation" is a term that usually has positive connotations; the intention is to give people the opportunity to act and experience things, rather than leaving them in the role of mere "spectators." This is, of course, a complex matter outside the protected enclave of the museum. For decades, people have been calling for "direct democracy" and thus for participation in state decision-making, while at the same time the consequences of personal action are becoming increasingly opaque. In light of increasing globalization in particular every trip to the supermarket, for example, could potentially foster exploitation and corruption elsewhere.

This also applies to the art world, because it is precisely the success of critical art on the international stage that brings it into closer contact with ominous financial backers, or essentially turns it into the product of private networks. Not to act and thus not to get bound up in power games and dependencies, seems therefore to be the ethically cleanest solution. The artists Anetta Mona Chişa and Lucia Tkáčová have written down a lengthy, personal dialog on this dilemma - line by line on 5-euro notes that are now being reintroduced into the money cycle. At several levels, their work is a game with the refusal to participate. On the one hand, we have the artistic piece that in our society is always subject to commercial utilization qua its status as a luxury commodity, extracted from the art market and transformed into a trivial means of payment. On the other, all those who have held one of these bills in their hands (involuntarily?) become participants in an art project and actors in a decentralized, nonlinear theater performance as soon as they read one of the sentences on the bank note. (JB)

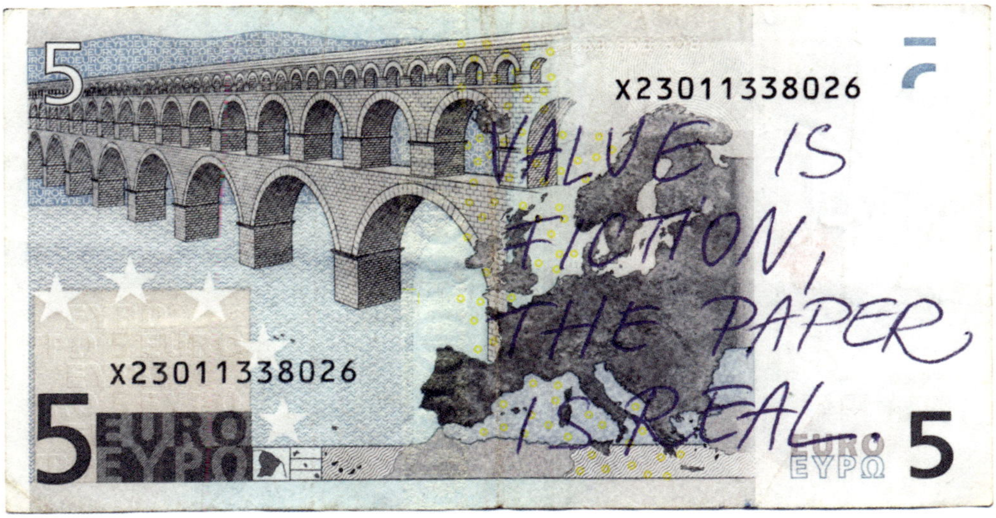

Minerva Cuevas

*1975 in Mexico City (MX), lives and works in Mexico City

Social Spectrum, 2011

GSM network and mixed-media installation,
in collaboration with Keith Whythe and Detlev Ernst
Produced in cooperation with ZKM | Karlsruhe

Minerva Cuevas' artistic practice is characterized by socially committed, site-specific actions that she carries out at a wide variety of venues - ranging from public spaces to museums and the Internet. During her period of residence at ZKM she created an interactive piece entitled *Social Spectrum* in which she explores the change in technological and social communication processes in the age of globalization and in so doing touches on ecological and social issues. An autonomous noncommercial network based on GSM within the museum building for the duration of the exhibition enabled visitors to communicate free of charge with one another via mobile phone or a using a land-line phone in the museum, even world-wide, thus forming a temporary network. By eliminating the mechanisms of inclusion and exclusion that still hold sway in the field of art, and at the same time ignoring and overcoming political and geographic boundaries, with her *Social Spectrum* installation Minerva Cuevas at least temporarily succeeded in initiating social interaction that went beyond the already networked art audience and linked up all sorts of different communities and individuals. (AM)

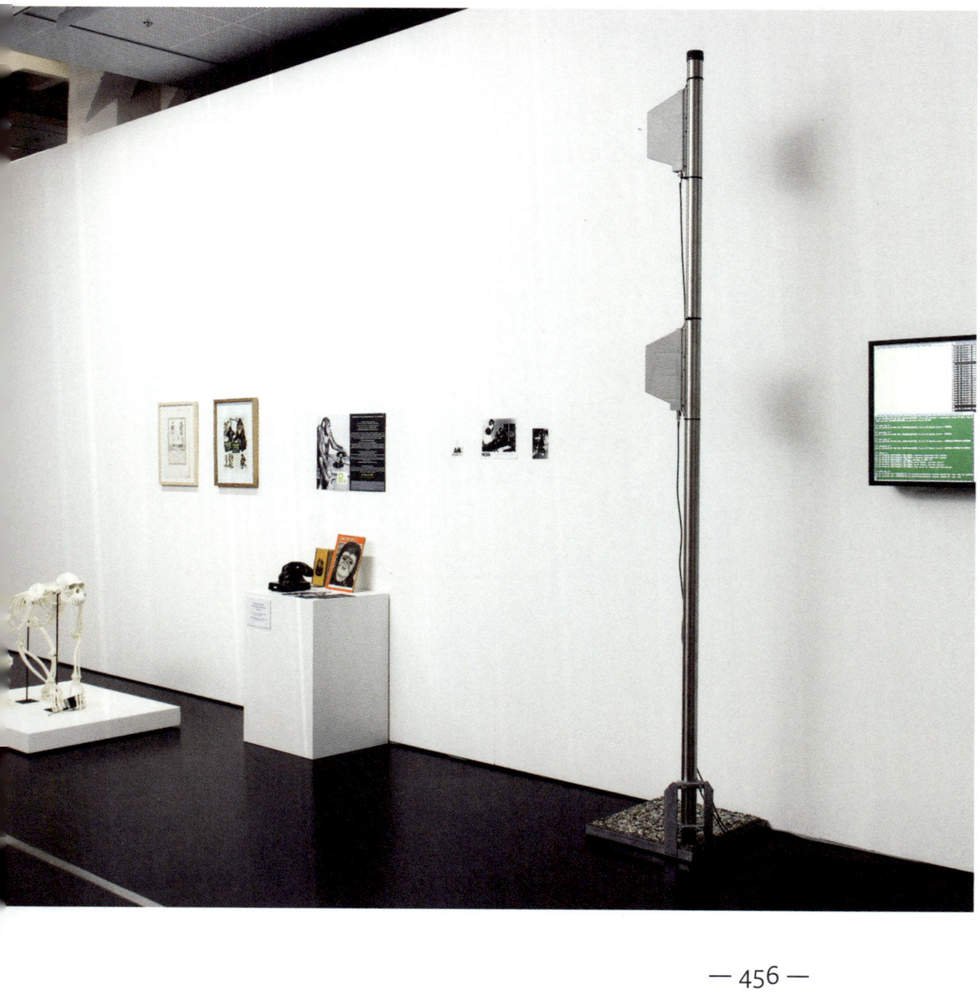

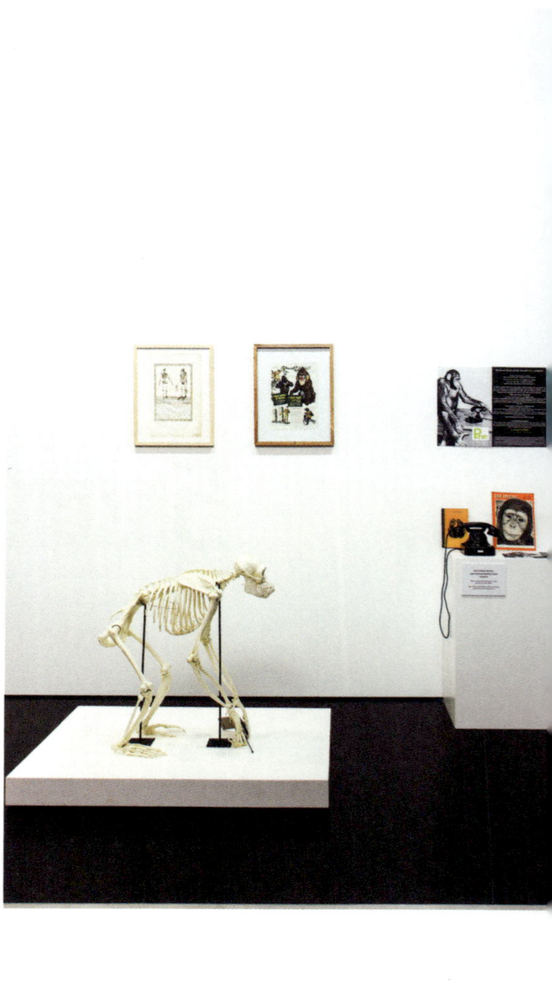

Ala Ebtekar

* 1978 in Berkeley, CA (US), lives and works in San Francisco, CA (US)

The dark midnight, fearful waves, and the tempestuous whirlpool, 2011
(selection from the upcoming book *Ayandeh-nameh*)

Mixed-media digital pigment prints
4 works, each 100 × 66 cm, framed,
1 work, 100 × 150 cm, framed

Paradise, 011
(selection from the upcoming book *Ayandeh-nameh*)

Mixed-media digital pigment prints
100 × 66 cm, 100 × 150 cm, 100 × 66 cm (triptych)

Untitled, 011
(from the upcoming book *Ayandeh-nameh*)

Mixed-media digital pigment print
100 × 150 cm

Produced in cooperation with
ZKM | Karlsruhe

Ala Ebtekar is renowned for his exceptional paintings, wall drawings, installations, and artist's books, which emerge at a visual crossroads between an equally vivid past, present, and future.

While at the ZKM in Karlsruhe, Ebtekar explored the process of painting and photomontage, with an overlay of popular Iranian visual culture. He studied the 1970s and contemporary Persian leisure, the dream of space flight, pageantry, celebrations, cultural heroes, and the concept of the nation as fantasy motifs. His investigation is part of *Ayandeh-nameh*, an edition of artist's books and mixtapes on Persian culture, curated by the artist Binta Ayofemi.

Ayandeh-nameh is a mash-up of 1970s Iran, pop music, fictional space programs, alternative futures, and competing nostalgias that extend into mythical pasts, all found in vivid storefronts, neighborhood parades, ritual events, pageantry, and festivities. What would a future Iran look like? What would be discarded and what remade? *Ayandeh-nameh* is divided into thematic chapters, including the "Wrestling Ring," "Disco," "Space flight," and "Epics."

Like fantasy, futuristic texts enact alternative realities, presenting entirely possible but previously untried modes of being such as time travel, technologies and new and different political or social systems (utopian and dystopian), situations and generative, hybrid platforms where organized society gives way to the new formations. Contemporary Iranian culture, whether in Los Angeles or Tehran, is being continually shaped by viewers, readers, and listeners. *Ayandeh-nameh* suggests a temporary world where memory, fantasy, and reality mingle. (AE)

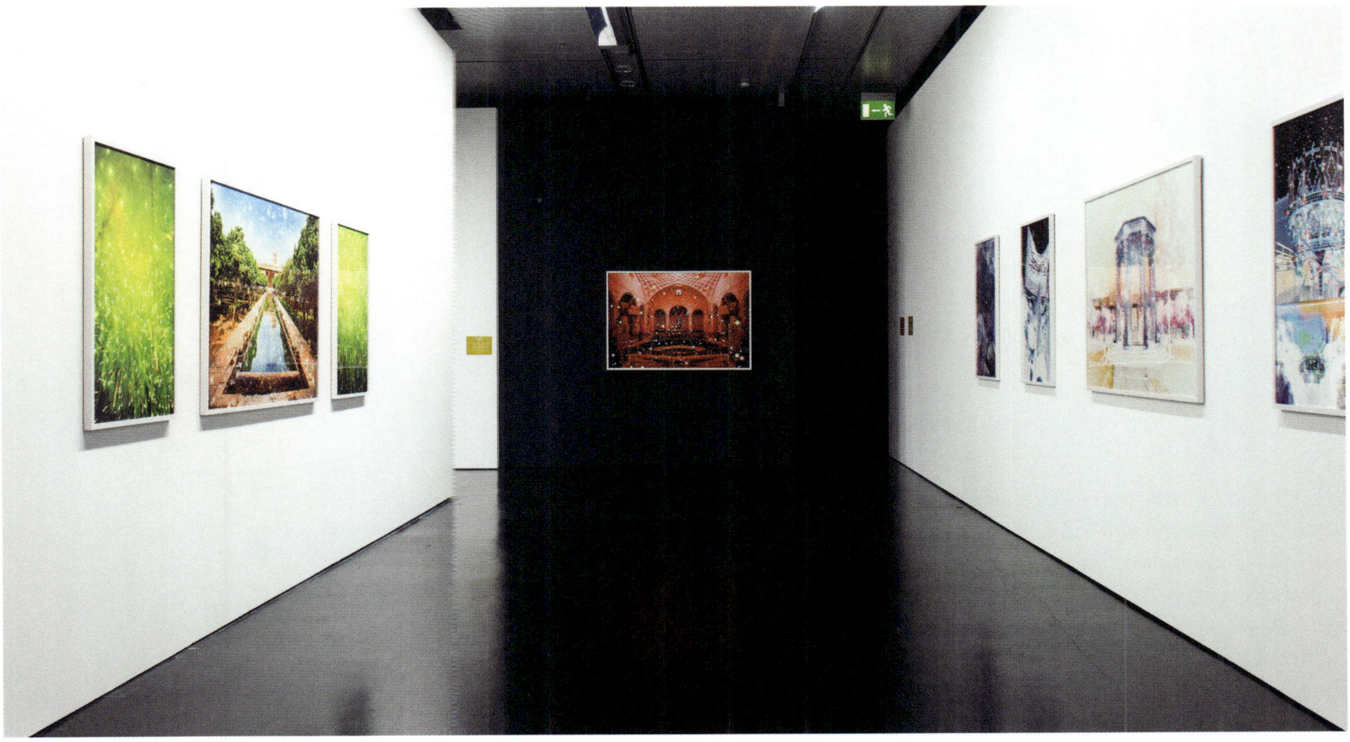

Yara El-Sherbini

* 1978 in London (UK), lives and works in London

A Weather House for the Current Climate, 2011

Mixed media, weather house, wood, plastic, metal, catgut, paper, string, 32 × 20 × 56 cm

Reproducing the Current Climate, 2011

Documentation of an intervention: reproduction of *A Weather House for the Current Climate* for sale at the Karlsruhe Christmas market
Mixed media, weather house, wood, plastic, catgut, paper, string, 16 × 10 × 28 cm

Produced in cooperation with ZKM | Karlsruhe

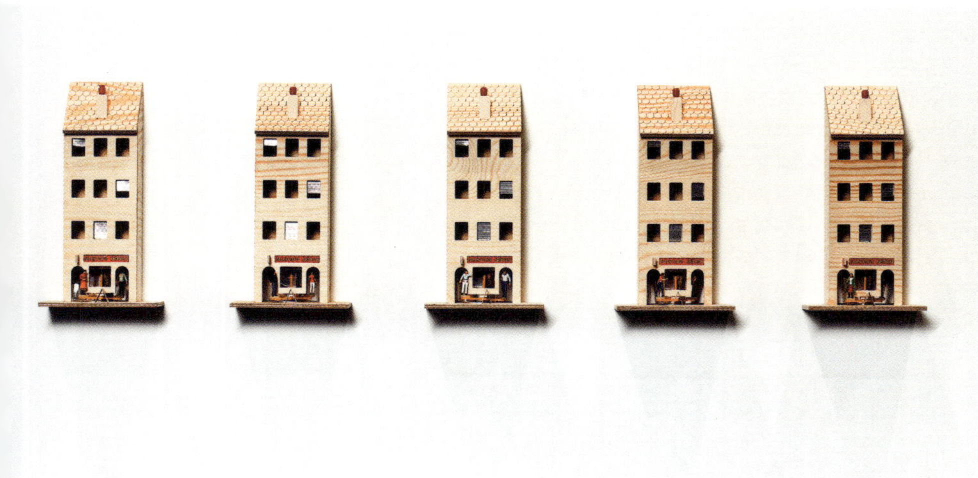

Humorously and playfully including her audience in her artistic processes is a strategy that Yara El-Sherbini has already used in earlier works, for example, when she exposed language as a tool for manipulating knowledge or investigated social and political systems in order to find out about their power structures. During her residency at Karlsruhe, she discovered the weather house as a typically German souvenir article from the Black Forest. By replacing the couple in Black Forest costumes with two persons clad in a more contemporary fashion idiom and by placing them in front of a kebab shop, she presents an updated image of cultural identity in our modern societies characterized by migration and globalization. And in fact, the döner kebab that has now become Germany's most popular fast food does not originate in Turkey but was invented in 1971 by a Turkish immigrant, Mahmut Aygun, in Berlin, and is already a piece of Turkish/German history and identity. As part of a subsequent attempt to sell ten serially produced copies (*Reproducing the Current Climate*) at the Karlsruhe Christmas market, El-Sherbini sought direct contact with the local public – and became involved in discussions about the relationship between originals and copies, the value of art, traditions and contemporary life as well as about the current status of culture. (AM)

Another Form of Regulation and Control, 2011

Hygro-thermograph, plastic, metal, paper, battery, 33 × 15 × 24 cm
Produced in cooperation with ZKM | Karlsruhe

With this work the artist is addressing various forms of control and influence exerted both on a curatorial and on an institutional or political level within the museum, processes that decide about the inclusion and exclusion of ideas and works. At the same time, these also control and influence political and social procedures in general. The work was produced as a direct response by the artist to an actual experience with the institution locally – one of her suggested projects which involved an intervention in the public sphere in connection with the activation of a fictitious partner town in Palestine was ultimately rejected by ZKM, partly for (local) political reasons. (AM)

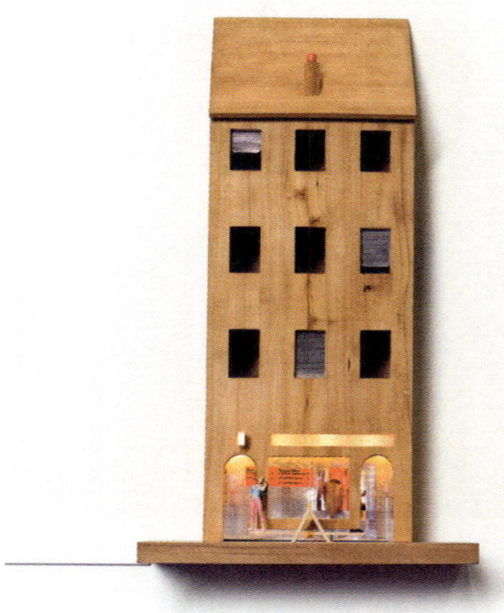

Brendan Fernandes

*1979 in Nairobi (KE), lives and works in New York, NY (US)

The Devil's Noise, 2011

Video, color, sound, 2:09 min,
Edited in collaboration with Moritz Büchner

Eyes on the Editor, 2011

Custom-made books, with Text on Table, dimensions variable

Symposium, I, II, III

3 Screen Prints, 50 × 65 cm

Language is power: not only because its use as act of speech shapes our reality, but also because a command of language brings us into direct contact with a specific culture; in other words, it furnishes us with an identity or refuses to allow us such. In the colonial South Africa of the 1970s, for example, Afrikaans, the language of the white minority, was designated the main teaching language in schools, and was thus an instrument that made access to education difficult for most of the population, who had never learned it. Pressure to use the language of the oppressors led in 1976 to the Soweto protests, crushed with much bloodshed by the Apartheid regime. Brendan Fernandes has taken this uprising as the subject for two pieces in which silence becomes a protest: "We Will Not Speak Your Devil Tongue" pinpoints the refusal to even consider the language of the oppressors as a means of communication. Turned into a poem, this historic slogan can be read on the spines of a long series of bound volumes. Inside the books is only black paper - bereft of writing and not fit for conventional writing, a library of the refusal to say anything. In the corresponding video the poem only crops up as a subtitle; the audio and visual levels are reduced to passages of hiss and the (devilish or protesting?) gestures by the artists. Fernandes juxtaposes these two pieces to the series of prints *Enconium*: transferred into Morse code and spread on sheets, what are actually sensuous words (*Love*, *Eros*, and *Desire*) become instructions or, if one thinks of the popular "deployment" of Morse code to signal an SOS, maybe even as a warning. (JB)

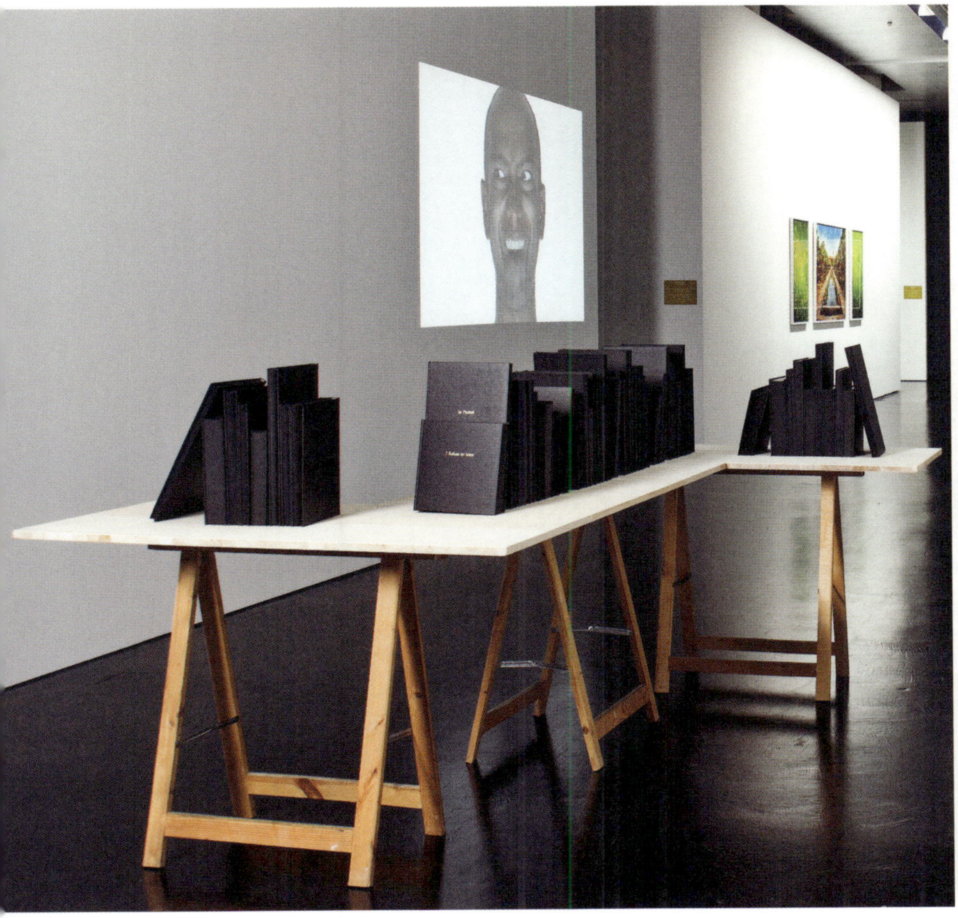

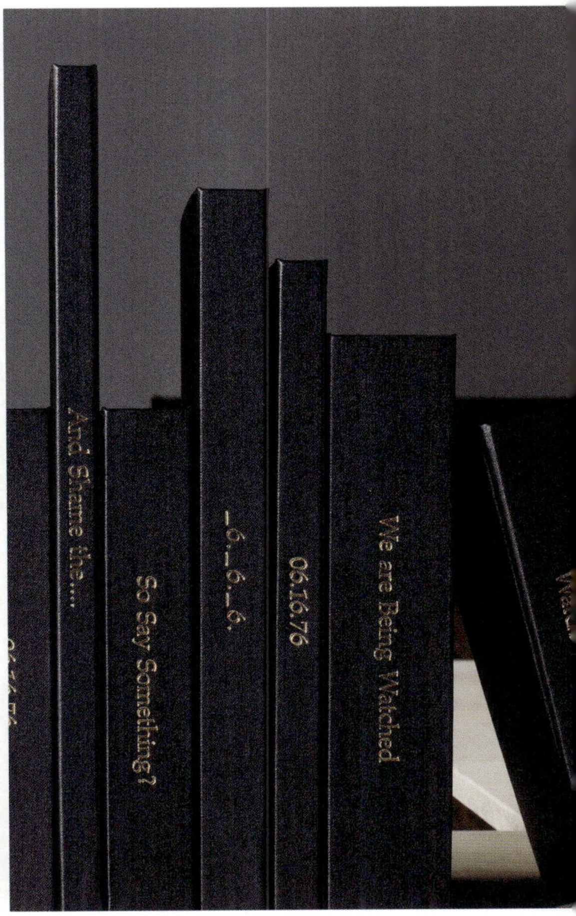

Will Kwan

*1978 in Hong Kong (CN), lives and works in Toronto (CA)

Two Signs Articulated, 2011

Vinyl wall text and backlit sign
Produced in cooperation with ZKM | Karlsruhe

Artists' Statement
Two Signs Articulated is an installation that appropriates the visual identity of Western Union and Art Basel, commercial enterprises that operate at polar ends of the global economy. The signs are "articulated" in two senses of the term. First, they are juxtaposed to mark the interdependence between the world of real labor and the world of symbolic labor, between economies of cash and systems of capital. Secondly, each sign has been modified to reveal its implicit cultural ambition or social reality. The bombastic language of Art Basel has been altered to express ambivalence and impermanence, while the Western Union logo has been converted into a phonetic system that points to the alterity of its clients and the intercultural economies that it profits from.
(Will Kwan)

Will Kwan moved with his family from Hong Kong to Toronto in 1981 when he was three. His practice is informed by a critical research on the homologation of culture in the age of globalization. By decontextualizing, manipulating and confronting internationally-known logos such as Art Basel's Un | Limited and Western Union, Kwan frames and investigates the imperialism of placeless visual signs. At the same time he questions the mechanisms of acceptance and expectation, which are at work in the acknowledgment of those images and symbols in particular contexts and situations. *Two Signs Articulated* is therefore a reflection on the production of meaning and consensus within the logic of an ephemeral yet pervasive "semiocapitalism." (SG)

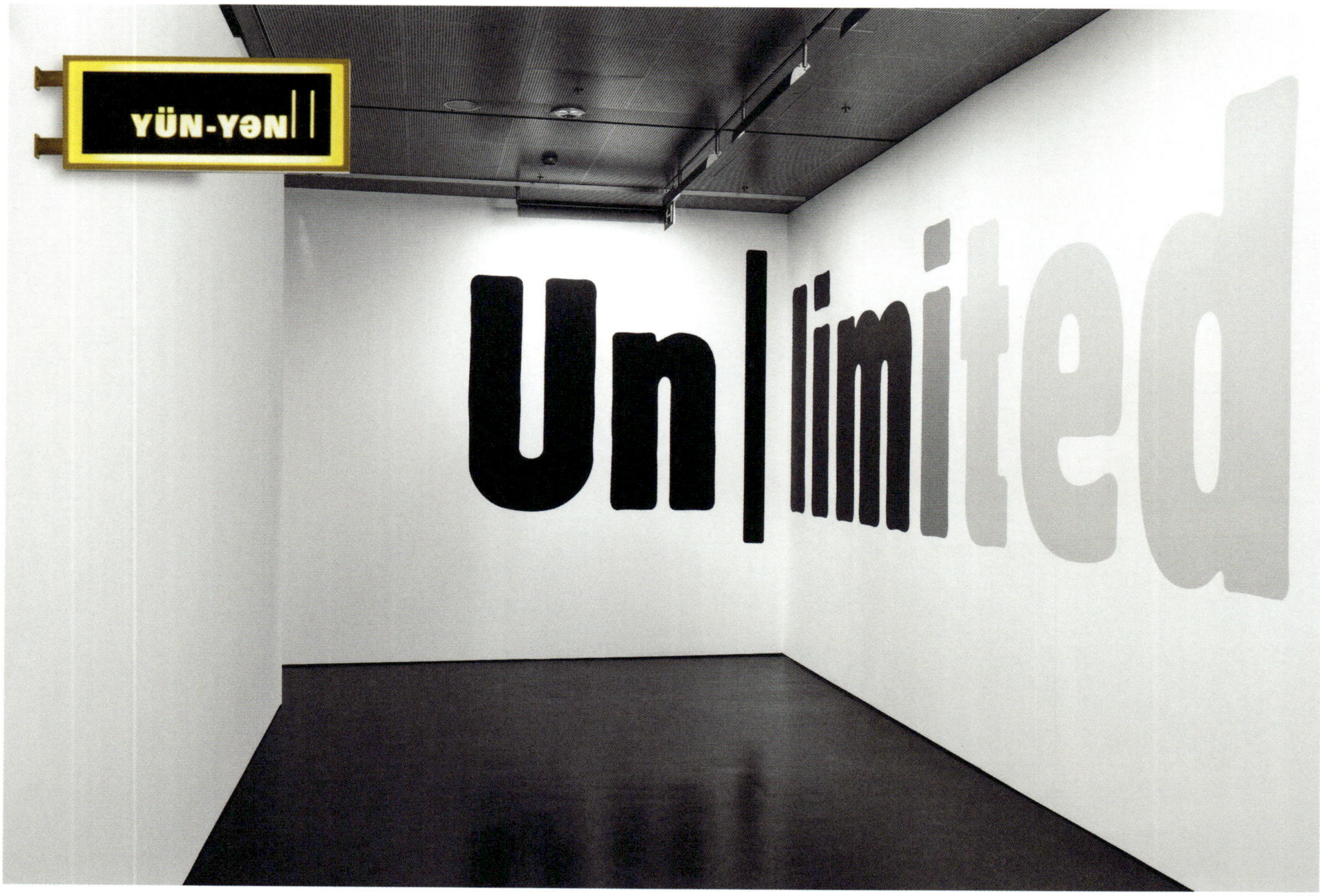

Pooneh Maghazehe

*1979 in New York, NY (US), lives and works in New York

Sandbox (work in progress), 2011

HD video (color, silent, 8 min), piano, sculpture, dimensions variable
Camera and editing in collaboration with Martin Lorenz, sculpture in collaboration with Silke Fehsenfeld
Produced in cooperation with ZKM | Karlsruhe

D.W. Griffith was the first American filmmaker commissioned to shoot a movie in a war zone. His film *Hearts of the World* (1918) depicts the story of two young lovers, ripped apart by the perturbations of the World War I. It was produced during the era when developments in photography and cinema began to inspire advancements in war technology and strategy. The film was commissioned by Great Britain, an effort to gain allied American support in the First World War I.

A significant portion of *Hearts of the World* was shot on the British war front with actual battle scenes. The complexities of the war heavily affected the production of the film. Army cameramen shot scenes; Griffith experienced surprise German artillery barrages and witnessed the deaths of escort soldiers. The final film, part war footage and the rest staged, severely impacted Griffith. Nonetheless, it was well received by American audiences.

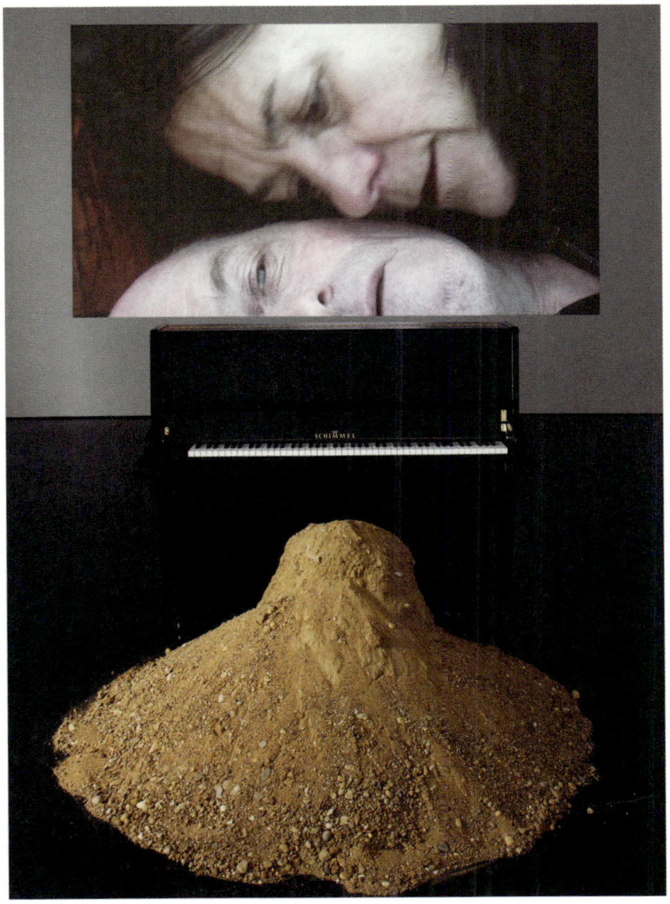

Sandbox[1] was shot in a vacant lot that was formerly the Karlsruhe DWM[2] munitions factory, a world leader in small arms at the time *Hearts of the World* was released. DWM armed soldiers worldwide with artillery that powered both world wars. As such, the empty pit, partially concealed by the crisp contours of a manicured lawn and protected by surrounding residential buildings and the ZKM, became an open anchor, an activated gap - the "sandbox" as an unrestricted game environment.

The initial motivations for *Sandbox* were to personify the dependent relationship between the rise of filmmaking and the advance of war technology through the ties between Lillian Gish, Dorothy Gish, and Robert Harron in *Hearts of the World*. *Sandbox* harbors a thick trace of incestuous history, an irresistible magnetic field of longing between two lovers.

The sandbox is heterotopic.
The sandbox is mimetic.
The sandbox is longing.
The sandbox is void.
The sandbox is trench.
The sandbox is hiccup.
The sandbox is archive.
The sandbox is desire.
The sandbox is grief.

(P. Maghazehe)

1 The term "sandbox" is used in game design to describe virtual environments that do not impose barriers or linear narratives on the players, but are open to various forms of interaction - inasmuch as this is allowed by the game's software.
2 Deutsche Waffen- und Munitionsfabriken Aktien-Gesellschaft [German Weapons and Munitions public limited company]

During the running time of the exhibition pianist Anna Zassimova accompanied the installation with live music performances.

Karen Mirza and Brad Butler

Karen Mirza, *1969 (UK), Brad Butler, *1973 (UK); live and work in London (UK)

A Common Stage, 2011

Mixed-media installation (HD video, color, sound, 7 min; neon sign, blackboard mural).
Produced in cooperation with ZKM | Karlsruhe

A museum is a place of order: The *ordering* of things in space and their *classification* - whether we understand these things as art or as historical artifacts, for example. The museum's order also refers to how one addresses things and accesses them; it's an order, in other words, that at times has to be asserted and that brings regulation with it on who may do what and what may be done, and who decides on such matters.

For their project, part of *The Global Contemporary*, Brad Butler and Karen Mirza started from the question: When can we talk about a place or a situation as a "shared stage" on which political issues can be voiced? This question actually applies to language itself, a vocabulary which may under certain circumstances not even permit certain political statements, thus condemning some to remain silent; moreover, it also relates to the place where people can speak. Such a place could, of course, be an art museum, a venue that today is often represented as a platform for knowledge transfer and free discourse. Yet rules also apply here as to when you can speak - and in what manner. For example, museum guardians as those responsible for compliance with the museum's rules, above all expect silence. Mirza and Butler placed a podium in their installation on which they join members of the ZKM's security service to discuss precisely these issues - and recorded this in a panel picture; it's a small shift in the museum's order, but one that exposes several assumed verities and power relationships within the institution of the museum. Can the guardians in a museum work in an artistic vein, and are they then still guardians or should they themselves then be placed under observation? (JB)

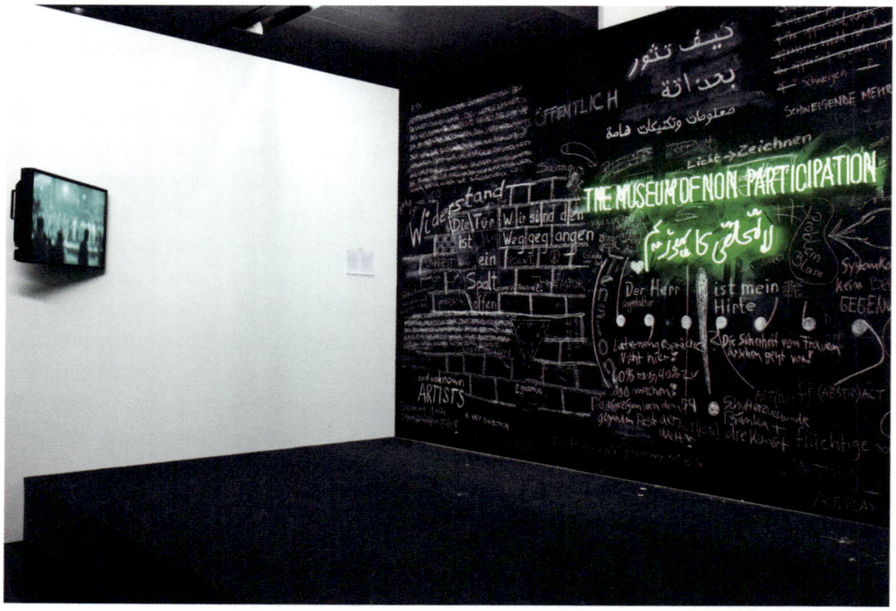

Artists' Statement

Our collaboration shifts across critical thought and direct action. In our art practice we site these "languages of resistance" within *The Museum of Non Participation*, a concept that speaks about both the boundaries of art institutions and the sets of social relations of an artistic practice. This we describe as a process of self-decolonization, focusing a critical view not only on the institution of art but also on wider social and political realms of cultural hegemony. Thus as part of our fictional museum we have been thinking through "what a possible collection might be" for a *Museum of Non Participation*: a museum interested in the archiving and production of gesture and action, a collecting of people around an action so that both the action and the gesture are what the museum collects.
(K. Mirza, B. Butler)

The Lack of A Common Stage

Workshop with: Brad Butler, Thomas Herzberger, Carolin Knebel, Stephan Krug, Karen Mirza, Philipp Sack, Rüdiger Stübler, and Norbert Werner, 2011

During a workshop that was part of *The Global Contemporary*, the ZKM museum attendants and gallery educators were invited to reflect, comment, and produce collectively an artwork on protest, speech, and silence. The resulting Blackboard mural serves as a background on which a neon sign acts both as a verb and a noun, a doing and a naming of the temporary and nomadic site of the *Museum of Non Participation*. The sign invokes a language of resistance that questions our paradoxical contemporary condition of participation and withdrawal. Its literal reading juxtaposes the Roman English and popular Urdu translation *larta lucki ka ajib ghar*, which when translated into English reads: "the museum of non participation, the house of the unexpected."

Eko Nugroho

* 1977 in Yogyakarta (ID), lives and works in Yogyakarta

ALIEN-NATION, 2011

Wall painting with emulsion paint, printed textile banner.

"Think global, act local": the popular dictum from the critical discourse on globalization shows us that we are responsible for the way we act in the context of world affairs. However, in a globalized art system that is permanently sending its protagonists and their works out on trips it is becoming increasingly difficult to pinpoint what is truly "local." This prompts the question why we identify ourselves as locals and what opportunities for what actions this fact involves.

For Eko Nugroho, this has long since become a part of his oeuvre. As a prominent figure on Yogyakarta's art scene he produces cartoons about the political situation there and, with his design project *Dagin Tumbuh*, establishes do-it-yourself practices as economically viable options for urban youth. These are strategies that do not transfer easily to the locations where Nugroho works as a protagonist of the globalized art scene. A number of weeks in a foreign city grants him a *tourist's* insights - a view of a place that both emphasizes its peculiarities and has a tendency to marvel at the kind of things that are decidedly a matter of course for the locals. For instance, the large mural he produced for *The Global Contemporary* with a pyramid and a monument to a prince, shows themes that must delight the tourist authorities as the inspiration for a visiting artist. By contrast, the figure of an older person with a forearm crutch is so much a feature of the cityscape that it only becomes visible when looked at by an outsider - a strange sight for the artist, because not in tune with the social structure in Yogyakarta: there, older people would not be out on the streets alone. The tourist's view, something that "global art" is often reproached for having, is here a vehicle for perception, when we gain new insights into our local reality through the eyes of a visitor. (JB)

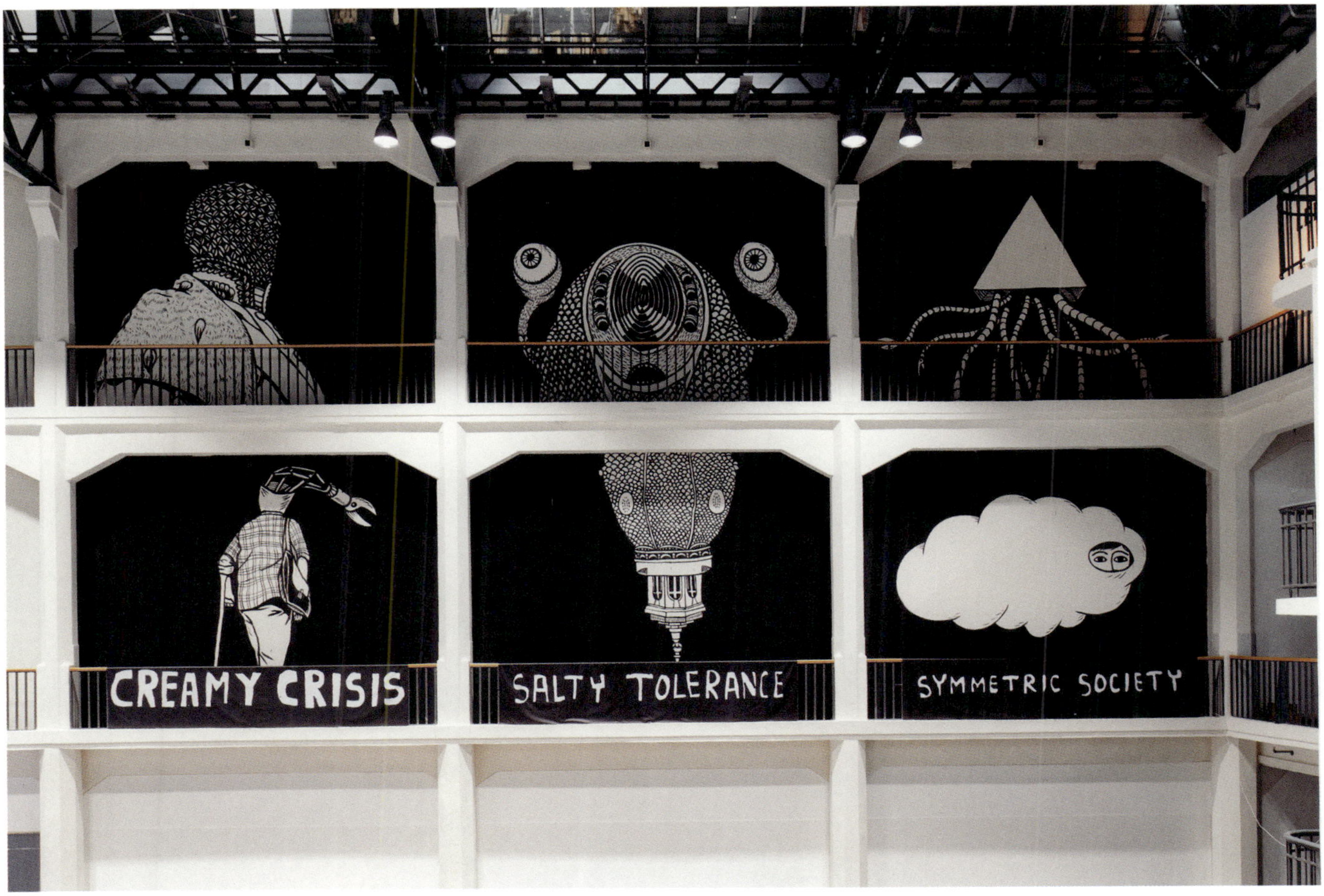

Ruth Sacks

* 1977 in Port Elizabeth (ZA), lives and works in Cape Town (ZA)

Legend Neutral, 2011

Ad in *Offenburger Tageblatt*, size variable, 1000 × A0 black-and-white poster, font set from Avoid Red Arrows
Produced in cooperation with ZKM | Karlsruhe

Is contemporary art a universal language? The fact that international biennials and residency programs are hosted in all manner of countries seems to suggest that art projects can indeed be construed as a globally mediated cultural technique, and that the sociopolitical edge of many works need (at least in terms of rhetoric) not shun a comparison with the claims of the "traditional" NGOs. That said, the notion of a universal language has its own history that, like any historiography, is also the product of conflict.

Artist Ruth Sacks often focuses in her work on the historical impact of language and writing, and tracked down one such language during her time in Karlsruhe: *Volapük*. Volapük is an artificial language primarily derived from English, which South German pastor and linguist Johann Martin Schleyer developed in the late nineteenth century. Despite the high goal he set himself, namely, to create a world language that would foster the emergence of a one-world community, Volapük was not accepted and was soon forgotten; it was hard to learn and it provided neither historical nor identity-forming roots. For example, J.R.R. Tolkien, the author of *Lord of the Rings*, decried artificial languages for being "deader" than Ancient languages because no legends were ever recorded in such artificial constructs. Ruth Sacks has now written a legend in Volapük which, in turn, tells the tale of another universalist project: the search for the "first plant." Like the idea of a "world language," the search for the original form of plant life falls into the category of local claims to power and the wish to subjugate the world to one's *own* interpretation. In an uncanny way this can also be related to the universal claims of the art scene that the world can be healed by drawing on art. (JB)

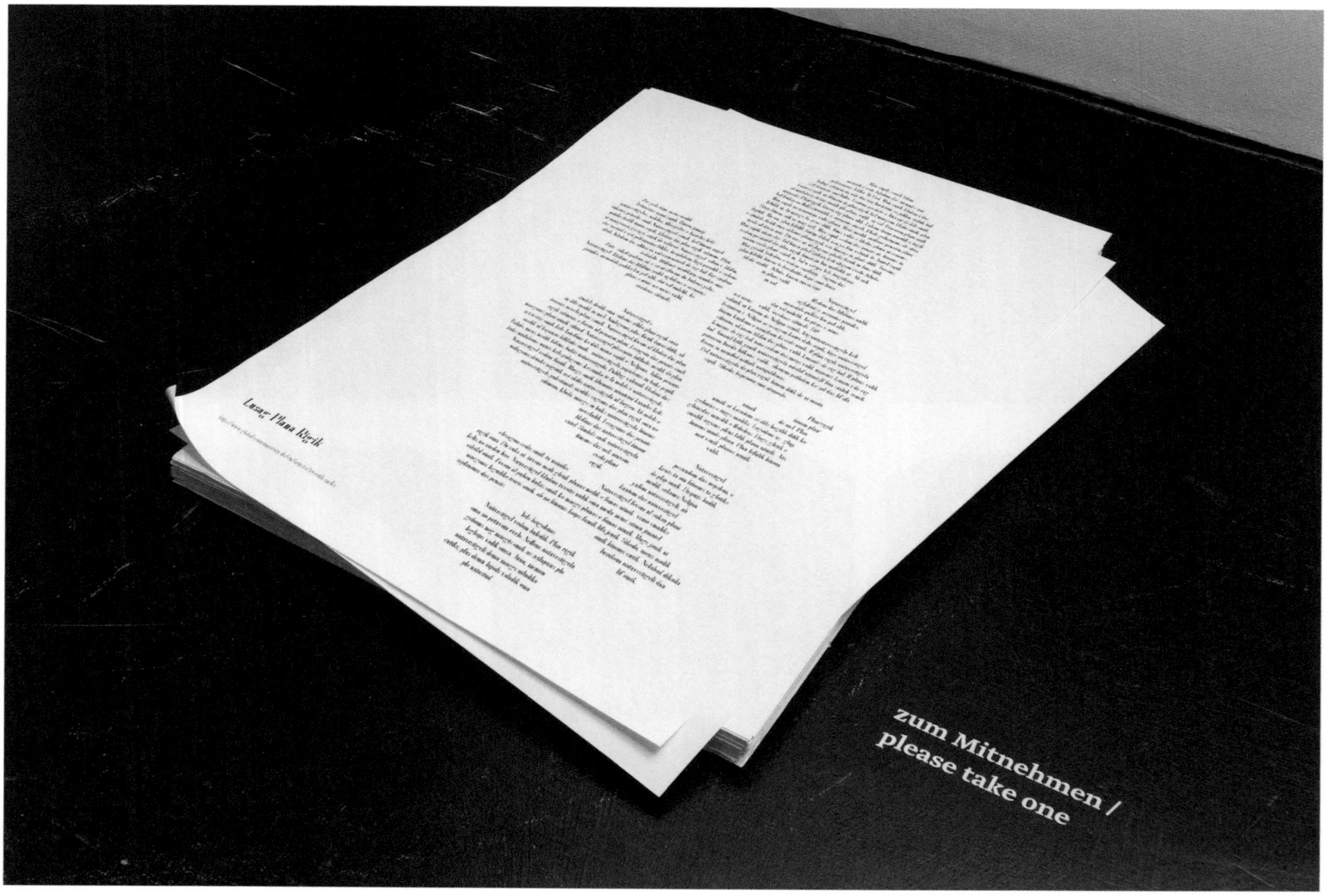

Tintin Wulia

* 1972 in Denpasar, Bali (ID), lives and works in Jakarta (ID) and Melbourne (AU)

The Butterfly Generator, 2012

Interactive Network Installation with Live Video Projection
Produced in cooperation with ZKM | Karlsruhe & Osage Art Foundation, Hong Kong.
This work is part of the artist's practice-based PhD research
at RMIT University, Australia

Descriptions of globalization processes hinge on two contradictory statements. On the one hand, globalization can mean that the number of opportunities is multiplied, since it makes more locations, more things and more knowledge available to more people. Yet, on the other, it can also represent a loss of opportunities, whenever ideas and products are standardized and simplified in order to reach the largest possible number of people. When criticizing the capitalist world view, for example, this latter situation is described as "McDonaldization" - a corporate strategy that attempts to uniformly cover the world with specific products and to squeeze out local alternatives.

The vision of a world where - for better or for worse - the same conditions prevail everywhere can be contrasted with visions of the globalized world as chaos. The "butterfly effect" in chaos theory says that the wings of a butterfly beating in Brazil can trigger a tornado in Texas and thus that small events in one place can engender unexpected consequences for the entire world. In *The Butterfly Generator*, Tintin Wulia has brought these two models of the world together. Almost entirely made of products from a popular furnishing store, her installation could be reproduced anywhere where this originally Swedish corporation has established one of its blue-and-yellow outposts. In fact, the installation is only complete with one identical counterpart, currently in Hong Kong; and in both locations it is possible to simultaneously see on a projection what is presently happening at the other location.

If you touch one of the pushbuttons on the installation an "atmospheric" reaction takes place, both on the installation before you and on its counterpart, and the insides of the object become agitated. At first glance, this supports the theory of the simultaneity and uniformity of shapes and events - but at second glance you realize that things are threatening to get out of control and that sometimes this can be rather uncanny, because, at the end of the day, we ourselves have no say in who happens to be operating the buttons on the other side of our planet, thus confusing both the own world and equally, that of the installation in front of us. (JB)

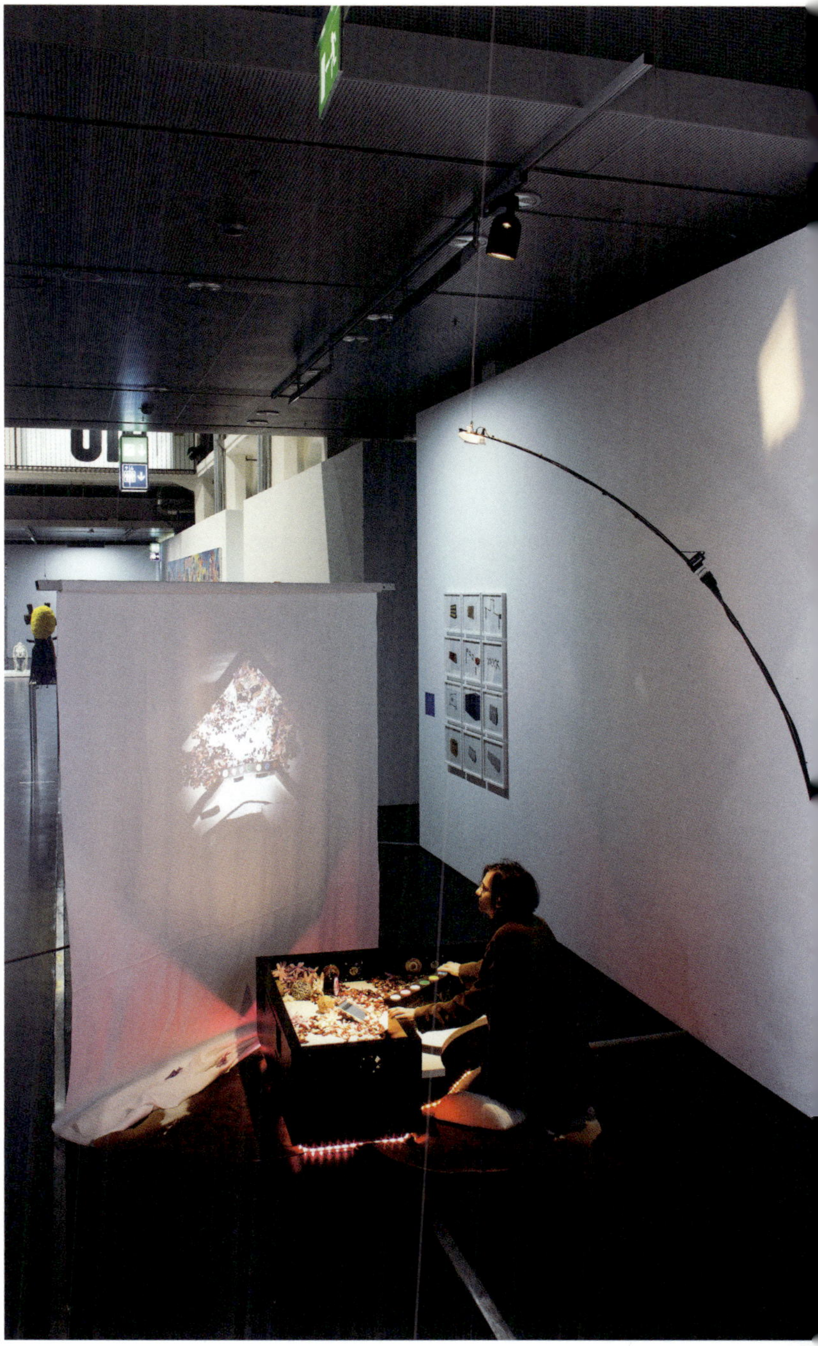

GAM | Education

The curatorial concept for the exhibition *The Global Contemporary. Art Worlds after 1989* was planned to integrate gallery education into the shaping of the exhibition. In addition to a pedagogical perspective on curatorial decision-making processes, this enabled various groups to participate early on in the exhibition through workshops, projects, and seminars. Inspired by visual culture studies as advanced by cultural analyst Mieke Bal, the focus of this work was based on the idea of collaborative knowledge production and detailed viewing, including a debate on artistic strategies and the conditions of exhibition production as well as the institution of the museum and the art market. In this process, gallery education aimed to facilitate the public's approach to the artistic works and the content of the exhibition and also, in engaging with contemporary art, to develop its own latitude for thought and action.

Reflective interaction with the exhibition was not only important for gallery education, but is also a central part of the exhibition itself. This became evident and assumed concrete form through establishing a "studio" in the exhibition where visitors could work with educators and artists on artistic educational projects and workshops, and in this way helped give shape to and continue *The Global Contemporary*. By working directly in the exhibition space, the creative processes not only became visible in the action on-site, but the educational work was documented in the exhibition itself in various ways and presented with the products that resulted.

Project Work

One main emphasis of GAM | Education, one that created the conditions for developing detailed viewing and collaborative knowledge production, was the intensive integration and collaboration with children, teenagers, and adults, which had begun a year before the exhibition opened. In cooperative projects with schools and

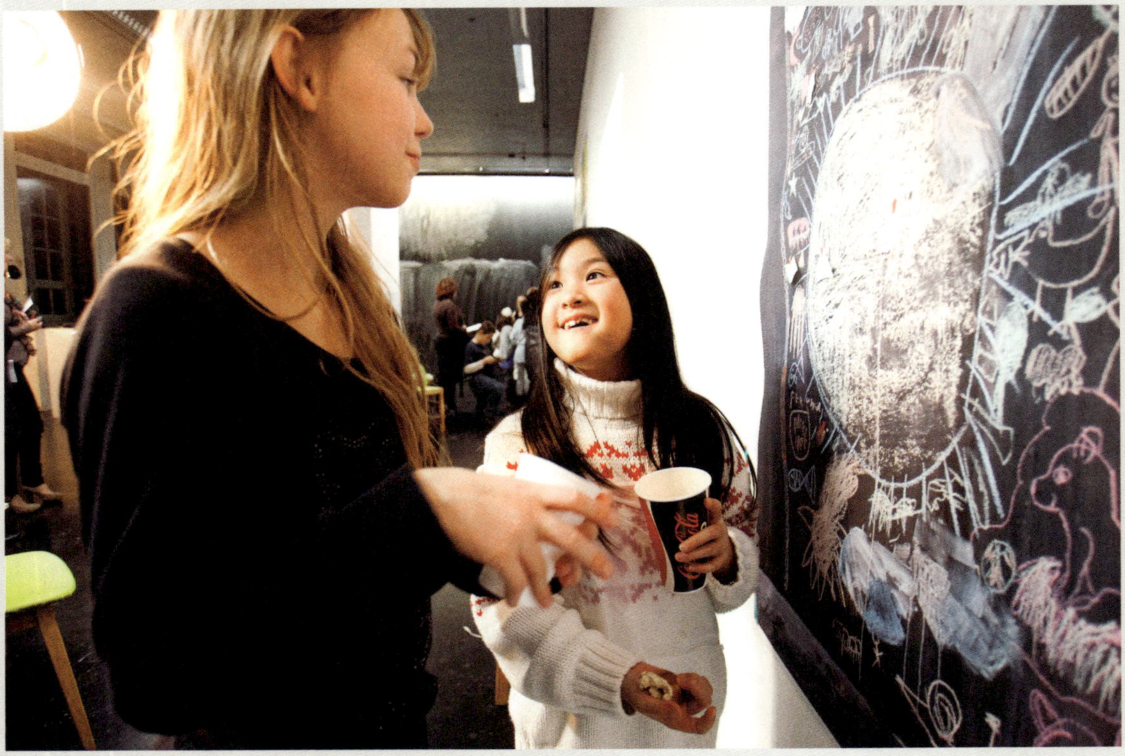

Closing event of "Globalization, Contemporary Art, and Forms of Artistic Mediation," a project on the interface of school and museum in collaboration with the University of Education Karlsruhe

various groups as well as in seminars at local universities, the themes and questions of the GAM research project and the exhibition *The Global Contemporary* were taken up and linked to the knowledge background, experience, and individual questions of the participants in each case. In addition to reflecting the content of the exhibition's themes, this was primarily about understanding current artistic strategies and determining art's relevance to today's society. Furthermore, the projects and seminars offered insights into areas of the museum that usually remain invisible to the general public. For example, storage areas were shown, and the public was admitted to see the installation of the exhibition; information was also communicated about curatorial decision-making processes and criteria crucially important to the creation of an exhibition. This kind of gallery education aimed to convey detailed information about the institution of the museum, the production of an exhibition, as well as to facilitate new ways for visitors to experience it.

One example of these projects is *microsglobe,* a one-and-a-half-year cooperation between a local elementary and middle school, and GAM | Education. GAM | Education worked with a class that had the preliminary goal of supporting children and young people who had only recently arrived in Germany to get to know their new living environment and learn the German language. As a result of their specific situation, the pupils had a particular perspective on and a special sensitivity to the phenomenon of migration, as well as specific knowledge about the lifestyles and effects of globalization processes in various countries. This knowledge nourished the *microsglobe* project. The pupils worked together with artists, teachers, and educators to connect contemporary art and aesthetic practices with their own experience and points of view to develop joint creative aesthetic contributions to the theme of globalization. Eventually, the result was presented as part of the exhibition *The Global Contemporary.*

The *microsglobe* project was based on the idea of developing a common process of communication and shaping without relying on a common language. The necessary translation work – which was done mainly

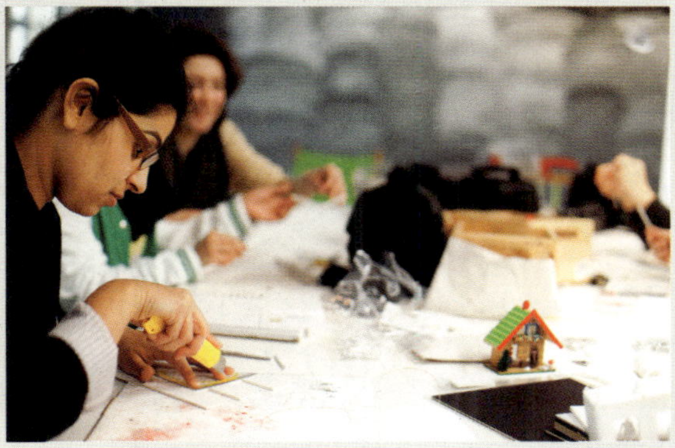

Workshop with Yara El-Sherbini

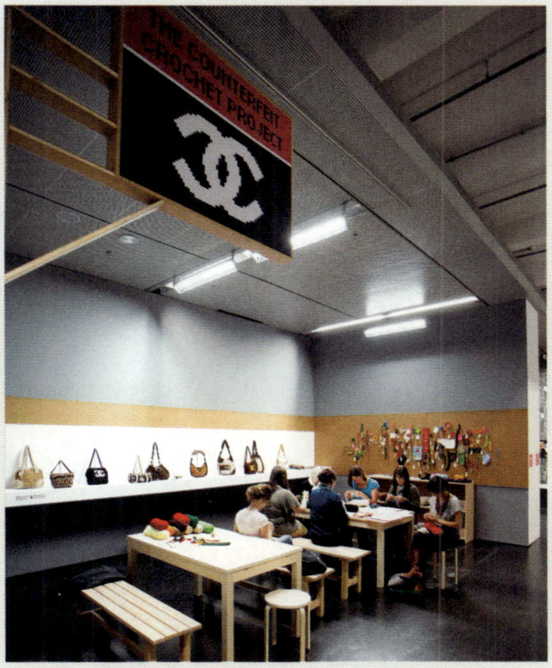

Workshop with Stephanie Syjuco

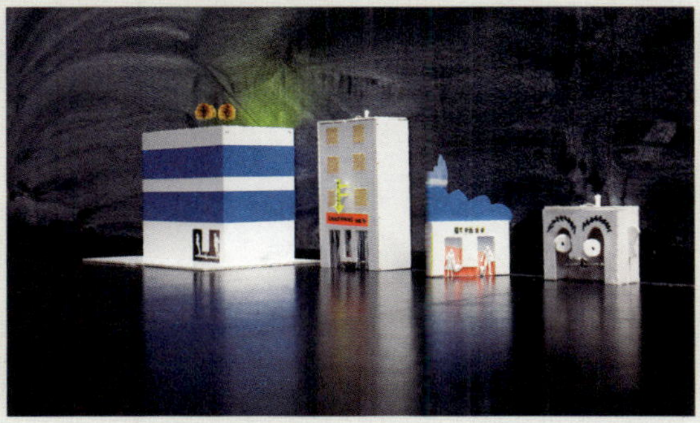

Workshop with Yara El-Sherbini

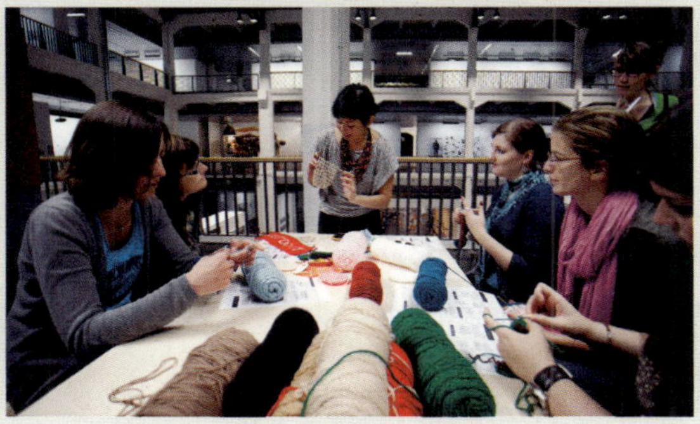

Workshop with Stephanie Syjuco

by the students - was thus an elementary part of the project work, whereby processes of communication slowed down, took detours, and often altered understanding. But these very aspects could be understood as a central challenge for education when the subject of globalization is reflected, namely, developing practices that enable collaborative action in and by means of difference.

Artist-in-Residence Program

The interplay between the production of the exhibition, gallery education, and an engagement with the local contexts of Karlsruhe was prominently realized in the artist-in-residence program, which coincided with the duration of the exhibition. Artists, whose artistic practice focuses specifically on performative or participatory strategies and who, in the process, integrate their local surroundings into their work, both in terms of subject matter and practice, or who permit different facets of participation, were invited to produce new artistic works on-site. For example, Indonesian artist Eko Nugroho designed a large mural in the exhibition, which portrayed his experiences with residents of Karlsruhe and the observations he made in the city. The intention was to create a dialog between the international production of art and the local audience, which was one central aspect of the residency program along with critically questioning and commenting on the exhibition.

Workshops with Artists

Several artists whose works were presented in the exhibition have an interest in the production of critical knowledge and the task of education. As a work of art itself already offers a direct contact with and specific knowledge of the exhibition's themes, the idea was to deepen this knowledge collaboratively by means of artist-led workshops.

For example, the artists' collective Pinky Show engaged interested participants in a creative exploration of self-education and independent media production in the age of globalization (*D.I.Y. Learning - Weapon: Context > Theory > Practice > Reflect (Repeat)*). Workshops by Ashley Hunt, Stephanie Syjuco, Nezaket Ekici, and RYBN.ORG, addressed such themes as economic (de-) privileging, illegalized forms of migration, as well as power relationships and contemporary art. Several workshops did not stay only in the museum, but reached out into the public space. (HP)

— —

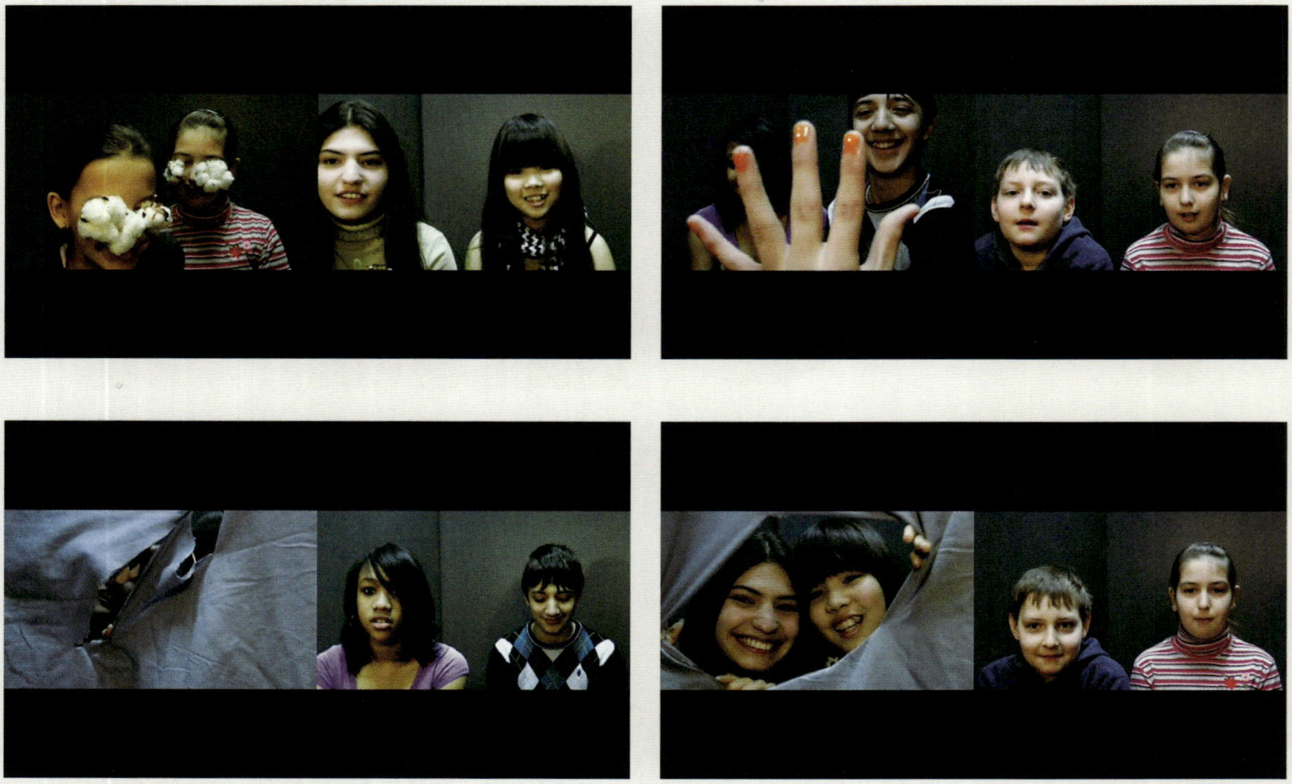

microsglobe Project

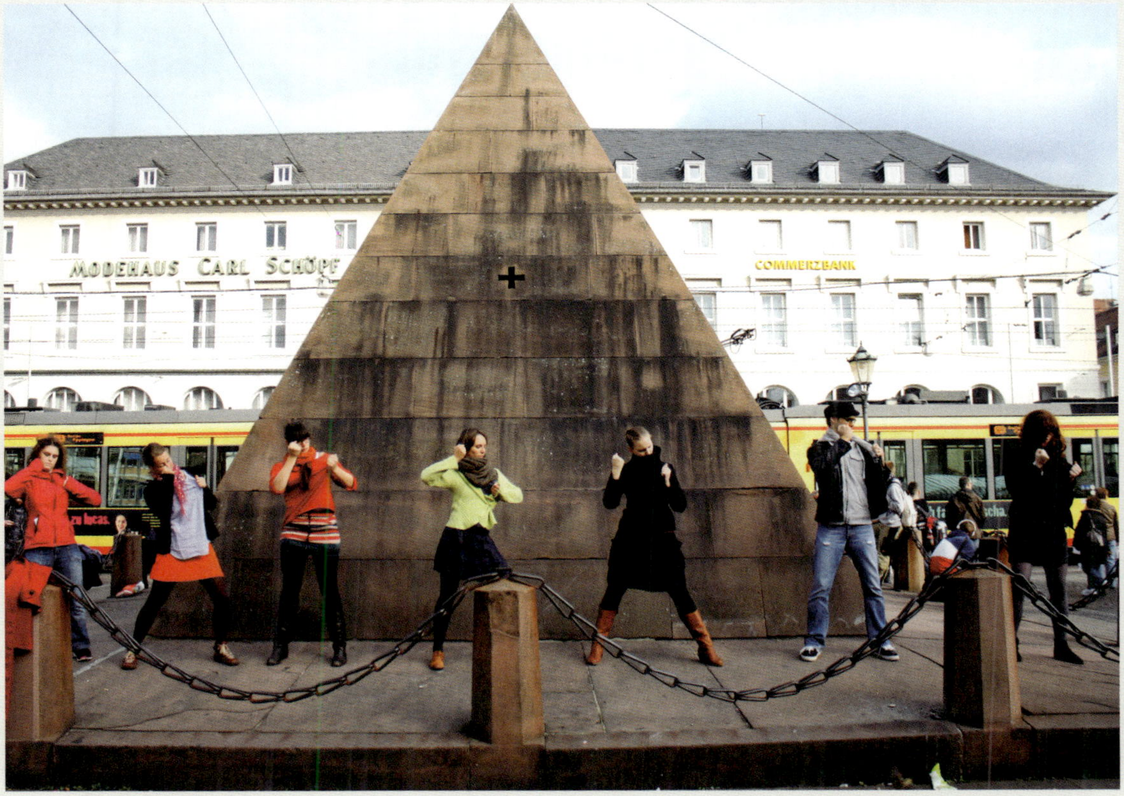

Workshop with Nezaket Ekici

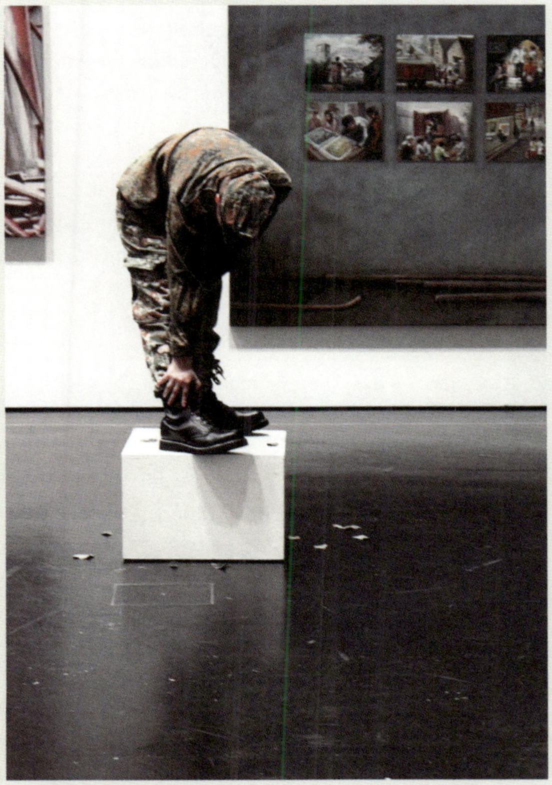

Workshop with Nezaket Ekici

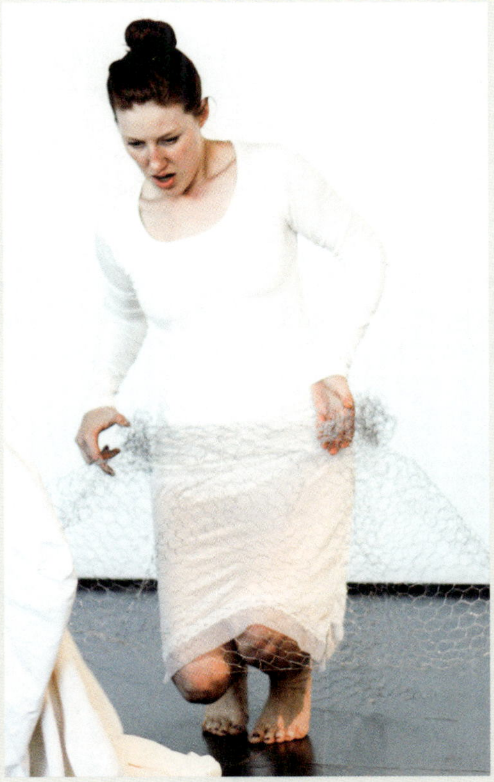

Workshop with Nezaket Ekici

Works in the Exhibition

◆◆◆

– **Bani Abidi**
Security Barriers A–L, 2008
12 inkjet prints, 28 × 44 cm each, framed
Courtesy of the artist & Green Cardamom

– **Bani Abidi**
...so he starts singing, 2000
Video, color, sound, 3:30 min, loop
Courtesy of the artist & Green Cardamom

– **AES Group**
Oasis, 2000
Mixed-media installation, dimensions variable
ZKM | Karlsruhe

– **Halim Al-Karim**
Hidden Prisoner, 1993
Lambda print, 158 × 369 cm (triptych)
Courtesy of AB Gallery

– **Halil Altindere**
My Mother Likes Pop Art Because Pop Art is Colorful, 1998
C-print on aluminum Dibond, 100 × 150 cm
Courtesy of the artist

– **Francis Alÿs**
Turista, Catedral Metropolitana, 1994
Color photograph, 29.8 × 23.6 cm, framed
Courtesy of the artist and Galerie Peter Kilchmann, Zurich

– **Rasheed Araeen**
The Reading Room, 1979–2011, 2011
Mixed-media installation (table of 36 wooden cubes from the installation *Vienna 36: Zero to Infinity*, 1968–2009, 50 × 50 × 50 cm and acrylic glass, Araeen's publicatios, 1 set of 110 issues of the journal *Third Text*, computer, monitor, wall text), dimensions variable
ZKM | Karlsruhe

– **Rasheed Araeen**
Golden Calf, 1987
Mixed media, 9 panels, 152 × 179 cm
Courtesy of the artist

– **Kader Attia**
Untitled (Plastic Bags), 2008–2011
Sculpture, empty plastic bags, dimensions variable
Courtesy of the artist, Galerie Krinzinger, and Galerie Christian Nagel

– **Yto Barrada**
Tectonic, 2004/2010
Wooden model with moveable continents, 122 × 200 cm
Courtesy of Sfeir-Semler Gallery, Hamburg/Beirut

– **Yto Barrada**
Bus, Tanger, 2004
4 C-prints, framed, 88 × 88 cm each
Courtesy of Galerie Sfeir-Semler, Hamburg/Beirut and Collection Kadist Art Foundation

– **Richard Bell**
Scientia E Metaphysica (Bell's Theorem), 2003
Synthetic polymer paint on canvas, 240 × 360 cm (6 panels, 240 × 60 cm each)
Courtesy of Museum and Art Gallery of the Northern Territory

– **Guy Ben-Ner**
Drop the Monkey, 2009
Video with German subtitles, color, sound, 8:30 min
Courtesy of Konrad Fischer Galerie

– **Tamy Ben-Tor**
Normal, 2006
Video, color, sound, 4:20 min
Courtesy of the artist and Zach Feuer Gallery, New York

– **Tamy Ben-Tor**
The End of Art, 2006
Video, color, sound, 7 min
Courtesy of the artist and Zach Feuer Gallery, New York

– **Tamy Ben-Tor**
Artist in Residence, 2005
Video, color, sound, 3:55 min
Courtesy of the artist and Zach Feuer Gallery, New York

– **Michael Bielicky and Kamila B. Richter**
The Garden of Error and Decay, 2010/2011
Web-based installation, computer graphic
Sound: Lorenz Schwarz
Courtesy of the artists

– **Ursula Biemann**
X-Mission, 2008
Video, color, sound, 40 min
Courtesy of the artist

– **Zander Blom**
The Drain of Progress, 2007
Photo series (selection), ultrachrome ink on cotton, 45 × 60 cm each (framed)
Courtesy of the artist & Stevenson, Cape Town/Johannesburg

Individual titles of the selected photographs:
Untitled or Like, Man. He was GOD to us, Bedroom 1, Corner 3, Time unknown, Sunday, 11 June 2006
Untitled, Lounge, Wall 4, 5.19 a.m., Saturday, 29 April 2006
Untitled or Study for a Nude, Bedroom 1, Corner 3, 6.20 p.m., Thursday, 17 August 2006
Untitled, Bedroom 1, Corner 3, 6.44 p.m., Wednesday, 9 August 2006
Untitled or Composition with Line, Corridor, Corner 2 and Ceiling, 4.28 p.m., Wednesday, 30 May 2007

Untitled, Bedroom 2, Wall 1, 11.50 a.m., Friday, 25 May 2007
Untitled of The Wreck of Hope, Bedroom 1, Wall 3, 10.50 a.m., Wednesday, 30 August 2006
Untitled, Bedroom 1, Corner 3, 4.38 p.m., Monday, 27 November 2006
Untitled or Unique Forms of Continuity in Space, Bedroom 1, Corner 2, 12.23 a.m., Sunday, 31 December 2006
Untitled, Bathroom, 2.01 a.m., Wednesday, 23 May 2007
Untitled, Bedroom 2, Wall 1, 8.35 p.m., Friday, 19 January 2007
Untitled, Bedroom 1, Wall 3, 8.40 a.m., Wednesday, 9 May 2007

– **Santiago Borja**
Diván, 2010
Digital print on cotton paper, 80 × 120 cm, framed
Courtesy of Caja Blanca

– **Santiago Borja**
Freud UXA-Aguila, 2010
Piezo print, carbon ink on cotton paper, 29 × 21 cm
Courtesy of Caja Blanca

– **Luchezar Boyadjiev**
GastARTbeiter, 2000–2007
Digital print on vinyl, 210 × 510 cm
Courtesy of the artist and Galerie FEINKOST, Berlin

– **Ondrej Brody and Kristofer Paetau**
Wang Bin Torture in Commercial Quality, High Quality and Museum Quality, 2010
3 paintings, oil on canvas, 110 × 160 cm each
Courtesy of the artists

– **Erik Bünger**
The Allens, 2004
Video, color, sound, 28 min
Courtesy of the artist

– **Roberto Cabot**
Favela Chic, 2008
Photograph from the series *E-Scapes*, 100 × 133.3 cm, framed, edition of 6
Courtesy of Galerie Brigitte Schenk

– **Roberto Cabot**
The UNO building in NY with Sugar Loaf reflected, 2008
Photograph from the series *E-Scapes*, 133.3 × 100 cm, framed
Courtesy of Galerie Brigitte Schenk

– **Cai Yuan and Jian Jun Xi**
Two Artists Piss on Duchamp's Urinal, 2000
Performance, Tate Modern, London, filmed by Eamon Lee
Video, color, sound, 1:35 min
Courtesy of the artists

– **Anetta Mona Chişa and Lucia Tkáčová**
The Importance of Doing Nothing (and Discussing Everything), 2011
Theater play written on 5-euro notes
Courtesy of the artists
Produced in cooperation with ZKM | Center for Art and Media Karlsruhe, artist-in-residence program of the exhibition *The Global Contemporary* (2011/2012)

– **Chto delat?**
The Tower: A Songspiel, 2010
HD video, color, sound, 36 min
Courtesy of the artists
The project has been realized by Tsaplya, Glucklya, Vilensky, and the composer M. KRUTIK.

– **Com&Com (Marcus Gossolt, Johannes M. Hedinger)**
Mocmoc & Mermer, 2006–2011
Mixed-media installation (2 mascots, 15 drawings, 30 × 35 cm each (framed), 3 videos, 1 publication), dimensions variable
Courtesy of the artists

Individual titles of the videos:
Mocmoc & Mermer, Episode I: The Secret Key, video DV, color, sound, English, 31 min
Mocmoc & Mermer, Episode II: The Right Way, video DV, color, sound, English, 34 min
Mocmoc (Swiss Television, 02/10/2004), video Beta, color, sound, Swiss German/German, English subtitles, 6 min

– **Minerva Cuevas**
Social Spectrum, 2011
GSM network and mixed-media installation
In collaboration with Keith Whythe and Detlev Ernst
Courtesy of the artist
Produced in cooperation with ZKM | Center for Art and Media Karlsruhe, artist-in-residence program of the exhibition *The Global Contemporary* (2011/2012)

– **Neil Cummings and Marysia Lewandowska**
Museum Futures: Distributed, 2008
Video, color, sound, 32 min
Courtesy of the artists

– **Pauline Curnier Jardin**
Ami, 2009
Video installation, color, sound, 7 min
Music: Leyland James Kirby
Courtesy of the artist

– **Manthia Diawara**
Édouard Glissant: Un monde en relation, 2009
Video, color, sound, 50 min
Courtesy of Manthia Diawara, Director

– **Ala Ebtekar**
The dark midnight, fearful waves, and the tempestuous whirlpool, 2011
(selection from the upcoming book *Ayandeh-nameh*)
Mixed media digital pigment prints, 4 works, each 100 × 66 cm, framed, 1 work, 100 × 150 cm, framed
Courtesy of the artist
Produced in cooperation with ZKM | Center for Art and Media Karlsruhe, artist-in-residence program of the exhibition *The Global Contemporary* (2011/2012)

– **Ala Ebtekar**
Paradise, 2011
(selection from the upcoming book *Ayandeh-nameh*)
Mixed media digital pigment prints, 100 × 66 cm, 100 × 150 cm, 100 × 66 cm (triptych) / Courtesy of the artist
Produced in cooperation with ZKM | Center for Art and Media Karlsruhe, artist-in-residence program of the exhibition *The Global Contemporary* (2011/2012)

– Ala Ebtekar
Untitled, 2011
(from the upcoming book *Ayandeh-nameh*)
Mixed media digital pigment print,
100 × 150 cm
Courtesy of the artist
Produced in cooperation with ZKM | Center for Art and Media Karlsruhe, artist-in-residence program of the exhibition *The Global Contemporary* (2011/2012)

– Nezaket Ekici
Work in progress – Personal Map, 2008 (ongoing)
Performance, mixed-media installation, ca. 4 × 3 m
Courtesy of the artist

– Elmgreen & Dragset
Prada Marfa, 2005
C-print, 160 × 204 cm
Courtesy of private collection

– Yara El-Sherbini
A Weather House for the Current Climate, 2011
Mixed-media weather house, wood, plastic, metal, catgut, paper, lace, 32 × 20 × 56 cm
Courtesy of the artist and La Caja Blanca
Produced in cooperation with ZKM | Center for Art and Media Karlsruhe, artist-in-residence program of the exhibition *The Global Contemporary* (2011/2012)

– Yara El-Sherbini
Reproducing the Current Climate, 2011
Documentation of an intervention: Reproductions of *A Weather House for the Current Climate* for sale at Karlsruhe's local Christmas market
Mixed-media weather houses wood, plastic, catgut, paper, lace, 16 × 10 × 28 cm
Courtesy of the artist and La Caja Blanca
Produced in cooperation with ZKM | Center for Art and Media Karlsruhe, artist-in-residence program of the exhibition *The Global Contemporary* (2011/2012)

– Yara El-Sherbini
Another Form of Regulation and Control, 2011
Hygrothermograph, plastic, metal, paper, battery, 33 × 15 × 24 cm
Courtesy of the artist and La Caja Blanca
Produced in cooperation with ZKM | Center for Art and Media Karlsruhe, artist-in-residence program of the exhibition *The Global Contemporary* (2011/2012)

– Erika & Javier
El Peso de la Memoria (The Weight of Memory), 2007
Digital print on vinyl, 315 × 210 cm
Courtesy of the artists

– Brendan Fernandes
The Devil's Noise, 2011
Video, color, sound, 02:09 min
Edited in collaboration with Moritz Büchner
Courtesy of the artist and Diaz Contemporary, Toronto
Produced in cooperation with ZKM | Center for Art and Media Karlsruhe, artist-in-residence program of the exhibition *The Global Contemporary* (2011/2012)

– Brendan Fernandes
Eyes on the Editor, 2011
Custom-made books, with text on table, dimensions variable
Courtesy of the artist and Diaz Contemporary, Toronto
Produced in cooperation with ZKM | Center for Art and Media Karlsruhe, artist-in-residence program of the exhibition *The Global Contemporary* (2011/2012)

– Brendan Fernandes
Symposium I, II, III, 2011
3 screen prints, 50 × 65 cm, Toronto
Courtesy of the artist and Diaz Contemporary
Produced in cooperation with ZKM | Center for Art and Media Karlsruhe, artist-in-residence program of the exhibition *The Global Contemporary* (2011/2012)

– Doug Fishbone
Elmina, 2010
Video, color, sound, 90 min
Direction: Emmanuel Apea, screenplay: Emmanuel Apea, John Apea, camera: Kofi Asante
Courtesy of the artist

– Meschac Gaba
Musée de l'Art de la Vie Active, 2010/2011
Performance and mixed-media installation, 30 wigs (braided synthetic hair and wire supports), 2 videos (performances in Cotonou and Karlsruhe)
Courtesy of the artist, Laboratorio Art Contemporain, Galleria Continua
Produced with Laboratorio Art Contemporain, Galleria Continua in cooperation with ZKM | Center for Art and Media Karlsruhe.

– Thierry Geoffroy/Colonel
Biennalist, 2011 (ongoing)
Performance and mixed-media installation (video, photograph, photo prints) dimensions variable
Courtesy of the artist
Produced in cooperation with ZKM | Center for Art and Media Karlsruhe

– Thierry Geoffroy/Colonel
Biennalist Mini Retrospective, 1989 (ongoing)
Mixed-media installation with video, photograph and photo prints, dimensions variable
Courtesy of the artist

– Ghana ThinkTank (John Ewing, Maria del Carmen Montoya, and Christopher Robbins)
Ghana ThinkTank in Karlsruhe, 2011
Mixed-media installation, dimensions variable
Courtesy of the artists
Produced in cooperation with ZKM | Center for Art and Media Karlsruhe

– Matthias Gommel
Untitled (Passage), 2011
Mixed-media installation, Tensabarrier posts, printed barrier tape, sound, dimensions variable
Courtesy of the artist
Produced in cooperation with ZKM | Center for Art and Media Karlsruhe

– Josh Greene with Yangzi
Red/Greene, 2011
Mixed-media installation, dimensions variable
Courtesy of the artist
Produced in cooperation with ZKM | Center for Art and Media Karlsruhe

– Anawana Haloba
The Greater G8 Advertising Market Stand, 2007–2009
Interactive sound installation, dimensions variable
Courtesy of the artist
This project was kindly supported by the Office for Contemporary Art, Norway and The Norwegian National Art Council (Norsk KulturraÅäd), Rijksakademie van Beeldende Kunsten, and Notamo2 Studios, Norway.

– Khosrow Hassanzadeh
Terrorist Series: Nadjibeh, Azimeh, Khosrow, 2004
3 silk screens, 200 × 320 cm each
Courtesy of Collection Tropenmuseum, Amsterdam, Netherlands

– Mona Hatoum
Measures of Distance, 1988
Video, color, sound, 15 min
Courtesy of Netherlands Media Art Institute, Amsterdam

– Antonia Hirsch
ARTnews Top 200, 2004
23 carat gold on paper, 102 × 67 cm
Courtesy of the artist

– Hong Hao
Kassel City Defense Vertical View, 1997
Mixed media, silk screen, 56 × 76 cm
Courtesy of Beijing Commune

– Pieter Hugo
Nollywood, 2008
Photo series, selection of 8 C-prints, each 102 × 102 cm (110 × 110 cm framed)
Courtesy of the artist & Stevenson, Cape Town/Johannesburg

Individual titles:
Escort Kama. Enugu, Nigeria, 2008
Chris Nkulo and Patience Umeh. Enugu, Nigeria, 2008
Emeka Onu. Enugu, Nigeria, 2008
Obechukwu Nwoye. Enugu, Nigeria, 2008
Pieter Hugo. Enugu, Nigeria, 2009
Princess Adaobi. Enugu, Nigeria, 2008
Fidelis Elenwa. Enugu, Nigeria, 2009
Mr Enblo. Enugu, Nigeria, 2008

– Ashley Hunt
A World Map: In Which We See..., 2004 (ongoing)
Mixed-media installation, 16 plates, ca. 60 × 100 cm each
Courtesy of the artist

– IRWIN and NSKSTATE.COM
NSK Folk Art, 2008 (ongoing)
Mixed-media installation, dimensions variable
Courtesy of the artists

– David Jablonowski
Kelly En Perles (3D) in Coop. With Cameroonian Artist, 2011
Hermès scarf, sound system (iPod, speaker), aluminum, 64 × 68 × 3 cm
Courtesy of Lüttgenmeijer, Berlin

– Melanie Jackson
From the Bank of Hell, 2008
Mixed-media installation, dimensions variable
Courtesy of the artist

– Christian Jankowski
Kunstmarkt TV, 2008
Video, color, sound, 45 min
Courtesy of Klosterfelde, Berlin

– Christian Jankowski
The China Painters, 2007/2008
Oil and acrylic on canvas (selection)
Courtesy of the artist, Klosterfelde, Berlin, and Lisson Gallery, London

Individual titles:
Abstract Picture, 119 × 88 cm
Bleak Dafen Future, 160 × 160 cm
Burlaks on Volga, 250 × 182 cm
Classical Flowers, 210 × 210 cm
Old Chair, 210 × 269 cm
Photo of Family, 300 × 214 cm
Story of Dafen, 230 × 174 cm
The Hero, 194 × 87 cm
Three Leaders, 64 × 228 cm
Wave, 180 × 200 cm

– Anna Jermolaewa
Kremlin Doppelgänger, 2008/2009
Photo series (selection), 50 × 35 cm each, framed
Courtesy of the artist

– Jin Shi
Retail Business: Karaoke, 2009
Mixed-media installation, 180 × 290 × 82 cm
Courtesy of Gao Magee Gallery, Madrid

– Jompet
Cortege of the Third Realm, 2010
24 life-size figures, electronics, video and sound installation, dimensions variable
Courtesy of Akili Museum of Art

– Martin Kippenberger
Ohne Titel, 1990
10 drawings (selection), mixed media on hotel stationary, with printer's imprint, 37.5 × 48.5 cm each
Courtesy of Landesbank Baden-Württemberg

– Agung Kurniawan
Souvenirs from the Third World, 1997–1999
5 objects of fiberglass, wood, aluminum, 70 × 35 × 35 cm each
Courtesy of the artist

– Surasi Kusolwong
50% OFF BOOKS (Never Mind Kapital = Never Mind Kunst), 2011
Performance
Courtesy of the artist

– Surasi Kusolwong
One Pound Turbo Market (You'll have a good time), 2006
Video, color, sound, 15:04 min, billboard, wall color, dimensions variable
Courtesy of the artist

– Will Kwan
Two Signs Articulated, 2011
Vinyl wall text and backlit sign
Courtesy of the artist
Produced in cooperation with ZKM | Center for Art and Media Karlsruhe, artist-in-residence program of the exhibition *The Global Contemporary* (2011/2012)

– Le Laboratoire de Déberlinisation
Mobil Exchange Office, 2011
Mixed-media installation (wooden exchange office, computer, 2 videos, color, sound, digital prints), dimensions variable

Courtesy of Le Laboratoire de Déberlinisation: Mansour Ciss Kanakassy, Baruch Gottlieb, Christian Hanussek

Individual titles of the digital prints:
Adieu Franc CFA, 2001–2011, 162 × 115 cm
Afro notre Monnaie, 2009, 111.5 × 89 cm
Europas Zukunft liegt in Afrika, 2009, 91.5 × 73 cm
Hommage à la Négritude, 2010, 29.7 × 42 cm
L'Afrique des Convoitises, 2011, 91.5 × 73 cm
Disques, 2011, 2 digital prints, 30 cm^2 each
Afrodisiac. Es geht um Geld, 2011, LP cover, 32.5 × 32,5 cm
Afrodisiac, vol. 2, 2011, LP cover, 32.5 × 32.5 cm
Cartographie Africa, 2011, 4 digital prints, 21 × 29.7 cm each
Afro Certificat, 2011, 3 digital prints, 29.7 × 42 cm each
Charte du Mandé, 2011, 4 digital prints, 21 × 29.7 cm each
Afro Organigrammes, 2011, 3 digital prints, 29.7 × 42 cm each
Courtesy of Mansour Ciss Kanakassy and Baruch Gottlieb

Black Star Line, 2008, 60 × 42 cm
Panafricanisme, 2011, 100 × 70 cm
Temporary Transitional Council, 2011, 100 × 70 cm
Charte de Kouroukan Fouga, 2011, 100 × 70 cm
Courtesy of Christian Hanussek

– **Moshekwa Langa**
Ohne Titel, 2003
2 × ink on paper, 140 × 100 cm each,
1 × pastel crayon on paper, 122 × 86 cm
Courtesy of Galerie Mikael Andersen, Berlin/Copenhagen

– **Ben Lewis**
The Great Contemporary Art Bubble, 2009
Video, color, sound, 90 min
© BLTV (Ben Lewis Television) Ltd.

– **Liu Ding**
Liu Ding's Store, 2008 (ongoing)
Mixed-media installation

Liu Ding's Store comprises 4 projects:
Take Home and Make Real the Priceless in Your Heart, 2010/2011
Mixed media (wooden shelf, 52 paintings, oil on canvas), 215 × 40 × 244 cm (shelf), 60 × 90 cm (paintings)
Courtesy of Galerie Urs Meile, Beijing-Lucerne
Courtesy of the artist (28 paintings)

The Utopian Future of Art, Our Reality, 2009
a) *A Container of Experience*, 2009
Mixed media, 200 × 80 × 60 cm (cabinet)
Courtesy of Sammlung Erlenmeyer-Stiftung, Switzerland
b) *The Perfect Sphere*, 2009
Mixed-media, 200 × 80 × 60 cm (cabinet)
Courtesy of Galerie Urs Meile, Beijing-Lucerne

Conversations, 2010/2011
C-print, paper, frames, dimensions variable
Courtesy of Galerie Urs Meile, Beijing-Lucerne

Friendship, 2010
a) *No. 2*, 2010
Wood, paint, stones, plant, terracotta pot, lamp, dimensions variable (wooden table 23.6 × 200 × 110 cm)
Courtesy of Galerie Urs Meile, Beijing-Lucerne
b) *No. 4*, 2010
Wood, paint, stones, plant, terracotta pot, lamp, dimensions variable (wooden table 15.6 × 200 × 110 cm)
Courtesy of Galerie Urs Meile, Beijing-Lucerne

– **Liu Ding**
Omission, 2009
Stone, book, marker, 34 × 34 × 30 cm
Courtesy of Galerie Urs Meile, Beijing-Lucerne

– **Rafael Lozano-Hemmer**
Please Empty Your Pockets, 2010
Interactive installation (conveyor belt, computer, HD projectors, HD camera), 273 × 42 × 124 cm (dimensions variable)
Copy 3/6, edition 6 + 1 AP
Courtesy of ZKM | Center for Art and Media Karlsruhe

– **James Luna**
The Artifact Piece, 1987/1990
C-print on aluminum Dibond, 180 × 116.5 cm
Courtesy of the artist

– **Pooneh Maghazehe**
Sandbox (work in progress), 2011
HD video (color, silent, 8 min), piano, sculpture, dimensions variable
Camera and editing in collaboration with Martin Lorenz
Sculpture in collaboration with Silke Fehsenfeld
Courtesy of the artist
Produced in cooperation with ZKM | Center for Art and Media Karlsruhe, artist-in-residence program of the exhibition *The Global Contemporary* (2011/2012)

– **Tirzo Martha**
The Invasion of The Netherlands supported by Chavez (Chavez had to stop at IKEA in Spain to buy himself a new presidential chair), 2008
Mixed-media installation, dimensions variable
Courtesy of the artist

– **Gabriele di Matteo**
China Made in Italy, 2008
Installation, 34 paintings, dimensions variable
Courtesy of the artist and Federico Luger Gallery

– **Miao Xiaochun**
The Last Judgment in Cyberspace – Where Will I Go?, 2006
3-D computer animation, b/w, sound, 7:15 min
Courtesy of Alexander Ochs Galleries Berlin | Beijing

– **Karen Mirza and Brad Butler**
A Common Stage, 2011
Mixed-media installation (HD video, color, sound, 7 min; neon sign, blackboard mural)
Courtesy of the artists
Produced in cooperation with ZKM | Center for Art and Media Karlsruhe, artist-in-residence program of the exhibition *The Global Contemporary* (2011/2012)

(The Lack of) A Common Stage
Workshop with: Brad Butler, Thomas Herzberger, Carolin Knebel, Stephan Krug, Karen Mirza, Philipp Sack, Rüdiger Stübler, Norbert Werner, 2011

– **Nástio Mosquito**
Africa, 2010
Video, color, sound, 1 min
Courtesy of DZZZZ Artworks

– **Nástio Mosquito**
America, 2010
Video, color, sound, 6:30 min
Courtesy of DZZZZ Artworks

– **Nástio Mosquito**
Europe, 2010
Video, color, sound, 3:30 min
Courtesy of DZZZZ Artworks

– **Krisna Murti**
For Odd For Ever, 2010
Digital print on board, 57 × 90 cm
Courtesy of the artist

– **Krisna Murti**
Shop Theater # 3, 2010
Digital print on board, 57 × 90 cm
Courtesy of the artist

– **Krisna Murti**
Street Theater, 2010
Digital print on board, 57 × 90 cm
Courtesy of the artist

– **Krisna Murti**
The Last Photograph, 2010
Digital print on canvas, 66 × 200 cm
Courtesy of the artist

– **Krisna Murti**
The Old and the Beauty, 2010
Digital print on board, 57 × 90 cm
Courtesy of the artist

– **Jun Nguyen-Hatsushiba**
The Ground, the Root and the Air: The Passing of the Bodhi Tree, 2007
1-channel video installation, HD, 14:30 min
Courtesy of the artist and Lehmann Maupin Gallery, New York

– **Ni Haifeng**
Para-Production, 2008
Mixed-media installation, textile shreds, 4–5 sewing machines, dimensions variable
Courtesy of the artist

– **Eko Nugroho**
ALIEN-NATION, 2011
Wall painting with emulsion paint, printed textile banner
Courtesy of the artist
Produced in cooperation with ZKM | Center for Art and Media Karlsruhe, artist-in-residence program of the exhibition *The Global Contemporary* (2011/2012)

– **Mattias Olofsson**
Culture Constructing Nature, 2004
3 C-prints, 70 × 100 cm each, framed
Courtesy of the artist

– **Tsuyoshi Ozawa**
Museum of Soy Sauce Art, 1998–2000
Mixed-media installation, wooden construction with drawings and objects, 2.50 × 9.25 × 1.85 m
Courtesy of Collection Lambert en Avignon

– **Adrian Paci**
Centro di Permanenza Temporanea, 2007
C-print on aluminum Dibond, 98 × 180 cm
Courtesy of Kaufmann Repetto, Milan

– **Leila Pazooki**
Moments of Glory, 2010
Neon tubes, transformers, 15 parts, length between 65 and 200 cm
Courtesy of the artist

– **Pavel Pepperstein**
The Gulf of Mexico oil spill disaster, 2011
Watercolor on paper, 4 drawings, 66 × 101 cm each, framed
Courtesy of Campoli Presti, London/Paris

– **Pinky Show**
Banked Into Submission (The Globalizationist's Guide to Developing Poverty), 2007
Comic and video, color, sound, 3:14 min
Courtesy of the artists

– **Pinky Show**
Defending Globalization ... a mission for the educated and enlightened, 2007
Comic and video, color, sound, 3:02 min
Courtesy of the artists

– **Pinky Show**
Globalization (and the metaphysics of control in a free market world), 2007
Comic and video, color, sound, 3:02 min
Courtesy of the artists

– **Tadej Pogačar**
MonApoly, A Human Trade Game, 2004
Mixed-media installation, board game (edition: 50), inkjet print on vinyl (249 × 249 cm), 3 *MonApoly* games
Courtesy of the artist & the P.A.R.A.S.I.T.E. Museum of Contemporary Art

– **Elodie Pong**
After the Empire, 2008
HD video, color, sound, 13:50 min
Courtesy of Freymond - Guth Fine Arts

– **Nusra Latif Qureshi**
Did you come here to find history?, 2009
20 digital prints on transparent film, 70 × 870 cm
Courtesy of the artist

– **Raqs Media Collective**
Escapement, 2009
Mixed-media installation, 27 clocks, high gloss aluminum with LED lights, 4 flat screen monitors, video and audio in loop, dimensions variable
Edition of 2
Courtesy of the artists and Frith Street Gallery, London

– **Araya Rasdjarmrearnsook**
Dow Song Duang (The Two Planets Series), 2008
Video, color, sound, 18:30 min
Courtesy of the artist and 100 Tonson Gallery

– **Navin Rawanchaikul**
SUPER CHINA!, 2009
Acrylic on canvas, 2.7 × 12.6 m
Courtesy of Tang Contemporary Art

– Navin Rawanchaikul
Curator Man and Navin, 2002
Painted fiberglass, 60 × 45 × 175 cm (Curator Man) 75 × 70 × 158 cm (Old Navin)
Courtesy of the artist

– RYBN.ORG
ADM VIII, 2011
Trading bot performance, panoramic installation
Courtesy of the artists
Realized in cooperation with ZKM | Institute for Visual Media
With the support of DICRéAM / French Ministry of Culture and Communication, CNC, CNL

– Ho-Yeol Ryu
Flughafen, 2005
Digital print, 100 × 150 cm
ZKM | Karlsruhe

– Ruth Sacks
Legend Neutral, 2011
Advertisement in the daily paper *Offenburger Tageblatt*, dimensions variable
Black and white posters, A0, edition of 1,000
Typeface by Avoid Red Arrows
Courtesy of the artist
Produced in cooperation with ZKM | Center for Art and Media Karlsruhe, artist-in-residence program of the exhibition *The Global Contemporary* (2011/2012)

– Chéri Samba
L'espoir fait vivre no. 2, 1997
Acrylic, sequines, photographs, glue on canvas, 130 × 194 cm
Courtesy of CAAC – The Pigozzi Collection, Geneva

– John Smith
Hotel Diaries, 2001–2007
Video, color, sound, 82 min
Courtesy of Tanya Leighton

Individual titles:
Frozen War, Ireland, October 8th 2001, 11 min
Museum Piece, Germany, October 14th 2004, 12 min
Throwing Stones, Switzerland, November 13th 2004, 11 min
B & B, UK, November 26th 2005, 6 min
Pyramids / Skunk, Netherlands, January 29th 2006 / January 29th 2007, 16 min
Dirty Pictures, Palestine, April 15th/16th 2007, 14 min
Six Years Later, Ireland, October 20th 2007, 9 min

– Stewart Smith, Robert Gerard Pietrusko, Bernd Lintermann
trans_actions: The Accelerated Art World 1989–2011, 2011
Installation for PanoramaScreen
Production: Project GAM, ZKM | Institute for Visual Media
Project management: Andrea Buddensieg, Bernd Lintermann
Concept: Hans Belting, Andrea Buddensieg, Anne Marie Buenker, Bernd Lintermann, Robert Gerard Pietrusko, Stewart Smith
Visual design and programming: Robert Gerard Pietrusko and Stewart Smith
Panorama Display Software: Bernd Lintermann
Sound: ZKM | Institute for Music and Acoustics, Holger Stenschke, Goetz Dipper, Ludger Brümmer
Scientific research: Anne Marie Buenker
Research assistance: Daria Mille, Sara Giannini
Scientific advisor: Clare McAndrew

Kindly supported by:
Eleonora Charans, Chiara di Stefano, Maria Vittoria Martini: Inter-University Doctoral School in History of Arts, Cá Foscari University in cooperation with IUAV University, Venice; Vinicius Spricigo, São Paulo; Berlin Biennale für Zeitgenössische Kunst; KW Institute for Contemporary Art, Berlin; documenta Archiv, Kassel; Arquivo Histórico Wanda Svevo, Bienal de São Paulo, Brasil; Biennale d'art contemporain de Lyon; Fukuoka Triennale, Japan; Fundacao Bienal do Mercosul, NDP; Núcleo de Documentacao Em Pesquisa, Porto Alegre; VentoSul, Bienal de Curitiba, Instituto Paranaense de Arte, Curitiba; T.I.C.A.B. – Tirana International Contemporary Art Biannual, Albania; Frances Mulhall Achilles Library, Whitney Museum of American Art, New York, USA; Regina Vogel, Daros Latinamerica AG, Zurich; Gwangju Biennale Foundation, Gwangju; Yuko Kawakami, Organizing Committee for Yokohama Triennale Office; Istanbul Biennale.

Sources:
Collection of Biennale catalogs at ZKM_Media Library; Asia Art Archive, "All You Want To Know
About International Art Biennials," www.aaa.org; hk/onlineprojects/bitri/en/index.aspx; Universes-in-Universe http://universes-in-universe.org; IFA, Biennalen-Datenbank www.ifa.de/?id=2753; Artnet, www.artnet.com/; Artprice, http://artprice.com/; ArtTactic, www.arttactic.com/Literature: Charlotte Bydler, *Global Art World, Inc. On the Globalization of Contemporary Art*, Figura Nova Series 32, Uppsala University Library, Uppsala, 2004; Elena Filipovic, Marieke van Hal, Solveig Øvstebø (eds.), *The Biennial Reader. An Anthology on Large-Scale Perrenial Exhibitions of Contemporary Art*, Hatje Cantz, Ostfildern, 2010; Noah Horowitz, *Art of the Deal. Contemporary Art in a Global Financial Market*, Princeton University Press, Princeton (NJ), 2011; Clare McAndrew, *Globalization and the Art Market. Emerging Economies and the Art Trade in 2008*, The European Fine Art Foundation, Helvoirt, 2008; Iain Robertson, *Understanding International Art Markets and Management*, Routledge, London/New York (NY), 2005; Sabine B. Vogel, *Biennalen – Kunst im Weltformat*, Springer, Wien/New York (NY), 2010

– Sean Snyder
Exhibition, 2008
Film, transferred to DVD, 7 min
Courtesy of the artist and Galerie Chantal Crousel, Paris

– Christa Sommerer & Laurent Mignonneau
The Value of Art (Unruhige See), 2010
Media installation, painting, 92 × 85 cm
© 2010, Christa Sommerer & Laurent Mignonneau, courtesy [DAM] Berlin

– SOSka group
Barter, 2007
3 C-prints, 100 × 150 cm each (on aluminum Dibond), 4 C-prints, 50 × 70 cm each (framed), video, color, sound, 6:50 min
Courtesy of the artists

– Michael Stevenson
The Fountain of Prosperity, 2006
Plexiglas, steel, brass, aluminum, rubber, cork, string, concrete, dyed water, pumps, and fluorescent lamps, 2.5 × 1.6 × 1 m
Courtesy of Vilma Gold, London

– Hito Steyerl
In Free Fall, 2010
HD video, color, sound, 32 min
Courtesy of the artist

– Mladen Stilinović
An artist who cannot speak English is no artist, 1994
Acrylic on artificial silk, 410 × 160 cm
Courtesy of the artist

– Jens M. Stober
1378 (km), 2010
Computer game installation for two players
Courtesy of the artist

– Jim Supangkat
Kamar Ibu Dan Anak (Bedroom of a Woman and her Child), 1975 (reconstruction 2006, 2011)
Mixed-media installation (wooden furniture), 3 × 3 m (bed 190 × 70 × 75 cm, closet 60 × 40 × 100 cm, chair 50 × 45 × 90 cm, table 100 × 45 × 157 cm, child's bed 80 × 40 × 100 cm)
Courtesy of the artist

– SUPERFLEX
FREE BEER & COUNTER-GAME STRATEGIES / ART WORLD MACHINE, 2007
(from the series *Counter-Game Strategies*)
Interactive installation for two or more players, dimensions variable
Courtesy of the artists

– Stephanie Syjuco
The Counterfeit Crochet Project (Critique of a Political Economy), 2008
Mixed-media installation, dimensions variable
Courtesy of the artist and Catharine Clark Gallery, San Francisco

– The Xijing Men
Welcome to Xijing - Xijing Olympics, 2008
Video, color, sound, 35 min, 2 flags, dimensions variable
Courtesy of the artists

– Tintin Wulia
The Butterfly Generator, 2012
Interactive network installation with live video projection
Courtesy of the artist
Produced in cooperation with ZKM | Center for Art and Media Karlsruhe, artist-in-residence program of the exhibition *The Global Contemporary* (2011/2012) & Osage Art Foundation, Hong Kong
This work is part of the artist's practice-based PhD research at RMIT University, Australia

– Xu Bing
Telephone, 1996–2006
Translation project, 10 written pages (paper), framed
Individual dimensions: 28 × 43 cm, 33.3 × 21.4 cm, 29.7 × 21 cm, 30.5 × 21.4 cm, 29.7 × 21.5 cm, 29.7 × 21 cm, 31 × 21.7 cm, 28 × 21.7 cm, 30.5 × 22.8 cm, 27.9 × 21.6 cm
Courtesy of Xu Bing Studio

– Zhou Tiehai
Press Conference, 1997
Photograph, digital print, 55 × 102 cm
Courtesy of the artist/Shanghart

– Zhou Tiehai
Will / We Must, 1996
35 mm film, transferred to DVD, b/w, silent, 9:17 min
Courtesy of the artist/Shanghart

Biographies of the Authors

Hans Belting was cofounder of the Karlsruhe University for Arts and Design (HfG) in Karlsruhe, Germany (1992) and professor of art history and media theory (until 2002). He previously held chairs of art history at the Universities of Heidelberg and Munich. He was visiting professor at Harvard (1984), Columbia University (1989), and Northwestern University (2004). In 2003, he lectured at the Collège de France, Paris, and received an honorary degree from the Courtauld Institute, London. From 2004 to 2007, he was director of the International Center for Cultural Science (IFK) in Vienna. At present, he is advisor of the project GAM - Global Art and the Museum at ZKM | Karlsruhe. He is a member of the American Philosophical Society, the American Academy of Arts and Sciences, the Medieval Academy of America, and the Academia Europea. Some of the many books he has written are available in English, including *The End of the History of Art?* (1987), *Max Beckmann. Modern Painting and Tradition* (1989), *The Image and its Public in the Middle Ages* (1990), *Likeness and Presence. A History of the Image Before the Era of Art* (1994), *The Germans and their Art. A Difficult Heritage* (2000), *The Invisible Masterpiece* (2001), *Bosch's Garden of Earthly Delights* (2003), *Art History after Modernism* (2003), *Thomas Struth: Museum Photographs* (2006), *Duchamp's Perspective: Duchamp. Sugimoto. Jeff Wall* (2009), *The Global Art World. Audiences, Markets, Museums* (coedited with Andrea Buddensieg, 2009), *Florence and Baghdad: Renaissance Art and Arab Science* (2011), *An Anthropology of Images: Picture, Medium, Body* (2011).

Jakob Birken is a writer and researcher with a focus on media theory and contemporary art. After studying at the Karlsruhe University for Arts and Design (HfG), he worked at the House of World Cultures in Berlin and the ZKM | Karlsruhe. He is currently a research assistant for "Images of Disasters," part of the research project Asia and Europe in a Global Context at Heidelberg University. Birken is also working on a PhD thesis on media representation of forbidden economies. Together with Martin Heus he curated several exhibitions for the Karlsruhe art space Morgenstrasse. He was cocurator of *The Global Contemporary. Art Worlds after 1989* (ZKM, 2011/2012). He is coeditor of *Mapping Contemporary Art and Culture* (2011) and *The Daniel Libeskind Research Studio* (2010).

Andrea Buddensieg is curator and project manager of the project GAM - Global Art and the Museum. She received her PhD in art history from the University of Bonn. She worked at KPM Porzellan Manufaktur Berlin and was part of the project management team for the exhibition *Iconoclash. Beyond the Image Wars in Science, Religion, and Art* from 2000-2001 at ZKM. From 2002 to 2006 she ran the Public Relations Department at ZKM. In 2011/2012 she curated together with Peter Weibel the exhibition *The Global Contemporary. Art Worlds after 1989* at ZKM. Her main research interests are twentieth-century design and contemporary art. She has lectured at several academies, and in 2008 she was guest scholar at CASVA, National Gallery of Art, in Washington D.C. She has contributed to exhibition catalogs and is coeditor of the books *Contemporary Art and the Museum. A Global Perspective* (2007), *The Global Art World. Audiences, Markets, Museums* (2009), and *Global Studies. Mapping Contemporary Art and Culture* (2011).

John Clark is professor of Asian art history at the University of Sydney. His book publications include *Modern Asian Art* (1998), *Modernities of Chinese Art* (2010) *Asian Modernities: Chinese and Thai Art in the 1980s and 1990s* (2010), Best Art Book Prize, Art Association of Australia and New Zealand, 2011), and *Modernities of Japanese Art* (2012).

Manthia Diawara is professor of comparative literature and film, and director of the Institute of African American Affairs at New York University. He has published articles on literature, film, and art in scholarly journals and popular magazines. Diawara is the founder and editor of *Black Renaissance/Renaissance Noire*, a bilingual review that publishes essays, fiction, reviews, and artwork relating to Africa and the Black diaspora. He has published several books on Black culture, film, and literature including *African Cinema: Politics and Culture* (1992), *Black American Cinema* (1993), *In Search of Africa* (1998) / *En quête d'Afrique* (2001), *We Won't Budge* (2003), *Bamako, Paris, New York: itinéraire d'un exilé* (2007), *African Film: New Forms of Aesthetics and Politics* (2010). Diawara's documentary films include the widely acclaimed *Rouch in Reverse* (1995), *Sembene Ousmane: The Making of African Cinema* (1993), *Conakry has* (2004; Awards: Golden Dhow, Zanzibar International Film Festival 2004; Grand Prix TV-Vidéo, FESPACO 2005), *Who Is Afraid of Ngugi?* (2006; Award: Prix spécial du Jury, Zanzibar International Film Festival 2007), *Maison Tropicale* (2008), *Édouard Glissant: A World in Relation* (2010).

Liu Ding, born in 1976 in Changzhou, is an artist and a curator based in Beijing. His artworks have been exhibited in numerous international art institutions, including the Turner Museum and the Arnolfini Gallery (UK), the Kunsthalle Wien in Vienna (AT), the Astrup Fearnley Modern Art Museum (NO), the São Paulo National Museum of Art (BR), the ZKM | Karlsruhe (DE), the

RasquArt Center (CH), the Seoul Museum of Art (KR), and the Shanghai Museum of Contemporary Art (CN). His conceptual art project *Liu Ding's Store* (2008–ongoing) discusses and presents the various visible and invisible mechanisms in the art system for the formation of value. In 2009, it was presented at the 53rd Venice Biennale. Liu Ding had his first solo exhibition in the USA at the Frye Art Museum in Seattle (2012), and was invited to participate in the launch event of the Tate Modern's new experimental program *The Tanks* the same year. With Carol Yinghua Lu he curated *Little Movements: Self-Practices in Contemporary Art*, an exhibition that premiered at the OCT Contemporary Art Terminal in Shenzhen (CN) in 2011, and began its international tour in 2012. He was cocurator of *Accidental Message: Art is Not a System, Not a World*, the 7th Shenzhen Sculpture Biennale (2012).

Thomas Fillitz is professor of social and cultural anthropology at the University of Vienna and has taught at various universities in Europe. He conducted ethnographic field research in Nigeria, Côte d'Ivoire, Bénin, London, Paris, and New York. His research activities include contemporary art in Africa, visual culture, transnational processes, and postcolonial theory. His regional focus is on Africa and Europe. Currently, Fillitz is analyzing the system of art biennials as "contested spaces" of a global culture, with a special interest in the biennial of Dakar (SN), the Dak'Art. His publications and writings include *Debating Authenticity. Concepts of Modernity in Anthropological Perspective* (2012), *Zeitgenössische Kunst aus Afrika. Vierzehn Künstler aus Côte d'Ivoire und Bénin* (2002), "The Mega-Event and the World Culture of Biennials: Dak'Art, the Biennale of Dakar," (2012), "Contemporary Art in Africa: Coevalness in the Global World," (2009).

Patrick D. Flores is professor of art studies at the Department of Art Studies at the University of the Philippines. He was a visiting fellow at the National Gallery of Art in Washington, D.C., an Asian Public Intellectuals Fellow, and grantee of the Asian Cultural Council. He is curator of the Jorge B. Vargas Museum and Filipina Research Center (Manila, PH) and adjunct curator at the National Art Gallery Singapore. He was one of the curators of the Gwangju Biennale in 2008 and of *Under Construction: New Dimensions in Asian Art* (2000). Flores was a member of the advisory board of the exhibition *The Global Contemporary. Art Worlds After 1989* (2011/2012) at the ZKM | Karlsruhe, and member of the Guggenheim Museum's Asian Art Council (2011). Among his publications are *Painting History: Revisions in Philippine Colonial Art* (1999), *Remarkable Collection: Art, History, and the National Museum* (2006), and *Past Peripheral: Curation in Southeast Asia* (2008). He coedited the Southeast Asian issue with Joan Kee for *Third Text* (2011).

Sara Giannini has been a research and curatorial fellow of GAM – Global Art and Museum since 2010. She was curatorial assistant of the project's exhibition *The Global Contemporary. Art Worlds after 1989* and cocurator of the show's documentation segment "Room of Histories." She is currently a PhD candidate at the Leiden University Institute for Arts in Society (LUCAS) with the project "Rearticulating Differences. Cannibalism and Contemporary Art." Since 2012 she is coordinator of the European research and artistic network OuUnPo, which curates artistic events in various cities of the world. She earned a BA in cultural studies from the University of Ferrara (IT) in 2007 and a MA in semiotics from the University of Bologna (IT) in 2010. For the completion of her MA thesis *One Thing Leads to Another. Art of Citation and Theory of Ex-citation in Ai Weiwei's Artistic Production* she was a visiting student researcher at the Galerie Urs Meile in Beijing (CN).

Thomas Hauschild was born in 1955. He holds a chair for social and cultural anthropology at the University of Halle-Wittenberg and is a member of the Heidelberg Academy of Sciences and Humanities. His anthropological fieldwork and publications focus on the confluence of religions in the Mediterranean, on ritual and healing, and on clientelism, localizing, and fascist political practices. His recent publications include *Power and Magic in Italy* (2011), *Von Vogelmenschen, Piloten und Schamanen. Kulturgeschichte und Technologien des Fliegens* (2011), *Weihnachtsmann. Die wahre Geschichte* (2012).

Oscar Ho Hing Kay was formerly the exhibition director of the Hong Kong Arts Centre and founding director of the Museum of Contemporary Art in Shanghai (CN). Since the late 1980s, he has curated many local and international exhibitions, including serving as guest curator for the 2nd and 3rd Asian Pacific Triennial and curator for the Asian section of the Container 96 at Copenhagen in 1996. He was a member of the Museum Advisory Group, which conceived the plan of 'M+' of the West Kowloon Cultural District, and a founding director of Asia Art Archive. He was also member of the International Committee of Documenta 13, and writes regularly on arts and culture for local and international publications such as *Art Forum*, *Art Journal*, and *Art in Asia Pacific* and is the founder of the Hong Kong chapter of the International Art Critics Association. Currently he is the program director of the MA program in cultural management at the Chinese University of Hong Kong and remains active as independent curator.

Carol Yinghua Lu was born in 1977 in Guangdong Province (CN). She is a curator and writer based in Beijing. Lu was a participant in the Critical Studies Program at Malmö Art Academy in Sweden. She is a contributing editor of *Frieze* magazine and writes frequently for international art journals including *e-flux journal*, *The Exhibitionist*, *Yishu*, and *Tate Etc*. She has started a column on visual art for the Chinese website of *New York Times*. From 2005 to 2007, she was the China researcher for Asia Art Archive. Lu was furthermore a jury member for the 2011 Venice Biennale's Golden Lion Award. *Little Movements: Self-Practices in Contemporary Art* is a research-based project she initiated and curated with Liu Ding, which was exhibited at the OCT Contemporary Art Terminal in 2011. She cocurated the 7th Shenzhen Sculpture Biennale 2012 titled *Accidental Message: Art Is Not a System, Not a World*. She is the coartistic director for the 9th Gwangju Biennale 2012. Lu is a member of the jury for the Future Generation Art

Prize 2012. Together with Liu Ding, she will be guest curator at Museion, Bolzano (IT) in 2013.

Antonia Marten, born 1976 in Friedrichshafen (DE), studied cultural studies, aesthetics, and applied arts at the University of Hildesheim and the University of Provence, Aix-Marseille (FR). She graduated with a thesis about transculturality in the arts and started to work at the ZKM | Karlsruhe in 2006. As assistant curator and project manager, Marten was involved in the conception and realization of various exhibitions at ZKM, such as *Bilder eines Reiches* (2006), *art_clips.ch.at.de* (video clip edition, 2006), *MindFrames. Media Study at Buffalo 1973–1990* (2006), *zwischen zwei toden / between two deaths* (2007), *Our Literal Speed. The Performative Discourse* (2008), *Vertrautes Terrain – Contemporary Art in/about Germany* (2008), and *Medium Religion* (2008/2009). She cocurated and managed *The Global Contemporary. Art Worlds After 1989* (2011/2012). Her published writing includes contributions to the exhibition catalogs *Buffalo Heads: Media Study, Media Practice, Media Pioneers, 1973–1990* (2008), *Vertrautes Terrain* (2009), *Medium Religion: Faith. Geopolitics. Art* (2011), and the book *Shift. Globalisierung, Medienkulturen, Aktuelle Kunst* (2012).

Jean-Hubert Martin, a graduate in art history, has been director of the Kunsthalle Bern (CH), the Musée national d'art modern of the Centre Pompidou, Paris, the Musée national des Arts d'Afrique et d'Océanie, Paris (FR), and the Museum Kunstpalast, Düsseldorf (DE). He was artistic director at the Château d'Oiron and the Padiglione d'Arte Contemporanea, Milan (IT). His interest in non-Western cultures has led him to devise exhibitions that cross boundaries, bringing together heterogeneous works to encourage new ways of seeing (*Artempo*, Museo Fortuny, Venice, IT, 2007, and *Theater Of The World*, MONA, Hobart, AU, 2012). He has curated many biennials and major exhibitions, including *Paris – Berlin* (1978), *Paris – Moscow* (1979), *Magiciens de la terre* (1989), and *Une image peut en cacher une autre* (2009). As head curator he was responsible for the exhibition *Dalí* at the Centre Georges Pompidou (November 21, 2012–March 25, 2013).

Clare McAndrew is a cultural economist, investment analyst, and author. She founded Arts Economics – a research and consulting firm focused exclusively on the art economy – in 2005. The company carries out bespoke research and analysis on all aspects of the fine and decorative art market for private and institutional clients. Clare completed her PhD in economics at Trinity College Dublin (IE) in 2001, where she also lectured and taught economics for four years. She then directed a number of research projects for the Arts Council England on the effects of regulation, taxation, and other issues in the visual arts market. In 2002, she joined US firm Kusin & Company, a boutique investment banking firm specializing in art investment, as chief economist. McAndrew returned to Europe in 2005 and set up Arts Economics to focus her efforts on art market research and analysis. She works with a network of private consultants and academic scholars in providing research and consulting services to the global art trade and financial sector. McAndrew has published widely on the economics of the art market, including her recent book entitled *Fine Art and High Finance* (2010) and her annual report on the global art market for TEFAF in Maastricht. She is a guest lecturer on the Masters program at Trinity College Dublin in the Trinity Irish Art Research Centre (TRIAC), lectures on regulatory and taxation issues in the art market at Christie's Education, as well as on a range of art market subjects for the Sotheby's Institute of Art in London.

Birgit Mersmann is professor for non-Western and European Art at the Jacobs University Bremen (DE). Previously, she was a senior researcher at the National Competence Centre of Research "Iconic Criticism" at the University of Basel (CH). Research foci include image and media theory, art theory and aesthetics, contemporary East Asian and Western art, global art history, transculturality, translation studies, and interrelations between script and image. Her most recent publications and writings include *Bild Macht Schrift. Schriftkulturen in bildkritischer Perspektive* (2011), *Transmission Image. Visual Translation and Cultural Agency* (ed. with A. Schneider, 2009), *Movens Bild. Zwischen Affekt und Evidenz* (2008), "Globalgeschichte der Kunstgeschichte. Ein kultur- und bildkritisches Manifest" (2012), "Bildkulturwissenschaft als Kulturbildwissenschaft? Von der Notwendigkeit eines inter- und transkulturellen Iconic Turn"(2004).

Gerardo Mosquera was born in Havana in 1945. Recipient of the Guggenheim Fellowship in 1990, he is an independent art critic, curator, historian, and writer, as well as advisor to various international art institutions, such as the Rijksakademie van Beeldende Kunsten (NL), Museo Universitario de Arte Contemporáneo (MX), and Art in General (US). He was a cofounder of the Havana Biennial (CU), curator at the New Museum, New York (NY), and artistic director of PhotoEspaña (2011–2013) in Madrid (ES). Mosquera is a member of the advisory board of several art journals, including *Art Nexus* (Bogota, CO), *Third Text* (London, UK), *Calabar* and *Nka* (New York, US). He has lectured extensively in Africa, Asia, Australia, Europe, Latin America, and North America. His recent publications include *Interfaces. Portraiture and Communication* (2011), *Caminar con el diablo. Textos sobre Arte, Internacionalizacion y Culturas* (2011), and *Copying Eden. Recent Art in Chile* (2006). The latest exhibitions he curated include *Face Contact* (2011), *1000 Faces / 0 Face / 1 Face. Cindy Sherman, Thomas Ruff, Frank Montero* (2011), *Fayum Portraits + Adrian Paci: No Visible Future* (2011), *Crisisss. Latin America, Art and Confrontation. 1910–2010* (2011), and *Denarrations, PanAmerican Art Projects* (2009).

Piotr Piotrowski is professor ordinarius at the Art History Department at the Adam Mickiewicz University in Poznań (PL) and its former chair (1999–2008). He was director of the National Museum in Warsaw (2009–2010), and visiting professor at the Humboldt-Universität zu Berlin (2011–2012), University of Warsaw (2011), Bard College (2001), and the Hebrew University of Jerusalem (2003). He was a fellow at numerous institutions including the Center for Advanced Studies in the Visual Arts, Washington D.C. (1989-1990), the Institute for Advanced Study, Princeton (2000), Collegium Budapest (2005-2006), and the Clark Art Institute (2009). He is the author of a dozen books including *In the Shadow of Yalta* (2009), and *Art and Democracy in Post-Communist Europe* (2012). In 2010 Piotrowski received the Igor Zabel Award for Culture and Theory.

Raqs Media Collective enjoys playing a plurality of roles: appearing as artists, as curators, and as philosophical agent provocateurs. They make contemporary art, curate exhibitions, edit books, stage events, collaborate with architects, computer programmers, and theater directors and have founded processes that have left deep impacts on contemporary culture in India. Raqs follows its self-declared imperative of "kinetic contemplation" to produce a trajectory that is restless in terms of the forms and methods it deploys even as it achieves a consistency of speculative procedures. See also: www.raqsmediacollective.net

Terry Smith is Andrew W. Mellon Professor of Contemporary Art History and Theory in the Department of the History of Art and Architecture at the University of Pittsburgh (US), and distinguished visiting professor at the National Institute for Experimental Arts, College of Fine Arts, University of New South Wales, Sydney. In 2010 he received the Mather Award for Art Criticism (College Art Association, USA) and the Australia Council Visual Arts Laureate Award (Commonwealth of Australia). He was a member of the Art & Language group (New York) and a founder of Union Media Services (Sydney). He is the author of *Making the Modern: Industry, Art and Design in America* (1993), *Transformations in Australian Art* (2002), *The Architecture of Aftermath* (2006), *What is Contemporary Art?* (2009), *Contemporary Art: World Currents* (2011), and *Thinking Contemporary Curating* (2012).

David Spalding is an American writer, curator, and editor based in Beijing. Over the last decade, he has published over one hundred texts on contemporary art. Spalding has served as a correspondent/contributing editor for *Art Papers*, *Artforum*, *Contemporary*, and *Flash Art International*, and was the founding editor-in-chief of *ARTINFO China*. Most recently, his writing was honored with an award from the Andy Warhol Foundation | Creative Capital. An active independent curator, Spalding was previously curator at the Ullens Center for Contemporary Art, Beijing (CN). He is currently at work editing *The King of Kowloon: The Art of Tsang Tsou Choi*, a monograph on Hong Kong's best known and least understood artist.

Jim Supangkat was born in Makassar, Indonesia in 1948. He entered the Faculty of Fine Art and Design, Bandung Institute of Technology, in 1970. From 1974 to 1975 he studied aesthetics under noted philosopher Dick Hartoko in the city of Yogyakarta (ID). After his graduation Supangkat founded the Indonesia New Art Movement, which proclaimed the redefinition of art and the search for an Indonesian subversive perception of art. The debate on the movement's principles continued for nearly ten years and is now considered the beginning of contemporary art discourse in Indonesia. In 1992, Supangkat decided to change direction. Aware of the need for professional curators in Indonesia, he stopped working as lecturer, even as an artist. As an independent curator he initiated several international contemporary art exhibitions in Indonesia, such as *Contemporary Art of the Non-Aligned Countries* (1995), CP Biennale I (2003), and CP Biennale II (2005). He has written several books and numerous essays introducing contemporary art in Asia and Indonesia to the international art world. In 1997, he received the Prince Claus Award for these endeavors.

Sabine B. Vogel was born in Essen (DE) and has lived in Austria since 1995. She received her doctorate from the University of Applied Arts Vienna with a thesis on the "History of Biennials." She has curated several exhibitions for well-known institutions, such as the Vienna Secession (1992), Kunsthalle Düsseldorf (1994), Kunstverein Vienna (1997-1999), Belvedere Vienna (2009), and the ifa galleries (2011). Her reviews have appeared in *Die Presse* (Vienna) and *Neue Züricher Zeitung* (Zurich). Vogel was New York correspondent for *Artforum*, and she launched the internet project www.kunstundbuecher.at. Since 2003 she lectures at the University of Applied Arts Vienna, and since 2008 she is president of AICA AUSTRIA, the international association of art critics in Austria. Vogel's publications include *Political Patterns - Ornament im Wandel* (2011), *Biennalen: Kunst im Weltformat* (2010), and *Die Macht des Ornaments* (2009).

Peter Weibel was born in Odessa in 1944. He studied literature, medicine, logic, philosophy, and film in Paris and Vienna. Since 1984 he is professor at the University of Applied Arts Vienna, and since 1999 CEO of the ZKM | Center for Art and Media Karlsruhe. As visiting professor he has taught at several international art schools and universities, inter alia at the State University of New York at Buffalo (Department for Media Study, 1984-1989) and the University of New South Wales in Sydney (2009-2012). In 1989 he founded the Institute for New Media at the Städelschule, Frankfurt am Main, and chaired the Institute until 1995. He was artistic director of the festival Ars Electronica (1986-1995), commissioner of the Austrian Pavilion at the Venice Biennale (1993-1999), chief curator of the Neuen Galerie in Graz (1993-2011), as well as artistic director of the International Biennial of Contemporary Art of Seville (2008) and the Moscow Biennial of Contemporary Art (2011).

Index

H

M

N

O

V

W

X

Y

Z

Symbols

The Global Contemporary. Art Worlds after 1989

Exhibition

ZKM | Center for Art and Media Karlsruhe
September 17, 2011 - February 5, 2012

Director and CEO
Peter Weibel

Curators
Andrea Buddensieg, Peter Weibel

Co-Curators
Jacob Birken, Antonia Marten

Scientific advisor
Hans Belting

Curatorial committee
N'Goné Fall, Patrick D. Flores, Carol Yinghua Lu, Jim Supangkat

Curator of education
Henrike Plegge

Project management
Andrea Buddensieg, Antonia Marten

Curatorial assistance
Anne Marie Buenker, Akvile Eglinskaite, Sara Giannini

Assistance education
Marlene Gauß

Exhibition architecture
Kuehn Malvezzi with Samuel Korn

Exhibition graphics
Boris Dworschak, Holger Jost

Room of Histories. A Documentation
Conception: Hans Belting, Andrea Buddensieg, Sara Giannini
Scientific research, assistance: Anne Marie Buenker, Daria Mille
Translations: Anne Marie Buenker, Nils Plath
Design: Boris Dworschak, Matthias Gommel

Studio
Design: Sanne Pawelzyk, Henrike Plegge

Registrar
Marianne Meister, Cathrin Langanke

Head of museum and exhibition technical services
Martin Häberle

Technical management
Anne Däuper

Technical staff
Volker Becker, Claudius Böhm, Mirco Frass, Rainer Gabler, Gregor Gaissmaier, Ronald Haas, Dirk Heesakker, Christof Hierholzer, Werner Hutzenlaub, Gisbert Laaber, Marco Preitschopf, Peter Schindler

Patrick Schmidt

Concern Art
Martin Boukhalfa, Lutz Fezer, Heiko Hoos
Jörg Baier, Berthold Dieterich, Christoph Dinges, Jean-Michel Dejasmin, Silke Fehsenfeld, Max Kosoric, Hubert Krauth, Skafte Kuhn, Manfred Schmieder, Esther Stephan, Daphne Walch, Harry Kresin

d&d art solutions
Raphael Dobler, TdS
Andreas Bordenach, Martin Brandt, Tino Brennenstuhl, Erdogan Coban, Max Darboven, Jörg Eisemann, Michael Feldbausch, Georg Müller, Silvan Hobert, Dirk Schiebel, Manfred Stürmlinger, Markus Zielke, Tobias Zilly

Conservation
Nahid Matin Pour, Ellen Kotthaus, Anna-Maria Virgin, Florence Babando

Office of museum technical services
Anna Reiß, Alexandra Kempf, Katrin Riedel

Video documentation, video editing
Christina Zartmann, Moritz Büchner, Jennifer Fluck

Website
Silke Altvater, Patrick Burkert, Frauke Schnoor (Blog)

Public relations
Dominika Szope, Stephanie Hock, Christina Hoffmann, Linda Mann, Denise Rothdiener, Elena Sánchez, Helene Schuller, Rebecca Zajonc

Museum communication
Janine Burger, Banu Beyer, Katharina Hauswaldt, Carolin Knebel, Marianne Spencer

Events
Hartmut Bruckner, Max Bäßler, Viola Gaiser, Hans Gass, Monika Weimer, Wolfgang Knapp, Manuel Weber

Media library
Andreas Brehmer, Claudia Gehrig, Hartmut Jörg, Christiane Minter, Stephanie Mayer, Petra Zimmermann

Institute for Visual Media
Bernd Lintermann, Moritz Büchner, Dimitrios Dermentzidis, Jennifer Fluck, Jan Gerigk, Manfred Hauffen, Julia Jochem, Silke Sutter, Christina Zartmann

Facility management
Angelika Obert, Peter Kuhn, Klaus Wirth, Hartmut Kampe, Martin Braun

IT-Support
Elena Lorenz, Joachim Schütze, Volker Sommerfeld

Funded by the German Federal Cultural Foundation
KULTURSTIFTUNG DES BUNDES
With the kind support of
EnBW
Hubert Burda Stiftung
GOETHE INSTITUT
Haus & Grund® Karlsruhe
Media partner
ikono

The Global Contemporary and the Rise of New Art Worlds

Publication

Editors
Hans Belting, Andrea Buddensieg, Peter Weibel

Editorial assistance Room of Histories
Sara Giannini

Editorial staff
ZKM | Publications: Jens Lutz, Miriam Stürner, Maraike Steding, Luise Pilz

Copy editing
Gloria Custance

Translations
Steven Lindberg, Jeremy Gaines, Imogen Forster, Elizabeth Volk, Christopher Winks

Graphic design
Renata Sas

Graphic design Room of Histories
Boris Dworschak

Lithography
COMYK Roland Merz, Karlsruhe
HK-Repro, Stuttgart (pp. 1-11, 32-33)

Authors of work descriptions and short texts
Evelyne Astner (EA), Karin Bellmann (KB), Hans Belting (HB), Jacob Birken (JB), Andrea Buddensieg (AB), Anne Marie Buerker (AMB), Akvile Eglinskaite (AE), Sara Giannini (SG), Carol Yinghua Lu (CL), Antonia Marten (AM), Daria Mille (DM), Henrike Plegge (HP), Isabel Seliger (IS)

Museum shop and Info counter
Petra Koger, Daniela Doermann, Tatjana Draskovic, Regine Frisch, Felicity Grobien, Gerlinde Lorch, Adriana Rys, Marina Siggelkow, Jutta Schuhmann

Printed and bound
Eberl Graphische Betriebe, Immenstadt, Germany

Typeface
Greta, Greta Sans, Theinhardt

Paper
Munken Lynx, 120 g/m², RT-Druckfein, 115 g/m²

MIT books may be purchased at special quantity discounts for business or sales promotional use. For information, please email special_sales@mitpress.mit.edu or write to Special Sales Department, The MIT Press, 55 Hayward Street, Cambridge, MA 02142.

ISBN:
978-0-262-51834-5 (P)

Library of Congress Control number:
2012954123

ZKM | Center for Art and Media Karlsruhe
Lorenzstr. 19, 76135 Karlsruhe, Germany
www.zkm.de

Founders of ZKM

Baden-Württemberg
MINISTERIUM FÜR WISSENSCHAFT, FORSCHUNG UND KUNST

Karlsruhe

Photo Credits

Photo ©

Afterall Books / König Books London: 68 left | Al-Ma'mal Foundation for Contemporary Art: 76 | Art Dubai: 118 | Arts Abu Dhabi/TDIC: 94-97 | Arts Council of Great Britain: 47 | Asia Art Archive: 70-71 | Athens Biennale: 115 bottom right | Bandjoun Station: 78 | Beirut Art Centre: 77 | Bibliotheque Kandinsky, Centre Pompidou: 66-67 | BMP Media Holdings: 64-65 | Centro Wilfredo Lam: 68 right | Collection of the 46th Venice Biennale: 199 (fishing boat) | Courtesy of Cemeti Art House: 79 | Courtesy Sharjah Art Foundation: 117| Dak'Art: 120 | Devi Art Foundation: 80 | Documenta: 73 | Edition Hazan, Paris and the artist: 213 | Editions de la Réunion des musées nationaux, Lyon: 217 | Fukuoka Asian Art Museum: 110 | Galerie Art&Public, Geneva: 198 | Galerie Perrotin: 416 | Galerie Peter Kilchmann: 436 | Galerie Urs Meile: 381 | Generali Foundation: 244 right | Giancarlo Politi Editore: 115 middle, top right | Greater Johannesburg Metropolitan Council: 121 | Guangdong Museum of Art, Guangzhou: 267-268 | Hayward Publishing: 69 | Hong Kong Arts Centre: 305, 307-309 | Inhotim: 81 | Institut du Monde Arabe, Paris: 214 | James Clifford: 242 | Jorge B. Vargas Museum: 91 | Kala Press, London: 44 | Kunstsammlung Nordrhein-Westfalen, Dumont, Cologne: 125 | L.A. Galerie, Frankfurt am Main: 269 | MAC USP: 82 | MIT Press: 115 top left | MoBY: 83 | MoMA, New York: 62 | MSU | Zagreb: 84 | Musée National des Arts d'Afrique et d'Océanie, Paris, et al.: 215 | Museum Kunstpalast, Düsseldorf: 218 | National Gallery of Australia, Canberra: 127 | Navin Production Co., Ltd.: 201 | OCAT: 85 | Padiglione d'Arte Contemporanea, Milan: 218 | Palgrave Macmillan: 144 | PERMM: 86 | Sàn Art: 87 | santralistanbul: 88 | SMBA, Amsterdam: 243 | SMCA: 89 | Sotheby's: 143 | steirischer herbst: 72 left | Sternberg Press, Berlin, New York: 123 right | TEFAF Maastricht: 130-136 | The Asia Society Galleries, New York, George Brazil er Publishers, New York: 124 | The Center for African Art and Prestel-Verlag: 63 | Today Art Museum: 90 | University of Chicago Press: 145 | University of Queensland Press, St. Lucia: 126 | Vilnius Contemporary Art Centre: 115 bottom left | Weltkulturen Museum, Frankfurt am Main: 244 left | West Kowloon District Hong Kong: 93 | Whitechapel Gallery: 122, 123 left (*Seven Stories about Modern Art in Africa*, catalog, text © Whitechapel Gallery and the authors; illustrations © Whitechapel Gallery and the owners; cover illustration: El Hadji Sy, *Untitled*, 1989, oil on canvas 103 x 90 cm, collection of Friedrich Axt) | Zinsou Foundation: 92 | ZKM | Karlsruhe: 1, 4-5, 6-11, 32 top left, 32 middle right, 32, bottom left, 33, top right, 34, 41, 50-51, 60-61, 74-75, 98-101, 128-129, 138, 140, 146-147, 208-211, 230, 261-266, 270, 316, 326-328, 331-332, 334-335, 344-345, 347-348, 249 top, 353-356, 362-364, 368, 370 right, 371, 373, 378, 380, 382 right, 384-385, 394, 397-401, 402 left, 403 bottom, 404-408, 409 left, bottom right, 414-415, 417, 418, 419, 421, 422, 432, 425 bottom, 426, 427, 428, 429, 430, 431, 439, 440, 441 top, 442, 444, 445, 446, 447, 448, 449, 450 left, 456, 457, 458, 459, 460, 462, 463, 464, 465, 461, 466, 467, 469

Photographers

Andrea Buddensieg: 33 bottom left | Anne Marie Buenker: 34 middle left | Timothy Brown: 285 | David Feinberg: 284 | Fidelis Fuchs: 1, 4-5, 146-147, 404-405, 461, 466, 467, 469 bottom left | Sara Giannini: 245 | Matthias Gommel: 330 | Wolfgang Günzel: 244 left | Steffen Harms: 6-11, 41, 50-51, 60-61, 74-75, 98-99, 100-101, 128-129, 138, 140, 230, 266, 270, 316, 326-328, 331 top, bottom, 332, 334-335, 344, 345, 347, 353-356, 362-364, 368, 370 right, 371, 373, 378, 380, 382 right, 384, 394, 397, 398, 399, 400, 401, 402 left, 403 bottom, 406, 407, 408, 409 left, bottom right, 414, 415, 417, 418, 419, 421 left, 422, 423, 425 bottom, 426, 427, 428, 430 right, 431, 439, 441 top, 442, 445, 446, 447, 448, 449, 450 left, 456, 457, 458, 459, 460, 462, 463, 464, 465 | Gina Kang: 286 | Joe Miletzki: cover illustration, 32 bottom left, 33 top right, 34 top, middle right, bottom left, 331 middle, 348-349 top, 421 right, 429, 430 left, 440 | ONUK, Karlsruhe: 32 top left, middle right | Gert Jan van Rooij: 243 | Renata Sas (design): 32 middle left, 33 top left | Margherita Spiluttini: 244 right | Schuyler Swenson: 283 | Yamamoto Tadasu, courtesy Cai Studio: 199 | Wolfgang Thaler: 43 | Timo Weiherich: 469 top

VG Bild-Kunst, Bonn 2013 for:
Kader Attia | Roberto Cabot | Elmgreen & Dragset | Meschac Gaba | Thierry Geoffroy/Colonel | Huang Yong Ping | Anna Jermolaewa | Rafael Lozano-Hemmer | John Smith | Hito Steyerl | SUPERFLEX